eighth
EDITION

An Introduction to
Management
Science

eighth
EDITION

An Introduction to Management Science

QUANTITATIVE APPROACHES TO DECISION MAKING

David R. Anderson

UNIVERSITY OF CINCINNATI

Dennis J. Sweeney

UNIVERSITY OF CINCINNATI

Thomas A. Williams

ROCHESTER INSTITUTE OF TECHNOLOGY

West Publishing Company
MINNEAPOLIS/ST. PAUL   NEW YORK   LOS ANGELES   SAN FRANCISCO

Design
David J. Farr/ImageSmythe

Copyediting
Cheryl Wilms

Composition and Prepress
Carlisle Communications

Artwork
Miyake Illustration

Indexing
Northwind Editorial Services

Production and Printing by
West Publishing Company

Dedication

To Our Parents

West's Commitment to the Environment

In 1906, West Publishing Company began recycling materials left over from the production of books. This began a tradition of efficient and responsible use of resources. Today, 100% of our legal bound volumes are printed on acid-free, recycled paper consisting of 50% new fibers. West recycles nearly 27,700,000 pounds of scrap paper annually—the equivalent of 229,300 trees. Since the 1960s, West has devised ways to capture and recycle waste inks, solvents, oils, and vapors created in the printing process. We also recycle plastics of all kinds, wood, glass, corrugated cardboard, and batteries, and have eliminated the use of polystyrene book packaging. We at West are proud of the longevity and the scope of our commitment to the environment. West pocket parts and advance sheets are printed on recyclable paper and can be collected and recycled with newspapers. Staples do not have to be removed. Bound volumes can be recycled after removing the cover.

 TEXT IS PRINTED ON 10% POST CONSUMER RECYCLED PAPER

British Library Cataloguing-in-Publication Data. A catalogue record for this book is available from the British Library.

04   03   02   01   00   99   98   97   8   7   6   5   4   3   2   1   0

Library of Congress Cataloging-in-Publication Data

Anderson, David Ray, 1941–
    An introduction to management science : quantitative approaches to decision making / David R. Anderson, Dennis J. Sweeney, Thomas A. Williams.—8th ed.
        p.   cm.
        Includes bibliographical references and index.
        ISBN 0–314–09687–6 (alk. paper)
        1. Management science.   I. Sweeny, Dennis J.   II. Williams, Thomas Arthur, 1944–   .   III. Title.
HD30.25.A53 1997
658—dc20   96-25601
                                                                    CIP

David R. Anderson   David R. Anderson is Professor of Quantitative Analysis in the College of Business Administration at the University of Cincinnati. Born in Grand Forks, North Dakota, he earned his B.S., M.S., and Ph.D. degrees from Purdue University. Professor Anderson has served as Head of the Department of Quantitative Analysis and as Associate Dean of the College of Business Administration. In addition, he was the coordinator of the College's first Executive Program.

At the University of Cincinnati, Professor Anderson has taught introductory statistics for business students as well as graduate level courses in regression analysis, multivariate analysis, and management science. He has also taught statistical courses at the Department of Labor in Washington, D.C. He has been honored with nominations and awards for excellence in teaching and excellence in service to student organizations.

Professor Anderson has coauthored seven textbooks in the areas of statistics, management science, linear programming, and production and operations management. He is an active consultant in the field of sampling and statistical methods.

Dennis J. Sweeney   Dennis J. Sweeney is Professor of Quantitative Analysis at the University of Cincinnati. Born in Des Moines, Iowa, he earned a B.S.B.A. degree from Drake University, graduating summa cum laude. He received his M.B.A. and D.B.A. degrees from Indiana University where he was an NDEA Fellow. Since receiving his doctorate in 1971, Professor Sweeney has spent all but 2 years at the University of Cincinnati. During 1978–79, he spent a year working in the management science group at Procter & Gamble; during 1981–82, he was a visiting professor at Duke University. Professor Sweeney served 5 years as Head of the Department of Quantitative Analysis and 4 years as Associate Dean at the University of Cincinnati.

Professor Sweeney has published over 30 articles in the general area of management science. The National Science Foundation, IBM, Procter & Gamble, and Cincinnati Gas & Electric have funded his research, which has been published in *Management Science, Operations Research, Mathematical Programming, Decision Sciences,* and other journals.

Professor Sweeney has coauthored seven textbooks in the areas of statistics, management science, linear programming, and production and operations management. His work with Procter & Gamble received an award in the 1996 Edelman competition sponsored by INFORMS.

Thomas A. Williams   Thomas A. Williams is Professor of Management Science and Team Leader for Decision Sciences in the College of Business at Rochester Institute of Technology. Born in Elmira, New York, he earned his B.S. degree at Clarkson University. He did his graduate work at Rensselaer Polytechnic Institute, where he received his M.S. and Ph.D. degrees.

Before joining the College of Business at RIT, Professor Williams served for 7 years as a faculty member in the College of Business Administration at the University of Cincinnati, where he developed the undergraduate program in Information Systems and then served as its coordinator. At RIT he was the first chairman of the Decision Sciences Department. He teaches courses in management science and statistics, as well as more advanced courses in regression and decision analysis.

Professor Williams is the coauthor of eight textbooks in the areas of management science, statistics, production and operations management, and mathematics. He has been a consultant for numerous Fortune 500 companies and has worked on projects ranging from the use of elementary data analysis to the development of large-scale regression models. His current research focuses on the application of total quality management in an academic setting.

Contents

CHAPTER THREE   Linear Programming: Formulation, Computer Solution, and Interpretation 81

CHAPTER FOUR   Linear Programming Applications 132

CHAPTER FIVE   Linear Programming: The Simplex Method 195

CHAPTER SIX   Simplex-Based Sensitivity Analysis and Duality 239

CHAPTER SEVEN   Transportation, Assignment, and Transshipment Problems 268

CHAPTER EIGHT

Integer Linear Programming 335

CHAPTER NINE   Network Models 372

CHAPTER TEN   Project Scheduling: PERT/CPM 401

CHAPTER ELEVEN   Inventory Models 439

CHAPTER TWELVE   Waiting Line Models 497

CHAPTER THIRTEEN   Simulation 535

CHAPTER FOURTEEN Decision Analysis 575

CHAPTER SEVENTEEN   Markov Processes 718

CHAPTER EIGHTEEN   Dynamic Programming 737

Appendixes A–1

Preface

Approximately 25 years ago, the three of us were assistant professors in the Department of Quantitative Analysis at the University of Cincinnati. Our graduate educations and experiences had convinced us of the valuable potential for management science and operations research techniques in business administration and related fields. We were committed to the challenge of writing a textbook that would help make the mathematical and technical concepts of management science understandable and useful to nonmathematicians. Judging from the responses from our teaching colleagues and thousands of students, we have successfully met that challenge. Thus, 25 years later, assisted by the helpful comments and suggestions of many users, we are pleased to offer the eighth edition of *An Introduction to Management Science.*

Our purpose continues to be to provide students with a sound conceptual understanding of the role that management science plays in the decision-making process. Written with the needs of the nonmathematician in mind, the text is applications oriented. As each new concept is introduced, a problem scenario or application is presented to help illustrate the topic; we then explain how management science assists in solving the problem. Using this style throughout the text, we describe the many quantitative methods that have been developed over the years, explain how they work, and show how they can be applied and interpreted. We have found that this approach helps to motivate the student by demonstrating not only how the procedure works, but also how it can contribute to the decision-making process.

Changes in the Eighth Edition

In preparing the eighth edition, we have been careful to maintain the overall format and approach of the previous editions. However, based on our own classroom experience and suggestions from users of previous editions, a number of changes have been made to enhance the content, managerial orientation, and readability of the text.

New Management Science in Practice Applications

End-of-chapter application sections provided by practitioners continue to be a feature of the text. We are pleased to be able to add recent management science applications from Procter & Gamble (Chapter 7) and Citibank (Chapter 12). These applications provide information about the company, the role of management science within the company, and an overview of a management science application that relates to the material the student has covered in the chapter. A total of 15 management science in practice applications now appear in the text.

Management Science in Action Vignettes

We have added more than 20 Management Science in Action vignettes throughout the text. They provide brief overviews of how the nearby text material has been used successfully in practice. Most are based on articles from *Interfaces*. The intent is to show the student that people actually are using the methods successfully. The vignettes complement the problem scenarios that are an integral part of the text and the chapter-ending applications prepared by practitioners.

Linear and Integer Programming

Chapter 4 has undergone a major revision. Two new applications have been added. One concerns the best mix of government securities for retiring future debt obligations. The other involves a company's decision about how much to produce on regular time and overtime versus how much to buy from outside suppliers. The section on data envelopment analysis has been completely rewritten to improve the pedagogy. Other chapter revisions involve more discussion concerning interpretation of computer output and sensitivity analysis.

Chapter 8 has been revised to show more types of applications of integer linear programming. A new section on fixed charge problems has been added. We show how to model production problems involving a setup cost and a variable cost per unit produced. This new material eases the transition into the plant location and distribution problem. A new case problem involving production scheduling with setup costs has also been added.

Chapter 5 on the simplex method has been shortened, and the branch-and-bound section has been dropped from the chapter on integer linear programming. These changes are in keeping with our increasing emphasis on managerial interpretation and computer solution of problems.

Project Scheduling: PERT/CPM

Chapter 10 has been revised to demonstrate the activity on node network representation of a project scheduling problem. We changed to this approach because the network model is easier to construct (no dummy arcs are necessary) and the crashing model is easier to develop. The changes enhance understanding without any loss of applicability.

Simulation

The chapter on simulation has been completely rewritten and modernized. The chapter begins with an application involving risk analysis and makes extensive use of spreadsheet output. An inventory simulation model and a waiting line simulation model are also covered. The use of spreadsheets has eliminated the dependence on using random number tables and performing simulation computations by hand. A chapter appendix shows how to use Microsoft Excel for simulation.

Spreadsheet Appendixes

Spreadsheet packages, such as Microsoft Excel and Lotus 1-2-3, have rapidly been adding management science solvers to their basic packages. Both Excel and Lotus 1-2-3 have the capability to solve linear programs. We added spreadsheet appendixes to six chapters to show how to use spreadsheets to implement some of the methods explained in the text. Microsoft Excel is used for the demonstrations, but users of other types of spreadsheets should have little difficulty adapting the material. For students and faculty who are comfortable with spreadsheets, these provide an alternative to the software tools provided by management science software packages. Of course, The Management Scientist and LINDO software packages are still described and illustrated in the text.

Other Changes

Many other changes, suggested by users, have been made. A number of student and instructor annotations have also been added and about 15 percent of the problems are new to this edition.

Prerequisite

The mathematical prerequisite for this text is a course in algebra. An introductory knowledge of probability and statistics would be desirable, but not necessary, for Chapters 10–14, 16, and 17.

Throughout the text, we have utilized generally accepted notation for the topic being covered. Thus, students who pursue study beyond the level of this text should find the difficulties of reading more advanced material minimized. To assist in further study, a bibliography is included in Appendix E of the book.

Course Outline Flexibility

The text has been designed to enhance the instructor's flexibility in selecting topics to meet specific course needs. The single-quarter and single-semester outlines that follow are a sampling of the many options available.

A one-quarter outline stressing linear programming, model development, and applications:

- Introduction (Chapter 1)
- Introduction to Linear Programming and Computer Solution (Chapters 2 and 3)
- Linear Programming Applications (selected portions of Chapters 4 and 7)
- Project Management: PERT/CPM (Chapter 10)
- Waiting Lines (Chapter 12)
- Computer Simulation (Chapter 13)
- Decision Analysis (Chapter 14)

The instructor in a one-semester course who wants to focus on model development and other applications could either spend more time on the applications in Chapter 4 or cover additional topics. One possible outline, stressing linear programming, model development, and applications, would be

- Introduction (Chapter 1)
- Introduction to Linear Programming (Chapters 2 and 3)
- Linear Programming Applications (Chapter 4)
- Simplex Method (Chapters 5 and 6)
- Transportation, Assignment, and Transshipment Models (Chapter 7)
- Integer Programming (Chapter 8)
- Project Management: PERT/CPM (Chapter 10)
- Inventory Models (Chapter 11)
- Waiting Lines (Chapter 12)
- Computer Simulation (Chapter 13)
- Decision Analysis (Chapter 14)
- Multicriteria Decision Making (Chapter 15)

Acknowledgments

We owe a debt to many of our colleagues and friends for their helpful comments and suggestions during the development of this and previous editions. Among these are Robert L. Armacost, E. Leonard Arnoff, John W. Auer, Uttarayan Bagchi, Edward Baker, Norman Baker, James Bartos, Richard Beckwith, Oded Berman, Jeanne Boeh, Stanley Brooking, Jeffrey Camm, Thomas Case, John Eatman, Ron Ebert, Don Edwards, Peter Ellis, Lawrence Ettkin, Jim Evans, Terri Friel, Robert Garfinkel, Damodar Golhar, Stephen Goodman, Jack Goodwin, Richard Gunther, Nicholas G. Hall, Michael E. Hanna, David Hott, Raymond Jackson, Muhannad Khawaja, Bharat Kolluri, Robert Landeros, Darlene Lanier, John Lawrence, Jr., Phillip Lowery, Prem Mann, William G. Marchal, Kamlesh Mathur, Joseph Mazzola, Cynthia S. McCahon, Richard McCready, Patrick McKeown, Constance McLaren, Edward Minieka, Richard C. Morey, Alan Neebe, Brian F. O'Neil, David Pentico, Gary Pickett, B. Madhusudan Rao, Handanhal V. Ravinder, Douglas V. Rippy, Donna Retzlaff-Roberts, Don R. Robinson, Richard Rosenthal, Sam H. Roy, Subhashish Samaddar, M.C. Sharman, Antoinette Somers, Carol Stamm, Christopher S. Tang, Giri Kumar Tayi, Willban Terpening, William Truscott, Charley Turner, James Vigen, Ed Winkofsky, Bruce Woodworth, M. Zafer Yakin, K. Paul Yoon, Sajjad Zahir, and Cathleen Zucco.

Our associates from organizations who supplied the Management Science in Practice applications made a major contribution to the text. These individuals are cited in a credit line on the first page of each application.

We are also indebted to our editor, Mary Schiller, production editor, Amy Hanson, promotion manager, John Tuvey, and others at West Publishing Company for their editorial counsel and support during the preparation of this text.

David R. Anderson
Dennis J. Sweeney
Thomas A. Williams

Introduction

Management science (MS), an approach to decision making based on the scientific method, makes extensive use of quantitative analysis. A variety of names exists for the body of knowledge involving quantitative approaches to decision making; in addition to management science, another widely known and accepted name is *operations research* (OR). Today, many use the terms *management science* and *operations research* interchangeably. We shall treat them as synonyms throughout the text.

The scientific management revolution of the early 1900s, initiated by Frederic W. Taylor, provided the foundation for MS/OR. But modern management science/operations research is generally considered to have originated during the World War II period, when teams were formed to deal with strategic and tactical problems faced by the military. These teams, which often consisted of people with diverse specialties (e.g., mathematicians, engineers, and behavioral scientists), were joined together to solve a common problem through the utilization of the scientific method. After the war, many of these team members continued their research on quantitative approaches to decision making.

Two developments that occurred during the post–World War II period led to the growth and use of management science in nonmilitary applications. First, continued research on quantitative approaches to decision making resulted in numerous methodological developments. Probably the most significant development was the discovery by George Dantzig, in 1947, of the simplex method for solving linear programming problems. Many more methodological developments followed, and in 1957 the first book on operations research was published by Churchman, Ackoff, and Arnoff.[1]

Concurrently with these methodological developments, there was a virtual explosion in computing power made available through digital computers. Computers enabled practitioners to use the methodological advances to solve successfully a large variety of problems. The computer technology explosion continues; personal computers are now more powerful than the mainframe computers of the 1970s. Today, variants of the post–World War II methodological developments are being used on personal computers to solve problems larger than those solved on mainframe computers in the 1980s.

---

[1]C. W. Churchman, R. L. Ackoff, and E. L. Arnoff, *Introduction to Operations Research* (New York: Wiley, 1957).

1.1 Problem Solving and Decision Making

Problem solving can be defined as the process of identifying a difference between the actual and the desired state of affairs and then taking action to resolve the difference. For problems important enough to justify the time and effort of careful analysis, the problem-solving process involves the following seven steps:

1. Identify and define the problem.
2. Determine the set of alternative solutions.
3. Determine the criterion or criteria that will be used to evaluate the alternatives.
4. Evaluate the alternatives.
5. Choose an alternative.
6. Implement the selected alternative.
7. Evaluate the results, and determine if a satisfactory solution has been obtained.

Decision making is the term generally associated with the first five steps of the problem-solving process. Thus, the first step of decision making is to identify and define the problem. Decision making ends with the choosing of an alternative, which is the act of making the decision.

Let us consider the following example of a decision-making process. For the moment assume that you will be graduating from college in the next few months, that you have completed the interviewing process, and that you have been lucky enough to receive job offers from four companies. Your problem is that you are currently unemployed and that you would like a position that will lead to a satisfying career.

Once the problem of obtaining a position that will lead to a satisfying career has been defined, the next step in the decision-making process is to identify the set of alternatives available. Assume that the alternatives available to you are these four job offers: one from a company located in Rochester, New York; one from a company located in Dallas, Texas; one from a company located in Greensboro, North Carolina; and one from a company located in Pittsburgh, Pennsylvania. Thus, the alternatives for your decision problem can be stated as follows:

1. Accept the position offered by the company located in Rochester, New York.
2. Accept the position offered by the company located in Dallas, Texas.
3. Accept the position offered by the company located in Greensboro, North Carolina.
4. Accept the position offered by the company located in Pittsburgh, Pennsylvania.

The next step of the problem-solving process involves determining the criterion or criteria that will be used to evaluate the four alternatives. Obviously, the starting salary is going to be a factor of some importance. If this were the only criterion of importance to you, the alternative selected as "best" would be the one with the highest starting salary. Problems in which the objective is to find the best solution with respect to one criterion are referred to as *single-criterion* decision problems.

For the current problem, suppose that you have also concluded that the potential for advancement and the location of the job are two other criteria of major importance. Thus, the three criteria in your decision problem are starting salary, potential for advancement, and location. Problems that involve more than one criterion are referred to as *multicriteria* decision problems.

The next step of the decision-making process is to evaluate each of the alternatives with respect to each criterion. For example, evaluating each alternative relative to the starting salary criterion is done simply by recording the starting salary for each job alternative. Evaluating each alternative with respect to the potential for advancement and

Table 1.1

Data for the Job Evaluation
Decision-Making Problem

Alternative	Starting Salary	Potential for Advancement	Job Location
Rochester	$28,500	Average	Average
Dallas	$26,000	Excellent	Good
Greensboro	$26,000	Good	Excellent
Pittsburgh	$27,000	Average	Good

the location of the job is more difficult to do, however, since these evaluations are based primarily on subjective factors that are often difficult to quantify. Assume for now that you have decided to measure potential for advancement and job location by rating each of these criteria as poor, fair, average, good, or excellent. The data that you have compiled are shown in Table 1.1.

You are now ready to make a choice from the available alternatives. What makes this choice phase so difficult is that the criteria are probably not all equally important, and no one alternative is "best" with regard to all criteria. Although we will present a method for dealing with situations like this later in the text, for now let us suppose that after a careful evaluation of the data in Table 1.1, you have decided to select alternative 3; alternative 3 is thus referred to as the *decision*.

At this point in time, the decision-making process is complete. In summary, we see that this process involves five steps:

1. Define the problem.
2. Identify the alternatives.
3. Determine the criteria.
4. Evaluate the alternatives.
5. Choose an alternative.

Note that missing from this list are the last two steps in the problem-solving process: implementing the selected alternative and evaluating the results to determine whether a satisfactory solution has been obtained. This is not meant to diminish the importance of each of these activities, but to emphasize the more limited scope of the term *decision making* as compared to the term *problem solving*. Figure 1.1 summarizes the relationship between these two concepts.

1.2 Quantitative Analysis and Decision Making

Consider the flowchart presented in Figure 1.2. Note that we have combined the first three steps of the decision-making process under the heading of "Structuring the Problem" and the latter two steps under the heading "Analyzing the Problem." Let us now consider in more detail how to carry out the set of activities that make up the decision-making process.

Figure 1.3 shows that the analysis phase of the decision-making process may take on two basic forms: qualitative and quantitative. Qualitative analysis is based primarily on the manager's judgment and experience; it includes the manager's intuitive "feel" for the problem and is more an art than a science. If the manager has had experience with similar problems, or if the problem is relatively simple, heavy emphasis may be placed upon a qualitative analysis. However, if the manager has had little experience with similar

Figure 1.1

The Relationship Between Problem Solving and Decision Making

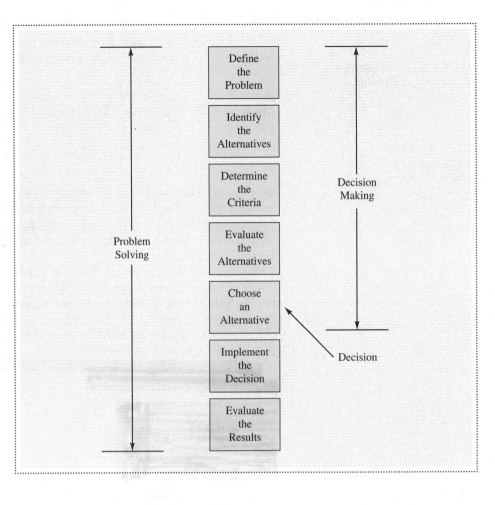

Figure 1.2

An Alternate Classification of the Decision-Making Process

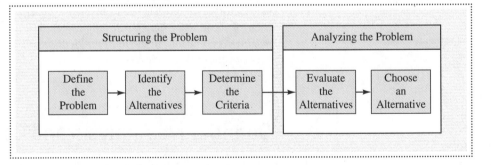

problems, or if the problem is sufficiently complex, then a quantitative analysis of the problem can be an especially important consideration in the manager's final decision.

When using the quantitative approach, an analyst will concentrate on the quantitative facts or data associated with the problem and develop mathematical expressions that describe the objectives, constraints, and other relationships that exist in the problem. Then, by using one or more quantitative methods, the analyst will make a recommendation based on the quantitative aspects of the problem.

While skills in the qualitative approach are inherent in the manager and usually increase with experience, the skills of the quantitative approach can be learned only by

Figure 1.3

The Role of Qualitative and Quantitative Analysis

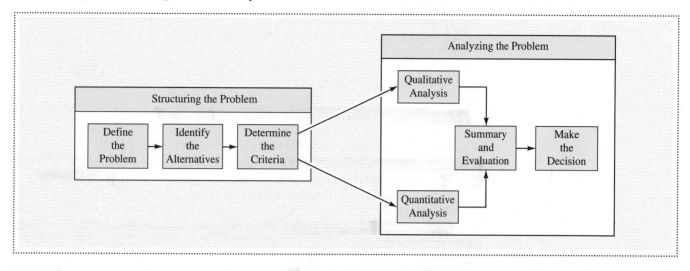

studying the assumptions and methods of management science. A manager can increase decision-making effectiveness by learning more about quantitative methodology and by better understanding its contribution to the decision-making process. The manager who is knowledgeable in quantitative decision-making procedures is in a much better position to compare and evaluate the qualitative and quantitative sources of recommendations and ultimately to combine the two sources in order to make the best possible decision.

The box in Figure 1.3 entitled "Quantitative Analysis" encompasses most of the subject matter of this text. We will consider a managerial problem, introduce the appropriate quantitative methodology, and then develop the recommended decision.

In closing this section, let us briefly state some of the reasons why a quantitative approach might be used in the decision-making process:

You should understand why quantitative approaches might be needed in a particular problem. Try Problem 4.

1. The problem is complex, and the manager cannot develop a good solution without the aid of quantitative analysis.
2. The problem is very important (e.g., a great deal of money is involved), and the manager desires a thorough analysis before attempting to make a decision.
3. The problem is new, and the manager has no previous experience from which to draw.
4. The problem is repetitive, and the manager saves time and effort by relying on quantitative procedures to make routine decision recommendations.

1.3 Quantitative Analysis

The problem definition step is a critical component in determining the success or failure of any quantitative approach to decision making. It usually takes imagination, teamwork, and considerable effort to transform a rather general problem description into a well-defined problem that can be approached quantitatively. For example, a broadly described excessive inventory problem must be clearly defined in terms of specific objectives and operating constraints before an analyst can begin the quantitative analysis process.

To successfully apply quantitative analysis to decision making, the management scientist must work closely with the manager or user of the results. When both the management scientist and the manager agree that the problem has been adequately defined, the management scientist will begin work on developing a model that can be used to represent the problem mathematically. Solution procedures can then be developed for the model in order to select the decision that "best" solves the problem.

Model Development

Models are representations of real objects or situations. These representations, or models, can be presented in various forms. For example, a scale model of an airplane is a representation of a real airplane. Similarly, a child's toy truck is a model of a real truck. The model airplane and toy truck are examples of models that are physical replicas of real objects. In modeling terminology, physical replicas are referred to as *iconic* models.

A second classification of models includes those that are physical in form but do not have the same physical appearance as the object being modeled. Such models are referred to as *analog* models. The speedometer of an automobile is an analog model; the position of the needle on the dial represents the speed of the automobile. A thermometer is another analog model representing temperature.

A third classification of models—the type we will primarily be studying—includes those that represent a problem by a system of symbols and mathematical relationships or expressions. Such models are referred to as *mathematical* models and are a critical part of any quantitative approach to decision making. For example, the total profit from the sale of a product can be determined by multiplying the profit per unit by the quantity sold. If we let x represent the number of units sold and P the total profit, then, with a profit of $10 per unit, the following mathematical model defines the total profit earned by selling x units:

$$P = 10x \tag{1.1}$$

The purpose, or value, of any model is that it enables us to make inferences about the real situation by studying and analyzing the model. For example, an airplane designer might test an iconic model of a new airplane in a wind tunnel to learn about the potential flying characteristics of the full-size airplane. Similarly, a mathematical model may be used to make inferences about how much profit will be earned if a specified quantity of a particular product is sold. According to the mathematical model of equation (1.1), we would expect selling three units of the product ($x = 3$) would provide a profit of $P = 10(3)$ = $30.

In general, experimenting with models requires less time and is less expensive than experimenting with the real object or situation. A model airplane is certainly quicker and less expensive to build and study than the full-size airplane. Similarly, the mathematical model in equation (1.1) allows a quick identification of profit expectations without actually requiring the manager to produce and sell x units. Models also have the advantage of reducing the risk associated with experimenting with the real situation. In particular, bad designs or bad decisions that cause the model airplane to crash or a mathematical model to project a $10,000 loss can be avoided in the real situation.

The value of model-based conclusions and decisions is dependent on how well the model represents the real situation. The more closely the scale model represents the real airplane, the more accurate the conclusions and predictions will be. Similarly, the more closely the mathematical model represents the company's true profit–volume relationship, the more accurate the profit projections will be.

Since this text deals with quantitative analysis based on mathematical models, let us look more closely at the mathematical modeling process. When initially considering a managerial problem, we usually find that the problem definition phase leads to a specific objective, such as maximization of profit or minimization of cost, and possibly a set of restrictions or *constraints,* such as production capacities. The success of the mathematical model and quantitative approach will depend heavily on how accurately the objective and constraints can be expressed in terms of mathematical equations or relationships.

A mathematical expression that describes the problem's objective is referred to as the *objective function.* For example, the profit equation $P = 10x$ would be an objective function for a firm attempting to maximize profit. A production capacity constraint would be necessary if, for instance, 5 hours are required to produce each unit and there are only 40 hours available per week. Let x indicate the number of units produced each week. The production time constraint is given by

$$5x \leq 40 \qquad (1.2)$$

The value of $5x$ is the total time required to produce x units; the symbol $\leq$ indicates that the production time required must be less than or equal to the 40 hours available.

The decision problem or question is the following: How many units of the product should be scheduled each week to maximize profit? A complete mathematical model for this simple production problem is

$$\text{Maximize} \qquad P = 10x \qquad \text{objective function}$$
subject to (s.t.)

$$\left. \begin{array}{r} 5x \leq 40 \\ x \geq 0 \end{array} \right\} \text{constraints}$$

The $x \geq 0$ constraint requires the production quantity x to be greater than or equal to zero, which simply recognizes the fact that it is not possible to manufacture a negative number of units. The optimal solution to this model can be easily calculated and is given by $x = 8$, with an associated profit of \$80. This model is an example of a linear programming model. In subsequent chapters we will discuss more complicated mathematical models and learn how to solve them in situations where the answers are not nearly so obvious.

In the preceding mathematical model, the profit per unit (\$10), the production time per unit (5 hours), and the production capacity (40 hours) are environmental factors that are not under the control of the manager or decision maker. Such environmental factors, which can affect both the objective function and the constraints, are referred to as *uncontrollable inputs* to the model. Inputs that are controlled or determined by the decision maker are referred to as *controllable inputs* to the model. In the example given, the production quantity x is the controllable input to the model. Controllable inputs are the decision alternatives specified by the manager and thus are also referred to as the *decision variables* of the model.

Once all controllable and uncontrollable inputs are specified, the objective function and constraints can be evaluated, and the output of the model determined. In this sense, the output of the model is simply the projection of what would happen if those particular environmental factors and decisions occurred in the real situation. A flowchart of how controllable and uncontrollable inputs are transformed by the mathematical model into output is shown in Figure 1.4. A similar flowchart showing the specific details of the production model is shown in Figure 1.5.

As stated earlier, the uncontrollable inputs are those the decision maker cannot influence. The specific controllable and uncontrollable inputs of a model depend on the particular problem or decision-making situation. In the production problem, the production time available (40), is an uncontrollable input. However, if it were possible to hire more employees or use overtime, the number of hours of production time would become a controllable input and therefore a decision variable in the model.

Figure 1.4
. . . .
**Flowchart of the Process of
Transforming Model Inputs into
Output**

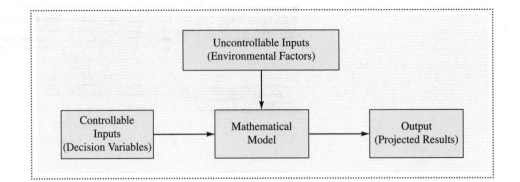

Figure 1.5
. . . .
Flowchart for the Production Model

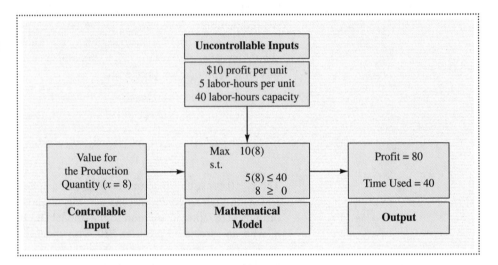

Uncontrollable inputs can either be known exactly or be uncertain and subject to variation. If all uncontrollable inputs to a model are known and cannot vary, the model is referred to as a *deterministic* model. Corporate income tax rates are not under the influence of the manager and thus constitute an uncontrollable input in many decision models. Since these rates are known and fixed (at least in the short run), a mathematical model with corporate income tax rates as the only uncontrollable input would be a deterministic model. The distinguishing feature of a deterministic model is that the uncontrollable input values are known in advance.

If any of the uncontrollable inputs are uncertain and subject to variation, the model is referred to as a *stochastic* or *probabilistic* model. An uncontrollable input to many production planning models is demand for the product. Since future demand may be any of a range of values, a mathematical model that treats demand with uncertainty would be called a stochastic model. In the production model, the number of hours of production time required per unit, the total hours available, and the unit profit were all uncontrollable inputs. Since the uncontrollable inputs were all known to take on fixed values, the model was deterministic. If, however, the number of hours of production time per unit could vary from 3 to 6 hours depending on the quality of the raw material, the model would be stochastic. The distinguishing feature of a stochastic model is that the value of the output cannot be determined even if the value of the controllable input is known because the specific values of the uncontrollable inputs are unknown. In this respect, stochastic models are often more difficult to analyze.

Data Preparation

Another step in the quantitative analysis of a problem is the preparation of the data required by the model. Data in this sense refer to the values of the uncontrollable inputs to the model. All uncontrollable inputs or data must be specified before we can analyze the model and recommend a decision or solution for the problem.

In the production model, the values of the uncontrollable inputs or data were $10 per unit for profit, 5 hours per unit for production time, and 40 hours for production capacity. In the development of the model, these data values were known and incorporated into the model as it was being developed. If the model is relatively small and the uncontrollable input values or data required are few, the quantitative analyst will probably combine model development and data preparation into one step. That is, in these situations the data values are inserted as the equations of the mathematical model are developed.

However, in many mathematical modeling situations, the data or uncontrollable input values are not readily available. In these situations the management scientist may know that the model will need profit per unit, production time, and production capacity data, but the values will not be known until the accounting, production, and engineering departments can be consulted. Rather than attempting to collect the required data as the model is being developed, the analyst will usually adopt a general notation for the model development step and then a separate data preparation step will be performed to obtain the uncontrollable input values required by the model.

Using the general notation

$$c = \text{profit per unit}$$
$$a = \text{production time in hours per unit}$$
$$b = \text{production capacity in hours}$$

the model development step of the production problem would result in the following general model:

$$\text{Max} \quad cx$$
$$\text{s.t.}$$
$$ax \leq b$$
$$x \geq 0$$

A separate data preparation step to identify the values for c, a, and b would then be necessary to complete the model.

Many inexperienced quantitative analysts assume that once the problem has been defined and a general model developed, the problem is essentially solved. These individuals tend to believe that data preparation is a trivial step in the process and can be easily handled by clerical staff. Actually, this assumption could not be farther from the truth, especially with large-scale models that have numerous data input values. For example, a moderate-size linear programming model with 50 decision variables and 25 constraints could have over 1300 data elements that must be identified in the data preparation step. The time required to prepare these data and the possibility of data collection errors will make the data preparation step a critical part of the quantitative analysis process. Often, a fairly large data base is needed to support a mathematical model, and information systems specialists also become involved in the data preparation step.

Table 1.2

Trial-and-Error Solution for the Production Model of Figure 1.5

Decision Alternative (Production Quantity) x	Projected Profit	Total Hours of Production	Feasible Solution? (capacity = 40)
0	0	0	Yes
2	20	10	Yes
4	40	20	Yes
6	60	30	Yes
8	80	40	Yes
10	100	50	No
12	120	60	No

Model Solution

Once the model development and data preparation steps have been completed, we can proceed to the model solution step. In this step, the analyst will attempt to identify the values of the decision variables that provide the "best" output for the model. The specific decision-variable value or values providing the "best" output will be referred to as the *optimal solution* for the model. For the production problem, the model solution step involves finding the value of the production quantity decision variable x that maximizes profit while not causing a violation of the production capacity constraint.

One procedure that might be used in the model solution step involves a trial-and-error approach in which the model is used to test and evaluate various decision alternatives. In the production model, this would mean testing and evaluating the model under various production quantities or values of x. Referring to Figure 1.5, note that we could input trial values for x and check the corresponding output for projected profit and satisfaction of the production capacity constraint. If a particular decision alternative does not satisfy one or more of the model constraints, the decision alternative is rejected as being *infeasible*, regardless of the objective function value. If all constraints are satisfied, the decision alternative is *feasible* and a candidate for the "best" solution or recommended decision. Through this trial-and-error process of evaluating selected decision alternatives, a decision maker can identify a good—and possibly the best—feasible solution to the problem. This solution would then be the recommended decision for the problem.

Table 1.2 shows the results of a trial-and-error approach to solving the production model of Figure 1.5. The recommended decision is a production quantity of 8 since the feasible solution with the highest projected profit occurs at $x = 8$.

While the trial-and-error solution process is often acceptable and can provide valuable information for the manager, it has the drawbacks of not necessarily providing the best solution and of being inefficient in terms of requiring numerous calculations if many decision alternatives are tried. Thus, quantitative analysts have developed special solution procedures for many models that are much more efficient than the trial-and-error approach. Throughout this text, you will be introduced to solution procedures that are applicable to the specific mathematical models that will be formulated. While some relatively small models or problems can be solved by hand computations, most practical applications require the use of a computer.

It is important to realize that the model development and model solution steps are not completely separable. While an analyst will want to develop an accurate model or representation of the actual problem situation, the analyst will also want to be able to find a solution to the model. If we approach the model development step by attempting to find the most accurate and realistic mathematical model, we may find the model so large and complex that it is impossible to obtain a solution. In this case, a simpler and perhaps more easily understood model with a readily available solution procedure is preferred even if the recommended solution is only a rough approximation of the best decision. As you learn more about quantitative solution procedures, you will have a better idea of the types of mathematical models that can be developed and solved.

After a model solution has been obtained, both the management scientist and the manager will be interested in determining how good the solution really is. While the analyst has undoubtedly taken many precautions to develop a realistic model, often the goodness or accuracy of the model cannot be assessed until model solutions are generated. Model testing and validation are frequently conducted with relatively small "test" problems that have known or at least expected solutions. If the model generates the expected solutions, and if other output information appears correct, the go-ahead may be given to use the model on the full-scale problem. However, if the model test and validation identify potential problems or inaccuracies inherent in the model, corrective action, such as model modification and/or collection of more accurate input data, may be taken. Whatever the corrective action, the model solution will not be used in practice until the model has satisfactorily passed testing and validation.

You should now understand the concept of a mathematical model and what is referred to as the optimal solution to the model. Try Problem 8.

Report Generation

An important part of the quantitative analysis process is the preparation of managerial reports based on the model's solution. Referring to Figure 1.3, we see that the solution based on the quantitative analysis of a problem is one of the inputs the manager considers before making a final decision. Thus, it is essential that the results of the model appear in a managerial report that can be easily understood by the decision maker. The report should include the recommended decision and other pertinent information about the results that may be helpful to the decision maker.

A Note Regarding Implementation

As discussed in Section 1.2, the manager is responsible for integrating the quantitative solution with qualitative considerations in order to make the best possible decision. After doing this, the manager must oversee the implementation and follow-up evaluation of the decision. During the implementation and follow-up, the manager should continue to monitor the contribution of the model. At times, this process may lead to requests for model expansion or refinement that will cause the management scientist to return to one of the earlier steps of the quantitative analysis process.

Successful implementation of results is of critical importance to the management scientist as well as the manager. If the results of the quantitative analysis process are not correctly implemented, the entire effort may be of no value. It doesn't take too many unsuccessful implementations before the management scientist is out of work. Because implementation often requires people to do things differently, it often meets with resistance. People want to know, "What's wrong with the way we've been doing it?" and so on. One of the most effective ways to ensure a successful implementation is to secure as much user involvement as possible throughout the modeling process. A user who feels involved in identifying the problem and developing the solution is much more likely to enthusiastically implement the results. The success rate for implementing the results of a management science project is much greater for those projects in which there has been extensive user involvement.

1.4 Models of Cost, Revenue, and Profit

Some of the most basic quantitative models arising in business and economic applications are those involving the relationship between a volume variable—such as production volume or sales volume—and cost, revenue, and profit. Through the use of these models, a manager can determine the projected cost, revenue, and/or profit associated with an established production quantity or a forecasted sales volume. Financial planning, production planning, sales quotas, and other areas of decision making can benefit from such cost, revenue, and profit models.

Cost and Volume Models

The cost of manufacturing or producing a product is a function of the volume produced. This cost can usually be defined as a sum of two costs: fixed cost and variable cost. *Fixed cost* is the portion of the total cost that does not depend on the production volume; this cost remains the same no matter how much is produced. *Variable cost,* on the other hand, is the portion of the total cost that is dependent on and varies with the production volume. For example, suppose that the setup cost for a production line is $3000. This is a fixed cost that is incurred regardless of the number of units eventually produced. In addition, suppose that variable labor and material costs are $2 for each unit produced. The cost–volume model for producing x units would be written as

$$C(x) = 3000 + 2x \qquad (1.3)$$

where

$$x = \text{production volume in units}$$
$$C(x) = \text{total cost of producing } x \text{ units}$$

Use of the model in equation (1.3) will determine the total production cost once the production volume is established. For example, a production volume of $x = 1200$ units would result in a total cost of $C(1200) = 3000 + 2(1200) = \$5400$.

Marginal cost is defined as the rate of change of the total cost with respect to volume. That is, it is the cost increase associated with a one-unit increase in the production volume. In the cost model of equation (1.3), we see that the total cost $C(x)$ will increase by $2 for each unit increase in the production volume. Thus, the marginal cost is $2. With more complex total cost models, marginal cost may depend on the production volume. In such cases, we could have marginal cost increasing or decreasing with the production volume x.

Revenue and Volume Models

A manager will also want information on the projected revenue associated with selling a specified number of units. Thus, a model of the relationship between revenue and volume is also needed. Suppose that the product in the preceding example sells for $5 per unit. The model for total revenue can be written as

$$R(x) = 5x \qquad (1.4)$$

where

$$x = \text{sales volume in units}$$
$$R(x) = \text{total revenue associated with selling } x \text{ units}$$

Marginal revenue is defined as the rate of change of total revenue with respect to sales volume. That is, it is the increase in total revenue resulting from a one-unit increase in sales volume. In the model of equation (1.4), we see that the marginal revenue is $5. In this case, marginal revenue is constant and does not vary with the sales volume. With more complex models, we may find that marginal revenue increases or decreases as the sales volume x increases.

Profit and Volume Models

One of the most important criteria for managerial decision making is profit. Managers need to be able to know the profit implications of their decisions. If we assume that we will only produce what can be sold, the production volume and sales volume will be equal. We can combine equations (1.3) and (1.4) to develop a profit–volume model that will determine profit associated with a specified production–sales volume. Since total profit is total revenue minus total cost, the following model provides the profit associated with producing and selling x units:

$$P(x) = R(x) - C(x)$$
$$= 5x - (3000 + 2x) = -3000 + 3x \qquad (1.5)$$

Thus, the model for profit $P(x)$ can be derived from the models of the revenue–volume and cost–volume relationships.

Break–Even Analysis

Using equation (1.5), we can now determine the profit associated with any production volume x. For example, suppose a demand forecast indicates that 500 units of the product can be sold. The decision to produce and sell the 500 units results in a projected profit of

$$P(500) = -3000 + 3(500) = -1500$$

In other words, a loss of $1500 is predicted. If sales are expected to be 500 units, the manager may decide against producing the product. However, a demand forecast of 1800 units would show a projected profit of

$$P(1800) = -3000 + 3(1800) = 2400$$

This profit may be enough to justify proceeding with the production and sale of the product.

We see that a volume of 500 units will yield a loss, whereas a volume of 1800 provides a profit. The volume that results in total revenue equaling total cost (providing $0 profit) is called the *break-even point*. If the break-even point is known, a manager can quickly infer that a volume above the break-even point will result in a profit, while a volume below the break-even point will result in a loss. Thus, the break-even point for a product provides valuable information for a manager who must make a yes/no decision concerning production of the product.

Let us now return to the example and show how the profit model in equation (1.5) can be used to compute the break-even point. The break-even point can be found by setting the profit expression equal to zero and solving for the production volume. Using equation (1.5), we have

$$P(x) = -3000 + 3x = 0$$
$$3x = 3000$$
$$x = 1000$$

Figure 1.6

**Graph of the Break-Even Analysis
for the Production Example**

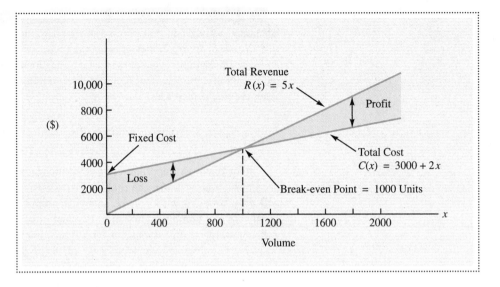

You should now be able to determine
the break-even point for a quantitative
model. Try Problem 15.

With this information, we know that production and sales of the product must be at least 1000 units before a profit can be expected. The graph of the total cost model, the total revenue model, and the location of the break-even point is shown in Figure 1.6.

1.5 Management Science in Practice

In this section we present a brief overview of the management science techniques covered in this text. We will then present the results of surveys that show which techniques have been used most frequently in practice and what needs to be done to enable you to successfully utilize quantitative approaches throughout your career.

Management Science Techniques

The following management science techniques are covered in this text.

Linear Programming   Linear programming is a problem-solving approach that has been developed for situations involving maximizing or minimizing a linear function subject to linear constraints that limit the degree to which the objective can be pursued. The production model developed in Section 1.3 (see Figure 1.5) is an example of a simple linear programming model.

Integer Linear Programming   Integer linear programming is an approach used for problems that can be set up as linear programs with the additional requirement that some or all of the decision recommendations be integer values.

Network Models   A network is a graphical description of a problem consisting of circles called nodes that are interconnected by lines called arcs. Specialized solution procedures exist for these types of problems, enabling us to quickly solve problems in such areas as transportation system design, information system design, and project scheduling.

Project Scheduling: PERT/CPM   In many situations, managers are responsible for planning, scheduling, and controlling projects that consist of numerous separate jobs or tasks performed by a variety of departments, individuals, and so forth. The PERT (Program Evaluation and Review Technique) and CPM (Critical Path Method) techniques help managers carry out their project scheduling responsibilities.

Inventory Models   Inventory models are used by managers faced with the dual problems of maintaining sufficient inventories to meet demand for goods and, at the same time, incurring the lowest possible inventory holding costs.

Waiting-Line or Queueing Models   Waiting-line or queueing models have been developed to help managers understand and make better decisions concerning the operation of systems involving waiting lines.

Computer Simulation   Computer simulation is a technique used to model the operation of a system. This technique employs a computer program to model the operation and perform simulation computations.

Decision Analysis   Decision analysis can be used to determine optimal strategies in situations involving several decision alternatives and an uncertain or risk-filled pattern of events.

Goal Programming   Goal programming is a technique for solving multicriteria decision problems, usually within the framework of linear programming.

Analytic Hierarchy Process   This multicriteria decision-making technique permits the inclusion of subjective factors in arriving at a recommended decision.

Forecasting   Forecasting methods are techniques that can be used to predict future aspects of a business operation.

Markov-Process Models   Markov-process models are useful in studying the evolution of certain systems over repeated trials. For example, Markov processes have been used to describe the probability that a machine, functioning in one period, will function or break down in another period.

Dynamic Programming   Dynamic programming is an approach that allows us to break up a large problem in such a fashion that once all the smaller problems have been solved, we are left with an optimal solution to the large problem.

Methods Used Most Frequently

A study of surveys by Lane, Mansour and Harpell indicated which management science techniques practitioners and educators have found to be the most important and most useful.[2] The three techniques that stand out as consistently being at the top of the list include statistical methods, linear programming, and simulation. The general preferences or ranking of management science methods are shown in Table 1.3. Multicriteria decision

---

[2] M. S. Lane, A. H. Mansour, and J. L. Harpell, "Operations Research Techniques," *Interfaces* 23:2, March–April 1993, pp. 63–68.

Table 1.3

A Ranking of the Importance and Usefulness of Management Science Techniques

Methodology
Statistical Methods
Mathematical Programming Methods
Linear Programming
Integer Linear Programming
Simulation
Network Models (Including PERT/CPM)
Decision Analysis
Waiting Line Models
Inventory Models
Dynamic Programming

problems including goal programming and the analytic hierarchy process, forecasting and Markov-process models were not specifically mentioned in the Lane, Mansour, and Harpell study but are additional management science techniques you will learn about in this text.

In a review of 12 company surveys and three practitioner surveys, Morgan provided further support for linear programming, simulation, and network models including PERT/CPM as being among the most frequently used management science techniques.[3] More importantly, Morgan concluded that (1) any firm just beginning to use management science techniques should locate analysts in functional areas, not in centralized units; (2) the initial use of management science should focus on the more frequently used and more useful techniques; and (3) the barriers to the use of management science can best be removed by increasing the manager's understanding of management science techniques. Furthermore, to gain the confidence and support of top management, MS/OR analysts must learn to sell their approaches and solutions, with particular emphasis placed on improving communications with managers.

Helping to bridge the gap between the manager and the MS/OR analyst is a major focus of this text. As authors and MS/OR practitioners, we want to help develop an understanding of what the management science techniques are, how they are used, and, most importantly, how they can assist managers in making better decisions.

NOTES & comments

1. Operations research analyst is listed by the Bureau of Labor Statistics as one of the fastest growing occupations for careers requiring a bachelor's degree; they predict a growth from 57,000 jobs in 1990 to 100,000 jobs in 2005, an increase of 73%.

2. The Institute for Operations Research and the Management Sciences (INFORMS) and the Decision Sciences Institute (DSI) are two professional societies that publish journals and newsletters dealing with current research and applications of operations research and management science techniques.

---

[3]C.L. Morgan, "A Survey of MS/OR Surveys," *Interfaces* 19:6, November–December 1989, pp. 95–103.

Summary

This is a book about how management science may be used to help managers make better decisions. The focus of this text is on the decision-making process and on the role of management science in that process. We have discussed the problem orientation of this process and in an overview have shown how mathematical models can be used in this type of analysis.

The difference between the model and the situation or managerial problem it represents is an important point. Mathematical models are abstractions of real-world situations and, as such, cannot capture all the aspects of the real situation. However, if a model can capture the major relevant aspects of the problem and can then provide a solution recommendation, it can be a valuable aid to decision making.

One of the characteristics of management science that will become increasingly apparent as we proceed through the text is the search for a best solution to the problem. In carrying out the quantitative analysis, we shall be attempting to develop procedures for finding the "best" or optimal solution.

Glossary

Problem solving The process of identifying a difference between the actual and the desired state of affairs and then taking action to resolve the difference.

Decision making The process of defining the problem, identifying the alternatives, determining the criteria, evaluating the alternatives, and choosing an alternative.

Single-criterion decision problem A problem in which the objective is to find the "best" solution with respect to just one criterion.

Multicriteria decision problem A problem that involves more than one criterion; the objective is to find the "best" solution, taking into account all the criteria.

Decision The alternative selected.

Model A representation of a real object or situation.

Iconic model A physical replica, or representation, of a real object.

Analog model While physical in form, an analog model does not have a physical appearance similar to the real object or situation it represents.

Mathematical model Mathematical symbols and expressions used to represent a real situation.

Constraints Restrictions or limitations imposed on a problem.

Objective function A mathematical expression used to represent the criterion for evaluating solutions to a problem.

Controllable input The decision alternatives or inputs that can be specified by the decision maker.

Decision variable Another term for controllable input.

Uncontrollable input The environmental factors or inputs that cannot be controlled by the decision maker.

Deterministic model A model in which all uncontrollable inputs are known and cannot vary.

Stochastic model A model in which at least one uncontrollable input is uncertain and subject to variation; stochastic models are also referred to as probabilistic models.

Optimal solution The specific decision variable value or values that provide the "best" output for the model.

Feasible solution A decision alternative or solution that satisfies all constraints.

Infeasible solution A decision alternative or solution that violates one or more constraints.

Fixed cost The portion of the total cost that does not depend on the volume; this cost remains the same no matter how much is produced.

Variable cost The portion of the total cost that is dependent on and varies with the volume.

Marginal cost The rate of change of the total cost with respect to volume.

Marginal revenue The rate of change of total revenue with respect to volume.

Break-even point The volume at which total revenue equals total cost.

Problems

1. Define the terms *management science* and *operations research.*
2. Describe the major reasons for the growth in the use of management science since World War II.
3. Discuss the different roles played by the qualitative and quantitative approaches to managerial decision making. Why is it important for a manager or decision maker to have a good understanding of both of these approaches to decision making?
4. **SELF**Test A firm has just completed a new plant that will produce more than 500 different products, using more than 50 different production lines and machines. The production scheduling decisions are critical in that sales will be lost if customer demands are not met on time. If no individual in the firm has had experience with this production operation, and if new production schedules must be generated each week, why should the firm consider a quantitative approach to the production scheduling problem?
5. List and discuss the steps of the decision making process.
6. Give an example of each of the three types of models discussed in this chapter: iconic, analog, and mathematical.
7. What are the advantages of analyzing and experimenting with a model as opposed to a real object or situation?
8. **SELF**Test Recall the production model from Section 1.3:

$$\text{Max} \quad 10x$$

$$\text{s.t.}$$

$$5x \leq 40$$

$$x \geq 0$$

Suppose the firm in this example considers a second product that has a unit profit of \$5 and requires 2 hours for each unit produced. Use y as the number of units of product 2 produced.
   a. Show the mathematical model when both products are considered simultaneously.
   b. Identify the controllable and uncontrollable inputs for this model.
   c. Draw the flowchart of the input–output process for this model (see Figure 1.5).
   d. What are the optimal solution values of x and $y?$
9. Is the model developed in Problem 8 a deterministic or a stochastic model? Explain.
10. Suppose we modify the model in Problem 8 to obtain the following mathematical model:

$$\text{Max} \quad 10x$$

$$\text{s.t.}$$

$$ax \leq 40$$

$$x \geq 0$$

where a is the number of hours required for each unit produced. With $a = 5$, the optimal solution is $x = 8$. If we have a stochastic model with $a = 3$, $a = 4$, $a = 5$, or $a = 6$ as the possible values for the number of hours required per unit, what is the optimal value for $x?$ What problems does this stochastic model cause?
11. A retail store in Des Moines, Iowa, receives shipments of a particular product from Kansas City and Minneapolis. Let

$$x = \text{units of product received from Kansas City}$$
$$y = \text{units of product received from Minneapolis}$$

   a. Write an expression for the total units of product received by the retail store in Des Moines.
   b. Shipments from Kansas City cost \$0.20 per unit, and shipments from Minneapolis cost \$0.25 per unit. Develop an objective function representing the total cost of shipments to Des Moines.

   c. Assuming the monthly demand at the retail store is 5000 units, develop a constraint that requires 5000 units to be shipped to Des Moines.
   d. No more than 4000 units can be shipped from Kansas City, and no more than 3000 units can be shipped from Minneapolis in a month. Develop constraints to model this situation.
   e. Of course, negative amounts cannot be shipped. Combine the objective function and constraints developed to state a mathematical model for satisfying the demand at the Des Moines retail store at minimum cost.

12. Suppose you are going on a weekend trip to a city that is d miles away. Develop a model that determines your round-trip gasoline costs. What assumptions or approximations are necessary to treat this model as a deterministic model? Are these assumptions or approximations acceptable to you?

13. For most products, higher prices result in a decreased demand, whereas lower prices result in an increased demand. Let

$$d = \text{annual demand for a product in units}$$
$$p = \text{price per unit}$$

Assume that a firm accepts the following price–demand relationship as being realistic:

$$d = 800 - 10p$$

where p must be between $20 and $70.
   a. How many units can the firm sell at the $20 per-unit price? At the $70 per-unit price?
   b. Show the mathematical model for the total revenue (TR), which is the annual demand multiplied by the unit price.
   c. Based on other considerations, the firm's management will only consider price alternatives of $30, $40, and $50. Use your model from part (b) to determine the price alternative that will maximize the total revenue.
   d. What are the expected annual demand and the total revenue according to your recommended price?

14. Suppose that a manager has a choice between the following two mathematical models of a given situation: (a) a relatively simple model that is a reasonable approximation of the real situation and (b) a thorough and complex model that is the most accurate mathematical representation of the real situation possible. Why might the model described in part (a) be preferred by the manager?

15. **SELF Test** The O'Neill Shoe Manufacturing Company will produce a special-style shoe if the order size is large enough to provide a reasonable profit. For each special-style order, the company incurs a fixed cost of $1000 for the production setup. The variable cost is $30 per pair, and each pair sells for $40.
   a. Let x indicate the number of pairs of shoes produced. Develop a mathematical model for the total cost of producing x pairs of shoes.
   b. Let P indicate the total profit. Develop a mathematical model for the total profit realized from an order for x pairs of shoes.
   c. How large must the shoe order be before O'Neill will break even?

16. Eastman Publishing Company is considering publishing a paperback textbook on spreadsheet applications for business. The fixed cost of manuscript preparation, textbook design, and production setup is estimated to be $80,000. Variable production and material costs are estimated to be $3 per book. Demand over the life of the book is estimated to be 4000 copies. The publisher plans to sell the text to college and university bookstores for $20 each.
   a. What is the break-even point?
   b. What profit or loss can be anticipated with a demand of 4000 copies?
   c. With a demand of 4000 copies, what is the minimum price per copy that the publisher must charge to break even?
   d. If the publisher believes that the price per copy could be increased to $25.95 and not affect the anticipated demand of 4000 copies, what action would you recommend? What profit or loss can be anticipated?

17. Preliminary plans are underway for the construction of a new stadium for a major league baseball team. City officials have questioned the number and profitability of the luxury corporate boxes planned for the upper deck of the stadium. Corporations and selected individuals may buy the boxes for $100,000 each. The fixed construction cost for the upper-deck area is estimated to be $1,500,000, with a variable cost of $50,000 for each box constructed.

   a. What is the break-even point for the number of luxury boxes in the new stadium?
   b. Preliminary drawings for the stadium show that space is available for the construction of up to 50 luxury boxes. Promoters indicate that buyers are available and that all 50 could be sold if constructed. What is your recommendation concerning the construction of luxury boxes? What profit is anticipated?

18. Financial Analysts, Inc., is an investment firm that manages stock portfolios for a number of clients. A new client has just requested that the firm handle an $80,000 portfolio. As an initial investment strategy, the client would like to restrict the portfolio to a mix of the following two stocks:

Stock	Price/ Share	Estimated Annual Return/Share	Maximum Possible Investment
Oil Alaska	$50	$6	$50,000
Southwest Petroleum	$30	$4	$45,000

   Let

   $$x = \text{number of shares of Oil Alaska}$$
   $$y = \text{number of shares of Southwest Petroleum}$$

   a. Develop the objective function, assuming that the client desires to maximize the total annual return.
   b. Show the mathematical expression for each of the following three constraints:
      (1) Total investment funds available are $80,000.
      (2) Maximum Oil Alaska investment is $50,000.
      (3) Maximum Southwest Petroleum investment is $45,000.

   Note: Adding the $x \geq 0$ and $y \geq 0$ constraints provides a linear programming model for the investment problem. A solution procedure for this model will be discussed in Chapter 2.

19. Models of inventory systems frequently consider the relationships among a beginning inventory, a production quantity, a demand or sales, and an ending inventory. For a given production period j, let

   s_{j-1} = ending inventory from the previous period (beginning inventory for period j)

   x_j = production quantity in period j

   d_j = demand in period j

   s_j = ending inventory for period j

   a. Write the mathematical relationship or model that describes how these four variables are related.
   b. What constraint should be added if production capacity for period j is given by C_j?
   c. What constraint should be added if safety stock requirements for period j mandate an ending inventory of at least I_j?

APPENDIX 1.1   Spreadsheets for Management Science

Spreadsheet software packages, such as Microsoft Excel and Lotus 1-2-3, are growing in popularity and have added capabilities so that they can be used in the application of many of the management science techniques introduced in this text. Generally, the user of the spreadsheet enters data from an application or problem directly into the spreadsheet. Formulas appearing in other cells of the spreadsheet are based on the appropriate quantitative method. The formulas supplemented by built-in functions convert the input data into the desired decision-making information, which is displayed on the spreadsheet.

Spreadsheet applications of Microsoft Excel are presented in appendixes to many chapters in this text, but they are optional. For the interested reader, the appendixes show the development of each spreadsheet application along with one or more examples based on the types of problems encountered in the chapter. If you have access to Microsoft Excel, Lotus 1-2-3, or another spreadsheet package, the appendixes will guide you in developing your own spreadsheet applications of management science. In the following discussion, we introduce spreadsheets by showing how to use Microsoft Excel to conduct the cost, profit, and break-even analysis presented in Section 1.4.

In each spreadsheet application, we will begin by showing a formula spreadsheet with the input data and the appropriate cell formulas clearly identified. Text information used for labels is screened, problem specific data is set in color type, and formulas all begin with an equal sign (=). Figure 1.7 shows the formula spreadsheet for the break-even analysis example. Two columns, labeled A and B, and 20 rows are used. As common to most spreadsheet applications, the cells in the spreadsheet are identified by a column letter and row number.

We first enter the selling price per unit, the fixed cost, the variable cost per unit, and the anticipated volume in cells B3, B6, B7, and B9, respectively. These inputs are shown in color. We then compute total revenue (B14), total cost (B15), profit or loss (B17), and the break-even point (B20), from the user input information. Note the appropriate cell formulas in those cells.

Figure 1.7

Formula Spreadsheet for Break-Even Analysis

	A	B
1	BREAK–EVEN ANALYSIS	
2		
3	SELLING PRICE/UNIT	5
4		
5	COST INFORMATION	
6	FIXED COST	3000
7	VARIABLE COST/UNIT	2
8		
9	VOLUME	500
10		
11		
12	PROFIT (LOSS) SUMMARY	
13		
14	TOTAL REVENUE	=B3*B9
15	TOTAL COST	=B6+B7*B9
16		
17	PROFIT (LOSS)	=B14-B15
18		
19		
20	BREAK–EVEN POINT	=B6 / (B3-B7)

Figure 1.8

Value Spreadsheet for Break-Even Analysis

	A	B
1	BREAK–EVEN ANALYSIS	
2		
3	SELLING PRICE/UNIT	$ 5
4		
5	COST INFORMATION	
6	FIXED COST	$ 3,000
7	VARIABLE COST/UNIT	$ 2
8		
9	VOLUME	500
10		
11		
12	PROFIT (LOSS) SUMMARY	
13		
14	TOTAL REVENUE	$ 2,500
15	TOTAL COST	$ 4,000
16		
17	PROFIT (LOSS)	$ (1,500)
18		
19		
20	BREAK–EVEN POINT	1000

For example, we compute total revenue as the selling price per unit times the volume. Thus, =B3*B9 is the formula for total revenue (see cell B14). The formula for total cost is simply the fixed cost plus the variable cost per unit times the volume. Thus, =B6+B7*B9 is the formula for total cost (see cell B15). The profit or loss formula is =B14−B15, which is the total revenue minus the total cost (see cell B17). The general formula for the break-even point is the fixed cell (B6) divided by the profit per unit (B3−B7), as shown in cell B20.

Figure 1.8 shows the value spreadsheet for this example. In a value spreadsheet each formula is replaced by a computed value. Currency formats are included for the monetary values in column B where appropriate. The volume of 500 units projects a total revenue of $5(500) = $2,500 and a corresponding total cost of $3,000 + $2(500) = $4,000. These results combine to provide a projected loss of $2,500 − $4,000 = ($1,500). Thus a volume of 500 units will result in a loss for the firm. The break-even point shows that the product will not break even until 1000 units are sold.

One big advantage of spreadsheet applications of management science is that we can input changes to the original data and, in effect, ask "what if" questions to learn how the profit, loss, and/or break-even point are affected by the changes. We can try different volumes, selling prices, and/or costs with the spreadsheet, which quickly and easily indicates the impact of these changes on the profitability of the product.

APPENDIX 1.2   The Management Scientist Software

Developments in computer technology have been a major factor in making management science techniques available to decision makers. A software package called *The Management Scientist* has been prepared to accompany this text. Version 4.0 is now available for Windows and Windows 95 systems. This software can be used to solve problems in the text as well as small-scale problems encountered in practice. Using The Management Scientist will give you an understanding and appreciation of the role of the computer in applying management science to decision problems.

The Management Scientist contains twelve modules, or programs, that will enable you to solve problems in the following areas:

Chapter 2–6	Linear programming
Chapter 7	Transportation and assignment
Chapter 8	Integer linear programming
Chapter 9	Shortest route and minimal spanning tree
Chapter 10	PERT/CPM
Chapter 11	Inventory models
Chapter 12	Waiting line models
Chapter 14	Decision analysis
Chapter 16	Forecasting
Chapter 17	Markov processes

Use of The Management Scientist with the text is optional. Occasionally, we insert a figure in the text that shows the output The Management Scientist provides for a problem. However, familiarity with the use of the software is not necessary to understand the figure and the text material. The remainder of this appendix provides an overview of the features and the use of the software.

Selecting a Module

After starting The Management Scientist, you will encounter the module selection screen as shown in Figure 1.9. The choices provide access to the 12 modules. Simply click the desired module and select OK to load the requested module into the computer's memory.

The File Menu

After a module is loaded, you will need to click the File menu to begin working with a problem. The File menu provides the following options.

New Select this option to begin a new problem. Dialog boxes and input templates will guide you through the data input process.

Open Select this option to retrieve a problem that has been previously saved. When the problem is selected it will be displayed on the screen so that you can verify the problem is the one you want to solve.

Figure 1.9

Module Selection Screen for The Management Scientist

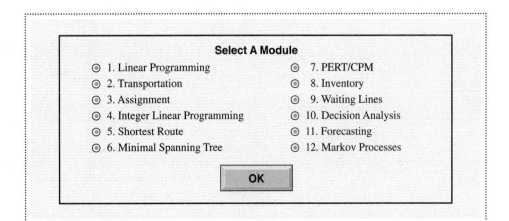

Save Once a new problem has been entered, you may want to save it for future use or modification. The Save option will guide you through the naming and saving process. If you create a folder named Problems, the Open and Save options will take you automatically to the Problems folder.

Change Modules This option returns control to the screen in Figure 1.9 and another module may be selected.

Exit This option will exit The Management Scientist.

The Edit Menu

After a new problem has been solved, you may want to make one or more modifications to the problem before resolving. The Edit menu provides the option to display the problem and then make revisions in the problem before solving or saving. In the linear and integer programming modules, the Edit menu also has options to change the problem size by adding or deleting variables and adding or deleting constraints. Similar options to change the problem size are provided in the Edit menu of the transportation and assignment modules.

The Solution Menu

The Solution menu provides two options.

Solve This option solves the current problem and displays the solution on the screen.

Print Solution Once the solution is on the screen, the Solution menu has the Print Solution option, which sends the solution to a printer or to a text file. If the text file option is used, the file can be accessed later by a word processor so that the solution output may be displayed as part of a solution report.

Advice about Data Input

Any time a new problem is selected, the appropriate module will provide dialog boxes and forms for describing the features of the problem and for entering data. When using The Management Scientist, you may find the following data input suggestions helpful.

1. Do not enter commas (,) with your input data. For example, the value 104,000 should be entered with the six digits: 104000.
2. Do not enter the dollar sign ($) for profit or cost data. For example, a cost of $20.00 should be entered as 20.
3. Do not enter the percent sign (%) if percentage is requested. For example, 25% should be entered as 25, not 25% or .25.
4. Occasionally, a model may be formulated with fractional values such as 1/4, 2/3, 5/6, and so on. The data input for The Management Scientist must be in decimal form. The fraction 1/4 can be entered as .25. However, fractions such as 2/3 and 5/6 have repeating decimal forms. In these cases, we recommend the convention of rounding to five places such as .66667 and .83333.
5. Finally, we recommend that in general you attempt to scale extremely large input data so that smaller numbers may be input and operated on by the computer. For example, costs such as $2,500,000 may be scaled to 2.5 with the understanding that the data used in the problem reflect millions of dollars.

Management Science in Practice Feature

Management Science in Practice write-ups prepared by practitioners are presented at the end of 14 chapters. We feel these provide a meaningful extension to the text material. The purpose of these application write-ups is to provide the reader with a better appreciation for the types of companies that use management science and the types of problems these companies are able to solve.

Each Management Science in Practice write-up begins with a description of the company involved and continues with a discussion of the areas where the company has successfully applied management science. The remainder of the write-up deals with an application that is closely related to the preceding chapter and/or part of the book. An effort has been made to avoid unnecessary technical detail and to focus on the managerial aspects and the value of the results to the company.

Since Chapter 1 is designed to provide an introduction to management science, we have not emphasized any particular solution methodology. Thus, we have placed the Mead Corporation write-up at the end of this first chapter because it provides an overview of several areas in which management science can be used effectively. It is evidence of the impact quantitative approaches to decision making are having at some companies.

MANAGEMENT SCIENCE in practice

Mead Corporation*
Dayton, Ohio

Mead is a major producer of papers for premium periodicals, books, commercial printing, and business forms, with special expertise in coating technologies. The company and its affiliates also produce pulp and lumber, a variety of specialty papers, and converted wood and paper products. Mead is a leader in the design and manufacture of packaging systems for beverage and other consumable markets. The company is a world leader in the production of coated board, and manufactures shipping containers and corrugating medium. Mead is a major manufacturer of paper-based school and office products, and operates a nationwide network of distribution centers for paper, packaging, and supplies.

Management Science at Mead Corporation

Management science applications at Mead are developed and implemented by the company's Decision Analysis (DA) Department. The DA Department provides timely, efficient internal consulting services to the operating groups and corporate staff in the functional areas of operations, finance, marketing, and human resources. The department assists decision makers by providing them with analytical tools of management science as well as personal analysis and recommendations. Through conversations and observations, the department recognizes needs where management science techniques are applicable, and it then recommends appropriate projects. In addition, the department provides a resource reservoir for information and assistance on quantitative methodology and assumes responsibility for keeping current in management science techniques that could produce efficiencies at Mead. This charter results in a variety of projects and applications that span the corporation. Four examples of management science applications at Mead are described here.

A Corporate Planning System

The DA Department built and maintains a corporate planning system. This system allows business units to create and evaluate their five-year plans in an interactive computer environment.

Once the individual business units have finished their planning, the system consolidates the information at a group level. The assumptions of the units and the group are evaluated and reconciled. The use of this computer model facilitates the process by ensuring uniformity of calculations and reporting by all the planning units. Ultimately, the information is consolidated and evaluated at a corporate level.

—Continued on next page

—Continued from previous page

A Timberland Financing Model

Another example of a management science application involves the development of a timberland financing model. Working directly with financial management, analysts assisted in the creation of a deterministic model that considered the major factors in a timberland financing arrangement. The model was used to examine the liability and profitability of timberland acquisition under various assumptions concerning forest growth rates, the inflation rate, and other financial considerations. By using the model, management was able to examine fully the acquisition and modify the financial arrangement as operating conditions warranted. The model is currently operated and modified by financial management and is considered a major tool in the examination of timberland financing.

Inventory Analysis

Inventory analysis is an area in which more sophisticated tools of management science have been used. Simulation models have been used to describe the major factors (e.g., demand or usage rates, lead times, and production rates) in an inventory system. Typically, an inventory model includes purchase, storage, ordering, stockout, and degradation costs. The simulation model is used to evaluate reorder points, safety stocks, customer service levels, review periods, and the response time of the inventory system to extraordinary events.

Once developed and in place, the model can be updated as economic and operating conditions change. Thus, the model can be used by management to evaluate its inventory system on an ongoing basis and to ensure that it is operating in a cost-efficient manner. These inventory simulation models are user friendly and can be operated and maintained by management with little formal computer training.

A Timber Harvesting Model

Mead also uses models to assist with the long-range management of the company's timberland. Through the use of large-scale linear programs, timber harvesting plans have been developed to cover a substantial time horizon. These models consider wood market conditions, mill pulpwood requirements, harvesting capacities, and general forest management principles. Within these constraints, the model develops an optimal harvesting and purchasing schedule based on discounted cash flow. Alternative schedules are developed to reflect various assumptions concerning forest growth, wood availability, and general economic conditions.

Quantitative methods are also used in the development of the inputs for the linear programming models already described. Timber prices and supplies as well as mill requirements must be forecast over the time horizon. Advanced sampling techniques are used to evaluate land holdings and to project forest growth. The harvest schedule is developed through the use of a number of management science techniques.

Summary

The applications briefly described here—although only a few of the many management science projects at Mead—convey the breadth of the activities currently in use within the company. The management scientist at Mead must be able to work in a number of different environments and be proficient in a wide range of quantitative methods. In addition, the analyst must possess exceptional oral and written communication skills. Only with this background will the analyst be able to achieve the major objective of management science at Mead—the development and implementation of user-friendly quantitative models that will support and enhance management decision making throughout the organization.

Questions

1. Which techniques listed in Table 1.3 are being used in the four management science applications described at the Mead Corporation?
2. Which of the Mead applications use a deterministic model, and which use a stochastic model? What conditions in the applications indicate a stochastic model is necessary?
3. Discuss how quantitative analysis described in Section 1.3 occurs in Mead's inventory analysis application.
4. Discuss the benefits associated with the management science applications at Mead.

....

*The authors are indebted to Dr. Edward P. Winkofsky, Mead Corporation, Dayton, Ohio, for providing this application.

two

Linear Programming: The Graphical Method

Linear programming is a problem-solving approach that has been developed to help managers make decisions. The following situations describe some typical applications of linear programming:

1. A manufacturer wants to develop a production schedule and an inventory policy that will satisfy sales demand in future periods. Ideally, the schedule and policy will enable the company to satisfy demand and at the same time *minimize* the total production and inventory costs.
2. A financial analyst must select an investment portfolio from a variety of stock and bond investment alternatives. The analyst would like to establish the portfolio that *maximizes* the return on investment.
3. A marketing manager wants to determine how best to allocate a fixed advertising budget among alternative advertising media such as radio, television, newspaper, and magazine. The manager would like to determine the media mix that *maximizes* advertising effectiveness.
4. A company has warehouses in a number of locations throughout the United States. Given a set of customer demands for its products, the company would like to determine which warehouse should ship how much product to which customers in order to *minimize* total transportation costs.

These are only a few examples of situations where linear programming has been used successfully, but they illustrate the diversity of linear programming applications. A close scrutiny reveals one basic property they all have in common. In each example, we were concerned with *maximizing* or *minimizing* some quantity. We wanted to minimize costs in example 1, we wanted to maximize return on investment in example 2, we wanted to maximize advertising effectiveness in example 3, and we wanted to minimize total transportation costs in example 4. *In all linear programming problems, the maximization or minimization of some quantity is the objective.*

Table 2.1

Production Requirements per Golf Bag

Perando

		Production Time (hours)			
Product		Cutting and Dyeing	Sewing	Finishing	Inspection and Packaging
Standard bag		$7/10$	$1/2$	1	$1/10$
Deluxe bag		1	$5/6$	$2/3$	$1/4$

A second property of all linear programming problems is restrictions or *constraints* that limit the degree to which the objective can be pursued. In example 1 the manufacturer is restricted by constraints requiring product demand to be satisfied and by the constraints limiting production capacity. The financial analyst's portfolio problem is constrained by the total amount of investment funds available and the maximum amounts that can be invested in each stock or bond. The marketing manager's media selection decision is constrained by a fixed advertising budget and the availability of the various media. In the transportation problem, the minimum-cost shipping schedule is constrained by the supply of product available at each warehouse. *Thus, constraints are another general feature of every linear programming problem.*

2.1 A Simple Maximization Problem

Par, Inc., is a small manufacturer of golf equipment and supplies whose management has decided to move into the market for medium- and high-priced golf bags. Par's distributor is enthusiastic about the new product line and has agreed to buy all the golf bags Par produces over the next 3 months.

After a thorough investigation of the steps involved in manufacturing a golf bag, management has determined that each golf bag produced will require the following operations:

1. Cutting and dyeing the material
2. Sewing
3. Finishing (inserting umbrella holder, club separators, etc.)
4. Inspection and packaging

The director of manufacturing has analyzed each of the operations and concluded that if the company produces a medium-priced standard model, each bag will require $7/10$ hour in the cutting and dyeing department, $1/2$ hour in the sewing department, 1 hour in the finishing department, and $1/10$ hour in the inspection and packaging department. The more expensive deluxe model will require 1 hour for cutting and dyeing, $5/6$ hour for sewing, $2/3$ hour for finishing, and $1/4$ hour for inspection and packaging. This production information is summarized in Table 2.1.

The accounting department has analyzed these production figures, assigned all relevant variable costs, and arrived at prices for both bags that will result in a profit contribution[1] of $10 for every standard bag and $9 for every deluxe bag produced.

---

[1] From an accounting perspective, this is more correctly described as the contribution margin per bag; for example, overhead and other shared costs have not been allocated.

In addition, after studying departmental work load projections, the director of manufacturing estimates that 630 hours for cutting and dyeing, 600 hours for sewing, 708 hours for finishing, and 135 hours for inspection and packaging will be available for the production of golf bags during the next 3 months.

The company's problem is to determine how many standard and deluxe bags it should produce to maximize the total profit contribution. If you were in charge of production scheduling for Par, Inc., what decision would you make? That is, how many standard and how many deluxe bags would you produce in the next 3 months? Write your decision below. Later you can check and see how well you did.

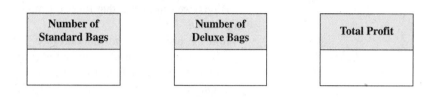

Number of Standard Bags	Number of Deluxe Bags	Total Profit

The Objective Function

Every linear programming problem has a maximization or minimization objective. For the Par problem, the objective is to maximize the total profit contribution. We can write this objective in mathematical form with the introduction of some simple notation. Let

$$x_1 = \text{number of standard bags Par, Inc., produces}$$
$$x_2 = \text{number of deluxe bags Par, Inc., produces}$$

Par's profit contribution will come from two sources: (1) the profit contribution made by producing x_1 standard bags and (2) the profit contribution made by producing x_2 deluxe bags. Since Par makes $10 for every standard bag produced, the company will make $10x_1$ if x_1 standard bags are produced. Also, since Par makes $9 for every deluxe bag produced, the company will make $9x_2$ if x_2 deluxe bags are produced. Denoting the total profit contribution by z, we have

$$\text{Total profit contribution} = z = \$10x_1 + \$9x_2$$

From now on we will assume that the profit contribution is measured in dollars and write the total profit contribution expression without the dollar signs. That is,

$$\text{Total profit contribution} = z = 10x_1 + 9x_2 \tag{2.1}$$

Par's problem can now be stated as one of choosing values for the variables x_1 and x_2 that will yield the highest possible value of z. In linear programming terminology, we refer to x_1 and x_2 as the *decision variables*. Since the objective—maximize total profit contribution—is a function of these decision variables, we refer to $10x_1 + 9x_2$ as the *objective function*. Using max as an abbreviation for maximize, Par's objective is written as follows:

$$\text{max } z = \text{max } 10x_1 + 9x_2 \tag{2.2}$$

In this problem, any particular production combination of standard and deluxe bags is referred to as a *solution* to the problem. However, only those solutions that satisfy *all* the constraints are referred to as *feasible solutions*. The particular feasible production combination (feasible solution) that results in the largest profit contribution will be referred to as the *optimal* production combination or, equivalently, as the *optimal solution.* At this point, however, we have no idea what the optimal solution will be. Indeed, we have not even developed a procedure for identifying feasible solutions. The procedure for determining feasible solutions requires us first to identify all the constraints of the problem.

The Constraints

Every standard and deluxe bag produced must go through four manufacturing operations. Since there is a limited amount of production time available for each of these operations, we can expect that four constraints will limit the total number of golf bags Par can produce.

From the production information (see Table 2.1), we know that every standard bag Par manufactures will use $7/10$ hour for cutting and dyeing. Hence, the total number of hours of cutting and dyeing time used in the manufacture of x_1 standard bags will be $7/10 x_1$. On the other hand, every deluxe bag Par produces will use 1 hour for cutting and dyeing; thus, x_2 deluxe bags will use $1x_2$ hours of cutting and dyeing time. The total cutting and dyeing time required for the production of x_1 standard bags and x_2 deluxe bags is given by

$$\text{Total cutting and dyeing time required} = 7/10\, x_1 + 1x_2$$

Since the director of manufacturing has stated that Par has at most 630 hours of cutting and dyeing time available, it follows that the product combination we select must satisfy the requirement

$$7/10\, x_1 + 1x_2 \leq 630 \tag{2.3}$$

where the symbol $\leq$ means *less than or equal to*. Relationship (2.3) is referred to as an inequality and denotes the fact that the total number of hours used for the cutting and dyeing operation in the production of x_1 standard bags and x_2 deluxe bags must be less than or equal to the maximum amount of cutting and dyeing time the company has available.

From Table 2.1 we also see that every standard bag manufactured will require $1/2$ hour for sewing and every deluxe bag will require $5/6$ hour for sewing. Since there are 600 hours of sewing time available, it follows that

$$1/2\, x_1 + 5/6\, x_2 \leq 600 \tag{2.4}$$

is the mathematical representation of the sewing constraint. Verify for yourself that the constraint for the finishing time available is

$$1x_1 + 2/3\, x_2 \leq 708 \tag{2.5}$$

and that the constraint for the inspection and packaging time available is

$$1/10\, x_1 + 1/4\, x_2 \leq 135 \tag{2.6}$$

We now have specified the mathematical relationships for the constraints associated with the four production operations. Are there any other constraints we have forgotten? Can Par produce a negative number of standard or deluxe bags? Clearly, the answer is no. Thus, to prevent the decision variables x_1 and x_2 from having negative values, two constraints

$$x_1 \geq 0 \quad \text{and} \quad x_2 \geq 0 \tag{2.7}$$

must be added. The symbol $\geq$ means *greater than or equal to*. These constraints ensure that the solution to the problem will contain nonnegative values for the decision variables and are thus referred to as the *nonnegativity constraints*. Nonnegativity constraints are a general feature of all linear programming problems and will be written in the following abbreviated form:

$$x_1, x_2 \geq 0$$

Mathematical Statement of the Par, Inc., Problem

You should be able to formulate a mathematical model for a maximization linear programming problem with less-than-or-equal-to constraints. Try Problem 22(a).

The mathematical statement or mathematical formulation of the Par, Inc., problem is now complete. We have succeeded in translating the objective and constraints of the problem into a set of mathematical relationships referred to as a *mathematical model*. The complete mathematical model for the Par problem is as follows:

$$\text{Max} \quad 10x_1 + 9x_2$$

subject to (s.t.)

$$\begin{array}{ll} \tfrac{7}{10}x_1 + 1x_2 \leq 630 & \text{Cutting and dyeing} \\ \tfrac{1}{2}x_1 + \tfrac{5}{6}x_2 \leq 600 & \text{Sewing} \\ 1x_1 + \tfrac{2}{3}x_2 \leq 708 & \text{Finishing} \\ \tfrac{1}{10}x_1 + \tfrac{1}{4}x_2 \leq 135 & \text{Inspection and packaging} \\ x_1, x_2 \geq 0 \end{array}$$

Our job now is to find the product mix (i.e., the combination of x_1 and x_2) that satisfies all the constraints and, at the same time, yields a value for the objective function that is greater than or equal to the value given by any other feasible solution. Once this is done, we will have found the optimal solution to the problem.

This mathematical model of the Par problem is a *linear program*. The problem has the objective and constraints that, as we said earlier, are common properties of all *linear programs*. But what is the special feature of this mathematical model that makes it a linear program? The special feature that makes it a linear program is that the objective function and all constraint functions (the left-hand sides of the constraint inequalities) are linear functions of the decision variables.

Mathematical functions in which each variable appears in a separate term and is raised to the first power are called *linear functions*. The objective function ($10x_1 + 9x_2$) is linear since each decision variable appears in a separate term and has an exponent of 1. If the objective function had appeared as $10x_1^2 + 9\sqrt{x_2}$, it would not have been a linear function, and we would not have a linear program. The amount of production time required in the cutting and dyeing department ($\tfrac{7}{10}x_1 + 1x_2$) is also a linear function of the decision variables for the same reason. Similarly, the functions on the left-hand side of all the constraint inequalities (the constraint functions) are linear functions. Thus, the mathematical formulation of this problem is referred to as a linear program.

You should now be able to recognize the types of mathematical relationships that can be found in a linear program. Try Problem 1.

Linear *programming* has nothing to do with computer programming. The use of the word *programming* here means "choosing a course of action." Linear programming involves choosing a course of action when the mathematical model of the problem contains only linear functions.

NOTES &comments

1. The three assumptions necessary for a linear programming model to be appropriate are proportionality, additivity, and divisibility. *Proportionality* means that the contribution to the objective function and the amount of resources used in each constraint are proportional to the value of each decision variable. *Additivity* means that the value of the objective function and the total resources used can be found by summing the objective function contribution and the resources used for all decision variables. *Divisibility* means that the decision variables are continuous. The divisibility assumption plus the nonnegativity constraints mean that decision variables can take on any value greater than or equal to zero.

2. Management scientists formulate and solve a variety of mathematical models that contain an objective function and a set of constraints. Models of this type are referred to as *mathematical programming models.* Linear programming models are a special type of mathematical programming model in that the objective function and all constraint functions are linear.

2.2 Graphical Solution

A linear programming problem involving only two decision variables can be solved using a graphical solution procedure. Let us begin the graphical solution procedure by developing a graph that displays the possible solutions (x_1 and x_2 values) for the Par problem. The graph (Figure 2.1) will have values of x_1 on the horizontal axis and values of x_2 on the vertical axis. Any point on the graph can be identified by the x_1 and x_2 values, which indicate the position of the point along the x_1 and x_2 axes, respectively. Since every point (x_1, x_2) corresponds to a possible solution, every point on the graph is called a *solution point.* The solution point where $x_1 = 0$ and $x_2 = 0$ is referred to as the origin.

The next step is to determine which of the solution points corresponds to feasible solutions for the linear program. Both x_1 and x_2 are required to be nonnegative, so we need only consider that portion of the graph where $x_1 \geq 0$ and $x_2 \geq 0$. In Figure 2.2 the arrows point to the portion of the solution region where these nonnegativity requirements are satisfied. Since linear programming decision variables are always required to be nonnegative, all future graphs will show only the portion of the solution region corresponding to nonnegative values for the decision variables.

Earlier, we saw that the inequality representing the cutting and dyeing constraint is

$$7/_{10}\, x_1 + 1x_2 \leq 630$$

To show all solution points that satisfy this relationship, we start by graphing the solution points satisfying the constraint as an equality. That is, the points where $7/_{10}\, x_1 + 1x_2 = 630$. Since the graph of this equation is a line, it can be obtained by identifying two points that satisfy the equation and then drawing a line through the points. Setting $x_1 = 0$ and solving for x_2, we see that the point ($x_1 = 0$, $x_2 = 630$) satisfies the above equation. To find a second point satisfying this equation, we set $x_2 = 0$ and solve for x_1. By doing this, we obtain $7/_{10}\, x_1 + 1(0) = 630$, or $x_1 = 900$. Thus, a second point satisfying the equation is

Figure 2.1

Solution Points for the Two-Variable Par, Inc., Problem

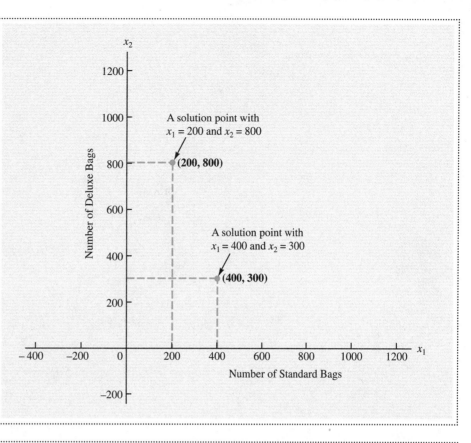

Figure 2.2

The Nonnegativity Constraints

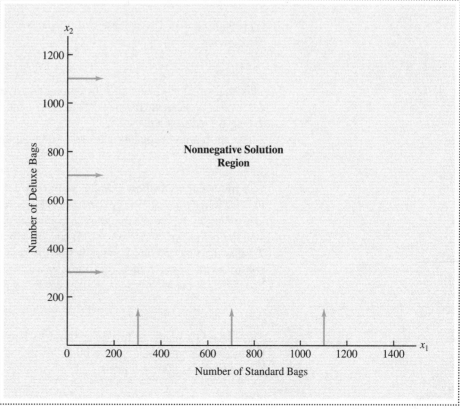

Figure 2.3
....

The Cutting and Dyeing Constraint Line

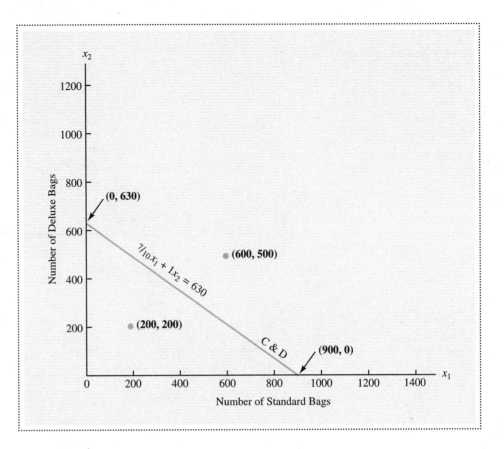

$(x_1 = 900, x_2 = 0)$. Given these two points, we can now graph the line corresponding to the equation

$$\tfrac{7}{10} x_1 + 1x_2 = 630$$

This line, which will be called the cutting and dyeing *constraint line,* is shown in Figure 2.3. We have labeled this line "C & D" to indicate that it represents the cutting and dyeing constraint line.

Recall that the inequality representing the cutting and dyeing constraint is

$$\tfrac{7}{10} x_1 + 1x_2 \leq 630$$

Can you identify all of the solution points that satisfy this constraint? Since all points on the line satisfy $\tfrac{7}{10} x_1 + 1x_2 = 630$, we know any point on this line must satisfy the constraint. But where are the solution points satisfying $\tfrac{7}{10} x_1 + 1x_2 < 630$? Consider two solution points: $(x_1 = 200, x_2 = 200)$ and $(x_1 = 600, x_2 = 500)$. You can see from Figure 2.3 that the first solution point is below the constraint line and the second is above the constraint line. Which of these solutions will satisfy the cutting and dyeing constraint? For the point $(x_1 = 200, x_2 = 200)$, we see that

$$\tfrac{7}{10} x_1 + 1x_2 = \tfrac{7}{10}(200) + 1(200) = 340$$

Since the 340 hours is less than the 630 hours available, the $(x_1 = 200, x_2 = 200)$ production combination, or solution point, satisfies the constraint. For the point $(x_1 = 600, x_2 = 500)$, we have

$$\tfrac{7}{10} x_1 + 1x_2 = \tfrac{7}{10}(600) + 1(500) = 920$$

Figure 2.4

Feasible Solutions for the Cutting and Dyeing Constraint Are Represented by the Shaded Region

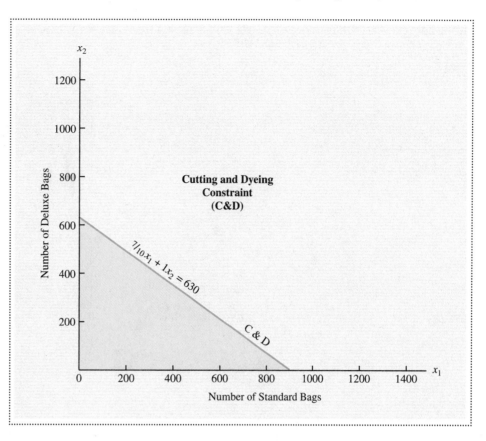

You should now be able to graph a constraint line and find the solution points that are feasible. Try Problem 2.

The 920 hours is greater than the 630 hours available, so the ($x_1 = 600$, $x_2 = 500$) solution point does not satisfy the constraint and is thus not feasible.

If a solution point is not feasible for a particular constraint, then all other solution points on the same side of that constraint line are not feasible. If a solution point is feasible for a particular constraint, then all other solution points on the same side of the constraint line are feasible for that constraint. Thus, one needs to evaluate the constraint function for only one solution point to determine which side of a constraint line is feasible. In Figure 2.4 we indicate all points satisfying the cutting and dyeing constraint by the shaded region.

We continue by identifying the solution points satisfying each of the other three constraints. The solutions that are feasible for each of these constraints are shown in Figure 2.5.

We now have four separate graphs showing the feasible solution points for each of the four constraints. In a linear programming problem, we need to identify the solution points that satisfy *all* the constraints *simultaneously*. To find these solution points, we can draw all four constraints on one graph and observe the region containing the points that do in fact satisfy all the constraints simultaneously.

You should now be able to find the feasible region given several constraints. Try Problem 7.

The graphs in Figures 2.4 and 2.5 can be superimposed to obtain one graph with all four constraints. This combined-constraint graph is shown in Figure 2.6. The shaded region in this figure includes every solution point that satisfies all the constraints simultaneously. Since solutions that satisfy all the constraints are termed *feasible solutions,* the shaded region is called the feasible solution region, or simply the *feasible region.* Any point on the boundary of the feasible region or within the feasible region is a *feasible solution point.*

Figure 2.5   Feasible Solutions for the Sewing, Finishing, and Inspection and Packaging Constraints Are Represented by the Shaded Regions

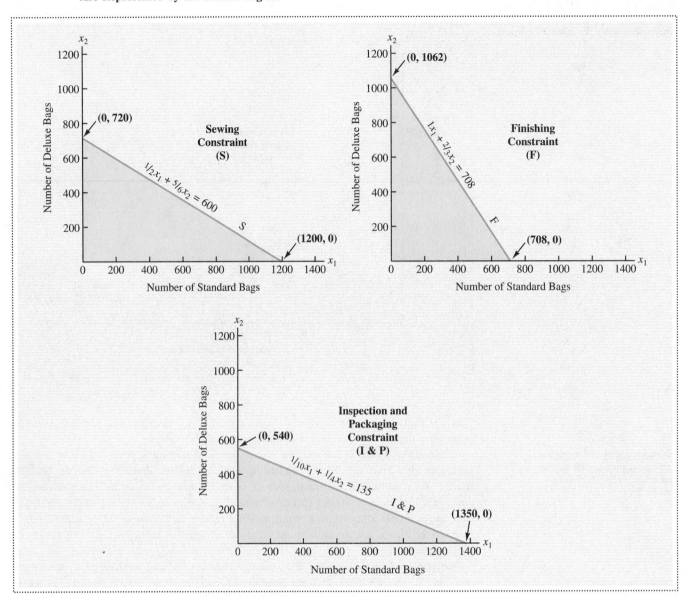

Now that we have identified the feasible region, we are ready to proceed with the graphical solution procedure and find the optimal solution to the Par, Inc., problem. Recall that the optimal solution for a linear programming problem is the feasible solution that provides the best possible value of the objective function. Let us start the optimizing step of the graphical solution procedure by redrawing the feasible region on a separate graph. The graph is shown in Figure 2.7.

One approach to finding the optimal solution would be to evaluate the objective function for each feasible solution; the optimal solution would then be the one yielding the largest value. The difficulty with this approach is that there are an infinite number of feasible solutions; thus, since it is not possible to evaluate an infinity of feasible solutions, this trial-and-error procedure cannot be used to identify the optimal solution.

Figure 2.6

Combined-Constraint Graph Showing the Feasible Solution Region for the Par, Inc., Problem

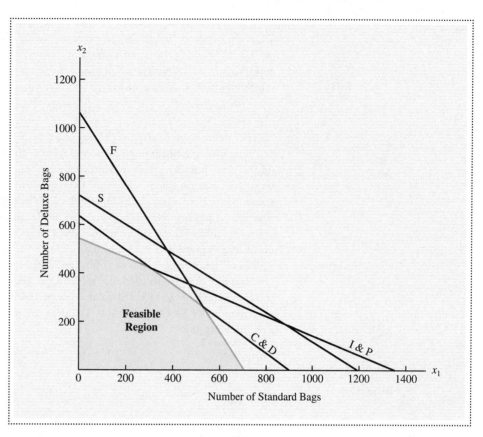

Figure 2.7

Feasible Solution Region for the Par, Inc., Problem

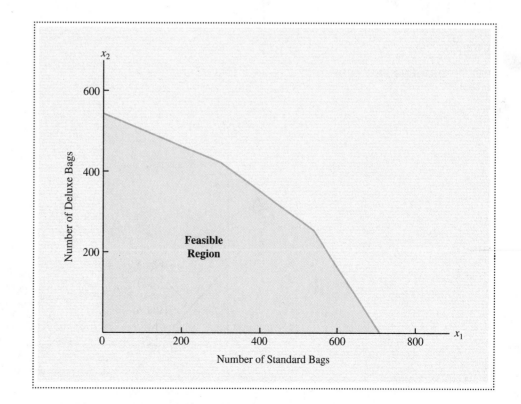

Rather than trying to compute the profit contribution for each feasible solution, we select an arbitrary value for profit contribution and identify all the feasible solutions (x_1, x_2) that yield the selected value. For example, what feasible solutions provide a profit contribution of $1800? These solutions are given by the values of x_1 and x_2 in the feasible region that will make the objective function

$$10x_1 + 9x_2 = 1800$$

This expression is simply the equation of a line. Thus, all feasible solution points (x_1, x_2) yielding a profit contribution of $1800 must be on the line. We learned earlier in this section how to graph a constraint line. The procedure for graphing the profit or objective function line is the same. Letting $x_1 = 0$, we see that x_2 must be 200; thus, the solution point $(x_1 = 0, x_2 = 200)$ is on the line. Similarly, by letting $x_2 = 0$, we see that the solution point $(x_1 = 180, x_2 = 0)$ is also on the line. Drawing the line through these two points identifies all the solutions that have a profit contribution of $1800. A graph of this profit line is presented in Figure 2.8.

Since the objective is to find the feasible solution yielding the largest profit contribution, let us proceed by selecting higher profit contributions and finding the solutions yielding the selected values. For instance, let us find all solutions yielding profit contributions of $3600 and $5400. To do so, we must find the x_1 and x_2 values that are on the following lines:

$$10x_1 + 9x_2 = 3600$$

and

$$10x_1 + 9x_2 = 5400$$

Using the previous procedure for graphing profit and constraint lines, we have drawn the $3600 and $5400 profit lines on the graph in Figure 2.9. While not all solution points

Figure 2.8
. . . .
$1800 Profit Line for the Par, Inc., Problem

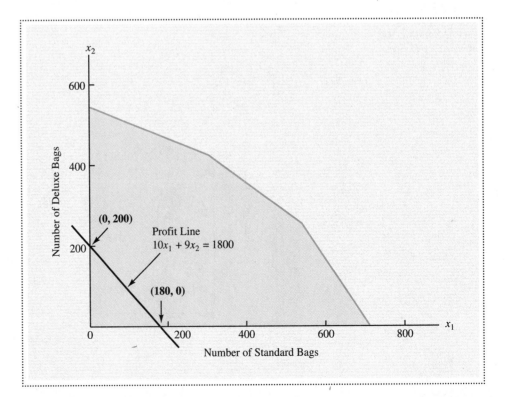

on the $5400 profit line are in the feasible region, at least some points on the line are, and it is therefore possible to obtain a feasible solution that provides a $5400 profit contribution.

Can we find a feasible solution yielding an even higher profit contribution? Look at Figure 2.9, and see what general observations you can make about the profit lines already drawn. Note the following: (1) the profit lines are *parallel* to each other, and (2) higher profit lines are obtained as we move farther from the origin. This can also be seen algebraically. Let z represent total profit. The objective function is

$$z = 10x_1 + 9x_2$$

Solving for x_2 in terms of x_1 and z, we obtain

$$9x_2 = -10x_1 + z$$

$$x_2 = -\tfrac{10}{9}x_1 + \tfrac{1}{9}z \qquad (2.8)$$

Equation (2.8) is the *slope–intercept form* of the linear equation relating x_1 and x_2. The coefficient of x_1, $-\tfrac{10}{9}$, is the slope of the line, and the term $\tfrac{1}{9}z$ is the x_2 intercept (i.e., the value of x_2 where the graph of equation (2.8) crosses the x_2 axis). Substituting the profit contributions of $z = 1800$, $z = 3600$, and $z = 5400$ into equation (2.8) yields the following slope–intercept equations for the profit lines shown in Figure 2.9:

For $z = 1800$,

$$x_2 = -\tfrac{10}{9}x_1 + 200$$

For $z = 3600$,

$$x_2 = -\tfrac{10}{9}x_1 + 400$$

For $z = 5400$,

$$x_2 = -\tfrac{10}{9}x_1 + 600$$

Figure 2.9

Selected Profit Lines for the Par, Inc., Problem

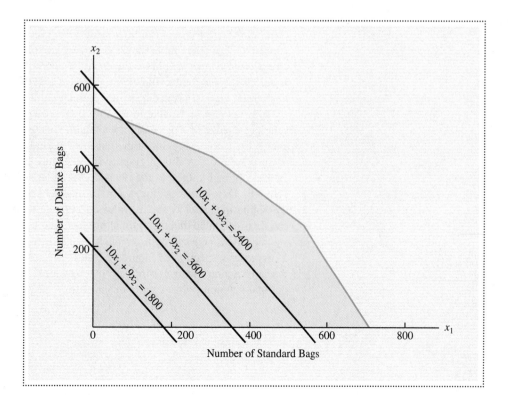

Figure 2.10

Optimal Solution for the Par, Inc., Problem

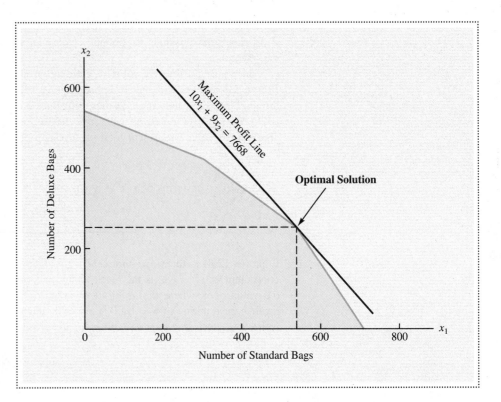

Can you graph the profit line for a linear program? Try Problem 6.

The slope $(-10/9)$ is the same for each profit line since the profit lines are parallel. Further, we see that the x_2 intercept increases with larger profit contributions. Thus, higher profit lines are farther from the origin.

Because the profit lines are parallel and higher profit lines are farther from the origin, we can obtain solutions that yield increasingly larger values for the objective function by continuing to move the profit line farther from the origin in such a fashion that it remains parallel to the other profit lines. However, at some point we will find that any further outward movement will place the profit line completely outside the feasible region. Since solutions outside the feasible region are unacceptable, the point in the feasible region that lies on the highest profit line is the optimal solution to the linear program.

You should now be able to identify the optimal solution point for this problem. Use a ruler or the edge of a piece of paper, and move the profit line as far from the origin as you can. What is the last point in the feasible region that you reach? This point, which is the optimal solution, is shown graphically in Figure 2.10.

The optimal values of the decision variables are the x_1 and x_2 values at the optimal solution. Depending on the accuracy of the graph, you may or may not be able to determine the *exact* x_1 and x_2 values. Referring to the graph in Figure 2.10, the best we can do is conclude that the optimal production combination consists of approximately 550 standard bags (x_1) and approximately 250 deluxe bags (x_2).

A closer inspection of Figures 2.6 and 2.10 shows that the optimal solution point is at the intersection of the cutting and dyeing and the finishing constraint lines. That is, the optimal solution point is on both the cutting and dyeing constraint line

$$\tfrac{7}{10} x_1 + 1x_2 = 630 \tag{2.9}$$

and the finishing constraint line

$$1x_1 + \tfrac{2}{3} x_2 = 708 \tag{2.10}$$

Thus, the optimal values of the decision variables x_1 and x_2 must satisfy both equations (2.9) and (2.10) simultaneously. Using equation (2.9) and solving for x_1 gives

$$\tfrac{7}{10} x_1 = 630 - 1x_2$$

or

$$x_1 = 900 - \tfrac{10}{7} x_2 \tag{2.11}$$

Substituting this expression for x_1 into equation (2.10) and solving for x_2 provides the following:

$$1(900 - \tfrac{10}{7} x_2) + \tfrac{2}{3} x_2 = 708$$

$$900 - \tfrac{10}{7} x_2 + \tfrac{2}{3} x_2 = 708$$

$$900 - \tfrac{30}{21} x_2 + \tfrac{14}{21} x_2 = 708$$

$$-\tfrac{16}{21} x_2 = -192$$

$$x_2 = \frac{192}{\tfrac{16}{21}} = 252$$

Using $x_2 = 252$ in equation (2.11) and solving for x_1, we obtain

$$x_1 = 900 - \tfrac{10}{7}(252)$$

$$= 900 - 360 = 540$$

The exact location of the optimal solution point is $x_1 = 540$ and $x_2 = 252$. Hence, the optimal production quantities for Par, Inc., are 540 standard bags and 252 deluxe bags, with a resulting profit contribution of $10(540) + 9(252) = \$7668$.

For a linear programming problem with two decision variables, the exact values of the decision variables can be determined by first using the graphical solution procedure to identify the optimal solution point and then solving the two simultaneous constraint equations associated with it.

You should now be able to use the graphical solution procedure to identify the optimal solution and find the exact values of the decision variables at the optimal solution. Try Problem 11.

A Note on Graphing Lines

An important aspect of the graphical method is the ability to graph lines showing the constraints and the objective function of the linear program. The procedure we have used for graphing the equation of a line is to find any two points satisfying the equation and then draw the line through the two points. For the Par, Inc., constraints, the two points were easily found by first setting $x_1 = 0$ and solving the constraint equation for x_2. Then we set $x_2 = 0$ and solved for x_1. For the cutting and dyeing constraint line

$$\tfrac{7}{10} x_1 + 1x_2 = 630$$

this procedure identified the two points ($x_1 = 0$, $x_2 = 630$) and ($x_1 = 900$, $x_2 = 0$). The cutting and dyeing constraint line was then graphed by drawing a line through these two points.

All constraint and objective function lines in two-variable linear programs can be graphed if two points on the line can be identified. However, finding the two points on the line is not always as easy as shown in the Par, Inc., problem. For example, consider the following constraint:

$$2x_1 - 1x_2 \leq 100$$

Figure 2.11

Feasible Solutions for the Constraint
$2x_1 - 1x_2 \leq 100$

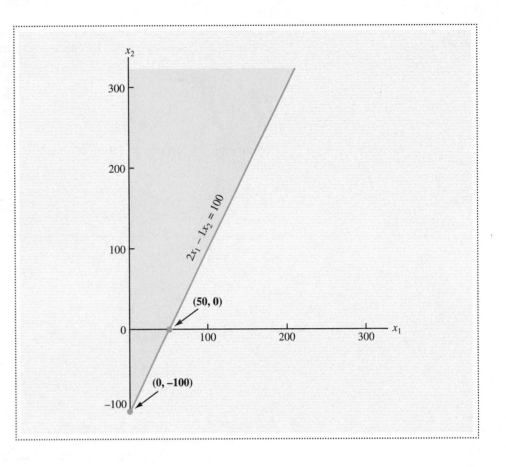

Using the equality form and setting $x_1 = 0$, we find the point ($x_1 = 0$, $x_2 = -100$) is on the constraint line. Setting $x_2 = 0$, we find a second point ($x_1 = 50$, $x_2 = 0$) on the constraint line. If we have drawn only the nonnegative ($x_1 \geq 0$, $x_2 \geq 0$) portion of the graph, the first point ($x_1 = 0$, $x_2 = -100$) cannot be plotted because $x_2 = -100$ is not on the graph. Whenever we have two points on the line, but one or both of the points cannot be plotted in the nonnegative portion of the graph, the simplest approach is to enlarge the graph to include the negative x_1 and/or x_2 axes. In this example, the point ($x_1 = 0$, $x_2 = -100$) can be plotted by extending the graph to include the negative x_2 axis. Once both points satisfying the constraint equation have been located, the line can be drawn. The constraint line and the feasible solutions for the constraint $2x_1 - 1x_2 \leq 100$ are shown in Figure 2.11.

As another example, let us consider a constraint of the form

$$1x_1 - 1x_2 \geq 0$$

To find all solutions satisfying the constraint as an equality, we first set $x_1 = 0$ and solve for x_2. This shows that the origin ($x_1 = 0$, $x_2 = 0$) is on the constraint line. Setting $x_2 = 0$ and solving for x_1 provides the same point. However, we can obtain a second point on the line by setting x_2 equal to any value other than zero and then solving for x_1. For instance, setting $x_2 = 100$ and solving for x_1, we find that the point ($x_1 = 100$, $x_2 = 100$) is on the line. With the two points ($x_1 = 0$, $x_2 = 0$) and ($x_1 = 100$, $x_2 = 100$), the constraint line $1x_1 - 1x_2 = 0$ and the feasible solutions for $1x_1 - 1x_2 \geq 0$ can be plotted as shown in Figure 2.12.

Figure 2.12

Feasible Solutions for the Constraint
$1x_1 - 1x_2 \geq 0$

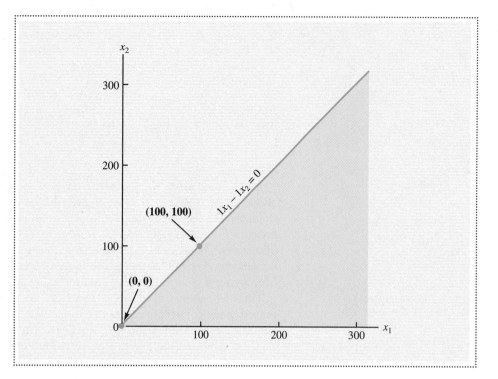

Summary of the Graphical Solution Procedure for Maximization Problems

As we have seen, the graphical solution procedure is a method for solving two-variable linear programming problems such as the Par, Inc., problem. The steps of the graphical solution procedure for a maximization problem are summarized here:

As additional practice in using the graphical solution procedure, try Problem 22(b), 22(c), and 22(d).

1. Prepare a graph of the feasible solutions for each of the constraints.
2. Determine the feasible region by identifying the solutions that satisfy all the constraints simultaneously.
3. Draw an objective function line showing the values of the x_1 and x_2 variables that yield a specified value of the objective function.
4. Move parallel objective function lines toward larger objective function values until further movement would take the line completely outside the feasible region.
5. Any feasible solution on the objective function line with the largest value is an optimal solution.

Slack Variables

In addition to the optimal solution and its associated profit contribution, Par's management will probably want information about the production time requirements for each production operation. We can determine this information by substituting the optimal solution values ($x_1 = 540, x_2 = 252$) into the constraints of the linear program.

Constraint	Hours Required for $x_1 = 540$ and $x_2 = 252$	Hours Available	Unused Hours
Cutting and dyeing	$7/10(540) + 1(252) = 630$	630	0
Sewing	$1/2(540) + 5/6(252) = 480$	600	120
Finishing	$1(540) + 2/3(252) = 708$	708	0
Inspection and packaging	$1/10(540) + 1/4(252) = 117$	135	18

Thus, the complete solution tells management that the production of 540 standard bags and 252 deluxe bags will require all available cutting and dyeing time (630 hours) and all available finishing time (708 hours), while 120 hours of sewing time (600 − 480) and 18 hours of inspection and packaging time (135 − 117) will remain idle. The 120 hours of unused sewing time and 18 hours of unused inspection and packaging time are referred to as *slack* for the two departments. In linear programming terminology, any unused or idle capacity for a $\leq$ constraint is referred to as the *slack* associated with the constraint.

Often variables, called *slack variables,* are added to the formulation of a linear programming problem to represent the slack, or idle capacity. Unused capacity makes no contribution to profit; thus, slack variables have coefficients of zero in the objective function. After the addition of slack variables to the mathematical statement of the Par, Inc., problem, the mathematical model becomes

$$\text{Max} \quad 10x_1 + 9x_2 + 0s_1 + 0s_2 + 0s_3 + 0s_4$$

s.t.

$$7/10\, x_1 + 1x_2 + 1s_1 \qquad\qquad\qquad = 630$$

$$1/2\, x_1 + 5/6\, x_2 \quad + 1s_2 \qquad\qquad = 600$$

$$1x_1 + 2/3\, x_2 \qquad\qquad + 1s_3 \qquad = 708$$

$$1/10\, x_1 + 1/4\, x_2 \qquad\qquad\qquad + 1s_4 = 135$$

$$x_1, x_2, s_1, s_2, s_3, s_4 \geq 0$$

Whenever a linear program is written in a form with all constraints expressed as equalities, it is said to be written in *standard form.*

Referring to the standard form of the Par, Inc., problem, we see that at the optimal solution ($x_1 = 540$ and $x_2 = 252$), the values for the slack variables are

Constraint	Value of Slack Variable
Cutting and dyeing	$s_1 = 0$
Sewing	$s_2 = 120$
Finishing	$s_3 = 0$
Inspection and packaging	$s_4 = 18$

Could we have used the graphical solution to provide some of this information? The answer is yes. By finding the optimal solution point on Figure 2.6, we can see that the cutting and dyeing and the finishing constraints restrict, or *bind,* the feasible region at this

Can you identify the slack associated with a constraint? Try Problem 22(e).

Can you write a linear program in standard form? Try Problem 18.

point. Thus, this solution requires the use of all available time for these two operations. In other words, the graph shows us that the cutting and dyeing and the finishing departments will have zero slack. On the other hand, since the sewing and the inspection and packaging constraints are not binding the feasible region at the optimal solution, we can expect some unused time or slack for these two operations.

As a final comment on the graphical analysis of this problem, we call your attention to the sewing capacity constraint as shown in Figure 2.6. Note, in particular, that this constraint did not affect the feasible region. That is, the feasible region would be the same whether the sewing capacity constraint were included or not. This tells us that there is enough sewing time available to accommodate any production level that can be achieved by the other three departments. Since the sewing constraint does not affect the feasible region and thus cannot affect the optimal solution, it is called a *redundant constraint.*

NOTES & comments

1. In the standard-form representation of a linear programming model, the objective function coefficients for slack variables are zero. This implies that slack variables, which represent unused resources, do not affect the value of the objective function. However, in some applications, unused resources can be sold and contribute to profit. In such cases, the corresponding slack variables become decision variables representing the amount of resources to be sold. For each of these variables, a nonzero coefficient in the objective function would reflect the profit associated with selling a unit of the corresponding resource.

2. Redundant constraints do not affect the feasible region; as a result, they can be removed from a linear programming model without affecting the optimal solution. However, if the linear programming model is to be resolved later, changes in some of the data might make a previously redundant constraint a binding constraint. Thus, we recommend keeping all constraints in the linear programming model even though at some point in time one or more of the constraints may be redundant.

2.3 Extreme Points and the Optimal Solution

Suppose that the profit contribution for Par's standard golf bag is reduced from \$10 to \$5 per bag, while the profit contribution for the deluxe golf bag and all the constraints remain unchanged. The complete linear programming model of this new problem is identical to the mathematical model in Section 2.1, except for the revised objective function:

$$\text{Max } 5x_1 + 9x_2$$

How does this change in the objective function affect the optimal solution to the Par, Inc., problem? Figure 2.13 shows the graphical solution of this new problem with the revised objective function. Note that since the constraints have not changed, the feasible region has not changed. However, the profit lines have been altered to reflect the new objective function.

Figure 2.13

• • • • • • • • • • •

Optimal Solution for the Par, Inc., Problem with an Objective Function of $5x_1 + 9x_2$

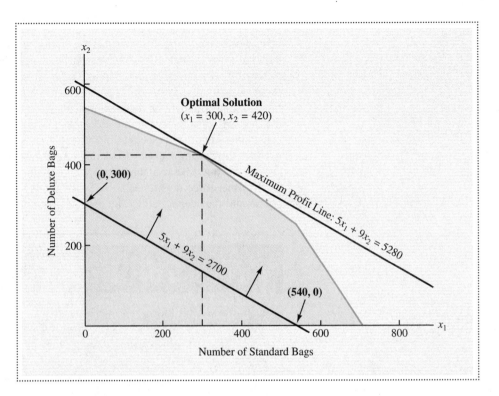

By moving the profit line in a parallel manner toward higher profit values, we find the optimal solution as shown in Figure 2.13. The values of the decision variables at this point are $x_1 = 300$ and $x_2 = 420$. The reduced profit contribution for the standard bag has caused a change in the optimal solution. In fact, as you may have suspected, we are cutting back the production of the lower-profit standard bags and increasing the production of the higher-profit deluxe bags.

What have you noticed about the location of the optimal solutions in the two linear programming problems that we have solved thus far? Look closely at the graphical solutions in Figures 2.10 and 2.13. An important observation that you should be able to make is that the optimal solutions occur at one of the vertices or "corners" of the feasible region. In linear programming terminology, these vertices are referred to as the *extreme points* of the feasible region. The Par, Inc., problem has five vertices, or five extreme points, for its feasible region (see Figure 2.14). We can now formally state our observation about the location of optimal solutions as follows:

> You should be able to identify the extreme points of the feasible region and determine the optimal solution by computing and comparing the objective function value at each extreme point. Try Problem 14.

An optimal solution to a linear programming problem can be found at an extreme point of the feasible region for the problem.[2]

This property means that if you are looking for the optimal solution to a linear programming problem, you do not have to evaluate all feasible solution points. In fact, you have to consider *only* the feasible solutions that occur at the extreme points of the

---

[2] We will see in Section 2.5 that there are two special cases (infeasibility and unboundedness) in linear programming where there is no optimal solution, and this statement does not apply.

Figure 2.14

The Five Extreme Points of the Feasible Region for the Par, Inc., Problem

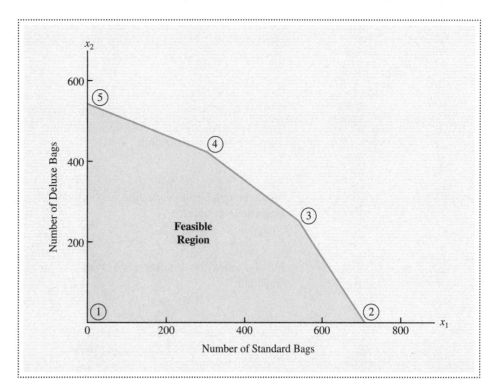

feasible region. Thus, for the Par, Inc., problem, instead of computing and comparing the profit contributions for all feasible solutions, we can find the optimal solution by evaluating the five extreme-point solutions and selecting the one that provides the largest profit contribution. Actually, the graphical solution procedure is nothing more than a convenient way of identifying an optimal extreme point for two-variable problems.

2.4 A Simple Minimization Problem

M&D Chemicals produces two products that are sold as raw materials to companies manufacturing bath soaps and laundry detergents. Based on an analysis of current inventory levels and potential demand for the coming month, M&D's management has specified that the combined production for products 1 and 2 must total at least 350 gallons. Separately, a major customer's order for 125 gallons of product 1 must also be satisfied. Product 1 requires 2 hours of processing time per gallon while product 2 requires 1 hour of processing time per gallon, and for the coming month, 600 hours of processing time are available. M&D's objective is to satisfy the above requirements at a minimum total production cost. Production costs are $2 per gallon for product 1 and $3 per gallon for product 2.

To find the minimum-cost production schedule, we will formulate the M&D Chemicals problem as a linear program. Following a procedure similar to the one used for Par, Inc., we first define the decision variables and the objective function for the problem. Let

x_1 = number of gallons of product 1 produced

x_2 = number of gallons of product 2 produced

Since the production costs are \$2 per gallon for product 1 and \$3 per gallon for product 2, the objective function which corresponds to the minimization of the total production cost can be written as

$$\text{Min } 2x_1 + 3x_2$$

Next consider the constraints placed on the M&D Chemicals problem. To satisfy the major customer's demand for 125 gallons of product 1, we know x_1 must be at least 125. Thus, we write the constraint

$$1x_1 \geq 125$$

Since the combined production for both products must total at least 350 gallons, we can write the constraint

$$1x_1 + 1x_2 \geq 350$$

Finally, since the limitation on available processing time is 600 hours, we add the constraint

$$2x_1 + 1x_2 \leq 600$$

After adding the nonnegativity constraints $(x_1, x_2 \geq 0)$, we have the following linear program for the M&D Chemicals problem:

$$\text{Min } \quad 2x_1 + 3x_2$$

s.t.

$$1x_1 \qquad\quad \geq 125 \quad \text{Demand for product 1}$$

$$1x_1 + 1x_2 \geq 350 \quad \text{Total production}$$

$$2x_1 + 1x_2 \leq 600 \quad \text{Processing time}$$

$$x_1, \; x_2 \geq 0$$

Since the linear programming model has only two decision variables, the graphical solution procedure can be used to find the optimal production quantities. The graphical method for this problem, just as in the Par problem, requires us to first graph the constraint lines to find the feasible region. By graphing each constraint line separately and then checking points on either side of the constraint line, the feasible solutions for each constraint can be identified. By combining the feasible solutions for each constraint on the same graph, we obtain the feasible region shown in Figure 2.15.

To find the minimum-cost solution, we now draw the objective function line corresponding to a particular total cost value. For example, we might start by drawing the line $2x_1 + 3x_2 = 1200$. This line is shown in Figure 2.16. Clearly there are points in the feasible region that would provide a total cost of \$1200. To find the values of x_1 and x_2 that provide smaller total cost values, we move the objective function line in a lower left direction until, if we moved it any farther, it would be entirely outside the feasible region. Note that the objective function line $2x_1 + 3x_2 = 800$ intersects the feasible region at the extreme point $x_1 = 250$ and $x_2 = 100$. This extreme point provides the minimum-cost solution with an objective function value of 800. From Figures 2.15 and 2.16, we can see that the total production constraint and the processing time constraint are binding. Just as in every linear programming problem, the optimal solution occurs at an extreme point of the feasible region.

Figure 2.15

The Feasible Region for the M&D Chemicals Problem

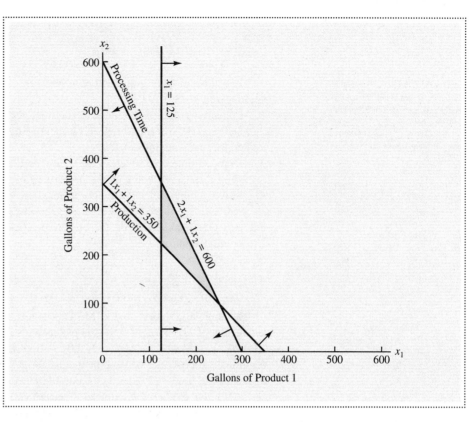

Figure 2.16

Graphical Solution for the M&D Chemicals Problem

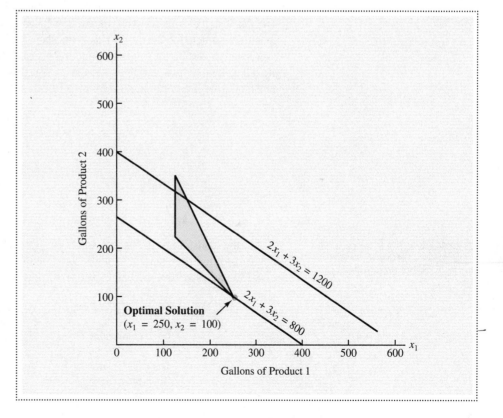

Summary of the Graphical Solution Procedure for Minimization Problems

Can you use the graphical solution procedure to determine the optimal solution for a minimization problem? Try Problem 29.

The steps of the graphical solution procedure for a minimization problem are summarized here:

1. Prepare a graph of the feasible solutions for each of the constraints.
2. Determine the feasible region by identifying the solutions that satisfy all the constraints simultaneously.
3. Draw an objective function line showing the values of the x_1 and x_2 variables that yield a specified value of the objective function.
4. Move parallel objective function lines toward smaller objective function values until further movement would take the line completely outside the feasible region.
5. Any feasible solution on the objective function line with the smallest value is an optimal solution.

Surplus Variables

The optimal solution to the M&D Chemicals problem shows that the desired total production of $1x_1 + 1x_2 = 350$ gallons has been achieved by using all available processing time of $2x_1 + 1x_2 = 2(250) + 1(100) = 600$ hours. In addition, note that the constraint requiring that product 1 demand be met has been satisfied with $x_1 = 250$ gallons. In fact, the production of product 1 exceeds its minimum level by $250 - 125 = 125$ gallons. This excess production for product 1 is referred to as *surplus*. In linear programming terminology, any excess quantity corresponding to a $\geq$ constraint is referred to as surplus.

Recall that with a $\leq$ constraint, a slack variable can be added to the left-hand side of the inequality to convert the constraint to equality form. With a $\geq$ constraint, a *surplus variable* can be subtracted from the left-hand side of the inequality to convert the constraint to equality form. Just as with slack variables, surplus variables are given a coefficient of zero in the objective function because they have no effect on its value. After including two surplus variables for the $\geq$ constraints and one slack variable for the $\leq$ constraint, the linear programming model of the M&D Chemicals problem becomes

$$\text{Min} \quad 2x_1 + 3x_2 + 0s_1 + 0s_2 + 0s_3$$
$$\text{s.t.}$$
$$1x_1 \qquad\quad - 1s_1 \qquad\qquad\qquad = 125$$
$$1x_1 + 1x_2 \qquad - 1s_2 \qquad\quad = 350$$
$$2x_1 + 1x_2 \qquad\qquad\quad + 1s_3 = 600$$
$$x_1, x_2, s_1, s_2, s_3 \geq 0$$

You should now be able to use slack and surplus variables to write a linear program in standard form. Try Problem 33.

All the constraints are now equalities. Hence, the preceding formulation is the standard-form representation of the M&D Chemicals problem. At the optimal solution of $x_1 = 250$ and $x_2 = 100$, the values of the surplus and slack variables are as follows:

Constraint	Value of Surplus or Slack Variables
Demand for product 1	$s_1 = 125$
Total production	$s_2 = 0$
Processing time	$s_3 = 0$

Refer to Figures 2.15 and 2.16. Note that the zero surplus and slack variables are associated with the constraints that are binding at the optimal solution—that is, the total production and processing time constraints. The surplus of 125 units is associated with the nonbinding constraint on the demand for product 1.

In the Par, Inc., problem all the constraints were of the $\leq$ type, and in the M&D Chemicals problem the constraints were a mixture of $\geq$ and $\leq$ types. The number and types of constraints encountered in a particular linear programming problem depends on the specific conditions existing in the problem. Linear programming problems may have some $\leq$ constraints, some $\geq$ constraints, and some $=$ constraints. For an equality constraint, feasible solutions must lie directly on the constraint line.

Try Problem 32 to practice solving a linear program with all three constraint forms.

An example of a linear program with all three constraint forms is given here:

$$\text{Min} \quad 2x_1 + 2x_2$$

$$\text{s.t.}$$

$$1x_1 + 3x_2 \leq 12$$

$$3x_1 + 1x_2 \geq 13$$

$$1x_1 - 1x_2 = 3$$

$$x_1, \ x_2 \geq 0$$

The standard-form representation of this problem is

$$\text{Min} \quad 2x_1 + 2x_2 + 0s_1 + 0s_2$$

$$\text{s.t.}$$

$$1x_1 + 3x_2 + 1s_1 \qquad = 12$$

$$3x_1 + 1x_2 \qquad - 1s_2 = 13$$

$$1x_1 - 1x_2 \qquad = 3$$

$$x_1, x_2, s_1, s_2 \geq 0$$

The standard form requires a slack variable for the $\leq$ constraint and a surplus variable for the $\geq$ constraint. However, neither a slack nor a surplus variable is required for the third constraint since it is already in equality form.

When solving linear programs graphically, it is not necessary to write the problem in its standard form. Nevertheless, you should be able to compute the values of the slack and surplus variables and understand what they mean. In Chapter 3 we will demonstrate that the values of slack and surplus variables are included in the computer solution of linear programs. In Chapter 5 we will introduce an algebraic solution procedure, the simplex method, which can be used to find optimal extreme-point solutions for linear programming problems with as many as several thousand decision variables. The mathematical steps of the simplex method involve solving simultaneous equations that represent the constraints of the linear program. Thus, in setting up a linear program for solution by the simplex method, we must have one linear equation for each constraint in the problem; therefore, the problem must be in its standard form.

A final point: The standard form of the linear programming problem is equivalent to the original formulation of the problem. That is, the optimal solution to any linear programming problem is the same as the optimal solution to the standard form of the problem. The standard form has not changed the basic problem; it has only changed how we write the constraints for the problem.

2.5 Special Cases

In this section we discuss three special situations that can arise when we attempt to solve linear programming problems.

Alternative Optimal Solutions

From our discussion of the graphical solution procedure, we know that optimal solutions can be found at the extreme points of the feasible region. Now let us consider the special case in which the optimal objective function line coincides with one of the binding constraint lines on the boundary of the feasible region. We will see that this can lead to the case of *alternative optimal solutions;* in such cases, more than one solution provides the optimal value for the objective function.

To illustrate the case of alternative optimal solutions, we return to the Par, Inc., problem. However, let us assume that the profit for the standard golf bag (x_1) has been decreased to $6.30. The revised objective function becomes $6.3x_1 + 9x_2$. The graphical solution of this problem is shown in Figure 2.17. Note that the optimal solution still occurs at an extreme point. In fact, it occurs at two extreme points: extreme point ④ ($x_1 = 300$, $x_2 = 420$) and extreme point ③ ($x_1 = 540$, $x_2 = 252$).

The objective function values at these two extreme points are identical; that is,

$$6.3x_1 + 9x_2 = 6.3(300) + 9(420) = 5670$$

and

$$6.3x_1 + 9x_2 = 6.3(540) + 9(252) = 5670$$

Figure 2.17

Par, Inc., Problem with an Objective Function of $6.3x_1 + 9x_2$ (Alternative Optimal Solutions)

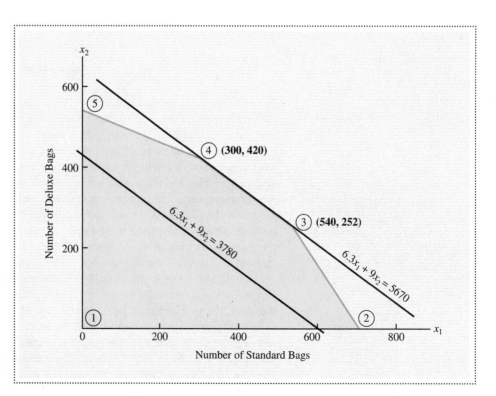

Furthermore, any point on the line connecting the two optimal extreme points also provides an optimal solution. For example, the solution point ($x_1 = 420$, $x_2 = 336$), which is halfway between the two extreme points, also provides the optimal objective function value of

$$6.3x_1 + 9x_2 = 6.3(420) + 9(336) = 5670$$

A linear programming problem with alternative optimal solutions is generally a good situation for the manager or decision maker. It means that several combinations of the decision variables are optimal and that the manager can select the specific optimal solution that is most desirable.

Infeasibility

Infeasibility means that no solution to the linear programming problem satisfies all the constraints, including the nonnegativity conditions $x_1, x_2 \geq 0$. Graphically, infeasibility means that a feasible region does not exist; that is, no points satisfy all the constraints and the nonnegativity conditions simultaneously. To illustrate this situation, let us look again at the problem faced by Par, Inc.

Suppose that management had specified that at least 500 of the standard bags and at least 360 of the deluxe bags must be manufactured. The graph of the solution region may now be constructed to reflect these new requirements (see Figure 2.18). The shaded area in the lower left-hand portion of the graph depicts those points satisfying the departmental constraints on the availability of time. The shaded area in the upper right-hand portion depicts those points satisfying the minimum production requirements of 500 standard and 360 deluxe bags. But there are no points satisfying both sets of constraints. Thus, we see that if management imposes these minimum production requirements, there will be no feasible solution to the linear programming model.

Figure 2.18

No Feasible Region for the Par, Inc., Problem with Minimum Production Requirements of 500 Standard and 360 Deluxe Bags

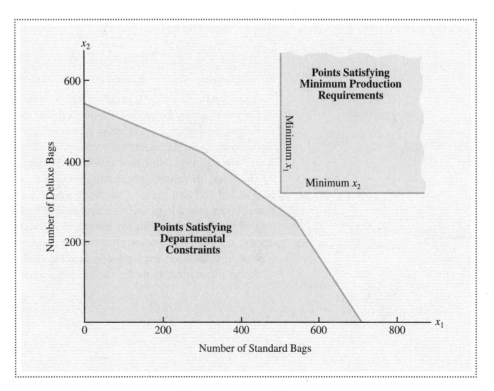

Table 2.2

Resources Needed to Manufacture 500 Standard Bags and 360 Deluxe Bags

Operation	Minimum Required Resources (hours)	Available Resources (hours)	Additional Resources Needed (hours)
Cutting and dyeing	$\frac{7}{10}(500) + 1(360) = 710$	630	80
Sewing	$\frac{1}{2}(500) + \frac{5}{6}(360) = 550$	600	None
Finishing	$1(500) + \frac{2}{3}(360) = 740$	708	32
Inspection and packaging	$\frac{1}{10}(500) + \frac{1}{4}(360) = 140$	135	5

How should we interpret infeasibility in terms of this current problem? First, we should tell management that given the resources available (i.e., production time for cutting and dyeing, sewing, finishing, and inspection and packaging), it is not possible to make 500 standard bags and 360 deluxe bags. Moreover, we can tell management exactly how much of each resource must be expended to make it possible to manufacture 500 standard and 360 deluxe bags. Table 2.2 shows the minimum amounts of resources that must be available, the amounts currently available, and additional amounts that would be required to accomplish this. Thus, we need 80 more hours for cutting and dyeing, 32 more hours for finishing, and 5 more hours for inspection and packaging to meet management's minimum production requirements.

If, after reviewing this information, management still wants to manufacture 500 standard and 360 deluxe bags, additional resources must be provided. Perhaps this will mean hiring another person to work in the cutting and dyeing department, transferring a person from elsewhere in the plant to work part-time in the finishing department, or having the sewing people help out periodically with the inspection and packaging. As you can see, there are many possibilities for corrective management action, once we discover that there is no feasible solution. The important thing to realize is that linear programming analysis can help determine whether management's plans are feasible. By analyzing the problem using linear programming, we are often able to point out infeasible conditions and initiate corrective action.

Unbounded

The solution to a maximization linear programming problem is *unbounded* if the value of the solution may be made infinitely large without violating any of the constraints; for a minimization problem, the solution is unbounded if the value may be made infinitely small. This condition might be termed *managerial utopia*; for example, if this condition were to occur in a profit maximization problem, the manager could achieve an unlimited profit.

However, in linear programming models of real problems, the occurrence of an unbounded solution means that the problem has been improperly formulated. We know that it is not possible to increase profits indefinitely. Therefore, we must conclude that if a profit maximization problem results in an unbounded solution, the mathematical model doesn't represent the real-world problem sufficiently. Usually, what has happened is that a constraint has been inadvertently omitted during problem formulation.

As an illustration, consider the simple numerical example:

$$\text{Max} \quad 20x_1 + 10x_2$$

$$\text{s.t.}$$
$$1x_1 \qquad \geq 2$$
$$1x_2 \leq 5$$
$$x_1, x_2 \geq 0$$

Figure 2.19

Example of an Unbounded Problem

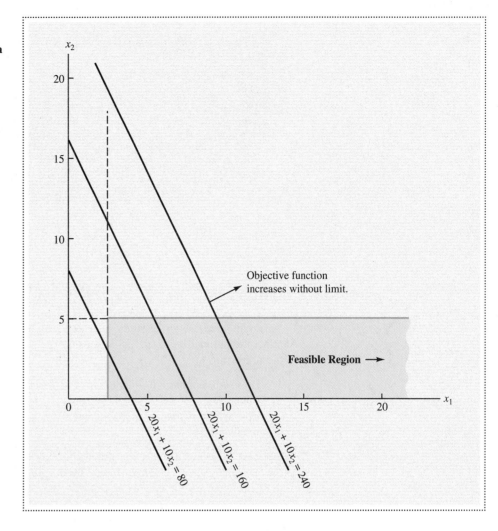

In Figure 2.19 we have graphed the feasible region associated with this problem. Note that we can only indicate part of the feasible region since the feasible region extends indefinitely in the direction of the x_1 axis. Looking at the objective function lines in Figure 2.19, we see that the solution to this problem may be made as large as we desire. That is, no matter what solution we pick, there will always be some feasible solution with a larger value. Thus, we say that the solution to this linear program is *unbounded*.

You should now be able to recognize whether a linear program involves alternative optimal solutions, infeasibility, or is unbounded. Try Problems 40 and 41.

NOTES & comments

1. Infeasibility is independent of the objective function. It exists because the constraints are so restrictive that there is no feasible region for the linear programming model. Thus, when you encounter infeasibility, making changes in the coefficients of the objective function will not help; the problem will remain infeasible.

—Continued

—Continued from previous page

2. The occurrence of an unbounded solution is often the result of a missing constraint. However, a change in the objective function may cause a previously unbounded problem to become bounded with an optimal solution. For example, the graph in Figure 2.19 shows an unbounded solution for the objective function max $20x_1 + 10x_2$. However, changing the objective function to max $-20x_1 - 10x_2$ will provide the optimal solution $x_1 = 2$ and $x_2 = 0$ even though no changes have been made in the constraints.

2.6 Introduction to Sensitivity Analysis

Sensitivity analysis is the study of how changes in the coefficients of a linear program affect the optimal solution. Using sensitivity analysis, we can answer questions such as the following:

1. How will a *change in a coefficient of the objective function* affect the optimal solution?
2. How will a *change in the right-hand-side value for a constraint* affect the optimal solution?

Since sensitivity analysis is concerned with how such changes affect the optimal solution, the analysis does not begin until the optimal solution to the original linear programming problem has been obtained. For this reason, sensitivity analysis is often referred to as *postoptimality analysis*.

Sensitivity analysis is important to decision makers because real problems exist in a dynamic environment. Prices of raw materials change, demand fluctuates, companies purchase new machinery to replace old, global labor markets cause changes in production costs, employee turnover occurs, and so on. If a linear programming model has been used in such an environment, we can expect some of the coefficients to change over time. A manager will want to determine how such changes affect the optimal solution to the original linear programming problem. Sensitivity analysis provides the information needed to respond to such changes without requiring the complete solution of a revised linear program.

Recall the Par, Inc., problem introduced in Section 2.1.

$$\text{Max} \quad 10x_1 + 9x_2$$

s.t.

$$
\begin{aligned}
\tfrac{7}{10}x_1 + 1x_2 &\le 630 \quad \text{Cutting and dyeing}\\
\tfrac{1}{2}x_1 + \tfrac{5}{6}x_2 &\le 600 \quad \text{Sewing}\\
1x_1 + \tfrac{2}{3}x_2 &\le 708 \quad \text{Finishing}\\
\tfrac{1}{10}x_1 + \tfrac{1}{4}x_2 &\le 135 \quad \text{Inspection and packaging}\\
x_1, x_2 &\ge 0
\end{aligned}
$$

The optimal solution, $x_1 = 540$ standard bags and $x_2 = 252$ deluxe bags, is based on profit figures of \$10 per standard bag and \$9 per deluxe bag. However, suppose we later learn that because of a price reduction the profit contribution per standard bag has been reduced to \$7. Sensitivity analysis can be used to determine whether the production schedule calling for 540 standard bags and 252 deluxe bags is still the best solution. If it is, there will be no need to solve a modified linear program with $7x_1 + 9x_2$ as the objective function.

Sensitivity analysis can also be used to determine which coefficients in a linear programming model are most critical. For instance, suppose Par's management believes that the \$9 profit contribution per deluxe bag is only a rough estimate of the profit contribution that will actually be obtained. If sensitivity analysis shows that 540 standard bags and 252 deluxe bags will be the optimal solution as long as the profit contribution for the deluxe bag is between \$5 and \$13, management should feel comfortable with the rough estimate of \$9 per bag and the recommended production quantities. However, if sensitivity analysis shows that 540 standard bags and 252 deluxe bags will be the optimal solution only if the profit contribution for the deluxe bag is between \$8.90 and \$9.25, management may want to review the accuracy of the \$9-per-bag profit estimate.

Another aspect of sensitivity analysis is concerned with changes in the right-hand sides of the constraints. Recall that in the Par, Inc., problem the optimal solution used all the cutting and dyeing time and all the finishing time. How would the optimal solution and the total profit contribution change if Par's management could obtain additional time for either of these operations? Sensitivity analysis can help determine how much each additional hour is worth and how many hours can be added before diminishing returns set in.

2.7 Graphical Sensitivity Analysis

For linear programming problems with two decision variables, graphical solution methods can be used to perform sensitivity analysis on the objective function coefficients and the right-hand-side values for the constraints.

Objective Function Coefficients

Let us consider how changes in the objective function coefficients might affect the optimal solution to the Par, Inc., problem. The current contribution to profit is \$10 per unit for the standard bag and \$9 per unit for the deluxe bag. It seems obvious that an increase in the profit contribution for one of the bags might lead management to increase production of that bag and a decrease in the profit contribution for one of the bags might lead management to decrease production of that bag. But it is not as obvious how much the profit contribution would have to change before management would want to change the production quantities.

The current optimal solution to this problem calls for producing 540 standard golf bags and 252 deluxe golf bags. The *range of optimality* for each objective function coefficient provides the range of values over which the current solution will remain optimal. Managerial attention should be focused on those objective function coefficients that have a narrow range of optimality and coefficients near the endpoints of the range. With these coefficients, a small change can necessitate modifying the optimal solution. Let us now compute the ranges of optimality for this problem.

Figure 2.20 shows the graphical solution. A careful inspection of this graph shows that as long as the slope of the objective function is between the slope of line A (which coincides with the cutting and dyeing constraint line) and the slope of line B (which coincides with the finishing constraint line), extreme point ③ with $x_1 = 540$ and $x_2 = 252$ will be optimal. Changing an objective function coefficient for x_1 or x_2 will cause the slope of the objective function to change. In Figure 2.20 we see that such changes cause the objective function line to rotate around extreme point ③. However, as long as the objective function line stays within the shaded region, extreme point ③ will remain optimal.

Rotating the objective function line *counterclockwise* causes the slope to become less negative, and the slope increases. When the objective function line has been rotated counterclockwise (slope increased) enough to coincide with line A, we obtain alternative optimal solutions between extreme points ③ and ④. Any further counterclockwise rotation of the objective function line will cause extreme point ③ to be nonoptimal. Hence, the slope of line A provides an upper limit for the slope of the objective function line.

Rotating the objective function line *clockwise* causes the slope to become more negative, and the slope decreases. When the objective function line has been rotated clockwise (slope decreased) enough to coincide with line B, we obtain alternative optimal solutions between extreme points ③ and ②. Any further clockwise rotation of the objective function line will cause extreme point ③ to be nonoptimal. Hence, the slope of line B provides a lower limit for the slope of the objective function line.

Figure 2.20

. . . .

Graphical Solution of Par, Inc., Problem with Slope of Objective Function between Slopes of Lines A and B; Extreme Point ③ Is Optimal

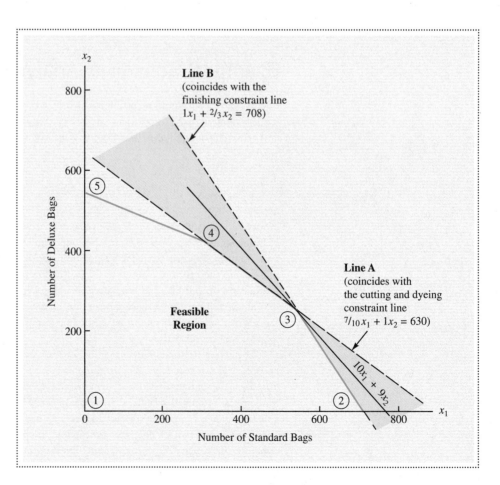

Thus, extreme point ③ will be the optimal solution as long as

Slope of line B ≤ slope of objective function line ≤ slope of line A

In Figure 2.20 we see that the equation for line A, the cutting and dyeing constraint line, is as follows:

$$\tfrac{7}{10}x_1 + 1x_2 = 630$$

By solving the above equation for x_2, we can write the equation for line A in its slope–intercept form. This yields

$$x_2 = -\tfrac{7}{10}x_1 + 630$$

↑   ↑

Slope of   Intercept of
line A   line A on
        x_2 axis

Thus, the slope for line A is $-\tfrac{7}{10}$, and its intercept on the x_2 axis is 630.

The equation for line B in Figure 2.20 is

$$1x_1 + \tfrac{2}{3}x_2 = 708$$

Solving for x_2 provides the slope–intercept form for line B. Doing so yields

$$\tfrac{2}{3}x_2 = -1x_1 + 708$$

$$x_2 = -\tfrac{3}{2}x_1 + 1062$$

Thus, the slope of line B is $-\tfrac{3}{2}$, and its intercept on the x_2 axis is 1062.

Now that the slopes of lines A and B have been computed, we see that for extreme point ③ to remain optimal we must have

$$-\tfrac{3}{2} \leq \text{slope of objective function} \leq -\tfrac{7}{10} \tag{2.12}$$

Let us now consider the general form of the slope of the objective function. Let c_1 denote the profit of a standard bag, c_2 denote the profit of a deluxe bag, and z denote the value of the objective function. Using this notation, the objective function can be written as

$$z = c_1x_1 + c_2x_2$$

Writing this equation in slope–intercept form, we obtain

$$c_2x_2 = -c_1x_1 + z$$

and

$$x_2 = -\frac{c_1}{c_2}x_1 + \frac{z}{c_2}$$

Thus, we see that the slope of the objective function is given by $-c_1/c_2$. Substituting $-c_1/c_2$ into expression (2.12), we see that extreme point ③ will be optimal as long as the following expression is satisfied:

$$-\tfrac{3}{2} \leq -\frac{c_1}{c_2} \leq -\tfrac{7}{10} \tag{2.13}$$

To compute the range of optimality for the standard-bag profit contribution, we hold the profit contribution for the deluxe bag fixed at its initial value $c_2 = 9$. Doing so in expression (2.13), we obtain

$$-\tfrac{3}{2} \leq -\frac{c_1}{9} \leq -\tfrac{7}{10}$$

From the left-hand inequality, we have

$$-\tfrac{3}{2} \leq -\frac{c_1}{9} \qquad \text{or} \qquad \tfrac{3}{2} \geq \frac{c_1}{9}$$

Thus,

$$\tfrac{27}{2} \geq c_1 \qquad \text{or} \qquad c_1 \leq \tfrac{27}{2} = 13.5$$

From the right-hand inequality, we have

$$-\frac{c_1}{9} \leq -\tfrac{7}{10} \qquad \text{or} \qquad \frac{c_1}{9} \geq \tfrac{7}{10}$$

Thus,

$$c_1 \geq \tfrac{63}{10} \qquad \text{or} \qquad c_1 \geq 6.3$$

You should now be able to compute the range of optimality using the graphical solution procedure. Try Problem 52.

Combining the calculated limits for c_1 provides the following range of optimality for the standard-bag profit contribution:

$$6.3 \leq c_1 \leq 13.5$$

In the original problem for Par, Inc., the standard bag had a profit contribution of $10. The resulting optimal solution was 540 standard bags and 252 deluxe bags. The range of optimality for c_1 tells Par's management that, with other coefficients unchanged, the profit contribution for the standard bag can be anywhere between $6.30 and $13.50 and the production quantities of 540 standard bags and 252 deluxe bags will remain optimal. Note, however, that while the production quantities will not change, the total profit contribution (value of objective function) will change due to the change in profit contribution per standard bag.

These computations can be repeated, holding the profit contribution for standard bags constant at $c_1 = 10$. In this case, the range of optimality for the deluxe-bag profit contribution can be determined. Check to see that this range is $6.67 \leq c_2 \leq 14.29$.

In cases where the rotation of the objective function line about an optimal extreme point causes the objective function line to become *vertical,* there will be either no upper limit or no lower limit for the slope as it appears in the form of expression (2.13). To show how this special situation can occur, suppose that the objective function for the Par, Inc. problem is $18x_1 + 9x_2$; in this case, extreme point ② in Figure 2.21 provides the optimal solution. Rotating the objective function line counterclockwise around extreme point ② provides an upper limit for the slope when the objective function line coincides with line B. Since we have previously seen that the slope of line B is $-\tfrac{3}{2}$, the upper limit for the slope of the objective function line must be $-\tfrac{3}{2}$. However, rotating the objective function line clockwise results in the slope becoming more and more negative, approaching a value of minus infinity as the objective function line becomes vertical; in this case, there is no lower limit for the slope of the objective function. Using the upper limit of $-\tfrac{3}{2}$, we can write

$$-\frac{c_1}{c_2} \leq -\tfrac{3}{2}$$

Slope of the $\nearrow$
objective function line

Following our previous procedure of holding c_2 constant at its original value, $c_2 = 9$, we have

$$-\frac{c_1}{9} \leq -\tfrac{3}{2} \qquad \text{or} \qquad \frac{c_1}{9} \geq \tfrac{3}{2}$$

Figure 2.21

Graphical Solution of Par, Inc., Problem with an Objective Function of $18x_1 + 9x_2$; Optimal Solution at Extreme Point ②

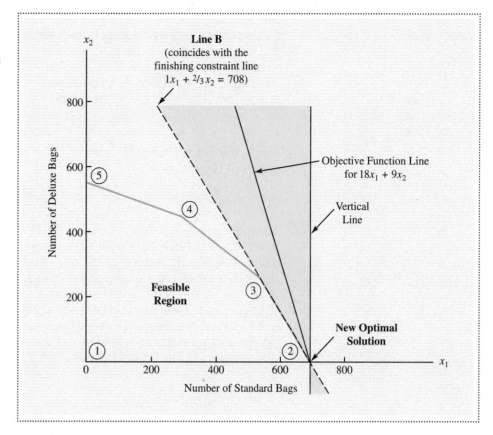

Solving for c_1 provides the following result:

$$c_1 \geq {}^{27}\!/_2 = 13.5$$

In reviewing Figure 2.21 we note that extreme point ② remains optimal for all values of c_1 above 13.5. Thus, we obtain the following range of optimality for c_1 at extreme point ②:

$$13.5 \leq c_1 < \infty$$

Simultaneous Changes   The range of optimality for objective function coefficients is only applicable for changes made to one coefficient at a time. All other coefficients are assumed to be fixed at their initial values. If two or more objective function coefficients are changed simultaneously, further analysis is necessary to determine whether the optimal solution will change. However, when solving two variable problems graphically, expression (2.13) suggests an easy way to determine whether simultaneous changes in both objective function coefficients will cause a change in the optimal solution. Simply compute the slope of the objective function ($-c_1/c_2$) for the new coefficient values. If this ratio is greater than or equal to the lower limit on the slope of the objective function and less than or equal to the upper limit, then the changes made will not cause a change in the optimal solution.

Consider changes in both of the objective function coefficients for the Par, Inc., problem. Suppose the profit contribution per standard bag is increased to \$13 and the profit contribution per deluxe bag is simultaneously reduced to \$8. Recall that the ranges of optimality for c_1 and c_2 (both computed in a one-at-a-time manner) are

$$6.3 \leq c_1 \leq 13.5 \tag{2.14}$$

$$6.67 \leq c_2 \leq 14.29 \tag{2.15}$$

For these ranges of optimality, we can conclude that changing either c_1 to \$13 or c_2 to \$8 (but not both) would not cause a change in the optimal solution of $x_1 = 540$ and $x_2 = 252$. But we cannot conclude from the ranges of optimality that changing both coefficients simultaneously would not result in a change in the optimal solution.

In expression (2.13) we showed that extreme point ③ remains optimal as long as

$$-\tfrac{3}{2} \le -\frac{c_1}{c_2} \le -\tfrac{7}{10}$$

If c_1 is changed to 13 and simultaneously c_2 is changed to 8, the new objective function slope will be given by

$$-\frac{c_1}{c_2} = -\frac{13}{8} = -1.625$$

Since this value is less than the lower limit of $-\tfrac{3}{2}$, the current solution of $x_1 = 540$ and $x_2 = 252$ will no longer be optimal. By resolving the problem with $c_1 = 13$ and $c_2 = 8$ we will find that extreme point ② is the new optimal solution.

Looking at the ranges of optimality, we concluded that changing either c_1 to \$13 or c_2 to \$8 (but not both) would not cause a change in the optimal solution. But in recomputing the slope of the objective function with simultaneous changes for both c_1 and c_2, we saw that the optimal solution did change. This emphasizes the fact that a range of optimality, by itself, can only be used to draw a conclusion about changes made to *one objective function coefficient at a time.*

Right–Hand Sides

Let us now consider how a change in the right-hand side for a constraint may affect the feasible region and perhaps cause a change in the optimal solution to the problem. To illustrate this aspect of sensitivity analysis, let us consider what happens if an additional 10 hours of production time becomes available in the cutting and dyeing department of Par, Inc. The right-hand side of the cutting and dyeing constraint is changed from 630 to 640, and the constraint is rewritten as

$$\tfrac{7}{10} x_1 + x_2 \le 640$$

By obtaining an additional 10 hours of cutting and dyeing time, we have expanded the feasible region for the problem, as shown in Figure 2.22. Since the feasible region has been enlarged, we now want to determine whether one of the new feasible solutions provides an improvement in the value of the objective function. Application of the graphical solution procedure to the problem with the enlarged feasible region shows that the extreme point with $x_1 = 527.5$ and $x_2 = 270.75$ now provides the optimal solution. The new value for the objective function is $10(527.5) + 9(270.75) = \$7711.75$; this provides an increase in profit of $\$7711.75 - \$7668.00 = \$43.75$. Thus, the increased profit occurs at a rate of $\$43.75/10$ hours $= \$4.375$ per hour added.

The *improvement* in the value of the optimal solution per unit increase in the right-hand side of the constraint is called the *dual price.* Here, the dual price for cutting and dyeing and production time is \$4.375 per hour; in other words, if we increase the right-hand side of the production and dyeing time constraint by 1 hour, the value of the objective function will improve by \$4.375. Conversely, if the right-hand side of the production and dyeing time constraint were to decrease by 1 hour, the objective function would get worse by \$4.375. The dual price can generally be used to determine what will happen to the value of the objective function when we make a one-unit change in the right-hand side of a constraint.

Can you compute and interpret the dual price for a constraint? Try Problem 53.

Figure 2.22

Effect of a 10-Unit Change in the Right-Hand Side of the Cutting and Dyeing Constraint

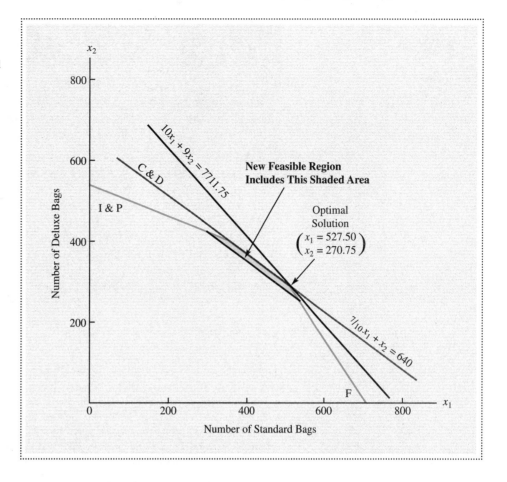

We caution here that the value of the dual price may be applicable only for small changes in the right-hand side. As more and more resources are obtained and the right-hand-side value continues to increase, other constraints will become binding and limit the change in the value of the objective function. For example, in the problem for Par, Inc., we would eventually reach a point where more cutting and dyeing time would be of no value; this would occur at the point where the cutting and dyeing constraint becomes nonbinding. At this point, the dual price would equal zero. In the next chapter we will show how to determine the range of values for a right-hand side over which the dual price will accurately predict the improvement in the objective function. Finally, we note that the dual price for any nonbinding constraint will be zero because an increase in the right-hand side of such a constraint will affect only the value of the slack or surplus variable for that constraint.

To illustrate the correct interpretation of dual prices for a minimization problem, suppose we had solved a problem involving the minimization of total cost and that the value of the optimal solution was $100. Furthermore, suppose that the dual price for a particular constraint was −$10. The *negative dual price* tells us that the objective function *will not improve* if the value of the right-hand side is increased by one unit. Thus, if the right-hand side of this constraint is increased by one unit, the value of the objective function will get worse by the amount of $10. Since becoming worse means an increase in the total cost, the value of the objective function will become $110 if the right-hand side is increased by one unit. Conversely, a decrease in the right-hand side of one unit will decrease the total cost by $10.

NOTES & comments

1. If two objective function coefficients change simultaneously, both may move outside their respective ranges of optimality and not affect the optimal solution. For instance, in a two-variable linear program, the slope of the objective function will not change at all if both coefficients are changed by the same percentage.

2. Some texts associate the term *shadow price* with each constraint. The concept of a shadow price is closely related to the concept of a dual price. The shadow price associated with a constraint is the *change* in the value of the optimal solution per unit increase in the right-hand side of the constraint. In general, the dual price and the shadow price are the *same* for all *maximization* linear programs. In *minimization* linear programs, the shadow price is the *negative* of the corresponding dual price.

Summary

Two problems, Par, Inc., and M&D Chemicals, were formulated as linear programs and solved by a graphical solution procedure. In studying the graphical solution procedure, we noted that if an optimal solution to a linear programming problem exists, it can be found at an extreme point.

In the process of formulating mathematical models of the problems presented in this chapter, the following general definition of a linear program was developed. A linear program is a mathematical model that has the following properties:

1. A linear objective function that is to be maximized or minimized
2. A set of linear constraints
3. Variables that are all restricted to nonnegative values

We have seen how slack variables can be used to write less-than-or-equal-to constraints in equality form and how surplus variables can be used to write greater-than-or-equal-to constraints in equality form. The value of a slack variable can usually be interpreted as the amount of unused resource, while the value of a surplus variable indicates the amount over and above some stated minimum requirement. When all constraints have been written as equalities, the linear program has been written in its standard form. In the special cases of infeasibility and unboundedness, we showed that there is no optimal solution to the problem. In the case of infeasibility, there are no feasible solutions; in the case of unboundedness, the objective function can be made infinitely large for a maximization problem and infinitely small for a minimization problem. A third special case, alternative optimal solutions, was also discussed. In this case, we have two optimal extreme points, and all the points on the line segment connecting them are also optimal.

The chapter concluded with a discussion of sensitivity analysis, the study of how changes in the coefficients of a linear program affect the optimal solution. We showed how a graphical solution method can be used to determine how a change in one of the objective function coefficients or a change in the right-hand-side value for a constraint will affect the optimal solution to the problem.

Glossary

Constraint An equation or inequality that rules out certain combinations of decision variables as feasible solutions.

Constraint function The left-hand side of a constraint (i.e., the portion of the constraint containing the variables).

Objective function All linear programs have a linear objective function that is to be either maximized or minimized. In many linear programming problems, the objective function will be used to measure the profit or cost of a particular solution.

Solution Any set of values for the variables.

Optimal solution A feasible solution that maximizes or minimizes the value of the objective function.

Nonnegativity constraints A set of constraints that requires all variables to be nonnegative.

Mathematical model A representation of a problem where the objective and all constraint conditions are described by mathematical expressions.

Linear program A mathematical model with a linear objective function, a set of linear constraints, and nonnegative variables.

Linear functions Mathematical expressions in which the variables appear in separate terms and are raised to the first power.

Feasible solution A solution that satisfies all the constraints.

Feasible region The set of all feasible solutions.

Slack variable A variable added to the left-hand side of a less-than-or-equal-to constraint to convert the constraint into an equality. The value of this variable can usually be interpreted as the amount of unused resource.

Standard form A linear program in which all the constraints are written as equalities. The optimal solution of the standard form of a linear program is the same as the optimal solution of the original formulation of the linear program.

Redundant constraint A constraint that does not affect the feasible region. If a constraint is redundant, it can be removed from the problem without affecting the feasible region.

Extreme point Graphically speaking, extreme points are the feasible solution points occurring at the vertices or "corners" of the feasible region. With two-variable problems, extreme points are determined by the intersection of the constraint lines.

Surplus variable A variable subtracted from the left-hand side of a greater-than-or-equal-to constraint to convert the constraint into an equality. The value of this variable can usually be interpreted as the amount over and above some required minimum level.

Alternative optimal solutions The case in which more than one solution provides the optimal value for the objective function.

Infeasibility The situation in which there is no solution to the linear programming problem that satisfies all the constraints.

Unbounded If the value of the solution may be made infinitely large in a maximization linear programming problem or infinitely small in a minimization problem without violating any of the constraints the problem is said to be unbounded.

Sensitivity analysis The evaluation of how changes in the coefficients of a linear programming problem affect the optimal solution to the problem.

Postoptimality analysis Another name for sensitivity analysis, indicating that the analysis is performed after the optimal solution to the original linear programming problem has been obtained.

Range of optimality The range of values over which an objective function coefficient may vary without causing any change in the values of the decision variables in the optimal solution.

Dual price The improvement in the value of the optimal solution per unit increase in a constraint right-hand-side value.

Problems

1. **SELFTest** Which of the following mathematical relationships could be found in a linear programming model, and which could not? For the relationships that are unacceptable for linear programs, state why.

a. $-1x_1 + 2x_2 - 1x_3 \leq 70$ yes

b. $2x_1 - 2x_3 = 50$ yes

violates proportionality

c. $1x_1 - 2x_2^2 + 4x_3 \leq 10$ NO
d. $3\sqrt{x_1} + 2x_2 - 1x_3 \geq 15$ NO
e. $1x_1 + 1x_2 + 1x_3 = 6$ YES
f. $2x_1 + 5x_2 + 1x_1x_2 \leq 25$ NO

2. **SELF Test** Find the feasible solution points for the following constraints:

a. $4x_1 + 2x_2 \leq 16$
b. $4x_1 + 2x_2 \geq 16$
c. $4x_1 + 2x_2 = 16$

3. Graphing constraint lines is an essential step in the graphical method. Show a separate graph of the constraint lines and feasible solutions for each of the following constraints:

a. $3x_1 + 2x_2 \leq 18$
b. $12x_1 + 8x_2 \geq 480$
c. $5x_1 + 10x_2 = 200$

4. Show a separate graph of the constraint lines and feasible solutions for each of the following constraints:

a. $3x_1 - 4x_2 \geq 60$
b. $-6x_1 + 5x_2 \leq 60$
c. $5x_1 - 2x_2 \leq 0$

5. Show a separate graph of the constraint lines and feasible solutions for each of the following constraints:

a. $x_1 \geq 0.25 (x_1 + x_2)$
b. $x_2 \leq 0.10 (x_1 + x_2)$
c. $x_1 \leq 0.50 (x_1 + x_2)$

6. **SELF Test** Three objective functions for linear programming problems are

$$z = 7x_1 + 10x_2$$
$$z = 6x_1 + 4x_2$$
$$z = -4x_1 + 7x_2$$

Determine the slope of each objective function. Show the graph of each of the three objective functions for $z = 420$.

7. **SELF Test** Identify the feasible region for the following set of constraints:

$$\tfrac{1}{2}x_1 + \tfrac{1}{4}x_2 \geq 30$$
$$1x_1 + 5x_2 \geq 250$$
$$\tfrac{1}{4}x_1 + \tfrac{1}{2}x_2 \leq 50$$
$$x_1, x_2 \geq 0$$

8. Identify the feasible region for the following set of constraints:

$$2x_1 - 1x_2 \leq 0$$
$$-1x_1 + 1.5x_2 \leq 200$$
$$x_1, x_2 \geq 0$$

9. Identify the feasible region for the following set of constraints:

$$3x_1 - 2x_2 \geq 0$$
$$2x_1 - 1x_2 \leq 200$$
$$1x_1 \leq 150$$
$$x_1, x_2 \geq 0$$

10. Solve the following linear program:

$$\text{Max} \quad 5x_1 + 5x_2$$

s.t.

$$1x_1 \qquad \le 100$$
$$1x_2 \le 80$$
$$2x_1 + 4x_2 \le 400$$
$$x_1, x_2 \ge 0$$

11. SELFTest Consider the following linear programming problem:

$$\text{Max} \quad 2x_1 + 3x_2$$

s.t.

$$1x_1 + 2x_2 \le 6$$
$$5x_1 + 3x_2 \le 15$$
$$x_1, x_2 \ge 0$$

Find the optimal solution. What is the value of the objective function at the optimal solution?

12. Consider the following linear programming problem:

$$\text{Max} \quad 3x_1 + 3x_2$$

s.t.

$$2x_1 + 4x_2 \le 12$$
$$6x_1 + 4x_2 \le 24$$
$$x_1, x_2 \ge 0$$

a. Find the optimal solution.
b. If the objective function is changed to $2x_1 + 6x_2$, what will the optimal solution be?
c. How many extreme points are there? What are the values of x_1 and x_2 at each extreme point?

13. Consider the following linear programming problem:

$$\text{Max} \quad 3x_1 + 2x_2$$

s.t.

$$2x_1 + 2x_2 \le 8$$
$$3x_1 + 2x_2 \le 12$$
$$1x_1 + 0.5x_2 \le 3$$
$$x_1, x_2 \ge 0$$

a. Find the optimal solution. What is the value of the objective function?
b. Does this problem have a redundant constraint? If so, what is it? Does the solution change if the redundant constraint is removed from the problem? Explain.

14. **SELF Test** Consider the following linear program:

$$\text{Max} \quad 1x_1 + 2x_2$$

s.t.

$$1x_1 \qquad \leq 5$$

$$1x_2 \leq 4$$

$$2x_1 + 2x_2 = 12$$

$$x_1, x_2 \geq 0$$

a. Show the feasible region.
b. What are the extreme points of the feasible region?
c. Find the optimal solution using the graphical procedure.

15. What constraint lines combine to form extreme point ④ of the Par, Inc., problem (see Figures 2.6 and 2.14)? Solve the simultaneous linear equations to show that the exact values of x_1 and x_2 at this extreme point are $x_1 = 300$ and $x_2 = 420$.

16. Suppose that Par's management encounters each of the following situations:
a. The accounting department revises its estimate of the profit contribution for the deluxe bag to $18 per bag.
b. A new low-cost material is available for the standard bag, and the profit contribution per standard bag can be increased to $20 per bag. (Assume the profit contribution of the deluxe bag is the original $9 value.)
c. New sewing equipment is available that would increase the sewing operation capacity to 750 hours. (Assume $10x_1 + 9x_2$ is the appropriate objective function.)
If each of the above conditions is encountered separately, what are the optimal solution and the total profit contribution for each situation?

17. Refer to the feasible region for the Par, Inc., problem in Figure 2.14.
a. Develop an objective function that will make extreme point ⑤ the optimal extreme point.
b. What is the optimal solution using the objective function you selected in part (a)?
c. What are the values of the slack variables associated with this solution?

18. **SELF Test** Write the following linear program in standard form:

$$\text{Max} \quad 5x_1 + 2x_2 + 8x_3$$

s.t.

$$1x_1 - 2x_2 + \tfrac{1}{2}x_3 \leq 420$$

$$2x_1 + 3x_2 - 1x_3 \leq 610$$

$$6x_1 - 1x_2 + 3x_3 \leq 125$$

$$x_1, x_2, x_3 \geq 0$$

19. For the linear program

$$\text{Max} \quad 4x_1 + 1x_2$$

s.t.

$$10x_1 + 2x_2 \leq 30$$

$$3x_1 + 2x_2 \leq 12$$

$$2x_1 + 2x_2 \leq 10$$

$$x_1, x_2 \geq 0$$

a. Write this problem in standard form.
b. Solve the problem.
c. What are the values of the three slack variables at the optimal solution?

20. Given the linear program

$$\text{Max} \quad 3x_1 + 4x_2$$

s.t.

$$-1x_1 + 2x_2 \leq 8$$

$$1x_1 + 2x_2 \leq 12$$

$$2x_1 + 1x_2 \leq 16$$

$$x_1, x_2 \geq 0$$

a. Write the problem in standard form.
b. Solve the problem.
c. What are the values of the three slack variables at the optimal solution?

21. RMC, Inc., is a small firm that produces a variety of chemical products. In a particular production process, three raw materials are blended (mixed together) to produce two products: a fuel additive and a solvent base. Each ton of fuel additive is a mixture of $2/5$ ton of material 1 and $3/5$ ton of material 3. A ton of solvent base is a mixture of $1/2$ ton of material 1, $1/5$ ton of material 2, and $3/10$ ton of material 3. After deducting relevant costs, the profit contribution is $40 for every ton of fuel additive produced and $30 for every ton of solvent base produced.

RMC's production is constrained by a limited availability of the three raw materials. For the current production period, RMC has available the following quantities of each raw material:

Raw Material	Amount Available for Production
Material 1	20 tons
Material 2	5 tons
Material 3	21 tons

Assuming that RMC is interested in maximizing the total profit contribution, answer the following:
a. What is the linear programming model for this problem?
b. Find the optimal solution. How many tons of each product should be produced, and what is the projected total profit contribution?
c. Is there any unused material? If so, how much?
d. Are there any redundant constraints? If so, which ones?

22. **SELF**Test Kelson Sporting Equipment, Inc., makes two different types of baseball gloves: a regular model and a catcher's model. The firm has 900 hours of production time available in its cutting and sewing department, 300 hours available in its finishing department, and 100 hours available in its packaging and shipping department. The production time requirements and the profit contribution per glove are given in the following table.

	Production Time (hours)			
Model	Cutting and Sewing	Finishing	Packaging and Shipping	Profit/Glove
Regular model	1	$1/2$	$1/8$	$5
Catcher's model	$3/2$	$1/3$	$1/4$	$8

Assuming that the company is interested in maximizing the total profit contribution, answer the following:

a. What is the linear programming model for this problem?

b. Find the optimal solution. How many gloves of each model should Kelson manufacture?

c. What is the total profit contribution Kelson can earn with the above production quantities?

d. How many hours of production time will be scheduled in each department?

e. What is the slack time in each department?

23. George Johnson recently inherited a large sum of money; he wants to use a portion of this money to set up a trust fund for his two children. The trust fund has two investment options: (1) a bond fund and (2) a stock fund. The projected returns over the life of the investments are 6% for the bond fund and 10% for the stock fund. Whatever portion of the inheritance he finally decides to commit to the trust fund, he wants to invest at least 30% of that amount in the bond fund. In addition, he wants to select a mix that will enable him to obtain a total return of at least 7.5%.

a. Formulate a linear programming model that can be used to determine the percentage that should be allocated to each of the possible investment alternatives.

b. Solve the problem using the graphical solution procedure.

24. The Sea Wharf Restaurant would like to determine the best way to allocate a monthly advertising budget of $1000 between newspaper advertising and radio advertising. Management has decided that at least 25% of the budget must be spent on each type of media, and that the amount of money spent on local newspaper advertising must be at least twice the amount spent on radio advertising. A marketing consultant has developed an index that measures audience exposure per dollar of advertising on a scale from 0 to 100, with higher values implying greater audience exposure. If the value of the index for local newspaper advertising is 50 and the value of the index for spot radio advertising is 80, how should the restaurant allocate its advertising budget in order to maximize the value of total audience exposure?

a. Formulate a linear programming model that can be used to determine how the restaurant should allocate its advertising budget in order to maximize the value of total audience exposure.

b. Solve the problem using the graphical solution procedure.

25. Investment Advisors, Inc., is a brokerage firm that manages stock portfolios for a number of clients. A new client has requested that the firm handle an $80,000 investment portfolio. As an initial investment strategy, the client would like to restrict the portfolio to a mix of the following stocks:

Stock	Price/Share	Estimated Annual Return/Share	Risk Index/Share
U.S. Oil	$25	$3	0.50
Hub Properties	$50	$5	0.25

The risk index for the stock is a rating of the relative risk of the two investment alternatives. For the data given, U.S. Oil is judged to be the riskier investment. By constraining the total risk for the portfolio, the investment firm avoids placing excessive amounts of the portfolio in potentially high-return, but also high-risk, investments. For the current portfolio, an upper limit of 700 has been set for the total risk index of all investments. The firm has also set an upper limit of 1000 shares for the more risky U.S. Oil stock. How many shares of each stock should be purchased to maximize the total annual return?

26. Tom's, Inc., produces various Mexican food products and sells them to Western Foods, a chain of grocery stores located in Texas and New Mexico. Tom's, Inc., makes two salsa products: Western Foods Salsa and Mexico City Salsa. Essentially, the two products have

different blends of whole tomatoes, tomato sauce, and tomato paste. The Western Foods Salsa is a blend of 50% whole tomatoes, 30% tomato sauce, and 20% tomato paste. The Mexico City Salsa, which has a thicker and chunkier consistency, consists of 70% whole tomatoes, 10% tomato sauce, and 20% tomato paste. Each jar of salsa produced weighs 10 ounces. For the current production period Tom's, Inc., can purchase up to 280 pounds of whole tomatoes, 130 pounds of tomato sauce, and 100 pounds of tomato paste; the price per pound for these ingredients is $0.96, $0.64, and $0.56, respectively. The cost of the spices and the other ingredients is approximately $0.10 per jar. Tom's, Inc., buys empty glass jars for $0.02 each, and labeling and filling costs are estimated to be $0.03 for each jar of salsa produced. Tom's contract with Western Foods results in sales revenue of $1.64 for each jar of Western Foods Salsa and $1.93 for each jar of Mexico City Salsa.

    a. Develop a linear programming model that will enable Tom's to determine the mix of salsa products that will maximize the total profit contribution.

    b. Graph the feasible region.

    c. Solve the appropriate simultaneous linear equations to determine the coordinates of each extreme point.

    d. Find the optimal solution.

27. The production editor for Rayburn Publishing Company has 1800 pages of manuscript that must be copyedited. Because of the short time frame involved, only two copyeditors are available: Erhan Mergen and Sue Smith. Erhan has 10 days available and Sue has 12 days available. Erhan can process 100 pages of manuscript per day and Sue can process 150 pages of manuscript per day. Rayburn Publishing has developed an index used to measure the overall quality of a copyeditor on a scale from 1 (worst) to 10 (best). Erhan's quality rating is 9 and Sue's quality rating is 6. In addition, Erhan charges $3 per page of copyedited manuscript and Sue charges $2 per page. If a budget of $4800 has been allocated for copyediting, how many pages should be assigned to each copyeditor in order to complete the project with the highest possible quality?

28. Car Phones, Inc., sells two models of car telephones: model x and model y. Records show that 3 hours of sales time are used for each model x phone that is sold and 5 hours of sales time for each model y phone. A total of 600 hours of sales time is available for the next 4-week period. In addition, management planning policies call for minimum sales goals of 25 units for both model x and model y.

    a. Show the feasible region for the Car Phones, Inc., problem.

    b. Assuming the company makes a $40 profit contribution for each model x sold and a $50 profit contribution for each model y sold, what is the optimal sales goal for the company for the next 4-week period?

    c. Develop a constraint and show the feasible region if management adds the restriction that Car Phones must sell at least as many model y phones as model x phones.

    d. What is the new optimal solution if the constraint in part (c) is added to the problem?

29. **SELF**Test Consider the following linear program:

$$\text{Min} \quad 3x_1 + 4x_2$$

s.t.

$$1x_1 + 3x_2 \geq 6$$

$$1x_1 + 1x_2 \geq 4$$

$$x_1, x_2 \geq 0$$

Identify the feasible region and find the optimal solution. What is the value of the objective function?

30. Identify the three extreme-point solutions for the M&D Chemicals problem (see Section 2.4). Identify the value of the objective function and the values of the slack and surplus variables at each extreme point.

31. Consider the following linear programming problem:

$$\text{Min} \quad x_1 + 2x_2$$

s.t.

$$x_1 + 4x_2 \leq 21$$

$$2x_1 + x_2 \geq 7$$

$$3x_1 + 1.5x_2 \leq 21$$

$$-2x_1 + 6x_2 \geq 0$$

$$x_1, x_2 \geq 0$$

a. Find the optimal solution and the value of the objective function.
b. Determine the amount of slack or surplus for each constraint.
c. Suppose the objective function is changed to max $5x_1 + 2x_2$. Find the optimal solution and the value of the objective function.

32. **SELF**Test   Consider the following linear program:

$$\text{Min} \quad 2x_1 + 2x_2$$

s.t.

$$1x_1 + 3x_2 \leq 12$$

$$3x_1 + 1x_2 \geq 13$$

$$1x_1 - 1x_2 = 3$$

$$x_1, x_2 \geq 0$$

a. Show the feasible region.
b. What are the extreme points of the feasible region?
c. Find the optimal solution using the graphical solution procedure.

33. **SELF**Test   For the linear program

$$\text{Min} \quad 6x_1 + 4x_2$$

s.t.

$$2x_1 + 1x_2 \geq 12$$

$$1x_1 + 1x_2 \geq 10$$

$$1x_2 \leq 4$$

$$x_1, x_2 \geq 0$$

a. Write the problem in standard form.
b. Solve the problem using the graphical solution procedure.
c. What are the values of the slack and surplus variables?

34. Greentree Kennels, Inc., provides overnight lodging for a variety of pets. A particular feature at Greentree is the quality of care the pets receive, including excellent food. The kennel's dog food is made by mixing two brand-name dog food products to obtain what the kennel calls the "well-balanced dog diet." The data for the two dog foods are as follows:

Dog Food	Cost/ Ounce	Protein (%)	Fat (%)
Bark Bits	$.06	30	15
Canine Chow	$.05	20	30

If Greentree wants to be sure that the dogs receive at least 5 ounces of protein and at least 3 ounces of fat per day, what is the minimum cost mix of the two dog food products?

35. The New England Cheese Company produces two cheese spreads by blending mild cheddar cheese with extra sharp cheddar cheese. The cheese spreads are packaged in 12-ounce containers, which are then sold to distributors throughout the Northeast. The Regular blend contains 80% mild cheddar and 20% extra sharp, and the Zesty blend contains 60% mild cheddar and 40% extra sharp. This year, a local dairy cooperative has offered to provide up to 8100 pounds of mild cheddar cheese for $1.20 per pound and up to 3000 pounds of extra sharp cheddar cheese for $1.40 per pound. The cost to blend and package the cheese spreads, excluding the cost of the cheese, is $0.20 per container. If each container of Regular is sold for $1.95 and each container of Zesty is sold for $2.20, how many containers of Regular and Zesty should New England Cheese produce?

36. Healthtech Food Products is considering developing a new low-fat snack food. It is to be a blend of two types of cereals, each of which has different fiber, fat, and protein characteristics. The following table shows these nutrition characteristics for one ounce of each type of cereal.

Cereal	Dietary Fiber (grams)	Fat (grams)	Protein (grams)
A	2	2	4
B	1.5	3	3

Note that each ounce of cereal A provides 2 grams of dietary fiber and that each ounce of cereal B provides 1.5 grams of dietary fiber. Thus, if Healthtech were to develop the new product using a mix consisting of 50% of cereal A and 50% cereal B, 1 ounce of the snack food would contain 1.75 grams of dietary fiber. Healthtech's nutrition requirements call for each ounce of the new food to have at least 1.7 grams of dietary fiber, no more than 2.8 grams of fat, and no more than 3.6 grams of protein. The cost of cereal A is $0.02 per ounce and the cost of cereal B is $0.025 per ounce. Healthtech wants to determine how much of each cereal is needed to produce 1 ounce of the new food product at the lowest possible cost.

a. Formulate a linear programming model for this situation.
b. Solve the problem using the graphical solution procedure.
c. What are the values of the slack and surplus variables?
d. If Healthtech markets the new snack food in an 8-ounce package, what is the cost per package?

37. Innis Investments manages funds for a number of companies and wealthy clients. The investment strategy is tailored to each client's needs. For a new client, Innis has been authorized to invest up to $1.2 million in two investment funds: a stock fund and a money market fund. Each unit of the stock fund costs $50 and provides an annual rate of return of 10%; each unit of the money market fund costs $100 and provides an annual rate of return of 4%.

The client wants to minimize risk subject to the requirement that the annual income from the investment be at least $60,000. According to Innis's risk measurement system, each unit invested in the stock fund has a risk index of 8, and each unit invested in the money market fund has a risk index of 3; the higher risk index associated with the stock fund simply indicates that it is the riskier investment. Innis's client has also specified that at least $300,000 be invested in the money market fund.

a. Determine how many units of each fund Innis should purchase for the client to minimize the total risk index for the portfolio.
b. How much annual income will this investment strategy generate?
c. Suppose the client desires to maximize annual return. How should the funds be invested?

38. Photo Chemicals produces two types of photographic developing fluids. Both products cost Photo Chemicals $1 per gallon to produce. Based on an analysis of current inventory levels and outstanding orders for the next month, Photo Chemicals' management has specified that at least 30 gallons of product 1 and at least 20 gallons of product 2 must be produced during the next 2 weeks. Management has also stated that an existing inventory of highly perishable raw material required in the production of both fluids must be used within the next 2 weeks. The current inventory of the perishable raw material is 80 pounds. While more of this raw material can be ordered if necessary, any of the current inventory that is not used within the next 2 weeks will spoil—hence, the management requirement that at least 80 pounds be used in the next 2 weeks. Furthermore, it is known that product 1 requires 1 pound of this perishable raw material per gallon and product 2 requires 2 pounds of the raw material per gallon. Since Photo Chemicals' objective is to keep its production costs at the minimum possible level, the firm's management is looking for a minimum-cost production plan that uses all the 80 pounds of perishable raw material and provides at least 30 gallons of product 1 and at least 20 gallons of product 2. What is the minimum-cost solution?

39. Bryant's Pizza, Inc., is a producer of frozen pizza products. The company makes a profit of $1.00 for each regular pizza it produces and $1.50 for each deluxe pizza produced. Each pizza includes a combination of dough mix and topping mix. The firm currently has 150 pounds of dough mix and 50 pounds of topping mix. Each regular pizza uses 1 pound of dough mix and 4 ounces of topping mix. Each deluxe pizza uses 1 pound of dough mix and 8 ounces of topping mix. Based on past demand, Bryant can sell at least 50 regular pizzas and at least 25 deluxe pizzas. How many regular and deluxe pizzas should the company make to maximize profits?
   a. What is the linear programming model for this problem?
   b. Write the linear program in standard form.
   c. Find the optimal solution.
   d. What are the values and interpretations of all slack and surplus variables?
   e. Which constraints are binding?

40. **SELF**Test Does the following linear program involve infeasibility, unbounded, and/or alternative optimal solutions? Explain.

$$\text{Max} \quad 4x_1 + 8x_2$$

s.t.

$$2x_1 + 2x_2 \leq 10$$

$$-1x_1 + 1x_2 \geq 8$$

$$x_1, x_2 \geq 0$$

41. **SELF**Test Does the following linear program involve infeasibility, unbounded, and/or alternative optimal solutions? Explain.

$$\text{Max} \quad 1x_1 + 1x_2$$

s.t.

$$8x_1 + 6x_2 \geq 24$$

$$4x_1 + 6x_2 \geq -12$$

$$2x_2 \geq 4$$

$$x_1, x_2 \geq 0$$

42. Consider the following linear program:

$$\text{Max} \quad 1x_1 + 1x_2$$

s.t.

$$5x_1 + 3x_2 \leq 15$$

$$3x_1 + 5x_2 \leq 15$$

$$x_1, x_2 \geq 0$$

a. What is the optimal solution for this problem?

b. Suppose that the objective function is changed to $1x_1 + 2x_2$. Find the new optimal solution.

c. By adjusting the coefficient of x_2 in the objective function, develop a new objective function that will make the solutions found in parts (a) and (b) alternative optimal solutions.

43. Consider the following linear program:

$$\text{Max} \quad 1x_1 - 2x_2$$

s.t.

$$-4x_1 + 3x_2 \leq 3$$

$$1x_1 - 1x_2 \leq 3$$

$$x_1, x_2 \geq 0$$

a. Graph the feasible region for the problem.

b. Is the feasible region unbounded? Explain.

c. Find the optimal solution.

d. Does an unbounded feasible region imply that the optimal solution to the linear program will be unbounded?

44. The manager of a small independent grocery store is trying to determine the best use of her shelf space for soft drinks. The store carries national and generic brands and currently has 200 square feet of shelf space available. The manager wants to allocate at least 60% of the space to the national brands and, regardless of the profitability, allocate at least 10% of the space to the generic brands. How many square feet of space should the manager allocate to the national brands and the generic brands if

a. The national brands are more profitable than the generic brands?

b. Both brands are equally profitable?

c. The generic brand is more profitable than the national brand?

45. Discuss what happens to the M&D Chemicals problem (see Section 2.4) if the cost per gallon for product 1 is increased to $3.00 per gallon. What would you recommend? Explain.

46. For the M&D Chemicals problem in Section 2.4, discuss the effect of management's requiring total production of 500 gallons for the two products. List two or three actions M&D should consider to correct the situation you encounter.

47. Reconsider the RMC situation in Problem 21.

a. Identify all the extreme points of the feasible region.

b. Suppose RMC discovers a way to increase the profit of solvent base to $60 per ton. Does this change the optimal solution? If so, how?

c. Suppose the profit for the solvent base is $50 per ton. What is the optimal solution now? Comment on any special characteristics that may exist with this profit for the solvent base.

48. Reconsider the RMC situation in Problem 21. Suppose that management adds the requirements that at least 30 tons of fuel additive and at least 15 tons of solvent base must be produced.

a. Graph the constraints for this revised RMC problem. What happens to the feasible region? Explain.

b. If there are no feasible solutions, explain what is needed to produce 30 tons of fuel additive and 15 tons of solvent base.

49. Reconsider the Kelson Sporting Equipment, Inc., production example in Problem 22. Discuss the concepts of infeasibility, unbounded solutions, and alternative optimal solutions as they occur in each of the following situations:

a. Management has requested that the production of baseball gloves (regular model plus catcher's model) be such that the total number of gloves produced is at least 750. That is, $1x_1 + 1x_2 \geq 750$.

    b. The original problem has to be solved again because the profit contribution for the regular model is adjusted downward to $4 per glove.

    c. What would have to happen for this problem to be unbounded?

50. Reconsider the RMC situation in Problem 21. Use the graphical sensitivity analysis approach to determine what ranges of values for the profit per ton of the fuel additive and solvent base can exist without causing RMC to change from the current optimal solution of 25 tons of fuel additive and 20 tons of solvent base.

51. For the RMC situation in Problem 21, use the graphical sensitivity analysis approach to determine what happens if an additional 3 tons of material 3 become available. What is the corresponding dual price?

52. **SELF**Test   Consider the linear program given below.

$$\text{Max} \quad 2x_1 + 3x_2$$

s.t.

$$x_1 + x_2 \leq 10$$
$$2x_1 + x_2 \geq 4$$
$$x_1 + 3x_2 \leq 24$$
$$2x_1 + x_2 \leq 16$$
$$x_1, x_2 \geq 0$$

    a. Solve this problem using the graphical solution procedure.

    b. Compute the range of optimality for c_1.

    c. Compute the range of optimality for c_2.

    d. Suppose c_1 is increased from 2 to 2.5. What is the new optimal solution?

    e. Suppose c_2 is decreased from 3 to 1. What is the new optimal solution?

53. **SELF**Test   Refer to Problem 52. Compute the dual prices for constraints 1 and 2 and interpret them.

54. Consider the linear program given below.

$$\text{Min} \quad x_1 + x_2$$

s.t.

$$x_1 + 2x_2 \geq 7$$
$$2x_1 + x_2 \geq 5$$
$$x_1 + 6x_2 \geq 11$$
$$x_1, x_2 \geq 0$$

    a. Solve this problem using the graphical solution procedure.

    b. Compute the range of optimality for c_1.

    c. Compute the range of optimality for c_2.

    d. Suppose c_1 is increased to 1.5. Find the new optimal solution.

    e. Suppose c_2 is decreased to $1/3$. Find the new optimal solution.

55. Refer to Problem 54. Compute and interpret the dual prices for the constraints.

56. Consider the linear program given below.

$$\text{Max} \quad 5x_1 + 7x_2$$

s.t.

$$2x_1 + x_2 \geq 3$$
$$-x_1 + 5x_2 \geq 4$$

$$2x_1 - 3x_2 \leq 6$$

$$3x_1 + 2x_2 \leq 35$$

$$\tfrac{3}{7}x_1 + x_2 \leq 10$$

$$x_1, x_2 \geq 0$$

a. Solve this problem using the graphical solution procedure.
b. Compute the range of optimality for c_1.
c. Compute the range of optimality for c_2.
d. Suppose c_1 is decreased to 2. What is the new optimal solution?
e. Suppose c_2 is increased to 10. What is the new optimal solution?

57. Refer to Problem 56. Suppose the objective function coefficient for c_2 is reduced to 3.
   a. Resolve using the graphical solution procedure.
   b. Compute the dual prices for constraints 2 and 3.

58. Refer again to Problem 52.
   a. Suppose c_1 is increased to 3 and c_2 is increased to 4. Find the new optimal solution.
   b. Suppose c_1 is increased to 3 and c_2 is decreased to 2. Find the new optimal solution.

59. Refer again to Problem 56.
   a. Suppose c_1 is decreased to 4 and c_2 is increased to 10. Find the new optimal solution.
   b. Suppose c_1 is decreased to 4 and c_2 is increased to 8. Find the new optimal solution.

60. Expedition Outfitters manufactures a variety of specialty clothing for hiking, skiing, and mountain climbing. They have decided to begin production on two new parkas designed for use in extremely cold weather; the names selected for the two models are the Mount Everest Parka and the Rocky Mountain Parka. Their manufacturing plant has 120 hours of cutting time and 120 hours of sewing time available for producing these two parkas. Each Mount Everest Parka requires 30 minutes of cutting time and 45 minutes of sewing time, and each Rocky Mountain Parka requires 20 minutes of cutting time and 15 minutes of sewing time. The labor and material cost is $150 for each Mount Everest Parka and $50 for each Rocky Mountain Parka, and the retail prices through the firm's mail order catalog are $250 for the Mount Everest Parka and $200 for the Rocky Mountain Parka. Because management believes that the Mount Everest Parka is a unique coat that will enhance the image of the firm, they have specified that at least 20% of the total production must consist of this model. Assuming that Expedition Outfitters can sell as many coats of each type as they can produce, how many units of each model should they manufacture to maximize the total profit contribution?

61. English Motors, Ltd. (EML), has developed a new all-wheel-drive sports utility vehicle. As part of the marketing campaign, EML has developed a video tape sales presentation which will be sent to both owners of current EML four-wheel-drive vehicles as well as to owners of four-wheel-drive sports utility vehicles offered by competitors; EML refers to these two target markets as the current customer market and the new customer market. Individuals who receive the new promotion video will also receive a coupon for a test drive of the new EML model for one weekend. A key factor in the success of the new promotion is the response rate, the percentage of individuals that receives the new promotion and test drives the new model. EML estimates that the response rate for the current customer market is 25% and the response rate for the new customer market is 20%. The sales rate is the percentage of individuals that receives the new promotion, takes the test drive, and makes a purchase. Marketing research studies indicate that the sales rate is 12% for the current customer market and 20% for the new customer market. The cost for each promotion, excluding the test drive costs, are $5 for each promotion sent to the current customer market and $4 for each promotion sent to the new customer market. Management has also specified that a minimum of 30,000 current customers should be sent the new promotion and a minimum of 10,000 new customers should be sent the new promotion. In addition, the number of current customers that test drives the new vehicle must be at least twice the number of new customers that test drives the new vehicle. If the marketing budget, excluding test drive costs, is $1,200,000, how many promotions should be sent to each group of customers in order to maximize total sales?

62. Creative Sports Designs (CSD) manufactures a standard-size racket and an oversize racket. The firm's rackets are extremely light due to the use of a magnesium–graphite alloy that was invented by the firm's founder. Each standard-size racket uses 0.125 kilograms of the alloy and each oversize racket uses 0.4 kilograms; over the next 2-week production period only 80 kilograms of the alloy are available. Each standard-size racket uses 10 minutes of manufacturing time and each oversize racket uses 12 minutes. The profit contributions are $10 for each standard-size racket and $15 for each oversize racket, and 40 hours of manufacturing time are available each week. Management has specified that at least 20% of the total production must be the standard-size racket. How many rackets of each type should CSD manufacture over the next 2 weeks to maximize the total profit contribution? Assume that because of the unique nature of their products, CSD can sell as many rackets as they can produce.

63. Management of High Tech Services (HTS) would like to develop a model that will help allocate their technicians' time between service calls to regular contract customers and new customers. A maximum of 80 hours of technician time is available over the 2-week planning period. To satisfy cash flow requirements, at least $800 in revenue (per technician) must be generated during the 2-week period. Technician time for regular customers generates $25 per hour. However, technician time for new customers only generates an average of $8 per hour because in many cases a new customer contact does not provide billable services. To ensure that new customer contacts are being maintained, the technician time spent on new customer contacts must be at least 60% of the time spent on regular customer contacts. Given the above revenue and policy requirements, HTS would like to determine how to allocate technician time between regular customers and new customers so that the total number of customers contacted during the 2-week period will be maximized. Technicians require an average of 50 minutes for each regular customer contact and 1 hour for each new customer contact.

  a. Develop a linear programming model that will enable HTS to allocate technician time between regular customers and new customers.

  b. Graph the feasible region.

  c. Solve the appropriate simultaneous linear equations to determine the values of x_1 and x_2 at each extreme point of the feasible region.

  d. Find the optimal solution.

64. Jackson Hole Manufacturing is a small manufacturer of plastic products used in the automotive and computer industries. One of its major contracts is with a large computer company and involves the production of plastic printer cases for the computer company's portable printers. The printer cases are produced on two injection molding machines. The M-100 machine has a production capacity of 20 printer cases per hour, and the M-200 machine has a production capacity of 40 cases per hour. Both machines use the same chemical material to produce the printer cases; the M-100 uses 40 pounds of the raw material per hour and the M-200 uses 50 pounds per hour. The computer company has asked Jackson Hole to produce as many of the cases during the upcoming week as possible and has said that it will pay $18 for each case Jackson Hole can deliver. However, next week is a regularly scheduled vacation period for most of Jackson Hole's production employees; during this time, annual maintenance is performed for all equipment in the plant. Because of the downtime for maintenance, the M-100 will be available for no more than 15 hours, and the M-200 will be available for no more than 10 hours. However, because of the high setup cost involved with both machines, management has a requirement that, if production is scheduled on either machine, the machine must be operated for at least 5 hours. The supplier of the chemical material used in the production process has informed Jackson Hole that a maximum of 1000 pounds of the chemical material will be available for next week's production; the cost for this raw material is $6 per pound. In addition to the raw material cost, Jackson Hole estimates that the hourly cost of operating the M-100 and the M-200 are $50 and $75, respectively.

  a. Formulate a linear programming model that can be used to maximize the contribution to profit.

  b. Solve the problem using the graphical solution procedure.

Case Problem: Advertising Strategy

Midtown Motors, Inc., has hired a marketing services firm to develop an advertising strategy for promoting Midtown's used-car sales. The marketing firm has recommended that Midtown use spot announcements on both television and radio as the advertising media for the proposed promotional campaign. Advertising strategy guidelines are expressed as follows:

1. Use at least 30 announcements for combined television and radio coverage.
2. Do not use more than 25 radio announcements.
3. The number of radio announcements cannot be less than the number of television announcements.

The television station has quoted a cost of $1200 per spot announcement, and the radio station has quoted a cost of $300 per spot announcement. Midtown's advertising budget has been set at $25,500. The marketing services firm has rated the various advertising media in terms of audience coverage and recall power of the advertisement. For Midtown's media alternatives, the television announcement is rated at 600, and the radio announcement is rated at 200. Midtown's president would like to know how many television and how many radio spot announcements should be used to maximize the overall rating of the advertising campaign.

Midtown's president believes the television station will consider running the Midtown spot announcement on its highly rated evening news program (at the same cost) if Midtown will consider using additional television announcements.

Managerial Report

Perform an analysis of advertising strategy for Midtown Motors, and prepare a report to Midtown's president presenting your findings and recommendations. Include (but do not limit your discussion to) a consideration of the following:

1. The recommended number of television and radio spot announcements
2. The relative merits of each advertising medium
3. The news program rating that would be necessary before it would make sense to increase the number of television spots
4. The number of television spots that should be purchased if the news program is rated highly enough to make increasing the number of television spots advisable
5. The restrictions placed on the advertising strategy that Midtown might want to consider relaxing or altering
6. The best use of any possible increase in the advertising budget
7. Any other information that may help Midtown's president make the advertising strategy decision

Include a copy of your linear programming model and graphical solution in the appendix to your report.

Case Problem: Production Strategy

Better Fitness, Inc. (BFI) manufactures exercise equipment at its plant in Freeport, Long Island. It recently designed two universal weight machines for the home exercise market. Both machines use BFI-patented technology that provides the user with an extremely wide range of motion capability for each type of exercise performed. Until now, such capabilities have been available only on expensive weight machines used primarily by physical therapists.

At a recent trade show, demonstrations of the machines resulted in significant dealer interest. In fact, the number of orders that BFI received at the trade show far exceeded its manufacturing capabilities for the current production period. As a result, management decided to begin production of the two machines. The two machines, which BFI has named the BodyPlus 100 and the BodyPlus 200, require different amounts of resources to produce.

The BodyPlus 100 consists of a frame unit, a press station, and a pec-dec station. Each frame produced uses 4 hours of machining and welding time and 2 hours of painting and finishing time. Each press station requires 2 hours of machining and welding time and 1 hour of painting and finishing time, and each pec-dec station uses 2 hours of machining and welding time and 2 hours of painting and finishing time. In addition, 2 hours are spent assembling, testing, and packaging each BodyPlus 100. The raw material costs are $450 for each frame, $300 for each press station, and $250 for each pec-dec station; packaging costs are estimated to be $50 per unit.

The BodyPlus 200 consists of a frame unit, a press station, a pec-dec station, and a leg-press station. Each frame produced uses 5 hours of machining and welding time and 4 hours of painting and finishing time. Each press station requires 3 hours of machining and welding time and 2 hours of painting and finishing time, each pec-dec station uses 2 hours of machining and welding time and 2 hours of painting and finishing time, and each leg-press station requires 2 hours of machining and welding time and 2 hours of painting and finishing time. In addition, 2 hours are spent assembling, testing, and packaging each BodyPlus 200. The raw material costs are $650 for each frame, $400 for each press station, $250 for each pec-dec station, and $200 for each leg-press station; packaging costs are estimated to be $75 per unit.

For the next production period, management estimates that 600 hours of machining and welding time, 450 hours of painting and finishing time, and 140 hours of assembly, testing, and packaging time will be available. Current labor costs are $20 per hour for machining and welding time, $15 per hour for painting and finishing time, and $12 per hour for assembly, testing, and packaging time. The market in which the two machines must compete suggests a retail price of $2400 for the BodyPlus 100 and $3500 for the BodyPlus 200, although some flexibility may be available to BFI because of the unique capabilities of the new machines. Authorized BFI dealers can purchase machines for 70% of the suggested retail price.

BFI's president believes that the unique capabilities of the BodyPlus 200 can help position BFI as one of the leaders in high-end exercise equipment. Consequently, he has stated that the number of units of the BodyPlus 200 produced must be at least 25% of the total production.

Managerial Report

Analyze Better Fitness, Inc.'s production problem and prepare a report to BFI's president presenting your findings and recommendations. Include (but do not limit your discussion to) a consideration of the following items:

1. The recommended number of BodyPlus 100 and BodyPlus 200 machines to produce
2. The effect on profits of the requirement that the number of units of the BodyPlus 200 produced must be at least 25% of the total production
3. Where efforts should be expended in order to increase profits

Include a copy of your linear programming model and graphical solution in an appendix to your report.

CHAPTER three

Linear Programming: Formulation, Computer Solution, and Interpretation

In this chapter we provide an introduction to the use of computers for solving linear programming problems. We begin by showing how to interpret computer output from The Management Scientist for the Par, Inc., and M&D Chemicals problems presented in Chapter 2. Then we extend the discussion by formulating and solving two slightly larger problems with three decision variables. In discussing the computer solution for each of these problems, we focus on the interpretation of the computer output including both the optimal solution and sensitivity analysis information. The final section provides both general guidelines for problem formulation and further practice in the formulation, computer solution, and interpretation of output for a problem involving four decision variables and various types of constraints. Three appendixes provide details on using The Management Scientist, LINDO/PC, and spreadsheets to solve linear programming problems.

3.1 Computer Solution of Linear Programs

Computer programs designed to solve linear programming problems are now widely available. Most companies and universities have access to these computer programs. After a short period of familiarization with the specific features of the package, users can usually solve linear programming problems with few difficulties. Problems involving thousands of variables and thousands of constraints are now routinely solved with computer packages. Most large linear programs can be solved with just a few minutes of computer time; small linear programs usually require only a few seconds.

More recently there has been a virtual explosion of software for personal computers. A large number of user-friendly computer programs that can solve linear programs are now available. These programs, developed by academicians and small software companies, are almost all easy to use. Most of these programs are designed to solve smaller linear programs (a few hundred variables). But, some can be used to solve problems involving thousands of variables and constraints. Linear programming solvers are now part of many spreadsheet packages. In Appendix 3.3, we show how to use the solver available with Microsoft Excel.

The Management Scientist, a software package developed by the authors of this text, contains a linear programming module. Let us demonstrate its usage by solving the Par, Inc., problem we introduced in Chapter 2. Since computer input must utilize decimal rather than fractional data values, we restate the problem with decimal coefficients:

$$\text{Max} \quad 10x_1 + \quad 9x_2$$

s.t.

$$0.7x_1 + \quad 1x_2 \le 630 \quad \text{Cutting and dyeing}$$

$$0.5x_1 + 0.83333x_2 \le 600 \quad \text{Sewing}$$

$$1.0x_1 + 0.66667x_2 \le 708 \quad \text{Finishing}$$

$$0.1x_1 + \quad 0.25x_2 \le 135 \quad \text{Inspection and packaging}$$

$$x_1, x_2 \ge 0$$

Note that in the preceding form, the coefficient of x_2 in the sewing constraint is written as 0.83333, which is the closest five-place decimal value to the fraction ⅚. A similar rounding occurs for the x_2 coefficient in the finishing constraint, where the decimal 0.66667 is used as the closest five-place decimal value to the fraction ⅔. When this rounding of the input data is required, we may expect the computer solution to be slightly different than the hand-calculated solution based on the exact fractional values. However, as you will see, the two solutions are extremely close, and the slight rounding of the input data causes no serious problem. The solution[1] generated by The Management Scientist is shown in Figure 3.1.

Interpretation of Computer Output

Let us look more closely at The Management Scientist output in Figure 3.1 and interpret the computer solution provided for the Par, Inc., problem. First, note the number 7667.99463, which appears to the right of Objective Function Value. Rounding this value, we can conclude that the optimal solution to this problem will provide a profit of $7668. Directly below the objective function value, we find the values of the decision variables at the optimal solution. After rounding we have $x_1 = 540$ standard bags and $x_2 = 252$ deluxe bags as the optimal production quantities.

The information in the Reduced Costs column indicates how much the objective function coefficient of each decision variable would have to improve[2] before it would be possible for that variable to assume a positive value in the optimal solution. If a decision variable is already positive in the optimal solution, its reduced cost is zero. For the Par, Inc., problem, the optimal solution is $x_1 = 540$ and $x_2 = 252$. Since both variables already have positive values, their corresponding reduced costs are zero. In Section 3.2 we will interpret the reduced cost for a decision variable that does not have a positive value in the optimal solution.

---

[1] The steps required to generate this solution are described in Appendix 3.1.
[2] For a maximization problem, improve means get bigger; for a minimization problem, improve means get smaller.

Figure 3.1

The Management Scientist Solution for the Par, Inc., Problem

```
     Objective Function Value =        7667.99463

          Variable            Value            Reduced Costs
        --------------    --------------    ------------------

            X1              539.99841              0.00000
            X2              252.00113              0.00000

         Constraint       Slack/Surplus         Dual Prices
        --------------    --------------    ------------------

             1                0.00000              4.37496
             2              120.00070              0.00000
             3                0.00000              6.93753
             4               17.99988              0.00000

     OBJECTIVE COEFFICIENT RANGES

        Variable       Lower Limit      Current Value      Upper Limit
       -----------    --------------    --------------    --------------

           X1             6.30000          10.00000          13.49993
           X2             6.66670           9.00000          14.28572

     RIGHT HAND SIDE RANGES

       Constraint      Lower Limit      Current Value      Upper Limit
       -----------    --------------    --------------    --------------

            1            495.59998         630.00000         682.36316
            2            479.99930         600.00000      No Upper Limit
            3            580.00146         708.00000         900.00000
            4            117.00012         135.00000      No Upper Limit
```

Immediately following the optimal x_1 and x_2 values and the reduced cost information, the computer output provides information about the status of the constraints. Recall that the Par, Inc., problem had four less-than-or-equal-to constraints corresponding to the hours available in each of four production departments. The information shown in the Slack/Surplus column provides the value of the slack variable for each of the departments. This information (after rounding) is summarized here:

Constraint Number	Constraint Name	Slack
1	Cutting and dyeing	0
2	Sewing	120
3	Finishing	0
4	Inspection and packaging	18

From this information, we see that the binding constraints (the cutting and dyeing and the finishing constraints) have zero slack at the optimal solution. The sewing department has 120 hours of slack, or unused capacity, and the inspection and packaging department has 18 hours of slack or unused capacity.

The Dual Prices column contains information about the marginal value of each of the four resources at the optimal solution. In Chapter 2 we defined the *dual price* as follows.

> The dual price associated with a constraint is the *improvement* in the value of the solution per-unit increase in the right-hand side of the constraint.

You should be able to use computer output to determine the optimal solution, and you should be able to interpret the values of the dual prices. Try Problem 1.

Thus, we see that the nonzero dual prices of 4.37496 for constraint 1 (cutting and dyeing constraint) and 6.93753 for constraint 3 (finishing constraint) tell us that an additional hour of cutting and dyeing time improves (increases) the value of the optimal solution by $4.37 and an additional hour of finishing time improves (increases) the value of the optimal solution by $6.94. Thus, if the cutting and dyeing time were increased from 630 to 631 hours, with all other coefficients in the problem remaining the same, Par's profit would be increased by $4.37 from $7668 to $7668 + $4.37 = $7672.37. A similar interpretation for the finishing constraint implies that an increase from 708 to 709 hours of available finishing time, with all other coefficients in the problem remaining the same, would increase Par's profit to $7668 + $6.94 = $7674.94. Since the sewing and the inspection and packaging constraints both have slack or unused capacity available, the dual prices of zero show that additional hours of these two resources will not improve the value of the objective function.

Referring again to the computer output in Figure 3.1, we see that after providing the constraint information on slack/surplus variables and dual prices, The Management Scientist prints ranges for the objective function coefficients and the right-hand sides of the constraints.

Considering the information provided under the computer output heading labeled OBJECTIVE COEFFICIENT RANGES, we see that variable x_1, which has a current profit coefficient of 10, has the following *range of optimality* for c_1:

$$6.30 \leq c_1 \leq 13.50$$

This tells us that as long as the profit contribution associated with the standard bag is between $6.30 and $13.50, the production of $x_1 = 540$ standard bags and $x_2 = 252$ deluxe bags will remain the optimal solution. Note that this is the range of optimality that we obtained by performing graphical sensitivity analysis for c_1 in Section 2.7.

Using the objective function coefficient range information for deluxe bags, we see that The Management Scientist has computed the following range of optimality:

$$6.67 \leq c_2 \leq 14.29$$

This tells us that as long as the profit contribution associated with the deluxe bag is between $6.67 and $14.29, the production of $x_1 = 540$ standard bags and $x_2 = 252$ deluxe bags will remain the optimal solution.

You should now be able to use computer output to determine the ranges of optimality and the ranges of feasibility. Try Problem 2.

The final section of the computer printout (RIGHT HAND SIDE RANGES) contains ranging information for the constraint right-hand sides. As long as the constraint right-hand side stays within this range, the associated dual price gives the improvement in the value of the optimal solution per-unit increase in the right-hand side. For example, let us consider the cutting and dyeing constraint with a current right-hand-side value of 630. Since the dual price for this constraint is $4.37, we can conclude that additional hours will increase the objective function by $4.37 per hour. It is also true that a reduction in the hours available will reduce the value of the objective function by $4.37 per hour. From the range information given, we see that the dual price of $4.37 is valid for increases up to 682.36316 and decreases down to 495.59998. A similar interpretation for the finishing constraint's right-hand side (constraint 3) shows that the dual price of $6.94 is applicable for increases up to 900 hours and decreases down to 580.00146 hours.

As mentioned, the right-hand-side ranges provide limits within which the dual prices are applicable. For changes outside the range, the problem must be resolved to find the new optimal solution and the new dual price. We shall call the range over which the dual price is applicable the *range of feasibility*. The ranges of feasibility for the Par, Inc., problem are summarized here:

Constraint	Min RHS	Max RHS
Cutting and dyeing	495.6	682.4
Sewing	480.0	No upper limit
Finishing	580.0	900.0
Inspection and packaging	117.0	No upper limit

As long as the values of the right-hand sides are within these ranges, the dual prices shown on the computer output will not change. Right-hand-side values outside these limits will result in changes in the dual price information.

Simultaneous Changes

The sensitivity analysis information in computer output is based on the assumption that only one coefficient changes; it is assumed that all other coefficients will remain as stated in the original problem. Thus, the ranges for the objective function coefficients and the constraint right-hand sides are only applicable for changes in a single coefficient. In many cases, however, we may be interested in what would happen if two or more coefficients are changed simultaneously. As we will demonstrate, some analysis of simultaneous changes is possible with the help of the *100 percent rule*.[3] We begin by showing how the 100 percent rule applies to simultaneous changes in the objective function coefficients.

Suppose that in the Par, Inc., problem the accounting department concluded that the original profit contributions of $10 and $9 for the standard and deluxe bags, respectively, were incorrectly computed; the correct values should have been $11.50 and $8.25. To determine what effect, if any, these simultaneous changes have on the optimal solution, we need to first define the terms "allowable increase" and "allowable decrease." For an objective function coefficient, the *allowable increase* is the maximum amount the coefficient may be increased without exceeding the upper limit of the range of optimality; the *allowable decrease* is the maximum amount the coefficient may be decreased without dropping below the lower limit of the range of optimality.

From Figure 3.1 we see that the upper limit for the objective function coefficient of x_1 is 13.49993; thus, the allowable increase is $3.49993 = 13.49993 - 10$. In terms of

---

[3] See S. P. Bradley, A. C. Hax, and T. L. Magnanti, *Applied Mathematical Programming* (Reading, Mass.: Addison-Wesley, 1977).

percentage change, the increase of $1.50 in the objective function coefficient (from 10 to 11.50) for the standard bags is $(1.50/3.49993)(100) = 42.86\%$ of the allowable increase. Given the lower limit of 6.66670 for x_2, the allowable decrease for x_2 is $2.33330 = 9 - 6.66670$. In terms of percentage change, the decrease of $0.75 in the objective function coefficient (from 9 to 8.25) for the deluxe bags is $(0.75/2.33330)(100) = 32.14\%$ of the allowable decrease. The sum of the percentage change of the allowable increase (42.86%) and the percentage change of the allowable decrease (32.14%) is 75.00%.

Let us now state the 100 percent rule as it applies to simultaneous changes in the objective function coefficients.

---

100 Percent Rule for Objective Function Coefficients

For all objective function coefficients that are changed, sum the percentages of the allowable increases and the allowable decreases represented by the changes. If the sum of the percentage changes does not exceed 100%, the optimal solution will not change.

Thus, since the sum of the two percentage changes in the objective function coefficients for the Par, Inc., problem is 75%, these simultaneous changes will not affect the optimal solution. Note, however, that although the optimal solution is still $x_1 = 539.99841$ and $x_2 = 252.00113$, the value of the optimal solution will change since the profit contribution for the standard bags has increased to $11.50 and the profit contribution of the deluxe bags has decreased to $8.25.

The 100 percent rule does not, however, say that the optimal solution will change if the sum of the percentage changes exceeds 100%. It is possible that the optimal solution will not change even though the sum of the percentage changes exceeds 100%. When the 100 percent rule is not satisfied, we must resolve the problem to determine what affect such changes will have on the optimal solution.

A similar version of the 100 percent rule also applies to simultaneous changes in the constraint right-hand sides.

---

100 Percent Rule for Constraint Right-Hand Sides

For all right-hand sides that are changed, sum the percentages of allowable increases and allowable decreases. If the sum of percentages does not exceed 100%, then the dual prices will not change.

Let us illustrate the 100 percent rule for constraint right-hand sides by considering simultaneous changes in the right-hand sides for the Par, Inc., problem. Suppose, for instance, that in this problem we could obtain 20 additional hours of cutting and dyeing time and 100 additional hours of finishing time. The allowable increase for cutting and dyeing time is $682.36316 - 630.0 = 52.36316$, and the allowable increase for finishing time is $900.0 - 708.0 = 192.0$ (see Figure 3.1). The 20 additional hours of cutting and dyeing time are $(20/52.36316)(100) = 38.19\%$ of the allowable increase in the constraint's right-hand side. The 100 additional hours of finishing time are $(100/192)(100) = 52.08\%$ of the allowable increase in the finishing time constraint's right-hand side. The sum of the percentage changes is 38.19% + 52.08% = 90.27%. Since the sum of the percentage changes does not exceed 100%, we can conclude that the dual prices are applicable and that the objective function will improve by (20)(4.37) + (100)(6.94) = 781.40.

Interpretation of Computer Output—A Second Example

As another example of interpreting computer output, let us reconsider the M&D Chemicals minimization problem introduced in Section 2.4. The linear programming model for this problem is restated as follows, where x_1 = number of gallons of product 1 and x_2 = number of gallons of product 2 and it is desired to minimize production cost.

$$\text{Min} \quad 2x_1 + 3x_2$$

$$\text{s.t.}$$
$$1x_1 \qquad\;\; \geq 125 \quad \text{Demand for product 1}$$
$$1x_1 + 1x_2 \geq 350 \quad \text{Total production}$$
$$2x_1 + 1x_2 \leq 600 \quad \text{Processing time}$$
$$x_1, x_2 \geq 0$$

The solution obtained using The Management Scientist is presented in Figure 3.2. The computer output shows that the minimum-cost solution yields an objective function value of \$800. The values of the decision variables show that 250 gallons of product 1 ($x_1 = 250$) and 100 gallons of product 2 ($x_2 = 100$) provide the minimum-cost solution.

The Slack/Surplus column shows that the $\geq$ constraint corresponding to the demand for product 1 (see constraint 1) has a surplus of 125 units. This tells us that production of product 1 in the optimal solution exceeds demand by 125 gallons. The Slack/Surplus values are zero for the total production requirement (constraint 2) and the processing time limitation (constraint 3); this indicates that these constraints are binding at the optimal solution.

The Dual Prices column again shows us the *improvement* in the value of the optimal solution per-unit increase in the right-hand side of the constraint. Focusing first on the dual price of 1.00 for the processing time constraint (constraint 3), we see that if we can increase the processing time from 600 to 601 hours, the objective function value will *improve* by \$1. Since the objective is to minimize costs, improvement in this case means a lowering of costs. Thus, if 601 hours of processing time are available, the value of the optimal solution will improve to \$800 − \$1 = \$799. The RIGHT HAND SIDE RANGES section of the output shows that the upper limit for the processing time constraint (constraint 3) is 700 hours. Thus, the dual price of \$1 per unit would be applicable for every additional hour of processing time up to a total of 700 hours.

Let us again return to the Dual Prices section of the output and consider the dual price for the total production constraint (constraint 2). The *negative dual price* tells us that the value of the optimal solution *will not improve* if the value of the right-hand side is increased by one unit. In fact, the dual price of − 4.00 tells us that if the right-hand side of the total production constraint is increased from 350 to 351 units, the value of the optimal solution will worsen by the amount of \$4. Since worsening means an increase in cost, the value of the optimal solution will become \$800 + \$4 = \$804 if the one-unit increase in the total production requirement is made.

Since the dual price refers to improvement in the value of the optimal solution per-unit increase in the right-hand side, a constraint with a negative dual price should not have its right-hand side increased. In fact, if the dual price is negative, efforts should be made to reduce the right-hand side of the constraint. If the right-hand side of the total production constraint were decreased from 350 to 349 units, the dual price tells us the total cost could be lowered by \$4 to \$800 − \$4 = \$796.

Figure 3.2

The Management Scientist Solution for the M&D Chemicals Problem

```
Objective Function Value =            800.000

        Variable            Value          Reduced Costs
    --------------      --------------    ------------------
        X1                250.000              0.000
        X2                100.000              0.000

        Constraint      Slack/Surplus       Dual Prices
    --------------      --------------    ------------------
        1                 125.000              0.000
        2                   0.000             -4.000
        3                   0.000              1.000

OBJECTIVE COEFFICIENT RANGES

    Variable      Lower Limit      Current Value      Upper Limit
   ------------   --------------   ---------------   ----------------
       X1         No Lower Limit       2.000               3.000
       X2              2.000           3.000         No Upper Limit

RIGHT HAND SIDE RANGES

    Constraint    Lower Limit      Current Value      Upper Limit
   ------------   --------------   ---------------   ----------------
        1         No Lower Limit      125.000            250.000
        2             300.000         350.000            475.000
        3             475.000         600.000            700.000
```

The dual price is the improvement in the value of the optimal solution per-unit increase in the right-hand side of a constraint. However, as we have seen, the interpretation of an *improvement* in the value of an objective function depends on whether we are solving a maximization or a minimization problem. The dual price for a $\leq$ constraint will always be greater than or equal to zero because increasing the right-hand side cannot make the value of the objective function worse. Similarly, the dual price for a $\geq$ constraint will always be less than or equal to zero because increasing the right-hand side cannot improve the value of the optimal solution.

Finally, consider the right-hand-side ranges provided in Figure 3.2. The ranges of feasibility for the M&D Chemicals problem are summarized here:

Constraint	Min RHS	Max RHS
Product 1 demand	No lower limit	250
Total production	300	475
Processing time	475	700

You should now be able to interpret the computer output for a minimization problem. Try Problem 6.

As long as the right-hand sides are within these ranges, the dual prices shown on the computer printout are applicable.

Cautionary Note on the Interpretation of Dual Prices

As stated previously, the dual price is the improvement in the value of the optimal solution per-unit increase in the right-hand side of a constraint. When the right-hand side of the constraint represents the amount of a resource available, the associated dual price is often interpreted as the maximum amount one should be willing to pay for one additional unit of the resource. However, such an interpretation is not always correct. To see why, we need to understand the difference between sunk and relevant costs. A *sunk cost* is one that is not affected by the decision made. It will be incurred no matter what values the decision variables assume. A *relevant cost* is one that depends on the decision made. The amount of a relevant cost will vary depending on the values of the decision variables.

Let us reconsider the Par, Inc., problem. The amount of cutting and dyeing time available is 630 hours. The cost of the time available is a sunk cost if it must be paid regardless of the number of standard and deluxe golf bags produced. It would be a relevant cost if Par only had to pay for the number of hours of cutting and dyeing time actually used to produce golf bags. All relevant costs should be reflected in the objective function of a linear program. Sunk costs should not be reflected in the objective function. For Par, Inc., we have been assuming that the company must pay its employees' wages whether or not their time on the job is completely utilized. Therefore, the cost of the labor-hours resource for Par, Inc., is a sunk cost and has not been reflected in the objective function.

When the cost of a resource is *sunk,* the dual price can be interpreted as the maximum amount the company should be willing to pay for one additional unit of the resource. When the cost of a resource used is relevant, the dual price can be interpreted as the amount by which the value of the resource exceeds its cost. Thus, when the resource cost is relevant, the dual price can be interpreted as the maximum premium over the normal cost that the company should be willing to pay for one unit of the resource.

NOTES & comments

1. Computer software packages for solving linear programs are readily available. Most of these provide the optimal solution, dual or shadow price information, the range of optimality for the objective function coefficients, and the range of feasibility for the right-hand sides. The labels used for the ranges of optimality and feasibility may vary, but the meaning is the same as what we have described here.

2. Whenever one of the right-hand sides is at an end point of its range of feasibility, the dual and shadow prices only provide one-sided information. In this case, they only predict the change in the optimal value of the objective function for changes toward the interior of the range.

3. A condition called *degeneracy* can cause a subtle difference in how we interpret changes in the objective function coefficients beyond the end points of the range of optimality. Degeneracy occurs when the dual price equals zero

—*Continued*

—*Continued from previous page*

for one of the binding constraints. Degeneracy does not affect the interpretation of changes toward the interior of the range of optimality. However, when degeneracy is present, changes beyond the end points of the range do not necessarily mean a different solution will be optimal. From a practical point of view, changes beyond the end points of the range of optimality necessitate resolving the problem.

4. The 100 percent rule permits an analysis of multiple changes in the right-hand sides or multiple changes in the objective function coefficients. But the 100 percent rule cannot be applied to changes in both objective function coefficients *and* right-hand sides at the same time. In order to consider simultaneous changes for *both* right-hand-side values and objective function coefficients, the problem must be resolved.

5. Managers are frequently called on to provide an economic justification for new technology. Often the new technology is developed, or purchased, in order to conserve resources. The dual price can be helpful in such cases because it can be used to determine the savings attributable to the new technology by showing the savings per unit of resource conserved.

3.2 More Than Two Decision Variables

The graphical solution procedure is useful only for linear programs involving two decision variables. Computer software packages are designed to handle linear programs involving large numbers of variables and constraints. In this section we discuss the formulation and computer solution for two linear programs with three decision variables. In doing so, we will show how to interpret the reduced-cost portion of the computer output and will also illustrate the interpretation of dual prices for constraints that involve percentages.

The Modified Par, Inc., Problem

In Section 3.1 we demonstrated how the linear programming module of The Management Scientist could be used to solve the Par, Inc., problem. The original problem is restated as follows with decimal coefficients:

$$\text{Max} \quad 10x_1 + 9x_2$$

s.t.

$$
\begin{array}{llll}
0.7x_1 + & 1x_2 & \leq 630 & \text{Cutting and dyeing} \\
0.5x_1 + & 0.83333x_2 & \leq 600 & \text{Sewing} \\
1x_1 + & 0.66667x_2 & \leq 708 & \text{Finishing} \\
0.1x_1 + & 0.25x_2 & \leq 135 & \text{Inspection and packaging}
\end{array}
$$

$$x_1, x_2 \geq 0$$

Recall that x_1 is the number of standard golf bags produced and x_2 is the number of deluxe golf bags produced. Suppose that management is also considering producing a lightweight model designed specifically for golfers who prefer to carry their bags. It is estimated that each new lightweight model will require 0.8 hours for cutting and dyeing, 1 hour for sewing, 1 hour for finishing, and 0.25 hours for inspection and packaging. Because of the unique capabilities designed into the new model, Par's management feels that they will realize a profit contribution of $12.85 for each lightweight model produced during the current production period.

Let us consider the modifications in the original linear programming model that are needed to incorporate the effect of this additional decision variable. We will let x_3 denote the number of lightweight bags produced. After adding x_3 to the objective function and to each of the four constraints, we obtain the following linear program for the modified problem:

$$\text{Max} \quad 10x_1 + \quad 9x_2 + 12.85x_3$$

s.t.

$$0.7x_1 + \quad 1x_2 + \quad 0.8x_3 \leq 630 \quad \text{Cutting and dyeing}$$

$$0.5x_1 + 0.83333x_2 + \quad 1x_3 \leq 600 \quad \text{Sewing}$$

$$1x_1 + 0.66667x_2 + \quad 1x_3 \leq 708 \quad \text{Finishing}$$

$$0.1x_1 + \quad 0.25x_2 + 0.25x_3 \leq 135 \quad \text{Inspection and packaging}$$

$$x_1, x_2, x_3 \geq 0$$

Figure 3.3 shows the solution to the modified problem using The Management Scientist. We see that the optimal solution calls for the production of 280 standard bags, 0 deluxe bags, and 428 of the new lightweight bags; the value of the optimal solution after rounding is $8299.80.

Let us now look at the information contained in the Reduced Costs column. Recall that the reduced costs indicate how much each objective function coefficient would have to improve before the corresponding decision variable could assume a positive value in the optimal solution. As the computer output shows, the reduced costs for x_1 and x_3 are zero since the corresponding decision variables already have positive values in the optimal solution. The reduced cost of 1.15003 for decision variable x_2 tells us that the profit contribution for the deluxe bag would have to increase to at least $9 + $1.15003 = $10.15003 before x_2 *could* assume a positive value in the optimal solution.[4] In other words, unless the profit contribution for x_2 increases by at least $1.15 the value of x_2 will remain at zero in the optimal solution.

Suppose we increase the coefficient of x_2 by exactly $1.15003 and then resolve the problem using The Management Scientist. Figure 3.4 shows the new solution. Note that although x_2 assumes a positive value in the new solution, the value of the optimal solution has not changed. In other words, increasing the profit contribution of x_2 by *exactly* the amount of the reduced cost has resulted in alternative optimal solutions. Using a different computer software package, you may not see x_2 assume a positive value if you resolve the problem with an objective function coefficient of exactly 10.15003 for x_2—that is, the software package may show a different alternative optimal solution. However, if the profit contribution of x_2 is increased by *more than* $1.15003, then x_2 will not remain at zero in the optimal solution.

----

[4] In the case of degeneracy, a variable may not assume a positive value in the optimal solution even when the improvement in the profit contribution exceeds the value of the reduced cost. Our definition of reduced costs, stated as "... *could* assume a positive value ...," provides for such special cases. More advanced texts on mathematical programming discuss these special types of situations.

Figure 3.3

The Management Scientist Solution for the Modified Par, Inc., Problem

```
Objective Function Value =        8299.80078

        Variable              Value          Reduced Costs
      --------------      --------------      ------------------
           X1              280.00000               0.00000
           X2                0.00000               1.15003
           X3              428.00000               0.00000

       Constraint        Slack/Surplus          Dual Prices
      --------------      --------------      ------------------
           1               91.60001               0.00000
           2               32.00000               0.00000
           3                0.00000               8.10000
           4                0.00000              19.00000

OBJECTIVE COEFFICIENT RANGES

      Variable       Lower Limit      Current Value      Upper Limit
     -----------    -------------    ---------------    ---------------
        X1             5.14000          10.00000          12.07007
        X2          No Lower Limit       9.00000          10.15003
        X3            11.90907          12.85000          25.00000

RIGHT HAND SIDE RANGES

     Constraint     Lower Limit      Current Value      Upper Limit
    -----------    -------------    ---------------    ---------------
        1            538.40002         630.00000       No Upper Limit
        2            568.00000         600.00000       No Upper Limit
        3            540.00000         708.00000         852.63159
        4             70.80000         135.00000         144.60001
```

We also note from Figure 3.3 that the dual prices for constraints 3 and 4 are 8.1 and 19, respectively, indicating that these two constraints are binding in the optimal solution. Thus, each additional labor-hour in the finishing department would increase the value of the optimal solution by $8.10 and each additional labor-hour in the inspection and packaging department would increase the value of the optimal solution by $19.00. Since there is a slack of 91.6 hours in the cutting and dyeing department and 32 hours in the sewing department (see Figure 3.3), management might want to consider the possibility of utilizing these unused labor-hours in the finishing or inspection and packaging departments. For example, some of the employees in the cutting and dyeing department could be used to perform certain operations in either the finishing department or the inspection and packaging department. In the future, Par's management may want to explore the possibility of cross-training employees so that unused capacity in one department could be shifted to other departments. In the next chapter we will consider modeling situations like this.

Figure 3.4

The Management Scientist Solution for the Modified Par, Inc., Problem with the Coefficient of x_2 Increased by \$1.15003

```
Objective Function Value =        8299.80078

      Variable            Value           Reduced Costs
      --------            -----           -------------
         X1             403.78317            0.00000
         X2             222.81198            0.00000
         X3             155.67476            0.00000

     Constraint       Slack/Surplus         Dual Prices
     ----------       -------------         -----------
         1              0.00000              0.00000
         2             56.75776              0.00000
         3              0.00000              8.10000
         4              0.00000             19.00000

OBJECTIVE COEFFICIENT RANGES

   Variable       Lower Limit      Current Value      Upper Limit
   --------       -----------      -------------      -----------
      X1           10.00000          10.00000          12.51072
      X2           10.15003          10.15003          15.40790
      X3           10.65313          12.85000          12.85000

RIGHT HAND SIDE RANGES

   Constraint     Lower Limit      Current Value      Upper Limit
   ----------     -----------      -------------      -----------
      1           538.40002         630.00000         682.36316
      2           543.24225         600.00000       No Upper Limit
      3           580.00140         708.00000         852.63159
      4           117.00012         135.00000         151.15410
```

Suppose that after reviewing the solution shown in Figure 3.3, management states that they will not consider any solution that does not include the production of some deluxe bags. Management then decides to add the requirement that the number of deluxe bags produced must be at least 30% of the number of standard bags produced. Writing this requirement using the decision variables x_1 and x_2, we obtain

$$x_2 \geq 0.3x_1$$

or

$$-0.3x_1 + x_2 \geq 0$$

Adding this new constraint to the modified Par, Inc., linear program and resolving the problem using The Management Scientist, we obtain the optimal solution shown in Figure 3.5.

Figure 3.5

The Management Scientist Solution for the Modified Par, Inc., Problem with the 30% Deluxe-Bag Requirement

```
    Objective Function Value =        8183.87793

        Variable              Value            Reduced Costs
        --------              -----            -------------
          X1                335.99933              0.00000
          X2                100.79980              0.00000
          X3                304.80048              0.00000


       Constraint         Slack/Surplus          Dual Prices
       ----------         -------------          -----------
          1                 50.16031              0.00000
          2                 43.20037              0.00000
          3                  0.00000              7.40998
          4                  0.00000             21.76006
          5                  0.00000             -1.38003


OBJECTIVE COEFFICIENT RANGES

     Variable        Lower Limit      Current Value      Upper Limit
     --------        -----------      -------------      -----------
       X1              6.29500          10.00000          12.07007
       X2             -3.35000           9.00000          10.15003
       X3             11.90907          12.85000          18.14286


RIGHT HAND SIDE RANGES

    Constraint       Lower Limit      Current Value      Upper Limit
    ----------       -----------      -------------      -----------
        1             579.83972         630.00000      No Upper Limit
        2             556.79962         600.00000      No Upper Limit
        3             540.00000         708.00000         765.00049
        4             103.24991         135.00000         147.00008
        5             -84.00000           0.00000         101.67704
```

Let us consider the interpretation of the dual price for constraint 5, the requirement that the number of deluxe bags produced must be at least 30% of the number of standard bags produced. The dual price of -1.38 indicates that a one-unit increase in the right-hand side of the constraint will lower profits by \$1.38. Thus, what the dual price of -1.38 is really telling us is what will happen to the value of the optimal solution if the constraint is changed to

$$x_2 \geq 0.3x_1 + 1$$

The correct interpretation of the dual price of -1.38 can now be stated as follows: If we are forced to produce one deluxe bag over and above the minimum 30% requirement, total profits will decrease by \$1.38. Conversely, if we relax the minimum 30% requirement by one bag ($x_2 \geq 0.3x_1 - 1$), total profits will increase by \$1.38.

The dual price for a percentage (or ratio) constraint such as this will not directly provide answers to questions concerning a percentage increase or decrease in the right-hand side of the constraint. For example, we might wonder what would happen to the value of the optimal solution if the number of deluxe bags has to be at least 31% of the number of standard bags. To answer such a question, we would resolve the problem using the constraint $-0.31x_1 + x_2 \geq 0$.

Because percentage (or ratio) constraints frequently occur in linear programming models, let us consider another example. For instance, suppose that Par's management states that the number of lightweight bags produced may not exceed 20% of the total golf bag production. Since the total production of golf bags is $x_1 + x_2 + x_3$, we can write this constraint as

$$x_3 \leq 0.2(x_1 + x_2 + x_3)$$
$$x_3 \leq 0.2x_1 + 0.2x_2 + 0.2x_3$$
$$-0.2x_1 - 0.2x_2 + 0.8x_3 \leq 0$$

The solution obtained using The Management Scientist for the model that incorporates both the effects of this new percentage requirement and the previous requirement ($-0.3x_1 + x_2 \geq 0$) is shown in Figure 3.6. After rounding, the dual price corresponding to the new constraint (constraint 6) is 0.89. Thus, every additional lightweight bag we are allowed to produce over the current 20% limit will increase the value of the objective function by \$0.89; moreover, the right-hand-side range for this constraint shows that this interpretation is valid for increases of up to 156 units.

The Bluegrass Farms Problem

To provide additional practice in formulating and interpreting the computer solution for linear programs involving more than two decision variables, we consider a minimization problem involving three decision variables. Bluegrass Farms, located in Lexington, Kentucky, has been experimenting with a special diet for its racehorses. The feed components available for the diet are a standard horse feed product, a vitamin-enriched oat product, and a new vitamin and mineral feed additive. The nutritional values in units per pound and the costs for the three feed components are summarized in Table 3.1; for example, each pound of the standard feed component contains 0.8 unit of ingredient A, 1 unit of ingredient B, and 0.1 unit of ingredient C. The minimum daily diet requirements for each horse are three units of ingredient A, six units of ingredient B, and four units of ingredient C. In addition, to control the weight of the horses, the total daily feed for a horse should not exceed 6 pounds. Bluegrass Farms would like to determine the minimum-cost mix that will satisfy the daily diet requirements.

Formulation of the Bluegrass Farms Problem

To formulate a linear programming model for the Bluegrass Farms problem, we introduce the following three decision variables:

x_1 = number of pounds of the standard horse feed product
x_2 = number of pounds of the enriched oat product
x_3 = number of pounds of the vitamin and mineral feed additive

Figure 3.6

The Management Scientist Solution for the Modified Par, Inc., Problem Incorporating the 20% Lightweight-Bag Requirement and the 30% Deluxe-Bag Requirement

```
Objective Function Value =        8044.25488

        Variable            Value            Reduced Costs
     --------------    ---------------     ------------------
          X1              403.44730               0.00000
          X2              222.20738               0.00000
          X3              156.41367               0.00000

       Constraint       Slack/Surplus          Dual Prices
     --------------    ---------------     ------------------
           1                0.24859               0.00000
           2               56.69057               0.00000
           3                0.00000               8.87330
           4                0.00000              13.05157
           5              101.17319               0.00000
           6                0.00000               0.89226

OBJECTIVE COEFFICIENT RANGES

      Variable        Lower Limit       Current Value       Upper Limit
    ------------     ---------------    ---------------    ---------------
         X1              3.13800           10.00000           12.07007
         X2              6.47670            9.00000           10.15003
         X3             11.90907           12.85000        No Upper Limit

RIGHT HAND SIDE RANGES

     Constraint       Lower Limit       Current Value       Upper Limit
    ------------     ---------------    ---------------    ---------------
         1             629.75140          630.00000       No Upper Limit
         2             543.30945          600.00000       No Upper Limit
         3             396.00146          708.00000          708.69653
         4             118.96714          135.00000          135.08900
         5          No Lower Limit          0.00000          101.17319
         6              -0.77936            0.00000          156.48053
```

Table 3.1

Nutritional Value and Cost Data for the Bluegrass Farms Problem

Feed Component	Standard	Enriched Oat	Additive
Ingredient A	0.8	0.2	0.0
Ingredient B	1.0	1.5	3.0
Ingredient C	0.1	0.6	2.0
Cost per pound	$0.25	$0.50	$3.00

Using the data in Table 3.1, the objective function for minimizing the total cost associated with the daily feed can be written as follows:

$$\min 0.25x_1 + 0.50x_2 + 3x_3$$

Since the minimum daily requirement for ingredient A is three units, we obtain the constraint

$$0.8x_1 + 0.2x_2 \geq 3$$

The constraint for ingredient B is

$$1.0x_1 + 1.5x_2 + 3.0x_3 \geq 6$$

and the constraint for ingredient C is

$$0.1x_1 + 0.6x_2 + 2.0x_3 \geq 4$$

Finally, the constraint that restricts the mix to at most 6 pounds is

$$x_1 + x_2 + x_3 \leq 6$$

Combining all the constraints with the nonnegativity requirements enables us to write the complete linear programming model for the Bluegrass Farms problem as follows:

$$\text{Min} \quad 0.25x_1 + 0.50x_2 + 3x_3$$

s.t.

$$
\begin{array}{llll}
0.8x_1 + & 0.2x_2 & & \geq 3 \quad \text{Ingredient A} \\
1.0x_1 + & 1.5x_2 + & 3.0x_3 & \geq 6 \quad \text{Ingredient B} \\
0.1x_1 + & 0.6x_2 + & 2.0x_3 & \geq 4 \quad \text{Ingredient C} \\
x_1 + & x_2 + & x_3 & \leq 6 \quad \text{Weight} \\
\end{array}
$$

$$x_1, x_2, x_3 \geq 0$$

Computer Solution and Interpretation for the Bluegrass Farms Problem

The output obtained using The Management Scientist to solve the Bluegrass Farms problem is shown in Figure 3.7. After rounding, we see that the optimal solution calls for a daily diet consisting of 3.51 pounds of the standard horse feed product, 0.95 pound of the enriched oat product, and 1.54 pounds of the vitamin and mineral feed additive. Thus, with feed component costs of $0.25, $0.50, and $3.00, the total cost of the optimal diet is

$$3.51 \text{ pounds @ } \$0.25 \text{ per pound} = \$0.88$$

$$0.95 \text{ pound @ } \$0.50 \text{ per pound} = 0.47$$

$$1.54 \text{ pounds @ } \$3.00 \text{ per pound} = \underline{4.62}$$

$$\text{Total cost} = \$5.97$$

Note that after rounding, this is the same as the objective function value in the computer output (Figure 3.7).

Looking at the Slack/Surplus section of the computer output, we find a value of 3.554 for constraint 2. Since constraint 2 is a greater-than-or-equal-to constraint, 3.554 is the surplus; the optimal solution exceeds the minimum daily diet requirement for ingredient

Figure 3.7

The Management Scientist Solution for the Bluegrass Farms Problem

```
Objective Function Value =            5.973

       Variable              Value            Reduced Costs
     --------------        --------------     ------------------

         X1                  3.514                 0.000
         X2                  0.946                 0.000
         X3                  1.541                 0.000

      Constraint         Slack/Surplus           Dual Prices
     --------------        --------------     ------------------

          1                  0.000                -1.216
          2                  3.554                 0.000
          3                  0.000                -1.959
          4                  0.000                 0.919

OBJECTIVE COEFFICIENT RANGES

    Variable        Lower Limit      Current Value      Upper Limit
  ------------    --------------    --------------    --------------

       X1               -0.393           0.250        No Upper Limit
       X2         No Lower Limit         0.500                 0.925
       X3                1.522           3.000        No Upper Limit

RIGHT HAND SIDE RANGES

   Constraint       Lower Limit      Current Value      Upper Limit
  ------------    --------------    --------------    --------------

       1                 1.143           3.000                 3.368
       2         No Lower Limit          6.000                 9.554
       3                 2.100           4.000                 4.875
       4                 5.562           6.000                 8.478
```

B (six units) by 3.554 units. Since the surplus values for constraints 1 and 3 are both zero, we see that the optimal diet just meets the minimum requirements for ingredients A and C; moreover, a slack value of zero for constraint 4 shows that the optimal solution provides a total daily feed weight of 6 pounds.

The dual price (after rounding) for the ingredient A constraint (constraint 1) is −1.22. To interpret this value properly, we first look at the sign; since it is negative, we know that increasing the right-hand side of constraint 1 will cause the solution value to worsen. Since this is a minimization problem, "worsen" means that the total daily cost will increase. A one-unit increase in the right-hand side of constraint 1 will increase the total cost of the daily diet by $1.22. Conversely, it is also correct to conclude that a decrease of one unit in the right-hand side will decrease the total cost by $1.22. Looking at the RIGHT HAND SIDE RANGES section of the computer output, we see that these interpretations are correct as long as the right-hand side is between 1.143 and 3.368.

Suppose that the Bluegrass management is willing to reconsider their position regarding the maximum weight of the daily diet. The dual price of 0.92 (after rounding) for constraint 4 shows that a one-unit increase in the right-hand side of constraint 4 will reduce total cost by $0.92. The RIGHT HAND SIDE RANGES section of the output shows that this interpretation is correct for increases in the right-hand side up to a maximum of 8.478 pounds. Thus, the effect of increasing the right-hand side of constraint 4 from 6 to 8 pounds is a decrease in the total daily cost of 2 × $0.92 or $1.84. Keep in mind that if this change were made, the feasible region would change, and we would obtain a new optimal solution.

The OBJECTIVE COEFFICIENT RANGES section of the computer output shows a lower limit of − 0.393 for x_1. Clearly, in a real problem, the objective function coefficient of x_1 (the cost of the standard horse feed product) cannot take on a negative value. So, from a practical point of view, we can think of the lower limit for the objective function coefficient of x_1 as being zero. We can thus conclude that no matter how much the cost of the standard mix were to decrease, the optimal solution would not change. Even if Bluegrass Farms could obtain the standard horse feed product for free, the optimal solution would still specify a daily diet of 3.51 pounds of the standard horse feed product, 0.95 pound of the enriched oat product, and 1.54 pounds of the vitamin and mineral feed additive. However, any decrease in the per-unit cost of the standard feed would result in a decrease in the total cost for the optimal daily diet.

Note that the objective function coefficient values for x_1 and x_3 have no upper limit. Even if the cost of x_3 were to increase, for example, from $3.00 to $13.00 per pound, the optimal solution would not change; the total cost of the solution, however, would increase by $10 (the amount of the increase) times 1.541 or $15.41. You must always keep in mind that the interpretations we have made using the sensitivity analysis information in the computer output are only appropriate if all other coefficients in the problem do not change. To consider simultaneous changes you must use the 100 percent rule or resolve the problem after making the changes.

3.3 Modeling

Modeling is the process of translating a verbal statement of a problem into a mathematical statement. In linear programming, the mathematical statement of the problem is a linear program. Up to this point, the problems that we have considered have been small and not particularly difficult to model. But, as problems become larger and more complex, some general guidelines for model formulation are useful.

Guidelines for Model Formulation

The process of formulating linear programming models is an art that can only be mastered with practice and experience. Although every problem has *some* unique features, most problems also have common features. As a result, some general guidelines for model formulation can be helpful, especially for beginners.

1. **Understand the problem thoroughly.**
    Read the problem description quickly to get a feel for what is involved. Identify those items that you feel should be included in the model. If the problem is especially complex, take notes; these notes will help you focus on the key ideas and facts.

2. **Write a verbal statement of the objective function and each constraint.**

Later you will translate these verbal statements into mathematical statements. At this step, you might write the objective function as, for instance, maximize profit or minimize monthly operating costs. You might write a constraint limiting funds borrowed as follows: funds borrowed ≤ line of credit. Even experienced management scientists find they sometimes make mistakes when skipping this step.

3. **Define the decision variables.**

Ask yourself what decisions the manager must make. What does she or he control? The decision variables should be chosen to represent these decisions. The decision variables should also be defined in such a fashion that writing a mathematical statement of the objective function and the left-hand side of the constraints is facilitated.

4. **Write the objective function in terms of the decision variables.**

Translate your verbal statement of the objective function developed in step 2 into a mathematical statement; the mathematical statement must be a linear function of the decision variables.

5. **Write the constraints in terms of the decision variables.**

Translate your verbal statement of each constraint developed in step 2 into a mathematical statement; the left-hand side of the resulting equation or inequality must be a linear function of the decision variables.

After carrying out these steps, we have a linear programming model that represents the problem, or application, under study. Solution of the model will provide the optimal

MANAGEMENT SCIENCE in action

An Optimal Wood Procurement Policy*

Wellborn Cabinet, Inc., operates an integrated sawmill and cabinet manufacturing system in Alabama. Its manufacturing facility consists of a sawmill, four dry kilns, and a wood cabinet assembly plant; the assembly plant includes a rough mill for producing cabinet components that are referred to as blanks. Because of the pressure to market quality products at competitive prices, a major concern for Wellborn Cabinet is to maintain consistency in product quality. A key factor in maintaining this quality depends on controlling the quality and costs of raw materials.

To produce blanks, Wellborn Cabinet purchases #1 and #2 grade hardwood logs, as well as #1 and #2 dry or green common grade lumber (note: higher numbers denote higher quality). During a typical five-day week of operation, the sawmill can process up to 1550 logs with a small-end diameter from 9 to 22 inches. Usually, the lumber is purchased in bundles containing random sizes. Both the logs processed by the sawmill and the green lumber purchased from outside suppliers are dried at the kilns to an average moisture content of 7%; the dried material is

then planed and converted into about 130 different sizes of blanks at the rough mill.

Wellborn developed a linear programming model of the blank production system. The objective was to determine a procurement plan that would minimize the total cost of producing blanks for a five-day work week. Constraints included capacities of the sawmill and dry kilns, the demand for blanks at the manufacturing plant, and the available supply of raw materials. The initial results indicate that the company can minimize the total cost of producing blanks by purchasing only #2 grade logs and #2 common green lumber; approximately 88% of the rough mill dry lumber requirements should come from #2 grade logs and the rest from purchased #2 common green lumber. The projected annual savings in raw material costs were $412,000.

....

*Based on Carino, H. F., and C. H. LeNoir, Jr., "Optimizing Wood Procurement in Cabinet Manufacturing." *Interfaces,* March–April 1988, pp. 10–19.

solution, the values of decision variables, the values of the slack/surplus variables, and a variety of information concerning the sensitivity analysis aspects of the problem. Proper interpretation of the solution can provide valuable decision-making information for the manager. The Management Science in Action: An Optimal Wood Procurement Policy describes how Wellborn Cabinet, Inc., realized projected annual savings of $412,000 by using a linear programming model to determine an optimal wood procurement policy.

Next we illustrate the modeling process for the Electronic Communications problem. After reading the written description of the problem, we encourage you to attempt a formulation following the preceding guidelines. Then, solve the problem using a linear programming software package, and compare your solution with the one provided.

The Electronic Communications Problem

Electronic Communications manufactures portable radio systems that can be used for two-way communications. The company's new product, which has a range of up to 25 miles, is particularly suitable for use in a variety of business and personal applications. The distribution channels for the new radio are as follows:

1. Marine equipment distributors
2. Business equipment distributors
3. National chain of retail stores
4. Mail order

Because of differing distribution and promotional costs, the profitability of the product will vary with the distribution channel. In addition, the advertising cost and the personal sales effort required will vary with the distribution channels. Table 3.2 summarizes the contribution to profit, advertising cost, and personal sales effort data pertaining to the Electronic Communications problem. The firm has set the advertising budget at $5000 and there is a maximum of 1800 hours of sales force time available for allocation to the sales effort. Management has also decided to produce exactly 600 units for the current production period. Finally, an ongoing contract with the national chain of retail stores requires that at least 150 units be distributed through this distribution channel.

Electronic Communications is now faced with the problem of establishing a strategy that will provide for the distribution of the radios in such a way that overall profitability of the new radio production will be maximized. Decisions must be made as to how many units should be allocated to each of the four distribution channels, as well as how to allocate the advertising budget and sales force effort to each of the four distribution channels.

Table 3.2	Distribution Channel	Profit per Unit Sold	Advertising Cost per Unit Sold	Personal Sales Effort per Unit Sold
Profit, Advertising Cost, and Personal Sales Time Data for the Electronic Communications Problem	Marine distributors	$90	$10	2 hours
	Business distributors	$84	$ 8	3 hours
	National retail stores	$70	$ 9	3 hours
	Mail order	$60	$15	None

Formulation of the Electronic Communications Problem

A written statement of the problem has been presented. Let us now attempt to write a verbal statement of the objective function and each constraint. For the objective function, we can write

Objective function: Maximize profit

There appear to be four constraints necessary for this problem. They are necessary because of (1) a limited advertising budget, (2) limited sales force availability, (3) a production requirement, and (4) a retail stores distribution requirement.

Constraint 1   Advertising expenditures $\leq$ Budget
Constraint 2   Sales time used $\leq$ Time available
Constraint 3   Radios produced $=$ Management requirement
Constraint 4   Retail distribution $\geq$ Contract requirement

This provides a verbal description of the objective function and the constraints. We are now ready to define the decision variables such that they represent the decisions that the manager must make.

For the Electronic Communications problem, we introduce the following four decision variables:

x_1 = the number of units produced for the marine equipment distribution channel

x_2 = the number of units produced for the business equipment distribution channel

x_3 = the number of units produced for the national retail chain distribution channel

x_4 = the number of units produced for the mail-order distribution channel

Using the data in Table 3.2, the objective function for maximizing the total contribution to profit associated with the radios can be written as follows:

$$\max 90x_1 + 84x_2 + 70x_3 + 60x_4$$

Let us now develop a mathematical statement of the constraints for the problem. Since the advertising budget has been set at $5000, the constraint that limits the amount of advertising expenditure can be written as follows:

$$10x_1 + 8x_2 + 9x_3 + 15x_4 \leq 5000$$

Similarly, since the sales time is limited to 1800 hours, we obtain the constraint

$$2x_1 + 3x_2 + 3x_3 \leq 1800$$

Management's decision to produce exactly 600 units during the current production period is expressed as

$$1x_1 + 1x_2 + 1x_3 + 1x_4 = 600$$

Finally, to account for the fact that the number of units distributed by the national chain of retail stores must be at least 150, we add the constraint

$$1x_3 \geq 150$$

Combining all of the constraints with the nonnegativity requirements enables us to write the complete linear programming model for the Electronic Communications problem as follows:

Figure 3.8

A Portion of the Management Scientist Computer Output for the Electronic Communications Problem

```
Objective Function Value =          48450.000

        Variable              Value            Reduced Costs
    --------------       ---------------      ------------------
        X1                  25.000                0.000
        X2                 425.000                0.000
        X3                 150.000                0.000
        X4                   0.000               45.000


        Constraint         Slack/Surplus          Dual Prices
    --------------       ---------------      ------------------
        1                    0.000                 3.000
        2                   25.000                 0.000
        3                    0.000                60.000
        4                    0.000               -17.000
```

$$\text{Max} \quad 90x_1 + 84x_2 + 70x_3 + 60x_4$$

s.t.

$$10x_1 + 8x_2 + 9x_3 + 15x_4 \leq 5000 \quad \text{Advertising budget}$$
$$2x_1 + 3x_2 + 3x_3 \qquad\quad \leq 1800 \quad \text{Sales force availability}$$
$$1x_1 + 1x_2 + 1x_3 + 1x_4 = 600 \quad \text{Production level}$$
$$1x_3 \qquad\qquad\quad \geq 150 \quad \text{Retail stores requirement}$$

$$x_1, x_2, x_3, x_4 \geq 0$$

Computer Solution and Interpretation for the Electronic Communications Problem

A portion of the output obtained using The Management Scientist to solve the Electronic Communications problem is shown in Figure 3.8. The Objective Function Value section shows that the optimal solution to the problem will provide a maximum profit of $48,450. The optimal values of the decision variables are given by $x_1 = 25$, $x_2 = 425$, $x_3 = 150$, and $x_4 = 0$. Thus, the optimal strategy for Electronic Communications is to concentrate on the business equipment distribution channel with $x_2 = 425$ units. In addition, the firm should allocate 25 units to the marine distribution channel ($x_1 = 25$) and meet its 150-unit commitment to the national retail chain store distribution channel ($x_3 = 150$). With $x_4 = 0$, the optimal solution indicates that the firm should not use the mail-order distribution channel.

Now consider the information contained in the Reduced Costs column. Recall that the reduced costs indicate how much each objective function coefficient would have to improve before the corresponding decision variable could assume a positive value in the optimal solution. As the computer output shows, the first three reduced costs are zero since the corresponding decision variables already have positive values in the optimal solution. However, the reduced cost of 45 for decision variable x_4 tells us that the profit for the new radios distributed via the mail-order channel would have to increase from its current value of $60 per unit to at least $60 + $45 = $105 per unit before it would be profitable to use the mail-order distribution channel.

The computer output information for the slack/surplus variables and the dual prices is restated here:

Constraint Number	Constraint Name	Type of Constraint	Slack or Surplus	Dual Price
1	Advertising budget	≤	0	3
2	Sales force availability	≤	25	0
3	Production level	=	0	60
4	Retail stores requirement	≥	0	−17

The advertising budget constraint has a slack of zero, indicating that the entire budget of $5000 has been used. The corresponding dual price of 3 tells us that an additional dollar added to the advertising budget will improve the objective function (increase the profit) by $3. Thus, the possibility of increasing the advertising budget should be seriously considered by the firm. The slack of 25 hours for the sales force availability constraint shows that the allocated 1800 hours of sales time are adequate to distribute the radios produced and that 25 hours of sales time will remain unused. Since the production level constraint is an equality, the zero slack/surplus shown on the output is expected. However, the dual price of 60 associated with this constraint shows that if the firm were to consider increasing the production level for the radios, the value of the objective function, or profit, would improve at the rate of $60 per radio produced. Finally, the surplus of zero associated with the retail store distribution channel commitment is a result of this constraint being binding. The negative dual price indicates that increasing the commitment from 150 to 151 units will actually decrease the profit by $17. Thus, Electronic Communications may want to consider reducing its commitment to the retail store distribution channel. A *decrease* in the commitment will actually improve profit at the rate of $17 per unit.

We now consider the additional sensitivity analysis information provided by the computer output shown in Figure 3.9. The ranges of optimality for the objective function coefficients are

$$84 \leq c_1 < \text{No upper limit}$$

$$50 \leq c_2 \leq 90$$

$$\text{No lower limit} < c_3 \leq 87$$

$$\text{No lower limit} < c_4 \leq 105$$

The current solution, or strategy, remains optimal, provided that the objective function coefficients remain in the given ranges of optimality. Note in particular the range of optimality associated with the mail-order distribution channel coefficient, c_4. This information is consistent with the earlier observation for the Reduced Costs portion of the output. In both instances, we see that the per-unit profit would have to increase to $105 before the mail-order distribution channel could be in the optimal solution with a positive value.

Figure 3.9

Objective Coefficient and Right-Hand-Side Ranges Provided by the Management Scientist for the Electronic Communications Problem

```
OBJECTIVE COEFFICIENT RANGES

    Variable        Lower Limit      Current Value      Upper Limit
    --------        -----------      -------------      -----------
      X1               84.000           90.000       No Upper Limit
      X2               50.000           84.000           90.000
      X3          No Lower Limit        70.000           87.000
      X4          No Lower Limit        60.000          105.000


RIGHT HAND SIDE RANGES

    Constraint      Lower Limit      Current Value      Upper Limit
    ----------      -----------      -------------      -----------
       1             4950.000         5000.000          5850.000
       2             1775.000         1800.000       No Upper Limit
       3              515.000          600.000           603.571
       4                0.000          150.000           200.000
```

Finally, the sensitivity analysis information on RIGHT HAND SIDE RANGES, as shown in Figure 3.9, provides the ranges of feasibility for the right-hand-side values.

Constraint	Min RHS	Current Value	Max RHS
Advertising budget	4950	5000	5850
Sales force	1775	1800	No upper limit
Production level	515	600	603.57
Retail stores requirement	0	150	200

Several interpretations of these ranges are possible. In particular, recall that the dual price for advertising budget enabled us to conclude that each $1 increase in the budget would improve the profit by $3. The range for the advertising budget shows that this statement about the value of increasing the budget is appropriate up to an advertising budget of $5850. Increases above this level would not necessarily be beneficial. Also note that the dual price of −17 for the retail stores requirement suggested the desirability of reducing this commitment. The range of feasibility for this constraint shows that the commitment could be reduced to zero and the value of the reduction would be at the rate of $17 per unit.

Again, the *sensitivity analysis* or *postoptimality analysis* provided by computer software packages for linear programming problems considers only *one change at a time*, with all other coefficients of the problem remaining as originally specified. As mentioned earlier, simultaneous changes can sometimes be analyzed without resolving the problem, provided that the cumulative changes are not large enough to violate the 100 percent rule.

Do you feel comfortable interpreting the computer output for problems involving more than two decision variables? Try Problems 8 and 9.

Finally, recall that the complete solution to the Electronic Communications problem requested information not only on the number of units to be distributed over each channel, but also on the allocation of the advertising budget and the sales force effort to each distribution channel. Since the optimal solution is $x_1 = 25$, $x_2 = 425$, $x_3 = 150$, and $x_4 = 0$, we can simply evaluate each term in a given constraint to determine how much of the constraint resource is allocated to each distribution channel. For example, the advertising budget constraint of

$$10x_1 + 8x_2 + 9x_3 + 15x_4 \le 5000$$

shows that $10x_1 = 10(25) = \$250$, $8x_2 = 8(425) = \$3400$, $9x_3 = 9(150) = \$1350$, and $15x_4 = 15(0) = \$0$. Thus, the advertising budget allocations are, respectively, $250, $3400,

Table 3.3

Profit-Maximizing Strategy for the Electronic Communications Problem

Distribution Channel	Volume	Advertising Allocation	Sales Force Allocation (hours)
Marine distributors	25	$ 250	50
Business distributors	425	3400	1275
National retail stores	150	1350	450
Mail order	0	0	0
Totals	600	$5000	1775

Projected total profit = $48,450

MANAGEMENT SCIENCE in action

Using Linear Programming for Traffic Control*

The Hanshin Expressway was the first urban toll expressway in Osaka, Japan. Although in 1964 its length was only 2.3 kilometers, today it is a large-scale urban expressway network of 200 kilometers. The Hanshin Expressway provides service for the Hanshin (Osaka-Kobe) area, the second-most populated area in Japan. An average of 828,000 vehicles use the expressway each day, with daily traffic sometimes exceeding 1,000,000 vehicles. In 1970, the Hanshin Expressway Public Corporation started using an automated traffic-control system in order to maximize the number of vehicles flowing into the expressway network.

The automated traffic-control system relies on two control methods: (1) limiting the number of cars that enter the expressway at each entrance ramp; and (2) providing drivers with up-to-date and accurate traffic information, including expected travel times and information about accidents. The approach used to limit the number of vehicles depends upon whether the expressway is in a normal or steady state of operation, or whether some type of unusual event, such as an accident or a breakdown, has occurred.

In the first phase of the steady-state case, the Hanshin system uses a linear programming model to maximize the total number of vehicles entering the system, while preventing traffic congestion and adverse effects on surrounding road networks. The data that drives the linear programming model is collected from detectors installed every 500 meters along the expressway and at all entrance and exit ramps. Every five minutes the real-time data collected from the detectors is used to update the model coefficients and a new linear program computes the maximum number of vehicles the expressway can accommodate.

The automated traffic control system has been very successful. According to surveys, traffic control has decreased the length of congested portions of the expressway by 30 percent and the duration by 20 percent. It has been shown to be an extremely cost effective, and drivers consider it an indispensable service.

....

*Based on Yoshino, T., T. Sasaki, and T. Hasegawa. "The Traffic-Control System on the Hanshin Expressway." *Interfaces*, January–February 1995, pp. 94–108.

$1350, and $0 for each of the four distribution channels. Making similar calculations for the sales force constraint results in the managerial summary of the Electronic Communications optimal solution as shown in Table 3.3.

Summary

In this chapter we have shown how computer software packages can be used to solve linear programming problems. Since the graphical method and graphical sensitivity analysis are limited to linear programs with two decision variables, a computer solution procedure was presented as a practical method of solving linear programming problems with any number of decision variables. Although many software packages are available for computer solution, we used The Management Scientist to illustrate linear programming solutions on a personal computer and showed the computer output for several example problems to demonstrate the use and interpretation of the results. In addition to the value of the objective function and the optimal values of the decision variables, the computer output provides a variety of additional information concerning slack, surplus, and dual prices, as well as objective function coefficient and right-hand-side ranges. In the final section of the chapter, we provided some general guidelines for model formulation and then applied them to a sample problem. In the chapter appendixes we show how The Management Scientist, LINDO/PC, a popular software package developed by Linus E. Schrage at the University of Chicago, and spreadsheet packages are used to solve linear programs.

The Management Science in Action: Using Linear Programming for Traffic Control provides another example of the widespread use of linear programming. It is being used all over the world for a wide variety of problems. In the next chapter we will see many more applications of linear programming.

Glossary

Reduced cost The amount by which an objective function coefficient would have to improve (increase for a maximization problem, decrease for a minimization problem), before it would be possible for the corresponding variable to assume a positive value in the optimal solution.

Dual price The improvement in the value of the objective function per-unit increase in a constraint right-hand side.

Range of optimality The range of values over which an objective function coefficient may vary without causing any change in the values of the decision variables in the optimal solution.

Range of feasibility The range of values over which a right-hand side may vary without changing the value and interpretation of the dual price.

100 percent rule A rule indicating when simultaneous changes in two or more objective function coefficients will not cause a change in the optimal values for the decision variables. It can also be applied to indicate when two or more right-hand-side changes will not cause a change in any of the dual prices.

Sunk cost A cost that is not affected by the decision made. It will be incurred no matter what values the decision variables assume.

Relevant cost A cost that depends upon the decision made. The amount of a relevant cost will vary depending on the values of the decision variables.

Modeling The process of translating a verbal statement of a problem into a mathematical statement.

Sensitivity analysis The evaluation of how changes in the coefficients of a linear programming problem affect the optimal solution to the problem.

Postoptimality analysis Another name for sensitivity analysis, indicating that the analysis is performed after the optimal solution to the original linear programming problem has been obtained.

Problems

1. 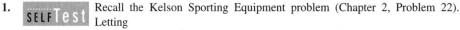 **SELF**Test Recall the Kelson Sporting Equipment problem (Chapter 2, Problem 22). Letting

$$x_1 = \text{number of regular gloves}$$
$$x_2 = \text{number of catcher's mitts}$$

leads to the following formulation:

$$\text{Max} \quad 5x_1 + 8x_2$$

s.t.

$$x_1 + \tfrac{3}{2}x_2 \leq 900 \quad \text{Cutting and sewing}$$

$$\tfrac{1}{2}x_1 + \tfrac{1}{3}x_2 \leq 300 \quad \text{Finishing}$$

$$\tfrac{1}{8}x_1 + \tfrac{1}{4}x_2 \leq 100 \quad \text{Packaging and shipping}$$

$$x_1, x_2 \geq 0$$

The computer solution obtained using The Management Scientist is shown in Figure 3.10.
   a. What is the optimal solution, and what is the value of the total profit contribution?
   b. Which constraints are binding?
   c. What are the dual prices for the resources? Interpret each.
   d. If overtime can be scheduled in one of the departments, where would you recommend doing so?

2. **SELF**Test Refer to the computer solution of the Kelson Sporting Equipment problem in Figure 3.10 (see Problem 1).
   a. Compute the ranges of optimality for the objective function coefficients.
   b. Interpret the ranges in part (a).
   c. Interpret the range of feasibility for the right-hand sides.
   d. How much will the value of the optimal solution improve if 20 extra hours of packaging and shipping time are made available?

3. Recall the Investment Advisors problem (Chapter 2, Problem 25). Letting

$$x_1 = \text{shares of U.S. Oil}$$
$$x_2 = \text{shares of Hub Properties}$$

leads to the following formulation:

$$\text{Max} \quad 3x_1 + \quad 5x_2 \qquad\qquad \text{Maximize total annual return}$$

s.t.

$$25x_1 + \quad 50x_2 \leq 80{,}000 \qquad \text{Funds available}$$

$$0.50x_1 + 0.25x_2 \leq \quad 700 \qquad \text{Risk maximum}$$

$$1x_1 \qquad\qquad \leq \quad 1000 \qquad \text{U.S. Oil maximum}$$

$$x_1, x_2 \geq 0$$

The computer solution of this problem is shown in Figure 3.11.
   a. What is the optimal solution, and what is the value of the total estimated annual return?
   b. Which constraints are binding? What is your interpretation of this in terms of the problem?
   c. What are the dual prices for the constraints? Interpret each.
   d. Would it be beneficial to relax the constraint on the amount invested in U.S. Oil? Why or why not?

Figure 3.10

The Management Scientist Solution for the Kelson Sporting Equipment Problem

```
Objective Function Value =        3700.00146

        Variable              Value              Reduced Costs
      --------------      --------------       --------------------

          X1               500.00153               0.00000
          X2               149.99924               0.00000


        Constraint          Slack/Surplus          Dual Prices
      --------------      --------------       --------------------

          1                174.99962               0.00000
          2                  0.00000               2.99999    $value/benefit
          3                  0.00000              28.00006


OBJECTIVE COEFFICIENT RANGES

      Variable      Lower Limit        Current Value       Upper Limit
    ------------    ------------      ---------------     ------------

        X1           4.00000             5.00000           12.00012
        X2           3.33330             8.00000           10.00000


RIGHT HAND SIDE RANGES

     Constraint     Lower Limit        Current Value       Upper Limit
    ------------    ------------      ---------------     ------------

        1          725.00037           900.00000       No Upper Limit
        2          133.33199           300.00000          400.00000   $binding
        3           75.00000           100.00000          134.99982
```

4. Refer to Figure 3.11, which shows the computer solution of Problem 3.
   a. How much would the estimated per-share return for U.S. Oil have to increase before it would be beneficial to increase the investment in this stock?
   b. How much would the estimated per-share return for Hub Properties have to decrease before it would be beneficial to reduce the investment in this stock?
   c. How much would the total annual return be reduced if the U.S. Oil maximum were reduced to 900 shares?

5. Recall the Tom's, Inc., problem (Chapter 2, Problem 26). Letting

$$x_1 = \text{jars of Western Foods Salsa produced}$$
$$x_2 = \text{jars of Mexico City Salsa produced}$$

   leads to the formulation:

$$\text{Max} \quad 1x_1 + 1.25x_2$$

   s.t.

$$
\begin{array}{llll}
5x_1 + & 7x_2 \le 4480 & \text{Whole tomatoes} \\
3x_1 + & 1x_2 \le 2080 & \text{Tomato sauce} \\
2x_1 + & 2x_2 \le 1600 & \text{Tomato paste} \\
x_1, x_2 \ge 0 &
\end{array}
$$

Figure 3.11

The Management Scientist Solution for the Investment Advisors Problem

```
Objective Function Value =            8400.000

        Variable              Value            Reduced Costs
     ---------------    ---------------    -------------------
          X1                 800.000                0.000
          X2                1200.000                0.000

       Constraint         Slack/Surplus          Dual Prices
     ---------------    ---------------    -------------------
           1                   0.000                0.093
           2                   0.000                1.333
           3                 200.000                0.000

OBJECTIVE COEFFICIENT RANGES

     Variable       Lower Limit      Current Value      Upper Limit
   ------------   ---------------   ---------------   ---------------
       X1               2.500             3.000            10.000
       X2               1.500             5.000             6.000

RIGHT HAND SIDE RANGES

    Constraint      Lower Limit      Current Value      Upper Limit
   ------------   ---------------   ---------------   ---------------
        1           65000.000         80000.000        140000.000
        2             400.000           700.000           775.000
        3             800.000          1000.000       No Upper Limit
```

The Management Scientist solution is shown in Figure 3.12.

  a. What is the optimal solution and what are the optimal production quantities?

  b. Specify the range of optimality for the objective function coefficients.

  c. What are the dual prices for each constraint? Interpret each.

  d. Identify the range of feasibility for each of the right-hand-side values.

6. **SELF**Test Recall the Innis Investments problem (Chapter 2, Problem 37). Letting

$$x_1 = \text{units purchased in the stock fund}$$
$$x_2 = \text{units purchased in the money market fund}$$

leads to the following formulation:

$$\text{Min} \quad 8x_1 + 3x_2$$

s.t.

$$50x_1 + 100x_2 \leq 1{,}200{,}000 \quad \text{Funds available}$$
$$5x_1 + 4x_2 \geq 60{,}000 \quad \text{Annual income}$$
$$x_2 \geq 3{,}000 \quad \text{Units in money market}$$
$$x_1, x_2 \geq 0$$

Figure 3.12

The Management Scientist Solution for the Tom's, Inc., Problem

```
OPTIMAL SOLUTION


Objective Function Value =              860.000


         Variable              Value              Reduced Costs
      --------------      ----------------      ------------------
           X1                 560.000                 0.000
           X2                 240.000                 0.000


        Constraint         Slack/Surplus           Dual Prices
      --------------      ----------------      ------------------
            1                   0.000                 0.125
            2                 160.000                 0.000
            3                   0.000                 0.187


OBJECTIVE COEFFICIENT RANGES

    Variable        Lower Limit       Current Value       Upper Limit
  ------------    ----------------   ---------------    ----------------
       X1              0.893             1.000               1.250
       X2              1.000             1.250               1.400


RIGHT HAND SIDE RANGES

   Constraint       Lower Limit       Current Value       Upper Limit
  ------------    ----------------   ---------------    ----------------
       1             4320.000           4480.000            5600.000
       2             1920.000           2080.000         No Upper Limit
       3             1280.000           1600.000            1640.000
```

The computer solution is shown in Figure 3.13.

a. What is the optimal solution, and what is the minimum total risk?

b. Specify the range of optimality for the objective function coefficients.

c. How much annual income will be earned by the portfolio?

d. What is the rate of return for the portfolio?

e. What is the dual price for the funds available constraint?

f. What is the marginal rate of return on extra funds added to the portfolio?

7. Refer to Problem 6 and the computer solution shown in Figure 3.13.

a. Suppose the risk index for the stock fund (the value of c_1) increases from its current value of 8 to 12. How does the optimal solution change, if at all?

b. Suppose the risk index for the money market fund (the value of c_2) increases from its current value of 3 to 3.5. How does the optimal solution change, if at all?

c. Suppose c_1 increases to 12 and c_2 increases to 3.3. How does the optimal solution change, if at all?

Figure 3.13

. . . .

The Management Scientist Solution for the Innis Investments Problem

```
Objective Function Value =          62000.000

      Variable              Value              Reduced Costs
  ---------------      ---------------      ------------------
        X1               4000.000                 0.000
        X2              10000.000                 0.000

     Constraint        Slack/Surplus           Dual Prices
  ---------------      ---------------      ------------------
         1                 0.000                  0.057
         2                 0.000                 -2.167
         3              7000.000                  0.000

OBJECTIVE COEFFICIENT RANGES

     Variable       Lower Limit      Current Value      Upper Limit
  ------------     ---------------   ---------------    ---------------
        X1               3.750           8.000        No Upper Limit
        X2         No Lower Limit        3.000              6.400

RIGHT HAND SIDE RANGES

    Constraint      Lower Limit      Current Value      Upper Limit
  ------------     ---------------   ---------------    ---------------
         1          780000.000       1200000.000       1500000.000
         2           48000.000         60000.000        102000.000
         3        No Lower Limit        3000.000         10000.000
```

8.   Suppose that in a product-mix problem x_1, x_2, x_3, and x_4 indicate the units of
products 1, 2, 3, and 4, respectively, and the linear program is

$$\text{Max} \quad 4x_1 + 6x_2 + 3x_3 + 1x_4$$

s.t.

$$1.5x_1 + 2x_2 + 4x_3 + 3x_4 \leq 550 \quad \text{Machine A hours}$$

$$4x_1 + 1x_2 + 2x_3 + 1x_4 \leq 700 \quad \text{Machine B hours}$$

$$2x_1 + 3x_2 + 1x_3 + 2x_4 \leq 200 \quad \text{Machine C hours}$$

$$x_1, x_2, x_3, x_4 \geq 0$$

The computer solution developed using The Management Scientist is shown in Figure 3.14.
a. What is the optimal solution, and what is the value of the objective function?
b. Which constraints are binding?

Figure 3.14
....

The Management Scientist Solution for Problem 8

```
Objective Function Value =          525.000

        Variable              Value            Reduced Costs
        --------            ---------          -------------
          X1                  0.000                0.050
          X2                 25.000                0.000
          X3                125.000                0.000
          X4                  0.000                3.500


       Constraint         Slack/Surplus          Dual Prices
       ----------         -------------          -----------
           1                  0.000                0.300
           2                425.000                0.000
           3                  0.000                1.800

OBJECTIVE COEFFICIENT RANGES

     Variable      Lower Limit      Current Value     Upper Limit
     --------      -----------      -------------     -----------
       X1        No Lower Limit         4.000            4.050
       X2             5.923             6.000            9.000
       X3             2.000             3.000           12.000
       X4        No Lower Limit         1.000            4.500

RIGHT HAND SIDE RANGES

    Constraint     Lower Limit      Current Value     Upper Limit
    ----------     -----------      -------------     -----------
        1            133.333           550.000          800.000
        2            275.000           700.000       No Upper Limit
        3            137.500           200.000          825.000
```

c. Which machines have excess capacity available? How much?

d. If the objective function coefficient of x_1 is increased by 0.50, will the optimal solution change?

9. **SELF Test** Refer to the computer solution of Problem 8 in Figure 3.14.

a. Identify the range of optimality for each objective function coefficient.

b. Suppose the objective function coefficient for x_1 is decreased by 3, the objective function coefficient of x_2 is increased by 1.5, and the objective function coefficient for x_4 is increased by 1. What will the new optimal solution be?

c. Identify the range of feasibility for the right-hand-side values.

d. If the number of hours available on machine A is increased by 300, will the dual price for that constraint change?

10. Consider the following linear program and computer solution shown in Figure 3.15.

$$\text{Min} \quad 15x_1 + 15x_2 + 16x_3$$

s.t.

$$1x_1 \quad\quad + \quad 1x_3 \leq 30$$
$$0.5x_1 - \quad 1x_2 + \quad 6x_3 \geq 15$$
$$3x_1 + \quad 4x_2 - \quad 1x_3 \geq 20$$
$$x_1, x_2, x_3 \geq 0$$

   a. What is the optimal solution, and what is the optimal value for the objective function?
   b. Which constraints are binding?
   c. What are the dual prices? Interpret each.
   d. If you could change the right-hand side of one constraint by one unit, which one would you choose? What would be the new value of the right-hand side?

11. Refer to the computer solution of Problem 10 in Figure 3.15.
   a. Interpret the ranges of optimality for the objective function coefficients.
   b. Suppose c_1 is increased by 0.25. What is the new optimal solution?
   c. Suppose c_1 is increased by 0.25 and c_2 is decreased by 0.25. What is the new optimal solution?

12. Supersport Footballs, Inc., has to determine the best number of All-Pro (x_1), College (x_2), and High School (x_3) models of footballs to produce in order to maximize profits. Constraints include production capacity limitations (time available in minutes) in each of three departments (cutting and dyeing, sewing, and inspection and packaging) as well as a constraint that requires the production of at least 1000 All-Pro footballs. The linear programming model of Supersport's problem is shown below:

$$\text{Max } 3x_1 + 5x_2 + \quad 4x_3$$

s.t.

$$12x_1 + 10x_2 + \quad 8x_3 \leq 18{,}000 \quad \text{Cutting and dyeing}$$
$$15x_1 + 15x_2 + 12x_3 \leq 18{,}000 \quad \text{Sewing}$$
$$3x_1 + \quad 4x_2 + \quad 2x_3 \leq \quad 9{,}000 \quad \text{Inspection and packaging}$$
$$1x_1 \quad\quad\quad\quad\quad \geq \quad 1{,}000 \quad \text{All-Pro model}$$
$$x_1, x_2, x_3 \geq 0$$

The computer solution to the Supersport problem is shown in Figure 3.16.
   a. How many footballs of each type should Supersport produce to maximize the total profit contribution?
   b. Which constraints are binding?
   c. Interpret the slack and/or surplus in each constraint.
   d. Interpret the ranges of optimality for the profit contributions of the three footballs.

13. Refer to the computer solution of Problem 12 (see Figure 3.16).
   a. Overtime rates in the sewing department are $12 per hour. Would you recommend that the company consider using overtime in that department? Explain.
   b. What is the dual price for the fourth constraint? Interpret its value for management.
   c. Note that the reduced cost for x_3 is zero, but x_3 is not in the solution at a positive value. What is your interpretation of this?
   d. Suppose that the profit contribution of the College ball is increased by $1. How do you expect the solution to change?

Note: **Problems 14–19 and the case problems require computer solution and interpretation of the results.**

Figure 3.15

The Management Scientist Solution for Problem 10

```
Objective Function Value =          139.730

        Variable            Value              Reduced Costs
        --------            -----              -------------
          X1              7.297                  0.000
          X2              0.000                  0.676
          X3              1.892                  0.000

        Constraint      Slack/Surplus           Dual Prices
        ----------      -------------           -----------
          1              20.811                  0.000
          2               0.000                 -3.405
          3               0.000                 -4.432

OBJECTIVE COEFFICIENT RANGES

   Variable      Lower Limit      Current Value      Upper Limit
   --------      -----------      -------------      -----------
     X1             1.333            15.000            15.543
     X2            14.324            15.000         No Upper Limit
     X3            13.500            16.000           180.000

RIGHT HAND SIDE RANGES

   Constraint    Lower Limit      Current Value      Upper Limit
   ----------    -----------      -------------      -----------
     1              9.189            30.000         No Upper Limit
     2              3.333            15.000           111.250
     3             -2.500            20.000            90.000
```

14. Better Products, Inc., manufactures three products on two machines. In a typical week, 40 hours are available on each machine. The profit contribution and production time in hours per unit are as follows:

Category	Product 1	Product 2	Product 3
Profit/unit	$30	$50	$20
Machine 1 time/unit	0.5	2.0	0.75
Machine 2 time/unit	1.0	1.0	0.5

Two operators are required for machine 1; thus, 2 hours of labor must be scheduled for each hour of machine 1 time. Only one operator is required for machine 2. A maximum of 100

Figure 3.16

....

The Management Scientist Solution for the Supersport Footballs Problem

```
Objective Function Value =              4000.000

          Variable              Value           Reduced Costs
      --------------       ---------------     -------------------

            X1                 1000.000               0.000
            X2                  200.000               0.000
            X3                    0.000               0.000


         Constraint         Slack/Surplus         Dual Prices
      --------------       ---------------     -------------------

             1                 4000.000               0.000
             2                    0.000               0.333
             3                 5200.000               0.000
             4                    0.000              -2.000
```

OBJECTIVE COEFFICIENT RANGES

Variable	Lower Limit	Current Value	Upper Limit
X1	No Lower Limit	3.000	5.000
X2	5.000	5.000	No Upper Limit
X3	No Lower Limit	4.000	4.000

RIGHT HAND SIDE RANGES

Constraint	Lower Limit	Current Value	Upper Limit
1	14000.000	18000.000	No Upper Limit
2	15000.000	18000.000	24000.000
3	3800.000	9000.000	No Upper Limit
4	0.000	1000.000	1200.000

labor hours is available for assignment to the machine during the coming week. Other production requirements are that product 1 cannot account for more than 50% of the units produced and that product 3 must account for at least 20% of the units produced.

a. How many units of each product should be produced to maximize the total profit contribution? What is the projected weekly profit associated with your solution?

b. How many hours of production time will be scheduled on each machine?

c. What is the value of an additional hour of labor?

d. Assume that labor capacity can be increased to 120 hours. Would you be interested in using the additional 20 hours available for this resource? Develop the optimal product mix assuming the extra hours are made available.

15. A manufacturer makes three components for sale to refrigeration companies. The components are processed on two machines: a shaper and a grinder. The times (in minutes) required on each machine are as follows:

	Machine	
Component	Shaper	Grinder
1	6	4
2	4	5
3	4	2

The shaper is available for 120 hours, and the grinder is available for 110 hours. No more than 200 units of component 3 can be sold, but up to 1000 units of each of the other components can be sold. In fact, the company already has orders for 600 units of component 1 that must be satisfied. The profit contributions for components 1, 2, and 3 are $8, $6, and $9, respectively.

a. Formulate and solve for the recommended production quantities. Use any computer code available.

b. What are the ranges of optimality for the profit contributions of the three components? Interpret these ranges for company management.

c. What are the ranges of feasibility for the right-hand sides? Interpret these ranges for company management.

d. If more time could be made available on the grinder, how much would it be worth?

e. If more units of component 3 can be sold by reducing the sales price by $4, should the company reduce the price?

16. National Insurance Associates carries an investment portfolio of stocks, bonds, and other investment alternatives. Currently $200,000 of funds are available and must be considered for new investment opportunities. The four stock options National is considering and the relevant financial data are as follows:

	Stock			
	A	B	C	D
Price per share	$100	$50	$80	$40
Annual rate of return	0.12	0.08	0.06	0.10
Risk measure per dollar invested	0.10	0.07	0.05	0.08

The risk measure indicates the relative uncertainty associated with the stock in terms of its realizing the projected annual return; higher values indicate greater risk. The risk measures are provided by the firm's top financial advisor.

National's top management has stipulated the following investment guidelines.

1. The annual rate of return for the portfolio must be at least 9%.

2. No one stock can account for more than 50% of the total dollar investment.

a. Use linear programming to develop an investment portfolio that minimizes risk.

b. If the firm ignores risk and uses a maximum return-on-investment strategy, what is the investment portfolio?

c. What is the dollar difference between the portfolios in parts (a) and (b)? Why might the company prefer the solution developed in part (a)?

17. The Carson Stapler Manufacturing Company forecasts a 5000-unit demand for its Sure-Hold model during the next quarter. This stapler is assembled from three major components: base, staple cartridge, and handle. Until now Carson has manufactured all three components. However, the forecast of 5000 units is a new high in sales volume, and the firm may not have sufficient production capacity to make all the components. The company is considering contracting with a local firm to produce at least some of the components. The production time requirements per unit are as follows:

| | Production Time (hours) | | | |
| | X_1 | X_2 | X_3 | Time Available |
Department	Base	Cartridge	Handle	(hours)
A	0.03	0.02	0.05	400
B	0.04	0.02	0.04	400
C	0.02	0.03	0.01	400

_5000_

Note that each component manufactured by Carson uses manufacturing time in each of three departments.

After considering the firm's overhead, material, and labor costs, the accounting department has determined the unit manufacturing cost for each component. These data, along with the purchase price quotations by the contracting firm, are as follows:

we buy from others

Component	Manufacturing Cost	Purchase Cost
Base	$0.75	$0.95
Cartridge	$0.40	$0.55
Handle	$1.10	$1.40

a. Determine the make-or-buy decision for Carson that will meet the 5000-unit demand at a minimum total cost. How many units of each component should be made and how many purchased?

b. Which departments are limiting the manufacturing volume? If overtime could be considered at the additional cost of $3 per hour, which department(s) should be allocated the overtime? Explain.

c. Suppose that up to 80 hours of overtime could be scheduled in department A. What would you recommend?

18. Golf Shafts, Inc. (GSI), produces graphite shafts for several manufacturers of golf clubs. Two GSI manufacturing facilities, one located in San Diego and the other in Tampa, have the capability to produce shafts in varying degrees of stiffness, ranging from regular models used primarily by average golfers to extra stiff models used primarily by low-handicap and professional golfers. GSI has just received a contract for the production of 200,000 regular shafts and 75,000 stiff shafts. Since both plants are currently producing shafts for previous orders, neither plant has sufficient capacity by itself to fill the new order. The San Diego plant can produce up to a total of 120,000 shafts and the Tampa plant can produce up to a total of 180,000 shafts. Because of equipment differences at each of the plants and differing labor costs, the per-unit production costs vary as shown here:

	San Diego Cost	Tampa Cost
Regular Shaft	$5.25	$4.95
Stiff Shaft	$5.45	$5.70

Min Z =

$X_1 = SD \quad Reg$
$\quad\quad\quad st.ff$
$X_2 = SD \quad Reg$
$X_3 = T \quad st.ff$
$X_4 = T$

$MIN \ Z = 5.25 X_1 + 5.45 X_2 + 4.95 X_3 + 5.70 X_4$

$X_1 + X_3 \leq 200,000$

$X_2 + X_4 \geq 75,000$

$X_1 + X_2 \leq 120,000$

$X_3 + X_4 \leq 180,000$

a. Formulate a linear programming model to determine how GSI should schedule production for the new order in order to minimize the total production cost.

b. Use any linear programming code to solve the model that you developed in part (a).

c. Suppose that some of the previous orders at the Tampa plant could be rescheduled in order to free up additional capacity for the new order. Would this be worthwhile? Explain.

d. Suppose that the cost to produce a stiff shaft in Tampa had been incorrectly computed, and that the correct cost is $5.30 per shaft. What effect, if any, would this have on the optimal solution developed in part (b)? What effect would this have on total production cost?

19. The Pfeiffer Company manages approximately $15 million for clients. For each client, Pfeiffer chooses a mix of three investment vehicles: a growth stock fund, an income fund, and a money market fund. Each client has different investment objectives and different tolerances for risk. To accommodate these differences, Pfeiffer places limits on the percentage of each portfolio that may be invested in the three funds and assigns a portfolio risk index to each client.

Here's how the system works for Dennis Hartmann, one of Pfeiffer's clients. Based on an evaluation of Hartmann's risk tolerance, Pfeiffer has assigned Hartmann's portfolio a risk index of 0.05. Furthermore, to maintain diversity, the fraction of Hartmann's portfolio invested in the growth and income funds must be at least 10% for each, and at least 20% must be in the money market fund.

The risk ratings for the growth, income, and money market funds are 0.10, 0.05, and 0.01, respectively. A portfolio risk index is computed as a weighted average of the risk ratings for the three funds where the weights are the fraction of the portfolio invested in each of the funds. Hartmann has given Pfeiffer $300,000 to manage. Pfeiffer is currently forecasting a yield of 20% on the growth fund, 10% on the income fund, and 6% on the money market fund.

a. Develop a linear programming model to select the best mix of investments for Hartmann's portfolio.

b. Use any linear programming computer code to solve the model you developed in part (a).

c. How much may the yields on the three funds vary before it will be necessary for Pfeiffer to modify Hartmann's portfolio?

d. If Hartmann were more risk tolerant, how much of a yield increase could he expect? For instance, what if his portfolio risk index is increased to 0.06?

e. If Pfeiffer revised his yield estimate for the growth fund downward to 0.10, how would you recommend modifying Hartmann's portfolio?

f. What information must Pfeiffer maintain on each client in order to use this system to manage client portfolios?

g. On a weekly basis Pfeiffer revises the yield estimates for the three funds. Suppose Pfeiffer has 50 clients. Describe how you would envision Pfeiffer making weekly modifications in each client's portfolio and allocating the total funds managed among the three investment funds.

20. La Jolla Beverage Products is considering producing a wine cooler that would be a blend of a white wine, a rosé wine, and fruit juice. To meet taste specifications, the wine cooler must consist of at least 50% white wine, at least 20% and no more than 30% rosé, and exactly 20% fruit juice. La Jolla purchases the wine from local wineries and the fruit juice from a processing plant in San Francisco. For the current production period, 10,000 gallons of white wine and 8000 gallons of rosé wine can be purchased; there is no limit on the amount of fruit juice that can be ordered. The costs for the wine are $1.00 per gallon for the white and $1.50 per gallon for the rosé; the fruit juice can be purchased for $0.50 per gallon. La Jolla Beverage Products can sell all of the wine cooler they can produce for $2.50 per gallon.

a. Is the cost of the wine and fruit juice a sunk cost or a relevant cost in this situation? Explain.

b. Formulate a linear program to determine the blend of the three ingredients that will maximize the total profit contribution. Solve the linear program to determine the number of gallons of each ingredient La Jolla should purchase and the total profit contribution they will realize from this blend.

c. If La Jolla could obtain additional amounts of the white wine, should they do so? If so, how much should they be willing to pay for each additional gallon, and how many additional gallons would they want to purchase?

d. If La Jolla Beverage Products could obtain additional amounts of the rosé wine, should they do so? If so, how much should they be willing to pay for each additional gallon, and how many additional gallons would they want to purchase?

e. Interpret the dual price for the constraint corresponding to the requirement that the wine cooler must contain at least 50% white wine. What is your advice to management given this dual price?

f. Interpret the dual price for the constraint corresponding to the requirement that the wine cooler must contain exactly 20% fruit juice. What is your advice to management given this dual price?

21. The program manager for Channel 10 would like to determine the best way to allocate the time for the 11:00–11:30 evening news broadcast. Specifically, she would like to determine the number of minutes of broadcast time to devote to local news, national news, weather, and sports. Over the 30-minute broadcast, 10 minutes are set aside for advertising. The station's broadcast policy states that at least 15% of the time available should be devoted to local news coverage; the time devoted to local news or national news must be at least 50% of the total broadcast time; the time devoted to the weather segment must be less than or equal to the time devoted to the sports segment; the time devoted to the sports segment should be no longer than the total time spent on the local and national news; and at least 20% of the time should be devoted to the weather segment. The production costs per minute are $300 for local news, $200 for national news, $100 for weather, and $100 for sports.

a. Formulate and solve a linear program that can determine how the 20 available minutes should be used to minimize the total cost of producing the program.

b. Interpret the dual price for the constraint corresponding to the available time. What advice would you give the station manager given this dual price?

c. Interpret the dual price for the constraint corresponding to the requirement that at least 15% of the available time should be devoted to local coverage. What advice would you give the station manager given this dual price?

d. Interpret the dual price for the constraint corresponding to the requirement that the time devoted to the local and the national news must be at least 50% of the total broadcast time. What advice would you give the station manager given this dual price?

e. Interpret the dual price for the constraint corresponding to the requirement that the time devoted to the weather segment must be less than or equal to the time devoted to the sports segment. What advice would you give the station manager given this dual price?

22. Gulf Coast Electronics is ready to award contracts for printing their annual report. For the past several years, the four-color annual report has been printed by Johnson Printing and Lakeside Litho. A new firm, Benson Printing, has inquired into the possibility of doing a portion of the printing. The quality and service level provided by Lakeside Litho has been extremely high; in fact, only 0.5% of their reports have had to be discarded because of quality problems. Johnson Printing has also had a high quality level historically, producing an average of only 1% unacceptable reports. Since Gulf Coast Electronics has had no experience with Benson Printing, they have estimated their defective rate to be 10%. Gulf Coast would like to determine how many reports should be printed by each firm to obtain 75,000 acceptable-quality reports. To ensure that Benson Printing will receive some of the contract, management has specified that the number of reports awarded to Benson Printing must be at least 10% of the volume given to Johnson Printing. In addition, the total volume assigned to Benson Printing, Johnson Printing, and Lakeside Litho should not exceed 30,000, 50,000, and 50,000 copies, respectively. Because of the long-term relationship that has developed with Lakeside Litho, management has also specified that at least 30,000 reports should be awarded to Lakeside Litho. The cost per copy is $2.45 for Benson Printing, $2.50 for Johnson Printing, and $2.75 for Lakeside Litho.

a. Formulate and solve a linear program for determining how many copies should be assigned to each printing firm to minimize the total cost of obtaining 75,000 acceptable-quality reports.

b. Suppose that the quality level for Benson Printing is much better than estimated. What effect, if any, would this have?

c. Suppose that management is willing to reconsider their requirement that Lakeside Litho be awarded at least 30,000 reports. What effect, if any, would this have?

Case Problem: Product Mix

TJ's, Inc., makes three nut mixes for sale to grocery chains located in the Southeast. The three mixes, referred to as the Regular Mix, the Deluxe Mix, and the Holiday Mix, are made by mixing different percentages of five types of nuts.

In preparation for the fall season, TJ's has just purchased the following shipments of nuts at the prices shown:

Type of Nut	Shipment Amount (pounds)	Cost per Shipment
Almond	6000	$7500
Brazil	7500	$7125
Filbert	7500	$6750
Pecan	6000	$7200
Walnut	7500	$7875

The Regular Mix consists of 15% almonds, 25% Brazil nuts, 25% filberts, 10% pecans, and 25% walnuts. The Deluxe Mix consists of 20% of each type of nut, and the Holiday Mix consists of 25% almonds, 15% Brazil nuts, 15% filberts, 25% pecans, and 20% walnuts.

TJ's accountant has analyzed the cost of packaging materials, sales price per pound, and so forth, and has determined that the profit contribution per pound is $1.65 for the Regular Mix, $2.00 for the Deluxe Mix, and $2.25 for the Holiday Mix. These figures do not include the cost of specific types of nuts in the different mixes because that cost can vary greatly in the commodity markets.

Customer orders already received are summarized below:

Type of Mix	Orders (pounds)
Regular	10,000
Deluxe	3,000
Holiday	5,000

Because demand is running high, it is expected that TJ's will receive many more orders than can be satisfied.

TJ's is committed to using the available nuts to maximize profit over the fall season; nuts not used will be given to the Free Store. But even if it is not profitable to do so, TJ's president has indicated that the orders already received must be satisfied.

Managerial Report

Perform an analysis of TJ's product-mix problem, and prepare a report for TJ's president that summarizes your findings. Be sure to include information and analysis on the following:

1. The cost per pound of the nuts included in the Regular, Deluxe, and Holiday mixes

2. The optimal product mix and the total profit contribution
3. Recommendations regarding how the total profit contribution can be increased if additional quantities of nuts can be purchased
4. A recommendation as to whether TJ's should purchase an additional 1000 pounds of almonds for $1000 from a supplier who overbought
5. Recommendations on how profit contribution could be increased (if at all) if TJ's does not satisfy all existing orders

Case Problem: Truck Leasing Strategy

Reep Construction has recently won a contract for the excavation and site preparation of a new rest area on the Pennsylvania turnpike. In preparing his bid for the job, Bob Reep, founder and president of Reep Construction, estimated that it would take 4 months to perform the work, and that the number of trucks needed in months 1 through 4 would be 10, 12, 14, and 8, respectively.

The firm currently has 20 trucks of the type that will be needed to perform the work on the new project. These trucks were obtained last year when Bob signed a long-term lease with PennState Leasing. While most of these trucks are currently being used on existing jobs, Bob estimates that one truck will be available for use on the new project in month 1, two trucks will be available in month 2, three trucks will be available in month 3, and one truck will be available in month 4. Thus, to complete the project, Bob will have to lease additional trucks.

The long-term leasing contract with PennState has a monthly cost of $600 per truck. Reep Construction pays their truck drivers $20 per hour, and daily fuel costs are approximately $100 per truck. All maintenance costs are paid by PennState Leasing. For planning purposes, Bob estimates that each truck used on the new project will be operating 8 hours per day, 5 days per week, and that there are approximately 4 weeks in each month.

Bob does not feel that current business conditions justify committing the firm to additional long-term leases. In discussing the short-term leasing possibilities with PennState Leasing, Bob has learned that he can obtain short-term leases of 1–4 months in length. Short-term leases differ from long-term leases in that the short-term leasing plans include the cost of both a truck and a driver. Maintenance costs for short-term leases are also paid by PennState Leasing. The following cost figures show the monthly leasing cost for each truck and driver:

Length of Lease (months)	Cost per Month
1	$4000
2	$3700
3	$3225
4	$3040

Bob Reep would like to acquire a lease that would minimize the cost of meeting the monthly trucking requirements for his new project, but he also takes great pride in the fact that his company has never laid off employees. Bob is committed to maintaining his no-layoff policy; that is, he will use his own drivers even if costs are higher.

Managerial Report

Perform an analysis of Reep Construction's leasing problem, and prepare a report for Bob Reep that summarizes your findings. Be sure to include information and analysis on the following:

1. The optimal leasing plan.
2. The costs associated with the optimal leasing plan.
3. Information as to what it will cost Reep Construction to maintain their current policy of no layoffs.

Figure 3.17
. . . .

Data Input for the Par, Inc., Problem Using The Management Scientist

Optimization Type: Maximize				
Variable Names: [Change if Desired]	X1	X2		
Objective Function Coefficients	10	9		
	Coefficients			
Subject To:	X1	X2	Relation (<, =, >)	Right Hand Side
Constraint 1	0.7	1	<	630
Constraint 2	0.5	0.83333	<	600
Constraint 3	1	0.66667	<	708
Constraint 4	0.1	0.25	<	135

APPENDIX 3.1   Solving Linear Programs with The Management Scientist

In this appendix we describe how The Management Scientist software package can be used to solve the Par, Inc., linear programming problem. After starting The Management Scientist, execute the following steps.

Step 1   Select the **Linear Programming** module
Step 2   Choose **New** from the **File Menu**
Step 3   When the **Problem Features** dialog box appears:
Enter 2 for **Number of Decision Variables**
Enter 4 for **Number of Constraints**
Select Maximize for **Optimization Type**
Select **OK**
Step 4   When the data input worksheet appears (see Figure 3.17):
Enter the objective function coefficients
For each constraint:
Enter the variable coefficients
Enter the relation type ($<$, $=$, $>$)
Enter the right-hand-side value
Step 5   Choose **Solve** from the **Solution menu**

The user entries in the data input worksheet are shown in color in Figure 3.17. The output from The Management Scientist is shown in Figure 3.1. In general, when entering the problem data, zero coefficients do not have to be entered. In addition, changes to the problem can be easily made by selecting the appropriate option from the Edit menu, and printed output can be obtained by selecting the Print Solution option from the Solution menu.

APPENDIX 3.2   Solving Linear Programs with LINDO/PC

LINDO/PC was developed by Linus E. Schrage at the University of Chicago. We will use the Par, Inc., problem to demonstrate LINDO/PC. The data input portion of a LINDO/PC computer session on an IBM Personal Computer is shown in Figure 3.18. The information keyed in by the user is shown in color, and the response from the computer package is shown in black.

Figure 3.18

Data Input Session with LINDO/PC (User Response Shown in Color)

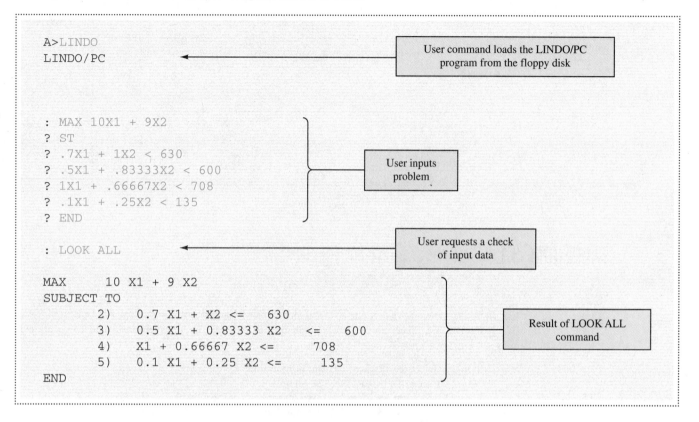

```
A>LINDO
LINDO/PC                                          User command loads the LINDO/PC
                                                  program from the floppy disk


: MAX 10X1 + 9X2
? ST
? .7X1 + 1X2 < 630
? .5X1 + .83333X2 < 600                           User inputs
? 1X1 + .66667X2 < 708                            problem
? .1X1 + .25X2 < 135
? END

: LOOK ALL                                        User requests a check
                                                  of input data

MAX      10 X1 + 9 X2
SUBJECT TO
      2)    0.7 X1 + X2 <=    630                  Result of LOOK ALL
      3)    0.5 X1 + 0.83333 X2  <=    600         command
      4)    X1 + 0.66667 X2 <=      708
      5)    0.1 X1 + 0.25 X2 <=     135
END
```

Note in particular the interactive nature of the system with the alternating user input and LINDO/PC response. Specific commands and symbols shown in Figure 3.18 are described as follows:

1. The "A>" is the user prompt for DOS systems on the IBM Personal Computer. The user command LINDO causes the LINDO/PC program to be loaded.
2. LINDO/PC begins by sending the symbol ":" to indicate that it is waiting for an instruction from the user.
3. The user keys in the objective function as it appears in the mathematical statement of the problem.
4. LINDO/PC then sends the symbol "?" to indicate that it is waiting for additional input concerning the linear program being solved.
5. The user input ST stands for *subject to*, notifying the program that information about the constraints is to follow.
6. After inputting each of the constraints with the symbol "<" (interpreted as $\leq$ by LINDO/PC) the user inputs END to signal that the data input is complete.
7. LINDO/PC again responds with ":" to indicate that it is waiting for an instruction.
8. The user inputs the optional instruction LOOK ALL; LINDO/PC then prints the linear programming problem that has been entered. LOOK ALL is not a required instruction, but using it provides an easy check on the accuracy of the input data. With LINDO/PC the objective function is identified as row 1. Thus, under the SUBJECT TO heading, we see the cutting and dyeing constraint identified as row 2, the sewing constraint as row 3, the finishing constraint as row 4, and the inspection and packaging constraint as row 5.

Figure 3.19

Par, Inc., Solution Using LINDO/PC

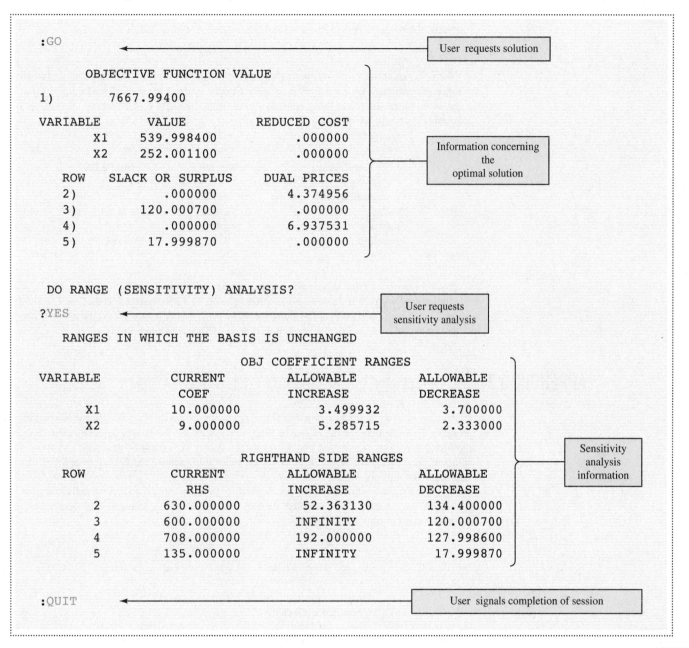

```
:GO                                                    ┌──────────────────────┐
                                                       │ User requests solution│
                                                       └──────────────────────┘

        OBJECTIVE FUNCTION VALUE

1)        7667.99400

VARIABLE        VALUE           REDUCED COST
      X1      539.998400            .000000        ┌──────────────────────┐
      X2      252.001100            .000000        │ Information concerning│
                                                   │         the           │
   ROW    SLACK OR SURPLUS     DUAL PRICES         │   optimal solution    │
   2)          .000000          4.374956           └──────────────────────┘
   3)        120.000700          .000000
   4)          .000000          6.937531
   5)         17.999870          .000000


DO RANGE (SENSITIVITY) ANALYSIS?
                                                   ┌──────────────────────┐
?YES                                               │   User requests      │
                                                   │ sensitivity analysis │
   RANGES IN WHICH THE BASIS IS UNCHANGED          └──────────────────────┘

                    OBJ COEFFICIENT RANGES
VARIABLE         CURRENT         ALLOWABLE       ALLOWABLE
                  COEF           INCREASE        DECREASE
      X1       10.000000          3.499932        3.700000
      X2        9.000000          5.285715        2.333000

                    RIGHTHAND SIDE RANGES            ┌──────────────────────┐
   ROW           CURRENT         ALLOWABLE       ALLOWABLE │ Sensitivity     │
                  RHS            INCREASE        DECREASE   │   analysis      │
     2         630.000000         52.363130      134.400000 │  information    │
     3         600.000000         INFINITY       120.000700 └──────────────────────┘
     4         708.000000        192.000000      127.998600
     5         135.000000         INFINITY        17.999870


:QUIT                                              ┌──────────────────────────────┐
                                                   │ User signals completion of session│
                                                   └──────────────────────────────┘
```

With the input data complete, the LINDO/PC package proceeds to develop the solution of the problem when given the command GO. The output from LINDO/PC is shown in Figure 3.19.

The first section of the output is self-explanatory. After printing the values of the slack variables and dual prices, LINDO/PC asks the user the following question: DO RANGE (SENSITIVITY) ANALYSIS? The user response of YES requests ranges on the objective function coefficients and the right-hand sides of the constraints.

Considering the information provided under the computer output heading labeled OBJ COEFFICIENT RANGES, we see that variable x_1, with a current profit coefficient of 10, has an allowable increase of 3.5 and an allowable decrease of 3.7. Adding 3.5 to and subtracting 3.7 from the current coefficient of 10 provides the following range of optimality for c_1:

$$6.3 \leq c_1 \leq 13.5$$

Similarly, the range of optimality for c_2 is found to be

$$6.67 \leq c_2 \leq 14.29$$

The information under the heading labeled RIGHT HAND SIDE RANGES permits computing the range of feasibility for each right-hand side. Simply subtract the allowable decrease from the current value to get the lower limit, and add the allowable increase to the current value to get the upper limit. Doing so, we obtain

Constraint	Min RHS	Max RHS
Cutting and dyeing	495.6	682.4
Sewing	480.0	No upper limit
Finishing	580.0	900.0
Inspecting and packaging	117.0	No upper limit

Note in Figure 3.19 that at the completion of the sensitivity analysis, LINDO/PC sends ":" and waits for another instruction. In this case, the user selected QUIT to signal the end of the LINDO/PC session. An optional instruction at this point would be ALT, which would enable the user to alter or modify one or more aspects of the problem and seek additional solution information.

APPENDIX 3.3   Spreadsheet Solution of Linear Programs

In this appendix we will show how Excel can be used to solve the Par, Inc., linear programming problem. First, the data for the objective function coefficients, the constraint coefficients, and the right-hand sides must be entered into a worksheet. Second, cells must be identified for storing the values of the decision variables, the value for the objective function, and the values of the left-hand sides of the constraints. Figure 3.20 shows a worksheet for the Par, Inc., problem in which the cells in the upper portion of the worksheet are reserved for problem input data and the cells in the lower portion of the worksheet are reserved for the solution output. The Input Data section of the worksheet contains the following values:

Input Value	Cell Location
Objective function coefficients	B11:C11
Constraint coefficients	B6:C9
Right-hand sides	D6:D9

The Solution Output section of the worksheet contains the following optimal solution values:

Output Value	Cell Location
Decision variables	B17:C17
Objective function	D18
Slack/Surplus	C22:C25

Figure 3.20

Excel Worksheet for the Par, Inc., Problem Data

	A	B	C	D
1				
2	**Input Data**			
3		**Production Time**		
4		(hours per unit)		
5	**Operation**	Standard bag	Deluxe bag	**Hours Available**
6	Cutting and dyeing	0.7	1	630
7	Sewing	0.5	0.83333	600
8	Finishing	1	0.66667	708
9	Inspection and packaging	0.1	0.25	135
10				
11	**Profit per unit**	10	9	
12				
13				
14	**Solution Output**			
15		**Decision Variables**		
16		Standard bag	Deluxe bag	**Total Profit**
17	**Number of units**			
18	**Profit**			
19				
20				
21	**Operation**	**Hours Used**	**Slack/Surplus**	
22	Cutting and dyeing			
23	Sewing			
24	Finishing			
25	Inspection and packaging			

To solve the Par, Inc., problem we will use Excel Solver, a general optimization and resource allocation tool. To use Solver, we must first write formulas that show how the values in the solution output section of the worksheet are related to the input data values. For instance, in the Par, Inc., problem, the profit contribution corresponding to the production of standard bags is 10 times the number of standard bags produced, and the profit contribution from the production of deluxe bags is 9 times the number of deluxe bags produced; thus, in cell B18 we entered the formula =B11*B17 (the contribution to profit from standard bags) and in cell C18 we entered the formula =C11*C17 (the contribution to profit from deluxe bags). Since the total contribution to profit is the sum of these two values, in cell D18 we entered the formula = B18+C18.

The total number of hours used of cutting and dyeing time is the product of the value in cell B6 (0.7) times the value in cell B17 (number of standard bags produced) plus the product of the value in cell C6(1) times the value in cell C17 (number of deluxe bags produced); thus, using the SUMPRODUCT function, we entered the following formula in cell B22:

$$=SUMPRODUCT(B6:C6,\$B\$17:\$C\$17)$$

After copying this formula to cells B23 through B25, these cells will also contain the formulas for the number of hours used for each of the other three operations in the Par, Inc., problem.

Finally, to compute the slack/surplus value for each operation, we subtract the number of hours used from the number of hours available. Thus, in cell C22 we entered the formula =D6−B22. After copying this formula to cells C23 through C25, these cells will also contain the formulas for the slack/surplus values for each of the other three operations. Figure 3.21 shows the formula worksheet for the Par, Inc., problem.

Figure 3.21

. . . .

Excel Formula Worksheet for the Par, Inc., Problem

	A	B	C	D
1				
2	**Input Data**			
3		**Production Time**		
4		(hours per unit)		
5	**Operation**	Standard bag	Deluxe bag	**Hours Available**
6	Cutting and dyeing	0.7	1	630
7	Sewing	0.5	0.83333	600
8	Finishing	1	0.66667	708
9	Inspection and packaging	0.1	0.25	135
10				
11	**Profit per unit**	10	9	
12				
13				
14	**Solution Output**			
15		**Decision Variables**		
16		Standard bag	Deluxe bag	**Total Profit**
17	**Number of units**			
18	**Profit**	=B11*B17	=C11*C17	=B18+C18
19				
20				
21	**Operation**	**Hours Used**	**Slack/Surplus**	
22	Cutting and dyeing	=SUMPRODUCT(B6:C6,$B$17:$C$17)	=D6–B22	
23	Sewing	=SUMPRODUCT(B7:C7,$B$17:$C$17)	=D7–B23	
24	Finishing	=SUMPRODUCT(B8:C8,$B$17:$C$17)	=D8–B24	
25	Inspection and packaging	=SUMPRODUCT(B9:C9,$B$17:$C$17)	=D9–B25	

We are now ready to use Solver to obtain an optimal solution to the problem. The following steps describe how to use Excel to obtain the optimal solution.

Step 1 Select the **Tools** pull-down menu

Step 2 Select the **Solver** option

Step 3 When the **Solver Parameters** dialog box appears
Enter D18 in the **Set Target Cell** box
Select the **Max** option
Enter B17:C17 in the **By Changing Cells** box
Choose **Add**

Step 4 When the **Add Constraint** dialog box appears
Enter $B$22:$B$25 in the **Cell Reference** box
Select <=
Enter $D$6:$D$9 in the **Constraint** box
Choose **ADD**
Enter $B$17:$C$17 in the **Cell Reference** box
Select >=
Enter 0 in the **Constraint** box
Select **OK**

Figure 3.22
....

Excel Solver Output for the Par, Inc., Problem

	A	B	C	D
1				
2	Input Data			
3		Production Time		
4		(hours per unit)		
5	Operation	Standard bag	Deluxe bag	Hours Available
6	Cutting and dyeing	0.7	1	630
7	Sewing	0.5	0.83333	600
8	Finishing	1	0.66667	708
9	Inspection and packaging	0.1	0.25	135
10				
11	Profit per unit	10	9	
12				
13				
14	Solution Output			
15		Decision Variables		
16		Standard bag	Deluxe bag	Total Profit
17	Number of units	539.988	252.001	
18	Profit	5399.984	2268.010	7667.994
19				
20				
21	Operation	Hours Used	Slack/Surplus	
22	Cutting and dyeing	630.000	0.000	
23	Sewing	479.999	120.001	
24	Finishing	708.000	0.000	
25	Inspection and packaging	117.000	18.000	

Step 5   When the **Solver Parameters** dialog box appears
Choose **Options**

Step 6   When the **Solver Options** dialog box appears
Select **Assume Linear Model** box
Select **OK**

Step 7   When the **Solver Parameters** dialog box appears
Choose **Solve**

Step 8   When the **Solver Results** dialog box appears
Select **Keep Solver Solution**
Select **OK** to produce the optimal solution output

Figure 3.22 shows the optimal solution output. Note that after rounding, the optimal solution of 540 standard bags and 252 deluxe bags is the same as we obtained using both the graphical solution procedure and The Management Scientist software package. In addition to the output information shown in Figure 3.22, Solver has an option to provide an answer report and sensitivity analysis information. In addition, note that we could simply change selected input data entries in the worksheet and then resolve the problem using Solver to identify the effect the changes would have on the optimal solution.

MANAGEMENT SCIENCE in practice

Eastman Kodak*
Rochester, New York

In 1880 entrepreneur/inventor George Eastman formed the East-man Dry Plate Company with a vision that it would become a worldwide manufacturer and marketer of photographic goods. Today, Eastman Kodak is a $20-billion enterprise with manufacturing operations on four continents, and customers in more than 150 countries. Headquartered in Rochester, New York, Kodak's imaging products include amateur roll film, photographic paper, medical and industrial X-ray film, motion picture film, and graphic arts materials. In addition, Kodak is a manufacturer of imaging equipment and chemicals.

Management Science at Kodak

Management science applications at Kodak can be traced back to pioneering efforts in the 1950s. Since then, management science has been employed to solve a variety of problems involving most of the operational areas of the company. Today, the majority of management science work is conducted by the Management Services Division, while a small group called Distribution Operations Research focuses on applying management science to worldwide logistics issues.

Assigning Products to Worldwide Facilities

The sensitizing operation is the heart of the manufacturing process for photographic paper and film. In this operation, a light-sensitive emulsion is coated on a base to produce a sensitized master roll. The sensitized master rolls are then sent to a finishing operation where they are cut into proper dimensions. The sensitizing operation, by virtue of its centrality to the overall process and the peculiarity of the manufacturing technologies required, receives a great deal of managerial attention, both at the operational and strategic levels.

One of Kodak's major planning issues involves the allocation of product to the various sensitizing facilities located throughout the world. The assignment of product to facilities is called the "world load." In determining the world load, Kodak is confronted with a number of interesting trade-offs. For instance, in terms of manufacturing costs, not all sensitizing facilities are equally efficient for all products. Some facilities tend to be more cost efficient over a broad range of products, but the margins by which they are better varies from product to product. However, there are many product–facility combinations that are essentially impossible because of unique product specifications and machine capabilities. Nonetheless, there is a choice of facilities for practically every product.

The product–facility manufacturing costs are only part of the picture. The cheapest place to sensitize a particular product might, for example, be Australia. But, if most of the customers for that product are in Europe, then Australia becomes less favorable because of the high transportation costs involved. Transportation costs are therefore among the costs considered in determining the world load.

Another cost that must be considered involves the duties and duty drawbacks for the various countries throughout the world. Duty drawback is the "forgiving" of duty for a manufacturer who brings a semifinished product into a country, adds value to it, and then ships it out of that country. The effects of duty and duty drawback can significantly affect the allocation decision.

To assist in determining the world load, Kodak developed a linear programming model that accounts for the physical nature of the distribution problem and the various cost elements already described. More specifically, the program's objective is to minimize total cost (manufacturing, transportation, and duties) subject to "natural" constraints such as satisfying demand and capacity constraints for each facility.

Sensitivity Analysis and Interpretation

The linear programming model is a static representation of the problem situation, and the real world is always changing. Thus, Kodak cannot simply solve the linear program and implement the optimal solution; the static linear programming model must be used in a dynamic way. For instance, when demand expectations change, the model can be used to determine the effect the change will have on the world load. Or, suppose that country A and country B tear down duty barriers between them; what effect will this have on the world load? Suppose that the currency of country A rises compared to the currency of country B; how should the world load be modified? These are but a few of the situations of how the world load must be reevaluated based on the impact of external stimuli.

In addition to using the linear programming model in a "how-to-react" mode, the model is useful in a more active mode by considering questions such as the following: Is it worthwhile for facility F to spend D dollars to lower the unit manufacturing cost of product P from X to Y? If such an investment is made, the effect may go well beyond the simple first-order impact at facility F; in fact, it is likely that the change at facility F will result in a reshuffling of the world load. The linear programming model helps evaluate the overall effect of possible changes at any facility.

—Continued on next page

—Continued from previous page

Managerial Use

The world-load model gives excellent directional advice and integrates the complex interaction of many factors, but there are many aspects of the world-load problem that do not fall neatly into specific cost categories. Although it might be possible to construct a model that would account for almost every aspect of the real-world situation, the time and cost needed to develop it would be prohibitive. Kodak has chosen to use a simpler world-load model; sensitivity analysis is then used to explore many of the questions that management may want to address. In the final analysis, managers recognize that they cannot use the model by simply turning it on, reading the results, and executing the solution. The model's recommendations combined with managerial judgment provide the final decisions and actions for world-load allocation.

Questions

1. What are some of the trade-offs associated with allocating the products to the various sensitizing facilities?
2. What costs are included in the objective function of the world-load model?
3. Briefly describe the role of sensitivity analysis in this application.
4. The world-load model does not account for all the various issues involved in assigning products to sensitizing facilities. What reason did Kodak have for not addressing *all* the issues, and what implications does this have for management?

....

*The authors are indebted to Greg Sampson of Eastman Kodak for providing this application.

four

Linear Programming Applications

In practice, linear programming has proven to be one of the most successful quantitative approaches to managerial decision making. Numerous applications have been reported in the chemical, airline, steel, paper, petroleum, and other industries. The problems that have been studied are diverse and have included production scheduling, media selection, financial planning, capital budgeting, transportation, plant location, product mix, staffing, blending, and many others.

As this variety of applications suggests, linear programming is a flexible problem-solving tool with applications in many disciplines. In this chapter we present several applications, including some from the areas of marketing, finance, and production management. Computer solutions obtained using The Management Scientist software package are presented for many of the examples.

4.1 Marketing Applications

Applications of linear programming in marketing are numerous. In this section we discuss applications in media selection and marketing research.

Media Selection

Media selection applications of linear programming are designed to help marketing managers allocate a fixed advertising budget to various advertising media. Potential media include newspapers, magazines, radio, television, and direct mail. In these applications, the objective is to maximize reach, frequency, and quality of exposure. Restrictions on the allowable allocation usually arise during consideration of company policy, contract requirements, and media availability. In the application that follows, we illustrate how a media selection problem might be formulated and solved using a linear programming model.

Relax-and-Enjoy Lake Development Corporation is developing a lakeside community at a privately owned lake. The primary market for the lakeside lots and homes they hope to sell includes all middle- and upper-income families within approximately 100 miles of the development. Relax-and-Enjoy has employed the advertising firm of Boone, Phillips and Jackson (BP&J) to design the promotional campaign for the project.

After considering possible advertising media and the market to be covered, BP&J has recommended that the first month's advertising be restricted to five media. At the end of the month, BP&J will then reevaluate its strategy based on the month's results. BP&J has collected data on the number of potential customers reached, the cost per advertisement, the maximum number of times each is available, and the exposure quality rating for each of the five media. The quality rating is measured in terms of an exposure quality unit, a measure of the relative value of one advertisement in each of the media. These measures, based on BP&J's experience in the advertising business, take into account factors such as audience demographics (age, income, and education of the audience reached), image presented, and quality of the advertisement. The information collected is presented in Table 4.1.

Relax-and-Enjoy provided BP&J with an advertising budget of $30,000 for the first month's campaign. In addition, Relax-and-Enjoy imposed the following restrictions on how BP&J may allocate these funds: at least 10 television commercials must be used, at least 50,000 potential customers must be reached, and no more than $18,000 may be spent on television advertisements. What advertising media selection plan should be recommended?

The decision to be made is how many times to use each medium. We begin by defining the decision variables:

$$DTV = \text{number of times daytime TV is used}$$
$$ETV = \text{number of times evening TV is used}$$
$$DN = \text{number of times daily newspaper is used}$$
$$SN = \text{number of times Sunday newspaper is used}$$
$$R = \text{number of times radio is used}$$

Table 4.1

Advertising Media Alternatives for the Relax-and-Enjoy Lake Development Corporation

Advertising Media	Number of Potential Customers Reached	Cost Per Advertisement	Maximum Times Available Per Month*	Exposure Quality Units
1. Daytime TV (1 min), station WKLA	1000	$1500	15	65
2. Evening TV (30 sec), station WKLA	2000	$3000	10	90
3. Daily newspaper (full page), *The Morning Journal*	1500	$ 400	25	40
4. Sunday newspaper magazine (½ page color), *The Sunday Press*	2500	$1000	4	60
5. Radio, 8:00 A.M. or 5:00 P.M. news (30 sec), station KNOP	300	$ 100	30	20

*The maximum number of times the medium is available is either the maximum number of times the advertising medium occurs (e.g., four Sundays for medium (4) or the maximum number of times BP&J recommends that the medium be used.

The data on quality of exposure in Table 4.1 show that each daytime TV (DTV) advertisement is rated at 65 exposure quality units. Thus, an advertising plan with DTV advertisements will provide a total of $65DTV$ exposure quality units. Continuing with the data in Table 4.1, we find evening TV (ETV) rated at 90 exposure quality units, daily newspaper (DN) rated at 40 exposure quality units, Sunday newspaper (SN) rated at 60 exposure quality units, and radio (R) rated at 20 exposure quality units. With the objective of maximizing the total exposure quality units for the overall media selection plan, the objective function becomes

$$\text{Max} \quad 65DTV + 90ETV + 40DN + 60SN + 20R \qquad \text{Exposure quality}$$

We now formulate the constraints for the model from the information given:

$$
\begin{aligned}
DTV &\quad & &\quad & &\quad & &\quad & &\leq 15 \quad \rbrace \\
&\quad ETV & &\quad & &\quad & &\quad & &\leq 10 \\
&\quad & DN &\quad & &\quad & &\quad & &\leq 25 \quad \text{Availability} \\
&\quad & &\quad SN & &\quad & &\quad & &\leq 4 \quad \text{of media} \\
&\quad & &\quad & & R &\leq 30
\end{aligned}
$$

$$1500DTV + 3000ETV + 400DN + 1000SN + 100R \leq 30{,}000 \quad \text{Budget}$$

$$DTV + ETV \geq 10 \quad \rbrace \; \text{Television}$$

$$1500DTV + 3000ETV \leq 18{,}000 \quad \text{restrictions}$$

$$1000DTV + 2000ETV + 1500DN + 2500SN + 300R \geq 50{,}000 \quad \text{Customers reached}$$

$$DTV, ETV, DN, SN, R \geq 0$$

Problem 1 provides practice at formulating a similar media selection model.

The computer solution to this five-variable, nine-constraint linear programming model is shown in Figure 4.1; a summary is presented in Table 4.2.

The optimal solution calls for advertisements to be distributed among daytime TV, daily newspaper, Sunday newspaper, and radio. The maximum number of exposure quality units is 2370 and the total number of customers reached is 61,500. The reduced costs column in Figure 4.1 indicates that the number of exposure quality units for evening TV would have to increase by at least 65 before this media alternative would appear in the optimal solution. Note that the budget constraint (constraint 6) has a dual price of 0.060. That is, a $1.00 increase in the advertising budget will lead to an increase of 0.06 exposure quality units. The dual price of −25.000 for constraint 7 indicates that reducing the number of television commercials will increase the exposure quality of the advertising plan. Thus, Relax-and-Enjoy should consider reducing the requirement of having at least 10 television commercials.

A possible shortcoming of this model is that, even if the exposure quality measure were not subject to error, there is no guarantee that maximization of total exposure quality will lead to a maximization of profit or of sales (a common surrogate for profit). However, this is not a shortcoming of linear programming; rather, it is a shortcoming of the use of exposure quality as a criterion. If we were able to measure directly the effect of an advertisement on profit, we could use total profit as the objective to be maximized.

Figure 4.1

The Management Scientist Solution for the Relax-and-Enjoy Lake Development Corporation Problem

```
Objective Function Value =            2370.000

      Variable                 Value              Reduced Costs
   --------------           --------------       ------------------
         DTV                   10.000                 0.000
         ETV                    0.000                65.000
         DN                    25.000                 0.000
         SN                     2.000                 0.000
         R                     30.000                 0.000


     Constraint            Slack/Surplus              Dual Prices
   --------------           --------------          ------------------
          1                    5.000                   0.000
          2                   10.000                   0.000
          3                    0.000                  16.000
          4                    2.000                   0.000
          5                    0.000                  14.000
          6                    0.000                   0.060
          7                    0.000                 -25.000
          8                 3000.000                   0.000
          9                11500.003                   0.000
```

Media Availability

Budget

Television Restrictions

Audience Coverage

Table 4.2

Advertising Plan for the Relax-and-Enjoy Lake Development Corporation

Media	Frequency	Budget
Daytime TV	10	$15,000
Daily newspaper	25	10,000
Sunday newspaper	2	2,000
Radio	30	3,000
		$30,000

Total customers reached = 61,500
Exposure quality units = 2,370

NOTES & comments

1. In previous chapters, we used the general notation x_1, x_2, and so on to denote the decision variables in a linear programming model. Practitioners often prefer using notation for the decision variables that is more descriptive and

—Continued on next page

—Continued from previous page

easier to interpret. For instance, in the Relax-and-Enjoy problem we used *DTV* for daytime TV, *ETV* for evening TV, *DN* for daily newspaper, *SN* for Sunday newspaper, and *R* for radio. The advantage of this notation is that it is easy to recall what each decision variable stands for when we review the computer output in Figure 4.1. We will use descriptive notation for decision variables for several other linear programming applications presented in this chapter.

2. The media selection model required subjective evaluations of the exposure quality for the media alternatives. Marketing managers may have substantial data concerning exposure quality, but the final coefficients used in the objective function may also include considerations based primarily on managerial judgment. Judgment is an acceptable way of obtaining input for a linear programming model.

3. The media selection model presented in this section uses exposure quality as the objective function and places a constraint on the number of customers reached. An alternative formulation of this problem would be to use the number of customers reached as the objective function and add a constraint indicating the minimum total exposure quality required for the media plan.

Marketing Research

An organization conducts marketing research to learn about consumer characteristics, attitudes, and preferences. Marketing research firms that specialize in providing such information often do the actual research for client organizations. Typical services offered by a marketing research firm include designing the study, conducting market surveys, analyzing the data collected, and providing summary reports and recommendations for the client. In the research design phase, targets or quotas may be established for the number and types of respondents to be surveyed. The marketing research firm's objective is to conduct the survey so as to meet the client's needs at a minimum cost.

Market Survey, Inc. (MSI), specializes in evaluating consumer reaction to new products, services, and advertising campaigns. A client firm has requested MSI's assistance in ascertaining consumer reaction to a recently marketed household product. During meetings with the client, MSI agreed to conduct door-to-door personal interviews to obtain responses from households with children and households without children. In addition, MSI agreed to conduct both day and evening interviews. Specifically, the client's contract called for MSI to conduct 1000 interviews under the following quota guidelines.

1. At least 400 households with children would be interviewed.
2. At least 400 households without children would be interviewed.
3. The total number of households interviewed during the evening would be at least as great as the number of households interviewed during the day.
4. At least 40% of the interviews for households with children would be conducted during the evening.
5. At least 60% of the interviews for households without children would be conducted during the evening.

Because the interviews for households with children take additional interviewer time and because evening interviewers are paid more than daytime interviewers, the cost varies with the type of interview. Based on previous research studies, estimates of the interview costs are as follows:

Household	Interview Cost	
	Day	Evening
Children	$20	$25
No children	$18	$20

What is the household, time-of-day interview plan that will satisfy the contract requirements at a minimum total interviewing cost?

In formulating the linear programming model for the MSI problem, we utilize the following decision-variable notation:

DC = the number of daytime interviews of households with children
EC = the number of evening interviews of households with children
DNC = the number of daytime interviews of households without children
ENC = the number of evening interviews of households without children

We begin the linear programming model formulation by using the cost-per-interview data to develop the objective function:

$$\text{Min} \quad 20DC + 25EC + 18DNC + 20ENC$$

The constraint requiring a total of 1000 interviews is

$$DC + EC + DNC + ENC = 1000$$

The five specifications concerning the types of interviews are as follows.

■ Households with children:

$$DC + EC \geq 400$$

■ Households without children:

$$DNC + ENC \geq 400$$

■ At least as many evening interviews as day interviews:

$$EC + ENC \geq DC + DNC$$

The usual format for linear programming model formulation and computer input places all decision variables on the left-hand side of the inequality and a constant (possibly zero) on the right-hand side. Thus, we rewrite this constraint as

$$-DC + EC - DNC + ENC \geq 0$$

■ At least 40% of interviews for households with children during the evening:

$$EC \geq 0.4(DC + EC) \quad \text{or} \quad -0.4DC + 0.6EC \geq 0$$

■ At least 60% of interviews for households without children during the evening:

$$ENC \geq 0.6(DNC + ENC) \quad \text{or} \quad -0.6DNC + 0.4ENC \geq 0$$

When we add the nonnegativity requirements, the four-variable and six-constraint linear programming model becomes

Min $20DC + 25EC + 18DNC + 20ENC$

s.t.

$DC +$	$EC +$	$DNC +$	ENC	$= 1000$	Total interviews
$DC +$	EC			≥ 400	Households with children
		$DNC +$	$ENC \geq$	400	Households without children
$-DC +$	$EC -$	$DNC +$	$ENC \geq$	0	Evening interviews
$-0.4DC + 0.6EC$				≥ 0	Evening households with children
		$-0.6DNC + 0.4ENC \geq$		0	Evening households without children

$DC, EC, DNC, ENC \geq 0$

The computer solution for this linear program is shown in Figure 4.2. The solution reveals that the minimum cost of $20,320 occurs with the following interview schedule.

	Number of Interviews		
Household	Day	Evening	**Totals**
Children	240	160	400
No children	240	360	600
Totals	480	520	1000

Figure 4.2

The Management Scientist Solution for the Market Survey Problem

```
Objective Function Value =          20320.000

        Variable              Value            Reduced Costs
        --------          --------------       --------------
          DC                240.000                0.000
          EC                160.000                0.000
          DNC               240.000                0.000
          ENC               360.000                0.000

        Constraint        Slack/Surplus          Dual Prices
        ----------        -------------          -----------
            1                 0.000                -19.200
            2                 0.000                 -2.800
            3               200.000                  0.000
            4                40.000                  0.000
            5                 0.000                 -5.000
            6                 0.000                 -2.000
```

Hence, 480 interviews will be scheduled during the day and 520 during the evening. Households with children will be covered by 400 interviews, and households without children will be covered by 600 interviews.

Selected sensitivity analysis information from Figure 4.2 shows a dual price of −19.200 for constraint 1. In other words, the objective function will get worse (the total interviewing cost will increase) by $19.20 if the number of interviews is increased from 1000 to 1001. Thus, $19.20 is the incremental cost of obtaining additional interviews. It also is the savings that could be realized by reducing the number of interviews from 1000 to 999.

The surplus variable, with a value of 200.000, for constraint 3 shows that 200 more households without children will be interviewed than required. Similarly, the surplus variable, with a value of 40.000, for constraint 4 shows that the number of evening interviews exceeds the number of daytime interviews by 40. The zero values for the surplus variables in constraints 5 and 6 indicate that the more expensive evening interviews are being held at a minimum. Indeed, the dual price of -5.000 for constraint 5 indicates that if one more household (with children) than the minimum requirement must be interviewed during the evening, the total interviewing cost will go up by $5.00. Similarly, constraint 6 shows that requiring one more household (without children) to be interviewed during the evening will increase costs by $2.00.

4.2 Financial Applications

In finance, linear programming has been applied in problem situations involving capital budgeting, make-or-buy decisions, asset allocation, portfolio selection, financial planning, and many more. In this section, we describe a portfolio selection problem and a problem involving funding of an early retirement program.

Portfolio Selection

Portfolio selection problems involve situations in which a financial manager must select specific investments—for example, stocks and bonds—from a variety of investment alternatives. Managers of mutual funds, credit unions, insurance companies, and banks frequently encounter this type of problem. The objective function for portfolio selection problems usually is maximization of expected return or minimization of risk. The constraints usually take the form of restrictions on the type of permissible investments, state laws, company policy, maximum permissible risk, and so on. Problems of this type have been formulated and solved using a variety of mathematical programming techniques. In this section we show how to formulate and solve a portfolio selection problem as a linear program.

Consider the case of Welte Mutual Funds, Inc., located in New York City. Welte has just obtained $100,000 by converting industrial bonds to cash and is now looking for other investment opportunities for these funds. Based on Welte's current investments, the firm's top financial analyst recommends that all new investments be made in the oil industry, steel industry, or in government bonds. Specifically, the analyst has identified five investment opportunities and projected their annual rates of return. The investments and rates of return are shown in Table 4.3.

Table 4.3

Investment Opportunities for Welte Mutual Funds

Investment	Projected Rate of Return (%)
Atlantic Oil	7.3
Pacific Oil	10.3
Midwest Steel	6.4
Huber Steel	7.5
Government bonds	4.5

Management of Welte has imposed the following investment guidelines.

1. Neither industry (oil or steel) should receive more than $50,000 of the total investment.
2. Government bonds should be at least 25% of the steel industry investments.
3. The investment in Pacific Oil, the high-return but high-risk investment, cannot be more than 60% of the total oil industry investment.

What portfolio recommendations—investments and amounts—should be made for the available $100,000? Given the objective of maximizing projected return subject to the budgetary and managerially imposed constraints, we can answer this question by formulating a linear programming model of the problem. The solution will provide investment recommendations for the management of Welte Mutual Funds.

Let

$$A = \text{dollars invested in Atlantic Oil}$$
$$P = \text{dollars invested in Pacific Oil}$$
$$M = \text{dollars invested in Midwest Steel}$$
$$H = \text{dollars invested in Huber Steel}$$
$$G = \text{dollars invested in government bonds}$$

Using the projected rates of return shown in Table 4.3, we write the objective function for maximizing the total return for the portfolio as

$$\text{Max}\quad 0.073A + 0.103P + 0.064M + 0.075H + 0.045G$$

The constraint specifying the available $100,000 is

$$A + P + M + H + G = 100{,}000$$

The requirements that neither the oil nor the steel industry should receive more than $50,000 are

$$A + P \leq 50{,}000$$
$$M + H \leq 50{,}000$$

The requirement that government bonds be at least 25% of the steel industry investment is expressed as

$$G \geq 0.25(M + H)\quad\text{or}\quad -0.25M - 0.25H + G \geq 0$$

Finally, the constraint that Pacific Oil cannot be more than 60% of the total oil industry investment is

$$P \leq 0.60(A + P)\quad\text{or}\quad -0.60A + 0.40P \leq 0$$

By adding the nonnegativity restrictions, we obtain the complete linear programming model for the Welte Mutual Fund investment problem:

$$\text{Max}\quad 0.073A + 0.103P + 0.064M + 0.075H + 0.045G$$

s.t.

$A +$	$P +$	$M +$	$H +$	G	$= 100{,}000$	Available funds
$A +$	P				$\leq 50{,}000$	Oil industry maximum
		$M +$	H		$\leq 50{,}000$	Steel industry maximum
		$-\ 0.25M -$	$0.25H +$	G	$\geq\quad 0$	Government bonds minimum
$-0.6A +$	$0.4P$				$\leq\quad 0$	Pacific Oil restriction

$$A, P, M, H, G \geq 0$$

Figure 4.3

The Management Scientist Solution for the Welte Mutual Funds Problem

```
        Objective Function Value =           8000.000

            Variable              Value           Reduced Costs
          --------------      --------------      ------------------
               A               20000.000               0.000
               P               30000.000               0.000
               M                   0.000               0.011
               H               40000.000               0.000
               G               10000.000               0.000

           Constraint        Slack/Surplus          Dual Prices
          --------------      --------------      ------------------
               1                   0.000               0.069
               2                   0.000               0.022
               3               10000.000               0.000
               4                   0.000              -0.024
               5                   0.000               0.030
```

Table 4.4

Optimal Portfolio Selection for Welte Mutual Funds

Investment	Amount	Expected Annual Return
Atlantic Oil	$ 20,000	$1,460
Pacific Oil	30,000	3,090
Huber Steel	40,000	3,000
Government bonds	10,000	450
Totals	$100,000	$8,000

Expected annual return of $8,000
Overall rate of return = 8%

We solved this problem using The Management Scientist; the output is shown in Figure 4.3. Table 4.4 shows how the funds are divided among the securities. Note that the optimal solution indicates that the portfolio should be diversified among all the investment opportunities except Midwest Steel. The projected annual return for this portfolio is $8000, which is an overall return of 8%.

The computer printout shows the dual price for constraint 3 is zero. The reason is that the steel industry maximum isn't a binding constraint; increases in the steel industry limit of $50,000 will not improve the value of the objective function. Indeed, the slack variable for this constraint shows that the current steel industry investment is $10,000 below its limit of $50,000. The dual prices for the other constraints are nonzero, indicating that these constraints are binding.

The dual price of 0.069 for constraint 1 shows that the objective function can be increased by 0.069 if one more dollar can be made available for the portfolio investment. If more funds can be obtained at a cost of less than 6.9%, management should consider obtaining them. However, if a return in excess of 6.9% can be obtained by investing funds elsewhere (other than in these five securities), management should question the wisdom of investing the entire $100,000 in this portfolio.

Similar interpretations can be given to the other dual prices. Note that the dual price for constraint 4 is negative at −0.024. This result indicates that increasing the value on the right-hand side of the constraint by one unit can be expected to worsen the objective function by 0.024. That is, in terms of the optimal portfolio, if Welte invests one more dollar in government bonds (beyond the minimum requirement) the total return will decrease by $0.024. To see why this is so, note again from the dual price for constraint 1 that the marginal return on the funds invested in the portfolio is 6.9% (the average return is 8%). The rate of return on government bonds is 4.5%. Thus, the cost of investing one more dollar in government bonds is the difference between the marginal return on the portfolio and the marginal return on government bonds: 6.9% − 4.5% = 2.4%.

Note that the optimal solution shows that Midwest Steel should not be included in the portfolio ($M = 0$). The associated reduced cost for M of 0.011 tells us that the objective function coefficient for Midwest Steel would have to increase by 0.011 before considering the Midwest Steel investment alternative would be advisable. With this increase the Midwest Steel return would be $0.064 + 0.011 = 0.075$, making this investment just as desirable as the currently used Huber Steel investment alternative.

Finally, a simple modification of the Welte linear programming model permits determining the fraction of available funds invested in each security. That is, we divide each of the right-hand-side values by 100,000. Then the optimal values for the variables will give the fraction of funds that should be invested in each security for a portfolio of any size.

Practice formulating a variation of the Welte problem by working Problem 9.

NOTES & comments

1. The optimal solution to the Welte Mutual Funds problem indicates that $20,000 is to be spent on the Atlantic Oil stock. If Atlantic Oil sells for $75 per share, we would have to purchase exactly $266\frac{2}{3}$ shares in order to spend exactly $20,000. The difficulty of purchasing fractional shares is usually handled by purchasing the largest possible integer number of shares with the allotted funds (e.g., 266 shares of Atlantic Oil). This approach guarantees that the budget constraint will not be violated. This approach, of course, introduces the possibility that the solution will no longer be optimal, but the danger is slight if a large number of securities are involved. In cases where the analyst believes that the decision variables *must* have integer values, the problem must be formulated as an integer linear programming model. Integer linear programming is the topic of Chapter 8.

2. Financial portfolio theory stresses obtaining a proper balance between risk and return. In the Welte problem, we explicitly considered return in the objective function. Risk is controlled by choosing constraints that ensure diversity among oil and steel stocks and a balance between government bonds and the steel industry investment.

MANAGEMENT SCIENCE in action

Using Linear Programming for Optimal Lease Structuring*

GE Capital is a $70-billion subsidiary of General Electric. As one of the nation's largest and most diverse financial services companies, GE Capital arranges leases in both domestic and international markets, including leases for telecommunications, data processing, construction, and fleets of cars, trucks, and commercial aircraft. To help allocate and schedule the rental and debt payments of a leveraged lease, GE Capital analysts have developed an optimization model, which is available as an optional component of the company's lease analysis proprietary software.

Leveraged leases are designed to provide financing for assets with economic lives of at least five years, which require large capital outlays. A leveraged lease represents an agreement among the lessor (the owner of the asset), the lessee (the user of the asset), and the lender who provides a nonrecourse loan of 50% to 80% of the lessor's purchase price. In a nonrecourse loan, the lenders cannot turn to the lessor for repayment in the event of default. As the lessor in such arrangements, GE Capital is able to claim ownership and realize income tax benefits, such as depreciation and interest deductions. These deductions usually produce tax losses during the early years of the lease, which reduces the total tax liability. Approximately 85% of all financial leases in the United States are leveraged leases.

In its simplest form, the leveraged lease structuring problem can be formulated as a linear program. The linear program models the after-tax cash flow for the lessor, taking into consideration rental receipts, borrowing and repaying of the loan, and income taxes. Constraints are formulated to ensure compliance with IRS guidelines and to enable customizing of leases to meet lessee and lessor requirements. The objective function can be entered in a custom fashion or selected from a predefined list. Typically, the objective is to minimize the lessee's cost, expressed as the net present value of rental payments, or to maximize the lessor's after-tax yield.

GE Capital developed an optimization approach that could be applied to single-investor lease structuring. In a study with the department most involved with these transactions, the optimization approach yielded substantial benefits. The approach has been used on a limited basis and has helped GE Capital win some single-investor transactions ranging in size from $1 million to $20 million.

....

*Based on Litty, C.J., "Optimal Lease Structuring at GE Capital." *Interfaces,* May–June, 1994, pp. 34–45.

Financial Planning

Linear programming has been used for a variety of financial planning applications. The Management Science in Action: Using Linear Programming for Optimal Lease Structuring describes how GE Captial used linear programming to optimize the structure of a leveraged lease.

Hewlitt Corporation has established an early retirement program as part of its corporate restructuring. At the close of the voluntary sign-up period, 68 employees had elected early retirement. As a result of these early retirements, the company has incurred the following obligations over the next 8 years. Cash requirements (in thousands of dollars) are due at the beginning of each year.

Year	1	2	3	4	5	6	7	8
Cash Requirement	430	210	222	231	240	195	225	255

The corporate treasurer must determine how much money has to be invested today to meet the 8-year financial obligations as they come due. The financing plan for the retirement program includes investments in government bonds as well as savings. The investments in government bonds are limited to three choices:

Bond	Price	Rate	Years to Maturity
1	$1150	8.875	5
2	1000	5.500	6
3	1350	11.750	7

The government bonds have a par value of $1000, which means that even with different prices each bond pays $1000 at maturity. The rates shown are based on the par value. For purposes of planning, the treasurer has assumed that any funds not invested in bonds will be placed in savings and earn interest at an annual rate of 4%.

We define the decision variables as follows:

F = total dollars required to meet the retirement plan's 8-year obligation
B_1 = units of bond 1 purchased (par value $1000)
B_2 = units of bond 2 purchased (par value $1000)
B_3 = units of bond 3 purchased (par value $1000)
S_i = investment in savings at the beginning of year i for $i = 1, \ldots, 8$

The objective function is to minimize the total dollars needed to meet the retirement plan's 8-year obligation, or

$$\text{Min} \quad F$$

A key feature of this type of financial planning problem is that there is a constraint for each year of the planning horizon. In general, each constraint takes the form:

$$\left(\begin{array}{c} \text{Funds available at} \\ \text{the beginning of the year} \end{array} \right) - \left(\begin{array}{c} \text{Funds invested in bonds} \\ \text{and saved} \end{array} \right) = \left(\begin{array}{c} \text{Cash obligation for} \\ \text{the current year} \end{array} \right)$$

We defined F to be the funds available at the beginning of year 1. With a current price of $1150 for bond 1 and investments expressed in thousands of dollars, the total investment for B_1 units of bond 1 would be $1.15B_1$. Similarly, the total investment in bonds 2 and 3 would be $1B_2$ and $1.35B_3$ respectively. The investment in savings for year 1 is S_1. Using these results and the first-year obligation of 430, we obtain the constraint for year 1:

$$F - 1.15B_1 - 1B_2 - 1.35B_3 - S_1 = 430 \qquad \text{Year 1}$$

Investments in bonds can take place only in this first year and the bonds will be held until maturity.

The funds available at the beginning of year 2 include the investment returns of 8.875% on the par value of bond 1, 5.5% on the par value of bond 2, 11.75% on the par value of bond 3, and 4% on savings. The new amount to be invested in savings for year 2 is S_2. With an obligation of 210, the constraint for year 2 is

$$0.08875B_1 + 0.055B_2 + 0.1175B_3 + 1.04S_1 - S_2 = 210 \quad \text{Year 2}$$

Similarly, the constraints for years 3 to 8 are

$$0.08875B_1 + 0.055B_2 + 0.1175B_3 + 1.04S_2 - S_3 = 222 \quad \text{Year 3}$$

$$0.08875B_1 + 0.055B_2 + 0.1175B_3 + 1.04S_3 - S_4 = 231 \quad \text{Year 4}$$

$$0.08875B_1 + 0.055B_2 + 0.1175B_3 + 1.04S_4 - S_5 = 240 \quad \text{Year 5}$$

$$1.08875B_1 + 0.055B_2 + 0.1175B_3 + 1.04S_5 - S_6 = 195 \quad \text{Year 6}$$

$$1.055B_2 + 0.1175B_3 + 1.04S_6 - S_7 = 225 \quad \text{Year 7}$$

$$1.1175B_3 + 1.04S_7 - S_8 = 255 \quad \text{Year 8}$$

Note that the constraint for year 6 shows that funds available from bond 1 are $1.08875B_1$. The coefficient of 1.08875 reflects the fact that bond 1 matures at the end of year 5. As a result, the par value plus the interest from bond 1 during year 5 is available at the beginning of year 6. Also, because bond 1 matures in year 5 and becomes available for use at the beginning of year 6, the variable B_1 does not appear in the constraints for years 7 and 8. Note the similar interpretation for bond 2, which matures at the end of year 6 and has the par value plus interest available at the beginning of year 7. In addition, bond 3 matures at the end of year 7 and has the par value plus interest available at the beginning of year 8.

Finally, note that a variable S_8 appears in the constraint for year 8. The retirement fund obligation will be completed at the beginning of year 8, so we anticipate that S_8 will be zero and no funds will be put into savings. However, the formulation includes S_8 in the event that the bond income plus interest from the savings in year 7 exceed the 255 cash requirement for year 8. Thus, S_8 is a surplus variable that shows any funds remaining after the 8-year cash requirements have been satisfied.

The solution to the 12 variable, 8 constraint linear program is shown in Figure 4.4. With an objective function value of 1728.79395, the total investment required to meet the

Figure 4.4

The Management Scientist Solution for the Hewlitt Corporation Cash Requirements Problem

```
Objective Function Value =            1728.79395

        Variable            Value            Reduced Costs
        --------            -----            -------------
           F             1728.79395              0.00000
           B1             144.98814              0.00000
           B2             187.85587              0.00000
           B3             228.18793              0.00000
           S1             636.14801              0.00000
           S2             501.60571              0.00000
           S3             349.68182              0.00000
           S4             182.68091              0.00000
           S5               0.00000              0.06403
           S6               0.00000              0.01261
           S7               0.00000              0.02132
           S8               0.00000              0.67084

        Constraint       Slack/Surplus         Dual Prices
        ----------       -------------         -----------
            1               0.00000             -1.00000
            2               0.00000             -0.96154
            3               0.00000             -0.92456
            4               0.00000             -0.88900
            5               0.00000             -0.85480
            6               0.00000             -0.76036
            7               0.00000             -0.71899
            8               0.00000             -0.67084
```

retirement plan's 8-year obligation is $1,728,794. Using the current prices of $1150, $1000, and $1350 for each of the bonds respectively, we can summarize the initial investments in the three bonds as follows:

Bond	Decision Variable Value	Investment Amount
1	$B_1 = 144.988$	$1150(144.988) = $166,736
2	$B_2 = 187.856$	$1000(187.856) = $187,856
3	$B_3 = 228.188$	$1350(228.188) = $308,054

The solution also shows that $636,148 (see S_1) will be placed in savings at the beginning of the first year. By starting with $1,728,794, the company can make the specified bond and savings investments and have enough left over to meet the retirement program's first-year cash requirement of $430,000.

The optimal solution in Figure 4.4 shows that the decision variables S_1, S_2, S_3, and S_4 all are greater than zero, indicating investments in savings are required in each of the first four years. However, interest from the bonds plus the bond maturity incomes will be sufficient to cover the retirement program's cash requirements in years 6 through 8.

The dual prices have an interesting interpretation in this application. Each right-hand-side value corresponds to the payment that must be made in that year. Note that the dual prices are negative, indicating that reducing the payment in any year would be beneficial because the total funds required for the retirement program's obligation would be less. Also note that the dual prices show that reductions are more beneficial in the early years, with decreasing benefits in subsequent years. As a result, Hewlitt would benefit by reducing cash requirements in the early years even if it had to make equivalently larger cash payments in later years.

NOTES & comments

1. The optimal solution for the Hewlitt Corporation problem shows fractional numbers of government bonds at 144.988, 187.856, and 228.188 units, respectively. However, fractional bond units usually are not available. If we were conservative and rounded up to 145, 188, and 229 units, respectively, the total funds required for the 8-year retirement program obligation would be approximately $1254 more than the total funds indicated by the objective function. Because of the magnitude of the funds involved, rounding up probably would provide a very workable solution. If an optimal integer solution were required, the methods of integer linear programming covered in Chapter 8 would have to be used.

2. We implicitly assumed that interest from the government bonds is paid annually. Investments such as treasury notes actually provide interest payments every 6 months. In such cases, the model can be reformulated with 6-month periods, with interest and/or cash payments occurring every 6 months.

Table 4.5

Manufacturing Costs and Purchase Prices for Janders' Calculator Components

| | Cost Per Unit | |
Component	Manufacture (Regular Time)	Purchase
Base	$0.50	$0.60
Financial cartridge	3.75	4.00
Technician cartridge	3.30	3.90
Financial top	0.60	0.65
Technician top	0.75	0.78

4.3 Production Management Applications

Many linear programming applications have been developed for production and operations management, including scheduling, staffing, inventory control, and capacity planning. In this section we describe examples with make-or-buy decisions, production scheduling, and work-force assignments.

A Make-or-Buy Decision

We illustrate the use of a linear programming model to determine how much of each of several component parts a company should manufacture and how much it should purchase from an outside supplier. Such a decision is referred to as a make-or-buy decision.

The Janders Company markets various business and engineering products. Currently, Janders is preparing to introduce two new calculators: one for the business market called the Financial Manager and one for the engineering market called the Technician. Each calculator has three components: a base, an electronic cartridge, and a face plate or top. The same base is used for both calculators, but the cartridges and tops are different. All components can be manufactured by the company or purchased from outside suppliers. The manufacturing costs and purchase prices for the components are summarized in Table 4.5.

Janders' forecasters indicate that 3000 Financial Manager calculators and 2000 Technician calculators will be needed. However, manufacturing capacity is limited. The company has 200 hours of regular manufacturing time and 50 hours of overtime that can be scheduled for the calculators. Overtime involves a premium at the additional cost of $9 per hour. Table 4.6 shows manufacturing times (in minutes) for the components.

The problem for Janders is to determine how many units of each component to manufacture and how many units of each component to purchase. We define the decision variables as follows:

$$BM = \text{number of bases manufactured}$$
$$BP = \text{number of bases purchased}$$
$$FCM = \text{number of Financial cartridges manufactured}$$
$$FCP = \text{number of Financial cartridges purchased}$$
$$TCM = \text{number of Technician cartridges manufactured}$$
$$TCP = \text{number of Technician cartridges purchased}$$
$$FTM = \text{number of Financial tops manufactured}$$
$$FTP = \text{number of Financial tops purchased}$$
$$TTM = \text{number of Technician tops manufactured}$$
$$TTP = \text{number of Technician tops purchased}$$

Table 4.6

Manufacturing Times in Minutes Per Unit for Janders' Calculator Components

Component	Manufacturing Time
Base	1.0
Financial cartridge	3.0
Technician cartridge	2.5
Financial top	1.0
Technician top	1.5

One additional decision variable is needed to determine the hours of overtime that must be scheduled:

$$OT = \text{number of hours of overtime to be scheduled}$$

The objective function is to minimize the total cost, including manufacturing costs, purchase costs and overtime costs. Using the cost per unit data in Table 4.5 and the overtime premium cost rate of $9 per hour, we write the objective function as

$$\text{Min} \quad 0.5BM + 0.6BP + 3.75FCM + 4FCP + 3.3TCM + 3.9TCP + 0.6FTM$$
$$+ 0.65FTP + 0.75TTM + 0.78TTP + 9OT$$

The first five constraints specify the number of each component that must be obtained to satisfy the demand for 3000 Financial Manager calculators and 2000 Technician calculators. A total of 5000 base components are needed, with the number of other components depending on the demand of the particular calculator. The five demand constraints are

$$
\begin{array}{lll}
BM + BP & = 5000 & \text{Bases} \\
FCM + FCP & = 3000 & \text{Financial cartridges} \\
TCM + TCP & = 2000 & \text{Technician cartridges} \\
FTM + FTP & = 3000 & \text{Financial tops} \\
TTM + TTP & = 2000 & \text{Technician tops}
\end{array}
$$

Two constraints are needed to guarantee that the manufacturing capacities for regular time and overtime cannot be exceeded. The first constraint limits overtime capacity to 50 hours, or

$$OT \leq 50$$

The second constraint states that the total manufacturing time required for all components must be less than or equal to the total manufacturing capacity, including regular time plus overtime. The manufacturing times for the components are expressed in minutes so we state the total manufacturing capacity constraint in minutes, with the 200 hours of regular time capacity becoming $60(200) = 12{,}000$ minutes. The actual overtime required is unknown at this point, so we write the overtime as $60OT$ minutes. Using the manufacturing times from Table 4.6, we have

$$BM + 3FCM + 2.5TCM + FTM + 1.5TTM \leq 12{,}000 + 60OT$$

Moving the decision variable for overtime to the left-hand side of the constraint provides the manufacturing capacity constraint:

$$BM + 3FCM + 2.5TCM + FTM + 1.5TTM - 60OT \leq 12{,}000$$

The complete formulation of Janders' make-or-buy problem with all decision variables greater than or equal to zero is

$$\text{Min} \quad 0.5BM + 0.6BP + 3.75FCM + 4FCP + 3.3TCM + 3.9TCP$$
$$+ 0.6FTM + 0.65FTP + 0.75TTM + 0.78TTP + 9OT$$

s.t.

$$
\begin{array}{llllll}
BM & & & & + BP & = & 5000 & \text{Bases} \\
& FCM & & & + FCP & = & 3000 & \text{Financial cartridges} \\
& & TCM & & + TCP & = & 2000 & \text{Technician cartridges} \\
& & & FTM & + FTP & = & 3000 & \text{Financial tops} \\
& & & TTM & + TTP & = & 2000 & \text{Technician tops} \\
& & & & OT & \leq & 50 & \text{Overtime hours} \\
BM + 3FCM + 2.5TCM + FTM + 1.5TTM & & & & - 60OT & \leq & 12{,}000 & \text{Manufacturing capacity}
\end{array}
$$

Figure 4.5

The Management Scientist Solution for the Janders Make-or-Buy Problem

```
Objective Function Value =          24443.332

        Variable              Value            Reduced Costs
     --------------       --------------      ------------------
          BM                5000.000                0.000
          BP                   0.000                0.017
          FCM                666.667                0.000
          FCP               2333.333                0.000
          TCM               2000.000                0.000
          TCP                  0.000                0.392
          FTM                  0.000                0.033
          FTP               3000.000                0.000
          TTM                  0.000                0.095
          TTP               2000.000                0.000
          OT                   0.000                4.000
        Constraint         Slack/Surplus         Dual Prices
     ------------        --------------      ------------------
           1                  0.000                -0.583
           2                  0.000                -4.000
           3                  0.000                -3.508
           4                  0.000                -0.650
           5                  0.000                -0.780
           6                 50.000                 0.000
           7                  0.000                 0.083


OBJECTIVE COEFFICIENT RANGES

Variable          Lower Limit       Current Value        Upper Limit
--------       ----------------    --------------      ---------------
   BM          No Lower Limit           0.500               0.517
   BP                   0.583           0.600         No Upper Limit
   FCM                  3.700           3.750               3.850
   FCP                  3.900           4.000               4.050
   TCM          No Lower Limit          3.300               3.692
   TCP                  3.508           3.900         No Upper Limit
   FTM                  0.567           0.600         No Upper Limit
   FTP          No Lower Limit          0.650               0.683
   TTM                  0.655           0.750         No Upper Limit
   TTP          No Lower Limit          0.780               0.875
   OT                   5.000           9.000         No Upper Limit

RIGHT HAND SIDE RANGES

Constraint        Lower Limit       Current Value        Upper Limit
----------      ----------------   --------------      ---------------
    1                  0.000          5000.000            7000.000
    2                666.667          3000.000        No Upper Limit
    3                  0.000          2000.000            2800.000
    4                  0.000          3000.000        No Upper Limit
    5                 -0.000          2000.000        No Upper Limit
    6                  0.000            50.000        No Upper Limit
    7              10000.000         12000.000           19000.000
```

The computer solution to this 11 variable, 7 constraint linear program is shown in Figure 4.5. The optimal solution indicates that all 5000 bases (*BM*), 667 Financial Manager cartridges (*FCM*), and 2000 Technician cartridges (*TCM*) should be manufactured. The remaining 2333 Financial Manager cartridges (*FCP*), all the Financial Manager tops (*FTP*), and all Technician tops (*TTP*) should be purchased. No overtime manufacturing is necessary, and the total cost associated with the optimal make-or-buy plan is $24,443.33.

Sensitivity analysis provides some additional information about the unused overtime capacity. The Reduced Costs column shows that the overtime (*OT*) premium would have to decrease by $4 per hour before overtime production should be considered. That is, if the overtime premium is $9 − $4 = $5 or less, Janders should replace some of the purchased components with components manufactured on overtime. Problem 12 at the end of the chapter asks you to reconsider the Janders problem with a lower overtime premium to show how the optimal make-or-buy solution changes.

The dual price for the manufacturing capacity constraint 7 is 0.083. This price indicates that an additional hour of manufacturing capacity is worth $0.083 per minute or ($0.083)(60) = $5 per hour. The range of feasibility for constraint 7 shows that this conclusion is valid until the amount of regular time increases to 19,000 minutes, or 316.7 hours.

Sensitivity analysis also indicates that a change in prices charged by the outside suppliers can affect the optimal solution. For instance, the range of optimality for the objective function coefficient for *BP* is 0.583 to no upper limit. If the purchase price for bases remains at $0.583 or more, the number of bases purchased (*BP*) will remain at zero. However, if the purchase price drops below $0.583, Janders should begin to purchase rather than manufacture the base component. Similar sensitivity analysis conclusions about the purchase price ranges can be drawn for the other components.

Try Problem 12 for practice with a variation of the Janders' make-or-buy problem.

NOTES & comments

The proper interpretation of the dual price for manufacturing capacity (constraint 7) in the Janders' problem is that an additional hour of manufacturing capacity is worth ($0.083)(60) = $5 per hour. Thus, the company should be willing to pay a premium of $5 per hour over and above the current regular time cost per hour, which is already included in the manufacturing cost of the product. Thus, if the regular time cost is $18 per hour, Janders' should be willing to pay up to $18 + $5 = $23 per hour to obtain additional manufacturing capacity.

Production Scheduling

One of the most important applications of linear programming deals with multiperiod planning, such as production scheduling. The solution to a production scheduling problem enables the manager to establish an efficient low-cost production schedule for one or more products over several time periods (weeks or months). Essentially, a production scheduling problem can be viewed as a product-mix problem for each of several periods in the future. The manager must determine the production levels that will allow the

Table 4.7	Component	April	May	June
Three-Month Demand Schedule for Bollinger Electronics Company	322A	1000	3000	5000
	802B	1000	500	3000

company to meet product demand requirements, given limitations on production capacity, labor capacity, and storage space, while minimizing total production costs.

One advantage of using linear programming for production scheduling problems is that they recur. A production schedule must be established for the current month, then again for the next month, for the month after that, and so on. When looking at the problem each month, the production manager will find that, although demand for the products have changed, production times, production capacities, storage space limitations, and so on are roughly the same. Thus, the production manager is basically resolving the same problem handled in previous months, and a general linear programming model of the production scheduling procedure may be frequently applied. Once the model has been formulated, the manager can simply supply the data—demand, capacities, and so on—for the given production period and use the linear programming model repeatedly to develop the production schedule.

Let us consider the case of the Bollinger Electronics Company, which produces two different electronic components for a major airplane engine manufacturer. The airplane engine manufacturer notifies the Bollinger sales office each quarter of its monthly requirements for components for each of the next 3 months. The monthly requirements for the components may vary considerably, depending on the type of engine the airplane engine manufacturer is producing. The order shown in Table 4.7 has just been received for the next 3-month period.

After the order is processed, a demand statement is sent to the production control department. The production control department must then develop a 3-month production plan for the components. In arriving at the desired schedule, the production manager will want to identify

1. total production cost,
2. inventory holding cost, and
3. change-in-production-level costs.

In the remainder of this section we show how to formulate a linear programming model of the production and inventory process for Bollinger Electronics to minimize the total cost.

To develop the model, we let x_{im} denote the production volume in units for product i in month m. Here $i = 1, 2,$ and $m = 1, 2, 3; i = 1$ refers to component 322A, $i = 2$ refers to component 802B, $m = 1$ refers to April, $m = 2$ refers to May, and $m = 3$ refers to June. The purpose of the double subscript is to provide a more descriptive notation. We could simply use x_6 to represent the number of units of product 2 produced in month 3, but x_{23} is more descriptive, identifying directly the product and month represented by the variable.

If component 322A costs $20 per unit produced and component 802B costs $10 per unit produced, the total production cost part of the objective function is

$$\text{Total production cost} = 20x_{11} + 20x_{12} + 20x_{13} + 10x_{21} + 10x_{22} + 10x_{23}$$

However, the production cost per unit is the same each month, so we don't need to include production costs in the objective function; that is, regardless of the production schedule selected, the total production cost will remain the same. In other words, production costs are not relevant costs for the production scheduling decision under consideration. In cases where the production cost per unit is expected to change each month, the variable production costs per unit per month must be included in the objective function. Since the solution for the Bollinger Electronics problem will be the same whether or not these costs are included, we included them so that the value of the linear programming objective function will include all the costs associated with the problem.

To incorporate the relevant inventory holding costs into the model, we let s_{im} denote the inventory level for product i at the end of month m. Bollinger has determined that on a monthly basis inventory holding costs are 1.5% of the cost of the product; that is, $(0.015)(\$20) = \$0.30$ per unit for component 322A and $(0.015)(\$10) = \$0.15$ per unit for component 802B. A common assumption made in using the linear programming approach to production scheduling is that monthly ending inventories are an acceptable approximation to the average inventory levels throughout the month. Making this assumption, we write the inventory holding cost portion of the objective function as

$$\text{Inventory holding cost} = 0.30s_{11} + 0.30s_{12} + 0.30s_{13} + 0.15s_{21} + 0.15s_{22} + 0.15s_{23}$$

To incorporate the costs of fluctuations in production levels from month to month, we need to define two additional variables:

$$I_m = \text{increase in the total production level necessary during month } m$$
$$D_m = \text{decrease in the total production level necessary during month } m$$

After estimating the effects of employee layoffs, turnovers, reassignment training costs, and other costs associated with fluctuating production levels, Bollinger estimates that the cost associated with increasing the production level for any month is $0.50 per unit increase. A similar cost associated with decreasing the production level for any month is $0.20 per unit. Thus, we write the third portion of the objective function as

$$\text{Change-in-production-level costs} = 0.50I_1 + 0.50I_2 + 0.50I_3$$
$$+ 0.20D_1 + 0.20D_2 + 0.20D_3$$

Note that the cost associated with changes in production level is a function of the change in the total number of units produced in month m compared to the total number of units produced in month $m - 1$. In other production scheduling applications, fluctuations in production level might be measured in terms of machine hours or labor-hours required rather than in terms of the total number of units produced.

Combining all three costs, the complete objective function becomes

$$\text{Min} \quad 20x_{11} + 20x_{12} + 20x_{13} + 10x_{21} + 10x_{22} + 10x_{23} + 0.30s_{11}$$
$$+ 0.30s_{12} + 0.30s_{13} + 0.15s_{21} + 0.15s_{22} + 0.15s_{23} + 0.50I_1$$
$$+ 0.50I_2 + 0.50I_3 + 0.20D_1 + 0.20D_2 + 0.20D_3$$

We now consider the constraints. First, we must guarantee that the schedule meets customer demand. Since the units shipped can come from the current month's production or from inventory carried over from previous months, the demand requirement takes the form

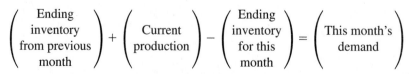

Suppose that the inventories at the beginning of the 3-month scheduling period were 500 units for component 322A and 200 units for component 802B. The demand for both

products in the first month (April) was 1000 units, so the constraints for meeting demand in the first month become

$$500 + x_{11} - s_{11} = 1000$$

$$200 + x_{21} - s_{21} = 1000$$

Moving the constants to the right-hand side, we have

$$x_{11} - s_{11} = 500$$

$$x_{21} - s_{21} = 800$$

Similarly, we need demand constraints for both products in the second and third months. We write them as follows.

Month 2

$$s_{11} + x_{12} - s_{12} = 3000$$

$$s_{21} + x_{22} - s_{22} = 500$$

Month 3

$$s_{12} + x_{13} - s_{13} = 5000$$

$$s_{22} + x_{23} - s_{23} = 3000$$

If the company specifies a minimum inventory level at the end of the 3-month period of at least 400 units of component 322A and at least 200 units of component 802B, we can add the constraints

$$s_{13} \geq 400$$

$$s_{23} \geq 200$$

Suppose that we have the additional information on machine, labor, and storage capacity shown in Table 4.8. Machine, labor, and storage space requirements are given in Table 4.9. To reflect these limitations, the following constraints are necessary.

Machine Capacity

$$0.10x_{11} + 0.08x_{21} \leq 400 \quad \text{Month 1}$$

$$0.10x_{12} + 0.08x_{22} \leq 500 \quad \text{Month 2}$$

$$0.10x_{13} + 0.08x_{23} \leq 600 \quad \text{Month 3}$$

Labor Capacity

$$0.05x_{11} + 0.07x_{21} \leq 300 \quad \text{Month 1}$$

$$0.05x_{12} + 0.07x_{22} \leq 300 \quad \text{Month 2}$$

$$0.05x_{13} + 0.07x_{23} \leq 300 \quad \text{Month 3}$$

Storage Capacity

$$2s_{11} + 3s_{21} \leq 10,000 \quad \text{Month 1}$$

$$2s_{12} + 3s_{22} \leq 10,000 \quad \text{Month 2}$$

$$2s_{13} + 3s_{23} \leq 10,000 \quad \text{Month 3}$$

One final set of constraints must be added to guarantee that I_m and D_m will reflect the increase or decrease in the total production level for month m. Suppose that the

Table 4.8
....

Machine, Labor, and Storage Capacities for Bollinger Electronics

Month	Machine Capacity (hours)	Labor Capacity (hours)	Storage Capacity (square feet)
April	400	300	10,000
May	500	300	10,000
June	600	300	10,000

Table 4.9
....

Machine, Labor, and Storage Requirements for Components 322A and 802B

Component	Machine (hours/unit)	Labor (hours/unit)	Storage (square feet/unit)
322A	0.10	0.05	2
802B	0.08	0.07	3

production levels for March, the month before the start of the current production scheduling period, had been 1500 units of component 322A and 1000 units of component 802B for a total production level of 1500 + 1000 = 2500 units. We can find the amount of the change in production for April from the relationship

$$\text{April production} - \text{March production} = \text{change}$$

Using the April production variables, x_{11} and x_{21}, and the March production of 2500 units, we have

$$(x_{11} + x_{21}) - 2500 = \text{Change}$$

Note that the change can be positive or negative. A positive change reflects an increase in the total production level, and a negative change reflects a decrease in the total production level. We can use the increase in production for April, I_1, and the decrease in production for April, D_1, to specify the constraint for the change in total production for the month of April:

$$(x_{11} + x_{21}) - 2500 = I_1 - D_1$$

Of course, we cannot have an increase in production and a decrease in production during the same 1-month period; thus, either I_1 or D_1 will be zero. If April requires 3000 units of production, $I_1 = 500$ and $D_1 = 0$. If April requires 2200 units of production, $I_1 = 0$ and $D_1 = 300$. This approach of denoting the change in production level as the difference between two nonnegative variables, I_1 and D_1, permits both positive and negative changes in the total production level. If a single variable (say, c_m) had been used to represent the change in production level, only positive changes would be possible because of the nonnegativity requirement.

Using the same approach in May and June (always subtracting the previous month's total production from the current month's total production), we obtain the constraints for the second and third months of the production scheduling period:

$$(x_{12} + x_{22}) - (x_{11} + x_{21}) = I_2 - D_2$$

$$(x_{13} + x_{23}) - (x_{12} + x_{22}) = I_3 - D_3$$

Figure 4.6
. . . .

The Management Scientist Solution for the Bollinger Electronics Problem

```
Objective Function Value =        225294.969

        Variable              Value           Reduced Costs
      --------------     ---------------    -------------------
           X11              500.000               0.000
           X12             3200.000               0.000
           X13             5200.000               0.000
           X21             2500.000               0.000
           X22             2000.000               0.000
           X23                0.000               0.128
           S11                0.000               0.172
           S12              200.000               0.000
           S13              400.000               0.000
           S21             1700.000               0.000
           S22             3200.000               0.000
           S23              200.000               0.000
           I1               500.000               0.000
           I2              2200.000               0.000
           I3                 0.000               0.072
           D1                 0.000               0.700
           D2                 0.000               0.700
           D3                 0.000               0.628

        Constraint         Slack/Surplus        Dual Prices
      --------------     ---------------    -------------------
            1                  0.000             -20.000
            2                  0.000             -10.000
            3                  0.000             -20.128
            4                  0.000             -10.150
            5                  0.000             -20.428
            6                  0.000             -10.300
            7                  0.000             -20.728
            8                  0.000             -10.450
            9                150.000               0.000
           10                 20.000               0.000
           11                 80.000               0.000
           12                100.000               0.000
           13                  0.000               1.111
           14                 40.000               0.000
           15               4899.999               0.000
           16                  0.000               0.000
           17               8599.999               0.000
           18                  0.000               0.500
           19                  0.000               0.500
           20                  0.000               0.428
```

Placing the variables on the left-hand side and the constants on the right-hand side yields the complete set of what are commonly referred to as production-smoothing constraints:

$$x_{11} + x_{21} \qquad\qquad\qquad - I_1 + D_1 = 2500$$

$$-x_{11} - x_{21} + x_{12} + x_{22} \qquad\qquad - I_2 + D_2 = 0$$

$$- x_{12} - x_{22} + x_{13} + x_{23} - I_3 + D_3 = 0$$

The initially rather small, 2-product, 3-month scheduling problem has now developed into an 18-variable, 20-constraint linear programming problem. Note that in this problem we were concerned only with one type of machine process, one type of labor, and one type of storage area. Actual production scheduling problems usually involve several machine types, several labor grades, and/or several storage areas, requiring large-scale linear programs. For instance, a problem involving 100 products over a 12-month period could have over 1000 variables and constraints.

Figure 4.6 shows the computer solution to the Bollinger Electronics production scheduling problem. Table 4.10 contains a portion of the managerial report based on the computer solution.

Consider the monthly variation in the production and inventory schedule shown in Table 4.10. Recall that the inventory cost for component 802B is one-half the inventory cost for component 322A. Therefore, as might be expected, component 802B is produced heavily in the first month (April) and then held in inventory for the demand that will occur in future months. Component 322A tends to be produced when needed, and only small amounts are carried in inventory.

The costs of increasing and decreasing the total production volume tend to smooth the monthly variations. In fact, the minimum-cost schedule calls for a 500-unit increase in total production in April and a 2200-unit increase in total production in May. The May production level of 5200 units is then maintained during June.

The machine usage section of the report shows ample machine capacity in all 3 months. However, labor capacity is at full utilization (slack = 0 for constraint 13 in Figure

Problem 19 involves a production scheduling application with labor-smoothing constraints.

Table 4.10

Minimum-Cost Production Schedule Information for the Bollinger Electronics Problem

Activity	April	May	June
Production			
Component 322A	500	3,200	5,200
Component 802B	2,500	2,000	0
Totals	3,000	5,200	5,200
Ending inventory			
Component 322A	0	200	400
Component 802B	1,700	3,200	200
Machine usage			
Scheduled hours	250	480	520
Slack capacity hours	150	20	80
Labor usage			
Scheduled hours	200	300	260
Slack capacity hours	100	0	40
Storage usage			
Scheduled storage	5,100	10,000	1,400
Slack capacity	4,900	0	8,600

Total production, inventory, and production-smoothing cost = $225,295

Libbey-Owens-Ford[*]

Libbey-Owens-Ford utilizes a large-scale linear programming model to achieve integrated production, distribution, and inventory planning for its flat glass products. The linear programming model is called FLAGPOL. Schedulers and planners in the flat-glass products group must coordinate production schedules for more than 200 different glass products. The products are made in 4 colors (clear, gray, bronze, and blue-green) and 26 thicknesses. Other options include 3 quality levels, 2 cutting classifications, 4 packaging modes, and various fabrication methods, including tempered glass and/or coated glass.

To integrate production, distribution, and inventory planning, company analysts developed a linear programming model that optimizes operations for all products over a 12-month planning horizon. The model is applied monthly, and its output helps planners react to unexpected changes in the operating environment and deal with strategic issues such as adding new plants and expanding capacity. A typical linear programming model has approximately 100,000 variables and 26,000 constraints. The computer solution for problems of this size can take 3 to 4 hours. The company estimates that the FLAGPOL model provides an annual savings of more than $2 million.

....

*Based on Martin, Clarence H., Denver C. Dent, and James C. Eckhart, "Integrated Production, Distribution and Inventory Planning at Libbey-Owens-Ford." *Interfaces,* May–June 1993, pp. 68–78.

4.6) in the month of May. The dual price shows that an additional hour of labor capacity in May will improve the objective function (lower cost) by approximately $1.11.

A linear programming model of a 2-product, 3-month production system can provide valuable information in terms of identifying a minimum-cost production schedule. In larger production systems, where the number of variables and constraints is too large to track manually, linear programming models can provide a significant advantage in developing cost-saving production schedules. The MS in Action: Libbey-Owens-Ford shows just how large linear programming models can be for applications involving production scheduling.

Work-Force Assignment

Work-force assignment problems frequently occur when production managers must make decisions involving staffing requirements for a given planning period. Work-force assignments often have some flexibility, and at least some personnel can be assigned to more than one department or work center. Such is the case when employees have been cross-trained on two or more jobs or, for instance, when sales personnel can be transferred between stores. In the following application we show how linear programming can be used to determine not only an optimal product mix, but also an optimal work-force assignment.

McCormick Manufacturing Company produces two products with contributions to profit per unit of $10 and $9, respectively. The labor requirements per unit produced and the total hours of labor available from personnel assigned to each of four departments are shown in Table 4.11. Assuming that the number of hours available in each department is fixed, we can formulate McCormick's problem as a standard product-mix linear program with the following decision variables:

$$P_1 = \text{units of product 1}$$
$$P_2 = \text{units of product 2}$$

Table 4.11

Departmental Labor-Hours Per Unit and Total Hours Available for the McCormick Manufacturing Company

| Department | Labor-Hours Per Unit | | |
	Product 1	Product 2	Total Hours Available
1	0.65	0.95	6500
2	0.45	0.85	6000
3	1.00	0.70	7000
4	0.15	0.30	1400

Figure 4.7

The Management Scientist Solution for the McCormick Manufacturing Company Problem with No Work-Force Transfers Permitted

```
        Objective Function Value =          73589.742

            Variable            Value          Reduced Costs
          --------------      --------------    ------------------
              P1                5743.590           0.000
              P2                1794.872           0.000

           Constraint        Slack/Surplus       Dual Prices
          --------------      --------------    ------------------
              1                1061.539           0.000
              2                1889.744           0.000
              3                   0.000           8.462
              4                   0.000          10.256
```

The linear program is

$$\text{Max} \quad 10P_1 + \quad 9P_2$$

s.t.

$$0.65P_1 + 0.95P_2 \leq 6500$$

$$0.45P_1 + 0.85P_2 \leq 6000$$

$$1.00P_1 + 0.70P_2 \leq 7000$$

$$0.15P_1 + 0.30P_2 \leq 1400$$

$$P_1, P_2 \geq 0$$

The optimal solution to the linear programming model is shown in Figure 4.7. After rounding, it calls for 5744 units of product 1, 1795 units of product 2, and a total profit of $73,590. With this optimal solution, departments 3 and 4 are operating at capacity, and departments 1 and 2 have a slack of approximately 1062 and 1890 hours, respectively. We would anticipate that the product mix would change and that the total profit would increase if the work-force assignment could be revised so that the slack, or unused hours, in departments 1 and 2 could be transferred to the departments currently working at

Table 4.12

Cross-Training Ability and Capacity Information

From Department	Cross-Training Transfers Permitted to Department				Maximum Hours Transferable
	1	2	3	4	
1	—	yes	yes	—	400
2	—	—	yes	yes	800
3	—	—	—	yes	100
4	yes	yes	—	—	200

capacity. However, the production manager may be uncertain as to how the work force should be reallocated among the four departments. Let us expand the linear programming model to include decision variables that will help determine the optimal work-force assignment in addition to the profit-maximizing product mix.

Suppose that McCormick has a cross-training program that enables some employees to be transferred between departments. By taking advantage of the cross-training skills, a limited number of employees and labor-hours may be transferred from one department to another. For example, suppose that the cross-training permits transfers as shown in Table 4.12. Row 1 of this table shows that some employees assigned to department 1 have cross-training skills that permit them to be transferred to department 2 or 3. The right-hand column shows that, for the current production planning period, a maximum of 400 hours can be transferred from department 1. Similar cross-training transfer capabilities and capacities are shown for departments 2, 3, and 4.

When work-force assignments are flexible, we do not automatically know how many hours of labor should be assigned to or transferred from each department. We need to add decision variables to the linear programming model to account for such changes.

$$b_i = \text{the labor-hours allocated to department } i \text{ for } i = 1, 2, 3, \text{ and } 4$$

$$t_{ij} = \text{the labor-hours transferred from department } i \text{ to department } j$$

With the addition of decision variables $b_1, b_2, b_3,$ and b_4, we write the capacity restrictions for the four departments as follows:

$$0.65P_1 + 0.95P_2 \leq b_1$$

$$0.45P_1 + 0.85P_2 \leq b_2$$

$$1.00P_1 + 0.70P_2 \leq b_3$$

$$0.15P_1 + 0.30P_2 \leq b_4$$

Since $b_1, b_2, b_3,$ and b_4 are now decision variables, we follow the standard practice of placing these variables on the left-hand side of the inequalities, and the first four constraints of the linear programming model become

$$0.65P_1 + 0.95P_2 - b_1 \qquad\qquad\qquad \leq 0$$

$$0.45P_1 + 0.85P_2 \qquad - b_2 \qquad\qquad \leq 0$$

$$1.00P_1 + 0.70P_2 \qquad\qquad - b_3 \qquad \leq 0$$

$$0.15P_1 + 0.30P_2 \qquad\qquad\qquad - b_4 \leq 0$$

The labor-hours ultimately allocated to each department must be determined by a series of labor balance equations, or constraints, that include the number of hours initially assigned to each department plus the number of hours transferred into the department minus the number of hours transferred out of the department. Using department 1 as an example, we determine the work-force allocation as follows:

$$b_1 = \begin{pmatrix} \text{Hours} \\ \text{initially in} \\ \text{department 1} \end{pmatrix} + \begin{pmatrix} \text{Hours} \\ \text{transferred into} \\ \text{department 1} \end{pmatrix} - \begin{pmatrix} \text{Hours} \\ \text{transferred out of} \\ \text{department 1} \end{pmatrix}$$

Table 4.11 shows 6500 hours initially assigned to department 1. We use the transfer decision variables t_{i1} to denote transfers into department 1 and t_{1j} to denote transfers from department 1. Table 4.12 shows that the cross-training capabilities involving department 1 are restricted to transfers from department 4 (variable t_{41}) and transfers to either department 2 or department 3 (variables t_{12} and t_{13}). Thus, we can express the total work-force allocation for department 1 as

$$b_1 = 6500 + t_{41} - t_{12} - t_{13}$$

Moving the decision variables for the work-force transfers to the left-hand side, we have the labor balance equation or constraint

$$b_1 - t_{41} + t_{12} + t_{13} = 6500$$

This form of constraint will be needed for each of the four departments. Thus, the following labor balance constraints for departments 2, 3, and 4 would be added to the model.

$$b_2 - t_{12} - t_{42} + t_{23} + t_{24} = 6000$$
$$b_3 - t_{13} - t_{23} + t_{34} = 7000$$
$$b_4 - t_{24} - t_{34} + t_{41} + t_{42} = 1400$$

Finally, since Table 4.12 shows that the number of hours that may be transferred from each department is limited, a transfer capacity constraint must be added for each of the four departments. The additional constraints are

$$t_{12} + t_{13} \leq 400$$
$$t_{23} + t_{24} \leq 800$$
$$t_{34} \leq 100$$
$$t_{41} + t_{42} \leq 200$$

The complete linear programming model has 2 product decision variables (P_1 and P_2), 4 department work-force assignment variables (b_1, b_2, b_3, and b_4), 7 transfer variables (t_{12}, t_{13}, t_{23}, t_{24}, t_{34}, t_{41}, and t_{42}), and 12 constraints. Figure 4.8 shows the optimal solution to this linear program provided by The Management Scientist software package.

McCormick's profit can be increased by \$10,421 to \$84,011 by taking advantage of cross-training and work-force transfers. The optimal product mix of 6825 units of product 1 and 1751 units of product 2 can be achieved if $t_{13} = 400$ hours are transferred from department 1 to department 3; $t_{23} = 751$ hours are transferred from department 2 to department 3; $t_{24} = 49$ hours are transferred from department 2 to department 4; and $t_{34} = 100$ hours are transferred from department 3 to department 4. The resulting work-force assignments for departments 1–4 would provide 6100, 5200, 8051, and 1549 hours, respectively.

If a manager has the flexibility to assign personnel to different departments, reduced work-force idle time, improved work-force utilization, and improved profit should result. The linear programming model in this section automatically assigns employees and labor-hours to the departments in the most profitable manner.

Figure 4.8

The Management Scientist Solution for the McCormick Manufacturing Company Problem

```
Objective Function Value =          84011.297

      Variable              Value            Reduced Costs
   --------------      ---------------      -------------------
        P1                6824.858              0.000
        P2                1751.413              0.000
        B1                6100.000              0.000
        B2                5200.000              0.000
        B3                8050.847              0.000
        B4                1549.153              0.000
        T41                  0.000              7.458
        T12                  0.000              8.249
        T13                400.000              0.000
        T42                  0.000              8.249
        T23                750.847              0.000
        T24                 49.153              0.000
        T34                100.000              0.000

     Constraint         Slack/Surplus          Dual Prices
   --------------      ---------------      -------------------
         1                  0.000               0.791
         2                640.113               0.000
         3                  0.000               8.249
         4                  0.000               8.249
         5                  0.000               0.791
         6                  0.000               0.000
         7                  0.000               8.249
         8                  0.000               8.249
         9                  0.000               7.458
        10                  0.000               8.249
        11                  0.000               0.000
        12                200.000               0.000
```

4.4 Blending Problems

Blending problems arise whenever a manager must decide how to blend two or more resources to produce one or more products. In these situations, the resources contain one or more essential ingredients that must be blended into final products that will contain specific percentages of each. In most of these applications, then, management must decide how much of each resource to purchase to satisfy product specifications and product demands at minimum cost.

Blending problems occur frequently in the petroleum industry (e.g., blending crude oil to produce different-octane gasolines), chemical industry (e.g., blending chemicals to

Table 4.13

Petroleum Cost and Supply for the Grand Strand Blending Problem

Petroleum Component	Cost/Gallon	Maximum Available
1	$0.50	5,000 gallons
2	$0.60	10,000 gallons
3	$0.84	10,000 gallons

produce fertilizers and weed killers), and food industry (e.g., blending ingredients to produce soft drinks and soups). In this section we illustrate how to apply linear programming to a blending problem in the petroleum industry.

The Grand Strand Oil Company produces regular and premium gasoline for independent service stations in the southeastern United States. The Grand Strand refinery manufactures the gasoline products by blending three petroleum components. The gasolines are sold at different prices, and the petroleum components have different costs. The firm wants to determine how to mix or blend the three components into the two gasoline products and maximize profits.

Data available show that regular gasoline can be sold for $1.00 per gallon and premium gasoline for $1.08 per gallon. For the current production planning period, Grand Strand can obtain the three petroleum components at the cost per gallon and in the quantities shown in Table 4.13.

The product specifications for the regular and premium gasolines restrict the amounts of each component that can be used in each gasoline product. Table 4.14 lists the product specifications. Current commitments to distributors require Grand Strand to produce at least 10,000 gallons of regular gasoline.

The Grand Strand blending problem is to determine how many gallons of each component should be used in the regular gasoline blend and how many should be used in the premium gasoline blend. The optimal blending solution should maximize the firm's profit, subject to the constraints on the available petroleum supplies shown in Table 4.13, the product specifications shown in Table 4.14, and the required 10,000 gallons of regular gasoline.

We define the decision variables as

$$x_{ij} = \text{gallons of component } i \text{ used in gasoline } j,$$
$$\text{where } i = 1, 2, \text{ or } 3 \text{ for components } 1, 2, \text{ or } 3,$$
$$\text{and } j = r \text{ if regular or } j = p \text{ if premium}$$

The six decision variables are

$$x_{1r} = \text{gallons of component 1 in regular gasoline}$$
$$x_{2r} = \text{gallons of component 2 in regular gasoline}$$
$$x_{3r} = \text{gallons of component 3 in regular gasoline}$$
$$x_{1p} = \text{gallons of component 1 in premium gasoline}$$
$$x_{2p} = \text{gallons of component 2 in premium gasoline}$$
$$x_{3p} = \text{gallons of component 3 in premium gasoline}$$

The total number of gallons of each type of gasoline produced is the sum of the number of gallons produced using each of the three petroleum components.

Total Gallons Produced

$$\text{Regular gasoline} = x_{1r} + x_{2r} + x_{3r}$$
$$\text{Premium gasoline} = x_{1p} + x_{2p} + x_{3p}$$

Table 4.14

Product Specifications for the Grand Strand Blending Problem

Product	Specifications
Regular gasoline	At most 30% component 1 At least 40% component 2 At most 20% component 3
Premium gasoline	At least 25% component 1 At most 40% component 2 At least 30% component 3

Similarly, the total gallons of each petroleum component are provided by

Total Petroleum Component Use

$$\text{Component } 1 = x_{1r} + x_{1p}$$

$$\text{Component } 2 = x_{2r} + x_{2p}$$

$$\text{Component } 3 = x_{3r} + x_{3p}$$

We develop the objective function of maximizing the profit contribution by identifying the difference between the total revenue from both gasolines and the total cost of the three petroleum components. By multiplying the \$1.00 per gallon price by the total gallons of regular gasoline, the \$1.08 per gallon price by the total gallons of premium gasoline, and the component cost per gallon figures in Table 4.13 by the total gallons of each component used, we obtain the objective function:

$$\text{Max} \quad 1.00(x_{1r} + x_{2r} + x_{3r}) + 1.08(x_{1p} + x_{2p} + x_{3p})$$

$$- 0.50(x_{1r} + x_{1p}) - 0.60(x_{2r} + x_{2p}) - 0.84(x_{3r} + x_{3p})$$

When we combine terms, the objective function becomes

$$\text{Max} \quad 0.50x_{1r} + 0.40x_{2r} + 0.16x_{3r} + 0.58x_{1p} + 0.48x_{2p} + 0.24x_{3p}$$

The limitations on the availability of the three petroleum components are

$$x_{1r} + x_{1p} \leq 5{,}000 \quad \text{Component 1}$$

$$x_{2r} + x_{2p} \leq 10{,}000 \quad \text{Component 2}$$

$$x_{3r} + x_{3p} \leq 10{,}000 \quad \text{Component 3}$$

Six constraints are now required to meet the product specifications stated in Table 4.14. The first specification states that component 1 can account for no more than 30% of the total gallons of regular gasoline produced. That is,

$$x_{1r} \leq 0.30(x_{1r} + x_{2r} + x_{3r})$$

Rewriting this constraint with the variables on the left-hand side and a constant on the right-hand side yields

$$0.70x_{1r} - 0.30x_{2r} - 0.30x_{3r} \leq 0$$

The second product specification listed in Table 4.14 becomes

$$x_{2r} \geq 0.40(x_{1r} + x_{2r} + x_{3r})$$

and thus,

$$-0.40x_{1r} + 0.60x_{2r} - 0.40x_{3r} \geq 0$$

Similarly, we write the four remaining blending specifications listed in Table 4.14 as

$$-0.20x_{1r} - 0.20x_{2r} + 0.80x_{3r} \leq 0$$

$$+0.75x_{1p} - 0.25x_{2p} - 0.25x_{3p} \geq 0$$

$$-0.40x_{1p} + 0.60x_{2p} - 0.40x_{3p} \leq 0$$

$$-0.30x_{1p} - 0.30x_{2p} + 0.70x_{3p} \geq 0$$

The constraint for at least 10,000 gallons of regular gasoline is

$$x_{1r} + x_{2r} + x_{3r} \geq 10,000$$

The complete linear programming model with 6 decision variables and 10 constraints is

Max $\quad 0.50x_{1r} + 0.40x_{2r} + 0.16x_{3r} + 0.58x_{1p} + 0.48x_{2p} + 0.24x_{3p}$

s.t.

$$
\begin{array}{llllll}
x_{1r} & & & + \ x_{1p} & & \leq \ 5{,}000 \\
& x_{2r} & & + \ x_{2p} & & \leq \ 10{,}000 \\
& & x_{3r} & + \ x_{3p} & & \leq \ 10{,}000 \\
0.70x_{1r} - 0.30x_{2r} - 0.30x_{3r} & & & & \leq \ 0 \\
-0.40x_{1r} + 0.60x_{2r} - 0.40x_{3r} & & & & \geq \ 0 \\
-0.20x_{1r} - 0.20x_{2r} + 0.80x_{3r} & & & & \leq \ 0 \\
0.75x_{1p} - 0.25x_{2p} - 0.25x_{3p} & & & & \geq \ 0 \\
-0.40x_{1p} + 0.60x_{2p} - 0.40x_{3p} & & & & \leq \ 0 \\
-0.30x_{1p} - 0.30x_{2p} + 0.70x_{3p} & & & & \geq \ 0 \\
x_{1r} + x_{2r} + x_{3r} & & & & \geq \ 10{,}000
\end{array}
$$

$$x_{1r}, x_{2r}, x_{3r}, x_{1p}, x_{2p}, x_{3p} \geq 0$$

Try Problem 15 as another example of a blending model.

The computer solution to the Grand Strand blending problem is shown in Figure 4.9. The optimal solution providing a profit of $9300 is summarized in Table 4.15. The optimal blending strategy shows that 10,000 gallons of regular gasoline should be produced. The regular gasoline will be manufactured as a blend of 1250 gallons of component 1, 6750 gallons of component 2, and 2000 gallons of component 3. The 15,000 gallons of premium gasoline will be manufactured as a blend of 3750 gallons of component 1, 3250 gallons of component 2, and 8000 gallons of component 3.

The interpretation of the slack and surplus variables associated with the product specification constraints (constraints 4–9) in Figure 4.9 needs some clarification. If the constraint is a $\leq$ constraint, the value of the slack variable can be interpreted as the gallons of component use below the maximum amount of the component use specified by

Figure 4.9

The Management Scientist Solution for the Grand Strand Blending Problem

```
Objective Function Value =            9300.000

        Variable              Value           Reduced Costs
     --------------      --------------     ------------------
          X1R                1250.000              0.000
          X2R                6750.000              0.000
          X3R                2000.000              0.000
          X1P                3750.000              0.000
          X2P                3250.000              0.000
          X3P                7999.999              0.000


       Constraint         Slack/Surplus         Dual Prices
     --------------      --------------     ------------------
            1                  0.000               0.580
            2                  0.000               0.480
            3                  0.000               0.240
            4               1750.000               0.000
            5               2750.000               0.000
            6                  0.000               0.000
            7                  0.000               0.000
            8               2750.000               0.000
            9               3499.999               0.000
           10                  0.000              -0.080
```

Table 4.15

Grand Strand Gasoline Blending Solution

	Gallons of Component (percentage)			
Gasoline	Component 1	Component 2	Component 3	**Total**
Regular	1250 (12.5%)	6750 (67.5%)	2000 (20%)	10,000
Premium	3750 (25%)	3250 (22%)	8000 (53%)	15,000

the constraint. For example, the slack of 1750.000 for constraint 4 shows that component 1 use is 1750 gallons below the maximum amount of component 1 that could have been used in the production of 10,000 gallons of regular gasoline. If the product specification constraint is a $\geq$ constraint, a surplus variable shows the gallons of component use above the minimum amount of component use specified by the blending constraint. For example, the surplus of 2750.000 for constraint 5 shows that component 2 use is 2750 gallons above the minimum amount of component 2 that must be used in the production of 10,000 gallons of regular gasoline.

NOTES & comments

A convenient way to define the decision variables in a blending problem is to use a matrix in which the rows correspond to the raw materials and the columns correspond to the final products. For example, in the Grand Strand blending problem, we could define the decision variables as follows:

		Final Products	
		Regular Gasoline	*Premium Gasoline*
Raw	*Component 1*	x_{1r}	x_{1p}
Materials	*Component 2*	x_{2r}	x_{2p}
	Component 3	x_{3r}	x_{3p}

This approach has two advantages: (1) it provides a systematic way to define the decision variables for any blending problem; and (2) it provides a visual image of the decision variables in terms of how they are related to the raw materials, products, and each other.

4.5 Data Envelopment Analysis

Data envelopment analysis (DEA) is an application of linear programming that has been used to measure the relative efficiency of operating units with the same goals and objectives. For example, DEA has been used within individual fast-food outlets in the same chain. In this case, the goal of DEA was to identify the inefficient outlets that should be targeted for further study and, if necessary, corrective action. Other applications of DEA have measured the relative efficiencies of hospitals, banks, courts, schools, and so on. In these applications, the performance of each institution or organization was measured relative to the performance of all operating units in the same system.

The operating units of most organizations have multiple inputs, such as staff size, salaries, hours of operation, and advertising budget, as well as multiple outputs, such as profit, market share, and growth rate. In these situations, it is often difficult for a manager to determine which operating units are inefficient in converting their multiple inputs into multiple outputs. This particular area is where data envelopment analysis has proven to be a helpful managerial tool. We will illustrate the application of data envelopment analysis by evaluating the performance of a group of four hospitals.

Evaluating the Performance of Hospitals

The hospital administrators at General Hospital, University Hospital, County Hospital, and State Hospital have been meeting to discuss ways in which they can help one another improve the performance at each of their hospitals. A consultant has suggested that they consider using DEA to measure the performance of each hospital relative to the

Table 4.16

Annual Resources Consumed (Inputs) for the Four Hospitals

Input Measure	Hospital			
	General	University	County	State
Full-time equivalent nonphysicians	285.20	162.30	275.70	210.40
Supply expense ($1000s)	123.80	128.70	348.50	154.10
Bed-days available (1000s)	106.72	64.21	104.10	104.04

Table 4.17

Annual Services Provided (Outputs) for the Four Hospitals

Output Measure	Hospital			
	General	University	County	State
Medicare patient-days (1000s)	48.14	34.62	36.72	33.16
Non-Medicare patient-days (1000s)	43.10	27.11	45.98	56.46
Nurses trained	253	148	175	160
Interns trained	41	27	23	84

performance of all four hospitals. In discussing how this could be done, the following three input measures and four output measures were identified:

Input Measures

1. The number of full-time equivalent (FTE) nonphysician personnel
2. The amount spent on supplies
3. The number of bed-days available

Output Measures

1. Patient-days of service under Medicare
2. Patient-days of service not under Medicare
3. Number of nurses trained
4. Number of interns trained

Summaries of the input and output measures for a 1-year period at each of the four hospitals are shown in Tables 4.16 and 4.17. Let us show how DEA can use these data to identify relatively inefficient hospitals.

An Overview of the DEA Approach

In this application of DEA, a linear programming model will be developed for each hospital whose efficiency is to be evaluated. To illustrate the modeling process, we will formulate a linear program that can be used to determine the relative efficiency of County Hospital.

First, using a linear programming model, we will construct a hypothetical composite hospital based on the outputs and inputs for all four hospitals. For each of the four output measures, the output for the composite hospital is determined by computing a weighted average of the corresponding outputs for all four hospitals. For each of the three input measures, the input for the composite hospital is determined by using the same weights to

Problem 26 will ask you to formulate and solve a linear program to assess the relative efficiency of General Hospital.

compute a weighted average of the corresponding inputs for all four hospitals. Constraints in the linear programming model require all outputs for the composite hospital to be *greater than or equal to* the outputs of County Hospital, the hospital being evaluated. If the inputs for the composite unit can be shown to be *less than* the inputs for County Hospital, the composite hospital will be shown to have the same, or more, output for *less input*. In this case, the model will show that the composite hospital is more efficient than County Hospital. In other words, the hospital being evaluated is *less efficient* than the composite hospital. Since the composite hospital is based on all four hospitals, the hospital being evaluated can be judged *relatively inefficient* when compared to the other hospitals in the group.

The DEA Linear Programming Model

To determine the weight that each hospital will have in computing the outputs and inputs for the composite hospital, we will use the following decision variables:

wg = weight applied to inputs and outputs for General Hospital
wu = weight applied to inputs and outputs for University Hospital
wc = weight applied to inputs and outputs for County Hospital
ws = weight applied to inputs and outputs for State Hospital

The DEA approach requires that the sum of these weights equal 1. Thus, the first constraint is

$$wg + wu + wc + ws = 1$$

In general, every DEA linear programming model will include a constraint that requires the weights for the operating units to sum to 1.

As we stated previously, for each output measure, the output for the composite hospital is determined by computing a weighted average of the corresponding outputs for all four hospitals. For instance, for output measure 1, the number of patient days of service under Medicare, the output for the composite hospital is

$$\begin{pmatrix} \text{Medicare Patient-Days} \\ \text{for Composite Hospital} \end{pmatrix} = \begin{pmatrix} \text{Medicare Patient-Days} \\ \text{for General Hospital} \end{pmatrix}wg + \begin{pmatrix} \text{Medicare Patient-Days} \\ \text{for University Hospital} \end{pmatrix}wu$$
$$+ \begin{pmatrix} \text{Medicare Patient-Days} \\ \text{for County Hospital} \end{pmatrix}wc + \begin{pmatrix} \text{Medicare Patient-Days} \\ \text{for State Hospital} \end{pmatrix}ws$$

Substituting the number of medicare patient-days for each hospital as shown in Table 4.17, we obtain the following expression:

$$\begin{pmatrix} \text{Medicare Patient-Days} \\ \text{for Composite Hospital} \end{pmatrix} = 48.14wg + 34.62wu + 36.72wc + 33.16ws$$

The other output measures for the composite hospital are computed in a similar fashion. Figure 4.10 provides a summary of the results.

For each of the four output measures, we need to write a constraint that requires the output for the composite hospital to be greater than or equal to the output for County Hospital. Thus, the general form of the output constraints is

$$\begin{pmatrix} \text{Output for the} \\ \text{Composite Hospital} \end{pmatrix} \geq \begin{pmatrix} \text{Output for} \\ \text{County Hospital} \end{pmatrix}$$

Since the number of medicare patient-days for County Hospital is 36.72, the output constraint corresponding to the number of medicare patient-days is

$$48.14wg + 34.62wu + 36.72wc + 33.16ws \geq 36.72$$

In a similar fashion, we formulated a constraint for each of the other three output measures, with the results as shown:

$$43.10wg + 27.11wu + 45.98wc + 56.46ws \geq 45.98 \quad \text{Non-Medicare}$$

$$253wg + 148wu + 175wc + 160ws \geq 175 \quad \text{Nurses}$$

$$41wg + 27wu + 23wc + 84ws \geq 23 \quad \text{Interns}$$

The four output constraints require the linear programming solution to provide weights that will make each output measure for the composite hospital greater than or equal to the corresponding output measure for County Hospital. Thus, if a solution satisfying the output constraints can be found, the composite hospital will have produced at least as much of each output as County Hospital.

Next, we need to consider the constraints needed to model the relationship between the inputs for the composite hospital and the resources available to the composite hospital. A constraint is required for each of the three input measures. The general form for the input constraints is as follows:

$$\begin{array}{c}\text{Input for the} \\ \text{Composite Hospital}\end{array} \leq \begin{array}{c}\text{Resources Available to} \\ \text{the Composite Hospital}\end{array}$$

For each input measure, the input for the composite hospital is a weighted average of the corresponding input for each of the four hospitals. Thus, for input measure 1, the number of full-time equivalent nonphysicians, the input for the composite hospital is

$$\begin{array}{c}\text{FTE Nonphysicians} \\ \text{for Composite} \\ \text{Hospital}\end{array} = \left(\begin{array}{c}\text{FTE Nonphysicians} \\ \text{for General Hospital}\end{array}\right)wg + \left(\begin{array}{c}\text{FTE Nonphysicians} \\ \text{for University Hospital}\end{array}\right)wu$$

$$+ \left(\begin{array}{c}\text{FTE Nonphysicians} \\ \text{for County Hospital}\end{array}\right)wc + \left(\begin{array}{c}\text{FTE Nonphysicians} \\ \text{for State Hospital}\end{array}\right)ws$$

Substituting the values for the number of medicare patient-days for each hospital as shown in Table 4.17, we obtain the following expression for the number of full-time equivalent nonphysicians for the composite hospital:

$$285.20wg + 162.30wu + 275.70wc + 210.40ws$$

Figure 4.10

Relationship between the Output Measures for the Four Hospitals and the Output Measures for the Composite Hospital

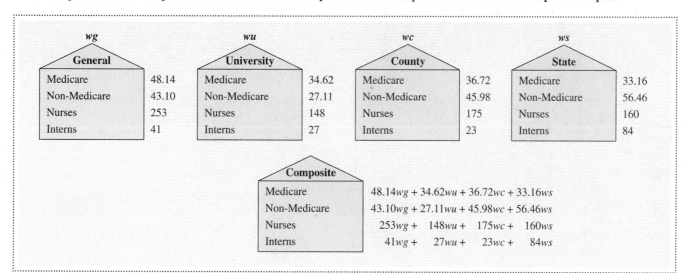

In a similar manner, we can write expressions for each of the other two input measures as shown in Figure 4.11.

To complete the formulation of the input constraints, we must write expressions for the right-hand-side values for each constraint. First, note that the right-hand side values are the resources available to the composite hospital. In the DEA approach, these right-hand-side values are a percentage of the input values for County Hospital. Thus, we must introduce the following decision variables:

E = the fraction of County Hospital's input available to the composite hospital

In order to illustrate the important role that E plays in the DEA approach, we will show how to write the expression for the number of FTE nonphysicians available to the composite hospital. Table 4.16 shows that the number of FTE nonphysicians used by County Hospital was 275.70; thus, 275.70E is the number of FTE nonphysicians available to the composite hospital. If $E = 1$, the number of FTE nonphysicians available to the composite hospital is 275.70, the same as the number of FTE nonphysicians used by County Hospital. However, if E is greater than 1, the composite hospital would have available proportionally more FTE nonphysicians, while if E is less than 1, the composite hospital would have available proportionally fewer FTE nonphysicians. Because of the effect that E has in determining the resources available to the composite hospital, E is referred to as the *efficiency index*.

We can now write the input constraint corresponding to the number of FTE nonphysicians available to the composite hospital:

$$285.20wg + 162.30wu + 275.70wc + 210.40ws \leq 275.70E$$

In a similar manner, we can write the input constraints for the supplies and bed-days available to the composite hospital. First, using the data in Table 4.16, we note that for each of these resources, the amount that is available to the composite hospital is 348.50E and 104.10E, respectively. Thus, the input constraints for the supplies and bed-days are written as follows:

$$123.80wg + 128.70wu + 348.50wc + 154.10ws \leq 348.50E \quad \text{Supplies}$$
$$106.72wg + 64.21wu + 104.10wc + 104.04ws \leq 104.10E \quad \text{Bed-days}$$

Figure 4.11

Relationship between the Input Measures for the Four Hospitals and the Input Measures for the Composite Hospital

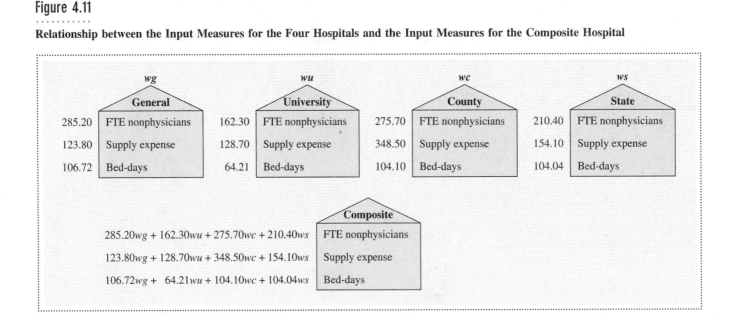

If a solution with $E < 1$ can be found, the composite hospital does not need as many resources as County Hospital needs to produce the same level of output.

The objective function for the DEA model is to minimize the value of E, which is equivalent to minimizing the input resources available to the composite hospital. Thus, the objective function is written as

$$\text{Min } E$$

The DEA efficiency conclusion is based on the optimal objective function value for E. The decision rule is as follows:

> If $E = 1$, the composite hospital requires *as much input* as County Hospital does. There is no evidence that County Hospital is inefficient.

> If $E < 1$, the composite hospital requires *less input* to obtain the output achieved by County Hospital. The composite hospital is more efficient; thus, County Hospital can be judged relatively inefficient.

The DEA linear programming model for the efficiency evaluation of County Hospital has five decision variables and eight constraints. The complete model is rewritten below:

Min E

s.t.

$$
\begin{aligned}
wg + \quad wu + \quad wc + \quad ws &= 1 \\
48.14wg + 34.62wu + 36.72wc + 33.16ws &\geq 36.72 \\
43.10wg + 27.11wu + 45.98wc + 56.46ws &\geq 45.98 \\
253wg + 148wu + 175wc + 160ws &\geq 175 \\
41wg + 27wu + 23wc + 84ws &\geq 23 \\
-275.50E + 285.20wg + 162.30wu + 275.70wc + 210.40ws &\leq 0 \\
-348.50E + 123.80wg + 128.70wu + 348.50wc + 154.10ws &\leq 0 \\
-104.10E + 106.72wg + 64.21wu + 104.10wc + 104.04ws &\leq 0 \\
E,\ wg,\ wu,\ wc,\ ws &\geq 0
\end{aligned}
$$

Note that in this formulation of the model, we have moved the terms involving E to the left-hand side of the three input constraints because E is a decision variable. This linear program was solved using The Management Scientist software package. The computer solution is shown in Figure 4.12.

We first note that the objective function shows that the efficiency score for County Hospital is 0.905. This tells us that the composite hospital can obtain at least the level of each output that County Hospital obtains by having available no more than 90.5% of the input resources required by County Hospital. Thus, the composite hospital is more efficient, and the DEA analysis has identified County Hospital as being relatively inefficient.

From the solution in Figure 4.12, we see that the composite hospital is formed from the weighted average of General Hospital ($wg = 0.212$), University Hospital ($wu = 0.260$), and State Hospital ($ws = 0.527$). Each input and output of the composite hospital is determined by the same weighted average of the inputs and outputs of these three hospitals.

Figure 4.12
. . . .

The Management Scientist Solution for the Data Envelopment Analysis County Hospital Problem

```
Objective Function Value =              0.905

        Variable            Value          Reduced Costs
     --------------      --------------    ------------------
         E                  0.905              0.000
        WG                  0.212              0.000
        WU                  0.260              0.000
        WC                  0.000              0.095
        WS                  0.527              0.000


        Constraint       Slack/Surplus        Dual Prices
     --------------      --------------     ------------------
         1                  0.000              0.239
         2                  0.000             -0.014
         3                  0.000             -0.014
         4                  1.615              0.000
         5                 37.027              0.000
         6                 35.643              0.000
         7                174.422              0.000
         8                  0.000              0.010
```

The Slack/Surplus column provides some additional information about the efficiency of County Hospital compared to the composite hospital. Specifically, the composite hospital has at least as much of each output as County Hospital has (constraints 2–5) and provides 1.6 more nurses trained (surplus for constraint 4) and 37 more interns trained (surplus for constraint 5). The slack of zero from constraint 8 shows that the composite hospital uses approximately 90.5% of the bed-days used by County Hospital. The slack values for constraints 6 and 7 show that less than 90.5% of the FTE nonphysician and the supplies expense resources used at County Hospital are used by the composite hospital.

It is clear that the composite hospital is more efficient than County Hospital and that we are justified in concluding that County Hospital is relatively inefficient compared to the hospitals in the group. Given the results of the DEA analysis, hospital administrators should examine operations to determine how County Hospital resources can be more effectively utilized.

Summary of the DEA Approach
. . . .

To use data envelopment analysis to measure the relative efficiency of County Hospital, we used a linear programming model to construct a hypothetical composite hospital based on the outputs and inputs for the four hospitals in the problem. The approach to solving other types of problems using DEA is similar. That is, for each operating unit that we want to measure the efficiency of, we must formulate and solve a linear programming model similar to the linear program we solved to measure the relative efficiency of County Hospital. The following step-by-step procedure should help you in formulating a linear programming model for other types of applications. Note that the operating unit that we want to measure the relative efficiency of is referred to as the jth operating unit.

Step 1   Define decision variables or weights (one for each operating unit) that can be used to determine the inputs and outputs for the composite operating unit.

Step 2   Write a constraint that requires the weights to sum to 1.

Step 3   For each output measure write a constraint that requires the output for the composite operating unit to be greater than or equal to the corresponding output for the jth operating unit.

Step 4   Define a decision variable, E, which determines the fraction of the jth operating unit's input available to the composite hospital.

Step 5   For each input measure write a constraint that requires the input for the composite operating unit to be less than or equal to the resources available to the composite operating unit.

Step 6   Write the objective function as Min E.

NOTES & COMMENTS

1. Remember that the goal of data envelopment analysis is to identify operating units that are relatively inefficient. The method *does not* necessarily identify the operating units that are *relatively efficient*. Just because the efficiency index is $E = 1$, we cannot conclude that the unit being analyzed is relatively efficient. Indeed, any unit that has the largest output on any one of the output measures cannot be judged relatively inefficient.

2. It is possible for DEA to show all but one unit to be relatively inefficient. Such would be the case if a unit producing the most of every output also consumes the least of every input. Such cases are extremely rare in practice.

3. In applying data envelopment analysis to problems involving a large group of operating units, practitioners have found that roughly 50% of the operating units can be identified as inefficient. Comparing each relatively inefficient unit to the units contributing to the composite unit may be helpful in understanding how the operation of each relatively inefficient unit can be improved.

Summary

In this chapter we presented a broad range of applications that demonstrate how to use linear programming to assist in the decision-making process. We formulated and solved problems from marketing, finance, and production management, and illustrated how linear programming can be applied to blending problems and data envelopment analysis.

Many of the illustrations presented in this chapter are scaled-down versions of actual situations in which linear programming has been applied. In real-world applications, the problem may not be so concisely stated, the data for the problem may not be as readily available, and the problem most likely will involve numerous decision variables and/or constraints. However, a thorough study of the applications in this chapter is a good place to begin in applying linear programming to real problems.

Problems

Note: The following problems have been designed to give you an understanding and appreciation of the broad range of problems that can be formulated as linear programs. You should be able to formulate a linear programming model for each of the problems. However, you will need access to a linear programming computer package to develop the solutions and make the requested interpretations.

1. **SELF** Test The Westchester Chamber of Commerce periodically sponsors public service seminars and programs. Currently, promotional plans are under way for this year's program. Advertising alternatives include television, radio, and newspaper. Audience estimates, costs, and maximum media usage limitations are as shown.

Constraint	Television	Radio	Newspaper
Audience per advertisement	100,000	18,000	40,000
Cost per advertisement	$2,000	$300	$600
Maximum media usage	10	20	10

To ensure a balanced use of advertising media, radio advertisements must not exceed 50% of the total number of advertisements authorized. In addition, television should account for at least 10% of the total number of advertisements authorized.

a. If the promotional budget is limited to $18,200, how many commercial messages should be run on each medium to maximize total audience contact? What is the allocation of the budget among the three media, and what is the total audience reached?

b. By how much would audience contact increase if an extra $100 were allocated to the advertising budget?

2. The Hartman Company is trying to determine how much of each of two products to produce over the coming planning period. The following information concerns labor availability, labor utilization, and product profitability.

Department	Product (hours/unit) 1	Product (hours/unit) 2	Labor-Hours Available
A	1.00	0.35	100
B	0.30	0.20	36
C	0.20	0.50	50
Profit contribution/unit	$30.00	$15.00	—

a. Develop a linear programming model of the Hartman Company problem. Solve the model to determine the optimal production quantities of products 1 and 2.

b. In computing the profit contribution per unit, Hartman doesn't deduct labor costs because they are considered fixed for the upcoming planning period. However, suppose that overtime can be scheduled in some of the departments. Which departments would you recommend scheduling for overtime? How much would you be willing to pay per hour of overtime in each department?

c. Suppose that 10, 6, and 8 hours of overtime may be scheduled in departments A, B, and C, respectively. The cost per hour of overtime is $18 in department A, $22.50 in department B, and $12 in department C. Formulate a linear programming model that can be used to determine the optimal production quantities if overtime is made available. What are the optimal production quantities and what is the revised total contribution to profit? How much overtime do you recommend using in each department? What is the increase in the total contribution to profit if overtime is used?

3. The employee credit union at State University is planning the allocation of funds for the coming year. The credit union makes four types of loans to its members. In addition, the credit union invests in risk-free securities to stabilize income. The various revenue-producing investments together with annual rates of return are as follows.

Type of Loan/Investment	Annual Rate of Return (%)
Automobile loans	8
Furniture loans	10
Other secured loans	11
Signature loans	12
Risk-free securities	9

The credit union will have $2,000,000 available for investment during the coming year. State laws and credit union policies impose the following restrictions on the composition of the loans and investments.

- Risk-free securities may not exceed 30% of the total funds available for investment.
- Signature loans may not exceed 10% of the funds invested in all loans (automobile, furniture, and other secured and signature loans).
- Furniture loans plus other secured loans may not exceed the automobile loans.
- Other secured loans plus signature loans may not exceed the funds invested in risk-free securities.

How should the $2,000,000 be allocated to each of the loan/investment alternatives to maximize total annual return? What is the projected total annual return?

4. Hilltop Coffee manufactures a coffee product by blending three types of coffee beans. The cost per pound and the available pounds of each bean are as follows.

Bean	Cost Per Pound	Available Pounds
1	$0.50	500
2	$0.70	600
3	$0.45	400

Consumer tests with coffee products were used to provide ratings on a scale of 0–100, with higher ratings indicating higher quality. Product quality standards for the blended coffee require a consumer rating for aroma to be at least 75 and a consumer rating for taste to be at least 80. The individual ratings of the aroma and taste for coffee made from 100% of each bean are as follows.

Bean	Aroma Rating	Taste Rating
1	75	86
2	85	88
3	60	75

Assume that the aroma and taste attributes of the coffee blend will be a weighted average of the attributes of the beans used in the blend.

a.   What is the minimum-cost blend that will meet the quality standards and provide 1000 pounds of the blended coffee product?

b.   What is the cost per pound for the coffee blend?

c.   Determine the aroma and taste ratings for the coffee blend.

d.   If additional coffee were to be produced, what would be the expected cost per pound?

5.   Ajax Fuels, Inc., is developing a new additive for airplane fuels. The additive is a mixture of three ingredients: A, B, and C. For proper performance, the total amount of additive (amount of A + amount of B + amount of C) must be at least 10 ounces per gallon of fuel. However, because of safety reasons, the amount of additive must not exceed 15 ounces per gallon of fuel. The mix or blend of the three ingredients is critical. At least 1 ounce of ingredient A must be used for every ounce of ingredient B. The amount of ingredient C must be greater than one-half the amount of ingredient A. If the costs per ounce for ingredients A, B, and C are $0.10, $0.03, and $0.09, respectively, find the minimum-cost mixture of A, B, and C for each gallon of airplane fuel.

6.   G. Kunz and Sons, Inc., manufactures two products used in the heavy equipment industry. Both products require manufacturing operations in two departments. The following are the production time (in hours) and profit contribution figures for the two products.

		Labor-Hours	
Product	Profit Per Unit	Dept. A	Dept. B
1	$25	6	12
2	$20	8	10

For the coming production period, Kunz has available a total of 900 hours of labor that can be allocated to either of the two departments. Find the production plan and labor allocation (hours assigned in each department) that will maximize the total contribution to profit.

7.   As part of the settlement for a class action lawsuit, Hoxworth Corporation must provide sufficient cash to make the following annual payments (in thousands of dollars).

Year	1	2	3	4	5	6
Payment	190	215	240	285	315	460

The annual payments must be made at the beginning of each year. The judge will approve an amount that, along with earnings on its investment, will cover the annual payments. Investment of the funds will be limited to savings (at 4% annually) and government securities, at prices and rates currently quoted in *The Wall Street Journal*.

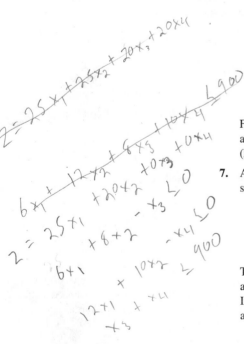

Hoxworth wants to develop a plan for making the annual payments by investing in the following securities (par value = $1000). Funds not invested in these securities will be placed in savings.

Security	Current Price	Rate (%)	Years to Maturity
1	$1055	6.750	3
2	$1000	5.125	4

Assume that interest is paid annually. The plan will be submitted to the judge and, if approved, Hoxworth will be required to pay a trustee the amount that will be required to fund the plan.

a. Use linear programming to find the minimum cash settlement necessary to fund the annual payments.

b. Use the dual price to determine how much more much Hoxworth should be willing to pay now to reduce the payment at the beginning of year 6 to $400,000.

c. Use the dual price to determine how much more Hoxworth should be willing to pay to reduce the year 1 payment to $150,000?

d. Suppose that the annual payments are to be made at the end of each year. Reformulate the model to accommodate this change. How much would Hoxworth save if this change could be negotiated?

8. The Clark County Sheriff's Department schedules police officers for 8-hour shifts. The beginning times for the shifts are 8:00 A.M., noon, 4:00 P.M., 8:00 P.M., midnight, and 4:00 A.M. An officer beginning a shift at one of the these times works for the next 8 hours. During normal weekday operations, the number of officers needed varies depending on the time of day. The department staffing guidelines require the following minimum number of officers on duty:

Time of Day	Minimum Officers on Duty
8:00 A.M.–noon	5
Noon–4:00 P.M.	6
4:00 P.M.–8:00 P.M.	10
8:00 P.M.–midnight	7
Midnight–4:00 A.M.	4
4:00 A.M.–8:00 A.M.	6

Determine the number of police officers that should be scheduled to begin the 8-hour shifts at each of the six times (8:00 A.M., noon, 4:00 P.M., 8:00 P.M., midnight, and 4:00 A.M.) to minimize the total number of officers required. (Hint: Let x_1 = the number of officers beginning work at 8:00 A.M., x_2 = the number of officers beginning work at noon, and so on.)

9. **SELF**Test Reconsider the Welte Mutual Funds problem from Section 4.2. Define your decision variables as the fraction of funds invested in each security. Also, modify the constraints limiting investments in the oil and steel industries as follows: No more than 50% of the total funds invested in stock (oil and steel) may be invested in the oil industry, and no more than 50% of the funds invested in stock (oil and steel) may be invested in the steel industry.

a. Solve the revised linear programming model. What fraction of the portfolio should be invested in each type of security?

b. How much should be invested in each type of security?

c. What are the total earnings for the portfolio?

d. What is the marginal rate of return on the portfolio? That is, how much more could be earned by investing one more dollar in the portfolio?

10. Lurix Electronics manufactures two products that can be produced on two different production lines. Both products have their lowest production costs when produced on the more modern of the two production lines. However, the modern production line does not have the capacity to handle the total production. As a result, some production will have to be routed to the older production line. The following data show total production requirements, production line capacities, and production costs.

| | Production Cost/Unit | | Minimum Production |
Product	Modern Line	Old Line	Requirements
1	$ 3.00	$ 5.00	500 units
2	$ 2.50	$ 4.00	700 units
Production line capacities	800	600	

Formulate a linear programming model that can be used to make the production routing decision. What is the recommended decision and the total cost?

11. Edwards Manufacturing Company purchases two component parts from three different suppliers. The suppliers have limited capacity, and no one supplier can meet all the company's needs. In addition, the suppliers charge different prices for the components. Component price data (in price/unit) are as follows.

| | Supplier | | |
Component	1	2	3
1	$12	$13	$14
2	$10	$11	$10

Each supplier has a limited capacity in terms of the total number of components it can supply. However, as long as Edwards provides sufficient advance orders, each supplier can devote its capacity to component 1, component 2, or any combination of the two components, if the total number of units ordered is within its capacity. Supplier capacities are as follows.

Supplier	1	2	3
Capacity	600	1000	800

If the Edwards production plan for the next period includes 1000 units of component 1 and 800 units of component 2, what purchases do you recommend? That is, how many units of each component should be ordered from each supplier? What is the total purchase cost for the components?

12. **SELFTest** Refer to the Janders application in Section 4.3. Consider each of the following variations of the original problem separately.

   a. Suppose that Janders' supplier lowers the price for the bases to $0.55 per unit. What is the new optimal solution and its value?

   b. Suppose that the supplier of the tops for the Technician calculator raises the unit price to $0.82. What is the new optimal solution and its value?

   c. If Janders' employees were willing to work overtime for an overtime premium of only $2 per hour, should Janders schedule overtime? Why or why not? What is the new optimal solution and its value?

13. Reconsider the McCormick Company Manufacturing problem in Section 4.3. Each of the following parts presents a variation of the original problem. Consider each question separately.

   a. Suppose that no more than 600 hours can be transferred from department 2. Based on the dual price information, how does the value of the optimal solution change?

   b. Modify the linear programming model to reflect the change described in part (a). Use a computer solution of the revised formulation to verify your conclusion in part (a). What transfers are recommended?

   c. Suppose that the employees transferred from department 1 to department 3 are only 80% as productive in department 3 as the employees originally assigned to that department. Reformulate the original model in Section 4.3 accordingly and use a computer solution. What is the new optimal solution? (Hint: Modify the labor balance equation for department 3.)

14. The production manager for the Classic Boat Corporation must determine how many units of the Classic 21 model to produce over the next four quarters. The company has a beginning inventory of 100 Classic 21 boats, and demand for the four quarters is 2000 units in quarter 1, 4000 units in quarter 2, 3000 units in quarter 3, and 1500 units in quarter 4. The firm has limited production capacity in each quarter. That is, up to 4000 units can be produced in quarter 1, 3000 units in quarter 2, 2000 units in quarter 3, and 4000 units in quarter 4. Each boat held in inventory in quarters 1 and 2 incurs an inventory holding cost of $250 per unit; the holding cost for quarters 3 and 4 is $300 per unit. The production costs for the first quarter are $10,000 per unit; these costs are expected to increase by 10% each quarter because of increases in labor and material costs. Management has specified that the ending inventory for quarter 4 must be at least 500 boats.

   a. Formulate a linear programming model that can be used to determine the production schedule that will minimize the total cost of meeting demand in each quarter subject to the production capacities in each quarter and also to the required ending inventory in quarter 4.

   b. Solve the linear program formulated in part (a); then develop a table that will show for each quarter the number of units to manufacture, the ending inventory, and the costs incurred.

   c. Interpret each of the dual prices corresponding to the constraints developed to meet demand in each quarter. Based on these dual prices what advice would you give the production manager?

   d. Interpret each of the dual prices corresponding to the production capacity in each quarter. Based on each of these dual prices what advice would you give the production manager?

15. **SELF Test**   Seastrand Oil Company produces two grades of gasoline: regular and high octane. Both gasolines are produced by blending two types of crude oil. Although both types of crude oil contain the two important ingredients required to produce both gasolines, the percentage of important ingredients in each type of crude oil differs, as does the cost per gallon. The percentage of ingredients A and B in each type of crude oil and the cost per gallon are shown.

Crude Oil	Cost	Ingredient A	Ingredient B
1	$0.10	20%	60%
2	$0.15	50%	30%

Crude oil 1 is 60% ingredient B

Each gallon of regular gasoline must contain at least 40% of ingredient A, whereas each gallon of high octane can contain at most 50% of ingredient B. Daily demand for regular and high-octane gasoline is 800,000 and 500,000 gallons, respectively. How many gallons of each type of crude oil should be used in the two gasolines to satisfy daily demand at a minimum cost?

16. The Ferguson Paper Company produces rolls of paper for use in adding machines, desk calculators, and cash registers. The rolls, which are 200 feet long, are produced in widths of $1\frac{1}{2}$, $2\frac{1}{2}$, and $3\frac{1}{2}$ inches. The production process provides 200-foot rolls in 10-inch widths only. The firm must therefore cut the rolls to the desired final product sizes. The seven cutting alternatives and the amount of waste generated by each are as follows.

Cutting Alternative	Number of Rolls			Waste (inches)
	$1\frac{1}{2}$ in.	$2\frac{1}{2}$ in.	$3\frac{1}{2}$ in.	
1	6	0	0	1
2	0	4	0	0
3	2	0	2	0
4	0	1	2	$\frac{1}{2}$
5	1	3	0	1
6	1	2	1	0
7	4	0	1	$\frac{1}{2}$

The minimum requirements for the three products are

Roll Width (inches)	$1\frac{1}{2}$	$2\frac{1}{2}$	$3\frac{1}{2}$
Units	1000	2000	4000

a. If the company wants to minimize the number of 10-inch rolls that must be manufactured, how many 10-inch rolls will be processed on each cutting alternative? How many rolls are required, and what is the total waste (inches)?

b. If the company wants to minimize the waste generated, how many 10-inch units will be processed on each cutting alternative? How many rolls are required, and what is the total waste (inches)?

c. What are the differences in approaches (a) and (b) to this problem? In this case, which objective do you prefer? Explain. What types of situations would make the other objective more desirable?

17. Frandec Company manufactures, assembles, and rebuilds material handling equipment used in warehouses and distribution centers. One product, called a Liftmaster, is assembled from four components: a frame, a motor, two supports, and a metal strap. Frandec's production schedule calls for 5000 Liftmasters to be made next month. Frandec purchases the motors from an outside supplier, but the frames, supports, and straps may either be manufactured by the company or purchased from an outside supplier. Manufacturing and purchase costs per unit are shown.

Component	Manufacturing Cost	Purchase Cost
Frame	$38.00	$51.00
Support	11.50	15.00
Strap	6.50	7.50

Three departments are involved in the production of these components. The time (in minutes per unit) required to process each component in each department is given, along with the available capacity (in hours) for the three departments.

	Department		
Component	Cutting	Milling	Shaping
Frame	3.5	2.2	3.1
Support	1.3	1.7	2.6
Strap	0.8	—	1.7
Capacity (hours)	350	420	680

a. Formulate and solve a linear programming model for this make-or-buy application. How many of each component should be manufactured and how many should be purchased?

b. What is the total cost of the manufacturing and purchasing plan?

c. How many hours of production time are used in each department?

d. How much should Frandec be willing to pay for an additional hour of time in the shaping department?

e. Another manufacturer has offered to sell frames to Frandec for $45.00 each. Could Frandec improve its position by pursuing this opportunity? Why or why not?

18. The Two-Rivers Oil Company near Pittsburgh transports gasoline to its distributors by truck. The company has recently contracted to supply gasoline distributors in southern Ohio, and it has $600,000 available to spend on the necessary expansion of its fleet of gasoline tank trucks. Three models of gasoline tank trucks are available.

Truck Model	Capacity (gallons)	Purchase Cost	Monthly Operating Cost, Including Depreciation
Super Tanker	5000	$67,000	$550
Regular Line	2500	$55,000	$425
Econo-Tanker	1000	$46,000	$350

The company estimates that the monthly demand for the region will be 550,000 gallons of gasoline. Because of the size and speed differences of the trucks, the number of deliveries or round trips possible per month for each truck model will vary. Trip capacities are estimated at 15 trips per month for the Super Tanker, 20 trips per month for the Regular Line, and 25 trips per month for the Econo-Tanker. Based on maintenance and driver availability, the firm does not want to add more than 15 new vehicles to its fleet. In addition, the company has decided to purchase at least three of the new Econo-Tankers for use on short-run, low-demand routes. As a final constraint, the company does not want more than half of the new models to be Super Tankers.

a. If the company wishes to satisfy the gasoline demand with a minimum monthly operating expense, how many models of each truck should be purchased?

b. If the company did not require at least three Econo-Tankers and did not limit the number of Super Tankers to at most half of the new models, how many models of each truck should be purchased?

19. **SELF Test** The Silver Star Bicycle Company will be manufacturing both men's and women's models for its Easy-Pedal 10-speed bicycles during the next 2 months. The company wants to develop a production schedule indicating how many bicycles of each model should be produced in each month. Current demand forecasts call for 150 men's and 125 women's models to be shipped during the first month and 200 men's and 150 women's models to be shipped during the second month. Additional data are shown.

Model	Production Costs	Labor Requirements (hours)		Current Inventory
		Manufacturing	Assembly	
Men's	$120	2.0	1.5	20
Women's	$ 90	1.6	1.0	30

Last month the company used a total of 1000 hours of labor. The company's labor relations policy will not allow the combined total hours of labor (manufacturing plus assembly) to increase or decrease by more than 100 hours from month to month. In addition, the company charges monthly inventory at the rate of 2% of the production cost based on the inventory levels at the end of the month. The company would like to have at least 25 units of each model in inventory at the end of the 2 months.

a. Establish a production schedule that minimizes production and inventory costs and satisfies the labor-smoothing, demand, and inventory requirements. What inventories will be maintained and what are the monthly labor requirements?

b. If the company changed the constraints so that monthly labor increases and decreases could not exceed 50 hours, what would happen to the production schedule? How much will the cost increase? What would you recommend?

20. Filtron Corporation produces filtration containers used in water treatment systems. Although business has been growing, the demand each month varies considerably. As a result, the company utilizes a mix of part-time and full-time employees to meet production demands. Although this approach provides Filtron with great flexibility, it has resulted in increased costs and morale problems among employees. For instance, if Filtron needs to increase production from one month to the next, additional part-time employees have to be hired and trained, and costs go up. If Filtron has to decrease production, the work force has to be reduced and Filtron incurs additional costs in terms of unemployment benefits and decreased morale. Best estimates are that increasing the number of units produced from one month to the next will increase production costs by $1.25 per unit, and that decreasing the number of units produced will increase production costs by $1.00 per unit. In February Filtron produced 10,000 filtration containers, but only sold 7500 units; 2500 units are currently in inventory. The sales forecasts for March, April, and May are for 12,000 units, 8,000 units, and 15,000 units, respectively. In addition, Filtron has the capacity to store up to 3000 filtration containers at the end of any month. Filtron would like to determine the number of units to be produced in March, April, and May that will minimize the total cost of the monthly production increases and decreases.

21. Greenville Cabinets has received a contract to produce speaker cabinets for a major speaker manufacturer. The contract calls for the production of 3300 bookshelf speakers and 4100 floor speakers over the next two months, with the following delivery schedule.

Model	Month 1	Month 2
Bookshelf	2100	1200
Floor	1500	2600

Greenville estimates that the production time for each bookshelf model is .7 hour and the production time for each floor model is 1 hour. The raw material costs are $10 for each bookshelf model and $12 for each floor model. Labor costs are $22 per hour using regular production time and $33 using overtime. Greenville has up to 2400 hours of regular production time available each month, and up to 1000 additional hours of overtime available each month. If production for either cabinet exceeds demand in month 1, the cabinets can be stored at a cost of $5 per cabinet. For each product, determine the number of units that should be manufactured each month on regular time and on overtime in order to minimize total production and storage costs.

22. The Williams Calculator Company manufactures two kinds of calculators: the TW100 and the TW200. The assembly process requires three people. The assembly times are as follows.

	Calculator		Maximum Labor Available
Assembler	TW100	TW200	(hours/day)
1	4 min	3 min	8
2	2 min	4 min	8
3	3½ min	3 min	8

The company policy is to balance workloads on all assembly jobs. In fact, management wants to schedule work so that no assembler will have more than 30 minutes more work per day than other assemblers. That is, in a regular 8-hour shift, all assemblers will be assigned at least 7½ hours of work. If the firm makes a $2.50 profit for each TW100 and a $3.50 profit for each TW200, how many units of each calculator should be produced per day? How much time will each assembler be assigned per day?

23. Multiperiod production and inventory planning models determine a production schedule and an ending inventory schedule for each of several periods that will maximize profit or minimize cost. Considering selling price, regular production costs, overtime costs, inventory carrying costs, and lost sales costs, develop a three-period production and inventory planning model for Allen Manufacturing Company. Use the following relevant information.

Period	Selling Price Per Unit	Production Cost Per Unit	Demand	Ending Inventory Cost Per Unit
1	$5.00	$2.80	500	$0.50
2	$5.00	$2.90	300	$0.50
3	$5.50	$3.00	400	$0.55

	Production Capacity (units)	
Period	Regular	Overtime
1	250	100
2	300	100
3	300	125

The overtime cost per unit in each period is 20% greater than the production cost per unit shown. The lost sales cost, which is $4 per unit in any period, accounts for lost customer goodwill, but does not account for the cost associated with the lost revenue. The beginning inventory for period 1 is 100 units. In addition, the firm wants to have at least 50 units in ending inventory for period 3 to prepare for period 4.

To account for the multiperiod aspects of the problem, each period t will require balance equations or constraints based on two relationships:

$$\text{Lost sales } (t) = \text{demand } (t) - \text{sales } (t)$$

$$\text{Ending inventory } (t) = \text{beginning inventory } (t) + \text{production } (t) - \text{sales } (t)$$

Develop a linear program that can be used to determine the optimal production and inventory schedule for Allen Manufacturing. Determine the sales, regular production, overtime production, ending inventory, and lost sales for each of the three periods. What is the net profit associated with your solution?

24. The Morton Financial Institution must decide on the percentage of available funds to commit to each of two investments, referred to as A and B, over the next four periods. The following table shows the amount of new funds available for each of the four periods, as well as the cash expenditure required for each investment (negative values) or the cash income from the investment (positive values). The data shown (in thousands of dollars) reflect the amount of expenditure or income if 100% of the funds available in any period are invested in either A or B. For example, if Morton decides to invest 100% of the funds available in any period in investment A, it will incur cash expenditures of $1000 in period 1, $800 in period 2, $200 in period 3, and income of $200 in period 4. Note, however, if Morton made the decision to invest 80% in investment A, the cash expenditures or income would be 80% of the values shown.

| | New Investment | Investment | |
Period	Funds Available	A	B
1	1500	−1000	−800
2	400	−800	−500
3	500	−200	−300
4	100	200	300

The amount of funds available in any period is the sum of the new investment funds for the period, the new loan funds, the savings from the previous period, the cash income from investment A, and the cash income from investment B. The funds available in any period can be used to pay the loan and interest from the previous period, placed in savings, used to pay the cash expenditures for investment A, or used to pay the cash expenditures for investment B.

Assume an interest rate of 10% per period for savings and an interest rate of 18% per period on borrowed funds. Let

$$S(t) = \text{the savings for period } t$$

$$L(t) = \text{the new loan funds for period } t$$

Then, in any period t, the savings income from the previous period is $1.1S(t − 1)$ and the loan and interest expenditure from the previous period is $1.18L(t − 1)$.

At the end of period 4, investment A is expected to have a cash value of $3200 (assuming a 100% investment in A), and investment B is expected to have a cash value of $2500 (assuming a 100% investment in B). Additional income and expenses at the end of period 4 will be income from savings in period 4 less the repayment of the period 4 loan plus interest.

Suppose that the decision variables are defined as

$$x_1 = \text{the proportion of investment A undertaken}$$

$$x_2 = \text{the proportion of investment B undertaken}$$

For example, if $x_1 = 0.5$, $500 would be invested in investment A during the first period, and all remaining cash flows and ending investment A values would be multiplied by 0.5. The same holds for investment B. The model must include constraints $x_1 \leq 1$ and $x_2 \leq 1$ to make sure that no more than 100% of the investments can be undertaken.

If no more than $200 can be borrowed in any period, determine the proportions of investments A and B and the amount of savings and borrowing in each period that will maximize the cash value for the firm at the end of the four periods.

25. Western Family Steakhouse offers a variety of low-cost meals and quick service. Other than management, the steakhouse operates with two full-time employees who work 8 hours per day. The rest of the employees are part-time employees who are scheduled for 4-hour shifts during peak meal times. On Saturdays the steakhouse is open from 11:00 A.M. to 10:00 P.M. Management wants to develop a schedule for part-time employees that will minimize labor costs and still provide excellent customer service. The average wage rate for the part-time employees is $4.60 per hour. The total number of full-time and part-time employees needed varies with the time of the day as shown as follows.

Time	Total Number of Employees Needed
11:00 A.M.–noon	9
Noon–1:00 P.M.	9
1:00 P.M.–2:00 P.M.	9
2:00 P.M.–3:00 P.M.	3
3:00 P.M.–4:00 P.M.	3
4:00 P.M.–5:00 P.M.	3
5:00 P.M.–6:00 P.M.	6
6:00 P.M.–7:00 P.M.	12
7:00 P.M.–8:00 P.M.	12
8:00 P.M.–9:00 P.M.	7
9:00 P.M.–10:00 P.M.	7

One of the full-time employees comes on duty at 11:00 A.M., works 4 hours, takes an hour off, and returns for another 4 hours. The other full-time employee comes to work at 1:00 P.M. and works the same 4-hours-on, 1-hour-off, 4-hours-on pattern.

a. Develop a minimum-cost schedule for part-time employees.

b. What is the total payroll for the part-time employees? How many part-time shifts are needed? Use the surplus variables to comment on the desirability of scheduling at least some of the part-time employees for 3-hour shifts.

c. Assume that part-time employees can be assigned either a 3-hour or 4-hour shift. Develop a minimum-cost schedule for the part-time employees. How many part-time shifts are needed and what is the cost savings compared to the previous schedule?

26. In Section 4.5 data envelopment analysis was used to evaluate the relative efficiencies of four hospitals. Data for three input measures and four output measures were provided in Tables 4.16 and 4.17.

a. Use these data to develop a linear programming model that could be used to evaluate the performance of General Hospital.

b. The computer solution obtained using The Management Scientist is shown below. Does the solution indicate that General Hospital is relatively inefficient?

c. Which hospital or hospitals make up the composite unit used to evaluate General Hospital? State why this is true.

```
Objective Function Value =   1.000000
```

Variable	Value	Reduced Costs
E	1.000	0.000
WG	1.000	0.000
WU	0.000	0.000
WC	0.000	0.331
WS	0.000	0.215

27. Data envelopment analysis has been used to measure the relative efficiency of a group of hospitals (H. David Sherman, "Hospital Efficiency Measurement and Evaluation," *Medical Care,* October 1984). Sherman's study involved seven teaching hospitals; data on three input measures and four output measures are contained in the following tables.

	Input Measures		
Hospital	Full-Time Equivalent Nonphysicians	Supply Expense ($1000s)	Bed-Days Available ($1000s)
A	310.0	134.60	116.00
B	278.5	114.30	106.80
C	165.6	131.30	65.52
D	250.0	316.00	94.40
E	206.4	151.20	102.10
F	384.0	217.00	153.70
G	530.1	770.80	215.00

	Output Measures			
Hospital	Patient-Days (65 or older) (1000s)	Patient-Days (under 65) (1000s)	Nurses Trained	Interns Trained
A	55.31	49.52	291	47
B	37.64	55.63	156	3
C	32.91	25.77	141	26
D	33.53	41.99	160	21
E	32.48	55.30	157	82
F	48.78	81.92	285	92
G	58.41	119.70	111	89

a. Formulate a linear programming model so that data envelopment analysis can be used to evaluate the performance of hospital D.

b. Solve the model using a computer software package.

c. Is hospital D relatively inefficient? What is the interpretation of the value of the objective function?

d. How many patient-days of each type are produced by the composite hospital?

e. Which hospitals would you recommend hospital D consider emulating to improve the efficiency of its operation?

28. Refer again to the data presented in Problem 27.

a. Formulate a linear programming model that can be used to perform data envelopment analysis for hospital E.

b. Solve the model using a computer software package.

c. Is hospital E relatively inefficient? What is the interpretation of the value of the objective function?

d. Which hospitals are involved in making up the composite hospital? Can you make a general statement about which hospitals will make up the composite unit associated with a unit that is not inefficient?

29. The Ranch House, Inc., operates five fast-food restaurants. Input measures for the restaurants include weekly hours of operation, full-time equivalent staff, and weekly supply expenses. Output measures of performance include average weekly contribution to profit, market share, and annual growth rate. Data for the input and output measures are shown in the following tables.

Restaurant	Input Measures		
	Hours of Operation	FTE Staff	Supplies ($)
Bardstown	96	16	850
Clarksville	110	22	1400
Jeffersonville	100	18	1200
New Albany	125	25	1500
St. Matthews	120	24	1600

Restaurant	Output Measures		
	Weekly Profit	Market Share (%)	Growth Rate (%)
Bardstown	$3800	25	8.0
Clarksville	$4600	32	8.5
Jeffersonville	$4400	35	8.0
New Albany	$6500	30	10.0
St. Matthews	$6000	28	9.0

a. Develop a linear programming model that can be used to evaluate the performance of the Clarksville Ranch House restaurant.
b. Solve the model using a computer software package.
c. Is the Clarksville Ranch House restaurant relatively inefficient? Discuss.
d. Where does the composite restaurant have more output than the Clarksville restaurant? How much less of each input resource does the composite restaurant require when compared to the Clarksville restaurant?
e. What other restaurants should be studied to find suggested ways for the Clarksville restaurant to improve its efficiency?

Case Problem: Environmental Protection

Skillings Industrial Chemicals, Inc., operates a refinery in southwestern Ohio near the Ohio River. The company's primary product is manufactured from a chemical process that requires the use of two raw materials—material A and material B. The production of 1 pound of the primary product requires the use of 1 pound of material A and 2 pounds of material B. The output of the chemical process is 1 pound of the primary product, 1 pound of liquid waste material, and 1 pound of solid waste by-product. The solid waste by-product is given to a local fertilizer plant as payment for picking it up and disposing of it. The liquid waste material has no market value, so the refinery has been dumping it directly into the Ohio River. The company's manufacturing process is shown schematically in Figure 4.13.

Figure 4.13
. . . .

Manufacturing Process at Skillings Industrial Chemicals, Inc.

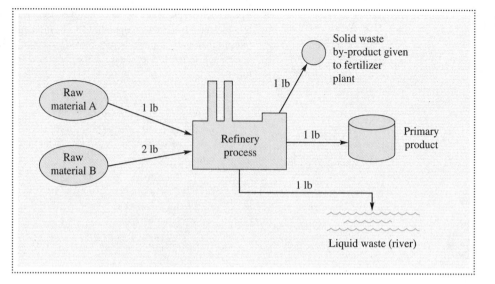

Figure 4.14
. . . .

Alternatives for Handling the Refinery Liquid Waste

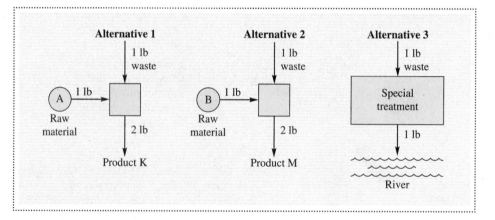

Government pollution guidelines established by the Environmental Protection Agency will no longer permit disposal of the liquid waste directly into the river. The refinery's research group has developed the following set of alternative uses for the liquid waste material.

1. Produce a secondary product K by adding 1 pound of raw material A to every pound of liquid waste.

2. Produce a secondary product M by adding 1 pound of raw material B to every pound of liquid waste.

3. Specially treat the liquid waste so that it meets pollution standards before dumping it into the river.

These three alternatives are depicted in Figure 4.14.

The company's management knows that the secondary products will be low in quality and may not be very profitable. However, management also recognizes that the special treatment alternative will be a relatively expensive operation. The company's problem is to determine how to satisfy the pollution regulations and still maintain the highest possible profit. How should the liquid waste material be handled? Should Skillings produce product K, produce product M, use the special treatment, or employ some combination of the three alternatives?

Last month 10,000 pounds of the company's primary product were produced. The accounting department has prepared a cost report showing the breakdown of fixed and variable expenses that were incurred during the month.

Cost Analysis for 10,000 Pounds of Primary Product	
Fixed costs	
Administrative expenses	$12,000
Refinery overhead	4,000
Variable costs	
Raw material A	15,000
Raw material B	16,000
Direct labor	5,000
Total	$52,000

In this cost analysis, the fixed-cost portion of the expenses is the same every month regardless of production level. Direct labor costs are expected to run $0.20 per pound for product K and $0.10 per pound for product M.

The company's primary product sells for $5.70 per pound. Secondary products K and M sell for $0.85 and $0.65 per pound, respectively. The special treatment of the liquid waste will cost $0.25 per pound.

One of the company's accountants believes that product K is too expensive to manufacture and cannot be sold at a price that recovers its material and labor cost. The accountant's recommendation is to eliminate product K as an alternative.

For the upcoming production period, 5000 pounds of raw material A and 7000 pounds of raw material B will be available.

Managerial Report

Develop an approach to the problem that will allow the company to determine how much primary product to produce, given the limitations on the amounts of the raw material available. Include recommendations as to how the company should dispose of the liquid waste to satisfy the environmental protection guidelines. How many pounds of product K should be produced? How many pounds of product M should be produced? How many pounds of liquid waste should be specially treated and dumped into the river? Include a discussion and analysis of the following in your report:

1. A cost analysis showing the profit contribution per pound for the primary product, product K, and product M.
2. The optimal production quantities and waste disposal plan, including the projected profit.
3. A discussion of the value of additional pounds of each raw material.
4. A discussion of the sensitivity analysis of the objective function coefficients.
5. Comments on the accountant's recommendation to eliminate product K as an alternative. Does the recommendation appear reasonable? What is your reaction to the recommendation? How would the optimal solution change if product K were eliminated?

Case Problem: Investment Strategy

J. D. Williams, Inc., is an investment advisory firm that manages more than $120 million in funds for its numerous clients. The company uses an asset allocation model that recommends the portion of each client's portfolio to be invested in a growth stock fund, an income fund, and a money market fund. To maintain diversity in each client's portfolio, the firm places limits on the percentage of each portfolio that may be invested in each of the three funds. General guidelines indicate that the amount invested in the growth fund must be between 20% and 40% of the total portfolio value. Similar percentages for the other two funds stipulate that between 20% and 50% of the total portfolio value must be in the income fund and at least 30% of the total portfolio value must be in the money market fund.

In addition, the company attempts to assess the risk tolerance of each client and adjust the portfolio to meet the needs of the individual investor. For example, Williams has just contracted with a new client who has $800,000 to invest. Based on an evaluation of the client's risk tolerance, Williams has assigned a maximum risk index of 0.05 for the client. The firm's risk indicators show the risk of the growth fund at 0.10, the income fund at 0.07, and the money market fund at 0.01. An overall portfolio risk index is computed as a weighted average of the risk rating for the three funds where the weights are the fraction of the client's portfolio invested in each of the funds.

Additionally, Williams is currently forecasting annual yields of 18% for the growth fund, 12.5% for the income fund, and 7.5% for the money market fund. Based on the information provided, how should the new client be advised to allocate the $800,000 among the growth, income, and money market funds? Develop a linear programming model that will provide the maximum yield for the portfolio. Use your model to develop a managerial report as described below.

Managerial Report

1. Recommend how much of the $800,000 should be invested in each of the three funds. What is the annual yield you anticipate for the investment recommendation?
2. Assume that the client's risk index could be increased to 0.055. How much would the yield increase and how would the investment recommendation change?
3. Refer again to the original situation where the client's risk index was assessed to be 0.05. How would your investment recommendation change if the annual yield for the growth fund were revised downward to 16% or even to 14%?
4. Assume that the client has expressed some concern about having too much money in the growth fund. How would the original recommendation change if the amount invested in the growth fund is not allowed to exceed the amount invested in the income fund?
5. The asset allocation model you have developed may be useful in modifying the portfolios for all of the firm's clients whenever the anticipated yields for the three funds are periodically revised. What is your recommendation as to whether this is possible?

Case Problem: Textile Mill Scheduling

The Scottsville Textile Mill* produces five different fabrics. Each fabric can be woven on one or more of the mill's 38 looms. The sales department has forecast demand for the next month. The demand data are shown in Table 4.18, along with data on the selling price per yard, variable cost per yard, and purchase price per yard. The mill operates 24 hours per day and is scheduled for 30 days during the coming month.

The mill has two types of looms: dobbie and regular. The dobbie looms are more versatile and can be used for all five fabrics. The regular looms can produce only three of the fabrics. There are a total of 38 looms—8 dobbie and 30 regular. The rate of production for each fabric on each type of loom is given in Table 4.19. The time required to change over from producing one fabric to another is negligible and does not have to be considered.

---

*This case is based on the Calhoun Textile Mill Case by Jeffery D. Camm, P.M. Dearing, and Suresh K. Tadisnia, 1987.

Table 4.18

Monthly Demand, Selling Price, Variable Cost, and Purchase Price Data for Scottsville Fabrics

Fabric	Demand (yards)	Selling Price ($/yard)	Variable Cost ($/yard)	Purchase Price ($/yard)
1	16,500	0.99	0.66	0.80
2	22,000	0.86	0.55	0.70
3	62,000	1.10	0.49	0.60
4	7,500	1.24	0.51	0.70
5	62,000	0.70	0.50	0.70

Table 4.19

Loom Production Rates for the Scottsville Textile Mill

	Loom Rate (yards/hour)	
Fabric	Dobbie	Regular
1	4.63	—
2	4.63	—
3	5.23	5.23
4	5.23	5.23
5	4.17	4.17

Note: Fabrics 1 and 2 can be manufactured only on the dobbie loom.

The Scottsville Textile Mill satisfies all demand with either its own fabric or fabric purchased from another mill. That is, fabrics that cannot be woven at the Scottsville Mill because of limited loom capacity will be purchased from another mill. The purchase price of each fabric is also shown in Table 4.18.

Managerial Report

Develop a model that can be used to schedule production for the Scottsville Textile Mill, and at the same time, determine how many yards of each fabric must be purchased from another mill. Include a discussion and analysis of the following items in your report.

1. The final production schedule and loom assignments for each fabric.
2. The projected total contribution to profit.
3. A discussion of the value of additional loom time. The mill is considering purchasing a ninth dobbie loom. What is your estimate of the monthly profit contribution of this additional loom?
4. A discussion of the ranges for the objective function coefficients.
5. A discussion of how the objective of minimizing total costs would provide a different model than the objective of maximizing total profit contribution. How would the interpretation of the ranges for the objective function coefficients differ for these two models?

APPENDIX 4.1 Spreadsheet Solution of Linear Programs

In Appendix 3.2 we showed how Excel can be used to solve the Par, Inc., linear programming problem. To illustrate the use of Excel in solving a more complex linear programming problem, we will show the solution to the Hewlitt financial planning problem presented in Section 4.2.

First, the data that represent the objective function and the constraints must be entered into a worksheet. Second, cells must be identified for storing the values of the decision variables, the value for the objective function, and the values of the left-hand sides of the constraints. Third, formulas must be written to show how the values for the left-hand sides of the constraints can be computed given the input data values and the values of the decision variables. Figure 4.15 shows the formula spreadsheet for the Hewlitt financial planning problem after completing these three steps. The decision values are stored in cells B5:M5, the value of the objective function is stored in cell B5, and cells N6:N13 show the formulas for the left-hand sides of the constraints. The SUMPRODUCT function is used for cells N6:N13. For instance, cell N6 contains the formula=SUMPRODUCT(B$5:M$5,B6:M6); this formula multiplies the values of the decision variables by the coefficients in the first constraint and adds them. Similar formula are used for cells N7 through N13.

Figure 4.15

Formula Spreadsheet for the Hewlitt Financial Planning Problem

	A	B	C	D	E	F	G	H	I	J	K	L	M	N	O
1		Funds	Gov't	Gov't	Gov't	Savings	Savings	Savings	Savings	Savings	Savings	Savings	Savings		
2		Required	Bond 1	Bond 2	Bond 3	Year 1	Year 2	Year 3	Year 4	Year 5	Year 6	Year 7	Year 8		
3		F	B1	B2	B3	S1	S2	S3	S4	S5	S6	S7	S8	Cash	Cash
4														Available	Req'd.
5															
6	Year 1	1	-1.15	-1	-1.35	-1								=SUMPRODUCT(B$5:M$5,B6:M6)	430
7	Year 2		0.08875	0.055	0.1175	1.04	-1							=SUMPRODUCT(B$5:M$5,B7:M7)	210
8	Year 3		0.08875	0.055	0.1175		1.04	-1						=SUMPRODUCT(B$5:M$5,B8:M8)	222
9	Year 4		0.08875	0.055	0.1175			1.04	-1					=SUMPRODUCT(B$5:M$5,B9:M9)	231
10	Year 5		0.08875	0.055	0.1175				1.04	-1				=SUMPRODUCT(B$5:M$5,B10:M10)	240
11	Year 6		1.08875	0.055	0.1175					1.04	-1			=SUMPRODUCT(B$5:M$5,B11:M11)	195
12	Year 7			1.055	0.1175						1.04	-1		=SUMPRODUCT(B$5:M$5,B12:M12)	225
13	Year 8				1.1175							1.04	-1	=SUMPRODUCT(B$5:M$5,B13:M13)	255

We are now ready to use the information in the worksheet to determine an optimal solution to the Hewlitt financial planning problem. The following steps describe how to use Excel Solver to obtain an optimal solution.

Step 1   Select the **Tools** pull-down menu

Step 2   Select the **Solver** option

Step 3   When the **Solver Parameters** dialog box appears
Enter B5 in the **Set Target Cell** box
Select the **Min** option
Enter B5:M5 in the **By Changing Cells** box
Choose **Add**

Step 4   When the **Add Constraint** dialog box appears
Enter N6:N13 in the **Cell Reference** box
Select =
Enter O6:O13 in the **Constraint** box
Choose **Add**
Enter C5:M5 in the **Cell Reference** box
Select >=
Enter 0 in the **Constraint** box
Select **OK**

Step 5   When the **Solver Parameters** dialog box appears
Choose **Options**

Step 6   When the **Solver Options** dialog box appears
Select **Assume Linear Model** box
Select **OK**

Step 7   When the **Solver Parameters** dialog box appears
Choose **Solve**

Step 8   When the **Solver Results** dialog box appears
Select **Keep Solver Solution**
Select **OK** to produce the optimal solution output

Figure 4.16

Value Spreadsheet for the Hewlitt Financial Planning Problem

	A	B	C	D	E	F	G	H	I	J	K	L	M	N	O
1		Funds	Gov't	Gov't	Gov't	Savings	Savings	Savings	Savings	Savings	Savings	Savings	Savings		
2		Required	Bond 1	Bond 2	Bond 3	Year 1	Year 2	Year 3	Year 4	Year 5	Year 6	Year 7	Year 8		
3		F	G1	G2	G3	S1	S2	S3	S4	S5	S6	S7	S8	Cash	Cash
4														Available	Req'd.
5		1728.794	144.988	187.855	228.1879	636.1479	501.6057	349.6818	182.680	0	0	0	0		
6	Year 1	1	−1.15	−1	−1.35	−1			9					430	430
7	Year 2		0.08875	0.055	0.1175	1.04	−1							210	210
8	Year 3		0.08875	0.055	0.1175		1.04	−1						222	222
9	Year 4		0.08875	0.055	0.1175			1.04	−1					231	231
10	Year 5		0.08875	0.055	0.1175				1.04	−1				240	240
11	Year 6		1.08875	.055	0.1175					1.04	−1			195	195
12	Year 7			1.055	0.1175						1.04	−1		225	225
13	Year 8				1.1175							1.04	−1	255	255

Figure 4.16 shows the optimal solution output. Except for some minor rounding differences, it is the same as the solution provided by The Management Scientist (see Figure 4.4). In addition to the solution shown in Figure 4.16, Excel Solver also provides options to obtain a variety of sensitivity analysis information; this information can be obtained by making appropriate selections from the Solver Results dialog box.

MANAGEMENT SCIENCE in practice

Marathon Oil Company*
Findlay, Ohio

Marathon Oil Company was founded in 1887 when 14 oilmen pooled their properties to organize an oil-producing company in the Trenton Rock oil fields of Ohio. In 1924 Marathon entered the refining and marketing phase of the petroleum industry. Today Marathon is a fully integrated oil company with significant international operations. In the United States the company markets petroleum products in 21 states, primarily in the Midwest and Southeast. Marathon is a unit of USX.

Quantitative Methods at Marathon Oil Company

Marathon Oil's Operations Research Department was formed in 1963 in order to aid problem solving and decision making in all areas of the company. Approximately 50% of the applications involve linear programming. Typical problems include refinery models, distribution models, gasoline and fuel oil blending models, and crude oil evaluation studies. Another 30% of the applications involve complex chemical engineering simulation models of process operations. The remaining applications involve solution techniques using nonlinear programming, network flow algorithms, and statistical techniques such as regression analysis.

—Continued on next page

—*Continued from previous page*

A Marketing Planning Model

Marathon Oil Company has four refineries within the United States, operates 50 light products terminals, and has product demand at over 95 locations. The Supply and Transportation Division is faced with the problem of determining which refinery should supply which terminal and, at the same time, determining which products should be transported via which pipeline, barge, or tanker in order to minimize cost. Product demand must be satisfied, and the supply capability of each refinery must not be exceeded. To help solve this difficult problem, Marathon's Operations Research Department developed a marketing planning model for the Operations Planning Department.

The marketing planning model is a large-scale linear programming model that takes into account sales not only at Marathon product terminals but also at all exchange locations. An exchange contract is an agreement with other oil product marketers that involves exchanging or trading Marathon's products for theirs at different locations. Thus, some geographic imbalance between supply and demand can be reduced. Both sides of the exchanges are represented since this not only affects the net requirements at a demand location, but in addition has important financial implications. All pipelines, barges, and tankers within Marathon's marketing area are also represented in the linear programming model. The objective of the linear programming model is to minimize the cost of meeting a given demand structure, taking into account sales price, pipeline tariffs, exchange contract costs, product demand, terminal operating costs, refining costs, and product purchases.

The marketing planning model is used to solve a wide variety of planning problems. These vary from evaluating gasoline blending economics to analyzing the economics of a new terminal or pipeline. Although the types of problems that can be solved are almost unlimited, the model is most effective in handling the following:

1. Evaluating additional product demand locations, pipelines, and exchange contracts
2. Determining profitability of shifting sales from one product demand location to another
3. Determining the effects on supply and distribution when a pipeline increases its tariff
4. Optimizing production of the grades at the five refineries based on distribution

The linear programming model not only solves these problems, but also gives the financial impact of each solution.

Benefits

With daily sales of about 10 million gallons of refined light product, a savings of even one-thousandth of a cent per gallon can result in significant long-term savings. At the same time, what may appear to be a savings in one area, such as refining or transportation, may actually add to overall costs when the effects are fully realized throughout the system. The marketing planning model allows a simultaneous examination of this total effect.

Questions

1. What is the primary objective of Marathon's marketing planning model?
2. Describe the types of problems the marketing planning model is most effective in handling.
3. If daily savings using the model are one-tenth of a cent per gallon sold, what is the projected daily savings?

....

The authors are indebted to Robert W. Wernert of Marathon Oil Company, Findlay, Ohio, for providing this application.

five

Linear Programming: The Simplex Method

In Chapter 2 we showed how the graphical solution procedure can be used to solve linear programming problems involving two decision variables. However, most linear programming problems are too large to be solved graphically, and an algebraic solution procedure must be employed. The most widely used algebraic procedure for solving linear programming problems is called the *simplex method.*[1] Computer programs based on this method can routinely solve linear programming problems with thousands of variables and constraints. The Management Science in Action: Fleet Assignment at Delta Airlines describes solving a linear program involving 60,000 variables and 40,000 constraints on a daily basis.

5.1 An Algebraic Overview of the Simplex Method

Let us introduce the problem we will use to demonstrate the simplex method. HighTech Industries imports electronic components that are used to assemble two different models of personal computers. One model is called the Deskpro, and the other model is called the Portable. HighTech's management is currently interested in developing a weekly production schedule for both products.

The Deskpro generates a profit contribution of $50 per unit, and the Portable generates a profit contribution of $40 per unit. For next week's production, a maximum of 150 hours of assembly time can be made available. Each unit of the Deskpro requires 3 hours of assembly time, and each unit of the Portable requires 5 hours of assembly time. In addition, HighTech currently has only 20 Portable display components in inventory; thus, no more than 20 units of the Portable may be assembled. Finally, only 300 square feet of

---

[1]Several computer codes also employ what are called interior point solution procedures. These appear to work well on many problems but, at this time, the simplex method is by far the most widely used.

Fleet Assignment at Delta Air Lines[*]

Delta Air Lines has recently begun to use linear and integer programming in its Coldstart project to solve its fleet assignment problem. The problem is to match aircraft to flight legs and fill seats with paying passengers. Airline profitability depends on being able to assign the right size of aircraft to the right leg at the right time of day. An airline seat is a perishable commodity; once a flight takes off with an empty seat the profit potential of that seat is gone forever. Primary objectives of the fleet assignment model are to minimize operating costs and lost passenger revenue. Constraints are aircraft availability, balancing arrivals and departures at airports, and maintenance requirements.

The successful implementation of the Coldstart model for assigning fleet types to flight legs shows the size of linear programs that can be solved today. The typical size of the daily Coldstart model is about 60,000 variables and 40,000 constraints. The first step in solving the fleet assignment problem is to solve the model as a linear program. The model developers report successfully solving these problems on a daily basis and contend that use of the Coldstart model will save Delta Air Lines $300 million over the next three years.

....

*Based on Subramanian, R., R. P. Scheff, Jr., J. D. Quillinan, D. S. Wiper, and R. E. Marsten, "Coldstart: Fleet Assignment at Delta Air Lines." *Interfaces*, January–February 1994, pp. 104–120.

warehouse space can be made available for new production. Assembly of each Deskpro requires 8 square feet of warehouse space; similarly, each Portable requires 5 square feet.

To develop a linear programming model for the HighTech problem, we will use the following decision variables:

$$x_1 = \text{number of units of the Deskpro}$$
$$x_2 = \text{number of units of the Portable}$$

The complete mathematical model for this problem is presented here.

$$\text{Max} \quad 50x_1 + 40x_2$$

s.t.

$$
\begin{aligned}
3x_1 + 5x_2 &\leq 150 \quad &\text{Assembly time}\\
1x_2 &\leq 20 \quad &\text{Portable display}\\
8x_1 + 5x_2 &\leq 300 \quad &\text{Warehouse capacity}\\
x_1, x_2 &\geq 0
\end{aligned}
$$

Adding a slack variable to each of the constraints permits us to write the problem in standard form.

$$\text{Max} \quad 50x_1 + 40x_2 + 0s_1 + 0s_2 + 0s_3 \tag{5.1}$$

s.t.

$$3x_1 + 5x_2 + 1s_1 \qquad\qquad = 150 \tag{5.2}$$
$$1x_2 \qquad + 1s_2 \qquad = 20 \tag{5.3}$$
$$8x_1 + 5x_2 \qquad\qquad + 1s_3 = 300 \tag{5.4}$$
$$x_1, x_2, s_1, s_2, s_3 \geq 0 \tag{5.5}$$

Algebraic Properties of the Simplex Method

Constraint equations (5.2) to (5.4) form a system of three simultaneous linear equations with five variables. Whenever a system of simultaneous linear equations has more variables than equations, we can expect an infinite number of solutions. The simplex method can be viewed as an algebraic procedure for finding the best solution to such a system of equations. In the preceding example, the best solution is the solution to equations (5.2) to (5.4) that maximizes the objective function (5.1) and satisfies the nonnegativity conditions given by (5.5).

Determining a Basic Solution

Since the HighTech Industries constraint equations have more variables (five) than equations (three), the simplex method finds solutions for these equations by assigning zero values to two of the variables and then solving for the values of the remaining three variables. For example, if we set $x_2 = 0$ and $s_1 = 0$, the system of constraint equations becomes

$$3x_1 \qquad\qquad\qquad = 150 \qquad\qquad (5.6)$$

$$1s_2 \qquad\qquad = 20 \qquad\qquad (5.7)$$

$$8x_1 \qquad\qquad + 1s_3 = 300 \qquad\qquad (5.8)$$

Using equation (5.6) to solve for x_1, we have

$$3x_1 = 150$$

and hence $x_1 = 150/3 = 50$. Equation (5.7) provides $s_2 = 20$. Finally, substituting $x_1 = 50$ into equation (5.8) results in

$$8(50) + 1s_3 = 300$$

Solving for s_3, we obtain $s_3 = -100$.

Thus, we have obtained the following solution to the three-equation, five-variable set of linear equations:

$$x_1 = \quad 50$$
$$x_2 = \quad 0$$
$$s_1 = \quad 0$$
$$s_2 = \quad 20$$
$$s_3 = -100$$

This solution is referred to as a *basic solution* for the HighTech linear programming problem. To state a general procedure for determining a basic solution, we must consider a standard-form linear programming problem consisting of n variables and m linear equations, where n is greater than m.

Basic Solution

To determine a basic solution, set $n - m$ of the variables equal to zero, and solve the m linear constraint equations for the remaining m variables.[2]

---

[2]There are cases where a unique solution cannot be found for a system of m equations and m variables. However, these cases will never be encountered when using the simplex method.

In terms of the HighTech problem, a basic solution can be obtained by setting any two variables equal to zero and then solving the system of three linear equations for the remaining three variables. We shall refer to the $n - m$ variables set equal to zero as the *nonbasic variables* and the remaining m variables as the *basic variables*. Thus, in the preceding example, x_2 and s_1 are the nonbasic variables, and x_1, s_2, and s_3 are the basic variables.

Basic Feasible Solutions

A basic solution can be either feasible or infeasible. A *basic feasible solution* is a basic solution that also satisfies the nonnegativity conditions. The basic solution found by setting x_2 and s_1 equal to zero and then solving for x_1, s_2, and s_3 is not a basic feasible solution because $s_3 = -100$. However, suppose that we had chosen to make x_1 and x_2 nonbasic variables by setting, $x_1 = 0$ and $x_2 = 0$. Solving for the corresponding basic solution is easy because with $x_1 = x_2 = 0$, the three constraint equations reduce to

$$1s_1 \qquad\qquad = 150$$
$$1s_2 \qquad = 20$$
$$1s_3 = 300$$

The complete solution with $x_1 = 0$ and $x_2 = 0$ is

$$x_1 = \quad 0$$
$$x_2 = \quad 0$$
$$s_1 = 150$$
$$s_2 = \quad 20$$
$$s_3 = 300$$

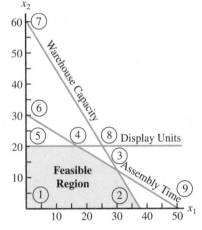

This solution is a basic feasible solution since all of the variables satisfy the nonnegativity conditions.

In Figure 5.1 we show a graph of the feasible region for the HighTech problem. We see that the basic feasible solution obtained by setting $x_1 = 0$ and $x_2 = 0$ corresponds to extreme point ① of the feasible region. This is not just a coincidence; all basic feasible solutions correspond to extreme points of the feasible region. Thus, for every extreme point of the feasible region of a linear programming problem, there is a corresponding basic feasible solution.

You should be able to find basic and basic feasible solutions to a system of equations at this point. Try Problem 1.

In Chapter 2 we showed that the optimal solution to a linear programming problem can be found at an extreme point. Since for every extreme point there is a corresponding basic feasible solution, we can now conclude that there is an optimal basic feasible solution.[3] The simplex method is an iterative procedure for moving from one basic feasible solution (extreme point) to another until the optimal solution is reached.

5.2 Tableau Form

A basic feasible solution to the system of m linear constraint equations and n variables is required as a starting point for the simplex method. The purpose of tableau form is to provide an initial basic feasible solution.

---

[3]We are only considering cases where there is an optimal solution. That is, in the cases of infeasibility and unboundedness, there is no optimal solution, so there cannot be an optimal basic feasible solution.

Figure 5.1

Feasible Region and Extreme Points for the HighTech Industries Problem

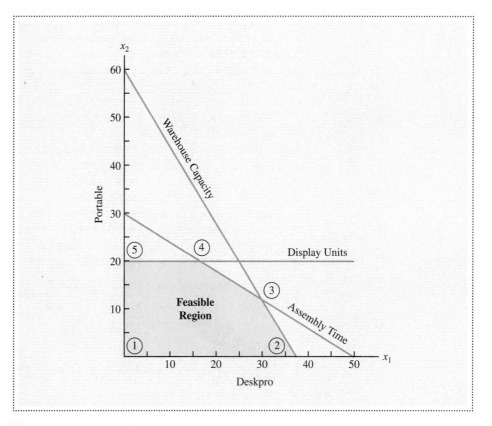

Recall that for the HighTech problem, the standard-form representation is

$$\text{Max} \quad 50x_1 + 40x_2 + 0s_1 + 0s_2 + 0s_3$$

s.t.

$$
\begin{aligned}
3x_1 + 5x_2 + 1s_1 \qquad\qquad\qquad &= 150 \\
1x_2 \qquad + 1s_2 \qquad\quad &= 20 \\
8x_1 + 5x_2 \qquad\qquad + 1s_3 &= 300 \\
x_1, x_2, s_1, s_2, s_3 &\geq 0
\end{aligned}
$$

When a linear programming problem with all less-than-or-equal-to constraints is written in standard form, it is easy to find a basic feasible solution. We simply set the decision variables equal to zero and solve for the values of the slack variables. Note that doing this sets the values of the slack variables equal to the right-hand-side values of the constraint equations. For the HighTech problem, this yields $x_1 = 0$, $x_2 = 0$, $s_1 = 150$, $s_2 = 20$, and $s_3 = 300$ as the initial basic feasible solution.

If we study the standard-form representation of the HighTech constraint equations closely, we can identify two properties that make it possible to find an initial basic feasible solution. The first property requires that the following conditions be satisfied:

a. For each constraint equation, the coefficient of one of the m basic variables in that equation must be 1, and the coefficients for all the remaining basic variables in that equation must be 0.

b. The coefficient for each basic variable must be 1 in only one constraint equation.

When these conditions are satisfied, there is exactly one basic variable with a coefficient of 1 associated with each constraint equation, and for each of the m constraint equations, it is a different basic variable. Thus, if the $n - m$ nonbasic variables are set equal to zero, the values of the basic variables are the values of the right-hand sides of the constraint equations.

The second property that enables us to find a basic feasible solution requires the values of the right-hand sides of the constraint equations be nonnegative. This ensures that the basic solution obtained by setting the basic variables equal to the values of the right-hand-sides will be feasible.

If a linear programming problem satisfies these two properties, it is said to be in *tableau form*. Thus, we see that the standard-form representation of the HighTech problem is already in tableau form. In fact, standard form and tableau form for linear programs that have all less-than-or-equal-to constraints and nonnegative right-hand-side values are the same. Later in this chapter we will show how to set up the tableau form for linear programming problems where the standard form and the tableau form are not the same.

To summarize, the following three steps are necessary to prepare a linear programming problem for solution using the simplex method:

Step 1   Formulate the problem.

Step 2   Set up the standard form by adding slack and/or subtracting surplus variables.

Step 3   Set up the tableau form.

5.3   Setting Up the Initial Simplex Tableau

After a linear programming problem has been converted to tableau form, we have an initial basic feasible solution that can be used to begin the simplex method. To provide a convenient means for performing the calculations required by the simplex solution procedure, we will first develop what is referred to as the initial *simplex tableau*.

Part of the initial simplex tableau is a table containing all the coefficients shown in the tableau form of a linear program. If we adopt the general notation

$$c_j = \text{objective function coefficient for variable } j$$
$$b_i = \text{right-hand-side value for constraint } i$$
$$a_{ij} = \text{coefficient associated with variable } j \text{ in constraint } i$$

we can show this portion of the initial simplex tableau as follows:

c_1	c_2	$\dots c_n$	
a_{11}	a_{12}	$\dots a_{1n}$	b_1
a_{21}	a_{22}	$\dots a_{2n}$	b_2
.	.	. . . .	.
.	.	. . . .	.
a_{m1}	a_{m2}	$\dots a_{mn}$	b_m

Thus, for the HighTech problem, we obtain the following partial initial simplex tableau:

50	40	0	0	0	
3	5	1	0	0	**150**
0	1	0	1	0	**20**
8	5	0	0	1	**300**

Later we may want to refer to the objective function coefficients, all the right-hand-side values, or all the coefficients in the constraints as a group. To do this, we will find the following general notation helpful:

c row = row of objective function coefficients

b column = column of right-hand-side values of the constraint equations

A matrix = m rows and n columns of coefficients of the variables in the constraint equations

Using this notation, we can show the above portion of the initial simplex tableau as follows:

c row	
A matrix	b column

To help us recall that each of the columns contains the coefficients for one of the variables, we write the variable associated with each column directly above the column. Doing this, we obtain

x_1	x_2	s_1	s_2	s_3	
50	40	0	0	0	
3	5	1	0	0	150
0	1	0	1	0	20
8	5	0	0	1	300

> **You should be able to set up the portion of the simplex tableau corresponding to the objective function and constraints at this point. Try Problem 4.**

This portion of the initial simplex tableau contains the tableau-form representation of the problem; thus, it is easy to identify the initial basic feasible solution. First, we note that for each basic variable, there is a corresponding column that has a 1 in the only nonzero position. Such columns are known as *unit columns* or *unit vectors*. Second, there is a row of the tableau associated with each basic variable. This row has a 1 in the unit column corresponding to the basic variable. The value of each basic variable is then given by the b_i value in the row associated with the basic variable. In the example, row 1 is associated with basic variable s_1 since this row has a 1 in the unit column corresponding to s_1. Thus, the value of s_1 is given by the right-hand-side value b_1: $s_1 = b_1 = 150$. In a similar fashion, $s_2 = b_2 = 20$, and $s_3 = b_3 = 300$.

To move from an initial basic feasible solution to a better basic feasible solution, the simplex method must generate a new basic feasible solution that yields a better value for the objective function. To do so requires changing the set of basic variables; this is accomplished by selecting one of the current nonbasic variables to be made basic and one of the current basic variables to be made nonbasic.

For computational convenience, we will add two new columns to the simplex tableau. One column is labeled "*Basis*" and the other column is labeled "c_B." In the *Basis* column, we list the current basic variables, and in the c_B column, we list the corresponding objective function coefficient for each of the basic variables. For the HighTech problem, this results in the following:

Basis	c_B	x_1	x_2	s_1	s_2	s_3	
		50	40	0	0	0	
s_1	0	3	5	1	0	0	150
s_2	0	0	1	0	1	0	20
s_3	0	8	5	0	0	1	300

Note that in the column labeled *Basis*, s_1 is listed as the first basic variable since its value is given by the right-hand-side value for the first equation. With s_2 listed second and s_3 listed third, the *Basis* column and right-hand-side values show the initial basic feasible solution has $s_1 = 150$, $s_2 = 20$, and $s_3 = 300$.

Can we improve the value of the objective function by moving to a new basic feasible solution? To find out whether this is possible, we add two rows to the bottom of the tableau. The first row, labeled z_j, represents the decrease in the value of the objective function that will result if one unit of the variable corresponding to the jth column of the A matrix is brought into the basis. The second row, labeled $c_j - z_j$, represents the net change in the value of the objective function if one unit of the variable corresponding to the jth column of the A matrix is brought into the solution. We refer to the $c_j - z_j$ row as the *net evaluation row*.

Let us first see how the entries in the z_j row are computed. Suppose that we consider increasing the value of the nonbasic variable x_1 by one unit—that is, from $x_1 = 0$ to $x_1 = 1$. In order to make this change and at the same time continue to satisfy the constraint equations, the values of some of the other variables will have to be changed. As we will show, the simplex method requires that the necessary changes be made to basic variables only. For example, in the first constraint we have

$$3x_1 + 5x_2 + 1s_1 = 150$$

The current basic variable in this constraint equation is s_1. Assuming that x_2 remains a nonbasic variable with a value of 0, if x_1 is increased in value by 1, then s_1 must be decreased by 3 for the constraint to be satisfied. Similarly, if we were to increase the value of x_1 by 1 (and keep $x_2 = 0$), we can see from the second and third equations that although s_2 would not decrease, s_3 would decrease by 8.

From analyzing all the constraint equations, we see that the coefficients in the x_1 column indicate the amount of decrease in the current basic variables when the nonbasic variable x_1 is increased from 0 to 1. In general, all the column coefficients can be interpreted this way. For instance, if we make x_2 a basic variable at a value of 1, s_1 will decrease by 5, s_2 will decrease by 1, and s_3 will decrease by 5.

Recall that the values in the c_B column of the simplex tableau are the objective function coefficients for the current basic variables. Hence, to compute the values in the z_j row (the decrease in value of the objective function when x_j is increased by one), we form the sum of the products obtained by multiplying the elements in the c_B column by the corresponding elements in the jth column of the A matrix. Doing this, we obtain

$$z_1 = 0(3) + 0(0) + 0(8) = 0$$

$$z_2 = 0(5) + 0(1) + 0(5) = 0$$

$$z_3 = 0(1) + 0(0) + 0(0) = 0$$

$$z_4 = 0(0) + 0(1) + 0(0) = 0$$

$$z_5 = 0(0) + 0(0) + 0(1) = 0$$

Since the objective function coefficient of x_1 is $c_1 = 50$, the value of $c_1 - z_1$ is $50 - 0 = 50$. This indicates that the net result of bringing one unit of x_1 into the current basis will be an increase in profit of $50. Hence, in the net evaluation row corresponding to x_1, we enter 50. In the same manner, we can calculate the $c_j - z_j$ values for the remaining variables. The result is the following initial simplex tableau:

Basis	c_B	x_1 50	x_2 40	s_1 0	s_2 0	s_3 0	
s_1	0	3	5	1	0	0	**150**
s_2	0	0	1	0	1	0	**20**
s_3	0	8	5	0	0	1	**300**
z_j		0	0	0	0	0	**0**
$c_j - z_j$		50	40	0	0	0	↑

Value of the
Objective Function

In this tableau we also see a boldfaced 0 in the z_j row in the last column. This zero is the value of the objective function associated with the current basic feasible solution. It was computed by multiplying the objective function coefficients in the c_B column by the corresponding values of the basic variables shown in the last column of the tableau—that is, $0(150) + 0(20) + 0(300) = 0$.

The initial simplex tableau is now complete. It shows that the initial basic feasible solution ($x_1 = 0$, $x_2 = 0$, $s_1 = 150$, $s_2 = 20$, and $s_3 = 300$) has an objective function value, or profit, of $0. In addition, the $c_j - z_j$ or net evaluation row has values that will guide us in improving the solution by moving to a better basic feasible solution.

You should now be able to set up the complete initial simplex tableau for a problem with less-than-or-equal constraints. Try Problem 5(a).

5.4 Improving the Solution

From the net evaluation row, we see that each unit of the Deskpro (x_1) increases the value of the objective function by 50 and each unit of the Portable (x_2) increases the value of the objective function by 40. Since x_1 causes the largest per-unit increase, we choose it as the variable to bring into the basis. We must next determine which of the current basic variables to make nonbasic.

In discussing how to compute the z_j values, we noted that each of the coefficients in the x_1 column indicates the amount of decrease in the corresponding basic variable that would result from increasing x_1 by one unit. Considering the first row, we see that every unit of the Deskpro produced will use 3 hours of assembly time, reducing s_1 by 3. In the current solution, $s_1 = 150$ and $x_1 = 0$. Thus—considering this row only—the maximum possible value of x_1 can be calculated by solving

$$3x_1 = 150$$

which provides

$$x_1 = 50$$

If x_1 is 50 (and x_2 remains a nonbasic variable with a value of 0), s_1 will have to be reduced to zero in order to satisfy the first constraint:

$$3x_1 + 5x_2 + 1s_1 = 150$$

Considering the second row, $0x_1 + 1x_2 + 1s_2 = 20$, we see that the coefficient of x_1 is 0. Thus, increasing x_1 will not have any effect on s_2; that is, increasing x_1 cannot drive the basic variable in the second row (s_2) to zero. Indeed, increases in x_1 will leave s_2 unchanged.

Finally, since the coefficient of x_1 is 8 in the third row, every unit that we increase x_1 will cause a decrease of eight units in s_3. Since the value of s_3 is currently 300, we can solve

$$8x_1 = 300$$

to find the maximum possible increase in x_1 before s_3 will become nonbasic at a value of zero; thus, we see that x_1 cannot be any larger than $^{300}/_8 = 37.5$.

Considering the three rows (constraints) simultaneously, we see that row 3 is the most restrictive. That is, producing 37.5 units of the Deskpro will force the corresponding slack variable to become nonbasic at a value of $s_3 = 0$.

In making the decision to produce as many Deskpro units as possible, we must change the set of variables in the basic feasible solution, which means obtaining a new basis. The simplex method moves from one basic feasible solution to another by selecting a nonbasic variable to replace one of the current basic variables. This process of moving from one basic feasible solution to another is called an *iteration*. We now summarize the rules for selecting a nonbasic variable to be made basic and for selecting a current basic variable to be made nonbasic.

Criterion for Entering a New Variable into the Basis

Look at the net evaluation row ($c_j - z_j$), and select the variable to enter the basis that will cause the largest per-unit improvement in the value of the objective function. In the case of a tie, follow the convention of selecting the variable to enter the basis that corresponds to the leftmost of the columns.

Criterion for Removing a Variable from the Current Basis (Minimum Ratio Test)

Suppose the incoming basic variable corresponds to column j in the A portion of the simplex tableau. For each row i, compute the ratio b_i/a_{ij} for each a_{ij} greater than zero. The basic variable that will be removed from the basis corresponds to the minimum of these ratios. In case of a tie, we follow the convention of selecting the variable that corresponds to the uppermost of the tied rows.

To illustrate the computations involved, we add an extra column to the right of the tableau showing the b_i/a_{ij} ratios.

Basis	c_B	x_1 50	x_2 40	s_1 0	s_2 0	s_3 0		$\dfrac{b_i}{a_{i1}}$
s_1	0	3	5	1	0	0	150	$\dfrac{150}{3} = 50$
s_2	0	0	1	0	1	0	20	—
s_3	0	⑧	5	0	0	1	300	$\dfrac{300}{8} = 37.5$
z_j		0	0	0	0	0	0	
$c_j - z_j$		50	40	0	0	0		

Any solution with x_1 or x_2 set equal to zero is not an optimal solution.

$ Amount increase by increasing x_1, x_2 by 1 unit.

We see that $c_1 - z_1 = 50$ is the largest positive value in the $c_j - z_j$ row. Hence, x_1 is selected to become the new basic variable. Checking the ratios b_i/a_{i1} for values of a_{i1} greater than zero, we see that $b_3/a_{31} = 300/8 = 37.5$ is the minimum of these ratios. Thus, the current basic variable associated with row 3 (s_3) is the variable selected to leave the basis. In the tableau we have circled $a_{31} = 8$ to indicate that the variable corresponding to the first column is to enter the basis and that the basic variable corresponding to the third row is to leave the basis. Adopting the usual linear programming terminology, we refer to this circled element as the *pivot element*. The column and the row containing the pivot element are called the *pivot column* and the *pivot row*, respectively.

To improve the current solution of $x_1 = 0$, $x_2 = 0$, $s_1 = 150$, $s_2 = 20$, and $s_3 = 300$, we should increase x_1 to 37.5. The production of 37.5 units of the Deskpro results in a profit of $50(37.5) = 1875$. In producing 37.5 units of the Deskpro, s_3 will be reduced to zero. Hence, x_1 will become the new basic variable, replacing s_3 in the previous basis.

5.5 Calculating the Next Tableau

We now want to update the simplex tableau in such a fashion that the column associated with the new basic variable is a unit column; in this way its value will be given by the right-hand-side value of the corresponding row. We would like the column in the new tableau corresponding to x_1 to look just like the column corresponding to s_3 in the original tableau, so our goal is to make the column in the A matrix corresponding to x_1 appear as

$$0$$
$$0$$
$$1$$

The way in which we transform the simplex tableau so that it still represents an equivalent system of constraint equations is to use the following *elementary row operations*.

Elementary Row Operations

1. Multiply any row (equation) by a nonzero number.
2. Replace any row (equation) by the result of adding or subtracting a multiple of another row (equation) to it.

The application of these elementary row operations to a system of simultaneous linear equations will not change the solution to the system of equations; however, the elementary row operations will change the coefficients of the variables and the values of the right-hand sides.

The objective in performing elementary row operations is to transform the system of constraint equations into a form that makes it easy to identify the new basic feasible solution. Consequently, we must perform the elementary row operations in such a manner that we transform the column for the variable entering the basis into a unit column. We emphasize that the feasible solutions to the original constraint equations are the same as the feasible solutions to the modified constraint equations obtained by performing elementary row operations. However, many of the numerical values in the simplex tableau will change as the result of performing these row operations. Thus, the present method of referring to elements in the simplex tableau may lead to confusion.

Up to now we have made no distinction between the A matrix and b column coefficients in the tableau form of the problem and the corresponding coefficients in the simplex tableau. Indeed, we showed that the initial simplex tableau is formed by properly placing the a_{ij}, c_j, and b_i elements as given in the tableau form of the problem into the simplex tableau. To avoid confusion in subsequent simplex tableaus, we will refer to the portion of the simplex tableau that initially contained the a_{ij} values with the symbol $\bar{A}$, and the portion of the tableau that initially contained the b_i values with the symbol $\bar{b}$. In terms of the simplex tableau, elements in $\bar{A}$ will be denoted by $\bar{a}_{ij}$, and elements in $\bar{b}$ will be denoted by $\bar{b}_i$. In subsequent simplex tableaus, elementary row operations will change the tableau elements. The overbar notation should avoid any confusion when we wish to distinguish between (1) the original constraint coefficient values a_{ij} and right-hand-side values b_i of the tableau form, and (2) the simplex tableau elements $\bar{a}_{ij}$ and $\bar{b}_i$.

Now let us see how elementary row operations are used to create the next simplex tableau for the HighTech problem. Recall that the goal is to transform the column in the $\bar{A}$ portion of the simplex tableau corresponding to x_1 to a unit column; that is,

$$\bar{a}_{11} = 0$$

$$\bar{a}_{21} = 0$$

$$\bar{a}_{31} = 1$$

To set $\bar{a}_{31} = 1$, we perform the first elementary row operation by multiplying the pivot row (row 3) by $\frac{1}{8}$ to obtain the equivalent equation

$$\tfrac{1}{8}(8x_1 + 5x_2 + 0s_1 + 0s_2 + 1s_3) = \tfrac{1}{8}(300)$$

or

$$1x_1 + \tfrac{5}{8}x_2 + 0s_1 + 0s_2 + \tfrac{1}{8}s_3 = \tfrac{75}{2} \tag{5.9}$$

We refer to equation (5.9) in the updated simplex tableau as the *new pivot row*.

To set $\bar{a}_{11} = 0$, we perform the second elementary row operation by first multiplying the new pivot row by 3 to obtain the equivalent equation

$$3(1x_1 + \tfrac{5}{8}x_2 + 0s_1 + 0s_2 + \tfrac{1}{8}s_3) = 3(\tfrac{75}{2})$$

or

$$3x_1 + \tfrac{15}{8}x_2 + 0s_1 + 0s_2 + \tfrac{3}{8}s_3 = \tfrac{225}{2} \tag{5.10}$$

Subtracting equation (5.10) from the equation represented by row 1 of the simplex tableau completes the application of the second elementary row operation; thus, after dropping the terms with zero coefficients, we obtain

$$(3x_1 + 5x_2 + 1s_1) - (3x_1 + \tfrac{15}{8}x_2 + \tfrac{3}{8}s_3) = 150 - \tfrac{225}{2}$$

or

$$0x_1 + \tfrac{25}{8}x_2 + 1s_1 - \tfrac{3}{8}s_3 = \tfrac{75}{2} \tag{5.11}$$

Since $\bar{a}_{21} = 0$, no row operations need be performed on the second row of the simplex tableau. Replacing rows 1 and 3 with the coefficients in equations (5.11) and (5.9), respectively, we obtain the new simplex tableau

Basis	c_B	x_1 50	x_2 40	s_1 0	s_2 0	s_3 0	
s_1	0	0	$25/8$	1	0	$-3/8$	$75/2$
s_2	0	0	1	0	1	0	20
x_1	50	1	$5/8$	0	0	$1/8$	$75/2$
z_j							1875
$c_j - z_j$							

Assigning zero values to the nonbasic variables x_2 and s_3 permits us to identify the following new basic feasible solution:

$$s_1 = 75/2$$
$$s_2 = 20$$
$$x_1 = 75/2$$

This solution is also provided by the last column in the new simplex tableau. The profit associated with this solution is obtained by multiplying the solution values for the basic variables as given in the $\bar{b}$ column by their corresponding objective function coefficients as given in the c_B column; that is,

$$0(75/2) + 0(20) + 50(75/2) = 1875$$

Interpreting the Results of an Iteration

In our example, the initial basic feasible solution was

$$x_1 = 0$$
$$x_2 = 0$$
$$s_1 = 150$$
$$s_2 = 20$$
$$s_3 = 300$$

with a corresponding profit of $0. One iteration of the simplex method moved us to another basic feasible solution with an objective function value of $1875. This new basic feasible solution is

$$x_1 = 75/2$$
$$x_2 = 0$$
$$s_1 = 75/2$$
$$s_2 = 20$$
$$s_3 = 0$$

In Figure 5.2 we see that the initial basic feasible solution corresponds to extreme point ①. The first iteration moved us in the direction of the greatest increase per unit in profit—that is, along the x_1 axis. We moved away from extreme point ① in the x_1 direction until we could not move farther without violating one of the constraints. The tableau we calculated after one iteration is the basic feasible solution corresponding to extreme point ②.

Figure 5.2

Feasible Region and Extreme Points for the HighTech Industries Problem

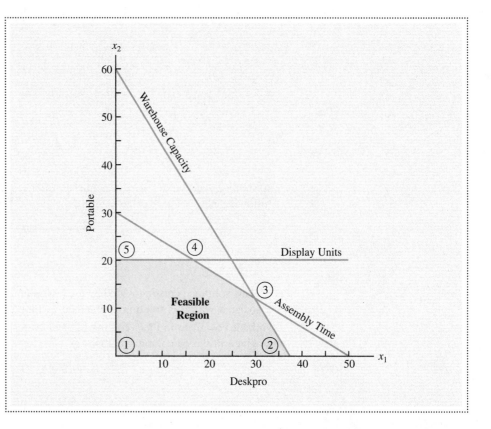

We note from Figure 5.2 that at extreme point ② the warehouse capacity constraint is binding with $s_3 = 0$ and that there is slack in the other two constraints. From the simplex tableau, we see that the amount of slack for these two constraints is given by $s_1 = {}^{75}/_2$ and $s_2 = 20$.

Moving toward a Better Solution

To see if a better basic feasible solution can be found, we need to calculate the z_j and $c_j - z_j$ rows for the new simplex tableau. Recall that the elements in the z_j row are the sum of the products obtained by multiplying the elements in the c_B column of the simplex tableau by the corresponding elements in the columns of the $\bar{A}$ matrix. Thus, we obtain

$$z_1 = 0(0) \quad + 0(0) + 50(1) = 50$$
$$z_2 = 0({}^{25}/_8) \quad + 0(1) + 50({}^5/_8) = {}^{250}/_8$$
$$z_3 = 0(1) \quad + 0(0) + 50(0) = 0$$
$$z_4 = 0(0) \quad + 0(1) + 50(0) = 0$$
$$z_5 = 0(-{}^3/_8) + 0(0) + 50({}^1/_8) = {}^{50}/_8$$

Subtracting z_j from c_j to compute the new net evaluation row, we obtain the following simplex tableau:

Basis	c_B	x_1 50	x_2 40	s_1 0	s_2 0	s_3 0	
s_1	0	0	$25/8$	1	0	$-3/8$	$75/2$
s_2	0	0	1	0	1	0	**20**
x_1	50	1	$5/8$	0	0	$1/8$	$75/2$
z_j		50	$250/8$	0	0	$50/8$	**1875**
$c_j - z_j$		0	$70/8$	0	0	$-50/8$	

Let us now analyze the $c_j - z_j$ row to see if we can introduce a new variable into the basis and continue to improve the value of the objective function. Using the rule for determining which variable should enter the basis next, we select x_2 since it has the highest positive coefficient in the $c_j - z_j$ row.

To determine which variable will be removed from the basis when x_2 enters, we must compute for each row i the ratio $\bar{b}_i / \bar{a}_{i2}$ (remember, though, that we should compute this ratio only if $\bar{a}_{i2}$ is greater than zero); then we select the variable to leave the basis that corresponds to the minimum ratio. As before, we will show these ratios in an extra column of the simplex tableau:

Basis	c_B	x_1 50	x_2 40	s_1 0	s_2 0	s_3 0		$\dfrac{\bar{b}_i}{\bar{a}_{i2}}$
s_1	0	0	$(25/8)$	1	0	$-3/8$	$75/2$	$\dfrac{75/2}{25/8} = 12$
s_2	0	0	1	0	1	0	**20**	$\dfrac{20}{1} = 20$
x_1	50	1	$5/8$	0	0	$1/8$	$75/2$	$\dfrac{75/2}{5/8} = 60$
z_j		50	$250/8$	0	0	$50/8$	**1875**	
$c_j - z_j$		0	$70/8$	0	0	$-50/8$		

Since 12 is the minimum ratio, s_1 will leave the basis. The pivot element is $\bar{a}_{12} = 25/8$, which is circled in the preceding tableau. The nonbasic variable x_2 must now be made a basic variable in row 1. This means that we must perform the elementary row operations that will convert the x_2 column into a unit column with a 1 in row 1; that is, we will have to transform the second column in the tableau to the form

$$1$$
$$0$$
$$0$$

We can do this by performing the following elementary row operations:

Step 1   Multiply every element in row 1 (the pivot row) by $8/25$ in order to make $\bar{a}_{12} = 1$.

Step 2   Subtract the new row 1 (the new pivot row) from row 2 to make $\bar{a}_{22} = 0$.

Step 3   Multiply the new pivot row by $5/8$, and subtract the result from row 3 to make $\bar{a}_{32} = 0$.

The new simplex tableau resulting from these row operations is as follows:

		x_1	x_2	s_1	s_2	s_3	
Basis	c_B	50	40	0	0	0	
x_2	40	0	1	$8/25$	0	$-3/25$	12
s_2	0	0	0	$-8/25$	1	$3/25$	8
x_1	50	1	0	$-5/25$	0	$5/25$	30
z_j		50	40	$14/5$	0	$26/5$	1980
$c_j - z_j$		0	0	$-14/5$	0	$-26/5$	

Note that the values of the basic variables are $x_2 = 12$, $s_2 = 8$, and $x_1 = 30$, and the corresponding profit is $40(12) + 0(8) + 50(30) = 1980$.

We must now determine whether or not to bring any other variable into the basis and thereby move to another basic feasible solution. Looking at the net evaluation row, we see that every element is zero or negative. Since $c_j - z_j$ is less than or equal to zero for both of the nonbasic variables s_1 and s_3, any attempt to bring a nonbasic variable into the basis at this point will result in a lowering of the current value of the objective function. Hence, this tableau represents the optimal solution. In general, the simplex method uses the following criterion to determine when the optimal solution has been obtained.

Optimality Criterion

The optimal solution to a linear programming problem has been reached when all of the entries in the net evaluation row ($c_j - z_j$) are zero or negative. In such cases, the optimal solution is the current basic feasible solution.

Referring to Figure 5.2, we can see graphically the process that the simplex method used to determine an optimal solution. The initial basic feasible solution corresponds to the origin ($x_1 = 0$, $x_2 = 0$, $s_1 = 150$, $s_2 = 20$, $s_3 = 300$). The first iteration caused x_1 to enter the basis and s_3 to leave. The second basic feasible solution corresponds to extreme point ② ($x_1 = 75/2$, $x_2 = 0$, $s_1 = 75/2$, $s_2 = 20$, $s_3 = 0$). At the next iteration, x_2 entered the basis and s_1 left. This brought us to extreme point ③ and the optimal solution ($x_1 = 30$, $x_2 = 12$, $s_1 = 0$, $s_2 = 8$, $s_3 = 0$).

For the HighTech problem with only two decision variables, we had a choice of using the graphical or simplex method. For problems with more than two vaiables, we shall always use the simplex method.

Interpreting the Optimal Solution

Using the final simplex tableau, we find the optimal solution to the HighTech problem consists of the basic variables x_1, x_2, and s_2 and nonbasic variables s_1 and s_3 with:

$$x_1 = 30$$
$$x_2 = 12$$
$$s_1 = 0$$
$$s_2 = 8$$
$$s_3 = 0$$

Figure 5.3

The Management Scientist Solution for the HighTech Industries Problem

```
OPTIMAL SOLUTION

Objective Function Value =            1980.000

        Variable            Value            Reduced Costs
      --------------      -------------      -----------------

           X1               30.000               0.000
           X2               12.000               0.000


       Constraint        Slack/Surplus          Dual Prices
      --------------      -------------      -----------------

           1                0.000                2.800
           2                8.000                0.000
           3                0.000                5.200
```

The value of the objective function is $1980. If management wants to maximize total profit contribution, HighTech should produce 30 units of the Deskpro and 12 units of the Portable. Since $s_2 = 8$, management should note that there will be eight unused Portable display units. Moreover, since $s_1 = 0$ and $s_3 = 0$, there is no slack associated with the assembly time constraint and the warehouse capacity constraint; in other words, these constraints are both binding. Consequently, if it is possible to obtain additional assembly time and/or additional warehouse space, management should consider doing so.

Figure 5.3 shows the computer solution to the HighTech problem using The Management Scientist software package. The optimal solution with $x_1 = 30$ and $x_2 = 12$ is shown to have an objective function value of $1980. The values of the slack variables complete the optimal solution with $s_1 = 0$, $s_2 = 8$ and $s_3 = 0$. The values in the reduced costs column are from the net evaluation row of the final simplex tableau. Note that the $c_j - z_j$ values in columns corresponding to x_1 and x_2 are both 0. The dual prices are the z_j values for the three slack variables in the final simplex tableau. Referring to the final tableau, we see that the dual price for constraint 1 is the z_j value corresponding to s_1 where $14/5 = 2.8$. Similarly, the dual price for constraint 2 is 0, and the dual price for constraint 3 is $26/5 = 5.2$. The use of the simplex method to compute dual prices will be discussed further when we cover sensitivity analysis in Chapter 6.

Summary of the Simplex Method

Let us now summarize the steps followed to solve a linear program using the simplex method. We assume that the problem has all less-than-or-equal-to constraints and involves maximization.

Step 1   Formulate a linear programming model of the problem.

Step 2   Add slack variables to each constraint to obtain standard form. This is also the tableau form necessary to identify an initial basic feasible solution for problems involving all less-than-or-equal-to constraints.

Step 3   Set up the initial simplex tableau.

Step 4   Choose the nonbasic variable with the largest entry in the net evaluation row to bring into the basis. This identifies the pivot column: the column associated with the incoming variable.

Step 5   Choose as the pivot row that row with the smallest ratio of $\bar{b}_i/\bar{a}_{ij}$ for $\bar{a}_{ij} > 0$ where j is the pivot column. This identifies the pivot row: the row of the variable leaving the basis when variable j enters.

Step 6   Perform the necessary elementary row operations to convert the column for the incoming variable to a unit column with a 1 in the pivot row.

    a.   Divide each element of the pivot row by the pivot element (the element in the pivot row and pivot column).

    b.   Obtain zeroes in all other positions of the pivot column by adding or subtracting an appropriate multiple of the new pivot row.
    Once the row operations have been completed, the value of the new basic feasible solution can be read from the $\bar{b}$ column of the tableau.

Step 7   Test for optimality. If $c_j - z_j \leq 0$ for all columns, we have the optimal solution. If not, return to step 4.

The algorithm is basically the same for problems with equality and greater-than-or-equal-to constraints except that setting up tableau form requires a little more work. We discuss what is involved in Section 5.6. The simple modification necessary for minimization problems is covered in Section 5.7.

You should now be able to solve a problem employing the simplex method. Try Problem 6.

NOTES & comments

The entries in the net evaluation row provide the reduced costs that appear in the computer solution to a linear program. Recall that in Chapter 3 we defined the reduced cost as the amount by which an objective function coefficient would have to improve before it would be possible for the corresponding variable to assume a positive value in the optimal solution. In general, the reduced costs are the absolute values of the entries in the net evaluation row.

5.6   Tableau Form: The General Case

When a linear program contains all less-than-or-equal-to constraints with nonnegative right-hand-side values, it is easy to set up the tableau form; we simply add a slack variable to each constraint. However, obtaining tableau form is somewhat more complex if the linear program contains greater-than-or-equal-to constraints, equality constraints, and/or negative right-hand-side values. In this section we describe how to develop tableau form for each of these situations and also how to solve linear programs involving equality and greater-than-or-equal-to constraints using the simplex method.

Greater-Than-or-Equal-to Constraints

Suppose that in the HighTech Industries problem, management wanted to ensure that the combined total production for both models would be at least 25 units. This requirement means that the following constraint must be added to the current linear program:

$$1x_1 + 1x_2 \geq 25$$

Adding this constraint results in the following modified problem:

Max $50x_1 + 40x_2$

s.t.

$$
\begin{array}{lll}
3x_1 + 5x_2 \leq 150 & \quad & \text{Assembly time} \\
1x_2 \leq 20 & & \text{Portable display} \\
8x_1 + 5x_2 \leq 300 & & \text{Warehouse space} \\
1x_1 + 1x_2 \geq 25 & & \text{Minimum total production}
\end{array}
$$

$$x_1, x_2 \geq 0$$

First, we use three slack variables and one surplus variable to write the problem in standard form. This provides the following:

Max $50x_1 + 40x_2 + 0s_1 + 0s_2 + 0s_3 + 0s_4$

s.t.

$$
\begin{array}{lll}
3x_1 + 5x_2 + 1s_1 & = 150 & \quad (5.12) \\
1x_2 + 1s_2 & = 20 & \quad (5.13) \\
8x_1 + 5x_2 + 1s_3 & = 300 & \quad (5.14) \\
1x_1 + 1x_2 - 1s_4 & = 25 & \quad (5.15)
\end{array}
$$

$$x_1, x_2, s_1, s_2, s_3, s_4 \geq 0$$

Now let us consider how we obtain an initial basic feasible solution to start the simplex method. Previously, we set $x_1 = 0$ and $x_2 = 0$ and selected the slack variables as the initial basic variables. The extension of this notion to the modified HighTech problem would suggest setting $x_1 = 0$ and $x_2 = 0$ and selecting the slack and surplus variables as the initial basic variables. Doing so results in the basic solution

$$
\begin{aligned}
x_1 &= 0 \\
x_2 &= 0 \\
s_1 &= 150 \\
s_2 &= 20 \\
s_3 &= 300 \\
s_4 &= -25
\end{aligned}
$$

Clearly this is not a basic feasible solution since $s_4 = -25$ violates the nonnegativity requirement. The difficulty is that the standard form and the tableau form are not equivalent when the problem contains greater-than-or-equal-to constraints.

To set up the tableau form, we shall resort to a mathematical "trick" that will enable us to find an initial basic feasible solution in terms of the slack variables s_1, s_2, and s_3 and a new variable we shall denote a_4. The new variable constitutes the mathematical trick. Variable a_4 really has nothing to do with the HighTech problem; it merely enables us to set up the tableau form and thus obtain an initial basic feasible solution. Since this new variable has been artificially created to start the simplex method, we will refer to it as an *artificial variable*.

The notation for artificial variables is similar to the notation used to refer to the elements of the A matrix. To avoid any confusion between the two, recall that the elements of the A matrix (constraint coefficients) always have two subscripts, whereas artificial variables only one subscript.

With the addition of an artificial variable, we can convert the standard form of the problem into tableau form. We add artificial variable a_4 to constraint equation (5.15) to obtain the following representation of the system of equations in tableau form:

$$
\begin{array}{rcrcrcrcrcrcr}
3x_1 &+& 5x_2 &+& 1s_1 & & & & & & & =& 150 \\
&& 1x_2 & & &+& 1s_2 & & & & & =& 20 \\
8x_1 &+& 5x_2 & & & & &+& 1s_3 & & & =& 300 \\
1x_1 &+& 1x_2 & & & & & & &-& 1s_4 &+& 1a_4 &=& 25
\end{array}
$$

Note that the subscript on the artificial variable identifies the constraint with which it is associated. Thus, a_4 is the artificial variable associated with the fourth constraint.

Since the variables s_1, s_2, s_3, and a_4 each appear in a different constraint with a coefficient of 1, and since the right-hand-side values are nonnegative, both requirements of the tableau form have been satisfied. We can now obtain an initial basic feasible solution by setting $x_1 = x_2 = s_4 = 0$. The complete solution is

$$
\begin{array}{rcr}
x_1 &=& 0 \\
x_2 &=& 0 \\
s_1 &=& 150 \\
s_2 &=& 20 \\
s_3 &=& 300 \\
s_4 &=& 0 \\
a_4 &=& 25
\end{array}
$$

Is this solution feasible in terms of the real HighTech problem? No, it is not. It does not satisfy the constraint 4 combined total production requirement of 25 units. We must make an important distinction between a basic feasible solution for the tableau form and a feasible solution for the real problem. A basic feasible solution for the tableau form of a linear programming problem is not always a feasible solution for the real problem.

The reason for creating the tableau form is to obtain the initial basic feasible solution that is required to start the simplex method. Thus, we see that whenever it is necessary to introduce artificial variables, the initial simplex solution will not in general be feasible for the real problem. This situation is not as difficult as it might seem, however, since the only time we must have a feasible solution for the real problem is at the last iteration of the simplex method. Thus, devising a way to guarantee that any artificial variable would be eliminated from the basic feasible solution before the optimal solution is reached would eliminate the difficulty.

The way in which we guarantee that artificial variables will be eliminated before the optimal solution is reached is to assign each artificial variable a very large cost in the objective function. For example, in the modified HighTech problem, we could assign a very large negative number as the profit coefficient for artificial variable a_4. Hence, if this variable is in the basis, it will substantially reduce profits. As a result, this variable will be eliminated from the basis as soon as possible, and this is precisely what we want to happen.

As an alternative to picking a large negative number such as $-100,000$ for the profit coefficient, we will denote the profit coefficient of each artificial variable by $-M$. Here it is assumed that M represents a very large number—in other words, a number of large magnitude and hence, the letter M. This notation will make it easier to keep track of the elements of the simplex tableau that depend on the profit coefficients of the artificial variables. Using $-M$ as the profit coefficient for artificial variable a_4 in the modified HighTech problem, we can write the objective function for the tableau form of the problem as follows:

$$\text{Max} \quad 50x_1 + 40x_2 + 0s_1 + 0s_2 + 0s_3 + 0s_4 - Ma_4$$

The initial simplex tableau for the problem is shown here.

		x_1	x_2	s_1	s_2	s_3	s_4	a_4	
Basis	c_B	50	40	0	0	0	0	$-M$	
s_1	0	3	5	1	0	0	0	0	150
s_2	0	0	1	0	1	0	0	0	20
s_3	0	8	5	0	0	1	0	0	300
a_4	$-M$	①	1	0	0	0	-1	1	25
z_j		$-M$	$-M$	0	0	0	M	$-M$	$-25M$
$c_j - z_j$		$50 + M$	$40 + M$	0	0	0	$-M$	0	

This tableau corresponds to the solution $s_1 = 150$, $s_2 = 20$, $s_3 = 300$, $a_4 = 25$, and $x_1 = x_2 = s_4 = 0$. In terms of the simplex tableau, this is a basic feasible solution since all the variables are greater than or equal to zero and $n - m = 7 - 4 = 3$ of the variables are equal to zero.

Since $c_1 - z_1 = 50 + M$ is the largest value in the net evaluation row, we see that x_1 will become a basic variable during the first iteration of the simplex method. Further calculations with the simplex method show that x_1 will replace a_4 in the basic solution. The simplex tableau after the first iteration is presented below.

Result of Iteration 1

		x_1	x_2	s_1	s_2	s_3	s_4	a_4	
Basis	c_B	50	40	0	0	0	0	$-M$	
s_1	0	0	2	1	0	0	3	-3	75
s_2	0	0	1	0	1	0	0	0	20
s_3	0	0	-3	0	0	1	8	-8	100
x_1	50	1	1	0	0	0	-1	1	25
z_j		50	50	0	0	0	-50	50	1250
$c_j - z_j$		0	-10	0	0	0	50	$-M - 50$	

Since the artificial variable $a_4 = 0$, we now have a situation in which the basic feasible solution contained in the simplex tableau is also a feasible solution to the real HighTech problem. In addition, since a_4 is an artificial variable that was added simply to obtain an initial basic feasible solution, we can now drop its associated column from the simplex tableau. Indeed, whenever artificial variables are used, they can be dropped from the simplex tableau as soon as they have been eliminated from the basic feasible solution.

When artificial variables are required to obtain an initial basic feasible solution, the iterations required to eliminate the artificial variables are referred to as *phase I* of the simplex method. When all the artificial variables have been eliminated from the basis, phase I is complete, and a basic feasible solution to the real problem has been obtained. Thus, by dropping the column associated with a_4 from the current tableau, we obtain the following simplex tableau at the end of phase I.

		x_1	x_2	s_1	s_2	s_3	s_4	
Basis	c_B	50	40	0	0	0	0	
s_1	0	0	2	1	0	0	3	75
s_2	0	0	1	0	1	0	0	20
s_3	0	0	-3	0	0	1	⑧	100
x_1	50	1	1	0	0	0	-1	25
z_j		50	50	0	0	0	-50	1250
$c_j - z_j$		0	-10	0	0	0	50	

We are now ready to begin phase II of the simplex method. This phase simply continues the simplex method computations after all artificial variables have been removed. At the next iteration, variable s_4 with $c_j - z_j = 50$ is entered into the solution, and variable s_3 is eliminated. The simplex tableau after this iteration is:

		x_1	x_2	s_1	s_2	s_3	s_4	
Basis	c_B	50	40	0	0	0	0	
s_1	0	0	㉕⁄₈	1	0	$-\frac{3}{8}$	0	$\frac{75}{2}$
s_2	0	0	1	0	1	0	0	20
s_4	0	0	$-\frac{3}{8}$	0	0	$\frac{1}{8}$	1	$\frac{25}{2}$
x_1	50	1	$\frac{5}{8}$	0	0	$\frac{1}{8}$	0	$\frac{75}{2}$
z_j		50	$\frac{250}{8}$	0	0	$\frac{50}{8}$	0	1875
$c_j - z_j$		0	$\frac{70}{8}$	0	0	$-\frac{50}{8}$	0	

One more iteration is required. This time x_2 comes into the solution, and s_1 is eliminated. After performing this iteration, the following simplex tableau shows that the optimal solution has been reached.

		x_1	x_2	s_1	s_2	s_3	s_4	
Basis	c_B	50	40	0	0	0	0	
x_2	40	0	1	$\frac{8}{25}$	0	$-\frac{3}{25}$	0	12
s_2	0	0	0	$-\frac{8}{25}$	1	$\frac{3}{25}$	0	8
s_4	0	0	0	$\frac{3}{25}$	0	$\frac{2}{25}$	1	17
x_1	50	1	0	$-\frac{5}{25}$	0	$\frac{5}{25}$	0	30
z_j		50	40	$\frac{14}{5}$	0	$\frac{26}{5}$	0	1980
$c_j - z_j$		0	0	$-\frac{14}{5}$	0	$-\frac{26}{5}$	0	

It turns out that the optimal solution to the modified HighTech problem is the same as the solution for the original problem. However, the simplex method required more iterations to reach this extreme point, because an extra iteration was needed to eliminate the artificial variable (a_4) in phase I.

Fortunately, once we obtain an initial simplex tableau using artificial variables, we need not concern ourselves with whether the basic solution at a particular iteration is feasible for the real problem. We need only follow the rules for the simplex method. If we reach the optimality criterion (all $c_j - z_j \leq 0$) and all the artificial variables have been eliminated from the solution, then we have found the optimal solution. On the other hand, if we reach the optimality criterion and one or more of the artificial variables remain in solution at a positive value, then there is no feasible solution to the problem. This special case will be discussed further in Section 5.8.

Equality Constraints

When an equality constraint occurs in a linear programming problem, we need to add an artificial variable to obtain tableau form and an initial basic feasible solution. For example, if constraint 1 is

$$6x_1 + 4x_2 - 5x_3 = 30$$

we would simply add an artificial variable a_1 to create a basic feasible solution in the initial simplex tableau. With the artificial variable, the constraint equation becomes

$$6x_1 + 4x_2 - 5x_3 + 1a_1 = 30$$

Now a_1 can be selected as the basic variable for this row, and its value is given by the right-hand side. Once we have created tableau form by adding an artificial variable to each equality constraint, the simplex method proceeds exactly as before.

Eliminating Negative Right-Hand-Side Values

One of the properties of the tableau form of a linear program is that the values on the right-hand sides of the constraints have to be nonnegative. In formulating a linear programming problem, we may find one or more of the constraints have negative right-hand-side values. To see how this might happen, suppose that the management of HighTech has specified that the number of units of the Portable model, x_2, has to be less than or equal to the number of units of the Deskpro model, x_1, after setting aside five units of the Deskpro for internal company use. We could formulate this constraint as

$$x_2 \leq x_1 - 5 \tag{5.16}$$

Subtracting x_1 from both sides of the inequality places both variables on the left-hand side of the inequality. Thus,

$$-x_1 + x_2 \leq -5 \tag{5.17}$$

Since this is a constraint with a negative right-hand-side value, we can develop an equivalent constraint with a nonnegative right-hand-side value by multiplying both sides of the constraint by -1. In doing so, we recognize that multiplying an inequality constraint by -1 changes the direction of the inequality.

Thus, to convert inequality (5.17) to an equivalent constraint with a nonnegative right-hand-side value, we multiply by -1 to obtain

$$x_1 - x_2 \geq 5 \tag{5.18}$$

We now have an acceptable nonnegative right-hand-side value. Tableau form for this constraint can now be obtained by subtracting a surplus variable and adding an artificial variable.

For a greater-than-or-equal-to constraint, multiplying by -1 creates an equivalent less-than-or-equal-to constraint. For example, suppose we had the following greater-than-or-equal-to constraint:

$$6x_1 + 3x_2 - 4x_3 \geq -20$$

Multiplying by -1 to obtain an equivalent constraint with a nonnegative right-hand-side value leads to the following less-than-or-equal-to constraint

$$-6x_1 - 3x_2 + 4x_3 \leq 20$$

Tableau form can be created for this constraint by adding a slack variable.

For an equality constraint with a negative right-hand-side value, we simply multiply by -1 to obtain an equivalent constraint with a nonnegative right-hand-side value. An artificial variable can then be added to create the tableau form.

Summary of the Steps to Create Tableau Form

Step 1   If the original formulation of the linear programming problem contains one or more constraints with negative right-hand-side values, multiply each of these constraints by -1. Doing this will change the direction of the inequalities. This step will provide an equivalent linear program with nonnegative right-hand-side values.

Step 2   For $\leq$ constraints, add a slack variable to obtain an equality constraint. The coefficient of the slack variable in the objective function is assigned a value of zero. This provides the tableau form for the constraint, and the slack variable becomes one of the basic variables in the initial basic feasible solution.

Step 3   For $\geq$ constraints, subtract a surplus variable to obtain an equality constraint, and then add an artificial variable to obtain the tableau form. The coefficient of the surplus variable in the objective function is assigned a value of zero. The coefficient of the artificial variable in the objective function is assigned a value of $-M$. The artificial variable becomes one of the basic variables in the initial basic feasible solution.

Step 4   For equality constraints, add an artificial variable to obtain the tableau form. The coefficient of the artificial variable in the objective function is assigned a value of $-M$. The artificial variable becomes one of the basic variables in the initial basic feasible solution.

To obtain some practice in applying these steps, convert the following example problem into tableau form, and then set up the initial simplex tableau:

$$\text{Max} \quad 6x_1 + 3x_2 + 4x_3 + 1x_4$$

s.t.

$$-2x_1 - \tfrac{1}{2}x_2 + 1x_3 - 6x_4 = -60$$

$$1x_1 \qquad\qquad + 1x_3 + \tfrac{2}{3}x_4 \leq 20$$

$$-\ 1x_2 - 5x_3 \qquad\qquad \leq -50$$

$$x_1, x_2, x_3, x_4 \geq 0$$

To eliminate the negative right-hand-side values in constraints 1 and 3, we apply step 1. Multiplying both constraints by -1, we obtain the following equivalent linear program:

$$\text{Max} \quad 6x_1 + 3x_2 + 4x_3 + 1x_4$$

s.t.

$$2x_1 + \tfrac{1}{2}x_2 - 1x_3 + 6x_4 = 60$$
$$1x_1 \qquad\quad + 1x_3 + \tfrac{2}{3}x_4 \le 20$$
$$1x_2 + 5x_3 \qquad\qquad \ge 50$$
$$x_1, x_2, x_3, x_4 \ge 0$$

Note that the direction of the $\le$ inequality in constraint 3 has been reversed as a result of multiplying the constraint by -1. By applying step 4 for constraint 1, step 2 for constraint 2, and step 3 for constraint 3, we obtain the following tableau form:

$$\text{Max} \quad 6x_1 + 3x_2 + 4x_3 + 1x_4 + 0s_2 + 0s_3 - Ma_1 - Ma_3$$

s.t.

$$2x_1 + \tfrac{1}{2}x_2 - 1x_3 + 6x_4 \qquad\qquad + 1a_1 \qquad = 60$$
$$1x_1 \qquad\quad + 1x_3 + \tfrac{2}{3}x_4 + 1s_2 \qquad\qquad = 20$$
$$1x_2 + 5x_3 \qquad\qquad - 1s_3 \qquad + 1a_3 = 50$$
$$x_1, x_2, x_3, x_4, s_2, s_3, a_1, a_3 \ge 0$$

The initial simplex tableau corresponding to this tableau form is

Basis	c_B	x_1 6	x_2 3	x_3 4	x_4 1	s_2 0	s_3 0	a_1 $-M$	a_3 $-M$	
a_1	$-M$	2	$\tfrac{1}{2}$	-1	⑥	0	0	1	0	60
s_2	0	1	0	1	$\tfrac{2}{3}$	1	0	0	0	20
a_3	$-M$	0	1	5	0	0	-1	0	1	50
z_j		$-2M$	$-\tfrac{3}{2}M$	$-4M$	$-6M$	0	M	$-M$	$-M$	$-110M$
$c_j - z_j$		$6 + 2M$	$3 + \tfrac{3}{2}M$	$4 + 4M$	$1 + 6M$	0	$-M$	0	0	

You should now be able to set up tableau form and develop the initial simplex tableau for problems with any constraint form. Try Problem 15.

Note that we have circled the pivot element indicating that x_4 will enter and a_1 will leave the basis at the first iteration.

NOTES & comments

We have shown how to convert constraints with negative right-hand sides to equivalent constraints with positive right-hand sides. Actually, there is nothing wrong with formulating a linear program and including negative right-hand sides. But if you want to use the ordinary simplex method to solve the linear program, you must first alter the constraints to eliminate the negative right-hand sides.

5.7 Solving a Minimization Problem

There are two ways in which we can use the simplex method to solve a minimization problem. The first approach requires that we change the rule used to introduce a variable into the basis. Recall that in the maximization case, we select the variable with the largest positive $c_j - z_j$ as the variable to introduce next into the basis, because the value of $c_j - z_j$ tells us the amount the objective function will increase if one unit of the variable in column j is brought into solution. To solve the minimization problem, we can simply reverse this rule. That is, we can select the variable with the most negative $c_j - z_j$ as the one to introduce next. Of course, this approach means the stopping rule for the optimal solution will also have to be changed. Using this approach to solve a minimization problem, we would stop when every value in the net evaluation row is zero or positive.

The second approach to solving a minimization problem is the one we shall employ in this book. It is based on the fact that any minimization problem can be converted to an equivalent maximization problem by multiplying the objective function by -1. Solving the resulting maximization problem will provide the optimal solution to the minimization problem.

Let us illustrate this second approach by using the simplex method to solve the M&D Chemicals problem introduced in Chapter 2. Recall that in this problem, management wanted to minimize the cost of producing two products subject to a demand constraint for product 1, a minimum total production quantity requirement, and a constraint on available processing time. The mathematical statement of the M&D Chemicals problem is shown below.

$$\text{Min} \quad 2x_1 + 3x_2$$

s.t.

$$
\begin{aligned}
1x_1 &\qquad\qquad \geq 125 & \text{Demand for product 1} \\
1x_1 &+ 1x_2 \geq 350 & \text{Total production} \\
2x_1 &+ 1x_2 \leq 600 & \text{Processing time} \\
x_1, x_2 &\geq 0
\end{aligned}
$$

To solve this problem using the simplex method, we first multiply the objective function by -1 to convert the minimization problem into the following equivalent maximization problem:

$$\text{Max} \quad -2x_1 - 3x_2$$

s.t.

$$
\begin{aligned}
1x_1 &\qquad\qquad \geq 125 & \text{Demand for product 1} \\
1x_1 &+ 1x_2 \geq 350 & \text{Total production} \\
2x_1 &+ 1x_2 \leq 600 & \text{Processing time} \\
x_1, x_2 &\geq 0
\end{aligned}
$$

The tableau form for this problem is as follows:

$$\text{Max} \quad -2x_1 - 3x_2 + 0s_1 + 0s_2 + 0s_3 - Ma_1 - Ma_2$$

s.t.

$$
\begin{aligned}
1x_1 \qquad\quad - 1s_1 \qquad\qquad\qquad + 1a_1 \qquad\quad &= 125 \\
1x_1 + 1x_2 \qquad\quad - 1s_2 \qquad\qquad\qquad + 1a_2 &= 350 \\
2x_1 + 1x_2 \qquad\qquad\qquad + 1s_3 \qquad\qquad\qquad &= 600 \\
x_1, x_2, s_1, s_2, s_3, a_1, a_2 &\geq 0
\end{aligned}
$$

The initial simplex tableau is shown here:

Basis	c_B	x_1 -2	x_2 -3	s_1 0	s_2 0	s_3 0	a_1 $-M$	a_2 $-M$	
a_1	$-M$	①	0	-1	0	0	1	0	125
a_2	$-M$	1	1	0	-1	0	0	1	350
s_3	0	2	1	0	0	1	0	0	600
z_j		$-2M$	$-M$	M	M	0	$-M$	$-M$	$-475M$
$c_j - z_j$		$-2 + 2M$	$-3 + M$	$-M$	$-M$	0	0	0	

At the first iteration, x_1 is brought into the basis and a_1 is removed. After dropping the a_1 column from the tableau, the result of the first iteration is as follows:

Basis	c_B	x_1 -2	x_2 -3	s_1 0	s_2 0	s_3 0	a_2 $-M$	
x_1	-2	1	0	-1	0	0	0	125
a_2	$-M$	0	1	1	-1	0	1	225
s_3	0	0	1	②	0	1	0	350
z_j		-2	$-M$	$2 - M$	M	0	$-M$	$-250 - 225M$
$c_j - z_j$		0	$-3 + M$	$-2 + M$	$-M$	0	0	

Continuing with two more iterations of the simplex method provides the following final simplex tableau:

Basis	c_B	x_1 -2	x_2 -3	s_1 0	s_2 0	s_3 0	
x_1	-2	1	0	0	1	1	250
x_2	-3	0	1	0	-2	-1	100
s_1	0	0	0	1	1	1	125
z_j		-2	-3	0	4	1	-800
$c_j - z_j$		0	0	0	-4	-1	

The value of the objective function -800 must be multiplied by -1 to obtain the value of the objective function for the original minimization problem. Thus, the minimum total cost of the optimal solution is $800.

You should now be able to solve a minimization problem with the simplex method. Try Problem 17.

In the next section we shall discuss some important special cases that may occur when trying to solve any linear programming problem. We will only consider the case for maximization problems, recognizing that all minimization problems may be placed into this form by multiplying the objective function by -1.

5.8 Special Cases

In Chapter 2 we discussed how infeasibility, unboundedness, and alternative optimal solutions could occur when solving linear programming problems using the graphical solution procedure. These special cases can also arise when using the simplex method. In addition, a special case referred to as *degeneracy* can theoretically cause difficulties for the simplex method. In this section we show how these special cases can be recognized and handled when the simplex method is used.

Infeasibility

Infeasibility occurs whenever there is no solution to the linear program that satisfies all the constraints, including the nonnegativity constraints. Let us now see how infeasibility is recognized when the simplex method is used.

In Section 5.6, when discussing artificial variables, we mentioned that infeasibility can be recognized when the optimality criterion indicates that an optimal solution has been obtained and one or more of the artificial variables remain in the solution at a positive value. As an illustration of this situation, let us consider another modification of the HighTech Industries problem. Suppose management had imposed a minimum combined total production requirement of 50 units. The revised problem formulation is shown below.

$$\text{Max} \quad 50x_1 + 40x_2$$
$$\text{s.t.}$$
$$3x_1 + 5x_2 \leq 150 \quad \text{Assembly time}$$
$$1x_2 \leq 20 \quad \text{Portable display}$$
$$8x_1 + 5x_2 \leq 300 \quad \text{Warehouse space}$$
$$1x_1 + 1x_2 \geq 50 \quad \text{Minimum total production}$$
$$x_1, x_2 \geq 0$$

Two iterations of the simplex method will provide the following tableau:

Basis	c_B	x_1 50	x_2 40	s_1 0	s_2 0	s_3 0	s_4 0	a_4 $-M$	
x_2	40	0	1	$8/25$	0	$-3/25$	0	0	**12**
s_2	0	0	0	$-8/25$	1	$3/25$	0	0	**8**
x_1	50	1	0	$-5/25$	0	$5/25$	0	0	**30**
a_4	$-M$	0	0	$-3/25$	0	$-2/25$	-1	1	**8**
z_j		50	40	$\dfrac{70 + 3M}{25}$	0	$\dfrac{130 + 2M}{25}$	M	$-M$	$1980 - 8M$
$c_j - z_j$		0	0	$\dfrac{-70 - 3M}{25}$	0	$\dfrac{-130 - 2M}{25}$	$-M$	0	

Note that $c_j - z_j \leq 0$ for all the variables; therefore, according to the optimality criterion, this should be the optimal solution. But this solution is *not feasible* for the modified HighTech problem because the artificial variable $a_4 = 8$ appears in the solution. The solution $x_1 = 30$ and $x_2 = 12$ results in a combined total production of 42 units instead of the constraint 4 requirement of at least 50 units. The fact that the artificial variable is in solution at a value of $a_4 = 8$ tells us that the final solution violates the fourth constraint $(1x_1 + 1x_2 \geq 50)$ by eight units.

If management is interested in knowing which of the first three constraints is preventing us from satisfying the total production requirement, a partial answer can be obtained from the final simplex tableau. Note that $s_2 = 8$, but that s_1 and s_3 are zero. This tells us that the assembly time and warehouse capacity constraints are binding. Since there are not enough assembly time and warehouse space available, we cannot satisfy the minimum combined total production requirement.

The management implications here are that additional assembly time and/or warehouse space must be made available to satisfy the total production requirement. If more time and/or space cannot be made available, management will have to relax the total production requirement by at least eight units.

In summary, a linear program is infeasible if there is no solution that satisfies all the constraints simultaneously. *We recognize infeasibility when one or more of the artificial variables remain in the final solution at a positive value.* In closing, we note that for linear programming problems with all $\leq$ constraints and nonnegative right-hand sides, there will always be a feasible solution. Since it is not necessary to introduce artificial variables to set up the initial simplex tableau for these types of problems, there cannot possibly be an artificial variable in the final solution.

You should now be able to recognize when there is no feasible solution to a problem using the simplex method. Try Problem 23.

Unboundedness

For maximization problems, we say that a linear program is unbounded if the value of the solution may be made infinitely large without violating any constraints. Thus, when unboundedness occurs, we can generally look for an error in the formulation of the problem.

The coefficients in the column of the $\bar{A}$ matrix associated with the incoming variable indicate how much each of the current basic variables will decrease if one unit of the incoming variable is brought into solution. Suppose then, that for a particular linear programming problem, we reach a point where the rule for determining which variable should enter the basis results in the decision to enter variable x_2. Assume that for this variable, $c_2 - z_2 = 5$, and that all $\bar{a}_{i2}$ in column 2 are ≤ 0. Thus, each unit of x_2 brought into solution increases the objective function by five units. Furthermore, since $\bar{a}_{i2} \leq 0$ for all i, this means that none of the current basic variables will be driven to zero, no matter how many units of x_2 we introduce. Thus, we can introduce an infinite amount of x_2 into solution and still maintain feasibility. Since each unit of x_2 increases the objective function by 5, we will have an unbounded solution. Hence, *the way we recognize the unbounded situation is that all the $\bar{a}_{ij}$ are less than or equal to zero in the column associated with the incoming variable.*

To illustrate this concept, let us consider the example of an unbounded problem we introduced in Chapter 2:

$$\text{Max} \quad 20x_1 + 10x_2$$

$$\text{s.t.} \quad 1x_1 \qquad \geq 2$$

$$1x_2 \leq 5$$

$$x_1, x_2 \geq 0$$

We subtract a surplus variable s_1 from the first constraint equation and add a slack variable s_2 to the second constraint equation to obtain the standard-form representation. We then add an artificial variable a_1 to the first constraint equation to obtain the tableau form and to set up the initial simplex tableau in terms of the basic variables a_1 and s_2. After bringing in x_1 and removing a_1 at the first iteration, the simplex tableau is as follows:

		x_1	x_2	s_1	s_2	
Basis	c_B	20	10	0	0	
x_1	20	1	0	-1	0	2
s_2	0	0	1	0	1	5
z_j		20	0	-20	0	40
$c_j - z_j$		0	10	20	0	

Since s_1 has the largest positive $c_j - z_j$, we know we can increase the value of the objective function most rapidly by bringing s_1 into the basis. But $\bar{a}_{13} = -1$ and $\bar{a}_{23} = 0$; hence, we cannot form the ratio $\bar{b}_i / \bar{a}_{i3}$ for any $\bar{a}_{i3} > 0$; there are no values of $\bar{a}_{i3}$ that are greater than zero. This is the indication that the solution to the linear program is unbounded. The reason the solution is unbounded is that each unit of s_1 that is brought into solution drives zero units of s_2 out of solution (since $\bar{a}_{23} = 0$) and provides one extra unit of x_1 (since $\bar{a}_{13} = -1$). The reason for this is that s_1 is a surplus variable and can be interpreted as the amount of x_1 over the minimum amount required. Since the simplex tableau indicates that we can introduce as much of s_1 as we desire without violating any constraints, this tells us that we can make as much as we want above the minimum amount of x_1 required. Since the objective function coefficient associated with x_1 is positive, there will be no upper bound on the value of the objective function.

In summary, a maximization linear program is unbounded if it is possible to make the value of the optimal solution as large as desired without violating any of the constraints. When employing the simplex solution procedure, an unbounded linear program exists if *at some iteration, the simplex method tells us to introduce variable j into the solution and all the $\bar{a}_{ij}$ are less than or equal to zero in the jth column.*

Try Problem 25 for another example of an unbounded problem.

We emphasize that the case of an unbounded solution will never occur in real cost minimization or profit maximization problems because it is not possible to reduce costs to minus infinity or to increase profits to plus infinity. Thus, if we encounter an unbounded solution to a linear programming problem, we should carefully reexamine the formulation of the problem to determine if a formulation error has occured.

Alternative Optimal Solutions

A linear program with two or more optimal solutions is said to have alternative optimal solutions. When using the simplex method, we cannot recognize that a linear program has alternative optimal solutions until the final simplex tableau is reached. Then if the linear program has alternative optimal solutions, $c_j - z_j$ will equal zero for one or more nonbasic variables.

To illustrate the case of alternative optimal solution when using the simplex method, consider changing the objective function for the HighTech problem from $50x_1 + 40x_2$ to $30x_1 + 50x_2$; in doing so, we obtain the revised linear program:

$$\text{Max} \quad 30x_1 + 50x_2$$

s.t.

$$3x_1 + 5x_2 \leq 150$$

$$1x_2 \leq 20$$

$$8x_1 + 5x_2 \leq 300$$

$$x_1, x_2 \geq 0$$

The final simplex tableau for this problem is shown here:

Basis	c_B	x_1 30	x_2 50	s_1 0	s_2 0	s_3 0	
x_2	50	0	1	0	1	0	**20**
s_3	0	0	0	$-8/3$	$25/3$	1	$200/3$
x_1	30	1	0	$1/3$	$-5/3$	0	$50/3$
z_j		30	50	10	0	0	**1500**
$c_j - z_j$		0	0	-10	0	0	

All values in the net evaluation row are less than or equal to zero, indicating that an optimal solution has been found. This solution is given by $x_1 = 50/3$, $x_2 = 20$, $s_1 = 0$, $s_2 = 0$, and $s_3 = 200/3$. The value of the objective function is 1500.

In looking at the net evaluation row in the optimal simplex tableau, we see that the $c_j - z_j$ value for nonbasic variable s_2 is equal to zero. This indicates that the linear program may have alternative optimal solutions. In other words, since the net evaluation row entry for s_2 is zero, we can introduce s_2 into the basis without changing the value of the solution. The tableau obtained after introducing s_2 follows:

Basis	c_B	x_1 30	x_2 50	s_1 0	s_2 0	s_3 0	
x_2	50	0	1	$8/25$	0	$-3/25$	**12**
s_2	0	0	0	$-8/25$	1	$3/25$	**8**
x_1	30	1	0	$-5/25$	0	$5/25$	**30**
z_j		30	50	10	0	0	**1500**
$c_j - z_j$		0	0	-10	0	0	

As shown, we have a different basic feasible solution: $x_1 = 30$, $x_2 = 12$, $s_1 = 0$, $s_2 = 8$, and $s_3 = 0$. However, this new solution is also optimal since $c_j - z_j \leq 0$ for all j. Another way to confirm that this solution is still optimal is to note that the value of the solution has remained equal to 1500.

Try Problem 24 for another example of alternative optimal solutions.

In summary, *when using the simplex method, we can recognize the possibility of alternative optimal solutions if $c_j - z_j$ equals zero for one or more of the nonbasic variables in the final simplex tableau.*

Degeneracy

A linear program is said to be *degenerate* if one or more of the basic variables have a value of zero. Degeneracy does not cause any particular difficulties for the graphical solution procedure; however, degeneracy can theoretically cause difficulties when the simplex method is used to solve a linear programming problem.

To see how a degenerate linear program could occur, consider a change in the right-hand-side value of the assembly time constraint for the HighTech problem. For example, what if the number of hours available had been 175 instead of 150? The modified linear program is shown below.

$$\text{Max} \quad 50x_1 + 40x_2$$

s.t.

$$3x_1 + 5x_2 \leq 175 \qquad \text{Assembly time increased to 175 hours}$$

$$1x_2 \leq 20 \qquad \text{Portable display}$$

$$8x_1 + 5x_2 \leq 300 \qquad \text{Warehouse space}$$

$$x_1, x_2 \geq 0$$

The simplex tableau after one iteration is as follows:

		x_1	x_2	s_1	s_2	s_3	
Basis	c_B	50	40	0	0	0	
s_1	0	0	25/8	1	0	$-3/8$	125/2
s_2	0	0	1	0	1	0	**20**
x_1	50	1	5/8	0	0	1/8	75/2
z_j		50	250/8	0	0	50/8	**1875**
$c_j - z_j$		0	70/8	0	0	$-50/8$	

The entries in the net evaluation row indicate that x_2 should enter the basis. By calculating the appropriate ratios to determine the pivot row, we obtain

$$\frac{\bar{b}_1}{\bar{a}_{12}} = \frac{125/2}{25/8} = 20$$

$$\frac{\bar{b}_2}{\bar{a}_{22}} = \frac{20}{1} = 20$$

$$\frac{\bar{b}_3}{\bar{a}_{32}} = \frac{75/2}{5/8} = 60$$

We see that there is a tie between the first and second rows. This is an indication that we will have a degenerate basic feasible solution at the next iteration. Recall that when there is a tie, we follow the convention of selecting the uppermost row as the pivot row. This means that s_1 will leave the basis. But from the tie for the minimum ratio we see that the basic variable in row 2, s_2, will also be driven to zero. Since it does not leave the basis, we will have a basic variable with a value of zero after performing this iteration. The simplex tableau after this iteration is as follows:

Basis	c_B	x_1 50	x_2 40	s_1 0	s_2 0	s_3 0	
x_2	40	0	1	$8/25$	0	$-3/25$	**20**
s_2	0	0	0	$-8/25$	1	$3/25$	**0**
x_1	50	1	0	$-5/25$	0	$5/25$	**25**
z_j		50	40	$70/25$	0	$130/25$	**2050**
$c_j - z_j$		0	0	$-70/25$	0	$-130/25$	

As expected, we have a basic feasible solution with one of the basic variables, s_2, equal to zero. Whenever we have a tie in the minimum $\bar{b}_i/\bar{a}_{ij}$ ratio, there will always be a basic variable equal to zero in the next tableau. Since we are at the optimal solution in the preceding case, we do not care that s_2 is in solution at a zero value. However, if degeneracy occurs at some iteration prior to reaching the optimal solution, it is theoretically possible for the simplex method to cycle; that is, the procedure could possibly alternate between the same set of nonoptimal basic feasible solutions and never reach the optimal solution. Cycling has not proven to be a significant difficulty in practice. Therefore, we do not recommend introducing any special steps into the simplex method to eliminate the possibility that degeneracy will occur. If while performing the iterations of the simplex algorithm a tie occurs for the minimum $\bar{b}_i/\bar{a}_{ij}$ ratio, then we recommend simply selecting the upper row as the pivot row.

NOTES & comments

1. We have stated that infeasibility is recognized when the stopping rule is encountered but one or more artificial variables are in solution at a positive value. This does not necessarily mean that all artificial variables must be nonbasic to have a feasible solution. An artificial variable could be in solution at a zero value.

2. An unbounded feasible region must exist for a problem to be unbounded, but this does not guarantee that a problem will be unbounded. A minimization problem may be bounded whereas a maximization problem is unbounded with the same feasible region.

Summary

In this chapter the simplex method was introduced as an algebraic procedure for solving linear programming problems. Although the simplex method can be used to solve small linear programs by hand calculations, this becomes too cumbersome as problems get larger. As a result, we must utilize a computer if we want to solve large linear programs in any reasonable length of time. The computational procedures of most computer software packages are based on the simplex method.

We described how developing the tableau form of a linear program is a necessary step in the simplex solution procedure, including how to convert greater-than-or-equal-to constraints, equality constraints, and constraints with negative right-hand-side values into tableau form.

For linear programs with greater-than-or-equal-to constraints and/or equality constraints, artificial variables are used to obtain tableau form. An objective function coefficient of $-M$, where M is a very large number, is assigned to each artificial variable. If there is a feasible solution to the real problem, all artificial variables will be driven out of solution (or to zero) before the simplex method reaches its optimality criterion. The iterations required to remove the artificial variables from solution constitute what is called phase I of the simplex method.

Two techniques were mentioned for solving minimization problems. The first approach involved changing the rule for introducing a variable into solution (choose the most negative $c_j - z_j$) and changing the optimality criterion (all $c_j - z_j \geq 0$). The second approach involved multiplying the objective function by -1 to obtain an equivalent maximization problem. With this change, any minimization problem can be solved using the steps required for a maximization problem, but the value of the optimal solution must be multiplied by (-1) to obtain the optimal value of the original minimization problem.

As a review of the material in this chapter we now present a detailed step-by-step procedure for solving linear programs using the simplex method.

Step 1   Formulate a linear programming model of the problem.

Step 2   Define an equivalent linear program by performing the following operations:

   a. Multiply each constraint with a negative right-hand-side value by -1, and change the direction of the constraint inequality.
   b. For a minimization problem, convert the problem to an equivalent maximization problem by multiplying the objective function by -1.

Step 3   Set up the standard form of the linear program by adding appropriate slack and surplus variables.

Step 4   Set up the tableau form of the linear program to obtain an initial basic feasible solution. All linear programs must be set up this way before the initial simplex tableau can be obtained.

Step 5   Set up the initial simplex tableau to keep track of the calculations required by the simplex method.

Step 6   Choose the nonbasic variable with the largest $c_j - z_j$ to bring into the basis. The column associated with that variable is the pivot column.

Step 7   Choose as the pivot row that row with the smallest ratio of $\bar{b}_i / \bar{a}_{ij}$ for $\bar{a}_{ij} > 0$. This ratio is used to determine which variable will leave the basis when variable j enters the basis. This ratio also indicates how many units of variable j can be introduced into solution before the basic variable in the ith row equals zero.

Step 8   Perform the necessary elementary row operations to convert the pivot column to a unit column.

   a. Divide each element in the pivot row by the pivot element. The result is a new pivot row containing a 1 in the pivot column.
   b. Obtain zeroes in all other positions of the pivot column by adding or subtracting an appropriate multiple of the new pivot row.

Step 9   Test for optimality. If $c_j - z_j \leq 0$ for all columns, we have the optimal solution. If not, return to step 6.

In Section 5.8 we discussed how the special cases of infeasibility, unboundedness, alternative optimal solutions, and degeneracy can occur when solving linear programming problems with the simplex method.

Glossary

Simplex method An algebraic procedure for solving linear programming problems. The simplex method uses elementary row operations to iterate from one basic feasible solution (extreme point) to another until the optimal solution is reached.

Basic solution Given a linear program in standard form, with n variables and m constraints, a basic solution is a solution obtained by setting $n - m$ of the variables equal to zero and solving the constraint equations for the values of the other m variables. If a unique solution exists, it is a basic solution.

Nonbasic variable One of $n - m$ variables set equal to zero in a basic solution.

Basic variable One of the m variables not required to equal zero in a basic solution.

Basic feasible solution A basic solution that is also feasible; that is, it satisfies the nonnegativity constraints. A basic feasible solution corresponds to an extreme point.

Tableau form The form in which a linear program must be written before setting up the initial simplex tableau. When a linear program is written in tableau form, its A matrix contains m unit columns corresponding to the basic variables, and the values of these basic variables are given by the values in the b column. A further requirement is that the entries in the b column be greater than or equal to zero.

Simplex tableau A table used to keep track of the calculations made when the simplex method is employed.

Unit vector or unit column A vector or column of a matrix that has a zero in every position except one. In the nonzero position there is a 1. There is a unit column in the simplex tableau for each basic variable.

Basis The set of variables that are not restricted to equal zero in the current basic solution. The variables that make up the basis are termed basic variables, and the remaining variables are called nonbasic variables.

Net evaluation row The row in the simplex tableau that contains the value of $c_j - z_j$ for every variable (column).

Elementary row operations Operations that may be performed on a system of simultaneous equations without changing the solution to the system of equations.

Iteration An iteration of the simplex method consists of the sequence of elementary row operations performed in moving from one basic feasible solution to another.

Pivot column The column in the simplex tableau corresponding to the nonbasic variable that is about to be introduced into solution.

Pivot row The row in the simplex tableau corresponding to the basic variable that will leave the solution.

Pivot element The element of the simplex tableau that is in both the pivot row and the pivot column.

Artificial variable A variable that has no physical meaning in terms of the original linear programming problem, but serves merely to enable a basic feasible solution to be created for starting the simplex method. Artificial variables are assigned an objective function coefficient of $-M$, where M is a very large number.

Phase I When artificial variables are present in the initial simplex tableau, phase I refers to the iterations of the simplex method that are used to drive the artificial variables out of solution. At the end of phase I, the basic feasible solution in the simplex tableau is also feasible for the real problem.

Degeneracy When one or more of the basic variables has a value of zero.

Problems

1. **SELFTest** Consider the following system of linear equations:

$$3x_1 + x_2 = 6$$
$$2x_1 + 4x_2 + x_3 = 12$$

    a. Find the basic solution with $x_1 = 0$.
    b. Find the basic solution with $x_2 = 0$.
    c. Find the basic solution with $x_3 = 0$.
    d. Which of the above would be basic feasible solutions for a linear program?

2. Consider the following linear program:

$$\text{Max} \quad x_1 + 2x_2$$

$$\text{s.t.}$$

$$x_1 + 5x_2 \leq 10$$

$$2x_1 + 6x_2 \leq 16$$

$$x_1, x_2 \geq 0$$

    a. Write the problem in standard form.
    b. How many variables will be set equal to zero in a basic solution for this problem?
    c. Find all the basic solutions, and indicate which are also feasible.
    d. Find the optimal solution by computing the value of each basic feasible solution.

3. Consider the following linear program:

$$\text{Max} \quad 5x_1 + 9x_2$$

$$\text{s.t.}$$

$$\tfrac{1}{2}x_1 + 1x_2 \leq 8$$

$$1x_1 + 1x_2 \geq 10$$

$$\tfrac{1}{4}x_1 + \tfrac{3}{2}x_2 \geq 6$$

$$x_1, x_2 \geq 0$$

    a. Write the problem in standard form.
    b. How many variables will be set equal to zero in a basic solution for this problem? Explain.
    c. Find the basic solution that corresponds to s_1 and s_2 equal to zero.
    d. Find the basic solution that corresponds to x_1 and s_3 equal to zero.
    e. Are your solutions for part (c) and/or (d) basic feasible solutions? Extreme-point solutions? Explain.
    f. Use the graphical approach to identify the solutions found in parts (c) and (d). Do the graphical results agree with your answer to part (e)? Explain.

4. **SELF Test** Consider the following linear programming problem:

$$\text{Max} \quad 60x_1 + 90x_2$$

$$\text{s.t.}$$

$$15x_1 + 45x_2 \leq 90$$

$$5x_1 + 5x_2 \leq 20$$

$$x_1, x_2 \geq 0$$

    a. Write the problem in standard form.
    b. Develop the portion of the simplex tableau involving the objective function coefficients, the coefficients of the variables in the constraints, and the constants for the right-hand sides.

5. A partially completed initial simplex tableau is given:

Basis	c_B	x_1	x_2	s_1	s_2	
		5	9	0	0	
s_1	0	10	9	1	0	90
s_2	0	-5	3	0	1	15
z_j						
$c_j - z_j$						

a. Complete the initial tableau.
b. Which variable would be brought into solution at the first iteration?
c. Write the original linear program.

6. The following partial initial simplex tableau is given:
a. Complete the initial tableau.
b. Write the problem in tableau form.
c. What is the initial basis? Does this correspond to the origin? Explain.
d. What is the value of the objective function at this initial solution?
e. For the next iteration, which variable should enter the basis, and which variable should leave the basis?
f. How many units of the entering variable will be in the next solution? Before making this first iteration, what do you think will be the value of the objective function after the first iteration?

Basis	c_B	x_1	x_2	x_3	s_1	s_2	s_3	
		5	20	25	0	0	0	
		2	1	0	1	0	0	40
		0	2	1	0	1	0	30
		3	0	$-\frac{1}{2}$	0	0	1	15
z_j								
$c_j - z_j$								

g. Find the optimal solution using the simplex method.

7. Solve the following linear program using the graphical approach:

$$\text{Max} \quad 4x_1 + 5x_2$$

s.t.

$$2x_1 + 2x_2 \leq 20$$

$$3x_1 + 7x_2 \leq 42$$

$$x_1, x_2 \geq 0$$

Put the linear program in tableau form, and solve using the simplex method. Show the sequence of extreme points generated by the simplex method on your graph.

8. Recall the problem for Par, Inc., introduced in Section 2.1. The mathematical model for this problem, is restated below:

$$\text{Max} \quad 10x_1 + 9x_2$$

s.t.

$$\begin{array}{ll} \frac{7}{10}x_1 + 1x_2 \leq 630 & \text{Cutting and dyeing} \\ \frac{1}{2}x_1 + \frac{5}{6}x_2 \leq 600 & \text{Sewing} \\ 1x_1 + \frac{2}{3}x_2 \leq 708 & \text{Finishing} \\ \frac{1}{10}x_1 + \frac{1}{4}x_2 \leq 135 & \text{Inspection and packaging} \\ x_1, x_2 \geq 0 \end{array}$$

where

x_1 = number of standard bags produced

x_2 = number of deluxe bags produced

   a. Use the simplex method to determine how many bags of each model Par should manufacture.
   b. What is the profit Par can earn with these production quantities?
   c. How many hours of production time will be scheduled for each operation?
   d. What is the slack time in each operation?

9. Solve the RMC problem (Chapter 2, Problem 21) using the simplex method. At each iteration, locate the basic feasible solution found by the simplex method on the graph of the feasible region. The problem formulation is shown below:

$$\text{Max} \quad 40x_1 + 30x_2$$

s.t.

$$\begin{array}{ll} \frac{2}{5}x_1 + \frac{1}{2}x_2 \leq 20 & \text{Material 1} \\ \frac{1}{5}x_2 \leq 5 & \text{Material 2} \\ \frac{3}{5}x_1 + \frac{3}{10}x_2 \leq 21 & \text{Material 3} \\ x_1, x_2 \geq 0 \end{array}$$

where

x_1 = tons of fuel additive produced

x_2 = tons of solvent base produced

10. Solve the following linear program:

$$\text{Max} \quad 5x_1 + 5x_2 + 24x_3$$

s.t.

$$\begin{array}{l} 15x_1 + 4x_2 + 12x_3 \leq 2800 \\ 15x_1 + 8x_2 \qquad\quad \leq 6000 \\ x_1 \qquad\quad + 8x_3 \leq 1200 \\ x_1, x_2, x_3 \geq 0 \end{array}$$

11. Solve the following linear program using both the graphical and the simplex methods:

$$\text{Max} \quad 2x_1 + 8x_2$$

s.t.

$$3x_1 + 9x_2 \leq 45$$

$$2x_1 + 1x_2 \geq 12$$

$$x_1, x_2 \geq 0$$

Show graphically how the simplex method moves from one basic feasible solution to another. Find the coordinates of all extreme points of the feasible region.

12. Suppose a company manufactures three products from two raw materials. The amount of raw material in each unit of each product is given.

Raw Material	Product A	Product B	Product C
I	7 lb	6 lb	3 lb
II	5 lb	4 lb	2 lb

If the company has available 100 pounds of material I and 200 pounds of material II, and if the profits for the three products are $20, $20, and $15 respectively, how much of each product should be produced to maximize profits?

13. Liva's Lumber, Inc., manufactures three types of plywood. The following table summarizes the production hours per unit in each of three production operations and other data for the problem.

Plywood	Operations (hours)			Profit/Unit
	I	II	III	
Grade A	2	2	4	$40
Grade B	5	5	2	$30
Grade X	10	3	2	$20
Maximum time available	900	400	600	

How many units of each grade of lumber should be produced?

14. Ye Olde Cording Winery in Peoria, Illinois, makes three kinds of authentic German wine: Heidelberg Sweet, Heidelberg Regular, and Deutschland Extra Dry. The raw materials, labor, and profit for a gallon of each of these wines are summarized here:

Wine	Grade A Grapes (bushels)	Grade B Grapes (bushels)	Sugar (pounds)	Labor (hours)	Profit/ Gallon
Heidelberg Sweet	1	1	2	2	$1.00
Heidelberg Regular	2	0	1	3	$1.20
Deutschland Extra Dry	0	2	0	1	$2.00

If the winery has 150 bushels of grade A grapes, 150 bushels of grade B grapes, 80 pounds of sugar, and 225 labor-hours available during the next week, what product mix of wines will maximize the company's profit?

a. Solve using the simplex method.

b. Interpret all slack variables.

c. An increase in what resources could improve the company's profit?

15. **SELF**Test Set up the tableau form for the following linear program (do not attempt to solve):

$$\text{Max} \quad 4x_1 + 2x_2 - 3x_3 + 5x_4$$

s.t.

$$2x_1 - 1x_2 + 1x_3 + 2x_4 \geq 50$$
$$3x_1 \qquad - 1x_3 + 2x_4 \leq 80$$
$$1x_1 + 1x_2 \qquad + 1x_4 = 60$$

$$x_1, x_2, x_3, x_4 \geq 0$$

16. Set up the tableau form for the following linear program (do not attempt to solve):

$$\text{Min} \quad 4x_1 + 5x_2 + 3x_3$$

s.t.

$$4x_1 \qquad + 2x_3 \geq 20$$
$$1x_2 - 1x_3 \leq -8$$
$$1x_1 - 2x_2 \qquad = -5$$
$$2x_1 + 1x_2 + 1x_3 \leq 12$$

$$x_1, x_2, x_3 \geq 0$$

17. **SELF**Test Solve the following linear program:

$$\text{Min} \quad 3x_1 + 4x_2 + 8x_3$$

s.t.

$$4x_1 + 2x_2 \qquad \geq 12$$
$$4x_2 + 8x_3 \geq 16$$

$$x_1, x_2, x_3 \geq 0$$

unbounded

18. Solve the following linear program:

$$\text{Min} \quad 84x_1 + 4x_2 + 30x_3$$

s.t.

$$8x_1 + 1x_2 + 3x_3 \leq 240$$
$$16x_1 + 1x_2 + 7x_3 \geq 480$$
$$8x_1 - 1x_2 + 4x_3 \geq 160$$

$$x_1, x_2, x_3 \geq 0$$

19. Captain John's Yachts, Inc., located in Fort Lauderdale, Florida, rents three types of ocean-going boats: sailboats, cabin cruisers, and Captain John's favorite, the luxury yachts. Captain John advertises his boats with his famous "you rent—we pilot" slogan, which means that the company supplies the captain and crew for each rented boat. Each rented boat has one captain, of course, but the crew sizes (deck hands, galley hands, etc.) differ. The crew requirements, in addition to a captain, are one for sailboats, two for cabin cruisers, and three for yachts. Ten employees are captains, and an additional 18 employees fill the various crew positions. Currently, Captain John has rental requests for all of his boats: four sailboats, eight cabin cruisers, and three luxury yachts. If Captain John's daily profit contribution is $50 for sailboats, $70 for cruisers, and $100 for luxury yachts, how many boats of each type should he rent?

20. The Our-Bags-Don't-Break (OBDB) plastic bag company manufactures three plastic refuse bags for home use: a 20-gallon garbage bag, a 30-gallon garbage bag, and a 33-gallon leaf-and-grass bag. Using purchased plastic material, three operations are required to produce each end product: cutting, sealing, and packaging. The production time required to process each type of bag in every operation and the maximum production time available for each operation are shown (note that the production time figures in this table are per box of each type of bag).

	Production Time (seconds/box)		
Type of Bag	Cutting	Sealing	Packaging
20 gallons	2	2	3
30 gallons	3	2	4
33 gallons	3	3	5
Time available	2 hours	3 hours	4 hours

If OBDB's profit contribution is $0.10 for each box of 20-gallon bags produced, $0.15 for each box of 30-gallon bags, and $0.20 for each box of 33-gallon bags, what is the optimal product mix?

21. Kirkman Brothers ice cream parlors sell three different flavors of Dairy Sweet ice milk: chocolate, vanilla, and banana. Due to extremely hot weather and a high demand for its products, Kirkman has run short of its supply of ingredients: milk, sugar, and cream. Hence, Kirkman will not be able to fill all the orders received from its retail outlets, the ice cream parlors. Due to these circumstances, Kirkman has decided to make the most profitable amounts of the three flavors, given the constraints on supply of the basic ingredients. The company will then ration the ice milk to the retail outlets.

Kirkman has collected the following data on profitability of the various flavors, availability of supplies, and amounts required for each flavor.

		Usage/Gallon		
Flavor	**Profit/ Gallon**	Milk (gallons)	Sugar (pounds)	Cream (gallons)
Chocolate	$1.00	0.45	0.50	0.10
Vanilla	$0.90	0.50	0.40	0.15
Banana	$0.95	0.40	0.40	0.20
Maximum available		200	150	60

Determine the optimal product mix for Kirkman Brothers. What additional resources could be used profitably?

22. Uforia Corporation sells two different brands of perfume: Incentive and Temptation No. 1. Uforia sells exclusively through department stores and employs a three-person sales staff to call on its customers. The amount of time necessary for each sales representative to sell one case of each product varies with experience and ability. Data on the average time for each of Uforia's three sales representatives is presented here.

Salesperson	Average Sales Time per Case (minutes)	
	Incentive	Temptation No. 1
John	10	15
Brenda	15	10
Red	12	6

Each sales representative spends approximately 80 hours per month in the actual selling of these two products. Cases of Incentive and Temptation No. 1 sell at profits of $30 and $25, respectively. How many cases of each perfume should each person sell during the next month to maximize the firm's profits? (Hint: Let x_1 = number of cases of Incentive sold by John, x_2 = number of cases of Temptation No. 1 sold by John, x_3 = number of cases of Incentive sold by Brenda, etc.)

Note: In Problems 23–29, we provide examples of linear programs that result in one or more of the following situations:
1. Optimal solution
2. Infeasible solution
3. Unbounded solution
4. Alternative optimal solutions
5. Degenerate solution

For each linear program, determine the solution situation that exists, and indicate how you identified each situation using the simplex method. For the problems with alternative optimal solutions, calculate at least two optimal solutions.

23.

$$\text{Max} \quad 4x_1 + 8x_2$$

s.t.

$$2x_1 + 2x_2 \le 10$$

$$-1x_1 + 1x_2 \ge 8$$

$$x_1, x_2 \ge 0$$

24.

$$\text{Min} \quad 3x_1 + 3x_2$$

s.t.

$$2x_1 + 0.5x_2 \ge 10$$

$$2x_1 \qquad \ge 4$$

$$4x_1 + 4x_2 \ge 32$$

$$x_1, x_2 \ge 0$$

25.

$$\text{Max} \quad 1x_1 + 1x_2$$

s.t.

$$8x_1 + 6x_2 \geq 24$$
$$4x_1 + 6x_2 \geq -12$$
$$2x_2 \geq 4$$
$$x_1, x_2 \geq 0$$

Unbounded

26.

$$\text{Max} \quad 2x_1 + 1x_2 + 1x_3$$

s.t.

$$4x_1 + 2x_2 + 2x_3 \geq 4$$
$$2x_1 + 4x_2 \leq 20$$
$$4x_1 + 8x_2 + 2x_3 \leq 16$$
$$x_1, x_2, x_3 \geq 0$$

optimal solution

27.

$$\text{Max} \quad 2x_1 + 4x_2$$

s.t.

$$1x_1 + \tfrac{1}{2}x_2 \leq 10$$
$$1x_1 + 1x_2 = 12$$
$$1x_1 + \tfrac{3}{2}x_2 \leq 18$$
$$x_1, x_2 \geq 0$$

Degenerous

28.

$$\text{Min} \quad -4x_1 + 5x_2 + 5x_3$$

s.t.

$$1x_2 + 1x_3 \geq 2$$
$$-1x_1 + 1x_2 + 1x_3 \geq 1$$
$$-1x_3 \geq 1$$
$$x_1, x_2, x_3 \geq 0$$

29. Solve the following linear program and identify any alternative solutions.

$$\text{Max} \quad 120x_1 + 80x_2 + 14x_3$$

s.t.

$$4x_1 + 8x_2 + x_3 \leq 200$$
$$2x_2 + 1x_3 \leq 300$$
$$32x_1 + 4x_2 + 2x_3 = 400$$
$$x_1, x_2, x_3 \geq 0$$

30. Supersport Footballs, Inc., manufactures three kinds of football: an All-Pro model, a College model, and a High School model. All three footballs require operations in the following departments: cutting and dyeing, sewing, and inspection and packaging. The production times and maximum production availabilities are shown below.

	Production Time (minutes)		
Model	Cutting and Dyeing	Sewing	Inspection and Packaging
All-Pro	12	15	3
College	10	15	4
High School	8	12	2
Time available	300 hours	200 hours	100 hours

Current orders indicate that at least 1000 All-Pro footballs must be manufactured.

a. If Supersport realizes a profit contribution of $3 for each All-Pro model, $5 for each College model, and $4 for each High School model, how many footballs of each type should be produced? What occurs in the solution of this problem? Why?

b. If Supersport can increase sewing time to 300 hours and inspection and packaging time to 150 hours by using overtime, what is your recommendation?

six

Simplex-Based Sensitivity Analysis and Duality

In Chapter 2 we defined sensitivity analysis as the study of how the optimal solution and the value of the optimal solution to a linear program change, given changes in the various coefficients of the problem. In this chapter we discuss how sensitivity analysis information such as the ranges for the objective function coefficients, dual prices, and the ranges for the right-hand-side values can be obtained from the final simplex tableau. The topic of duality is also introduced. We will see that associated with every linear programming problem is a dual problem that has an interesting economic interpretation.

6.1 Sensitivity Analysis with the Simplex Tableau

The usual sensitivity analysis for linear programs involves computing ranges for the objective function coefficients and the right-hand-side values, as well as the dual prices.

Objective Function Coefficients

Sensitivity analysis for an objective function coefficient involves placing a range on the coefficient's value. We call this range the *range of optimality*. As long as the actual value of the objective function coefficient is within the range of optimality, *the current basic feasible solution will remain optimal.* The range of optimality for a basic variable defines the objective function coefficient values for which that variable will remain part of the current optimal basic feasible solution. The range of optimality for a nonbasic variable defines the objective function coefficient values for which that variable will remain nonbasic.

In computing the range of optimality for an objective function coefficient, all other coefficients in the problem are assumed to remain at their original values; in other words, *only one coefficient is allowed to change at a time.* To illustrate the process of computing ranges for objective function coefficients, recall the HighTech Industries problem introduced in Chapter 5. The linear program for this problem is restated as follows:

$$\text{Max} \quad 50x_1 + 40x_2$$

s.t.

$$3x_1 + 5x_2 \leq 150 \quad \text{Assembly time}$$
$$1x_2 \leq 20 \quad \text{Portable display}$$
$$8x_1 + 5x_2 \leq 300 \quad \text{Warehouse capacity}$$
$$x_1, x_2 \geq 0$$

where

$$x_1 = \text{number of units of the Deskpro}$$
$$x_2 = \text{number of units of the Portable}$$

The final simplex tableau for the HighTech problem is as follows.

Basis	c_B	x_1 50	x_2 40	s_1 0	s_2 0	s_3 0	
x_2	40	0	1	$8/25$	0	$-3/25$	**12**
s_2	0	0	0	$-8/25$	1	$3/25$	**8**
x_1	50	1	0	$-5/25$	0	$5/25$	**30**
z_j		50	40	$14/5$	0	$26/5$	**1980**
$c_j - z_j$		0	0	$-14/5$	0	$-26/5$	

Recall that when the simplex method is used to solve a linear program, an optimal solution is recognized when all entries in the net evaluation row ($c_j - z_j$) are ≤ 0. Since the preceding simplex tableau satisfies this criterion, the solution shown is optimal. However, if a change in one of the objective function coefficients were to cause one or more of the $c_j - z_j$ values to become positive, then the current solution would no longer be optimal; in such a case, one or more additional simplex iterations would be necessary to find the new optimal solution. *The range of optimality for an objective function coefficient, then, is determined by those coefficient values that maintain*

$$c_j - z_j \leq 0 \tag{6.1}$$

for all values of j.

Let us illustrate this approach by computing the range of optimality for c_1, the profit contribution per unit of the Deskpro. Using c_1 (instead of 50) as the objective function coefficient of x_1, the final simplex tableau is as follows:

Basis	c_B	x_1 c_1	x_2 40	s_1 0	s_2 0	s_3 0	
x_2	40	0	1	$8/25$	0	$-3/25$	**12**
s_2	0	0	0	$-8/25$	1	$3/25$	**8**
x_1	c_1	1	0	$-5/25$	0	$5/25$	**30**
z_j		c_1	40	$\dfrac{64 - c_1}{5}$	0	$\dfrac{c_1 - 24}{5}$	**$480 + 30c_1$**
$c_j - z_j$		0	0	$\dfrac{c_1 - 64}{5}$	0	$\dfrac{24 - c_1}{5}$	

Note that this tableau is the same as the previous optimal tableau except that c_1 replaces 50. Thus, we have a c_1 in the objective function coefficient row and the c_B column, and the z_j and $c_j - z_j$ rows have been recomputed using c_1 instead of 50. The current solution will remain optimal as long as the value of c_1 results in all $c_j - z_j \leq 0$. Hence, from the column for s_1, we must have

$$\frac{c_1 - 64}{5} \leq 0$$

and from the column for s_3, we must have

$$\frac{24 - c_1}{5} \leq 0$$

Using the first inequality, we obtain

$$c_1 - 64 \leq 0$$

or

$$c_1 \leq 64 \tag{6.2}$$

Similarly, from the second inequality, we obtain

$$24 - c_1 \leq 0$$

or

$$24 \leq c_1 \tag{6.3}$$

Since c_1 must satisfy both (6.2) and (6.3), the range of optimality for c_1 is given by

$$24 \leq c_1 \leq 64 \tag{6.4}$$

To see how management of HighTech can make use of this sensitivity analysis information, suppose an increase in material costs reduces the profit contribution per unit for the Deskpro to \$30. The range of optimality indicates that the current solution ($x_1 = 30$, $x_2 = 12$, $s_1 = 0$, $s_2 = 8$, $s_3 = 0$) is still optimal. To verify this, let us recompute the final simplex tableau after reducing the value of c_1 to 30.

		x_1	x_2	s_1	s_2	s_3	
Basis	c_B	30	40	0	0	0	
x_2	40	0	1	$8/25$	0	$-3/25$	12
s_2	0	0	0	$-8/25$	1	$3/25$	8
x_1	30	1	0	$-5/25$	0	$5/25$	30
z_j		30	40	$34/5$	0	$6/5$	1380
$c_j - z_j$		0	0	$-34/5$	0	$-6/5$	

Since $c_j - z_j \leq 0$ for all variables, the solution with $x_1 = 30$, $x_2 = 12$, $s_1 = 0$, $s_2 = 8$, and $s_3 = 0$ is still optimal. That is, the optimal solution with $c_1 = 30$ is the same as the optimal solution with $c_1 = 50$. Note, however, that the decrease in profit contribution per unit of the Deskpro has caused a reduction in total profit from \$1980 to \$1380.

What if the profit contribution per unit were reduced even further—say, to \$20? Referring to the range of optimality for c_1 given by expression (6.4), we see that $c_1 = 20$ is outside the range; thus, we know that a change this large will cause a new basis to be optimal. To verify this, we have modified the final simplex tableau by replacing c_1 by 20.

		x_1	x_2	s_1	s_2	s_3	
Basis	c_B	20	40	0	0	0	
x_2	40	0	1	$8/25$	0	$-3/25$	12
s_2	0	0	0	$-8/25$	1	$3/25$	8
x_1	20	1	0	$-5/25$	0	$5/25$	30
z_j		20	40	$44/5$	0	$-4/5$	1080
$c_j - z_j$		0	0	$-44/5$	0	$4/5$	

As expected, the current solution ($x_1 = 30$, $x_2 = 12$, $s_1 = 0$, $s_2 = 8$, and $s_3 = 0$) is no longer optimal since the entry in the s_3 column of the net evaluation row is greater than zero. This implies that at least one more simplex iteration must be performed to reach the optimal solution. Continue to perform the simplex iterations in the previous tableau to verify that the new optimal solution will require the production of $16\frac{2}{3}$ units of the Deskpro and 20 units of the Portable.

The procedure we used to compute the range of optimality for c_1 can be used for any basic variable. The procedure for computing the range of optimality for nonbasic variables is even easier since a change in the objective function coefficient for a nonbasic variable causes only the corresponding $c_j - z_j$ entry to change in the final simplex tableau. To illustrate the approach, we show the following final simplex tableau for the original HighTech problem after replacing 0, the objective function coefficient for s_1, with the coefficient c_{s_1}:

Basis	c_B	x_1 50	x_2 40	s_1 c_{s_1}	s_2 0	s_3 0	
x_2	40	0	1	$8/25$	0	$-3/25$	12
s_2	0	0	0	$-8/25$	1	$3/25$	8
x_1	50	1	0	$-5/25$	0	$5/25$	30
z_j		50	40	$14/5$	0	$26/5$	1980
$c_j - z_j$		0	0	$c_{s_1} - 14/5$	0	$-26/5$	

Note that the only changes in the tableau are in the s_1 column. In applying inequality (6.1) to compute the range of optimality, we get

$$c_{s_1} - 14/5 \leq 0$$

and hence

$$c_{s_1} \leq 14/5$$

Therefore, as long as the objective function coefficient for s_1 is less than or equal to $14/5$, the current solution will be optimal. Since there is no lower bound on how much the coefficient may be decreased, we write the range of optimality for c_{s_1} as

$$c_{s_1} \leq 14/5$$

The same approach works for all nonbasic variables. In a maximization problem, there is no lower limit on the range of optimality, and the upper limit is given by z_j. Thus, the range of optimality for the objective function coefficient of any nonbasic variable is given by

$$c_j \leq z_j \tag{6.5}$$

Let us summarize the steps necessary to compute the range of optimality for objective function coefficients. In stating the following steps, we assume that computing the range of optimality for c_k, the coefficient of x_k, in a maximization problem is the desired goal. Keep in mind that x_k in this context may refer to one of the original decision variables, a slack variable, or a surplus variable.

Steps to Compute the Range of Optimality

Step 1   Replace the numerical value of the objective function coefficient for x_k with c_k everywhere it appears in the final simplex tableau.

Step 2   Recompute $c_j - z_j$ for each nonbasic variable (if x_k is a nonbasic variable, it is only necessary to recompute $c_k - z_k$).

Step 3   Requiring that $c_j - z_j \leq 0$, solve each inequality for any upper or lower bounds on c_k. If there are two or more upper bounds on c_k, the smaller of these is the upper bound on the range of optimality. If there are two or more lower bounds, the largest of these is the lower bound on the range of optimality.

Step 4   If the original problem is a minimization problem that was converted to a maximization problem in order to apply the simplex method, multiply the inequalities obtained in step 3 by -1, and change the direction of the inequalities to obtain the ranges of optimality for the original minimization problem.

You should now be able to compute the range of optimality for objective function coefficients by working with the final simplex tableau. Try Problem 1.

By using the range of optimality to determine whether a change in an objective function coefficient is large enough to cause a change in the optimal solution, we can often avoid the process of formulating and solving a modified linear programming problem.

Right–Hand–Side Values

In many linear programming problems, we can interpret the right-hand-side values (the b_i's) as the resources available. For instance, in the HighTech Industries problem, the right-hand side of constraint 1 represents the available assembly time, the right-hand side of constraint 2 represents the available Portable displays, and the right-hand side of constraint 3 represents the available warehouse space. Dual prices provide information on the value of additional resources in these cases; the ranges over which these dual prices are valid are given by the ranges for the right-hand-side values.

Dual Prices   In Chapter 2 we stated that the improvement in value of the optimal solution per-unit increase in a constraint's right-hand-side value is called a *dual price*.[1] When the simplex method is used to solve a linear programming problem, the values of the dual prices are easy to obtain. They are found in the z_j row of the final simplex tableau. To illustrate this point, the final simplex tableau for the HighTech problem is again shown.

Basis	c_B	x_1 50	x_2 40	s_1 0	s_2 0	s_3 0	
x_2	40	0	1	$8/25$	0	$-3/25$	**12**
s_2	0	0	0	$-8/25$	1	$3/25$	**8**
x_1	50	1	0	$-5/25$	0	$5/25$	**30**
z_j		50	40	$14/5$	0	$26/5$	**1980**
$c_j - z_j$		0	0	$-14/5$	0	$-26/5$	

The z_j values for the three slack variables are $14/5$, 0, and $26/5$, respectively. Thus, the dual prices for the assembly time constraint, Portable display constraint, and warehouse capacity constraint are respectively $14/5 = \$2.80$, 0.00, and $26/5 = \$5.20$. The dual price of $5.20 shows that more warehouse space will have the biggest positive impact on HighTech's profit.

To see why the z_j values for the slack variables in the final simplex tableau are the dual prices, let us first consider the case for slack variables that are part of the optimal basic feasible solution. Each of these slack variables will have a z_j value of zero, implying a dual price of zero for the corresponding constraint. For example, consider slack variable s_2, a basic variable in the HighTech problem. Since $s_2 = 8$ in the optimal solution, HighTech will have eight Portable display units unused. Consequently, how much would management of HighTech Industries be willing to pay to obtain additional Portable

[1]The closely related term *shadow price* is used by some authors. The shadow price is the same as the dual price for maximization problems; for minimization problems, the dual and shadow prices are equal in absolute value but have opposite signs. LINDO/PC and The Management Scientist provide dual prices as part of the computer output. Some software packages provide shadow prices.

display units? Clearly the answer is nothing since at the optimal solution HighTech has an excess of this particular component. Additional amounts of this resource are of no value to the company, and, consequently, the dual price for this constraint is zero. In general, if a slack variable is a basic variable in the optimal solution, the value of z_j—and hence, the dual price of the corresponding resource—is zero.

Consider now the nonbasic slack variables—for example, s_1. In the previous subsection we determined that the current solution will remain optimal as long as the objective function coefficient for s_1 (denoted c_{s_1}) stays in the following range:

$$c_{s_1} \leq {}^{14}\!/_5$$

This implies that the variable s_1 should not be increased from its current value of zero unless it is worth more than ${}^{14}\!/_5 = \$2.80$ to do so. We can conclude then that $\$2.80$ is the marginal value to HighTech of 1 hour of assembly time used in the production of Deskpro and Portable computers. Thus, if additional time can be obtained, HighTech should be willing to pay up to $\$2.80$ per hour for it. A similar interpretation can be given to the z_j value for each of the nonbasic slack variables.

With a greater-than-or-equal-to constraint, the value of the dual price will be less than or equal to zero because a one-unit increase in the value of the right-hand side cannot be helpful; a one-unit increase makes it more difficult to satisfy the constraint. For a maximization problem, then, the optimal value can be expected to decrease when the right-hand side of a greater-than-or-equal-to constraint is increased. The dual price gives the amount of the expected improvement—a negative number, since we expect a decrease. As a result, the dual price for a greater-than-or-equal-to constraint is given by the negative of the z_j entry for the corresponding surplus variable in the optimal simplex tableau.

Finally, it is possible to compute dual prices for equality constraints. They are given by the z_j values for the corresponding artificial variables. We will not develop this case in detail here since we have recommended dropping each artificial variable column from the simplex tableau as soon as the corresponding artificial variable leaves the basis.

To summarize, when the simplex method is used to solve a linear programming problem, the dual prices for the constraints are contained in the final simplex tableau. Table 6.1 summarizes the rules for determining the dual prices for the various constraint types in a maximization problem solved by the simplex method.

Recall that we convert a minimization problem to a maximization problem by multiplying the objective function by -1 before using the simplex method. Nevertheless, the dual price is given by the same z_j values since improvement for a minimization problem is a decrease in the optimal value.

To illustrate the approach for computing dual prices for a minimization problem, recall the M&D Chemicals problem that we solved in Section 5.7 as an equivalent maximization problem by multiplying the objective function by -1. The linear programming

Try Problem 3, parts (a), (b), and (c) for practice at finding dual prices from the optimal simplex tableau.

Table 6.1

Tableau Location of Dual Price by Constraint Type

Constraint Type	Dual Price Given by
$\leq$	z_j value for the slack variable associated with the constraint
$\geq$	Negative of the z_j value for the surplus variable associated with the constraint
$=$	z_j value for the artificial variable associated with the constraint

model for this problem and the final simplex tableau are restated as follows, with x_1 and x_2 representing manufacturing quantities of products 1 and 2, respectively.

$$\text{Min} \quad 2x_1 + 3x_2$$

s.t.

$$
\begin{aligned}
1x_1 &\qquad\qquad \geq 125 \quad \text{Demand for product 1} \\
1x_1 &+ 1x_2 \geq 350 \quad \text{Total production} \\
2x_1 &+ 1x_2 \leq 600 \quad \text{Processing time}
\end{aligned}
$$

$$x_1, x_2 \geq 0$$

		x_1	x_2	s_1	s_2	s_3	
Basis	c_B	-2	-3	0	0	0	
x_1	-2	1	0	0	1	1	**250**
x_2	-3	0	1	0	-2	-1	**100**
s_1	0	0	0	1	1	1	125
	z_j	-2	-3	0	4	1	-800
	$c_j - z_j$	0	0	0	-4	-1	

Following the rules in Table 6.1 for identifying the dual price for each constraint type, the dual prices for the constraints in the M&D Chemicals problem are given in Table 6.2. Since constraint 1 is not binding, its dual price is zero. The dual price for constraint 2 shows that the marginal cost of increasing the total production requirement is $4 per unit. Finally, the dual price of one for the third constraint shows that the per-unit value of additional processing time is $1.

Range of Feasibility   As we have just seen, the z_j row in the final simplex tableau can be used to determine the dual price and, as a result, predict the change in the value of the objective function corresponding to a unit change in a b_i. This interpretation is only valid, however, as long as the change in b_i is not large enough to make the current basic solution infeasible. Thus, we will be interested in calculating a range of values over which a particular b_i can vary without any of the current basic variables becoming infeasible (i.e., less than zero). This range of values will be referred to as the *range of feasibility*.

To demonstrate the effect of changing a b_i, consider increasing the amount of assembly time available in the HighTech problem from 150 to 160 hours. Will the current basis still yield a feasible solution? If so, given the dual price of $2.80 for the assembly time

Table 6.2

Dual Prices for M&D Chemicals Problem

Constraint	Constraint Type	Dual Price
Demand for product 1	$\geq$	0
Total production	$\geq$	-4
Processing time	$\leq$	1

constraint, we can expect an increase in the value of the solution of $10(2.80) = 28$. The final simplex tableau corresponding to an increase in the assembly time of 10 hours is shown here.

Basis	c_B	x_1 50	x_2 40	s_1 0	s_2 0	s_3 0	
x_2	40	0	1	$8/25$	0	$-3/25$	**15.2**
s_2	0	0	0	$-8/25$	1	$3/25$	**4.8**
x_1	50	1	0	$-5/25$	0	$5/25$	**28.0**
z_j		50	40	$14/5$	0	$26/5$	**2008**
$c_j - z_j$		0	0	$-14/5$	0	$-26/5$	

The same basis, consisting of the basic variables x_2, s_2, and x_1, is feasible since all the basic variables are nonnegative. Note also that, just as we predicted using the dual price, the value of the optimal solution has increased by $10(\$2.80) = \$28$, from \$1980 to \$2008.

You may wonder whether we had to resolve the problem completely to find this new solution. The answer is no! The only changes in the final simplex tableau (as compared with the final simplex tableau with $b_1 = 150$) are the differences in the values of the basic variables and the value of the objective function. That is, only the last column of the simplex tableau has changed. The entries in this new last column of the simplex tableau were obtained by adding 10 times the first four entries in the s_1 column to the last column in the previous tableau:

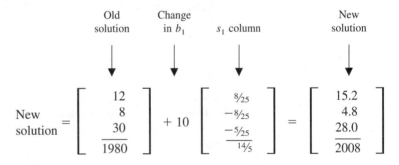

Let us now consider why this procedure can be used to find the new solution. First, recall that each of the coefficients in the s_1 column indicates the amount of decrease in a basic variable that would result from increasing s_1 by one unit. In other words, these coefficients tell us how many units of each of the current basic variables will be driven out of solution if one unit of variable s_1 is brought into solution. Bringing one unit of s_1 into solution, however, is the same as reducing the availability of assembly time (decreasing b_1) by one unit; increasing b_1, the available assembly time, by one unit has just the opposite effect. Therefore, the entries in the s_1 column can also be interpreted as the changes in the values of the current basic variables corresponding to a one-unit increase in b_1.

The change in the value of the objective function corresponding to a one-unit increase in b_1 is given by the value of z_j in that column (the dual price). In the foregoing case, the availability of assembly time increased by 10 units; thus, we multiplied the first four entries in the s_1 column by 10 to obtain the change in the value of the basic variables and the optimal value.

You should now be able to find the new solution after a change in a right-hand side without resolving the problem when the same basis remains feasible. Try Problem 3, parts (d) and (e).

How do we know when a change in b_1 is so large that the current basis will become infeasible? We shall first answer this question specifically for the HighTech Industries problem and then state the general procedure for less-than-or-equal-to constraints. The approach taken with greater-than-or-equal-to and equality constraints will then be discussed.

We begin by showing how to compute upper and lower bounds for the maximum amount that b_1 can be changed before the current optimal basis becomes infeasible. We have seen how to find the new basic feasible solution values, given a 10-unit increase in b_1. In general, given a change in b_1 of Δb_1, the new values for the basic variables in the HighTech problem are given by

$$\begin{bmatrix} x_2 \\ s_2 \\ x_1 \end{bmatrix} = \begin{bmatrix} 12 \\ 8 \\ 30 \end{bmatrix} + \Delta b_1 \begin{bmatrix} 8/25 \\ -8/25 \\ -5/25 \end{bmatrix} = \begin{bmatrix} 12 + 8/25\, \Delta b_1 \\ 8 - 8/25\, \Delta b_1 \\ 30 - 5/25\, \Delta b_1 \end{bmatrix} \qquad (6.6)$$

As long as the new value of each basic variable remains nonnegative, the current basis will remain feasible and therefore optimal. We can keep the basic variables nonnegative by limiting the change in b_1 (i.e., Δb_1) so that we satisfy each of the following conditions:

$$12 + 8/25\, \Delta b_1 \geq 0 \qquad (6.7)$$

$$8 - 8/25\, \Delta b_1 \geq 0 \qquad (6.8)$$

$$30 - 5/25\, \Delta b_1 \geq 0 \qquad (6.9)$$

The left-hand sides of these inequalities represent the new values of the basic variables after b_1 has been changed by Δb_1.

Solving for Δb_1 in inequalities (6.7), (6.8), and (6.9), we obtain

$$\Delta b_1 \geq (\ 25/8)(-12) = -37.5$$

$$\Delta b_1 \leq (-25/8)(-8) = 25$$

$$\Delta b_1 \leq (-25/5)(-30) = 150$$

Since all three inequalities must be satisfied, the most restrictive limits on b_1 must be satisfied for all the current basic variables to remain nonnegative. Therefore, Δb_1 must satisfy

$$-37.5 \leq \Delta b_1 \leq 25 \qquad (6.10)$$

The initial amount of assembly time available was 150 hours. Therefore, $b_1 = 150 + \Delta b_1$, where b_1 is the amount of assembly time available. We add 150 to each of the three terms in expression (6.10) to obtain

$$150 - 37.5 \leq 150 + \Delta b_1 \leq 150 + 25 \qquad (6.11)$$

Replacing $150 + \Delta b_1$ with b_1, we obtain the range of feasibility for b_1:

$$112.5 \leq b_1 \leq 175$$

This range of feasibility for b_1 indicates that as long as the available assembly time is between 112.5 and 175 hours, the current optimal basis will remain feasible. This is why we call this range the range of feasibility.

Since the dual price for b_1 (assembly time) is $14/5$, we know profit can be increased by \$2.80 by obtaining an additional hour of assembly time. Suppose then that we increase b_1 by 25; that is, we increase b_1 to the upper limit of its range of feasibility, 175. The profit will increase to $1980 + ($2.80)25 = $2050, and the values of the optimal basic variables become

$$x_2 = 12 + 25(8/25) \quad = 20$$
$$s_2 = 8 + 25(-8/25) = 0$$
$$x_1 = 30 + 25(-5/25) = 25$$

What has happened to the solution? The increased assembly time has caused a revision in the optimal production plan. HighTech should produce more of the Portable and less of the Deskpro. Overall, the profit will be increased by ($2.80)(25) = $70. Note that although the optimal solution has changed, the basic variables that were optimal before are still optimal.

The procedure for determining the range of feasibility has been illustrated with the assembly time constraint. The procedure for calculating the range of feasibility for the right-hand side of any less-than-or-equal-to constraint is the same. The first step for a general constraint i is to calculate the range of values for b_i that satisfy the inequalities shown below.

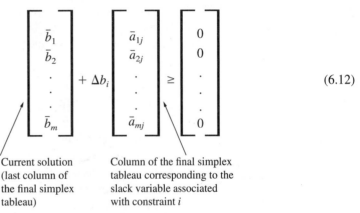

$$\begin{bmatrix} \bar{b}_1 \\ \bar{b}_2 \\ \cdot \\ \cdot \\ \cdot \\ \bar{b}_m \end{bmatrix} + \Delta b_i \begin{bmatrix} \bar{a}_{1j} \\ \bar{a}_{2j} \\ \cdot \\ \cdot \\ \cdot \\ \bar{a}_{mj} \end{bmatrix} \geq \begin{bmatrix} 0 \\ 0 \\ \cdot \\ \cdot \\ \cdot \\ 0 \end{bmatrix} \qquad (6.12)$$

Current solution (last column of the final simplex tableau)

Column of the final simplex tableau corresponding to the slack variable associated with constraint i

The inequalities are used to identify lower and upper limits on Δb_i. The range of feasibility can then be established by the maximum of the lower limits and the minimum of the upper limits.

Similar arguments can be used to develop a procedure for determining the range of feasibility for the right-hand-side value of a greater-than-or-equal-to constraint. Essentially the procedure is the same, with the column corresponding to the surplus variable associated with the constraint playing the central role. For a general greater-than-or-equal-to constraint i, we first calculate the range of values for Δb_i that satisfy the inequalities shown in equation (6.13).

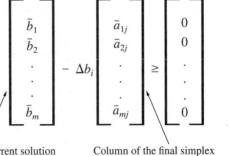

$$\begin{bmatrix} \bar{b}_1 \\ \bar{b}_2 \\ \cdot \\ \cdot \\ \cdot \\ \bar{b}_m \end{bmatrix} - \Delta b_i \begin{bmatrix} \bar{a}_{1j} \\ \bar{a}_{2j} \\ \cdot \\ \cdot \\ \cdot \\ \bar{a}_{mj} \end{bmatrix} \geq \begin{bmatrix} 0 \\ 0 \\ \cdot \\ \cdot \\ \cdot \\ 0 \end{bmatrix} \qquad (6.13)$$

Current solution (last column of the final simplex tableau)

Column of the final simplex tableau corresponding to the surplus variable associated with constraint i

Once again, these inequalities establish lower and upper limits on Δb_i. Given these limits, the range of feasibility is easily determined.

A range of feasibility for the right-hand side of an equality constraint can also be computed. To do so for equality constraint i, one could use the column of the final simplex tableau corresponding to the artificial variable associated with constraint i in equation (6.12). Since we have suggested dropping the artificial variable columns from the simplex tableau as soon as the artificial variable becomes nonbasic, these columns will not be available in the final tableau. Thus, more involved calculations are required to compute a range of feasibility for equality constraints. Details may be found in more advanced texts.

As long as the change in a right-hand-side value is such that b_i stays within its range of feasibility, the same basis will remain feasible and optimal. Changes that force b_i outside its range of feasibility will force us to resolve the problem to find the new optimal solution consisting of a different set of basic variables. (More advanced linear programming texts show how this can be done without completely resolving the problem.) In any case, the calculation of the range of feasibility for each b_i is valuable management information and should be included as part of the management report on any linear programming project. The range of feasibility is typically made available as part of the computer solution to the problem.

Try Problem 4 to make sure you can compute the range of feasibility by working with the final simplex tableau.

Simultaneous Changes

In reviewing the procedures for developing the range of optimality and the range of feasibility, we note that only one coefficient at a time was permitted to vary. That is why our statements concerning changes within these ranges were made with the understanding that no other coefficients are permitted to change. However, sometimes we can make the same statements when either two or more objective function coefficients or two or more right-hand sides are varied simultaneously. When the simultaneous changes satisfy the 100 percent rule, the same statements are applicable. The 100 percent rule was explained in Chapter 3, but we will briefly review it here.

Let us define allowable increase as the amount a coefficient can be increased before reaching the upper limit of its range, and allowable decrease as the amount a coefficient can be decreased before reaching the lower limit of its range. Now suppose simultaneous changes are made in two or more objective function coefficients. For each coefficient changed, we compute the percentage of the allowable increase, or allowable decrease, represented by the change. If the sum of the percentages for all changes does not exceed 100%, we say that the 100 percent rule is satisfied and that the simultaneous changes will not cause a change in the optimal solution. However, just as with a single objective function coefficient change, the value of the solution will change because of the change in the coefficients.

Similarly, if two or more changes in constraint right-hand-side values are made, we again compute the percentage of allowable increase or allowable decrease represented by each change. If the sum of the percentages for all changes does not exceed 100%, we say that the 100 percent rule is satisfied. The dual prices are then valid for determining the change in value of the objective function associated with the right-hand-side changes.

NOTES & comments

1. Sometimes, interpreting dual prices and choosing the appropriate sign can be confusing. It often helps to think of this process as follows. Relaxing a $\geq$ constraint means decreasing its right-hand side, and relaxing a $\leq$ constraint means increasing its right-hand side. Relaxing a constraint permits improvement in value; restricting a constraint (decreasing the right-hand side of a $\leq$ constraint or increasing the right-hand side of a $\geq$ constraint) has the opposite effect. In every case, the absolute value of the dual price gives the improvement in the optimal value associated with relaxing the constraint.

2. The Notes & Comments in Chapters 2 and 3 concerning sensitivity analysis are also applicable here. In particular, recall that the 100 percent rule cannot be applied to simultaneous changes in the objective function *and* the right-hand sides; it applies only to simultaneous changes in one or the other. Also note that this rule *does not* mean that simultaneous changes that do not satisfy the rule will necessarily cause a change in the solution. For instance, any proportional change in *all* the objective function coefficients will leave the optimal solution unchanged, and any proportional change in *all* the right-hand sides will leave the dual prices unchanged.

6.2 Duality

Every linear programming problem has an associated linear programming problem called the *dual*. Referring to the original formulation of the linear programming problem as the *primal,* we will see how the primal can be converted into its corresponding dual. Then we will solve the dual linear programming problem and interpret the results. A fundamental property of the primal–dual relationship is that the optimal solution to either the primal or the dual problem also provides the optimal solution to the other. In cases where the primal and the dual problems differ in terms of computational difficulty, we can choose the easier problem to solve.

Let us return to the HighTech Industries problem. The original formulation—the primal—is as follows:

$$\text{Max} \quad 50x_1 + 40x_2$$

s.t.

$$3x_1 + 5x_2 \leq 150 \quad \text{Assembly time}$$

$$1x_2 \leq 20 \quad \text{Portable display}$$

$$8x_1 + 5x_2 \leq 300 \quad \text{Warehouse space}$$

$$x_1, x_2 \geq 0$$

A maximization problem with all less-than-or-equal-to constraints and nonnegativity requirements for the variables is said to be in *canonical form*. For a maximization problem in canonical form, such as the HighTech Industries problem, the conversion to the associated dual linear program is relatively easy. Let us state the dual of the HighTech problem and then identify the steps taken to make the primal–dual conversion. The HighTech dual problem is as follows:

$$\text{Min} \quad 150u_1 + 20u_2 + 300u_3$$

s.t.

$$3u_1 \qquad\quad + \quad 8u_3 \geq 50$$

$$5u_1 + 1u_2 + \quad 5u_3 \geq 40$$

$$u_1, u_2, u_3 \geq 0$$

This is *canonical form for a minimization problem:* a minimization problem with all greater-than-or-equal-to constraints and nonnegativity requirements for the variables. Thus, the dual of a maximization problem in canonical form is a minimization problem in canonical form. The variables u_1, u_2, and u_3 are referred to as *dual variables*.

With the preceding example in mind, we make the following general statements about the *dual of a maximization problem in canonical form.*

1.   The dual is a minimization problem in canonical form.
2.   When the primal has *n* decision variables ($n = 2$ in the HighTech problem), the dual will have *n* constraints. The first constraint of the dual is associated with variable x_1 in the primal, the second constraint in the dual is associated with variable x_2 in the primal, and so on.
3.   When the primal has *m* constraints ($m = 3$ in the HighTech problem), the dual will have *m* decision variables. Dual variable u_1 is associated with the first primal constraint, dual variable u_2 is associated with the second primal constraint, and so on.
4.   The right-hand sides of the primal constraints become the objective function coefficients in the dual.
5.   The objective function coefficients of the primal become the right-hand sides of the dual constraints.
6.   The constraint coefficients of the *i*th primal variable become the coefficients in the *i*th constraint of the dual.

Try part (a) of Problem 17 for practice in finding the dual of a maximization problem in canonical form.

These six statements are the general requirements that must be satisfied when converting a maximization problem in canonical form to its associated dual: a minimization problem in canonical form. While these requirements may seem cumbersome at first, practice with a few simple problems will show that the primal–dual conversion process is relatively easy to implement.

Since we have formulated the HighTech dual linear programming problem, let us now proceed to solve it. With three variables in the dual, we will use the simplex method. After subtracting surplus variables s_1 and s_2 to obtain the standard form, adding artificial variables a_1 and a_2 to obtain the tableau form, and multiplying the objective function by -1 to convert the dual problem to an equivalent maximization problem, we arrive at the following initial simplex tableau.

Basis	c_B	u_1 -150	u_2 -20	u_3 -300	s_1 0	s_2 0	a_1 $-M$	a_2 $-M$	
a_1	$-M$	3	0	⑧	-1	0	1	0	**50**
a_2	$-M$	5	1	5	0	-1	0	1	**40**
z_j		$-8M$	$-M$	$-13M$	M	M	$-M$	$-M$	$-90M$
$c_j - z_j$		$-150+8M$	$-20+M$	$-300+13M$	$-M$	$-M$	0	0	

At the first iteration, u_3 is brought into the basis, and a_1 is removed. At the second iteration, u_1 is brought into the basis, and a_2 is removed. At this point, the simplex tableau appears as follows.

Basis	c_B	u_1 -150	u_2 -20	u_3 -300	s_1 0	s_2 0	
u_3	-300	0	$-3/25$	1	$-5/25$	$3/25$	$26/5$
u_1	-150	1	$8/25$	0	$5/25$	$-8/25$	$14/5$
z_j		-150	-12	-300	30	12	-1980
$c_j - z_j$		0	-8	0	-30	-12	

Since all the entries in the net evaluation row are less than or equal to zero, the optimal solution has been reached; it is $u_1 = 14/5$, $u_2 = 0$, $u_3 = 26/5$, $s_1 = 0$, and $s_2 = 0$. Since we have been maximizing the negative of the dual objective function, the value of the objective function for the optimal dual solution must be $-(-1980) = 1980$.

The final simplex tableau for the original HighTech Industries problem is shown here.

Basis	c_B	x_1 50	x_2 40	s_1 0	s_2 0	s_3 0	
x_2	40	0	1	$8/25$	0	$-3/25$	**12**
s_2	0	0	0	$-8/25$	1	$3/25$	**8**
x_1	50	1	0	$-5/25$	0	$5/25$	**30**
z_j		50	40	$14/5$	0	$26/5$	**1980**
$c_j - z_j$		0	0	$-14/5$	0	$-26/5$	

The optimal solution to the primal problem is $x_1 = 30$, $x_2 = 12$, $s_1 = 0$, $s_2 = 8$, and $s_3 = 0$. The optimal value of the objective function is 1980.

What observation can we make about the relationship between the optimal value of the objective function in the primal and the optimal value in the dual for the HighTech problem? The optimal value of the objective function is the same (1980) for both. This relationship is true for all primal and dual linear programming problems and is stated as property 1.

Property 1

If the dual problem has an optimal solution, the primal problem has an optimal solution, and vice versa. Furthermore, the values of the optimal solutions to the dual and primal problems are equal.

This property tells us that if we had solved only the dual problem, we would have known that HighTech could make a maximum of $1980.

Economic Interpretation of the Dual Variables

Before making further observations about the relationship between the primal and the dual solutions, let us consider the meaning or interpretation of the dual variables u_1, u_2, and u_3. Remember that in setting up the dual problem, each dual variable is associated with one of the constraints in the primal. Specifically, u_1 is associated with the assembly time constraint, u_2 with the Portable display constraint, and u_3 with the warehouse space constraint.

To understand and interpret these dual variables, let us return to property 1 of the primal–dual relationship, which stated that the objective function values for the primal and dual problems must be equal. At the optimal solution, the primal objective function results in

$$50x_1 + 40x_2 = 1980 \tag{6.14}$$

while the dual objective function is

$$150u_1 + 20u_2 + 300u_3 = 1980 \tag{6.15}$$

Using equation (6.14), let us restrict our interest to the interpretation of the primal objective function. Since x_1 and x_2 are the number of units of the Deskpro and the Portable that are assembled respectively, we have

$$\begin{pmatrix} \text{Dollar value} \\ \text{per unit of} \\ \text{Deskpro} \end{pmatrix} \begin{pmatrix} \text{Number of} \\ \text{units of} \\ \text{Deskpro} \end{pmatrix} + \begin{pmatrix} \text{Dollar value} \\ \text{per unit of} \\ \text{Portable} \end{pmatrix} \begin{pmatrix} \text{Number of} \\ \text{units of} \\ \text{Portable} \end{pmatrix} = \begin{matrix} \text{Total dollar} \\ \text{value of} \\ \text{production} \end{matrix}$$

From equation (6.15), we see that the coefficients of the dual objective function (150, 20, and 300) can be interpreted as the number of units of resources available. Thus, since the primal and dual objective functions are equal at optimality, we have

$$\begin{pmatrix} \text{Units of} \\ \text{resource} \\ 1 \end{pmatrix} u_1 + \begin{pmatrix} \text{Units of} \\ \text{resource} \\ 2 \end{pmatrix} u_2 + \begin{pmatrix} \text{Units of} \\ \text{resource} \\ 3 \end{pmatrix} u_3 = \begin{matrix} \text{Total dollar value} \\ \text{of production} \end{matrix}$$

Thus, we see that the dual variables must carry the interpretation of being the value per unit of resource. For the HighTech problem,

$$u_1 = \text{dollar value per hour of assembly time}$$
$$u_2 = \text{dollar value per unit of the Portable display}$$
$$u_3 = \text{dollar value per square foot of warehouse space}$$

Have we attempted to identify the value of these resources previously? Recall that in Section 6.1, when we considered sensitivity analysis of the right-hand sides, we identified the value of an additional unit of each resource. These values were called dual prices and are helpful to the decision maker in determining whether additional units of the resources should be made available.

The analysis in Section 6.1 led to the following dual prices for the resources in the HighTech problem.

Resource	Value per Additional Unit (dual price)
Assembly time	$2.80
Portable display	$0.00
Warehouse space	$5.20

Let us now return to the optimal solution for the HighTech dual problem. The values of the dual variables at the optimal solution are $u_1 = 14/5 = 2.80$, $u_2 = 0$, and $u_3 = 26/5 = 5.20$. For this maximization problem, the values of the dual variables and the dual prices are the same. For a minimization problem, the dual prices and the dual variables are the same in absolute value but have opposite signs. Thus, the optimal values of the dual variables identify the dual prices of each additional resource or input unit at the optimal solution.

In light of the preceding discussion, the following interpretation of the primal and dual problems can be made when the primal is a product-mix problem.

Primal Problem   Given a per-unit value of each product, determine how much of each should be produced to maximize the value of the total production. Constraints require the amount of each resource used to be less than or equal to the amount available.

Dual Problem   Given the availability of each resource, determine the per-unit value such that the total value of the resources used is minimized. Constraints require the resource value per unit be greater than or equal to the value of each unit of output.

Using the Dual to Identify the Primal Solution

At the beginning of this section, we mentioned that an important feature of the primal–dual relationship is that when an optimal solution is reached, the value of the optimal solution for the primal problem is the same as the value of the optimal solution for the dual problem; see property 1. However, the question remains: If we solve only the dual problem, can we identify the optimal values for the primal variables?

Recall that in Section 6.1 we showed that when a primal problem is solved by the simplex method, the optimal values of the primal variables appear in the right-most column of the final tableau, and the dual prices (values of the dual variables) are found in the z_j row. Since the final simplex tableau of the dual problem provides the optimal values of the dual variables, the values of the primal variables should be found in the z_j row of the optimal dual tableau. This is, in fact, the case and is formally stated as property 2.

Property 2

Given the simplex tableau corresponding to the optimal dual solution, the optimal values of the primal decision variables are given by the z_j entries for the surplus variables; furthermore, the optimal values of the primal slack variables are given by the negative of the $c_j - z_j$ entries for the u_j variables.

You should now be able to find the primal solution from the optimal simplex tableau for the dual and also be able to interpret the dual variables. Try parts (b) and (c) of Problem 17.

This property enables us to use the final simplex tableau for the dual of the HighTech problem to determine the optimal primal solution of $x_1 = 30$ units of the Deskpro and $x_2 = 12$ units of the Portable. These optimal values of x_1 and x_2, as well as the values for all primal slack variables, are given in the z_j and $c_j - z_j$ rows of the final simplex tableau of the dual problem, which is shown again here.

Basis	c_B	u_1 -150	u_2 -20	u_3 -300	s_1 0	s_2 0	
u_3	-300	0	$-3/25$	1	$-5/25$	$3/25$	$26/5$
u_1	-150	1	$8/25$	0	$5/25$	$-8/25$	$14/5$
	z_j	-150	-12	-300	30	12	-1980
	$c_j - z_j$	0	-8	0	-30	-12	

Finding the Dual of Any Primal Problem

The HighTech Industries primal problem provided a good introduction to the concept of duality since it was formulated as a maximization problem in canonical form. For this form of primal problem, we have seen that conversion to the dual problem is rather easy. If the primal problem is a minimization problem in canonical form, then the dual is a maximization problem in canonical form. Therefore, finding the dual of a minimization problem in canonical form is also easy. Consider the following linear program in canonical form for a minimization problem:

$$\text{Min} \quad 6x_1 + 2x_2$$

s.t.

$$5x_1 - 1x_2 \geq 13$$
$$3x_1 + 7x_2 \geq 9$$
$$x_1, x_2 \geq 0$$

The dual is the following maximization problem in canonical form:

$$\text{Max} \quad 13u_1 + 9u_2$$

s.t.

$$5u_1 + 3u_2 \leq 6$$
$$-1u_1 + 7u_2 \leq 2$$
$$u_1, u_2 \geq 0$$

Try Problem 18 for practice in finding the dual of a minimization problem in canonical form.

While we could state a special set of rules for converting each type of primal problem into its associated dual, we believe it is easier to first convert any primal problem into an equivalent problem in canonical form. Then, we follow the procedures already established for finding the dual of a maximization or minimization problem in canonical form.

Let us illustrate the procedure for finding the dual of any linear programming problem by finding the dual of the following minimization problem:

$$\text{Min} \quad 2x_1 - 3x_2$$

s.t.

$$1x_1 + 2x_2 \leq 12$$
$$4x_1 - 2x_2 \geq 3$$
$$6x_1 - 1x_2 = 10$$
$$x_1, x_2 \geq 0$$

Since this is a minimization problem, we obtain the canonical form by converting all constraints to greater-than-or-equal-to form. For this problem, the necessary steps are as follows:

1. Convert the first constraint to greater-than-or-equal-to form by multiplying both sides of the inequality by (−1). Doing so yields

$$-x_1 - 2x_2 \geq -12$$

2. Constraint 3 is an equality constraint. For an equality constraint, we first create two inequalities: one with ≤ form, the other with ≥ form. Doing so yields

$$6x_1 - 1x_2 \geq 10$$
$$6x_1 - 1x_2 \leq 10$$

Then, we multiply the ≤ constraint by (−1) to get two ≥ constraints.

$$6x_1 - 1x_2 \geq 10$$
$$-6x_1 + 1x_2 \geq -10$$

Now the original primal problem has been restated in the following equivalent form:

$$\text{Min} \quad 2x_1 - 3x_2$$

s.t.

$$-1x_1 - 2x_2 \geq -12$$
$$4x_1 - 2x_2 \geq 3$$
$$6x_1 - 1x_2 \geq 10$$
$$-6x_1 + 1x_2 \geq -10$$
$$x_1, x_2 \geq 0$$

With the primal problem now in canonical form for a minimization problem, we can easily convert to the dual problem by the primal–dual procedure presented earlier in this section. The dual becomes[2]

$$\text{Max} \quad -12u_1 + 3u_2 + 10u_3' - 10u_3''$$

s.t.

$$-1u_1 + 4u_2 + 6u_3' - 6u_3'' \leq 2$$
$$-2u_1 - 2u_2 - 1u_3' + 1u_3'' \leq -3$$
$$u_1, u_2, u_3', u_3'' \geq 0$$

---

[2]Note that the right-hand side of the second constraint is negative. Thus, we must multiply both sides of the constraint by −1 to obtain a positive value for the right-hand side before attempting to solve the problem with the simplex method.

You should now be able to write the dual of any linear programming problem. Try Problem 19.

Since the equality primal constraint required two $\geq$ constraints, we denote the dual variables associated with these constraints as u_3' and u_3''. This reminds us that u_3' and u_3'' both refer to the third constraint in the initial primal problem. Since there are two dual variables associated with an equality constraint, the interpretation of the dual variable must be modified slightly. The dual variable for the equality constraint $6x_1 - x_2 = 10$ is given by the value of $u_3' - u_3''$ in the optimal solution to the dual. Hence, the dual variable for an equality constraint can be negative.

Summary

In this chapter we showed how sensitivity analysis can be performed using the information in the final simplex tableau. This included computing the range of optimality for objective function coefficients, dual prices, and the range of feasibility for the right-hand sides. This sensitivity information is routinely made available as part of the solution report provided by most linear programming computer packages.

We stress here that the sensitivity analysis is based on the assumption that only one coefficient is allowed to change at a time; all other coefficients are assumed to remain at their original values. It is possible to do some limited sensitivity analysis on the effect of changing more than one coefficient at a time; the 100 percent rule was mentioned as being useful in this context.

In studying duality, we saw how the original linear programming problem, called the primal, can be converted into its associated dual linear programming problem. Solving either the primal or the dual provides the solution to the other. We learned that the value of the dual variable identifies the economic contribution or value of additional resources in the primal problem.

Glossary

Range of optimality The range of values over which an objective function coefficient may vary without causing any change in the optimal solution (i.e., the values of all the variables will remain the same, but the value of the objective function will change).

Dual price The improvement in value of the optimal solution per-unit increase in the value of the right-hand side associated with a linear programming constraint.

Range of feasibility The range of values over which a b_i may vary without causing the current basic solution to become infeasible. The values of the variables in solution will change, but the same variables will remain basic. The dual prices for constraints do not change within these ranges.

Dual problem A linear programming problem related to the primal problem. Solution of the dual also provides the solution to the primal.

Primal problem The original formulation of a linear programming problem.

Canonical form for a maximization problem A maximization problem with all less-than-or-equal-to constraints and nonnegativity requirements for the decision variables.

Canonical form for a minimization problem A minimization problem with all greater-than-or-equal-to constraints and nonnegativity requirements for the decision variables.

Dual variable The variable in a dual linear programming problem. Its optimal value provides the dual price for the associated primal resource.

Problems

1. **SELF Test** Consider the linear programming problem given below.

$$\text{Max} \quad 5x_1 + 6x_2 + 4x_3$$

s.t.

$$3x_1 + 4x_2 + 2x_3 \le 120$$

$$x_1 + 2x_2 + x_3 \le 50$$

$$x_1 + 2x_2 + 3x_3 \ge 30$$

$$x_1, x_2, x_3 \ge 0$$

The optimal simplex tableau is as follows:

		x_1	x_2	x_3	s_1	s_2	s_3	
Basic	c_B	5	6	4	0	0	0	
s_3	0	0	4	0	-2	7	1	**80**
x_3	4	0	2	1	-1	3	0	**30**
x_1	5	1	0	0	1	-2	0	**20**
z_j		5	8	4	1	2	0	**220**
$c_j - z_j$		0	-2	0	-1	-2	0	

   a. Compute the range of optimality for c_1.
   b. Compute the range of optimality for c_2.
   c. Compute the range of optimality for c_{s_1}.

2. For the HighTech problem, we found the range of optimality for c_1, the profit contribution per unit of the Deskpro. The final simplex tableau is given in Section 6.1. Find the following:
   a. The range of optimality for c_2.
   b. The range of optimality for c_{s_2}.
   c. The range of optimality for c_{s_3}.
   d. Suppose the per-unit profit contribution of the Portable (c_2) dropped to \$35. How would the optimal solution change? What is the new value for total profit?

3. **SELF Test** Refer to the problem formulation and optimal simplex tableau given in Problem 1.
   a. Find the dual price for the first constraint.
   b. Find the dual price for the second constraint.
   c. Find the dual price for the third constraint.
   d. Suppose the right-hand side of the first constraint is increased from 120 to 125. Find the new optimal solution and its value.
   e. Suppose the right-hand side of the first constraint is decreased from 120 to 110. Find the new optimal solution and its value.

4. **SELF Test** Refer again to the problem formulation and optimal simplex tableau given in Problem 1.
   a. Find the range of feasibility for b_1.
   b. Find the range of feasibility for b_2.
   c. Find the range of feasibility for b_3.

5. For the HighTech problem, we found the range of feasibility for b_1, the assembly time available (see Section 6.1).
   a. Find the range of feasibility for b_2.

    b. Find the range of feasibility for b_3.

    c. How much will HighTech's profit increase if there is a 20-square-foot increase in the amount of warehouse space available (b_3)?

6. Recall the Par, Inc., problem introduced in Chapter 2. The linear program for this problem is

$$\text{Max} \quad 10x_1 + 9x_2$$

s.t.

$$\tfrac{7}{10}x_1 + 1x_2 \le 630 \quad \text{Cutting and dyeing time}$$

$$\tfrac{1}{2}x_1 + \tfrac{5}{6}x_2 \le 600 \quad \text{Sewing time}$$

$$1x_1 + \tfrac{2}{3}x_2 \le 708 \quad \text{Finishing time}$$

$$\tfrac{1}{10}x_1 + \tfrac{1}{4}x_2 \le 135 \quad \text{Inspection and packaging time}$$

$$x_1, x_2 \ge 0$$

where

$$x_1 = \text{number of standard bags produced}$$
$$x_2 = \text{number of deluxe bags produced}$$

The final simplex tableau is

Basis	c_B	x_1 10	x_2 9	s_1 0	s_2 0	s_3 0	s_4 0	
x_2	9	0	1	$\tfrac{30}{16}$	0	$-\tfrac{21}{16}$	0	**252**
s_2	0	0	0	$-\tfrac{15}{16}$	1	$\tfrac{5}{32}$	0	**120**
x_1	10	1	0	$-\tfrac{20}{16}$	0	$\tfrac{30}{16}$	0	**540**
s_4	0	0	0	$-\tfrac{11}{32}$	0	$\tfrac{9}{64}$	1	**18**
z_j		10	9	$\tfrac{70}{16}$	0	$\tfrac{111}{16}$	0	**7668**
$c_j - z_j$		0	0	$-\tfrac{70}{16}$	0	$-\tfrac{111}{16}$	0	

    a. Calculate the range of optimality for the profit contribution, c_1, of the standard bag.

    b. Calculate the range of optimality for the profit contribution, c_2, of the deluxe bag.

    c. If the profit contribution per deluxe bag drops to $7 per unit, how will the optimal solution be affected?

    d. What unit profit contribution would be necessary for the deluxe bag before Par, Inc., would consider changing its current production plan?

    e. If the profit contribution of the deluxe bags can be increased to $15 per unit, what is the optimal production plan? State what you think will happen before you compute the new optimal solution.

7. For the Par, Inc., problem (Problem 6):

    a. Calculate the range of feasibility for b_1 (cutting and dyeing capacity).

    b. Calculate the range of feasibility for b_2 (sewing capacity).

    c. Calculate the range of feasibility for b_3 (finishing capacity).

    d. Calculate the range of feasibility for b_4 (inspection and packaging capacity).

    e. Which of these four departments are you interested in scheduling for overtime? Explain.

8. **a.** Calculate the final simplex tableau for the Par, Inc., problem (Problem 6) after increasing b_1 from 630 to $682\tfrac{4}{11}$.

    b. Would the current basis be optimal if b_1 were increased further? If not, what would be the new optimal basis?

9. Also for the Par, Inc., problem (Problem 6):
   a. How much would profit increase if an additional 30 hours became available in the cutting and dyeing department (i.e., if b_1 were increased from 630 to 660)?
   b. How much would profit decrease if 40 hours were removed from the sewing department?
   c. How much would profit decrease if, because of an employee accident, there were only 570 hours instead of 630 available in the cutting and dyeing department?

10. The following are additional conditions encountered by Par, Inc. (Problem 6).
   a. Suppose because of some new machinery Par, Inc., was able to make a small reduction in the amount of time it took to do the cutting and dyeing (constraint 1) for a standard bag. What effect would this have on the objective function?
   b. Management believes that by buying a new sewing machine, the sewing time for standard bags can be reduced from $\frac{1}{2}$ to $\frac{1}{3}$ hour. Do you think this machine would be a good investment? Why?

11. Recall the RMC problem (Chapter 2, Problem 21). Letting

$$x_1 = \text{tons of fuel additive produced}$$
$$x_2 = \text{tons of solvent base produced}$$

leads to the following formulation of the RMC problem:

$$\text{Max} \quad 40x_1 + 30x_2$$

s.t.

$$\frac{2}{5}x_1 + \frac{1}{2}x_2 \leq 20 \quad \text{Material 1}$$
$$\frac{1}{5}x_2 \leq 5 \quad \text{Material 2}$$
$$\frac{3}{5}x_1 + \frac{3}{10}x_2 \leq 21 \quad \text{Material 3}$$
$$x_1, x_2 \geq 0$$

The final simplex tableau is shown here.

		x_1	x_2	s_1	s_2	s_3	
Basis	c_B	40	30	0	0	0	
x_2	30	0	1	$\frac{10}{3}$	0	$-\frac{20}{9}$	20
s_2	0	0	0	$-\frac{2}{3}$	1	$\frac{4}{9}$	1
x_1	40	1	0	$-\frac{5}{3}$	0	$\frac{25}{9}$	25
z_j		40	30	$\frac{100}{3}$	0	$\frac{400}{9}$	1600
$c_j - z_j$		0	0	$-\frac{100}{3}$	0	$-\frac{400}{9}$	

   a. Compute the ranges of optimality for c_1 and c_2.
   b. Suppose that because of an increase in production costs, the profit per ton on the fuel additive is reduced to $30 per ton. What effect will this have on the optimal solution?
   c. What is the dual price for the material 1 constraint? What is the interpretation?
   d. If RMC had an opportunity to purchase additional materials, which material would be the most valuable? How much should the company be willing to pay for this material?

12. Refer to Problem 11.
   a. Compute the range of feasibility for b_1 (material 1 availability).
   b. Compute the range of feasibility for b_2 (material 2 availability).
   c. Compute the range of feasibility for b_3 (material 3 availability).
   d. What is the dual price for material 3? Over what range of values for b_3 is this dual price valid?

13. Consider the following linear program:

$$\text{Max} \quad 3x_1 + 1x_2 + 5x_3 + 3x_4$$

s.t.

$$3x_1 + 1x_2 + 2x_3 \qquad = 30$$
$$2x_1 + 1x_2 + 3x_3 + 1x_4 \geq 15$$
$$2x_2 \qquad + 3x_4 \leq 25$$
$$x_1, x_2, x_3, x_4 \geq 0$$

   a. Find the optimal solution.
   b. Calculate the range of optimality for c_3.
   c. What would be the effect of a four-unit decrease in c_3 (from 5 to 1) on the optimal solution and the value of that solution?
   d. Calculate the range of optimality for c_2.
   e. What would be the effect of a three-unit increase in c_2 (from 1 to 4) on the optimal solution and the value of that solution?

14. Consider the final simplex tableau shown here.

		x_1	x_2	x_3	x_4	s_1	s_2	s_3	
Basis	c_B	4	6	3	1	0	0	0	
x_3	3	$3/60$	0	1	$1/2$	$3/10$	0	$-6/30$	**125**
s_2	0	$195/60$	0	0	$-1/2$	$-5/10$	1	-1	**425**
x_2	6	$39/60$	1	0	$1/2$	$-1/10$	0	$12/30$	**25**
z_j		$81/20$	6	3	$9/2$	$3/10$	0	$54/30$	**525**
$c_j - z_j$		$-1/20$	0	0	$-7/2$	$-3/10$	0	$-54/30$	

The original right-hand-side values were $b_1 = 550$, $b_2 = 700$, and $b_3 = 200$.
   a. Calculate the range of feasibility for b_1.
   b. Calculate the range of feasibility for b_2.
   c. Calculate the range of feasibility for b_3.

15. Consider the following linear program:

$$\text{Max} \quad 15x_1 + 30x_2 + 20x_3$$

s.t.

$$1x_1 \qquad + 1x_3 \leq 4$$
$$0.5x_1 + 2x_2 + 1x_3 \leq 3$$
$$1x_1 + 1x_2 + 2x_3 \leq 6$$
$$x_1, x_2, x_3 \geq 0$$

Solve using the simplex method, and answer the following questions:
   a. What is the optimal solution?
   b. What is the value of the objective function?
   c. Which constraints are the binding constraints?
   d. How much slack is available in the nonbinding constraints?
   e. What are the dual prices associated with the three constraints? Which right-hand-side value would have the greatest effect on the value of the objective function if it could be changed?

f. Develop the appropriate ranges for the coefficients of the objective function. What is your interpretation of these ranges?

g. Develop and interpret the ranges of feasibility for the right-hand-side values.

16. Recall the Innis Investments problem (Chapter 2, Problem 37). Letting

$$x_1 = \text{units purchased in the stock fund}$$
$$x_2 = \text{units purchased in the money market fund}$$

leads to the following formulation:

$$\text{Min} \quad 8x_1 + 3x_2 \qquad\qquad \text{Total risk}$$

s.t.

$$50x_1 + 100x_2 \leq 1{,}200{,}000 \quad \text{Funds available}$$
$$5x_1 + 4x_2 \geq 60{,}000 \quad \text{Annual income}$$
$$1x_2 \geq 3{,}000 \quad \text{Minimum units in money market}$$
$$x_1, x_2 \geq 0$$

a. Solve this problem using the simplex method.

b. The value of the optimal solution is a measure of the riskiness of the portfolio. What effect will increasing the annual income requirement have on the riskiness of the portfolio?

c. Find the range of feasibility for b_2.

d. How will the optimal solution and its value change if the annual income requirement is increased from \$60,000 to \$65,000?

e. How will the optimal solution and its value change if the risk measure for the stock fund is increased from 8 to 9?

17. **SELFTest** Suppose that in a product-mix problem x_1, x_2, x_3, and x_4 indicate the units of products 1, 2, 3, and 4, respectively, and we have

$$\text{Max} \quad 4x_1 + 6x_2 + 3x_3 + 1x_4$$

s.t.

$$1.5x_1 + 2x_2 + 4x_3 + 3x_4 \leq 550 \quad \text{Machine A hours}$$
$$4x_1 + 1x_2 + 2x_3 + 1x_4 \leq 700 \quad \text{Machine B hours}$$
$$2x_1 + 3x_2 + 1x_3 + 2x_4 \leq 200 \quad \text{Machine C hours}$$
$$x_1, x_2, x_3, x_4 \geq 0$$

a. Formulate the dual to this problem.

b. Solve the dual. Use the dual solution to show that the profit-maximizing product mix is $x_1 = 0$, $x_2 = 25$, $x_3 = 125$, and $x_4 = 0$.

c. Use the dual variables to identify the machine or machines that are producing at maximum capacity. If the manager can select one machine for additional production capacity, which machine should have priority? Why?

18. **SELFTest** Find the dual for the following linear program:

$$\text{Min} \quad 2800x_1 + 6000x_2 + 1200x_3$$

s.t.

$$15x_1 + 15x_2 + 1x_3 \geq 5$$
$$4x_1 + 8x_2 \geq 5$$
$$12x_1 + 8x_3 \geq 24$$
$$x_1, x_2, x_3 \geq 0$$

19. Write the following primal problem in canonical form, and find its dual.

SELFTest

$$\text{Max} \quad 3x_1 + 1x_2 + 5x_3 + 3x_4$$

s.t.

$$3x_1 + 1x_2 + 2x_3 \qquad\qquad = 30$$

$$2x_1 + 1x_2 + 3x_3 + 1x_4 \geq 15$$

$$2x_2 + \qquad 3x_4 \leq 25$$

$$x_1, x_2, x_3, x_4 \geq 0$$

20. Photo Chemicals produces two types of photograph-developing fluids at a cost of $1.00 per gallon. Let

$$x_1 = \text{gallons of product 1}$$
$$x_2 = \text{gallons of product 2}$$

Photo Chemicals management has required that at least 30 gallons of product 1 and at least 20 gallons of product 2 be produced. They have also required that at least 80 pounds of a perishable raw material be used in production. A linear programming formulation of the problem is as follows:

$$\text{Min} \quad 1x_1 + 1x_2$$

s.t.

$$1x_1 \qquad\qquad \geq 30 \quad \text{Minimum product 1}$$

$$1x_2 \geq 20 \quad \text{Minimum product 2}$$

$$1x_1 + 2x_2 \geq 80 \quad \text{Minimum raw material}$$

$$x_1, x_2 \geq 0$$

a. Show the dual problem.
b. Solve the dual problem, and show from it that the optimal production plan is $x_1 = 30$ and $x_2 = 25$.
c. The third constraint involves a management request that the current 80 pounds of a perishable raw material be used. However, after learning that the optimal solution calls for an excess production of five units of product 2, management is reconsidering the raw material requirement. Specifically, you have been asked to identify the cost effect if this constraint is relaxed. Use the dual variable to indicate the change in the cost if only 79 pounds of raw material have to be used.

21. Consider the following linear programming problem:

$$\text{Min} \quad 4x_1 + 3x_2 + 6x_3$$

s.t.

$$1x_1 + 0.5x_2 + 1x_3 \geq 15$$

$$2x_2 + 1x_3 \geq 30$$

$$1x_1 + 1x_2 + 2x_3 \geq 20$$

$$x_1, x_2, x_3 \geq 0$$

a. Write the dual problem.
b. Solve the dual.
c. Use the dual solution to identify the optimal solution to the original primal problem.
d. Verify that the optimal values for the primal and dual problems are equal.

22. A sales representative who sells two products is trying to determine the number of sales calls that should be made during the next month to promote each product. Based on past experience, there is an average $10 commission for every call on product 1 and a $5 commission for every call on product 2. The company requires at least 20 calls per month for each product and not more than 100 calls per month on any one product. In addition, the sales representative spends about 3 hours on each call for product 1 and 1 hour on each call for product 2. If there are a total of 175 selling hours available next month, how many calls should be made for each of the two products to maximize the commission?

   a. Formulate a linear program for this problem.
   b. Formulate and solve the dual problem.
   c. Use the final simplex tableau for the dual to determine the optimal number of calls for the products. What is the maximum commission?
   d. Interpret the values of the dual variables.

23. Consider the linear program

$$\text{Max} \quad 3x_1 + 2x_2$$

s.t.

$$1x_1 + 2x_2 \leq 8$$

$$2x_1 + 1x_2 \leq 10$$

$$x_1, x_2 \geq 0$$

   a. Solve this problem using the simplex method. Keep a record of the value of the objective function at each extreme point.
   b. Formulate and solve the dual of this problem using the graphical procedure.
   c. Compute the value of the dual objective function for each extreme-point solution of the dual problem.
   d. Compare the values of the objective functions for each primal and dual extreme-point solution.
   e. Can a dual feasible solution yield a value less than a primal feasible solution? Can you state a result concerning bounds on the value of the primal solution provided by any feasible solution to the dual problem?

24. Suppose the optimal solution to a three-variable linear programming problem has $x_1 = 10$, $x_2 = 30$, and $x_3 = 15$. It is later discovered that the following two constraints were inadvertently omitted when formulating the problem.

$$6x_1 + 4x_2 - 1x_3 \leq 170$$

$$\tfrac{1}{4}x_1 + 1x_2 \qquad \geq \quad 25$$

Find the new optimal solution if possible. If this is not possible, state that it is not possible and why.

MANAGEMENT SCIENCE in practice

Performance Analysis Corporation*
Chapel Hill, North Carolina

Performance Analysis Corporation, founded in 1979, is a management consulting company that specializes in the use of management science to design more efficient and effective operations for a wide variety of chain stores. Performance Analysis Corporation has evaluated the operation of banks, savings and loans, and grocery chains. Recently, the company has been involved in evaluating the efficiency of fast-food outlets. In the following application, we describe how linear programming methodology has been used to provide an evaluation model for a chain of fast-food restaurants.

Fast-Food Business

The fast-food business for a chain such as McDonald's or Kentucky Fried Chicken is characterized by hundreds, or even thousands, of individual restaurants, some of which are company owned and some of which are franchised. A typical restaurant may gross close to a million dollars annually; thus, the impact of relatively minor improvements at a large proportion of the restaurants can have a substantial effect on a chain's profitability and market share.

Although each individual restaurant in a given chain usually offers the same type of menu (with some minor geographical variations), they must often deal with vastly different environments and competition. In addition, the age of the restaurant, facade used, ease of access and egress, hours of operation, scale of operation, and so on can vary substantially from restaurant to restaurant.

A major objective of company management in the fast-food industry involves the performance evaluations of managers of individual restaurants in the chain. These evaluations are the basis for awarding year-end bonuses and for personal advancement purposes. Unfortunately, there is not a single measure of performance such as profit that can be used as the basis for the evaluation since other measures such as market share and rate of growth are also important.

A Linear Programming Evaluation Model

One approach to the store evaluation problem utilizes the concept of Pareto optimality. According to this concept, a restaurant in a given chain is *relatively* inefficient if there are other restaurants in the same chain that have the following characteristics:

1. Have the same or worse environment.
2. Produce at least the same levels of *all* outputs.
3. Utilize no more of *any* resource and *less* of at least one of the resources.

The mechanism for discovering which of the restaurants are Pareto inefficient involves the development and solution of a linear programming model.** Constraints on the problem involve requirements concerning the minimum acceptable levels of output (e.g., profit and market share) and conditions imposed by uncontrollable elements in the environment. The objective function calls for the minimization of the resources necessary to produce the output. Solution of the model produces the following output for each restaurant:

1. A score that assesses the level of so-called relative technical efficiency achieved by the particular restaurant over the time period in question.
2. The reduction in controllable resources and/or the augmentation of outputs over the time period in question for an inefficient restaurant to have been rated as efficient.
3. A peer group of other restaurants with which each restaurant can be compared in the future.

Sensitivity analysis, especially that concerning the dual prices, provides important managerial information. For each constraint concerning a minimum acceptable output level, the dual price tells the manager how much one more unit of output would increase his/her efficiency measure. Analysis of the ranges for each of the constraint coefficients (the a_{ij} values) provides information concerning how much outputs could be reduced or inputs increased before the restaurant would become inefficient.

Types of Factors Utilized

The approach is capable of handling three types of factors: quantitative controllable factors, such as salaries paid or local advertising expenditures; noncontrollable quantitative factors, such as the median income in the geographic area served by the restaurant or the unemployment rate; and qualitative factors, such as the degree of competition or appearance of restaurant. The outputs include total sales of various types (e.g., by time of day), profits, market share, rate of growth of sales, and so forth.

—Continued on next page

—Continued from previous page

Benefits

The analysis typically identifies 40–50% of the restaurants as underperforming, given the previously stated conditions concerning the inputs available and outputs produced. Performance Analysis Corporation has found that if all of the relative inefficiencies identified are eliminated simultaneously, the resulting increase in corporate profits is typically in the neighborhood of 5–10%. This is truly a substantial increase given the large scale of operations involved.

The district manager has an objective score card for each restaurant manager that indicates areas (e.g., overtime salary) where improvements may be in order. The efficient restaurants can be used to generate a set of best practices that can be models for other restaurants. Of primary benefit are the reactions of restaurant managers who appreciate that the evaluation process they are subject to recognizes the environment they are forced to operate within; deals with noncommensurability of outputs involved; is theory based and nonpolitical; and is defensible, understandable, and equitable.

Questions

1. State in your own words what it means for one restaurant in a chain to be relatively inefficient when compared to another restaurant in the same chain.
2. Suppose the evaluation model showed that for a particular restaurant the resource mix necessary to produce a given output mix was 90% of what another restaurant was using to produce that same mix of output. Would you conclude that the restaurant was relatively efficient or inefficient? Why?

....

The authors are indebted to Richard C. Morey for providing this application.
**The model used is the data envelopment analysis model discussed in Section 4.5.*

seven

CHAPTER

Transportation, Assignment, and Transshipment Problems

Transportation, assignment, and transshipment problems belong to a special class of linear programming problems called *network flow problems*. A separate chapter is devoted to these problems for two reasons. First, a wide variety of applications can be modeled as transportation, assignment, or transshipment problems. Second, these problems have a mathematical structure that has enabled management scientists to develop efficient specialized solution procedures for solving them; as a result, even large problems can be solved with just a few seconds of computer time.

We will approach the network flow problems by illustrating each problem with a specific application. We first develop a graphical representation, called a *network*, of the problem and then show how each can be formulated and solved as a linear program. We present special-purpose solution procedures for the transportation and assignment problems in the last two sections of the chapter.

An applications-oriented introduction to the transportation, assignment, and transshipment problems can be obtained by covering Sections 7.1–7.4. Sections 7.5 and 7.6, involving special-purpose algorithms, are optional and can be skipped without loss of continuity.

7.1 The Transportation Problem: The Network Model and a Linear Programming Formulation

The *transportation problem* arises frequently in planning for the distribution of goods and services from several supply locations to several demand locations. Typically, the quantity of goods available at each supply location (origin) is limited, and the quantity of goods needed at each of several demand locations (destinations) is known. The usual objective in a transportation problem is to minimize the cost of shipping goods from the origins to the destinations.

Let us illustrate by considering a transportation problem faced by Foster Generators. This problem involves the transportation of a product from three plants to four distribution centers. Foster Generators has plants in Cleveland, Ohio; Bedford, Indiana; and York, Pennsylvania. Production capacities over the next 3-month planning period for one particular type of generator are as follows:

Origin	Plant	3-Month Production Capacity (units)
1	Cleveland	5,000
2	Bedford	6,000
3	York	2,500
	Total	13,500

The firm distributes its generators through four regional distribution centers located in Boston, Chicago, St. Louis, and Lexington; the 3-month forecast of demand for the distribution centers is as follows:

Destination	Distribution Center	3-Month Demand Forecast (units)
1	Boston	6,000
2	Chicago	4,000
3	St. Louis	2,000
4	Lexington	1,500
	Total	13,500

Management would like to determine how much of its production should be shipped from each plant to each distribution center. Figure 7.1 shows graphically the 12 distribution routes Foster can use. Such a graph is called a *network;* the circles are referred to as *nodes* and the lines connecting the nodes as *arcs.* Each origin and destination is represented by a node, and each possible shipping route is represented by an arc. The amount of the supply is written next to each origin node, and the amount of the demand is written next to each destination node. The goods shipped from the origins to the destinations represent the flow in the network. Note that the direction of flow (from origin to destination) is indicated by the arrows.

Try Problem 1 for practice in developing a network model of a transportation problem.

For Foster's transportation problem, the objective is to determine the routes to be used and the quantity to be shipped via each route that will provide the minimum total transportation cost. The cost for each unit shipped on each route is given in Table 7.1 and is shown on each arc in Figure 7.1.

A linear programming model can be used to solve this transportation problem. We will use double-subscripted decision variables, with x_{11} denoting the number of units shipped from origin 1 (Cleveland) to destination 1 (Boston), x_{12} denoting the number of units shipped from origin 1 (Cleveland) to destination 2 (Chicago), and so on. In general, the

Figure 7.1

The Network Representation of the Foster Generators Transportation Problem

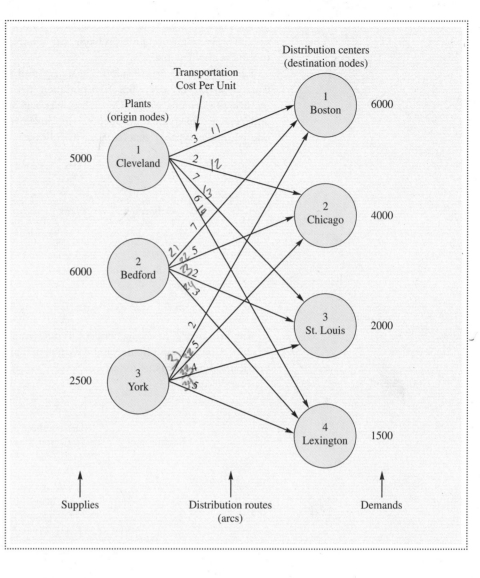

Table 7.1

Transportation Cost Per Unit for the Foster Generators Transportation Problem

	Destination			
Origin	Boston	Chicago	St. Louis	Lexington
Cleveland	3	2	7	6
Bedford	7	5	2	3
York	2	5	4	5

decision variables for a transportation problem having m origins and n destinations are written as follows:

$$x_{ij} = \text{number of units shipped from origin } i \text{ to destination } j$$
$$\text{where } i = 1, 2, \ldots, m \text{ and } j = 1, 2, \ldots, n$$

Since the objective of the transportation problem is to minimize the total transportation cost, we can use the cost data in Table 7.1 or on the arcs in Figure 7.1 to develop the following cost expressions:

Transportation costs for
units shipped from Cleveland $= 3x_{11} + 2x_{12} + 7x_{13} + 6x_{14}$

Transportation costs for
units shipped from Bedford $= 7x_{21} + 5x_{22} + 2x_{23} + 3x_{24}$

Transportation costs for
units shipped from York $= 2x_{31} + 5x_{32} + 4x_{33} + 5x_{34}$

The sum of the these expressions provides the objective function showing the total transportation cost for Foster Generators.

Transportation problems need constraints because each origin has a limited supply and each destination has a specific demand. We will consider the supply constraints first. The capacity at the Cleveland plant is 5000 units. With the total number of units shipped from the Cleveland plant expressed as $x_{11} + x_{12} + x_{13} + x_{14}$, the supply constraint for the Cleveland plant is

$$x_{11} + x_{12} + x_{13} + x_{14} \leq 5000 \quad \text{Cleveland supply}$$

With three origins (plants), the Foster transportation problem has three supply constraints. Given the capacity of 6000 units at the Bedford plant and 2500 units at the York plant, the two additional supply constraints are

$$x_{21} + x_{22} + x_{23} + x_{24} \leq 6000 \quad \text{Bedford supply}$$

$$x_{31} + x_{32} + x_{33} + x_{34} \leq 2500 \quad \text{York supply}$$

With the four distribution centers as the destinations, four demand constraints are needed to ensure that destination demands will be satisfied:

$$x_{11} + x_{21} + x_{31} = 6000 \quad \text{Boston demand}$$

$$x_{12} + x_{22} + x_{32} = 4000 \quad \text{Chicago demand}$$

$$x_{13} + x_{23} + x_{33} = 2000 \quad \text{St. Louis demand}$$

$$x_{14} + x_{24} + x_{34} = 1500 \quad \text{Lexington demand}$$

Combining the objective function and constraints into one model provides a 12-variable, 7-constraint linear programming formulation of the Foster Generators transportation problem:

Min $3x_{11} + 2x_{12} + 7x_{13} + 6x_{14} + 7x_{21} + 5x_{22} + 2x_{23} + 3x_{24} + 2x_{31} + 5x_{32} + 4x_{33} + 5x_{34}$

s.t.

$$
\begin{array}{l}
x_{11} + x_{12} + x_{13} + x_{14} \leq 5000 \\
\qquad x_{21} + x_{22} + x_{23} + x_{24} \leq 6000 \\
\qquad\qquad x_{31} + x_{32} + x_{33} + x_{34} \leq 2500 \\
x_{11} \qquad + x_{21} \qquad + x_{31} \qquad = 6000 \\
\quad x_{12} \qquad + x_{22} \qquad + x_{32} \qquad = 4000 \\
\quad\quad x_{13} \qquad + x_{23} \qquad + x_{33} \qquad = 2000 \\
\quad\quad\quad x_{14} \qquad + x_{24} \qquad + x_{34} = 1500
\end{array}
$$

$x_{ij} \geq 0 \quad$ for $i = 1, 2, 3$ and $j = 1, 2, 3, 4$

You should now be able to use the computer to solve a linear programming model of a transportation problem. Try Problem 2.

Comparing the linear programming formulation to the network in Figure 7.1 leads to several observations. All the information needed for the linear programming formulation is on the network. Each node has one constraint and each arc has one variable. The sum of the variables corresponding to arcs from an origin node must be less than or equal to the origin's supply, and the sum of the variables corresponding to the arcs into a destination node must be equal to the destination's demand.

We solved the Foster Generators problem with the linear programming module of The Management Scientist. The computer solution (see Figure 7.2) shows that the minimum total transportation cost is $39,500. The values for the decision variables show the optimal amounts to ship over each route. For example, with $x_{11} = 3500$, 3500 units should be shipped from Cleveland to Boston, and with $x_{12} = 1500$, 1500 units should be shipped from Cleveland to Chicago. Other values of the decision variables indicate the remaining shipping quantities and routes. Table 7.2 shows the minimum-cost transportation schedule and Figure 7.3 summarizes the optimal solution on the network.

Figure 7.2   **The Management Scientist Solution for the Foster Generators Transportation Problem**

```
        Objective Function Value =        39500.000

            Variable              Value            Reduced Costs
            --------            --------           -------------
              X11              3500.000                0.000
              X12              1500.000                0.000
              X13                 0.000                8.000
              X14                 0.000                6.000
              X21                 0.000                1.000
              X22              2500.000                0.000
              X23              2000.000                0.000
              X24              1500.000                0.000
              X31              2500.000                0.000
              X32                 0.000                4.000
              X33                 0.000                6.000
              X34                 0.000                6.000
```

Table 7.2

Optimal Solution to the Foster Generators Transportation Problem

| Route | | Units | Cost | Total |
From	To	Shipped	Per Unit	Cost
Cleveland	Boston	3500	$3	$10,500
Cleveland	Chicago	1500	$2	3,000
Bedford	Chicago	2500	$5	12,500
Bedford	St. Louis	2000	$2	4,000
Bedford	Lexington	1500	$3	4,500
York	Boston	2500	$2	5,000
				$39,500

Figure 7.3

Optimal Solution to the Foster Generators Transportation Problem

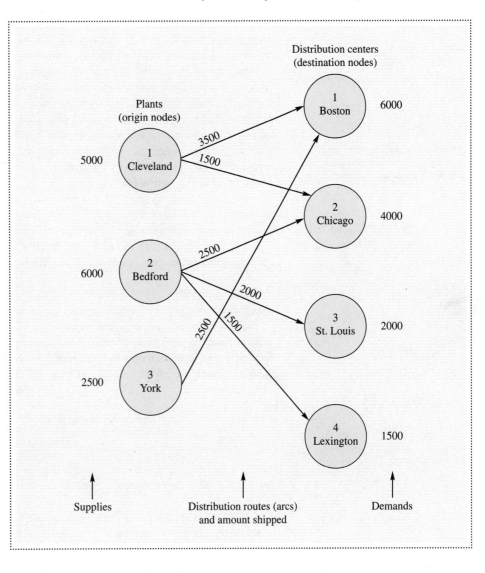

Problem Variations

The Foster Generators problem illustrates use of the basic transportation model. Variations of the basic transportation problem may involve one or more of the following situations:

1. total supply not equal to total demand
2. maximization objective function
3. route capacities or route minimums
4. unacceptable routes

With slight modifications in the linear programming model, you can easily accommodate these situations.

Total Supply Not Equal to Total Demand   Often *the total supply is not equal to the total demand.* If total supply exceeds total demand, no modification in the linear programming formulation is necessary. Excess supply will appear as slack in the linear programming solution. Slack for any particular origin can be interpreted as the unused supply or amount not shipped from the origin.

Try Problem 8 to see if you can handle a case where demand is greater than supply with a maximization objective.

If total supply is less than total demand, the linear programming model of a transportation problem will not have a feasible solution. In this case, we modify the network representation by adding a *dummy origin* with a supply equal to the difference between the total demand and the total supply. With the addition of the dummy origin, and an arc from the dummy origin to each destination, the linear programming model will have a feasible solution. A zero cost per unit is assigned to each arc leaving the dummy origin so that the value of the optimal solution for the revised problem will represent the shipping cost for the units actually shipped (no shipments actually will be made from the dummy origin). When the optimal solution is implemented, the destinations showing shipments being received from the dummy origin will be the destinations experiencing a shortfall or unsatisfied demand.

Maximization Objective Function   In some transportation problems, the objective is to find a solution that maximizes profit or revenue. Using the values for profit or revenue per unit as coefficients in the objective function, we simply solve a maximization rather than a minimization linear program. This change does not affect the constraints.

Route Capacities and/or Route Minimums   The linear programming formulation of the transportation problem also can accommodate capacities and/or minimum quantities for one or more of the routes. For example, suppose that in the Foster Generators problem the York–Boston route (origin 3 to destination 1) had a capacity of 1000 units because of limited space availability on its normal mode of transportation. With x_{31} denoting the amount shipped from York to Boston, the route capacity constraint for the York–Boston route would be

$$x_{31} \leq 1000$$

Similarly, route minimums can be specified. For example,

$$x_{22} \geq 2000$$

would guarantee that a previously committed order for a Bedford–Chicago delivery of at least 2000 units would be maintained in the optimal solution.

Unacceptable Routes   Finally, establishing a route from every origin to every destination may not be possible. To handle this situation, we simply drop the corresponding arc from the network and remove the corresponding variable from the linear programming formulation. For example, if the Cleveland–St. Louis route were unacceptable or unusable, the arc from Cleveland to St. Louis could be dropped in Figure 7.1, and x_{13} could be removed from the linear programming formulation. Solving the resulting 11-variable, 7-constraint model would provide the optimal solution while guaranteeing that the Cleveland–St. Louis route is not used.

A General Linear Programming Model of the Transportation Problem

To show the general linear programming model of the transportation problem, we use the notation:

i = index for origins, $i = 1, 2, \ldots, m$

j = index for destinations, $j = 1, 2, \ldots, n$

x_{ij} = number of units shipped from origin i to destination j

c_{ij} = cost per unit of shipping from origin i to destination j

s_i = supply or capacity in units at origin i

d_j = demand in units at destination j

The general linear programming model of the m-origin, n-destination transportation problem is

$$\text{Min} \quad \sum_{i=1}^{m} \sum_{j=1}^{n} c_{ij} x_{ij}$$

s.t.

$$\sum_{j=1}^{n} x_{ij} \leq s_i \qquad i = 1, 2, \ldots, m \quad \text{Supply}$$

$$\sum_{i=1}^{m} x_{ij} = d_j \qquad j = 1, 2, \ldots, n \quad \text{Demand}$$

$$x_{ij} \geq 0 \qquad \text{for all } i \text{ and } j$$

As mentioned previously, we can add additional constraints of the form $x_{ij} \leq L_{ij}$ if the route from origin i to destination j has capacity L_{ij}. A transportation problem that includes constraints of this type is called a *capacitated transportation problem*. Similarly, we can add route minimum constraints of the form $x_{ij} \geq M_{ij}$ if the route from origin i to destination j must handle at least M_{ij} units.

NOTES & comments

1. Transportation problems encountered in practice usually lead to very large linear programs. Transportation problems with 100 origins and 100 destinations are not unusual. Such a problem would involve (100)(100) = 10,000 variables. For such a problem, special-purpose solution procedures (see Section 7.5) are much more efficient than general-purpose linear programming codes. But if speed is not an issue, a general-purpose linear programming code that has the capability to solve large problems will solve most transportation problems.

2. To handle a situation in which some routes may be unacceptable, we stated that you could drop the corresponding arc from the network and remove the corresponding variable from the linear programming formulation. Another approach often used is to assign an extremely large objective function cost coefficient to any unacceptable arc. If the problem has already been formulated, another option is to add a constraint to the formulation that sets the variable you want to remove equal to zero.

3. The optimal solution to a transportation model will consist of integer values for the decision variables as long as all supply and demand values are integers. The reason is the special mathematical structure of the linear programming model. Each variable appears in exactly one supply and one demand constraint, and all coefficients in the constraint equations are 1's and 0's.

4. Although many transportation problems involve minimizing the cost of transporting goods between locations, many other applications of the transportation model exist. The Management Science in Action: Marine Corps Mobilization illustrates the use of a transportation model to send Marine Corps officers to billets.

MANAGEMENT SCIENCE in action

Marine Corps Mobilization*

The U.S. Marine Corps has developed a network model for mobilizing its officers in the event of a world crisis or war. The problem is to send officers to billets (duty assignments) as quickly as possible. The model developed to solve this problem is a transportation model much like the ones discussed in this chapter, only much larger. The origins or supply nodes represent the officers available, and the destinations or demand nodes represent the billets. A realistic implementation might involve as many as 40,000 officers and 25,000 billets. If all officer-to-billets arc combinations are permitted, the transportation problem would have 1 billion arcs. To reduce the problem size, officers with similar qualifications are aggregated into the same supply node and similar duty assignments are aggregated into the same demand nodes. Using this approach and methods for eliminating infeasible arcs, the Marine Corps has solved

problems involving 27,000 officers and 10,000 billets in 10 seconds on a personal computer.

Excellent results in sending officers of appropriate grade and job qualifications to the desired billets have been obtained. In a crisis, the availability and use of this system can make the difference between an appropriate response and disaster. The prior system required 2–4 days to produce a complete mobilization plan and provided a lower quality match between officer qualifications and billet needs. The Marine Corps is now using the mobilization model to enhance its peace-time capability.

....

*Based on Bausch, D. O., G. G. Brown, D. R. Hundley, S. H. Rapp, and R. E. Rosenthal, "Mobilizing Marine Corps Officers." *Interfaces*, July–August 1991, pp. 26–38.

7.2 The Assignment Problem: The Network Model and a Linear Programming Formulation

The *assignment problem* arises in a variety of decision-making situations; typical assignment problems involve assigning jobs to machines, agents to tasks, sales personnel to sales territories, contracts to bidders, and so on. A distinguishing feature of the assignment problem is that *one* agent is assigned to *one and only one* task. Specifically, we look for the set of assignments that will optimize a stated objective, such as minimize cost, minimize time, or maximize profits.

To illustrate the assignment problem, let us consider the case of Fowle Marketing Research, which has just received requests for market research studies from three new clients. The company faces the task of assigning a project leader (agent) to each client (task). Currently, three individuals have no other commitments and are available for the project leader assignments. Fowle's management realizes, however, that the time required to complete each study will depend on the experience and ability of the project leader assigned. The three projects have approximately the same priority, and the company wants to assign project leaders to minimize the total number of days required to complete all three projects. If a project leader is to be assigned to one client only, what assignments should be made?

To answer the assignment question, Fowle's management must first consider all possible project leader–client assignments and then estimate the corresponding project completion times. With three project leaders and three clients, nine assignment alternatives are possible. The alternatives and the estimated project completion times in days are summarized in Table 7.3.

Table 7.3

Estimated Project Completion Times (Days) for the Fowle Marketing Research Assignment Problem

	Client		
Project Leader	**1**	**2**	**3**
1. Terry	10	15	9
2. Carle	9	18	5
3. McClymonds	6	14	3

Figure 7.4

A Network Model of the Fowle Marketing Research Assignment Problem

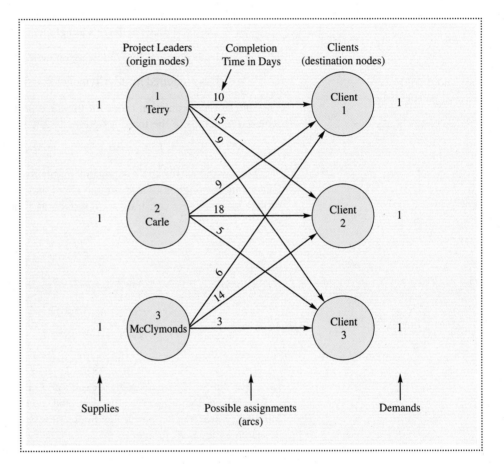

Try part (a) of Problem 12 to see if you can develop a network model for an assignment problem.

Figure 7.4 shows the network representation of Fowle's assignment problem. The nodes correspond to the project leaders and clients, and the arcs represent the possible assignments of project leaders to clients. The supply at each origin node and the demand at each destination node are 1; the cost of assigning a project leader to a client is the time it takes that project leader to complete the client's task. Note the similarity between the network models of the assignment problem (Figure 7.4) and the transportation problem (Figure 7.1). The assignment problem is a special case of the transportation problem in which all supply and demand values equal 1 and the amount shipped over each arc is either 0 or 1.

Since the assignment problem is a special case of the transportation problem, a linear programming formulation can be developed. Again, we need a constraint for each node and a variable for each arc. As in the transportation problem, we use double-subscripted decision variables, with x_{11} denoting the assignment of project leader 1 (Terry) to client 1, x_{12} denoting the assignment of project leader 1 (Terry) to client 2, and so on. Thus, we define the decision variables for Fowle's assignment problem as

$$x_{ij} = \begin{cases} 1 & \text{if project leader } i \text{ is assigned to client } j \\ 0 & \text{otherwise} \end{cases}$$

where $i = 1, 2, 3$, and $j = 1, 2, 3$

Using this notation and the completion time data in Table 7.3, we develop completion time expressions:

$$\text{Days required for Terry's assignment} = 10x_{11} + 15x_{12} + 9x_{13}$$

$$\text{Days required for Carle's assignment} = 9x_{21} + 18x_{22} + 5x_{23}$$

$$\text{Days required for McClymonds's assignment} = 6x_{31} + 14x_{32} + 3x_{33}$$

The sum of the completion times for the three project leaders will provide the total days required to complete the three assignments. Thus, the objective function is

$$\text{Min} \quad 10x_{11} + 15x_{12} + 9x_{13} + 9x_{21} + 18x_{22} + 5x_{23} + 6x_{31} + 14x_{32} + 3x_{33}$$

The constraints for the assignment problem reflect the conditions that each project leader can be assigned to at most one client and that each client must have one assigned project leader. These constraints are written as follows:

$$
\begin{array}{ll}
x_{11} + x_{12} + x_{13} \le 1 & \text{Terry's assignment} \\
x_{21} + x_{22} + x_{23} \le 1 & \text{Carle's assignment} \\
x_{31} + x_{32} + x_{33} \le 1 & \text{McClymonds's assignment} \\
x_{11} + x_{21} + x_{31} = 1 & \text{Client 1} \\
x_{12} + x_{22} + x_{32} = 1 & \text{Client 2} \\
x_{13} + x_{23} + x_{33} = 1 & \text{Client 3}
\end{array}
$$

Note that there is one constraint for each node in Figure 7.4.

Combining the objective function and constraints into one model provides the following 9-variable, 6-constraint linear programming model of the Fowle Marketing Research assignment problem.

$$\text{Min} \quad 10x_{11} + 15x_{12} + 9x_{13} + 9x_{21} + 18x_{22} + 5x_{23} + 6x_{31} + 14x_{32} + 3x_{33}$$

s.t.

At this point, you should be able to formulate and solve a linear programming model for an assignment problem on the computer. Try part (b) of Problem 12.

$$
\begin{array}{ll}
x_{11} + x_{12} + x_{13} & \le 1 \\
x_{21} + x_{22} + x_{23} & \le 1 \\
x_{31} + x_{32} + x_{33} & \le 1 \\
x_{11} + x_{21} + x_{31} & = 1 \\
x_{12} + x_{22} + x_{32} & = 1 \\
x_{13} + x_{23} + x_{33} & = 1
\end{array}
$$

$$x_{ij} \ge 0 \quad \text{for } i = 1, 2, 3; \, j = 1, 2, 3$$

Figure 7.5   The Management Scientist Solution for the Fowle Marketing Research Assignment Problem

```
        Objective Function Value =              26.000

            Variable            Value            Reduced Costs
        --------------      ---------------      ------------------
              X11              0.000                  0.000
              X12              1.000                  0.000
              X13              0.000                  3.000
              X21              0.000                  0.000
              X22              0.000                  4.000
              X23              1.000                  0.000
              X31              1.000                  0.000
              X32              0.000                  3.000
              X33              0.000                  1.000
```

Table 7.4

Optimal Project Leader
Assignments for the Fowle
Marketing Research Problem

Project Leader	Assigned Client	Days
Terry	2	15
Carle	3	5
McClymonds	1	6
	Total	26

Figure 7.5 shows the computer solution for this model. Terry is assigned to client 2 ($x_{12} = 1$), Carle is assigned to client 3 ($x_{23} = 1$), and McClymonds is assigned to client 1 ($x_{31} = 1$). The total completion time required is 26 days. This solution is summarized in Table 7.4.

Problem Variations

Because the assignment problem can be viewed as a special case of the transportation problem, the problem variations that may arise in an assignment problem parallel those for the transportation problem. Specifically, we can handle

1. total number of agents (supply) not equal to the total number of tasks (demand)
2. a maximization objective function
3. unacceptable assignments

The situation in which the number of agents does not equal the number of tasks is analogous to total supply not equaling total demand in a transportation problem. If the number of agents exceeds the number of tasks, the extra agents simply remain unassigned in the linear programming model. If the number of tasks exceeds the number of agents, the linear programming model will not have a feasible solution. In this situation, a simple modification is to add enough dummy agents to equalize the number of agents and the number of tasks. For instance, in the Fowle problem we might have had five clients (tasks) and only three project leaders (agents). By adding two dummy project leaders, we can create a new assignment problem with the number of project leaders equal to the number of clients. The objective function coefficients for the assignment of dummy project leaders would be zero so that the value of the optimal solution would represent the total number of days required by the assignments actually made (no assignments will actually be made to the clients receiving dummy project leaders).

If the assignment alternatives are evaluated in terms of revenue or profit rather than time or cost, the linear programming formulation can be solved as a maximization rather than a minimization problem. In addition, if one or more assignments are unacceptable, the corresponding decision variable can be removed from the linear programming formulation. This could happen, for example, if an agent did not have the experience necessary for one or more of the tasks.

A General Linear Programming Model of the Assignment Problem

The general assignment problem involves m agents and n tasks. If we let $x_{ij} = 1$ or 0 according to whether agent i is assigned to task j or not, and if c_{ij} denotes the cost of assigning agent i to task j, we can write the general assignment model as

$$\text{Min} \quad \sum_{i=1}^{m} \sum_{j=1}^{n} c_{ij} x_{ij}$$

s.t.

$$\sum_{j=1}^{n} x_{ij} \leq 1 \qquad i = 1, 2, \ldots, m \quad \text{Agents}$$

$$\sum_{i=1}^{m} x_{ij} = 1 \qquad j = 1, 2, \ldots, n \quad \text{Tasks}$$

$$x_{ij} \geq 0 \qquad \text{for all } i \text{ and } j$$

Multiple Assignments

At the beginning of this section, we indicated that a distinguishing feature of the assignment problem is that *one* agent is assigned to *one and only one* task. In generalizations of the assignment problem where one agent can be assigned to two or more tasks, the linear programming formulation of the problem can be easily modified. For example, let us assume that in the Fowle Marketing Research problem Terry could be assigned up to two clients; in this case, the constraint representing Terry's assignment would be $x_{11} + x_{12} + x_{13} \leq 2$. In general, if a_i denotes the upper limit for the number of tasks to which agent i can be assigned, we write the agent constraints as

$$\sum_{j=1}^{n} x_{ij} \leq a_i \qquad i = 1, 2, \ldots, m$$

Thus, we see that one advantage of formulating and solving assignment problems as linear programs is that special cases such as the situation involving multiple assignments can be easily handled.

NOTES & comments

1. As noted, the assignment model is a special case of the transportation model. We stated in the notes and comments at the end of the preceding section that the optimal solution to the transportation problem will consist of integer values for the decision variables as long as the supplies and demands are integers. For the assignment problem, all supplies and demands equal 1; thus, the optimal solution must be integer valued and the integer values must be 0 or 1.

2. Combining the method for handling multiple assignments with the notion of a dummy agent provides another means of dealing with situations when the number of tasks exceeds the number of agents. That is, we add one dummy agent, but provide the dummy agent with the capability to handle multiple tasks. The number of tasks the dummy agent can handle is equal to the difference between the number of tasks and the number of agents.

7.3 The Transshipment Problem: The Network Model and a Linear Programming Formulation

The *transshipment problem* is an extension of the transportation problem in which intermediate nodes, referred to as *transshipment nodes,* are added to account for locations such as warehouses. In this more general type of distribution problem, shipments may be made between any pair of the three general types of nodes: origin nodes, transshipment nodes, and destination nodes. For example, the transshipment problem permits shipments of goods from origins to transshipment nodes and on to destinations, from one origin to another origin, from one transshipment location to another, from one destination location to another, and directly from origins to destinations.

As was true for the transportation problem, the supply available at each origin is limited and the demand at each destination is specified. The objective in the transshipment problem is to determine how many units should be shipped over each arc in the network so that all destination demands are satisfied with the minimum possible transportation cost.

Try part (a) of Problem 23 for practice in developing a network representation of a transshipment problem.

Let us consider the transshipment problem faced by Ryan Electronics. Ryan is an electronics company with production facilities in Denver and Atlanta. Components produced at either facility may be shipped to either of the firm's regional warehouses, which are located in Kansas City and Louisville. From the regional warehouses, the firm supplies retail outlets in Detroit, Miami, Dallas, and New Orleans. The key features of the problem are shown in the network model depicted in Figure 7.6. Note that the supply at each origin and demand at each destination are shown in the left and right margins, respectively. Nodes 1 and 2 are the origin nodes; nodes 3 and 4 are the transshipment nodes; and nodes 5, 6, 7, and 8 are the destination nodes. The transportation cost per unit for each distribution route is shown in Table 7.5 and on the arcs of the network model in Figure 7.6.

As with the transportation and assignment problems, we can formulate a linear programming model of the transshipment problem from a network representation. Again,

Figure 7.6

Network Representation of the Ryan Electronics Transshipment Problem

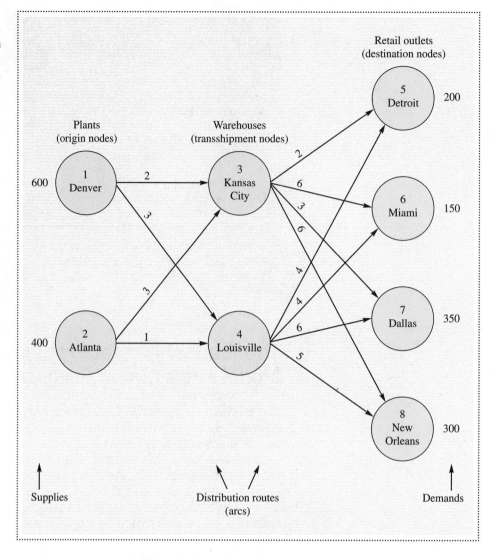

Table 7.5

Transportation Costs Per Unit for the Ryan Electronics Transshipment Problem

	Warehouse	
Plant	Kansas City	Louisville
Denver	2	3
Atlanta	3	1

	Retail Outlet			
Warehouse	Detroit	Miami	Dallas	New Orleans
Kansas City	2	6	3	6
Louisville	4	4	6	5

we need a constraint for each node and a variable for each arc. Let x_{ij} denote the number of units shipped from node i to node j. For example, x_{13} denotes the number of units shipped from the Denver plant to the Kansas City warehouse, x_{14} denotes the number of units shipped from the Denver plant to the Louisville warehouse, and so on. Since the supply at the Denver plant is 600 units, the amount shipped from the Denver plant must be less than or equal to 600. Mathematically, we write this supply constraint as

$$x_{13} + x_{14} \leq 600$$

Similarly, for the Atlanta plant we have

$$x_{23} + x_{24} \leq 400$$

We now consider how to write the constraints corresponding to the two transshipment nodes. For node 3 (the Kansas City warehouse), we must guarantee that the number of units shipped out must equal the number of units shipped into the warehouse. Since

Number of units
shipped out of node 3 $= x_{35} + x_{36} + x_{37} + x_{38}$

and

Number of units
shipped into node 3 $= x_{13} + x_{23}$

we obtain

$$x_{35} + x_{36} + x_{37} + x_{38} = x_{13} + x_{23}$$

Placing all the variables on the left-hand side provides the constraint corresponding to node 3 as

$$-x_{13} - x_{23} + x_{35} + x_{36} + x_{37} + x_{38} = 0$$

Similarly, the constraint corresponding to node 4 is

$$-x_{14} - x_{24} + x_{45} + x_{46} + x_{47} + x_{48} = 0$$

To develop the constraints associated with the destination nodes, we recognize that for each node the amount shipped to the destination must equal the demand. For example, to satisfy the demand for 200 units at node 5 (the Detroit retail outlet), we write

$$x_{35} + x_{45} = 200$$

Similarly, for nodes 6, 7, and 8, we have

$$x_{36} + x_{46} = 150$$
$$x_{37} + x_{47} = 350$$
$$x_{38} + x_{48} = 300$$

As usual, the objective function reflects the total shipping cost over the 12 shipping routes. Combining the objective function and constraints leads to a 12-variable, 8-constraint linear programming model of the Ryan Electronics transshipment problem (see Figure 7.7). We used the linear programming module of The Management Scientist to obtain the optimal solution. Figure 7.8 shows the computer output, and Table 7.6 summarizes the optimal solution.

As mentioned at the beginning of this section, in the transshipment problem arcs may connect any pair of nodes. All such shipping patterns are possible in a transshipment

Try parts (b) and (c) of Problem 23 for practice in developing the linear programming model and in solving a transshipment problem on the computer.

Figure 7.7　Linear Programming Formulation of the Ryan Electronics Transshipment Problem

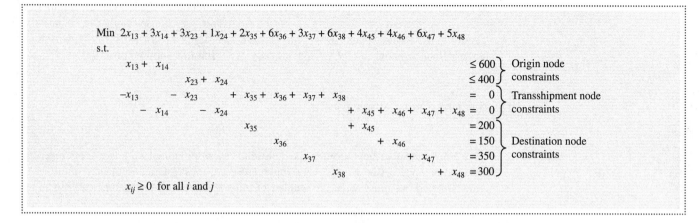

Figure 7.8　The Management Scientist Solution for the Ryan Electronics Transshipment Problem

```
Objective Function Value =          5200.000

        Variable            Value            Reduced Costs
      --------------    ---------------    -------------------
           X13             550.000              0.000
           X14              50.000              0.000
           X23               0.000              3.000
           X24             400.000              0.000
           X35             200.000              0.000
           X36               0.000              1.000
           X37             350.000              0.000
           X38               0.000              0.000
           X45               0.000              3.000
           X46             150.000              0.000
           X47               0.000              4.000
           X48             300.000              0.000
```

Table 7.6

Optimal Solution to the Ryan Electronics Transshipment Problem

| Route | | | | |
From	To	Units Shipped	Cost Per Unit	Total Cost
Denver	Kansas City	550	$2	$1100
Denver	Louisville	50	$3	150
Atlanta	Louisville	400	$1	400
Kansas City	Detroit	200	$2	400
Kansas City	Dallas	350	$3	1050
Louisville	Miami	150	$4	600
Louisville	New Orleans	300	$5	1500
				$5200

Figure 7.9

Network Representation of the Modified Ryan Electronics Transshipment Problem

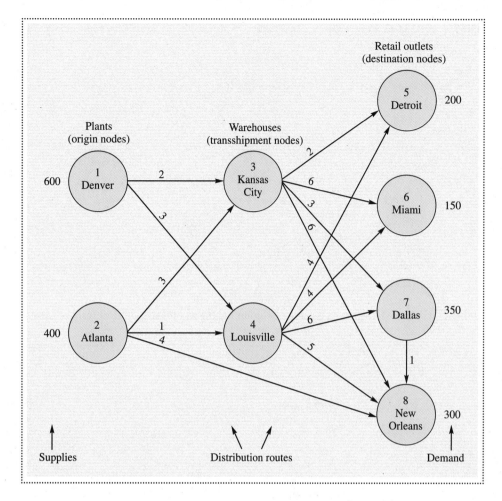

problem. We still require only one constraint per node, but the constraint must include a variable for every arc entering or leaving the node. For origin nodes, the sum of the shipments out minus the sum of the shipments in must be less than or equal to the origin supply. For destination nodes, the sum of the shipments in minus the sum of the shipments out must equal demand. For transshipment nodes, the sum of the shipments out must equal the sum of the shipments in, as before.

For an illustration of this more general type of transshipment problem, let us modify the Ryan Electronics problem. Suppose that it is possible to ship directly from Atlanta to New Orleans at $4 per unit and from Dallas to New Orleans at $1 per unit. The network model corresponding to this modified Ryan Electronics problem is shown in Figure 7.9, the linear programming formulation is shown in Figure 7.10, and the computer solution is shown in Figure 7.11.

In Figure 7.9 we added two new arcs to the network model. Thus, two new variables are necessary in the linear programming formulation. Figure 7.10 shows that the new variables x_{28} and x_{78}, appear in the objective function and in the constraints corresponding to the nodes to which the new arcs are connected. Figure 7.11 shows that the value of the optimal solution has been reduced $600 by adding the two new shipping routes; $x_{28} = 250$ units are being shipped directly from Atlanta to New Orleans, and $x_{78} = 50$ units are being shipped from Dallas to New Orleans.

Try Problem 24 for practice working with transshipment problems with this more general structure.

Figure 7.10   Linear Programming Formulation of the Modified Ryan Electronics Transshipment Problem

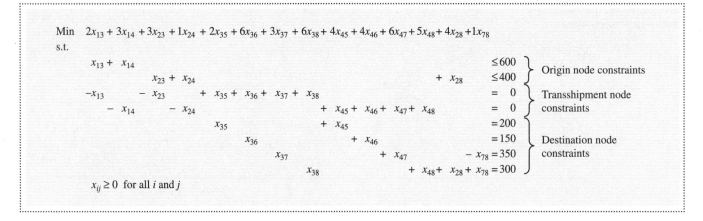

Figure 7.11   The Management Scientist Solution for the Modified Ryan Electronics Transshipment Problem

```
               Objective Function Value =           4600.000

                  Variable              Value             Reduced Costs
               --------------      ----------------      ------------------
                     X13             600.000                 0.000
                     X14               0.000                 0.000
                     X23               0.000                 3.000
                     X24             150.000                 0.000
                     X35             200.000                 0.000
                     X36               0.000                 1.000
                     X37             400.000                 0.000
                     X38               0.000                 2.000
                     X45               0.000                 3.000
                     X46             150.000                 0.000
                     X47               0.000                 4.000
                     X48               0.000                 2.000
                     X28             250.000                 0.000
                     X78              50.000                 0.000
```

Problem Variations

As with transportation and assignment problems, transshipment problems may be formulated with several variations, including

1. total supply not equal to total demand
2. maximization objective function
3. route capacities or route minimums
4. unacceptable routes

The linear programming model modifications required to accommodate these variations are identical to the modifications required for the transportation problem described in Section 7.1. When we add one or more constraints of the form $x_{ij} \leq L_{ij}$ to show that the route from node i to node j has capacity L_{ij}, we refer to the transshipment problem as a *capacitated transshipment problem*.

A General Linear Programming Model of the Transshipment Problem

The general linear programming model of the transshipment problem is

$$\text{Min} \quad \sum_{\text{all arcs}} c_{ij} x_{ij}$$

s.t.

$$\sum_{\text{arcs out}} x_{ij} - \sum_{\text{arcs in}} x_{ij} \leq s_i \qquad \text{Origin nodes } i$$

$$\sum_{\text{arcs out}} x_{ij} - \sum_{\text{arcs in}} x_{ij} = 0 \qquad \text{Transshipment nodes}$$

$$\sum_{\text{arcs in}} x_{ij} - \sum_{\text{arcs out}} x_{ij} = d_j \qquad \text{Destination nodes } j$$

$$x_{ij} \geq 0 \text{ for all } i \text{ and } j$$

where

x_{ij} = number of units shipped from node i to node j

c_{ij} = cost per unit of shipping from node i to node j

s_i = supply at origin node i

d_j = demand at destination node j

NOTES & comments

1. In more advanced treatments of linear programming and network flow problems, the capacitated transshipment problem is called the pure network flow problem. Efficient special-purpose solution procedures are available for network flow problems and their special cases.

2. In the general linear programming formulation of the transshipment problem, the constraints for the destination nodes are often written as

$$\sum_{\text{arcs out}} x_{ij} - \sum_{\text{arcs in}} x_{ij} = -d_j$$

The advantage of writing the constraints this way is that the left-hand side of each constraint then represents the flow out of the node minus the flow in. But such constraints would then have to be multiplied by -1 to obtain nonnegative right-hand sides before solving the problem by most linear programming codes.

7.4 A Production and Inventory Application

The introduction to the transportation and transshipment problems in Sections 7.1 and 7.3 involved applications for the shipment of goods from several supply locations or origins to several demand sites or destinations. Although the shipment of goods is the subject of many transportation and transshipment problems, transportation and/or transshipment models can be developed for applications that have nothing to do with the physical shipment of goods from origins to destinations. In this section we show how to use a transshipment model to solve a production scheduling and inventory problem.

Contois Carpets is a small manufacturer of carpeting for home and office installations. Production capacity, demand, production cost per square yard, and inventory holding cost per square yard for the next four quarters are shown in Table 7.7. Note that production capacity, demand, and production costs vary by quarter, whereas the cost of carrying inventory from one quarter to the next is constant at $0.25 per yard. Contois wants to determine how many yards of carpeting to manufacture each quarter to minimize the total production and inventory cost for the four-quarter period.

We begin by developing a network representation of the problem. First, we create four nodes corresponding to the production in each quarter and four nodes corresponding to the demand in each quarter. Each production node is connected by an outgoing arc to the demand node for the same period. The flow on the arc represents the number of square yards of carpet manufactured for the period. For each demand node, an outgoing arc represents the amount of inventory (square yards of carpet) carried over to the demand node for the next period. Figure 7.12 shows the network model. Note that nodes 1–4 represent the production for each quarter and that nodes 5–8 represent the demand for each quarter. The quarterly production capacities are shown in the left margin, and the quarterly demands are shown in the right margin.

The objective is to determine a production scheduling and inventory policy that will minimize the total production and inventory cost for the four quarters. Constraints involve production capacity and demand in each quarter. As usual, a linear programming model can be developed from the network by establishing a constraint for each node and a variable for each arc.

Let x_{15} denote the number of square yards of carpet manufactured in quarter 1. The capacity of the facility is 600 square yards in quarter 1, so the production capacity constraint is

$$x_{15} \leq 600$$

Using similar decision variables, we obtain the production capacities for quarters 2–4:

$$x_{26} \leq 300$$

$$x_{37} \leq 500$$

$$x_{48} \leq 400$$

Table 7.7

Production, Demand, and Cost Estimates for Contois Carpets

Quarter	Production Capacity (square yards)	Demand (square yards)	Production Cost ($/square yard)	Inventory Cost ($/square yard)
1	600	400	2	0.25
2	300	500	5	0.25
3	500	400	3	0.25
4	400	400	3	0.25

Figure 7.12

Network Representation of the Contois Carpets Problem

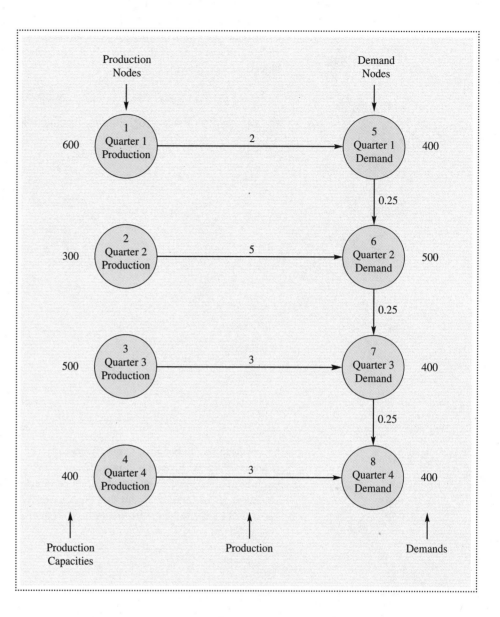

We now consider the development of the constraints for each of the demand nodes. For node 5, one arc enters the node, which represents the number of square yards of carpet produced in quarter 1, and one arc leaves the node, which represents the number of square yards of carpet that will not be sold in quarter 1 and will be carried over for possible sale in quarter 2. In general, for each quarter the beginning inventory plus the production minus the ending inventory must equal demand. However, for quarter 1 there is no beginning inventory; thus, the constraint for node 5 is

$$x_{15} - x_{56} = 400$$

The constraints associated with the demand nodes in quarters 2, 3, and 4 are

$$x_{56} + x_{26} - x_{67} = 500$$
$$x_{67} + x_{37} - x_{78} = 400$$
$$x_{78} + x_{48} = 400$$

Note that the constraint for node 8 (fourth-quarter demand) involves only two variables as there is no provision for holding inventory for a fifth quarter.

The objective is to minimize total production and inventory cost, so we write the objective function as

$$\text{Min} \quad 2x_{15} + 5x_{26} + 3x_{37} + 3x_{48} + 0.25x_{56} + 0.25x_{67} + 0.25x_{78}$$

The complete linear programming formulation of the Contois Carpets problem is

$$\text{Min} \quad 2x_{15} + 5x_{26} + 3x_{37} + 3x_{48} + 0.25x_{56} + 0.25x_{67} + 0.25x_{78}$$

s.t.

$$
\begin{aligned}
x_{15} & & & & & & & & \leq 600 \\
& x_{26} & & & & & & & \leq 300 \\
& & x_{37} & & & & & & \leq 500 \\
& & & x_{48} & & & & & \leq 400 \\
x_{15} & & & & - x_{56} & & & & = 400 \\
& x_{26} & & & + x_{56} & - x_{67} & & & = 500 \\
& & x_{37} & & & + x_{67} & - x_{78} & & = 400 \\
& & & x_{48} & & & + x_{78} & & = 400 \\
\end{aligned}
$$

$$x_{ij} \geq 0 \quad \text{for all } i \text{ and } j$$

We used the linear programming module of The Management Scientist to solve the Contois Carpets problem. Figure 7.13 shows the results: Contois Carpets should manufacture 600 square yards of carpet in quarter 1, 300 square yards in quarter 2, 400 square yards in quarter 3, and 400 square yards in quarter 4. Note also that 200 square yards will be carried over from quarter 1 to quarter 2. The total production and inventory cost is $5150.

Figure 7.13   The Management Scientist Solution for the Contois Carpets Problem

```
         Objective Function Value =        5150.000

         Variable            Value            Reduced Costs
         ---------------     ---------------   -------------------
             X15              600.000               0.000
             X26              300.000               0.000
             X37              400.000               0.000
             X48              400.000               0.000
             X56              200.000               0.000
             X67                0.000               2.250
             X78                0.000               0.000
```

NOTES & comments

1. Often the same problem can be modeled in different ways. In this section we modeled the Contois Carpets problem as a transshipment problem. It also can be modeled as a transportation problem. In Problem 39 at the end of the chapter, we ask you to develop such a model.

2. In the network model we developed for the transshipment problem, the amount leaving the starting node for an arc is always equal to the amount entering the ending node for that arc. An extension of such a network model is the case where a gain or a loss occurs as an arc is traversed. The amount entering the destination node may be greater or smaller than the amount leaving the origin node. For instance, if cash is the commodity flowing across an arc, the cash earns interest from one period to the next. Thus, the amount of cash entering the next period is greater than the amount leaving the previous period by the amount of interest earned. Networks with gains or losses are treated in more advanced texts on network flow programming.

7.5 The Transportation Simplex Method: A Special-Purpose Solution Procedure (Optional)

Solving transportation problems with a general-purpose linear programming code is fine for small- to medium-sized problems. However, these problems often grow very large (a problem with 100 origins and 1000 destinations would have 100,000 variables), and more efficient solution procedures are needed. The special network structure of the transportation problem has enabled management scientists to develop special-purpose solution procedures that greatly simplify the computations.

In Section 7.1 we introduced the Foster Generators, Inc., transportation problem and showed how to formulate and solve it as a linear program. The linear programming formulation involved 12 variables and 7 constraints. In this section we describe a special-purpose solution procedure, called the *transportation simplex method,* that takes advantage of the network structure of the transportation problem and makes possible the solution of large transportation problems efficiently on a computer and small transportation problems by hand.

The transportation simplex method, like the simplex method for linear programs, is a two-phase procedure; it involves first finding an initial feasible solution and then proceeding iteratively to make improvements in the solution until an optimal solution is reached. To summarize the data conveniently and to keep track of the calculations, we utilize a *transportation tableau.* The transportation tableau for the Foster Generators problem is presented in Table 7.8.

Note that the 12 *cells* in the tableau correspond to the 12 arcs shown in Figure 7.1; that is, each cell corresponds to the route from one origin to one destination. Thus, each cell in the transportation tableau corresponds to a variable in the linear programming formulation. The entries in the right-hand margin of the tableau indicate the supply at

Table 7.8

Transportation Tableau for the Foster Generators Transportation Problem

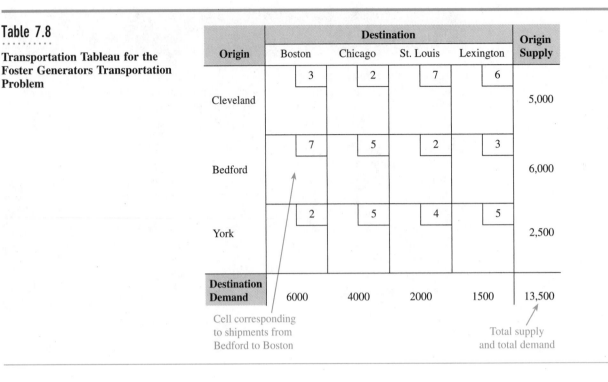

Origin	Destination				Origin Supply
	Boston	Chicago	St. Louis	Lexington	
Cleveland	3	2	7	6	5,000
Bedford	7	5	2	3	6,000
York	2	5	4	5	2,500
Destination Demand	6000	4000	2000	1500	13,500

Cell corresponding to shipments from Bedford to Boston

Total supply and total demand

each origin, and the entries in the bottom margin indicate the demand at each destination. Each row corresponds to a supply node, and each column corresponds to a demand node in the network model of the problem. The number of rows plus the number of columns equals the number of constraints in the linear programming formulation of the problem. The entries in the upper right-hand corner of each cell show the transportation cost per unit shipped over the corresponding route. Note also that for the Foster Generators problem total supply equals total demand. The transportation simplex method can be applied only to a balanced (total supply = total demand) problem; if a problem is not balanced, a dummy origin or dummy destination must be added. The use of dummy origins and destinations will be discussed later in this section.

Phase I: Finding An Initial Feasible Solution

The first phase of the transportation simplex method involves finding an initial feasible solution. Such a solution provides arc flows that satisfy each demand constraint without shipping more from any origin node than the supply available. The procedures most often used to find an initial feasible solution to a transportation problem are called heuristics. A *heuristic* is a common-sense procedure for quickly finding a solution to a problem.

Several heuristics have been developed to find an initial feasible solution to a transportation problem. Although some heuristics can find an initial feasible solution quickly, often the solution they find is not very good in terms of minimizing total cost. Other heuristics may not find an initial feasible solution as quickly, but the solution they find is often very good in terms of minimizing total cost. The heuristic we describe for finding an initial feasible solution to a transportation problem is called *the minimum-cost method*. This heuristic strikes a compromise between finding a feasible solution quickly and finding a feasible solution that is close to the optimal solution.

Table 7.9

Transportation Tableau after One Iteration of the Minimum-Cost Method

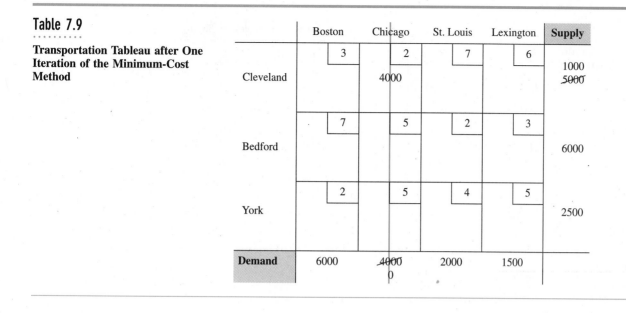

	Boston	Chicago	St. Louis	Lexington	Supply
Cleveland	3	2	7	6	1000 ~~5000~~
		4000			
Bedford	7	5	2	3	6000
York	2	5	4	5	2500
Demand	6000	~~4000~~ 0	2000	1500	

We begin by allocating as much flow as possible to the minimum-cost arc. In Table 7.8 we see that the Cleveland–Chicago, Bedford–St. Louis, and York–Boston routes each qualify as the minimum-cost arc since they each have a transportation cost of $2 per unit. When ties such as this occur, we follow the convention of selecting the arc to which the most flow can be allocated. In this case it corresponds to shipping 4000 units from Cleveland to Chicago, so we write 4000 in the Cleveland–Chicago cell of the transportation tableau. This selection reduces the supply at Cleveland from 5000 to 1000; hence, we cross out the 5000-unit supply value and replace it with the reduced value of 1000. In addition, allocating 4000 units to this arc satisfies the demand at Chicago, so we reduce the Chicago demand to zero and eliminate the corresponding column from further consideration by drawing a line through it. The transportation tableau now appears as shown in Table 7.9.

Now we look at the reduced tableau consisting of all unlined cells to identify the next minimum-cost arc. There is a tie between the Bedford–St. Louis and York–Boston routes with a transportation cost of $2 per unit. More units of flow can be allocated to the York–Boston route, so we choose it for the next allocation. This results in an allocation of 2500 units over the York–Boston route. To update the tableau, we reduce the Boston demand by 2500 units to 3500, reduce the York supply to zero, and eliminate this row from further consideration by lining through it. Continuing the process results in an allocation of 2000 units over the Bedford–St. Louis route and the elimination of the St. Louis column because its demand goes to zero. The transportation tableau obtained after carrying out the second and third iterations is shown in Table 7.10.

We now have two arcs that qualify for the minimum-cost arc with a value of 3: Cleveland–Boston and Bedford–Lexington. We can allocate a flow of 1000 units to the Cleveland–Boston route and a flow of 1500 to the Bedford–Lexington route, so we allocate 1500 units to the Bedford–Lexington route. Doing so results in a demand of zero at Lexington and eliminates this column. The next minimum-cost allocation is 1000 over the Cleveland–Boston route. After we make these two allocations, the transportation tableau appears as shown in Table 7.11.

The only remaining unlined cell is Bedford–Boston. Allocating 2500 units to the corresponding arc uses up the remaining supply at Bedford and satisfies all the demand at Boston. The resulting tableau is shown in Table 7.12.

Table 7.10

Transportation Tableau after Three Iterations of the Minimum-Cost Method

	Boston	Chicago	St. Louis	Lexington	**Supply**
Cleveland	3	2	7	6	1000 ~~5000~~
		4000			
Bedford	7	5	2	3	4000 ~~6000~~
			2000		
York	2	5	4	5	0 ~~2500~~
	2500				
Demand	~~6000~~ 3500	~~4000~~ 0	~~2000~~ 0	1500	

Table 7.11

Transportation Tableau after Five Iterations of the Minimum-Cost Method

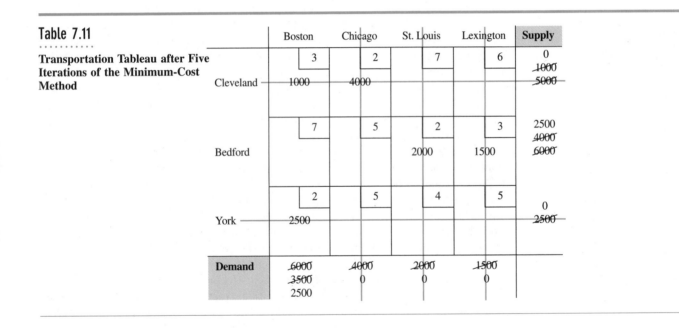

	Boston	Chicago	St. Louis	Lexington	**Supply**
Cleveland	3	2	7	6	0 ~~1000~~ ~~5000~~
	1000	4000			
Bedford	7	5	2	3	2500 ~~4000~~ ~~6000~~
			2000	1500	
York	2	5	4	5	0 ~~2500~~
	2500				
Demand	~~6000~~ ~~3500~~ 2500	~~4000~~ 0	~~2000~~ 0	~~1500~~ 0	

This solution is feasible because all the demand is satisfied and all the supply is used. The total transportation cost resulting from this initial feasible solution is calculated in Table 7.13. Phase I of the transportation simplex method is now complete; we have an initial feasible solution. The total transportation cost associated with this solution is $42,000.

Summary of the Minimum-Cost Method Before applying phase II of the transportation simplex method, let us summarize the steps for obtaining an initial feasible solution using the minimum-cost method.

Table 7.12

Final Tableau Showing the Initial Feasible Solution Obtained Using the Minimum-Cost Method

	Boston	Chicago	St. Louis	Lexington	Supply
Cleveland	3 1000	2 4000	7	6	0 ~~1000~~ ~~5000~~
Bedford	7 2500	5	2 2000	3 1500	0 ~~2500~~ ~~4000~~ ~~6000~~
York	2 2500	5	4	5	0 ~~2500~~
Demand	~~6000~~ ~~3500~~ ~~2500~~ 0	~~4000~~ 0	~~2000~~ 0	~~1500~~ 0	

Table 7.13

Total Cost of the Initial Feasible Solution Obtained Using the Minimum-Cost Method

| Route | | Units | Cost | |
From	To	Shipped	Per Unit	Total Cost
Cleveland	Boston	1000	$3	$ 3,000
Cleveland	Chicago	4000	$2	8,000
Bedford	Boston	2500	$7	17,500
Bedford	St. Louis	2000	$2	4,000
Bedford	Lexington	1500	$3	4,500
York	Boston	2500	$2	5,000
				$42,000

Step 1 Identify the cell in the transportation tableau with the lowest cost, and allocate as much flow as possible to this cell. In case of a tie, choose the cell corresponding to the arc over which the most units can be shipped. If ties still exist, choose any of the tied cells.

Step 2 Reduce the row supply and the column demand by the amount of flow allocated to the cell identified in step 1.

Step 3 If *all* row supplies and column demands have been exhausted, then stop; the allocations made will provide an initial feasible solution. Otherwise, continue with step 4.

You should be able to use the minimum-cost method to find an initial feasible solution. Try part (a) of Problem 34.

Step 4 If the row supply is now zero, eliminate the row from further consideration by drawing a line through it. If the column demand is now zero, eliminate the column by drawing a line through it.

Step 5 Continue with step 1 for all unlined rows and columns.

Phase II: Iterating to the Optimal Solution

Phase II of the transportation simplex method is a procedure for iterating from the initial feasible solution identified in phase I to the optimal solution. Recall that each cell in the transportation tableau corresponds to an arc (route) in the network model of the transportation problem. The first step at each iteration of phase II is to identify an incoming arc. The *incoming arc* is the currently unused route (unoccupied cell) where making a flow allocation will cause the largest per-unit reduction in total cost. Flow is then assigned to the incoming arc, and the amounts being shipped over all other arcs to which flow had previously been assigned (occupied cells) are adjusted as necessary to maintain a feasible solution. In the process of adjusting the flow assigned to the occupied cells, we identify and drop an *outgoing arc* from the solution. Thus, at each iteration in phase II, we bring a currently unused arc (unoccupied cell) into the solution, and remove an arc to which flow had previously been assigned (occupied cell) from the solution.

To show how phase II of the transportation simplex method works, we must explain how to identify the incoming arc (cell), how to make the adjustments to the other occupied cells when flow is allocated to the incoming arc, and how to identify the outgoing arc (cell). We first consider identifying the incoming arc.

As mentioned, the incoming arc is the one that will cause the largest reduction per unit in the total cost of the current solution. To identify this arc, we must compute for each unused arc the amount by which total cost will be reduced by shipping one unit over that arc. The *mo*dified *di*stribution or *MODI method* is a way to make this computation.

The MODI method requires that we define an index u_i for each row of the tableau and an index v_j for each column of the tableau. Computing these row and column indices requires that the cost coefficient for each occupied cell equal $u_i + v_j$. Thus, if c_{ij} is the cost per unit from origin i to destination j, $u_i + v_j = c_{ij}$ for each occupied cell. Let us return to the initial feasible solution for the Foster Generators problem, which we found using the minimum-cost method (see Table 7.14), and use the MODI method to identify the incoming arc.

Table 7.14

Initial Feasible Solution to the Foster Generators Problem

	Boston	Chicago	St. Louis	Lexington	Supply
Cleveland	3 / 1000	2 / 4000	7	6	5000
Bedford	7 / 2500	5	2 / 2000	3 / 1500	6000
York	2 / 2500	5	4	5	2500
Demand	6000	4000	2000	1500	

Requiring that $u_i + v_j = c_{ij}$ for all the occupied cells in the initial feasible solution leads to a system of six equations and seven indices, or variables:

Occupied Cell	$u_i + v_j = c_{ij}$
Cleveland–Boston	$u_1 + v_1 = 3$
Cleveland–Chicago	$u_1 + v_2 = 2$
Bedford–Boston	$u_2 + v_1 = 7$
Bedford–St. Louis	$u_2 + v_3 = 2$
Bedford–Lexington	$u_2 + v_4 = 3$
York–Boston	$u_3 + v_1 = 2$

With one more index (variable) than equation in this system, we can freely pick a value for one of the indices and then solve for the others. We will always choose $u_1 = 0$ and then solve for the values of the other indices. Setting $u_1 = 0$, we obtain

$$0 + v_1 = 3$$

$$0 + v_2 = 2$$

$$u_2 + v_1 = 7$$

$$u_2 + v_3 = 2$$

$$u_2 + v_4 = 3$$

$$u_3 + v_1 = 2$$

Solving these equations leads to the following values for $u_1, u_2, u_3, v_1, v_2, v_3,$ and v_4:

$$u_1 = 0 \qquad v_1 = 3$$

$$u_2 = 4 \qquad v_2 = 2$$

$$u_3 = -1 \qquad v_3 = -2$$

$$ v_4 = -1$$

Management scientists have shown that for each *unoccupied* cell, $e_{ij} = c_{ij} - u_i - v_j$ provides the change in total cost per unit that will be obtained by allocating one unit of flow to the corresponding arc. Thus, we will call e_{ij} the *net evaluation index*. Because of the way u_i and v_j are computed, the net evaluation index for each occupied cell equals zero.

Rewriting the tableau containing the initial feasible solution for the Foster Generators problem and replacing the previous marginal information with the values of u_i and v_j, we obtain Table 7.15. We computed the net evaluation index (e_{ij}) for each unoccupied cell, which is the circled number in the cell. Thus, shipping one unit over the route from origin 1 to destination 3 (Cleveland–St. Louis) will increase total cost by $9; shipping one unit from origin 1 to destination 4 (Cleveland–Lexington) will increase total cost by $7; shipping one unit from origin 2 to destination 2 (Bedford–Chicago) will decrease total cost by $1; and so on.

On the basis of the net evaluation indices, the best arc in terms of cost reduction (a net evaluation index of −1) is associated with the Bedford–Chicago route (origin 2–destination 2); thus, the cell in row 2 and column 2 is chosen as the incoming cell. There will be a $1 decrease in total cost for every unit of flow assigned to this arc. The question now is: How much flow should we assign to this arc? Because the total cost

Table 7.15

Cost Per Unit Changes for the Initial Feasible Solution to the Foster Generators Problem Computed Using the MODI Method

u_i	v_j			
	3	2	−2	−1
0	3 1000	2 4000	7 ⑨	6 ⑦
4	7 2500	5 ⊝1	2 2000	3 1500
−1	2 2500	5 ④	4 ⑦	5 ⑦

Table 7.16

Cycle of Adjustments in Occupied Cells Necessary to Maintain Feasibility When Shipping One Unit from Bedford to Chicago

	Boston	Chicago	St. Louis	Lexington	**Supply**
Cleveland	3 1001 ~~1000~~	2 3999 ~~4000~~	7	6	5000
Bedford	7 2499 ~~2500~~	5 1	2 2000	3 1500	6000
York	2 2500	5	4	5	2500
Demand	6000	4000	2000	1500	

decreases by $1 per unit assigned, we want to allocate the maximum possible flow. To find that maximum, we must recognize that, to maintain feasibility, each unit of flow assigned to this arc will require adjustments in the flow over the other currently used arcs. The *stepping-stone method* can be used to determine the adjustments necessary and to identify an outgoing arc.

The Stepping-Stone Method   Suppose that we allocate one unit of flow to the incoming arc (the Bedford–Chicago route). To maintain feasibility—that is, not exceed the number of units to be shipped to Chicago—we would have to reduce the flow assigned to the Cleveland–Chicago arc to 3999. But then we would have to increase the flow on the Cleveland–Boston arc to 1001 so that the total Cleveland supply of 5000 units could be shipped. Finally, we would have to reduce the flow on the Bedford–Boston arc by 1 to satisfy the Boston demand. Table 7.16 summarizes this cycle of adjustments.

Table 7.17

Stepping-Stone Path with the
Bedford–Chicago Route as the
Incoming Arc

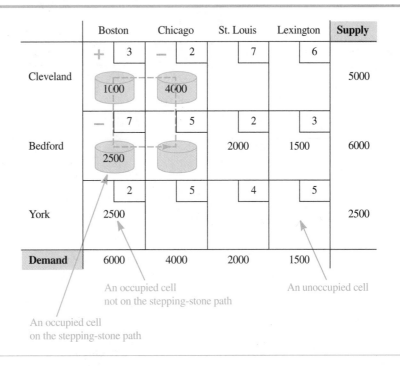

	Boston	Chicago	St. Louis	Lexington	Supply
Cleveland	+ 3 / 1000	− 2 / 4000	7	6	5000
Bedford	− 7 / 2500	5	2 / 2000	3 / 1500	6000
York	2 / 2500	5	4	5	2500
Demand	6000	4000	2000	1500	

An occupied cell
not on the stepping-stone path

An unoccupied cell

An occupied cell
on the stepping-stone path

The cycle of adjustments needed in making an allocation to the Bedford–Chicago cell required changes in four cells: the incoming cell (Bedford–Chicago) and three currently occupied cells. We can view these four cells as forming a stepping-stone path in the tableau, where the corners of the path are currently occupied cells. The idea behind the stepping-stone path name is to view the tableau as a pond with the occupied cells as stones sticking up in it. To identify the stepping-stone path for an incoming cell, we start at the incoming cell and move horizontally and vertically using occupied cells as the stones at the corners of the path; the objective is to step from stone to stone and return to the incoming cell where we started. To focus attention on which occupied cells are part of the stepping-stone path, we draw each occupied cell in the stepping-stone path as a cylinder, which should reinforce the image of these cells as stones sticking up in the pond. Table 7.17 depicts the stepping-stone path associated with the incoming arc of the Bedford–Chicago route.

In Table 7.17 we placed a plus sign (+) or a minus sign (−) in each occupied cell on the stepping-stone path. A plus sign indicates that the allocation to that cell will increase by the same amount we allocate to the incoming cell. A minus sign indicates that the allocation to that cell will decrease by the amount allocated to the incoming cell. Thus, to determine the maximum amount that may be allocated to the incoming cell, we simply look to the cells on the stepping-stone path identified with a minus sign. Because no arc can have a negative flow, the minus-sign cell with the *smallest amount* allocated to it will determine the maximum amount that can be allocated to the incoming cell. After allocating this maximum amount to the incoming cell, we then make all the adjustments necessary on the stepping-stone path to maintain feasibility. The incoming cell becomes an occupied cell, and the outgoing cell is dropped from the current solution.

In the Foster Generators problem, the Bedford–Boston and Cleveland–Chicago cells are the ones where the allocation will decrease (the ones with a minus sign) as flow is allocated to the incoming arc (Bedford–Chicago). The 2500 units currently assigned to

Table 7.18

New Solution After One Iteration in Phase II of the Transportation Simplex Method

	Boston	Chicago	St. Louis	Lexington	Supply
Cleveland	3 3500	2 1500	7	6	5000
Bedford	7	5 2500	2 2000	3 1500	6000
York	2 2500	5	4	5	2500
Demand	6000	4000	2000	1500	

Bedford–Boston is less than the 4000 units assigned to Cleveland–Chicago, so we identify Bedford–Boston as the outgoing arc. We then obtain the new solution by allocating 2500 units to the Bedford–Chicago arc, making the appropriate adjustments on the stepping-stone path and dropping Bedford–Boston from the solution (its allocation has been driven to zero). Table 7.18 shows the tableau associated with the new solution. Note that the only changes from the previous tableau are located on the stepping-stone path originating in the Bedford–Chicago cell.

We now try to improve on the current solution. Again, the first step is to apply the MODI method to find the best incoming arc, so we recompute the row and column indices by requiring that $u_i + v_j = c_{ij}$ for all occupied cells. The values of u_i and v_j can easily be computed directly on the tableau. Recall that we begin the MODI method by setting $u_1 = 0$. Thus, for the two occupied cells in row 1 of the table, $v_j = c_{1j}$; as a result, $v_1 = 3$ and $v_2 = 2$. Moving down the column associated with each newly computed column index, we compute the row index associated with each occupied cell in that column by subtracting v_j from c_{ij}. Doing so for the newly found column indices, v_1 and v_2, we find that $u_3 = 2 - 3 = -1$ and that $u_2 = 5 - 2 = 3$. Next, we use these row indices to compute the column indices for occupied cells in the associated rows, obtaining $v_3 = 2 - 3 = -1$ and $v_4 = 3 - 3 = 0$. Table 7.19 shows these new row and column indices.

Also shown in Table 7.19 are the net changes (the circled numbers) in the value of the solution that will result from allocating one unit to each unoccupied cell. Recall that these are the net evaluation indices given by $e_{ij} = c_{ij} - u_i - v_j$. Note that the net evaluation index for every unoccupied cell is now greater than or equal to zero. This condition shows that if current unoccupied cells are used, the cost will actually increase. Without an arc to which flow can be assigned to decrease the total cost, we have reached the optimal solution. Table 7.20 summarizes the optimal solution and shows its total cost. As expected, this solution is exactly the same as the one obtained using the linear programming solution approach (Figure 7.2).

Maintaining $m + n - 1$ Occupied Cells   Recall that m represents the number of origins and n represents the number of destinations. A solution to a transportation problem that has less than $m + n - 1$ cells with positive allocations is said to be *degenerate*. The solution to the Foster Generators problem is not degenerate; six cells are occupied and $m +$

Table 7.19

MODI Evaluation of Each Cell in Solution

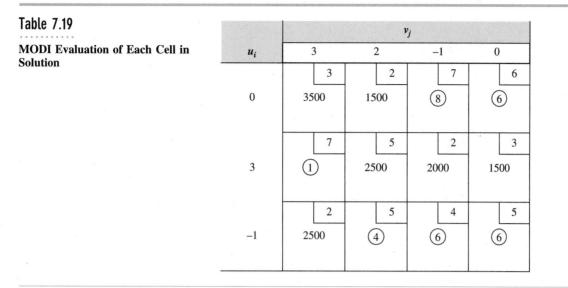

Table 7.20

Optimal Solution to the Foster Generators Transportation Problem

Route				
From	To	Units Shipped	Cost/Unit	Total Cost
Cleveland	Boston	3500	$3	$10,500
Cleveland	Chicago	1500	$2	3,000
Bedford	Chicago	2500	$5	12,500
Bedford	St. Louis	2000	$2	4,000
Bedford	Lexington	1500	$3	4,500
York	Boston	2500	$2	5,000
				$39,500

$n - 1 = 3 + 4 - 1 = 6$. The problem with degeneracy is that $m + n - 1$ occupied cells are required by the MODI method to compute all the row and column indices. When degeneracy occurs, we must artificially create an occupied cell in order to compute the row and column indices. Let us illustrate how degeneracy could occur and how to deal with it.

Table 7.21 shows the initial feasible solution obtained using the minimum-cost method for a transportation problem involving $m = 3$ origins and $n = 3$ destinations. To use the MODI method for this problem, we must have $m + n - 1 = 3 + 3 - 1 = 5$ occupied cells. Since the initial feasible solution has only four occupied cells, the solution is degenerate.

Suppose that we try to use the MODI method to compute row and column indices to begin phase II for this problem. Setting $u_1 = 0$ and computing the column indices for each occupied cell in row 1, we obtain $v_1 = 3$ and $v_2 = 6$ (see Table 7.21). Continuing, we then compute the row indices for all occupied cells in columns 1 and 2. Doing so yields $u_2 = 5 - 6 = -1$. At this point, we cannot compute any more row and column indices because there are no occupied cells in rows 1 or 2 of column 3.

To compute all the row and column indices when there are less than $m + n - 1$ occupied cells, we must create one or more "artificially" occupied cells with a flow of zero. In Table 7.21 we must create one artificially occupied cell to have five occupied

Table 7.21

Transportation Tableau with a Degenerate Initial Feasible Solution

u_i	v_j 3	6		Supply
0	3 35	6 25	7	60
−1	8	5 30	7	30
	4	9	11 30	30
Demand	35	55	30	

Table 7.22

Transportation Tableau with an Artificial Cell in Row 2 and Column 3

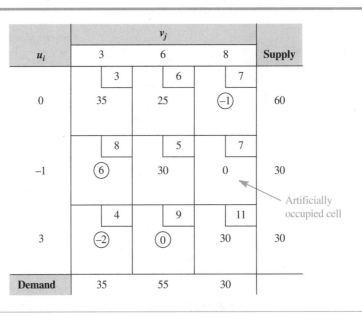

u_i	v_j 3	6	8	Supply
0	3 35	6 25	7 (−1)	60
−1	8 (6)	5 30	7 0	30
3	4 (−2)	9 (0)	11 30	30
Demand	35	55	30	

Artificially occupied cell

cells. Any currently unoccupied cell can be made an artificially occupied cell if doing so makes it possible to compute the remaining row and column indices. For instance, treating the cell in row 2 and column 3 of Table 7.21 as an artificially occupied cell will enable us to compute v_3 and u_3, but placing it in row 2 and column 1 will not.

As we previously stated, whenever an artificially occupied cell is created, we assign a flow of zero to the corresponding arc. Table 7.22 shows the results of creating an artificially occupied cell in row 2 and column 3 of Table 7.21. Creation of the artificially occupied cell results in five occupied cells, so we can now compute the remaining row

Table 7.23

Stepping-Stone Path for the
Incoming Cell in Row 3 and
Column 1

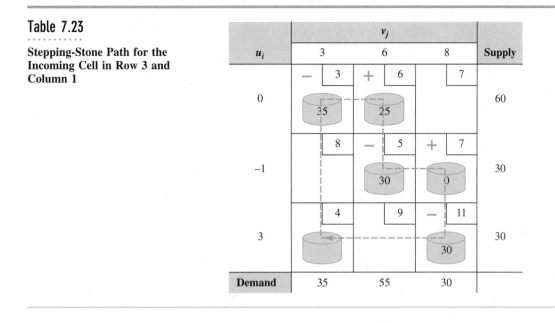

u_i	v_j			
	3	6	8	Supply
0	− 3 / 35	+ 6 / 25	7	60
−1	8	− 5 / 30	+ 7 / 0	30
3	4	9	− 11 / 30	30
Demand	35	55	30	

and column indices. Using the row 2 index ($u_2 = -1$) and the artificially occupied cell in row 2, we compute the column index for column 3; thus, $v_3 = c_{23} - u_2 = 7 - (-1) = 8$. Then, using the column 3 index ($v_3 = 8$) and the occupied cell in row 3 and column 3 of the tableau, we compute the row 3 index: $u_3 = c_{33} - v_3 = 11 - 8 = 3$. Table 7.22 shows the complete set of row and column indices and the net evaluation index for each unoccupied cell.

Reviewing the net evaluation indices in Table 7.22, we identify the cell in row 3 and column 1 (net evaluation index = −2) as the incoming cell. The stepping-stone path and the adjustments necessary to maintain feasibility are shown in Table 7.23. Note that the stepping-stone path can be more complex than the simple one obtained for the incoming cell in the Foster Generators problem. The path in Table 7.23 requires adjustments in all five occupied cells to maintain feasibility. Again, the plus- and minus-sign labels simply show where increases and decreases in the allocation will occur as units of flow are added to the incoming cell. The smallest flow in a decreasing cell is a tie between the cell in row 2 and column 2 and the cell in row 3 and column 3.

Since the smallest amount in a decreasing cell is 30, the allocation we make to the incoming cell is 30 units. However, when 30 units are allocated to the incoming cell and the appropriate adjustments are made to the occupied cells on the stepping-stone path, the allocations to two cells go to zero (row 2, column 2 and row 3, column 3). We may choose either one as the outgoing cell, but not both. One will be treated as unoccupied; the other will become an artificially occupied cell with a flow of zero allocated to it. The reason we cannot let both become unoccupied cells is that doing so would lead to a degenerate solution, and as before, we could not use the MODI method to compute the row and column indices for the next iteration. When ties occur in choosing the outgoing cell, we can choose any one of the tied cells as the artificially occupied cell and then use the MODI method to recompute the row and column indices. As long as no more than one cell is dropped at each iteration, the MODI method will work.

The solution obtained after allocating 30 units to the incoming cell in row 3 and column 1 and making the appropriate adjustments on the stepping-stone path leads to the tableau shown in Table 7.24. Note that we treated the cell in row 2 and column 2 as the

Table 7.24

New Row and Column Indices Obtained after Allocating 30 Units to the Incoming Cell

u_i	v_j 3	6	8	Supply
0	3 ⌐ 5	6 ⌐ 55	7 ⌐ Ⓝ(-1)	60
-1	8 ⌐ Ⓝ6	5 ⌐ 0	7 ⌐ 30	30
1	4 ⌐ 30	9 ⌐ Ⓝ2	11 ⌐ Ⓝ2	30
Demand	35	55	30	

Table 7.25

Stepping-Stone Path Associated with the Incoming Cell in Row 1 and Column 3

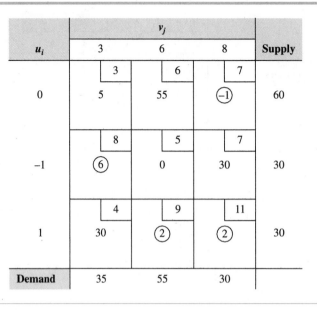

u_i	v_j 3	6	8	Supply
0	3	6 − 55	7	60
-1	8 + 0	5 − 30	7	30
1	4	9	11	30
Demand	35	55	30	

artificially occupied cell. After computing the new row and column indices, we see that the cell in row 1 and column 3 will be the next incoming cell. Each unit allocated to this cell will further decrease the value of the solution by 1. The stepping-stone path associated with this incoming cell is shown in Table 7.25. The cell in row 2 and column 3 is the outgoing cell; the tableau after this iteration is shown in Table 7.26. Note that we have found the optimal solution and that, even though several earlier iterations were degenerate, the final solution is not degenerate.

Table 7.26

**Optimal Solution to a Problem with
a Degenerate Initial Feasible
Solution**

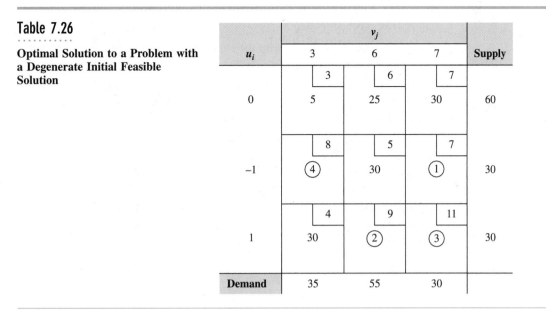

u_i	v_j 3	6	7	Supply
0	[3] 5	[6] 25	[7] 30	60
−1	[8] ④	[5] 30	[7] ①	30
1	[4] 30	[9] ②	[11] ③	30
Demand	35	55	30	

Summary of the Transportation Simplex Method

The transportation simplex method is a special-purpose solution procedure applicable to any network model having the special structure of the transportation problem. It is actually a clever implementation of the general simplex method for linear programming that takes advantage of the special mathematical structure of the transportation problem; but because of the special structure, the transportation simplex method is hundreds of times faster than the general simplex method.

To apply the transportation simplex method, you must have a transportation problem with total supply equal to total demand; thus, for some problems you may need to add a dummy origin or dummy destination to put the problem in this form. The transportation simplex method takes the problem in this form and applies a two-phase solution procedure. In phase I, apply the minimum-cost method to find an initial feasible solution. In phase II, begin with the initial feasible solution and iterate until you reach an optimal solution. The steps of the transportation simplex method for a minimization problem are summarized as follows.

Try part (b) of Problem 34 for practice using the transportation simplex method.

Phase I
Find an initial feasible solution using the minimum-cost method.

Phase II

Step 1   If the initial feasible solution is degenerate with less than $m + n - 1$ occupied cells, add an artificially occupied cell or cells so that $m + n - 1$ occupied cells exist in locations that enable use of the MODI method.

Step 2   Use the MODI method to compute the row indicies, u_i, and the column indices, v_j.

Step 3   Compute the net evaluation index $e_{ij} = c_{ij} - u_i - v_j$ for each unoccupied cell.

Step 4   If $e_{ij} \geq 0$ for all unoccupied cells, stop; you have reached the optimal solution. Otherwise, proceed to step 5.

Step 5   Identify the unoccupied cell with the smallest (most negative) net evaluation index as the incoming cell.

Step 6   Find the stepping-stone path associated with the incoming cell. Label each cell on the stepping-stone path whose flow will increase with a plus sign and each cell whose flow will decrease with a minus sign.

Step 7   Choose as the outgoing cell the minus-sign cell on the stepping-stone path with the smallest flow. If there is a tie, choose any one of the tied cells. The tied cells that are not chosen will be artificially occupied with a flow of zero at the next iteration.

Step 8   Allocate to the incoming cell the amount of flow currently given to the outgoing cell; make the appropriate adjustments to all cells on the stepping-stone path, and continue with step 2.

Problem Variations

The following problem variations can be handled, with slight adaptations, by the transportation simplex method:

1.   Total supply not equal to total demand
2.   Maximization objective function
3.   Unacceptable routes

[handwritten annotation: All should be Negative or Zero]

The case where the total supply is not equal to the total demand can be handled easily by the transportation simplex method if we first introduce a dummy origin or a dummy destination. If total supply is greater than total demand, we introduce a *dummy destination* with demand equal to the excess of supply over demand. Similarly, if total demand is greater than total supply, we introduce a *dummy origin* with supply equal to the excess of demand over supply. In either case, the use of a dummy destination or a dummy origin will equalize total supply and total demand so that we can use the transportation simplex method. When a dummy destination or origin is present, we assign cost coefficients of zero to every arc into a dummy destination and to every arc out of a dummy origin. The reason is that no shipments will actually be made from a dummy origin or to a dummy destination when the solution is implemented and thus a zero cost per unit is appropriate.

The transportation simplex method also can be used to solve maximization problems. The only modification necessary involves the selection of an incoming cell. Instead of picking the cell with the smallest or most negative e_{ij} value, we pick that cell for which e_{ij} is largest. That is, we pick the cell that will cause the largest increase per unit in the objective function. If $e_{ij} \leq 0$ for all unoccupied cells, we stop; the maximization solution has been reached.

To handle unacceptable routes in a minimization problem, infeasible arcs must carry an extremely high cost, denoted M, to keep them out of the solution. Thus, if we have a route (arc) from an origin to a destination that for some reason cannot be used, we simply assign this arc a cost per unit of M, and it will not enter the solution. Unacceptable arcs would be assigned a profit per unit of $-M$ in a maximization problem.

NOTES &comments

1. Much research in the 1970s and 1980s was devoted to developing efficient special-purpose solution procedures for network problems. The transportation simplex method is generally recognized as one of the best; it is used in The Management Scientist software package. A simple extension of this method also can be used to solve transshipment problems.

2. As we have previously noted, each cell in the transportation tableau corresponds to an arc (route) in the network model of the problem and a variable in the linear programming formulation. Phase II of the transportation simplex method is thus the same as phase II of the simplex method for linear programming. At each iteration, one variable is brought into solution and another variable is dropped from solution. The reason the method works so much better for transportation problems is that the special mathematical structure of the constraint equations means that only addition and subtraction operations are necessary. We can implement the entire procedure in a transportation tableau that has one row for each origin and one column for each destination. A simplex tableau for such a problem would require a row for each origin, a row for each destination, and a column for each arc; thus, the simplex tableau would be much larger.

7.6 The Assignment Problem: A Special-Purpose Solution Procedure (Optional)

As mentioned previously, the assignment problem is a special case of the transportation problem. Thus, the transportation simplex method can be used to solve the assignment problem. However, the assignment problem has an even more special structure: All supplies and demands equal 1. Because of this additional special structure, special-purpose solution procedures have been specifically designed to solve the assignment problem; one such procedure is called the *Hungarian method*. In this section we will show how the Hungarian method can be used to solve the Fowle Marketing Research problem.

Recall that the Fowle problem (see Section 7.2) involved assigning project leaders to clients; three project leaders were available and three research projects were to be completed for three clients. Fowle's assignment alternatives and estimated project completion times in days are restated in Table 7.27.

The Hungarian method involves what is called *matrix reduction*. Subtracting and adding appropriate values in the matrix yields an optimal solution to the assignment problem. Three major steps are associated with the procedure. Step 1 involves row and column reduction.

Step 1   Reduce the initial matrix by subtracting the smallest element in each row from every element in that row. Then, using the row-reduced matrix, subtract the smallest element in each column from every element in that column.

Table 7.27

Estimated Project Completion Times (Days) for the Fowle Assignment Problem

	Client		
Project Leader	1	2	3
Terry	10	15	9
Carle	9	18	5
McClymonds	6	14	3

Thus, we first reduce the matrix in Table 7.27 by subtracting the minimum value in each row from each element in the row. With the minimum values of 9 for row 1, 5 for row 2, and 3 for row 3, the row-reduced matrix becomes

	1	2	3
Terry	1	6	0
Carle	4	13	0
McClymonds	3	11	0

The assignment problem represented by this reduced matrix is equivalent to the original assignment problem in the sense that the same solution will be optimal. To understand why, first note that the row 1 minimum element, 9, has been subtracted from every element in the first row. Since Terry must still be assigned to one of the clients, the only change is that in this revised problem the time for any assignment will be 9 days less. Similarly, Carle and McClymonds are shown with completion times requiring 5 and 3 fewer days, respectively.

Continuing with step 1 in the matrix reduction process, we now subtract the minimum element in each column of the row-reduced matrix from every element in the column. This operation also leads to an equivalent assignment problem; that is, the same solution will still be optimal, but the times required to complete each project are reduced. With the minimum values of 1 for column 1, 6 for column 2, and 0 for column 3, the reduced matrix becomes

	1	2	3
Terry	0	0	0
Carle	3	7	0
McClymonds	2	5	0

The goal of the Hungarian method is to continue reducing the matrix until the value of one of the solutions is zero—that is, until an assignment of project leaders to clients can be made that, in terms of the reduced matrix, requires a total time expenditure of zero days. Then, as long as there are no negative elements in the matrix, the zero-valued solution will be optimal. The way in which we perform this further reduction and recognize when we have reached an optimal solution is described in the following two steps.

Step 2   Find the minimum number of straight lines that must be drawn through the rows and the columns of the current matrix so that all the zeros in the matrix will be covered. If the minimum number of straight lines is the same as the number of rows (or equivalently, columns), an optimal assignment with a value of zero can be made. If the minimum number of lines is less than the number of rows, go to step 3.

Applying step 2, we see that the minimum number of lines required to cover all the zeros is 2. Thus, we must continue to step 3.

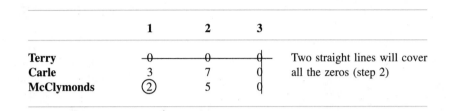

	1	2	3	
Terry	0	0	0	Two straight lines will cover
Carle	3	7	0	all the zeros (step 2)
McClymonds	②	5	0	

Step 3   Subtract the value of the smallest unlined element from every unlined element, and add this same value to every element at the intersection of two lines. All other elements remain unchanged. Return to step 2, and continue until the minimum number of lines necessary to cover all the zeros in the matrix is equal to the number of rows.

The minimum unlined element is 2. In the preceding matrix we circled this element. Subtracting 2 from all unlined elements and adding 2 to the intersection element for Terry and client 3 produces the new matrix:

	1	2	3
Terry	0	0	2
Carle	1	5	0
McClymonds	0	3	0

Returning to step 2, we find that the minimum number of straight lines required to cover all the zeros in the current matrix is 3. The following matrix illustrates the step 2 calculations.

	1	2	3	
Terry	0	0	2	Three lines must be drawn to
Carle	1	5	0	cover all zeros; therefore, the opti-
McClymonds	0	3	0	mal solution has been reached

According to step 2, then, it must be possible to find an assignment with a value of zero. To do so we first locate any row or column that contains only one zero. If all have more than one zero, we choose the assignment with the fewest assignments tied with it. We draw a square around the zero, indicating an assignment, and eliminate that row and column from further consideration. Row 2 has only one zero in the Fowle problem, so we assign Carle to client 3 and eliminate row 2 and column 3 from further consideration. McClymonds must then be assigned to client 1 (the only remaining zero in row 3) and, finally, Terry to client 2. The solution to the Fowle problem, in terms of the reduced matrix, requires a time expenditure of zero days, as follows:

	1	2	3
Terry	0	[0]	2
Carle	1	5	[0]
McClymonds	[0]	3	0

We obtain the value of the optimal assignment by referring to the original assignment problem and summing the solution times associated with the optimal assignment—in this case, Terry to client 2, Carle to client 3, and McClymonds to client 1. Thus, we obtain the solution time of 15 + 5 + 6 = 26 days.

Finding the Minimum Number of Lines

Sometimes it is not obvious how the lines should be drawn through rows and columns of the matrix in order to cover all the zeros with the smallest number of lines. In these cases, the following heuristic works well. Choose any row or column with a single zero. If it is a row, draw a line through the column the zero is in; if it is a column, draw a line through the row the zero is in. Continue in this fashion until you cover all the zeros.

If you make the mistake of drawing too many lines to cover the zeros in the reduced matrix and thus conclude incorrectly that you have reached an optimal solution, you will be unable to identify a zero-value assignment. Thus, if you think you have reached the optimal solution, but cannot find a set of zero-value assignments, go back to the preceding step and check to see if you can cover all the zeros with fewer lines.

You should be able to solve an assignment problem using the Hungarian method. Try Problem 40.

Problem Variations

We now discuss how to handle the following problem variations with the Hungarian method:

1. Number of agents not equal to number of tasks
2. Maximization objective function
3. Unacceptable assignments

Number of Agents Not Equal to Number of Tasks   The Hungarian method requires that the number of rows (agents) equal the number of columns (tasks). Suppose that in the Fowle problem four project leaders (agents) had been available for assignment to the three new clients (tasks). Fowle still faces the same basic problem, namely, which project leaders should be assigned to which clients to minimize the total days required. Table 7.28 shows the project completion time estimates with a fourth project leader.

We know how to apply the Hungarian method when the number of rows and the number of columns are equal. We can apply the same procedure if we can add a new client. Since we do not have another client, we simply add a *dummy column,* or a dummy client. This dummy client is nonexistent, so the project leader assigned to the dummy client in the optimal assignment solution, in effect, will be the unassigned project leader.

What project completion time estimates should we show in this new dummy column? Since the dummy client assignment will not actually take place, a zero project completion

Table 7.28

Estimated Project Completion Time (Days) for the Fowle Assignment Problem with Four Project Leaders

	Client		
Project Leader	1	2	3
Terry	10	15	9
Carle	9	18	5
McClymonds	6	14	3
Higley	8	16	6

Table 7.29

Estimated Project Completion Time (Days) for the Fowle Assignment Problem with a Dummy Client

	Client				Dummy client
Project Leader	1	2	3	D	↙
Terry	10	15	9	0	
Carle	9	18	5	0	
McClymonds	6	14	3	0	
Higley	8	16	6	0	

Table 7.30

Estimated Annual Profit (Thousands of Dollars) for Each Department–Location Combination

	Location			
Department	1	2	3	4
Shoe	10	6	12	8
Toy	15	18	5	11
Auto parts	17	10	13	16
Housewares	14	12	13	10
Video	14	16	6	12

time for all project leaders seems logical. Table 7.29 shows the Fowle assignment problem with a dummy client, labeled D. (Problem 42 at the end of the chapter asks you to use the Hungarian method to determine the optimal solution to this problem.)

Note that if we had considered the case of four new clients and only three project leaders, we would have had to add a *dummy row* (dummy project leader) in order to apply the Hungarian method. The client receiving the dummy leader would not actually be assigned a project leader immediately and would have to wait until one becomes available. To obtain a problem form compatible with the solution algorithm, adding several dummy rows or dummy columns, but never both, may be necessary.

Maximization Objective   To illustrate how maximization assignment problems can be handled, let us consider the problem facing management of Salisbury Discounts, Inc. Suppose that Salisbury Discounts has just leased a new store and is attempting to determine where various departments should be located within the store. The store manager has four locations that have not yet been assigned a department and is considering five departments that might occupy the four locations. The departments under consideration are shoes, toys, auto parts, housewares, and videos. After a careful study of the layout of the remainder of the store, the store manager has made estimates of the expected annual profit for each department in each location. These are presented in Table 7.30.

Table 7.31

Estimated Annual Profit (Thousands of Dollars) for Each Department–Location Combination, Including a Dummy Location

Department	Location 1	2	3	4	5 (Dummy location)
Shoe	10	6	12	8	0
Toy	15	18	5	11	0
Auto parts	17	10	13	16	0
Housewares	14	12	13	10	0
Video	14	16	6	12	0

Table 7.32

Opportunity Loss (Thousands of Dollars) for Each Department–Location Combination

Department	Location 1	2	3	4	5 (Dummy location)
Shoe	7	12	1	8	0
Toy	2	0	8	5	0
Auto parts	0	8	0	0	0
Housewares	3	6	0	6	0
Video	3	2	7	4	0

This assignment problem requires a maximization objective. However, the problem also involves more rows than columns. Thus, we must first add a dummy column, corresponding to a dummy or fictitious location, in order to apply the Hungarian method. After adding a dummy column, we obtain the 5 × 5 Salisbury Discounts, Inc., assignment problem shown in Table 7.31.

We can obtain an equivalent minimization assignment problem by converting all the elements in the matrix to *opportunity losses*. We do so by subtracting every element in each column from the largest element in the column. Finding the assignment that minimizes opportunity loss leads to the same solution that maximizes the value of the assignment in the original problem. Thus, any maximization assignment problem can be converted to a minimization problem by converting the assignment matrix to one in which the elements represent opportunity losses. Hence, we begin the solution to this maximization assignment problem by developing an assignment matrix in which each element represents the opportunity loss for not making the "best" assignment. Table 7.32 presents the opportunity losses.

The opportunity loss from putting the shoe department in location 1 is $7000. That is, if we put the shoe department, instead of the best department (auto parts), in that location, we forgo the opportunity to make an additional $7000 in profit. The opportunity loss associated with putting the toy department in location 2 is zero because it yields the highest profit in that location. What about the opportunity losses associated with the dummy column? The assignment of a department to this dummy location means that the department will not be assigned a store location in the optimal solution. As all departments earn the same amount from this dummy location, zero, the opportunity loss for each department is zero.

Following steps 1, 2, and 3 of the Hungarian method on Table 7.32 will minimize opportunity loss and determine the maximum profit assignment.

Unacceptable Assignments   As an illustration of how we can handle unacceptable assignments, suppose that in the Salisbury Discounts, Inc., assignment problem the store

Try Problem 43 for practice in using the Hungarian method for a maximization problem.

Table 7.33

Estimated Profit for the Salisbury Department–Location Combinations

Department	Location				
	1	2	3	4	5
Shoe	10	6	12	8	0
Toy	15	$-M$	5	11	0
Auto parts	17	10	13	$-M$	0
Housewares	14	12	13	10	0
Video	14	16	6	12	0

manager believed that the toy department should not be considered for location 2 and that the auto parts department should not be considered for location 4. Essentially the store manager is saying that, based on other considerations, such as size of the area, adjacent departments, and so on, these two assignments are unacceptable alternatives.

Using the same approach for the assignment problem as we did for the transportation problem, we define a value of M for unacceptable minimization assignments and a value of $-M$ for unacceptable maximization assignments, where M is an arbitrarily large value. In fact, we assume M to be so large that M plus or minus any value is still extremely large. Thus, an M-valued cell in an assignment matrix retains its M value throughout the matrix reduction calculations. An M-valued cell can never be zero, so it can never be an assignment in the final solution.

The Salisbury Discounts, Inc., assignment problem with the two unacceptable assignments is shown in Table 7.33. When this assignment matrix is converted to an opportunity loss matrix, the $-M$ profit value will be changed to M. (Problem 44 at the end of this chapter asks you to solve this assignment problem.)

Summary

In this chapter we introduced transportation, assignment, and transshipment problems. All three types of problems belong to the special category of linear programs called *network flow problems*. The network model of a transportation problem consists of nodes representing a set of origins and a set of destinations. In the basic model, an arc is used to represent the route from each origin to each destination. Each origin has a supply and each destination has a demand. The problem is to determine the optimal amount to ship from each origin to each destination.

The assignment model is a special case of the transportation model in which all supply and all demand values are equal to 1. We represent each agent as an origin node and each task as a destination node. The transshipment model is an extension of the transportation model to distribution problems involving transfer points referred to as transshipment nodes. In this more general model, we allow arcs between any pair of nodes. A variation of the transshipment problem allows for placing capacities on the arcs. This variation, called the *capacitated transshipment problem,* is also known in the network flow literature as the pure network problem.

We showed how each of these network flow problems could be modeled as a linear program, and we solved each using a general-purpose linear programming computer package. However, many practical applications of network flow models lead to very large problems for which general-purpose linear programming codes are not efficient. The transportation simplex method was presented as an efficient special-purpose solution procedure for solving transportation problems. The procedure, and its extension to the transshipment problem, is hundreds of times faster than the general-purpose simplex method for large transportation and transshipment problems. The Hungarian method was presented as a special-purpose solution procedure for assignment problems.

In network flow problems, the optimal solution will be integral as long as all supplies and demands are integral. Therefore, when solving any transportation, assignment, or transshipment problem in which the supplies and demands are integral, we can expect to obtain an integer-valued solution.

Glossary

Transportation problem A network flow problem that often involves minimizing the cost of shipping goods from a set of origins to a set of destinations; it can be formulated and solved as a linear program by including a variable for each arc and a constraint for each node.

Network A graphical representation of a problem consisting of numbered circles (nodes) interconnected by a series of lines (arcs); arrowheads on the arcs show the direction of flow. Transportation, assignment, and transshipment problems are network flow problems.

Nodes The intersection or junction points of a network.

Arcs The lines connecting the nodes in a network.

Capacitated transportation problem A variation of the basic transportation problem in which there are capacities on some or all of the arcs.

Assignment problem A network flow problem that often involves the assignment of agents to tasks; it can be formulated as a linear program and is a special case of the transportation problem.

Transshipment problem An extension of the transportation problem to distribution problems involving transfer points and possible shipments between any pair of nodes.

Capacitated transshipment problem A variation of the transshipment problem in which there are capacities on some or all of the arcs.

Transportation simplex method A special-purpose solution procedure for the transportation problem.

Heuristic A commonsense procedure for quickly finding a solution to a problem. Heuristics are used to find initial feasible solutions for the transportation simplex method and in other applications.

Minimum-cost method A heuristic used to find an initial feasible solution to a transportation problem; it is easy to use and usually provides a good (but not optimal) solution.

Incoming arc The unused arc (represented by an unoccupied cell in the transportation tableau) to which flow is assigned during an iteration of the transportation simplex method.

MODI method The modified distribution method is a procedure for determining the net evaluation index for unused arcs in the transportation simplex method.

Net evaluation index The per-unit change in the objective function associated with assigning flow to an unused arc in the transportation simplex method.

Stepping-stone path The sequence of occupied cells that receive flow adjustments when flow is assigned to an unused arc in the transportation simplex method.

Outgoing arc The arc corresponding to an occupied cell that is dropped from solution during an iteration of the transportation simplex method.

Degenerate solution A solution to a transportation problem in which fewer than $m + n - 1$ arcs (cells) have positive flow; m is the number of origins and n is the number of destinations.

Dummy destination A destination added to a transportation problem to make the total supply equal to the total demand. The demand assigned to the dummy destination is the difference between the total supply and the total demand.

Dummy origin An origin added to a transportation problem in order to make the total supply equal to the total demand. The supply assigned to the dummy origin is the difference between the total demand and the total supply.

Hungarian method A special-purpose solution procedure for solving an assignment problem.

Opportunity loss For each cell in an assignment matrix, the difference between the largest value in the column and the value in the cell. The entries in the cells of an assignment matrix must be converted to opportunity losses to solve maximization problems using the Hungarian method.

Problems

Note: For Problems 1–32 a variety of solution methods can be used. In many cases, we ask you to formulate and solve the problem as a linear program. Where the solution method is not specified, you may also use the transportation or assignment modules of The Management Scientist or some other software package. Problems 33–45 are intended to be solved using the special-purpose algorithms of Sections 7.5 and 7.6. These special-purpose algorithms could also be used for many of the first 32 problems.

1. **SELF Test** A company imports goods at two ports: Philadelphia and New Orleans. Shipments of one of its products are made to customers in Atlanta, Dallas, Columbus, and Boston. For the next planning period, the supplies at each port, customer demands, and the shipping costs per case from each port to each customer are as follows:

| | Customers | | | | |
| | 1 | 2 | 3 | 4 | Port |
Port	Atlanta	Dallas	Columbus	Boston	Supply
1 Philadelphia	2	6	6	2	5000
2 New Orleans	1	2	5	7	3000
Demand	1400	3200	2000	1400	

Develop a network model of the distribution system (transportation problem).

2. **SELF Test** Consider the following network representation of a transportation problem:

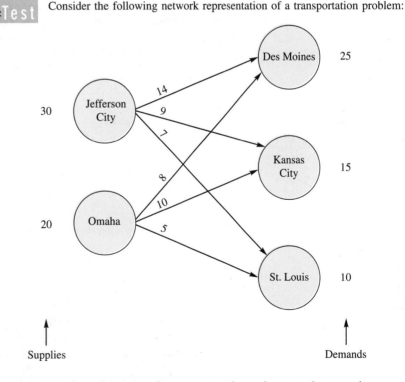

Supplies   Demands

The supplies, demands, and transportation costs per unit are shown on the network.
a. Develop a linear programming model for this problem; be sure to define the variables in your model.
b. Solve the linear program to determine the optimal solution.

3. Reconsider the distribution system described in Problem 1.
   a. Develop a linear programming model that can be solved to minimize transportation cost.
   b. Solve the linear program to determine the minimum-cost shipping schedule.

4. A product is produced at three plants and shipped to three warehouses (the transportation costs per unit are shown in the following table).

Plant	Warehouse W_1	W_2	W_3	Plant Capacity
P_1	20	16	24	300
P_2	10	10	8	500
P_3	12	18	10	100
Warehouse demand	200	400	300	

   a. Show a network representation of the problem.
   b. Develop a linear programming model for minimizing transportation costs; solve this model to determine the minimum-cost solution.
   c. Suppose that the entries in the table represent profit per unit produced at plant i and sold to warehouse j. How does the model formulation change from that in part (b)?

5. Tri-County Utilities, Inc., supplies natural gas to customers in a three-county area. The company purchases natural gas from two companies: Southern Gas and Northwest Gas. Demand forecasts for the coming winter season are Hamilton County, 400 units; Butler County, 200 units; and Clermont County, 300 units. Contracts to provide the following quantities have been written: Southern Gas, 500 units; and Northwest Gas, 400 units. Distribution costs for the counties vary, depending upon the location of the suppliers. The distribution costs per unit (in thousands of dollars) are as follows:

From	To Hamilton	Butler	Clermont
Southern Gas	10	20	15
Northwest Gas	12	15	18

   a. Develop a network representation of this problem.
   b. Develop a linear programming model that can be used to determine the plan that will minimize total distribution costs.
   c. Describe the distribution plan and show the total distribution cost.
   d. Recent residential and industrial growth in Butler County has the potential for increasing demand by as much as 100 units. Which supplier should Tri-County contract with to supply the additional capacity?

6. Arnoff Enterprises manufactures the central processing unit (CPU) for a line of personal computers. The CPUs are manufactured in Seattle, Columbus, and New York and shipped to warehouses in Pittsburgh, Mobile, Denver, Los Angeles, and Washington, D.C., for further distribution. The following transportation tableau shows the number of CPUs available at each plant and the number of CPUs required by each warehouse. The shipping costs (dollars per unit) are also shown in each cell.

Plant	Warehouse					CPUs Available
	Pittsburgh	Mobile	Denver	Los Angeles	Washington	
Seattle	10	20	5	9	10	9000
Columbus	2	10	8	30	6	4000
New York	1	20	7	10	4	8000
CPUs Required	3000	5000	4000	6000	3000	21,000

a. Develop a network representation of this problem.

b. Determine the amount that should be shipped from each plant to each warehouse to minimize the total shipping cost.

c. The Pittsburgh warehouse has just increased its order by 1000 units, and Arnoff has authorized the Columbus plant to increase its production by 1000 units. Will this lead to an increase or decrease in total shipping costs? Solve for the new optimal solution.

7. Premier Consulting has two consultants, Avery and Baker, who can be scheduled to work for clients up to a maximum of 160 hours each over the next four weeks. A third consultant, Campbell, has some administrative assignments already planned and is available for clients up to a maximum of 140 hours over the next four weeks. The company has four clients with projects in process. The estimated hourly requirements for each of the clients over the four-week period are

Client	Hours
A	180
B	75
C	100
D	85

Hourly rates vary for the consultant–client combination and are based on several factors, including project type and the consultant's experience. The rates (dollars per hour) for each consultant–client combination are

Consultant	Client A	Client B	Client C	Client D
Avery	100	125	115	100
Baker	120	135	115	120
Campbell	155	150	140	130

a. Develop a network representation of the problem.

b. Formulate the problem as a linear program, with the optimal solution providing the hours each consultant should be scheduled for each client in order to maximize the consulting firm's billings. What is the schedule and what is the total billing?

c. New information shows that Avery doesn't have the experience to be scheduled for client B. If this consulting assignment is not permitted, what impact does it have on total billings? What is the revised schedule?

8. **SELF Test** Klein Chemicals, Inc., produces a special oil-base material that is currently in short supply. Four of Klein's customers have already placed orders that together exceed the combined capacity of Klein's two plants. Klein's management faces the problem of deciding how many units it should supply to each customer. Since the four customers are in different industries, different prices can be charged because of the various industry pricing structures. However, slightly different production costs at the two plants and varying transportation costs between the plants and customers make a "sell to the highest bidder" strategy unacceptable. After considering price, production costs, and transportation costs, Klein has established the following profit per unit for each plant–customer alternative.

| | Customer | | | |
Plant	D_1	D_2	D_3	D_4
Clifton Springs	$32	$34	$32	$40
Danville	$34	$30	$28	$38

The plant capacities and customer orders are as follows:

Plant Capacity (units)	Distributor Orders (units)
Clifton Springs 5000	D_1 2000
	D_2 5000
Danville 3000	D_3 3000
	D_4 2000

How many units should each plant produce for each customer to maximize profits? Which customer demands will not be met? Show your network model and linear programming formulation.

9. Sound Electronics, Inc., produces a battery-operated tape recorder at plants located in Martinsville, North Carolina; Plymouth, New York; and Franklin, Missouri. The unit transportation cost for shipments from the three plants to distribution centers in Chicago, Dallas, and New York are as follows:

| | To | | |
From	Chicago	Dallas	New York
Martinsville	1.45	1.60	1.40
Plymouth	1.10	2.25	0.60
Franklin	1.20	1.20	1.80

After considering transportation costs, management has decided that under no circumstances will it use the Plymouth–Dallas route. The plant capacities and distributor orders for the next month are as follows:

Plant	Capacity (units)	Distributor	Orders (units)
Martinsville	400	Chicago	400
Plymouth	600	Dallas	400
Franklin	300	New York	400

Because of different wage scales at the three plants, the unit production cost varies from plant to plant. Assuming the costs are $29.50 per unit at Martinsville, $31.20 per unit at Plymouth, and $30.35 per unit at Franklin, find the production and distribution plan that minimizes production and transportation costs.

10. The Ace Manufacturing Company has orders for three similar products:

Product	Orders (units)
A	2000
B	500
C	1200

Three machines are available for the manufacturing operations. All three machines can produce all the products at the same production rate. However, due to varying defect percentages of each product on each machine, the unit costs of the products vary depending on the machine used. Machine capacities for the next week, and the unit costs, are as follows:

Machine	Capacity (units)
1	1500
2	1500
3	1000

Machine	Product A	Product B	Product C
1	$1.00	$1.20	$0.90
2	$1.30	$1.40	$1.20
3	$1.10	$1.00	$1.20

Use the transportation model to develop the minimum-cost production schedule for the products and machines. Show the linear programming formulation.

11. Forbelt Corporation has a one-year contract to supply motors for all refrigerators produced by the Ice Age Corporation. Ice Age manufactures the refrigerators at four locations around the country: Boston, Dallas, Los Angeles, and St. Paul. Plans call for the following number (in thousands) of refrigerators to be produced at each location.

Boston	50
Dallas	70
Los Angeles	60
St. Paul	80

Forbelt has three plants that are capable of producing the motors. The plants and production capacities (in thousands) are

Denver	100
Atlanta	100
Chicago	150

Because of varying production and transportation costs, the profit that Forbelt earns on each lot of 1000 units depends on which plant produced the lot and which destination it was shipped to. The following table gives the accounting department estimates of the profit per unit (shipments will be made in lots of 1000 units).

	Shipped To			
Produced At	Boston	Dallas	Los Angeles	St. Paul
Denver	7	11	8	13
Atlanta	20	17	12	10
Chicago	8	18	13	16

With profit maximization as a criterion, Forbelt wants to determine how many motors should be produced at each plant and how many motors should be shipped from each plant to each destination.
a. Develop a network representation of this problem.
b. Find the optimal solution.

12. **SELF** **Test** Scott and Associates, Inc., is an accounting firm that has three new clients. Project leaders will be assigned to the three clients. Based on the different backgrounds and experiences of the leaders, the various leader–client assignments differ in terms of projected completion times. The possible assignments and the estimated completion times in days are

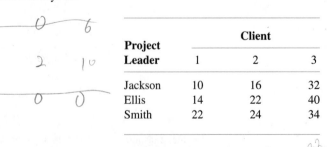

Project Leader	Client		
	1	2	3
Jackson	10	16	32
Ellis	14	22	40
Smith	22	24	34

a. Develop a network representation of this problem.
b. Formulate the problem as a linear program, and solve. What is the total time required?

13. Assume that in Problem 12 an additional employee is available for possible assignment. The following table shows the assignment alternatives and the estimated completion times.

Project Leader	Client		
	1	2	3
Jackson	10	16	32
Ellis	14	22	40
Smith	22	24	34
Burton	14	18	36

   a. What is the optimal assignment?
   b. How did the assignment change compared to the best assignment possible in Problem 12? Was there any savings associated with considering Burton as one of the possible project leaders?
   c. Which project leader remains unassigned?

14. Wilson Distributors, Inc., is opening two new sales territories in the western states. Three individuals currently selling in the Midwest and the East are being considered for promotion to regional sales manager positions in the new sales territories. Management has estimated total annual sales (in thousands of dollars) for the assignment of each individual to each sales territory. The management sales projections are as follows:

Regional Managers	Sales Region	
	Northwest	Southwest
Bostock	$100	$95
McMahon	$ 85	$80
Miller	$ 90	$75

   a. Develop a network representation of the problem.
   b. Formulate and solve a linear programming model to obtain the optimal solution to this problem.

15. Fowle Marketing Research has four project leaders available for assignment to three clients. Find the assignment of project leaders to clients that will minimize the total time to complete all projects. The estimated project completion times in days are as follows:

Project Leader	Client		
	1	2	3
Terry	10	15	9
Carle	9	18	5
McClymonds	6	14	3
Higley	8	16	6

16. a. Develop a network representation of the Salisbury Discount, Inc., department–location assignment problem using the estimated annual profit data provided in Table 7.30.
   b. Formulate a linear programming model, and solve for the department–location assignment that maximizes profit.

17. Consider the Salisbury Discount, Inc., assignment problem with two unacceptable assignments (see Table 7.33).
    a. Develop a network representation of the problem.
    b. Formulate and solve a linear programming model.

18. In a job shop operation, four jobs may be performed on any of four machines. The numbers of hours required for each job on each machine are summarized in the table. What is the minimum total time job–machine assignment?

| | Machine | | | |
Job	A	B	C	D
1	32	18	32	26
2	22	24	12	16
3	24	30	26	24
4	26	30	28	20

19. Mayfax Distributors, Inc., has four sales territories, each of which must be assigned a sales representative. From past experience the firm's sales manager has estimated the annual sales volume (in thousands of dollars) for each sales representative in each sales territory. Find the sales representative–territory assignments that will maximize sales.

| | Sales Territory | | | |
Sales Representative	A	B	C	D
Washington	44	80	52	60
Benson	60	56	40	72
Fredricks	36	60	48	48
Hodson	52	76	36	40

20. The department head of a management science department at a major midwestern university will be scheduling faculty to teach courses during the coming autumn term. Four core courses need to be covered. The four courses are at the UG, MBA, MS, and Ph.D. levels. Four professors will be assigned to the courses, with each professor receiving one of the courses. Student evaluations of professors are available from previous terms. Based on a rating scale of 4 (excellent), 3 (very good), 2 (average), 1 (fair), and 0 (poor), the average student evaluations for each professor are shown. Professor D does not have a Ph.D. and cannot be assigned to teach the Ph.D.-level course. If the department head makes teaching assignments based on maximizing the student evaluation ratings over all four courses, what staffing assignments should be made?

| | Course | | | |
Professor	UG	MBA	MS	Ph.D.
A	2.8	2.2	3.3	3.0
B	3.2	3.0	3.6	3.6
C	3.3	3.2	3.5	3.5
D	3.2	2.8	2.5	—

21. A market research firm has three clients who have each requested that the firm conduct a sample survey. Four available statisticians can be assigned to these three projects; however, all

four statisticians are busy, and therefore each can handle only one of the clients. The following data show the number of hours required for each statistician to complete each job; the differences in time are based on experience and ability of the statisticians.

Statistician	Client		
	A	B	C
1	150	210	270
2	170	230	220
3	180	230	225
4	160	240	230

a. Formulate and solve a linear programming model for this problem.
b. Suppose that the time it takes statistician 4 to complete the job for client A is increased from 160 to 165 hours. What effect will this have on the solution?
c. Suppose that the time it takes statistician 4 to complete the job for client A is decreased to 140 hours. What effect will this have on the solution?
d. Suppose that the time it takes statistician 3 to complete the job for client B increases to 250 hours. What effect will this have on the solution?

22. Hatcher Enterprises uses a chemical called Rbase in production operations at five divisions. There are only six suppliers of Rbase that meet Hatcher's quality control standards. All six of the suppliers can produce Rbase in sufficient quantities to accommodate the needs of each division. The quantity of Rbase needed by each of Hatcher's divisions and the price per gallon charged by each supplier are as follows:

Division	Demand (1000s of gallons)
1	40
2	45
3	50
4	35
5	45

Supplier	Price Per Gallon ($)
1	12.60
2	14.00
3	10.20
4	14.20
5	12.00
6	13.00

The cost per gallon ($) for shipping from each supplier to each division is provided in the following table.

Division	Supplier					
	1	2	3	4	5	6
1	2.75	2.50	3.15	2.80	2.75	2.75
2	0.80	0.20	5.40	1.20	3.40	1.00
3	4.70	2.60	5.30	2.80	6.00	5.60
4	2.60	1.80	4.40	2.40	5.00	2.80
5	3.40	0.40	5.00	1.20	2.60	3.60

Hatcher believes in spreading its business among suppliers so that the company will be less affected by supplier problems (e.g., labor strikes or resource availability). Company policy requires that each division have a separate supplier.
a. For each supplier–division combination, compute the total cost of supplying the division's demand.
b. Determine the optimal assignment of suppliers to divisions.

23. **SELF Test** The distribution system for the Herman Company consists of three plants, two warehouses, and four customers. Plant capacities and shipping costs (in $) from each plant to each warehouse are

	Warehouse		
Plant	1	2	Capacity
1	4	7	450
2	8	5	600
3	5	6	380

Customer demand and shipping costs per unit (in $) from each warehouse to each customer are

	Customer			
Warehouse	1	2	3	4
1	6	4	8	4
2	3	6	7	7
Demand	300	300	300	400

  a. Develop a network model of this problem.
  b. Formulate a linear programming model of the problem.
  c. Use a computer code (e.g., The Management Scientist) to find the optimal shipping plan.

24. Refer to Problem 23. Suppose that shipments between the two warehouses are permitted at $2 per unit and that direct shipments can be made from plant 3 to customer 4 at a cost of $7 per unit.
  a. Develop a network model of this problem.
  b. Formulate a linear programming model of this problem.
  c. Use a computer code (e.g., The Management Scientist) to find the optimal shipping plan.

25. A company has two plants (P₁ and P₂), one regional warehouse (W), and two retail outlets (R₁ and R₂). The plant capacities, retail outlet demands, and per-unit shipping costs are shown in the following network.

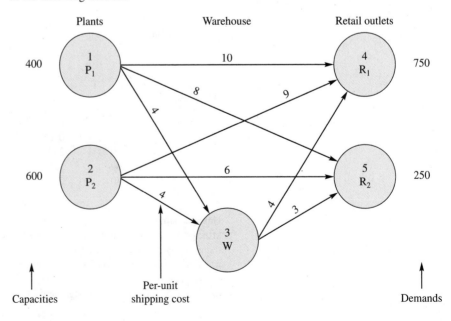

a. Formulate a linear programming model to minimize shipping costs for this problem.

b. If you have access to a linear programming computer code, determine the optimal solution for the model formulated in part (a).

c. What change would have to be made in the linear programming model if the maximum amount of goods that can be shipped from W to R_1 is 500? How would this change the optimal solution?

26. Adirondack Paper Mills, Inc., has paper plants in Augusta, Maine, and Tupper Lake, New York. Warehouse facilities are located in Albany, New York, and Portsmouth, New Hampshire. Distributors are located in Boston, New York, and Philadelphia. The plant capacities and distributor demands for the next month are as follows:

Plant	Capacity (units)	Distributor	Demand (units)
Augusta	300	Boston	150
Tupper Lake	100	New York	100
		Philadelphia	150

The unit transportation costs ($) for shipments from the two plants to the two warehouses and from the two warehouses to the three distributors are as follows:

	Warehouse	
Plant	Albany	Portsmouth
Augusta	7	5
Tupper Lake	3	4

	Distributor		
Warehouse	Boston	New York	Philadelphia
Albany	8	5	7
Portsmouth	5	6	10

a. Draw the network representation of the Adirondack Paper Mills problem.

b. Formulate the Adirondack Paper Mills problem as a linear programming problem.

c. If you have access to a linear programming computer code, determine the minimum-cost shipping schedule for the problem.

27. Consider a transshipment problem consisting of three origin nodes, two transshipment nodes, and four destination nodes. The supplies at the origin nodes and the demands at the destination nodes are as follows:

Origin	Supply	Destination	Demand
1	400	1	200
2	450	2	500
3	350	3	300
		4	200

The shipping costs per unit are provided in the following table.

From		To					
		Transshipment		Destination			
		1	2	1	2	3	4
Origin	1	6	8	—	—	—	—
	2	8	12	—	—	—	—
	3	10	5	—	—	—	—
Transshipment	1	—	—	9	7	6	10
	2	—	—	7	9	6	8

a. Draw the network representation of this problem.
b. Formulate this as a linear programming problem.
c. Solve for the optimal solution.

28. The Moore & Harman Company is in the business of buying and selling grain. An important aspect of the company's business is arranging for the purchased grain to be shipped to customers. If the company can keep freight costs low, profitability will be improved.

Currently, the company has purchased three rail cars of grain at Muncie, Indiana; six rail cars at Brazil, Indiana; and five rail cars at Xenia, Ohio. Twelve carloads of grain have been sold. The locations and the amount sold at each location are as follows:

Location	Number of Rail Car Loads
Macon, Ga.	2
Greenwood, S.C.	4
Concord, S.C.	3
Chatham, N.C.	3

All shipments must be routed through either Louisville or Cincinnati. Shown are the shipping costs per bushel (in cents) from the origins to Louisville and Cincinnati and the costs per bushel to ship from Louisville and Cincinnati to the destinations.

From	To	
	Louisville	Cincinnati
Muncie	8	6 ← Cost per bushel
Brazil	3	8 from Muncie to
Xenia	9	3 Cincinnati is 6¢

From	To			
	Macon	Greenwood	Concord	Chatham
Louisville	44	34	34	32
Cincinnati	57	35	28	24

Cost per bushel from
Cincinnati to Greenwood is 35¢

Determine a shipping schedule that will minimize the freight costs necessary to satisfy demand. Which (if any) rail cars of grain must be held at the origin until buyers can be found?

29. A rental car company has an imbalance of cars at seven of its locations. The following network shows the locations of concern (the nodes) and the cost to move a car between locations. A positive number by a node indicates an excess supply at the node, and a negative number indicates an excess demand.

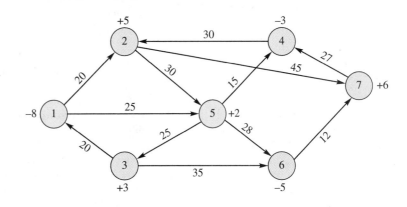

a. Develop a linear programming model of this problem.
b. Solve the model formulated in part (a) to determine how the cars should be redistributed among the locations.

30. The following linear programming formulation is for a transshipment problem.

$$\text{Min} \quad 11x_{13} + 12x_{14} + 10x_{21} + 8x_{34} + 10x_{35} + 11x_{42} + 9x_{45} + 12x_{52}$$

s.t.

$$
\begin{array}{rl}
x_{13} + x_{14} - x_{21} & \leq 5 \\
x_{21} \quad\quad - x_{42} \quad - x_{52} & \leq 3 \\
x_{13} \quad\quad - x_{34} - x_{35} & = 6 \\
- x_{14} \quad - x_{34} \quad + x_{42} + x_{45} & \leq 2 \\
x_{35} \quad + x_{45} - x_{52} & = 4 \\
\end{array}
$$

$$x_{ij} \geq 0 \quad \text{for all } i, j$$

Show the network representation of this problem.

31. Refer to the Contois Carpets problem for which the network representation is shown in Figure 7.12. Suppose that Contois has a beginning inventory of 50 yards of carpet and requires an inventory of 100 yards at the end of quarter 4.
a. Develop a network representation of this modified problem.
b. Develop a linear programming model, and solve for the optimal solution.

32. Sanders Fishing Supply of Naples, Florida, manufactures a variety of fishing equipment, which it sells throughout the United States. For the next three months, Sanders estimates demand for a particular product at 150, 250, and 300 units, respectively. Sanders can supply this demand by producing on regular time or overtime. Because of other commitments and anticipated cost increases in month 3, the production capacities in units and the production costs per unit are as follows:

Production	Capacity (units)	Cost Per Unit
Month 1—Regular	275	$ 50
Month 1—Overtime	100	80
Month 2—Regular	200	50
Month 2—Overtime	50	80
Month 3—Regular	100	60
Month 3—Overtime	50	100

Inventory may be carried from one month to the next, but the cost is $20 per unit per month. For example, regular production from month 1 used to meet demand in month 2 would cost Sanders $50 + $20 = $70 per unit. This same month 1 production used to meet demand in month 3 would cost Sanders $50 + 2($20) = $90 per unit.

a. Develop a network representation of this production scheduling problem as a transportation problem. (Hint: Use six origin nodes; the supply for origin node 1 is the maximum that can be produced in month 1 on regular time, and so on.)

b. Develop a linear programming model that can be used to schedule regular and overtime production for each of the three months.

c. What is the production schedule, how many units are carried in inventory each month, and what is the total cost?

d. Is there any unused production capacity? If so, where?

Note: The remaining problems involve the use of the special-purpose algorithms described in Sections 7.5 and 7.6 for solving transportation and assignment problems.

33. Consider the following transportation tableau with four origins and four destinations.

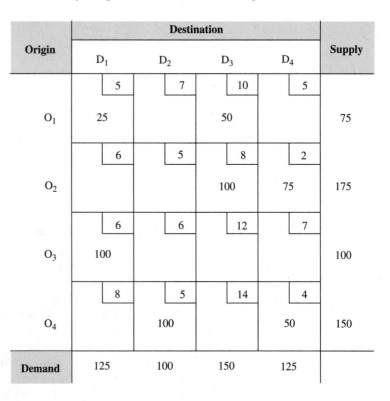

Origin	Destination				Supply
	D_1	D_2	D_3	D_4	
O_1	5 / 25	7	10 / 50	5	75
O_2	6	5	8 / 100	2 / 75	175
O_3	6 / 100	6	12	7	100
O_4	8	5 / 100	14	4 / 50	150
Demand	125	100	150	125	

a. Use the MODI method to determine whether this solution provides the minimum transportation cost. If it is not the minimum cost solution, find that solution. If it is the minimum cost solution, what is the total transportation cost?

b. Does an alternative optimal solution exist? Explain. If so, find the alternative optimal solution. What is the total transportation cost associated with this solution?

34. .... **SELF Test**   Consider the following minimum-cost transportation problem.

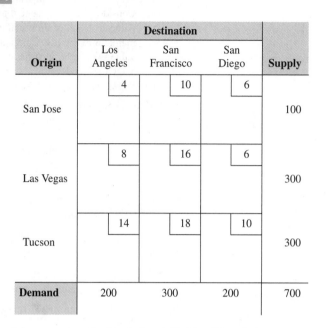

Origin	Destination			Supply
	Los Angeles	San Francisco	San Diego	
San Jose	4	10	6	100
Las Vegas	8	16	6	300
Tucson	14	18	10	300
Demand	200	300	200	700

a. Use the minimum-cost method to find an initial feasible solution.
b. Use the transportation simplex method to find an optimal solution.
c. How would the optimal solution change if you must ship 100 units on the Tucson–San Diego route?
d. Because of road construction, the Las Vegas–San Diego route is now unacceptable. Resolve the initial problem.

35. Refer to Problem 2.
   a. Set up the transportation tableau for the problem.
   b. Use the minimum-cost method to find an initial feasible solution.

36. Refer to Problem 4. Use the transportation simplex method to find an optimal solution.

37. Consider the following minimum-cost transportation problem.

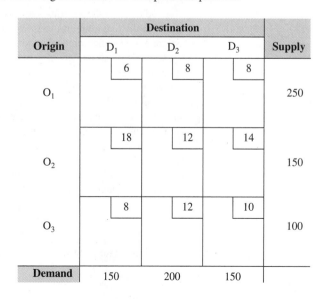

Origin	Destination			Supply
	D_1	D_2	D_3	
O_1	6	8	8	250
O_2	18	12	14	150
O_3	8	12	10	100
Demand	150	200	150	

a. Use the minimum-cost method to find an initial feasible solution.

b. Use the transportation simplex method to find an optimal solution.

c. Using your solution to part (b), identify an alternative optimal solution.

38. Use the per-unit cost changes for each unoccupied cell shown in Table 7.15 to do the following:

a. Consider the arc connecting Bedford and Chicago as a candidate for the incoming arc. Allocate 1 unit of flow, and make the necessary adjustments on the stepping-stone path to maintain feasibility. Compute the value of the new solution, and show that the change in value is exactly what has been indicated by the cost change per unit obtained using the MODI method.

b. Repeat part (a) for the arc connecting York and Lexington.

39. Refer again to the Contois Carpets problem for which the network representation is shown in Figure 7.12. This problem can also be formulated and solved as a transportation problem.

a. Develop a network representation of this as a transportation problem. (Hint: Eliminate the inventory arcs, and add arcs showing that quarterly production can be used to satisfy demand in the current quarter and all future quarters.)

b. Solve the problem using the transportation simplex method.

40. **SELF Test** Refer to Problem 12. Using the Hungarian method, obtain the optimal solution.

41. Refer to Problem 14. Use the Hungarian method to obtain the optimal solution.

42. Refer to Problem 15. Use the Hungarian method to obtain the optimal solution.

43. **SELF Test** Use the Hungarian method to solve the Salisbury Discount, Inc., problem by using the profit data in Table 7.30.

44. Use the Hungarian method to solve the Salisbury Discount, Inc., problem as described in Problem 17.

45. Refer to Problem 19. Use the Hungarian method to find an optimal solution.

Case Problem: Assigning Umpire Crews [*]

The American Baseball League consists of 14 professional baseball teams organized into three divisions: the West Division with Seattle, Oakland, California, and Texas; the Central Division with Kansas City, Minnesota, Chicago, Milwaukee, and Cleveland; and the East Division with Detroit, Toronto, Baltimore, New York, and Boston.

In addition to the schedules for each team, the American League must determine the best way to assign the umpire crews to the various games played throughout the league. Umpire crews are assigned to specific home-team cities for the two-, three-, or four-game series in that city, but are not assigned on an individual-game basis. Since there are 14 American League teams, there can be as many as seven games being played at the same time (double-headers count as one game in assigning crews); hence, seven umpire crews must be assigned.

Several considerations are important in making the umpire crew assignments. Because of the amount of travel required, airline costs can be substantial. Thus, from a cost point of view, umpire crew assignments with minimum travel distances are desirable. However, a second consideration in the assignment of the umpire crews is that there should be a balance such that each crew works approximately the same number of games with each team and in each city. The considerations of minimizing travel distances and, at the same time, balancing the crew assignments among the teams and cities are in conflict.

---

*The authors are indebted to James R. Evans, consultant to the American League, New York, N.Y., for providing this case problem.

In addition to these considerations, a number of requirements must be satisfied. The most important of these are

1. A crew cannot travel from city A to city B if the last game in city A is a night game and the first game in city B is an afternoon game on the next day.

2. A crew cannot travel from a West Coast location (Seattle, Oakland, or California) to Chicago, Milwaukee, Cleveland, or any East Division city without a day off.

3. Because of flight scheduling difficulties, a crew traveling into or out of Toronto must have a day off unless coming from or going to New York, Boston, Detroit, or Cleveland.

4. Any crew traveling from a night game in Seattle, Oakland, or California cannot be assigned to Kansas City or Texas for a game on the next day.

5. No crew should be assigned to the same team for more than two series in a row.

The umpire crews have already been scheduled for the first four series of the five-series schedule shown in Table 7.34. Table 7.35 summarizes the crew assignments for the first four series in the schedule and shows the pairings for the fifth series. The superscript next to each team identification indicates the umpire crew assigned for that pairing. For example, for the fourth series, crew 1 is assigned to the Boston–Toronto games, crew 2 is assigned to the Detroit–California games, and so on.

Table 7.36 shows the distances from the cities where the fourth series is being played to the cities where the fifth series is being played. There are some other issues league management would like considered in assigning crews to the next series. Over the past nine series, crew 4 has umpired three series with Kansas City and three series with Milwaukee. Also, crew 5 has not been assigned to any games with New York, Toronto, or Detroit over the past month.

Table 7.34   Segment of the American League Schedule Showing Five Series

		Home Team													
Series	Date	SEA	OAK	CAL	TEX	KC	MIN	CHI	MKE	DET	CLE	TOR	BAL	NY	BOS
1	Mon.		CAL*		BOS*		SEA		TOR*	NY*			CHI*		
	Tues.		CAL*		BOS*		SEA		TOR*	NY*	KC*		CHI*		
	Wed.		CAL		BOS*		SEA		TOR*	NY	KC*		CHI*		
2	Thurs.	DET*		MKE*	KC*						CHI*		TOR*		MIN*
	Fri.	DET*	NY*	MKE*	KC*						CHI*		TOR*		MIN*
	Sat.	DET*	NY	MKE*	KC*						CHI		TOR*		MIN*
	Sun.	DET	NY(2)	MKE	KC*						CHI		TOR		MIN*
3	Mon.	MKE*		NY*		BOS*							MIN*		
	Tues.	MKE*	DET*	NY*	CHI*	BOS*						CLE*	MIN*		
	Wed.	MKE*	DET*	NY*	CHI*	BOS*						CLE*	MIN*		
	Thurs.	MKE*	DET	NY*	CHI*							CLE*			
4	Fri.	NY*	MKE*	DET*	BAL*		CLE*	KC*					BOS*		
	Sat.	NY*	MKE	DET*	BAL*		CLE*	KC*					BOS		
	Sun.	NY*	MKE	DET	BAL*		CLE	KC					BOS		
5	Mon.					TEX*		CLE*					BOS*		
	Tues.					TEX*	BOS*	CLE*	CAL*	SEA*			BAL*	OAK*	
	Wed.					TEX*	BOS*	CLE*	CAL*	SEA*			BAL*	OAK*	
	Thurs.					TEX*	BOS		CAL	SEA*			BAL*	OAK*	

*Denotes night game or early-evening start.   (2)Denotes doubleheader (two games in one day).

Table 7.35　Umpire Crew Assignments for the First Four Series Are Shown as Superscripts

						Home Team								
Series	SEA	OAK	CAL	TEX	KC	MIN	CHI	MKE	DET	CLE	TOR	BAL	NY	BOS
1		CAL^5		BOS^3		SEA^7		TOR^4	NY^1	KC^6		CHI^2		
2	DET^3	NY^2	MKE^7	KC^5						CHI^6		TOR^4		MIN^1
3	MKE^2	DET^7	NY^3	CHI^6	BOS^5						CLE^1	MIN^4		
4	NY^7	MKE^3	DET^2	BAL^6		CLE^5	KC^4				BOS^1			
5					TEX	BOS	CLE	CAL	SEA		BAL		OAK	

For the fourth series, umpire crew 1 is assigned to the Boston at Toronto series

Table 7.36

Distance Cost Matrix for Umpire Crew Assignments (Series 5)

Crew From	To						
	KC	MIN	CHI	MKE	DET	TOR	NY
SEA(7)	1825	1399	2007	1694	1939	2124	2421
OAK(3)	1498	1589	2125	1845	2079	2286	2586
CAL(2)	1363	1536	2035	1756	1979	2175	2475
TEX(6)	506	853	798	843	982	1186	1383
MIN(5)	394	0	334	297	528	780	1028
CHI(4)	403	334	0	74	235	430	740
TOR(1)	968	897	497	583	206	0	366

Note: The numbers in parentheses reference umpire crews.

Managerial Report

Prepare a written recommendation to league management concerning the assignment of umpire crews to the fifth series that will minimize the distance traveled.

Case Problem:　Distribution System Design

The Darby Company manufactures and distributes meters used to measure electric power consumption. The company started with a small production plant in El Paso and gradually built a customer base throughout Texas. A distribution center was established in Ft. Worth, Texas, and later, as business expanded to the north, a second distribution center was established in Santa Fe, New Mexico.

The El Paso plant was expanded when the company began marketing its meters in Arizona, California, Nevada, and Utah. With the growth of the West Coast business, the Darby Company opened a third distribution center in Las Vegas and just two years ago opened a second production plant in San Bernardino, California.

Table 7.37

Shipping Cost Per Unit from Production Plants to Distribution Centers (in $)

	Distribution Center		
Plant	Ft. Worth	Santa Fe	Las Vegas
El Paso	3.20	2.20	4.20
San Bernardino	—	3.90	1.20

Table 7.38

Quarterly Demand Forecast

Customer Zone	Demand (meters)
Dallas	6300
San Antonio	4880
Wichita	2130
Kansas City	1210
Denver	6120
Salt Lake City	4830
Phoenix	2750
Los Angeles	8580
San Diego	4460

Table 7.39

Shipping Cost from the Distribution Centers to the Customer Zones

	Customer Zone								
Distribution Center	Dallas	San Antonio	Wichita	Kansas City	Denver	Salt Lake City	Phoenix	Los Angeles	San Diego
Ft. Worth	0.3	2.1	3.1	4.4	6.0	—	—	—	—
Santa Fe	5.2	5.4	4.5	6.0	2.7	4.7	3.4	3.3	2.7
Las Vegas	—	—	—	—	5.4	3.3	2.4	2.1	2.5

Manufacturing costs differ between the company's production plants. The cost of each meter produced at the El Paso plant is $10.50. The San Bernardino plant utilizes newer and more efficient equipment; as a result, manufacturing costs are $0.50 per meter less than at the El Paso plant.

Due to the company's rapid growth, not much attention had been paid to the efficiency of the distribution system, but Darby's management has decided that it is time to address this issue. The cost of shipping a meter from each of the two plants to each of the three distribution centers is shown in Table 7.37.

The quarterly production capacity is 30,000 meters at the older El Paso plant and 20,000 meters at the San Bernardino plant. Note that no shipments are allowed from the San Bernardino plant to the Ft. Worth distribution center.

The company serves nine customer zones from the three distribution centers. The forecast of the number of meters needed in each customer zone for the next quarter is shown in Table 7.38.

The cost per unit of shipping from each distribution center to each customer zone is given in Table 7.39; note that some of the distribution centers cannot serve certain customer zones.

In the current distribution system, demand at the Dallas, San Antonio, Wichita, and Kansas City customer zones is satisfied by shipments from the Ft. Worth distribution center. In a similar manner, the Denver, Salt Lake City, and Phoenix customer zones are served by the Santa Fe distribution center, and the Los Angeles and San Diego customer zones are served by the Las Vegas distribution center. To determine how many units to ship from each plant, the quarterly customer demandforecasts are aggregated at the distribution centers, and a transportation model is used to minimize the cost of shipping from the production plants to the distribution centers.

Managerial Report

You have been called in to make recommendations for improving the distribution system. Your report should address, but not be limited to, the following issues.

1. If the company does not change its current distribution strategy, what will its distribution costs be for the following quarter?
2. Suppose that the company is willing to consider dropping the distribution center limitations; that is, customers could be served by any of the distribution centers. Can costs be reduced? By how much?
3. The company wants to explore the possibility of satisfying some of the customer demand directly from the production plants. In particular, the shipping cost is $0.30 per unit from San Bernardino to Los Angeles and $0.70 from San Bernardino to San Diego. The cost for direct shipments from El Paso to San Antonio is $3.50 per unit. Can distribution costs be further reduced by considering these direct plant–customer shipments?
4. Over the next five years, Darby is anticipating moderate growth (5000 meters) to the North and West. Would you recommend that they consider plant expansion at this time?

MANAGEMENT SCIENCE in practice

Procter & Gamble*

Procter & Gamble (P&G) is in the consumer-products business worldwide. P&G produces and markets such products as detergents, disposable diapers, coffee, over-the-counter pharmaceuticals, dentifrices, bar soaps, mouthwashes, and paper towels. It has the leading brand in more categories than any other consumer-products company in the United States.

In order to maintain its leadership position in its many markets, P&G makes extensive use of management science. Some of the methodologies employed include probability and risk analysis, linear and integer programming, network flow analysis, and simulation. The individuals employing these methodologies are scattered throughout P&G's numerous divisions with perhaps the largest concentration being in the management systems division. P&G employs engineers, operations researchers, computer scientists, and businesspeople who are skilled in employing quantitative methodologies.

Recently P&G embarked on a major strategic planning initiative: the North American Product Sourcing Study. P&G was interested in consolidating its product sources and optimizing its distribution system design throughout North America. One of the decision support systems that proved to be a great aid in this project was called the Product Sourcing Heuristic (PSH). This heuristic was based on a transshipment model much like the ones described in this chapter.

In a preprocessing phase, the many P&G products were aggregated into groups that shared the same technology and could be made at the same plant. The PSH was used by product strategy teams that had responsibility for developing product sourcing options for the separate product groups. The various plants that could produce the product group were source nodes, the company's regional distribution centers were the transshipment nodes, and P&G's customer zones were the destinations. Direct shipments to customer zones as well as shipments through distribution centers were employed.

The product strategy teams used the heuristic interactively to explore a variety of questions concerning product sourcing and distribution. For instance, the team might be interested in the impact of closing two plants and consolidating production in three remaining plants. The product sourcing heuristic would then delete the source nodes corresponding to the two closed plants, make any capacity modifications recommended to the sources corresponding to the remaining three plants, and resolve the transshipment problem. The product strategy team could then examine the new solution, make some more modifications, solve again, and so on.

The Product Sourcing Heuristic was viewed as a valuable decision support system by all who used it. Probably the most valuable feature was that the model permitted a rapid evaluation of a variety of strategic options. A feature that was viewed as a big plus by all who used it was that solutions provided by the PSH were displayed on a map of North America using a geographic information system. This enabled strategic planners to review immediately the impact of their sourcing decisions across North America. The PSH has proven so successful that P&G is considering using it in other markets around the world.

....

*The authors are indebted to Mr. Franz Dill and Mr. Tom Chorman of Procter & Gamble for providing this application.

eight

CHAPTER

Integer Linear Programming

In this chapter we discuss a class of problems that are modeled as linear programs with the additional requirement that some or all of the decision variables must be integer. If all the variables are required to be integer, we have an *all-integer linear program*. If some, but not necessarily all, of the decision variables in a problem are required to be integer, we have a *mixed-integer linear program*. In most practical applications of linear programming, the integer variables are permitted to assume only the values 0 or 1. In such cases we have a *binary* or *0–1 integer linear program;* you may recall that we encountered these types of decision variables when we formulated a linear programming model of the assignment problem in Chapter 7.

The use of integer variables—especially *0–1* integer variables—provides additional modeling flexibility. As a result, the number of practical applications that can be addressed with linear programming methodology is greater. For instance, the Management Science in Action: Scheduling Employees at McDonald's Restaurants describes an employee scheduling application. The cost of the added modeling flexibility is that problems involving integer variables usually are much more difficult to solve. In fact, although linear programming problems involving several thousand continuous variables can be routinely solved with commercial linear programming codes, the solution of all-integer linear programming problems involving less than 100 variables can cause great difficulty. Experienced quantitative analysts usually can identify the types of integer linear programs that are easiest to solve; in such cases, problems with hundreds (and sometimes thousands) of *0–1* integer variables can be solved with available computer codes, such as IBM's MPSX-MIP, OSL, CPLEX, and LINDO. Spreadsheets with integer capabilities are now also available. For instance, the standard version of Microsoft Excel has the capability to solve integer problems.

Our objective in this chapter is to provide an applications-oriented introduction to integer linear programming. We begin with a short section describing the different types of integer linear programming models. In the following section we introduce an

MANAGEMENT SCIENCE in action

Scheduling Employees at McDonald's Restaurants*

The owner and operator of four McDonald's restaurants in the Cumberland, Maryland, area was spending more than eight hours every week manually preparing employee work schedules. He had to forecast sales by hour and then convert the hourly forecasts into personnel requirements for the grill, counter, and drive-through work areas. Then, he had to match the employees' available work hours and job skills with the hourly requirements to develop a work schedule for each employee. The scheduling process is further complicated by the following: Employee needs vary dramatically over the course of each day, the fast-food industry has no standard work shifts, the availability of student and other part-time employees is limited, and employee qualifications vary.

A typical McDonald's Restaurant has three work areas (grill, counter, and drive-through), 150 employees, and 30 work shifts. A complete integer linear programming model for scheduling employees in this situation would involve approximately 100,000 integer variables and 3000 constraints. The company's management wanted to obtain a solution in 15 minutes or less on a personal computer, so using the complete model to obtain a

solution was impossible. As a result, quantitative analysts decomposed the problem into two subproblems. The solution to the first subproblem determines the shift requirements that minimize surplus scheduled hours, and the solution to the second subproblem determines the assignment of employees to meet the shift requirements from the first subproblem. The analysts developed specialized solution algorithms that enabled a restaurant manager to develop a schedule in about 15 minutes.

Using the new system, restaurant managers can generate employee schedules in only 10–20% of the time formerly needed to do so. The system satisfies half-hourly labor requirements while minimizing surplus scheduled hours and reducing direct labor costs. Additionally, employees are more likely to get their preferred work hours and the work areas where they perform best.

....

*Based on Love, R., Jr., and J. M. Hovey, "Management Science Improves Fast-Food Operations." *Interfaces,* March–April 1990, pp. 21–29.

application that requires the formulation of an all-integer linear program. After showing how a graphical solution procedure can be used to obtain an optimal integer solution, we show the computer solution provided by the integer programming module of The Management Scientist.

We discuss four applications that make use of *0–1* integer variables: a capital budgeting problem, a fixed-charge problem, a distribution systems design problem, and a bank location problem. The objective is to provide additional practice involving the development of models involving integer variables. Our focus is on applications and not on the details of the solution procedure; we show how to use The Management Scientist software package and LINDO to provide optimal integer solutions. The last section of the chapter provides additional illustrations of the modeling flexibility provided by *0–1* integer variables.

8.1 Types of Integer Linear Programming Models

The only difference between the problems studied in this chapter and the ones studied in the earlier chapters on linear programming is that some of the variables are required to be integer. If all the variables are required to be integer, we have an *all-integer linear program.* The following is a two-variable, all-integer linear programming model.

$$\text{Max} \quad 2x_1 + 3x_2$$

s.t.

$$3x_1 + 3x_2 \leq 12$$

$$\tfrac{2}{3}x_1 + 1x_2 \leq 4$$

$$1x_1 + 2x_2 \leq 6$$

$$x_1, x_2 \geq 0 \text{ and integer}$$

Note that if we drop the phrase "and integer" from this model, we have the familiar two-variable linear program. The linear program that results from dropping the integer requirements for the decision variables is referred to as the *LP* (linear programming) *Relaxation* of the integer linear program.

If some, but not necessarily all, of the decision variables in a problem are required to be integer, we have a *mixed-integer linear program.* The following is a two-variable, mixed-integer linear program.

$$\text{Max} \quad 3x_1 + 4x_2$$

s.t.

$$-1x_1 + 2x_2 \leq 8$$

$$1x_1 + 2x_2 \leq 12$$

$$2x_1 + 1x_2 \leq 16$$

$$x_1, x_2 \geq 0 \text{ and } x_2 \text{ integer}$$

We obtain The LP Relaxation of this mixed-integer linear program by dropping the requirement that x_2 be integer. Sometimes the variables required to assume integer values are called *discrete variables;* the others are said to be *continuous.*

In most practical applications of integer linear programming, the integer variables are permitted to assume only the values 0 or 1. In such cases, we have a *binary* or a *0–1 integer linear program.* Such *0–1* problems may be of either the all-integer or the mixed-integer type. The capital budgeting, distribution system design, and bank location problems discussed later in this chapter all make use of *0–1* variables.

You should now be able to recognize the various types of integer programs and their LP Relaxations. Try Problem 1.

NOTES & comments

1. The general linear programming formulation of the assignment problem (see Chapter 7) actually is a *0–1* integer linear program. However, the special structure of the assignment problem allows the problem to be solved as a regular linear program and still obtain integer values for the decision variables.

2. The optimal solution to a transportation or transshipment problem with integer values for the supply and demand nodes always will be integer valued. Thus, these problems can be modeled as general linear programs or as integer programs.

8.2 Graphical and Computer Solution for an All-Integer Linear Program

Security Realty Investors currently has $1,365,000 available for new rental property investments. After an initial screening, Security has reduced the investment alternatives to a series of townhouses and a group of apartment buildings in a large apartment complex. The townhouses can be purchased in blocks of three for $195,000 per block, but only four blocks of townhouses are available at this time. Each building in the apartment complex contains 12 dwelling units and sells for $273,000. The individual apartment buildings can be purchased separately, and the complex developer has agreed to build as many 12-unit buildings as Security Realty would like to purchase.

Security's property manager can devote 140 hours per month to these investments. Each block of townhouses will require 4 hours of the property manager's time each month, and each apartment building will require 40 hours per month. The yearly cash flow after deducting mortgage payments and operating expenses, is estimated at $2000 per block of townhouses and $3000 per apartment building. Security wants to allocate its investment funds to townhouses and apartment buildings so as to maximize yearly cash flow.

To develop an appropriate mathematical model for this problem, we define the decision variables as

$$x_1 = \text{number of blocks of townhouses purchased}$$
$$x_2 = \text{number of apartment buildings purchased}$$

The objective function, measuring cash flow in thousands of dollars, is

$$\text{Max} \quad 2x_1 + 3x_2$$

Three constraints must be satisfied:

$$195x_1 + 273x_2 \leq 1365 \quad \text{Funds available in thousands of dollars}$$
$$4x_1 + 40x_2 \leq 140 \quad \text{Manager's time in hours}$$
$$x_1 \leq 4 \quad \text{Townhouse availability in blocks}$$

These variables must be restricted to nonnegative values. Also, as fractional values for the blocks of townhouses and/or number of apartment buildings are unacceptable, the decision variables x_1 and x_2 must be integer. Thus, the proper model for the Security Realty problem is the following all-integer linear program.

$$\text{Max} \quad 2x_1 + 3x_2$$
$$\text{s.t.}$$
$$195x_1 + 273x_2 \leq 1365$$
$$4x_1 + 40x_2 \leq 140$$
$$x_1 \leq 4$$
$$x_1, x_2 \geq 0 \text{ and integer}$$

Graphical Solution Procedure

A first approach to solving such a problem might be to drop the integer requirements and solve the resulting LP Relaxation. You might then round the decision variables in an attempt to find the optimal solution to the integer linear program. However, such an approach may not yield the optimal solution. In fact, rounding values of the decision variables can result in an infeasible solution.

The linear program resulting from dropping the integer requirements for the decision variables (the LP Relaxation) in the Security Realty problem is as follows:

$$\text{Max} \quad 2x_1 + 3x_2$$

s.t.

$$195x_1 + 273x_2 \leq 1365$$

$$4x_1 + 40x_2 \leq 140$$

$$x_1 \leq 4$$

$$x_1, x_2 \geq 0$$

The optimal solution to the LP Relaxation (see Figure 8.1) is $x_1 = 2.44$ and $x_2 = 3.26$. The objective function value for this solution is 14.66, corresponding to a cash flow of $14,660. However, this solution is not feasible for the integer linear programming problem because the decision variables have fractional values.

Rounding the decision variables to the nearest integer value yields a solution of $x_1 = 2$ and $x_2 = 3$ for an objective function value of 13, or a $13,000 annual cash flow. In Figure 8.2 we show the feasible solution points that provide integer values for x_1 and x_2. Is the rounded solution of $x_1 = 2$ and $x_2 = 3$ the optimal integer solution? The answer is no! As Figure 8.2 shows, the optimal integer solution is $x_1 = 4$ and $x_2 = 2$, with an objective function value of 14.00, or a $14,000 annual cash flow. For Security Realty, the approach

Figure 8.1

Graphical Solution to the LP Relaxation of the Security Realty Problem

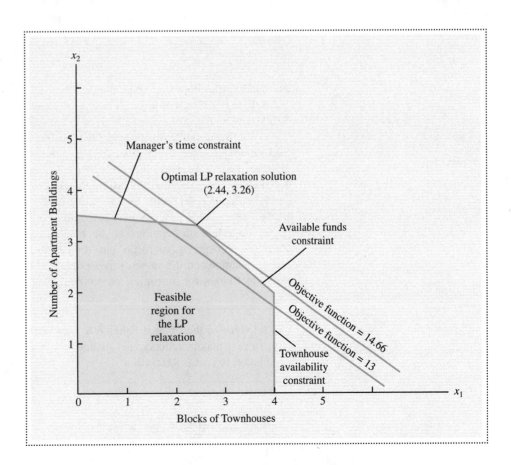

Figure 8.2

The Integer Solution to the Security Realty Problem

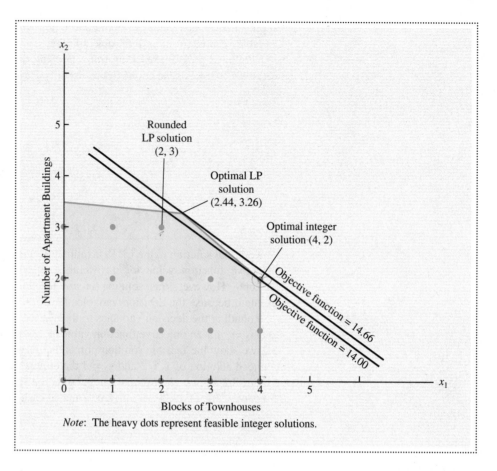

Note: The heavy dots represent feasible integer solutions.

Try Problem 2 for practice in solving an integer programming problem graphically.

of rounding the linear programming solution to the nearest integer solution was not a good strategy. The rounded solution of $x_1 = 2$ and $x_2 = 3$ would have cost Security Realty $1000 a year in cash flow.

As the Security Realty problem demonstrates, the graphical procedure for solving two-variable integer linear programs is quite similar to the graphical procedure for solving linear programs. First, construct a graph of the feasible region for the LP Relaxation. Then, denote the feasible integer points with heavy dots. Finally, locate the integer solution point on the best objective function line; this point is the optimal solution to the integer linear programming program.

An important observation can be made from the analysis of the Security Realty Investors problem; it has to do with the relationship between the value of the optimal integer solution and the value of the optimal LP Relaxation solution. This observation is stated as follows for maximization problems.[1]

> The value of the optimal solution to any integer or mixed-integer linear program involving maximization yields a value *less than or equal to* the value of the optimal solution to its LP Relaxation.

---

[1]For minimization problems, the observation would be stated with "greater than or equal to" substituted for "less than or equal to."

Try Problem 5 to see how to solve a mixed-integer program graphically.

To understand better the significance of this observation, refer again to the two objective function lines in Figure 8.2. The value of the optimal solution to the LP Relaxation for the Security Realty Investors problem is on the highest objective function line, with a value of $14.66; note that the optimal solution consists of 2.44 blocks of townhouses and 3.26 apartment buildings. If, by chance, this solution had been integer, the solution also would have been the optimal solution to the original integer linear program. However, as Figure 8.2 also shows, the optimal integer solution to the Security Realty Investors Problem is on a lower objective function line, with a value of $14.00. In general, you can find an *upper bound* on the value of any maximization integer or mixed-integer linear program by solving its associated LP Relaxation. If you can round the LP solution and obtain a feasible solution almost as good, you know that it is, at least, close to being optimal.

Computer Solution

As mentioned in the chapter introduction, computer packages for solving integer linear programs are now widely available. Generally, commercial codes are reliable for problems involving up to 100 or so integer variables and often are used to solve specially structured problems with several thousand variables.

The Management Scientist can be used to solve integer linear programs with a small number of variables. To use The Management Scientist to solve the Security Realty problem, the data input worksheet is completed in the same way as for solving a linear program (see Appendix 3.1). However, after instructing the computer to solve the problem, the user will be asked to indicate which variables are integer and whether they

MANAGEMENT SCIENCE in action

Cutting Photographic Color Paper Rolls[*]

At Kodak (Australasia) Pty. Ltd. (or simply Kodak), photographic color paper is available in the form of bulk rolls in widths of 42 inches and 52.5 inches and in lengths up to 8750 feet. Because of certain characteristics of the coating process, each bulk roll has a slightly different color response; as a result, the bulk rolls are grouped into blends that have an equivalent response when exposed to light. The majority of Kodak customers, such as the operators of one-hour processing shops, purchase rolls from Kodak ranging in widths from 3.5 inches to 11 inches, and usually in lengths of 275, 575, 775, and 1150 feet. A particular combination of width and length is referred to as a customer roll size or product.

To produce customer rolls from bulk rolls, Kodak must select a combination of customer widths that do not exceed the width of the bulk roll, the *slitting design* (SD), and a mix of customer lengths that do not exceed the length of the bulk roll, a *length combination* (LC). *Diagramming* refers to the process of deciding the match of SD and LC for a set of bulk rolls and a *diagram* is the SD and LC for one bulk roll. The problem of diagramming

is complex because of the high cost associated with waste, the existence of blends, and the fact that customer rolls of 1150 feet can be spliced.

To determine the best cutting pattern, a two-stage integer programming approach is used. In stage 1, a set of good alternative cutting plans (based on the proportion of waste) is developed. In stage 2, a *0–1* integer programming model is solved to choose a feasible cutting plan that minimizes waste for the bulk rolls being processed. Use of the integer programming model has reduced side- and end-trim waste to approximately 50% of previous levels, productivity of the cutting operation has increased, planning effort for diagramming has been reduced, and Kodak has been able to better match production to customer requirements. In the first 12 months of operation the savings in waste exceeded $2 million.

....

*Based on A. A. Farley, "Planning the Cutting of Photographic Color Paper Rolls for Kodak (Australasia), Pty. Ltd." *Interfaces,* January–February 1991, pp. 92–106.

Figure 8.3
. . . .

**The Management Scientist Solution
for the Security Realty Problem**

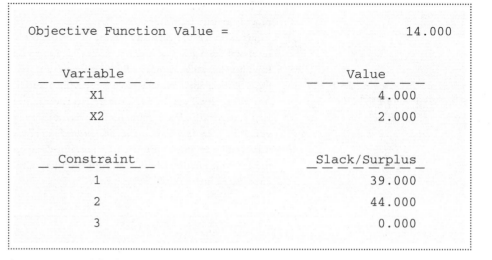

```
Objective Function Value =                          14.000


       Variable                              Value
    _ _ _ _ _ _ _ _                      _ _ _ _ _ _ _ _
          X1                             4.000
          X2                             2.000


      Constraint                         Slack/Surplus
    _ _ _ _ _ _ _ _                    _ _ _ _ _ _ _ _ _ _
          1                              39.000
          2                              44.000
          3                              0.000
```

are restricted to *0–1* values. Figure 8.3 shows the solution generated by The Management Scientist. The computer solution obtained using The Management Scientist is the same as the solution obtained using the graphical solution procedure.

NOTES & comments

1. Although we illustrated the graphical solution procedure only for an all-integer linear program, mixed-integer linear programs with two decision variables can be solved by a simple modification of the graphical procedure for an all-integer linear program.

2. The Management Science in Action: Cutting Photographic Color Paper Rolls describes how Kodak of Australasia used integer programming to decrease costs by $2 million.

8.3 Applications

In the preceding section we illustrated an all-integer linear program: the Security Realty Investors problem. In this section we discuss four applications involving *0–1,* or binary, integer variables: the capital budgeting problem, a problem involving fixed costs, a distribution system design problem, and a bank location problem.

Capital Budgeting

The Ice-Cold Refrigerator Company is considering a variety of projects with varying capital requirements over the next four years. Faced with limited capital resources, the company must select the most profitable projects for the capital expenditures.

Table 8.1

Project Net Present Values, Capital
Requirements, and Available Capital
Projections for the Ice-Cold
Refrigerator Company

Project	Estimated Net Present Value ($)	Capital Requirements ($)			
		Year 1	Year 2	Year 3	Year 4
Plant expansion	90,000	15,000	20,000	20,000	15,000
Warehouse expansion	40,000	10,000	15,000	20,000	5,000
New machinery	10,000	10,000	0	0	4,000
New product research	37,000	15,000	10,000	10,000	10,000
Available capital funds		40,000	50,000	40,000	35,000

The estimated net present values of the projects, the capital requirements, and the available capital projections[2] are shown in Table 8.1.

We define the decision variables as:

$x_1 = 1$ if the plant expansion project is accepted; 0 if rejected

$x_2 = 1$ if the warehouse expansion project is accepted; 0 if rejected

$x_3 = 1$ if the new machinery project is accepted; 0 if rejected

$x_4 = 1$ if the new product research project is accepted; 0 if rejected

The linear programming relaxation of this capital budgeting problem has a separate constraint for each year's available funds and a separate constraint requiring each variable to be less than or equal to 1. The linear programming relaxation follows (units are thousands of dollars).

$$\text{Max} \quad 90x_1 + 40x_2 + 10x_3 + 37x_4$$

s.t.

$$15x_1 + 10x_2 + 10x_3 + 15x_4 \leq 40$$

$$20x_1 + 15x_2 \qquad\quad + 10x_4 \leq 50$$

$$20x_1 + 20x_2 \qquad\quad + 10x_4 \leq 40$$

$$15x_1 + 5x_2 + 4x_3 + 10x_4 \leq 35$$

$$x_1 \qquad\qquad\qquad\qquad\quad \leq 1$$

$$x_2 \qquad\qquad\qquad\quad \leq 1$$

$$x_3 \qquad\qquad\quad \leq 1$$

$$x_4 \leq 1$$

$$x_1, x_2, x_3, x_4 \geq 0$$

The optimal solution to this linear program is $x_1 = 1$, $x_2 = 0.5$, $x_3 = 0.5$, and $x_4 = 1$, with a total estimated net present value of $152,000. The difficulty with a linear programming approach to the capital budgeting problem is now readily apparent. Unless it is possible

---

[2]The estimated net present value is the net return for the project discounted back to the beginning of year 1.

to implement the warehouse expansion and new machinery projects in 50% increments, the current solution is not feasible.

The *0–1* integer linear programming formulation of the Ice-Cold Refrigerator Company problem is

$$\text{Max} \quad 90x_1 + 40x_2 + 10x_3 + 37x_4$$

s.t.

$$15x_1 + 10x_2 + 10x_3 + 15x_4 \leq 40$$

$$20x_1 + 15x_2 \qquad\quad + 10x_4 \leq 50$$

$$20x_1 + 20x_2 \qquad\quad + 10x_4 \leq 40$$

$$15x_1 + 5x_2 + 4x_3 + 10x_4 \leq 35$$

$$x_1, x_2, x_3, x_4 = 0, 1$$

Using the integer programming module of The Management Scientist, we obtained the optimal integer solution of $x_1 = 1$, $x_2 = 1$, $x_3 = 1$, and $x_4 = 0$, with a total estimated net present value of $140,000. Note that we could not have discovered this optimal solution by simply rounding the linear programming solution. In fact, the best feasible solution that can be found by considering all possible roundings of the fractional variables in the linear programming solution is $x_1 = 1$, $x_2 = 0$, $x_3 = 0$, $x_4 = 1$, with a total estimated net present value of $127,000. This result is substantially less than the value of the optimal integer solution to the capital budgeting problem.

The ability to avoid fractional values is one of two main reasons that an integer programming formulation (as opposed to a linear programming formulation) is usually preferred for capital budgeting problems. The second reason that most management scientists prefer a *0–1* integer programming model for the capital budgeting problem is the flexibility provided in developing certain nonbudgetary constraints. These constraints often are important in capital budgeting problems and can be formulated only through the use of *0–1* (sometimes called logical) variables. We discuss how this is accomplished in the following subsections, and in more detail in Section 8.4.

Models Involving Fixed Costs

The cost of production often involves two components: a setup cost (fixed cost) that is not related to volume and a variable cost per unit. For instance, let us consider the RMC problem. Three raw materials are used to produce three products: a fuel additive, a solvent base, and a carpet cleaning fluid. We define the decision variables as follows:

$$x_1 = \text{number of tons of fuel additive produced}$$
$$x_2 = \text{number of tons of solvent base produced}$$
$$x_3 = \text{number of tons of cleaning fluid produced}$$

The fuel additive is a mixture of 40% material 1 and 60% material 2. The solvent base is a mixture of 50% material 1, 20% material 2, and 30% material 3. The cleaning fluid is a mixture of 60% material 1, 10% material 2, and 30% material 3. The profit contributions are $40 for every ton of fuel additive produced, $30 for every ton of solvent base produced, and $50 for every ton of carpet cleaning fluid produced.

A linear programming model of the RMC problem is shown here.

$$\text{Max} \quad 40x_1 + 30x_2 + 50x_3$$

s.t.

$$0.4x_1 + 0.5x_2 + 0.6x_3 \leq 20 \quad \text{Material 1}$$

$$0.2x_2 + 0.1x_3 \leq 5 \quad \text{Material 2}$$

$$0.6x_1 + 0.3x_2 + 0.3x_3 \leq 21 \quad \text{Material 3}$$

$$x_1, x_2, x_3 \geq 0$$

Using the linear programming module of The Management Scientist, we obtained an optimal solution consisting of 27.5 tons of fuel additive, 0 tons of solvent base, and 15 tons of carpet cleaning fluid, with a value of $1850.

Suppose that, in reviewing the solution, a manager had noted that setup costs (the labor costs required to install the different filters required for each product and to adjust the mixing and packaging equipment) had not been taken into account. They were $200 for the fuel additive, $50 for the solvent base, and $400 for the carpet cleaning fluid.

The modeling flexibility provided by $0-1$ integer variables provides a way to handle setup costs. For instance, suppose that we define the $0-1$ integer variables as follows:

$$y_1 = \begin{cases} 0 & \text{if no fuel additive is produced} \\ 1 & \text{if fuel additive is produced} \end{cases}$$

$$y_2 = \begin{cases} 0 & \text{if no solvent base is produced} \\ 1 & \text{if solvent base is produced} \end{cases}$$

$$y_3 = \begin{cases} 0 & \text{if no carpet cleaning fluid is produced} \\ 1 & \text{if carpet cleaning fluid is produced} \end{cases}$$

With these $0-1$ variables, we write the total setup cost as

$$200y_1 + 50y_2 + 400y_3$$

Thus, the objective function for the fixed-cost RMC problem is

$$\text{Max} \quad 40x_1 + 30x_2 + 50x_3 - 200y_1 - 50y_2 - 400y_3$$

Now, we must write constraints so that, when $y_i = 0$, the corresponding $x_i = 0$, and, when $y_i = 1$, production of the corresponding product is permitted. To do so we must first find an upper bound on the permissible values for $x_1, x_2,$ and x_3.

Suppose, for the moment, that the values of x_2 and x_3 are both 0. In this case, the first constraint (amount of material 1) limits the amount of x_1 that can be produced to 20/0.4 = 50 tons. Because the fuel additive does not require material 2, the second constraint does not limit the value of x_1. Finally, the third constraint limits the amount of x_1 that can be produced to 21/0.6 = 35 tons. Thus, considering all three constraints, the maximum permissible value of x_1 alone is 35. As the maximum amount of fuel additive that can be produced is 35 tons, the constraint relating x_1 and y_1 is

$$x_1 \leq 35y_1$$

Note that if $y_1 = 0$, corresponding to a decision to not produce fuel additive, the constraint becomes $x_1 \leq 0$. However, if $y_1 = 1$, a decision to produce fuel additive, the constraint becomes $x_1 \leq 35$. Thus, the production of fuel additive can take place only if $y_1 = 1$.

Since the maximum amount of solvent base (x_2) that can be produced is 25 tons (limit corresponds to constraint 2) and the maximum amount of carpet cleaning fluid (x_3) that can be produced is 33.33 tons (limit corresponds to constraint 1), we add the following two constraints relating x_2 to y_2 and x_3 to y_3:

$$x_2 \leq 25y_2$$

$$x_3 \leq 33.33y_3$$

The complete model, incorporating the fixed setup cost for RMC, is a mixed-integer linear program.

Max $40x_1 + 30x_2 + 50x_3 - 200y_1 - 50y_2 - 400y_3$

s.t.

$0.4x_1 + 0.5x_2 + 0.6x_3$		≤ 20	Material 1
$0.2x_2 + 0.1x_3$		≤ 5	Material 2
$0.6x_1 + 0.3x_2 + 0.3x_3$		≤ 21	Material 3
x_1	$- 35y_1$	≤ 0	Max x_1
x_2	$- 25y_2$	≤ 0	Max x_2
x_3	$- 33.33y_3$	≤ 0	Max x_3

$x_1, x_2, x_3 \geq 0$; $y_1, y_2, y_3 = 0, 1$

Using the integer linear programming module of The Management Scientist we obtained an optimal solution consisting of 25 tons of fuel additive, 20 tons of solvent base, and 0 tons of carpet cleaning fluid, with a value of $1350. Thus, when the setup costs are included in the objective function, the high setup cost associated with producing the carpet cleaning fluid ($400) offsets its relatively large profit contribution ($50) and the new optimal solution does not include the production of carpet cleaning fluid.

Distribution System Design

The Martin-Beck Company is in the process of planning new production facilities and developing a more efficient distribution system. At present it has one plant in St. Louis with a capacity of 30,000 units that supplies regional distribution centers located in Boston, Atlanta, and Houston. But, because of increased demand, management is considering four potential new plant sites: Detroit, Toledo, Denver, and Kansas City. Table 8.2 summarizes the projected plant capacities (in thousands of units), the cost per unit (in dollars) of shipping from each plant to each distribution center, and the demand forecasts at each distribution center (in thousands of units) for a one-year planning horizon. The estimated annual fixed costs for the new plants (in thousands) are

Detroit	$175
Toledo	$300
Denver	$375
Kansas City	$500

The Martin-Beck Company wants to minimize the total cost of plant operation and distribution of goods.

Table 8.2

Projected Plant Capacities, Shipping Costs Per Unit, and Demand Forecasts for the Martin-Beck Company Distribution System Problem

| | Destination | | | |
Plant Site	Boston	Atlanta	Houston	Capacity (1000s)
Detroit	5	2	3	10
Toledo	4	3	4	20
Denver	9	7	5	30
Kansas City	10	4	2	40
St. Louis	8	4	3	30
Demand (1000s)	30	20	20	

For the moment, let us suppose that Martin-Beck already had plants at Detroit, Toledo, Denver, and Kansas City and that the objective was to minimize the cost of shipping goods from the five plants to the three distribution centers. Note that this situation is simply a transportation problem of the type encountered in Chapter 7. The network representation for this problem is shown in Figure 8.4. If we let x_{ij} = number of units shipped (in thousands) from plant i ($i = 1, 2, \ldots, 5$) to distribution center j ($j = 1, 2, 3$), we write the linear programming formulation for this transportation problem as follows:

$$\text{Min} \quad 5x_{11} + 2x_{12} + 3x_{13} + 4x_{21} + 3x_{22} + 4x_{23} + 9x_{31} + 7x_{32} + 5x_{33} + 10x_{41} + 4x_{42}$$
$$+ 2x_{43} + 8x_{51} + 4x_{52} + 3x_{53}$$

s.t.

$$x_{11} + x_{12} + x_{13} \leq 10 \quad \text{Detroit Capacity}$$

$$x_{21} + x_{22} + x_{23} \leq 20 \quad \text{Toledo Capacity}$$

$$x_{31} + x_{32} + x_{33} \leq 30 \quad \text{Denver Capacity}$$

$$x_{41} + x_{42} + x_{43} \leq 40 \quad \text{Kansas City Capacity}$$

$$x_{51} + x_{52} + x_{53} \leq 30 \quad \text{St. Louis Capacity}$$

$$x_{11} + x_{21} + x_{31} + x_{41} + x_{51} = 30 \quad \text{Boston Demand}$$

$$x_{12} + x_{22} + x_{32} + x_{42} + x_{52} = 20 \quad \text{Atlanta Demand}$$

$$x_{13} + x_{23} + x_{33} + x_{43} + x_{53} = 20 \quad \text{Houston Demand}$$

$$x_{ij} \geq 0 \text{ for all } i \text{ and } j$$

We solved this transportation linear program using The Management Scientist. The optimal solution calls for the shipment of 10,000 units from Detroit to Boston, 20,000 units from Toledo to Boston, 20,000 units from Kansas City to Atlanta, and 20,000 units from Kansas City to Houston; the total transportation cost of this solution is $250,000.

As the Martin-Beck Company does not actually have plants in Detroit, Toledo, Denver, and Kansas City, the solution to the preceding transportation problem isn't feasible. Let us consider then how we can modify that linear program in order to decide which plants to build. To begin, we will consider the changes needed to assess the possibility of constructing a plant in Detroit. The procedure is similar to the one described in the previous subsection.

Figure 8.4

The Network Representation of the Martin-Beck Company Distribution System Problem

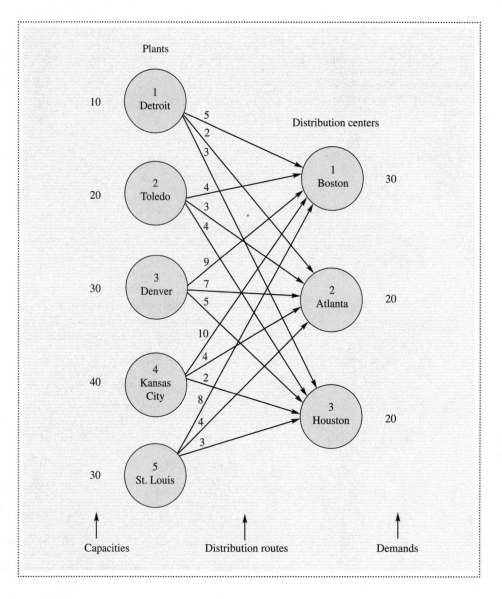

We first need to introduce a $0{-}1$ integer variable that will indicate whether a plant is constructed in Detroit. Let

$$y_1 = 1 \text{ if a plant is constructed in Detroit; 0 if not}$$

Using this $0{-}1$ integer variable, we can represent the constraint that nothing can be shipped from Detroit unless a plant is constructed there as follows:

$$x_{11} + x_{12} + x_{13} \leq 10y_1 \tag{8.1}$$

Note that if a plant is not constructed at Detroit, $y_1 = 0$ and equation (8.1) becomes

$$x_{11} + x_{12} + x_{13} \leq 0$$

Because all the decision variables must be nonnegative, this constraint is equivalent to

$$x_{11} + x_{12} + x_{13} = 0$$

If a plant is constructed at Detroit, $y_1 = 1$ and equation (8.1) becomes

$$x_{11} + x_{12} + x_{13} \leq 10$$

Similarly, we can introduce decision variables y_2, y_3, and y_4 to account for the possibility of plants in Toledo, Denver, and Kansas City; the corresponding constraints are

$$x_{21} + x_{22} + x_{23} \leq 20y_2 \qquad (8.2)$$

$$x_{31} + x_{32} + x_{33} \leq 30y_3 \qquad (8.3)$$

$$x_{41} + x_{42} + x_{43} \leq 40y_4 \qquad (8.4)$$

In the transportation linear program initially developed, the objective function represented the total shipping cost based on the assumption that Martin-Beck actually had plants at each site. To include the fixed costs associated with new plants, we must add the following costs to the objective function:

$$175y_1 + 300y_2 + 375y_3 + 500y_4$$

The following mixed-integer linear program now represents the complete model for the Martin-Beck Company distribution system problem.

Min $\quad 5x_{11} + 2x_{12} + 3x_{13} + 4x_{21} + 3x_{22} + 4x_{23} + 9x_{31} + 7x_{32} + 5x_{33} + 10x_{41} + 4x_{42}$

$\qquad + 2x_{43} + 8x_{51} + 4x_{52} + 3x_{53} + 175y_1 + 300y_2 + 375y_3 + 500y_4$

s.t.

$$\begin{array}{lll}
x_{11} + x_{12} + x_{13} & \leq 10y_1 & \text{Detroit Capacity} \\
x_{21} + x_{22} + x_{23} & \leq 20y_2 & \text{Toledo Capacity} \\
x_{31} + x_{32} + x_{33} & \leq 30y_3 & \text{Denver Capacity} \\
x_{41} + x_{42} + x_{43} & \leq 40y_4 & \text{Kansas City Capacity} \\
x_{51} + x_{52} + x_{53} & \leq 30 & \text{St. Louis Capacity} \\
x_{11} + x_{21} + x_{31} + x_{41} + x_{51} & = 30 & \text{Boston Demand} \\
x_{12} + x_{22} + x_{32} + x_{42} + x_{52} & = 20 & \text{Atlanta Demand} \\
x_{13} + x_{23} + x_{33} + x_{43} + x_{53} & = 20 & \text{Houston Demand}
\end{array}$$

$$x_{ij} \geq 0 \text{ for all } i \text{ and } j; \ y_1, y_2, y_3, y_4 = 0, 1$$

Using the integer linear programming module of The Management Scientist, we obtained the solution shown in Figure 8.5. The optimal solution calls for the construction of a plant in Kansas City ($y_4 = 1$); 20,000 units will be shipped from Kansas City to Atlanta ($x_{42} = 20$), 20,000 units will be shipped from Kansas City to Houston ($x_{43} = 20$), and 30,000 units will be shipped from St. Louis to Boston ($x_{51} = 30$). Note that the total cost of this solution including the fixed cost of $500,000 to construct the plant in Kansas City is $860,000.

This basic model can be expanded to accommodate distribution systems involving direct shipments from plants to warehouses, from plants to retail outlets, and multiple products.[3] Using the special properties of $0-1$ variables, the model can also be expanded

Try Problem 15 for practice in formulating a distribution system problem involving 0–1 variables.

---

[3]For computational reasons, it is usually preferable to replace the m plant capacity constraints with mn shipping route capacity constraints of the form $x_{ij} \leq \text{Min} \{s_i, d_j\} \, y_i$ for $i = 1, \ldots, m$ and $j = 1, \ldots, n$. The coefficient for y_i in each of these constraints is the smaller of the origin capacity (s_i) or the destination demand (d_j). These additional constraints often cause the solution of the LP Relaxation to be integer.

Figure 8.5

....

**The Management Scientist Solution
for the Martin-Beck Company
Distribution System Problem**

```
OPTIMAL SOLUTION

Objective Function Value =                      860.000

     Variable                              Value
       X11                                 0.000
       X12                                 0.000
       X13                                 0.000
       X21                                 0.000
       X22                                 0.000
       X23                                 0.000
       X31                                 0.000
       X32                                 0.000
       X33                                 0.000
       X41                                 0.000
       X42                                20.000
       X43                                20.000
       X51                                30.000
       X52                                 0.000
       X53                                 0.000
       Y1                                  0.000
       Y2                                  0.000
       Y3                                  0.000
       Y4                                  1.000

     Constraint                        Slack/Surplus
        1                                  0.000
        2                                  0.000
        3                                  0.000
        4                                  0.000
        5                                  0.000
        6                                  0.000
        7                                  0.000
        8                                  0.000
```

to accommodate a variety of configuration constraints on the plant locations. For example, suppose in another problem, site 1 was in Dallas and site 2 was in Fort Worth. A company might not want to locate plants in both Dallas and Fort Worth because the cities are so close together. To prevent this result, the following constraint can be added to the model:

$$y_1 + y_2 \leq 1$$

This constraint allows either y_1 or y_2 to equal 1, but not both. If we had written the constraint as an equality, it would require that a plant be located in either Dallas or Fort Worth.

A Bank Location Application

....

The long-range planning department for the Ohio Trust Company is considering expanding its operation into a 20-county region in northeastern Ohio (see Figure 8.6). Currently, Ohio Trust does not have a principal place of business in any of the 20 counties

Figure 8.6

The 20-County Area in Northeastern Ohio

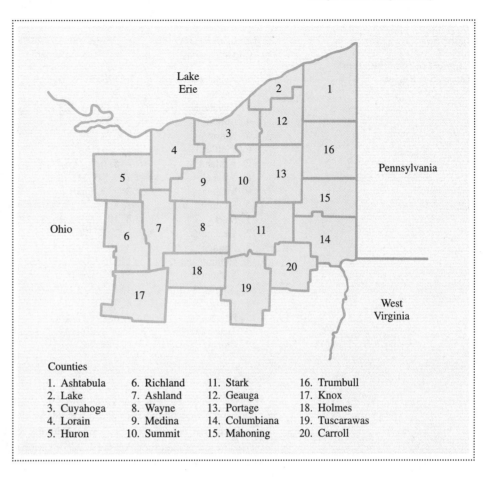

Counties

1. Ashtabula	6. Richland	11. Stark	16. Trumbull
2. Lake	7. Ashland	12. Geauga	17. Knox
3. Cuyahoga	8. Wayne	13. Portage	18. Holmes
4. Lorain	9. Medina	14. Columbiana	19. Tuscarawas
5. Huron	10. Summit	15. Mahoning	20. Carroll

under consideration. According to the banking laws in Ohio, if a bank establishes a principal place of business (PPB) in any county, branch banks can be established in that county and in any adjacent county. However, to establish a new principal place of business, Ohio Trust must either obtain approval for a new bank from the state's superintendent of banks or purchase an existing bank.

Table 8.3 lists the 20 counties in the region and adjacent counties. For example, Ashtabula County is adjacent to Lake, Geauga, and Trumbull counties; Lake County is adjacent to Ashtabula, Cuyahoga, and Geauga counties; and so on.

As an initial step in its planning, Ohio Trust would like to determine the minimum number of PPBs necessary to do business throughout the 20-county region. A $0-1$ integer programming model can be used to solve this problem for Ohio Trust. We define the variables as

$$x_i = 1 \text{ if a PPB is established in county } i; 0 \text{ otherwise}$$

To minimize the number of PPBs needed, we write the objective function as

$$\text{Min} \quad x_1 + x_2 + \cdots + x_{20}$$

The bank may locate branches in a county if the county contains a PPB or is adjacent to another county with a PPB. Thus, there will be one constraint for each county. For example, the constraint for Ashtabula County is

$$x_1 + x_2 + x_{12} + x_{16} \geq 1 \qquad \text{Ashtabula}$$

Table 8.3
··········
Counties in the Ohio Trust Expansion Region

Counties Under Consideration	Adjacent Counties (by Number)
1. Ashtabula	2, 12, 16
2. Lake	1, 3, 12
3. Cuyahoga	2, 4, 9, 10, 12, 13
4. Lorain	3, 5, 7, 9
5. Huron	4, 6, 7
6. Richland	5, 7, 17
7. Ashland	4, 5, 6, 8, 9, 17, 18
8. Wayne	7, 9, 10, 11, 18
9. Medina	3, 4, 7, 8, 10
10. Summit	3, 8, 9, 11, 12, 13
11. Stark	8, 10, 13, 14, 15, 18, 19, 20
12. Geauga	1, 2, 3, 10, 13, 16
13. Portage	3, 10, 11, 12, 15, 16
14. Columbiana	11, 15, 20
15. Mahoning	11, 13, 14, 16
16. Trumbull	1, 12, 13, 15
17. Knox	6, 7, 18
18. Holmes	7, 8, 11, 17, 19
19. Tuscarawas	11, 18, 20
20. Carroll	11, 14, 19

Note that satisfaction of this constraint ensures that a PPB will be placed in Ashtabula County *or* in one or more of the adjacent counties. This constraint thus guarantees that Ohio Trust will be able to place branch banks in Ashtabula County.

The complete statement of the bank location problem is

$$\text{Min} \quad x_1 + x_2 + \quad \cdots \quad + x_{20}$$

s.t.

$$x_1 + x_2 \quad + x_{12} + x_{16} \quad \geq 1 \quad \text{Ashtabula}$$

$$x_1 + x_2 + x_3 + x_{12} \quad \geq 1 \quad \text{Lake}$$

$$\vdots \qquad\qquad\qquad \vdots$$

$$x_{11} + x_{14} + x_{19} + x_{20} \geq 1 \quad \text{Carroll}$$

$$x_i = 0, 1 \quad i = 1, 2, \ldots, 20$$

We used LINDO/PC to solve this 20-variable, 20-constraint problem formulation. In Figure 8.7 we show a portion of the computer output. Note that the variable names correspond to the first four letters in the name of each county. Using the output, we see that the optimal solution calls for principal places of business in Ashland, Stark, and Geauga counties. With PPBs in these three counties, Ohio Trust can place branch banks in all 20 counties (see Figure 8.8). All other decision variables have an optimal value of zero, indicating that a PPB should not be placed in these counties. Clearly the integer programming model could be enlarged to allow for expansion into a larger area or throughout the entire state.[4]

---

[4]A model of this type allowing for expansion throughout the state and some other variations is presented in Sweeney, D. J., L. Mairose, and R. Martin, "Strategic Planning in Bank Location," *Decision Sciences Proceedings,* November 1979.

Figure 8.7

LINDO/PC Solution for the Bank Location Problem

```
          OBJECTIVE FUNCTION VALUE

     1)    3.00000000

          VARIABLE          VALUE        REDUCED COST
              ASHT        .000000            .000000
              LAKE        .000000            .000000
              CUYA        .000000            .000000
              LORA        .000000            .000000
              HURO        .000000            .000000
              RICH        .000000           1.000000
              ASHL       1.000000            .000000
              WAYN        .000000            .000000
              MEDI        .000000            .000000
              SUMM        .000000            .000000
              STAR       1.000000            .000000
              GEAU       1.000000            .000000
              PORT        .000000            .000000
              COLU        .000000            .000000
              MAHO        .000000            .000000
              TRUM        .000000            .000000
              KNOX        .000000           1.000000
              HOLM        .000000            .000000
              TUSC        .000000            .000000
              CARR        .000000            .000000
```

Figure 8.8

Principal Place of Business Counties for Ohio Trust

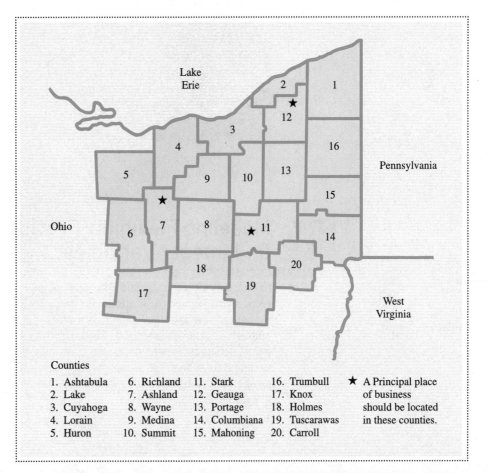

Counties

1. Ashtabula	6. Richland	11. Stark	16. Trumbull	★ A Principal place
2. Lake	7. Ashland	12. Geauga	17. Knox	of business
3. Cuyahoga	8. Wayne	13. Portage	18. Holmes	should be located
4. Lorain	9. Medina	14. Columbiana	19. Tuscarawas	in these counties.
5. Huron	10. Summit	15. Mahoning	20. Carroll	

NOTES & comments

1. Most practical applications of integer linear programming involve only *0–1* integer variables. Indeed, some mixed-integer computer codes are designed to handle only integer variables with binary values. However, if a clever mathematical trick is employed, these codes can still be used for problems involving general integer variables. The trick is called *binary expansion* and requires that an upper bound be established for each integer variable. More advanced texts on integer programming show how this can be done.

2. The Management Science in Action: Analyzing Price Quotations Under Business Volume Discounts describes how *0–1* variables can be used in a model designed to take advantage of business volume discounts. Bellcore clients have saved millions of dollars by using a mixed-integer programming model.

3. General-purpose mixed-integer linear programming codes and some spreadsheet packages can be used for linear programming problems, all-integer problems, and problems involving some continuous and some integer variables. General-purpose codes are seldom the fastest for solving problems with special structure (such as the transportation, assignment, and transshipment problems); however, unless the problems are very large, speed is usually not a critical issue. Thus, for most practitioners, it is probably better to become familiar with one general-purpose computer package that can be used on a variety of problems than to maintain a variety of computer codes designed for special problems.

4. Several computer software packages can provide solutions to both general linear programming problems and integer linear programming problems. Note, however, that the sensitivity analysis information for integer linear programs shown in some of these software outputs does not have the same meaning as it does for linear programming problems and should ordinarily be disregarded.

8.4 Modeling Flexibility Provided by *0–1* Integer Variables

In Section 8.3 we presented four applications involving *0–1* integer variables. In this section we continue the discussion of the use of *0–1* integer variables in modeling. First, we will show how *0–1* integer variables can be used to model multiple-choice and mutually exclusive constraints. Then, we show how *0–1* integer variables can be used to model situations in which k projects of a set of n projects must be selected, as well as situations in which the acceptance of one project is conditional on the acceptance of another. We close the section with a cautionary note on the role of sensitivity analysis in integer linear programming.

MANAGEMENT SCIENCE in action

Analyzing Price Quotations under Business Volume Discounts*

Bellcore was formed in 1984 to provide various support services for the regional Bell operating telephone companies. In order to reduce the cost of buying goods and services, Bellcore client companies are increasingly requesting business volume discounts from suppliers in place of traditional quantity discounts. With traditional quantity discounts, the price of each item purchased is discounted on the basis of how much of that item is purchased. Business volume discounts differ from single-item quantity discounts in that the supplier discounts the price of each item by a percentage that is based on the total dollar volume of business over all items awarded to the supplier; whatever this percentage, it remains the same for each item. In general, a firm can realize lower overall purchasing costs with business volume discounts and a supplier can increase total revenues by obtaining a larger volume of that firm's business. However, business volume discounts greatly increase the complexity of the procurement process because the discount obtained depends on the purchase quantities and prices of all products purchased.

To assist Bellcore client companies in using business volume discounts, Bellcore developed the procurement decision support-system (PDSS), a PC-based decision support program that uses a mixed-integer programming model to minimize the total cost of purchases. The model uses $0-1$ integer variables to model the discount categories applicable to the problem and includes a variety of constraints involving factors such as supplier capacity and limits on the dollar amount awarded to a supplier. Since 1990, one Bellcore client company has reported two savings, one of $4.5 million and another of $15 million; these figures represent approximately 10% on the cost of purchases. Another client company has realized a reduction of approximately 80% in the cost of analyzing quotations, and users generally believe that PDSS is a useful tool in identifying opportunities in negotiations with suppliers.

....

*Based on Katz, P., A. Sadrian, and P. Tendick, "Telephone Companies Analyze Price Quotations with Bellcore's PDSS Software." *Interfaces*, January–February 1994, pp. 50–63.

Multiple-Choice and Mutually Exclusive Constraints

Recall the Ice-Cold Refrigerator capital budgeting problem introduced in Section 8.3. We defined the decision variables for that problem as

$x_1 = 1$ if the plant expansion project is accepted; 0 if rejected

$x_2 = 1$ if the warehouse expansion project is accepted; 0 if rejected

$x_3 = 1$ if the new machinery project is accepted; 0 if rejected

$x_4 = 1$ if the new product research project is accepted; 0 if rejected

Suppose that, instead of one warehouse expansion project, the Ice-Cold Refrigerator Company actually has three warehouse expansion projects under consideration. One of the warehouses *must* be expanded because of increasing product demand, but new demand isn't sufficient to make expansion of more than one warehouse necessary. The following variable definitions and *multiple-choice constraint* could be incorporated into the previous $0-1$ integer linear programming model to reflect this situation. Let

$x_2 = 1$ if the original warehouse expansion project is accepted; 0 if rejected

$x_5 = 1$ if the second warehouse expansion project is accepted; 0 if rejected

$x_6 = 1$ if the third warehouse expansion project is accepted; 0 if rejected

The multiple-choice constraint reflecting the requirement that exactly one of these projects may be selected is

$$x_2 + x_5 + x_6 = 1$$

You can easily see why this is called a multiple-choice constraint. Since x_2, x_5, and x_6 are allowed to assume only the values 0 or 1, one and only one of these projects must be selected from among the three choices. Note that if fractional values (as in linear programming) were allowed for the decision variables, we could not enforce the requirement of selecting one and only one project (e.g., $x_2 = \frac{1}{3}$, $x_5 = \frac{1}{3}$, $x_6 = \frac{1}{3}$ would satisfy the constraint).

If the requirement that one warehouse must be expanded did not exist, the multiple-choice constraint could be modified as follows:

$$x_2 + x_5 + x_6 \leq 1$$

This modification allows for the case of no warehouse expansion ($x_2 = x_5 = x_6 = 0$) but does not permit more than one warehouse to be expanded. This type of constraint is often called a *mutually exclusive constraint.*

k Out of n Alternatives Constraint

An extension of the notion of a multiple-choice constraint can be used to model situations in which *k out of a set of n* projects must be selected. Suppose that x_2, x_5, x_6, x_7, and x_8 represent five potential warehouse expansion projects and that two of the five projects must be accepted. The constraint that satisfies this new requirement is

$$x_2 + x_5 + x_6 + x_7 + x_8 = 2$$

If no more than two of the projects are to be selected, we would use the following less-than-or-equal-to constraint:

$$x_2 + x_5 + x_6 + x_7 + x_8 \leq 2$$

Again, each of these variables must be restricted to *0–1* values.

Conditional and Corequisite Constraints

Sometimes the acceptance of one project is conditional on the acceptance of another. For example, suppose for the Ice-Cold Refrigerator Company that the warehouse expansion project was conditional on the plant expansion project. That is, the company will not consider expanding the warehouse unless the plant is expanded. With x_1 representing plant expansion and x_2 representing warehouse expansion, a *conditional constraint* could be introduced to enforce this requirement:

$$x_2 \leq x_1$$

As both x_1 and x_2 must be 0 or 1, whenever x_1 is 0, x_2 will be forced to 0. When x_1 is 1, x_2 is also allowed to be 1; thus, both the plant and the warehouse can be expanded. However, we note that the preceding constraint does not force the warehouse expansion project (x_2) to be accepted if the plant expansion project (x_1) is accepted.

If the warehouse expansion project had to be accepted whenever the plant expansion project was, and vice versa, we would say that x_1 and x_2 represented *corequisite* projects. To model such a situation, we simply write the preceding constraint as an equality:

$$x_2 = x_1$$

Try Problem 7 for practice with the modeling flexibility provided by *0–1* variables.

This constraint forces x_1 and x_2 to take on the same value.

A Cautionary Note on Sensitivity Analysis

Sensitivity analysis often is more crucial for integer linear programming problems than for linear programming problems. A very small change in one of the coefficients in the constraints can cause a relatively large change in the value of the optimal solution. To understand why, consider the following integer programming model of a simple capital budgeting problem involving four projects and a budgetary constraint for a single time period:

$$\text{Max} \quad 40x_1 + 60x_2 + 70x_3 + 160x_4$$

$$\text{s.t.}$$

$$16x_1 + 35x_2 + 45x_3 + 85x_4 \leq 100$$

$$x_1, x_2, x_3, x_4 = 0, 1$$

We obtain the optimal solution to this problem by enumerating the alternatives. It is $x_1 = 1$, $x_2 = 1$, $x_3 = 1$, and $x_4 = 0$, with an objective function value of \$170. However, note that if the budget available is increased by \$1 (from \$100 to \$101), the optimal solution changes to $x_1 = 1$, $x_2 = 0$, $x_3 = 0$, and $x_4 = 1$, with an objective function value of \$200. That is, one additional dollar in the budget would lead to a \$30 increase in the return. Surely management, when faced with such a situation, would increase the budget by \$1. Because of the extreme sensitivity of the value of the optimal solution to the constraint coefficients, practitioners usually recommend resolving the integer linear program several times with slight variations in the coefficients before attempting to choose an optimal solution for implementation.

Summary

We have introduced an important extension of the linear programming model: the integer linear program. The only difference between the integer linear programming problem and the linear programming problem studied in previous chapters is the added restriction on some of the variables. If all the variables are required to be integer, we have an all-integer linear program; if some, but not necessarily all, the variables are required to be integer, we have a mixed-integer linear program. Finally, in case the integer variables are permitted to assume only the values 0 or 1, we have a *0–1* (binary) integer linear program. Binary integer linear programs may be either all integer or mixed integer.

There are two primary reasons for studying integer linear programming. First, in many applications, fractional values of the decision variables are not permitted. Since rounding the linear programming solution can provide poor results, methods for finding the optimal integer solution are needed. A second reason for studying integer linear programming is that it increases modeling flexibility through the use of *0–1* variables. In the discussion of the capital budgeting, fixed-cost, distribution system, and bank location problems, we showed how integer variables can be used to represent important managerial considerations.

In recent years, with the availability of commercial integer linear programming computer codes, the use of integer linear programming has grown rapidly. As researchers develop solution procedures capable of solving integer linear programs with larger numbers of variables and as computer speeds increase, a continuation of this growth and the development of new applications can be expected.

Glossary

Integer linear program A linear program with the additional requirement that some or all of the decision variables must be integer.

All-integer linear program An integer linear program in which all the decision variables are required to be integer.

LP Relaxation The linear program that results from dropping the integer requirements for the decision variables. For a maximization problem, the value of the optimal solution to the LP Relaxation is an upper bound on the value of the optimal integer solution.

Mixed-integer linear program An integer linear program in which some, but not all, of the decision variables are required to be integer.

Discrete variable Another name for a variable that may assume only integer values.

Continuous variable A variable that may take on any real number as a value. The variables in a linear program are continuous.

0–1 integer linear program Also called *binary integer program.* An all-integer or mixed-integer linear program in which the integer variables are only permitted to assume the values 0 or 1.

Multiple-choice constraint A constraint requiring that the sum of two or more *0–1* variables equal 1. Thus, any feasible solution makes a choice of one of these variables to set equal to 1.

Mutually exclusive constraint A constraint requiring that the sum of two or more *0–1* variables be less than or equal to 1. Thus, if one of the variables equals 1, the others must equal 0. However, all variables could equal 0.

k out of n alternatives constraint An extension of the multiple-choice constraint. This constraint requires that the sum of *n 0–1* variables equal *k*.

Conditional constraints Constraints involving *0–1* variables that do not allow certain variables to equal 1 unless certain other variables are equal to 1.

Corequisite constraint A constraint requiring that two *0–1* variables be equal. Thus, they are both in or out of solution together.

Problems

1. **SELF** Test Indicate which of the following are all-integer linear programs, which are mixed-integer linear programs, and which are ordinary linear programs. For each of the all-integer and mixed-integer linear programs, write the LP Relaxation. (Do not attempt to solve.)

a. Max $30x_1 + 25x_2$

s.t.

$$3x_1 + 1.5x_2 \leq 400$$

$$1.5x_1 + 2x_2 \leq 250$$

$$1x_1 + 1x_2 \leq 150$$

$$x_1, x_2 \geq 0 \text{ and } x_2 \text{ integer}$$

b. Min $3x_1 + 4x_2$

s.t.

$$2x_1 + 4x_2 \geq 8$$

$$2x_1 + 6x_2 \geq 12$$

$$x_1, x_2 \geq 0 \text{ and integer}$$

c. Min $30x_1 + 4x_2$

s.t.

$$3x_1 + 2x_2 \geq 50$$

$$0.1x_1 + 0.2x_2 \geq 2$$

$$x_1, x_2 \geq 0 \text{ and } x_1 \text{ integer}$$

d. Max $3x_1 + 4x_2$

s.t.

$$-1x_1 + 2x_2 \leq 8$$

$$1x_1 + 2x_2 \leq 12$$

$$2x_1 + 1x_2 \leq 16$$

$$x_1, x_2 \geq 0 \text{ and integer}$$

e. Max $20x_1 + 5x_2$

s.t.

$$5x_1 + 1x_2 \leq 15$$

$$6x_1 + 4x_2 \leq 24$$

$$1x_1 + 1x_2 \leq 5$$

$$x_1, x_2 \geq 0$$

2. **SELF**Test   Consider the following all-integer linear program.

$$\text{Max}   5x_1 + 8x_2$$

s.t.

$$6x_1 + 5x_2 \leq 30$$

$$9x_1 + 4x_2 \leq 36$$

$$1x_1 + 2x_2 \leq 10$$

$$x_1, x_2 \geq 0 \text{ and integer}$$

a. Graph the constraints for this problem. Use heavy dots to indicate all the feasible integer solutions.
b. Find the optimal solution to the LP Relaxation. Round down to find a feasible integer solution.
c. Find the optimal integer solution. Is it the same as the solution obtained in part (b) by rounding down?

3. Consider the following all-integer linear program.

$$\text{Max}   1x_1 + 1x_2$$

s.t.

$$4x_1 + 6x_2 \leq 22$$

$$1x_1 + 5x_2 \leq 15$$

$$2x_1 + 1x_2 \leq 9$$

$$x_1, x_2 \geq 0 \text{ and integer}$$

a. Graph the constraints for this problem. Use heavy dots to indicate all the feasible integer solutions.

b. Solve the LP Relaxation of this problem.

c. Find the optimal integer solution.

4. Consider the following all-integer linear program.

$$\text{Max} \quad 10x_1 + 3x_2$$

s.t.

$$6x_1 + 7x_2 \leq 40$$

$$3x_1 + 1x_2 \leq 11$$

$$x_1, x_2 \geq 0 \text{ and integer}$$

a. Formulate and solve the LP Relaxation of the problem. Solve it graphically, and round down to find a feasible solution. Specify upper and lower bounds on the value of the optimal solution.

b. Solve the integer linear program graphically. Compare the value of this solution with the solution obtained in part (a).

c. Suppose the objective function changes to Max $3x_1 + 6x_2$. Repeat parts (a) and (b).

5. **SELF**Test   Consider the following mixed-integer linear program.

$$\text{Max} \quad 2x_1 + 3x_2$$

s.t.

$$4x_1 + 9x_2 \leq 36$$

$$7x_1 + 5x_2 \leq 35$$

$$x_1, x_2 \geq 0 \text{ and } x_1 \text{ integer}$$

a. Graph the constraints for this problem. Indicate on your graph all feasible mixed-integer solutions.

b. Find the optimal solution to the LP Relaxation. Round the value of x_1 down to find a feasible mixed-integer solution. Is this solution optimal? Why or why not?

c. Find the optimal solution for the mixed-integer linear program.

6. Consider the following mixed-integer linear program.

$$\text{Max} \quad 1x_1 + 1x_2$$

s.t.

$$7x_1 + 9x_2 \leq 63$$

$$9x_1 + 5x_2 \leq 45$$

$$3x_1 + 1x_2 \leq 12$$

$$x_1, x_2 \geq 0 \text{ and } x_2 \text{ integer}$$

a. Graph the constraints for this problem. Indicate on your graph all feasible mixed-integer solutions.

b. Find the optimal solution to the LP Relaxation. Round the value of x_2 down to find a feasible mixed-integer solution. Specify upper and lower bounds on the value of the optimal solution to the mixed-integer linear program.

c. Find the optimal solution to the mixed-integer linear program.

7. **SELF**Test The following questions refer to a capital budgeting problem with six projects represented by $0-1$ variables x_1, x_2, x_3, x_4, x_5, and x_6.

   a. Write a constraint modeling a situation in which two of the projects 1, 3, 5, and 6 must be undertaken.

   b. Write a constraint modeling a situation in which projects 3 and 5 must be undertaken simultaneously.

   c. Write a constraint modeling a situation in which project 1 or 4 must be undertaken, but not both.

   d. Write constraints modeling a situation where project 4 cannot be undertaken unless projects 1 and 3 also are undertaken.

   e. Revise the requirement in part (d) to accommodate the case in which, when projects 1 and 3 are undertaken, project 4 also must be undertaken.

8. Spencer Enterprises is attempting to choose among a series of new investment alternatives. The potential investment alternatives, the net present value of the future stream of returns, the capital requirements, and the available capital funds over the next 3 years are summarized as follows:

	Net Present Value ($)	Capital Requirements ($)		
Alternative		Year 1	Year 2	Year 3
Limited warehouse expansion	4,000	3,000	1,000	4,000
Extensive warehouse expansion	6,000	2,500	3,500	3,500
Test market new product	10,500	6,000	4,000	5,000
Advertising campaign	4,000	2,000	1,500	1,800
Basic research	8,000	5,000	1,000	4,000
Purchase new equipment	3,000	1,000	500	900
Capital funds available		10,500	7,000	8,750

   a. Develop and solve an integer programming model for maximizing the net present value.

   b. Assume that only one of the warehouse expansion projects can be implemented. Modify your model of part (a).

   c. Suppose that, if the test marketing of the new product is carried out, the advertising campaign also must be conducted. Modify your formulation of part (b) to reflect this new situation.

9. The following is the integer programming formulation of the Ice-Cold Refrigerator Company capital budgeting problem.

$$\text{Max} \quad 90x_1 + 40x_2 + 10x_3 + 37x_4$$

s.t.

$$15x_1 + 10x_2 + 10x_3 + 15x_4 \leq 40$$

$$20x_1 + 15x_2 \qquad\quad + 10x_4 \leq 50$$

$$20x_1 + 20x_2 \qquad\quad + 10x_4 \leq 40$$

$$15x_1 + 5x_2 + 4x_3 + 10x_4 \leq 35$$

$$x_1, x_2, x_3, x_4 = 0, 1$$

   a. Solve by trial and error.

   b. If you have a computer code for solving integer programs, use it to solve the problem.

10. Snow Cinemas is considering four options for the seating capacity of a new movie theater: 100, 150, 250, and 400 seats. Let

$x_1 = 1$ if a seating capacity of 100 is selected; 0 otherwise

$x_2 = 1$ if a seating capacity of 150 is selected; 0 otherwise

$x_3 = 1$ if a seating capacity of 250 is selected; 0 otherwise

$x_4 = 1$ if a seating capacity of 400 is selected; 0 otherwise

a. Let z = capacity of the movie theater that Snow Cinemas decides to build. Write constraints that will ensure that the capacity chosen will be either 100, 150, 250, or 400.

b. Write constraints that will ensure that the capacity chosen will be 100, 150, 250, or 400 if Snow Cinemas does build the new theater, or 0 if the company does not build the new theater.

11. Hawkins Manufacturing Company produces connecting rods for 4- and 6-cylinder automobile engines using the same production line. The cost required to set up the production line to produce the 4-cylinder connecting rods is $2000, and the cost required to set up the production line for the 6-cylinder connecting rods is $3500. Manufacturing costs are $15 for each 4-cylinder connecting rod and $18 for each 6-cylinder connecting rod. Hawkins makes a decision at the end of each week as to which product will be manufactured the following week. If there is a production changeover from one week to the next, the weekend is used to reconfigure the production line. Once the line has been set up, the weekly production capacities are 6000 6-cylinder connecting rods and 8000 4-cylinder connecting rods. Let

x_4 = the number of 4-cylinder connecting rods produced next week

x_6 = the number of 6-cylinder connecting rods produced next week

$s_4 = 1$ if the production line is set up to produce the 4-cylinder connecting rods; 0 otherwise

$s_6 = 1$ if the production line is set up to produce the 6-cylinder connecting rods; 0 otherwise

a. Using the decision variables x_4 and s_4, write a constraint that limits next week's production of the 4-cylinder connecting rods to either 0 or 8000 units.

b. Using the decision variables x_6 and s_6, write a constraint that limits next week's production of the 6-cylinder connecting rods to either 0 or 6000 units.

c. Write 3 constraints that, taken together, limit the production of connecting rods for next week.

d. Write an objective function for minimizing the cost of production for next week.

12. Grave City is considering the relocation of several police substations to obtain better enforcement in high-crime areas. The locations under consideration together with the areas that can be covered from these locations are given in the following table.

Potential Locations for Substations	Areas Covered
A	1, 5, 7
B	1, 2, 5, 7
C	1, 3, 5
D	2, 4, 5
E	3, 4, 6
F	4, 5, 6
G	1, 5, 6, 7

a. Formulate an integer programming model that could be used to find the minimum number of locations necessary to provide coverage to all areas.

b. Solve the problem in part (a) by using any means at your disposal.

13. Hart Manufacturing makes three products. Each product requires manufacturing operations in three departments: A, B, and C. The labor-hour requirements, by department, are

Department	Product 1	Product 2	Product 3
A	1.50	3.00	2.00
B	2.00	1.00	2.50
C	0.25	0.25	0.25

During the next production period, the labor-hours available are 450 in department A, 350 in department B, and 50 in department C. The profit contributions per unit are $25 for product 1, $28 for product 2, and $30 for product 3.
   a. Formulate a linear programming model for maximizing total profit contribution.
   b. Solve the linear program formulated in part (a). How much of each product should be produced and what is the projected total profit contribution?
   c. After evaluating the solution obtained in part (b), one of the production supervisors noted that production setup costs had not been taken into account. She noted that setup costs are $400 for product 1, $550 for product 2, and $600 for product 3. If the solution developed in part (b) is to be used, what is the total profit contribution after taking into account the setup costs?
   d. Management realized that the optimal product mix, taking setup costs into account, might be different from the one recommended in part (b). Formulate a mixed-integer linear program that takes setup costs into account.
   e. Use a computer code to solve the mixed integer linear program formulated in part (d). How much of each product should be produced and what is the projected total profit contribution? Compare this profit contribution to that obtained in part (c).

14. Yates Company supplies road salt to county highway departments. The company has three trucks, and the dispatcher is trying to schedule tomorrow's deliveries to Polk, Dallas, and Jasper counties. Two of the trucks have 15-ton capacities and the third truck has a 30-ton capacity. Based on these truck capacities, two of the counties will receive 15 tons and the third will receive 30 tons of road salt. The dispatcher wants to determine how much to ship to each county. Let

$$x_1 = \text{amount shipped to Polk County}$$

$$x_2 = \text{amount shipped to Dallas County}$$

$$x_3 = \text{amount shipped to Jasper County}$$

and

$$y_i = \begin{cases} 1 \text{ if the 30-ton truck is assigned to county } i \\ 0 \text{ otherwise} \end{cases}$$

   a. Use these variable definitions and write constraints that appropriately restrict the amount shipped to each county.
   b. The cost of assigning the 30-ton truck to the three counties is $100 to Polk, $85 to Dallas, and $50 to Jasper. Formulate and solve a mixed-integer linear program to determine how much to ship to each county.

15. **SELF Test** Recall the Martin-Beck Company distribution system problem in Section 8.3.
   a. Modify the formulation shown in Section 8.3 to account for the policy restriction that one plant, but not two, must be located either in Detroit or in Toledo.
   b. Modify the formulation shown in Section 8.3 to account for the policy restriction that no more than two plants can be located in Denver, Kansas City, and St. Louis.

16. An automobile manufacturer has five outdated plants: one each in Michigan, Ohio, and California and two in New York. Management is considering modernizing these plants in order to manufacture engine blocks and transmissions for a new model car. The cost to modernize each plant and the manufacturing capacity after modernization are as follows:

Plant	Cost (millions)	Engine Blocks (1000s)	Transmissions (1000s)
Michigan	25	500	300
New York	35	800	400
New York	35	400	800
Ohio	40	900	600
California	20	200	300

The projected needs are for total capacities of 900,000 engine blocks and 900,000 transmissions. Management wants to determine which plants to modernize to meet projected manufacturing needs and, at the same time, minimize the total cost of modernization.

a. Develop a table that lists every possible option available to management. As part of your table, indicate the total engine block capacity and transmission capacity for each possible option, whether the option is feasible based on the projected needs, and the total modernization cost for each option.

b. Based on your analysis in part (a), what recommendation would you provide management?

c. Formulate a *0–1* integer programming model that could be used to determine the optimal solution to the modernization question facing management.

d. Solve the model formulated in part (c) to provide a recommendation for management.

17. CHB, Inc., is a bank holding company that is evaluating the potential for expanding into a 13-county region in the southwestern part of the state. State law permits establishing branches in any county that is adjacent to a county in which a PPB (principal place of business) is located. Following is a map of the 13-county region with the population of each county indicated.

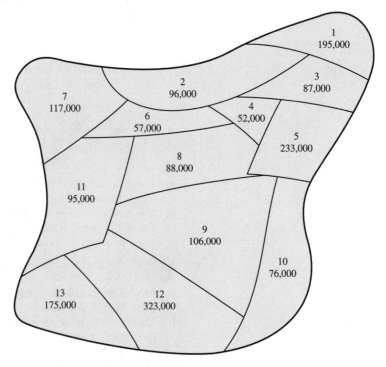

a. Assume that only one PPB can be established in the region. Where should it be located to maximize the population served? (Hint: Review the Ohio Trust formulation in Section 8.3. Consider minimizing the population not served, and introduce variable $y_i = 1$ if it is not possible to establish a branch in county i, and $y_i = 0$ otherwise.)

b. Suppose that two PPBs can be established in the region. Where should they be located to maximize the population served?

c. Management has learned that a bank located in county 5 is considering selling. If CHB purchases this bank, the requisite PPB will be established in county 5, and a base for beginning expansion in the region will also be established. What advice would you give the management of CHB?

18. The Northshore Bank is working to develop an efficient work schedule for full-time and part-time tellers. The schedule must provide for efficient operation of the bank including adequate customer service, employee breaks, and so on. On Fridays the bank is open from 9:00 A.M. to 7:00 P.M. The number of tellers necessary to provide adequate customer service during each hour of operation is summarized here.

Time	Number of Tellers	Time	Number of Tellers
9:00 am–10:00 am	6	2:00 pm–3:00 pm	6
10:00 am–11:00 am	4	3:00 pm–4:00 pm	4
11:00 am–Noon	8	4:00 pm–5:00 pm	7
Noon–1:00 pm	10	5:00 pm–6:00 pm	6
1:00 pm–2:00 pm	9	6:00 pm–7:00 pm	6

Each full-time employee starts on the hour and works a four-hour shift, followed by one hour for lunch and then a three-hour shift. Part-time employees work one four-hour shift beginning on the hour. Considering salary and fringe benefits, full-time employees cost the bank $15 per hour ($105 per day), and part-time employees cost the bank $8 per hour ($32 per day).

a. Formulate an integer programming model that can be used to develop a schedule that will satisfy customer service needs at a minimum employee cost. (Hint: Let x_i = number of full-time employees coming on duty at the beginning of hour i and y_i = number of part-time employees coming on duty at the beginning of hour i.)

b. Solve the LP Relaxation of your model in part (a).

c. Solve for the optimal schedule of tellers. Comment on the solution.

d. After reviewing the solution to part (c), the bank manager has realized that some additional requirements must be specified. Specifically, she wants to ensure that one full-time employee is on duty at all times and that there is a staff of at least five full-time employees. Revise your model to incorporate these additional requirements and solve for the optimal solution.

19. Refer to the Ohio Trust bank location problem introduced in Section 8.3. Table 8.3 shows the counties under consideration and the adjacent counties.

a. Write the complete integer programming model for expansion into the following counties only: Lorain, Huron, Richland, Ashland, Wayne, Medina, and Knox.

b. Use trial and error to solve the problem in part (a).

c. If you have a computer code for integer programs, use it to solve the problem.

20. Refer to Problem 16. Suppose that management determined that its cost estimates to modernize the New York plants were too low. Specifically, suppose that the actual cost is $40 million to modernize each plant.

a. What changes in your previous $0-1$ integer linear programming model are needed to incorporate these changes in costs?

b. For these cost changes, what recommendations would you now provide management regarding the modernization plan?

c. Reconsider the solution obtained using the revised cost figures. Suppose that management decides that closing two plants in the same state is not acceptable. How could this policy restriction be added to your *0–1* integer programming model?

d. Based on the cost revisions and the policy restrictions presented in part (c), what recommendations would you now provide management regarding the modernization plan?

21. The Bayside Art Gallery is considering installing a video camera security system to reduce its insurance premiums. A diagram of the eight display rooms that Bayside uses for exhibitions is shown in Figure 8.9; the openings between the rooms are numbered 1–13. A security firm has proposed that two-way cameras be installed at some of the room openings. Each camera has the ability to monitor the two rooms between which the camera is located. For example, if a camera were located at opening number 4, rooms 1 and 4 would be covered; if a camera were located at opening 11, rooms 7 and 8 would be covered; and so on. Bayside has decided

Figure 8.9

Diagram of Display Rooms for Problem 21

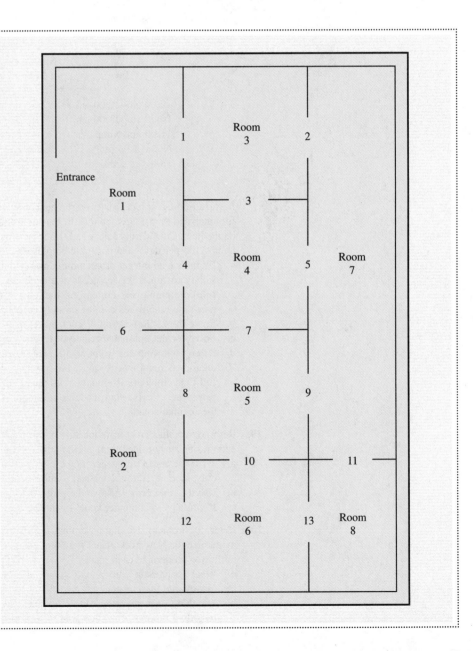

not to locate a camera system at the entrance to the display rooms. Bayside's objective is to provide security coverage for all eight rooms using the minimum number of two-way cameras.

a. Formulate a *0–1* integer linear programming model that will enable Bayside to determine the locations for the camera systems.

b. Solve the model formulated in part (a) to determine how many two-way systems Bayside will need to purchase and where they should be located.

c. Suppose that management wants to provide additional security coverage for room 7. Specifically, management wants room 7 to be covered by two cameras. How would your model formulated in part (a) have to change to accommodate this policy restriction?

d. With the policy restriction specified in part (c), determine how many two-way camera systems Bayside will need to purchase and where they will be located.

22. The Delta Group is a management consulting firm specializing in the health care industry. A team is being formed to study possible new markets and a linear programming model has been developed for selecting team members. But one of the constraints the president has imposed is a team size of three, five, or seven members. The staff can't figure out how to incorporate this requirement in the model. The current model requires that team members be selected from three departments and uses the following variable definitions.

$$x_1 = \text{the number of employees selected from department 1}$$

$$x_2 = \text{the number of employees selected from department 2}$$

$$x_3 = \text{the number of employees selected from department 3}$$

Show the staff how to write constraints that will ensure that the team will consist of three, five, or seven employees. The following integer variables should be helpful.

$$y_1 = \begin{cases} 1 & \text{if team size is 3} \\ 0 & \text{otherwise} \end{cases}$$

$$y_2 = \begin{cases} 1 & \text{if team size is 5} \\ 0 & \text{otherwise} \end{cases}$$

$$y_3 = \begin{cases} 1 & \text{if team size is 7} \\ 0 & \text{otherwise} \end{cases}$$

Case Problem: Textbook Publishing

ASW Publishing, Inc., a small publisher of college textbooks, must make a decision regarding which books to publish next year. The books under consideration are listed in the following table, along with the projected three-year sales expected from each book.

Book Subject	Type of Book	Projected Sales (1000s)
Business calculus	New	20
Finite mathematics	Revision	30
General statistics	New	15
Mathematical statistics	New	10
Business statistics	Revision	25
Finance	New	18
Financial accounting	New	25
Managerial accounting	Revision	50
English literature	New	20
German	New	30

The books that are listed as revisions are texts that ASW already has under contract; these texts are being considered for publication as new editions. The books that are listed as new have been reviewed by the company, but contracts have not yet been signed.

The company has three individuals who can be assigned to these projects, all of whom have varying amounts of time available; John has 60 days available, and Susan and Monica both have 40 days available. The days required by each person to complete each project are shown in the following table. For instance, if the business calculus book is published, it will require 30 days of John's time and 40 days of Susan's time. An "X" indicates that the person will not be used on the project. Note that at least two staff members will be assigned to each project except the finance book.

Book Subject	John	Susan	Monica
Business calculus	30	40	X
Finite mathematics	16	24	X
General statistics	24	X	30
Mathematical statistics	20	X	24
Business statistics	10	X	16
Finance	X	X	14
Financial accounting	X	24	26
Managerial accounting	X	28	30
English literature	40	34	30
German	X	50	36

ASW will not publish more than two statistics books or more than one accounting text in a single year. In addition, management has decided that one of the mathematics books (business calculus or finite math) must be published, but not both.

Managerial Report

Prepare a report for the general manager of ASW that describes your findings and recommendations regarding the best publication strategy for next year. In carrying out your analysis, assume that the fixed costs and the sales revenues per unit are approximately equal for all books; management is interested primarily in maximizing the total sales volume.

The general manager has also asked that you include recommendations regarding the following possible changes.

1. If it would be advantageous to do so, Susan can be moved off another project to allow her to work 12 more days.
2. If it would be advantageous to do so, Monica can also be made available for another 10 days.
3. If one or more of the revisions could be postponed for another year, should they be? Clearly the company will risk losing market share by postponing a revision.

Include details of your analysis in an appendix to your report.

Case Problem: Production Scheduling with Changeover Costs

Buckeye Manufacturing produces heads for engines used in the manufacture of trucks. The production line is highly complex, and measures 900 feet in length. Two types of engine heads are produced on this line: the P-Head and the H-Head. The P-Head is used in heavy-duty trucks and the H-Head is used in smaller trucks. Because only one type of head can be produced at a time, the line is either set up to manufacture the P-Head or the H-Head, but not both. Changeovers are made over the weekend; costs are $1000 in going from a setup for the P-Head to a setup for the H-Head, and vice-versa. When set up for the P-Head the maximum production rate is 1000 units per week and when set up for the H-Head the maximum production rate is 800 units per week.

Buckeye has just shut down for the week; the line has been producing the P-Head. The manager wants to plan production and changeovers for the next 8 weeks. Currently, Buckeye has an inventory of 1247 P-Heads and 1430 H-Heads. Inventory carrying costs are charged at an annual rate of 19.5% of the value of inventory. The production cost for the P-Head is $225, and the production cost for the H-Head is $310. The objective in developing a production schedule is to minimize the sum of production cost, plus inventory carrying cost, plus changeover cost.

Buckeye has received the following requirements schedule from its customer (an engine assembly plant) for the next 9 weeks.

	Product Demand	
Week	P-Head	H-Head
1	550	380
2	550	380
3	440	300
4	0	0
5	450	480
6	450	480
7	360	580
8	350	570
9	350	580

Safety stock requirements are such that week-ending inventory must provide for at least 80% of the next week's demand.

Managerial Report

Prepare a report for Buckeye's management with a production and changeover schedule for the next 8 weeks. Be sure to note how much of the total cost is due to production, how much is due to inventory, and how much is due to changeover.

MANAGEMENT SCIENCE in practice

Ketron*
Arlington, Virginia

Ketron Division of The Bionetics Corporation is an operations research organization with offices throughout the United States. An important part of Ketron's business involves work for local, state, and national governmental agencies.

The Ketron Management Science group is responsible for the development, enhancement, marketing, and support of MPSIII, a proprietary mathematical programming system that runs on a wide range of computers—from PC's to mainframes. Ketron Management Science provides consulting services for the design and implementation of mathematical programming applications. One such mixed-integer programming (MIP) application developed for a major sporting equipment company is outlined in the following sections.

A Customer Order Allocation Model

A major sporting equipment company satisfies demand for its products by making shipments from its factories and other locations around the country where inventories are maintained. The company markets approximately 300 products and has about 30 sources of supply (factory and warehouse locations). The problem of interest is to determine how best to allocate customer orders to the various sources of supply such that the total manufacturing cost is minimized. Although transportation cost is not directly considered, it can be accounted for indirectly by not including variables corresponding to shipments from distant locations. Figure 8.10 provides a graphical representation of this problem. Note in the figure that each customer can receive shipments from only a few of the various sources of supply. For example, we see that customer 1 may be supplied by source A or B, customer 2 may be supplied only by source A, and so on.

The customer order allocation problem is solved periodically. In a typical period, there are between 30 and 40 customers to be supplied. Since most customers require several products, there are usually between 600 and 800 orders that must be assigned to the sources of supply.

The sporting equipment company classifies each customer order as either a "guaranteed" or a "secondary" order. Guaranteed orders are single-source orders in that they must be filled by a single supplier to ensure that the complete order will be delivered to the customer at one time. It is this single-source requirement that necessitates the use of integer variables in the model. Approximately 80% of the company's orders are guaranteed orders.

Figure 8.10

Graphical Representation of the Customer Order Allocation Problem

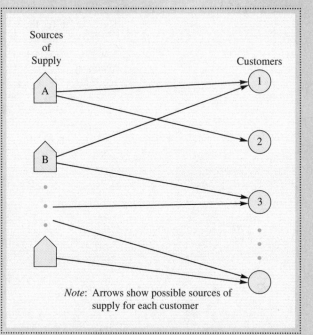

Note: Arrows show possible sources of supply for each customer

Secondary orders can be split among the various sources of supply. These orders are made by customers restocking inventory, and there is no problem in receiving partial shipments from different sources at different times. The total of all secondary orders for a given product is treated as a goal or target in the model formulation. Deviations below the goal are permitted, but a penalty cost is associated with these deviations in the objective function. When deviations occur in the optimal solution, the secondary orders will not be completely satisfied; the shortfall is spread among customers in specified proportions.

Manufacturing considerations are such that raw material availability and the type of process used constrain the amount of production. In addition, groups of items that are similar may belong to a "model group" that must be jointly constrained at some factories. There are also several restrictions on international shipping. For various policy reasons, shipments between sources and customers in certain countries may not be made. This reduces the number of variables in the model, but necessitates extensive data checking to ensure that all guaranteed orders have a permissible source. If they do not, some means must be found to make the problem feasible before beginning to solve the mixed-integer programming model.

—Continued on next page

—Continued from previous page

The primary objective of the model is to minimize the total manufacturing costs subject to the requirement that the guaranteed orders be met. As indicated previously, the deviations below the secondary demand goals are dealt with by defining shortfall-variables with an associated cost. This cost represents a penalty for not having the item in inventory when it is required.

A description of the constraints and the objective function for the model follows.

Constraints

Guaranteed orders: Each customer's order for each product is assigned to a single supplier. (This is a multiple-choice constraint.)

Secondary orders: For each product, the total amount of secondary demand assigned plus the shortfall must equal the total demand goal (target).

Raw material capacities: The amount of each type of raw material used at a supply source cannot exceed the amount available.

Manufacturing capacities: At each supply source, the capacity for each type of production process cannot be exceeded.

Individual product capacities: The amount of product produced at a site cannot exceed that site's capacity for the product.

Group capacities: The total production for a group of similar products at a site cannot exceed that site's capacity for the group of products.

Objective Function

The objective is to minimize the sum of (1) the manufacturing cost for guaranteed orders, (2) the manufacturing cost for secondary orders, and (3) the penalty cost for unsatisfied secondary demand.

Model Solution

It is unreasonable to expect to obtain an optimal solution for a problem of this complexity. Furthermore, the goal programming methodology for handling the secondary demand means that an "optimum" is of questionable interpretation. What is needed is a "good" feasible mixed-integer solution. If an integer solution is found whose value is within a few percent of the value of the lower bound, the room for improvement is obviously small.

A fairly typical problem has about 800 constraints, 2000 $0-1$ assignment variables for the guaranteed orders, and 500 continuous variables associated with the secondary orders. This model is solved using Ketron's MPSIII system.

Implementation Notes

In large-scale applications such as this, considerable systems work is involved in generating the data for the model and the managerial reports. Special data processing languages are often available to ease the programming burden of these phases. The DATAFORM language facility of MPSIII is used to generate the data for this model and to prepare the reports.

In this application, it is necessary to make a completely separate preprocessing run to check for internal consistency and errors in the data. Only when the data appear logically error-free is the model generated and solved. Although tedious, this kind of preprocessing effort is critical for mixed-integer models since the cost of solving the wrong model can be significant. Furthermore, in some cases the data preprocessing step permits the size of the model to be reduced. Such a reduction is possible in this application when a demand for a product has only one legitimate source. The computational benefits of such reductions can be substantial.

Questions

1. Discuss the relationship between the method for handling secondary orders and feasibility.
2. It is mentioned that an "optimum" is of questionable interpretation. Discuss what is meant by this statement. Does it mean that any feasible solution is acceptable?

....

The authors are indebted to J. A. Tomlin for providing this application.

CHAPTER nine

Network Models

Many managerial problems in areas such as transportation systems design, information systems design, and project scheduling have been successfully solved with the aid of network models and network analysis techniques. In Chapter 7 we showed how *networks* consisting of nodes and arcs can be used to provide graphical representations of transportation, assignment, and transshipment problems. In this chapter we present three additional network problems: the shortest-route problem, the minimal spanning tree problem, and the maximal flow problem. In each case, we will show how a network model can be developed and solved in order to provide an optimal solution to the problem.

9.1 The Shortest-Route Problem

In this section we consider a network application in which the primary objective is to determine the *shortest route* or *path* between any pair of nodes in a network. Let us demonstrate the shortest-route problem by considering the situation facing the Gorman Construction Company. Gorman has several construction projects located throughout a three-county area. Construction sites are sometimes located as far as 50 miles from Gorman's main office. With multiple daily trips carrying personnel, equipment, and supplies to and from the construction locations, the costs associated with transportation activities are substantial. For any given construction site, the travel alternatives between the site and the office can be described by a network of roads, streets, and highways. The network shown in Figure 9.1 describes the travel alternatives to and from six of Gorman's newest construction sites. The circles or *nodes* of the network correspond to the site locations. The roads, streets, and highways appear as the *arcs* in the network. The distances between the sites are shown above the corresponding arcs. Gorman would like to determine the routes or paths that will minimize the total travel distance from the office to each site.

Figure 9.1

Road Network for the Gorman Company Shortest-Route Problem

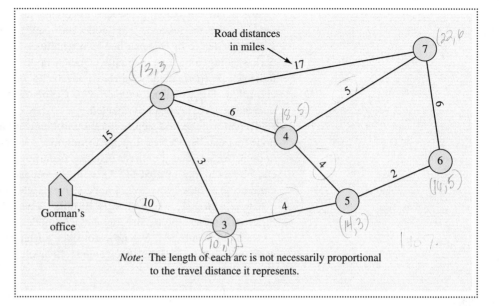

Road distances in miles → 17

Note: The length of each arc is not necessarily proportional to the travel distance it represents.

Figure 9.2

An Example of a Node Label

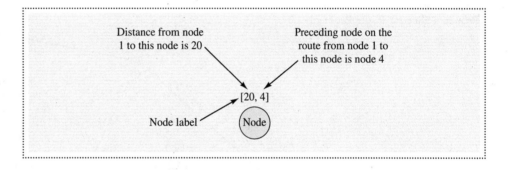

Distance from node 1 to this node is 20

Preceding node on the route from node 1 to this node is node 4

[20, 4]

Node label → Node

A Shortest-Route Algorithm

To solve Gorman's problem, we need to determine the shortest route from Gorman's office, node 1, to each of the other nodes in the network. The algorithm we present uses a labeling procedure to find the shortest distance from node 1 to each of the other nodes. As we perform the steps of the labeling procedure, we will identify a *label* consisting of two numbers enclosed in brackets for each node. The first number in the label for a particular node indicates the distance from node 1 to that node, while the second number indicates the preceding node on the route from node 1 to that node. We will show the label for each node directly above or below the node in the network. For example, a label for a particular node might appear as shown in Figure 9.2.

At any step of the labeling procedure, a node is said to be either labeled or unlabeled. A labeled node is any node for which we have identified a path from node 1 to that node, and an unlabeled node is any node for which a path has not yet been identified. A labeled node is also said to be either permanently or tentatively labeled. That is, whenever the algorithm has determined the *shortest* distance from node 1 to a particular node, the node is said to have a *permanent* label. If, however, the shortest distance from node 1 to a particular labeled node has not yet been determined, the node is said to have a *tentative* label. Now let us show how labels are computed and how the labeling process can be used to determine the shortest route to each of the nodes in the network.

We begin the labeling process by giving node 1 the permanent label [0,S]. The 0 indicates that the distance from node 1 to itself is zero and the S identifies node 1 as the starting node. To distinguish between tentatively and permanently labeled nodes, we use dark shading for all permanently labeled nodes in the network. In addition, an arrow indicates the permanently labeled node being investigated at each step of the labeling algorithm. The initial identification of Gorman's network is shown in Figure 9.3 when only node 1 is permanently labeled.

To perform the first step or iteration of the labeling procedure, we must consider every node that can be reached directly from node 1; hence, we look first at node 2 and then at node 3. We see that the direct distance from node 1 to node 2 is 15 miles. Thus, node 2 can be tentatively labeled [15,1], with the second number indicating that the preceding node on this route to node 2 is node 1. Next, we consider node 3 and find that the direct distance from node 1 to node 3 is 10 miles. Thus, the tentative label at node 3 is [10,1]. Figure 9.4 shows the results thus far with nodes 2 and 3 tentatively labeled.

Refer to Figure 9.4. We now consider all tentatively labeled nodes and identify the node with the smallest distance value in its label; thus, node 3 with a travel distance of 10

Figure 9.3

Initial Network Identification for Gorman's Shortest-Route Problem

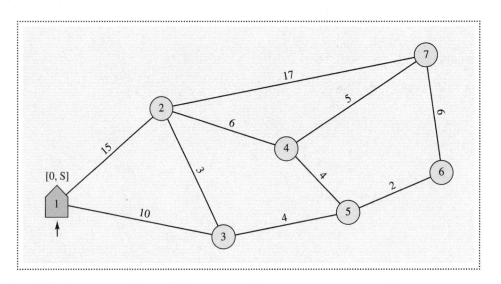

Figure 9.4

Gorman's Network with Tentative Labels for Nodes 2 and 3

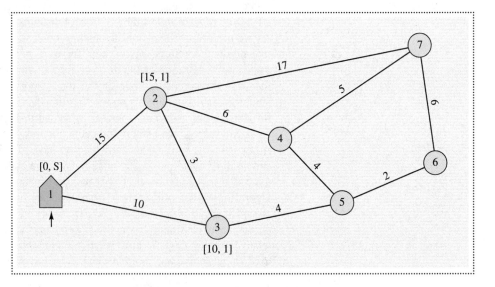

miles is selected. Could we get to node 3 following a shorter route? Since any other route to node 3 would require passing through other nodes, and since the distance from node 1 to all other nodes is greater than or equal to 10, a shorter route to node 3 cannot be found. Accordingly, node 3 is permanently labeled with a distance of 10 miles. Dark shading indicates that node 3 is a permanently labeled node and the arrow indicates that node 3 will be used to start the next step of the labeling process; the result of these steps is shown in Figure 9.5.

We proceed by considering all nodes that are not permanently labeled and that can be reached directly from node 3; these are nodes 2 and 5. Note that the direct distance is 3 miles from node 3 to node 2 and it is 4 miles from node 3 to node 5. Since node 3's permanent label indicates that the shortest distance to node 3 is 10 miles, we see that we can reach node 2 in 10 + 3 = 13 miles and node 5 in 10 + 4 = 14 miles. Thus, the tentative label at node 2 is revised to [13,3] to indicate that we have now found a route from node 1 to node 2 that has a distance of 13 miles and passes through node 3. The tentative label for node 5 is set to [14,3]. Figure 9.6 shows the network computations up to this point.

Figure 9.5

Gorman's Network with Node 3 Identified as a Permanently Labeled Node

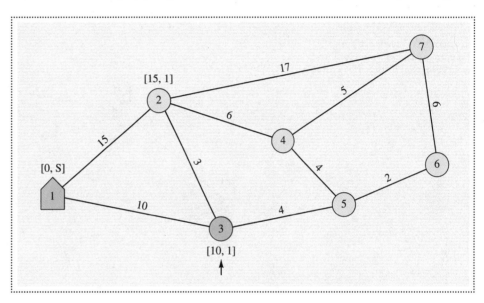

Figure 9.6

Gorman's Network with New Tentative Labels for Nodes 2 and 5

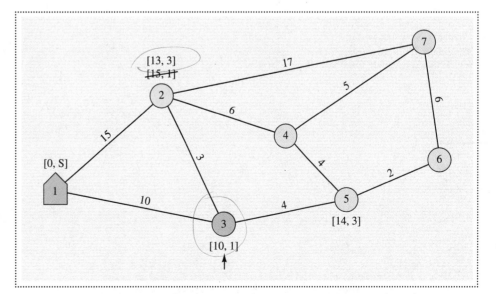

We next consider all tentatively labeled nodes in order to find the node with the smallest distance value in its label. From Figure 9.6 we see that this is node 2 with a distance of 13 miles. Node 2 is now permanently labeled because we know that it can be reached from node 1 in the shortest possible distance of 13 miles by going through node 3.

The next step or iteration begins at node 2, the most recently permanently labeled node. As before, we consider every nonpermanently labeled node that can be reached directly from node 2; that is, nodes 4 and 7. Starting with the distance value of 13 in the permanent label at node 2 and adding the direct distance from node 2 to both nodes 4 and 7, we see that node 4 can be reached in $13 + 6 = 19$ miles, while node 7 can be reached in $13 + 17 = 30$ miles. Thus, the tentative labels at nodes 4 and 7 are as shown in Figure 9.7.

From among the tentatively labeled nodes (nodes 4, 5, and 7), we select the node with the smallest distance value and declare that node permanently labeled. Thus node 5, with a distance of 14, becomes the new permanently labeled node. From node 5, then, we

Figure 9.7

Gorman's Network with a Permanent Label at Node 2 and New Tentative Labels for Nodes 4 and 7

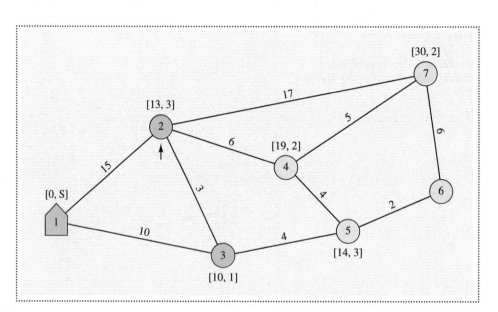

Figure 9.8

Gorman's Network with a Permanent Label at Node 5 and New Tentative Labels for Nodes 4 and 6

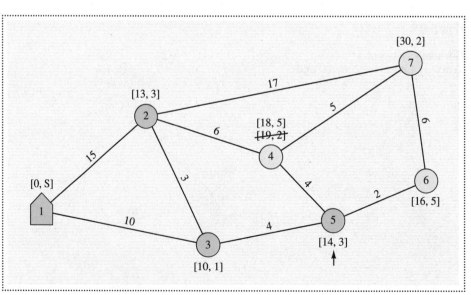

consider all nonpermanently labeled nodes that can be reached directly from node 5. Thus, the tentative label on node 4 is revised, and node 6 is tentatively labeled. Figure 9.8 depicts these calculations.

The smallest distance is again identified for the remaining tentatively labeled nodes, and this results in node 6 being permanently labeled. From node 6 we can determine a new tentative label with a distance value of 22 for node 7. After this step, the network appears as shown in Figure 9.9.

We now have only two remaining nonpermanently labeled nodes. Since the distance value at node 4 is smaller than that at node 7, node 4 becomes the new permanently labeled node. Since node 7 is the only nonpermanently labeled node that can be reached directly from node 4, we compare its distance value of 22 with the sum of the distance value at node 4 and the direct distance from node 4 to node 7, that is, 18 + 5 = 23. Since the [22,6] tentative label at node 7 is smaller, it remains unchanged. Figure 9.10 shows the network at this point.

Figure 9.9

Gorman's Network with a Permanent Label at Node 6 and a New Tentative Label for Node 7

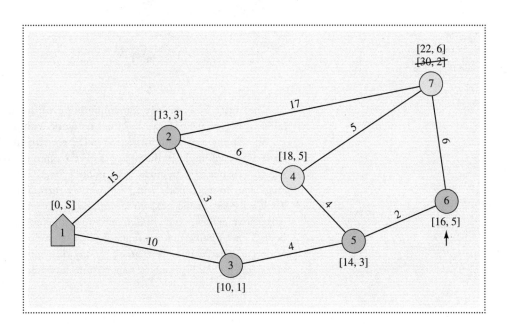

Figure 9.10

Gorman's Network with a Permanent Label at Node 4

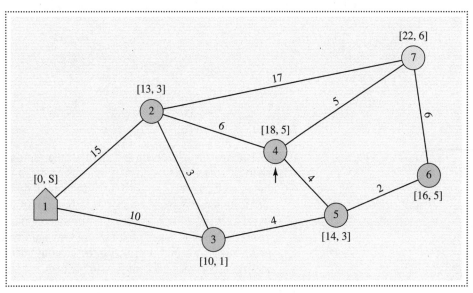

Figure 9.11

Gorman's Network with All Nodes Permanently Labeled

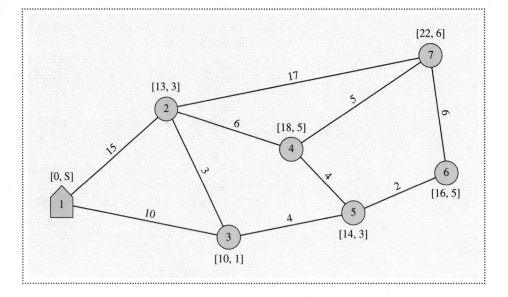

Since node 7 is the only remaining node with a tentative label, it is now permanently labeled. Figure 9.11 shows the final network with all nodes permanently labeled.

We can now use the information in the permanent labels to find the shortest route from node 1 to each node in the network. For example, node 7's permanent label tells us the shortest distance from node 1 to node 7 is 22 miles. To find the particular route that enables us to reach node 7 in 22 miles, we *start* at node 7 and work back to node 1. Node 7's label gives us the next direct link—node 6—and node 6's label indicates that node 5 is the next shortest-route link. Continuing this process, we note that we reach node 5 from node 3 and, finally, that we reach node 3 from node 1. Therefore, the shortest route from node 1 to node 7 is 1−3−5−6−7. Using this approach, the following shortest routes are identified for the Gorman transportation network:

Node	Shortest Route from Node 1	Distance in Miles
2	1−3−2	13
3	1−3	10
4	1−3−5−4	18
5	1−3−5	14
6	1−3−5−6	16
7	1−3−5−6−7	22

Perhaps for a problem as small as the Gorman problem you could have found the shortest routes just as fast, if not faster, by inspection. However, when we begin to investigate problems with 15 to 20 or more nodes, it becomes time-consuming to find the shortest routes by inspection. In fact, because of the increased number of alternate routes in a larger network, it is easy to miss one or more routes and come up with the wrong answer. Thus, for larger problems a systematic procedure such as the preceding labeling procedure is required. Even with the labeling method, we find that as the networks grow in size, it becomes necessary to implement the algorithm on a computer.

As we summarize the shortest-route algorithm, think of a network consisting of N nodes. The following procedure can be used to find the shortest route from node 1 to each of the other nodes in the network:

Step 1 Assign node 1 the permanent label [0, S]; The 0 indicates that the distance from node 1 to itself is zero and the S indicates that node 1 is the starting node.

Step 2 Compute tentative labels for the nodes that can be reached directly from node 1. The first number in each label is the direct distance from node 1 to the node in question; we refer to this portion of the label as the distance value. The second number in each label, which we refer to as the preceding-node value, indicates the preceding node on the route from node 1 to the node in question; thus, in this step the preceding-node value is 1 since we are only considering nodes that can be directly reached from node 1.

Step 3 Identify the tentatively labeled node with the smallest distance value, and declare that node permanently labeled. If all nodes are permanently labeled, go to step 5.

Step 4 Consider the remaining nodes that are not permanently labeled and that can be reached directly from the new permanently labeled node identified in step 3. Compute new tentative labels for these nodes as follows:

   a. If the node in question has a tentative label, add the distance value at the new permanently labeled node to the direct distance from the new permanently labeled node to the node in question. If this sum is less than the distance value for the node in question, set the distance value for this node equal to this sum; in addition, set the preceding-node value equal to the new permanently labeled node that provided the smaller distance. Go to step 3.

   b. If the node in question is not yet labeled, create a tentative label by adding the distance value at the new permanently labeled node to the direct distance from the new permanently labeled node to the node in question. The preceding-node value is set equal to the new permanently labeled node. Go to step 3.

Step 5 The permanent labels identify both the shortest distance from node 1 to each node and the preceding node on the shortest route. The shortest route to a given node can be found by starting at the given node and moving to its preceding node. Continuing this backward movement through the network will provide the shortest route from node 1 to the node in question.

This algorithm will determine the shortest distance from node 1 to each of the other nodes in the network. Note that $N - 1$ iterations of the algorithm are required to find the shortest distance to all other nodes. If the shortest distance to every node is not needed, the algorithm can be stopped when those nodes of interest have been permanently labeled. The algorithm can also be easily modified to find the shortest distance from any node, say node k, to all other nodes in the network. To make such a change, we would merely begin by labeling node k with the permanent label [0,S]. Then by applying the steps of the algorithm, we can find the shortest route from node k to each of the other nodes in the network.

The personal computer package, The Management Scientist, can be used to solve small shortest-route problems. Input for the program includes the number of nodes, the number of arcs, and the length of each arc. The output shown in Figure 9.12 provides the shortest route from node 1 to node 7 for the Gorman problem.

You should now be able to use the labeling algorithm to solve a shortest-route problem. Try Problem 1.

Figure 9.12

The Management Scientist Solution of the Gorman Shortest-Route Problem

```
        ****   NETWORK DESCRIPTION   ****

              7 NODES AND 10 ARCS

     ARC     START NODE     END NODE     DISTANCE
     ---     ----------     --------     --------
      1          1             2            15
      2          1             3            10
      3          2             3             3
      4          2             4             6
      5          2             7            17
      6          3             5             4
      7          4             5             4
      8          4             7             5
      9          5             6             2
     10          6             7             6


     THE SHORTEST ROUTE FROM NODE 1 TO NODE 7
     *******************************************


     START NODE         END NODE         DISTANCE
     ----------         --------         --------
         1                 3                10
         3                 5                 4
         5                 6                 2
         6                 7                 6

          TOTAL DISTANCE                   22
```

NOTES & comments

1. Many applications of the shortest-route algorithm involve criteria such as time or cost instead of distance. In these cases, the shortest-route algorithm provides the minimum-time or minimum-cost solution. However, since the shortest-route algorithm always identifies a minimum-value solution, it would not make sense to apply the algorithm to problems that involve a profit criterion.

2. In some applications, the value associated with an arc may be negative. For example, in situations where cost is the criterion, a negative arc value would denote a negative cost; in other words, a profit would be realized by traversing the arc. The shortest-route algorithm presented in this section can only be applied to networks with nonnegative arc values. More advanced texts discuss algorithms that can solve problems with negative arc values.

9.2 The Minimal Spanning Tree Problem

In network terminology, the minimal spanning tree problem involves using the arcs of the network to reach *all* nodes of the network in such a fashion that the total length of all the arcs used is minimized. To better understand this problem, let us consider the communications system design problem encountered by a regional computer center.

The Southwestern Regional Computer Center must have special computer communications lines installed to connect five satellite users with a new central computer. The telephone company will install the new communications network. However, the installation is an expensive operation. To reduce costs, the center's management group wants the total length of the new communications lines to be as small as possible. While the central computer could be connected directly to each user, it appears to be more economical to install a direct line to some users and let other users tap into the system by linking them with users already connected to the system. The determination of this minimal length communications system design is an example of the *minimal spanning tree* problem. The network for this problem with possible connection alternatives and distances is shown in Figure 9.13. An algorithm that can be used to solve this network model is explained in the following subsection.

A Minimal Spanning Tree Algorithm

A *spanning tree* for an *N*-node network is a set of *N* − 1 arcs that connects every node to every other node. A minimal spanning tree is the set of arcs that does this at minimal total arc cost, distance, etc. The network algorithm that can be used to solve the minimal spanning tree problem is simple. The steps of the algorithm are as follows:

Step 1 Arbitrarily begin at any node and connect it to the closest node in terms of the criterion being used (e.g., time, cost, or distance). The two nodes are referred to as *connected* nodes, and the remaining nodes are referred to as *unconnected* nodes.

Step 2 Identify the unconnected node that is closest to one of the connected nodes. Break ties arbitrarily if two or more nodes qualify as the closest node. Add this new node to the set of connected nodes. Repeat this step until all nodes have been connected.

Figure 9.13

Communications Network for the Regional Computer System

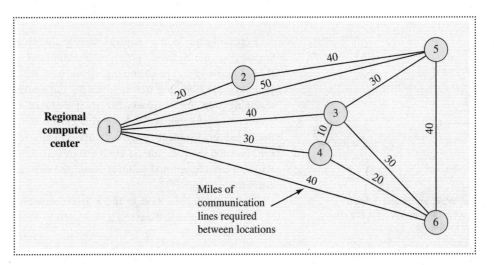

This network algorithm is easily implemented by making the connection decisions directly on the network.

Referring to the communications network for the regional computer center and arbitrarily beginning at node 1, we find the closest node is node 2 with a distance of 20. Using a bold line to connect nodes 1 and 2, step 1 of the algorithm provides the following result:

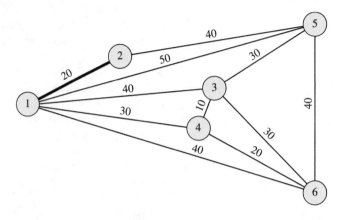

In step 2 of the algorithm, we find that the unconnected node closest to one of the connected nodes is node 4, with a distance of 30 miles from node 1. Adding node 4 to the set of connected nodes provides the following result:

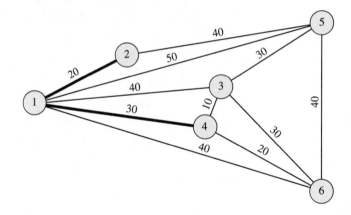

Repeating the step of always adding the closest unconnected node to the connected segment of the network provides the minimal spanning tree solution shown in Figure 9.14. Follow the steps of the algorithm, and see if you obtain this solution. The minimal length of the spanning tree is given by the sum of the distances on the arcs forming the spanning tree. In this case, the total distance is 110 miles for the computer center's communications network. Note that while the computer center's network arcs were measured in distance, other network models may measure the arcs in terms of other criteria such as cost, time, and so on. In such cases, the minimal spanning tree algorithm will identify the optimal solution (minimal cost, minimal time, etc.) for the criterion being considered.

The computer solution to the regional computer center's problem is shown in Figure 9.15. The Management Scientist was used to obtain the minimal spanning tree solution of 110 miles.

You should now be able to find a minimal spanning tree for a network. Try Problem 10.

Figure 9.14
....

**Minimal Spanning Tree
Communications Network for the
Regional Computer Center**

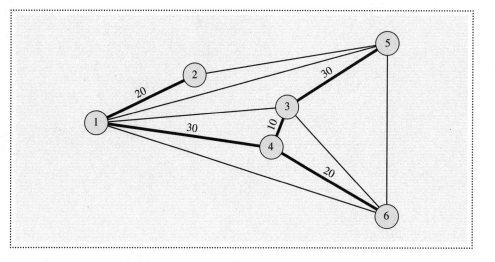

Figure 9.15
....

**The Management Scientist Solution
for the Regional Computer Center
Minimal Spanning Tree Problem**

```
     ****   NETWORK DESCRIPTION   ****
            6 NODES AND 11 ARCS

  ARC     START NODE      END NODE      DISTANCE
  ---     ----------      --------      --------

   1          1              2             20
   2          1              3             40
   3          1              4             30
   4          1              5             50
   5          1              6             40
   6          2              5             40
   7          3              4             10
   8          3              5             30
   9          3              6             30
  10          4              6             20
  11          5              6             40

           MINIMAL SPANNING TREE
         ********************

  START NODE         END NODE         DISTANCE
  ----------         --------         --------
      1                 2                20
      1                 4                30
      4                 3                10
      4                 6                20
      3                 5                30

        TOTAL LENGTH              110
```

NOTES & comments

The minimal spanning tree algorithm is considered a *greedy algorithm* since at each stage we can be "greedy" and take the best action available at that stage. Following this strategy at each successive stage will provide the overall optimal solution. Cases such as this, where a greedy algorithm provides the optimal solution, are rare. For many problems, however, greedy algorithms are excellent heuristics.

9.3 The Maximal Flow Problem

Consider a network with one input or *source* node and one output or *sink* node. The *maximal flow* problem asks: What is the maximum amount of flow (vehicles, messages, fluid, etc.) that can enter and exit the network system in a given period of time? In this problem, we attempt to transmit flow through all arcs of the network as efficiently as possible. The amount of flow is limited due to capacity restrictions on the various arcs of the network. For example, highway types limit vehicle flow in a transportation system, while pipe sizes limit oil flow in an oil distribution system. The maximum or upper limit on the flow in an arc is referred to as the *flow capacity* of the arc. While we do not specify capacities for the nodes, we do assume that the flow out of a node is equal to the flow into the node.

As an example of the maximal flow problem, consider the north–south interstate highway system passing through Cincinnati, Ohio. The north–south vehicle flow reaches a level of 15,000 vehicles per hour at peak times. Due to a summer highway maintenance program, which calls for the temporary closing of lanes and lower speed limits, a network of alternate routes through Cincinnati has been proposed by a transportation planning committee. The alternate routes include other highways as well as city streets. Because of differences in speed limits and traffic patterns, flow capacities vary, depending on the particular streets or roads used. The proposed network with arc flow capacities is shown in Figure 9.16.

The flow capacities are based on the direction of the flow. For example, highway section or arc 1–2 shows a capacity of 5000 vehicles per hour in the 1–2 direction; however, a zero capacity exists in the 2–1 direction. This means that the highway network planners do not want vehicles flowing from node 2 into node 1. Logically speaking, since node 1 is the input, or source, and a potential traffic jam location, it would be undesirable to permit traffic flow into the node 1 intersection from node 2. The directional capacities on arc 1–2 can also be interpreted as indicating a one-way street leading from the node 1 intersection. In any case, this example shows that the flow capacities of arcs can be dependent on the direction of the flow. Do you believe the highway system network shown in Figure 9.16 can accommodate the north–southmaximum flow of 15,000 vehicles per hour? What is the maximal flow in vehicles per hour for the network? How much flow should go over each arc?

Figure 9.16

Network of Highway System and
Flow Capacities (1000's/Hour) for
Cincinnati

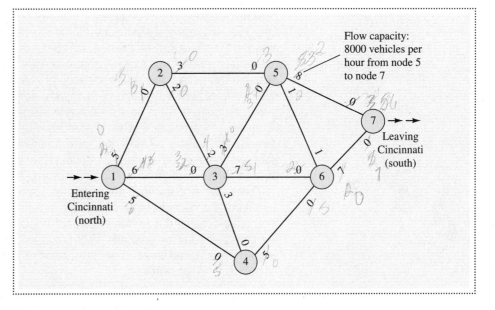

A Maximal Flow Algorithm

As we shall see, the maximal flow algorithm presented in this section uses the following commonsense approach:

1. Find any path from the input (source) node to the output (sink) node that has flow capacities in the direction of the flow greater than zero for all arcs on the path.
2. Increase the flow along the path by as much as possible.
3. Continue looking for source-to-sink paths that have remaining flow capacities in the direction of the flow greater than zero for all arcs, and increase the flow along these paths as much as possible.
4. Stop when it is no longer possible to find a source-to-sink path with flow capacities in the direction of the flow greater than zero for all arcs on the path.

Before presenting the details of the maximal flow algorithm, let us briefly discuss a procedure that will ensure that these intuitive steps result in an optimal solution to this maximal flow problem.

The procedure permits previously assigned flow to take an alternate route by permitting fictional flows in the reverse direction. For example, consider the 3–6 arc:

Here we see that the initial flow capacity in the 3–6 direction is 7000 vehicles per hour, while no flow is permitted in the 6–3 direction.

If we choose to let 6000 vehicles per hour flow in the 3–6 direction, we will revise the flow capacities as follows:

Note that we have decreased the flow capacity in the 3–6 direction by 6000 vehicles per hour and simultaneously increased the flow capacity in the 6–3 direction by the same amount. The revised flow capacity of 1000 vehicles per hour in the 3–6 direction is readily interpreted as the remaining flow capacity for the arc. However, note that the 6–3 direction that had an initial flow capacity of zero now shows a revised flow capacity of 6000 vehicles per hour. This revised capacity in the 6–3 direction is actually indicating that a fictitious flow of up to 6000 vehicles per hour is permitted in this direction. Fictitious flow would not actually send vehicles in the 6–3 direction but would rather decrease the amount of flow originally committed to the 3–6 arc direction. In effect, fictitious flow in the 6–3 direction would result in diverting flow originally committed to the 3–6 direction to other arcs in the network.

This process of tracking flow capacities is an important part of the maximal flow algorithm. For example, in an earlier step of the algorithm, we might commit flow along a certain arc. Later, due to flows identified in other arcs, it may be desirable to decrease the flow along the original arc. This procedure will identify the extent to which our original decision to commit some flow needs to be revised in order to increase the total flow through the network.

Let us now look at the steps of the maximal flow algorithm.

Step 1   Find any path from the source (input) node to the sink (output) node that has flow capacities in the direction of the flow greater than zero for all arcs on the path. If no path is available, the optimal solution has been reached.

Step 2   Find the smallest arc capacity, P_f, on the path selected in step 1. Increase the flow through the network by sending an amount P_f over the path selected in step 1.

Step 3   For the path selected in step 1, reduce all arc flow capacities in the direction of flow by P_f, and increase all arc flow capacities in the reverse direction by P_f. Go to step 1.

While the procedure will vary depending on the analyst's choice of paths in step 1, the algorithm will eventually provide the maximal flow solution. Our calculations for the highway flow network are as follows:

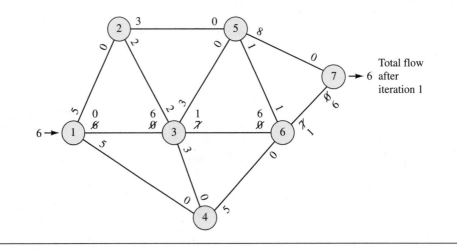

Iteration 1

The path selected is 1–3–6–7; P_f, determined by arc 1–3, is 6. The revised network is as follows:

Total flow → 6 after iteration 1

Iteration 2

The path selected is 1–2–5–7; P_f, determined by arc 2–5, is 3. The revised network is as follows:

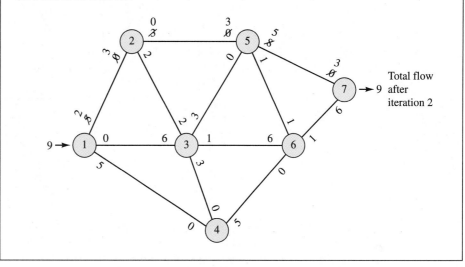

The total flow through the network at each iteration can be found by summing the P_f values from all iterations.

While we will not show the revised network after each iteration, you should attempt to update the network flow capacities as you follow the discussion. For example, what will this network look like after the following three iterations?

Iteration 3

The path selected is 1–2–3–5–7; P_f, determined by arc 1–2 (or 2–3), is 2.

Iteration 4

The path selected is 1–4–6–7; P_f, determined by arc 6–7, is 1.

Iteration 5

The path selected is 1–4–6–5–7; P_f, determined by arc 6–5, is 1.

At this point, we have a total flow of 13,000 vehicles per hour, and the revised network capacities are as follows:

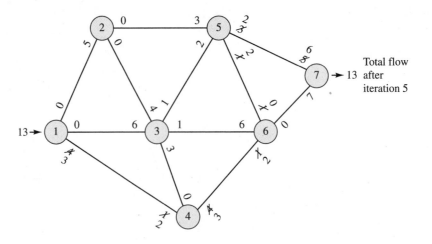

Total flow
13 after
iteration 5

Are there any other paths from node 1 to node 7 that have flow capacities in the direction of the flow greater than zero? Try 1–4–6–3–5–7, with a flow of $P_f = 1$ determined by arc 3–5. This increases the flow to 14,000 vehicles per hour. However, as you can see from the following revised network, there are no more paths from node 1 to node 7 that have flow capacities greater than zero on all arcs of the path; thus, 14,000 vehicles per hour is the maximal flow for this network.

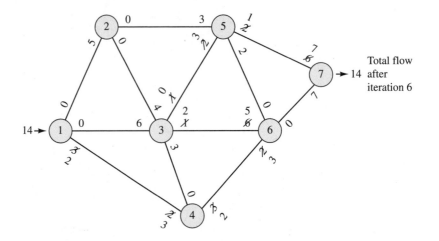

Total flow
14 after
iteration 6

Note that in iteration 6 a flow of 1000 vehicles per hour was permitted in the 6–3 direction. From the initial network, however, we know that the flow capacity in the 6–3 direction is zero; thus, the 1000 units of flow in the 6–3 direction represent a fictitious flow. The real effect of this flow is to divert 1000 units of flow originally committed to the 3–6 arc in iteration 1 along the 3–5 arc to enable us to get 1000 units more of flow through the network. Let us now determine the amount and direction of flow in each arc so that the total flow of 14,000 vehicles per hour can be attained.

Arc flows for the maximal flow solution can be found by comparing the final arc flow capacities with the initial arc flow capacities. If the final flow capacity is *less* than the initial flow capacity, flow is occurring over the arc with an amount equal to the difference between the initial and final flow capacities. For example, consider the 3–6 arc with initial and final flow capacities as follows.

Initial Capacities

Final Capacities

Since the final flow capacity in the 3–6 direction is less than the initial flow capacity, the arc has a flow of $7 - 2 = 5$ in the 3–6 direction. This arc flow is summarized as follows:

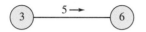

Comparing final and initial arc flow capacities for all arcs in the network enables us to determine the final flow pattern as shown in Figure 9.17.

The results of the maximal flow analysis indicate that the planned highway network system will not handle the peak flow of 15,000 vehicles per hour. The transportation planners will have to expand the highway network, increase current arc flow capacities, or be prepared for serious traffic jam problems. If the network is extended or modified, another maximal flow analysis will determine the extent of any improved flow.

Try Problem 15 for practice in solving a maximal flow problem.

Figure 9.17

Maximal Flow Pattern for the Highway System Network

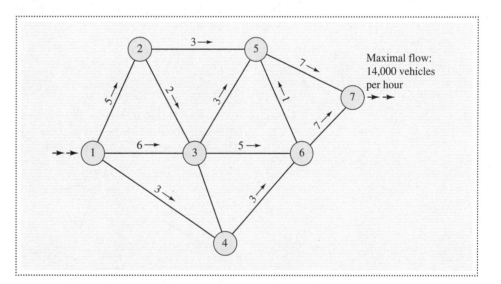

N O T E S & comments

Network models can be used to describe a variety of management science problems. Unfortunately, no one network solution algorithm or computer code can be used to solve every network problem. It is important to recognize the specific type of problem being modeled in order to select the correct specialized solution algorithm and computer code.

Summary

In this chapter we extended the discussion of the use of network models in managerial decision making. We introduced the shortest-route, minimal spanning tree, and maximal flow problems and presented specialized solution algorithms for each. The key to success in network approaches to problem solving is in seeing how the problem can be represented as a network model. While some network formulations are obvious, other problems may require substantial ingenuity to develop the appropriate network representation. In any case, once the network representation has been developed, specialized solution algorithms are available to solve the problem.

Glossary

Shortest route Shortest path between two nodes in a network.

Spanning tree A set of $N - 1$ arcs that connect every node in the network with all other nodes where N is the number of nodes.

Minimal spanning tree The spanning tree with the minimum length.

Arc capacity The maximum flow for an arc of the network. The arc capacity in one direction may not equal the arc capacity in the reverse direction.

Source A node that generates flow; flow can only move away from it and never into it.

Sink A node that absorbs flow; flow can only move into it and never away from it.

Maximal flow The maximum amount of flow that can enter and exit a network system during a given period of time.

Problems

1. **SELF**Test Find the shortest route from node 1 to each of the other nodes in the transportation network shown.

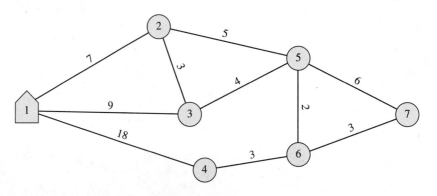

2. For the Gorman Construction Company problem (see Figure 9.1), assume that node 7 is the company's warehouse and supply center. Several daily trips are commonly made from node 7 to the other nodes or construction sites. Using node 7 as the starting node, find the shortest route from this node to each of the other nodes in the network.

3. In the original Gorman Construction Company problem, we found the shortest distance from the office (node 1) to each of the other nodes or construction sites. Because some of the roads are highways and others are city streets, the shortest-distance routes between the office and the construction sites may not necessarily provide the quickest or shortest-time routes. Shown

here is the Gorman road network with travel time values rather than distance values. Find the shortest route from Gorman's office to each of the construction sites if the objective is to minimize travel time rather than distance.

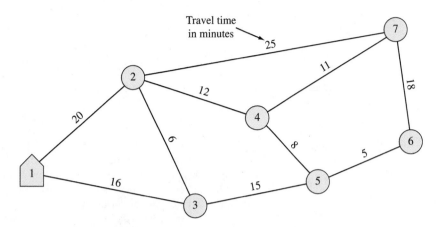

4. Find the shortest route between nodes 1 and 8 in the following network:

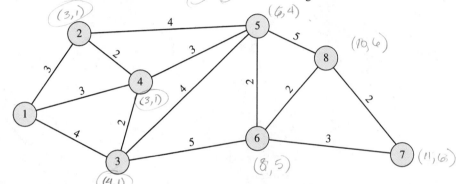

5. Find the shortest route between nodes 1 and 10 in the following network:

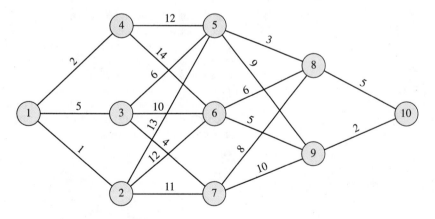

6. Morgan Trucking Company operates a special fast-service pickup and delivery service between Chicago and 10 other cities located in a four-state area. When Morgan receives a request for service, it dispatches a truck from Chicago to the city requesting service as soon as possible. Since both fast service and minimum travel costs are objectives for Morgan, it is important that the dispatched truck take the shortest route from Chicago to the specified city. Assume that the following network (not drawn to scale) with distances given in miles represents the highway network for this problem, and find the shortest-route distances from Chicago to all 10 cities.

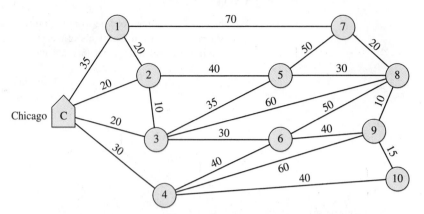

7. City Cab Company has identified 10 primary pickup and drop locations for cab riders in New York City. In an effort to minimize travel time and improve customer service and the utilization of the company's fleet of cabs, management would like the cab drivers to take the shortest route between locations whenever possible. Using the network of roads and streets shown below, what is the route a driver beginning at location 1 should take to reach location 10? The travel times in minutes are shown on the arcs of the network.

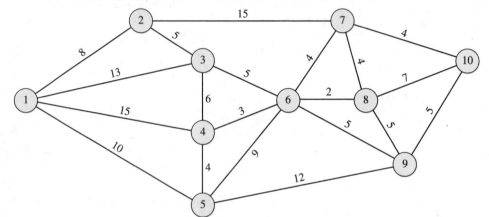

8. The Wisman Candy Company manufactures a variety of candy products. Company trucks are used to deliver local orders directly to retail outlets. When the business was small, the drivers of the trucks were free to take routes of their choice as they made the delivery rounds to the retail outlets. However, as the business has grown, transportation and delivery costs have become significant. In an effort to improve the efficiency of the delivery operation, Wisman's management would like to determine the shortest delivery routes between retail outlets. For example, the following network shows the roads that may be taken between a retail outlet at node 1 and a retail outlet at node 11. Determine the shortest route for a truck that must make deliveries to both outlets.

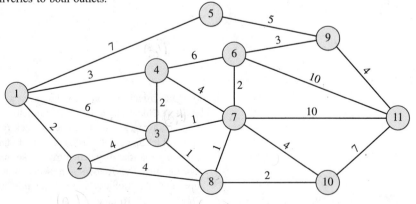

9. The five nodes in the following network represent points 1 year apart over a 4-year period. Each node indicates a time when a decision is made to keep or replace a firm's computer equipment. If a decision is made to replace the equipment, a decision must also be made as to how long the new equipment will be used. The arc from node 0 to node 1 represents the decision to keep the current equipment 1 year and replace it at the end of the year. The arc from node 0 to node 2 represents the decision to keep the current equipment 2 years and replace it at the end of year 2. The numbers above the arcs indicate the total cost associated with the equipment replacement decisions. These costs include discounted purchase price, trade-in value, operating costs, and maintenance costs. Determine the minimum-cost equipment replacement policy for the 4-year period.

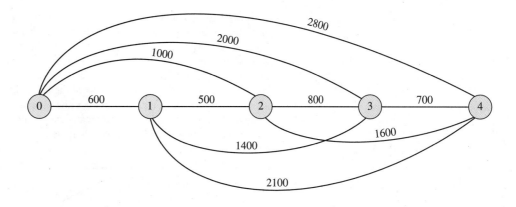

10. **SELF**Test The State of Ohio recently purchased land for a new state park, and park planners have identified the ideal locations for the lodge, cabins, picnic groves, boat dock, and scenic points of interest. These locations are represented by the nodes of the following network. The arcs of the network represent possible road alternatives in the park. If the state park designers want to minimize the total road miles that must be constructed in the park and still permit access to all facilities (nodes), which road alternatives should be constructed?

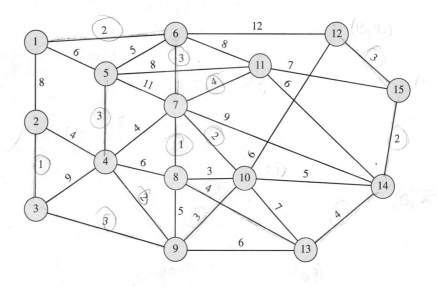

11. Develop the minimal spanning tree solution for the following emergency communications network.

1, 3   2
3, 4   2
~~4, 5~~   3
5, ~~3~~ ~~6~~   ~~3~~ 3
~~5, 7~~
5, 2   2
~~7, 6~~
8, 7   2
7, 6   3
          ~~19~~
          17

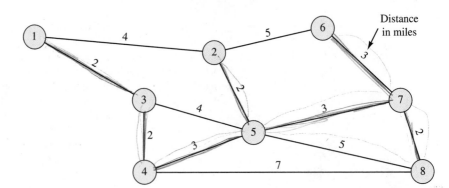

12. In a large soap products plant, quality control inspectors take samples of various products from the different production areas and deliver them to the lab for analysis. The inspection process is slow, and the inspectors spend substantial time transporting samples from the production areas to the lab. The company is considering installing a pneumatic tube conveyor system that could transport the samples between the production areas and the lab. The following network shows the locations of the lab and the production areas (nodes) where the samples must be collected. The arcs are the alternatives being considered for the conveyor system. What is the minimum total length and layout of the conveyor system that will enable all production areas to send samples to the lab?

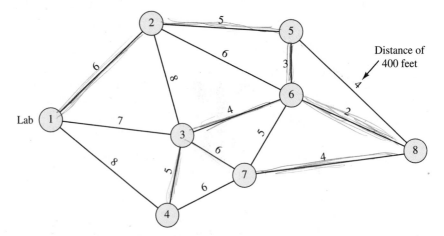

13. Midwest University is installing an electronic mail system. The following network shows the possible electronic connections among the offices. Distances between offices are shown in thousands of feet. Develop a design for the office communication system that will enable all offices to have access to the electronic mail service. Provide the design that minimizes the total length of connections among the eight offices.

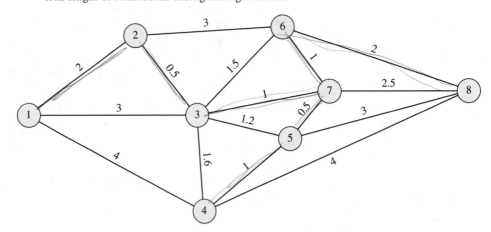

14. The Metrovision Cable Company has just received approval to begin providing cable television service to a suburb of Memphis, Tennessee. The nodes of the following network show the distribution points that must be reached by the company's primary cable lines. The arcs of the network show the number of miles between the distribution points. Determine the solution that will enable the company to reach all distribution points with the minimum length of primary cable line.

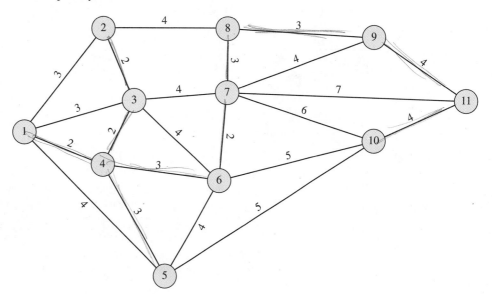

15. **SELFTest** The north–south highway system passing through Albany, New York, can accommodate the capacities shown.

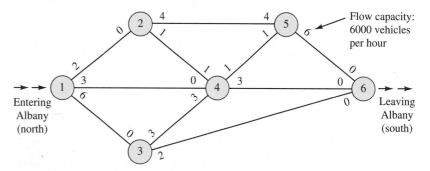

Can the highway system accommodate a north–south flow of 10,000 vehicles per hour?

16. If the Albany highway system problem (see Problem 15) has revised flow capacities as shown in the following network, what is the maximal flow in vehicles per hour through the system? How many vehicles per hour must travel over each road (arc) to obtain this maximal flow?

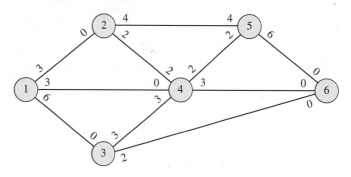

17. A long-distance telephone company uses an underground cable network of communication lines to provide high-quality audio communication between two major cities. Calls are carried through series cable lines and connecting nodes in the network as shown here.

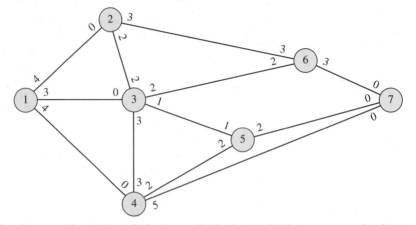

Also shown are the number of telephone calls (in thousands) that may occur simultaneously at any point in time. What is the maximum number of telephone calls that can be transmitted simultaneously between the two cities? What are the connecting nodes and cable flows when the system is operating at capacity?

18. The High-Price Oil Company owns a pipeline network that is used to convey oil from its source to several storage locations. A portion of the network is as follows:

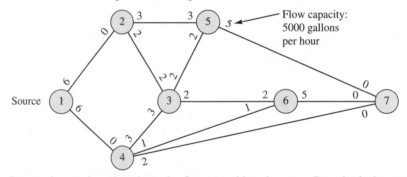

Due to the varying pipe sizes, the flow capacities also vary. By selectively opening and closing sections of the pipeline network, the firm can supply any of the storage locations.

a. If the firm wants to supply storage location 7 and fully utilize the system capacity, how long will it take to satisfy a location 7 demand of 100,000 gallons? What is the maximal flow for this pipeline system?

b. If a break occurs on line 2–3 and it is closed down, what is the maximal flow for the system? How long will it take to transmit 100,000 gallons to location 7?

19. For the following highway network system, determine the maximal flow in vehicles per hour.

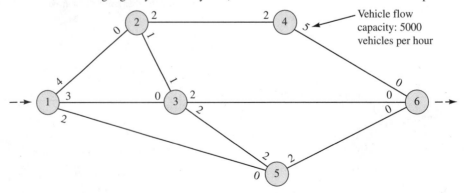

The highway commission is considering adding highway section 3–4 to permit a flow of 2000 vehicles per hour or, at an additional cost, a flow of 3000 vehicles per hour. What is your recommendation for the 3–4 arc of the network?

20. A chemical processing plant has a network of pipes that are used to transfer liquid chemical products from one part of the plant to another. The following pipe network has pipe flow capacities in gallons per minute as shown. What is the maximum flow capacity for the system if the company wishes to transfer as much liquid chemical as possible from location 1 to location 9? How much of the chemical will flow through the section of pipe from node 3 to node 5?

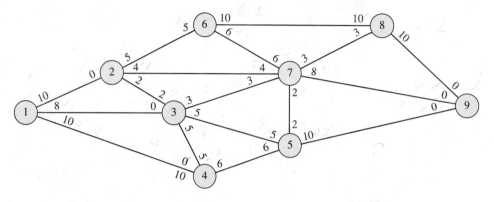

Case Problem: Ambulance Routing

The city of Binghamton is served by two major hospitals: Western Medical and Binghamton General. Western Medical is located in the southwest part of the city, and Binghamton General is in the northeast.

Bob Jones, the hospital administrator at Western Medical, has been discussing the problem of scheduling and routing ambulances with Margaret Johnson, the hospital administrator at Binghamton General. Both administrators feel that some type of system needs to be developed to better coordinate the use of the ambulance services at the two hospitals so that together they can provide the fastest possible emergency service for the city.

A proposal being considered is for all ambulance service calls to be handled through a central dispatcher, who would assign a call to the hospital capable of providing the fastest service. In studying this proposal, a project team consisting of employees from both hospitals met and decided that the best approach would be to divide the city into 20 service zones. In the proposed configuration, Western Medical would be located in zone 1 and Binghamton General in zone 20. A map showing the placement of the 20 zones and the travel time (in minutes) between adjacent zones is provided in Figure 9.18.

According to the proposed operating procedure, incoming emergency calls would be identified by zone number, and an ambulance from the hospital closest to that zone would be assigned the service call. However, if all ambulances from the closest hospital were occupied with other emergencies, the service call would be assigned to the other hospital. Regardless of which hospital responded to the service call, the individual or individuals requiring the emergency service would be taken to the closest hospital.

To make the coordinated service as efficient as possible, the ambulance drivers must know in advance the quickest route to take to each zone, which hospital the individual or individuals in that zone should be taken to, and the quickest route to that hospital.

Figure 9.18

Network for Proposed Ambulance Service

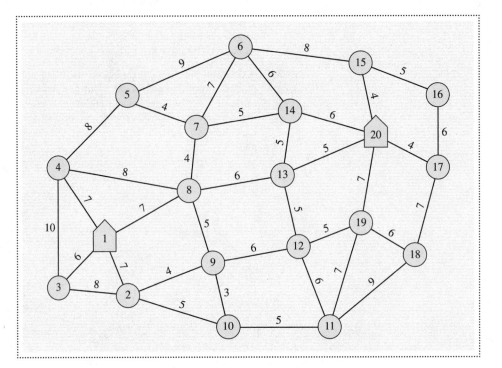

Managerial Report

Prepare a report for the two hospital administrators describing your analysis of the problem. Include in your report recommendations regarding the following items:

1. A chart for the dispatcher that identifies the primary hospital ambulance service for every zone in the city.
2. A chart for the Western Medical ambulance drivers that provides the minimum-time routes from Western Medical to every zone in the city, including Binghamton General. Include a chart that tells Western Medical drivers which hospital the individuals should be taken to and the route that should be followed.
3. A chart for the Binghamton General ambulance drivers that provides the minimum-time routes from Binghamton General to every zone in the city, including Western Medical. Include a chart that tells Binghamton General drivers which hospital the individuals should be taken to and the route that should be followed.
4. Include recommendations regarding how the system could be modified to take into account varying traffic conditions that occur throughout the day and/or changes in driving conditions resulting from temporary road construction projects.

MANAGEMENT SCIENCE in practice

EDS
Plano, Texas*

EDS is a global leader in providing information technology services. For more than 30 years, the company has provided hardware, software, communications, and process solutions to companies and governments around the world. Headquartered in Plano, Texas, EDS helps customers become more competitive by focusing technology on business goals. Customers come from a variety of industries and include leaders in the automotive, government services, financial, insurance, communications, manufacturing, retail, energy, distribution, transportation, utili-

ties, and health care industries. In 1984, EDS was acquired by the world's leading auto manufacturer, General Motors, and became an independently-operated subsidiary.

Minimal Spanning Tree Network Problem

EDS designs communication systems and information networks for many of its customers. In one application, a customer had 64 locations that needed to be linked together for information flow, information processing, and communications. Interactive data including voice, video, and digital data had to be accommodated in the information flow between the various sites. The customer's locations included approximately 50 offices and information centers in the continental United States; they ranged from Connecticut to Florida to Michigan to Texas to

Figure 9.19

A Portion of the Information Network Designed by EDS

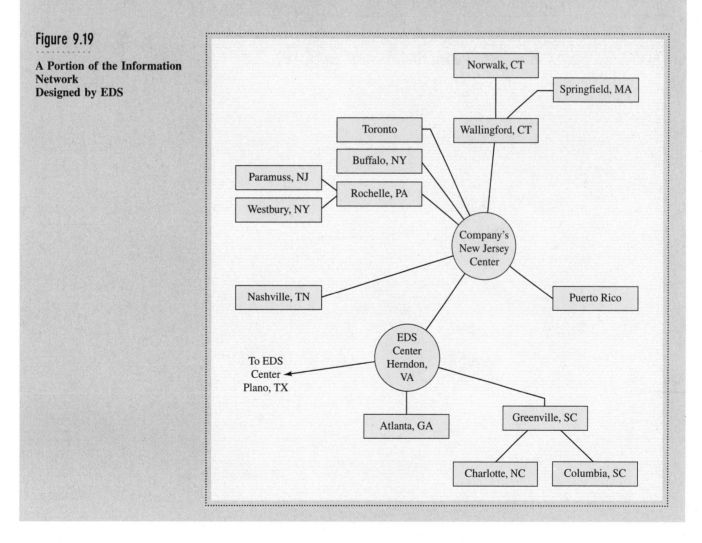

—Continued from previous page

California. Additional locations existed in Canada, Mexico, Hawaii, and Puerto Rico. The total of 64 company locations formed the nodes of the information network.

EDS's task was to span the network by finding the most cost-effective way to link 64 customer locations or nodes with the other customer locations as well as with existing EDS data centers. The arcs of the network were formed by connecting pairs of nodes in the network. In cases where land communication lines were available, the arcs consisted of fiber optic telephone lines. In other cases, the arcs were formed by satellite communication connections.

Using cost as the criterion, the information network design was a minimal spanning tree problem with the ultimate goal being the development of a minimum-cost network design such that all locations (nodes) could communicate with all other locations (nodes). Figure 9.19 shows a portion of the information network developed by EDS. With a communication arc between the company's New Jersey center and the EDS center in Herndon, Virginia, the network enabled the company to communicate through Herndon with locations in Texas, Arizona, California, Hawaii, and Mexico by taking advantage of the existing EDS center in Plano, Texas. The use of the EDS centers in Herndon and Plano meant that the client could span its network without developing its own independent information network. An effective and economical communication system was developed for the customer.

Questions

1. What were the nodes and the arcs of the information network?
2. Where does the minimal spanning tree problem enter into design of the information network?
3. Why were the number of nodes expanded to include existing EDS centers in addition to the 64 company locations? What advantages did this provide in developing the minimum-cost network design?

. . . .

* The authors are indebted to Greg A. Dennis of EDS for providing this application.

Project Scheduling: PERT/CPM

In many situations, managers are responsible for planning, scheduling, and controlling projects that consist of numerous separate jobs or tasks performed by a variety of departments and individuals. Often these projects are so large and/or complex that the manager cannot possibly remember all the information pertaining to the plan, schedule, and progress of the project. In these situations the *program evaluation and review technique* (PERT) and the *critical path method* (CPM) have proven to be extremely valuable.

PERT and CPM have been used to plan, schedule, and control a wide variety of projects, such as

1. research and development of new products and processes;
2. construction of plants, buildings, and highways;
3. maintenance of large and complex equipment; and
4. design and installation of new systems.

In projects such as these, project managers must schedule and coordinate the various jobs or activities so that the entire project is completed on time. A complicating factor in carrying out this task is the interdependence of the activities; for example, some activities depend on the completion of other activities before they can be started. Projects may have as many as several thousand activities, so project managers look for procedures that will help them answer questions such as the following.

1. What is the total time to complete the project?
2. What are the scheduled start and finish dates for each specific activity?
3. Which activities are "critical" and must be completed *exactly* as scheduled in order to keep the project on schedule?
4. How long can "noncritical" activities be delayed before they cause an increase in the total project completion time?

PERT and CPM can help answer these questions.

Although PERT and CPM have the same general purpose and utilize much of the same terminology, the techniques were developed independently. PERT was developed in the late 1950s specifically for the Polaris missile project. Many of the activities associated with this project had never been attempted previously, so PERT was developed to handle uncertain activity times. CPM was developed primarily for industrial projects for which activity times generally were known. CPM offered the option of reducing activity times by adding more workers and/or resources, usually at an increased cost. Thus, a distinguishing feature of CPM was that it identified trade-offs between time and cost for various project activities.

Today's computerized versions of PERT and CPM have combined the best features of both approaches. Thus, the distinction between the two techniques is no longer necessary. As a result, we will refer to the project scheduling procedures covered in this chapter as PERT/CPM. We begin the discussion of PERT/CPM by considering a project for the expansion of the Western Hills Shopping Center.

10.1   Project Scheduling with Known Activity Times

The owner of the Western Hills Shopping Center is planning to modernize and expand the current 32-business shopping center complex. The project is expected to provide room for 8 to 10 new businesses. Financing has been arranged through a private investor. All that remains is for the owner of the shopping center to plan, schedule and complete the expansion project. Let us show how PERT/CPM can help.

The first step in the PERT/CPM scheduling process is to develop a list of the activities that make up the project. Table 10.1 shows the list of activities for the Western Hills Shopping Center expansion project. Nine activities are described and denoted A through I for later reference. Additional information in Table 10.1 includes immediate predecessor and activity times (in weeks). For a given activity, the *immediate predecessor* column identifies the activities that must be completed *immediately prior* to the start of that activity. Activities A and B do not have immediate predecessors and can be started as soon as the project begins; thus, a dash is written in the immediate predecessor column for these activities. The other entries in the immediate predecessor column show that activities

Table 10.1

List of Activities for the Western Hills Shopping Center Project

Activity	Activity Description	Immediate Predecessor	Activity Time
A	Prepare architectural drawings	—	5
B	Identify potential new tenants	—	6
C	Develop prospectus for tenants	A	4
D	Select contractor	A	3
E	Prepare building permits	A	1
F	Obtain approval for building permits	E	4
G	Perform construction	D, F	14
H	Finalize contracts with tenants	B, C	12
I	Tenants move in	G, H	2
			Total 51

Figure 10.1   **Project Network for the Western Hills Shopping Center**

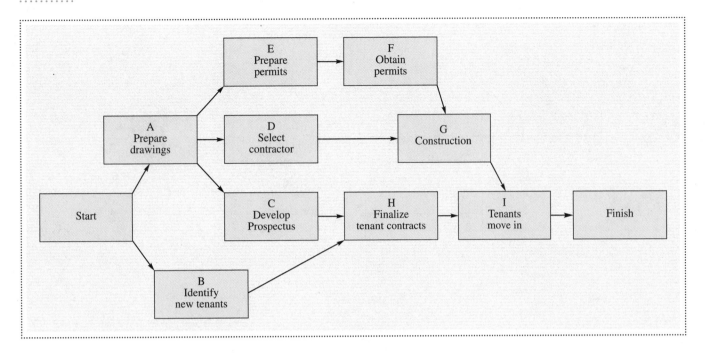

C, D, and E cannot be started until activity A has been completed, activity F cannot be started until activity E has been completed, activity G cannot be started until both activities D and F have been completed, activity H cannot be started until both activities B and C have been completed, and, finally, activity I cannot be started until both activities G and H have been completed. The project is finished when activity I is completed.

The last column in Table 10.1 shows the number of weeks required to complete each activity. For example, activity A takes 5 weeks, activity B takes 6 weeks, and so on. The sum of activity times is 51. As a result, you may think that the total time required to complete the project is 51 weeks. However, as we will show, two or more activities often may be scheduled concurrently, thus shortening the completion time for the project. Ultimately, PERT/CPM will provide a detailed activity schedule for completing the project in the shortest time possible.

Using the immediate predecessor information in Table 10.1, we can construct a graphical representation of the project, or the *project network*. Figure 10.1 depicts the project network for Western Hills shopping center. The activities correspond to the *nodes* of the network (drawn as rectangles) and the *arcs* (the lines with arrows) show the precedence relationships among the activities. In addition, nodes have been added to the network to denote the start and the finish of the project. A project network will help a manager visualize the activity relationships and provide a basis for carrying out the PERT/CPM computations.

Try Problem 3. This problem provides the immediate predecessor information for a project with seven activities and asks you to develop the project network.

The Concept of a Critical Path

To facilitate the PERT/CPM computations, we modified the project network as shown in Figure 10.2. Note that the upper left-hand corner of each node contains the corresponding activity letter. The activity time appears immediately below the letter.

Figure 10.2 Western Hills Shopping Center Project Network with Activity Times

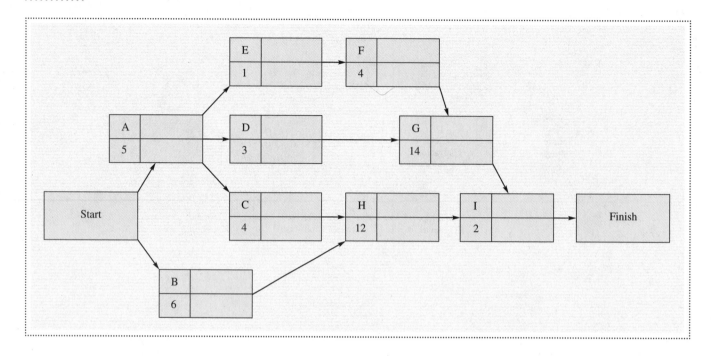

In order to determine the project completion time, we have to analyze the network and identify what is called the *critical path* for the network. However, before doing so, we need to define the concept of a path through the network. A *path* is a sequence of connected nodes that leads from the Start node to the Finish node. For instance, one path for the network in Figure 10.2 is defined by the sequence of nodes A–E–F–G–I. By inspection, we see that other paths are possible, such as A–D–G–I, A–C–H–I, and B–H–I. All paths in the network must be traversed in order to complete the project, so we will look for the path that requires the most time. Since all other paths are shorter in duration, this *longest* path determines the total time required to complete the project. If activities on the longest path are delayed, the entire project will be delayed. Thus, the longest path is the *critical path*. Activities on the critical path are referred to as the *critical activities* for the project. The following discussion presents a step-by-step algorithm for finding the critical path in a project network.

Determining the Critical Path

We begin by finding the *earliest start time* and a *latest start time* for all activities in the network. Let

$$ES = \text{earliest start time for an activity}$$
$$EF = \text{earliest finish time for an activity}$$
$$t = \text{activity time}$$

The earliest finish time for any activity, then, is

$$EF = ES + t \tag{10.1}$$

Activity A can start as soon as the project starts, so we set the earliest start time for activity A equal to 0. With an activity time of 5 weeks, the earliest finish time for activity A is $EF = ES + t = 0 + 5 = 5$.

We will write the earliest start and earliest finish times in the node to the right of the activity letter. Using activity A as an example, we have

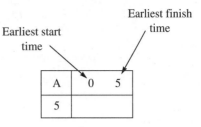

Since an activity cannot be started until *all* immediately preceding activities have been finished, the following rule can be used to determine the earliest start time for each activity.

Earliest Start Time Rule

The earliest start time for an activity is equal to the *largest* of the earliest finish times for all of its immediate predecessors.

Let us apply the earliest start time rule to the portion of the network involving nodes A, B, C, and H, as shown in Figure 10.3. With an earliest start time of 0 and an activity time of 6 for activity B, we show $ES = 0$ and $EF = ES + t = 0 + 6 = 6$ in the node for activity B. Looking at node C, we note that activity A is the only immediate predecessor for activity C. The earliest finish time for activity A is 5, so the earliest start time for activity C must be $ES = 5$. Thus, with an activity time of 4, the earliest finish time for activity C is $EF = ES + t = 5 + 4 = 9$. Both the earliest starting time and the earliest finish time can be shown in the node for activity C (see Figure 10.4).

Continuing with Figure 10.4, we move on to activity H and apply the earliest start time rule for this activity. With both activities B and C as immediate predecessors, the earliest start time for activity H must be equal to the largest of the earliest finish times for activities B and C. Thus, with $EF = 6$ for activity B and $EF = 9$ for activity C, we select the largest value, 9, as the earliest start time for activity H ($ES = 9$). With an activity time of 12 as shown in the node for activity H, the earliest finish time is $EF = ES + t = 9 + 12 = 21$. The $ES = 9$ and $EF = 21$ values can now be entered in the node for activity H in Figure 10.4.

Continuing with this *forward pass* through the network, we can establish the earliest start times and the earliest finish times for all activities in the network. Figure 10.5 shows the Western Hills Shopping Center project network with the ES and EF values for each activity. Note that the earliest finish time for activity I, the last activity in the project, is 26 weeks. Therefore we now know that the total completion time for the project is 26 weeks.

We now continue the algorithm for finding the critical path by making a *backward pass* through the network. Since the project can be completed in 26 weeks, we will begin

Figure 10.3

A Portion of the Western Hills Shopping Center Project Network, Showing Activities A, B, C, and H

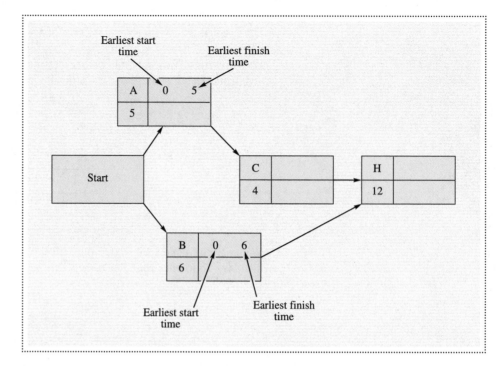

Figure 10.4

Determining the Earliest Start Time for Activity H

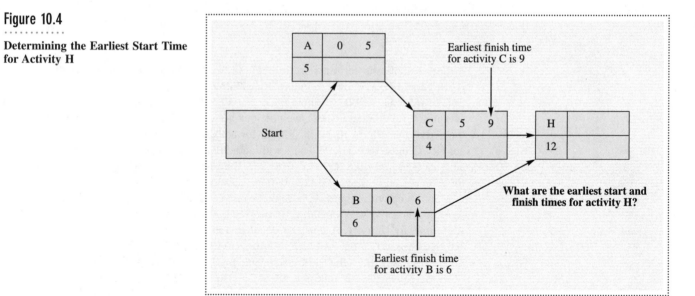

the backward pass with a *latest finish time* of 26 for activity I. Once the latest finish time for an activity is known, the *latest start time* for an activity can be computed as follows. Let

$$LS = \text{latest start time for an activity}$$
$$LF = \text{latest finish time for an activity}$$

then

$$LS = LF - t \qquad (10.2)$$

Figure 10.5 **Western Hills Shopping Center Project Network with Earliest Start and Earliest Finish Times Shown for All Activities**

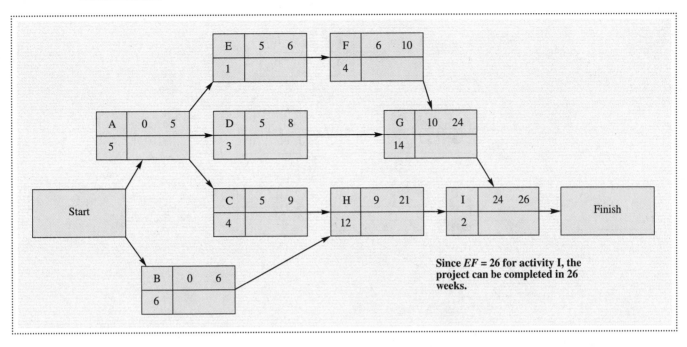

Since *EF* = 26 for activity I, the project can be completed in 26 weeks.

Beginning the backward pass with activity I, we know that the latest finish time is *LF* = 26 and that the activity time is *t* = 2. Thus, the latest start time for activity I is *LS* = *LF* − *t* = 26 − 2 = 24. We will write the *LS* and *LF* values in the node directly below the earliest start (*ES*) and earliest finish (*EF*) times. Thus, for node I, we have

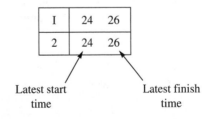

The following rule can be used to determine the latest finish time for each activity in the network.

Latest Finish Time Rule

The latest finish time for an activity is the *smallest* of the latest start times for all activities that immediately follow the activity.

Logically, this rule states that the latest time an activity can be finished equals the earliest (smallest) value for the latest start time of following activities. Figure 10.6 shows the complete project network with the *LS* and *LF* backward pass results. We can use the latest

Figure 10.6   Western Hills Shopping Center Project Network with Latest Start and Latest Finish Times Shown in Each Node

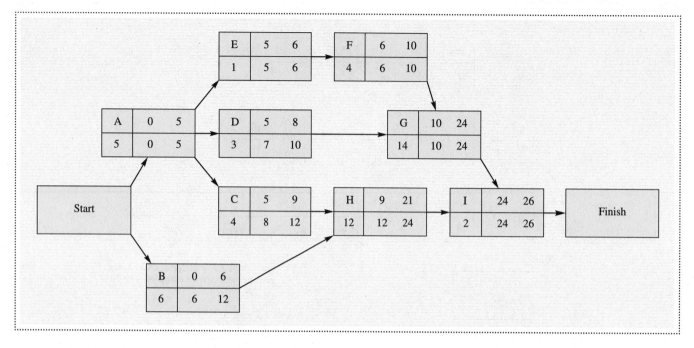

finish time rule to verify the *LS* and *LF* values shown for activity H. The latest finish time for activity H must be the latest start time for activity I. Thus, we set $LF = 24$ for activity H. Using equation (10.2), we find that $LS = LF - t = 24 - 12 = 12$ as the latest start time for activity H. These values are shown in the node for activity H in Figure 10.6.

Activity A requires a more involved application of the latest start time rule. First, note that three activities (C, D, and E) immediately follow activity A. Figure 10.6 shows that the latest start times for activities C, D, and E are $LS = 8, LS = 7$, and $LS = 5$, respectively. The latest finish time rule for activity A states that the *LF* for activity A is the smallest of the latest start times for activities C, D, and E. With the smallest value being 5 for activity E, we set the latest finish time for activity A to $LF = 5$. Verify this result and the other latest start times and latest finish times shown in the nodes in Figure 10.6.

After we have completed the forward and backward passes, we can determine the amount of slack associated with each activity. *Slack* is defined as the length of time an activity can be delayed without increasing the project completion time. The amount of slack for an activity is computed as follows:

$$Slack = LS - ES = LF - EF \qquad (10.3)$$

For example, the slack associated with activity C is $LS - ES = 8 - 5 = 3$ weeks. Hence, activity C can be delayed up to 3 weeks and the entire project can still be completed in 26 weeks. In this sense, activity C is not critical to the completion of the entire project in 26 weeks. Next, we consider activity E. Using the information in Figure 10.6, we find that the slack is $LS - ES = 5 - 5 = 0$. Thus, activity E has zero, or no, slack. Thus, this activity cannot be delayed without increasing the completion time for the entire project. In other words, completing activity E exactly as scheduled is critical in terms of keeping the project on schedule. Thus, activity E is a critical activity. In general, the *critical activities* are the activities with zero slack.

Table 10.2
....

Activity Schedule for the Western Hills Shopping Center Project

Activity	Earliest Start (ES)	Latest Start (LS)	Earliest Finish (EF)	Latest Finish (LF)	Slack (LS−ES)	Critical Path?
A	0	0	5	5	0	Yes
B	0	6	6	12	6	
C	5	8	9	12	3	
D	5	7	8	10	2	
E	5	5	6	6	0	Yes
F	6	6	10	10	0	Yes
G	10	10	24	24	0	Yes
H	9	12	21	24	3	
I	24	24	26	26	0	Yes

The start and finish times shown in Figure 10.6 can be used to develop a detailed start time and finish time schedule for all activities. Putting this information in tabular form provides the activity schedule shown in Table 10.2. Note that the slack column shows that activities A, E, F, G, and I have zero slack. Hence, these activities are the critical activities for the project. The path formed by nodes A–E–F–G–I is the *critical path* in the Western Hills Shopping Center project network. The detailed schedule shown in Table 10.2 indicates the slack or delay that can be tolerated for the noncritical activities before these activities will increase project completion time.

Contributions of PERT/CPM
....

Previously, we stated that project managers look for procedures that will help answer important questions regarding the planning, scheduling, and controlling of projects. Let us reconsider these questions in light of the information that the critical path calculations have given us.

1. How long will the project take to complete?
   Answer: The project can be completed in 26 weeks if each activity is completed on schedule.
2. What are the scheduled start and completion times for each activity?
   Answer: The activity schedule (see Table 10.2) shows the earliest start, latest start, earliest finish, and latest finish times for each activity.
3. Which activities are critical and must be completed *exactly* as scheduled in order to keep the project on schedule?
   Answer: A, E, F, G, and I are the critical path activities.
4. How long can noncritical activities be delayed before they cause an increase in the completion time for the project?
   Answer: The activity schedule (see Table 10.2) shows the slack associated with each activity.

Such information is valuable in managing any project. Although larger projects may increase substantially the time required to make the necessary calculations, the procedure and contributions of PERT/CPM to larger projects are identical to those for the shopping center expansion project. Furthermore, computer packages may be used to carry out the steps of the PERT/CPM procedure. Figure 10.7 shows the activity schedule for the

MANAGEMENT SCIENCE in action

Project Management on the PC[*]

More than 100 project management software packages are available for personal computers (PCs). A survey of users of well-known project management software packages for PCs identified applications such as the construction of a $20 million sawmill, the installation of a new software system in a hospital, the development of a communications satellite, the production of an electronic device, and the relocation of a facility. These projects ranged in size from 1000 activities for the sawmill construction project to 6500 activities for the facility relocation project.

At the low end of the market, packages generally cost less than $500. In this group, Harvard Total Project Manager, Microsoft Project, SuperProject Plus, and Time Line account for the majority of sales. These packages have modest memory requirements and the ability to analyze projects with as many as 1000 activities, and can produce a wide range of reports. At the high end of the market, prices generally exceed $2000; this group includes packages such as OPEN, PLAN, PMS-II Professional, Primavera Project Planner, and PROMIS. These more sophisticated systems are designed to handle projects with as many as 10,000 activities and have the ability to produce presentation-quality graphics.

....

*Based on Wasil, E., and A. A. Assad, "Project Management on the PC: Software, Applications, and Trends." *Interfaces,* March–April 1988, pp. 75–84.

Figure 10.7 **The Management Scientist Activity Schedule for the Western Hills Shopping Center Project**

```
              ***    ACTIVITY SCHEDULE    ***

             EARLIEST  LATEST  EARLIEST  LATEST            CRITICAL
  ACTIVITY   START     START   FINISH    FINISH  SLACK     ACTIVITY
  -------------------------------------------------------------------
     A          0         0       5         5       0        YES
     B          0         6       6        12       6
     C          5         8       9        12       3
     D          5         7       8        10       2
     E          5         5       6         6       0        YES
     F          6         6      10        10       0        YES
     G         10        10      24        24       0        YES
     H          9        12      21        24       3
     I         24        24      26        26       0        YES
  -------------------------------------------------------------------

     CRITICAL PATH:  A-E-F-G-I

     PROJECT COMPLETION TIME = 26
```

shopping center expansion project developed by The Management Scientist software package. Input to the program included the activities, their immediate predecessors, and the expected activity times. Only a few minutes were required to input the information and generate the critical path and activity schedule. The Management Science in Action: Project Management on the PC describes the important role software packages play in the management of projects with 1000 or more activities.

Summary of the PERT/CPM Critical Path Procedure

Before leaving this section, let us summarize the PERT/CPM critical path procedure.

Step 1   Develop a list of the activities that make up the project.

Step 2   Determine the immediate predecessors for each activity in the project.

Step 3   Estimate the completion time for each activity.

Step 4   Draw a project network depicting the activities and immediate predecessors listed in steps 1 and 2.

Step 5   Use the project network and the activity time estimates to determine the earliest start and the earliest finish time for each activity by making a forward pass through the network. The earliest finish time for the last activity in the project identifies the total time required to complete the project.

Step 6   Use the project completion time identified in step 5 as the latest finish time for the last activity and make a backward pass through the network to identify the latest start and latest finish time for each activity.

Step 7   Use the difference between the latest start time and the earliest start time for each activity to determine the slack for the activity.

Step 8   Find the activities with zero slack; these are the critical path activities.

Step 9   Use the information from steps 5 and 6 to develop the activity schedule for the project.

NOTES & comments

If after analyzing a PERT/CPM network and finding that the project completion time is unacceptable (i.e., the project is going to take too long), a manager must take one or both of the following steps. First, review the original PERT/CPM network to see if the immediate predecessor relationships can be modified so that at least some of the critical path activities can be done simultaneously. Second, consider adding resources to critical path activities in an attempt to shorten the critical path; we discuss this alternative, referred to as *crashing,* in Section 10.3.

10.2 Project Scheduling with Uncertain Activity Times

In this section we consider the details of project scheduling for a problem involving new-product research and development. Because many of the activities in this project have never been attempted, the project manager wants to account for uncertainties in the activity times. Let us show how project scheduling can be conducted with uncertain activity times.

The Daugherty Porta-Vac Project

The H. S. Daugherty Company has manufactured industrial vacuum cleaning systems for many years. Recently, a member of the company's new-product research team submitted a report suggesting that the company consider manufacturing a cordless vacuum cleaner. The new product, referred to as a Porta-Vac, could contribute to Daugherty's expansion into the household market. Management hopes that it can be manufactured at a reasonable cost and that its portability and no-cord convenience will make it extremely attractive.

Daugherty's management wants to study the feasibility of manufacturing the Porta-Vac product. The feasibility study will recommend the action to be taken. To complete this study, information must be obtained from the firm's research and development (R&D), product testing, manufacturing, cost estimating, and market research groups. How long will this feasibility study take? In the following discussion, we will show how to answer this question and provide an activity schedule for the project.

Again, the first step in the project scheduling process is to identify all the activities that make up the project and then determine the immediate predecessors for each activity. Table 10.3 shows these data for the Porta-Vac project.

The Porta-Vac project network is shown in Figure 10.8. Verify that the network does in fact maintain the immediate predecessor relationships shown in Table 10.3.

Table 10.3

Activity List for the Porta-Vac Project

Activity	Description	Immediate Predecessor
A	Develop product design	—
B	Plan market research	—
C	Prepare routing (manufacturing engineering)	A
D	Build prototype model	A
E	Prepare marketing brochure	A
F	Prepare cost estimates (industrial engineering)	C
G	Do preliminary product testing	D
H	Complete market survey	B, E
I	Prepare pricing and forecast report	H
J	Prepare final report	F, G, I

Figure 10.8   **Porta-Vac Cordless Vacuum Cleaner Project Network**

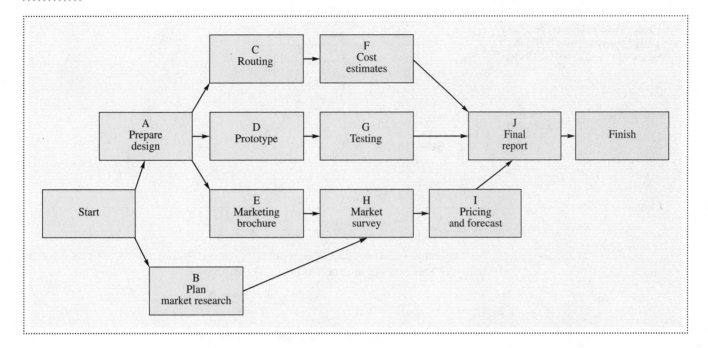

Uncertain Activity Times

Once we have developed the project network, we will need information on the time required to complete each activity. This information will be used in the calculation of the total time required to complete the project and in the scheduling of specific activities. For repeat projects, such as construction and maintenance projects, managers may have the experience and historical data necessary to provide accurate activity time estimates. However, for new or unique projects, estimating the time for each activity may be quite difficult. In fact, in many cases, activity times are uncertain and are best described by a range of possible values rather than by one specific time estimate. In these instances, the uncertain activity times are treated as random variables with associated probability distributions. As a result, probability statements will be provided about the ability to meet a specific project completion date.

To incorporate uncertain activity times into the analysis, we need to obtain three time estimates for each activity:

> Optimistic time a = the minimum activity time if everything progresses ideally
> Most probable time m = the most probable activity time under normal conditions
> Pessimistic time b = the maximum activity time if significant delays are encountered

To illustrate the PERT/CPM procedure with uncertain activity times, let us consider the optimistic, most probable, and pessimistic time estimates for the Porta-Vac activities as presented in Table 10.4. Using activity A as an example, we see that the most probable time is 5 weeks with a range from 4 weeks (optimistic) to 12 weeks (pessimistic). If the

Table 10.4

Optimistic, Most Probable, and Pessimistic Activity Time Estimates (in Weeks) for the Porta-Vac Project

Activity	Optimistic (a)	Most Probable (m)	Pessimistic (b)
A	4	5	12
B	1	1.5	5
C	2	3	4
D	3	4	11
E	2	3	4
F	1.5	2	2.5
G	1.5	3	4.5
H	2.5	3.5	7.5
I	1.5	2	2.5
J	1	2	3

activity could be repeated a large number of times, what is the average time for the activity? This average or *expected time* (t) is as follows:

$$t = \frac{a + 4m + b}{6} \tag{10.4}$$

For activity A we have an average or expected time of

$$t_A = \frac{4 + 4(5) + 12}{6} = \frac{36}{6} = 6 \text{ weeks}$$

With uncertain activity times, we can use the *variance* to describe the dispersion or variation in the activity time values. The variance of the activity time is given by the formula[1]

$$\sigma^2 = \left(\frac{b - a}{6}\right)^2 \tag{10.5}$$

The difference between the pessimistic (b) and optimistic (a) time estimates greatly affects the value of the variance. Large differences in these two values reflect a high degree of uncertainty in the activity time. Using equation (10.5), we obtain the measure of uncertainty—that is, the variance—of activity A, denoted σ_A^2:

$$\sigma_A^2 = \left(\frac{12 - 4}{6}\right)^2 = \left(\frac{8}{6}\right)^2 = 1.78$$

Equations (10.4) and (10.5) are based on the assumption that the activity time distribution can be described by a *beta probability distribution*.[2] With this assumption, the probability distribution for the time to complete activity A is as shown in Figure 10.9. Using equations (10.4) and (10.5) and the data in Table 10.4, we calculated the expected times and variances for all of the Porta-Vac activities; the results are summarized in Table 10.5. The Porta-Vac project network with expected activity times is shown in Figure 10.10.

---

[1] The variance equation is based on the notion that a standard deviation is approximately ⅙ of the difference between the extreme values of the distribution: ($b - a$)/6. The variance is the square of the standard deviation.

[2] The equations for t and σ^2 require additional assumptions about the parameters of the beta probability distribution. However, even when these additional assumptions are not made, the equations still provide very good approximations of t and σ^2.

Figure 10.9

Activity Time Distribution for Project Design Activity A of the Porta-Vac Project

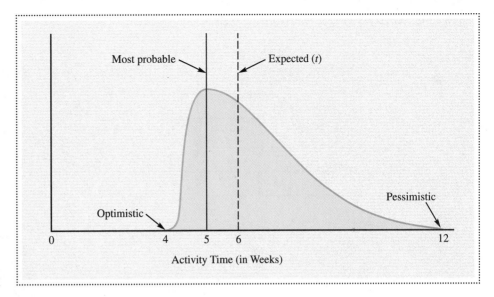

Table 10.5

Expected Times and Variances for the Porta-Vac Project Activities

Activity	Expected Time (weeks)	Variance
A	6	1.78
B	2	0.44
C	3	0.11
D	5	1.78
E	3	0.11
F	2	0.03
G	3	0.25
H	4	0.69
I	2	0.03
J	2	0.11
	Total 32	

The Critical Path

When we have the project network and the expected activity times, we are ready to proceed with the critical path calculations necessary to determine the expected time required to complete the project and determine the activity schedule. In these calculations, we will treat the expected activity times (Table 10.5) as the *fixed length* or *known duration* of each activity. As a result, we can use the PERT/CPM critical path procedure introduced in Section 10.1 to find the critical path for the Porta-Vac project. After the critical activities and the expected time to complete the project have been determined, we will analyze the effect of the activity time variability.

Proceeding with a forward pass through the network shown in Figure 10.10, we can establish the earliest start (*ES*) and earliest finish (*EF*) times for each activity. Figure 10.11 shows the project network with the *ES* and *EF* values. Note that the earliest finish time for activity J, the last activity, is 17 weeks. Thus, the expected completion time for

Figure 10.10 **Porta-Vac Project Network with Expected Activity Times**

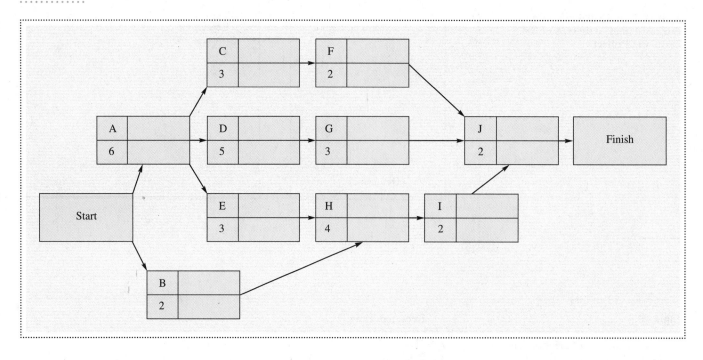

Figure 10.11 **Porta-Vac Project Network with Earliest Start and Earliest Finish Times**

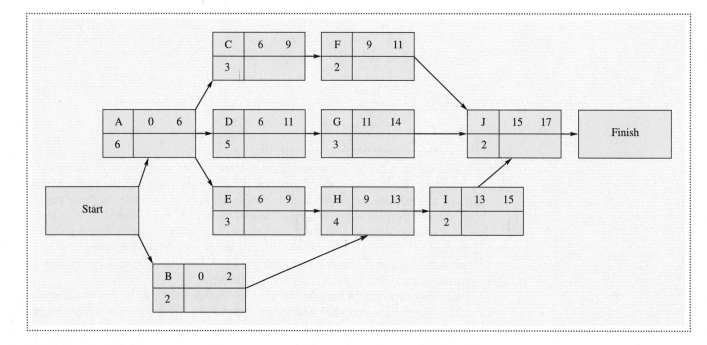

Figure 10.12 Porta-Vac Project Network with Latest Start and Latest Finish Times

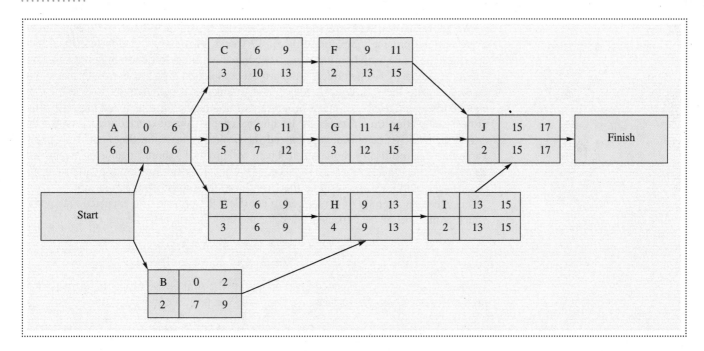

Table 10.6

Activity Schedule for the Porta-Vac Project

Activity	Earliest Start (ES)	Latest Start (LS)	Earliest Finish (EF)	Latest Finish (LF)	Slack (LS−ES)	Critical Path?
A	0	0	6	6	0	Yes
B	0	7	2	9	7	
C	6	10	9	13	4	
D	6	7	11	12	1	
E	6	6	9	9	0	Yes
F	9	13	11	15	4	
G	11	12	14	15	1	
H	9	9	13	13	0	Yes
I	13	13	15	15	0	Yes
J	15	15	17	17	0	Yes

the project is 17 weeks. Next, we make a backward pass through the network. The backward pass provides the latest start (*LS*) and latest finish (*LF*) times shown in Figure 10.12.

The activity schedule for the Porta-Vac project is shown in Table 10.6. Note that the slack time (*LS* − *ES*) is also shown for each activity. The activities with zero slack (A, E, H, I, and J) form the critical path for the Porta-Vac project network.

Variability in Project Completion Time

We know that for the Porta-Vac project the critical path of A–E–H–I–J resulted in an expected total project completion time of 17 weeks. However, variation in critical path activities can cause variation in the project completion time. Variation in noncritical path activities ordinarily has no effect on the project completion time because of the slack time associated with these activities. However, if a noncritical path activity is delayed long enough to expend its slack time, it becomes part of a new critical path and may affect the project completion time. Variability leading to a longer-than-expected total time for the critical path activities will always extend the project completion time, and conversely, variability that results in a shorter critical path will produce a shorter-than-expected project completion time, unless other activities become critical. Let us now use the variance in the critical path activities to determine the variance in the project completion time.

Let T denote the total time required to complete the project. The expected value of T, which is the sum of the expected times for the critical path activities is

$$E(T) = t_A + t_E + t_H + t_I + t_J$$
$$= 6 + 3 + 4 + 2 + 2 = 17 \text{ weeks}$$

The variance in the project completion time is the sum of the variances of the critical path activities. Thus, the variance for the Porta-Vac project completion time is

$$\sigma^2 = \sigma_A^2, + \sigma_E^2, + \sigma_H^2, + \sigma_I^2, + \sigma_J^2$$
$$= 1.78 + 0.11 + 0.69 + 0.03 + 0.11 = 2.72$$

where σ_A^2, σ_E^2, σ_H^2, σ_I^2, and σ_J^2 are the variances of the critical path activities.

The formula for σ^2 is based on the assumption that the activity times are independent. If two or more activities are dependent, the formula provides only an approximation to the variance of the project completion time. The closer the activities are to being independent, the better the approximation is.

Knowing that the standard deviation is the square root of the variance, we compute the standard deviation σ for the Porta-Vac project completion time as

$$\sigma = \sqrt{\sigma^2} = \sqrt{2.72} = 1.65$$

Assuming that the distribution of the project completion time T follows a normal or bell-shaped distribution[3] allows us to draw the distribution shown in Figure 10.13. With this distribution, we can compute the probability of meeting a specified project completion date. For example, suppose that management has allotted 20 weeks for the Porta-Vac project. What is the probability that we will meet the 20-week deadline? Using the normal probability distribution shown in Figure 10.14, we are asking for the probability that $T \leq 20$; this probability is shown graphically as the shaded area in the figure. The z value for the normal probability distribution at $T = 20$ is

$$z = \frac{20 - 17}{1.65} = 1.82$$

Using $z = 1.82$ and the table for the normal distribution (see Appendix A), we find that the probability of the project meeting the 20-week deadline is $0.4656 + 0.5000 = 0.9656$. Thus, even though activity time variability may cause the completion time to exceed 17 weeks, there is an excellent chance that the project will be completed before the 20-week deadline. Similar probability calculations can be made for other project deadline alternatives.

Problem 10 involves a project with uncertain activity times and asks you to compute the expected completion time and the variance for the project.

---

[3]The use of the normal distribution as an approximation is based on the central limit theorem, which indicates that the sum of independent random variables (activity times) follows a normal distribution as the number of random variables becomes large.

Figure 10.13

Normal Distribution of the Project Completion Time for the Porta-Vac Project

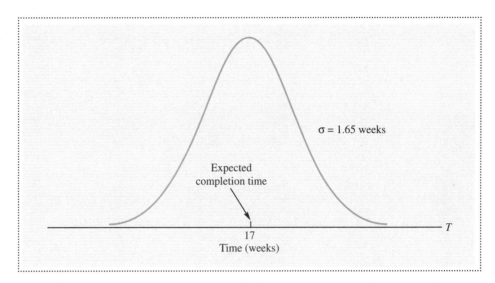

Figure 10.14

Probability of a Porta-Vac Project Completion Date Prior to the 20-Week Deadline

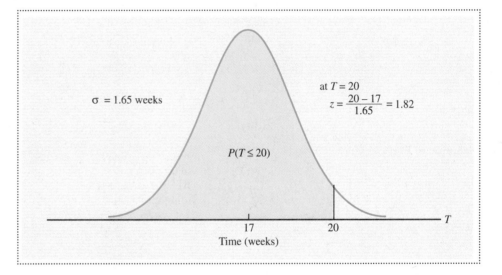

NOTES & comments

For projects involving uncertain activity times, the probability that the project can be completed within a specified amount of time is helpful managerial information. However, remember that this probability estimate is based *only* on the critical path activities. When uncertain activity times exist, longer-than-expected completion times for one or more noncritical path activities may cause an original noncritical path to become critical and hence increase the time required to complete the project. By frequently monitoring the progress of the project to make sure all activities are on schedule, the project manager will be better prepared to take corrective action if a noncritical activity begins to lengthen the duration of the project.

10.3 Considering Time–Cost Trade-Offs

The original developers of CPM provided the project manager with the option of adding resources to selected activities to reduce project completion time. Added resources (such as more workers, overtime, and so on) generally increase project costs, so the decision to reduce activity times must take into consideration the additional cost involved. In effect, the project manager has to make a decision that involves trading reduced activity time for additional project cost.

Table 10.7 defines a two-machine maintenance project consisting of five activities. Since management has had substantial experience with similar projects, the times for maintenance activities are considered to be known; hence, a single time estimate is given for each activity. The project network is shown in Figure 10.15.

The procedure for making critical path calculations for the maintenance project network is the same one we used to find the critical path in the networks for both the Western Hills Shopping Center expansion project and the Porta-Vac project. Making the forward pass and backward pass calculations for the network in Figure 10.15, we obtained the activity schedule shown in Table 10.8. The zero slack times, and thus the critical path, are associated with activities A–B–E. The length of the critical path, and thus the total time required to complete the project, is 12 days.

Table 10.7

Activity List for the Two-Machine Maintenance Project

Activity	Description	Immediate Predecessor	Expected Time (days)
A	Overhaul machine I	—	7
B	Adjust machine I	A	3
C	Overhaul machine II	—	6
D	Adjust machine II	C	3
E	Test system	B, D	2

Figure 10.15 **Two-Machine Maintenance Project Network**

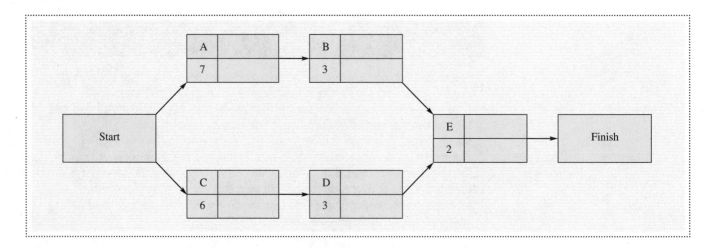

Table 10.8

Activity Schedule for the Two-Machine Maintenance Project

Activity	Earliest Start (ES)	Latest Start (LS)	Earliest Finish (EF)	Latest Finish (LF)	Slack (LS−ES)	Critical Path?
A	0	0	7	7	0	Yes
B	7	7	10	10	0	Yes
C	0	1	6	7	1	
D	6	7	9	10	1	
E	10	10	12	12	0	Yes

Crashing Activity Times

Now suppose that the current production levels make it imperative for the maintenance project to be completed within 10 days. By looking at the length of the critical path of the network (12 days), we realize that meeting the desired project completion time is impossible unless we can shorten selected activity times. This shortening of activity times, which usually can be achieved by adding resources, is referred to as *crashing*. However, the added resources associated with crashing activity times usually result in added project costs, so we will want to identify the activities that cost the least to crash and then crash those activities only the amount necessary to meet the desired project completion time.

To determine just where and how much to crash activity times, we need information on how much each activity can be crashed and how much the crashing process costs. Hence, we must ask for the following information:

1. Estimated activity cost under the normal or expected activity time
2. Estimated time to complete the activity under maximum crashing (i.e., the shortest possible activity time)
3. Estimated activity cost under maximum crashing

Let

τ_i = expected time for activity i

τ_i' = time for activity j under maximum crashing

M_i = maximum possible reduction in time for activity i due to crashing

Given τ_i and τ_i', we can compute M_i:

$$M_i = \tau_i - \tau_i' \tag{10.6}$$

Next, let C_i denote the estimated cost for activity i under the normal or expected activity time and C_i' denote the estimated cost for activity i under maximum crashing. Thus, per unit of time (e.g., per day), the crashing cost K_i for each activity is given by

$$K_i = \frac{C_i' - C_i}{M_i} \tag{10.7}$$

For example, if the normal or expected time for activity A is 7 days at a cost of $C_A = \$500$ and the time under maximum crashing is 4 days at a cost of $C_A' = \$800$, equations (10.6) and (10.7) show that the maximum possible reduction in time for activity A is

$$M_A = 7 - 4 = 3 \text{ days}$$

with a crashing cost of

$$K_A = \frac{C'_A - C_A}{M_A} = \frac{800 - 500}{3} = \frac{300}{3} = \$100 \text{ per day}$$

We will make the assumption that any portion or fraction of the activity crash time can be achieved for a corresponding portion of the activity crashing cost. For example, if we decided to crash activity A by only 1½ days, the added cost would be 1½($100) = $150, which results in a total activity cost of $500 + $150 = $650. Figure 10.16 shows the graph of the time–cost relationship for activity A. The complete normal and crash activity data for the two-machine maintenance project are given in Table 10.9.

Which activities should be crashed—and by how much—to meet the 10-day project completion deadline at minimum cost? Your first reaction to this question may be to consider crashing the critical path activities—A, B, or E. Activity A has the lowest crashing cost of the three, and crashing this activity by 2 days will reduce the A–B–E path to the desired 10 days. Keep in mind, however, that as you crash the current critical path activities, other paths may become critical. Thus, you will need to check the critical path

Figure 10.16

Time–Cost Relationship for Activity A

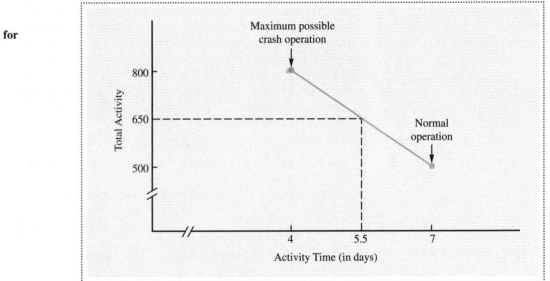

Table 10.9

Normal and Crash Activity Data for the Two-Machine Maintenance Project

Activity	Time (days) Normal	Time (days) Crash	Total Cost Normal(C_i)	Total Cost Crash(C'_i)	Maximum Reduction in Time (M_i)	Crash Cost Per day $\left(K_i = \dfrac{C'_i - C_i}{M_i}\right)$
A	7	4	$ 500	$ 800	3	$100
B	3	2	200	350	1	150
C	6	4	500	900	2	200
D	3	1	200	500	2	150
E	2	1	300	550	1	250
			$1700	$3100		

in the revised network and perhaps either identify additional activities to crash or modify your initial crashing decision. For a small network, this trial-and-error approach can be used to make crashing decisions; in larger networks, however, a mathematical procedure is required to determine the optimal crashing decisions. The following discussion shows how linear programming can be used to solve the network crashing problem.

A Linear Programming Model for Crashing Decisions

In the PERT/CPM procedure, we used

$$EF = ES + t$$

to determine the earliest finish time for an activity. Note that if ES, the earliest start time for an activity, is known, the effect of crashing a particular activity will be to reduce t and hence EF, the earliest finish time. In essence, we will use linear programming to determine which activities to crash and how much they should be crashed.

Consider activity A, which has a normal time of 7 days. Let x_A = earliest finish time for activity A and y_A = amount of time activity A is crashed. If we assume that the project begins at time 0, the earliest start time for activity A is 0. Since the time for activity A is reduced by the amount of time that activity A is crashed, the earliest finish time for activity A is

$$x_A \geq 0 + (7 - y_A)$$

Moving y_A to the left-hand side,

$$x_A + y_A \geq 7$$

In general, let

$$x_i = \text{the earliest finish time for activity } i \qquad i = A, B, C, D, E$$
$$y_i = \text{the amount of time activity } i \text{ is crashed} \quad i = A, B, C, D, E$$

If we follow the same approach that we used for activity A, the constraint corresponding to the earliest finish time for activity C (expected time = 6 days) is

$$x_C \geq 0 + (6 - y_C) \qquad \text{or} \qquad x_C + y_C \geq 6$$

Continuing with the forward pass of the PERT/CPM procedure, we see that the earliest start time for activity B is x_A, the earliest finish time for activity A. Thus, the constraint corresponding to the earliest finish time for activity B is

$$x_B \geq x_A + (3 - y_B) \qquad \text{or} \qquad x_B + y_B - x_A \geq 3$$

Similarly, we obtain the constraint for the earliest finish time for activity D:

$$x_D \geq x_C + (3 - y_D) \qquad \text{or} \qquad x_D + y_D - x_C \geq 3$$

Finally, we consider activity E. The earliest start time for activity E equals the *largest* of the earliest finish times for activities B and D. Because the earliest finish times for both activities B and D will be determined by the crashing procedure, we must write two constraints for activity E, one based on the earliest finish time for activity B and one based upon the earliest finish time for activity D:

$$x_E + y_E - x_B \geq 2 \qquad \text{and} \qquad x_E + y_E - x_D \geq 2$$

Recall that the current production levels made it imperative for the maintenance project to be completed within 10 days. Thus, the constraint for the earliest finish time for activity E is

$$x_E \leq 10$$

In addition, we must add the following five constraints corresponding to the maximum allowable crashing time for each activity:

$$y_A \leq 3, \qquad y_B \leq 1, \qquad y_C \leq 2, \qquad y_D \leq 2, \qquad \text{and} \qquad y_E \leq 1$$

As with all linear programs, we add the usual nonnegativity requirements for the decision variables.

All that remains is to develop an objective function for the model. Since the total project cost for a normal completion time is fixed at \$1700 (see Table 10.9), we can minimize the total project cost (normal cost plus crashing cost) by minimizing the total crashing costs. Thus, the linear programming objective function becomes

$$\text{Min} \quad 100y_A + 150y_B + 200y_C + 150y_D + 250y_E$$

NOTES & comments

Note that the two-machine maintenance project network for the crashing illustration (see Figure 10.15) has only one activity, activity E, leading directly to the Finish node. As a result, the project completion time is equal to the completion time for activity E. Thus, the linear programming constraint requiring the project completion in 10 days or less could be written $x_E \leq 10$.

If two or more activities lead directly to the Finish node of a project network, a slight modification is required in the linear programming model for crashing. Consider the following portion of a project network:

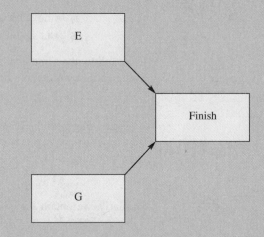

In this case, we suggest creating an additional variable, x_{FIN}, which indicates the finish or completion time for the entire project. The fact that the project cannot be finished until both activities E and G are completed can be modeled by the two constraints

$$x_{FIN} \geq x_E \quad \text{or} \quad x_{FIN} - x_E \geq 0$$
$$x_{FIN} \geq x_G \quad \text{or} \quad x_{FIN} - x_G \geq 0$$

The constraint that the project must be finished by time T can be added as $x_{FIN} \leq T$. Self-test Problem 22 will give you practice with this type of project network.

Thus, to determine the optimal crashing for each of the activities, we must solve a 10-variable, 12-constraint linear programming model. The linear programming module of The Management Scientist provides the optimal solution of crashing activity A by 1 week and activity E by 1 week, with a total crashing cost of $350. We can now develop a detailed activity schedule by using $7 - 1 = 6$ as the revised time for activity A and $2 - 1 = 1$ day as the revised time for activity E.

Summary

In this chapter we showed how PERT/CPM can be used to plan, schedule, and control a wide variety of projects. The key to this approach to project scheduling is the development of a PERT/CPM project network that depicts the activities and their precedence relationships. From this project network and activity time estimates, the critical path for the network and the associated critical path activities can be identified. In the process, an activity schedule showing the earliest start and finish times, the latest start and finish times, and the slack for each activity can be identified.

We showed how we can include capabilities for handling variable or uncertain activity times and how to use this information to provide a probability statement about the chances the project can be completed in a specified period of time. We introduced crashing as a procedure for reducing activity times to meet project completion deadlines. A linear programming model can be used to determine the crashing decisions that will minimize the cost of reducing the project completion time.

Glossary

Program evaluation and review technique (PERT) A network-based project scheduling procedure.

Critical path method (CPM) A network-based project scheduling procedure.

Activities Specific jobs or tasks that are components of a project. They are represented by nodes in a project network.

Immediate predecessors The activities that must be completed immediately prior to the start of a given activity.

Project network A graphical representation of a project that depicts the activities and shows the predecessor relationships among the activities.

Critical path The longest path in a project network.

Path A sequence of connected nodes that leads from the Start node to the Finish node.

Critical path activities The activities on the longest path in the network.

Earliest start time The earliest time an activity may begin.

Earliest finish time The earliest time an activity may be completed.

Forward pass Part of the PERT/CPM procedure that involves moving forward through the project network to determine the earliest start and earliest finish times for each activity.

Latest start time The latest time an activity may begin without increasing the project completion time.

Latest finish time The latest time an activity may be completed without increasing the project completion time.

Backward pass Part of the PERT/CPM procedure that involves moving backward through the network to determine the latest start and latest finish times for each activity.

Optimistic time The minimum activity time if everything progresses ideally.

Most probable time The most probable activity time under normal conditions.

Pessimistic time The maximum activity time if significant delays are encountered.

Expected time The average activity time.

Beta distribution A probability distribution used to describe activity times.

Slack The length of time an activity can be delayed without affecting the project completion time.

Crashing The process of reducing an activity time by adding resources and hence usually increasing cost.

Problems

1. The Mohawk Discount Store is designing a management training program for individuals at its corporate headquarters. The company wants to design the program so that the trainees can complete it as quickly as possible. Important precedence relationships must be maintained between assignments or activities in the program. For example, a trainee cannot serve as an assistant to the store manager until the trainee has obtained experience in the credit department and at least one sales department. The activities shown are the assignments that must be completed by each trainee in the program.

Activity	A	B	C	D	E	F	G	H
Immediate Predecessor	—	—	A	A, B	A, B	C	D, F	E, G

Construct a project network for this problem. Do not perform any further analysis.

2. Bridge City Developers is coordinating the construction of an office complex. As part of the planning process, the company generated the following activity list. Draw a project network that can be used to assist in the scheduling of the project activities.

Activity	A	B	C	D	E	F	G	H	I	J
Immediate Predecessor	—	—	—	A, B	A, B	D	E	C	C	F, G, H, I

3. **SELF Test** Construct a project network for the following project.

Activity	A	B	C	D	E	F	G
Immediate Predecessor	—	—	A	A	C, B	C, B	D, E

The project is completed when activities F and G are both complete.

4. Assume that the project in Problem 3 has the following activity times (in months).

Activity	A	B	C	D	E	F	G
Time	4	6	2	6	3	3	5

a. Find the critical path.
b. The project must be completed in 1½ years. Do you anticipate difficulty in meeting the deadline? Explain.

5. Management Decision Systems (MDS) is a consulting company that specializes in the development of decision support systems. MDS has just obtained a contract to develop a computer system to assist the management of a large company in formulating its capital expenditure plan. The project leader has developed the following list of activities and immediate predecessors.

Activity	A	B	C	D	E	F	G	H	I	J
Immediate Predecessor	—	—	—	B	A	B	C, D	B, E	F, G	H

Construct a project network for this problem.

6. **SELF**Test   Consider the following project network and activity times (in weeks).

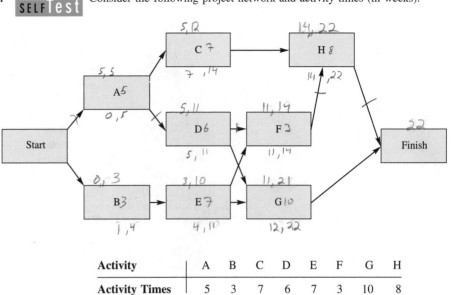

Activity	A	B	C	D	E	F	G	H
Activity Times	5	3	7	6	7	3	10	8
Slack	0	1	2	0	1	0	1	0

a. Identify the critical path.

b. How long will it take to complete this project?

c. Can activity D be delayed without delaying the entire project? If so, by how many weeks?

d. Can activity C be delayed without delaying the entire project? If so, by how many weeks?

e. What is the schedule for activity E?

7. A project involving the installation of a computer system comprises eight activities. The immediate predecessors and activity times (in weeks) are shown.

Activity	Immediate Predecessor	Time
A	—	3
B	—	6
C	A	2
D	B, C	5
E	D	4
F	E	3
G	B, C	9
H	F, G	3

a. Draw a project network.

b. What are the critical path activities?

c. What is the expected project completion time?

8. Colonial State College is considering building a new multipurpose athletic complex on campus. The complex would provide a new gymnasium for intercollegiate basketball games, expanded office space, classrooms, and intramural facilities. The following activities would have to be undertaken before construction can begin.

Activity	Description	Immediate Predecessor	Time (weeks)
A	Survey building site	—	6
B	Develop initial design	—	8
C	Obtain board approval	A, B	12
D	Select architect	C	4
E	Establish budget	C	6
F	Finalize design	D, E	15
G	Obtain financing	E	12
H	Hire contractor	F, G	8

a. Draw a project network.
b. Identify the critical path.
c. Develop the activity schedule for the project.
d. Does it appear reasonable that construction of the athletic complex could begin 1 year after the decision to begin the project with the site survey and initial design plans? What is the expected completion time for the project?

9. Hamilton County Parks is planning to develop a new park and recreational area on a recently purchased 100-acre tract. Project development activities include clearing playground and picnic areas, constructing roads, constructing a shelter house, purchasing picnic equipment, and so on. The following network and activity times (in weeks) are being used in the planning, scheduling, and controlling of this project.

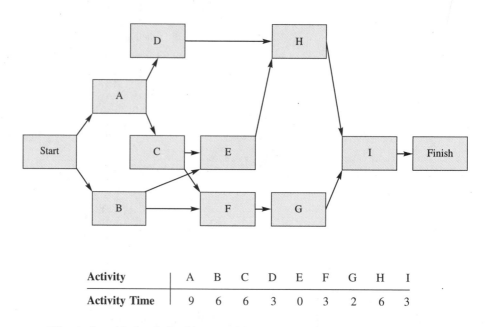

Activity	A	B	C	D	E	F	G	H	I
Activity Time	9	6	6	3	0	3	2	6	3

a. What is the critical path for this network?
b. Show the activity schedule for this project.
c. The park commissioner would like to open the park to the public within 6 months from the time the work on the project is started. Does this opening date appear to be feasible? Explain.

10. **SELF**Test The following estimates of activity times (in days) are available for a small project.

Activity	Optimistic	Most Probable	Pessimistic
A	4	5.0	6
B	8	9.0	10
C	7	7.5	11
D	7	9.0	10
E	6	7.0	9
F	5	6.0	7

a. Compute the expected activity completion times and the variance for each activity.

b. An analyst determined that the critical path consists of activities B–D–F. Compute the expected project completion time and the variance.

11. Building a backyard swimming pool consists of nine major activities. The activities and their immediate predecessors are shown. Develop the project network.

Activity	A	B	C	D	E	F	G	H	I
Immediate Predecessor	—	—	A, B	A, B	B	C	D	D, F	E, G, H

12. Assume that the activity time estimates (in days) for the swimming pool construction project in Problem 11 are

Activity	Optimistic	Most Probable	Pessimistic
A	3	5	6
B	2	4	6
C	5	6	7
D	7	9	10
E	2	4	6
F	1	2	3
G	5	8	10
H	6	8	10
I	3	4	5

a. What are the critical path activities?

b. What is the expected time to complete the project?

c. What is the probability that the project can be completed in 25 days or less?

13. **SELF**Test   Suppose that the following estimates of activity times (in weeks) were provided for the network shown in Problem 6.

Activity	Optimistic	Most Probable	Pessimistic
A	4.0	5.0	6.0
B	2.5	3.0	3.5
C	6.0	7.0	8.0
D	5.0	5.5	9.0
E	5.0	7.0	9.0
F	2.0	3.0	4.0
G	8.0	10.0	12.0
H	6.0	7.0	14.0

What is the probability that the project will be completed
a. Within 21 weeks?
b. Within 22 weeks?
c. Within 25 weeks?

14. Consider the following project network.

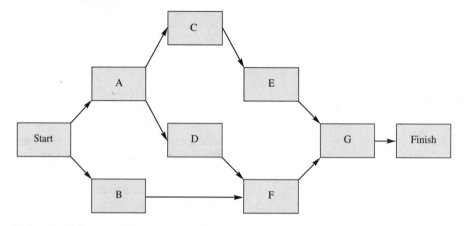

Estimates of the optimistic, most probable, and pessimistic times (in days) for the activities are

Activity	Optimistic	Most Probable	Pessimistic
A	5	6	7
B	5	12	13
C	6	8	10
D	4	10	10
E	5	6	13
F	7	7	10
G	4	7	10

a. Find the critical path.
b. How much slack time, if any, is there in activity C?
c. Determine the expected project completion time and the variance.
d. Find the probability that the project will be completed in 30 days or less.

15. Doug Casey is in charge of planning and coordinating next spring's sales management training program for his company. Doug has listed the following activity information for this project.

Activity	Description	Immediate Predecessor	Time (weeks) Optimistic	Most Probable	Pessimistic
A	Plan topic	—	1.5	2.0	2.5
B	Obtain speakers	A	2.0	2.5	6.0
C	List meeting locations	—	1.0	2.0	3.0
D	Select location	C	1.5	2.0	2.5
E	Finalize speaker travel plans	B, D	0.5	1.0	1.5
F	Make final check with speakers	E	1.0	2.0	3.0
G	Prepare and mail brochure	B, D	3.0	3.5	7.0
H	Take reservations	G	3.0	4.0	5.0
I	Handle last-minute details	F, H	1.5	2.0	2.5

    a. Draw a project network.

    b. Prepare an activity schedule.

    c. What are the critical path activities and the expected project completion time?

    d. If Doug wants a 0.99 probability of completing the project on time, how far ahead of the scheduled meeting date should he begin working on the project?

16. The Daugherty Porta-Vac project discussed in Section 10.2 had an expected project completion time of 17 weeks. The probability that the project could be completed in 20 weeks or less was found to be 0.9656. The noncritical paths in the Porta-Vac project network are

A–D–G–J

A–C–F–J

B–H–I–J

    a. Use the information in Table 10.5 to compute the expected time and variance for each of the paths shown.

    b. Compute the probability that each path will be completed in the desired 20-week period.

    c. Why is the computation of the probability of completing a project on time based on the analysis of the critical path? In what case, if any, would making the probability computation for a noncritical path be desirable?

17. The Porsche Shop, founded in 1985 by Dale Jensen, specializes in the restoration of vintage Porsche automobiles. One of Jensen's regular customers asked him to prepare an estimate for the restoration of a 1964 model 356SC Porsche. To estimate the time and cost to perform such a restoration, Jensen broke the restoration process into four separate activities: disassembly and initial preparation work (A), body restoration (B), engine restoration (C), and final assembly (D). Once activity A has been completed, activities B and C can be performed independently of each other; however, activity D can be started only if both activities B and C have been completed. Based on his inspection of the car, Jensen believes that the following time estimates (in days) are applicable.

Activity	Optimistic	Most Probable	Pessimistic
A	3	4	8
B	5	8	11
C	2	4	6
D	4	5	12

Jensen estimates that the parts needed to restore the body will cost $3000 and that the parts needed to restore the engine will cost $5000. His current labor costs are $400 per day.

    a. Develop a project network.

    b. What is the expected project completion time?

    c. Jensen's business philosophy is based on making decisions using a best and worst case scenario. Develop cost estimates for completing the restoration based on both a best and worst case analysis. Assume that the total restoration cost is the sum of the labor cost plus the material cost.

    d. If Jensen obtains the job with a bid that is based on the costs associated with an expected completion time, what is the probability that he will lose money on the job?

    e. If Jensen obtains the job based on a bid of $16,800, what is the probability that he will lose money on the job?

18. The manager of the Oak Hills Swimming Club is planning the club's swimming team program. The first team practice is scheduled for May 1. The activities, their immediate predecessors, and the activity time estimates (in weeks) are as follows.

Activity	Description	Immediate Predecessor	Time		
			Optimistic	Most Probable	Pessimistic
A	Meet with board	—	1	1	2
B	Hire coaches	A	4	6	8
C	Reserve pool	A	2	4	6
D	Announce program	B, C	1	2	3
E	Meet with coaches	B	2	3	4
F	Order team suits	A	1	2	3
G	Register swimmers	D	1	2	3
H	Collect fees	G	1	2	3
I	Plan first practice	E, H, F	1	1	1

a. Show the project network.

b. Develop an activity schedule.

c. What are the critical path activities and what is the expected project completion time?

d. If the club manager plans to start the project on February 1, what is the probability the swimming program will be ready by the scheduled May 1 date (13 weeks)? Should the manager begin planning the swimming program before February 1?

19. The product development group at Landon Corporation has been working on a new computer software product that has the potential to capture a large market share. Through outside sources, Landon's management has learned that a competitor is working to introduce a similar product. As a result, Landon's top management has increased its pressure on the product development group. The group's leader has turned to PERT/CPM as an aid to scheduling the activities remaining before the new product can be brought to the market. The project network is as follows.

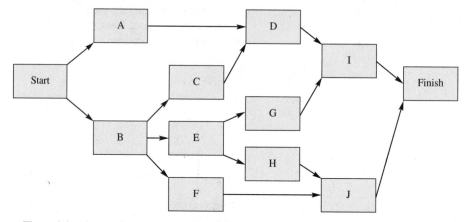

The activity time estimates (in weeks) are

Activity	Optimistic	Most Probable	Pessimistic
A	3.0	4.0	5.0
B	3.0	3.5	7.0
C	4.0	5.0	6.0
D	2.0	3.0	4.0
E	6.0	10.0	14.0
F	7.5	8.5	12.5
G	4.5	6.0	7.5
H	5.0	6.0	13.0
I	2.0	2.5	6.0
J	4.0	5.0	6.0

a. Develop an activity schedule for this project and identify the critical path activities.
b. What is the probability that the project will be completed so that Landon Corporation may introduce the new product within 25 weeks? Within 30 weeks?

20. Return to the computer installation project in Problem 7 and assume that the project has to be completed in 16 weeks. Crashing of the project is necessary. Relevant information is shown.

Activity	Time (weeks)		Cost ($)	
	Normal	Crash	Normal	Crash
A	3	1	900	1700
B	6	3	2000	4000
C	2	1	500	1000
D	5	3	1800	2400
E	4	3	1500	1850
F	3	1	3000	3900
G	9	4	8000	9800
H	3	2	1000	2000

a. Formulate a linear programming model that can be used to make the crashing decisions for this project.
b. Solve the linear programming model and make the minimum-cost crashing decisions. What is the added cost of meeting the 16-week completion time?
c. Develop a complete activity schedule based on the crashed activity times.

21. **SELF Test** Consider the following project network and activity times (in days).

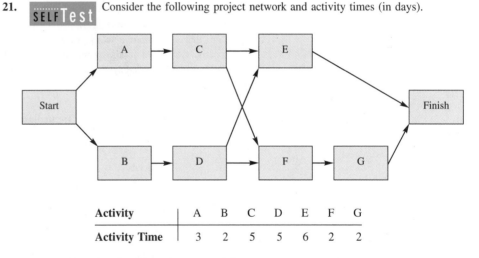

Activity	A	B	C	D	E	F	G
Activity Time	3	2	5	5	6	2	2

The crashing data for this project are as follows.

Activity	Time (days)		Total Cost ($)	
	Normal	Crash	Normal	Crash
A	3	2	800	1400
B	2	1	1200	1900
C	5	3	2000	2800
D	5	3	1500	2300
E	6	4	1800	2800
F	2	1	600	1000
G	2	1	500	1000

a. Find the critical path and the expected project completion time.
b. What is the total project cost using the normal times?

22. **SELFTest** Refer to Problem 21. Assume that management desires a 12-day project completion time.
    a. Formulate a linear programming model that can be used to assist with the crashing decisions.
    b. What activities should be crashed?
    c. What is the total project cost for the 12-day completion time?

23. Consider the project network shown. Note that the normal or expected activity times are denoted τ_i, $i = A, B, \ldots, I$. Let x_i = the earliest finish time for activity i. Formulate a linear programming model that can be used to determine the length of the critical path.

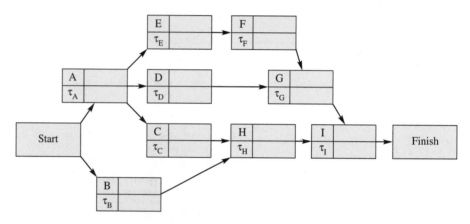

24. Office Automation, Inc., has developed a proposal for introducing a new computerized office system that will improve word processing and interoffice communications for a particular company. Contained in the proposal is a list of activities that must be accomplished to complete the new office system project. Shown is relevant information about the activities.

Activity	Description	Immediate Predecessor	Time (weeks)		Cost ($1000s)	
			Normal	Crash	Normal	Crash
A	Plan needs	—	10	8	30	70
B	Order equipment	A	8	6	120	150
C	Install equipment	B	10	7	100	160
D	Set up training lab	A	7	6	40	50
E	Conduct training course	D	10	8	50	75
F	Test system	C, E	3	3	60	—

a. Show the project network.
b. Develop an activity schedule.
c. What are the critical path activities and what is the expected project completion time?
d. Assume that the company wants to complete the project in 6 months or 26 weeks. What crashing decisions would be recommended to meet the desired completion time at the least possible cost? Work through the network and attempt to make the crashing decisions by inspection.
e. Develop an activity schedule for the crashed project.
f. What added project cost is required to meet the 6-month completion time?

25. Because Landon Corporation (see Problem 19) is being pressured to complete the product development project at the earliest possible date, the project leader has requested that the possibility of crashing the project be evaluated.

    a. Formulate a linear programming model that could be used in making the crashing decisions.

    b. What information would have to be provided before the linear programming model could be implemented?

Case Problem   Warehouse Expansion

R. C. Coleman distributes a variety of food products that are sold through grocery store and supermarket outlets. The company receives orders directly from the individual outlets, with a typical order requesting the delivery of several cases of anywhere from 20 to 50 different products. Under the company's current warehouse operation, warehouse clerks dispatch order-picking personnel to fill each order and have the goods moved to the warehouse shipping area. Because of the high labor costs and relatively low productivity of hand order-picking, the company has decided to automate the warehouse operation by installing a computer-controlled order-picking system, along with a conveyor system for moving goods from storage to the warehouse shipping area.

R. C. Coleman's director of material management has been named the project manager in charge of the automated warehouse system. After consulting with members of the engineering staff and warehouse management personnel, the director has compiled a list of activities associated with the project. The optimistic, most probable, and pessimistic times (in weeks) have also been provided for each activity.

Activity	Description	Immediate Predecessor
A	Determine equipment needs	—
B	Obtain vendor proposals	—
C	Select vendor	A, B
D	Order system	C
E	Design new warehouse layout	C
F	Design warehouse	E
G	Design computer interface	C
H	Interface computer	D, F, G
I	Install system	D, F
J	Train system operators	H
K	Test system	I, J

Activity	Time		
	Optimistic	Most Probable	Pessimistic
A	4	6	8
B	6	8	16
C	2	4	6
D	8	10	24
E	7	10	13
F	4	6	8
G	4	6	20
H	4	6	8
I	4	6	14
J	3	4	5
K	2	4	6

Managerial Report

· ·

Develop a report that presents the activity schedule and expected project completion time for the warehouse expansion project. Include a project network in the report. In addition, take into consideration the following issues.

1. R. C. Coleman's top management has established a required 40-week completion time for the project. Can this completion time be achieved? Include probability information in your discussion. What recommendations do you have if the 40-week completion time is required?
2. Suppose that management requests that activity times be shortened to provide an 80% chance of meeting the 40-week completion time. If the variance in the project completion time is the same as you found in part (a), how much should the expected project completion time be shortened to achieve the goal of an 80% chance of completion within 40 weeks?
3. Using the expected activity times as the normal times and the following crashing information, determine the activity crashing decisions and revised activity schedule for the warehouse expansion project.

Activity	Crashed Activity Time (weeks)	Cost ($) Normal	Cost ($) Crashed
A	4	1,000	1,900
B	7	1,000	1,800
C	2	1,500	2,700
D	8	2,000	3,200
E	7	5,000	8,000
F	4	3,000	4,100
G	5	8,000	10,250
H	4	5,000	6,400
I	4	10,000	12,400
J	3	4,000	4,400
K	3	5,000	5,500

MANAGEMENT SCIENCE in practice

· ·

Seasongood & Mayer
Cincinnati, Ohio

Seasongood & Mayer, established in 1887, is an investment securities firm that engages in the following areas of municipal finance:

1. Underwriting new issues of municipal bonds
2. Trading—for example, acting as a market maker for the buying and selling of previously issued bonds
3. Investment banking—that is, the process of obtaining money from the capital markets at the lowest possible cost

The major applications of management science at Seasongood & Mayer are in the investment banking area. One particular application involved the use of PERT/CPM in the introduction of a $31 million hospital revenue bond issue.

Scheduling the Introduction of a Bond Issue

In any major building project there are certain common steps:

1. Defining the project
2. Determining the cost of the project
3. Financing the project

The investment banker's role in building projects is to develop the method of financing that will result in the owner's receiving

—Continued on next page

—Continued from previous page

the necessary funds in a timely manner. In a hospital building project, such as the one we will be discussing, the typical method of financing is tax-free hospital revenue bonds.

The construction cost for the building project is an important factor in determining the best approach to financing. Normally, the construction cost is based on a bid submitted by a contractor or a construction manager. However, this cost is usually guaranteed only for a specified period of time, such as 60–90 days. The major function of the hospital's investment banker is to arrange the timing of the financing in such a way that the proceeds of the bond issue can be made available within the time limit of the guaranteed-price construction bid. Since most hospitals must have the proceeds of their permanent long-term financing in hand prior to committing to major construction contracts, the investment banker's role is a significant one.

To arrange for the financing, the investment banker must coordinate the activities of hospital attorneys, the bond counsel, and so on. The cooperation of all parties and the coordination of project activities are best achieved if everyone recognizes the interdependency of the activities and the necessity of completing individual tasks in a timely manner. Seasongood & Mayer has found PERT/CPM to be useful in scheduling and coordinating such a project.

As managing underwriter for a $31,050,000 issue of Hospital Facilities Revenue Bonds for Providence Hospital in Hamilton County, Ohio, Seasongood & Mayer used the PERT/CPM critical path procedure to coordinate and schedule the project financing activities. Descriptions of the activities, times required, and immediate predecessors are given in Table 10.10. The project network is shown in Figure 10.17. The critical path activities K–L–M–N–P–Q–R–S–U–W resulted in a scheduled project completion time of 29.14 weeks. Specific schedules showing start and finish times for all activities were used to keep the entire project on track. The use of PERT/CPM was instrumental in helping Seasongood & Mayer obtain financing for this project within the time specified in the construction bid.

Questions

1. What is the role of the investment banker in building projects?
2. For the hospital project described, what is the primary objective of the investment banker?
3. Perform the critical path calculations for the project network shown in Figure 10.17. Is there more than one critical path? Discuss.

—Continued on next page

Figure 10.17 Seasongood & Mayer Project Network

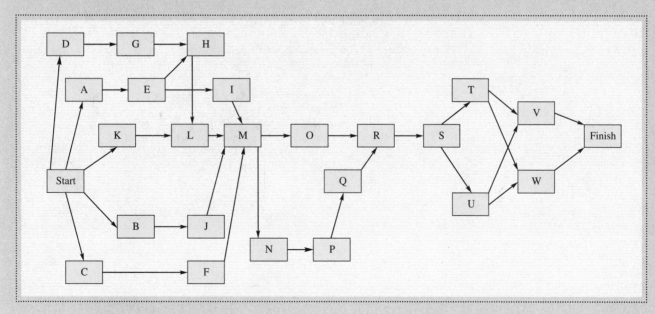

—Continued from previous page

Table 10.10

Activities for the Seasongood & Mayer Project

Activity	Time Required (weeks)	Description of Activity	Immediate Predecessor
A	4	Drafting and distribution of legal documents	—
B	3	Preparation and distribution of unaudited financial statements of hospital	—
C	2	Drafting and distribution of hospital history, description of services, and existing facilities for Preliminary Official Statement (POS)	—
D	8	Drafting and distribution of demand portion of feasibility study	—
E	4	Review (additions/deletions) and approval as to form of legal documents	A
F	1	Review (additions/deletions) and approval of history, etc., for POS	C
G	4	Review (additions/deletions) and approval of demand portion of feasibility study	D
H	2	Drafting and distribution of financial portion (as to form) of feasibility study	E, G
I	2	Drafting and distribution of plan of financing and all pertinent facts relevant to the bond transaction for POS	E
J	0.5	Review and approval of unaudited financial statements	B
K	20	Receipt of firm price for project	—
L	1	Review (additions/deletions), approval, and completion of financial portion of feasibility study	H, K
M	1	Drafting of POS completed	F, I, J, L
N	0.14	Distribution of all material to bond rating services	M
O	0.28	Printing and distribution of POS to all interested parties	M
P	1	Presentation to bond rating services (Standard & Poor's, Moody's)	N
Q	1	Receipt of bond rating	P
R	2	Marketing of bonds	O, Q
S	0	Execution of Purchase Contract	R
T	0.14	Authorization and completion of Final Official Statement, completion of legal documents	S
U	3	Fulfillment of all terms and conditions of Purchase Contract	S
V	0	Bond proceeds available to hospital	T, U
W	0	Hospital able to sign construction contract	T, U

Inventory Models

Inventory refers to idle goods or materials that are held by an organization for use sometime in the future. Items carried in inventory include raw materials, purchased parts, components, subassemblies, work-in-process, finished goods, and supplies. One reason organizations maintain inventory is that it is rarely possible to predict sales levels, production times, demand, and usage needs exactly. Thus, inventory serves as a buffer against uncertain and fluctuating usage and keeps a supply of items available in case the items are needed by the organization or its customers. While inventory serves an important and essential role, the expense associated with financing and maintaining inventories is a substantial part of the cost of doing business. In large organizations, the cost associated with inventory can run into the millions of dollars.

Two important questions that must be answered in order to effectively manage inventories are as follows:

1. *How much* should be ordered when the inventory for an item is replenished?
2. *When* should the inventory be replenished?

The purpose of this chapter is to show how quantitative models can assist in making these decisions.

We will first consider *deterministic* inventory models in which we assume that the rate of demand for the item is constant or nearly constant. Later we will consider *probabilistic* inventory models in which the demand for the item fluctuates and can be described only in probabilistic terms. In addition, we will describe an inventory management procedure referred to as *material requirements planning* (MRP); this approach is suited for managing inventories of raw materials, subassemblies, and components whose demand is directly dependent on the demand for the final products in the inventory system. Finally, in the last section of the chapter, we discuss a philosophy of material management and control known as *just-in-time* (JIT); the primary objective of JIT is to eliminate all sources of waste, including unnecessary inventory.

11.1   Economic Order Quantity (EOQ) Model

The *economic order quantity (EOQ) model* is applicable when the demand for an item has a constant, or nearly constant, rate and when the entire quantity ordered arrives in inventory at one point in time. The *constant demand rate* assumption means that the same number of units is taken from inventory each period of time, such as 5 units every day, 25 units every week, 100 units every 4-week period, and so on.

To illustrate the EOQ model, let us consider the situation faced by the R & B Beverage Company. R & B Beverage is a distributor of beer, wine, and soft drink products. From a main warehouse located in Columbus, Ohio, R & B supplies nearly 1000 retail stores with beverage products. The beer inventory, which constitutes about 40% of the company's total inventory, averages approximately 50,000 cases. With an average cost per case of approximately $8, R & B estimates the value of its beer inventory to be $400,000.

The warehouse manager has decided to do a detailed study of the inventory costs associated with Bub Beer, the number-one-selling R & B beer. The purpose of the study is to establish the *how-much*-to-order and the *when*-to-order decisions for Bub Beer that will result in the lowest possible total cost. As the first step in the study, the warehouse manager has obtained the following demand data for the past 10 weeks:

Week	Demand (cases)
1	2,000
2	2,025
3	1,950
4	2,000
5	2,100
6	2,050
7	2,000
8	1,975
9	1,900
10	2,000
Total cases	20,000
Average cases per week	2,000

Strictly speaking, these weekly demand figures do not show a constant demand rate. However, given the relatively low variability exhibited by the weekly demand, inventory planning with a constant demand rate of 2000 cases per week appears acceptable. In practice, you will find that the actual inventory situation seldom, if ever, satisfies the assumptions of the model exactly. Thus, in any particular application, the manager must determine whether the model assumptions are close enough to reality for the model to be useful. In this situation, since demand varies from a low of 1900 cases to a high of 2100 cases, the assumption of constant demand of 2000 cases per week appears to be a reasonable approximation.

The how-much-to-order decision involves selecting an order quantity that draws a compromise between (1) keeping small inventories and ordering frequently and (2) keeping large inventories and ordering infrequently. The first alternative can result in undesirably high ordering costs, while the second alternative can result in undesirably high inventory holding costs. To find an optimal compromise between these conflicting alternatives, let us consider a mathematical model that will show the total cost as the sum of the holding cost and the ordering cost.[1]

Holding costs are the costs associated with maintaining or carrying a given level of inventory; these costs depend on the size of the inventory. First, there is the cost of financing the inventory investment. When a firm borrows money, it incurs an interest charge; if the firm uses its own money, it experiences an opportunity cost associated with not being able to use the money for other investments. In either case, an interest cost exists for the capital tied up in inventory. This *cost of capital* is usually expressed as a percentage of the amount invested. R & B estimates its cost of capital at an annual rate of 18%.

There are a number of other holding costs, such as insurance, taxes, breakage, pilferage, and warehouse overhead, that also depend on the value of the inventory. R & B estimates these other costs at an annual rate of approximately 7% of the value of its inventory. Thus, the total holding cost for the R & B beer inventory is 25% of the value of the inventory.

Assume that the cost of one case of Bub Beer is $8. Since R & B estimates its annual holding cost to be 25% of the value of its inventory, the cost of holding one case of Bub Beer in inventory for 1 year is 0.25($8) = $2.00. Note that defining the holding cost as a percentage of the value of the product is convenient because it is easily transferable to other products. For example, a case of Carle's Red Ribbon Beer, which costs $7.00 per case, would have an annual holding cost of 0.25($7.00) = $1.75 per case.

The next step in the inventory analysis is to determine the *ordering cost*. This cost, which is considered fixed regardless of the order quantity, covers the preparation of the voucher, the processing of the order including payment, postage, telephone, transportation, invoice verification, receiving, and so on. For R & B Beverage, the largest portion of the ordering cost involves the salaries of the purchasers. An analysis of the purchasing process showed that a purchaser spends approximately 45 minutes preparing and processing an order for Bub Beer. With a wage rate and fringe benefit cost for purchasers of $20 per hour, the labor portion of the ordering cost is $15. Making allowances for paper, postage, telephone, transportation, and receiving costs at $17 per order, the manager estimates that the ordering cost is $32 per order. That is, R & B is paying $32 per order regardless of the quantity requested in the order.

The holding cost, ordering cost, and demand information are the three data items that must be known prior to the use of the EOQ model. Since these data have now been developed for the R & B problem, let us see how they are used to develop a total-cost model. We begin by defining Q to be the order quantity. Thus, the how-much-to-order decision involves finding the value of Q that will minimize the sum of holding and ordering costs.

The inventory level for Bub will have a maximum value of Q units when an order of size Q is received from the supplier. R & B will then satisfy customer demand from inventory until the inventory is depleted, at which time another shipment of Q units will be received. Suppose that R & B is open 5 days each week. Thus, assuming a constant demand rate of 2000 cases per week or 400 cases per day, the graph of the inventory level for Bub Beer is as shown in Figure 11.1. Note that the graph indicates an average inventory level of $\frac{1}{2}Q$ for the period in question. This should appear reasonable since the maximum inventory level is Q, the minimum is zero, and the inventory level declines at a constant rate over the period.

---

[1]While management scientists typically refer to "total-cost" models for inventory systems, often these models describe only the total *variable* or total *relevant* costs for the decision being considered. Costs that are not affected by the how-much-to-order decision are considered fixed or constant and are not included in the model.

Figure 11.1 shows the inventory pattern during one order cycle of length T. As time goes on, this pattern will repeat. The complete inventory pattern is shown in Figure 11.2. If the average inventory during each cycle is $\frac{1}{2}Q$, the average inventory level over any number of cycles is also $\frac{1}{2}Q$.

The holding cost can be calculated using the average inventory level. That is, we can calculate the holding cost by multiplying the average inventory level by the cost of carrying one unit in inventory for the stated period. The period selected for the model is up to you; it could be 1 week, 1 month, 1 year, or more. However, since the holding cost for many industries and businesses is expressed as an *annual* percentage, most inventory models are developed on an *annual cost* basis.

Let

I = annual holding cost rate
C = unit cost of the inventory item
C_h = annual cost of holding one unit in inventory

The annual cost of holding one unit in inventory is

$$C_h = IC \tag{11.1}$$

Figure 11.1

Inventory Level for Bub Beer

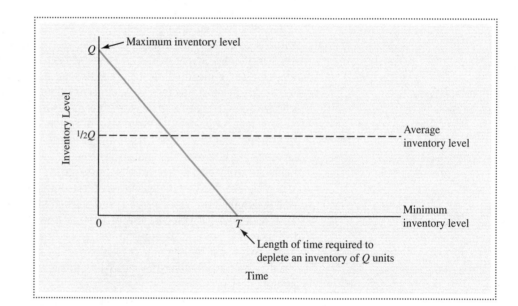

Figure 11.2

Inventory Pattern for the EOQ Inventory Model

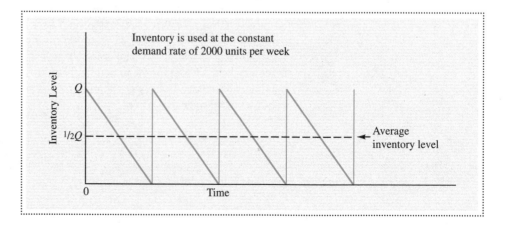

The general equation for the annual holding cost for the average inventory of $\frac{1}{2}Q$ units is as follows:

$$\text{Annual} \atop \text{holding cost} = \left(\begin{matrix} \text{Average} \\ \text{inventory} \\ \text{level} \end{matrix} \right) \left(\begin{matrix} \text{Annual holding} \\ \text{cost} \\ \text{per unit} \end{matrix} \right)$$

$$= \frac{1}{2}QC_h \qquad (11.2)$$

To complete the total-cost model, we must now include the annual ordering cost. The goal is to express the annual ordering cost in terms of the order quantity Q. The first question is, How many orders will be placed during the year? Let D denote the annual demand for the product. For R & B Beverage, $D =$ (52 weeks)(2000 cases per week) = 104,000 cases per year. We know that by ordering Q units every time we order, we will have to place D/Q orders per year. If C_o is the cost of placing one order, the general equation for the annual ordering cost is as follows:

$$\text{Annual} \atop \text{ordering cost} = \left(\begin{matrix} \text{Number of} \\ \text{orders} \\ \text{per year} \end{matrix} \right) \left(\begin{matrix} \text{Cost} \\ \text{per} \\ \text{order} \end{matrix} \right)$$

$$= \left(\frac{D}{Q} \right) C_o \qquad (11.3)$$

Thus, the total annual cost, denoted TC, can be expressed as follows:

$$\text{Total} \atop \text{annual} \atop \text{cost} = \text{Annual} \atop \text{holding} \atop \text{cost} + \text{Annual} \atop \text{ordering} \atop \text{cost}$$

$$TC = \frac{1}{2}QC_h + \frac{D}{Q}C_o \qquad (11.4)$$

Using the Bub Beer data ($C_h = IC = (0.25)(\$8) = \$2$, $C_o = \$32$, and $D = 104,000$), the total annual cost model is

$$TC = \frac{1}{2}Q(\$2) + \frac{104,000}{Q}(\$32) = Q + \frac{3,328,000}{Q}$$

The development of the total-cost model has gone a long way toward solving the inventory problem. We now are able to express the total annual cost as a function of *how much* should be ordered. The development of a realistic total-cost model is perhaps the most important part of the application of management science to inventory decision making. Equation (11.4) is the general total-cost equation for inventory situations in which the assumptions of the economic order quantity model are valid.

The How-Much-to-Order Decision

The next step is to find the order quantity Q that will minimize the total annual cost for Bub Beer. Using a trial-and-error approach, we can compute the total annual cost for several possible order quantities. As a starting point, let us consider $Q = 8000$. The total annual cost for Bub Beer is

$$TC = Q + \frac{3,328,000}{Q}$$

$$= 8000 + \frac{3,328,000}{8000} = \$8416$$

A trial order quantity of 5000 gives

$$TC = 5000 + \frac{3,328,000}{5000} = \$5666$$

The results of several other trial order quantities are shown in Table 11.1. As can be seen, the lowest cost solution is around 2000 cases. Graphs of the annual holding and ordering costs, and total annual costs are shown in Figure 11.3.

The advantage of the trial-and-error approach is that it is rather easy to do and provides the total annual cost for a number of possible order quantity decisions. In this case, the minimum-cost order quantity appears to be approximately 2000 cases. The disadvantage of this approach, however, is that it does not provide the exact minimum-cost order quantity.

Refer to Figure 11.3. The minimum total-cost order quantity is denoted by an order size of Q^*. By using differential calculus, it can be shown (see Appendix 11.1) that the value of Q^* that minimizes the total annual cost is given by the formula

$$Q^* = \sqrt{\frac{2DC_o}{C_h}} \tag{11.5}$$

Table 11.1

Annual Holding, Ordering, and Total Costs for Various Order Quantities of Bub Beer

| | **Annual Cost** | | |
Order Quantity	Holding	Ordering	Total
5000	$5000	$ 666	$5666
4000	4000	832	4832
3000	3000	1109	4109
2000	2000	1664	3664
1000	1000	3328	4328

Figure 11.3

Annual Holding, Ordering, and Total Costs for Bub Beer

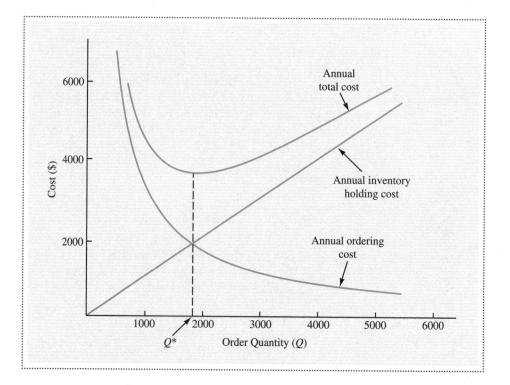

This formula is referred to as the *economic order quantity (EOQ) formula*.

Using equation (11.5), the minimum total-annual-cost order quantity for Bub Beer is

$$Q^* = \sqrt{\frac{2(104{,}000)32}{2}} = 1824 \text{ cases}$$

The use of an order quantity of 1824 in equation (11.4) shows that the minimum-cost inventory policy for Bub Beer has a total annual cost of \$3649. Note that $Q^* = 1824$ has balanced the holding and ordering costs. Check for yourself to see that these costs are equal.[2] (Problem 2 at the end of the chapter will ask you to show that equal holding and ordering costs is a property of the EOQ model.)

The When-to-Order Decision

Now that we know how much to order, we want to address the question of *when* to order. To answer this question, we need to introduce the concept of inventory position. The *inventory position* for an item is defined as the amount of inventory on hand plus the amount of inventory on order. The when-to-order decision is expressed in terms of a *reorder point*—the inventory position at which a new order should be placed.

The manufacturer of Bub Beer guarantees a 2-day delivery on any order placed by R & B Beverage. Hence, assuming a constant demand rate of 2000 cases per week or 400 cases per day, we expect (2 days)(400 cases/day) = 800 cases of Bub to be sold during the 2 days it takes a new order to reach the R & B warehouse. In inventory terminology, the 2-day delivery period is referred to as the *lead time* for a new order, and the 800-case demand anticipated during this period is referred to as the *lead-time demand*. Thus, R & B should order a new shipment of Bub Beer from the manufacturer when the inventory level reaches 800 cases. For inventory systems using the constant demand rate assumption and a fixed lead time, the reorder point is the same as the lead-time demand. For these systems, the general expression for the reorder point is as follows:

$$r = dm \tag{11.6}$$

where

$$r = \text{reorder point}$$
$$d = \text{demand per day}$$
$$m = \text{lead time for a new order in days}$$

The question of how frequently the order will be placed can now be answered. The period between orders is referred to as the *cycle time*. Previously in equation (11.2), we defined D/Q as the number of orders that will be placed in a year. Thus, $D/Q^* = 104{,}000/1824 = 57$ is the number of orders R & B Beverage will place for Bub Beer each year. If R & B places 57 orders over 250 working days, it will order approximately every $250/57 = 4.4$ working days. Thus, the cycle time is 4.4 working days. The general expression for a cycle time[3] of T days is given by

$$T = \frac{250}{D/Q^*} = \frac{250Q^*}{D} \tag{11.7}$$

---

[2]Actually, Q^* from equation (11.5) is 1824.28, but since we cannot order fractional cases of beer, a Q^* of 1824 is shown. This value of Q^* may cause a few cents deviation between the two costs. If Q^* is used at its exact value, the holding and ordering costs will be exactly the same.

[3] This general expression for cycle time is based on 250 working days per year. If the firm operated 300 working days per year and wanted to express cycle time in terms of working days, the cycle time would be given by $T = 300Q^*/D$.

Sensitivity Analysis in the EOQ Model

Even though substantial time may have been spent in arriving at the cost per order ($32) and the holding cost rate (25%), we should realize that these figures are at best good estimates. Thus, we may want to consider how much the recommended order quantity would change if the estimated ordering and holding costs had been different. To determine this, we can calculate the recommended order quantity under several different cost conditions; Table 11.2 shows the minimum total-cost order quantity for several cost possibilities. As you can see from the table, the value of $Q*$ appears relatively stable, even with some variations in the cost estimates. Based on these results, it appears that the best order quantity for Bub Beer is somewhere around 1700–2000 cases. If operated properly, the total cost for the Bub Beer inventory system should be close to $3400–$3800 per year. We also note that there is very little risk associated with implementing the calculated order quantity of 1824. For example, if holding cost rate = 24%, $C_o = \$34$, and the true optimal order quantity $Q* = 1919$, there is only a $5 increase in the total annual cost; that is, $3690 − $3685 = $5, with $Q = 1824$.

From the preceding analysis, we would say that this EOQ model is insensitive to small variations or errors in the cost estimates. This is a property of EOQ models in general, which indicates that if we have at least reasonable estimates of ordering cost and holding cost, we can expect to obtain a good approximation of the true minimum-cost order quantity.

The Manager's Use of the EOQ Model

The EOQ model results in a recommended order quantity of 1824 units. Is this the final decision, or should the manager's judgment enter into the establishment of the final inventory policy? Although the model has provided a good order-quantity recommendation, it may not have taken into account all aspects of the inventory situation. As a result, the decision maker may want to modify the final order-quantity recommendation to meet the unique circumstances of his or her inventory situation. In this case, the warehouse manager felt that it would be desirable to increase the order quantity from 1824 cases to 2000 cases in order to have an order quantity equal to 5 working days' demand. By doing so, R & B Beverage can maintain a weekly order cycle.

The warehouse manager also realized that the EOQ model was based on the constant demand rate assumption of 2000 cases per week. While this is a good approximation, we must also recognize that sometimes the demand exceeds 2000 cases per week. If a reorder point of 800 cases is used, we would be expecting an 800-case demand during the lead time and the new order to arrive exactly when the inventory level reached zero. Such

Table 11.2	Possible Inventory Holding Cost (%)	Possible Cost Per Order	Optimal Order Quantity ($Q*$)	Projected Total Annual Cost	
				Using $Q*$	Using $Q = 1824$
Optimal Order Quantities for Several Cost Possibilities	24	$30	1803	$3461	$3462
	24	34	1919	3685	3690
	26	30	1732	3603	3607
	26	34	1844	3835	3836

close timing would have little room for error, and the scheduling of arrivals would be critical if stockouts were to be avoided. To protect against shortages due to higher-than-expected demands or slightly delayed incoming orders, the warehouse manager recommended a 1200-case reorder point. Thus, under normal conditions, R & B Beverage will order 2000 cases of Bub whenever the current inventory reaches 1200 cases. During the expected 2-day lead time, 800 cases should be demanded, and 400 cases should be in inventory when an order arrives. The extra 400 cases serve as a safety precaution against a higher-than-expected demand or a delayed incoming order. In general, the amount by which the reorder point exceeds the expected lead-time demand is referred to as *safety stock.*

The decisions to adjust the order quantity and reorder point were purely judgment decisions and were not necessarily made with a minimum-cost objective in mind. However, they are examples of how managerial judgment might interface with the inventory decision model to arrive at a sound inventory policy. The final decision of $Q =$ 2000 with a 400-case safety stock resulted in a total annual cost of $4464.[4]

How Has the EOQ Decision Model Helped?

The EOQ model has objectively included holding and ordering costs and, with the aid of some management judgment, has led to a low-cost inventory policy. In addition, the general optimal order-quantity model, equation (11.5), is potentially applicable to other R & B products. For example, Red Ribbon Beer ($7/case), which has an ordering cost of $32, a constant demand rate of 1200 cases per week (62,400 cases/year), and a 2-day lead-time period, has a recommended order quantity of

$$Q* = \sqrt{\frac{2(62,400)(32)}{(0.25)(7)}} = 1511 \text{ cases}$$

a cycle time of $T = [250(1511)]/62,400 = 6.05$ days, and a reorder point of $r = (240)(2) = 480$ cases.

Problem 1 provides practice in applying the EOQ model to another R & B product.

A Summary of the EOQ Model Assumptions

To use the optimal order-quantity and reorder-point model described here, an analyst must make assumptions about how the inventory system operates. The EOQ model with its economic order quantity formula is based on some specific assumptions about the R & B inventory system. A summary of the assumptions for this model is provided in Table 11.3. Before using the EOQ formula, you should carefully review these assumptions to ensure that they are applicable to the inventory system being analyzed. If the assumptions are not reasonable, a different inventory model should be sought.

There are various types of inventory systems in practice, and the inventory models presented in the following sections alter one or more of the EOQ model assumptions shown in Table 11.3 to meet the needs of the different systems. When the assumptions change, a different inventory model with different optimal operating policies becomes necessary.

---

[4]A Q of 2000 units resulted in a total cost of $3664 (see Table 11.1). The additional safety stock inventory of 400 units increases the average inventory by 400 units since it is on hand all year long. Thus, the inventory carrying charge is increased by 2(400) = $800, the total cost of the revised policy is $3664 + $800 = $4464.

Table 11.3

Summary of the EOQ Model Assumptions

1. Demand D is deterministic and occurs at a constant rate.
2. The order quantity Q is the same for each order. The inventory level increases by Q units each time an order is received.
3. The cost per order, C_o, is constant and does not depend on the quantity ordered.
4. The purchase cost per unit, C, is constant and does not depend on the quantity ordered.
5. The inventory holding cost per unit per time period, C_h, is constant. The total inventory holding cost depends on both C_h and the size of the inventory.
6. Shortages such as stockouts or backorders are not permitted.
7. The lead time for an order is constant.
8. The inventory position is reviewed continuously. As a result, an order is placed as soon as the inventory position reaches the reorder point.

NOTES & comments

With relatively long lead times, the lead-time demand and the resulting reorder point r, determined by equation (11.6), may exceed Q^*. If this condition occurs, there will be at least one order outstanding when a new order is placed. For example, assume that Bub Beer has a lead time of $m = 6$ days. With a daily demand of $d = 400$ cases, equation (11.6) shows that the reorder point would be $r = dm = 6 \times 400 = 2400$ cases. Thus, a new order for Bub Beer should be placed whenever the inventory position (the amount of inventory on hand plus the amount of inventory on order) reaches 2400. With an economic order quantity of $Q^* = 1824$ cases, the inventory position of 2400 cases occurs when one order of 1824 cases is outstanding and $2400 - 1824 = 576$ cases are on hand.

11.2 Economic Production Lot Size Model

The inventory model presented in this section is similar to the EOQ model in that we are attempting to determine *how much* we should order and *when* the order should be placed. We will again assume a constant demand rate. However, instead of assuming that the goods arrive in a shipment of size Q^*, as in the EOQ model, we will assume that units are supplied to inventory at a constant rate over several days or several weeks. The *constant supply rate* assumption implies that the same number of units is supplied to inventory each period of time (e.g., 10 units every day or 50 units every week). This model is designed for production situations in which, once an order is placed, production begins and a constant number of units is added to inventory each day until the production run has been completed.

If we have a production system that produces 50 units per day and we decide to schedule 10 days of production, we have a $50(10) = 500$-unit production lot size. In general, if we let Q indicate the production lot size, the approach to the inventory decisions will be similar to the EOQ model; that is, we will attempt to build a holding and

Figure 11.4
. . . .
**Inventory Pattern for the
Production Lot Size Inventory
Model**

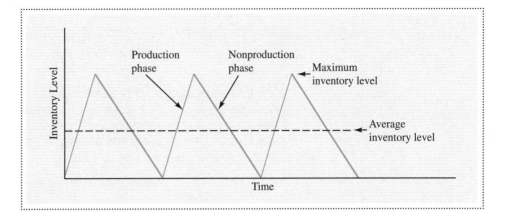

ordering cost model that expresses the total cost as a function of the production lot size. Then we will attempt to find the production lot size that minimizes the total cost.

One other condition that should be mentioned at this time is that the model will only apply to situations where the production rate is greater than the demand rate; the production system must be able to satisfy demand. For instance, if the constant demand rate is 2000 units per week, the production rate must be at least 2000 units per week to satisfy demand.

During the production run, demand will be reducing the inventory while production will be adding to inventory. Since we have assumed that the production rate exceeds the demand rate, each day during a production run we will be producing more units than are demanded. Thus, the excess production will cause a gradual inventory buildup during the production period. When the production run is completed, the continuing demand will cause the inventory to gradually decline until a new production run is started. The inventory pattern for this system is shown in Figure 11.4.

As in the EOQ model, we are now dealing with two costs, the holding cost and the ordering cost. While the holding cost is identical to the definition in the EOQ model, the interpretation of the ordering cost is slightly different. In fact, in a production situation the ordering cost is more correctly referred to as the production *setup cost*. This cost, which includes labor, material, and lost production costs incurred while preparing the production system for operation, is a fixed cost that occurs for every production run regardless of the production lot size.

The Total Cost Model
. . . .

Let us begin building the production lot size model by writing the holding cost in terms of the production lot size Q. Again, the approach will be to develop an expression for average inventory and then establish the holding costs associated with the average inventory level. We will use a 1-year time period and an annual cost for the model.

In the EOQ model the average inventory is one-half the maximum inventory or $\frac{1}{2}Q$. Figure 11.4 shows that for a production lot size model there is a constant inventory buildup rate during the production run and a constant inventory depletion rate during the nonproduction period; thus, the average inventory will be one-half of the maximum inventory level. However, in this inventory system the production lot size Q does not go into inventory at one point in time, and thus the inventory level never reaches a level of Q units.

To show how we can compute the maximum inventory level, let

d = daily demand rate for the product
p = daily production rate for the product
t = number of days for a production run

Since we are assuming p will be larger than d, the daily inventory buildup rate during the production phase is $p - d$. If we run production for t days and place $p - d$ units in inventory each day, the inventory level at the end of the production run will be $(p - d)t$. From Figure 11.4 we can see that the inventory level at the end of the production run is also the maximum inventory level. Thus

$$\text{Maximum inventory level} = (p - d)t \tag{11.8}$$

If we know we are producing a production lot size of Q units at a daily production rate of p units, then $Q = pt$, and the length of the production run t must be

$$t = \frac{Q}{p} \text{ days} \tag{11.9}$$

Thus

$$\text{Maximum inventory level} = (p - d)t = (p - d)\left(\frac{Q}{p}\right)$$

$$= \left(1 - \frac{d}{p}\right)Q \tag{11.10}$$

The average inventory level, which is one-half of the maximum inventory level, is given by

$$\text{Average inventory level} = \frac{1}{2}\left(1 - \frac{d}{p}\right)Q \tag{11.11}$$

With an annual per unit holding cost of C_h, the general equation for annual holding cost is as follows:

$$\begin{pmatrix} \text{Annual} \\ \text{holding cost} \end{pmatrix} = \begin{pmatrix} \text{Average} \\ \text{inventory} \\ \text{level} \end{pmatrix}\begin{pmatrix} \text{Annual holding} \\ \text{cost} \\ \text{per unit} \end{pmatrix}$$

$$= \frac{1}{2}\left(1 - \frac{d}{p}\right)QC_h \tag{11.12}$$

If D is the annual demand for the product and C_o is the setup cost for a production run, then the annual setup cost, which takes the place of the annual ordering cost in the EOQ model, is as follows:

$$\text{Annual setup cost} = \begin{pmatrix} \text{Number of production} \\ \text{runs per year} \end{pmatrix}\begin{pmatrix} \text{Setup cost} \\ \text{per run} \end{pmatrix} \tag{11.13}$$

$$= \frac{D}{Q}C_o$$

Thus, the total annual cost (TC) model is

$$TC = \frac{1}{2}\left(1 - \frac{d}{p}\right)QC_h + \frac{D}{Q}C_o \tag{11.14}$$

Suppose that a production facility operates 250 days per year; 115 days are idle due to weekends and holidays. Then we can write daily demand d in terms of annual demand D as follows:

$$d = \frac{D}{250}$$

Now let P denote the annual production for the product if the product were produced every day. Then

$$P = 250p \quad \text{and} \quad p = \frac{P}{250}$$

Thus[5]

$$\frac{d}{p} = \frac{D/250}{P/250} = \frac{D}{P}$$

Therefore, we can write the total annual cost model as follows:

$$TC = \frac{1}{2}\left(1 - \frac{D}{P}\right)QC_h + \frac{D}{Q}C_o \quad (11.15)$$

Equations (11.14) and (11.15) are equivalent. However, equation (11.15) may be used more frequently since an *annual* cost model tends to make the analyst think in terms of collecting *annual* demand data (D) and *annual* production data (P) rather than daily data.

Finding the Economic Production Lot Size

Given estimates of the holding cost (C_h), setup cost, (C_o), annual demand rate (D), and annual production rate (P), we could use a trial-and-error approach to compute the total annual cost for various production lot sizes (Q). However, this is not necessary; we can use the minimum-cost formula for $Q*$ that has been developed using differential calculus (see Appendix 11.3). The equation is as follows:

$$Q* = \sqrt{\frac{2DC_o}{(1 - D/P)C_h}} \quad (11.16)$$

An Example   Beauty Bar Soap is produced on a production line that has an annual capacity of 60,000 cases. The annual demand is estimated at 26,000 cases, with the demand rate essentially constant throughout the year. The cleaning, preparation, and setup of the production line cost approximately $135. The manufacturing cost per case is $4.50, and the annual holding cost is figured at a 24% rate. Thus, $C_h = IC = 0.24(\$4.50) = \$1.08$. What is the recommended production lot size?

Using equation (11.16), we have

$$Q* = \sqrt{\frac{2(26,000)(135)}{(1 - 26,000/60,000)(1.08)}} = 3387$$

The total annual cost using equation (11.15) and $Q* = 3387$ is $2073.

Other relevant data include a 1-week lead time to schedule and set up a production run. Thus, the lead-time demand of $26,000/52 = 500$ cases is the reorder point. The cycle time is the time between production runs. Using equation (11.7), the cycle time is estimated to be $T = 250Q*/D = [(250)(3387)]/26,000$, or about 33 working days. Thus, we should plan a production run of 3387 units about every 33 working days.

Work Problem 13 as an example of an economic production lot size model.

---

[5]The ratio $d/p = D/P$ regardless of the number of days of operation; 250 days is used here merely as an illustration.

Certainly the manager will want to review the model recommendations. Adjusting the recommended $Q* = 3387$ to a slightly different figure and/or adding safety stock may be desirable.

11.3 An Inventory Model with Planned Shortages

A shortage or stockout is a demand that cannot be supplied. In many situations, shortages are undesirable and should be avoided if at all possible. However, there are other cases in which it may be desirable—from an economic point of view—to plan for and allow shortages. In practice, these types of situations are most commonly found where the value of the inventory per unit is very high and hence the holding cost is high. An example of this type of situation is a new-car dealer's inventory. Often a specific car that a customer wants may not be in stock. However, if the customer is willing to wait a few weeks, the dealer is usually able to order it.

The model developed in this section takes into account a type of shortage known as a *backorder*. In a backorder situation, we assume that when a customer places an order and discovers that the supplier is out of stock, the customer waits until the new shipment arrives, and then the order is filled. Frequently, the waiting period in backordering situations is relatively short; thus, by promising the customer top priority and immediate delivery when the goods become available, companies may be able to convince the customer to wait until the order arrives. In these cases, the backorder assumption is valid.

The backorder model that we will develop is an extension of the EOQ model presented in Section 11.1. We will use the EOQ model in which the goods arrive in inventory all at one time and there is a constant demand rate (see Table 11.3 for a summary of the EOQ model assumptions). If we let S indicate the number of backorders that are accumulated when a new shipment of size Q is received, then the inventory system for the backorder case has the following characteristics:

■ If S backorders exist when a new shipment of size Q arrives, the S backorders are shipped to the appropriate customers, and the remaining $Q - S$ units are placed in inventory. Therefore, $Q - S$ is the maximum inventory level.
■ The inventory cycle of T days is divided into two distinct phases; t_1 days when inventory is on hand and orders are filled as they occur, and t_2 days when there are stockouts and all new orders are placed on backorder.

The inventory pattern for the inventory model with backorders, where negative inventory represents the number of backorders, is shown in Figure 11.5.

With the inventory pattern now defined, we can proceed with the basic step of all inventory models—namely, the development of a total-cost model. For the inventory model with backorders, we will encounter the usual holding costs and ordering costs. We will also incur a backorder cost in terms of the labor and special delivery costs directly associated with the handling of the backorders. Another portion of the backorder cost accounts for the loss of goodwill due to the fact that some customers will have to wait for their orders. Since the *goodwill cost* depends on how long the customer has to wait, it is customary to adopt the convention of expressing backorder cost in terms of the cost of having a unit on backorder for a stated period of time. This method of costing backorders on a time basis is similar to the method used to compute the inventory holding cost, and we can use it to compute a total annual cost of backorders once the average backorder level and the backorder cost per unit per period are known.

Let us begin the development of a total-cost model by calculating the inventory holding costs for a small hypothetical problem. If we have an average inventory of two

Figure 11.5

....

Inventory Pattern for an Inventory Model with Backorders

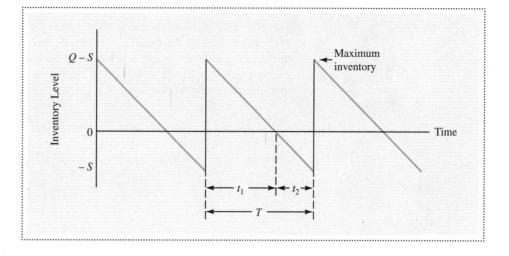

units for 3 days and no inventory on the fourth day, what is the average inventory level over the 4-day period? It is

$$\frac{2 \text{ units (3 days)} + 0 \text{ units (1 day)}}{4 \text{ days}} = \frac{6}{4} = 1.5 \text{ units}$$

Refer to Figure 11.5. You can see that this situation is what happens in the backorder model. With a maximum inventory of $Q - S$ units, the t_1 days we have inventory on hand will have an average inventory of $(Q - S)/2$. No inventory is carried for the t_2 days in which we experience backorders. Thus, over the total cycle time of $T = t_1 + t_2$ days, we can compute the average inventory level as follows:

$$\text{Average inventory level} = \frac{\frac{1}{2}(Q - S)t_1 + 0t_2}{t_1 + t_2} = \frac{\frac{1}{2}(Q - S)t_1}{T} \qquad (11.17)$$

Can we find other ways of expressing t_1 and T? Since we know that the maximum inventory is $Q - S$ and that d represents the constant daily demand, we have

$$t_1 = \frac{Q - S}{d} \text{ days} \qquad (11.18)$$

That is, the maximum inventory level of $Q - S$ units will be used up in $(Q - S)/d$ days. Since Q units are ordered each cycle, we know the length of a cycle must be

$$T = \frac{Q}{d} \text{ days} \qquad (11.19)$$

Combining equations (11.18) and (11.19) with equation (11.17), we can compute the average inventory level as follows:

$$\text{Average inventory level} = \frac{\frac{1}{2}(Q - S)[(Q - S)/d]}{Q/d} = \frac{(Q - S)^2}{2Q} \qquad (11.20)$$

Thus, the average inventory level is expressed in terms of two inventory decisions: how much we will order (Q) and the maximum number of backorders we will allow (S).

The formula for the annual number of orders placed using this model is identical to that for the EOQ model. With D representing the annual demand, we have

$$\text{Annual number of orders} = \frac{D}{Q} \qquad (11.21)$$

The next step is to develop an expression for the average backorder level. Since there is a maximum of S backorders, we can use the same logic we used to establish average inventory in finding the average number of backorders. We have an average number of backorders during the period t_2 of $\frac{1}{2}$ the maximum number of backorders or $\frac{1}{2}S$. Since we do not have any backorders during the t_1 days we have inventory, we can calculate the average backorder level in a manner similar to equation (11.17). Using this approach, we have

$$\text{Average backorder level} = \frac{0t_1 + (S/2)t_2}{T} = \frac{(S/2)t_2}{T} \tag{11.22}$$

Since we let the maximum number of backorders reach an amount S at a daily rate of d, the length of the backorder portion of the inventory cycle is

$$t_2 = \frac{S}{d} \tag{11.23}$$

Using equations (11.23) and (11.19) in equation (11.22), we have

$$\text{Average backorder level} = \frac{(S/2)(S/d)}{Q/d} = \frac{S^2}{2Q} \tag{11.24}$$

Let

C_h = cost to maintain one unit in inventory for 1 year
C_o = cost per order
C_b = cost to maintain one unit on backorder for 1 year

The total annual cost (TC) for the inventory model with backorders becomes

$$TC = \frac{(Q - S)^2}{2Q}C_h + \frac{D}{Q}C_o + \frac{S^2}{2Q}C_b \tag{11.25}$$

Given the cost estimates C_h, C_o, and C_b and the annual demand D, the minimum-cost values for the order quantity Q^* and the planned backorders S^* are as follows (see Appendix 11.4):

$$Q^* = \sqrt{\frac{2DC_o}{C_h}\left(\frac{C_h + C_b}{C_b}\right)} \tag{11.26}$$

$$S^* = Q^*\left(\frac{C_h}{C_h + C_b}\right) \tag{11.27}$$

An Example   Suppose the Higley Radio Components Company has a product for which the assumptions of the inventory model with backorders are valid. Information obtained by the company is as follows:

D = 2000 units per year
I = 0.20
C = \$50 per unit
$C_h = IC = (0.20)(\$50) = \$10$ per unit per year
C_o = \$25 per order

The company is considering the possibility of allowing some backorders to occur for the product. The annual backorder cost has been estimated to be \$30 per unit per year. Using equations (11.26) and (11.27), we have

$$Q^* = \sqrt{\frac{2(2000)(25)}{10}\left(\frac{10 + 30}{30}\right)} = 115$$

and

$$S^* = 115\left(\frac{10}{10 + 30}\right) = 29$$

An inventory situation that incorporates backorder costs is considered in Problem 15.

If this solution is implemented, the system will operate with the following properties:

$$\text{Maximum inventory} = Q - S = 115 - 29 = 86$$

$$\text{Cycle time} = T = \frac{Q}{D}(250) = \frac{115}{2000}(250) = 14.4 \text{ working days}$$

The total annual cost is

$$\text{Holding cost} = \frac{(86)^2}{2(115)}(10) = \$322$$

$$\text{Ordering cost} = \frac{2000}{115}(25) \quad = \$435$$

$$\text{Backorder cost} = \frac{(29)^2}{2(115)}(30) = \underline{\$110}$$

$$\text{Total cost} \quad = \$867$$

If the company had chosen to prohibit backorders and had adopted the regular EOQ model, the recommended inventory decision would have been

$$Q^* = \sqrt{\frac{2(2000)(25)}{10}} = \sqrt{10,000} = 100$$

This order quantity would have resulted in a holding cost and an ordering cost of \$500 each or a total annual cost of \$1000. Thus, in this problem, allowing backorders is projecting a \$1000 − \$867 =\$133 or 13.3% savings in cost from the no-stockout EOQ model. The preceding comparison and conclusion are based on the assumption that the backorder model with an annual cost per backordered unit of \$30 is a valid model for the actual inventory situation. If the company is concerned that stockouts might lead to lost sales, then the savings might not be enough to warrant switching to an inventory policy that allowed for planned shortages.

NOTES & comments

Equation (11.27) shows that the optimal number of planned backorders S^* is proportional to the ratio $C_h/(C_h + C_b)$, where C_h is the annual holding cost per unit and C_b is the annual backorder cost per unit. Whenever C_h increases, this ratio becomes larger, and the number of planned backorders increases. This explains why items that have a high per-unit cost and a correspondingly high annual holding cost are more economically handled on a backorder basis. On the other hand, whenever the backorder cost C_b increases, the ratio becomes smaller, and the number of planned backorders decreases. Thus, the model provides the intuitive result that items with high backordering costs will be handled with few backorders. In fact, with high backorder costs, the backorder model and the EOQ model with no backordering allowed provide similar inventory policies.

11.4 Quantity Discounts for the EOQ Model

Quantity discounts occur in numerous situations where suppliers provide an incentive for large order quantities by offering a lower purchase cost when items are ordered in larger lots or quantities. In this section we show how the EOQ model can be used when quantity discounts are available.

Assume that we have a product where the basic EOQ model (see Table 11.3) is applicable, but instead of a fixed unit cost, the supplier quotes the following discount schedule:

Discount Category	Order Size	Discount (%)	Unit Cost
1	0 to 999	0	$5.00
2	1000 to 2499	3	4.85
3	2500 and over	5	4.75

The 5% discount for the 2500-unit minimum order quantity looks tempting; however, realizing that higher order quantities result in higher inventory holding costs, we should prepare a thorough cost analysis before making a final ordering and inventory policy recommendation.

Suppose the data and cost analyses show an annual holding cost rate of 20%, an ordering cost of $49 per order, and an annual demand of 5000 units; what order quantity should we select? The following three-step procedure shows the calculations necessary to make this decision. In the preliminary calculations, we will use Q_1 to indicate the order quantity for discount category 1, Q_2 for discount category 2, and Q_3 for discount category 3.

Step 1 For each discount category, compute a $Q*$ using the EOQ formula based on the unit cost associated with the discount category.

Recall that the EOQ model provides $Q* = \sqrt{2DC_o/C_h}$, where $C_h = IC = (0.20)C$. With three discount categories providing three different unit costs C, we obtain

$$Q_1^* = \sqrt{\frac{2(5000)49}{(0.20)(5.00)}} = 700$$

$$Q_2^* = \sqrt{\frac{2(5000)49}{(0.20)(4.85)}} = 711$$

$$Q_3^* = \sqrt{\frac{2(5000)49}{(0.20)(4.75)}} = 718$$

Since the only differences in the EOQ formulas are slight differences in the holding cost, the economic order quantities resulting from this step will be approximately the same. However, these order quantities will usually not all be of the size necessary to qualify for

Table 11.4

Total Annual Cost Calculations for the EOQ Model with Quantity Discounts

| Discount Category | Unit Cost | Order Quantity | Annual Cost | | | |
			Holding	Ordering	Purchase	Total
1	$5.00	700	$ 350	$350	$25,000	$25,700
2	4.85	1000	485	245	24,250	24,980
3	4.75	2500	1188	98	23,750	25,036

the discount price assumed. In the preceding case, both Q_2^* and Q_3^* are insufficient order quantities to obtain their assumed discounted costs of $4.85 and $4.75, respectively. For those order quantities for which the assumed price cannot be obtained, the following procedure must be used.

Step 2 For the Q^* that is too small to qualify for the assumed discount price, adjust the order quantity upward to the nearest order quantity that will allow the product to be purchased at the assumed price.

In our example, this causes us to set

$$Q_2^* = 1000$$

and

$$Q_3^* = 2500$$

If a calculated Q^* for a given discount price is large enough to qualify for a bigger discount, that value of Q^* cannot lead to an optimal solution. While the reason may not be obvious, it does turn out to be a property of the EOQ quantity discount model. Problem 23 at the end of the chapter will ask you to show that this property is true.

In the previous inventory models considered, the annual purchase cost of the item was not included because it was constant and never affected by the inventory-order policy decision. However, in the quantity discount model, the annual purchase cost depends on the order-quantity and the associated unit cost. Thus, annual purchase cost (annual demand $D \times$ unit cost C) is included in the equation for total cost as shown here.

$$TC = \frac{Q}{2}C_h + \frac{D}{Q}C_o + DC \qquad (11.28)$$

Using this total-cost formula, we can determine the optimal order quantity for the EOQ discount model in step 3.

Step 3 For each of the order quantities resulting from steps 1 and 2, compute the total annual cost using the unit price from the appropriate discount category and equation (11.28). The order quantity yielding the minimum total annual cost is the optimal order quantity.

Problem 21 will give you practice in applying the EOQ model to situations with quantity discounts.

The step 3 calculations for the example problem are summarized in Table 11.4. As you can see, a decision to order 1000 units at the 3% discount rate yields the minimum-cost solution. While the 2500-unit order quantity would result in a 5% discount, its excessive holding cost makes it the second best solution. Figure 11.6 shows the total-cost curve for each of the three discount categories. Note that $Q^* = 1000$ provides the minimum-cost order quantity.

Figure 11.6

Total-Cost Curves for the Three Discount Categories

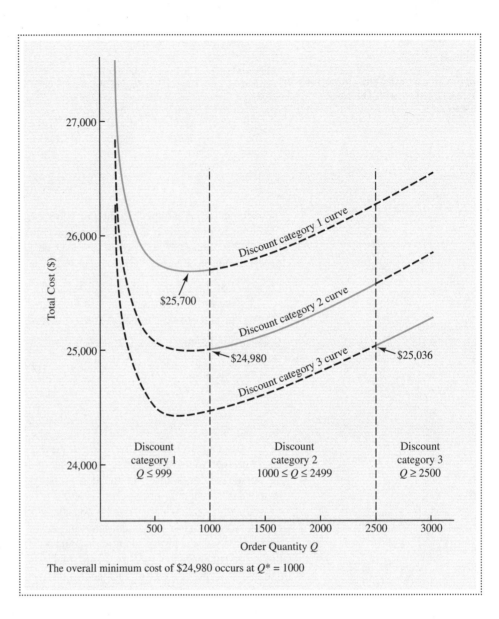

The overall minimum cost of $24,980 occurs at $Q^* = 1000$

11.5   A Single-Period Inventory Model with Probabilistic Demand

The inventory models that we have discussed thus far have been based on the assumption that the demand rate is constant and *deterministic* throughout the year. We developed minimum-cost order quantity and reorder-point policies based on this assumption. In situations where the demand rate is not deterministic, models have been developed that treat demand as *probabilistic* and best described by a probability distribution. In this section we consider a *single-period* inventory model with probabilistic demand.

The single-period inventory model refers to inventory situations in which *one* order is placed for the product; at the end of the period, the product has either sold out, or there is a surplus of unsold items that will be sold for a salvage value. The single-period inventory model is applicable in situations involving seasonal or perishable items that cannot be carried in inventory and sold in future periods. Seasonal clothing (such as bathing suits and winter coats) are typically handled in a single-period manner. In these situations, a buyer places one preseason order for each item and then experiences a stockout or holds a clearance sale on the surplus stock at the end of the season. No items are carried in inventory and sold the following year. Newspapers are another example of a product that is ordered one time and is either sold or not sold during the single period. While newspapers are ordered daily, they cannot be carried in inventory and sold in later periods. Thus, newspaper orders may be treated as a sequence of single-period models; that is, each day or period is separate, and a single-period inventory decision must be made each period (day). Since we order only once for the period, the only inventory decision we must make is *how much* of the product to order at the start of the period. Because newspaper sales is an excellent example of a single-period situation, the single-period inventory problem is sometimes referred to as the *newsboy problem.*

Obviously, if the demand were known for a single-period inventory situation, the solution would be easy; we would simply order the amount we knew would be demanded. However, in most single-period models, the exact demand is not known. In fact, forecasts may show that demand can have a wide variety of values. If we are going to analyze this type of inventory problem in a quantitative manner, we will need information about the probabilities associated with the various demand values. Thus, the single-period model presented in this section is based on probabilistic demand.

The Johnson Shoe Company Problem

Let us consider a single-period inventory model that could be used to make a how-much-to-order decision for the Johnson Shoe Company. The buyer for the Johnson Shoe Company has decided to order a shoe for men that has just been shown at a buyers' meeting in New York City. The shoe will be part of the company's spring-summer promotion and will be sold through nine retail stores in the Chicago area. Since the shoe is designed for spring and summer months, it cannot be expected to sell in the fall. Johnson plans to hold a special August clearance sale in an attempt to sell all shoes that have not been sold by July 31. The shoes cost $40 per pair and retail for $60 per pair. At the sale price of $30 per pair, it is expected that all surplus shoes can be sold during the August sale. If you were the buyer for the Johnson Shoe Company, how many pairs of the shoes would you order?

An obvious question at this time is, What are the possible values of demand for the shoe? We will need this information to answer the question of how much to order. Let us suppose that the uniform probability distribution shown in Figure 11.7 can be used to

Figure 11.7

Uniform Probability Distribution of Demand for the Johnson Shoe Company Problem

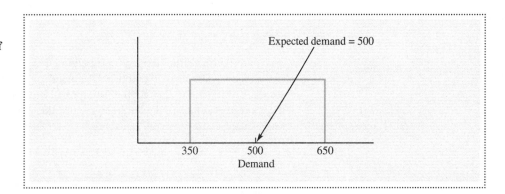

describe the demand for the size 10D shoes. In particular, note that the range of demand is from 350 to 650 pairs of shoes, with an average, or expected, demand of 500 pairs of shoes.

Incremental analysis is a method that can be used to determine the optimal order quantity for a single-period inventory model. Incremental analysis addresses the how-much-to-order question by comparing the cost or loss of *ordering one additional unit* with the cost or loss of *not ordering one additional unit*. The costs involved are defined as follows:

c_o = cost per unit of *overestimating* demand. This cost represents the loss of ordering one additional unit and finding that it cannot be sold.

c_u = cost per unit of *underestimating* demand. This cost represents the opportunity loss of not ordering one additional unit and finding that it could have been sold.

In the Johnson Shoe Company problem, the company will incur the cost of overestimating demand whenever it orders too much and has to sell the extra shoes during the August sale. Thus, the cost per unit of overestimating demand is equal to the purchase cost per unit minus the August sales price per unit; that is, $c_o = \$40 - \$30 = \$10$. Therefore, Johnson will lose $10 for each pair of shoes that it orders over the quantity demanded. The cost of underestimating demand is the lost profit due to the fact that a pair of shoes that could have been sold was not available in inventory. Thus, the per-unit cost of underestimating demand is the difference between the regular selling price per unit and the purchase cost per unit; that is, $c_u = \$60 - \$40 = \$20$.

Since the exact level of demand for the size 10D shoes is unknown, we will have to consider the probability of demand and thus the probability of obtaining the associated costs or losses. For example, let us assume that the Johnson Shoe Company wishes to consider an order quantity equal to the average or expected demand for 500 pairs of shoes. In incremental analysis, we will consider the possible losses associated with an order quantity of 501 (ordering one additional unit) and an order quantity of 500 (not ordering one additional unit). The order-quantity alternatives and the possible losses are summarized here.

Order-Quantity Alternatives	Loss Occurs If	Possible Loss	Probability Loss Occurs
$Q = 501$	Demand overestimated; the additional unit *cannot* be sold.	$c_o = \$10$	$P(\text{demand} \leq 500)$
$Q = 500$	Demand underestimated; an additional unit *could have* been sold.	$c_u = \$20$	$P(\text{demand} > 500)$

By looking at the demand probability distribution in Figure 11.7, we see that $P(\text{demand} \leq 500) = 0.50$ and that $P(\text{demand} > 500) = 0.50$. By multiplying the possible losses, $c_o = \$10$ and $c_u = \$20$, by the probability of obtaining the loss, we can compute the expected value of the loss, or simply the *expected loss* (EL), associated with the order-quantity alternatives. Thus

$$\text{EL}(Q = 501) = c_o\, P(\text{demand} \leq 500) = \$10(0.50) = \$5$$

$$\text{EL}(Q = 500) = c_u\, P(\text{demand} > 500) = \$20(0.50) = \$10$$

Based on these expected losses, do you prefer an order quantity of 501 or 500 pairs of shoes? Since the expected loss is greater for $Q = 500$, and since we want to avoid this higher cost or loss, we should make $Q = 501$ the preferred decision. We could now consider incrementing the order quantity one additional unit to $Q = 502$ and repeating the expected loss calculations.

While we could continue this unit-by-unit analysis, it would be time-consuming and cumbersome. We would have to evaluate $Q = 502$, $Q = 503$, $Q = 504$, and so on, until we found the value of Q where the expected loss of ordering one incremental unit is equal to the expected loss of not ordering one incremental unit; that is, the optimal order quantity Q^* occurs when the incremental analysis shows that

$$EL(Q^* + 1) = EL(Q^*) \tag{11.29}$$

When this relationship holds, there is no economic advantage to increasing the order quantity by one additional unit. Using the logic with which we computed the expected losses for the order quantities of 501 and 500, the general expressions for $EL(Q^* + 1)$ and $EL(Q^*)$ can be written

$$EL(Q^* + 1) = c_o\, P(\text{demand} \le Q^*) \tag{11.30}$$

$$EL(Q^*) = c_u\, P(\text{demand} > Q^*) \tag{11.31}$$

Since we know from basic probability that

$$P(\text{demand} \le Q^*) + P(\text{demand} > Q^*) = 1 \tag{11.32}$$

we can write

$$P(\text{demand} > Q^*) = 1 - P(\text{demand} \le Q^*) \tag{11.33}$$

Using this expression, equation (11.31) can be rewritten as

$$EL(Q^*) = c_u[1 - P(\text{demand} \le Q^*)] \tag{11.34}$$

Equations (11.30) and (11.34) can be used to show that $EL(Q^* + 1) = EL(Q^*)$ whenever

$$c_o\, P(\text{demand} \le Q^*) = c_u[1 - P(\text{demand} \le Q^*)] \tag{11.35}$$

Solving for $P(\text{demand} \le Q^*)$, we have

$$P(\text{demand} \le Q^*) = \frac{c_u}{c_u + c_o} \tag{11.36}$$

This expression provides the general condition for the optimal order quantity Q^* in the single-period inventory model.

In the Johnson Shoe Company problem, $c_o = \$10$ and $c_u = \$20$. Thus, equation (11.36) shows that the optimal order size for Johnson shoes must satisfy the following condition:

$$P(\text{demand} \le Q^*) = \frac{c_u}{c_u + c_o} = \frac{20}{20 + 10} = \frac{20}{30} = \frac{2}{3}$$

We can find the optimal order quantity Q^* by referring to the assumed probability distribution shown in Figure 11.7 and finding the value of Q that will provide $P(\text{demand}$

≤ Q^*) = ⅔. To do this, we note that in the uniform distribution the probability is evenly distributed over the entire range of 350–650 pairs of shoes. Thus, we can satisfy the expression for Q^* by moving two-thirds of the way from 350 to 650. Since this is a range of 650 – 350 = 300, we move 200 units from 350 toward 650. Doing so provides the optimal order quantity of 550 pairs of size 10D shoes.

In summary, the key to establishing an optimal order quantity for single-period inventory models is to identify the probability distribution that describes the demand for the item and the costs of overestimation and underestimation. Then, using the information for the costs of overestimation and underestimation, equation (11.36) can be used to find the location of Q^* in the probability distribution.

The Kremer Chemical Company Problem

As another example of a single-period inventory model with probabilistic demand, consider the situation faced by the Kremer Chemical Company. Kremer has a contract with one of its customers to supply a unique liquid chemical product. Historically, the customer places orders approximately every 6 months. Since a 2-month aging condition exists for the product, Kremer will have to make its production quantity decision before the customer places an order. Kremer's inventory problem is to determine the number of pounds of the chemical to produce in anticipation of the customer's order.

Kremer's manufacturing costs for the chemical are $15 per pound, and the product sells at the fixed contract price of $20 per pound. If Kremer underproduces, it will be unable to satisfy the customer's demand. When this condition occurs, Kremer has agreed to absorb the added cost of filling the order by purchasing a higher-quality substitute product from another chemical firm. The substitute product, including additional transportation expenses, will cost Kremer $19 per pound. If Kremer overproduces, it will have more product in inventory than the customer requires. Because of the spoilage potential for the product, Kremer cannot store excess production until the customer's next order. As a result, Kremer reprocesses the excess production and sells the surplus for $5 per pound.

Based on previous experience with the customer's orders, Kremer believes that the normal probability distribution shown in Figure 11.8 best describes the possible demand. Note that the normal distribution shows an average or expected demand of $\mu = 1000$

Figure 11.8

Normal Probability Distribution of Demand for the Kremer Chemical Company Problem

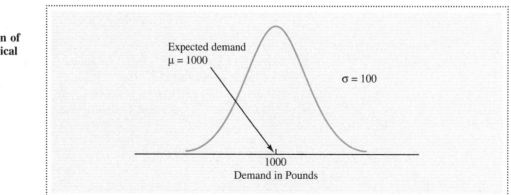

pounds with a standard deviation of $\sigma = 100$ pounds. Using Kremer's price and cost data as well as the probability distribution of demand shown in Figure 11.8, how much production should Kremer plan for in anticipation of the customer's order for the liquid chemical?

Let us compute the cost of underestimation, c_u, and the cost of overestimation, c_o, as required for equation (11.36). First, if Kremer underproduces, it will have to purchase a substitute product at a higher cost per unit to satisfy the customer's demand for the product. Since the substitute product costs $19 per pound and Kremer could have manufactured the product for $15 per pound, a cost of $c_u = \$19 - \$15 = \$4$ exists for every pound of underestimated demand. If Kremer overestimates demand, the company incurs a cost of $15 per pound to manufacture the product and then sells the reprocessed excess product for $5 per pound. Thus, Kremer has a per-unit cost of $c_o = \$15 - \$5 = \$10$ for overestimating demand.

Applying equation (11.36) indicates that the optimal order quantity must satisfy the following condition:

$$P(\text{demand} \leq Q^*) = \frac{c_u}{c_u + c_o} = \frac{4}{4 + 10} = 0.29$$

We can use the normal probability distribution for demand as shown in Figure 11.9 to find the order quantity that satisfies the condition that $P(\text{demand} \leq Q^*) = 0.29$. From Appendix A, we see that 0.29 of the area in the left tail of the curve of the normal probability distribution occurs at $z = 0.55$ standard deviations *below* the mean. Since the mean or expected demand is given by $\mu = 1000$ and the standard deviation is $\sigma = 100$, we have

$$Q^* = \mu - 0.55\sigma$$
$$= 1000 - 0.55(100) = 945$$

An example of a single-period inventory model with probabilistic demand described by a normal probability distribution is considered in Problem 25.

Thus, with the assumed normal probability distribution of demand, the Kremer Chemical Company should produce 945 pounds of the chemical in anticipation of the customer's order. Note that in this case the cost of underestimation is less than the cost of overestimation. Thus, Kremer is willing to risk a higher probability of underestimation and hence a higher probability of a stockout. In fact, Kremer's optimal order quantity has a 0.29 probability of having a surplus and a $1 - 0.29 = 0.71$ probability of a stockout.

Figure 11.9

Probability Distribution of Demand for the Kremer Chemical Company Problem Showing the Location of the Optimal Order Quantity Q^*

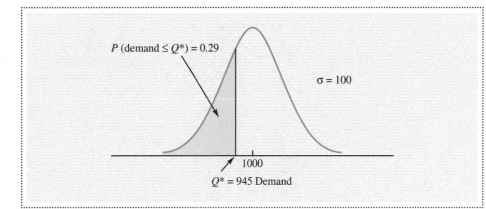

NOTES & comments

1. In any probabilistic inventory model, the assumption about the probability distribution for demand is critical and can affect the recommended inventory decision. In the problems presented in this section, we used the uniform and the normal probability distributions to describe demand. In some situations, other probability distributions may be more appropriate. In using probabilistic inventory models, we must exercise care in selecting the probability distribution that most realistically describes demand.

2. In the single-period inventory model, the value of $c_u/(c_u + c_o)$ plays a critical role in selecting the order quantity (see equation (11.36)). Whenever $c_u = c_o$, $c_u/(c_u + c_o)$ equals 0.50; in this case, we should select an order quantity corresponding to the median demand. With this choice, it is just as likely to have a stockout as it is to have a surplus; this makes sense because the two costs are equal. However, whenever $c_u < c_o$, a smaller order quantity will be recommended. In this case, there will be a higher probability of a stockout; however, the more expensive cost of overestimating demand and having a surplus will tend to be avoided. Finally, whenever $c_u > c_o$, a larger order quantity will be recommended. In this case, the larger order quantity provides a lower probability of a stockout in an attempt to avoid the more expensive cost of underestimating demand and experiencing a stockout.

11.6 An Order-Quantity, Reorder-Point Model with Probabilistic Demand

In the previous section we considered a single-period inventory model with probabilistic demand. In this section we extend our discussion to a multiperiod order-quantity, reorder-point inventory model with probabilistic demand. In the multiperiod model, the inventory system operates continuously with many repeating periods or cycles; inventory can be carried from one period to the next. Whenever the inventory position reaches the reorder point, an order for Q units is placed. Since demand is probabilistic, the time the reorder point will be reached, the time between orders, and the time the order of Q units will arrive in inventory cannot be determined in advance.

The inventory pattern for the order-quantity, reorder-point model with probabilistic demand will have the general appearance shown in Figure 11.10. Note that the increases or jumps in the inventory level occur whenever an order of Q units arrives. The inventory level decreases at a nonconstant rate based on the probabilistic demand. A new order is placed whenever the reorder point is reached. At times, the order quantity of Q units will arrive before inventory reaches zero. However, at other times, higher demand will cause a stockout before a new order is received. As with other order-quantity, reorder-point models, the manager must determine the order quantity Q and the reorder point r for the inventory system.

The exact mathematical formulation of an order-quantity, reorder-point inventory model with probabilistic demand is beyond the scope of this text. However, we will

Figure 11.10

Inventory Pattern for an Order-Quantity, Reorder-Point Model with Probabilistic Demand

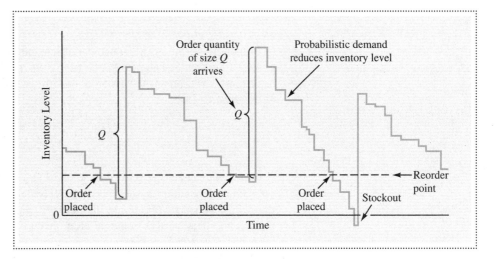

Figure 11.11

Lead-Time Demand Probability Distribution for Dabco Light Bulbs

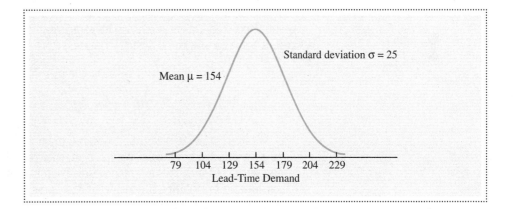

present a procedure that can be used to obtain good, workable order-quantity and reorder-point inventory policies. While the solution procedure can be expected to provide only an approximation of the optimal solution, it has been found to yield very good solutions in many practical situations.

Let us consider the inventory problem of Dabco Industrial Lighting Distributors. Dabco purchases a special high-intensity light bulb for industrial lighting systems from a well-known light bulb manufacturer. Dabco would like a recommendation on how much to order and when to order so that a low-cost inventory policy can be maintained. Pertinent facts are that the ordering cost is $12 per order, one bulb costs $6, and Dabco uses a 20% annual holding cost rate for its inventory ($C_h = IC = 0.20 \times \$6 = \$1.20$). Dabco, which has over 1000 different customers, experiences a probabilistic demand; in fact, the number of units demanded varies considerably from day to day and from week to week. The lead time for a new order of light bulbs is 1 week. Historical sales data indicate that demand during a 1-week lead time can be described by a normal probability distribution with a mean of 154 light bulbs and a standard deviation of 25 light bulbs. The normal distribution of demand during the lead time is shown in Figure 11.11. Since the mean demand during 1-week is 154 units, Dabco can anticipate a mean or expected annual demand of 154 units per week $\times$ 52 weeks per year $=8008$ units per year.

The How-Much-to-Order Decision

Although we are in a probabilistic demand situation, we have an estimate of the expected annual demand of 8008 units. We can apply the EOQ model from Section 11.1 as an approximation of the best order quantity, with the expected annual demand used for D. In Dabco's case

$$Q^* = \sqrt{\frac{2DC_o}{C_h}} = \sqrt{\frac{2(8008)(12)}{(1.20)}} = 400 \text{ units}$$

When we studied the sensitivity of the EOQ model, we learned that the total cost of operating an inventory system was relatively insensitive to order quantities that were in the neighborhood of Q^*. Using this knowledge, we expect 400 units per order to be a good approximation of the optimal order quantity. Even if annual demand were as low as 7000 units or as high as 9000 units, an order quantity of 400 units should be a relatively good low-cost order size. Thus, given our best estimate of annual demand at 8008 units, we will use $Q^* = 400$.

We have established the 400-unit order quantity by ignoring the fact that demand is probabilistic. Using $Q^* = 400$, Dabco can anticipate placing approximately $D/Q^* = 8008/400 = 20$ orders per year with an average of approximately $250/20 = 12.5$ working days between orders.

The When-to-Order Decision

We now want to establish a when-to-order decision rule or reorder point that will trigger the ordering process. With a mean lead-time demand of 154 units, you might first suggest a 154-unit reorder point. However, it now becomes extremely important to consider the probability of demand. If 154 is the mean lead-time demand, and if demand is symmetrically distributed about 154, then the lead-time demand will be more than 154 units roughly 50% of the time. When the demand during the 1-week lead time exceeds 154 units, Dabco will experience a shortage or stockout. Thus, using a reorder point of 154 units, approximately 50% of the time (10 of the 20 orders a year) Dabco will be short of bulbs before the new supply arrives. This shortage rate would most likely be viewed as unacceptable.

Refer to the *lead-time demand distribution* shown in Figure 11.11. Given this distribution, we can now determine how the reorder point r affects the probability of a stockout. Since stockouts occur whenever the demand during the lead time exceeds the reorder point, we can find the probability of a stockout by using the lead-time demand distribution to compute the probability that demand will exceed r.

We could now approach the when-to-order problem by defining a cost per stockout and then attempting to include this cost in a total-cost equation. Alternatively, we can ask management to specify the average number of stockouts that can be tolerated per year; this number is referred to as the service level. If demand for a product is probabilistic, a manager who will never tolerate a stockout is being somewhat unrealistic because attempting to avoid stockouts completely will require high reorder points, high inventory levels, and an associated high holding cost.

Suppose in this case that Dabco management is willing to tolerate an average of one stockout per year. Since Dabco places 20 orders per year, this implies management is willing to allow demand during lead time to exceed the reorder point one time in 20, or

Figure 11.12

....

Reorder Point *r* That Allows a 5% Chance of a Stockout for Dabco Light Bulbs

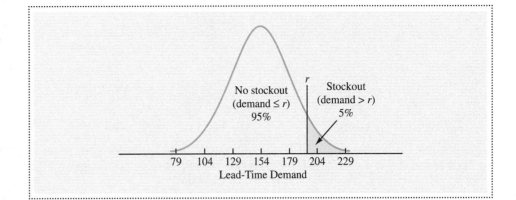

5% of the time. This suggests that the reorder point *r* can be found by using the lead-time demand distribution to find the value of *r* for which there is only a 5% chance of having a lead-time demand that will exceed it. This situation is shown graphically in Figure 11.12.

From the standard normal probability distribution table in Appendix A, we see that the *r* value is 1.645 standard deviations above the mean. Therefore, for the assumed normal distribution for lead-time demand with $\mu = 154$ and $\sigma = 25$, the reorder point *r* is

$$r = 154 + 1.645(25) = 195$$

If a normal distribution is used for lead-time demand, the general equation for *r* is

$$r = \mu + z\sigma \qquad (11.37)$$

where *z* is the number of standard deviations necessary to obtain the acceptable stockout probability.

Thus, the recommended inventory decision is to order 400 units whenever the inventory level reaches the reorder point of 195. Since the mean or expected demand during the lead time is 154 units, the $195 - 154 = 41$ units serve as a safety stock, which absorbs higher-than-usual demand during the lead time. Roughly 95% of the time, the 195 units will be able to satisfy demand during the lead time. The anticipated annual cost for this system is as follows:

Ordering cost	$(D/Q)C_o = (8000/400)12 =$	\$240.00
Holding cost, normal inventory	$(Q/2)C_h = (400/2)(1.20) =$	\$240.00
Holding cost, safety stock	$(41)C_h = 41(1.20) \quad\;\; =$	\$ 49.20
	Total	\$529.20

Try Problem 29 as an example of an order-quantity, reorder-point model with probabilistic demand.

If Dabco could have assumed that a known, constant demand rate of 8008 units per year existed for the light bulbs, then $Q^* = 400$, $r = 154$, and a total annual cost of $\$240 + \$240 = \$480$ would have been optimal. When demand is uncertain and can only be expressed in probabilistic terms, a larger total cost can be expected. The larger cost occurs in the form of larger holding costs due to the fact that more inventory must be maintained to limit the number of stockouts. For Dabco, this additional inventory or safety stock was 41 units, with an additional annual holding cost of \$49.20. The Management Science in Action article describes how a warehouser in the Netherlands has implemented an order-quantity, reorder point system with probabilistic demand.

MANAGEMENT SCIENCE in action

Information from a Netherlands Supplier Lowers Inventory Cost*

In the Netherlands, companies such as Philips, Rank Xerox, and Fokker have followed the trend of developing closer relations between the firm and its suppliers. As teamwork, coordination, and informatin sharing improve, opportunities are available for better cost control in the operation of inventory systems.

One Dutch public warehouser has a contract with its supplier under which the supplier routinely provides information regarding the status and schedule of upcoming production runs. The warehouser's inventory system operates as an order-quantity, reorder-point system with probabalistic demand. When the order-quantity, Q, has been determined, the warehouser selects the desired reorder point for the product. The distribution of the lead-time demand is essential in determining the reorder point. Usually, the lead-time demand distribution is approximated

directly, taking into account both the probablilistic demand and the probabilistic length of the lead-time period.

The supplier's information concerning scheduled production runs provides the warehouser with a better understanding of the lead time involved for a product and the resulting lead-time demand distribution. With this information, the warehouse can modify the reorder point accordingly. Information sharing by the supplier thus enables the order-quantity, reorder-point system to operate with a lower inventory holding cost.

....

*Source: van der Duyn Schouten, F. A., M. J. G. van Eijs, and R. M. J. Heuts, "The Value of Supplier Information to Improve Management of a Retailer's Inventory." *Decision Sciences,* vol. 25, no. 1, January–February 1994, pp. 1–14.

11.7 A Periodic-Review Model with Probabilistic Demand

The order-quantity, reorder-point inventory models previously discussed require a *continuous-review* inventory system. In a continuous-review inventory system, the inventory position is monitored continuously so that an order can be placed whenever the reorder point is reached. Computerized inventory systems can easily provide the continuous review required by the order-quantity, reorder-point models.

An alternative to the continuous-review system is the *periodic-review* system. With a periodic-review system, the inventory level is checked and reordering is done only at specified points in time. For example, inventory levels may be checked and orders placed on a weekly, biweekly, monthly, or some other periodic basis. When a firm or business handles multiple products, the periodic-review system has the advantage of requiring that the orders for several items be placed at the same preset periodic-review time. With this type of inventory system, the shipping and receiving of orders for multiple products are easily coordinated. Under the previously discussed order-quantity, reorder-point systems, the reorder points for various products can be encountered at substantially different points in time, making the coordination of orders for multiple products more difficult.

To illustrate this system, let us consider Dollar Discounts, a firm with several retail stores that carry a wide variety of products for household use. The company operates its inventory system with a two-week periodic review. Under this system, a retail store manager may order any number of units of any product from the Dollar Discounts central warehouse every two weeks. The orders for all products going to a particular store are combined into one shipment. When making the order-quantity decision for each product

Figure 11.13

Inventory Pattern for Periodic-Review Model with Probabilistic Demand

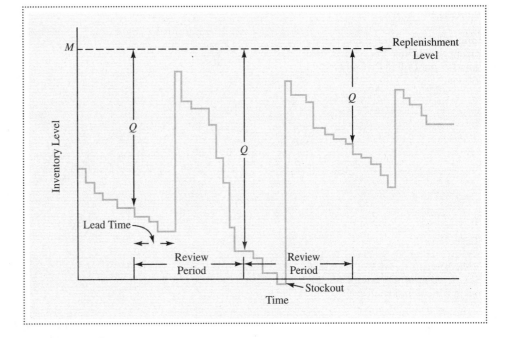

at a given review period, the store manager knows that a reorder for the product cannot be made until the next review period.

Assuming that the lead time is less than the length of the review period, an order placed at a review period will be received prior to the next review period. In this case, the how-much-to-order decision at any review period is determined using the following:

$$Q = M - H \tag{11.38}$$

where

$$Q = \text{the order quantity}$$
$$M = \text{the replenishment level}$$
$$H = \text{the inventory on hand at the review period}$$

Since the demand is probabilistic, the inventory on hand at the review period, H, will vary. Thus, the order quantity that must be sufficient to bring the inventory position back to its maximum or replenishment level M can be expected to vary each period. For example, if the replenishment level for a particular product is 50 units, and the inventory on hand at the review period is $H = 12$ units, an order of $Q = M - H = 50 - 12 = 38$ units should be made. Thus, under the periodic-review model, enough units are ordered each review period to bring the inventory position back up to the replenishment level.

A typical inventory pattern for a periodic-review system with probabilistic demand is shown in Figure 11.13. Note that the time between periodic reviews is predetermined and fixed. The order quantity Q at each review period can vary and is shown to be the difference between the replenishment level and the inventory on hand. Finally, as with other probabilistic models, an unusually high demand can result in an occasional stockout.

The decision variable in the periodic-review model is the replenishment level M. To determine M, we could begin by developing a total-cost model, including holding, ordering, and stockout costs. Instead, we will describe an approach that is often used in practice. In this approach, the objective is to determine a replenishment level that will

Figure 11.14
. . . .

Probability Distribution of Demand During the Review Period and Lead Time for the Dollar Discounts Problem

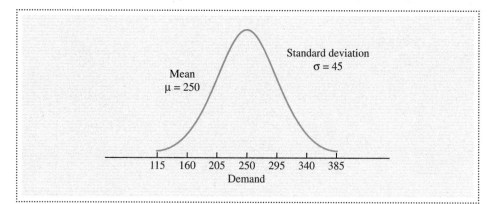

Figure 11.15
. . . .

Replenishment Level *M* That Allows a 1% Chance of a Stockout for the Dollar Discounts Problem

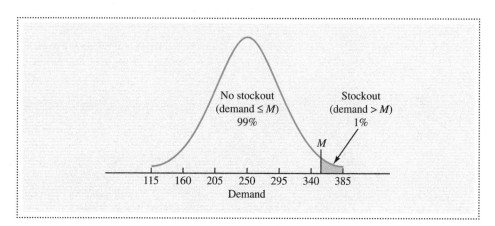

meet a desired performance level, such as a reasonably low probability of stockout or a reasonably low number of stockouts per year.

In the Dollar Discounts problem, we will assume that management's objective is to determine the replenishment level for which there is only a 1% chance of a stockout. In the periodic-review model, the order quantity at each review period must be sufficient to cover demand for the *review period plus the demand for the following lead time.* That is, the order quantity that brings the inventory position up to the replenishment level *M* must last until the order made at the next review period is received in inventory. The length of this time is equal to the review period plus the lead time. Figure 11.14 shows the normal probability distribution of demand during the review period plus the lead-time period for one of the Dollar Discounts products. The mean demand is 250 units, and the standard deviation of demand is 45 units. Given this situation, the logic used to establish *M* is similar to the logic used to establish the reorder point in Section 11.6. Figure 11.15 shows the replenishment level *M*, for which there is a 1% chance that demand will exceed that replenishment level. In other words, Figure 11.15 shows the replenishment level that allows a 1% chance of a stockout associated with the replenishment decision. Using the normal probability distribution table in Appendix A, we see that a value of *M* that is 2.33 standard deviations above the mean will allow stockouts with a 1% probability. Therefore, for the assumed normal probability distribution with $\mu = 250$ and $\sigma = 45$, the replenishment level is determined by

$$M = 250 + 2.33(45) = 355$$

Problem 33 will give you practice in computing the replenishment level for a periodic-review model with probabilistic demand.

While other probability distributions can be used to express the demand during the review period plus the lead-time period, if the normal probability distribution is used, the general expression for M is

$$M = \mu + z\sigma \tag{11.39}$$

where z is the number of standard deviations necessary to obtain the acceptable stockout probability.

If demand had been deterministic rather than probabilistic, the replenishment level would have been the demand during the review period plus the demand during the lead-time period. In this case, the replenishment level would have been 250 units, and no stockout would have occurred. However, with the probabilistic demand, we have seen that higher inventory levels are necessary to allow for uncertain demand and to control the probability of a stockout. In the Dollar Discounts problem, $355 - 250 = 105$ is the safety stock that is necessary to absorb any higher-than-usual demand during the review period plus the demand during the lead-time period. It is this safety stock that limits the probability of a stockout to 1%. The Management Science in Action article describes a periodic-review inventory system at Hewlett-Packard.

More Complex Periodic-Review Models

The periodic-review model that we have just discussed is one approach to determining a replenishment level for the periodic-review inventory system with probabilistic demand. More complex versions of the periodic-review model incorporate a reorder point

MANAGEMENT SCIENCE in action

Inventory Model Helps Hewlett-Packard's Product Design for Worldwide Markets*

Product design always affects the efficiency of manufacturing operations. At Hewlett-Packard's Vancouver, Washington, division, managers are also learning how product design affects product customization, distribution, and delivery to worldwide markets. In most cases, different markets require different product configurations because of language, environment, and/or government regulations. Should Hewlett-Packard design variations of each product to meet the unique requirements of each market, or should it design a more general product with product customization being completed in the local market area?

An inventory model was used to study the inventory levels and costs associated with the product design alternatives for the Hewlett-Packard Deskjet-Plus printer. Inventory levels for the printer are maintained on a periodic-review basis. Planners review the inventory position (on-hand inventory plus inventory in the pipeline) weekly. Orders are placed for quantities needed to return the inventory position to the target inventory level. Demand during the lead time is assumed to follow a normal probability distribution.

The inventory model projected the inventory cost associated with each product design alternative. As a result, Hewlett-Packard's Vancouver, Washington, division redesigned its products to support final customization of the product at the local distribution center level. The inventory model projected an 18% reduction in the total inventory investment, which saved millions of dollars.

....

*Source: Lee, H. L., C. Billington, and B. Carter, "Hewlett-Packard Gains Control of Inventory and Service through Design for Localization." *Interfaces*, vol. 23, no. 4, July–August 1993, pp. 1–11.

as another decision variable. That is, instead of ordering at every periodic review, a reorder point is established. If the inventory on hand at the periodic review is at or below the reorder point, a decision is made to order up to the replenishment level. However, if the inventory on hand at the periodic review is greater than the reorder level, such an order is not placed, and the system continues until the next periodic review. In this case, the cost of ordering is a relevant cost and can be included in a cost model along with holding and stockout costs. Optimal policies can be reached based on minimizing the expected total cost. Situations with lead times longer than the review period add to the complexity of the model. The mathematical level required to treat these more extensive periodic-review models is beyond the scope of this text.

NOTES & comments

1. The periodic-review model presented in this section is based on the assumption that the lead time for an order is less than the periodic-review period. Most periodic-review systems operate under this condition. However, the case in which the lead time is longer than the review period can be handled by defining H in equation (11.38) as the inventory position, where H includes the inventory on hand plus the inventory on order. In this case, the order quantity at any review period is the amount needed for the inventory on hand plus *all* outstanding orders needed to reach the replenishment level.

2. In the order-quantity, reorder-point model discussed in Section 11.6, a continuous review was used to initiate an order whenever the reorder point was reached. The safety stock for this model was based on the probabilistic demand during the lead time. The periodic-review model presented in this section also determined a recommended safety stock. However, since the inventory review was only periodic, the safety stock was based on the probabilistic demand during the *review period plus the lead-time period.* This longer period for the safety stock computation means that periodic-review systems tend to require a larger safety stock than do continuous-review systems.

11.8   Material Requirements Planning

The inventory models we have discussed thus far have been found to be most appropriate for managing the inventories of finished goods. Finished goods are characterized as having *independent demands* that may be forecast. In this section we focus on the planning and controlling of manufacturing inventories such as raw materials, components, and subassemblies. The demand for these types of items is *dependent* on the amounts of finished goods that are scheduled to be produced and can be *calculated* from the forecasts and scheduled production of finished goods. A technique that can be used to manage dependent-demand inventories is called *material requirements planning* (MRP).

Dependent Demand and the MRP Concept

To illustrate dependent demand and the MRP concept, consider a finished product that is manufactured using a single component that is purchased from an outside supplier. The demand for the finished product consists of many independent demands from many customers. Since these demands occur somewhat randomly, the demand rate is often fairly constant, and the assumptions of the production lot size model are reasonable. The inventory level for the finished product is shown at the top of Figure 11.16. When production of the finished product is initiated (point A on the time axis), the component parts are withdrawn from inventory in order to meet the manufacturing needs. The inventory level of the component part is shown at the bottom of Figure 11.16. When the component inventory level falls below its reorder point, an order for the component is placed with the supplier. The shipment is received at point B, and the component inventory is replenished. However, note that the component is not needed again until the next production run for the finished product, which is scheduled to occur at point C. Clearly, the investment in the component inventory from points B to C is unnecessary. We can eliminate this unnecessary component inventory by "backing up" from point C according to the purchase lead time so that the components will arrive just at time C. This situation is illustrated in Figure 11.17. Note that the component inventory level and corresponding inventory investment are less in Figure 11.17 than in Figure 11.16.

The philosophy of basing component inventory orders on the demand and production needs of other items is the approach followed by MRP. When operating properly, the MRP system will reduce inventory investment, improve work flow, reduce the shortage of materials and components, and help achieve more reliable delivery schedules.

Figure 11.16

Finished Product and Component Part Inventory Levels without an MRP System

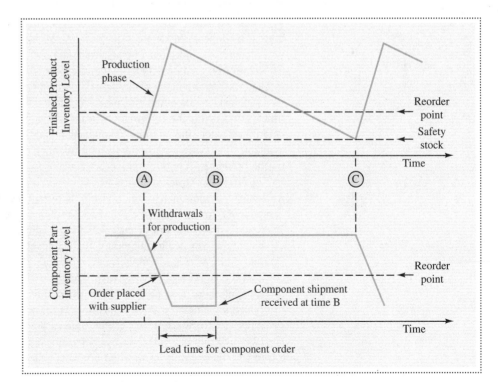

Figure 11.17

Finished Product and Component Part Inventory Levels with an MRP System

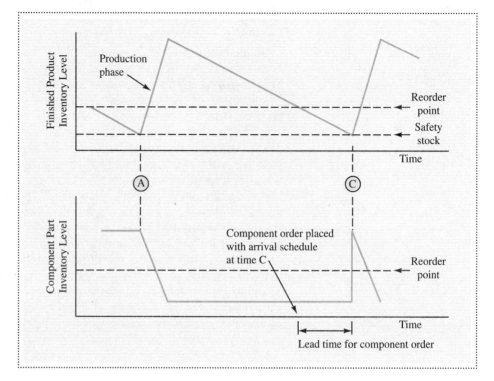

Information System for MRP

What makes the MRP process difficult to implement is that many finished products consist of dozens or hundreds of parts, many of which are in turn dependent on other parts. Therefore, there must be accurate data and a reliable computer information system to perform the many calculations required for MRP.

Material requirements planning calculations begin with the *master production schedule,* which states the number of units of each finished product to be produced during each time period. With the information in the master production schedule, we can begin to determine when the various components that make up the final products must be available. Thus, the next step will be to identify the list of components that are required by the products. This information is available from the *bill of materials* (BOM).

The BOM is a structured parts list; however, it differs from an ordinary parts list in that it shows the hierarchical relationship between the finished product and its various components. An example of a BOM for the Spiecker Company is shown in Figure 11.18. This figure shows the bill of materials for a 14-inch snowblower. The finished product is shown at the top of the hierarchy (called level 0). It consists of one main housing assembly, one wheel assembly, one engine assembly, and one handle assembly. If we consider the BOM as a "family tree," then the 14-inch snowblower is the "parent" item for each of these assemblies. These assemblies, in turn, are parent items for all the components included in them. Thus, the wheel assembly is the parent item of one blade assembly and two wheels. In general, items at level *k* are parent items for components at level *k* + 1. From the BOM, we can determine exactly how many components are needed to produce the quantity of finished products stated in the master production schedule.

A schematic diagram of an MRP information system is given in Figure 11.19. Forecasts and orders are used to develop the master production schedule. The master

Figure 11.18

Bill of Materials for the Spiecker 14-inch Snowblower

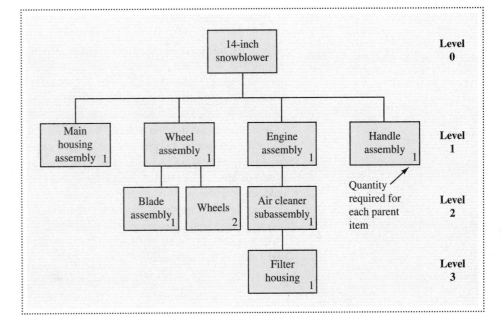

Figure 11.19

An MRP System

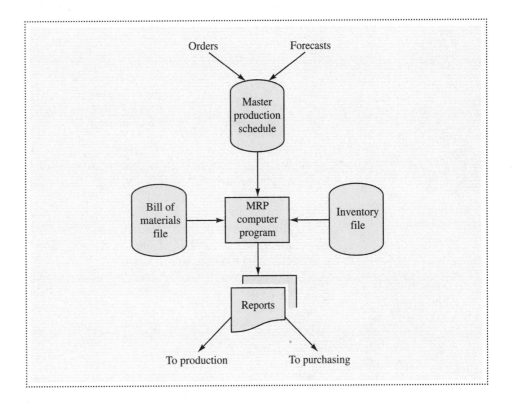

production schedule, BOM, and current inventory files are the inputs needed to begin the MRP computations. The outputs from the MRP system are the requirements for each item in the BOM along with the dates each item is needed. This information is used to plan order releases for production and purchasing. To illustrate how these calculations are performed, let us consider an MRP system for the Spiecker snowblower problem.

MRP Calculations

In MRP terminology, the time periods, which are called *buckets,* are often 1 week in length. Buckets, such as 1 week, are good for scheduling production over a short time horizon but may be too precise for long-range planning; larger buckets are used as the planning horizon gets longer. However, for the Spiecker Manufacturing problem, we assume that all buckets are 1 week in length.

The master production schedule calls for the final assembly of 1250 units of the 14-inch snowblower during week 21 of the current planning period. The assembly lead time is 1 week; thus, to meet this schedule, the four main assemblies in the bill of materials must be completed no later than the end of week 20. We now examine the production and inventory control aspects for the engine assembly in detail, concentrating on how the MRP approach can be applied. Relevant data regarding the number of units in inventory and lead time are given in Table 11.5.

Before the advent of MRP, the net requirement for each component was often found using the following formula:

$$\text{Net component requirement} = \begin{pmatrix} \text{Number of components} \\ \text{required to meet} \\ \text{demand for} \\ \text{finished good} \end{pmatrix} - \begin{pmatrix} \text{Number of} \\ \text{components} \\ \text{in inventory} \end{pmatrix}$$

Thus, the net requirements based on 1250 snowblowers are calculated as follows:

Components	Number of Components Required to Meet Demand for 1250 Snowblowers	−	Number in Inventory	=	Net Requirement
Engines	1250	−	450	=	800
Air cleaners	1250	−	250	=	1000
Filter housings	1250	−	500	=	750

However, note that this approach does not recognize the nature of dependent demand; for example, the number of filter housings required is dependent on the number of air cleaners produced, and so on.

The approach to determining net requirements whenever a dependent demand situation exists is

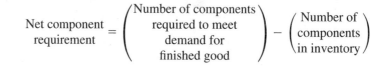

$$\text{Net component requirement} = \begin{pmatrix} \text{Gross component} \\ \text{requirement} \end{pmatrix} - \begin{pmatrix} \text{Scheduled} \\ \text{receipts} \end{pmatrix} - \begin{pmatrix} \text{Number of} \\ \text{components} \\ \text{in inventory} \end{pmatrix}$$

Table 11.5

Inventory on Hand and Lead Time for the Spiecker Manufacturing Problem

Component	Units in Inventory	Lead Time (weeks)
Engine assembly	450	4
Air cleaner subassembly	250	1
Filter housing	500	2

where the gross component requirement is the quantity of the component needed to support production at the next higher level of assembly. For example, the gross component requirement for the filter housing is the number of filter housings required to meet the net requirement for the air cleaner subassembly; the gross component requirement for the air cleaner subassembly is the number of air cleaners needed to meet the net requirement for the engine assembly; and so on. Let us see how these requirements can be computed for Spiecker Manufacturing. (We assume, for simplicity, that scheduled receipts are zero.)

The computation of MRP net requirements is the subject of Problem 37.

	Units	
Quantity of snowblowers to be produced:	1250	
Gross requirements, engines:	1250	
Less engines in inventory:	450	
Net requirements, engines:	800	← Engines
Gross requirements, air cleaners:	800	
Less air cleaners in inventory:	250	
Net requirements, air cleaners:	550	← Air cleaners
Gross requirements, filter housings:	550	
Less filter housings in inventory:	500	
Net requirements, filter housings:	50	← Filter housings

While the net requirement for engines under the MRP approach is still 800 units, note how MRP has used the dependent-demand information to show that fewer air cleaners and filter housings will be needed. In addition to considering dependent demand in the determination of net requirements for components, an MRP system also determines when the net requirements are needed. MRP handles this aspect of production and inventory control using the *time-phasing* concept. By starting with the time that the finished product must be completed, we can work backward to determine when an order for each component must be placed. For example, the time-phasing calculations for the Spiecker snowblower problem might appear as follows:

	Week	
Complete order for engines:	20	
Minus lead time for engines:	4	
Place an order for engines:	16	← Order engines
Complete order for air cleaners:	16	
Minus lead time for air cleaners:	1	
Place an order for air cleaners:	15	← Order air cleaners
Complete order for filter housings:	15	
Minus lead time for filter housings:	2	
Place an order for filter housings:	13	← Order filter housings

The components are scheduled so that they are made available only when required for the next higher level of assembly. Similar calculations can be made for all the other components of the snowblower, and if the bill of materials is exploded into detailed part requirements, a complete schedule for shop orders and purchase requisitions is available.

Until the development of large-scale computers, the sheer volume of calculations prohibited the implementation of an MRP system. For example, even in our small illustration, you can begin to appreciate the complexity involved in keeping track of the production and inventory status for every component.

11.9 The Just-in-Time Approach to Inventory Management

The Japanese have captured a sizable share of world markets for many products because of the progress they have made in manufacturing. Among the reasons for this success are the Japanese style of management, the development of new technologies, and the use of new methods of material management and control. One method that has received much attention is known as *just-in-time* (JIT). JIT represents a philosophy whose objective is the elimination of all sources of waste including unnecessary inventory.

The fundamental principle of JIT is to produce the right units in the right quantity at the right time. With JIT, units are produced only when they are required. Inventories are not needed, or are at least minimized. For JIT to function effectively, fundamental changes in traditional production systems must take place. These changes require modifications in the production layout design and material flow process; in addition, setup times must be reduced.

Poor equipment layout is one of the major causes of inefficiencies in manufacturing. In a typical U.S. manufacturing environment, material is transported from the supplier to the warehouse and then to the plant. Within the plant, material may be transported from department to department. When production is completed, the finished goods may be returned to the warehouse, where they are stored until later distribution to the customer. Even with optimal inventory models, inventory and material handling costs can be substantial. The JIT approach helps reduce inventory and material handling costs by providing a flow of raw materials and finished goods in which material introduced at one end of the manufacturing process moves without delays into the finished products.

The driving force behind JIT production is the coordination of successive production activities. A key component of this coordination is an information system called a *Kanban*—the Japanese word for *card*. The type and number of units required by the production process are written on Kanbans, which are used to initiate the withdrawal and the production of units through the production process. By beginning at the final assembly, the Kanban "pulls" parts and components from preceding work stations. Thus, the entire manufacturing operation is synchronized to the final assembly stage. In this fashion, JIT prohibits earlier sources of supply and production from "pushing" units forward and building unnecessary and excessive inventories.

It is important to realize that the total quality concept is critical in the implementation of the JIT philosophy. Since lot sizes are small and inventory levels are minimal, there is no safety stock to replace nonconforming or defective units. Any quality problems disrupt the flow of materials throughout the plant and can be disastrous to the JIT system.

Finally, the coordination of the materials flow from suppliers to the manufacturer is another critical component of JIT. The JIT philosophy does not permit the shipment of large lots from suppliers that would build unnecessarily high inventory levels and costs. To maintain the smooth flow required by JIT, suppliers must make just-in-time deliveries.

Instead of the large shipments that must be counted, inspected, and stored, suppliers make smaller deliveries on a daily basis or even more frequently as necessary to accommodate the manufacturer's daily production schedule. JIT requires a close partnership between the suppliers and the manufacturer to enable materials to be obtained on time and with zero defects.

The benefits of JIT are improved profits, resulting from reduced inventory costs, and improved quality. In the area of inventory management, the more obvious benefits of JIT are the reduced inventory levels, the increased inventory turnover, and the overall lower holding costs.

Summary

In this chapter we presented some of the approaches management scientists use to assist managers in establishing low-cost inventory policies. We first considered cases where the demand rate for the product is constant. In analyzing these inventory systems, total-cost models were developed, which included ordering costs, holding costs, and, in some cases, backordering costs. Then minimum-cost formulas for the order quantity Q were presented. A reorder point r can be established by considering the lead-time demand for the item.

In addition, we discussed inventory models where a deterministic and constant rate could not be assumed, and thus, demand was described by a probability distribution. A critical issue with these probabilistic inventory models is obtaining a probability distribution that most realistically approximates the demand distribution for the item. We first described a single-period model where only one order is placed for the product and, at the end of the period, either the product has sold out or there is a surplus of unsold products that will be sold for a salvage value. Solution procedures were then presented for multiperiod models based on either an order-quantity, reorder-point, continuous-review system or a replenishment-level, periodic-review system.

We pointed out that the models presented in the earlier sections of the chapter are for independent-demand situations and are most applicable for managing finished goods inventory. For manufacturing inventories of subassemblies and component parts, where dependent demand exists, methods such as material requirements planning (MRP) offer significant advantages. Finally, we discussed the just-in-time philosophy that has evolved from the Japanese approach to material management and control. In inventory management, JIT is directed at reducing inventory levels and increasing inventory turnover.

In closing this chapter, we reemphasize that inventory and inventory systems can be an expensive phase of a firm's operation. It is of utmost economic importance for managers to be aware of the cost of inventory systems and to make the best possible operating policy decisions for the inventory system. Inventory models, as presented in this chapter, can help managers to develop good inventory policies.

Glossary

Economic order quantity (EOQ) The order quantity that minimizes the annual holding cost plus the annual ordering cost.

Constant demand rate An assumption of many inventory models that states that the same number of units are taken from inventory each period of time.

Holding cost The cost associated with maintaining an inventory investment, including the cost of the capital investment in the inventory, insurance, taxes, warehouse overhead, and so on. This cost may be stated as a percentage of the inventory investment or as a cost per unit.

Cost of capital The cost a firm incurs in order to obtain capital for investment. It may be stated as an annual percentage rate, and is part of the holding cost associated with maintaining inventory levels.

Ordering cost The fixed cost (salaries, paper, transportation, etc.) associated with placing an order for an item.

Setup cost The fixed cost (labor, materials, lost production) associated with preparing for a new production run.

Inventory position The inventory on hand plus the inventory on order.

Reorder point The inventory position at which a new order should be placed.

Lead time The time between the placing of an order and its receipt in the inventory system.

Lead-time demand The number of units demanded during the lead-time period.

Cycle time The length of time between the placing of two consecutive orders.

Safety stock Inventory maintained in order to reduce the number of stockouts resulting from higher-than-expected demand.

Constant supply rate The situation in which the inventory is built up at a constant rate over a period of time.

Backorder The receipt of an order for a product when there are no units in inventory. These backorders become shortages, which are eventually satisfied when a new supply of the product becomes available.

Goodwill cost A cost associated with a backorder, a lost sale, or any form of stockout or unsatisfied demand. This cost may be used to reflect the loss of future profits due to the fact a customer experienced an unsatisfied demand.

Quantity discounts Discounts or lower unit costs offered by the manufacturer when a customer purchases larger quantities of the product.

Deterministic demand rate A demand for an inventory item that is considered known and not subject to uncertainty.

Probabilistic demand rate When the demand for the inventory item is not known exactly, probabilities must be associated with the possible values for demand.

Single-period inventory models Inventory models in which only one order is placed for the product, and at the end of the period either the item has sold out, or there is a surplus of unsold items that will be sold for a salvage value.

Incremental analysis A method used to determine an optimal order quantity by comparing the cost of ordering an additional unit with the cost of not ordering an additional unit.

Lead-time demand distribution The distribution of demand that occurs during the lead-time period.

Service level The average number of stockouts tolerated per year.

Continuous review When the inventory position is monitored or reviewed on a continuous basis so that a new order can be placed as soon as the reorder point is reached.

Periodic review When the inventory position is checked or reviewed at predetermined periodic points in time. Reorders are placed only at periodic-review points.

Independent demand Demand for an item that is independent of the demand for other products or items. Usually independent demand is generated by customers placing orders for finished goods.

Dependent demand Demand for a product, component, subassembly, or item that is dependent on the demand for another product or item.

Material requirements planning (MRP) A computerized inventory management system whose functions are to schedule production and to control the level of inventory for components with dependent demand.

Master production schedule A statement of how many finished items are to be produced, and when.

Bill of materials (BOM) A structured parts list that shows the manner in which the product is put together.

Time phasing Adding the dimension of time to inventory status data in an MRP environment.

Just-in-time A philosophy that encourages the elimination of waste in time and resources. In inventory management, JIT works to reduce inventory levels and increase inventory turnover.

Kanban The Japanese word for *card*, which refers to the information system used for implementing JIT.

Problems

1. Suppose that the R & B Beverage Company has a soft-drink product that has a constant annual demand rate of 3600 cases. A case of the soft drink costs R & B $3. Ordering costs are $20 per order and holding costs are 25% of the value of the inventory. There are 250 working days per year and the lead time is 5 days. Identify the following aspects of the inventory policy.
   a. Economic order quantity
   b. Reorder point
   c. Cycle time
   d. Total annual cost

2. A general property of the EOQ inventory model is that total inventory holding and total ordering costs are equal at the optimal solution. Use the data in Problem 1 to show that this result is true. Use equations (11.1), (11.2), and (11.3) to show that, in general, total holding costs and total ordering costs are equal whenever Q^* is used.

3. The reorder point (see equation (11.6)) is defined as the lead-time demand for the item. In cases of long lead times, the lead-time demand and thus the reorder point may exceed the economic order quantity Q^*. In such cases, the inventory position will not equal the inventory on hand when an order is placed and the reorder point may be expressed in terms of either the inventory position or the inventory on hand. Consider the economic order quantity model with $D = 5000$, $C_o = \$32$, $C_h = \$2$, and 250 working days per year. Identify the reorder point in terms of the inventory position and in terms of the inventory on hand for each of the following lead times.
   a. 5 days
   b. 15 days
   c. 25 days
   d. 45 days

4. Westside Auto purchases a component used in the manufacture of automobile generators directly from the supplier. Westside's generator production operation, which is operated at a constant rate, will require 1000 components per month throughout the year (12,000 units annually). Assume that the ordering costs are $25 per order, the unit cost is $2.50 per component, and that annual holding costs are 20% of the value of the inventory. There are 250 working days per year and the lead time is 5 days. Answer the following inventory policy questions.
   a. What is the EOQ for this component?
   b. What is the reorder point?
   c. What is the cycle time?
   d. What are the total annual holding and ordering costs associated with your recommended EOQ?

5. Suppose that Westside's management in Problem 4 likes the operational efficiency of ordering once each month and in quantities of 1000 units. How much more expensive would this policy be than your EOQ recommendation? Would you recommend in favor of the 1000-unit order quantity? Explain. What would the reorder point be if the 1000-unit quantity were acceptable?

6. Tele-Reco is a new specialty store that sells television sets, videotape recorders, video games, and other television-related products. A new Japanese-manufactured videotape recorder costs Tele-Reco $600 per unit. Tele-Reco's annual holding cost rate is 22%. Ordering costs are estimated to be $70 per order.
   a. If demand for the new videotape recorder is expected to be constant with a rate of 20 units per month, what is the recommended order quantity for the videotape recorder?
   b. What are the estimated annual inventory holding and ordering costs associated with this product?
   c. How many orders will be placed per year?
   d. With 250 working days per year, what is the cycle time for this product?

7. A large distributor of oil-well drilling equipment has operated over the past 2 years with EOQ policies based on an annual holding cost rate of 22%. Under the EOQ policy, a particular product has been ordered with a $Q^* = 80$. A recent evaluation of holding costs shows that because of an increase in the interest rate associated with bank loans, the annual holding cost rate should be 27%.

a. What is the new economic order quantity for the product?

b. Develop a general expression showing how the economic order quantity changes when the annual holding cost rate is changed from I to I'.

8. Nation-Wide Bus Lines is proud of its 6-week bus driver training program that it conducts for all new Nation-Wide drivers. As long as the class size remains less than or equal to 35, a 6-week training program costs Nation-Wide $22,000 for instructors, equipment, and so on. The Nation-Wide training program must provide the company with approximately five new drivers per month. After completing the training program, new drivers are paid $1600 per month but do not work until a full-time driver position is open. Nation-Wide views the $1600 per month paid to each idle new driver as a holding cost necessary to maintain a supply of newly trained drivers available for immediate service. Viewing new drivers as inventory-type units, how large should the training classes be to minimize Nation-Wide's total annual training and new driver idle-time costs? How many training classes should the company hold each year? What is the total annual cost associated with your recommendation?

9. Cress Electronic Products manufactures components used in the automotive industry. Cress purchases parts for use in its manufacturing operation from a variety of different suppliers. One particular supplier provides a part where the assumptions of the EOQ model are realistic. The annual demand is 5000 units, the ordering cost is $80 per order, and the annual holding cost rate is 25%.

a. If the cost of the part is $20 per unit, what is the economic order quantity?

b. Assume 250 days of operation per year. If the lead time for an order is 12 days, what is the reorder point?

c. If the lead time for the part is 7 weeks (35 days), what is the reorder point?

d. What is the reorder point for part (c) if the reorder point is expressed in terms of the inventory on hand rather than the inventory position?

10. All-Star Bat Manufacturing, Inc., supplies baseball bats to major and minor league baseball teams. After an initial order in January, demand over the 6-month baseball season is approximately constant at 1000 bats per month. Assuming that the bat production process can handle up to 4000 bats per month, the bat production setup costs are $150 per setup, the production cost is $10 per bat, and that holding costs have a monthly rate of 2%, what production lot size would you recommend to meet the demand during the baseball season? If All-Star operates 20 days per month, how often will the production process operate, and what is the length of a production run?

11. Assume that a production line operates such that the production lot size model of Section 11.2 is applicable. Given $D = 6400$ units per year, $C_o = 100, and $C_h = 2 per unit per year, compute the minimum-cost production lot size for each of the following production rates:

a. 8000 units per year   **c.** 32,000 units per year

b. 10,000 units per year   **d.** 100,000 units per year

Compute the EOQ recommended lot size using equation (11.5). What two observations can you make about the relationship between the EOQ model and the production lot size model?

12. Assume that you are reviewing the production lot size decision associated with a production operation where $P = 8000$ units per year, $D = 2000$ units per year, $C_o = 300, and $C_h = 1.60 per unit per year. Also assume that current practice calls for production runs of 500 units every 3 months. Would you recommend changing the current production lot size? Why or why not? How much could be saved by converting to your production lot size recommendation?

13. **SELF**Test Wilson Publishing Company produces books for the retail market. Demand for a current book is expected to occur at a constant annual rate of 7200 copies. The cost of one copy of the book is $14.50. The holding cost is based on an 18% annual rate, and production setup costs are $150 per setup. The equipment on which the book is produced has an annual production volume of 25,000 copies. There are 250 working days

per year and the lead time for a production run is 15 days. Use the production lot size model to compute the following values:

a. Minimum-cost production lot size
b. Number of production runs per year
c. Cycle time
d. Length of a production run

e. Maximum inventory level
f. Total annual cost
g. Reorder point

14. A well-known manufacturer of several brands of toothpaste uses the production lot size model to determine production quantities for its various products. The product known as Extra White is currently being produced in production lot sizes of 5000 units. The length of the production run for this quantity is 10 days. Because of a recent shortage of a particular raw material, the supplier of the material has announced a cost increase that will be passed along to the manufacturer of Extra White. Current estimates are that the new raw material cost will increase the manufacturing cost of the toothpaste products by 23% per unit. What will be the effect of this price increase on the production lot sizes for Extra White?

15. **SELF**Test Suppose that Westside Auto of Problem 4, with $D = 12{,}000$ units per year, $C_h = (2.50)(0.20) = \$0.50$, and $C_o = \$25$, decided to operate with a backorder inventory policy. Backorder costs are estimated to be \$5 per unit per year. Identify the following:

a. Minimum-cost order quantity
b. Maximum number of backorders
c. Maximum inventory level

d. Cycle time
e. Total annual cost

16. Assuming 250 days of operation per year and a lead time of 5 days, what is the reorder point for Westside Auto in Problem 15? Show the general formula for the reorder point for the EOQ model with backorders. In general, is the reorder point when backorders are allowed greater than or less than the reorder point when backorders are not allowed? Explain.

17. A manager of an inventory system believes that inventory models are important decision-making aids. While often using an EOQ policy, the manager has never considered a backorder model because of the assumption that backorders were "bad" and should be avoided. However, with upper management's continued pressure for cost reduction, you have been asked to analyze the economics of a backordering policy for some products that can possibly be backordered. For a specific product with $D = 800$ units per year, $C_o = \$150$, $C_h = \$3$, and $C_b = \$20$, what is the difference in total annual cost between the EOQ model and the planned shortage or backorder model? If the manager adds constraints that no more than 25% of the units can be backordered and that no customer will have to wait more than 15 days for an order, should the backorder inventory policy be adopted? Assume 250 working days per year.

18. If the lead time for new orders is 20 days for the inventory system discussed in Problem 17, find the reorder point for both the EOQ and the backorder models.

19. The A&M Hobby Shop carries a line of radio-controlled model racing cars. Demand for the cars is assumed to be constant at a rate of 40 cars per month. The cars cost \$60 each, and ordering costs are approximately \$15 per order, regardless of the order size. The annual holding cost rate is 20%.

a. Determine the economic order quantity and total annual cost under the assumption that no backorders are permitted.
b. Using a \$45 per unit per year backorder cost, determine the minimum-cost inventory policy and total annual cost for the model racing cars.
c. What is the maximum number of days a customer would have to wait for a backorder under the policy in part (b)? Assume that the Hobby Shop is open for business 300 days per year.
d. Would you recommend a no-backorder or a backorder inventory policy for this product? Explain.
e. If the lead time is 6 days, what is the reorder point for both the no-backorder and backorder inventory policies?

20. Assume that the following quantity discount schedule is appropriate:

Order Size	Discount (%)	Unit Cost
0 to 49	0	$30.00
50 to 99	5	28.50
100 or more	10	27.00

If annual demand is 120 units, ordering costs are $20 per order, and the annual holding cost rate is 25%, what order quantity would you recommend?

21. **SELF Test** Apply the EOQ model to the following quantity discount situation where $D = 500$ units per year, $C_o = \$40$, and an annual holding cost rate of 20% are given:

Discount Category	Order Size	Discount (%)	Unit Cost
1	0 to 99	0	$10.00
2	100 or more	3	9.70

What order quantity do you recommend?

22. Keith Shoe Stores carries a basic black dress shoe for men that sells at an approximate constant rate of 500 pairs of shoes every 3 months. Keith's current buying policy is to order 500 pairs each time an order is placed. It costs Keith $30 to place an order. The annual holding cost rate is 20%. With the order quantity of 500, Keith obtains the shoes at the lowest possible unit cost of $28 per pair. Other quantity discounts offered by the manufacturer are as follows:

Order Quantity	Price Per Pair
0–99	$36
100–199	32
200–299	30
300 or more	28

What is the minimum-cost order quantity for the shoes? What are the annual savings of your inventory policy over the policy currently being used by Keith?

23. In the EOQ model with quantity discounts, we stated that if the Q^* for a price category is larger than necessary to qualify for the category price, the category cannot be optimal. Use the two discount categories in Problem 21 to show that this is true. That is, plot the total-cost curves for the two categories and show that if the category 2 minimum cost Q is an acceptable solution, we do not have to consider category 1.

24. The J&B Card Shop sells calendars with different Colonial pictures shown for each month. The once-a-year order for each year's calendar arrives in September. From past experience, the September-to-July demand for the calendars can be approximated by a normal probability distribution with $\mu = 500$ and $\sigma = 120$. The calendars cost $1.50 each, and J&B sells them for $3 each.
   a. If J&B throws out all unsold calendars at the end of July (i.e., salvage value is zero), how many calendars should be ordered?
   b. If J&B reduces the calendar price to $1 at the end of July and can sell all surplus calendars at this price, how many calendars should be ordered?

25. **SELFTest** The Gilbert Air-Conditioning Company is considering the purchase of a special shipment of portable air conditioners manufactured in Japan. Each unit will cost Gilbert $80 and it will be sold for $125. Gilbert does not want to carry surplus air conditioners over until the following year. Thus, all surplus air conditioners will be sold to a wholesaler for $50 per unit. Assume that the air conditioner demand follows a normal probability distribution with $\mu = 20$ and $\sigma = 8$.
   a. What is the recommended order quantity?
   b. What is the probability that Gilbert will sell all units it orders?

26. A popular newsstand in a large metropolitan area is attempting to determine how many copies of the Sunday paper it should purchase each week. Demand for the newspaper on Sundays can be approximated by a normal probability distribution with $\mu = 450$ and $\sigma = 100$. The newspaper costs the newsstand 35¢ a copy and sells for 50¢ a copy. The newsstand does not receive any value from surplus papers and thus absorbs a 100% loss on all unsold papers.
   a. How many copies of the Sunday paper should be purchased each week?
   b. What is the probability that the newsstand will have a stockout?
   c. The manager of the newsstand is concerned about the newsstand's image if the probability of stockout is high. The customers often purchase other items after coming to the newsstand for the Sunday paper. Frequent stockouts would cause customers to go to another newsstand. The manager agrees that a 50¢ goodwill cost should be assigned to any stockout. What is the new recommended order quantity and the new probability of a stockout?

27. A perishable dairy product is ordered daily at a particular supermarket. The product, which costs $1.19 per unit, sells for $1.65 per unit. If units are unsold at the end of the day, the supplier takes them back at a rebate of $1 per unit. Assume that daily demand is approximately normally distributed with $\mu = 150$ and $\sigma = 30$.
   a. What is your recommended daily order quantity for the supermarket?
   b. What is the probability that the supermarket will sell all the units it orders?
   c. In problems such as these, why would the supplier offer a rebate as high as $1? For example, why not offer a nominal rebate of, say, 25¢ per unit? What happens to the supermarket order quantity as the rebate is reduced?

28. A retail outlet sells a seasonal product for $10 per unit. The cost of the product is $8 per unit. All units not sold during the regular season are sold for half the retail price in an end-of-season clearance sale. Assume that demand for the product is uniformly distributed between 200 and 800.
   a. What is the recommended order quantity?
   b. What is the probability that at least some customers will ask to purchase the product after the outlet is sold out? That is, what is the probability of a stockout using your order quantity in part (a)?
   c. To keep customers happy and returning to the store later, the owner feels that stockouts should be avoided if at all possible. What is your recommended order quantity if the owner is willing to tolerate a 0.15 probability of a stockout?
   d. Using your answer to part (c), what is the goodwill cost you are assigning to a stockout?

29. **SELFTest** Floyd Distributors, Inc., provides a variety of auto parts to small local garages. Floyd purchases parts from manufacturers according to the EOQ model and then ships the parts from a regional warehouse direct to its customers. For a particular type of muffler, Floyd's EOQ analysis recommends orders with $Q^* = 25$ to satisfy an annual demand of 200 mufflers. There are 250 working days per year and the lead time averages 15 days.
   a. What is the reorder point if Floyd assumes a constant demand rate?
   b. Suppose that an analysis of Floyd's muffler demand shows that the lead-time demand follows a normal probability distribution with $\mu = 12$ and $\sigma = 2.5$. If Floyd's management can tolerate one stockout per year, what is the revised reorder point?
   c. What is the safety stock for part (b)? If $C_h = \$5$/unit/year, what is the extra cost due to the uncertainty of demand?

30. For Floyd Distributors in Problem 29, we were given $Q^* = 25$, $D = 200$, $C_h = \$5$, and a normal lead-time demand distribution with $\mu = 12$ and $\sigma = 2.5$.

a. What is Floyd's reorder point if the firm is willing to tolerate two stockouts during the year?

b. What is Floyd's reorder point if the firm wants to restrict the probability of a stockout on any one cycle to at most 1%?

c. What are the safety stock levels and the annual safety stock costs for the reorder points found in parts (a) and (b)?

31. A product with an annual demand of 1000 units has $C_o = \$25.50$ and $C_h = \$8$. The demand exhibits some variability such that the lead-time demand follows a normal probability distribution with $\mu = 25$ and $\sigma = 5$.

a. What is the recommended order quantity?

b. What are the reorder point and safety stock if the firm desires at most a 2% probability of stockout on any given order cycle?

c. If a manager sets the reorder point at 30, what is the probability of a stockout on any given order cycle? How many times would you expect to stockout during the year if this reorder point were used?

32. The B&S Novelty and Craft Shop in Bennington, Vermont, sells a variety of quality handmade items to tourists. B&S will sell 300 hand-carved miniature replicas of a Colonial soldier each year, but the demand pattern during the year is uncertain. The replicas sell for $20 each, and B&S uses a 15% annual inventory holding cost rate. Ordering costs are $5 per order, and demand during the lead time follows a normal probability distribution with $\mu = 15$ and $\sigma = 6$.

a. What is the recommended order quantity?

b. If B&S is willing to accept a stockout roughly twice a year, what reorder point would you recommend? What is the probability that B&S will have a stockout in any one order cycle?

c. What are the safety stock and annual safety stock costs for this product?

33. **SELFTest** A firm uses a 1-week periodic review inventory system. There is a 2-day lead time for any order, and the firm is willing to tolerate an average of one stockout per year.

a. Using the firm's service guideline, what is the probability of a stockout associated with each replenishment decision?

b. What is the replenishment level if demand during the review period plus lead-time period is normally distributed with a mean of 60 units and a standard deviation of 12 units?

c. What is the replenishment level if demand during the review period plus lead-time period is uniformly distributed between 35 and 85 units?

34. Foster Drugs, Inc., handles a variety of health and beauty aid products. A particular hair conditioner product costs Foster Drugs $2.95 per unit. The annual holding cost rate is 20%. An order-quantity, reorder-point inventory model recommends an order quantity of 300 units per order.

a. Lead time is one week and the lead-time demand is normally distributed with a mean of 150 units and a standard deviation of 40 units. What is the reorder point if the firm is willing to tolerate a 1% chance of stockout on any one cycle?

b. What safety stock and annual safety stock cost is associated with your recommendation in part (a)?

c. The order-quantity, reorder-point model requires a continuous-review system. Foster is considering making a transition to a periodic-review system in an attempt to coordinate ordering for many of its products. The demand during the proposed two-week review period and the one-week lead-time period is normally distributed with a mean of 450 units and a standard deviation of 70 units. What is the recommended replenishment level for this periodic-review system if the firm is willing to tolerate the same 1% chance of stockout associated with any replenishment decision?

d. What safety stock and annual safety stock cost is associated with your recommendation in part (c)?

e. Compare your answers to parts (b) and (d). The company is seriously considering the periodic-review system. Would you support this decision? Explain.

f. Would you tend to favor the continuous-review system for more expensive items? For example, assume that the product in the above example sold for $295 per unit. Explain.

35. Statewide Auto Parts uses a 4-week periodic-review system to reorder parts for its inventory stock. A 1-week lead time is required to fill the order. Demand for one particular part during the 5-week replenishment period is normally distributed with a mean of 18 units and a standard deviation of 6 units.

    a. At a particular periodic review, 8 units are in inventory. The parts manager places an order for 16 units. What is the probability that this part will have a stockout before an order that is placed at the next 4-week review period arrives?

    b. Assume that the company is willing to tolerate a 2.5% chance of a stockout associated with a replenishment decision. How many parts should the manager have ordered in part (a)? What is the replenishment level for the 4-week periodic-review system?

36. Rose Office Supplies, Inc., which is open 6 days a week, uses a 2-week periodic review for its store inventory. On alternating Monday mornings, the store manager fills out an order sheet requiring a shipment of various items from the company's warehouse. A particular three-ring notebook sells at an average rate of 16 notebooks per week. The standard deviation in sales is 5 notebooks per week. The lead time for a new shipment is 3 days. The mean lead time demand is 8 notebooks with a standard deviation of 3.5.

    a. What is the mean or expected demand during the review period plus the lead-time period?

    b. Under the assumption of independent demand from week to week, the variances in demands are additive. Thus, the variance of the demand during the review period plus the lead-time period is equal to the variance of demand during the first week plus the variance of demand during the second week plus the variance of demand during the lead-time period. What is the variance of demand during the review period plus the lead-time period? What is the standard deviation of demand during the review period plus the lead-time period?

    c. Assuming that demand has a normal probability distribution, what is the replenishment level that will provide an expected stockout rate of one per year?

    d. On Monday, March 22, 18 notebooks remain in inventory at the store. How many notebooks should the store manager order?

37. **SELFTest** Consider the Spiecker Manufacturing problem of Section 11.8. Determine the net requirements for the engine assembly, the air cleaner subassembly, and the filter housing if the number of units in inventory were 2000, 1500, and 1000, respectively. Assume that 5000 units of the 14-inch snowblower are required in week 21.

38. For the Spiecker Manufacturing problem of Section 11.8, determine the effect on time phasing if lead times were 10 for the engine assembly, 3 for the air cleaner subassembly, and 5 for the filter housing.

39. C & D Lawn Products manufactures a rotary spreader for applying fertilizer. A portion of the bill of materials is shown as follows:

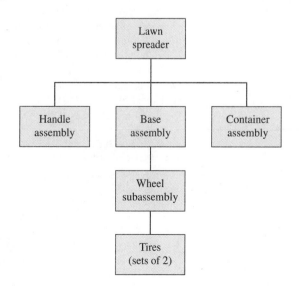

If 3000 lawn spreaders are needed to satisfy a customer's order, determine the net requirements for the base assembly, wheel subassembly, and tires (sets of two). Assume that 1000 base assemblies, 1500 wheel subassemblies, and 800 tires (sets of two) are currently in inventory.

40. In Problem 39, assume that the lead time for the base assembly, wheel subassembly, and tires are 2 weeks, 4 weeks, and 5 weeks, respectively. If all components must be completed no later than week 15 of the current production period, determine when orders must be placed to meet the production schedule.

Case Problem: A Make-or-Buy Analysis

Wagner Fabricating Company is reviewing the economic feasibility of manufacturing a part that it currently purchases from a supplier. Forecasted annual demand for the part is 3200 units. Wagner operates 250 days per year.

Wagner's financial analysts have established a cost of capital of 14% for the use of funds for investments within the company. In addition, over the past year $600,000 has been the average investment in the company's inventory. Accounting information shows that a total of $24,000 was spent on taxes and insurance related to the company's inventory. In addition, it has been estimated that $9000 was lost due to inventory shrinkage, which included damaged goods as well as pilferage. A remaining $15,000 was spent on warehouse overhead, including utility expenses for heating and lighting.

An analysis of the purchasing operation shows that approximately 2 hours are required to process and coordinate an order for the part regardless of the quantity ordered. Purchasing salaries average $28 per hour, including employee benefits. In addition, a detailed analysis of 125 orders showed that $2375 was spent on telephone, paper, and postage directly related to the ordering process.

A 1-week lead time is required to obtain the part from the supplier. An analysis of demand during the lead time shows that lead-time demand is approximately normally distributed with a mean of 64 units and a standard deviation of 10 units. Service level guidelines indicate that one stockout per year is acceptable.

Currently, the company has a contract to purchase the part from a supplier at a cost of $18 per unit. However, over the past few months, the company's production capacity has been expanded. As a result, excess capacity is now available in certain production departments and the company is considering the alternative of producing the parts itself.

Forecasted utilization of equipment shows that production capacity will be available for the part being considered. The production capacity is available at the rate of 1000 units per month, with up to 5 months of production time available. It is felt that with a 2-week lead time, schedules can be arranged so that the part can be produced whenever needed. The demand during the 2-week lead time is approximately normally distributed, with a mean of 128 units and a standard deviation of 20 units. Production costs are expected to be $17 per part.

A concern of management is that setup costs will be significant. The total cost of labor and lost production time is estimated to be $50 per hour, and it will take a full 8-hour shift to set up the equipment for producing the part.

Managerial Report

Develop a report for management of Wagner Fabricating that will address the question of whether the company should continue to purchase the part from the supplier or should begin to produce the part itself. Include the following factors in your report:

1. An analysis of the holding costs, including the appropriate annual holding cost rate.
2. An analysis of ordering costs, including the appropriate cost per order from the supplier.

3. An analysis of setup costs for the production operation.
4. A development of the inventory policy for the following two alternatives:
   a. Ordering a fixed quantity Q from the supplier
   b. Ordering a fixed quantity Q from in-plant production
5. Include the following in the policies of parts 4(a) and 4(b) above.
   a. Optimal quantity $Q*$
   b. Number of order or production runs per year
   c. Cycle time
   d. Reorder point
   e. Amount of safety stock
   f. Expected maximum inventory level
   g. Average inventory level
   h. Annual holding cost
   i. Annual ordering cost
   j. Annual cost of the units purchased or manufactured
   k. Total annual cost of the purchase policy and the total annual cost of the production policy
6. Make a recommendation as to whether the company should purchase or manufacture the part. What is the saving associated with your recommendation as compared with the other alternative?

APPENDIX 11.1   Inventory Models with Spreadsheets

In this appendix we demonstrate the use of spreadsheets to implement the economic order quantity inventory model. The approach demonstrated for the EOQ model can be modified to accommodate the other inventory models presented in this chapter.

Figure 11.20 shows the formula spreadsheet for the R&B Beverage Company EOQ model introduced in Section 11.1. The annual demand, cost per unit, inventory holding cost rate, cost per order, days per year, and lead time in days are placed in spreadsheet cells B3–B8. The values shown in color in Figure 11.20 correspond to the Bub Beer data. The economic order quantity, $Q*$, is computed by the formula in cell B11. Cell B12 then uses the economic order quantity from cell B11 to compute the total annual cost. The formula in cell B14 assumes implementation of the recommended economic order quantity in cell B11. The remaining spreadsheet formulas provide additional information that will help the manager understand the inventory operation and determine the final order quantity to be used. In addition to the breakdown of the total annual cost into annual inventory and annual ordering costs, the results show inventory levels that can be anticipated, the reorder point, the number of orders per year, and the cycle time. The general equations for these aspects of the inventory operation were presented in Section 11.1. The corresponding spreadsheet formulas appear in cells B16–B24.

Figure 11.21 is the value spreadsheet for the Bub Beer EOQ problem. The economic order quantity of 1824.28 cases, with a minimum total annual cost of $3,648.56, is shown. The spreadsheet enables the user to view the economic order quantity and then evaluate alternative order quantities. For example, assume that the inventory manager believes that, operationally, an order quantity of 2000 cases would be easier to implement. The analyst simply enters 2000 cases as the requested order quantity in cell B14. The spreadsheet will then automatically recompute the inventory system characteristics. Figure 11.22 shows the results based on the order quantity of 2000 cases. In particular note that the last two entries on the spreadsheet show that the added cost is only $15.44 per year, or a 0.42% increase. The manager may prefer the 2000-case order quantity with its slight cost increase over the EOQ model's solution.

Finally, as with most other spreadsheet applications, the manager may change or vary one or more of the model's inputs and quickly learn how the changes affect the inventory cost and optimal solution. For example, changing the inventory holding cost and/or ordering cost would show how sensitive the recommended EOQ and total annual cost are to these values.

Figure 11.20

Formula Spreadsheet for the Economic Order Quantity Model

	A	B
1	ECONOMIC ORDER QUANTITY MODEL	
2		
3	ANNUAL DEMAND	104000
4	COST PER UNIT	8
5	HOLDING COST RATE %	25
6	COST PER ORDER	32
7	DAYS PER YEAR	250
8	LEAD TIME (DAYS)	2
9		
10		
11	MINIMUM COST EOQ	=SQRT(2*B3*B6/(B4*B5/100))
12	TOTAL ANNUAL COST	= (B11/2)*(B4*B5/100)+B3*B6/B11
13		
14	REQUESTED ORDER QUANTITY	=B11
15		
16	ANNUAL INVENTORY COST	= (B14/2)*(B4*B5/100)
17	ANNUAL ORDER COST	= (B3/B14)*B6
18	TOTAL ANNUAL COST	=B16+B17
19		
20	MAXIMUM INVENTORY	=B14
21	AVERAGE INVENTORY	=B20/2
22	REORDER POINT	= (B3/B7)*B8
23	NUMBER ORDERS PER YEAR	=B3/B14
24	CYCLE TIME (DAYS)	=B7/B23
25		
26	ANNUAL COST OVER EOQ	=B18-B12
27	PERCENTAGE	=B26/B12

Figure 11.21

Value Spreadsheet for the Economic Order Quantity Model

	A	B
1	ECONOMIC ORDER QUANTITY MODEL	
2		
3	ANNUAL DEMAND	104000
4	COST PER UNIT	8
5	HOLDING COST RATE %	25
6	COST PER ORDER	32
7	DAYS PER YEAR	250
8	LEAD TIME (DAYS)	2
9		
10		
11	MINIMUM COST EOQ	1824.28
12	TOTAL ANNUAL COST	$3,648.56
13		
14	REQUESTED ORDER QUANTITY	1824.28
15		
16	ANNUAL INVENTORY COST	$1,824.28
17	ANNUAL ORDER COST	$1,824.28
18	TOTAL ANNUAL COST	$3,648.56
19		
20	MAXIMUM INVENTORY	
21	AVERAGE INVENTORY	1824.28
22	REORDER POINT	912.14
23	NUMBER ORDERS PER YEAR	832.00
24	CYCLE TIME (DAYS)	57.01
25		4.39
26	ANNUAL COST OVER EOQ	$0.00
27	PERCENTAGE	0.00%

Figure 11.22

....

Value Spreadsheet for the Economic Order Quantity Model with a Requested Quantity of 2000 Cases

	A	B
1	ECONOMIC ORDER QUANTITY MODEL	
2		
3	ANNUAL DEMAND	104000
4	COST PER UNIT	8
5	HOLDING COST RATE %	25
6	COST PER ORDER	32
7	DAYS PER YEAR	250
8	LEAD TIME (DAYS)	2
9		
10		
11	MINIMUM COST EOQ	1824.28
12	TOTAL ANNUAL COST	$3,648.56
13		
14	REQUESTED ORDER QUANTITY	2000.00
15		
16	ANNUAL INVENTORY COST	$2,000.00
17	ANNUAL ORDER COST	$1,664.00
18	TOTAL ANNUAL COST	$3,664.00
19		
20	MAXIMUM INVENTORY	2000.00
21	AVERAGE INVENTORY	1000.00
22	REORDER POINT	832.00
23	NUMBER ORDERS PER YEAR	52.00
24	CYCLE TIME (DAYS)	4.81
25		
26	ANNUAL COST OVER EOQ	$15.44
27	PERCENTAGE	0.42%

APPENDIX 11.2 Development of the Optimal Order-Quantity (Q^*) Formula for the EOQ Model

Given equation (11.4) as the total annual cost for the EOQ model,

$$TC = \frac{1}{2}QC_h + \frac{D}{Q}C_o \tag{11.4}$$

we can find the order quantity Q that minimizes the total cost by setting the derivative, dTC/dQ, equal to zero and solving for Q^*.

$$\frac{dTC}{dQ} = \frac{1}{2}C_h - \frac{D}{Q^2}C_o = 0$$

$$\frac{1}{2}C_h = \frac{D}{Q^2}C_o$$

$$C_h Q^2 = 2DC_o$$

$$Q^2 = \frac{2DC_o}{C_h}$$

Hence,

$$Q^* = \sqrt{\frac{2DC_o}{C_h}} \tag{11.5}$$

The second derivative is

$$\frac{d^2TC}{dQ^2} = \frac{2D}{Q^3}C_o$$

Since the value of the second derivative is greater than zero for D, C_o, and Q greater than zero, Q^* from equation (11.5) is the minimum-cost solution.

APPENDIX 11.3 Development of the Optimal Lot Size (Q^*) Formula for the Production Lot Size Model

Given equation (11.15) as the total annual cost for the production lot size model,

$$TC = \frac{1}{2}\left(1 - \frac{D}{P}\right)QC_h + \frac{D}{Q}C_o \tag{11.15}$$

we can find the order quantity Q that minimizes the total cost by setting the derivative, dTC/dQ, equal to zero and solving for Q^*.

$$\frac{dTC}{dQ} = \frac{1}{2}\left(1 - \frac{D}{P}\right)C_h - \frac{D}{Q^2}C_o = 0$$

Solving for Q^*, we have

$$\frac{1}{2}\left(1 - \frac{D}{P}\right)C_h = \frac{D}{Q^2}C_o$$

$$\left(1 - \frac{D}{P}\right)C_h Q^2 = 2DC_o$$

$$Q^2 = \frac{2DC_o}{(1 - D/P)C_h}$$

Hence,

$$Q^* = \sqrt{\frac{2DC_o}{(1 - D/P)C_h}} \tag{11.28}$$

The second derivative is

$$\frac{d^2TC}{dQ^2} = \frac{2DC_o}{Q^3}$$

Since the value of the second derivative is greater than zero for D, C_o, and Q greater than zero, Q^* from equation (11.16) is a minimum-cost solution.

APPENDIX 11.4 Development of the Optimal Order-Quantity (Q^*) and Optimal Backorder (S^*) Formulas for the Planned Shortage Model

Given equation (11.25) as the total annual cost for the planned shortage model,

$$TC = \frac{(Q - S)^2}{2Q}C_h + \frac{D}{Q}C_o + \frac{S^2}{2Q}C_b \tag{11.25}$$

we have two inventory decision variables, Q and S. To find the Q and S values that minimize equation (11.25), we must set the two partial derivatives, $\partial TC/\partial Q$ and $\partial TC/\partial S$, equal to zero.

First, let us rewrite equation (11.25) as follows:

$$TC = \left(\frac{Q^2 - 2QS + S^2}{2Q}\right)C_h + \frac{D}{Q}C_o + \frac{S^2}{2Q}C_b$$

$$= \frac{Q}{2}C_h - SC_h + \frac{C_h}{2Q}S^2 + \frac{DC_o}{Q} + \frac{C_b}{2Q}S^2$$

$$= \left(\frac{C_h + C_b}{2Q}\right)S^2 - SC_h + \frac{QC_h}{2} + \frac{DC_o}{Q}$$

Then, setting $\partial TC/\partial S = 0$, we obtain

$$\frac{\partial TC}{\partial S} = \left(\frac{C_h + C_b}{Q}\right)S - C_h = 0$$

Solving for S^*, we have

$$\left(\frac{C_h + C_b}{Q}\right)S = C_h$$

Thus

$$S^* = Q\left(\frac{C_h}{C_h + C_b}\right) \qquad (11.27)$$

Setting $\partial TC/\partial Q = 0$, we obtain

$$\frac{\partial TC}{\partial Q} = \frac{-(C_h + C_b)S^2}{2Q^2} + \frac{C_h}{2} - \frac{DC_o}{Q^2} = 0$$

Substituting S^* of equation (11.27), we have

$$\frac{\partial TC}{\partial Q} = \frac{-(C_h + C_b)Q^2(C_h)^2/(C_h + C_b)^2}{2Q^2} + \frac{C_h}{2} - \frac{DC_o}{Q^2} = 0$$

We can solve for Q^* as follows:

$$\frac{-C_h^2}{2(C_h + C_b)} + \frac{C_h}{2} = \frac{DC_o}{Q^2}$$

$$\frac{-C_h^2 + C_h(C_h + C_b)}{2(C_h + C_b)} = \frac{DC_o}{Q^2}$$

$$Q^2 = \frac{2(C_h + C_b)DC_o}{C_h C_b}$$

$$Q^2 = \frac{2C_h DC_o}{C_h C_b} + \frac{2C_b DC_o}{C_h C_b}$$

$$Q^2 = \frac{2DC_o}{C_h}\left(\frac{C_h}{C_b} + \frac{C_b}{C_b}\right)$$

Hence

$$Q^* = \sqrt{\frac{2DC_o}{C_h}\left(\frac{C_h + C_b}{C_b}\right)} \qquad (11.26)$$

The second-order conditions will show that equations (11.26) and (11.27) are the minimum-cost solutions.

MANAGEMENT SCIENCE in practice

SupeRx, Inc.*
Cincinnati, Ohio

SupeRx, Inc., is a chain of drugstores with locations in 15 states. The company operates a total of 345 stores that are part of Hook-SupeRx, Inc., which operates more than 1100 stores, primarily in the Midwest and Northeast. As in any retail business, the company's primary functions and concerns revolve around sales growth, profit margins, expense control, and inventory management.

Inventory management is undergoing a rapid transformation from an art to a science. No longer can any retail business expect to operate profitably without a sound inventory management program, and SupeRx has recognized this. A key consideration for the company is product movement information that in turn determines reorder quantities at both the store and warehouse levels. Seasonal fluctuations and advertising can affect product movement, and their effects must be measured using historical data rather than seat-of-the-pants guesswork.

General inventory management for SupeRx involves several product categories: basic products carried on an everyday basis, seasonal products carried only during certain times of the year (such as fruitcakes during Christmas), and special items bought on an in-and-out basis throughout the year.

By far the most critical inventory issue is the replenishment of basic products. At SupeRx, as at most retail drug chains, this type of product is ordered under a periodic-review inventory system, with the review period being 1 week. The weekly review uses electronic ordering equipment that scans an order label affixed to the shelf. Such a label is located on the shelf directly below each item. Among other information on this label is the "order-to quantity." (*Note:* This is the replenishment level referred to in the periodic-review inventory model of Section 11.7.) The store employee placing the order determines the quantity to order by subtracting the number of units of product on the shelf from the order-to quantity (OTQ). For example, if the OTQ is 6 and there are two units of product on the shelf, the quantity ordered would be 4. The OTQ is the key factor in inventory control for basic products.

Several factors are considered in determining individual item OTQs. The most obvious is average weekly demand or movement. SupeRx uses movement figures from the warehouse to the stores. Suppose, for example, an item averages two units per week per store in warehouse deliveries. Setting the OTQ equal to 2 would not allow for sales fluctuations that exceeded the average of 2. To compensate for this and to avoid stockouts, SupeRx sets the OTQ equal to a 3-week demand or movement. Thus, in our example, the OTQ would become 6.

Another factor to consider is whether an item can be ordered in units or cases. In some instances, it is not feasible for the warehouse to deliver in anything less than case quantities. An example would be candy bars. Stores must order a minimum of one case (36 units), no matter what the movement indicates. Thus, the OTQ is 36 or a multiple of 36 to accommodate the case order restriction. Merchandising esthetics must also be considered when determining an OTQ. If an item has four facings or open positions on the shelf, but the optimum OTQ determined by movement is 3, there would be one space without product. This would create an out-of-stock impression to the customer, and, thus, the OTQ would be increased to at least 4. Seasonal fluctuations in movement must be considered when OTQs are determined. For example, the OTQ for a cough and cold item would be significantly higher in January than it would be in July. Adhesive bandages would be just the opposite, with higher usage in the summer than in the winter.

SupeRx is in the process of taking advantage of new technological breakthroughs in inventory management. Today, its OTQs are based on average company warehouse movement into the stores. Soon SupeRx will have a program in place to produce OTQs by item by individual store, based on that store's movement, rather than on the company movement. Once that is in place, SupeRx will be able to accommodate seasonal fluctuations by individual store as well.

The chain drug industry is well behind other retail industries (most notably the grocery industry) in the ability to capture point-of-sale information with the use of scanning registers. SupeRx is in the process of installing them, and once they are in place, the company will be able to use actual point-of-sale product information instead of warehouse movement. These

—Continued on next page

—Continued from previous page

scanning registers also have the ability to place an order to the warehouse automatically, based on what is actually sold that week, so the inventory movement management can only continue to improve.

Good inventory management does not occur in a vacuum, but must be interrelated with sales, gross margin, and expense control objectives. SupeRx is fortunate in that it has had planning software in place for some time. This system allows SupeRx merchandisers to act out "what if" scenarios relating to OTQs, product costs, retail sales prices, inventory carrying costs, sales, and other factors. As an example, optimum order-to quantities normally result in some percentage of missed sales due to individual item movement fluctuations. On the other hand, increasing the OTQs to maximize sales also increases inventory, decreases inventory turnover, and thus ties up capital that could otherwise be used for building new stores, remodeling existing locations, and so on. By using the new inventory-management techniques, SupeRx can maximize both sales and

inventory turnover. Rapidly becoming a necessity rather than a luxury, the use of this modern technology ensures the maximization of sales, profits, and inventory turnovers that ultimately determine the success or failure of a drug chain.

Questions

1. Does SupeRx use a continuous-review or a periodic-review inventory system? Why would this system be preferred for a retail business such as SupeRx?
2. What is the decision rule that SupeRx uses to provide a safety stock and minimize stockouts?
3. What is SupeRx doing to obtain information that will help continue to improve inventory management?

············

*The authors are indebted to Bob Carver of SupeRx, Inc., for providing this application.

Waiting Line Models

ecall the last time that you had to wait at a supermarket checkout counter, for a teller at your local bank, or to be served at a fast-food restaurant. In these and many other waiting line situations, the time spent waiting is undesirable. Adding more checkout clerks, bank tellers, or servers is not always the most economical strategy for improving service, so businesses need to determine ways to keep waiting times within tolerable limits.

Models have been developed to help managers understand and make better decisions concerning the operation of waiting lines. In management science terminology, a waiting line is also known as a *queue,* and the body of knowledge dealing with waiting lines is known as *queuing theory.* In the early 1900s A. K. Erlang, a Danish telephone engineer, began a study of the congestion and waiting times occurring in the completion of telephone calls. Since then, queuing theory has grown far more sophisticated and has been applied to a wide variety of waiting line situations.

Waiting line models consist of mathematical formulas and relationships that can be used to determine the *operating characteristics* (performance measures) for a waiting line. Some of the operating characteristics of interest are

1. the probability that there are no units in the system,
2. the average number of units in the waiting line,
3. the average number of units in the system (the number of units in the waiting line plus the number of units being served),
4. the average time a unit spends in the waiting line,
5. the average time a unit spends in the system (the waiting time plus the service time),
6. the probability that an arriving unit has to wait for service, and
7. the probability of *n* units in the system.

Managers who have such information are better able to make decisions that balance desirable service levels against the cost of providing the service.

12.1 The Structure of a Waiting Line System

To illustrate the basic features of a waiting line model, we consider the waiting line at the Burger Dome fast-food restaurant. Burger Dome sells hamburgers, cheeseburgers, french fries, soft drinks, and milk shakes, as well as a limited number of specialty items and dessert selections. Although Burger Dome would like to serve each customer immediately, at times more customers arrive than can be handled by the Burger Dome food-service staff. Thus, customers wait in line to place and receive their orders.

Burger Dome is concerned that the methods they are currently using to serve customers are resulting in excessive waiting times. Management has asked that a waiting line study be performed to help determine the best approach to reducing waiting times and improving service.

The Single-Channel Waiting Line

In the current Burger Dome operation, a server takes the customer's order, determines the total cost of the order, takes the money from the customer, and then fills the order. Once the first customer's order is filled, the server takes the order of the next customer waiting for service. This operation is an example of a *single-channel* waiting line. By this, we mean that each customer entering the Burger Dome restaurant must pass through the *one* channel—one order-taking and order-filling station—to place an order, pay the bill, and receive the food. When more customers arrive than can be served immediately, they form a waiting line and wait for the order-taking and order-filling station to become available. A diagram of the Burger Dome single-channel waiting line is shown in Figure 12.1.

The Distribution of Arrivals

Defining the arrival process for a waiting line involves determining the probability distribution for the number of arrivals in a given period of time. For many waiting line situations, the arrivals occur *randomly* and *independently* of other arrivals, and we cannot predict when an arrival will occur. In such cases, management scientist have found that the *Poisson probability distribution* provides a good description of the arrival pattern.

Figure 12.1

The Burger Dome Single-Channel Waiting Line

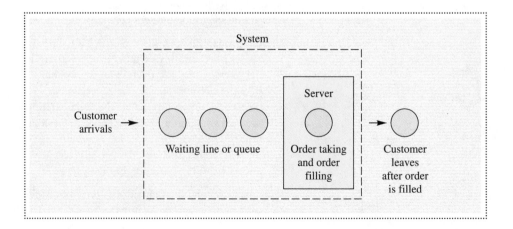

The Poisson probability function[1] defines the probability of x arrivals in a specific time period as

$$P(x) = \frac{\lambda^x e^{-\lambda}}{x!} \quad \text{for } x = 0, 1, 2, \ldots \tag{12.1}$$

where

x = the number of arrivals in the time period
λ = the average or mean number of arrivals per time period
e = 2.71828

Values of $e^{-\lambda}$ can be found by using a calculator or by using Appendix C.

Suppose that Burger Dome has analyzed data on customer arrivals and has concluded that the mean arrival rate is 45 customers per hour. For a 1-minute period, the mean number of arrivals would be $\lambda = 45/60 = 0.75$ arrivals per minute. Thus, we can use the following Poisson probability function to compute the probability of x arrivals during a 1-minute period:

$$P(x) = \frac{\lambda^x e^{-\lambda}}{x!} = \frac{0.75^x e^{-0.75}}{x!} \tag{12.2}$$

Thus, the probabilities of 0, 1, and 2 arrivals during a 1-minute period are

$$P(0) = \frac{(0.75)^0 e^{-0.75}}{0!} = e^{-0.75} = 0.4724$$

$$P(1) = \frac{(0.75)^1 e^{-0.75}}{1!} = 0.75e^{-0.75} = 0.75(0.4724) = 0.3543$$

$$P(2) = \frac{(0.75)^2 e^{-0.75}}{2!} = \frac{(0.75)^2 e^{-0.75}}{2!} = \frac{(0.5625)(0.4724)}{2} = 0.1329$$

The probability of no arrivals in a 1-minute period is 0.4724, the probability of 1 arrival in a 1-minute period is 0.3543, and the probability of 2 arrivals in a 1-minute period is 0.1329. Table 12.1 shows the Poisson probability distribution of arrivals during a 1-minute period.

The waiting line models presented in Sections 12.2 and 12.3 use the Poisson probability distribution to describe the customer arrivals at Burger Dome. In practice, you should record the actual number of arrivals per time period for several days or weeks and compare the frequency distribution of the observed number of arrivals to the Poisson probability distribution to determine whether the Poisson probability distribution provides a reasonable approximation of the arrival distribution.

Table 12.1

Poisson Probabilities for the Number of Arrivals at a Burger Dome Restaurant During a 1-Minute Period ($\lambda = 0.75$)

Number of Arrivals	Probability
0	0.4724
1	0.3543
2	0.1329
3	0.0332
4	0.0062
5 or more	0.0010

The Distribution of Service Times

The service time is the time the customer spends at the service facility once the service has started. At Burger Dome, the service time starts when the customer begins to place the order with the food server and continues until the customer has received the order. Service times are rarely constant. At Burger Dome, the number of items ordered and the mix of items ordered vary considerably from one customer to the next. Small orders can be handled in a matter of seconds, but larger orders may require more than 2 minutes to process.

---

[1] The term $x!$, x *factorial*, is defined as $x! = x(x-1)(x-2) \ldots (2)(1)$. For example, $4! = (4)(3)(2)(1) = 24$. For the special case of $x = 0$, $0! = 1$ by definition.

Management scientists have found that, if service times can be assumed to have (or at least can be approximated by) an *exponential probability distribution,* formulas are available for providing useful information about the operation of the waiting line. If the probability distribution for the service times follows an exponential probability distribution, the probability that the service time will be less than or equal to a time of length t is

$$P(\text{service time} \le t) = 1 - e^{-\mu t} \tag{12.3}$$

where

μ = the average or mean number of units that can be served per time period

Suppose that Burger Dome has studied the order-taking and order-filling process and has found that the single food server can process an average of 60 customer orders per hour. On a 1-minute basis, the average or mean service rate would be $\mu = 60/60 = 1$ customer per minute. For example, with $\mu = 1$, we can use equation (12.3) to compute probabilities such as the probability an order can be processed in ½ minute or less, 1 minute or less, and 2 minutes or less. These computations are

$$P(\text{service time} \le 0.5 \text{ min.}) = 1 - e^{-1(0.5)} = 1 - 0.6065 = 0.3935$$

$$P(\text{service time} \le 1.0 \text{ min.}) = 1 - e^{-1(1.0)} = 1 - 0.3679 = 0.6321$$

$$P(\text{service time} \le 2.0 \text{ min.}) = 1 - e^{-1(2.0)} = 1 - 0.1353 = 0.8647$$

Thus, we would conclude that there is a 0.3935 probability that an order can be processed in ½ minute or less, a 0.6321 probability that it can be processed in 1 minute or less, and a 0.8647 probability that it can be processed in 2 minutes or less.

In several of the waiting line models presented in this chapter, we will assume that the probability distributions for the service times follow an exponential probability distribution. In practice, you should collect data on actual service times to see whether the exponential probability distribution is a reasonable approximation of the service times for your application.

Queue Discipline

In describing a waiting line system, we must define the manner in which the waiting units are arranged for service. For the Burger Dome waiting line, and in general for most customer-oriented waiting lines, the units waiting for service are arranged on a *first-come, first-served* basis; this approach is referred to as an *FCFS* queue discipline. However, some situations call for different queue disciplines. For example, when people wait for an elevator, the last one on the elevator is usually the first one to complete service (i.e., the first to leave the elevator). Other types of queue disciplines assign priorities to the waiting units and then serve the unit with the highest priority first. In this chapter we consider only waiting lines based on a first-come, first-served queue discipline.

Steady–State Operation

When the Burger Dome restaurant opens in the morning, no customers are in the restaurant. Gradually, activity builds up to a normal or steady state. The beginning or start-up period is referred to as the *transient period.* The transient period ends when the system reaches the normal or *steady-state* operation. Waiting line models describe the steady-state operating characteristics of the waiting line.

12.2 The Single-Channel Waiting Line Model with Poisson Arrivals and Exponential Service Times

In this section we will present formulas that can be used to determine the steady-state operating characteristics for a single-channel waiting line. The formulas should be used only if the following assumptions are reasonable.

1. The waiting line has a single channel.
2. The arrivals follow a Poisson probability distribution.
3. The service times follow an exponential probability distribution.
4. The queue discipline is first-come, first-served (FCFS).

As these assumptions apply to the Burger Dome waiting line problem introduced in Section 12.1, we will show how formulas can be used to determine Burger Dome's operating characteristics and thus provide management with helpful decision-making information.

The mathematical methodology used to derive the formulas for the operating characteristics of waiting lines is rather complex. However, our purpose in this chapter is not to provide the theoretical development of waiting line models, but rather to show how the formulas that have been developed can provide information about operating characteristics of the waiting line. Readers interested in the mathematical development of the formulas can consult any of the specialized texts listed in the References and Bibliography section at the end of the text.

The Operating Characteristics

The following formulas can be used to develop the steady-state operating characteristics for a single-channel waiting line with Poisson arrivals and exponential service times, where

λ = the mean or average number of arrivals per time period (the mean arrival rate)

μ = the mean or average number of services per time period (the mean service rate)

1. The probability that there are no units in the system:

$$P_0 = 1 - \frac{\lambda}{\mu} \tag{12.4}$$

2. The average number of units in the waiting line:

$$L_q = \frac{\lambda^2}{\mu(\mu - \lambda)} \tag{12.5}$$

3. The average number of units in the system:

$$L = L_q + \frac{\lambda}{\mu} \tag{12.6}$$

4. The average time a unit spends in the waiting line:

$$W_q = \frac{L_q}{\lambda} \tag{12.7}$$

5. The average time a unit spends in the system:

$$W = W_q + \frac{1}{\mu} \tag{12.8}$$

6. The probability that an arriving unit has to wait for service:

$$P_w = \frac{\lambda}{\mu} \tag{12.9}$$

7. The probability of n units in the system:

$$P_n = \left(\frac{\lambda}{\mu}\right)^n P_0 \tag{12.10}$$

The values of the *mean arrival rate* λ and the *mean service rate* μ are clearly important components in determining the operating characteristics. Equation (12.9) shows that the ratio of the mean arrival rate to the mean service rate, λ/μ, provides the probability that an arriving unit has to wait because the service facility is busy. Hence, λ/μ often is referred to as the *utilization factor* for the service facility.

The operating characteristics presented in equations (12.4) through (12.10) are applicable only when the mean service rate μ is *greater than* the mean arrival rate λ—in other words, when $\lambda/\mu < 1$. If this condition does not exist, the waiting line will continue to grow without limit because the service facility does not have sufficient capacity to handle the arriving units. Thus, in using equations (12.4) through (12.10), we must have $\mu > \lambda$.

Operating Characteristics for the Burger Dome Problem

Recall that for the Burger Dome problem we had a mean arrival rate of $\lambda = 0.75$ customers per minute and a mean service rate of $\mu = 1$ customer per minute. Thus, with $\mu > \lambda$, equations (12.4) through (12.10) can be used to provide operating characteristics for the Burger Dome single-channel waiting line:

$$P_0 = 1 - \frac{\lambda}{\mu} = 1 - \frac{0.75}{1} = 0.25$$

$$L_q = \frac{\lambda^2}{\mu(\mu - \lambda)} = \frac{0.75^2}{1(1 - 0.75)} = 2.25 \text{ customers}$$

$$L = L_q + \frac{\lambda}{\mu} = 2.25 + \frac{0.75}{1} = 3 \text{ customers}$$

$$W_q = \frac{L_q}{\lambda} = \frac{2.25}{0.75} = 3 \text{ minutes}$$

$$W = W_q + \frac{1}{\mu} = 3 + \frac{1}{1} = 4 \text{ minutes}$$

$$P_w = \frac{\lambda}{\mu} = \frac{0.75}{1} = 0.75$$

Problem 5 asks you to compute the operating characteristics for a single-channel waiting line application.

Equation (12.10) can be used to determine the probability of any number of customers in the system. Applying it provides the probability information summarized in Table 12.2.

Table 12.2

The Probability of *n* Customers in the System for the Burger Dome Waiting Line Problem

Number of Customers	Probability
0	0.2500
1	0.1875
2	0.1406
3	0.1055
4	0.0791
5	0.0593
6	0.0445
7 or more	0.1335

The Manager's Use of Waiting Line Models

The results of the single-channel waiting line for Burger Dome show several important things about the operation of the waiting line. In particular, customers wait an average of 3 minutes before beginning to place an order, which appears somewhat long for a business based on fast service. In addition, the facts that the average number of customers waiting in line is 2.25 and that 75% of the arriving customers have to wait for service are indicators that something should be done to improve the waiting line operation. Table 12.2 shows that there is a 0.1335 probability that seven or more customers are in the Burger Dome system at one time. This condition indicates a fairly high probability that Burger Dome will experience some long waiting lines if it continues to use the single-channel operation.

If the operating characteristics are unsatisfactory in terms of meeting company standards for service, Burger Dome's management should consider alternative designs or plans for improving the waiting line operation.

Improving the Waiting Line Operation

After reviewing the operating characteristics provided by the waiting line model, Burger Dome's management concluded that improvements designed to reduce waiting times are desirable. Improvements in the waiting line operation most often focus on ways to improve the service rate. Generally, service improvements are made by the following:

1. Increase the mean service rate μ by making a creative design change or by using new technology.
2. Add service channels so that more units can be served simultaneously.

Assume that in considering alternative 1, Burger Dome's management decides to employ an order filler who will assist the order taker at the cash register. The customer begins the service process by placing the order with the order taker. As the order is placed, the order taker announces the order over an intercom system, and the order filler begins filling the order. When the order is completed, the order taker handles the money, while the order filler continues to fill the order. With this design, Burger Dome's management estimates the mean service rate can be increased from the current service rate of 60 customers per hour to 75 customers per hour. Thus, the mean service rate for the revised system is $\mu = 75/60 = 1.25$ customers per minute. For $\lambda = 0.75$ and $\mu = 1.25$, equations (12.4) through (12.10) provide the operating characteristics summarized in Table 12.3.

Table 12.3

Operating Characteristics for the Burger Dome System with the Mean Service Rate Increased to $\mu = 1.25$ Customers per Minute

Probability of no units in the system	0.400
Average number of units in the waiting line	0.900
Average number of units in the system	1.500
Average time in the waiting line	1.200 minutes
Average time in the system	2.000 minutes
Probability that an arriving unit has to wait	0.600
Probability that seven or more are in system	0.028

Table 12.3 indicates that all the operating characteristics have improved because of the increased service rate provided by the order filler. In particular, the average time in the system has been reduced from 4 to 2 minutes. Are other alternatives possible for increasing the service rate? If so—and if the mean service rate μ can be identified for these alternatives—equations (12.4) through (12.10) will provide the information needed to assess the amount of improvement for the proposed alternatives. The added cost of any proposed change can be compared to the corresponding service improvements to help the manager determine whether the proposed service improvements are worthwhile.

As mentioned previously, another option that is usually available is to provide one or more additional service channels so that more than one customer may be served at the same time. The extension of the single-channel waiting line model to the multiple-channel waiting line model is the topic of the next section.

Problem 11 asks you to determine whether a change in the mean service rate will meet the company's service guideline for its customers.

NOTES & comments

1. The assumption that arrivals follow a Poisson probability distribution is equivalent to the assumption that the time between arrivals has an exponential probability distribution. For example, if the arrivals for a waiting line follow a Poisson probability distribution with a mean of 20 arrivals per hour, the time between arrivals will follow an exponential probability distribution, with a mean time between arrivals of $\frac{1}{20}$ or 0.05 hour.

2. Many individuals believe that whenever the mean service rate μ is greater than the mean arrival rate λ, the system should be able to handle or serve all arrivals. However, as the Burger Dome example shows, the variability of arrival times and service times may result in long waiting times even when the mean service rate exceeds the mean arrival rate. A contribution of waiting line models is that they can point out undesirable waiting line operating characteristics even when the $\mu > \lambda$ condition appears satisfactory.

12.3   The Multiple-Channel Waiting Line Model with Poisson Arrivals and Exponential Service Times

A *multiple-channel* waiting line consists of two or more channels or service locations that are assumed to be identical in terms of service capability. In the multiple-channel system, arriving units wait in a single waiting line and then move to the first available channel to be served.

The single-channel Burger Dome operation could be expanded to a two-channel system by opening a second service channel. Figure 12.2 shows a diagram of the Burger Dome two-channel waiting line.

In this section we present formulas that can be used to determine the steady-state operating characteristics for a multiple-channel waiting line. These formulas are applicable if

1. the waiting line has two or more channels,
2. the arrivals follow a Poisson probability distribution,

Figure 12.2
. . . .

**The Burger Dome Two-Channel
Waiting Line**

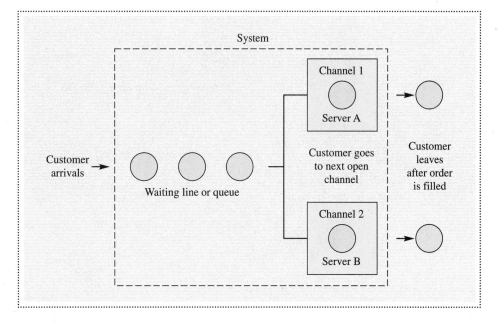

3. the service time for each channel follows an exponential probability distribution,
4. the mean service rate μ is the same for each channel,
5. the arrivals wait in a single waiting line and then move to the first open channel for service, and
6. the queue discipline is first-come, first-served (FCFS).

The Operating Characteristics
. . . .

The following formulas can be used to compute the steady-state operating characteristics for multiple-channel waiting lines, where

$$\lambda = \text{the mean arrival rate for the system}$$
$$\mu = \text{the mean service rate for } each \text{ channel}$$
$$k = \text{the number of channels}$$

1. The probability that there are no units in the system:

$$P_0 = \frac{1}{\displaystyle\sum_{n=0}^{k-1} \frac{(\lambda/\mu)^n}{n!} + \frac{(\lambda/\mu)^k}{k!}\left(\frac{k\mu}{k\mu-\lambda}\right)} \qquad (12.11)$$

2. The average number of units in the waiting line:

$$L_q = \frac{(\lambda/\mu)^k \lambda\mu}{(k-1)!(k\mu-\lambda)^2} P_0 \qquad (12.12)$$

3. The average number of units in the system:

$$L = L_q + \frac{\lambda}{\mu} \qquad (12.13)$$

4. The average time a unit spends in the waiting line:

$$W_q = \frac{L_q}{\lambda} \tag{12.14}$$

5. The average time a unit spends in the system:

$$W = W_q + \frac{1}{\mu} \tag{12.15}$$

6. The probability that an arriving unit has to wait:

$$P_w = \frac{1}{k!}\left(\frac{\lambda}{\mu}\right)^k\left(\frac{k\mu}{k\mu - \lambda}\right)P_0 \tag{12.16}$$

7. The probability of n units in the system:

$$P_n = \frac{(\lambda/\mu)^n}{n!}P_0 \quad \text{for } n \le k \tag{12.17}$$

$$P_n = \frac{(\lambda/\mu)^n}{k!k^{(n-k)}}P_0 \quad \text{for } n > k \tag{12.18}$$

Because μ is the mean service rate for each channel, $k\mu$ is the mean service rate for the multiple-channel system. As was true for the single-channel waiting line model, the formulas for the operating characteristics of multiple-channel waiting lines can be applied only in situations where the mean service rate for the system is greater than the mean arrival rate for the system; in other words, the formulas are applicable only if $k\mu$ is greater than λ.

Some of the expressions for the operating characteristics of multiple-channel waiting lines are more complex than their single-channel counterparts. However, equations (12.11) through (12.18) provide the same information as provided by the single-channel model. To help simplify the use of the multiple-channel equations, Table 12.4 contains values of P_0 for selected values of λ/μ and k. The values provided in the table correspond to cases where $k\mu > \lambda$, and hence the service rate is sufficient to process all arrivals.

Operating Characteristics for the Burger Dome Problem

To illustrate the multiple-channel waiting line model, we return to the Burger Dome fast-food restaurant waiting line problem. Suppose that management wants to evaluate the desirability of opening a second order-processing station so that two customers can be served simultaneously. Assume that there will be a single waiting line with the next customer in line moving to the first available server, giving Burger Dome a two-channel waiting line. Let us evaluate the operating characteristics for this two-channel system.

We will use equations (12.12) through (12.18) for the $k = 2$ channel system. For a mean arrival rate of $\lambda = 0.75$ customers per minute and mean service rate of $\mu = 1$ customer per minute for each channel, we obtain the operating characteristics:

$$P_0 = 0.4545 \quad \text{(from Table 12.4 with } \lambda/\mu = 0.75)$$

$$L_q = \frac{(0.75/1)^2(0.75)(1)}{(2 - 1)![2(1) - 0.75]^2}(0.4545) = 0.1227 \text{ customer}$$

Table 12.4

Values of P_0 for Multiple-Channel Waiting Lines with Poisson Arrivals and Exponential Service Times

Ratio λ/μ	Number of Channels (k)			
	2	3	4	5
0.15	0.8605	0.8607	0.8607	0.8607
0.20	0.8182	0.8187	0.8187	0.8187
0.25	0.7778	0.7788	0.7788	0.7788
0.30	0.7391	0.7407	0.7408	0.7408
0.35	0.7021	0.7046	0.7047	0.7047
0.40	0.6667	0.6701	0.6703	0.6703
0.45	0.6327	0.6373	0.6376	0.6376
0.50	0.6000	0.6061	0.6065	0.6065
0.55	0.5686	0.5763	0.5769	0.5769
0.60	0.5385	0.5479	0.5487	0.5488
0.65	0.5094	0.5209	0.5219	0.5220
0.70	0.4815	0.4952	0.4965	0.4966
0.75	0.4545	0.4706	0.4722	0.4724
0.80	0.4286	0.4472	0.4491	0.4493
0.85	0.4035	0.4248	0.4271	0.4274
0.90	0.3793	0.4035	0.4062	0.4065
0.95	0.3559	0.3831	0.3863	0.3867
1.00	0.3333	0.3636	0.3673	0.3678
1.20	0.2500	0.2941	0.3002	0.3011
1.40	0.1765	0.2360	0.2449	0.2463
1.60	0.1111	0.1872	0.1993	0.2014
1.80	0.0526	0.1460	0.1616	0.1646
2.00		0.1111	0.1304	0.1343
2.20		0.0815	0.1046	0.1094
2.40		0.0562	0.0831	0.0889
2.60		0.0345	0.0651	0.0721
2.80		0.0160	0.0521	0.0581
3.00			0.0377	0.0466
3.20			0.0273	0.0372
3.40			0.0186	0.0293
3.60			0.0113	0.0228
3.80			0.0051	0.0174
4.00				0.0130
4.20				0.0093
4.40				0.0063
4.60				0.0038
4.80				0.0017

$$L = L_q + \frac{\lambda}{\mu} = 0.1227 + \frac{0.75}{1} = 0.8727 \text{ customer}$$

$$W_q = \frac{L_q}{\lambda} = \frac{0.1227}{0.75} = 0.16 \text{ minute}$$

$$W = W_q + \frac{1}{\mu} = 0.16 + \frac{1}{1} = 1.16 \text{ minutes}$$

$$P_w = \frac{1}{2!}\left(\frac{0.75}{1}\right)^2\left[\frac{2(1)}{2(1) - 0.75}\right](0.4545) = 0.2045$$

Try Problem 19, which will give you practice in determining the operating characteristics for a two-channel waiting line.

Table 12.5

· · · · · · · · · · ·

The Probability of *n* Customers in the System for the Burger Dome Two-Channel Waiting Line

Number of Customers	Probability
0	0.4545
1	0.3409
2	0.1278
3	0.0479
4	0.0180
5 or more	0.0109

Using equations (12.17) and (12.18), we can compute the probabilities of *n* customers in the system. The results from these computations are summarized in Table 12.5.

We can now compare the steady-state operating characteristics of the two-channel system to the operating characteristics of the original single-channel system discussed in Section 12.2.

1. The average time a customer spends in the system (waiting time plus service time) is reduced from $W = 4$ minutes to $W = 1.16$ minutes.
2. The average number of customers in the waiting line is reduced from $L_q = 2.25$ customers to $L_q = 0.1227$ customers.
3. The average time a customer spends in the waiting line is reduced from $W_q = 3$ minutes to $W_q = 0.16$ minutes.
4. The probability that a customer has to wait for service is reduced from $P_w = 0.75$ to $P_w = 0.2045$.

Clearly the two-channel system will significantly improve the operating characteristics of the waiting line. However, adding an order filler at each service station would further increase the mean service rate and improve the operating characteristics. The final decision regarding the staffing policy at Burger Dome rests with the Burger Dome management. The waiting line study has simply provided the operating characteristics that can be anticipated under three configurations: a single-channel system with one employee, a single-channel system with two employees, and a two-channel system with an employee for each channel. After considering these results, what action would you recommend? In this case, Burger Dome adopted the following policy statement: For periods when customer arrivals are expected to average 45 customers per hour, Burger Dome will open two order-processing stations with one employee assigned to each station.

By changing the mean arrival rate λ to reflect arrival rates at different times of the day, and then computing the operating characteristics, Burger Dome's management can establish guidelines and policies that tell the store managers when they should schedule service operations with a single channel, two channels, or perhaps even three or more channels. The Management Science in Action article for Lourdes Hospital shows how a multiple-channel waiting line model has been used to make hospital staffing decisions.

NOTES & comments

The multiple-channel waiting line model is based on a single waiting line. You may have also encountered situations where each of the *k* channels has its own waiting line. Management scientists have shown that the operating characteristics of multiple-channel systems are better if a single waiting line is used. People like them better also; no one who comes in after you can be served ahead of you. Thus, when possible, banks, airline reservation counters, food-service establishments, and other businesses typically use a single waiting line for a multiple-channel system.

MANAGEMENT SCIENCE in action

Hospital Staffing Based on a Multiple-Channel Waiting Line Model[*]

Lourdes Hospital in Binghamton, New York, uses a centralized staff to schedule appointments for the hospital's outpatient, inpatient, and ambulance services. Physicians, their staffs, hospital personnel, and patients contact the centralized scheduling office by telephone in order to establish desired appointment times.

Efficiency of the scheduling process depends on the department's staff being able to process incoming telephone calls in a timely manner. Periodically, incoming requests for services overload the staff's ability to answer the telephone and process the appointments. As a result, users reported undesirable delays and lengthy waiting times. Management used a waiting line model to study the operation and suggest staffing changes that could improve the efficiency of the centralized scheduling process.

Data were collected on the number of telephone calls that arrived during each 15-minute period. The calls were random, not depending on the day of the week. A Poisson probability distribution was a good description of the random arrivals, with peak arrival times occurring between 9:00 A.M. and 11:30 A.M.

and between 2:00 P.M. and 3:45 P.M. each day. An investigation of service times found that, although service times were not exactly exponential, the exponential probability distribution provided a reasonable approximation.

In effect, the hospital's scheduling service was viewed as a multiple-channel waiting line with Poisson arrivals and exponential service times. The number of channels was simply the number of individuals on the scheduling staff. With the mean arrival rate adjusted for the different periods of the day, a waiting line model with k channels was used to estimate the probability that an arriving call would have to wait for service. The staff size was determined by selecting the number of channels that kept the steady state probability of waiting to no more than 10%. Staff schedules and workloads were adjusted, efficiency improved, and the number of complaints about waiting for service declined.

....

*Based on Agnihothri, S. R., and P. F. Taylor, "Staffing a Centralized Appointment Scheduling Department in Lourdes Hospital." *Interfaces,* vol. 21, no. 5, September–October 1991, pp. 1–11.

12.4 Some General Relationships for Waiting Line Models

In Sections 12.2 and 12.3 we presented formulas for computing the operating characteristics for single-channel and multiple-channel waiting lines with Poisson arrivals and exponential service times. The operating characteristics of interest included

$L_q =$ the average number of units in the waiting line

$L =$ the average number of units in the system

$W_q =$ the average time a unit spends in the waiting line

$W =$ the average time a unit spends in the system

John D. C. Little showed that several relationships exist among these four characteristics and that these relationships apply to a variety of different waiting line systems. Two of the relationships, referred to as *Little's flow equations,* are

$$L = \lambda W \tag{12.19}$$

$$L_q = \lambda W_q \tag{12.20}$$

Equation (12.19) shows that the average number of units in the system, L, can be found by multiplying the mean arrival rate, λ, by the average time a unit spends in the system, W. Equation (12.20) shows that the same relationship holds between the average number of units in the waiting line, L_q, and the average time a unit spends in the waiting line, W_q.

Using equation (12.20) and solving for W_q, we obtain

$$W_q = \frac{L_q}{\lambda} \tag{12.21}$$

Equation (12.21) follows directly from Little's second flow equation. We used it for the single-channel waiting line model in Section 12.2 and the multiple-channel waiting line model in Section 12.3 (see equations (12.7) and (12.14)). Once L_q is computed for either of these models, equation (12.21) can then be used to compute W_q.

Another general expression that applies to waiting line models is that the average time in the system, W, is equal to the average time in the waiting line, W_q, plus the average service time. For a system with a mean service rate μ, the average or mean service time is $1/\mu$. Thus, we have the general relationship

$$W = W_q + \frac{1}{\mu} \tag{12.22}$$

Recall that we used equation (12.22) to provide the average time in the system for both the single- and multiple-channel waiting line models (see equations (12.8) and (12.15)).

The importance of Little's flow equations is that they apply to *any waiting line model* regardless of whether arrivals follow the Poisson probability distribution and regardless of whether service times follow the exponential probability distribution. For example, in a study of the grocery checkout counters at Murphy's Foodliner, an analyst concluded that arrivals follow the Poisson probability distribution with the mean arrival rate of 24 customers per hour or $\lambda = 24/60 = 0.40$ customers per minute. However, the analyst found that service times follow a normal probability distribution rather than an exponential probability distribution. The mean service rate was found to be 30 customers per hour or $\mu = 30/60 = 0.50$ customers per minute. A time study of actual customer waiting times showed that, on average, a customer spends 4.5 minutes in the system (waiting time plus checkout time); that is, $W = 4.5$. Using the waiting line relationships discussed in this section, we can now compute other operating characteristics for this waiting line.

First, using equation (12.22) and solving for W_q, we have

$$W_q = W - \frac{1}{\mu} = 4.5 - \frac{1}{0.50} = 2.5 \text{ minutes}$$

With both W and W_q known, we can use Little's flow equations, (12.19) and (12.20), to compute

The application of Little's flow equations are demonstrated in Problem 25.

$$L = \lambda W = 0.40(4.5) = 1.8 \text{ customers}$$

$$L_q = \lambda W_q = 0.40(2.5) = 1 \text{ customer}$$

The manager of Murphy's Foodliner can now review these operating characteristics to see if action should be taken to improve the service and to reduce the waiting time and the length of the waiting line.

12.5 Economic Analysis of Waiting Lines

Frequently, the decisions involving the design of waiting lines will be based on a subjective evaluation of the operating characteristics of the waiting line. For example, a manager may decide that an average waiting time of 1 minute or less and an average of two customers or less in the system are reasonable goals. The waiting line models presented in the preceding sections can be used to determine the number of channels that will meet the manager's waiting line performance goals.

On the other hand, a manager may want to identify the cost of operating the waiting line system and then base the decision regarding system design on a minimum hourly or daily operating cost. Before an economic analysis of a waiting line can be conducted, a total-cost model, which includes the cost of waiting and the cost of service, must be developed.

To develop a total-cost model for a waiting line, we begin by defining the notation to be used:

c_w = the waiting cost per time period for each unit
L = the average number of units in the system
c_s = the service cost per time period for each channel
k = the number of channels
TC = the total cost per time period

The total cost is the sum of the waiting cost and the service cost; that is,

$$TC = c_w L + c_s k \qquad (12.23)$$

To conduct an economic analysis of a waiting line, we must obtain reasonable estimates of the waiting cost and the service cost. Of these two costs, the waiting cost is usually the more difficult to evaluate. In the Burger Dome restaurant problem, the waiting cost would be the cost per minute for a customer waiting for service. This cost is not a direct cost to Burger Dome. However, if Burger Dome ignores this cost and allows long waiting lines, customers ultimately will take their business elsewhere. Thus, Burger Dome will experience lost sales and, in effect, incur a cost.

The service cost is generally easier to determine. This cost is the relevant cost associated with operating each service channel. In the Burger Dome problem, this cost would include the server's wages, benefits, and any other direct costs associated with operating the service channel. At Burger Dome, this cost is estimated to be $7 per hour.

To demonstrate the use of equation (12.23), we assume that Burger Dome is willing to assign a cost of $10 per hour for customer waiting time. We use the average number of units in the system, L, as computed in Sections 12.2 and 12.3 to obtain the total hourly cost for the single-channel and two-channel systems:

Single-channel system ($L = 3$ customers)

$$TC = c_w L + c_s k$$

$$TC = \$10(3) + \$7(1) = \$37.00 \text{ per hour}$$

Two-channel system ($L = 0.8727$ customer):

$$TC = c_w L + c_s k$$

$$= \$10(0.8727) + \$7(2) = \$22.73 \text{ per hour}$$

Thus, based on the cost data provided by Burger Dome, the two-channel system provides the most economical operation.

Figure 12.3 shows the general shapes of the cost curves in the economic analysis of waiting lines. The service cost increases as the number of channels is increased. However, with more channels, the service is better. As a result, waiting time and cost decrease as the number of channels is increased. The number of channels that will provide a good approximation of the minimum total-cost design can be found by evaluating the total cost for several design alternatives.

Working Problem 21 will give you the chance to test your ability to conduct an economic analysis of proposed single-channel and two-channel waiting line systems.

Figure 12.3

The General Shape of Waiting Cost, Service Cost, and Total-Cost Curves in Waiting Line Models

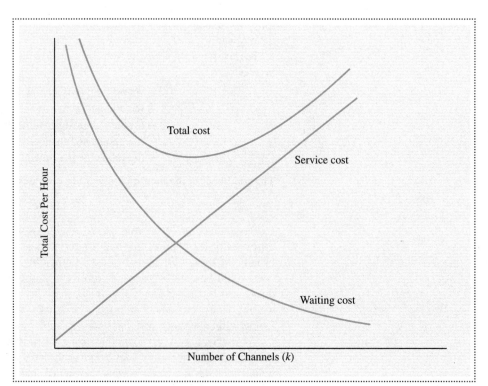

NOTES & comments

1. In dealing with government agencies and utility companies, customers may not be able to take their business elsewhere. In these situations, no lost business occurs when long waiting times are encountered. This condition is one of the reasons why service in such organizations may be poor, and why customers in such situations may experience long waiting times.

2. In some instances, the organization providing the service also employs the units waiting for the service. For example, consider the case of a company that owns and operates the trucks used to deliver goods to and from its manufacturing plant. In addition to the costs associated with the trucks waiting to be loaded or unloaded, the firm also pays the wages of the truck loaders and unloaders who operate the service channel. In this case, the cost of having the trucks wait and the cost of operating the service channel are direct expenses to the firm. An economic analysis of the waiting line system is highly recommended for these types of situations.

12.6   Other Waiting Line Models

D. G. Kendall suggested a notation that is helpful in classifying the wide variety of different waiting line models that have been developed. The three-symbol Kendall notation is as follows:

$$A/B/s$$

where

    A denotes the probability distribution for the arrivals
    B denotes the probability distribution for the service time
    s denotes the number of channels

Depending on the value of the letter appearing in the A or B position, a wide variety of waiting line systems can be described. The values for A and B that are commonly used are as follows:

    M designates a Poisson probability distribution for the arrivals or an exponential probability distribution for service time
    D designates that the arrivals or the service time is deterministic or constant
    G designates that the arrivals or the service time has a general probability distribution with a known mean and variance

Using the Kendall notation, the single-channel waiting line model with Poisson arrivals and exponential service times is classified as an $M/M/1$ model. The 2-channel waiting line model with Poisson arrivals and exponential service times presented in Section 12.3 would be classified as an $M/M/2$ model.

NOTES & comments

In some cases, the Kendall notation is extended to five symbols. The fourth symbol indicates the largest number of units that can be in the system, and the fifth symbol indicates the size of the input or calling population. The fourth symbol is used in situations where the waiting line can hold a finite or maximum number of units, and the fifth symbol is necessary when the population of arriving units or customers is finite. When the fourth and fifth symbols of the Kendall notation are omitted, the waiting line system is assumed to have infinite capacity, and the calling population is assumed to be infinite.

12.7 The Single-Channel Waiting Line Model with Poisson Arrivals and Arbitrary Service Times

Let us return to the single-channel waiting line model where arrivals are described by a Poisson probability distribution. However, we now assume that the probability distribution for the service times is not an exponential probability distribution. Thus, using the Kendall notation, the waiting line model that is appropriate is an *M/G/*1 model, where *G* denotes a general or unspecified probability distribution.

Operating Characteristics for the *M/G/*1 Model

The notation used to describe the operating characteristics for the *M/G/*1 model is

λ = the mean arrival rate

μ = the mean service rate

$\dfrac{1}{\mu}$ = the average or mean service time

σ = the standard deviation of the service time

Some of the steady-state operating characteristics of the *M/G/*1 waiting line model are as follows:

1. The probability that there are no units in the system:

$$P_0 = 1 - \frac{\lambda}{\mu} \tag{12.24}$$

2. The average number of units in the waiting line:

$$L_q = \frac{\lambda^2 \sigma^2 + (\lambda/\mu)^2}{2(1 - \lambda/\mu)} \tag{12.25}$$

3. The average number of units in the system:

$$L = L_q + \frac{\lambda}{\mu} \tag{12.26}$$

4. The average time a unit spends in the waiting line:

$$W_q = \frac{L_q}{\lambda} \tag{12.27}$$

5. The average time a unit spends in the system:

$$W = W_q + \frac{1}{\mu} \tag{12.28}$$

6. The probability that an arriving unit has to wait:

$$P_w = \frac{\lambda}{\mu} \tag{12.29}$$

Note that the relationships for L, W_q, and W are the same as the relationships used for the waiting line models in Sections 12.2 and 12.3. They also are based on Little's flow equations.

An Example   Retail sales at Hartlage's Seafood Supply are handled by one clerk. Customer arrivals are random, and the average arrival rate is 21 customers per hour or $\lambda = 21/60 = 0.35$ customers per minute. A study of the service process shows that the average or mean service time is 2 minutes per customer, with a standard deviation of $\sigma = 1.2$ minutes. The mean time of 2 minutes per customer shows that the clerk has a mean service rate of $\mu = \frac{1}{2} = 0.50$ customers per minute. The operating characteristics of this $M/G/1$ waiting line system are

$$P_0 = 1 - \frac{\lambda}{\mu} = 1 - \frac{0.35}{0.50} = 0.30$$

$$L_q = \frac{(0.35)^2(1.2)^2 + (0.35/0.50)^2}{2(1 - 0.35/0.50)} = 1.11 \text{ customers}$$

$$L = L_q + \frac{\lambda}{\mu} = 1.11 + \frac{0.35}{0.50} = 1.81 \text{ customers}$$

$$W_q = \frac{L_q}{\lambda} = \frac{1.11}{0.35} = 3.17 \text{ minutes}$$

$$W = W_q + \frac{1}{\mu} = 3.17 + \frac{1}{0.50} = 5.17 \text{ minutes}$$

$$P_w = \frac{\lambda}{\mu} = \frac{0.35}{0.50} = 0.70$$

Problem 27 provides another application of a single-channel waiting line with Poisson arrivals and arbitrary service times.

Hartlage's manager can review these operating characteristics to determine whether scheduling a second clerk appears to be worthwhile.

Constant Service Times

We need to comment briefly on the single-channel waiting line model that assumes random arrivals but constant service times. Such a waiting line can occur in production and manufacturing environments where machine-controlled service times are constant. This waiting line is described by the $M/D/1$ model, with the D referring to the deterministic service times. With the $M/D/1$ model, the average number of units in the waiting line, L_q, can be found by using equation (12.25) with the condition that the standard deviation of the constant service time is $\sigma = 0$. Thus, the expression for the average number of units in the waiting line for the $M/D/1$ waiting line becomes

$$L_q = \frac{(\lambda/\mu)^2}{2(1 - \lambda/\mu)} \tag{12.30}$$

The other expressions presented earlier in this section can be used to determine additional operating characteristics of the $M/D/1$ system.

NOTES &comments

Whenever the operating characteristics of a waiting line are unacceptable, managers often try to improve service by increasing the mean service rate μ. This is a good idea, but equation (12.25) shows that the variation in the service times also affects the operating characteristics of the waiting line. Because the standard deviation of service times, σ, appears in the numerator of equation (12.25), a larger variation in service times results in a larger average number of units in the waiting line. Hence, another alternative for improving the service capabilities of a waiting line is to reduce the variation in the service times. Thus, even when the mean service rate of the service facility cannot be increased, a reduction in σ will reduce the average number of units in the waiting line and, in general, improve the other operating characteristics of the system.

12.8 A Multiple-Channel Model with Poisson Arrivals, Arbitrary Service Times, and No Waiting Line

An interesting variation of the waiting line models discussed so far involves a system in which no waiting is allowed. Arriving units or customers seek service from one of several service channels. If all the channels are busy, arriving units are denied access to the system. In waiting line terminology, the arrivals occurring when the system is full are *blocked* and cleared from the system. Such customers may be lost or may attempt a return to the system later.

The specific model considered in this section is based on the following assumptions.

1. The system has k channels.
2. The arrivals follow a Poisson probability distribution, with mean arrival rate λ.
3. The service times for each channel may have any probability distribution.
4. The mean service rate μ is the same for each channel.
5. The arrivals enter the system only if at least one of the k channels is available. Arrivals occurring when all channels are busy are blocked—that is, denied service and not allowed to enter the system.

With G denoting a general or unspecified probability distribution for service times, the appropriate model for this situation is referred to as an $M/G/k$ model with "blocked customers cleared." The question addressed in this type of situation is, How many channels or servers should be utilized?

One of the primary applications of this model involves the design of telephone and other communication systems where the arrivals are the calls and the channels are the number of telephone or communication lines available. In such a system, the calls are made to one telephone number, with each call automatically switched to an open channel if possible. When all channels are busy, additional calls receive a busy signal and are denied access to the system.

The Operating Characteristics for the *M/G/k* Model with Blocked Customers Cleared

We approach the problem of selecting the best number of channels by computing the steady-state probabilities that j of the k channels will be busy. These probabilities are

$$P_j = \frac{(\lambda/\mu)^j/j!}{\sum_{i=0}^{k} (\lambda/\mu)^i/i!} \tag{12.31}$$

where

λ = the mean arrival rate
μ = the mean service rate for each channel
k = the number of channels
P_j = the probability that j of the k channels are busy
    for $j = 0, 1, 2, \ldots, k$

The most important probability value is P_k, which is the probability that all k channels are busy. On a percentage basis, P_k indicates the percentage of arrivals that are blocked and denied access to the system.

Another operating characteristic of interest is the average number of units in the system; note that this is equivalent to the average number of channels in use. Letting L denote the average number of units in the system, we have

$$L = \frac{\lambda}{\mu}(1 - P_k) \tag{12.32}$$

An Example   Microdata Software, Inc., uses a telephone ordering system for its computer software products. Callers place orders with Microdata by using the company's 800 telephone number. Assume that calls to this telephone number arrive at an average rate of 12 per hour. The time required to process a telephone order varies considerably from order to order. However, each Microdata sales representative can be expected to handle an average of six calls per hour. Currently, the Microdata 800 telephone number has three internal lines or channels, each operated by a separate sales representative. Calls received on the 800 number are automatically transferred to one of the open lines or channels if available.

Whenever all three lines are busy, callers receive a busy signal. In the past, Microdata has assumed that callers receiving a busy signal will call back later. However, recent research on telephone ordering has shown that a substantial number of callers who are denied access do not call back later. These lost calls represent lost revenues for the firm, so Microdata's management has requested an analysis of the telephone ordering system.

Specifically, management wants to know the percentage of callers who are getting busy signals and are being blocked from the system. If management's goal is to provide sufficient capacity to handle 90% of the callers, how many telephone lines and sales representatives should Microdata use?

We can demonstrate the use of equation (12.31) by computing P_3, the probability that all three of the currently available telephone lines will be in use and additional callers will be blocked:

$$P_3 = \frac{(12/6)^3/3!}{(12/6)^0/0! + (12/6)^1/1! + (12/6)^2/2! + (12/6)^3/3!} = \frac{1.3333}{6.3333} = 0.2105$$

With $P_3 = 0.2105$, approximately 21% of the calls, or slightly more than one in five calls, are being blocked. Only 79% of the calls are being handled immediately by the 3-line system.

Let us assume Microdata expands to a 4-line system. Then, the probability that all four channels will be in use and that callers will be blocked is

$$P_4 = \frac{(12/6)^4/4!}{(12/6)^0/0! + (12/6)^1/1! + (12/6)^2/2! + (12/6)^3/3! + (12/6)^4/4!} = \frac{0.6667}{7} = 0.0952$$

Try Problem 30 to obtain practice in multiple-channel systems with no waiting line.

With only 9.52% of the callers blocked, 90.48% of the callers will reach the Microdata sales representatives. Thus, Microdata should expand its order-processing operation to 4 lines to meet management's goal of providing sufficient capacity to handle at least 90% of the callers. The average number of calls in the 4-line system and thus the average number of lines and sales representatives that will be busy is

$$L = \lambda/\mu(1 - P_4) = 12/6(1 - 0.0952) = 1.81$$

Although an average of less than 2 lines will be busy, the 4-line system is necessary to provide the capacity to handle at least 90% of the callers. We used equation (12.31) to calculate the probability that 0, 1, 2, 3, or 4 lines will be busy. These probabilities are summarized in Table 12.6.

As we discussed in Section 12.5, an economic analysis of waiting lines can be used to guide the system design decisions. In the Microdata system, the cost of the additional line and additional sales representative should be relatively easy to establish. This cost can be balanced against the cost of the blocked calls. With 9.52% of the calls blocked and $\lambda = 12$ calls per hour, an 8-hour day will have an average of $8(12)(0.0952) = 9.1$ blocked calls. If Microdata can estimate the cost of possible lost sales, the cost of these blocked calls can be established. The economic analysis based on the service cost and the blocked-call cost can assist in determining the optimal number of lines for the system.

Table 12.6

Probabilities of Busy Lines for the Microdata 4-Line System

Number of Busy Lines	Probability
0	0.1429
1	0.2857
2	0.2857
3	0.1905
4	0.0952

NOTES & comments

Many of the operating characteristics we have considered in previous sections are not relevant for the $M/G/k$ model with blocked customers cleared. In particular, the average time in the waiting line, W_q, and the average number of units in the waiting line, L_q, are no longer considered because waiting is not permitted in this type of system.

12.9 Waiting Line Models with Finite Calling Populations

For the waiting line models introduced so far, the population of units or customers arriving for service has been considered to be unlimited. In technical terms, when no limit is placed on how many units may seek service, the model is said to have an *infinite calling population*. Under this assumption, the mean arrival rate λ remains constant regardless of how many units are in the waiting line system. This assumption of an infinite calling population is made in most waiting line models.

In other cases, the maximum number of units or customers that may seek service is assumed to be finite. In this situation, the mean arrival rate for the system changes, depending on the number of units in the waiting line, and the waiting line model is said to have a *finite calling population*. The formulas for the operating characteristics of the previous waiting line models must be modified to account for the effect of the finite calling population.

The finite calling population model discussed in this section is based on the following assumptions.

1. The waiting line has a single channel.
2. The population of units that may seek service is finite.
3. The arrivals for *each unit* follow a Poisson probability distribution, with mean arrival rate λ.
4. The service times follow an exponential probability distribution, with mean service rate μ.
5. The queue discipline is first-come, first-served (FCFS).

The waiting line model that is appropriate in such cases is referred to as an *M/M/*1 model with a finite calling population.

The mean arrival rate for the *M/M/*1 model with a finite calling population is defined in terms of how often *each unit* arrives or seeks service. This situation differs from that for previous waiting line models in which λ denoted the mean arrival rate for the system. With a finite calling population, the mean arrival rate for the system varies, depending on how many units are in the system. Instead of adjusting for the changing system arrival rate, in the finite calling population model λ indicates the mean arrival rate for each unit.

The Operating Characteristics for the *M/M/1* Model with a Finite Calling Population

The following formulas are used to determine the steady-state operating characteristics for an *M/M/*1 model with a finite calling population, where

$$\lambda = \text{the mean arrival rate for each unit}$$
$$\mu = \text{the mean service rate}$$
$$N = \text{the size of the population}$$

1. The probability that there are no units in the system:

$$P_0 = \frac{1}{\displaystyle\sum_{n=0}^{N} \frac{N!}{(N-n)!} \left(\frac{\lambda}{\mu}\right)^n} \tag{12.33}$$

2. The average number of units in the waiting line:

$$L_q = N - \frac{\lambda + \mu}{\lambda}(1 - P_0) \tag{12.34}$$

3. The average number of units in the system:

$$L = L_q + (1 - P_0) \tag{12.35}$$

4. The average waiting time in the waiting line:

$$W_q = \frac{L_q}{(N - L)\lambda} \tag{12.36}$$

5. The average waiting time in the system:

$$W = W_q + \frac{1}{\mu} \tag{12.37}$$

6. The probability of n units in the system:

$$P_n = \frac{N!}{(N - n)!}\left(\frac{\lambda}{\mu}\right)^n P_0 \qquad \text{for } n = 0, 1, \ldots, N \tag{12.38}$$

One of the primary applications of the $M/M/1$ model with a finite calling population is referred to as the machine repair problem. In this problem, a group of machines is considered to be the finite population of "customers" that may request repair service. Whenever a machine breaks down, an arrival occurs in the sense that a new repair request is initiated. If another machine breaks down before the repair work has been completed on the first machine, the second machine begins to form a "waiting line" for the repair service. Additional breakdowns by other machines will add to the length of the waiting line. The assumption of first-come, first-served indicates that machines are repaired in the order they break down. The $M/M/1$ model shows that one person or one channel is available to perform the repair service. To return the machine to operation, each machine with a breakdown must be handled by the single-channel repair operation.

An Example   The Kolkmeyer Manufacturing Company has a group of six identical machines; each machine operates an average of 20 hours between breakdowns. Thus, the mean arrival rate or request for repair service for each individual machine is $\lambda = \frac{1}{20} = 0.05$ machine per hour. With randomly occurring breakdowns, the Poisson probability distribution is used to describe the machine breakdown arrival process. One person from the maintenance department provides the single-channel repair service for the six machines. The exponentially distributed service times have a mean of 2 hours per machine or a mean service rate of $\mu = \frac{1}{2} = 0.50$ machines per hour.

With $\lambda = 0.05$ and $\mu = 0.50$, we use equations (12.33) through (12.37) to compute the operating characteristics for this system. Note that the use of equation (12.33) makes the computations involved somewhat cumbersome. Confirm for yourself that equation (12.30) provides the value $P_0 = 0.4845$. The computations for the other operating characteristics are

$$L_q = 6 - \left(\frac{0.05 + 0.50}{0.05}\right)(1 - 0.4845) = 0.3295 \text{ machine}$$

$$L = 0.3295 + (1 - 0.4845) = 0.845 \text{ machine}$$

$$W_q = \frac{0.3295}{(6 - 0.845)0.05} = 1.28 \text{ hours}$$

$$W = 1.28 + \frac{1}{0.50} = 3.28 \text{ hours}$$

Operating characteristics of an *M/M/1* waiting line with a finite calling population are considered in Problem 34.

Finally, equation (12.38) can be used to compute the probabilities of any number of machines being in the repair system.

As with other waiting line models, the operating characteristics provide the manager with information about the waiting line operation. Whether these operating characteristics suggest that better repair service is needed depends on the cost of the idle machine waiting time compared to the cost of assigning an additional person to make the repair operation either a two-channel system or a faster one-channel system.

Computations for the multiple-channel finite calling population model are more complex than those for the single-channel model. A computer solution is virtually mandatory in this case. The Management Scientist software package that accompanies this text has the capability of analyzing the finite calling population model. The computer output for the Kolkmeyer machine repair problem with a two-person, two-channel, repair system is shown in Figure 12.4. By considering the cost of machine waiting or down time and the cost of repair personnel, management can determine whether the two-channel system is cost effective.

Figure 12.4   **The Management Scientist Printout for the Kolkmeyer Two-Channel Machine Repair Problem**

```
WAITING LINE MODELS
*******************
    NUMBER OF CHANNELS = 2
    POISSON ARRIVALS WITH MEAN RATE = .05
    EXPONENTIAL SERVICE TIMES WITH MEAN RATE = .5 PER CHANNEL
    FINITE CALLING POPULATION OF SIZE = 6

OPERATING CHARACTERISTICS
-------------------------
THE PROBABILITY OF NO UNITS IN THE SYSTEM              0.5602
THE AVERAGE NUMBER OF UNITS IN THE WAITING LINE        0.0227
THE AVERAGE NUMBER OF UNITS IN THE SYSTEM              0.5661
THE AVERAGE TIME A UNIT SPENDS IN THE WAITING LINE     0.0834
THE AVERAGE TIME A UNIT SPENDS IN THE SYSTEM           2.0834
THE PROBABILITY THAT AN ARRIVING UNIT HAS TO WAIT      0.1036


Number of Units in the System          Probability
-----------------------------          -----------
            0                            0.5602
            1                            0.3361
            2                            0.0840
            3                            0.0168
            4                            0.0025
            5                            0.0003
            6                            0.0000
```

Summary

In this chapter we presented a variety of waiting line models that have been developed to help managers make better decisions concerning the operation of waiting lines. For each model, we presented formulas that could be used to develop operating characteristics for the system being studied. Some of the operating characteristics presented were the

1. probability that there are no units in the system,
2. average number of units in the waiting line,
3. average number of units in the system,
4. average time a unit spends in the waiting line,
5. average time a unit spends in the system,
6. probability that arriving units will have to wait for service, and
7. probability that the service facility is in use.

We also showed how an economic analysis of the waiting line could be conducted by developing a total-cost model that includes the cost associated with units waiting for service and the cost required to operate the service facility.

As many of the examples in this chapter show, the most obvious applications of waiting line models are situations in which customers arrive for service, such as at a grocery checkout counter, bank, or restaurant. However, with a little creativity, waiting line models can be applied to many different situations, such as telephone calls waiting for connections, mail orders waiting for processing, machines waiting for repairs, manufacturing jobs waiting to be processed, and money waiting to be spent or invested. The Management Science in Action article describes how a waiting line model provided the basis for improving productivity of a fire department in New Haven, Connecticut.

The complexity and diversity of waiting line systems found in practice often prevents an analyst from finding an existing waiting line model that fits the specific application being studied. Computer simulation, the topic discussed in the next chapter, provides another approach to determining the operating characteristics of waiting line systems.

MANAGEMENT SCIENCE in action

Improving Fire Department Productivity*

The New Haven, Connecticut, Fire Department implemented a reorganization plan with cross-trained fire and medical personnel responding to both fire and medical emergencies. A waiting line model provided the basis for the reorganization by demonstrating that substantial improvements in emergency medical response time could be achieved with only a small reduction in fire protection. Annual savings were reported to be $1.4 million.

The model was based on Poisson arrivals and exponential service times for both fire and medical emergencies. It was used to estimate the average time that a person placing a call would have to wait for the appropriate emergency unit to arrive at the location. Waiting times were estimated by the model's prediction of the average travel time to reach each of the city's 28 census tracts.

The model was first applied to the original system of 16 fire units and 4 emergency medical units that operated independently. It was then applied to the proposed reorganization plan that involved cross-trained department personnel qualified to respond to both fire and medical emergencies. Results from the model demonstrated that average travel times could be reduced under the reorganization plan. Various facility location alternatives also were evaluated. When implemented the reorganization plan both reduced operating cost and improved public safety services.

....

*Based on Sweeney, A. J., L. Goldring, and E. D. Geyer, "Improving Fire Department Productivity: Merging Fire and Emergency Medical Units in New Haven." *Interfaces*, vol. 23, no. 1, January–February 1993, pp. 109–129.

Glossary

Queue A waiting line.

Queuing theory The body of knowledge dealing with waiting lines.

Single channel A waiting line with only one service facility.

Poisson probability distribution The probability distribution used to describe the arrival pattern for some waiting line models.

Exponential probability distribution The probability distribution used to describe the service time for some waiting line models.

FCFS The queue discipline that serves waiting units on a first-come, first-served basis.

Transient period The start-up period for a waiting line, occurring before the waiting line reaches a normal or steady-state operation.

Steady-state The normal operation of the waiting line after it has gone through a start-up or transient period. General operating characteristics of waiting lines are computed for steady-state conditions.

Mean arrival rate The average number of customers or units arriving in a given period.

Mean service rate The average number of customers or units that can be served by one service facility in a given period.

Multiple channel A waiting line with two or more parallel service facilities.

Blocking When arriving units cannot enter the waiting line because the system is full. Blocking can occur when waiting lines are not allowed or when waiting lines have a finite capacity.

Infinite calling population The population of customers or units who may seek service has no specified upper limit.

Finite calling population The population of customers or units who may seek service has a fixed and finite value.

Problems

1. Willow Brook National Bank operates a drive-up teller window that allows customers to complete bank transactions without getting out of their cars. On weekday mornings, arrivals to the drive-up teller window occur at random, with a mean arrival rate of 24 customers per hour or 0.4 customer per minute.
   a. What is the mean or expected number of customers that will arrive in a 5-minute period?
   b. Assume that the Poisson probability distribution can be used to describe the arrival process. Use the mean arrival rate in part (a) and compute the probabilities that exactly 0, 1, 2, and 3 customers will arrive during a 5-minute period.
   c. Delays are expected if more than 3 customers arrive during any 5-minute period. What is the probability that delay will occur?

2. In the Willow Brook National Bank waiting line system (see Problem 1), assume that the service times for the drive-up teller follow an exponential probability distribution with a mean service rate of 36 customers per hour or 0.6 customer per minute. Use the exponential probability distribution to answer the following questions.
   a. What is the probability that the service time is 1 minute or less?
   b. What is the probability that the service time is 2 minutes or less?
   c. What is the probability that the service time is more than 2 minutes?

3. Use the single-channel drive-up bank teller operation referred to in Problems 1 and 2 to determine the following operating characteristics for the system.
   a. The probability that there are no customers in the system
   b. The average number of customers waiting
   c. The average number of customers in the system
   d. The average time a customer spends waiting
   e. The average time a customer spends in the system
   f. The probability that arriving customers will have to wait for service

4. Use the single-channel drive-up bank teller operation referred to in Problems 1–3 and find the probabilities of 0, 1, 2, and 3 customers in the system. What is the probability that more than 3 customers will be in the drive-up teller system at the same time?

5. **SELFTest** The reference desk of a university library receives requests for assistance. Assume that a Poisson probability distribution with a mean rate of 10 requests per hour can be used to describe the arrival pattern and that service times follow the exponential probability distribution with a mean service rate of 12 requests per hour.
   a. What is the probability that there are no requests for assistance in the system?
   b. What is the average number of requests that will be waiting for service?
   c. What is the average waiting time in minutes before service begins?
   d. What is the average time at the reference desk in minutes (waiting time plus service time)?
   e. What is the probability that a new arrival has to wait for service?

6. Trucks using a single-channel loading dock arrive according to the Poisson probability distribution. The time required to load/unload follows the exponential probability distribution. The mean arrival rate is 12 trucks per day, and the mean service rate is 18 trucks per day.
   a. What is the probability that there are no trucks in the system?
   b. What is the average number of trucks waiting for service?
   c. What is the average time a truck waits for the loading/unloading service to begin?
   d. What is the probability that a new arrival will have to wait?

7. A mail-order nursery specializes in European beech trees. New orders, which are processed by a single shipping clerk, have a mean arrival rate of 6 per day and a mean service rate of 8 per day. Assume that arrivals follow a Poisson probability distribution and that service times follow an exponential probability distribution.
   a. What is the average number of orders in the system?
   b. What is the average time that an order spends waiting before the clerk is available to begin service?
   c. What is the average time an order spends in the system?

8. For the Burger Dome single-channel waiting line in Section 12.2, assume that the arrival rate is increased to 1 customer per minute and the mean service rate is increased to 1.25 customers per minute. Compute the following operating characteristics for the new system: P_0, L_q, L, W_q, W, and P_w. Does this system provide better or poorer service compared to the original system? Discuss any differences and the reason for these differences.

9. Marty's Barber Shop has one barber. Customers arrive at the rate of 2.2 customers per hour, and haircuts are given at the average rate of 5 per hour. Use the Poisson arrivals and exponential service times model to answer the following questions.
   a. What is the probability that there are no units in the system?
   b. What is the probability that 1 customer is receiving a haircut and no one is waiting?
   c. What is the probability that 1 customer is receiving a haircut and 1 customer is waiting?
   d. What is the probability that 1 customer is receiving a haircut and 2 customers are waiting?
   e. What is the probability that more than 2 customers are waiting?
   f. What is the average time a customer waits for service?

10. Trosper Tire Company has decided to hire a new mechanic to handle all tire changes for customers ordering a new set of tires. Two mechanics have applied for the job. One mechanic has limited experience, can be hired for $14 per hour, and can service an average of 3 customers per hour. The other mechanic has several years of experience, can service an average of 4 customers per hour, but must be paid $20 per hour. Assume that customers arrive at the Trosper garage at the rate of 2 customers per hour.
   a. Compute the waiting line characteristics for each mechanic, assuming Poisson arrivals and exponential service times.
   b. If the company assigns a customer waiting cost of $30 per hour, which mechanic provides the lower operating cost?

11. **SELF Test** Agan Interior Design provides home and office decorating assistance to its customers. In normal operation, an average of 2.5 customers arrive each hour. One design consultant is available to answer customer questions and make product recommendations. The consultant averages 10 minutes with each customer.

   a. Compute the operating characteristics of the customer waiting line, assuming Poisson arrivals and exponential service times.

   b. Service goals dictate that an arriving customer should not wait for service more than an average of 5 minutes. Is this goal being met? If not, what action do you recommend?

   c. If the consultant can reduce the average time spent per customer to 8 minutes, what is the mean service rate? Will the service goal be met?

12. Pete's Market is a small local grocery store with only one checkout counter. Assume that shoppers arrive at the checkout lane according to the Poisson probability distribution, with a mean arrival rate of 15 customers per hour. The checkout service times follow an exponential probability distribution, with a mean service rate of 20 customers per hour.

   a. Compute the operating characteristics for this waiting line.

   b. If the manager's service goal is to limit the waiting time prior to beginning the checkout process to no more than 5 minutes, what recommendations would you provide regarding the current checkout system?

13. After reviewing the waiting line analysis of Problem 12, the manager of Pete's Market wants to consider one of the following alternatives for improving service. What alternative would you recommend? Justify your recommendation.

   a. Hire a second person to bag the groceries while the cash register operator is entering the cost data and collecting money from the customer. With this improved single-channel operation, the mean service rate could be increased to 30 customers per hour.

   b. Hire a second person to operate a second checkout counter. The two-channel operation would have a mean service rate of 20 customers per hour for each channel.

14. Keuka Park Savings and Loan currently has one drive-up teller window. The arrivals follow a Poisson probability distribution, with a mean arrival rate of 10 cars per hour. The service times follow an exponential probability distribution, with a mean service rate of 12 cars per hour.

   a. What is the probability that no customers are in the system?

   b. If you were to drive up to the facility, how many cars would you expect to see waiting and being served?

   c. What is the probability that at least one car will be waiting to be served?

   d. What is the average time in the queue waiting for service?

   e. As a potential customer of the system, would you be satisfied with the given waiting line characteristics? Why or why not?

15. To improve customer service, Keuka Park Savings and Loan (see Problem 14) wants to investigate the effect of a second drive-up teller window. Assume a mean arrival rate of 10 cars per hour and a mean service rate of 12 cars per hour for each drive-up window. What effect would the addition of a new teller window have on the system? Does this system appear acceptable?

16. The new Fore and Aft Marina is to be located on the Ohio River near Madison, Indiana. Assume that Fore and Aft has decided to build a docking facility where one boat at a time can stop for gas and servicing. Assume that arrivals follow a Poisson probability distribution, with a mean of 5 boats per hour, and that service times follow an exponential probability distribution, with a mean of 10 boats per hour. Answer the following questions.

   a. What is the probability that no boats are in the system?

   b. What is the average number of boats that will be waiting for service?

   c. What is the average time a boat will spend waiting for service?

   d. What is the average time a boat will spend at the dock?

   e. If you were the management of Fore and Aft Marina, would you be satisfied with the service level your system will be providing? Why or why not?

17. The management of the Fore and Aft Marina in Problem 16 wants to investigate the possibility of enlarging the docking facility so that two boats can stop for gas and servicing simultaneously. Assume that the mean arrival rate is 5 boats per hour and that the mean service rate for each of the channels is 10 boats per hour.

a. What is the probability that the boat dock will be idle?

b. What is the average number of boats that will be waiting for service?

c. What is the average time a boat will spend waiting for service?

d. What is the average time a boat will spend at the dock?

e. If you were the manager of Fore and Aft Marina, would you be satisfied with the service level your system will be providing? Why or why not?

18. The City Beverage Drive-Thru is considering a two-channel service system. Cars arrive according to the Poisson probability distribution, with a mean arrival rate of 6 cars per hour. The service times have an exponential probability distribution, with a mean service rate of 10 cars per hour for each channel.

a. What is the probability no cars are in the system?

b. What is the average number of cars waiting for service?

c. What is the average time waiting for service?

d. What is the average time in the system?

e. What is the probability that an arrival will have to wait for service?

19. **SELFTest** Consider a two-channel waiting line with Poisson arrivals and exponential service times. The mean arrival rate is 14 units per hour, and the mean service rate is 10 units per hour for each channel.

a. What is the probability that no units are in the system?

b. What is the average number of units in the system?

c. What is the average time a unit waits for service?

d. What is the average time a unit is in the system?

e. What is the probability of having to wait for service?

20. Refer to Problem 19. Assume that the system is expanded to a three-channel operation.

a. Compute the operating characteristics for this waiting line system.

b. If the service goal is to provide sufficient capacity so that no more than 25% of the customers have to wait for service, is the two- or three-channel system preferred?

21. **SELFTest** Refer to the Agan Interior Design situation in Problem 11. Agan would like to evaluate two alternatives:

• Use one consultant with an average service time of 8 minutes per customer.

• Expand to two consultants, each of whom has an average service time of 10 minutes per customer.

If the consultants are paid $16 per hour and the customer waiting time is valued at $25 per hour for waiting time prior to service, should Agan expand to the two-consultant system? Explain.

22. A fast-food franchise is considering operating a drive-up window food-service operation. Assume that customer arrivals follow a Poisson probability distribution, with a mean arrival rate of 24 cars per hour, and that service times follow an exponential probability distribution. Arriving customers place orders at an intercom station at the back of the parking lot and then drive to the service window to pay for and receive their orders. The following three service alternatives are being considered.

• A single-channel operation in which one employee fills the order and takes the money from the customer. The average service time for this alternative is 2 minutes.

• A single-channel operation in which one employee fills the order while a second employee takes the money from the customer. The average service time for this alternative is 1.25 minutes.

• A two-channel operation with two service windows and two employees. The employee stationed at each window fills the order and takes the money for customers arriving at the window. The average service time for this alternative is 2 minutes for each channel.

Answer the following questions and recommend an alternative design for the fast-food franchise.

a. What is the probability that no customers are in the system?

b. What is the average number of cars waiting for service?

c. What is the average time a car waits for service?

d. What is the average time in the system?

e. What is the average number of cars in the system?

f. What is the probability an arriving car will have to wait for service?

23. The following cost information is available for the fast-food franchise in Problem 22.

- Customer waiting time is valued at $25 per hour to reflect the fact that waiting time is costly to the fast-food business.
- The cost of each employee is $6.50 per hour.
- To account for equipment and space, an additional cost of $20 per hour is attributable to each channel.

What is the lowest-cost design for the fast-food business?

24. Patients arrive at a dentist's office at a mean rate of 2.8 patients per hour. The dentist can treat patients at the mean rate of 3 patients per hour. A study of patient waiting times shows that, on average, a patient waits 30 minutes before seeing the dentist.

a. What are the mean arrival and treatment rates in terms of patients per minute?

b. What is the average number of patients in the waiting room?

c. If a patient arrives at 10:10 A.M., at what time is the patient expected to leave the office?

25. **SELF**Test A study of the multichannel food-service operation at the Red Birds' baseball park shows that the average time between the arrival of a customer at the food-service counter and his or her departure with a filled order is 10 minutes. During the game, customers arrive at the average rate of 4 per minute. The food-service operation requires an average of 2 minutes per customer order.

a. What is the mean service rate per channel in terms of customers per minute?

b. What is average waiting time in the line prior to placing an order?

c. On average, how many customers are in the food-service system?

26. Manning Autos operates an automotive service counter. While completing the repair work, Manning mechanics arrive at the company's parts department counter at the mean rate of 4 per hour. The parts coordinator spends an average of 6 minutes with each mechanic, discussing the parts the mechanic needs and retrieving the parts from inventory.

a. Currently, there is one parts coordinator. On average, each mechanic waits 4 minutes before the parts coordinator is available to answer questions and/or retrieve parts from inventory. Find L_q, W, and L for this single-channel parts operation.

b. A trial period with a second parts coordinator showed that, on average, each mechanic waited only 1 minute before a parts coordinator was available. Find L_q, W, and L for this two-channel parts operation.

c. If the cost of each mechanic is $20 per hour and the cost of each parts coordinator is $12 per hour, is the one-channel or the two-channel system the more economical?

27. **SELF**Test Gubser Welding, Inc., operates a welding service for construction and automotive repair jobs. Assume that the arrival of jobs at the company's office can be described by a Poisson probability distribution with a mean arrival rate of 2 jobs per 8-hour day. The time required to complete the jobs follows a normal probability distribution with a mean time of 3.2 hours and a standard deviation of 2 hours. Answer the following questions, assuming that Gubser uses one welder to complete all jobs.

a. What is the mean arrival rate in jobs per hour?

b. What is the mean service rate in jobs per hour?

c. What is the average number of jobs waiting for service?

d. What is the average time a job waits before the welder can begin working on it?

e. What is the average number of hours between when a job is received and when it is completed?

f. What percentage of the time is Gubser's welder busy?

28. Jobs arrive randomly at a particular assembly plant; assume that the mean arrival rate is 5 jobs per hour. Service times (in minutes per job) do not follow the exponential probability distribution. Two proposed designs for the plant's assembly operation are shown.

	Service Time	
Design	*Mean*	*Standard Deviation*
A	6.0	3.0
B	6.25	0.6

  a. What is the mean service rate in jobs per hour for each of the designs?

  b. For the mean service rates in part (a), what design appears to provide the best or fastest service rate?

  c. What are the standard deviations of the service times in hours?

  d. Use the *M/G/*1 model in Section 12.7 to compute the operating characteristics for each of the designs.

  e. Which design provides the best operating characteristics? Why?

29. The Robotics Manufacturing Company operates an equipment repair business where emergency jobs arrive randomly at the rate of 3 jobs per 8-hour day. The company's repair facility is a single-channel system operated by a repair technician. The service time varies with a mean repair time of 2 hours and a standard deviation of 1.5 hours. The company's cost of the repair operation is $28 per hour. In the economic analysis of the waiting line system, Robotics uses $35 per hour cost for customers waiting during the repair process.

  a. What are the arrival rate and service rate in jobs per hour?

  b. What is the hourly cost of the repair operation?

  c. The company is considering purchasing a computer-based equipment repair system that would enable a constant repair time of 2 hours. For practical purposes, the standard deviation is 0. Because of the computer-based equipment, the company's cost of the new operation would be $32 per hour. The firm's director of operations has said no to the new equipment because the hourly cost is $4 higher and the mean repair time is the same 2 hours. Do you agree? What effect will the new system have on the waiting line characteristics of the repair service?

  d. Does it make econo:.ic sense to pay for the computer-based system in order to reduce the variation in service time? How much will the new system save the company during a 40-hour work week?

30. **SELF**Test A large insurance company has a central computing system that contains a variety of information about customer accounts. Insurance agents in a six-state area use telephone lines to access the customer information data base. Currently, the company's central computer system allows 3 users to access the central computer simultaneously. Agents who attempt to use the system when it is full are denied access; no waiting is allowed. The company realizes that with its expanding business, more requests will be made to the central information system. Being denied access to the system is inefficient as well as annoying for the agents. Access requests follow a Poisson probability distribution, with a mean of 42 calls per hour. The mean service rate per line is 20 calls per hour.

  a. What is the probability that 0, 1, 2, and 3 access lines will be in use?

  b. What is the probability that an agent will be denied access to the system?

  c. What is the average number of access lines in use?

  d. In planning for the future, the company wants to be able to handle $\lambda = 50$ calls per hour; in addition, the probability that an agent will be denied access to the system should be no greater than your answer to part (b). How many access lines should this system have?

31. Mid-West Publishing Company publishes college textbooks. The company operates an 800 telephone number whereby potential adopters can ask questions about forthcoming texts, request examination copies of texts, and place orders. Currently, two extension lines are used, with two representatives handling the telephone inquiries. Calls occurring when both extension lines are being used receive a busy signal; no waiting is allowed. Each representative can accommodate an average of 12 calls per hour.
    a. If the mean arrival rate is 20 calls per hour, what percentage of the calls receive a busy signal?
    b. How many extensions should be used if the company wants to handle 90% of the calls immediately?
    c. What is the average number of extensions that will be busy if your recommendation in part (b) is used?

32. City Cab, Inc., uses two dispatchers to handle requests for service and dispatch the cabs. The telephone calls that are made to City Cab use a common telephone number. When both dispatchers are busy, the caller hears a busy signal; no waiting is allowed. Callers who receive a busy signal can call back later or call another cab service. Assume that the arrival of calls follows a Poisson probability distribution, with a mean of 40 calls per hour, and that each dispatcher can handle a mean of 30 calls per hour.
    a. What percentage of the time are both dispatchers idle?
    b. What percentage of the time are both dispatchers busy?
    c. What is the probability callers will receive a busy signal if 2, 3, or 4 dispatchers are used?
    d. If the company wants no more than 12% of the callers to receive a busy signal, how many dispatchers should be used?

33. Kolkmeyer Manufacturing Company (see Section 12.9) is considering adding 2 machines to its manufacturing operations; this will bring the number of machines to 8. Mr. Andrews, the president of Kolkmeyer, has asked for a study of the need to add a second employee to the repair process. The mean arrival rate is 0.05 machine per hour for each machine, and the mean service rate for each individual assigned to the repair operation is 0.50 machine per hour.
    a. Compute the following operating characteristics if the company retains the single-employee repair service.
        • The probability that all machines are in operation and the repair person is idle
        • The average number of machines waiting for repair
        • The average number of machines down (those waiting plus those being serviced)
        • The average waiting time before repair can begin
        • The average down time (waiting time plus servicing time)
    b. Use The Management Scientist software package to compute the same characteristics if a second employee is added to the machine repair operation.
    c. Each employee assigned to the service operation is paid $20 per hour. Machine down time is valued at $80 per hour. From an economic point of view, should one or two employees handle the machine repair operation? Explain.

34. **SELF Test** Five secretaries use an office copier. The average time between arrivals for each secretary is 40 minutes, which is equivalent to a mean arrival rate of $1/40 = 0.025$ arrivals per minute. The mean time each secretary spends at the copier is 5 minutes, which is equivalent to a mean service rate of $\frac{1}{5} = 0.20$ users per minute. Use the $M/M/1$ model with a finite calling population to determine the following:
    a. The probability that the copier is idle
    b. The average number of secretaries in the waiting line
    c. The average number of secretaries at the copier
    d. The average time a secretary spends waiting for the copier
    e. The average time a secretary spends at the copier.
    f. During an 8-hour day, how many minutes does a secretary spend at the copier? How much of this time is waiting time?
    g. Should the company consider purchasing a second copier? Explain.

Case Problem: Airline Reservations

Regional Airlines is establishing a new telephone system for handling flight reservations. During the 10:00 A.M. to 11:00 A.M. time period, calls to the reservation agent occur randomly at an average of one call every 3.75 minutes. Historical service time data show that a reservation agent spends an average of 3 minutes with each customer. The waiting line model assumptions of Poisson arrivals and exponential service times appear reasonable for the telephone reservation system.

Regional Airlines' management believes that offering an efficient telephone reservation system is an important part of establishing an image as a service-oriented airline. If the system is properly implemented, Regional Airlines will establish good customer relations, which in the long run will increase business. However, if the telephone reservation system is frequently overloaded and customers have difficulty contacting an agent, a negative customer reaction may lead to an eventual loss of business. The cost of a ticket reservation agent is $20 per hour. Thus, management wants to provide good service, but does not want to incur the cost of overstaffing the telephone reservation operation by using more agents than necessary.

At a planning meeting, Regional's management team agreed that an acceptable customer service goal is to answer at least 85% of the incoming calls immediately. During the planning meeting, Regional's vice-president of administration pointed out that the data show that the average service rate for an agent is faster than the average arrival rate of the telephone calls. His conclusion was that the personnel costs could be minimized by using one agent and that the single agent should be able to handle the telephone reservations and still have some idle time. The vice-president of marketing restated the importance of customer service and expressed support for at least two reservation agents.

The current telephone reservation system design does not allow callers to wait. Callers who attempt to reach a reservation agent when all agents are occupied receive a busy signal and are blocked from the system. A representative from the telephone company suggested that Regional Airlines consider an expanded system that accommodates waiting. In the expanded system, when a customer calls and all agents are busy, a recorded message tells the customer that the call is being held in the order received and that an agent will be available shortly. The customer can stay on the line and listen to background music while waiting for an agent. Regional's management will need more information before switching to the expanded system.

Managerial Report

Prepare a managerial report for Regional Airlines analyzing the telephone reservation system. Evaluate both the system that does not allow waiting and the expanded system that allows waiting. Include the following information in your report.

1. A detailed analysis of the operating characteristics of the reservation system with one agent as proposed by the vice-president of administration. What is your recommendation concerning a single-agent system?
2. A detailed analysis of the operating characteristics of the reservation system based on your recommendation regarding the number of agents Regional should use and whether the system should allow customers to wait.
3. What appear to be the advantages or disadvantages of the expanded system? Discuss the number of waiting callers the expanded system would need to accommodate.
4. The telephone arrival data presented are for the 10:00 A.M. to 11:00 A.M. time period; however, the arrival rate of incoming calls is expected to change from hour to hour. Describe how your waiting line analysis could be used to develop a ticket agent staffing plan that would enable the company to provide different levels of staffing for the ticket reservation system at different times during the day. Indicate the information that you would need to develop this staffing plan.

APPENDIX 12.1 Waiting Line Models with Spreadsheets

Spreadsheets provide a capability for quickly and easily evaluating waiting line formulas and determining the operating characteristics of a waiting line model. Figure 12.5 shows the formula spreadsheet for a single-channel waiting line with Poisson arrivals and exponential service times. You must input the mean arrival rate, λ, and the mean service rate, μ, in cells B4 and B6, respectively. The input values shown with $\lambda = 0.75$ and $\mu = 1$ are the values used for the Burger Dome single-channel waiting line model presented in Section 12.2.

Equations (12.4) through (12.9) provide the operating characteristics for a single-channel waiting line model with Poisson arrivals and exponential service times. You can obtain a spreadsheet evaluation of this waiting line model by placing these equations (as formulas) in selected cells. In Figure 12.5 cell B10 contains the formula =1-B4/B6. With λ entered in cell B4 and μ entered in cell B6, cell B10 contains the probability of no units in the system, given by 1 − (λ/μ) in equation (12.4). Verify that the formula in cell B12 determines the average number of units in the waiting line as given by equation (12.5):

$$L_q = \frac{\lambda^2}{\mu(\mu - \lambda)}$$

Note that the average number of units in the system in cell B14 is given by equation (12.6), where $L = L_q + (\lambda/\mu)$. Thus, B14 contains the formula =B12+B4/B6. As L_q has already been computed in cell B12, the formula in cell B14 takes advantage of the computation made in cell B12 in arriving at the average number of units in the system. Continuing with the formula spreadsheet, equations (12.7) through (12.9) for the single-channel model have been entered as the formulas for cells B16, B18, and B20, respectively.

Figure 12.5

Formula Spreadsheet for a Single-Channel Waiting Line Model

	A	B
1	SINGLE CHANNEL WAITING LINE	
2		
3		
4	MEAN ARRIVAL RATE	0.75
5		
6	MEAN SERVICE RATE	1
7		
8		
9		
10	PROBABILITY OF NO UNITS	=1-B4/B6
11		
12	AVERAGE NUMBER IN WAITING LINE	=B4^2/(B6*(B6-B4))
13		
14	AVERAGE NUMBER IN SYSTEM	=B12+B4/B6
15		
16	AVERAGE TIME IN WAITING LINE	=B12/B4
17		
18	AVERAGE TIME IN SYSTEM	=B16+1/B6
19		
20	PROBABILITY OF WAITING	=B4/B6

Figure 12.6

. . . .

Value Spreadsheet Results for the Burger Dome Waiting Line Model

	A	B
1	SINGLE CHANNEL WAITING LINE	
2		
3		
4	MEAN ARRIVAL RATE	0.75
5		
6	MEAN SERVICE RATE	1.00
7		
8		
9		
10	PROBABILITY OF NO UNITS	0.25
11		
12	AVERAGE NUMBER IN WAITING LINE	2.25
13		
14	AVERAGE NUMBER IN SYSTEM	3.00
15		
16	AVERAGE TIME IN WAITING LINE	3.00
17		
18	AVERAGE TIME IN SYSTEM	4.00
19		
20	PROBABILITY OF WAITING	0.75

For the mean arrival rate of 0.75 and the mean service rate of 1.00, the value spreadsheet in Figure 12.6 provides the operating characteristics for the Burger Dome single-channel waiting line model. Note that these are the same as those computed in Section 12.2.

After you have developed the spreadsheet, you can easily change input parameters and automatically adjust the operating characteristics throughout the spreadsheet. In Section 12.2 we discussed the design alternative of increasing the mean service rate at Burger Dome to $\mu = 1.25$ by using a combined order-taker, order-filler system. Thus, if you simply change the mean service rate to 1.25, the new operating characteristics, as previously shown in Table 12.3, will appear. Thus a spreadsheet enables you to ask "what-if" questions and immediately learn how changes in design will affect the operating characteristics of the system.

You will have to develop a similar, but slightly different, spreadsheet for each different waiting line model. For example, the multiple-channel waiting line model in Section 12.3 could be placed in a formula spreadsheet similar to that in Figure 12.5. In addition to the mean arrival rate and mean service rate, the multiple-channel spreadsheet would require a third input cell indicating the number of channels in the waiting line. The operating characteristic formulas of Figure 12.5 currently based on equations (12.4) through (12.9) would have to be modified to accommodate equations (12.11) through (12.16) for the multiple-channel model. Additional input cells for the cost of a service channel and the cost of waiting could be used to create another cell formula to compute the total cost of operating the waiting line system.

MANAGEMENT SCIENCE in practice

Citibank*
Long Island City, New York

Citibank, a major subsidiary of Citicorp, makes available a wide range of financial services, including checking and savings accounts, loans and mortgages, insurance, and investment services, within the framework of a unique strategy for delivering those services called Citibanking. Citibanking entails a consistent brand identity all over the world, consistent product offerings, and a high level of customer service. Citibanking lets you manage your money anytime, anywhere, anyway you choose. Whether you need to save for the future or borrow for today, you can do it all at Citibank.

Citibanking's state-of-the-art automatic teller machines (ATMs) located in Citicard Banking Centers (CBCs), let customers do all their banking in one place with the touch of a finger, 24 hours a day, 7 days a week. More than 150 different banking functions from deposits to managing investments can be performed with ease. Citibanking ATMs are so much more than just cash machines that customers today use them for 80% of their transactions.

A Waiting Line Application

The New York franchise of U.S. Citibanking operates approximately 250 CBCs. Each CBC provides customers with one or more ATMs, called customer activated terminals (or CATs), which are capable of performing a variety of banking transactions. Approximately 70% of the CBCs are located in Manhattan, the Bronx, Brooklyn, Queens, and Staten Island. The remaining 30% are suburban CBCs located in Nassau, Suffolk, Orange, Rockland, and Westchester counties. Measuring performance and service capacity at each of the CBCs is an important part of Citibank's emphasis on providing superior access and convenience for its customers.

Each Citibank CBC operates as a waiting line system with randomly arriving customers seeking service at a CAT. Based on the use at each site, the number of CATs ranges from 1 to 20 with each site operating with a single queue. If 1 CAT is present, the system operates as a single-channel waiting line, with arriving customers waiting whenever the CAT is being used by another customer. At most of the CBC sites multiple CATs provide a multiple-channel waiting line system.

A periodic CBC capacity study is used to determine the capacity needed at each center. The hardware supply at the center is measured in terms of the transactional volume the site is capable of supporting for a standard number of transactions per CAT per hour. The customer demand is measured in terms of the peak number of arrivals per hour at the site. Comparing supply and demand enables Citibank to classify each CBC as either

■ Highly endangered—average peak hour waiting time exceeds 5 minutes.
■ Borderline—average peak hour waiting time is 3–5 minutes.
■ Sufficient—average peak hour waiting time is 3 minutes or less.

In a recent capacity study, demand data suggested approximately 6% of the CBCs should be classified as endangered and approximately 8% should be classified as borderline. In total, 34 sites were listed as candidates for possible capacity expansion with incremental CATs desired.

In order to make recommendations on the number of CATs to add at the selected sites, management needed additional information concerning the customer service levels at each of the sites. Operating characteristics information provided by a waiting line model would be helpful in determining the number of CATs each center should have. Typical information provided by the model included:

■ The average number of customers in the waiting line
■ The average number of customers in the system
■ The average time a customer spends in the waiting line
■ The average time a customer spends in the system
■ The probability that an arriving customer has to wait

In-house management information system (MIS) data on arrival rates and service times were collected to determine whether a multiple-channel waiting line model with Poisson arrivals and exponential service time could be used to model a CBC waiting line system. Customer arrivals were indeed random and adequately represented by a Poisson probability distribution. The mean arrival rate varied, depending on time of day and day of week. However, it was important for the operating characteristic information to be developed for the peak or high demand periods. An average of the top 10 hourly demands was used to determine the mean arrival rate for each CBC site. Observed service times showed that the exponential probability distribution provided a reasonable approximation of the service time distribution.

—Continued on next page

....

*The authors are indebted to Stacey Karter, Citibank, for providing this application.

—Continued from previous page

For example, one midtown Manhattan branch site was classified as an endangered center operating with 5 CATs. On-site observations were conducted to verify the MIS data and the peak arrival rate of 172 customers per hour. From the observed session times of 2 minutes per customer, the mean service rate per CAT was estimated to be 30 per hour. Five CATs were insufficient to meet this peak demand. A multiple-channel waiting line model with an expansion to 6 CATs showed that 88% of the customers would still have to wait and that the average waiting time would be 6 to 7 minutes. Expansion to 6 CATs still provided an unacceptable level of service. Expansion to 7 CATs provided acceptable service levels with an average of 2.4 customers in the waiting line. Hence, expansion to 8 CATs was not necessary at that time.

Even though peak demand periods were not always long enough to reach the steady-state conditions projected by the waiting line model, the operating characteristics indicated by the model provided general guidelines for capacity decisions. Use of the observed mean arrival and service rates unique to each site enabled the waiting line model to provide useful information for making the incremental CAT decisions at each CBC location.

Questions

1. How did Citibank's CBCs operate as a waiting line system?
2. How did Citibank ensure appropriate arrival and service time rates for the CBC waiting line operation?
3. What information did the waiting line model provide? How was this information helpful in making the incremental CAT decisions for each site?

thirteen

CHAPTER

Simulation

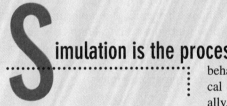 imulation is the process of studying the behavior of a real system by using a model that replicates the behavior of the system. A simulation model is constructed by identifying the mathematical expressions and logical relationships that describe how the system operates. Generally, a computer is used to perform the computations required by the simulation model.

Simulation is one of the most frequently used techniques of management science. When a system is complex, simulation may be the best and perhaps only way to model the system. The variety of simulation applications is extensive and includes the following examples:

1. Simulating the flow of traffic through a busy intersection. The objective is to determine whether installing left-turn signals at the intersection will improve traffic flow.
2. Simulating an inventory system. The objective is to determine the order quantity and reorder point that will provide a low operating cost and still meet acceptable service reliability requirements.
3. Simulating the operation of a manufacturing facility. The objective is to determine the benefits of an expanded or redesigned production operation.
4. Simulating arriving and departing flights at a major metropolitan airport. The objective is to determine the impact of scheduling changes on the waiting time for passengers who must catch connecting flights.

While simulation is not an optimization technique, it can be used to establish good operating policies and/or design characteristics for a system. Through a series of computer runs, or experiments, data can be obtained about the performance of the system using various operating policies or system design alternatives. In each case studied, the simulation data will predict how such design alternatives affect the performance of the system. By reviewing the simulation data, an analyst can recommend policy or design changes that appear to have the best chance of achieving the desired operation of the system.

In this chapter we introduce simulation by showing how it can be used to study the financial risks associated with the introduction of a new product and how it can be used to select a profitable inventory policy for a product. In addition, we use simulation to study the behavior of a waiting line system at an automatic bank-teller station. The appendix shows how Excel can be used to obtain the simulation results shown throughout the chapter.

13.1 Using Simulation for Risk Analysis

Whenever a proposed project may significantly impact the profit or loss for an organization, an evaluation of the financial risks is advisable before making a final decision to go ahead with the project. Risk analysis is especially important whenever one or more of the variables affecting profit or loss is difficult to determine with certainty. Such variables, called *random variables,* may include factors such as the cost of labor, the cost of raw materials, the level of demand, the interest rate, and so on. Ultimately, the profit or loss for the project will depend upon the future values of these random variables.

The term *risk* focuses on the potential for loss. Projects with a low probability or small magnitude of loss may be judged to have a relatively low risk. However, projects with a high probability or high magnitude of loss may be judged to be too risky for implementation. In this setting, an evaluation of the loss potential of a project is referred to as *risk analysis.* In the following example, we will introduce simulation as a valuable technique in providing risk analysis for a project whose profit or loss is subject to one or more random variables. In the process, we shall demonstrate how risk analysis provides the basis for determining whether to accept or reject a proposed project.

The PortaCom Portable Printer

PortaCom, Inc., manufacturers personal computers and printers sold by mailorder. PortaCom's product design group has developed a proposal for a high quality portable printer with a 30-page paper feeder. The new printer has an innovative design and the potential to capture a significant share of the portable printer market. Preliminary financial analyses indicate that the following price and cost values can be expected.

Selling price = $249 per unit

Administrative Costs = $400,000 per year

Advertising Costs = $600,000 per year

The cost of direct labor, the cost of parts, and the demand for the portable printer, are not known with certainty and are the random variables for the project. The following information has been provided about these random variables:

- Direct Labor Cost: This cost ranges from $33 to $37 per unit and is described by the discrete probability distribution shown in Table 13.1. Thus, we see there is only a 0.1 probability that the direct labor cost will be as low as $33 per unit. The highest probability of 0.4 is associated with the direct labor cost of $35 per unit.

- Parts Cost: This cost depends upon the general economy, the overall demand for parts, and the pricing strategy of PortaCom's parts suppliers. This cost ranges from $80 to $100 per unit and is described by the uniform probability distribution shown in Figure 13.1.

Table 13.1

Probability Distribution for Direct Labor Cost per Unit for the PortaCom Portable Printer

Direct Labor Cost per Unit	Probability
$33	0.1
$34	0.2
$35	0.4
$36	0.2
$37	0.1

Figure 13.1

Uniform Probability Distribution for Parts Cost per Unit for the PortaCom Portable Printer

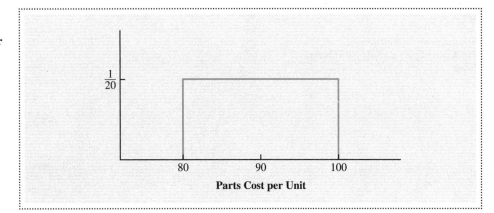

Figure 13.2

Normal Probability Distribution of Demand for the PortaCom Portable Printer

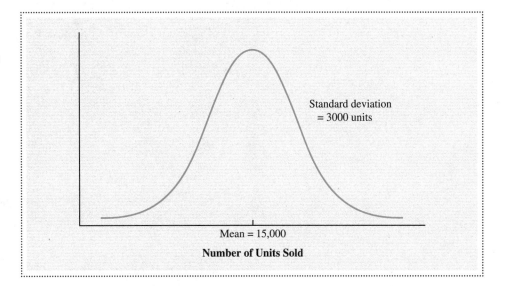

■ Demand: Demand is described by the normal probability distribution shown in Figure 13.2. The uncertain demand has an expected value or mean of 15,000 units per year. The standard deviation of 3000 units describes the variability or uncertainty in the demand for the portable printer.

In the PortaCom example, the selling price, administrative cost, advertising cost, direct labor cost per unit, parts cost per unit, and demand will be combined to determine the profit or loss for the product. The uncertainty associated with the direct labor cost, the parts cost, and the demand random variables means that different profit and loss levels will be realized based on the different values these random variables take on. Combining all this information into a model that predicts the possible profit or loss for the product requires the development of a simulation model.

The PortaCom Simulation Model

In order to simulate any system we must develop the mathematical expressions and logical relationships that describe how the system behaves or operates. The set of mathematical expressions and logical relationships is referred to as the *simulation model*.

Figure 13.3
. . . .
Flowchart Showing the Logic of the PortaCom Risk Analysis Simulation Model

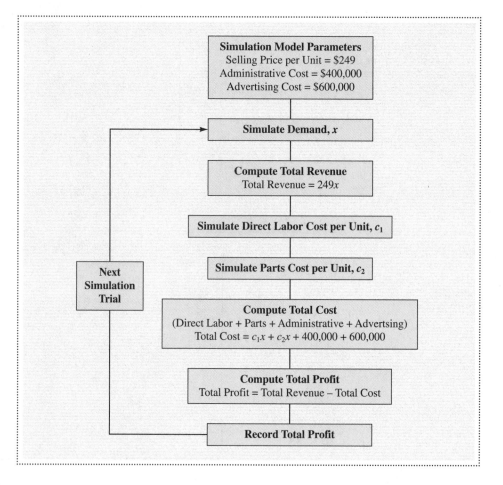

The system under study is the profit generating system for the PortaCom portable printer. The simulation model is developed by showing how the selling price, administrative cost, advertising cost, direct labor cost per unit, parts cost per unit, and demand are combined to determine the profit or loss. The Portacom simulation model is depicted by the flowchart in Figure 13.3.

Following the logic described by the flowchart, we see that the selling price, administrative cost, and advertising cost are fixed parameters of the model as set at $249, $400,000, and $600,000, respectively. Next the value for the random variable demand, x, is generated. Total revenue is then computed by multiplying the price per unit by the demand. Thus,

$$\text{Total Revenue} = 249x \tag{13.1}$$

The variable cost of the project requires first determining the values of the two random variables: direct labor cost per unit (c_1) and parts cost per unit (c_2). Multiplying these cost-per-unit values by the demand provides the following total variable cost expression.

$$\text{Total Variable Cost} = c_1x + c_2x \tag{13.2}$$

Adding the fixed administrative and advertising costs provides the following total cost expression for the model.

$$\text{Total Cost} = c_1x + c_2x + 400,000 + 600,000$$
$$= c_1x + c_2x + 1,000,000 \tag{13.3}$$

Using equations (13.1) and (13.3), the total profit is computed as follows:

$$\text{Total Profit} = \text{Total Revenue} - \text{Total Cost} \qquad (13.4)$$

The total profit is the measure of performance for the project. Obviously, the higher the total profit, the better. A negative total profit reflects the amount of any loss.

Random Numbers and Simulating Values of Random Variables

In the preceding model, values of the random variables denoted by demand (x), direct labor cost per unit (c_1), and parts cost per unit (c_2) will have to be determined in order to compute the total profit. The simulation procedure will use random numbers and the corresponding probability distribution to determine values of these random variables.

In order to simulate values of any random variables, we will use computer-generated random numbers that are randomly generated from the set of all possible numbers over the range from 0 up to, but not including 1; in other words, a number between 0 and 1. These values, referred to as uniformly distributed random numbers, can be obtained by using built-in functions that are available in most computer programming languages and spreadsheet packages.[1] For instance, placing the Excel function RAND() in a cell of a spreadsheet will result in a random number between 0 and 1 being placed in that cell.

To generate a value for the direct labor cost per unit for the PortaCom simulation model, we must associate an interval of random numbers with each possible value of the direct labor cost per unit so that the probability of generating a random number in the interval will be equal to the probability of the corresponding direct labor cost per unit. Table 13.2 shows how this is done for the direct labor cost per unit in the PortaCom simulation model. Note that the probability of obtaining a random number in any interval of random numbers is equal to the probability of obtaining the corresponding direct labor cost per unit. For example, the data in Table 13.2 show that the probability of a direct labor cost of $33 per unit is 0.10. Thus, the table shows that we have assigned the random

Table 13.2	Direct Labor Cost per Unit	Probability	Cumulative Probability	Interval of Random Numbers
Random Number Intervals for Simulating Direct Labor Cost per Unit for PortaCom	$33	0.1	0.1	0.0 but less than 0.1
	$34	0.2	0.3	0.1 but less than 0.3
	$35	0.4	0.7	0.3 but less than 0.7
	$36	0.2	0.9	0.7 but less than 0.9
	$37	0.1	1.0	0.9 but less than 1.0

[1]Originally, mechanical devices were used to generate random numbers. Today, computer-generated random numbers use mathematical procedures to provide random numbers between 0 and 1. Since these numbers are generated through a series of mathematical computations, they are referred to as *pseudorandom* numbers. Since the difference between random numbers and pseudorandom numbers is primarily philosophical, we shall use the term *random numbers* regardless of whether they are generated by the computer.

numbers from 0.0 to less than 0.1 to the direct labor cost \$33 per unit. Since 10% of all uniformly distributed random numbers are in the interval 0.0 but less than 0.1, the probability that a random number is in this interval and the direct labor cost is \$33 per unit is the desired 0.1. Similarly, the 0.20 probability of the direct labor cost of \$34 per unit is reflected by the fact that 20% of the random numbers fall in the interval from 0.1 but less than 0.3. The random numbers associated with each possible value of the direct labor cost per unit are shown in Table 13.2.

Let us now show how a value of a random variable can be selected in a simulation model. First we will use the computer's random number procedure to generate a random number between 0 and 1. Assume that the random number for the direct labor cost per unit is 0.9109. Table 13.2 shows that the simulated direct labor cost is \$37 per unit.

Let us now determine a simulated value for the parts cost per unit based on the uniform probability distribution shown in Figure 13.1. Since this random variable has a different probability distribution than direct labor cost per unit, we will use random numbers in a slightly different way to determine the value for the parts cost per unit. From Figure 13.1, we see that the parts cost per unit is uniformly distributed between \$80 and \$100. Thus, we want the computer-generated random number to identify a value for the parts cost between these two values. With a uniform probability distribution, the random number r generates the following value of the random variable:

Problem 1 will give you the opportunity to establish intervals of random numbers and simulate demand for the product.

$$\text{Value} = a + r(b - a) \tag{13.5}$$

where

$$r = \text{random number between 0 and 1}$$
$$a = \text{smallest value for the parts cost}$$
$$b = \text{largest value for the parts cost}$$

For the PortaCom product's parts cost per unit, $a = 80$ and $b = 100$. Thus, equation (13.5) becomes Value $= 80 + r(100 - 80) = 80 + 20r$. In effect, the random number r will generate a parts cost per unit between 80 and 100. Thus, a random number of 0.2680 would provide a simulated parts cost per unit of $80 + 20(0.2680) = \$85.36$.

Finally, we need to use a similar random number procedure that will generate a value for the random variable demand based on the probability distribution shown in Figure 13.2. In this case, demand is shown to be normally distributed with a mean of 15,000 units and a standard deviation of 3000 units. Because of the mathematical complexity of using the normal probability distribution, a discussion of the detailed procedure for generating random values for a normally distributed random variable is beyond the scope of this text. However, most computer software and spreadsheet packages include a built-in routine or function that provides the randomly generated value from a normal probability distribution. For example, using Excel the following statement can be used

$$=\text{NORMINV(RAND(), Mean, Standard Deviation)}$$

For the PortaCom demand random variable with a mean of 15,000 and a standard deviation of 3000, the Excel statement

$$=\text{NORMINV(RAND(), 15000, 3000)} \tag{13.6}$$

will provide a simulated value for demand. For example, if RAND() generates the random number 0.7849, the Excel function indicates the demand random variable takes on a value of 17,367 units.

Using the Simulation Model

Using the simulation model involves using the model's fixed input data values and simulated values of the random variables to compute performance measures for the system. For the PortaCom project, we will use the fixed input data values of selling price ($249 per unit), administrative cost ($400,000), and advertising cost ($600,000), along with the simulated random variable values of $37 per unit for the direct labor cost, $85.36 per unit for the parts cost, and 17,367 units for the demand to compute the overall simulated value of profit or loss for the product.

Using the simulation model equations as shown in (13.1), (13.3), and (13.4), we have the following computations:

$$\text{Total Revenue} = 249x = 249(17{,}367) = \$4{,}324{,}383$$

$$\text{Total Cost} = 37x + 85.36x + 400{,}000 + 600{,}000$$

$$= 37(17{,}367) + 85.36(17{,}367) + 1{,}000{,}000 = \$3{,}125{,}026$$

$$\text{Total Profit} = \text{Total Revenue} - \text{Total Cost}$$

$$= \$4{,}324{,}383 - \$3{,}125{,}026 = \$1{,}199{,}357$$

Thus, the simulated profit for the PortaCom product if the direct labor cost is $37 per unit, the parts cost is $85.36 per unit, and demand is 17,367 units is $1,199,357. Management should be encouraged by this simulation result. However, one simulation trial does not provide a complete understanding of the possible profit and loss levels. Since other values are possible for the random variables, we can benefit from another simulation iteration. Assume that this time random numbers of 0.2841, 0.5842, 0.2421 resulted in simulated values of $34 per unit for the direct labor cost, $91.68 per unit for the parts cost, and 12,901 units for demand. Show that these values provide a simulated profit of $590,951.

Repetition of the simulation process with different random variables is the essence of simulation. Through the repeated trials, management will begin to understand what might happen when the project is implemented in the real world. We have shown the results of ten simulation trials in Table 13.3. For these ten cases we find a profit as high as $1,755,930 for the 6th trial, but a loss of $290,390 for the 9th trial. Thus, we see that in some situations, the product will result in a profit while in other cases the product will result in a loss.

Table 13.3   Simulation Results for Ten Trials

Trial	Direct Labor Cost per Unit	Parts Cost per Unit	Number of Units Sold	Total Revenue	Total Cost	Contribution to Profit
1	$37	$85.36	17,367	$4,324,383	$3,125,026	$1,199,357
2	34	91.68	12,901	3,212,349	2,621,398	590,951
3	35	93.35	20,686	5,150,814	3,655,048	1,495,766
4	33	98.56	10,889	2,711,361	2,432,557	278,804
5	35	88.36	14,260	3,550,740	2,759,114	791,626
6	34	94.68	22,905	5,703,345	3,947,415	1,755,930
7	35	88.65	15,732	3,917,268	2,945,262	972,006
8	35	82.37	17,805	4,433,445	3,089,773	1,343,672
9	35	93.89	5,908	1,471,092	1,761,482	−290,390
10	36	95.74	12,919	3,216,831	2,701,949	514,882

Simulation Results

In practice, analysts run the simulation for numerous trials in order to learn more about what may happen to total profit. Using the Excel spreadsheet system, we simulated the PortaCom model 500 times. A histogram of the simulated total profit is shown in Figure 13.4. Some standard descriptive statistics for the simulated profit are shown in Table 13.4 Interpretation of the simulation results provides the financial risk information the manager is seeking.

Risk Analysis Conclusions

Risk analysis suggests that we look at the extremes of the project's possible outcomes. Table 13.4 shows the maximum profit for the 500 simulations was $2,380,950, and the maximum loss was $818,899. While these outcomes would be rare in practice, they give the manager a range of possible profit levels. Further analysis focuses on the mean profit of $809,296 and median profit of $784,941 as the representative central values for profit. The histogram in Figure 13.4 shows that the mode, or most frequently projected profit, occurs in the $750,000 to $1,000,000 range. Finally, only 20 of the 500 simulation trials resulted in a loss. Thus we estimate a $20/500 = 0.04$ probability that the product will result in a loss and 0.96 probability that the product will result in a profit.

The risk analysis conclusions provided by the simulation results should help the manager better understand the profit/loss potential of the PortaCom portable printer. The 0.96 probability of a profit, with an anticipated most likely profit in the $750,000 to $1,000,000 range, is helpful information in supporting the manager's decision to produce the PortaCom portable printer.

Table 13.4

Descriptive Statistics for 500 Trials for the PortaCom Simulation

Mean Profit	$809,296
Median Profit	$784,941
Standard deviation	$499,972
Maximum Profit	$2,380,950
Minimum Profit	−$818,899

Figure 13.4

Simulated Profit for 500 Trials

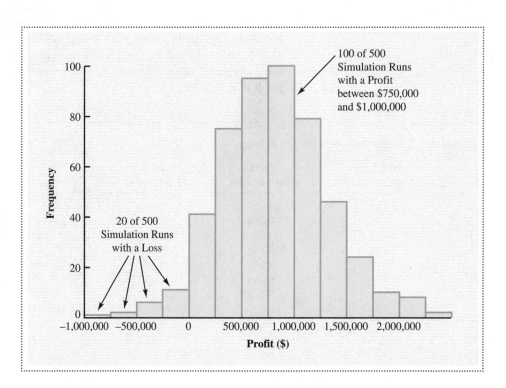

Some Simulation Terminology

Try Problem 3. This is another example in setting up and simulating demand. A slightly more complicated simulation application is discussed in Problem 15.

Note that while we have simulated the PortaCom project 500 times, each simulation trial was *independent;* that is, what happened during one simulation trial was not affected by what happened in a previous simulation trial. Such simulations are referred to as *Monte Carlo simulations.* The inventory simulation model in Section 13.2 is another example of Monte Carlo simulation. In other simulation studies, a model is needed to describe how a system *evolves over time.* In these models, the *state of the system* at one point in time is dependent upon the state of the system at previous points of time. This type of simulation, referred to as *discrete-event simulation*, is covered in the discussion of the simulation of a waiting line system in Section 13.3.

NOTES &comments

1. In many situations the probability distribution used to generate values for a random variable in a simulation model is developed using historical data. For instance, suppose that an analysis of daily sales values at new car dealership for the past 50 days showed that on 2 of the 50 days no cars were sold; on 5 of the 50 days 1 car was sold; on 9 days 2 cars were sold; on 24 days 3 cars were sold; on 7 days 4 cars were sold; and on 3 of the 50 days 5 cars were sold. We can estimate the probability distribution of daily demand using the relative frequency distribution for the observed data. Thus, an estimate of the probability that no cars are sold on a given day is 2/50 = .04, an estimate of the probability that 1 car is sold is 5/50 = .10, and so on. The probability distribution of daily demand obtained is as follows:

Daily Sales	0	1	2	3	4	5
Probability	0.04	0.10	0.18	0.48	0.14	0.06

2. Spreadsheet add-in packages such as @RISK and Crystal Ball have been developed to make spreadsheet simulation a simple process. For instance, using Crystal Ball we could simulate the PortaCom problem by first entering the equations that show the relationships among the problem variables. Then, after selecting the probability distribution type for each random variable from a menu of distributions, Crystal Ball will generate random values for each of the random variables, compute the total cost and contribution to profit, and repeat the simulation process for as many trials as desired. The final simulation results are displayed graphically, and numerical descriptive statistics can be easily obtained.

13.2 An Inventory Simulation Model

In this section we describe how Monte Carlo simulation can be used to establish a profitable inventory policy for a product that has an uncertain monthly demand. The product is a home ventilation fan distributed by the Butler Electrical Supply Company.

Butler carries more than 2000 electrical products, which it sells to building contractors and individual homeowners. To coordinate the ordering of the fans with its other products, Butler replenishes its inventory of fans to a level Q at the beginning of each month. Each fan costs $75 per unit, has a selling price of $125 per unit, and provides a profit contribution of $125 $-$ $75 $=$ $50 per unit. Monthly demand is described by a normal probability distribution with a mean demand of 100 units and a standard deviation of 20 units. If monthly demand is less than the beginning inventory level Q, a surplus inventory exists at the end of the month. An inventory holding cost of $15 per unit is charged for the surplus inventory. If monthly demand is greater than the beginning inventory level Q, a stockout or shortage occurs during the month. A shortage cost of $30 per unit is charged to reflect the lost customer goodwill due to the unsatisfied demand. Given the data on the profit contribution per unit, the monthly demand probability distribution, the inventory holding cost, and the shortage cost, what beginning monthly inventory level Q should Butler use to maximize the profitability of the home ventilation fans?

Figure 13.5 shows the logic of the simulation of the profit generation process for the Butler inventory system. Once the profit contribution, inventory holding cost, and shortage cost parameters are established, the simulation process begins with the selection

Figure 13.5
....

Simulation Model for the Butler Inventory System

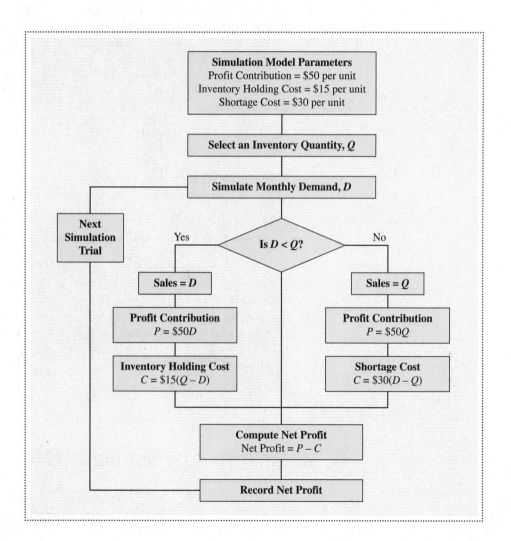

Table 13.5

......

Butler Inventory Simulation Results for Five Trials with $Q = 100$

Trial	Simulated Demand	Sales	Profit Contribution	Holding Cost	Shortage Cost	Net Profit
1	79	79	$3950	$315	$ 0	$3635
2	111	100	5000	0	330	4670
3	93	93	4650	105	0	4545
4	100	100	5000	0	0	5000
5	118	100	5000	0	540	4460

of a beginning inventory quantity Q. Then a random number procedure is used to simulate the monthly demand D. If monthly demand D is less than the inventory quantity Q, the company sells D units with a profit contribution of $50D. In this case, the excess inventory of $(Q - D)$ units incurs an inventory holding cost of $15(Q - D)$. On the other hand, if monthly demand D is greater than or equal to the inventory quantity Q, the company can only sell the Q units it has in inventory with a profit contribution of $50Q. In this case, the shortage of $(D - Q)$ units incurs a shortage cost of $30(D - Q)$. In both cases, the profit contribution less the appropriate inventory holding cost or shortage cost is used to determine the net profit for the month. Multiple simulation trials are used to learn about the profit associated with the inventory quantity Q selected by the manager.

Let us assume that the manager selects an inventory quantity $Q = 100$ units. Table 13.5 shows the results of five simulation trials. These simulation results were obtained by using an Excel spreadsheet. Details regarding the Excel commands are shown in Appendix 13.1. Referring to Table 13.5, we see that the simulated demand for the first trial is 79 units. In this case, demand is less than $Q = 100$. The sale of 79 units results in a profit contribution of $50(79) = $3950. The surplus of $100 - 79 = 21$ units incurs an inventory holding cost of $15(21) = $315. The result of the first trial is a simulated net profit of $3950 - $315 = $3635. The simulated demand for the second trial in Table 13.5 is 111 units. In this case, demand is greater than $Q = 100$. The sale of the 100 units from inventory results in a profit contribution of $50(100) = $5000. The shortage of $111 - 100 = 11$ units incurs a shortage cost of $30(11) = $330. The result of the second trial is a simulated net profit of $5000 - $330 = $4670.

We continued the Butler inventory simulation for a total of 100 trials. The average net profit for the 100 trials was $4271. We are now ready to use the simulation model to consider other levels of inventory that may improve the projected net profit. Specifically, we conducted a series of simulation experiments by repeating the Butler inventory simulation with alternative beginning inventory quantities of 110, 120, 130, and 140 units. In each case, we simulated the operation of the inventory system for 100 trials. The average monthly net profit for each inventory quantity is shown in Table 13.6. The best average profit of $4610 per month occurred for the inventory level of $Q = 120$ units. Thus the simulation results lead to the recommendation that Butler begin each month with 120 units in inventory.

Experimental simulation studies such as the Butler inventory system example can help identify good operating policies and decisions. However, simulation is not an optimization technique in the sense that it cannot guarantee the optimal inventory quantity has been obtained. Perhaps a manager would like to consider additional simulation runs with inventory quantities such as $Q = 115$ and $Q = 125$ units to search for an even better inventory policy. However, the data in Table 13.6 indicate that an inventory policy with $Q = 120$ units is a good solution and should generate an average monthly profit of approximately $4600.

Table 13.6

....

Butler Inventory Simulation Results Showing the Average Net Profit for 100 Trials

Inventory Quantity Q	Average Net Profit
100	$4271
110	4523
120	4610
130	4598
140	4505

13.3 A Waiting Line Simulation Model

The simulation models discussed thus far have been based on independent trials in which what happens during one trial is not affected by what happens in previous trials. In this sense, the system being modeled does not change or evolve over time. With random numbers employed to simulate at least one random variable, the simulation process is referred to as Monte Carlo simulation. In this section, we present a simulation model of a waiting line system in which the state of the system, including the number of individuals in the waiting line and whether the service facility is busy, changes or evolves over time. Arrivals of new individuals into the waiting line as well as departures of individuals who have completed service are referred to as *events*. Since these events occur at discrete points in time, the simulation process is referred to as *discrete-event simulation*. In this section we show how an Excel spreadsheet can be used to conduct a discrete-event simulation of the single-channel waiting line for the Hammondsport Savings and Loan Bank automatic teller machine.

The Hammondsport Savings and Loan Waiting Line

The Hammondsport Savings and Loan plans to open several new branch banks during the coming year. Each new branch bank location is designed to have one automatic teller machine (ATM). Once the bank is opened for business, customers will arrive at the bank seeking the ATM service. If the ATM is in use, an arriving customer will have to wait until all preceding customers are finished before accessing the ATM. During busy periods, several customers may have to wait for the ATM service.

The bank's vice-president wants to determine whether one ATM will be sufficient at branches where a high volume of customers is anticipated. The bank has published service guidelines for its ATM system stating that the average customer waiting time for an ATM should be one minute or less. In this section, we develop a simulation model that can be used to determine whether a particular branch can satisfy the bank's customer service guideline with one ATM.

Customer Arrival Times

One of the components of the ATM waiting line system that will have to be simulated is the arrival times of the customers seeking the ATM service. In the study of waiting lines, the arrival times are determined by simulating the time between successive customer arrivals, referred to as the *interarrival time*. For example, suppose that for one Hammondsport Savings and Loan branch bank, the customer interarrival times are assumed to be uniformly distributed between 0 and 5 minutes as shown in Figure 13.6. With r denoting a random number between 0 and 1, an interarrival time for two successive customers can be simulated by using the formula for a uniform probability distribution as previously presented in Section 13.1.

$$\text{Interarrival Time} = a + r(b - a)$$

where

r = random number between 0 and 1
a = minimum interarrival time
b = maximum interarrival time

Figure 13.6

Uniform Probability Distribution of Customer Interarrival Times for the ATM Waiting Line System

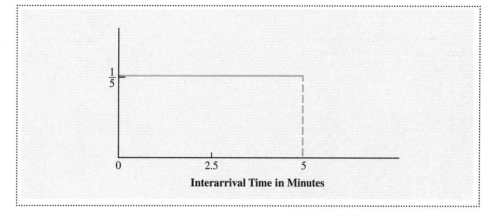

For the Hammondsport ATM system with a minimum interarrival time of $a = 0$ minutes and a maximum interarrival time of $b = 5$ minutes, we have

$$\text{Interarrival Time} = 0 + r(5 - 0) = 5r$$

Assuming the simulation process begins at time 0, a random number of $r = 0.28$ would indicate an interarrival time of $0.28(5) = 1.4$ minutes for customer 1. Thus, customer 1 arrives 1.4 minutes after the simulation process begins. A second random number of $r = 0.26$ simulates an interarrival time of $0.26(5) = 1.3$ minutes indicating that customer 2 arrives 1.3 minutes after customer 1. Thus, customer 2 arrives $1.4 + 1.3 = 2.7$ minutes after the ATM simulation process begins. Continuing this process, we note that a random number of $r = 0.98$ would indicate that customer 3 arrives 4.9 minutes after customer 2, which is 7.6 minutes after the simulation process begins. While probability distributions other than a uniform probability distribution can be used to describe the interarrival time distribution, the simulation of interarrival times and the determination of the corresponding arrival times are essential components of any waiting line simulation process.

Customer Service Times

Another random component that exists in most waiting line models is the time it takes the customer to obtain the service once the customer reaches the server (the ATM). In the Hammondsport simulation model, the customer *service time* is the time a customer spends using the ATM. Past data from similar ATMs indicates that a normal probability distribution with a mean of two minutes and a standard deviation of 0.5 minutes as shown in Figure 13.7 can be used to describe the customer service times. As discussed in Section 13.1, values from this normal probability distribution can be simulated using the Excel command =NORMINV(RAND(),2,0.5). Here, RAND() is the random number generated, 2 is the mean of the normal probability distribution, and 0.5 is its standard deviation. For example, the random number of 0.7257 would simulate a customer service time of 2.3 minutes. While probability distributions other than a normal probability distribution can be used to describe the service time distribution, the simulation of service times is another essential component of a waiting line simulation process.

Figure 13.7

Normal Probability Distribution of Service Times for the ATM Waiting Line System

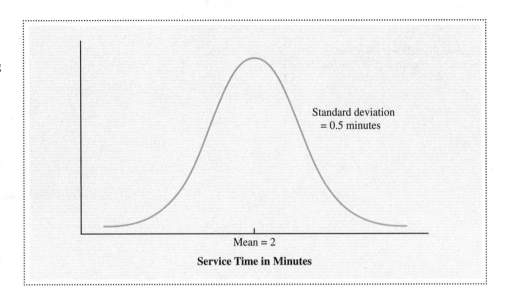

The Simulation Model

The flowchart of the simulation model for the Hammondsport ATM waiting line system is shown in Figure 13.8. The flowchart uses the following notation:

IAT = Simulated Interarrival Time
Arrival Time(i) = Arrival time for customer i
Start Time(i) = Time service is started for customer i
Wait Time(i) = Time customer i waits prior to starting service
ST = Simulated Service Time
Completion Time(i) = Time service is completed for customer i
System Time(i) = Time customer i spends in the system (waiting time + service time)

After the simulation model has been initialized, the simulation is conducted on a customer-by-customer basis. When a new customer is identified, the interarrival time between the new customer and the preceding customer is simulated. The arrival time for the new customer is computed by adding the interarrival time to the arrival time of the preceding customer.

The diamond shaped "?" step in Figure 13.8 shows that the arrival time for the new customer must be compared to the completion time of the preceding customer to determine if the ATM is idle or busy. If the arrival time of the new customer is greater than the completion time of the preceding customer, the preceding customer will have already finished with the ATM service before the new customer arrives. In this case, the ATM will be idle; the new customer can begin service immediately with a service starting time equal to the arrival time. However, if the arrival time for the new customer is not greater than the completion time of the preceding customer, the new customer has arrived before the preceding customer has finished the ATM service. In this case, the ATM is busy; the new customer must wait and cannot begin service until the preceding customer has completed service. Thus, the service starting time for the new customer is equal to the completion time of the preceding customer.

The time the new customer waits for the ATM service can be computed as the difference between the customer's starting time and the customer's arrival time. At this

Figure 13.8   Flowchart of the Hammondsport Saving and Loan ATM Waiting Line Simulation Model

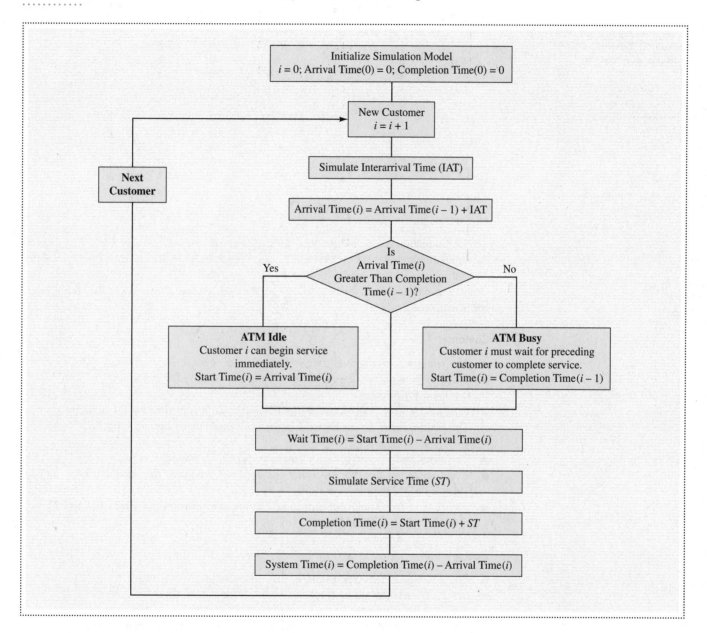

point, the customer is ready to use the ATM and the simulation process continues with the simulation of the customer's service time. The starting time plus the service time determine the customer's completion time. Finally, the total time the customer spent in the system can be computed as the difference between the customer's completion time and the customer's arrival time. At this point, the simulation computations are complete for the current customer, and the simulation process continues with the introduction of the next customer. The simulation process is continued until a specified number of customers have been served by the ATM.

Table 13.7

Simulation Results for Ten Customers for the ATM Waiting Line System

Customer	Interarrival Time	Arrival Time	Service Start Time	Waiting Time	Service Time	Completion Time	Time in System
1	1.4	1.4	1.4	0.0	2.3	3.7	2.3
2	1.3	2.7	3.7	1.0	1.5	5.2	2.5
3	4.9	7.6	7.6	0.0	2.2	9.8	2.2
4	3.5	11.1	11.1	0.0	2.5	13.6	2.5
5	0.7	11.8	13.6	1.8	1.8	15.4	3.6
6	2.8	14.6	15.4	0.8	2.4	17.8	3.2
7	2.1	16.7	17.8	1.1	2.1	19.9	3.2
8	0.6	17.3	19.9	2.6	1.8	21.7	4.4
9	2.5	19.8	21.7	1.9	2.0	23.7	3.9
10	1.9	21.7	23.7	2.0	2.3	26.0	4.3

The simulation results for the first ten customers are shown in Table 13.7. We describe the simulation process for the first three customers in order to demonstrate the logic of the simulation model and show how the data in Table 13.7 are generated. Since the simulation calculations will be carried out for each customer, we begin by seeing what happens to customer 1.

Customer 1

- The simulated interarrival time is $IAT = 1.4$ minutes.
- Since the simulation begins at time 0, the arrival time for customer 1 is $0 + 1.4 = 1.4$ minutes.
- Customer 1 may begin service immediately with a start time of 1.4 minutes.
- The waiting time for customer 1 is the start time minus the arrival time: $1.4 - 1.4 = 0$ minutes.
- The simulated service time for customer 1 is 2.3 minutes.
- The completion time for customer 1 is the start time plus the service time: $1.4 + 2.3 = 3.7$ minutes.
- The time in the system for customer 1 is the completion time minus the arrival time: $3.7 - 1.4 = 2.3$ minutes.

Customer 2

- The simulated interarrival time is $IAT = 1.3$ minutes.
- Since the arrival time of customer 1 is 1.4, the arrival time for customer 2 is $1.4 + 1.3 = 2.7$ minutes.
- Since the completion time of customer 1 is 3.7 minutes, the arrival time for customer 2 is not greater than the completion time of customer 1; thus, the ATM is busy when customer 2 arrives.
- Customer 2 must wait for customer 1 to complete service before beginning service. Since customer 1 completes service at 3.7 minutes, the starting time for customer 2 is 3.7 minutes.
- The waiting time for customer 2 is the start time minus the arrival time: $3.7 - 2.7 = 1$ minute.
- The simulated service time for customer 2 is 1.5 minutes.
- The completion time for customer 2 is the start time plus the service time: $3.7 + 1.5 = 5.2$ minutes.

- The time in the system for customer 2 is the completion time minus the arrival time: $5.2 - 2.7 = 2.5$ minutes.

Customer 3

- The simulated interarrival time is $IAT = 4.9$ minutes.
- Since the arrival time of customer 2 is 2.7 minutes, the arrival time for customer 3 is $2.7 + 4.9 = 7.6$ minutes.
- Since the completion time of customer 2 is 5.2 minutes, the arrival time for customer 3 is greater than the completion time of customer 2; thus, the ATM is idle when customer 3 arrives.
- Customer 3 may begin service immediately with a start time of 7.6 minutes.
- The waiting time for customer 3 is the start time minus the arrival time: $7.6 - 7.6 = 0$ minutes.
- The simulated service time for customer 3 is 2.2 minutes.
- The completion time for customer 3 is the start time plus the service time: $7.6 + 2.2 = 9.8$ minutes.
- The time in the system for customer 3 is the completion time minus the arrival time: $9.8 - 7.6 = 2.2$ minutes.

Fortunately, the Excel spreadsheet can be used to keep track of the simulation calculation and provide the customer-by-customer simulation results as shown in Table 13.7. The details regarding the Excel commands necessary to produce the simulation results are shown in Appendix 13.1.

Simulation Results

The results shown in Table 13.7 are far are too limited to permit any general conclusions about the operation of the ATM waiting line system. Thus, we continued the simulation process until a total of 1000 customers had completed the ATM service. The final Excel spreadsheet produced 1000 rows of simulation data similar to those shown in Table 13.7

Before analyzing the data for the 1000 customers, let us point out that most simulation studies of systems that evolve over time focus on the operation of the system during its normal, or steady-state, operation. *Steady-state* refers to the behavior of the system after it has been operating long enough for the effect of any start-up conditions to have dissipated. Remember we started the ATM waiting line simulation with no customers waiting and with the ATM idle. Perhaps the waiting line system operates better during the start-up phase than it does after reaching steady-state operation.

To avoid the start-up difficulties, a simulation is usually run for a specified period without collecting any data about the operation of the system. The length of time of the start-up period can vary depending upon the application, but it is generally selected to be sufficient for the system to have stabilized at its normal or steady-state operation. For the Hammondsport waiting line simulation, we treated the results for the first 100 customers as the start-up period. This start-up period required 274.5 minutes of simulated ATM waiting line operation.

Simulation data were summarized for the next 900 customers. Figure 13.9 shows a histogram of the customer waiting times for these customers, with 56.3% of the customers experiencing waiting times of 1 minute or less. Thus, 43.7% of the customers experienced waiting times of more than 1 minute. Five percent of the customers

Figure 13.9
· · · · · · · · · · · ·
Histogram Showing the Waiting Time for 900 ATM Customers

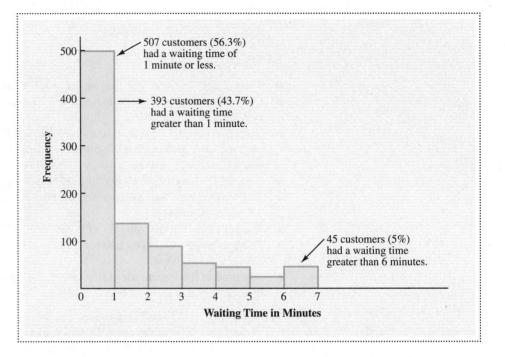

experienced waiting time of more than 6 minutes. The average waiting time for the 900 customers was 1.59 minutes.

Excel commands can be used to summarize the simulation data and provide further insight into the performance of the waiting line system. For example, Excel can be used to count the number of customers who had a waiting time of 0.0 and thus did not wait for service. Doing so showed that 351 of the 900 customers did not have to wait. This tells us that 351/900 = 0.39 or 39% of the customers did not wait, while 549/900 = 0.61 or 61% of the customers experienced a wait.

In addition, we note that the simulation time for all 1000 customers ended with the completion time for the 1000th customer at 2536.4 minutes of simulated operation. Since the 100-customer start-up period ended at 274.5 minutes, we have a steady-state simulation period of 2536.4 − 274.5 = 2261.9 minutes. Summing the spreadsheet column of service times shows that the 900 customers used 1777.2 minutes of ATM service time. Thus, the utilization of the ATM was 1777.2/2261.9 = 0.786, indicating that the ATM was in use 78.6% of the time. Thus, the ATM was idle only 21.4% of the time.

In general, these simulation data support the conclusion that the branch has a busy ATM operation. With an average customer waiting time of 1.59 minutes, the branch does not satisfy the bank's customer service guideline. This branch is a good candidate for installation of a second ATM.

The ATM waiting line simulation model that we have developed can now be used to study the ATM operation at other branch banks. In each case, assumptions must be made about the appropriate customer interarrival time and customer service time probability distributions. However, once these assumptions have been made, the Excel spreadsheet can quickly carry out the simulation calculations that will determine the operating characteristics of the ATM waiting line system. The Red Cross simulation model described in the Management Science in Action possesses many of the same characteristics as the ATM simulation model. These similarities are common in simulation models of waiting lines.

MANAGEMENT SCIENCE in action

Red Cross Uses Simulation to Improve Bloodmobile Services[*]

The American Red Cross collects more than 6 million units of blood each year in the United States, making it the largest blood-product supplier in the country. Blood is collected daily at some 400 fixed and mobile sites.

The Red Cross relies heavily on repeat donations by the same group of individuals. A particular concern to the Red Cross was the length of the waiting times occurring at bloodmobile temporary sites sponsored by businesses, schools, and community groups. If bloodmobile waiting lines and times are excessive, blood donor dissatisfaction with the process could significantly decrease the number of future blood donations.

The Red Cross bloodmobile operation was simulated to study ways of reducing the waiting line and waiting times. Data were collected on the number of donor arrivals during 30-minute periods of time. The donors selected their own times to visit the bloodmobile, with these nonscheduled (random) visits described by a nonstationary Poisson probability distribution. Data on arrival rates and service times at the bloodmobile were based on the study of actual bloodmobile operations in Atlanta, Charlotte, and Washington, D.C.

The GPSS computer simulation language was used to model the waiting line at the bloodmobile. After testing and validating the simulation model, the project team varied setup procedures, staff allocation, and work rules to determine how each change would affect the waiting line characteristics at the bloodmobile. Through a series of experiments with the simulation model, the project team developed recommendations for improving processing. Implementation of the recommendations markedly reduced waiting times. Improved blood donor satisfaction was noted, with the majority of donors reporting both less waiting time and less processing time compared to previous visits.

....

*Based on Brennan, J. F., B. L. Golden, and H. K. Rappoport, "Go with the Flow: Improving Red Cross Bloodmobiles Using Simulation Analysis." *Interfaces*, vol. 22, no. 5, September–October 1992, pp. 1–13.

NOTES & comments

1. The ATM waiting line model was based on uniformly distributed interarrival times and normally distributed service times. One of the advantages of simulation is its flexibility in accommodating a variety of different probability distributions. If we believe exponentially distributed interarrival times are more appropriate, the ATM simulation could be repeated by simply changing the way the interarrival times are generated. Simulation can also accommodate empirical probability distributions. For example, we could collect data on actual interarrival times and actual service times at existing ATM locations. Empirical probability distributions based on these data could replace any assumed uniform, exponential, or normal probability distribution. In fact, many would view a simulation model based on empirical interarrival times and empirical service times as being more representative of the actual waiting line system.

—continued

—Continued from previous page

2. At the beginning of this section we defined discrete-event simulation as a technique used to simulate a system that evolves over discrete points in time. With this method, the simulation computations focus on the sequence of events as they occur at discrete points in time. In the ATM waiting line example, customer arrivals and customer service completions were the events of the simulation process. Referring to the arrival times and completion times in Table 13.7, we see that the first five discrete events for the ATM waiting line simulation were as follows:

Event	Description	Time Event Occurred
1	Customer 1 arrives	1.4
2	Customer 2 arrives	2.7
3	Customer 1 completes service	3.7
4	Customer 2 completes service	5.2
5	Customer 3 arrives	7.6

The Excel spreadsheet provides a convenient way to identify the events and keep track of the discrete-event simulation process.

13.4 Other Issues

In this section, we comment on several additional aspects of simulation studies including selecting a simulation language, verifying and validating the simulation model, and keeping track of time in more complex discrete-event simulation models. At the end of the section we comment on some of the advantages and disadvantages of using simulation to study a real system.

Selecting a Simulation Language

The computer simulation models presented in this chapter have demonstrated how spreadsheets can be used to describe the logic of a simulation model, perform the necessary simulation calculations, generate the simulation data and provide a summary of the simulation results. While spreadsheets can be valuable in conducting simulation studies, they are generally limited to smaller and less complex simulation models. As a system grows in complexity, other computer procedures may be necessary to adequately model the system and carry out the simulation calculations.

General-purpose computer programming languages such as BASIC, FORTRAN, PASCAL, and C can be used to develop a computer program that will model the system and perform the simulation computations. The advantage of using a general-purpose programming language rather than a spreadsheet is that general-purpose languages have greater flexibility in terms of being able to model more complex systems.

Based on the growth of simulation applications, both users of simulation and developers of computer software began to realize that computer simulations had many common features, including generating values from probability distributions, maintaining a record of what happens during the simulation process, recording simulation data, and summarizing the simulation results. Thus, software manufacturers saw the advantage of developing special-purpose simulation languages such as GPSS, SIMAN, SIMSCRIPT, and SLAM. These languages enable analysts and programmers to simplify the process of writing the computer program of the simulation model. In particular, these special-purpose simulation languages have automatic or built-in simulation clocks, simplified procedures for generating probabilistic components, and procedures that will collect and summarize the simulation data. One programming statement for a special-purpose simulation language often performs the computations and record keeping tasks that would require several BASIC, FORTRAN, PASCAL, or C statements to duplicate.

As part of a simulation application, an analyst will have to consider the relative merits of a spreadsheet, a general-purpose language, and a special-purpose language in order to select the computer procedure that is easiest to develop while still providing an adequate representation of the system being studied.

Verification and Validation

An important aspect in any simulation study involves confirming that the simulation model accurately describes the behavior of the real system. Inaccurate models cannot be expected to provide worthwhile information. Thus, before using simulation results to draw conclusions about a real system, an analyst must take steps to verify and validate the simulation model.

Verification refers to the process of determining that the computer program or computer spreadsheet that performs the simulation calculations is working correctly. Verification is largely a computer debugging task designed to make sure that there are no errors in the computer program that implements the simulation model. In some cases, an analyst may compare the computer results for a limited number of events with independent hand calculations of the same simulation circumstances. In other cases, test runs with the computer program may be performed to determine whether the assumed probabilistic components are being simulated correctly and if the output from the simulation model appears reasonable. The verification step is not complete until there is a high degree of confidence that the computer procedure is operating as it is intended.

Validation refers to the process of assuring that the simulation model provides an accurate representation of the real system. Validation includes an agreement among analysts and managers that the logic and assumptions used in the design of the simulation model accurately reflect how the real system operates. The first phase of the validation process is done prior to or in conjunction with the development of the computer program for the simulation process. The validation step continues after the computer program has been developed with the analyst reviewing the simulation output and attempting to conclude that the simulation results closely approximate the performance of the real system. In an ideal validation, the output of the simulation model is compared to the output of an existing real system to make sure that the simulation output closely approximates the performance of the real system. If this form of validation cannot be done, an analyst can still experiment with the simulation model and have one or more individuals experienced with the operation of the real system review the simulation output to determine whether it is a reasonable approximation of how the real system operates.

In any case, verification and validation are not trivial tasks that can be taken lightly. They are key aspects of any simulation study and are necessary to ensure that decisions and conclusions drawn from the simulation are appropriate for the real system.

Keeping Track of Time

A common aspect of most discrete-event simulation models is the use of a computer-programmed *simulation clock* that keeps track of time as the simulation proceeds. The two approaches for advancing the simulation clock are called the *next-event time advance* and the *fixed-increment time advance* methods. The next-event time advance method is used in all major special-purpose simulation languages and is preferred by most programmers using a general-purpose language. With this approach, the simulation clock is advanced to the time of the next occurring event and the state of the system is updated depending upon what happens to the system when the event occurs. In waiting line models, the events include customer arrivals and customer service completions. In these models, the simulation clock is advanced to the most imminent or first of the future events that will occur. If a customer arrival is most imminent, the simulation clock will be advanced to the time of the arrival and the status of the waiting line system will be updated accordingly. The updating process includes revising the state of the system and identifying the time of future events so that the advancement of the simulation clock to the time of the next event is possible. Using this method, the increment of the clock advance varies and depends upon when the simulaton events occur.

In the fixed-increment time advance method, the simulation clock is advanced with a fixed increment of time such as a minute, hour, day, month, or other convenient period of time for the system being simulated. The status of the system is reviewed at each time increment, and the state of the system is updated whenever an event corresponds to the current time increment. Since the fixed-increment time advance requires a review of the status of the system at every time increment, simulation calculations are made repeatedly whether or not an event takes place. In this sense, the fixed-increment time advance method can take more computer time than the next-event time advance method.

Advantages and Disadvantages

A primary advantage of simulation is that it can be used to model complex systems that would be difficult to evaluate analytically. Simulation models are more flexible and can be used to describe complex systems without requiring simplifying assumptions or approximations that might be required by mathematical models. In general, the larger the number of probabilistic components a system has, the more likely it is that a simulation model will provide the best approach for studying the system. Another advantage of computer simulation is that a simulation model provides a convenient experimental laboratory for the real system. Changing assumptions or operating policies in the simulation model can predict how such changes will affect the operation of the real system. In fact, computer simulations can be used to study how a system operates over a long time period. Experimenting directly with a real system for such a long time period would not be feasible. The Management Science in Action describes how simulation was used in this manner to select manufacturing configurations and the design of new plants at Mexico's Vilpac Truck Company.

However, simulation is not without some disadvantages. First of all, someone must have the expertise to develop a simulation model and implement it on a computer. For complex systems, the process of developing, verifying, and validating a simulation model can be time consuming and expensive. In addition, each simulation run only provides a sample of how the real system will operate. As such, the summary of the simulation data only provides estimates or approximations about the real system; thus, computer simulation does not guarantee an optimal solution to a problem. Nonetheless, the danger

MANAGEMENT SCIENCE in action

Simulation at Mexico's Vilpac Truck Company[*]

Manufacturing has gone global, with U.S. firms joining diverse geographical and cultural partners in Western Europe, Asia, and Mexico to capitalize on one anothers' advantages and remain competitive in the world markets. Mexico, the United States' third largest trading partner, offers a unique opportunity for integrating manufacturing operations. For example, Mexican and U.S. firms have been working together to turn the Mexican truck company, Vilpac, into a world-class manufacturing firm.

The selection of manufacturing configurations and the design of new plants at Vilpac is being guided by a simulation model of the firm's manufacturing operations. A network simulation language, SIMNET II, has been used to model the manufacturing system that comprises some 95 machines and 1900 parts. Various simulation runs were used to validate the model. When applied to a plant that was producing 20 trucks per day, the simulation model accurately predicted production at 19.8 trucks per day.

The three interrelated modules of the simulation model include operations, corrective maintenance, and preventive maintenance. Various components of the model include capabilities for handling changes in customer demand, manufacturing cost, capacity, and work-in-process and inventory levels. Experimentation with the model investigated capacity requirements, product-mix effects, new products, inventory policies, product flow, setup times, production planning and control strategies, plant expansion, and new plant design. Tangible benefits include an increase in production of 260%, a reduction in work-in-process of 70%, and an increase in market share.

....

*Based on Nuno, J. P., D. L. Shunk, J. M. Padillo, and B. Beltran, "Mexico's Vilpac Truck Company Uses a CIM Implementation to Become a World Class Manufacturer." *Interfaces,* vol. 23, no. 1, January–February 1993, pp. 59–75.

of obtaining bad solutions is slight if the analyst exercises good judgment in developing the simulation model and if the simulation process is run long enough under a wide variety of conditions so that the analyst has sufficient data to predict how the real system will operate.

Summary

Simulation is a method that can be used to study the behavior of a real system by using a model that "behaves like" or simulates the real system. Some of the reasons computer simulation is one of the most frequently used techniques in management science are as follows:

1. It can be used for a large variety of practical problems.
2. It can be used to obtain good solutions to problems that are too complex to be modeled and solved with analytical procedures.
3. The simulation approach is straightforward and hence relatively easy to explain and understand. As a result, management confidence is increased, and acceptance of the model is more easily obtained.
4. Computer software firms have developed special-purpose programming languages, thus facilitating the use of simulation in practice.

In this chapter we showed how simulation can be used to evaluate the risks associated with introducing a new product, to select a profitable beginning inventory level for a product, and to study the behavior of a waiting line system. In each case we began by developing a model that simulated the system being studied. Then, through a computer run, or experiment, we collected simulation data about the behavior of the system. A summary of these data provides a better understanding of the system and helps select an appropriate course of action.

Glossary

Simulation A method used to study the behavior of a system by using a model that "behaves like" or simulates the real system.

Risk analysis An analysis of the potential for loss when a decision must be made in presence of an uncertain future.

Simulation model The collection of mathematical expressions and logical relationships that describe how a real system behaves or operates.

Monte Carlo simulation A simulation with one or more random variables where the evolution of the system over time is not relevant. Each simulation trial is an independent repetition and what happens during one simulation trial is not affected by what happened in previous simulation trials.

State of the system The values for a collection of variables used to describe a system at a particular point in time.

Event An instantaneous occurrence that changes the state of the system in a simulation model.

Discrete-event simulation A simulation that describes how a system evolves over time. In these simulations, the state of the system at one point in time is dependent upon the state of the system at previous points of time. Events that occur at discrete points in time are used to update the state of the system.

Steady state The normal operation of a system after the effects of start-up conditions have dissipated.

Verification The process of determining that a computer program implements a simulation model as it is intended.

Validation The process of determining that a simulation model provides an accurate representation of a real system.

Simulation clock A computer-programmed clock that keeps track of time during a simulation run.

Next-event time advance A method that advances a simulation clock to the time of the most imminent or next event in a simulation process.

Fixed-increment time advance A method that advances a simulation clock in fixed time increments such as a minute, hour, day, month, or other convenient time period. The state of the system is monitored at each time increment.

Problems

1. **SELF Test** A retail store has experienced the following historical daily demand for a particular product.

Sales (units)	0	1	2	3	4	5	6
Frequency (days)	4	6	14	12	7	5	2

   a. Use the historical data to estimate the probability distribution of sales.
   b. Using the probability distribution that you developed in part (a), compute the mean or expected value of daily sales.
   c. Suppose that the following random numbers were obtained using Excel:

   0.46 0.27 0.68 0.74 0.53 0.44 0.79 0.06 0.71 0.22

   Use these random numbers to simulate daily sales for a 10-day period.
   d. What is the average number of cars sold per day for the 10-day simulation. Compare this value with the mean that you computed in part (b).

2. An automated photo processing laboratory has several machines that are used for developing and printing. A significant factor in meeting customer delivery schedules is the number of breakdowns that occur because of paper jams. The following data show the number of breakdowns per day for the past 100 days of operation

Number of Breakdowns	0	1	2	3	4
Number of Occurrences	12	24	37	19	8

   a. Use the historical data to estimate the probability distribution for the number of breakdowns that occur per day.
   b. Using the probability distribution that you developed in part (a), compute the mean or expected value of the number of breakdowns that occur per day.
   c. Suppose that the following uniformly distributed random numbers were obtained using Excel:

   0.08   0.61   0.22

   Use these random numbers to simulate the number of breakdowns for the next three days.
   d. Using a spreadsheet, simulate the number of breakdowns for 100 days.
   e. What is the average number of breakdowns per day for the 100-day simulation. Compare this value with the mean that you computed in part (b).

3. **SELF Test** A car rental agency has collected the following data on the demand for luxury automobiles over the past 25 days.

Daily Demand	7	8	9	10	11
Number of Days	2	5	8	7	3

   Because customers drop cars at another location, the agency only has nine cars available currently.
   a. Use the following five random numbers to generate 5 days of demand for the rental agency:

   0.15   0.48   0.71   0.56   0.90

   b. What is the average number of cars rented for the 5 days?
   c. How many rentals will be lost over the 5 days?
   d. What is the average daily demand for the 5 days?
   e. Using a spreadsheet, simulate the number of cars that will be demanded for 100 days. How many rentals will be lost over the 100 days, and what is the average daily demand for the 100 days?

4. Decca Industries has experienced the following weekly absenteeism over the past 20 weeks.

Number of Employees Absent	1	2	3	4	5	6
Number of Weeks	2	4	7	3	2	2

   a. Use the historical data to estimate the probability distribution for the number of employees absent.
   b. Use the following random numbers to simulate weekly absenteeism for a 10-week period:

   0.09   0.99   0.6   0.48   0.1   0.56   0.6   0.26   0.11   0.21

   c. Use a spreadsheet to simulate weekly absenteeism for a 52-week period. What is the average number of employees absent per week for the 52-week period?

5. Shown are 50 weeks of historical sales data for cars sold by Domoy Motors, Inc., a new car dealer in Newton, Ohio.

Weekly Sales	0	1	2	3	4	5
Number of Weeks	2	5	8	22	10	3

   a. Use the historical data to estimate the probability distribution for weekly sales.

   b. Use the following random numbers to simulate weekly sales for a 10-week period:

   0.03   0.29   0.92   0.45   0.17   0.18   0.62   0.14   0.66   0.67

   c. Use a spreadsheet to simulate weekly sales for 52 weeks. What is the average weekly sales for the 52 weeks?

6. **SELF Test** Suppose that the account balance for credit card customers who are behind by one month or more in their monthly payments is uniformly distributed between $2000 and $8000. Use the following random numbers to generate five account balances for this group of customers:

   0.14   0.56   0.08   0.89   0.44

   What is the average account balance for the five randomly selected accounts.

7. Jacobs Supplies is a mail-order firm that specializes in outdoor clothing and camping equipment. Suppose that the length of time required to process a customer order by phone is uniformly distributed between 1 and 3 minutes. Use the following random numbers to generate the processing time for 10 customers:

   0.05   0.36   0.96   0.04   0.37   0.52   0.66   0.28   0.91   0.33

   What is the average processing time for the 10 customers?

8. **SELF Test** Carolina Resort Rentals has an 800 toll-free number customers can call for information and to request a brochure that shows pictures of the condominiums available for rent, along with information such as price, number of bedrooms, special features, and so on. Suppose that the number of requests for a brochure is normally distributed with a mean of 400 brochures per month and a standard deviation of 50. Use a spreadsheet package to simulate the number of brochures that will be requested over the next 12 months.

9. Bob's Auto Service sells and installs tires. Suppose that the amount of time required to balance and install a new set of four tires is normally distributed with a mean of 50 minutes and a standard deviation of 7 minutes. Use a spreadsheet package to simulate the length of time to balance and install a set of tires for the next 25 customers. What is the average length of time observed for the sample of 25 customers?

10. Charlestown Electric Company is building a new generator for its Mount Washington plant. Even with good maintenance procedures, the generator will have periodic failures or breakdowns. Historical data for similar generators indicate that the relative frequency of failures during a year is as follows:

Number of Failures	0	1	2	3
Relative Frequency	0.80	0.15	0.04	0.01

   Assume that the useful lifetime of the generator is 25 years. Use simulation to estimate the number of breakdowns that will occur in the 25 years of operation. Are five or more consecutive years of operation without a failure common?

11. A service technician for a major photocopier company is trained to service two copiers: the X100 and the Y200. Approximately 60% of the technician's service calls are for the X100, and 40% are for the Y200. The service time distributions for the two copiers are as follows:

X100 Copier		Y200 Copier	
Time (minutes)	Probability	Time (minutes)	Probability
25	0.50	20	0.40
30	0.25	25	0.40
35	0.15	30	0.10
40	0.10	35	0.10

Simulate 20 service calls. What is the total time spent on the 20 calls?

12. Bushnell's Sand and Gravel (BSG) is a small firm that supplies sand, gravel, and topsoil to contractors and landscaping firms. BSG maintains an inventory of high-quality screened topsoil that is used to supply the weekly orders for two companies: Bath Landscaping Service and Pittsford Lawn Care, Inc. BSG must determine how many cubic yards of screened topsoil to have in inventory at the beginning of each week to satisfy the needs of both its customers. BSG would like to select the lowest possible inventory level that would have a 0.95 probability of satisfying the combined weekly orders from both customers. The demand distributions for the two customers are as follows:

Customer	Weekly Demand (cubic yards)	Probability
Bath Landscaping	10	0.20
	15	0.35
	20	0.30
	25	0.10
	30	0.05
Pittsford Lawn Care	30	0.20
	40	0.40
	50	0.30
	60	0.10

Simulate 20 weeks of operation for beginning inventories of 70 and 80 cubic yards. Based on your limited simulation results, how many cubic yards should BSG maintain in inventory? Discuss what you would want to do in a full-scale simulation of this problem.

13. Baseball's World Series is a maximum 7 games, with the winner being the first team to win 4 games. Assume that the Toronto Blue Jays are in the World Series and that the first 2 games are to be played in Toronto, the next 3 games (the third one only if necessary) at the opponent's ball park, and the last 2 games, only if necessary, back in Toronto. Taking into account the projected starting pitchers for each game and homefield advantage that favors the home team, the probabilities of Toronto winning each game are as follows:

Game	1	2	3	4	5	6	7
Probability	0.60	0.55	0.48	0.45	0.47	0.55	0.50

Develop a spreadsheet model that can be used to simulate the World Series results, including the number of games played and the winner. Use the results of 100 trials to estimate the overall probability of Toronto winning the series, as well as the most likely number of games in the series.

14. Brinkley Corporation is interested in using a simulation model to determine the cost and profit associated with a new product. Uncertainty is present in terms of raw materials cost, labor cost, and transportation cost. The probability distributions for the costs per unit are as follows:

Purchase Cost	Probability	Assembly Labor Cost	Probability	Transportation Cost	Probability
$10	0.25	$20	0.10	$3	0.75
$11	0.45	$22	0.25	$5	0.25
$12	0.30	$24	0.35		
		$25	0.30		

a. Use the random numbers 0.37, 0.58, and 0.82 to simulate the total cost per unit. If the unit sells for $45 per unit, what is the simulated profit?
b. Repeat part (a) using the random numbers 0.18, 0.74, and 0.61.
c. Perform 100 trials of the simulation process to determine the average or expected profit.
d. How can the simulated probability distribution of profit help the company determine the product's selling price?

15. **SELF Test** Three discount pharmacies (Super Z, Devco, and Floorgreen) compete for business in a suburban area. Customers often make a purchase at one of the stores and then make their next purchase at another store. The following table shows the probability that a customer will switch stores from one purchase to the next.

Current Purchase	Next Purchase		
	Super Z	Devco	Floorgreen
Super Z	0.70	0.10	0.20
Devco	0.30	0.55	0.15
Floorgreen	0.10	0.10	0.80

a. Gary Hatcher made his last purchase at Super Z. Use the following four random numbers to simulate the store at which he makes his next four purchases: 0.42, 0.81, 0.16, and 0.57.
b. Suppose that Hatcher's last purchase in part (a) had been made at Devco. Use the same four random numbers to generate his next four purchases.
c. If the simulation were conducted for a large number of purchases, the fraction of Hatcher's purchases from each store would be about the same regardless of which store he made his last purchase from. This is what it means to reach steady state. Use your results from parts (a) and (b) to comment on whether simulating four purchases is enough to reach steady state.

16. The historical sales data for a door-to-door magazine salesperson shows that if the salesperson talks to the woman of the house, there is a 15% chance of making a sale. Furthermore, if the salesperson convinces the woman of the house to purchase some magazines, the relative frequency distribution for the number of the subscriptions ordered is as follows:

Number of Subscriptions	1	2	3
Relative Frequency	0.60	0.30	0.10

However, if the man of the house answers the door, the salesperson's chances of making a sale are 25%. In addition, the relative frequency distribution for the number of subscriptions ordered is as follows:

Number of Subscriptions	1	2	3	4
Relative Frequency	0.10	0.40	0.30	0.20

The salesperson has found that no one answers the door at about 30% of the houses contacted. However, of the people who do answer the door, 80% are women and 20% are men. The salesperson's profit is $2 for each subscription sold.

a. Use simulation to show the house-by-house results for 25 calls.

b. What is the total profit projected for the 25 calls?

c. Based on your results from part (b), how many subscriptions should the salesperson expect to sell by calling on 100 houses per day? What is the salesperson's expected daily profit?

17. A project has four activities (A, B, C, and D) that must be performed sequentially to complete the project. The probability distribution for the time required to complete each of the activities is as follows:

Activity	Activity Time (weeks)	Probability
A	5	0.25
	6	0.30
	7	0.30
	8	0.15
B	3	0.20
	5	0.55
	7	0.25
C	10	0.10
	12	0.25
	14	0.40
	16	0.20
	18	0.05
D	8	0.60
	10	0.40

a. Simulate the completion time for each activity. Sum the activity times to establish a completion time for the entire project.

b. Simulate 20 completions of this project. Show the distribution of completion times, and estimate the probability that the project can be completed in 35 weeks or less.

18. A New York City newsstand orders 250 copies of *The New York Times* daily. Primarily due to weather conditions, the demand for newspapers varies from day to day. The probability distribution of the demand for newspapers is as follows:

Number of Newspapers	150	175	200	225	250
Probability	0.10	0.30	0.30	0.20	0.10

The newsstand makes a $0.15 profit on every paper sold, but it loses $0.10 on every paper unsold by the end of the day. Use 10 days of simulated results to determine whether the newsstand should order 200, 225, or 250 papers per day. What is the average daily profit the newsstand can anticipate based on your recommendation?

19. Geosystems, Inc., specializes in the development of customized geographic information systems. For the most recent quarter, sales revenues were $850,000, consisting of $600,000 from the sale of the firm's software package, $200,000 from consulting services, and $50,000 from training. Quarterly software revenue is decreasing at a rate uniformly distributed between 1% and 3% per quarter; consulting revenue is increasing at a rate uniformly distributed between 5% and 8% per quarter; and training revenue is increasing at a rate uniformly distributed between 5% and 10% per quarter. Develop a spreadsheet model that can be used to simulate total annual revenues for the next four quarters. Rerun the simulation for 100 trials and briefly summarize your findings. Note that each of the 100 trials in your simulation will show the simulated results for the next four quarters; your summary should provide information for management regarding what type of revenues are likely over the next four quarters.

20. Bristol Bikes, Inc., wants to develop an order-quantity and reorder-point policy that would minimize the total costs associated with the company's inventory of exercise bikes. The relative frequency distribution for weekly retail demand is

Demand	0	1	2	3	4	5
Probability	0.20	0.50	0.10	0.10	0.05	0.05

The relative frequency distribution for lead time is

Lead Time (weeks)	1	2	3	4
Relative Frequency	0.10	0.25	0.60	0.05

The holding cost is $1 per unit per week, the ordering cost is $20 per order, the shortage cost is $25 per unit, and the beginning inventory is 7 units. For an order quantity of 12 and a reorder point of 5, simulate 10 weeks of operation of this inventory system.

21. Stollar's Bakery Shop wants to determine how many 10-inch white cakes it should produce each day to maximize profits. The production cost is $2.50 per cake, and the selling price is $4.50. Any cakes that are not sold at the end of the day are sold for $1.50 to a local store that specializes in day-old goods. The following data show the daily demand during the past month (20 days of operation).

Daily Demand	0	1	2	3	4	5	6	7	8
Frequency	1	2	1	2	3	6	3	1	1

Develop a spreadsheet model that can be used to simulate the system for production sizes ranging from 1 to 8 cakes per day. Run the simulation for a period of 100 days. What appears to be the best production size?

22. Marianne Haverly is a sales representative for a major paper company. She receives a monthly base salary of $1500 plus a commission equal to five percent of her gross monthly sales. Although her company provides a company car, she is responsible for covering all other expenses. Suppose that she believes that gross monthly sales are normally distributed with a mean of $100,000 and a standard deviation of $15,000, and that her monthly expenses are uniformly distributed between $1000 and $2000 per month. Develop a spreadsheet model that can be used to simulate monthly gross sales and monthly expenses. Run the simulation for a period of 60 months, and compute the average monthly net income.

23. Domoy Motors, Inc., purchases a certain model automobile for $5778. To finance the purchase of these cars, Domoy must pay an 18% annual interest rate on borrowed capital. This interest rate amounts to approximately $20 per car per week. Orders for additional cars can be placed each week, but a minimum order size of 5 cars is required. Receiving a new shipment of cars after the order is placed currently takes 3 weeks. The cost of placing an order is $50. If Domoy runs out of cars in inventory, a shortage cost of $300 per car is incurred. Currently,

Domoy has 20 cars of this model in inventory. Historical data showing the weekly demand are as follows:

Weekly Sales	0	1	2	3	4	5
Number of Weeks	2	5	8	22	10	3

a. Assuming an order quantity of 15 cars and a reorder point of 10 cars, perform a 12-week simulation of Domoy's operation.

b. Determine the order policy that appears to minimize Domoy's overall costs.

24. A national chain of hotels and motels is interested in learning where individuals prefer to stay when on business trips. Three competing hotel and motel chains are included in the study. They are the Marimont Inn, the Harrison Inn, and the Hinton Hotel. The study revealed that where an individual stays on one trip is a good predictor of where the individual will stay the next trip. However, the study showed that sometimes individuals switch from one chain to another. The probabilities of staying at each chain are shown. For example, if an individual stayed at the Marimont Inn on one trip, there is a 0.70 probability of staying at the Marimont Inn the next trip, a 0.10 probability of staying at the Harrison Inn the next trip, and a 0.20 probability of staying at the Hinton Hotel the next trip. Similar probability values are shown for individuals staying at the Harrison Inn and the Hinton Hotel on a particular trip.

Currently Staying at	Probability of Staying the Next Trip at		
	Marimont	Harrison	Hinton
Marimont	0.70	0.10	0.20
Harrison	0.20	0.60	0.20
Hinton	0.15	0.05	0.80

a. Assume that an individual most recently stayed at the Marimont Inn. Simulate where the individual would stay on the next 50 business trips. What percentage of time will the person select each chain? Which appears to be the most popular chain?

b. Repeat the simulation in part (a) starting with an individual most recently staying at the Harrison Inn. Repeat part (a) again with the individual most recently staying at the Hinton Hotel. Which is the most popular chain based on these simulation results?

25. Shown is the probability distribution for the number of pins a bowler knocks down with a first ball.

Number of Pins	6	7	8	9	10
Probability	0.02	0.08	0.20	0.30	0.40

The probability table showing the number of pins obtained on a second ball is as follows:

If Number of Pins on First Ball Is	Number of Pins on Second Ball Is				
	0	1	2	3	4
6	0.01	0.03	0.20	0.26	0.50
7	0.04	0.10	0.36	0.50	
8	0.05	0.25	0.70		
9	0.15	0.85			

a. Using this information, simulate a game of bowling. What is the bowler's score?

b. Develop a spreadsheet model for this problem, and simulate several games of bowling. What is an estimate of the bowler's average score?

26. Mount Washington Service Station sells regular and unleaded gasoline. Pump 1 is self-service for customers who want to pump their own gas. Pump 2 is full-service for customers who are willing to pay a higher cost per gallon to have an attendant pump the gas, check the oil, and so on. Both pumps can serve 1 car at a time. Based on past data, the owner estimates that 70% of the customers select the self-service pump and 30% want full service. The arrival rate of cars for each minute of operation is given by the following probability distribution.

Number of Arrivals	0	1	2	3	4
Probability	0.10	0.20	0.35	0.30	0.05

The time (in minutes) required to serve a car depends on whether the self-service or the full-service facility is used and is given by the following probability distribution.

Self-Service Pump		Full-Service Pump	
Service Time	Probability	Service Time	Probability
2	0.10	3	0.20
3	0.20	4	0.30
4	0.60	5	0.35
5	0.10	6	0.10
Total	1.00	7	0.05
		Total	1.00

Use simulation to study a 10-minute operation of the system. As part of your analysis, consider the following questions: What is the average number of cars waiting for service per minute at both facilities? What is the average amount of time a car must wait for service? Prepare a brief report for Mount Washington's owner that describes your analysis and any conclusions.

27. Bob's Auto Store sells automotive parts and supplies to individuals and automotive repair shops. Sales to individuals are all cash transactions, and sales to automotive repair shops are a mix of cash and credit. Suppose that monthly cash sales are normally distributed with a mean of $20,000 and a standard deviation of $4000, and that monthly credit sales are normally distributed with a mean of $75,000 and a standard deviation of $8000. At the beginning of each month a certain percentage of the total accounts receivable is collected. For instance, suppose that this percentage is 70% and that the total amount of accounts receivable at the beginning of the month is $100,000; in this case, $70,000 of the beginning accounts receivable is collected. If credit sales for the month were $60,000, the ending accounts receivable would be equal to $100,000 + $60,000 − $70,000 = $90,000. In general, the Ending Accounts Receivable = Beginning Accounts Receivable + Credit Sales − Collections. The store's owner has observed that the percentage of total accounts receivable that is collected has been decreasing over the past year. Suppose that the following probability distribution describes what is expected over the next year.

Percentage Collected	Probability
50%	.1
60%	.3
70%	.4
80%	.2

Assuming that the ending accounts receivable from the previous month is $50,000, develop a spreadsheet model that can be used to compute the ending accounts receivable for the next 12 months.

28. A medical consulting firm has been asked to determine the facilities required in the X-ray laboratory of a new hospital. In particular, the firm should provide recommendations on the number of X-ray units for the laboratory. How could computer simulation assist in reaching a good decision? What factors would you consider in developing a simulation model of this problem?

29. Consider a medium-sized community that currently has only one fire station. You have been hired by the city manager to help determine the best location for a second fire station. What would be your objective for this problem? Explain how you might use computer simulation to evaluate alternative locations and help identify the best location.

30. A bus company is considering adding a new 10-stop route to its operation. The bus will be scheduled to complete the route once each hour. If the company has determined the approximate demand distribution for each location, discuss how computer simulation might be used to project the hourly profit associated with the new route. If the company can assign a regular bus or a more economical minibus to this route, discuss how computer simulation might help management make this decision. Note that with the minibus the company's management is concerned about being unable to pick up customers if the bus is already full.

Case Problem: County Beverage Drive-Thru

County Beverage Drive-Thru, Inc., operates a chain of beverage supply stores in northern Illinois. Each store has a single service lane; cars enter at one end of the store and exit at the other end. Customers pick up soft drinks, beer, snacks, and party supplies without getting out of their cars. When a new customer arrives at the store, he/she waits until the preceding customer's order is complete and then drives into the store for service.

Typically, three employees operate each store during peak periods; two clerks take and fill orders, and a third clerk serves as a cashier and store supervisor. County Beverage is considering a revised store design in which computerized order taking and payment are integrated with specialized warehousing equipment. Management hopes that the new design will permit operating each store with one clerk. To determine if the new design is beneficial, County Beverage has decided to build a new store using the revised design.

County Beverage's new store will be located near a major shopping center. Based on their experience at other locations, County Beverage believes that during the peak late afternoon and evening hours, the time between arrivals follows an exponential probability distribution with a mean of 6 minutes. Sales records from the company's other stores show variability in the order size. Orders are classified as small, medium, and large, with approximately 40% small orders, 50% medium orders, and 10% large orders. Management estimates that the average time to fill an order if one clerk operates the store is 3 minutes for a small order, 6 minutes for a medium order, and 9 minutes for a large order. If necessary, an additional clerk could be used to assist in filling orders; County Beverage estimates that using two clerks will reduce the service time to 2 minutes for a small order, 5 minutes for a medium order, and 7 minutes for a large order. The projected average contribution to profit, excluding employee wages, is $1.50 per small order, $3.00 per medium order, and $6.00 per large order. The hourly cost of each employee, including overhead, is $9.00.

County Beverage would like you to develop a spreadsheet simulation model of the new system and use it to compare the behavior of the system when one employee operates the system with the behavior when two employees are used. Management is especially concerned with how long customers have to wait for service as well as how long they will spend in the system. Expected profits and costs are also factors they would like you to investigate.

Managerial Report

Prepare a report that discusses the general development of the spreadsheet simulation model, and make any recommendations that you have regarding the best decision for County Beverage. Include the following items:

1. List the information the spreadsheet simulation model should generate so that a decision can be made about the desired number of clerks.
2. Run the simulation for 500 customers, for both the case of one employee and the case of two employees. *Note:* Values from an exponential probability distribution with mean μ can be generated in Excel using the following function:
    $$= -\mu * LN(RAND())$$
3. Compute the average waiting time and contribution to profit for each case.

Case Problem: Machine Repair

Jerry Masters, president of Pacific Plastics, Inc. (PPI), has become concerned with reports that downtime for PPI's plastic injection-molding machines has been increasing. A machine's downtime includes the time the machine must wait for a repair service technician to arrive after a breakdown plus the actual repair time. Currently, PPI has three plastic injection-molding machines, which are repaired by one service technician. However, because of an increase in business, PPI is considering the purchase of three additional machines. Masters is concerned that, with the additional machines, downtime will increase.

An analysis of historical data shows that the probability of each machine breaking down during 1 hour of operation is 0.10. In addition, the distribution of the repair time (in hours) for a machine that breaks down is as follows:

Repair Time	1	2	3	4	5
Probability	0.20	0.35	0.25	0.15	0.05

The loss in revenue associated with a machine being down for 1 hour is $100. PPI pays its service technician $22 per hour and believes that it can hire additional service technicians at the same wage rate.

In reviewing the breakdown problem, Masters decided that the best way to learn about the machine repair operation would be to simulate the performance of the system. In considering the potential use of computer simulation, he indicated that PPI must deal with the two conflicting sources of cost: the cost of the service technician(s) and the cost of machine downtime. He indicated that PPI could minimize salaries by employing only one service technician. Conversely, PPI could minimize the cost of machine downtime by hiring so many service technicians that a machine could be serviced immediately after a breakdown.

Masters wants you to develop a computer simulation model of the machine repair operation and use it to determine how many service technicians PPI should employ to minimize its total cost. When developing the model, you can assume that if a machine breaks down, the breakdown can be treated as occurring at the beginning of the hour of operation—that is, if a machine breaks down in hour 4, count the entire hour as downtime. If 1 hour is spent waiting for a service technician and the length of time required to service the machine is 2 hours, the machine will be down during hours 4, 5, and 6 and then ready for operation at the beginning of hour 7. You can also assume that the probability of any machine breakdown is independent of the breakdown of any other machine and that each service time also is independent of other service times.

Managerial Report

Prepare a report that discusses the general development of the computer simulation model, the conclusions that you plan to draw by using the model, and any recommendations that you have regarding the best decision for PPI. Include the following items:

1. List the information the computer simulation model should generate so that a decision can be made about the desired number of service technicians.
2. Set up a flowchart of the machine repair operation for one machine and one service technician.
3. Use random numbers and hand computations to demonstrate the simulation of the machine repair operation with three machines and one service technician.
4. Discuss how simulation can be used to make a recommendation about the number of service technicians that PPI should employ.

APPENDIX 13.1   Simulation with Spreadsheets

Spreadsheets enable small and moderate-sized simulation models to be implemented relatively easily and quickly. If a person is somewhat familiar with spreadsheets, the advantage of using spreadsheets is that there is no need to learn a general-purpose language or a special-purpose simulation language to develop and run a simulation model. In this appendix we show the Excel spreadsheets for the three simulation models presented in this chapter.

The PortaCom Simulation Model

The probability distribution for the direct labor cost per unit in the PortaCom simulation model is shown in Table 13.8. In Section 13.1 we defined intervals of random numbers that could be used to simulate the direct labor cost per unit. These intervals are shown again in Table 13.9. Since there is a 0.1 probability that a random number will be in the interval of 0.0 but less than 0.1, there is a 0.1 probability that the direct labor cost will be $33 per unit. Similarly since there is a 0.2 probability that a random number will be in the interval of 0.1 but less than 0.3, there is a 0.2 probability that the direct labor cost will be $34 per unit. Continuing in this fashion, we see that the random number intervals shown in Table 13.9 can be used to simulate the direct labor cost per unit consistent with its probability distribution.[1] Developing a table of random number intervals in the form shown here is necessary for Excel to simulate values from any tabular probability distribution.

Figure 13.10 shows the excel spreadsheet with the first five trials of the PortaCom risk analysis simulation. Note that the random number intervals and their associated direct labor cost per unit appear in the upper left-hand corner of the spreadsheet. While this table can be placed anywhere in the spreadsheet, it will have to be referred to whenever the model requests a simulated value for the direct labor cost.

Figure 13.11 shows the formula spreadsheet for the PortaCom simulation model. The function =VLOOKUP(RAND(),$A$3:$C$7,3) in column B is used to simulate values for the direct labor cost. The VLOOKUP function works as follows. The RAND() portion of the function instructs the computer to select a random number between 0.0 and 1.0. The $A$3:$C$7 entry tells the computer where the direct labor cost per unit table is located in the spreadsheet. For

Table 13.8

Probability Distribution for Direct Labor Cost per Unit for PortaCom

Direct Labor Cost per Unit	Probability
$33	0.1
$34	0.2
$35	0.4
$36	0.2
$37	0.1

[1] When Excel references the direct labor cost table, it will use random numbers of 0.0 *but less than* 0.1 for $33, 0.1 *but less than* 0.3 for $34, 0.3 *but less than* 0.7 for $35, and so on. Thus, there is no chance that the boundary random numbers of exactly 0.1, exactly 0.3, exactly 0.7 and so on will refer to two different direct labor costs.

Table 13.9

Random Number Intervals for the Simulation of the Direct Labor Cost per Unit in the PortaCom Simulation Model

Lower Random Number	Upper Random Number	Direct Labor Cost per Unit	Probability
0.0	0.1	$33	0.1
0.1	0.3	$34	0.2
0.3	0.7	$35	0.4
0.7	0.9	$36	0.2
0.9	1.0	$37	0.1

Figure 13.10 A Portion of the Excel Spreadsheet for the PortaCom Simulation Model

	A	B	C	D	E	F	G
1	Lower	Upper	Direct				
2	Random No.	Random No.	Labor Cost				
3	0.0	0.1	33				
4	0.1	0.3	34				
5	0.3	0.7	35				
6	0.7	0.9	36				
7	0.9	1.0	37				
8							
9		Direct Labor	Parts	Number of	Total	Total	Contribution
10	Trial	Cost Per Unit	Cost Per Unit	Units Sold	Revenue	Cost	to Profit
11	1	$37	$85.36	17367	$4,324,383	$3,125,026	$1,199,357
12	2	$34	$91.68	12901	$3,212,349	$2,621,398	$590,951
13	3	$35	$93.35	20686	$5,150,814	$3,655,048	$1,495,766
14	4	$33	$98.56	10889	$2,711,361	$2,432,557	$278,804
15	5	$35	$88.36	14260	$3,550,740	$2,759,114	$791,626

Figure 13.11 The Formula Spreadsheet for the PortaCom Simulation Model

	A	B	C	D	E	F	G
1	Lower	Upper	Direct				
2	Random No.	Random No.	Labor Cost				
3	0.0	0.1	33				
4	0.1	0.3	34				
5	0.3	0.7	35				
6	0.7	0.9	36				
7	0.9	1.0	37				
8							
9		Direct Labor	Parts	Number of	Total	Total	Contribution
10	Trial	Cost Per Unit	Cost Per Unit	Units Sold	Revenue	Cost	to Profit
11	1	=VLOOKUP(RAND(),$A$3:$C$7,3)	=80+20*RAND()	=NORMINV(RAND(),15000,300)	=249*D11	=B11*D11+C11*D11+100000	=E11–F11
12	2	=VLOOKUP(RAND(),$A$3:$C$7,3)	=80+20*RAND()	=NORMINV(RAND(),15000,300)	=249*D12	=B12*D12+C12*D12+100000	=E12–F12
13	3	=VLOOKUP(RAND(),$A$3:$C$7,3)	=80+20*RAND()	=NORMINV(RAND(),15000,300)	=249*D13	=B13*D13+C13*D13+100000	=E13–F13
14	4	=VLOOKUP(RAND(),$A$3:$C$7,3)	=80+20*RAND()	=NORMINV(RAND(),15000,300)	=249*D14	=B14*D14+C14*D14+100000	=E14–F14
15	5	=VLOOKUP(RAND(),$A$3:$C$7,3)	=80+20*RAND()	=NORMINV(RAND(),15000,300)	=249*D15	=B15*D15+C15*D15+100000	=E15–F15

example, if the random number is 0.7308, the VLOOKUP function will determine that 0.7308 is in the interval of 0.7 but less than 0.9, corresponding to row 4 of the table. The 3 at the end of the function =VLOOKUP(RAND()),$A$3:$C$7,3) indicates that the corresponding direct labor cost per unit appears in the *third* column of the selected row. Thus, the random number 0.7308 provides the simulated direct labor cost of $36 per unit.

The parts cost per unit (column C) and number of units sold (column D) are generated by the functions for the uniform probability distribution and the normal probability distribution as discussed in Section 13.1. Finally, the total revenue (column E), total cost (column F), and contribution to profit (column G) are computed using the standard spreadsheet cell formulas that correspond to the total revenue, total cost, and contribution to profit formulas presented in Section 13.1.

Any number of simulation trials can be quickly carried out simply by selecting the first trial row of the spreadsheet and dragging the fill handle for as many rows or simulation trials as desired. When the fill handle is released, the simulation rows will be inserted in the spreadsheet automatically. Unless the simulation model is extremely complex, these simulation calculations should be completed fairly quickly.

The standard Excel spreadsheet functions can be used to compute summary statistics for the simulation results. In Table 13.4, we used the mean, median, standard deviation, and maximum and minimum values of the contribution-to-profit data in column G to help evaluate the risk for the PortaCom project. In Figure 13.4, we provided a histogram of the contribution-to-profit data. Exactly how the simulation data are summarized depends upon the application. Generally, the user selects the summary measures that provide the best understanding of how the system operates.

Finally, the F9 key can be used to perform another complete simulation of the PortaCom project. In this case, the entire spreadsheet will be recalculated and a set of new simulation results will be provided. Any data summaries, measures, or functions that have been built into the spreadsheet earlier will be updated automatically.

The Butler Inventory Simulation Model

The formula spreadsheet for the Butler inventory simulation model from Section 13.2 is shown in Figure 13.12. Any beginning inventory quantity of interest can be entered in cell B1. Demand (column B) is simulated by using the normal probability distribution function with a mean of 100 units and a standard deviation of 20 units. The statement =IF(B5<$B$1,B5,$B$1) shows that if the simulated demand in cell B5 is less than the inventory quantity entered in cell B1, sales will be equal to the simulated demand in cell B5. However, if the simulated demand in cell B5 is not less than the inventory quantity entered in cell B1, sales will be equal to the inventory quantity in cell B1. Once the number of units sold has been determined, the profit contribution (column D) is simply $50 times the number of units sold (column C). An IF function is used to compute the inventory holding cost (column E). The function =IF(B5<$B$1,15*($B$1-B5),0) in cell E5 checks to see if demand in cell B5 is less than the inventory quantity in cell B1. If it is, an inventory holding of $15 times the inventory surplus ($B$1 - B5) is computed. If demand in cell B5 is not less than inventory quantity in cell B1, there will be a stockout and the inventory holding cost will be 0.

Another IF function is used to compute the shortage cost (column F). With =IF(B5<$B$1,0,30*(B5-$B$1)) in cell F5, we see that if demand in cell B5 is less than the inventory quantity in cell B1, there will not be a stockout and the shortage cost will be 0. However, if this is not the case, a shortage cost of $30 times the number of units short (B5-$B$1) will be incurred. Finally, the net profit (column G) is computed from the spreadsheet commands that take the profit contribution (column D) and subtract the holding cost (column E) and the shortage cost (column F). As we did for the PortaCom simulation model, the first simulation row or trial can be selected and dragged to create as many rows of simulation trials as desired.

Experimentation with the inventory simulation model can be carried out by changing the quantity appearing in cell B1. For each quantity considered, the user can press the F9 key and recalculate the spreadsheet. A corresponding revised set of simulation results will be provided. By comparing the outputs of the various simulation experiments, the user should be able to learn about the performance of the system and select a good beginning inventory quantity.

Figure 13.12 The Formula Spreadsheet for the Butler Inventory Simulation Model

	A	B	C	D	E	F	G
1	Quantity =	100					
2							
3		Simulated		Profit	Holding	Shortage	Net
4	Trial	Demand	Sales	Contribution	Cost	Cost	Profit
5	1	=NORMINV(RAND(),100,20)	=IF(B5<$B$1,B5,$B$1)	=50*C5	=IF(B5<$B$1,15*($B$1−B5),0)	=IF(B5<$B$1,0,30*(B5−$B$1))	=D5−E5−F5
6	2	=NORMINV(RAND(),100,20)	=IF(B6<$B$1,B6,$B$1)	=50*C6	=IF(B6<$B$1,15*($B$1−B6),0)	=IF(B6<$B$1,0,30*(B6−$B$1))	=D6−E6−F6
7	3	=NORMINV(RAND(),100,20)	=IF(B7<$B$1,B7,$B$1)	=50*C7	=IF(B7<$B$1,15*($B$1−B7),0)	=IF(B7<$B$1,0,30*(B7−$B$1))	=D7−E7−F7
8	4	=NORMINV(RAND(),100,20)	=IF(B8<$B$1,B8,$B$1)	=50*C8	=IF(B8<$B$1,15*($B$1−B8),0)	=IF(B8<$B$1,0,30*(B8−$B$1))	=D8−E8−F8
9	5	=NORMINV(RAND(),100,20)	=IF(B9<$B$1,B9,$B$1)	=50*C9	=IF(B9<$B$1,15*($B$1−B9),0)	=IF(B9<$B$1,0,30*(B9−$B$1))	=D9−E9−F9

Figure 13.13 The Formula Spreadsheet for the ATM Waiting Line Simulation Model

	A	B	C	D	E	F	G	H
1		Interarrival	Arrival	Service	Waiting	Service	Completion	Time
2	Customer	Time	Time	Start Time	Time	Time	Time	in System
3	1	=RAND()*5	=B3	=C3	=D3−C3	=NORMINV(RAND(),2,0.5)	=D3+F3	=G3−C3
4	2	=RAND()*5	=C3+B4	=IF(C4>G3,C4,G3)	=D4−C4	=NORMINV(RAND(),2,0.5)	=D4+F4	=G4−C4
5	3	=RAND()*5	=C4+B5	=IF(C5>G4,C5,G4)	=D5−C5	=NORMINV(RAND(),2,0.5)	=D5+F5	=G5−C5
6	4	=RAND()*5	=C5+B6	=IF(C6>G5,C6,G5)	=D6−C6	=NORMINV(RAND(),2,0.5)	=D6+F6	=G6−C6
7	5	=RAND()*5	=C6+B7	=IF(C7>G6,C7,G6)	=D7−C7	=NORMINV(RAND(),2,0.5)	=D7+F7	=G7−C7

The Hammondsport ATM Waiting Line Simulation Model

The formula spreadsheet for the Hammondsport ATM waiting line simulation model from Section 13.3 is shown in Figure 13.13. The rows correspond to the customers who arrive at the bank for the ATM service. The customer interarrival times are simulated by the uniform probability distribution function =RAND()*5 in column B. Each customer arrival time in column C is computed by adding the interarrival time in column B to the arrival time of the preceding customer, which appears one row earlier in column C. The service start time will be shown in column D. Using customer 2 (row 4) as an example, we see that the function =IF(C4>G3,C4,G3) appears in cell D4. Thus, if the arrival time of customer 2 in cell C4 is greater than the completion time of the preceding customer 1 in cell G3, customer 1 has already completed service when customer 2 arrives. As a result, the start time for customer 2 is the customer's arrival time, which appears in cell C4. However, if C4>G3 is not true, customer 1 has not completed service when customer 2 arrives. As a result, customer 2 cannot start service until customer 1 has completed service. Thus, the start time for customer 2 is set equal to the completion time for customer 1 shown in cell G3.

Waiting time (column E) is the difference between the service start time (column D) and the arrival time (column C). Service time (column F) is simulated by using the function for the normal probability distribution with a mean of 2 minutes and a standard deviation of 0.5 minutes. The completion time (column G) is the sum of the start time (column D) and the service time (column F). Finally, the time in the system (column H) is the difference between the completion time (column G) and the arrival time (column C).

In this spreadsheet, the simulation row for customer 2 can be selected and dragged to create as many rows of simulated customer arrivals as desired. As with the other simulation models, the F9 key can be used any time to recalculate the spreadsheet and provide a completely new set of simulation results.

MANAGEMENT SCIENCE in practice

The Upjohn Company*
Kalamazoo, Michigan

The Upjohn Company is a worldwide supplier of high-quality, innovative pharmaceutical products. While its largest business is in prescription pharmaceutical products, Upjohn also operates related businesses in animal health care products, agronomic and vegetable seeds, and specialty chemical products. Founded in 1886, Upjohn had sales of $3.6 billion in 1992. The company has approximately 19,000 employees worldwide, with major manufacturing facilities in Kalamazoo, Puerto Rico, and Belgium, and research laboratories in Kalamazoo, England, and Japan. Committed to total quality improvement—in service to its customers, its products, and its performance in the work place—Upjohn is also dedicated to conducting businesses in an environmentally and socially responsible manner.

Management Science at Upjohn

The management science function at Upjohn is part of the Management Information and Office Services organization and offers a high-quality, professional problem-solving service to any part of the corporation. The mission of the group is to provide decision-making support for the company's customers, strategies, and priorities by using quantitative techniques to solve business problems and exploit business opportunities in a cost-effective manner. The primary areas of application are problem definition and analysis, modeling and simulation, capacity planning, resource allocation, scheduling, and project management.

A Computer Simulation Application

Demand for one of Upjohn's long-standing products had remained stable for several years at a level easily satisfied by the company's manufacturing facility. However, changes in market conditions caused an increase in demand to a level beyond the capacity of the current facility. In the discussion that follows, we describe a simulation study successfully undertaken to determine the most cost-effective means of increasing production to meet the new level of demand.

The production process is shown in Figure 13.14. It consists of three independent subprocesses: raw material processing, bulk processing, and spent material reprocessing. Raw material processing takes purchased material as input and transforms it into material that can be used in bulk processing. Bulk processing (shown within the dashed line in Figure 13.14), which involves initial processing, assay, and final processing, converts the raw materials into a finished product. The key step occurs when an

Figure 13.14

A Production Process at Upjohn

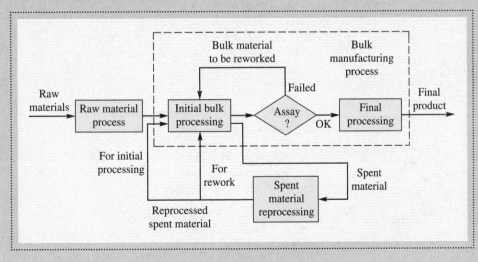

—Continued on next page

—Continued from previous page

assay of the initial bulk processing output or intermediate is performed to determine whether the lot is ready for final processing. If the assay is acceptable, the lot proceeds to final processing and completion. If the assay is not acceptable, the intermediate is returned to initial bulk processing and several steps are repeated. The new intermediate material, which is input during the repeat processing, is obtained by reprocessing one of the spent materials generated during a prior initial bulk processing.

Each time the initial bulk process is run, a quantity of spent material is generated for possible reprocessing. Although the primary use of the reprocessed material is as input for repeat bulk processing, it also can be used as a replacement for the original raw material at the start of the bulk processing. Since the cost of the reprocessed material is significantly less than the cost of new raw material, it is beneficial to use as much reprocessed material as possible.

A simulation model of the production process was developed, and these questions were addressed:

1. What is the maximum throughput of the existing facility?
2. How can the production process be modified to increase the throughput of the existing facility?
3. How much equipment (tanks and centrifuges) must be added to the current facility to increase the capacity to meet the forecasted demand?
4. How should the reprocessed spent material be used to minimize the total production cost?
5. If a new facility is required, what is the optimal size and configuration?

The scope of the simulation model included the raw material, bulk- and spent-material processes already defined. The model was built in a modular flexible manner that allowed for the evaluation of resource levels within the facility, staffing levels and hours, changes in process times or equipment usage, changes in lot size, and/or yield changes. The logic of the process flow served as the core of the model and was developed in collaboration with the lead operators and supervisors of the production area. Since a good logical model is the key to good simulation results, a significant amount of time was spent defining the logic of the process flow. The model development process provided a secondary benefit in that production personnel got to review and evaluate the process as they explained it.

The computer simulation model has been used on several occasions over the past two years. Simulation results have assisted management in addressing capacity, resource allocation, and operating policy issues. Each time a request to evaluate an issue is made, a detailed experimental design is developed that defines the alternatives to be evaluated. The appropriate simulation runs are made, the results evaluated and presented to production management and personnel, and follow-up actions defined.

The computer simulation model was developed using the SLAMSYSTEM Version 3.0 simulation language from the Pritsker Corporation. All simulation runs were made on a personal computer.

Benefits of the Simulation Model

The ongoing investigation of the production process using computer simulation has resulted in numerous benefits to the company, including the following:

1. Optimizing the use of reprocessed spent material to replace fresh raw material. Total material costs were reduced by approximately $3 million per year.
2. Demonstrating that the current facility, with some operating policy improvements, was large enough to satisfy the increased demand for the next several years. Expansion to a new facility was not necessary.
3. Determining the impact on facility throughput from alternative process changes. Numerous potential changes were investigated. The simulation model predicted how each change would affect total facility throughput. One change was identified that would increase throughput beyond what was needed for the 5-year forecasted demand.
4. Determining appropriate staffing levels within the facility. The model determined the number of operators that will be required as the production level increases in the future. This ensures that the proper number of operators will be trained by the time they are needed.
5. Determining the required size and configuration for a new facility. Although the current facility was found adequate to meet demand, the model still allowed management to determine the cost required to build a new facility.

The final actions taken based on the simulation results included alterations in policies for using reprocessed spent material, priority implementation of the process change that most impacted increasing facility throughput, establishment of appropriate staffing levels, and cost minimization because the expense of building a new or expanded facility was avoided.

Questions

1. Briefly describe the Upjohn production operation.
2. What is the primary reason Upjohn conducted a study of this operation?
3. Describe some of the factors that had to be included in the simulation model.
4. What were the advantages of computer simulation to Upjohn?

....

The authors are indebted to Dr. David B. Magerlein, Dr. James M. Magerlein, and Mr. Michael J. Goodrich of The Upjohn Company for providing this application.

Decision Analysis

Decision analysis can be used to determine optimal strategies when a decision maker is faced with several decision alternatives and an uncertain or risk-filled pattern of future events. For example, a manufacturer of a new line of seasonal clothing would like to manufacture large quantities if consumer acceptance and consequent demand for the product are going to be high. However, the manufacturer would like to produce much smaller quantities if consumer acceptance and demand for the product are going to be low. Unfortunately, seasonal clothing items require the manufacturer to make a production–volume decision before the demand is known. Actual consumer acceptance of the product will not be determined until the items have been placed in the stores and buyers have had the opportunity to purchase them. Selection of the best production–volume decision from among several alternatives when the decision maker is faced with the uncertainty of future demand is a problem suited for decision analysis.

We begin the study of decision analysis by considering problems in which there are reasonably few decision alternatives and reasonably few possible future events. We introduce the concepts of a payoff table and a decision tree to provide a structure for this type of decision situation and illustrate the fundamentals of decision analysis. We then extend the discussion to show how additional information obtained through experimentation can be combined with the decision maker's preliminary information to develop an optimal decision strategy.

The last section of the chapter introduces the concepts of utility and the expected utility criterion. Utility takes into account the decision maker's attitude toward the profit, loss, and risk associated with an outcome. In situations where the decision maker feels that monetary values do not adequately reflect the preferences for the payoffs, a utility analysis of the problem should be considered.

14.1 Structuring the Decision Problem

Pittsburgh Development Corporation (PDC) has purchased land for a luxury, riverfront condominium complex. The site provides a spectacular view of downtown Pittsburgh and the Golden Triangle where the Allegheny and Monongahela rivers meet to form the Ohio River. The individual units will be priced from $300,000 to $1,200,000, depending on the floor the unit is located on, the square footage of the unit, and optional features such as fireplaces and large balconies.

The company has had preliminary architectural drawings developed for three different project sizes: 6 floors with 30 units, 12 floors with 60 units, and 18 floors with 90 units. The financial success of the project will depend heavily on the decision that PDC makes regarding the size of the condominium project. Let us consider how decision analysis can help PDC determine which size project to develop.

The first step in the decision analysis approach is to identify the decision alternatives that are being considered. For PDC, there are three:

d_1 = a small condominium complex with 6 floors and 30 units
d_2 = a medium condominium complex with 12 floors and 60 units
d_3 = a large condominium complex with 18 floors and 90 units

A key factor in selecting one of these decision alternatives involves management's assessment of the demand for the condominiums.

When asked about possible market acceptance of the condominium project, management viewed the possible acceptance of the project as an all-or-nothing situation. That is, management believes that the market acceptance will be one of two possibilities: high market acceptance of the project and hence a substantial demand for the condominiums, or low market acceptance of the project and hence a limited demand for the condominiums. Although management can exercise some influence over market acceptance with advertising, the high prices for the units mean that demand will likely depend on a variety of other factors over which PDC will have no control.

In decision analysis, events that may occur but which the decision maker cannot control are referred to as *states of nature*. The list of possible states of nature includes everything that can happen, and individual states of nature are defined so that only one will actually occur. For the PDC condominium project, the two states of nature are

s_1 = high market acceptance and hence a substantial demand for the units
s_2 = low market acceptance and hence a limited demand for the units

Payoff Tables

Given the three decision alternatives and the two states of nature, which condominium size should PDC select? To answer this question, PDC will need information on the profit associated with each combination of a decision alternative and a state of nature. For example, what profit would PDC realize if it constructs a large condominium complex (d_3) and market acceptance turns out to be high (s_1)? But what would happen to the profit if PDC constructs a large condominium complex (d_3) and the market acceptance turns out to be low (s_2)? In decision analysis, we refer to the outcome that results from a specific decision alternative and the occurrence of a particular state of nature as a *payoff*. A table showing the payoffs for all combinations of the decision alternatives and states of nature is a *payoff table*.

Table 14.1

Payoff Table for the PDC Condominium Project (Payoffs in $ Million)

| | State of Nature | |
| | High Acceptance | Low Acceptance |
Decision Alternative	s_1	s_2
Small complex, d_1	8	7
Medium complex, d_2	14	5
Large complex, d_3	20	−9

Using the best information available, management has estimated the payoffs, or profits, for the PDC condominium project. These estimates, with profits expressed in millions of dollars, are presented in Table 14.1. In general, entries in a payoff table can be stated in terms of profit, cost, time, distance, or any other measure of output that may be appropriate for the situation being analyzed. We will refer to the payoff associated with decision alternative i and state of nature j as V_{ij}. For example, Table 14.1 shows that $V_{31} = 20$, indicating that a $20 million profit is anticipated if the large complex is constructed (d_3) and a high market acceptance (s_1) occurs. However, $V_{32} = -9$ shows an anticipated loss of $9 million if the large complex is constructed (d_3) and a low market acceptance (s_2) occurs.

Decision Trees

A *decision tree* provides a graphical representation of the decision-making process. Figure 14.1 presents a decision tree for the PDC problem. Note that the decision tree shows the natural or logical progression that will occur over time. First, PDC must make a decision regarding the size of the condominium complex (d_1, d_2, or d_3). Then, after the decision is implemented, either state of nature s_1 or s_2 will occur. The number at each end point of the tree indicates the payoff associated with a particular sequence. For example the topmost payoff of 8 indicates that an $8 million profit is anticipated if PDC constructs a small condominium complex (d_1) and market acceptance turns out to be high (s_1). The next payoff of 7 indicates an anticipated profit of $7 million if PDC constructs a small condominium complex (d_1) and market acceptance turns out to be low (s_2). Thus, the decision tree shows graphically the sequences of decision alternatives and states of nature that provide the six possible outcomes and payoffs for PDC.

We refer to an intersection or junction point of the decision tree as a *node* and the arc or connector between nodes as a *branch*. Figure 14.1 shows the PDC decision tree with the nodes numbered 1–4. When the branches *leaving* a node are decision branches, we refer to the node as a *decision node* and represent it by a square. Similarly, when the branches leaving a node are state-of-nature branches, we refer to the node as a *state-of-nature node* and represent it by a circle. Hence, node 1 is a decision node, whereas nodes 2, 3, and 4 are state-of-nature nodes.

The identification of the decision alternatives, the states of nature, and the payoff associated with each decision alternative and state-of-nature combination are the first three steps in the decision analysis process. The question we now turn to is: How can the decision maker best utilize the information presented in the payoff table or the decision tree to arrive at a decision? Several approaches may be used.

If you have a payoff table, you should be able to develop a decision tree. Try Problem 1(a).

Figure 14.1

Decision Tree for the PDC Condominium Project (Payoffs in $ Million)

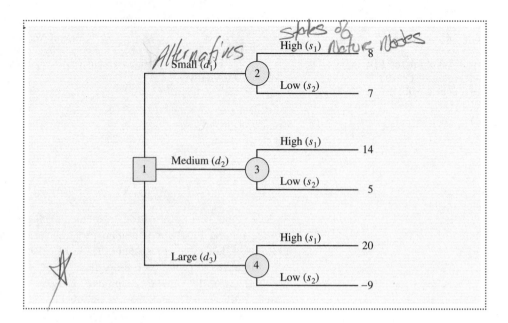

N O T E S & **comments**

1. Experts in problem solving agree that the first step in solving a complex problem is to decompose it into a series of smaller subproblems. Decision trees provide a useful way to show how the problem can be decomposed and the sequential nature of the decision process.

2. People often view the same problem from different perspectives. Thus, the discussion regarding the development of a decision tree may provide additional insight about the problem.

14.2 Decision Making without Probabilities

In this section we consider approaches to decision making that do not require knowledge of the probabilities of the states of nature. These approaches are appropriate in situations where the decision maker has little confidence in his or her ability to assess the probabilities of the various states of nature, or where considering best and worst case analyses that are independent of state-of-nature probabilities is desirable. Because different approaches sometimes lead to different decision recommendations, the decision maker needs to understand the approaches available and then select the specific approach that, according to the decision maker's judgment, is the most appropriate.

Optimistic Approach

The *optimistic approach* evaluates each decision alternative in terms of the *best* payoff that can occur. The decision alternative that is recommended is the one that provides the best possible payoff. For a problem in which maximum profit is desired, as in the PDC problem, the optimistic approach would lead the decision maker to choose the alternative corresponding to the largest profit. For problems involving minimization, this approach leads to choosing the alternative with the smallest payoff.

To illustrate the optimistic approach, we will use it to develop a recommendation for the PDC problem. First, we determine the maximum payoff for each of the decision alternatives; then we select the decision alternative that provides the overall maximum payoff. These steps systematically identify the decision alternative that provides the largest possible profit. Table 14.2 illustrates these steps.

Since 20, corresponding to d_3, is the largest payoff, the decision to construct the large condominium complex is the recommended decision alternative using the optimistic approach.

Conservative Approach

The *conservative approach* evaluates each decision alternative in terms of the *worst* payoff that can occur. The decision alternative recommended is the one that provides the best of the worst possible payoffs. For a problem in which the output measure is profit, as in the PDC problem, the conservative approach would lead the decision maker to choose the alternative that maximizes the minimum possible profit that could be obtained. For problems involving minimization, this approach identifies the alternative that will minimize the maximum payoff.

To illustrate the conservative approach, we will use it to develop a recommendation for the PDC problem. First, we identify the minimum payoff for each of the decision alternatives; then we select the decision alternative that maximizes the minimum payoff. Table 14.3 illustrates these steps for the PDC problem.

Table 14.2

Maximum Payoff for Each PDC Decision Alternative

Decision Alternative	Maximum Payoff	
Small complex, d_1	8	
Medium complex, d_2	14	
Large complex, d_3	20	← Maximum of the maximum payoff values

Table 14.3

Minimum Payoff for Each PDC Decision Alternative

Decision Alternative	Minimum Payoff	
Small complex, d_1	7	← Maximum of the minimum payoff values
Medium complex, d_2	5	
Large complex, d_3	−9	

Since 7, corresponding to d_1, yields the maximum of the minimum payoffs, the decision alternative of a small condominium complex is recommended. This decision approach is considered conservative because it identifies the worst possible payoffs and then recommends the decision alternative that avoids the possibility of extremely "bad" payoffs. In the conservative approach, PDC is guaranteed a profit of at least $7 million. Although PDC may make more, it *cannot* make less than $7 million.

Minimax Regret Approach

Minimax regret is an approach to decision making that is neither purely optimistic nor purely conservative. Let us illustrate the minimax regret approach by showing how it can be used to select a decision alternative for the PDC problem.

Suppose that the PDC constructs a small condominium complex (d_1) and market acceptance turns out to be high (s_1). Table 14.1 shows that the resulting profit for PDC would be $8 million. However, we now know that the high acceptance state of nature (s_1) has occurred, so we realize that the decision to construct a large condominium complex (d_3), yielding a profit of $20 million, would have been the best decision. The difference between the payoff for the best decision alternative ($20 million) and the payoff for the decision to construct a small condominium complex ($8 million) is the *opportunity loss,* or *regret,* associated with decision alternative d_1 when state of nature s_1 occurs; thus, for this case, the opportunity loss or regret is $20 million – $8 million = $12 million. Similarly, if PDC makes the decision to construct a medium condominium complex (d_2) and the high acceptance state of nature (s_1) occurs, the opportunity loss, or regret, associated with d_2 would be $20 million – $14 million = $6 million.

In general the following expression represents the opportunity loss, or regret.

O p p o r t u n i t y   L o s s ,   o r   R e g r e t

$$R_{ij} = |V_j^* - V_{ij}| \qquad (14.1)$$

where

R_{ij} = the regret associated with decision alternative d_i and state of nature s_j
V_j^* = the payoff value[1] corresponding to the best decision for state of nature s_j
V_{ij} = the payoff corresponding to decision alternative d_i and state of nature s_j

---

Note the role of the absolute value in equation (14.1). That is, for minimization problems, the best payoff, V_j^*, is the smallest entry in column j. Because this value always is less than or equal to V_{ij}, the absolute value of the difference between V_j^* and V_{ij} ensures that the regret is always the magnitude of the difference.

Using equation (14.1) and the payoffs in Table 14.1, we can compute the regret associated with each combination of decision alternative d_i and state of nature s_j. Since the PDC problem is a maximization problem, V_j^* will be the largest entry in column j of

---

[1]In maximization problems, V_j^* will be the largest entry in column j of the payoff table. In minimization problems, V_j^* will be the smallest entry in column j of the payoff table.

Table 14.4

....

Opportunity Loss, or Regret, Table for the PDC Condominium Project ($ Million)

	State of Nature	
Decision Alternative	High Acceptance s_1	Low Acceptance s_2
Small complex, d_1	12	0
Medium complex, d_2	6	2
Large complex, d_3	0	16

Table 14.5

....

Maximum Regret for Each PDC Decision Alternative

Decision Alternative	Maximum Regret	
Small complex, d_1	12	
Medium complex, d_2	6	◄—— Minimum of the maximum regret
Large complex, d_3	16	

the payoff table. Thus, to compute the regret, we simply subtract each entry in a column from the largest entry in the column. Table 14.4 shows the opportunity loss, or regret, table for the PDC problem.

The next step in applying the minimax regret approach is to list the maximum regret for each decision alternative; Table 14.5 shows the results for the PDC problem. Selecting the decision alternative with the *minimum* of the *maximum* regret values—hence, the name *minimax regret*—yields the minimax regret decision. For the PDC problem, the alternative to construct the medium condominium complex, with a corresponding maximum regret of $6 million, is the recommended minimax regret decision.

Note that the three approaches discussed in this section provide different recommendations, which in itself isn't bad. It simply reflects the difference in decision-making philosophies that underlie the various approaches. Ultimately, the decision maker will have to choose the most appropriate approach and then make the final decision accordingly. The main criticism of the approaches discussed in this section is that they do not consider any information about the probabilities of the various states of nature. In the next section we discuss an approach that utilizes probability information in selecting a decision alternative.

You should be able to develop a decision recommendation using the optimistic, conservative, and minimax regret approaches. Try Problem 1(b).

14.3   Decision Making with Probabilities

In many decision-making situations, we can obtain probability estimates for each of the states of nature. When such probabilities are available, we can use the *expected value approach* to identify the best decision alternative. Let us first define the expected value of a decision alternative and then apply it to the PDC problem.

Let

$$N = \text{the number of states of nature}$$
$$P(s_j) = \text{the probability of state of nature } s_j$$

Since one and only one of the N states of nature can occur, the probabilities must satisfy two conditions:

$$P(s_j) \geq 0 \qquad \text{for all states of nature} \tag{14.2}$$

$$\sum_{j=1}^{N} P(s_j) = P(s_1) + P(s_2) + \cdots + P(s_N) = 1 \tag{14.3}$$

The *expected value* (EV) of decision alternative d_i is defined as follows.

Expected Value of Decision Alternative d_i

$$\text{EV}(d_i) = \sum_{j=1}^{N} P(s_j)V_{ij} \tag{14.4}$$

In words, the expected value of a decision alternative is the sum of weighted payoffs for the decision alternative. The weight for a payoff is the probability of the associated state of nature and therefore the probability that the payoff will occur. Let us return to the PDC problem to see how the expected value approach can be applied.

PDC is optimistic about the potential for the luxury high-rise condominium complex. Suppose that this optimism provides an initial subjective probability assessment of 0.8 that market acceptance will be high (s_1) and a corresponding probability of 0.2 that market acceptance will be low (s_2). Thus, $P(s_1) = 0.8$ and $P(s_2) = 0.2$. Using the payoff values in Table 14.1 and equation (14.4), we compute the expected value for each of the three decision alternatives as follows:

$$\text{EV}(d_1) = 0.8(8) + 0.2(7) = 7.8$$

$$\text{EV}(d_2) = 0.8(14) + 0.2(5) = 12.2$$

$$\text{EV}(d_3) = 0.8(20) + 0.2(-9) = 14.2$$

Thus, using the expected value approach, we find that the large condominium complex, with an expected value of \$14.2 million, is the recommended decision.

The calculations required to identify the decision alternative with the best expected value can be conveniently carried out on a decision tree. Figure 14.2 shows the decision tree for the PDC problem with state-of-nature branch probabilities. Working backward through the decision tree, we first compute the expected value at each state-of-nature node. That is, at each state-of-nature node, we weight each possible payoff by its chance of occurrence. By doing so, we obtain the expected values for nodes 2, 3, and 4, as shown in Figure 14.3.

Since the decision maker controls the branch leaving decision node 1 and since we are trying to maximize the expected profit, the best decision branch at node 1 is d_3. Thus, the decision tree analysis leads to a recommendation of d_3 with an expected value of \$14.2 million. Note that this is the same recommendation obtained with the expected value approach in conjunction with the payoff table.

Other decision problems may be substantially more complex than the PDC problem, but if there are a reasonable number of decision alternatives and states of nature, you can

You should now be able to use the expected value approach to develop a decision recommendation. Try Problem 5.

Figure 14.2

PDC Decision Tree with State-of-Nature Branch Probabilities

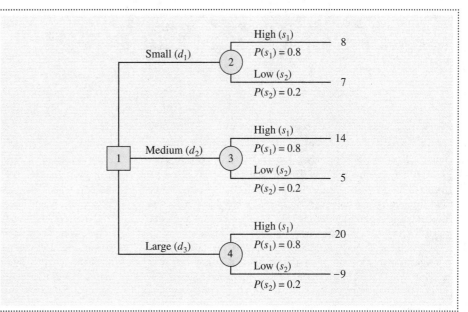

Figure 14.3

Applying the Expected Value Approach Using Decision Trees

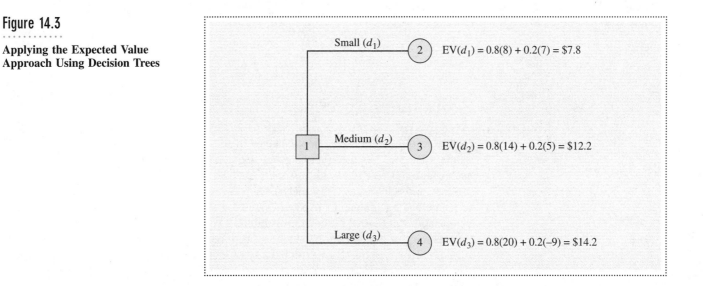

use the decision tree approach outlined here. First, draw a decision tree consisting of decision and state-of-nature nodes and branches that describe the sequential nature of the problem. If you use the expected value approach, the next step is to determine the probabilities for each of the state-of-nature branches and compute the expected value at each state-of-nature node. Then select the decision branch leading to the state-of-nature node with the best expected value. The decision alternative associated with this branch is the recommended decision. The Management Science in Action article on decision analysis and the selection of home mortgages describes how the decision analysis approach can be used to help home buyers select the best type of mortgage.

MANAGEMENT SCIENCE in action

Decision Analysis and the Selection
of Home Mortgages[*]

Purchasing a new home can be a stressful experience, especially when it may commit the new owners to a mortgage contract for the next 20–30 years. The decision is further complicated by the fact that mortgages have varying interest rates that range from traditional fixed-rate mortgages (FRM) to adjustable-rate mortgages (ARM) with a wide variety of special features.

A decision analysis approach to selecting the best type of mortgage involves the development of a decision tree that includes one branch for each of the mortgage alternatives available. For example, if the buyer is considering three different mortgage contracts—fixed rate, variable rate with a 3-year adjustment, and variable rate with a 5-year adjustment—the decision tree begins with three decision alternative branches.

The future events that indicate what can happen to interest rates over time are the states of nature branches for the decision tree. For instance, variable-rate mortgage branches have state-of-nature branches that indicate possible interest rate increases and decreases. The complete decision tree shows the outcomes for each mortgage alternative and its associated cost.

Using decision analysis criteria reflecting a conservative or an optimistic perspective, a prospective home buyer can select a recommended mortgage alternative. If probability estimates are available for the future mortgage rates, the expected value approach will use the probability information to recommend the best mortgage alternative.

....

*Source: Luna, Robert E., and Richard A. Reid, "Mortgage Selection Using a Decision Tree Approach." *Interfaces,* vol. 16, no. 3, May–June 1986, pp. 73–81.

14.4 Sensitivity Analysis

In this section we consider how changes in the probability estimates for the states of nature affect or alter the recommended decision alternative. The study of the effect of such changes is referred to as *sensitivity analysis.*

One approach to sensitivity analysis is to consider different probabilities for the states of nature and recompute the expected value for each decision alternative. Repeating this computation for several different probabilities, we can begin to learn how changes in the probabilities for the states of nature affect the recommended decision. For example, in the PDC problem, suppose that the probability of high acceptance is reduced to 0.2 and that the probability of low acceptance is increased to 0.8. Using $P(s_1) = 0.2$, $P(s_2) = 0.8$, and equation (14.4), we obtain the expected value for each decision alternative:

$$EV(d_1) = 0.2(8) + 0.8(7) = 7.2$$

$$EV(d_2) = 0.2(14) + 0.8(5) = 6.8$$

$$EV(d_3) = 0.2(20) + 0.8(-9) = -3.2$$

Thus, with these probabilities the recommended decision alternative is to construct a small condominium complex (d_1), with an expected value of $7.2 million. The probability of high acceptance is only 0.2, so constructing the large condominium complex (d_3) is the least preferred alternative, with an expected value or loss of $3.2 million.

Thus, when the probability of high acceptance is large, PDC should build the large complex; when the probability of high acceptance is small, PDC should build the small complex. Obviously, we could continue to modify the probabilities of the states of nature and learn even more about how changes in the probabilities affect the recommended decision alternative. The only drawback to this approach is the numerous calculations required to evaluate the effect of several possible changes in the state-of-nature probabilities.

For the special case of two states of nature, a graphical procedure substantially eases the sensitivity analysis computations. To demonstrate this procedure, we let p denote the probability of state of nature s_1; that is, $P(s_1) = p$. With only two states of nature in the PDC problem, the probability of state of nature s_2 is

$$P(s_2) = 1 - P(s_1) = 1 - p$$

Using equation (14.4) and the payoff values in Table 14.1, we determine the expected value for decision alternative d_1 as follows:

$$EV(d_1) = P(s_1)(8) + P(s_2)(7)$$

$$= p(8) + (1 - p)(7)$$

$$= 8p + 7 - 7p = p + 7 \qquad (14.5)$$

Repeating the expected value computations for decision alternatives d_2 and d_3, we obtain expressions for the expected value of each decision alternative as a function of p:

$$EV(d_2) = 9p + 5 \qquad (14.6)$$

$$EV(d_3) = 29p - 9 \qquad (14.7)$$

Thus, we have developed three equations that show the expected value of the three decision alternatives as a function of the probability of state of nature s_1.

We continue by developing a graph with values of p on the horizontal axis and the associated EVs on the vertical axis. Because equations (14.5), (14.6), and (14.7) are linear equations, the graph of each equation is a straight line. For each equation, then, we can obtain the line by identifying two points that satisfy the equation and drawing a line through the points. For instance, if we let $p = 0$ in equation (14.5), $EV(d_1) = 7$. Then, letting $p = 1$, $EV(d_1) = 8$. Connecting these two points, $(0, 7)$ and $(1, 8)$, provides the line labeled $EV(d_1)$ in Figure 14.4. Similarly, we obtain the lines labeled $EV(d_2)$ and $EV(d_3)$; these lines are the graphs of equations (14.6) and (14.7), respectively.

Figure 14.4 shows how the recommended decision changes as p, the probability of the high acceptance state of nature (s_1), changes. Note that for small values of p, decision alternative d_1 (small complex) provides the largest expected value and is thus the recommended decision. When the value of p increases to a certain point, decision alternative d_2 (medium complex) provides the largest expected value and is the recommended decision. Finally, for large values of p, decision alternative d_3 (large complex) becomes the recommended decision.

The value of p for which the expected values of d_1 and d_2 are equal is the value of p corresponding to the intersection of the $EV(d_1)$ and the $EV(d_2)$ lines. To determine this value, we set $EV(d_1) = EV(d_2)$ and solve for the value of p:

$$p + 7 = 9p + 5$$

$$8p = 2$$

$$p = \frac{2}{8} = 0.25$$

Hence, whenever $p = 0.25$, decision alternatives d_1 and d_2 provide the same expected value. Repeating this calculation for the value of p corresponding to the intersection of the $EV(d_2)$ and $EV(d_3)$ lines we obtain $p = 0.70$.

Figure 14.4
. . . .
Expected Value for the PDC Decision Alternatives as a Function of p

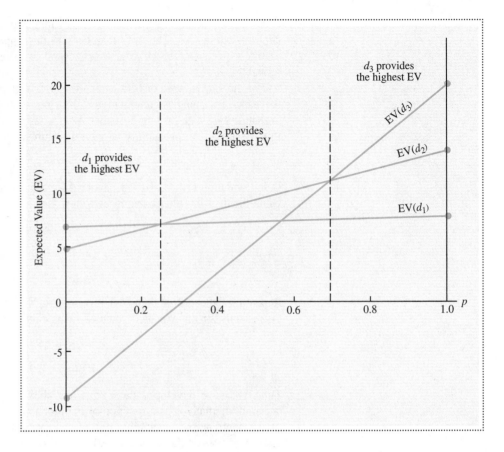

Using Figure 14.4, we can conclude that decision alternative d_1 provides the largest expected value for $p < 0.25$, decision alternative d_2 provides the largest expected value for $0.25 < p < 0.70$, and decision alternative d_3 provides the largest expected value for $p > 0.70$. Since p is simply the probability of state of nature s_1 and $(1-p)$ is the probability of state of nature s_2, we now have the sensitivity analysis information that tells us how changes in the state-of-nature probabilities affect the recommended decision alternative.

The benefit of performing sensitivity analysis is that it can provide a better perspective on management's original judgment regarding the state-of-nature probabilities. Management originally estimated the probability of high customer acceptance as $P(s_1) = 0.8$. As a result, decision alternative d_3 was recommended. After carrying out the sensitivity analysis, we can now tell management that as long as $P(s_1) > 0.70$, the d_3 decision alternative remains optimal.

The graphical sensitivity analysis procedure just described for the PDC problem applies only to decision analysis problems with two states of nature. However, sensitivity analysis also is important in problems with more than two states of nature. In these cases, a spreadsheet or computer software package can be used to assist with the computations. Basically, we return to the approach of testing a variety of likely changes for the state-of-nature probabilities. The spreadsheet or software package is helpful in making the necessary expected value computations and providing the decision alternative recommendations with a minimum of time and effort.

You should now be able to use graphical sensitivity analysis to determine how changes in the probability estimates affect the recommended decision. Try Problem 8.

14.5   Expected Value of Perfect Information

Suppose that PDC has the opportunity to conduct a market research study that would help evaluate buyer interest in the condominium project and provide information that management could use to improve the probability assessments for the states of nature. To determine the potential value of this information, we begin by assuming that the study could provide *perfect information* regarding the states of nature; that is, we assume for the moment that PDC could determine with certainty which state of nature is going to occur. To make use of this perfect information, we will develop a decision strategy that PDC should follow once it knows which state of nature will occur. As we will show, a decision strategy is simply a decision rule that specifies the decision alternative to be selected after the new information becomes available.

To help determine the decision strategy for PDC, we have reproduced PDC's payoff table as Table 14.6. Note that, if PDC knew for sure that state of nature s_1 would occur, the best decision alternative would be d_3, with a payoff of $20 million. Similarly, if PDC knew for sure that state of nature s_2 would occur, the best decision alternative would be d_1, with a payoff of $7 million. Thus, we can state PDC's optimal decision strategy based on perfect information as follows:

If s_1, select d_3.

If s_2, select d_1.

What is the expected value for this decision strategy? To compute the expected value with perfect information, we return to the original probability estimates for the states of nature: $P(s_1) = 0.8$, and $P(s_2) = 0.2$. Based on these probabilities, there is a 0.8 probability that the perfect information will indicate state of nature s_1. In this case, the resulting decision alternative d_3 will provide a $20 million profit. Similarly, with a 0.2 probability for state of nature s_2, the resulting decision alternative d_1 will provide a $7 million profit. Thus, from equation (14.4), the expected value of the decision strategy that uses perfect information is

$$0.8(20) + 0.2(7) = 17.4$$

We refer to the expected value of $17.4 million as the *expected value with perfect information* (EVwPI).

Recall from Section 14.3 that the recommended decision using the expected value approach is decision alternative d_3, with an expected value of $14.2 million. Because this decision recommendation and expected value computation were made without the benefit of perfect information, $14.2 million is referred to as the *expected value without perfect information* (EVwoPI).

Table 14.6

Payoff Table for the PDC Condominium Project ($ Million)

Decision Alternative	State of Nature	
	High Acceptance s_1	Low Acceptance s_2
Small complex, d_1	8	7
Medium complex, d_2	14	5
Large complex, d_3	20	−9

Figure 14.5

The Expected Value of Perfect Information

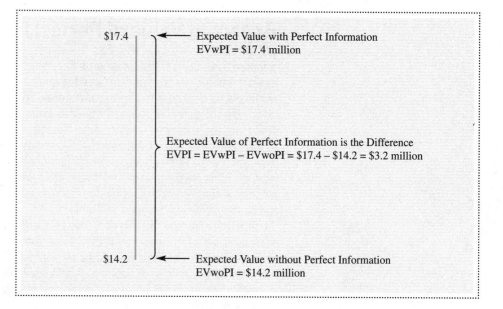

The expected value with perfect information is $17.4 million and the expected value without perfect information is $14.2; therefore, the expected value of the perfect information (EVPI) is $17.4 − $14.2 = $3.2 million. In other words, $3.2 million represents the additional expected value that can be obtained if perfect information were available about the states of nature. Figure 14.5 provides a summary of the computation of EVPI for the PDC problem.

Generally speaking, a market research study will not provide "perfect" information; however, if the market research study is a good one, the information gathered might be worth a sizable portion of the $3.2 million. Given the EVPI of $3.2 million, PDC should seriously consider the market survey as a way to obtain more information about the states of nature.

In general, the expected value of perfect information is computed as follows.

E x p e c t e d   V a l u e   o f   P e r f e c t   I n f o r m a t i o n

$$EVPI = |EVwPI - EVwoPI| \qquad (14.8)$$

where

EVPI = expected value of perfect information

EVwPI = expected value *with* perfect information about the states of nature

EVwoPI = expected value *without* perfect information about the states of nature

---

You should be able to determine the expected value of perfect information. Try Problem 12(d).

Note the role of the absolute value in equation (14.8). That is, for minimization problems the expected value with perfect information is always less than or equal to the expected value without perfect information. In this case, EVPI is the magnitude of the difference between EVwPI and EVwoPI, or the absolute value of the difference as shown in equation (14.8).

NOTES & comments

We restate the *opportunity loss*, or *regret*, table for the PDC problem (see Table 14.4) as follows.

Decision Alternative	State of Nature	
	High Acceptance s_1	Low Acceptance s_2
Small complex, d_1	12	0
Medium complex, d_2	6	2
Large complex, d_3	0	16

Using $P(s_1)$, $P(s_2)$, and the opportunity loss values, we can compute the *expected opportunity loss* (EOL) for each decision alternative. With $P(s_1) = 0.8$ and $P(s_2) = 0.2$, the expected opportunity loss for each of the three decision alternatives is

$$EOL(d_1) = 0.8(12) + 0.2(0) = 9.6$$

$$EOL(d_2) = 0.8(6) + 0.2(2) = 5.2$$

$$EOL(d_3) = 0.8(0) + 0.2(16) = 3.2$$

Regardless of whether the decision analysis involves maximization or minimization, the *minimum* expected opportunity loss always provides the best decision alternative. Thus, with $EOL(d_3) = 3.2$, d_3 is the recommended decision. In addition, the minimum expected opportunity loss always is *equal to the expected value of perfect information.* That is, EOL(best decision) = EVPI; for the PDC problem, this value is $3.2 million.

14.6 Decision Analysis with Sample Information

In applying the expected value approach, we have shown how probability information about the states of nature affects the expected value calculations and thus the decision recommendation. Frequently, decision makers have preliminary or prior probability estimates for the states of nature that are the best probability values available. However, to make the best possible decision, the decision maker may want to seek additional information about the states of nature. This new information can be used to revise or update the prior probabilities so that the final decision is based on more accurate probability estimates for the states of nature.

Most often, additional information is obtained through experiments designed to provide sample information about the states of nature. Raw material sampling, product testing, and market research studies are examples of experiments that may enable management to revise or update the state-of-nature probabilities. In the following

Figure 14.6

Probability Revision Based on New Information

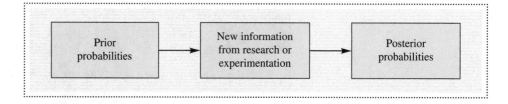

discussion, we will reconsider the PDC problem and show how to use sample information to revise the state-of-nature probabilities. We will then show how to use the revised probabilities to develop an optimal decision strategy for PDC.

Recall that PDC's management provided initial subjective probability estimates of 0.8 for high market acceptance and 0.2 for low market acceptance. Since $P(s_1) = 0.8$ and $P(s_2) = 0.2$ were estimates developed prior to the collection of any sample information, they are referred to as the *prior probabilities* for the states of nature. Recall that, using these prior probabilities, we determined that d_3, the decision to construct the large condominium complex, was optimal, yielding an expected value of $14.2 million. Calculation of the expected value of perfect information showed that new information about the states of nature could potentially be worth as much as $3.2 million.

Suppose that PDC considers undertaking a six-month market research study designed to evaluate market acceptance and ultimately buyer interest in purchasing the condominium units. The market research will provide new information that can be combined with the prior probabilities through a Bayesian procedure to obtain updated or revised probability estimates for the states of nature. These *revised* probabilities are called *posterior probabilities*. Figure 14.6 depicts the process of revising probabilities.

We will refer to the new information obtained through research or experimentation as an *indicator*. In many cases the experiment conducted to obtain the additional information will consist of taking a statistical sample, so the new information also is often referred to as *sample information*.

Using the indicator terminology, we can denote the outcomes of the PDC market research study as

I_1 = favorable market research report (i.e., the individuals contacted generally express interest in purchasing a PDC condominium)

I_2 = unfavorable market research report (i.e., the individuals contacted generally express little interest in purchasing a PDC condominium)

Given one of these possible indicators, the objective is to provide improved estimates of the probabilities of the two states of nature. The end result of the *Bayesian revision* process depicted in Figure 14.6 is a set of posterior probabilities of the form $P(s_j \mid I_k)$, where $P(s_j \mid I_k)$ represents the conditional probability that state of nature s_j will occur given that the outcome of the market research study is indicator I_k.

To make effective use of this indicator information, we must know something about the probability relationships between the indicators and the states of nature. For example, in the PDC problem, given that the state of nature ultimately turns out to be high acceptance, what is the probability that the market research study will result in a favorable report? In this case, we are asking about the conditional probability of indicator I_1 given state of nature s_1, written $P(I_1 \mid s_1)$. To carry out the analysis, we will need conditional probabilities for all indicators given all states of nature, that is, $P(I_1 \mid s_1)$, $P(I_1 \mid s_2)$, $P(I_2 \mid s_1)$, and $P(I_2 \mid s_2)$.

In the PDC problem, we assume that the following estimates are available for the conditional probabilities.

State of Nature	Market Research	
	Favorable, I_1	Unfavorable, I_2
High acceptance, s_1	$P(I_1 \mid s_1) = 0.90$	$P(I_2 \mid s_1) = 0.10$
Low acceptance, s_2	$P(I_1 \mid s_2) = 0.25$	$P(I_2 \mid s_2) = 0.75$

Note that these probability estimates provide a reasonable degree of confidence in the market research study. If the true state of nature is s_1, the probability of a favorable market research report (I_1) is 0.90 and the probability of an unfavorable market research report (I_2) is 0.10. If the true state of nature is s_2, the probability of a favorable market research report is 0.25 and the probability of an unfavorable market research report is 0.75. The reason for a 0.25 probability of a potentially misleading favorable market research report for state of nature s_2 is that when some potential buyers first hear about the new condominium project, their enthusiasm may lead them to overstate their real interest in it. A potential buyer's initial favorable response can change quickly to a "no thank you" when later faced with the reality of signing a purchase contract and making a down payment.

14.7 Developing a Decision Strategy

A decision strategy is a rule that is to be followed by the decision maker. In the PDC problem, a decision strategy is a rule that recommends a particular decision based on whether the market research report is favorable or unfavorable. We will use a decision tree analysis to find the optimal decision strategy for PDC.

Figure 14.7 shows the decision tree for the PDC problem if a market research study is conducted. Note that, from left to right, the tree shows the natural or logical order that will occur in the decision-making process. First, PDC will obtain the market research indicator (I_1 or I_2); then a decision (d_1, d_2, or d_3) will be made; finally, the state of nature (s_1 or s_2) will occur. The decision and the state of nature combine to provide the final profit or payoff.

Using decision tree terminology, we have now introduced an *indicator node,* node 1, and *indicator branches,* I_1 and I_2. Since the branches emanating from indicator nodes are not under the control of the decision maker, but are determined by chance, these nodes are represented by a circle as we did for the state-of-nature nodes. Nodes 2 and 3 are decision nodes, whereas nodes 4, 5, 6, 7, 8, and 9 are state-of-nature nodes. For decision nodes, the decision maker must select the specific branch d_1, d_2, or d_3 that will be taken. Selecting the best decision branch is equivalent to making the best decision. However, as the indicator and state-of-nature branches are not controlled by the decision maker, the specific branch leaving an indicator or a state-of-nature node will depend on the probability associated with the branch. Thus, before we can carry out an analysis of the decision tree and develop a decision strategy, we must compute the probability of each indicator branch and the probability of each state-of-nature branch. Note from the decision tree that the state-of-nature branches occur *after* the indicator branches. Thus, when we attempt to compute state-of-nature branch probabilities, we will need to consider which indicator was previously observed. That is, we will express the state-of-nature probabilities in terms of the probability of state of nature s_j *given* that indicator I_k was observed. Thus, all state-of-nature probabilities will be expressed in a $P(s_j \mid I_k)$ form.

Figure 14.7

PDC Decision Tree Incorporating
the Results of the Market Research
Study (Payoffs in $ Million)

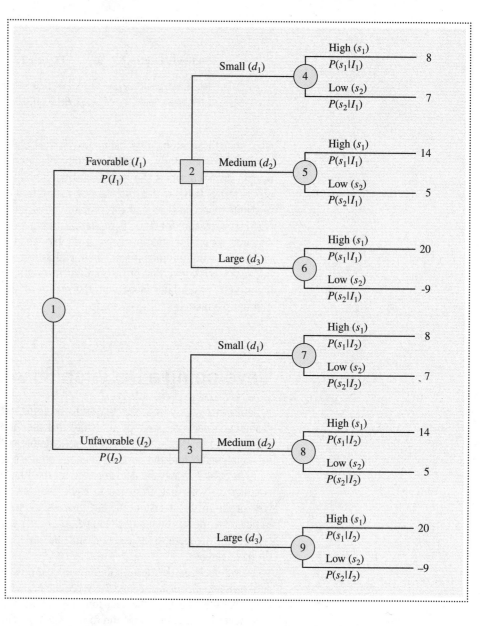

Computing Branch Probabilities

Recall that the prior probabilities for PDC are $P(s_1) = 0.8$ and $P(s_2) = 0.2$. In Section 14.6 we identified the relationships between the market research indicators and states of nature with the conditional probabilities

$$P(I_1 \mid s_1) = 0.90 \qquad P(I_2 \mid s_1) = 0.10$$
$$P(I_1 \mid s_2) = 0.25 \qquad P(I_2 \mid s_2) = 0.75$$

To develop a decision strategy utilizing the decision tree in Figure 14.7, we need indicator branch probabilities $P(I_k)$ and state-of-nature branch probabilities $P(s_j \mid I_k)$. The problem now is to determine how to use the prior probability estimates $P(s_j)$ and the conditional probability estimates $P(I_k \mid s_j)$ to calculate the branch probabilities $P(I_k)$ and $P(s_j \mid I_k)$. In

Table 14.7

Branch Probabilities for the PDC Condominium Project Based on Indicator I_1, a Favorable Market Research Report

States of Nature s_j	Prior Probabilities $P(s_j)$	Conditional Probabilities $P(I_1 \mid s_j)$	Joint Probabilities $P(I_1 \cap s_j)$	Posterior Probabilities $P(s_j \mid I_1)$
s_1	0.8	0.90	0.72	0.9351
s_2	0.2	0.25	0.05	0.0649
			$P(I_1) = 0.77$	

Table 14.8

Branch Probabilities for the PDC Condominium Project Based on Indicator I_2, an Unfavorable Market Research Report

States of Nature s_j	Prior Probabilities $P(s_j)$	Conditional Probabilities $P(I_2 \mid s_j)$	Joint Probabilities $P(I_2 \cap s_j)$	Posterior Probabilities $P(s_j \mid I_2)$
s_1	0.8	0.10	0.08	0.3478
s_2	0.2	0.75	0.15	0.6522
			$P(I_2) = 0.23$	

this section we will show how to use a Bayesian revision process to calculate the branch probabilities $P(I_k)$ and $P(s_j \mid I_k)$.

A probability relationship or formula known as Bayes' Theorem can be used to revise or update the prior probability values based on new information from research or experimentation. In the following discussion we present a tabular approach as a convenient method for carrying out the computations to obtain the revised or posterior probabilities. We will use this tabular approach to compute the branch probabilities for the PDC decision tree. The computations for the PDC problem based on a favorable market research report (I_1) are summarized in Table 14.7. The steps used to develop this table are as follows.

Step 1   In column 1 enter the states of nature. In column 2 enter the prior probabilities for the states of nature. In column 3 enter the conditional probabilities of indicator I_1 for each state of nature.

Step 2   In column 4 compute the joint probabilities for each state of nature–indicator combination by multiplying the prior probability entry in column 2 by the corresponding conditional probability entry in column 3.

Step 3   Sum the joint probabilities in column 4 to obtain $P(I_1)$, the probability of indicator I_1.

Step 4   Compute the posterior probabilities in column 5 by dividing each joint probability entry in column 4 by $P(I_1) = 0.77$.

Table 14.7 shows that the probability of obtaining a favorable market research report is $P(I_1) = 0.77$. In addition, $P(s_1 \mid I_1) = 0.9351$ and $P(s_2 \mid I_1) = 0.0649$ show the posterior probabilities of the states of nature based on a favorable market report. In particular, note that if the market report is favorable, there is a 0.9351 probability of a high market acceptance (s_1) of the condominium project. A favorable market research report will encourage PDC to go ahead with plans to build the large condominium complex.

The tabular procedure must be repeated for each possible indicator. Table 14.8 shows the computations of the branch probabilities for the PDC problem based on an

Figure 14.8

Decision Tree with Branch Probabilities

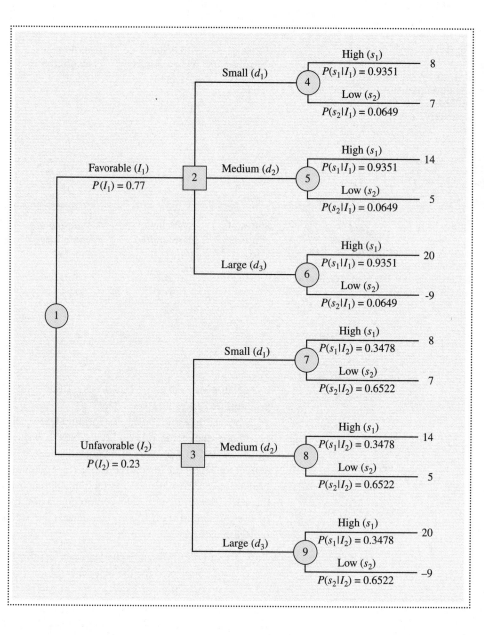

You should now be able to compute revised or posterior probabilities. Try Problem 14.

unfavorable market research report (I_2). Note that the probability of obtaining an unfavorable market research report is $P(I_2) = 0.23$. If an unfavorable report is obtained, the posterior probability of a high market acceptance (s_1) is 0.3478 and of a low market acceptance (s_2) is 0.6522. The branch probabilities from Table 14.7 and 14.8 are shown on the PDC decision tree in Figure 14.8.

An Optimal Decision Strategy

After we have computed the branch probabilities, we can use the expected value approach to determine the optimal decision strategy. Working *backward* through the decision tree in Figure 14.8, we first compute the expected value at each state-of-nature

Figure 14.9

Developing a Decision Strategy for the PDC Problem

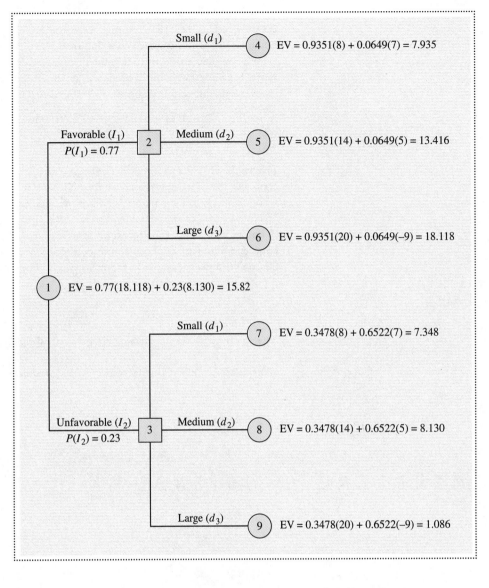

node. That is, at each state-of-nature node, we weight the possible payoffs by their chance of occurring. Thus, the expected values for nodes 4–9 are

$$EV(\text{node } 4) = 0.9351(8) + 0.0649(7) = 7.935$$

$$EV(\text{node } 5) = 0.9351(14) + 0.0649(5) = 13.416$$

$$EV(\text{node } 6) = 0.9351(20) + 0.0649(-9) = 18.118$$

$$EV(\text{node } 7) = 0.3478(8) + 0.6522(7) = 7.348$$

$$EV(\text{node } 8) = 0.3478(14) + 0.6522(5) = 8.130$$

$$EV(\text{node } 9) = 0.3478(20) + 0.6522(-9) = 1.086$$

Figure 14.9 shows these calculations on the decision tree. Since the decision maker controls the branch leaving a decision node and is trying to maximize expected profit, the optimal decision at node 2 is d_3, with an expected value of 18.118. Thus, we write EV(node 2) as 18.118. A similar analysis at node 3 shows that the optimal decision branch is d_2, with an expected value of 8.130. Thus, EV(node 3) = 8.130.

We continue working backward in order to determine the expected value of node 1. Node 1 has two probability branches leaving it, corresponding to indicators I_1 and I_2. We must use the branch probabilities, $P(I_1)$ and $P(I_2)$, to compute the overall expected value:

$$EV(\text{node 1}) = (0.77)EV(\text{node 2}) + (0.23)EV(\text{node 3})$$

$$= (0.77)(18.118) + (0.23)(8.130) = 15.82$$

The value $15.82 million is the expected value of the optimal decision strategy if PDC conducts the market research study and uses the resulting information to determine a recommended size for the condominium complex.

Note that PDC has not yet determined the size for the complex. Management will need to know the results of the market research study before deciding whether to construct the large complex (d_3) or the medium complex (d_2). The results of the decision analysis at this point, however, provide the following optimal decision strategy.

If	Then
Market research report is favorable (I_1),	Construct the large condominium complex (d_3).
Market research report is unfavorable (I_2),	Construct the medium condominium complex (d_2).

MANAGEMENT SCIENCE in action

Decision Analysis and Drug Testing for Student Athletes[*]

The athletic governing board of Santa Clara University considered whether to implement a drug-testing program for the university's intercollegiate athletes. The decision analysis framework contains two decision alternatives: implement a drug-testing program and do not implement a drug-testing program. Each student athlete is either a drug user or not a drug user, so these two possibilities are considered to be the states of nature for the problem.

If the drug-testing program is implemented, student athletes will be required to take a drug-screening test. Results of the test will be either positive (test indicates a potential drug user) or negative (test does not indicate a potential drug user). The test outcomes are considered to be the indicators in the decision problem. If the test result is negative, no follow-up action will be

taken. However, if the test result is positive, follow-up action will be taken to determine whether the student athlete actually is a drug user. The payoffs include the cost of not identifying a drug user and the cost of falsely identifying a nonuser.

Decision analysis showed that if the test result is positive, there is still a reasonably high probability that the student athlete is not a drug user. The cost and other problems associated with this type of misleading test result were considered significant. Consequently, the athletic governing board decided not to implement the drug-testing program.

....

*Source: Feinstein, Charles D., "Deciding Whether to Test Student Athletes for Drug Use." *Interfaces,* vol. 20, no. 3, May–June 1990, pp. 80–87.

Although other decision analysis problems may not be as simple as the PDC problem, the optimal decision strategy approach outlined is still applicable. First, draw a decision tree consisting of indicator, decision, and state-of-nature nodes and branches that describes the sequential nature of the problem. Make posterior probability calculations to establish indicator and state-of-nature branch probabilities. Then, by working backward through the tree, computing expected values at state-of-nature and indicator nodes, and selecting the best decision branch at decision nodes, determine an optimal decision strategy and its associated expected value. The Management Science in Action article on drug testing for student athletes describes how Santa Clara University used decision analysis to make a decision regarding whether to implement a drug-testing program for student athletes.

14.8 Expected Value of Sample Information

The optimal decision strategy developed in the preceding section shows that if the market research report is favorable, PDC should construct the large condominium complex. However, if the market research report is unfavorable, PDC should construct the medium condominium complex. The expected value of this optimal decision strategy, $15.82 million, is the *expected value with sample information* (EVwSI).

In Section 14.3 we used the expected value approach to recommend a decision alternative based on PDC's original probability estimates of $P(s_1) = 0.8$ and $P(s_2) = 0.2$. That analysis showed that d_3, with an expected value of $14.2 million, is the best decision. However, that recommendation lacked the benefit of sample information, so the $14.2 million result is the *expected value without sample information* (EVwoSI).

Since the expected value with sample information is $15.82 million and the expected value without sample information is $14.2 million, the expected value of the sample information (EVSI) is $15.82 − $14.2 = $1.62 million. In other words, $1.62 million is the increase in the expected value based on the sample information. In general, the expected value of sample information is computed as follows.

> ## Expected Value of Sample Information
> $$EVSI = |\,EVwSI - EVwoSI\,| \qquad (14.9)$$
> where
>
>   EVSI = expected value of sample information
> EVwSI = expected value *with* sample information about the states of nature
> EVwoSI = expected value *without* sample information about the states of nature

Note the role of the absolute value in equation (14.9). That is, for minimization problems the expected value with sample information always is less than or equal to the expected value without sample information. In this case, EVSI is the magnitude of the difference between EVwSI and EVwoSI; thus, by taking the absolute value of the difference as shown in equation (14.9), we can handle both the maximization and minimization cases with one equation.

Efficiency of Sample Information

In Section 14.5 we showed that the expected value of perfect information (EVPI) for the PDC problem is $3.2 million. We never anticipated that the market research report would obtain perfect information, but we can use an *efficiency* measure to express the value of the market research information. With perfect information having an efficiency rating of 100%, the efficiency rating E for sample information is computed as follows.

Efficiency of Sample Information

$$E = \frac{EVSI}{EVPI} \times 100 \qquad (14.10)$$

For the PDC problem,

$$E = \frac{1.62}{3.2} \times 100 = 50.6\%$$

In other words, the information from the market research study is 50.6% as efficient as perfect information.

Low efficiency ratings for sample information might lead the decision maker to look for other types of information. However, high efficiency ratings indicate that the sample information is almost as good as perfect information and that additional sources of information would not yield significantly better results.

NOTES & comments

1. The use of microcomputer software packages for decision analysis is becoming commonplace. The ARBORIST, a software package available from Texas Instruments, allows the user to develop a graph of the decision tree on the screen; the package will then perform all the decision analysis calculations. Another product, SUPERTREE, from SDG Decision Systems, requires the user to specify the tree in a manner similar to that used in PERT/CPM problems; that is, the user provides the system with the nodes and their immediate predecessors, and the software package develops the resulting decision tree. Although packages such as the ARBORIST and SUPERTREE are not needed for problems as small as those introduced in this chapter, computer support is necessary for larger decision problems.

2. The expected value without perfect information (EVwoPI) defined in Section 14.5 and the expected value without sample information (EVwoSI) defined in Section 14.8 are the same. This value simply represents the expected value of the best decision based on prior probabilities.

14.9 Utility and Decision Making

In the previous sections of this chapter we expressed the payoffs in terms of monetary values. When probability information was available about the states of nature, we recommended selecting the decision alternative with the best expected monetary value. However, in some situations the decision alternative with the best expected monetary value may not be the most desirable decision.

By the most desirable decision we mean the one that is preferred by the decision maker after taking into account not only monetary value, but also other factors such as the risk associated with the outcomes. Examples of situations in which selecting the decision alternative with the best expected monetary value may not lead to the selection of the most preferred decision are numerous. One such example is the decision to buy house insurance. Clearly, buying insurance for a house does not provide a higher expected monetary value than not buying such insurance. Otherwise, insurance companies could not pay expenses and make a profit. Similarly, many people buy tickets for state lotteries even though the expected monetary value of such a decision is negative.

Should we conclude that persons or businesses that buy insurance or participate in lotteries do so because they are unable to determine which decision alternative leads to the best expected monetary value? On the contrary, we take the view that in these cases monetary value is not the sole measure of the true worth of the outcome to the decision maker.

We will see that in cases where expected monetary value does not lead to the most preferred decision alternative, expressing the value (or worth) of an outcome in terms of its *utility* will permit the use of *expected utility* to identify the most desirable decision.

The Meaning of Utility

Utility is a measure of the total worth of a particular outcome; it reflects the decision maker's attitude toward a collection of factors such as profit, loss, and risk. As an example of a case where utility can help in selecting the best decision alternative, let us consider the problem faced by Swofford, Inc., a relatively small real estate investment firm located in Atlanta, Georgia. Swofford currently has two investment opportunities, which require approximately the same cash outlay. The cash requirements necessary prohibit Swofford from making more than one investment at this time. Consequently, there are three possible decision alternatives that may be considered.

The three decision alternatives, denoted by d_1, d_2, and d_3, are as follows:

$$d_1 = \text{make investment A}$$
$$d_2 = \text{make investment B}$$
$$d_3 = \text{do not invest}$$

The monetary payoffs associated with the investment opportunities depend largely on what happens to the real estate market during the next 6 months. Real estate prices will go up, remain stable, or go down. Thus, the states of nature, denoted by s_1, s_2, and s_3, are as follows:

$$s_1 = \text{real estate prices go up}$$
$$s_2 = \text{real estate prices remain stable}$$
$$s_3 = \text{real estate prices go down}$$

Table 14.9

Payoff Table for Swofford, Inc. (Profit in $)

		State of Nature		
Decision Alternative		Prices Up s_1	Prices Stable s_2	Prices Down s_3
Investment A,	d_1	30,000	20,000	−50,000
Investment B,	d_2	50,000	−20,000	−30,000
Do not invest,	d_3	0	0	0

Using the best information available, Swofford has estimated the profits or payoffs associated with each decision alternative and state-of-nature combination. The resulting payoff table is show in Table 14.9.

The best estimate of the probability that prices will go up is 0.3, the best estimate of the probability that prices will remain stable is 0.5, and the best estimate of the probability that real estate prices will go down is 0.2. Thus, the expected values for the three decision alternatives are

$$EV(d_1) = 0.3(\$30,000) + 0.5(\$20,000) + 0.2(-\$50,000) = \$9,000$$

$$EV(d_2) = 0.3(\$50,000) + 0.5(-\$20,000) + 0.2(-\$30,000) = -\$1,000$$

$$EV(d_3) = 0.3(\$0) + 0.5(\$0) + 0.2(\$0) = \$0$$

Using the expected value approach, the optimal decision is to select investment A, with an expected monetary value of $9000. Is this really the best decision alternative? Let us consider some other relevant factors that relate to Swofford's capability for absorbing the $50,000 loss if investment A is made and real estate prices go down.

It turns out that Swofford's financial position is very weak. This was partly reflected in Swofford's ability to undertake, at most, one investment at the current time. More important, however, the firm's president feels that if the next investment results in substantial losses, Swofford's future will be in jeopardy. Although the expected value approach leads to a recommendation for d_1, do you think this is the decision the firm's president would prefer? We suspect that d_2 or d_3 would be selected to avoid the possibility of incurring a $50,000 loss. In fact, it is reasonable to believe that if a loss as great as even $30,000 could drive Swofford out of business, the president would select d_3, feeling that both investment A and investment B are too risky for Swofford's current financial position.

The way we resolve Swofford's dilemma is first to determine Swofford's utility for the various monetary outcomes. Recall that the utility of any outcome is the total worth of that outcome, taking into account the risks and payoffs involved. If the utilities for the various outcomes are assessed correctly, then the decision alternative with the highest expected utility is the most preferred or best alternative.

Developing Utilities for Payoffs

The procedure we will use to establish utility values for the payoffs requires that we first assign a utility value to the best and worst possible payoffs in the decision situation. Any values will work as long as the utility assigned to the best payoff is greater than the utility assigned to the worst payoff. In Swofford's case, Table 14.9 shows that $50,000 is the best payoff and −$50,000 is the worst payoff. Suppose, then, that we arbitrarily make the following assignments of these two payoffs:

$$\text{Utility of } -\$50,000 = U(-\$50,000) = 0$$

$$\text{Utility of } \$50,000 = U(\$50,000) = 10$$

Now let us see how we can determine the utility associated with every other payoff.

Consider the process of establishing the utility of a payoff of $30,000. First, we ask Swofford's president to state a preference between a guaranteed $30,000 payoff and the opportunity to engage in the following *lottery,* or bet:

Lottery: Swofford obtains a payoff of $50,000 with probability p
and a payoff of −$50,000 with probability $(1 - p)$.

If p is very close to 1, Swofford's president would prefer the lottery to the certain payoff of $30,000 since the firm would virtually guarantee itself a payoff of $50,000. On the other hand, if p is very close to 0, the president would clearly prefer the guarantee of $30,000. In any event, as p changes continuously from 0 to 1, the preference for the guaranteed payoff of $30,000 will change at some point into a preference for the lottery. At this value of p, there is no greater preference for the guaranteed payoff of $30,000 than for the lottery. For example, let us assume that when $p = 0.95$, the president is indifferent between the certain payoff of $30,000 and the lottery. Given this value of $p,$ we can compute the utility of a $30,000 payoff as follows:

$$U(\$30,000) = pU(\$50,000) + (1 - p)U(-\$50,000)$$

$$= 0.95(10) + (0.05)(0)$$

$$= 9.5$$

Obviously, if we had started with a different assignment of utilities for payoffs of $50,000 and −$50,000, we would have ended up with a different utility for $30,000. Hence, we must conclude that the utility assigned to each payoff is not unique, but merely depends on the initial choice of utilities for the best and worst payoffs. We will discuss this further at the end of this section. For now, however, we will continue to use a value of 10 for the utility of $50,000 and a value of 0 for the utility of −$50,000.

Before computing the utility for the other payoffs, let us consider the significance of assigning a utility of 9.5 to a payoff of $30,000. Clearly, when $p = 0.95$, the expected value of the lottery is

$$\text{EV(lottery)} = 0.95(\$50,000) + 0.05(-\$50,000)$$

$$= \$47,500 - \$2,500$$

$$= \$45,000$$

We see that although the expected value of the lottery when $p = 0.95$ is $45,000, Swofford's president would just as soon take a guaranteed payoff of $30,000 and thus take a conservative, or risk-avoiding, viewpoint. That is, the president would rather have $30,000 for certain than risk anything greater than a 5% chance of incurring a loss of $50,000. One can view the difference between the EV of $45,000 for the lottery and the $30,000 guaranteed payoff as the risk premium that the president would be willing to pay to avoid the 5% chance of losing $50,000.

To compute the utility associated with a payoff of −$20,000, we must ask Swofford's president to state a preference between a guaranteed −$20,000 payoff and the opportunity to engage in the following lottery.

Lottery: Swofford obtains a payoff of $50,000 with probability p and a payoff of −$50,000 with probability $(1 − p)$.

Note that this is exactly the same lottery we used to establish the utility of a payoff of $30,000. In fact, this will be the lottery used to establish the utility for any monetary value in the Swofford payoff table. Using this lottery, then, we must ask the president to state the value of p that provides an indifference between a guaranteed payoff of −$20,000 and the lottery. For example, we might begin by asking the president to choose between a certain loss of $20,000 and the lottery with a payoff of $50,000 with probability $p = 0.90$ and a payoff of − $50,000 with probability $(1 − p) = 0.10$. What answer do you think we would get? Surely, with this high probability of obtaining a payoff of $50,000, the president would elect the lottery. Next, we might ask if $p = 0.85$ would result in indifference between the loss of $20,000 for certain and the lottery. Again, the president might tell us that the lottery would be preferred. Suppose that we continue in this fashion until we get to $p = 0.55$, where we find that with this value of p, the president is indifferent between the payoff of − $20,000 and the lottery. That is, for any value of p less than 0.55, the president would rather take a loss of $20,000 for certain than risk the potential loss of $50,000 with the lottery; for any value of p above 0.55, the president would elect the lottery. Thus, the utility assigned to a payoff of −$20,000 is

$$U(-\$20,000) = pU(50,000) + (1 − p)U(-\$50,000)$$

$$= 0.55(10) + 0.45(0)$$

$$= 5.5$$

Again, let us examine the significance of this assignment as compared with the expected value approach. When $p = 0.55$, the expected value of the lottery is

$$EV(lottery) = 0.55(\$50,000) + 0.45(-\$50,000)$$

$$= \$27,500 − \$22,500$$

$$= \$5,000$$

Thus, the president would just as soon absorb a loss of $20,000 for certain as take the lottery, even though the expected value of the lottery is $5000. Once again we see the conservative, or risk-avoiding, point of view of Swofford's president.

In the two preceding examples where we computed the utility for a specific monetary payoff, M, we first found the probability p where the decision maker was indifferent between a guaranteed payoff of M and a lottery with a payoff of $50,000 with probability p and −$50,000 with probability $(1 − p)$. The utility of M was then computed as

$$U(M) = pU(\$50,000) + (1 − p)U(-\$50,000)$$

$$= p(10) + (1 − p)0$$

$$= 10p$$

Using the above procedure, utility values for the rest of the payoffs in Swofford's problem were developed. The results are presented in Table 14.10.

Now that we have determined the utility value of each of the possible monetary values, we can write the original payoff table in terms of utility values. Table 14.11 shows the utility for the various outcomes in the Swofford problem. The notation we will use for the

Table 14.10

Utility of Monetary Payoffs for the Swofford, Inc., Problem

Monetary Value	Indifference Value of p	Utility Value
$ 50,000	Does not apply	10.0
30,000	0.95	9.5
20,000	0.90	9.0
0	0.75	7.5
−20,000	0.55	5.5
−30,000	0.40	4.0
−50,000	Does not apply	0.0

Table 14.11

Utility Table for Swofford, Inc., Problem

	State of Nature		
	Prices Up	Prices Stable	Prices Down
Decision Alternative	s_1	s_2	s_3
Investment A, d_1	9.5	9.0	0.0
Investment B, d_2	10.0	5.5	4.0
Do not invest, d_3	7.5	7.5	7.5

entries in the utility table is U_{ij}, which denotes the utility associated with decision alternative d_i and state of nature s_j. Using this notation, we see that $U_{23}, = 4.0$.

The Expected Utility Approach

We can now apply the expected value computations introduced in Section 14.3 to the payoffs in Table 14.11 in order to select an optimal decision alternative for Swofford, Inc. However, since utility values represent such a special case of expected value, we will refer to the expected value when applied to utility values as the *expected utility* (EU). In this way, we will avoid any possible confusion between the expected value for the original payoff table and the expected value for the payoff table consisting of *utility values*. Thus, the expected utility approach requires the analyst to compute the expected utility for each decision alternative and then select the alternative yielding the best expected utility. If there are N possible states of nature, the expected utility of a decision alternative d_i is given by

$$\text{EU}(d_i) = \sum_{j=1}^{N} P(s_j)U_{ij} \tag{14.11}$$

The expected utility for each of the decision alternatives in the Swofford problem is computed as follows:

$$\text{EU}(d_1) = 0.3(9.5) + 0.5(9.0) + 0.2(0) \quad = 7.35$$

$$\text{EU}(d_2) = 0.3(10) \ + 0.5(5.5) + 0.2(4.0) = 6.55$$

$$\text{EU}(d_3) = 0.3(7.5) + 0.5(7.5) + 0.2(7.5) = 7.50$$

We see that the optimal decision using the expected utility approach is d_3, do not invest. The ranking of alternatives according to the president's utility assignments and the associated monetary values is as follows:

You should now be able to use the expected utility approach to determine the optimal decision. Try Problem 30.

Ranking of Decision Alternatives	Expected Utility	Expected Monetary Value
Do not invest	7.50	$ 0
Investment A	7.35	9000
Investment B	6.55	−1000

Note that whereas investment A had the highest expected monetary value of $9000, the analysis indicates that Swofford should decline this investment. The rationale behind not selecting Investment A is that the 0.2 probability of a $50,000 loss was considered by Swofford's president to involve a serious risk. The seriousness of this risk and its associated impact on the company were not adequately reflected by the expected monetary value of investment A. It was necessary to assess the utility for each payoff to adequately take this risk into account.

Unfortunately, the determination of the appropriate utilities is not a trivial task. As we have seen, measuring utility requires a degree of subjectivity on the part of the decision maker, and different decision makers will have different utility functions. This aspect of utility often causes decision makers to feel uncomfortable about using the expected utility approach. However, if we encounter a decision situation in which we are convinced monetary value is not the only relevant measure of performance, utility analysis should be considered.

NOTES & comments

1. In the Swofford problem, we used a utility of 10 for the largest possible payoff and 0 for the smallest. Had we chosen 1 for the utility of the largest payoff and 0 for the utility of the smallest, the utility for any monetary value M would have been the value of p at which the decision maker was indifferent between a certain payoff of M and a lottery in which the best payoff is obtained with probability of p and the worst payoff is obtained with probability $(1 - p)$. Thus the utility for any monetary value would have been equal to the probability of earning the highest payoff. Often, this choice is made because of the ease in computation. We chose not to do so to emphasize the distinction between the utility values and the indifference probabilities for the lottery.

2. Generally, when the payoffs for a particular decision-making problem fall into a reasonable range—the best is not too good and the worst is not too bad—decision makers tend to express preferences in agreement with the expected value approach. Thus, as a guideline we suggest asking the decision maker to consider the best and worst possible payoffs for a problem and assess their reasonableness. If the decision maker believes they are in the reasonable range, the expected monetary value criterion can be used. However, if the payoffs appear unreasonably large or unreasonably small and if the decision maker feels monetary values do not adequately reflect the true preferences for the payoffs, a utility analysis of the problem should be considered.

Summary

In this chapter we showed how decision analysis can be used to solve problems with a reasonable number of decision alternatives and a reasonable number of states of nature. The goal of decision analysis is to identify the best decision alternative in the face of uncertain or risk-filled future events (i.e., states of nature).

We presented three approaches to decision making without probabilities and discussed the use of the expected value approach for decision making with probabilities. Then we showed how to use additional information about the states of nature to revise or update the probability estimates and develop an optimal decision strategy. We utilized the concepts of expected value of sample information, expected value of perfect information, and efficiency of information to evaluate the contribution of the sample information.

We suggested that the expected utility approach should be used in situations in which monetary value is not the only relevant measure of performance. Unlike monetary value, utility is a measure of the total worth of an outcome resulting from the choice of a decision alternative and the occurrence of a state of nature. As such, utility takes into account the decision maker's attitude toward the profit, loss, and risk associated with an outcome. In the examples, we have seen how the use of utility analysis can lead to decision recommendations that differ from those that would be selected using the expected monetary value approach.

Glossary

States of nature The uncontrollable future events that affect the payoff associated with a decision alternative.

Payoff The outcome measure, such as profit, cost, and time. Each combination of a decision alternative and a state of nature has an associated payoff.

Payoff table A tabular representation of the payoffs for a decision problem.

Decision tree A graphical representation of the decision problem that shows the sequential nature of the decision-making situation.

Node An intersection or junction point of a decision tree.

Branch A line or arc connecting nodes of a decision tree.

Optimistic approach An approach to choosing a decision alternative without using probabilities. For a maximization problem, it leads to choosing the decision alternative corresponding to the largest payoff; for a minimization problem, it leads to choosing the decision alternative corresponding to the smallest payoff.

Conservative approach An approach to choosing a decision alternative without using probabilities. For a maximization problem, it leads to choosing the decision alternative that maximizes the minimum payoff; for a minimization problem, it leads to choosing the decision alternative that minimizes the maximum payoff.

Minimax regret approach An approach to choosing a decision alternative without using probabilities. For each alternative, the maximum regret is computed. This approach leads to choosing the decision alternative that minimizes the maximum regret.

Opportunity loss, or regret The amount of loss (lower profit or higher cost) from not making the best decision for each state of nature.

Expected value approach An approach to choosing a decision alternative that is based upon the expected value of each decision alternative. The recommended decision alternative is the one that provides the best expected value.

Expected value (EV) For a decision alternative, it is the weighted average of the payoffs. The weights are the state-of-nature probabilities.

Sensitivity analysis The study of how changes in the probability estimates for the states of nature affect the recommended decision alternative.

Expected value of perfect information (EVPI) The expected value of information that would tell the decision maker exactly which state of nature is going to occur (i.e., perfect information).

Prior probabilities The probabilities of the states of nature prior to obtaining sample information.

Posterior (revised) probabilities The probabilities of the states of nature after revising the prior probabilities based on given indicator information.

Indicator Information about a state of nature. An indicator may be the result of a sample.

Bayesian revision The process of revising prior probabilities to create the posterior probabilities based on sample information.

Expected value of sample information (EVSI) The difference between the expected value of an optimal strategy based on sample information and the "best" expected value without any sample information.

Efficiency The ratio of EVSI to EVPI; perfect information is 100% efficient.

Utility A measure of the total worth of an outcome reflecting a decision maker's attitude toward considerations such as profit and loss, and intangibles such as risk.

Lottery A hypothetical investment alternative with a probability p of obtaining the best possible payoff and a probability of $(1 - p)$ of obtaining the worst possible payoff.

Expected utility approach An approach that considers the expected utility for each decision alternative and then selects the decision alternative yielding the highest expected utility.

Problems

1. **SELF Test** The payoff table showing profit for a decision analysis problem with two decisions and three states of nature is shown.

	State of Nature		
Decision Alternative	s_1	s_2	s_3
d_1	250	100	25
d_2	100	100	75

a. Construct a decision tree for this problem.
b. If the decision maker knows nothing about the probabilities of the three states of nature, what is the recommended decision using the optimistic, conservative, and minimax regret approaches?

2. Suppose that a decision maker faced with four decision alternatives and four states of nature develops the following profit payoff table.

	State of Nature			
Decision Alternative	s_1	s_2	s_3	s_4
d_1	14	9	10	5
d_2	11	10	8	7
d_3	9	10	10	11
d_4	8	10	11	13

a. If the decision maker knows nothing about the probabilities of the four states of nature, what is the recommended decision using the optimistic, conservative, and minimax regret approaches?

b. Which approach do you prefer? Explain. Is it important for the decision maker to establish the most appropriate approach before analyzing the problem? Explain.

c. Assume that the payoff table provides *cost* rather than profit payoffs. What is the recommended decision using the optimistic, conservative, and minimax regret approaches?

3. Southland Corporation's decision to produce a new line of recreational products has resulted in the need to construct either a small plant or a large plant. The selection of plant size depends on how the marketplace reacts to the new product line. To conduct an analysis, marketing management has decided to view the possible long-run demand as either low, medium, or high. The following payoff table shows the projected profit in millions of dollars:

	Long-Run Demand		
Decision Alternative	Low	Medium	High
Small plant	150	200	200
Large plant	50	200	500

a. Construct a decision tree for this problem.

b. Recommend a decision based on the use of the optimistic, conservative, and minimax regret approaches.

4. Investment Advisors, Inc., has three investment strategies under consideration. Profits from the strategies will depend on what happens to the prime interest rate over the next three months. Payoffs (in thousand of dollars) are shown.

	State of Nature		
Decision Alternative	Rate Decrease, s_1	No Change, s_2	Rate Increase, s_3
Strategy, d_1	50	70	40
Strategy, d_2	55	35	80
Strategy, d_3	15	60	70

What investment strategy would you recommend based on the use of the optimistic, pessimistic, and minimax regret approaches?

5. **SELF Test** The payoff table presented in Problem 1 is repeated here.

	State of Nature		
Decision Alternative	s_1 .65	s_2 .15	s_3 .2
d_1	250	100	25
d_2	100	100	75

Suppose that the decision maker has obtained the following probability estimates: $P(s_1) = 0.65$, $P(s_2) = 0.15$, and $P(s_3) = 0.20$. Use the expected value approach to determine the optimal decision.

6. The profit payoff table presented in Problem 2 is repeated here.

	State of Nature			
Decision Alternative	s_1	s_2	s_3	s_4
d_1	14	9	10	5
d_2	11	10	8	7
d_3	9	10	10	11
d_4	8	10	11	13

(handwritten annotations: .5 14 + .2 9 + .2 10 + .0 5)

Suppose that the decision maker obtains information that enables the following probability estimates to be made: $P(s_1) = 0.5$, $P(s_2) = 0.2$, $P(s_3) = 0.2$, and $P(s_4) = 0.1$.

a. Use the expected value approach to determine the optimal decision.

b. Now assume that the entries in the payoff table are costs; use the expected value approach to determine the optimal decision.

7. A firm is considering three options for managing its data processing operation: continuing with its own staff, hiring an outside vendor to do the managing (referred to as *outsourcing*), or a combination of its own staff and outside vendor. The cost of the operation depends on future demand. The annual cost of each decision alternative and state of nature (in thousands of dollars) is as follows.

	State of Nature		
Decision Alternative	High Demand, s_1	Medium Demand, s_2	Low Demand, s_3
Own staff, d_1	650	650	600
Vendor, d_2	900	600	300
Combination, d_3	800	650	500

If the demand probabilities are 0.2, 0.5, and 0.3, which decision alternative will minimize the expected cost of the data processing operation? What is the expected annual cost associated with that recommendation?

8. **SELFTest** The following payoff table shows the profit for a decision problem with two states of nature and two decision alternatives.

	State of Nature	
Decision Alternative	s_1	s_2
d_1	10	1
d_2	4	3

Use graphical sensitivity analysis to determine the probability of state of nature s_1 for which each of the decision alternatives has the largest expected value.

9. The following payoff table shows the profit for a decision problem with two states of nature and three decision alternatives.

	State of Nature	
Decision Alternative	s_1	s_2
d_1	80	50
d_2	65	85
d_3	30	100

Use graphical sensitivity analysis to determine the values of the probability of state of nature s_1 for which each of the decision alternatives has the largest expected value.

10. Political Systems, Inc., is a new firm specializing in information services such as surveys and data analysis for individual running for political office. The firm is opening its headquarters in Chicago and is considering three office locations, which differ in cost due to square footage and office equipment requirements. The profit projections shown (in thousands of dollars) for each location were based on both high demand and low demand states of nature.

	State of Nature	
	High Demand, s_1	Low Demand, s_2
Decision Alternative		
Location A	200	−20
Location B	120	10
Location C	100	60

a. Initially, management is uncomfortable stating probabilities for the states of nature. Let p denote the probability of the high demand state of nature. What does graphical sensitivity analysis tell management about location preferences? Can any location be dropped from consideration? Why or why not?

b. After further review, management estimated the probability of a high demand at 0.65. Based on the results in part (a), which location should be selected? What is the expected value associated with that decision?

11. Six months ago, Doug Reynolds paid $25,000 for an option to purchase a tract of land that he is considering developing. Another investor has offered to purchase Doug's option for $275,000. If Doug does not accept the investor's offer, he will purchase the property, clear the land, and prepare the site for building. He believes that once the site is prepared he can sell the land to a home builder. However, the success of the investment depends on the real estate market at the time he sells the property. If the real estate market is down, Doug believes that he will lose $1.5 million. If market conditions stay at their current level, he estimates that his profit will be $1 million; if market conditions are up at the time he sells, he estimates a profit of $4 million. Because of other commitments Doug does not consider it feasible to hold the land once he has developed it; thus, the only two alternatives are to sell the option or to develop the land. Suppose that the probabilities of the real estate market being down, at the current level, or up are 0.6, 0.3, and 0.1, respectively.

a. What decision should Doug make using the expected value approach?

b. Suppose that the probabilities of the real estate market being down, at the current level, or up are 0.5, 0.3, and 0.2, respectively. What decision should Doug make based on the expected value approach? What if the probabilities are 0.4, 0.4, and 0.2? What do the results suggest regarding the proposed investment?

c. Suppose that, after further consideration, Doug concludes that 0.1 is a good estimate of the probability of the real estate market being up. However, he is unable to reach any definite conclusions regarding the probabilities for the other two states of nature. What would the probability of the market being down have to be for the expected value approach to recommend that he should sell his option for $275,000? Would this information help Doug make a decision regarding whether to sell the option or develop the site? Explain.

12. The payoff table presented in Problems 1 and 5 is repeated here.

| | State of Nature | | |
Decision Alternative	s_1	s_2	s_3
d_1	250	100	25
d_2	100	100	75

The probabilities for the states of nature are: $P(s_1) = 0.65$, $P(s_2) = 0.15$, and $P(s_3) = 0.20$.
a. What is the optimal decision strategy if perfect information were available?
b. What is the expected value for the decision strategy developed in part (a)?
c. Using the expected value approach, what is the recommended decision? What is its expected value?
d. What is the expected value of perfect information?

13. The profit payoff table presented in Problems 2 and 6 is repeated here.

| | State of Nature | | | |
Decision Alternative	s_1	s_2	s_3	s_4
d_1	14	9	10	5
d_2	11	10	8	7
d_3	9	10	10	11
d_4	8	10	11	13

The probabilities are $P(s_1) = 0.5$, $P(s_2) = 0.2$, $P(s_3) = 0.2$, and $P(s_4) = 0.1$.
a. What is the optimal decision strategy if perfect information were available?
b. What is the expected value for the decision strategy developed in part (a)?
c. Using the expected value approach, what is the recommended decision? What is its expected value?
d. What is the expected value of perfect information?

14. Suppose that you are given a decision situation with three possible states of nature: s_1, s_2, and s_3. The prior probabilities are $P(s_1) = 0.2$, $P(s_2) = 0.5$, and $P(s_3) = 0.3$. With indicator information I, $P(I \mid s_1) = 0.1$, $P(I \mid s_2) = 0.05$, and $P(I \mid s_3) = 0.2$. Compute the revised or posterior probabilities: $P(s_1 \mid I)$, $P(s_2 \mid I)$, and $P(s_3 \mid I)$.

15. In the following profit payoff table for a decision problem with two states of nature and three decision alternatives, the prior probabilities for s_1 and s_2 are $P(s_1) = 0.8$ and $P(s_2) = 0.2$.

| | State of Nature | |
Decision Alternatives	s_1	s_2
d_1	15	10
d_2	10	12
d_3	8	20

a. Use only the prior probabilities and the expected value approach to find the optimal decision.
b. Use graphical sensitivity analysis to determine the values of the probability of state of nature s_1 for which each of the decision alternatives has the largest expected value.
c. Find the EVPI.
d. Suppose indicator information I is obtained, with $P(I \mid s_1) = 0.2$ and $P(I \mid s_2) = 0.75$. Find the posterior probabilities $P(s_1 \mid I)$ and $P(s_2 \mid I)$. Recommend a decision alternative based on these probabilities.

16. Consider the following decision tree representation of a decision analysis problem with two iindicators, two decision alternatives, and two states of nature.

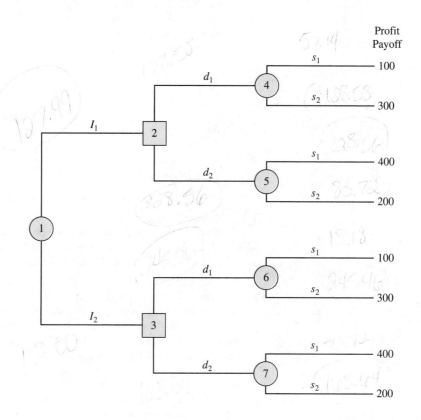

The probabilities are

$$P(s_1) = 0.4 \qquad P(I_1 \mid s_1) = 0.8 \qquad P(I_2 \mid s_1) = 0.2$$

$$P(s_2) = 0.6 \qquad P(I_1 \mid s_2) = 0.4 \qquad P(I_2 \mid s_2) = 0.6$$

a. What are the values for $P(I_1)$ and $P(I_2)$?
b. What are the values of $P(s_1 \mid I_1)$, $P(s_2 \mid I_1)$, $P(s_1 \mid I_2)$, and $P(s_2 \mid I_2)$?
c. Using the decision tree approach, determine the optimal decision strategy and its expected value.

17. A real estate investor has the opportunity to purchase land that is currently zoned residential. If the county board approves a request to rezone the property as commercial within the next year, the investor will be able to lease the land to a large discount firm that wants to open a new store on the property. However, if the zoning change is not approved, the investor will have to sell the property at a loss. Profits (in thousands of dollars) are shown in the following payoff table.

	State of Nature	
Decision Alternative	Rezoning Approved, s_1	Rezoning Not Approved, s_2
Purchase, d_1	600	−200
Do not purchase, d_2	0	0

a. If the probability that the rezoning will be approved is 0.5, what decision is recommended? What is the expected profit?

b. The investor can purchase an option to buy the land. Under the option, the investor maintains the rights to purchase the land anytime during the next 3 months while learning more about possible resistance to the rezoning proposal from area residents. Historical probabilities about such resistance by area residents for each state of nature are as follows.

	High Resistance, I_1	Low Resistance, I_2
Rezoning approved, s_1	0.2	0.8
Rezoning not approved, s_2	0.9	0.1

What is the optimal decision strategy if the investor uses the option period to learn more about the resistance from area residents before making the purchase decision?

c. If the option will cost the investor an additional $10,000, should the investor purchase the option? Why or why not? What is the maximum that the investor should be willing to pay for the option?

18. McHuffter Condominiums, Inc., of Pensacola, Florida, recently purchased land near the Gulf of Mexico and is attempting to determine the size of the condominium development it should build. It is considering three sizes of developments: small, d_1; medium, d_2; and large, d_3. At the same time, an uncertain economy makes ascertaining the demand for the new condominiums difficult. McHuffter's management realizes that a large development followed by low demand could be very costly to the company. However, if McHuffter makes a conservative small-development decision and then finds a high demand, the firm's profits will be lower than they might have been. With the three levels of demand—low, medium, and high—McHuffter's management has prepared the following profit (in thousands of dollars) payoff table.

	Demand		
Decision Alternative	Low, s_1	Medium, s_2	High, s_3
Small, d_1	400	400	400
Medium, d_2	100	600	600
Large, d_3	−300	300	900

a. Construct a decision tree for this problem.

b. If nothing is known about the demand probabilities, what are the recommended decisions using the optimistic, conservative, and minimax regret approaches?

c. If $P(\text{low}) = 0.20$, $P(\text{medium}) = 0.35$, and $P(\text{high}) = 0.45$, what is the recommended decision using the expected value approach?

d. What is the expected value of perfect information?

Suppose that McHuffter Condominiums conducts a survey to help evaluate the demand for the new condominium development. The survey reports on three indicators of demand: weak (I_1), average (I_2), or strong (I_3). The conditional probabilities are shown here:

	$P(I_k \mid s_k)$		
	I_1	I_2	I_3
s_1	0.6	0.3	0.1
s_2	0.4	0.4	0.2
s_3	0.1	0.4	0.5

e. What is McHuffter's optimal strategy?

f. What is the value of the survey information?

g. What are the EVPI and the efficiency of the survey information?

19. Hale's TV Productions is considering producing a pilot for a comedy series for a major television network. The network may reject the pilot and the series, but it may also purchase the program for 1 or 2 years. Hale may decide to produce the pilot or transfer the rights for the series to a competitor for $100,000. Hale's profits are summarized in the following profit (in thousands of dollars) payoff table.

	State of Nature		
Decision Alternative	Reject, s_1	1 Year, s_2	2 Years, s_3
Produce pilot, d_1	−100	50	150
Sell to competitor, d_2	100	100	100

a. If the probability estimates for the states of nature are $P(\text{reject}) = 0.2$, $P(1 \text{ year}) = 0.3$, and $P(2 \text{ years}) = 0.5$, what should the company do?

b. What is the maximum that Hale should be willing to pay for inside information on what the network will do?

For a consulting fee of $2500, an agency will review the plans for the comedy series and indicate the overall chances of a favorable network reaction to the series. If the special agency review results in a favorable (I_1) or an unfavorable (I_2) evaluation, what should Hale's decision strategy be? Assume that Hale believes that the following conditional probabilities are realistic appraisals of the agency's evaluation accuracy.

$$P(I_1 \mid s_1) = 0.3 \qquad P(I_2 \mid s_1) = 0.7$$

$$P(I_1 \mid s_2) = 0.6 \qquad P(I_2 \mid s_2) = 0.4$$

$$P(I_1 \mid s_3) = 0.9 \qquad P(I_2 \mid s_3) = 0.1$$

c. Show the decision tree for this problem.

d. What is the recommended decision strategy and the expected value, assuming that the agency information is obtained?

e. What is the EVSI? Is the agency's information worth the $2500 consulting fee? What is the maximum that Hale should be willing to pay for the information?

20. Martin's Service Station is considering investing in a heavy-duty snowplow this fall. Martin has analyzed the situation carefully and believes that it would be a profitable investment if the snowfall is heavy. Martin could still make a small profit if the snowfall is moderate, but he

would lose money if the snowfall is light. Specifically, Martin forecasts a profit of $7000 if the snowfall is heavy and $2000 if it is moderate and a $9000 loss if the snowfall is light. Based on the weather bureau's long-range forecast, Martin estimates that $P(\text{heavy snowfall}) = 0.4$, $P(\text{moderate snowfall}) = 0.3$, and $P(\text{light snowfall}) = 0.3$.

a. Prepare a decision tree for Martin's problem.

b. What is the expected value at each state-of-nature node?

c. Would the expected value approach recommend that Martin invest in the snowplow?

Suppose that Martin can purchase a blade to attach to his service truck that can also be used to plow driveways and parking lots. This truck must also be available to start cars, so Martin will not be able to generate as much revenue plowing snow if he chooses this alternative. But his loss will be smaller if the snowfall is light. Under this alternative, Martin forecasts a profit of $3500 if the snowfall is heavy and $1000 if it is moderate and a $1500 loss if the snowfall is light.

d. Prepare a new decision tree showing all three alternatives.

e. What is the optimal decision using the expected value approach?

f. What is the expected value of perfect information?

Suppose that Martin decides to wait to check the September temperature pattern before making a final decision. Estimates of the probabilities associated with an unseasonably cold September (I_1) are $P(I_1 \mid s_1) = 0.30$, $P(I_1 \mid s_2) = 0.20$, and $P(I_1 \mid s_3) = 0.05$.

g. If Martin observes an unseasonably cold September, what is the recommended decision?

h. If Martin does not observe an unseasonably cold September (I_2), what is the recommended decision?

21. Joseph Software, Inc. (JSI), has been investigating the possibility of developing a grammar-and-style checker for use on microcomputers. Based on its experience with other software projects, JSI estimates that the total cost to develop a prototype is $200,000. If the performance of the prototype is somewhat better than existing software, referred to as a *moderate success,* JSI believes that it could sell the rights to the software to a larger software developer for $600,000. If the performance of the prototype is significantly better than existing software, referred to as a *major success,* JSI believes that it can sell the software for $1.2 million. However, if the performance of the prototype does not exceed the performance of existing software, referred to as a *failure,* JSI will not be able to sell the software and hence will lose all its development costs.

a. Prepare a decision tree for JSI.

b. If the best estimates of the states of nature are $P(\text{failure}) = 0.70$, $P(\text{moderate success}) = 0.20$, and $P(\text{major success}) = 0.10$, what should JSI do if it uses the expected value approach?

Suppose that JSI can hire an independent consultant to review its ideas for the new software. For a fee of $5000, the consultant will make a recommendation as to whether JSI should develop a prototype. Based on previous experience with this consultant, JSI has assigned conditional probabilities:

$$P(I_1 \mid s_1) = 0.2$$

$$P(I_1 \mid s_2) = 0.6$$

$$P(I_1 \mid s_3) = 0.9$$

where

$$I_1 = \text{recommendation to develop a prototype}$$

$$s_1 = \text{failure}$$

$$s_2 = \text{moderate success}$$

$$s_3 = \text{major success}$$

c. Should JSI hire the consultant? Explain.

22. Milford Trucking Company of Chicago has requests to haul two shipments, one to St. Louis and one to Detroit. Because of a scheduling problem, Milford will be able to accept only one of these assignments. The St. Louis customer has guaranteed a return shipment, but the Detroit customer has not. Thus, if Milford accepts the Detroit shipment and cannot find a Detroit–Chicago return shipment, the truck will return to Chicago empty. The payoff table showing profit is as follows.

Shipment	Return Shipment from Detroit, s_1	No Return Shipment from Detroit, s_2
St. Louis, d_1	2000	2000
Detroit, d_2	2500	1000

a. If the probability of a Detroit return shipment is 0.4, what should Milford do?
b. Use graphical sensitivity analysis to determine the values of the probability of state of nature s_1 for which d_1 has the largest expected value.
c. What is the expected value of perfect information that would tell Milford Trucking whether Detroit has a return shipment?

Milford can phone a Detroit truck dispatch center and determine whether the general Detroit shipping activity is busy (I_1) or slow (I_2). If the report is busy, the chances of obtaining a return shipment will increase. Suppose that the conditional probabilities are

$$P(I_1 \mid s_1) = 0.6 \qquad P(I_2 \mid s_1) = 0.4$$

$$P(I_1 \mid s_2) = 0.3 \qquad P(I_2 \mid s_2) = 0.7$$

d. What should Milford do?
e. If the general Detroit shipping activity is busy (I_1), what is the probability that Milford will obtain a return shipment if it makes the trip to Detroit?
f. What is the efficiency of the phone information?

23. Lawson's Department Store faces a buying decision for a seasonal product for which demand can be high, medium, and low. The purchaser for Lawson's can order 1, 2, or 3 lots of the product before the season begins but cannot reorder later. Profit projections (in thousands of dollars) are shown.

	State of Nature		
Decision Alternative	High Demand, s_1	Medium Demand, s_2	Low Demand, s_3
Order 1 lot, d_1	60	60	50
Order 2 lots, d_2	80	80	30
Order 3 lots, d_3	100	70	10

a. If the prior probabilities for the three states of nature are 0.3, 0.3, and 0.4, respectively, what is the recommended order quantity?
b. At each preseason sales meeting, the vice-president of sales provides his personal opinion regarding potential demand for this product. Because of his enthusiasm and optimistic nature, his predictions of market conditions have always been either "excellent" (I_1) or "very good" (I_2). Conditional probabilities for each state of nature are as follows.

	Prediction	
State of Nature	Excellent, I_1	Very Good, I_2
High demand, s_1	0.80	0.20
Medium demand, s_2	0.75	0.25
Low demand, s_3	0.60	0.40

What are the revised probabilities of each state of nature for each of the vice-president's predictions?

c. What is the optimal decision strategy for the vice-president's predictions?

d. Use the efficiency of sample information and discuss whether the firm should consider a consulting expert who could provide independent forecasts of market conditions for the product.

24. To save on gasoline expenses, Rona and Jerry agreed to form a carpool for traveling to and from work. After limiting the travel routes to two alternatives, they couldn't agree on the best way to travel to work. Jerry preferred the expressway because it usually was the fastest; however, Rona pointed out that traffic jams on the expressway sometimes led to long delays. Rona preferred the somewhat longer but more consistent Queen City Avenue. Although Jerry preferred the expressway, he agreed with Rona that they should take Queen City Avenue if the expressway had a traffic jam. Unfortunately, they do not know the state of the expressway ahead of time. The following payoff table provides the one-way time estimates in minutes for traveling to or from work.

	State of Nature	
Route	Expressway Open, s_1	Expressway Jammed, s_2
Expressway, d_1	25	45
Queen City Avenue, d_2	30	30

a. After driving to work on the expressway for 1 month (20 days), they found the expressway jammed three times. Assuming that these days are representative of future days, should they continue to use the expressway for traveling to work? Explain.

b. Use graphical sensitivity analysis to determine the values of the probability of state of nature s_1 for which d_1 has the best expected value.

c. Would not using the expected value approach for this particular problem make sense? Explain.

After a period of time, Rona and Jerry noted that the weather seemed to affect traffic conditions on the expressway. They identified three weather conditions (indicators) and gave them conditional probabilities:

$$I_1 = \text{clear} \qquad I_2 = \text{overcast} \qquad I_3 = \text{rain}$$

$$P(I_1 \mid s_1) = 0.8 \qquad P(I_2 \mid s_1) = 0.2 \qquad P(I_3 \mid s_1) = 0$$

$$P(I_1 \mid s_2) = 0.1 \qquad P(I_2 \mid s_2) = 0.3 \qquad P(I_3 \mid s_2) = 0.6$$

d. Show the decision tree for the problem of traveling to work.

e. What is the optimal decision strategy and the expected travel time?

f. What is the efficiency of the weather information?

25. The Gorman Manufacturing Company must decide whether to purchase a component from a supplier or manufacture the component at its Milan, Michigan, plant. If demand is high, Gorman could profitably manufacture the component. However, if demand is low, Gorman's unit manufacturing cost would be high due to underutilization of equipment. The following table shows the projected profit (in thousands of dollars) for Gorman's make-or-buy decision.

	Demand		
	Low,	Medium,	High,
Decision Alternative	s_1	s_2	s_3
Manufacture component, d_1	−20	40	100
Purchase component, d_2	10	45	70

The states of nature probabilities are $P(\text{low}) = 0.35$, $P(\text{medium}) = 0.35$, and $P(\text{high}) = 0.30$.
a. Use a decision tree to recommend a decision.
b. Use EVPI to determine whether Gorman should attempt to obtain a better estimate of demand.

A test market study of the potential demand for the product is expected to report either a favorable (I_1) or unfavorable (I_2) condition. The relevant conditional probabilities are as follows:

$$P(I_1 \mid s_1) = 0.10 \quad P(I_2 \mid s_1) = 0.90$$
$$P(I_1 \mid s_2) = 0.40 \quad P(I_2 \mid s_2) = 0.60$$
$$P(I_1 \mid s_3) = 0.60 \quad P(I_2 \mid s_3) = 0.40$$

c. What is the probability that the market research report will be favorable?
d. What is Gorman's optimal decision strategy?
e. What is the expected value of the market research information?
f. What is the efficiency of the information?

26. A quality control procedure involves 100% inspection of parts received from a supplier. Historical records indicate the following defective rates:

Percent Defective	Probability
0	0.15
1	0.25
2	0.40
3	0.20

The cost to inspect 100% of the parts received is $250 for each shipment of 500 parts. If the shipment is not 100% inspected, defective parts will cause rework problems later in the production process. The rework cost is $25 for each defective part.
a. Complete the following payoff table, where the entries represent the total cost of inspection and reworking.

	Percent Defective			
Inspection	0, s_1	1, s_2	2, s_3	3, s_4
100% inspection, d_1	$250	$250	$250	$250
No inspection, d_2				

b. The plant manager is considering eliminating the inspection process to save the $250 inspection cost per shipment. Do you support this action? Use expected value to justify your answer.

c. Show the decision tree for this problem.

d. Suppose that a sample of five parts is selected from the shipment and one defect is found. Let $I = 1$ defect in a sample of 5. Use the binomial probability distribution to compute $P(I \mid s_1)$, $P(I \mid s_2)$, $P(I \mid s_3)$, and $P(I \mid s_4)$. The binomial probability function is as follows:

$$f(x) = \frac{n!}{x!(n-x)!} p^x (1-p)^{n-x}$$

where

n = the sample size
x = the number of defects
p = the proportion defective

In this problem, $n = 5$, $x = 1$, and $p = 0, 0.01, 0.02$, and 0.03.

e. If I occurs, what are the revised probabilities for the states of nature?

f. Should the entire shipment be 100% inspected whenever 1 defect is found in a sample of size 5?

g. What is the cost savings associated with the sample information?

27. A food processor considers daily production runs of 100, 200, and 300 cases. Possible demands for the product are 100, 200, and 300 cases. The payoff table is as follows:

	Demand		
Production	100, s_1	200, s_2	300, s_3
100, d_1	500	200	-100
200, d_2	-400	800	700
300, d_3	-1000	-200	1600

a. If $P(s_1) = 0.2$, $P(s_2) = 0.2$, and $P(s_3) = 0.6$, what is the recommended production quantity?

b. On some days the firm receives phone calls for advance orders, and on some days it doesn't. Suppose that I_1 = advance orders are received and I_2 = no advance orders are received. If $P(I_2 \mid s_1) = 0.8$, $P(I_2 \mid s_2) = 0.4$, and $P(I_2 \mid s_3) = 0.1$, what is the recommended production quantity for days the company doesn't receive any advance orders?

28. **SELFTest** Three decision makers have assessed utilities for the following decision problem (payoff in dollars).

	State of Nature		
Decision Alternative	s_1	s_2	s_3
d_1	20	50	-20
d_2	80	100	-100

The indifference probabilities are as follows.

	Indifference Probability (p)		
Payoff	Risk Avoider	Risk Taker	Risk Neutral
100	1.00	1.00	1.00
80	0.95	0.70	0.90
50	0.90	0.60	0.75
20	0.70	0.45	0.60
−20	0.50	0.25	0.40
−100	0.00	0.00	0.00

For the payoff of 20, what is the premium that the risk avoider will pay to avoid risk? What is the premium that the risk taker will pay to have the opportunity of the high payoff?

29. In Problem 28, if $P(s_1) = 0.25$, $P(s_2) = 0.50$, and $P(s_3) = 0.25$, find a recommended decision for each of the three decision makers. Note that for the same decision problem, different utilities can lead to different decisions.

30. **SELF Test** A firm has three investment alternatives. The payoff table (in $1000s) and associated probabilities are as follows:

	Economic Condition		
Investment	Up	Stable	Down
d_1	100	25	0
d_2	75	50	25
d_3	50	50	50
Probabilities	0.40	0.30	0.30

a. Using the expected value approach, which decision is preferred?
b. For the lottery having a payoff of $100,000 with probability p and $0 with probability $(1 - p)$, two decision makers expressed the following indifference probabilities:

	Indifference Probability (p)	
Profit	Decision Maker A	Decision Maker B
$75,000	0.80	0.60
50,000	0.60	0.30
25,000	0.30	0.15

Find the most preferred decision for each decision maker using the expected utility approach.
c. Why don't decision makers A and B select the same decision alternative?

31. In a certain state lottery, a lottery ticket costs $2. In terms of the decision to purchase or not to purchase a lottery ticket, suppose the following payoff table (in $) applies:

	State of Nature	
Decision Alternative	Win s_1	Lose s_2
Purchase lottery ticket, d_1	300,000	−2
Do not purchase lottery ticket, d_2	0	0

a. If a realistic estimate of the chances of winning are 1 in 250,000, use the expected value approach to recommend a decision.
b. If a particular decision maker assigns an indifference probability of 0.000001 to the $0 payoff, would this individual purchase a lottery ticket? Use expected utility to justify your answer.

32. Alexander Industries is considering purchasing an insurance policy for its new office building in St. Louis. The policy has an annual cost of $10,000. If Alexander Industries does not purchase the insurance and minor fire damage occurs to the office building, a cost of $100,000 is anticipated; the cost if major or total destruction occurs is $200,000. The payoff table in ($), including the state-of-nature probabilities, is as follows:

	Damage		
Decision Alternative	None s_1	Minor s_2	Major s_3
Purchase insurance, d_1	10,000	10,000	10,000
Do not purchase insurance, d_2	0	100,000	200,000
Probabilities	0.96	0.03	0.01

a. Using the expected value approach, what decision do you recommend?
b. What lottery would you use to assess utilities? (Note that since the data are costs, the best payoff is $0.)
c. Assume we found the following indifference probabilities for the lottery defined in part (b):

Cost	Indifference Probability (p)
$ 10,000	0.99
100,000	0.60

What decision would you recommend?
d. Do you favor using expected value or expected utility for this decision problem? Why?

33. Suppose that the point spread for a particular sporting event is 10 points and that with this spread you are convinced you would have a 0.6 probability of winning a bet on your team. However, the local bookie will accept only a $1000 bet. Assuming that such bets are legal, would you bet on your team? (Disregard any commission charged by the bookie.) Remember that *you* must pay losses out of your own pocket. Your payoff table (in $) is as follows:

| Decision Alternative | State of Nature | |
	You Win s_1	You Lose s_2
Bet, d_1	1000	−1000
Don't bet, d_2	0	0

a. What decision does the expected value approach recommend?
b. What is *your* indifference probability for the $0 payoff? (While this is not easy, be as realistic as possible. Remember, this is required if we are to do an analysis that reflects your attitude toward risk.)
c. What decision would you make based on the expected utility approach?
d. Would other individuals assess the same utility values you do? Explain.
e. If your decision in part (c) was to place the bet, repeat the analysis, assuming a minimum bet of $10,000.

34. There are two different routes for traveling between two cities. Route A normally takes 60 minutes, while route B normally takes 45 minutes. If traffic problems are encountered on route A, the travel time increases to 70 minutes; traffic problems on route B increase travel time to 90 minutes. The probability of the delay is 0.2 for route A and 0.3 for route B.
a. Using the expected value approach, what is the recommended route?
b. If utilities are to be assigned to the travel times, what is the appropriate lottery? Note that the smaller times should reflect higher utilities.
c. Using the lottery of part (b), assume the decision maker expresses indifference probabilities of

$$p = 0.8 \quad \text{for 60 minutes}$$
$$p = 0.6 \quad \text{for 70 minutes}$$

What route should this decision maker select?

35. A new product has the following profit projections and associated probabilities:

Profit	Probability
150,000	0.10
100,000	0.25
50,000	0.20
0	0.15
−50,000	0.20
−100,000	0.10

a. Use the expected value approach to make the decision of whether to market the new product.
b. Because of the high dollar values involved, especially the possibility of a $100,000 loss, the marketing vice president has expressed some concern about the use of the expected value approach. As a consequence, if a utility analysis is performed, what is the appropriate lottery? Assume the following indifference probabilities are assigned:

Profit	Indifference Probability (p)
$ 100,000	0.95
50,000	0.70
0	0.50
−50,000	0.25

    c. Use expected utility to make a recommended decision.

    d. Should the decision maker feel comfortable with the final decision recommended by the analysis?

36. A Las Vegas roulette wheel has 38 different numerical values. If an individual bets on one number and wins, the payoff is 35 to 1.

    a. Show a payoff table for a $10 bet on one number using decision alternatives of bet and do not bet.

    b. What is the recommended decision using the expected value approach?

    c. What range of utility values would a decision maker have to assign to the $0 payoff to have expected utility justify his or her decision to place the $10 bet?

Case Problem: Property Purchase Strategy

Glenn Foreman, president of Oceanview Development Corporation, is considering submitting a bid to purchase property that will be sold by sealed bid at a county tax foreclosure. Glenn's initial judgment is to submit a bid of $5 million. From past experience, Glenn estimates that a bid of $5 million will have a 0.2 probability of being the highest bid and securing the property for Oceanview. The current date is June 1. Sealed bids for the property must be submitted by August 15. The winning bid will be announced on September 1.

If Oceanview submits the highest bid and obtains the property, the firm plans to build and sell a complex of luxury condominiums. However, a complicating factor is that the property is currently zoned for single-family residences only. Glenn believes that a referendum could be placed on the voting ballot in time for the November election. Passage of the referendum would change the zoning of the property and permit construction of the condominiums.

The sealed-bid procedure requires the bid to be submitted with a certified check for 10% of the amount bid. If the bid is rejected, the deposit is refunded. If the bid is accepted, the deposit is the down payment for the property. However, if the bid is accepted and the bidder does not follow through with the purchase and meet the remainder of the financial obligation within 6 months, the deposit will be forfeited. In this case, the county will offer the property to the next highest bidder.

To determine whether Oceanview should submit the $5 million bid, Glenn has done some preliminary analysis. This preliminary work provided an estimate of 0.3 for the probability that the referendum for a zoning change will be approved and resulted in the following estimates of the costs and revenues that will be incurred if the condominiums are built.

Cost and Revenue Estimates	
Revenue from condominium sales	$15,000,000
Cost	
Property	$5,000,000
Construction expenses	$8,000,000

If Oceanview obtains the property and the zoning change is not approved in November, Glenn believes that the best option would be for the firm not to complete the purchase of the property. In this case, Oceanview would forfeit the 10% deposit that accompanied the bid.

Because the likelihood that the zoning referendum will be approved is such an important factor in the decision process, Glenn has suggested that the firm hire a market research service to conduct a survey of voters. The survey would provide a better estimate of the likelihood that the referendum for a zoning change would be approved. The market research firm that Oceanview Development has worked with in the past has agreed to do the study for $15,000. The results of the study will be available August 1, so that Oceanview will have this information before the August 15 bid deadline. The results of the survey will be either a prediction that the zoning change will be approved or a prediction that the zoning change will not be approved. After considering the record of the market research service in previous studies conducted for Oceanview, Glenn has developed the following probability estimates concerning the accuracy of the market research information.

$$P(I_1 \mid s_1) = 0.9 \qquad P(I_2 \mid s_1) = 0.1$$
$$P(I_1 \mid s_2) = 0.2 \qquad P(I_2 \mid s_2) = 0.8$$

where

$I_1 =$ prediction that the zoning change will be approved

$I_2 =$ prediction that the zoning change will not be approved

$s_1 =$ the zoning change is approved by the voters

$s_2 =$ the zoning change is not approved by the voters

Managerial Report

Perform an analysis of the problem facing the Oceanview Development Corporation, and prepare a report that summarizes your findings and recommendations. Include the following items in your report:

1. A decision tree that shows the logical sequence of the decision problem
2. A recommendation regarding what Oceanview should do if the market research information is not available
3. A decision strategy that Oceanview should follow if the market research is conducted
4. A recommendation as to whether Oceanview should employ the market research firm, along with the value of the information provided by the market research firm. Include the details of your analysis as an appendix to your report.

APPENDIX 14.1 Decision Analysis and Spreadsheets

A spreadsheet provides a convenient way to perform the basic decision analysis computations. A spreadsheet may be designed for any of the decision analysis approaches described in this chapter. We will demonstrate use of the spreadsheet in decision analysis by solving the PDC condominium problem using the expected value approach.

Figure 14.10 shows the formula spreadsheet for the PDC problem. The values in color are the payoffs and the state of nature probabilities that the user must enter directly into the spreadsheet. In the EXPECTED VALUE column, we show the cell formulas used in the spreadsheet computations. For example, the expected value for decision alternative 1 is provided by the cell formula =$B$11*B7+$C$11*C7.

In addition to making the expected value computation for all three decision alternatives, the cell D14 formula =MAX(D7:D9) indicates that this cell will contain the maximum of the computed expected values. This computation indicates the expected value under the best decision alternative.

Figure 14.10 Formula Spreadsheet for the Expected Value of the PDC Decision Problem

	A	B	C	D
1	PDC DECISION PROBLEM			
2				
3				
4			STATE	EXPECTED
5		HIGH	LOW	VALUE
6				
7	SMALL	8	7	=$B$11*B7+$C$11*C7
8	MEDIUM	14	5	=$B$11*B8+$C$11*C8
9	LARGE	20	−9	=$B$11*B9+$C$11*C9
10				
11	PROBABILITY	0.8	0.2	
12				
13				
14	MAXIMUM EXPECTED VALUE			=MAX (D7:D9)
15				
16	EV OF PERFECT INFORMATION			=B11*MAX (B7:B9) +C11*MAX (C7:C9) −D14

Figure 14.11

Value Spreadsheet for the Expected Value of the PDC Decision Problem

	A	B	C	D
1	PDC DECISION PROBLEM			
2				
3				
4			STATE	EXPECTED
5		HIGH	LOW	VALUE
6				
7	SMALL	8	7	7.8
8	MEDIUM	14	5	12.2
9	LARGE	20	−9	14.2
10				
11	PROBABILITY	0.8	0.2	
12				
13				
14	MAXIMUM EXPECTED VALUE			14.2
15				
16	EV OF PERFECT INFORMATION			3.2

Finally, the cell D16 formula provides the computation of expected value of perfect information, EVPI. Probabilities $P(s_1)$ and $P(s_2)$ are multiplied by the best payoff in column 1, MAX(B7:B9), and the best payoff column 2, MAX(C7:C9), to obtain the expected value with perfect information. Subtracting the value in cell D14 provides the EVPI.

Figure 14.11 shows the value spreadsheet for the PDC decision problem. The recommended decision alternative is the large complex with a maximum expected value of $14.2 million. The EVPI is $3.2 million, as computed previously in Section 14.5.

One of the advantages of the spreadsheet is its use in sensitivity analysis. For example, Figure 14.12 shows the solution under the assumption that the probabilities of the states of nature are changed to $P(s_1) = 0.2$ and $P(s_2) = 0.8$. Making these two data modifications provides the results shown. In this situation, the small complex is the recommended decision, with the maximum expected value reduced to $7.2 million. Similarly, further sensitivity analysis of other states of nature and/or modified payoff values can be quickly and easily considered.

Figure 14.13 shows the formula spreadsheet for the computation of the decision tree branch probabilities based on Bayes' Theorem. With this spreadsheet design we have to input only the prior probabilities and the conditional probabilities, as shown in color. Branch probabilities are provided by P(I1), P(I2), and four posterior probabilities (POSTERIOR PROBS). Note that the prior probabilities have to be entered only once because the cell formulas of =B6 and =B8 in the PRIOR PROBS column for INDICATOR 2 show that the same prior probabilities of 0.8 and 0.2 will be used for the INDICATOR 2 probability revision process. Figure 14.14 shows the value spreadsheet. Determine whether you can follow the logic of the formula spreadsheet and verify that the results shown in Figure 14.14 are identical to the hand computation of the branch probabilities, as presented in Section 14.7.

Figure 14.12

Value Spreadsheet for the PDC Decision Problem with $P(s_1) = 0.2$ and $P(s_2) = 0.8$

	A	B	C	D
1	PDC DECISION PROBLEM			
2				
3				
4		STATE		EXPECTED
5		HIGH	LOW	VALUE
6				
7	SMALL	8	7	7.2
8	MEDIUM	14	5	6.8
9	LARGE	20	−9	−3.2
10				
11	PROBABILITY	0.2	0.8	
12				
13				
14	MAXIMUM EXPECTED VALUE			7.2
15				
16	EV OF PERFECT INFORMATION			2.4

Figure 14.13 Formula Spreadsheet for Computing Branch Probabilities for the PDC Decision Problem

	A	B	C	D	E
1	INDICATOR 1				
2					
3	STATES OF	PRIOR	COND	JOINT	POSTERIOR
4	NATURE	PROBS	PROBS	PROBS	PROBS
5					
6	S1	0.8	0.9	=B6*C6	=D6/D10
7					
8	S2	0.2	0.25	=B8*C8	=D8/D10
9					
10			P(I1) =	=SUM (D6 : D8)	
11					
12					
13	INDICATOR 2				
14					
15	STATES OF	PRIOR	COND	JOINT	POSTERIOR
16	NATURE	PROBS	PROBS	PROBS	PROBS
17					
18	S1	=B6	0.1	=B18*C18	=D18/D22
19					
20	S2	=B8	0.75	=B20*C20	=D20/D22
21					
22			P(I2) =	=SUM (D18 : D20)	

Figure 14.14

Value Spreadsheet of Branch Probabilities for the PDC Decision Problem

	A	B	C	D	E
1	INDICATOR 1				
2					
3	STATES OF	PRIOR	COND	JOINT	POSTERIOR
4	NATURE	PROBS	PROBS	PROBS	PROBS
5					
6	S1	0.8	0.90	0.72	0.9351
7					
8	S2	0.2	0.25	0.05	0.0649
9					
10			P(I1) =	0.77	
11					
12					
13	INDICATOR 2				
14					
15	STATES OF	PRIOR	COND	JOINT	POSTERIOR
16	NATURE	PROBS	PROBS	PROBS	PROBS
17					
18	S1	0.8	0.10	0.08	0.3478
19					
20	S2	0.2	0.75	0.15	0.6522
21					
22			P(I2) =	0.23	

MANAGEMENT SCIENCE in practice

Ohio Edison Company*
Akron, Ohio

Ohio Edison Company is an investor-owned electric utility headquartered in northeastern Ohio. Ohio Edison and a Pennsylvania subsidiary provide electrical service to more than 2 million people. Most of this electricity is generated by coal-fired power plants. To meet evolving air-quality standards, Ohio Edison replaced existing particulate control equipment at most of its generating plants with more efficient equipment. The combination of this program to upgrade air-quality control equipment with the continuing need to construct new generating plants to meet future power requirements resulted in a large capital investment program.

Management science activities at Ohio Edison are distributed throughout the company rather than centralized in a specific department, and are more or less evenly divided among the following areas: fossil and nuclear fuel planning, environmental studies, capacity planning, large equipment evaluation, and corporate planning. Applications include decision analysis, optimal ordering strategies, computer modeling, and simulation.

A Decision Analysis Application

The flue gas emitted by coal-fired power plants contains small ash particles and sulfur dioxide (SO_2). Federal and state regulatory agencies have established emission limits for both particulates and sulfur dioxide. In the late 1970s, Ohio Edison developed a plan to comply with new air-quality standards at one of its largest power plants. This plant, which consists of seven coal-fired units (most of which were constructed in the 1960s), constitutes about one-third of the generating capacity of Ohio Edison and its subsidiary company. Although all the units were initially constructed with particulate emission control equipment, that equipment was no longer capable of meeting new particulate emission requirements.

A decision had already been made to burn low-sulfur coal in four of the smaller units (units 1–4) at the plant in order to meet SO_2 emission standards. Fabric filters were to be installed on these units to control particulate emissions. Fabric filters, also known as baghouses, use thousands of fabric bags to filter out the particulates; they function in much the same way as a household vacuum cleaner.

It was considered likely, although not certain, that the three larger units (units 5–7) at this plant would burn medium- to high-sulfur coal. A method of controlling particulate emissions at these units had not yet been selected. Preliminary studies narrowed the particulate control equipment choice to a decision between fabric filters and electrostatic precipitators (which remove particulates suspended in the flue gas by passing the flue gas through a strong electric field). This decision was affected by a number of uncertainties, including the following:

- Uncertainty in the way some air-quality laws and regulations might be interpreted
- Potential requirements that either low-sulfur coal or high-sulfur Ohio coal (or neither) be burned in units 5–7
- Potential future changes to air quality laws and regulations
- An overall plant reliability improvement program already under way at this plant
- The outcome of this program itself, which would affect the operating costs of whichever pollution control technology was installed in these units
- Uncertain construction costs of the equipment, particularly since limited space at the plant site made it necessary to install the equipment on a massive bridge deck over a four-lane highway immediately adjacent to the power plant
- Uncertain costs associated with replacing the electrical power required to operate the particulate control equipment
- Various other factors, including potential accidents and chronic operating problems that could increase the costs of operating the generating units (the degree to which each of these factors could affect operating costs varied with the choice of technology and with the sulfur content of the coal).

Particulate Control Decision

The air-quality program involved a choice between two types of particulate control equipment (fabric filters and electrostatic precipitators) for units 5–7. Because of the complexity of the problem, the high degree of uncertainty associated with factors affecting the decision, and the importance (because of potential reliability and cost impact on Ohio Edison) of the choice, decision analysis was used in the selection process.

The decision measure used to evaluate the outcomes of the particulate technology decision analysis was the annual revenue requirements for the three large units over their remaining lifetime. Revenue requirements are the monies that would have to be collected from the utility customers to recover costs resulting from the decision. They include not only direct costs, but also the cost of capital and return on investment.

- - - - - - - - - - -

*The authors are indebted to Thomas J. Madden and M. S. Hyrnick of Ohio Edison Company, Akron, Ohio, for providing this application.

—*Continued from previous page*

Figure 14.15

Simplified Particulate Control Equipment Decision Tree

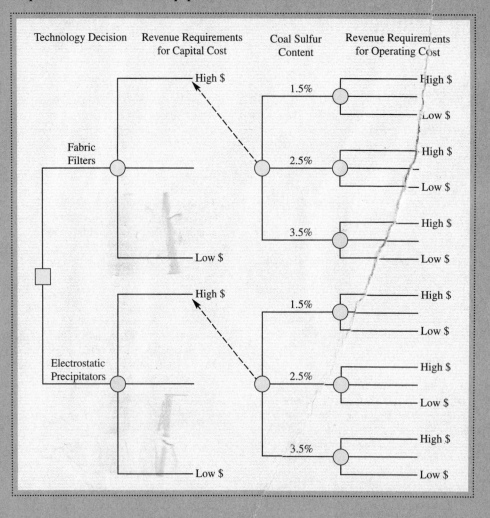

A decision tree was constructed to represent the particulate control decision and its uncertainties and costs. A simplified version of this decision tree is shown in Figure 14.15. The decision and state-of-nature nodes are indicated. Note that to conserve space, a type of shorthand notation is used. The coal sulfur content state-of-nature node should actually be located at the end of each branch of the capital cost state-of-nature node, as the dashed lines indicate. Each of the state-of-nature nodes actually represents several probabilistic cost models or submodels. The total revenue requirements are the sum of the revenue requirements for capital and operating costs. Costs associated with these models were obtained from engineering calculations or estimates. Probabilities were obtained from existing data or the subjective assessments of knowledgeable persons.

—Continued from previous page

A decision tree similar to that shown in Figure 14.15 was used to generate cumulative probability distributions for the annual revenue requirements outcomes calculated for each of the two particulate control alternatives. Careful study of these results led to the following conclusions:

The expected value of annual revenue requirements for the electrostatic precipitator technology was approximately $1 million lower than that for the fabric filters.

The fabric filter alternative had a higher upside risk—that is, a higher probability of high revenue requirements—than did the precipitator alternative.

The precipitator technology had nearly an 80% probability of lower annual revenue requirements than the fabric filters.

Although the capital cost of the fabric filter equipment (the cost of installing the equipment) was lower than for the precipitator, this was more than offset by the higher operating costs associated with the fabric filter.

These results led Ohio Edison to select the electrostatic precipitator technology for the generating units in question. Had the decision analysis not been performed, the particulate control decision might have been based chiefly on capital cost, a decision measure that would have favored the fabric filter equipment. Decision analysis offers a means for effectively analyzing the uncertainties involved in a decision. Because of this, it is felt that the use of decision analysis methodology in this application resulted in a decision that yielded both lower expected revenue requirements and lower risk.

Questions

1. Why was decision analysis used in the selection of particulate control equipment for units 5, 6, and 7?
2. List the decision alternatives for the decision analysis problem developed by Ohio Edison.
3. What were the benefits of using decision analysis in this application?

Multicriteria Decision Problems

In previous chapters we have shown how a variety of management science methods can help managers make better decisions. In each case, whenever we desired an optimal solution, we utilized a single criterion (e.g., maximize profit, minimize cost, or minimize expected cost). In this chapter we discuss techniques that are appropriate for situations in which the decision maker needs to consider multiple criteria in arriving at the overall best decision. For example, consider a company involved in selecting a location for a new manufacturing plant. The cost of land and construction may vary from location to location, so one criterion in selecting the best site could be the cost involved in building the plant; if cost were the sole criterion of interest, management would simply select the location that minimizes land cost plus construction cost. Before making any decision, however, management might also want to consider additional criteria such as the availability of transportation from the plant to the firm's distribution centers, the attractiveness of the proposed location in terms of hiring and retaining employees, energy costs at the proposed site, and state and local taxes. In such situations the complexity of the problem increases because one location may be more desirable in terms of one criterion and less desirable in terms of one or more of the other criteria.

To introduce the topic of multicriteria decision making, we will first consider a technique referred to as *goal programming*. This technique was developed to handle multicriteria situations within the general framework of linear programming. The other approach we will consider, referred to as the *analytic hierarchy process* (AHP), permits the inclusion of subjective factors in arriving at a decision. In this approach, the decision maker must make judgments about the relative importance of each of the criteria and then specify a preference for each alternative relative to each criterion; the output is a prioritized ranking indicating the overall preference for each of the decision alternatives.

15.1 Goal Programming: Formulation and Graphical Solution

To illustrate the goal programming approach to multicriteria decision problems, let us consider a problem facing Nicolo Investment Advisors. A particular client has $80,000 to invest and, as an initial strategy, would like the investment portfolio restricted to two stocks:

Stock	Price/Share	Estimated Annual Return/Share	Risk Index/Share
U.S. Oil	$25	$3	0.50
Hub Properties	$50	$5	0.25

U.S. Oil, which has a return of $3 on a $25 share price, provides an annual rate of return of 12%, whereas Hub Properties provides an annual rate of return of 10%. The risk index per share, 0.50 for U.S. Oil and 0.25 for Hub Properties, is a rating Nicolo has assigned to measure the relative risk of the two investments. Higher risk index values imply greater risk; hence, Nicolo has judged U.S. Oil to be the riskier investment. By specifying a maximum portfolio risk index, Nicolo will avoid placing too much of the portfolio in high-risk investments.

To illustrate how to use the risk index per share to measure the total portfolio risk, suppose that Nicolo chooses a portfolio that invests all $80,000 in U.S. Oil, the higher-risk, but higher-return, investment. Nicolo could purchase $80,000/$25 = 3200 shares of U.S. Oil, and the portfolio would have a risk index of 3200(0.50) = 1600. Conversely, if Nicolo purchases no shares of either stock, there will be no risk, but no return. Thus, the portfolio risk index will vary from 0 (least risk) to 1600 (most risk).

Nicolo's client would like to avoid a high-risk portfolio; thus, investing all funds in U.S. Oil would not be desirable. However, the client agreed that an acceptable level of risk would correspond to portfolios with a maximum total risk index of 700. Thus, considering only risk, one *goal* is to find a portfolio with a risk index of 700 or less.

Another goal of the client is to obtain an annual return of at least $9000. This goal can be achieved with a portfolio consisting of 2000 shares of U.S. Oil (at a cost of 2000($25) = $50,000) and 600 shares of Hub Properties (at a cost of 600($50) = $30,000); the annual return in this case would be 2000($3) + 600($5) = $9000. Note, however, that the portfolio risk index for this investment strategy would be 2000(0.50) + 600(0.25) = 1150; thus, this portfolio achieves the annual return goal but does not satisfy the portfolio risk index goal.

Thus, the portfolio selection problem is a multicriteria decision problem involving two conflicting goals: one dealing with risk and one dealing with annual return. The goal programming approach was developed precisely for this kind of problem. Goal programming can be used to identify a portfolio that comes closest to achieving both goals. Before applying the methodology, the client must determine which, if either, goal is more important.

Suppose that the client's top-priority goal is restricting the risk; that is, keeping the portfolio risk index at 700 or less is so important that the client is not willing to trade the achievement of this goal for any amount of an increase in annual return. But, as long as the portfolio risk index does not exceed 700, the client seeks the best possible return. Based on this statement of priorities, the goals for the problem are as follows:

Primary Goal (Priority Level 1)

Goal 1:   Find a portfolio that has a risk index of 700 or less.

Secondary Goal (Priority Level 2)

Goal 2:   Find a portfolio that will provide an annual return of at least $9000.

The primary goal is called a priority level 1 goal, and the secondary goal is called a priority level 2 goal. In goal programming terminology, these are called *preemptive priorities* because the decision maker is not willing to sacrifice any amount of achievement of the priority level 1 goal for the lower priority goal. The portfolio risk index of 700 is the *target value* for the priority level 1 (primary) goal, and the annual return of $9000 is the target value for the priority level 2 (secondary) goal. The difficulty in finding a solution that will achieve these goals is that only $80,000 is available for investment.

Developing the Constraints and the Goal Equations

We begin by defining the decision variables:

$$x_1 = \text{number of shares of U.S. Oil purchased}$$
$$x_2 = \text{number of shares of Hub Properties purchased}$$

Constraints for goal programming problems are handled in the same way as in an ordinary linear programming problem. In the Nicolo Investment Advisors problem there is only one constraint corresponding to the funds available. Since each share of U.S. Oil costs $25 and each share of Hub Properties costs $50, the constraint representing the funds available is

$$25x_1 + 50x_2 \leq 80,000$$

To complete the formulation of the model, we must develop a *goal equation* for each goal. Let us begin by writing the goal equation for the primary goal. Since each share of U.S. Oil has a risk index of 0.50 and each share of Hub Properties has a risk index of 0.25, the portfolio risk index is $0.50x_1 + 0.25x_2$. Depending on the values of x_1 and x_2, the portfolio risk index may be less than, equal to, or greater than the target value of 700. To represent these possibilities mathematically, we create the goal equation

$$0.50x_1 + 0.25x_2 = 700 + d_1^+ - d_1^-$$

where

$d_1^+ = $ the amount by which the portfolio risk index exceeds the target value of 700

$d_1^- = $ the amount by which the portfolio risk index is less than the target value of 700

In goal programming, d_1^+ and d_1^- are called *deviation variables*. The purpose of deviation variables is to allow for the possibility of not meeting the target value exactly. Consider, for example, a portfolio that consists of $x_1 = 2000$ shares of U.S. Oil and $x_2 = 0$ shares of Hub Properties. The portfolio risk index is $0.50(2000) + 0.25(0) = 1000$. In this case, $d_1^+ = 300$ reflects the fact that the portfolio risk index exceeds the target value by 300 units; note also that since d_1^+ is greater than zero, the value of d_1^- must be zero. For a portfolio consisting of $x_1 = 0$ shares of U.S. Oil and $x_2 = 1000$ shares of Hub Properties, the portfolio risk index would be $0.50(0) + 0.25(1000) = 250$. In this case, $d_1^- = 450$ and $d_1^+ = 0$, indicating that the solution provides a portfolio risk index of 450 less than the target value of 700.

In general, the letter d is used for deviation variables in a goal programming model. A superscript of plus ($+$) or minus ($-$) is used to indicate whether the variable corresponds to a positive or negative deviation from the target value. If we bring the deviation variables to the left-hand side, we can rewrite the goal equation for the primary goal as

$$0.50x_1 + 0.25x_2 - d_1^+ + d_1^- = 700$$

Note that the value on the right-hand side of the goal equation is the target value for the goal. The left-hand side of the goal equation consists of two parts:

1. a function that defines the amount of goal achievement in terms of the decision variables (e.g., $0.50x_1 + 0.25x_2$); and
2. deviation variables representing the difference between the target value for the goal and the level achieved.

To develop a goal equation for the secondary goal, we begin by writing a function representing the annual return for the investment:

$$\text{Annual return} = 3x_1 + 5x_2$$

Then we define two deviation variables that represent the amount of over- or under-achievement of the goal. Doing so, we obtain

$d_2^+ =$ the amount by which the annual return for the portfolio is greater than the target value of \$9000

$d_2^- =$ the amount by which the annual return for the portfolio is less than the target value of \$9000

Using these two deviation variables, we write the goal equation for goal 2 as

$$3x_1 + 5x_2 = 9000 + d_2^+ - d_2^-$$

or

$$3x_1 + 5x_2 - d_2^+ + d_2^- = 9000$$

This step completes the development of the goal equations and the constraints for the Nicolo portfolio problem. We are now ready to develop an appropriate objective function for the problem.

Developing an Objective Function with Preemptive Priorities

The objective function in a goal programming model calls for minimizing a function of the deviation variables. In the portfolio selection problem, the most important goal, denoted P_1, is to find a portfolio with a risk index of 700 or less. There are only two goals in the problem, and the client is unwilling to incur a portfolio risk index greater than 700 to achieve the secondary annual return goal. Therefore, the secondary goal is denoted P_2. These goal priorities are referred to as preemptive priorities in goal programming terminology because the satisfaction of a higher level goal cannot be traded for the satisfaction of a lower level goal.

Goal programming problems with preemptive priorities are solved by treating priority level 1 goals (P_1) first in an objective function. The idea is to start by finding a solution that comes closest to satisfying the priority level 1 goals. This solution is then modified by solving a problem with an objective function involving only priority level 2 goals (P_2); however, revisions in the solution are permitted only if they do not hinder achievement of the P_1 goals. In general, solving a goal programming problem with preemptive priorities involves a sequence of linear programs with different objective functions; P_1 goals are considered first, P_2 goals second, P_3 goals third, and so on. At each stage of the procedure, a revision in the solution is permitted only if it causes no reduction in the achievement of a higher priority goal.

The number of linear programs that we must solve in sequence to develop the solution to a goal programming problem is determined by the number of priority levels. One linear program must be solved for each priority level. We will call the first linear program solved the priority level 1 problem, the second linear program solved the priority level 2 problem, and so on. Each of the linear programs is obtained from the one at the next higher level by changing the objective function and adding a constraint.

We first formulate the objective function for the priority level 1 problem. The client has stated that the portfolio risk index should not exceed 700. Is underachieving the target value of 700 a concern? Clearly, the answer is no because values of less than 700 correspond to less risk. Is overachieving the target value of 700 a concern? The answer is yes because portfolios with a risk index greater than 700 correspond to unacceptable levels of risk. Thus, the objective function corresponding to the priority level 1 linear program should minimize the value of d_1^+.

The goal equations and the funds available constraint have already been developed. Thus, the priority level 1 linear program can now be stated.

P_1 Problem

$$\text{Min} \quad d_1^+$$

s.t.

$$
\begin{array}{llll}
25x_1 + 50x_2 & & \leq 80{,}000 & \text{Funds available} \\
0.50x_1 + 0.25x_2 - d_1^+ + d_1^- & = 700 & P_1 \text{ goal} \\
3x_1 + 5x_2 & -d_2^+ + d_2^- = 9000 & P_2 \text{ goal} \\
\end{array}
$$

$$x_1, x_2, d_1^+, d_1^-, d_2^+, d_2^- \geq 0$$

The Graphical Solution Procedure

The graphical solution procedure for goal programming is similar to that for linear programming presented in Chapter 2. The only difference is that the procedure for goal programming involves a separate solution for each priority level. Recall that the linear programming graphical solution procedure uses a graph to display the values for the decision variables. Because the decision variables are nonnegative, we consider only that portion of the graph where $x_1 \geq 0$ and $x_2 \geq 0$. Recall also that every point on the graph is called a *solution point*.

We begin the graphical solution procedure for the Nicolo Investment problem by identifying all solution points that satisfy the available funds constraint:

$$25x_1 + 50x_2 \leq 80{,}000$$

Figure 15.1

Portfolios That Satisfy the Available Funds Constraint

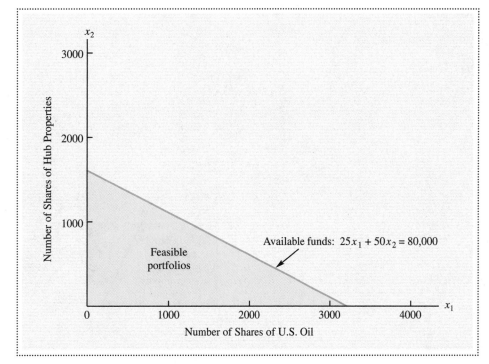

The shaded region in Figure 15.1, feasible portfolios, consists of all points that satisfy this constraint—that is, values of x_1 and x_2 for which $25x_1 + 50x_2 \leq 80,000$.

The objective for the priority level 1 linear program is to minimize d_1^+, the amount by which the portfolio index exceeds the target value of 700. Recall that the P_1 goal equation is

$$0.50x_1 + 0.25x_2 - d_1^+ + d_1^- = 700$$

When the P_1 goal is met exactly, $d_1^+ = 0$ and $d_1^- = 0$; the goal equation then reduces to $0.50x_1 + 0.25x_2 = 700$. Figure 15.2 shows the graph of this equation; the shaded region identifies all solution points that satisfy the available funds constraint and also result in the value of $d_1^+ = 0$. Since any solution point for which $d_1^+ = 0$ will achieve the priority level 1 goal, the shaded region contains all the feasible solution points that correspond to portfolios with a risk index of 700 or less.

At this point, we have solved the priority level 1 problem. Note that there are alternative optimal solutions; in fact, all solution points in the shaded region in Figure 15.2 maintain a portfolio risk index of 700 or less, and hence $d_1^+ = 0$.

The priority level 2 goal for the Nicolo Investment problem is to find a portfolio that will provide an annual return of at least \$9000. Is overachieving the target value of \$9000 a concern? Clearly, the answer is no because portfolios with an annual return of more than \$9000 correspond to higher returns. Is underachieving the target value of \$9000 a concern? The answer is yes because portfolios with an annual return of less than \$9000 are not acceptable to the client. Thus, the objective function corresponding to the priority level 2 linear program should minimize the value of d_2^-. However, since goal 2 is a secondary goal, the solution to the priority level 2 linear program must not degrade the optimal solution to the priority level 1 problem. Thus, the priority level 2 linear program can now be stated.

Figure 15.2

Portfolios That Satisfy the P_1 Goal

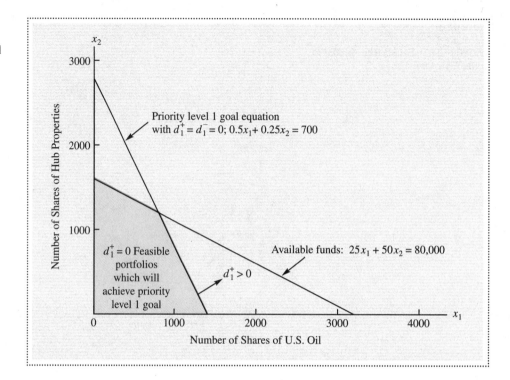

P_2 Problem

Min d_2^-

s.t.

$$25x_1 + 50x_2   \leq 80{,}000 \quad \text{Funds available}$$

$$0.50x_1 + 0.25x_2 - d_1^+ + d_1^- = 700 \quad P_1 \text{ goal}$$

$$3x_1 + 5x_2 - d_2^+ + d_2^- = 9{,}000 \quad P_2 \text{ goal}$$

$$d_1^+ = 0 \quad \begin{array}{l}\text{Maintain achievement}\\ \text{of } P_1 \text{ goal}\end{array}$$

$$x_1, x_2, d_1^+, d_1^-, d_2^+, d_2^- \geq 0$$

Note that the priority level 2 linear program differs from the priority level 1 linear program in two ways. The objective function involves minimizing the amount by which the portfolio annual return underachieves the level 2 goal, and another constraint has been added to ensure that no amount of achievement of the priority level 1 goal is sacrificed.

Let us now continue the graphical solution procedure. The goal equation for the priority level 2 goal is

$$3x_1 + 5x_2 - d_2^+ + d_2^- = 9000$$

When both d_2^+ and d_2^- equal zero, this equation reduces to $3x_1 + 5x_2 = 9000$; we show the graph with this equation in Figure 15.3.

At this stage, we cannot consider any solution point that will degrade the achievement of the priority level 1 goal. Figure 15.3 shows that there are no solution points that will achieve the priority level 2 goal and maintain the values we were able to achieve for the priority level 1 goal. In fact, the best solution that can be obtained when considering the

Figure 15.3
. . . .

Best Solution with Respect to Both Goals (Solution to P_2 Problem)

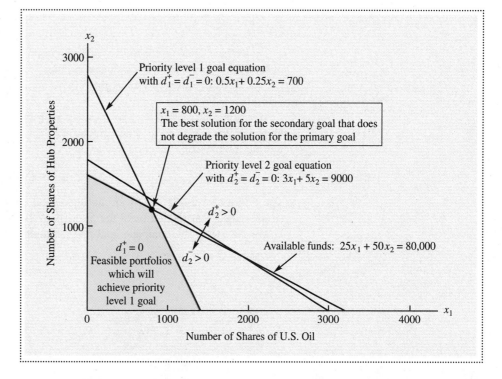

priority level 2 goal is given by the point ($x_1 = 800$, $x_2 = 1200$); in other words, this point comes the closest to satisfying the priority level 2 goal from among those solutions satisfying the priority level 1 goal. Since the annual return corresponding to this solution point is $3(800) + $5(1200) = 8400, identifying a portfolio that will satisfy both the priority level 1 and the priority level 2 goals is impossible; in fact, the best solution point underachieves goal 2 by $d_2^- = $9000 - $8400 = 600.

Thus, the goal programming solution for the Nicolo Investment problem recommends that the $80,000 available for investment be used to purchase 800 shares of U.S. Oil and 1200 shares of Hub Properties. Note that the priority level 1 goal of a portfolio risk index of 700 or less has been achieved. However, the priority level 2 goal of at least a $9000 annual return is not achievable. The recommended portfolio projects an $8400 annual return.

In summary, the graphical solution procedure for goal programming involves the following steps.

1. Identify the feasible solution points; these are the ones that satisfy the problem constraints.
2. Identify all feasible solutions that achieve the highest-priority goal; if there are no feasible solutions that will achieve the highest-priority goal, identify the solution(s) that comes closest to achieving it.
3. Move down one priority level, and determine the "best" solution possible without sacrificing any achievement of higher priority goals.
4. Repeat step 3 until all priority levels have been considered.

You should be able to formulate a goal programming model and use the graphical solution procedure to obtain a solution. Try Problem 2.

Although the graphical solution procedure is a convenient method for solving goal programming problems involving two decision variables, the solution of larger problems requires a computer-aided approach. In Section 15.2 we will illustrate how to use a computer software package to solve more complex goal programming problems.

The Goal Programming Model

As we have stated, preemptive goal programming problems are solved as a sequence of linear programs; there is one linear program for each priority level. However, having a notation that permits writing a goal programming problem in one concise statement is helpful.

In writing the overall objective for the portfolio selection problem, we must write the objective function in a way that reminds us of the preemptive priorities. We can do so by writing the objective function as

$$\text{Min } P_1(d_1^+) + P_2(d_2^-)$$

The priority levels P_1 and P_2 are not numerical weights on the deviation variables, but simply labels that remind us of the priority levels for the goals.

We now write the complete goal programming model as

$$\text{Min} \quad P_1(d_1^+) + P_2(d_2^-)$$

s.t.

$$
\begin{aligned}
25x_1 + 50x_2 && \leq 80{,}000 \quad &\text{Funds available} \\
0.50x_1 + 0.25x_2 - d_1^+ + d_1^- && = 700 \quad &P_1 \text{ goal} \\
3x_1 + 5x_2 \qquad - d_2^+ + d_2^- &= 9000 \quad &P_2 \text{ goal} \\
x_1, x_2, d_1^+, d_1^-, d_2^+, d_2^- \geq 0
\end{aligned}
$$

With the exception of the P_1 and P_2 priority levels in the objective function, this model is a linear programming model. The solution of this linear program involves solving a sequence of linear programs involving goals at decreasing priority levels.

We now summarize the procedure used to develop a goal programming model.

1. Identify the goals and any constraints that reflect resource capacities or other restrictions that may prevent achievement of the goals.
2. Determine the priority level of each goal; goals with priority level P_1 are most important, those with priority level P_2 are next most important, and so on.
3. Define the decision variables.
4. Formulate the constraints in the usual linear programming fashion.
5. For each goal, develop a goal equation, with the right-hand side specifying the target value for the goal. Deviation variables d_i^+ and d_i^- are included in each goal equation to reflect the possible deviations above or below the target value.
6. Write the objective function in terms of minimizing a prioritized function of the deviation variables.

NOTES & comments

1. The constraints in the general goal programming model are of two types: goal equations and ordinary linear programming constraints. Some analysts call the goal equations *goal constraints* and the ordinary linear programming constraints *system constraints*.

—*Continued*

—*Continued from previous page*

2. You might think of the general goal programming model as having "hard" and "soft" constraints. The hard constraints are the ordinary linear programming constraints that cannot be violated. The soft constraints are the ones resulting from the goal equations. Soft constraints can be violated, but there is a penalty for doing so. The penalty is reflected by the coefficient of the deviation variable in the objective function; in Section 15.2 we illustrate this point with a problem that has a coefficient of 2 for one of the deviation variables.

3. Note that the constraint added in moving from the linear programming problem at one priority level to the linear programming problem at the next lower priority level becomes a hard constraint. No amount of achievement of a higher priority goal may be sacrificed to achieve a lower priority goal.

15.2 Goal Programming: Solving More Complex Problems

In Section 15.1 we formulated and solved a goal programming model that involved one priority level 1 goal and one priority level 2 goal. In this section we show how to formulate and solve goal programming models that involve multiple goals within the same priority level. Although computer programs have been specially developed to solve goal programming models, these programs are not as readily available as general purpose linear programming software packages. Thus, the computer solution procedure outlined in this section develops a solution to a goal programming model by solving a sequence of linear programming models with a general purpose linear programming software package.

The Suncoast Office Supplies Problem

The management of Suncoast Office Supplies establishes monthly goals, or quotas, for the types of customers contacted. For the next 4 weeks, Suncoast's customer contact strategy calls for the sales force, which consists of four salespeople, to make 200 contacts with customers who have previously purchased supplies from the firm. In addition, the strategy calls for 120 contacts of new customers. The purpose of this latter goal is to ensure that the sales force is continuing to investigate new sources of sales.

Making allowances for travel and waiting time, as well as for demonstration and direct sales time, Suncoast has allocated 2 hours of sales force effort to each contact of a previous customer. New customer contacts tend to take longer and require 3 hours per contact. Normally, each salesperson works 40 hours per week, or 160 hours over the 4-week planning horizon; under a normal work schedule, the four salespeople will have $4(160) = 640$ hours of sales force time available for customer contacts.

Management is willing to use some overtime, if needed, but is also willing to accept a solution that uses less than the scheduled 640 hours available. However, management wants both overtime and underutilization of the work force limited to no more than 40 hours over the 4-week period. Thus, in terms of overtime, management's goal is to use no more than $640 + 40 = 680$ hours of sales force time, and in terms of labor utilization, management's goal is to use at least $640 - 40 = 600$ hours of sales-force time.

In addition to the customer contact goals, Suncoast has established a goal regarding sales volume. Based on past experience, Suncoast estimates that each previous customer contacted will generate $250 of sales and that each new customer contacted will generate $125 of sales. Management wants to generate sales revenue of at least $70,000 for the next month.

Given Suncoast's small sales force and the short time frame involved, management has decided that the overtime goal and the labor utilization goal are both priority level 1 goals. Management also concluded that the $70,000 sales revenue goal should be a priority level 2 goal and that the two customer contact goals should be priority level 3 goals. Based on these priorities, we can now summarize the goals.

Priority Level 1 Goals

Goal 1:   Do not use any more than 680 hours of sales force time.

Goal 2:   Do not use any less than 600 hours of sales force time.

Priority Level 2 Goal

Goal 3:   Generate sales revenue of at least $70,000.

Priority Level 3 Goals

Goal 4:   Call on at least 200 previous customers.

Goal 5:   Call on at least 120 new customers.

Formulating the Goal Equations

Next, we must define the decision variables whose values will be used to determine whether we are able to achieve the goals. Let

$$x_1 = \text{the number of previous customers contacted}$$
$$x_2 = \text{the number of new customers contacted}$$

Using these decision variables and appropriate deviation variables, we can develop a goal equation for each goal. The procedure used parallels the approach introduced in the preceding section. A summary of the results obtained is shown for each goal.

Goal 1

$$2x_1 + 3x_2 - d_1^+ + d_1^- = 680$$

where

$d_1^+ = $ the amount by which the number of hours used by the sales force is greater than the target value of 680 hours

$d_1^- = $ the amount by which the number of hours used by the sales force is less than the target value of 680 hours

Goal 2

$$2x_1 + 3x_2 - d_2^+ + d_2^- = 600$$

where

d_2^+ = the amount by which the number of hours used by the sales force is greater than the target value of 600 hours

d_2^- = the amount by which the number of hours used by the sales force is less than the target value of 600 hours

Goal 3

$$250x_1 + 125x_2 - d_3^+ + d_3^- = 70,000$$

where

d_3^+ = the amount by which the sales revenue is greater than the target value of \$70,000

d_3^- = the amount by which the sales revenue is less than the target value of \$70,000

Goal 4

$$x_1 - d_4^+ + d_4^- = 200$$

where

d_4^+ = the amount by which the number of previous customer contacts is greater than the target value of 200 previous customer contacts

d_4^- = the amount by which the number of previous customer contacts is less than the target value of 200 previous customer contacts

Goal 5

$$x_2 - d_5^+ + d_5^- = 120$$

where

d_5^+ = the amount by which the number of new customer contacts is greater than the target value of 120 new customer contacts

d_5^- = the amount by which the number of new customer contacts is less than the target value of 120 new customer contacts

Formulating the Objective Function

To develop the objective function for the Suncoast Office Supplies problem, we begin by considering the priority level 1 goals. When considering goal 1, if $d_1^+ = 0$, we will have found a solution that uses no more than 680 hours of sales-force time. Since solutions for which d_1^+ is greater than zero represent overtime beyond the desired level, the objective function should minimize the value of d_1^+. When considering goal 2, if $d_2^- = 0$, we will have found a solution that uses *at least* 600 hours of sales-force time. If

d_2^- is greater than zero, however, labor utilization will not have reached the acceptable level. Thus, the objective function for the priority level 1 goals should minimize the value of d_2^-. Because both of these priority level 1 goals are equally important, the objective function for the priority level 1 problem is

$$\text{Min } d_1^+ + d_2^-$$

In considering the priority level 2 goal, we note that management wants to achieve sales revenues of at least \$70,000. If $d_3^- = 0$, Suncoast will achieve revenues of *at least* \$70,000, and if $d_3^- > 0$, revenues of less than \$70,000 will be obtained. Thus, the objective function for the priority level 2 problem is

$$\text{Min } d_3^-$$

Next, we consider what the objective function must be for the priority level 3 problem. When considering goal 4, if $d_4^- = 0$, we will have found a solution with *at least* 200 previous customer contacts; however, if $d_4^- > 0$, we will have underachieved the goal of contacting at least 200 previous customers. Thus, for goal 4 the objective is to minimize d_4^-. When considering goal 5, if $d_5^- = 0$, we will have found a solution with *at least* 120 new customer contacts; however, if $d_5^- > 0$, we will have underachieved the goal of contacting at least 120 new customers. Thus, for goal 5 the objective is to minimize d_5^-. If both goals 4 and 5 are equal in importance, the objective function for the priority level 3 problem would be

$$\text{Min } d_4^- + d_5^-$$

However, suppose that management believes that generating new customers is vital to the long-run success of the firm and that goal 5 should be weighted more than goal 4. If management believes that goal 5 is twice as important as goal 4, the objective function for the priority level 3 problem would be

$$\text{Min } d_4^- + 2d_5^-$$

Combining the objective functions for all three priority levels, we obtain the overall objective function for the Suncoast Office Supplies problem:

$$\text{Min } P_1(d_1^+) + P_1(d_2^-) + P_2(d_3^-) + P_3(d_4^-) + P_3(2d_5^-)$$

As we indicated previously, P_1, P_2, and P_3 are simply labels that remind us that goals 1 and 2 are the priority level 1 goals, goal 3 is the priority level 2 goal, and goals 4 and 5 are the priority level 3 goals. We can now write the complete goal programming model for the Suncoast Office Supplies problem as follows:

$$\text{Min } P_1(d_1^+) + P_1(d_2^-) + P_2(d_3^-) + P_3(d_4^-) + P_3(2d_5^-)$$

s.t.

$$
\begin{array}{llll}
2x_1 + 3x_2 - d_1^+ + d_1^- & = & 680 & \text{Goal 1} \\
2x_1 + 3x_2 - d_2^+ + d_2^- & = & 600 & \text{Goal 2} \\
250x_1 + 125x_2 - d_3^+ + d_3^- & = & 70{,}000 & \text{Goal 3} \\
x_1 - d_4^+ + d_4^- & = & 200 & \text{Goal 4} \\
x_2 - d_5^+ + d_5^- & = & 120 & \text{Goal 5} \\
\end{array}
$$

$$x_1, x_2, d_1^+, d_1^-, d_2^+, d_2^-, d_3^+, d_3^-, d_4^+, d_4^-, d_5^+, d_5^- \geq 0$$

Computer Solution

•••

The computer procedure develops a solution to a goal programming model by solving a sequence of linear programming problems. The first problem comprises all the constraints and all the goal equations for the complete goal programming model; however, the objective function for this problem involves only the P_1 priority level goals. Again, we refer to this problem as the P_1 problem.

Whatever the solution is to the P_1 problem, a P_2 problem is formed by adding a constraint to the P_1 model that ensures that subsequent problems will not degrade the solution obtained for the P_1 problem. The objective function for the priority level 2 problem takes into consideration only the P_2 goals. We continue the process until we have considered all priority levels. We will illustrate the procedure for the Suncoast Office Supplies problem using LINDO/PC.

To solve the Suncoast Office Supplies problem, we begin by solving the P_1 problem:

$$\text{Min} \quad d_1^+ + d_2^-$$

s.t.

$$
\begin{array}{rcll}
2x_1 + 3x_2 - d_1^+ + d_1^- & = & 680 & \text{Goal 1} \\
2x_1 + 3x_2 - d_2^+ + d_2^- & = & 600 & \text{Goal 2} \\
250x_1 + 125x_2 - d_3^+ + d_3^- & = & 70{,}000 & \text{Goal 3} \\
x_1 - d_4^+ + d_4^- & = & 200 & \text{Goal 4} \\
x_2 - d_5^+ + d_5^- & = & 120 & \text{Goal 5}
\end{array}
$$

$$x_1, x_2, d_1^+, d_1^-, d_2^+, d_2^-, d_3^+, d_3^-, d_4^+, d_4^-, d_5^+, d_5^- \geq 0$$

In Figure 15.4 we show the LINDO/PC solution for this linear program. Note that D1MINUS refers to d_1^-, D1PLUS refers to d_1^+, D2MINUS refers to d_2^-, and so on. The solution consisting of $x_1 = 200$ previous customer contacts and $x_2 = 66.67$ new customer contacts achieves both goals 1 and 2 because D1PLUS and D2MINUS are equal to zero; alternatively, the objective function value of D1PLUS + D2MINUS = 0 also confirms that both priority level 1 goals have been achieved. Note that this solution underachieves the sales revenue goal by D3MINUS = \$11,666.67, achieves goal 4, and underachieves goal 5 by D5MINUS = 53.33 new customers. Most importantly, however, we now know that a solution exists that achieves the priority level 1 goals.

The model for the P_2 problem is formed by adding a constraint to the P_1 problem that ensures that subsequent solutions will not degrade the solution already obtained for the priority level 1 goals. We can do this by requiring that all future solutions satisfy the constraint $d_1^+ + d_2^- = 0$. Adding this constraint to the model and writing the objective function in terms of the priority level 2 goal, we obtain the linear program and LINDO/PC solution shown in Figure 15.5.

The optimal solution to the P_2 problem is to contact $x_1 = 270$ previous customers and $x_2 = 20$ new customers. Since D3MINUS = 0, we now know that achieving both the P_1 and the P_2 level goals is possible. In other words, a solution can be found that will achieve the labor utilization goals and also generate sales revenues of at least \$70,000. Note, however, that this solution overachieves the previous customer contact goal by D4PLUS = 70 previous customers and falls short of the new customer contact goal by D5MINUS = 100 new customers.

Figure 15.4
. . . .
The LINDO/PC Solution of the P_1 Problem

```
                    OBJECTIVE FUNCTION VALUE

        1)                 .00000000


          VARIABLE              VALUE        REDUCED COST

            D1PLUS            .000000          1.000000
           D2MINUS            .000000          1.000000
                X1         200.000000           .000000
                X2          66.666660           .000000
           D1MINUS          80.000000           .000000
            D2PLUS            .000000           .000000
            D3PLUS            .000000           .000000
           D3MINUS       11666.670000           .000000
            D4PLUS            .000000           .000000
           D4MINUS            .000000           .000000
            D5PLUS            .000000           .000000
           D5MINUS          53.333330           .000000
```

Figure 15.5
. . . .
The LINDO/PC Solution of the P_2 Problem

```
MIN    D3MINUS
SUBJECT TO
        2)  - D1PLUS + 2 X1 + 3 X2 + D1MINUS =      680
        3)    D2MINUS + 2 X1 + 3 X2 - D2PLUS =      600
        4)    250 X1 + 125 X2 - D3PLUS + D3MINUS =      70000
        5)    X1 - D4PLUS + D4MINUS =      200
        6)    X2 - D5PLUS + D5MINUS =      120
        7)    D1PLUS + D2MINUS =     0
END
                OBJECTIVE FUNCTION VALUE

    1)                .00000000

    VARIABLE              VALUE        REDUCED COST

      D1PLUS             .000000          .000000
     D2MINUS             .000000          .000000
          X1          270.000000          .000000
          X2           20.000000          .000000
     D1MINUS           80.000000          .000000
      D2PLUS             .000000          .000000
      D3PLUS             .000000          .000000
     D3MINUS             .000000         1.000000
      D4PLUS           70.000000          .000000
     D4MINUS             .000000          .000000
      D5PLUS             .000000          .000000
     D5MINUS          100.000000          .000000
```

Figure 15.6

The LINDO/PC Solution of the P_3 Problem

```
MIN     D4MINUS + 2 D5MINUS
SUBJECT TO
        2)  - D1PLUS + 2 X1 + 3 X2 + D1MINUS =     680
        3)    D2MINUS + 2 X1 + 3 X2 - D2PLUS =     600
        4)    250 X1 + 125 X2 - D3PLUS + D3MINUS =     70000
        5)    X1 - D4PLUS + D4MINUS =    200
        6)    X2 - D5PLUS + D5MINUS =    120
        7)    D1PLUS + D2MINUS =    0
        8)    D3MINUS =    0
END
                OBJECTIVE FUNCTION VALUE

 1)             120.000000


     VARIABLE            VALUE         REDUCED COST

      D1PLUS           .000000          .000000
     D2MINUS           .000000         1.000000
          X1        250.000000          .000000
          X2         60.000000          .000000
     D1MINUS           .000000         1.000000
      D2PLUS         80.000000          .000000
      D3PLUS           .000000          .000000
     D3MINUS           .000000          .000000
      D4PLUS         50.000000          .000000
     D4MINUS           .000000         1.000000
      D5PLUS           .000000         2.000000
     D5MINUS         60.000000          .000000
```

The third linear programming problem requires adding a constraint to the P_2 problem that will ensure that the P_2 sales revenue goal will continue to be achieved. Note that this can be done by adding the constraint $d_3^- = 0$. With the addition of this constraint and the objective function corresponding to the P_3 priority level goals, we obtain the priority level 3 linear program and LINDO/PC solution shown in Figure 15.6. The optimal solution consisting of $x_1 = 250$ previous customer contacts and $x_2 = 60$ new customer contacts overachieves goal 4 by D4PLUS = 50 previous customers; however, this solution underachieves goal 5 by D5MINUS = 60 new customers.

All the priority levels have been considered, so the solution procedure is finished. The optimal solution for Suncoast is to contact 250 previous customers and 60 new customers. Although this solution will not achieve management's goal of contacting at least 120 new customers, it does achieve each of the other goals specified. If management isn't happy with this solution, a different set of priorities could be considered. Management must keep in mind, however, that in any situation involving multiple goals at different priority levels, rarely will all the goals be achieved with existing resources.

NOTES & comments

1. Not all goal programming problems involve multiple priority levels. For problems with one priority level, only one linear program needs to be solved to obtain the goal programming solution. The analyst simply minimizes the weighted deviations from the goals. Trade-offs are permitted among the goals because they are all at the same priority level.

2. The goal programming approach can be used when the analyst is confronted with an infeasible solution to an ordinary linear program. Reformulating some of the constraints as goal equations with deviation variables allows a solution that minimizes the weighted sum of the deviation variables. Often, this approach will suggest a reasonable solution.

3. The approach that we utilized to solve goal programming problems with multiple priority levels is to solve a sequence of linear programs. These linear programs are closely related so that complete reformulation and solution are not necessary. By changing the objective function and adding a constraint, we can go from one linear program to the next.

15.3 The Analytic Hierarchy Process

The analytic hierarchy process (AHP), developed by Thomas L. Saaty,[1] is designed to solve complex problems involving multiple criteria. The process requires the decision maker to provide judgments about the relative importance of each criterion and then specify a preference on each criterion for each decision alternative. The output of AHP is a prioritized ranking indicating the overall preference for each of the decision alternatives. The Management Science in Action: Using AHP and Goal Programming to Plan Facility Locations describes how the University of Missouri-Rolla used AHP and goal programming to allocate floor space in a new facility.

To introduce AHP, we consider the problem facing Diane Payne, who is planning to purchase a new car. After a preliminary analysis of the makes and models available, she has narrowed the list of decision alternatives to three cars, A, B, and C. Table 15.1 provides a summary of the information that she has collected regarding these cars.

Based on the information in Table 15.1—as well as her own personal feelings resulting from driving each car—Payne decided that she needed to consider several criteria in making the purchase decision. After some thought, she selected purchase price, miles per gallon (MPG), comfort, and style as the four criteria to consider. Quantitative data regarding the purchase price and MPG criteria are provided directly in Table 15.1. However, measures of comfort and style cannot be specified so easily. Payne will need to

---

[1]Saaty, T. L., *The Analytic Hierarchy Process.* New York: McGraw-Hill, 1980.

MANAGEMENT SCIENCE in action

Using AHP and Goal Programming to Plan Facility Locations*

The department of engineering management at the University of Missouri-Rolla needed to determine how 5072 square feet of floor space for a new computer-integrated manufacturing (CIM) laboratory should be allocated to best achieve the objectives of the university. An in-house planning team identified a list of 15 sections (e.g., production machines, physical simulation lab, robot system, etc.) to be located in the CIM laboratory. The floor space required for all 15 sections, however, totaled 6035 square feet. Thus, the team needed to find a method for allocating the available space among the sections.

The team identified five goals that reflected the teaching, research, and extension objectives of the university. Goal 1: increase student use of the new facilities; Goal 2: develop new courses; Goal 3: stimulate research; Goal 4: increase industry awareness of CIM concepts; and Goal 5: enhance the univer-

sity's image. The team used AHP to develop priority weights for each objective (teaching, research, and extension) and each goal. It incorporated the weights derived through the AHP analysis in a linear goal programming model that determined the fractions of the 5072 square feet of floor space to be allocated to each section.

The team found "the AHP methodology effective in eliciting judgment from the members of the facilities-planning task force in a systematic and consistent manner. It helped obtain group consensus in a highly political environment in a timely manner for a fairly complex institutional planning problem."

....

*Based on Benjamin, C. O., I. C. Ehie, and Y. Omurtag, "Planning Facilities at the University of Missouri-Rolla." Interfaces, July–August 1992, pp. 95–105.

Table 15.1

Information for the Car-Selection Problem

Category	Car A	Car B	Car C
Price	$13,100	$11,200	$9500
MPG	18	23	29
Interior	Deluxe	Above average	Standard
Body	4-door midsize	2-door sport	2-door compact
Radio	AM/FM, tape	AM/FM	AM/FM
Engine	6-cylinder	4-cylinder turbo	4-cylinder

consider factors such as car interior, type of radio, ease of entry and exit, and seat-adjustment features to determine the comfort level of each car. The style criterion will need to be measured in terms of Payne's subjective evaluation of each car.

Even when we deal with a criterion as easily measured as purchase price, however, subjectivity becomes an issue whenever a particular decision maker indicates a personal preference. For instance, car A costs $3600 more than car C; this difference might represent a great deal of money to one person, but not very much money to another person. Thus, whether car A is considered extremely more expensive than car C or only moderately more expensive is a subjective judgment that will depend primarily on the financial status of the person making the comparison. An advantage of AHP is that it is designed to handle situations such as this, in which the subjective judgments of individuals constitute an important part of the decision process.

Figure 15.7

Hierarchy for the Car-Selection Problem

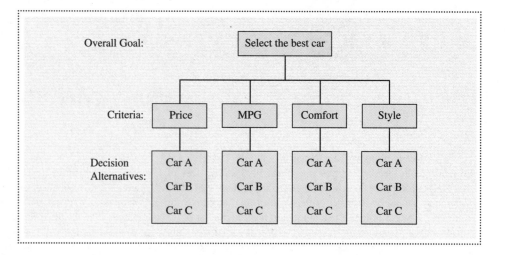

Developing the Hierarchy

The first step in AHP is to develop a graphical representation of the problem in terms of the *overall goal, criteria,* and *decision alternatives.* Such a graph depicts the *hierarchy* for the problem. Figure 15.7 shows the hierarchy for the car-selection problem. Note that the first level of the hierarchy shows that the overall goal is to select the best car. At the second level, the four criteria (purchase price, MPG, comfort, and style) will contribute to the achievement of the overall goal. Finally, at the third level, each decision alternative (car A, car B, and car C) contributes to each criterion in a unique way.

AHP has the decision maker specify judgments about the relative importance of each criterion in terms of its contribution to the achievement of the overall goal. At the next level, AHP asks the decision maker to indicate a preference or priority for each decision alternative in terms of how it contributes to each criterion. For example, in the car-selection problem, Payne will need to specify her judgment about the relative importance of each of the four criteria. She will also need to indicate her preference for each of the three cars relative to each criterion. A mathematical process is used to synthesize the information on relative importance and preferences and provide a priority ranking of the three cars in terms of their overall preference.

15.4 Establishing Priorities Using AHP

In this section we will show how AHP utilizes pairwise comparisons to establish priority measures for both the criteria and the decision alternatives. What needs to be determined in the car-selection problem are the priorities of

1. the four criteria in terms of the overall goal,
2. the three cars in terms of the purchase price criterion,
3. the three cars in terms of the MPG criterion,
4. the three cars in terms of the comfort criterion, and
5. the three cars in terms of the style criterion.

In the following discussion, we will demonstrate how to establish priorities for the three cars in terms of the *comfort* criterion. The other sets of priorities can be determined similarly.

Pairwise Comparisons

Pairwise comparisons are fundamental building blocks of AHP. In establishing the priorities for the three cars in terms of comfort, we will ask Diane Payne to state a preference for the comfort of the cars when the cars are considered two at a time (pairwise). That is, she must compare the comfort of car A to car B, car A to car C, and car B to car C in three separate comparisons.

AHP uses an underlying scale with values 1–9 to rate the relative preferences for two items. Table 15.2 provides the numerical ratings recommended for the verbal preferences expressed by the decision maker. Research and experience have confirmed the 9-unit scale as a reasonable basis for discriminating between the preferences for two items.

In the car-selection problem, suppose that Payne has compared the comfort of car A with the comfort of car B and is convinced that car A is more comfortable. She is then asked to state her preference for the comfort of car A compared to that of car B using one of the verbal descriptions shown in Table 15.2. If she *moderately* prefers car A to car B, a value of 3 is utilized in AHP; if she *strongly* perfers car A, a value of 5 is utilized; if she *very strongly* prefers car A, a value of 7 is utilized; if she *extremely* prefers car A, a value of 9 is utilized. Values of 2, 4, 6, and 8 are the intermediate values for the preference scale. A value of 1 is reserved for the case where the two items are judged to be *equally* preferred.

Suppose that when asked her preference between cars A and B with respect to the comfort criterion, Payne states that she prefers car A equally to moderately more than car B; the numerical measure that reflects this judgment is 2. She is then asked to state her preference between car A and car C. Suppose that in this case she states that she prefers car A very strongly to extremely more than car C; this corresponds to a numerical rating of 8. Finally, Payne is asked to state her preference for car B compared to car C. Suppose in this case that she indicates that she prefers car B strongly to very strongly to car C; AHP would assign a numerical rating of 6.

The Pairwise Comparison Matrix

To develop the priorities for the three cars in terms of the comfort criterion, we need to construct a matrix of the pairwise comparison ratings. Three cars are being considered, so the pairwise comparison matrix will consist of three rows and three columns. Shown is a portion of the *pairwise comparison matrix* based on the preferences that Diane Payne has specified.

| | Comfort | | |
	Car A	Car B	Car C
Car A		2	8
Car B			6
Car C			

The value in the matrix that corresponds to comparing car A with car B is 2, comparing car A with car C is 8, and comparing car B with car C is 6.

To determine the remaining entries in the pairwise comparison matrix, first note that when we compare any car against itself, the judgment must be "equally preferred." Thus, based on the scale shown in Table 15.2, the rating of car A compared to car A, car B to

Table 15.2

Pairwise Comparison Scale for AHP Preferences

Verbal Judgment of Preference	Numerical Rating
Extremely preferred	9
Very strongly to extremely	8
Very strongly preferred	7
Strongly to very strongly	6
Strongly preferred	5
Moderately to strongly	4
Moderately preferred	3
Equally to moderately	2
Equally preferred	1

car B, and car C to car C must be 1. Hence, AHP assigns a 1 to all elements on the diagonal of the pairwise comparison matrix.

All that remains is to determine the rating for car B compared to car A, car C compared to car A, and car C compared to car B. Obviously, we could follow the same procedure and ask Payne to state her preferences for these pairwise comparisons. However, we already know that her rated preference for car A compared to car B is 2, so there is no need for her to make another pairwise comparison of these two cars. In fact, we will conclude that the preference rating for car B compared to car A is simply the reciprocal of the preference rating for car A compared to car B, or ½. Hence, AHP obtains the preference rating of car B compared to car A by computing the reciprocal of the rating of car A to car B. Using this inverse, or reciprocal, relationship, we find that the rating of car C compared to car A is ⅛ and the rating of car C to car B is ⅙. These numerical values of preference yield the complete pairwise comparison matrix for the comfort criterion, as shown in Table 15.3.

Synthesis

After we have developed the matrix of pairwise comparisons, we can calculate the *priority* of each of the elements being compared. For example, we now want to use the pairwise comparison information in Table 15.3 to estimate the relative priority for each of the cars in terms of the comfort criterion. This part of AHP is referred to as *synthesization.*

The exact mathematical procedure required to perform this synthesization involves the computation of eigenvalues and eigenvectors and is beyond the scope of this text. However, the following three-step procedure provides a good approximation of the synthesized priorities.

Procedure for Synthesizing Judgments

Step 1   Sum the values in each column of the pairwise comparison matrix.

Step 2   Divide each element in the pairwise comparison matrix by its column total; the resulting matrix is referred to as the *normalized pairwise comparison matrix.*

Step 3   Compute the average of the elements in each row of the normalized matrix; these averages provide an estimate of the relative priorities of the elements being compared.

To show how the synthesization process works, we carry out the three-step procedure for the pairwise comparison matrix shown in Table 15.3.

Step 1   Sum the values in each column.

Table 15.3

Pairwise Comparison Matrix Showing Preferences for the Three Cars in Terms of Comfort

	Comfort		
	Car A	Car B	Car C
Car A	1	2	8
Car B	1/2	1	6
Car C	1/8	1/6	1

	Comfort		
	Car A	Car B	Car C
Car A	1	2	8
Car B	1/2	1	6
Car C	1/8	1/6	1
Totals	13/8	19/6	15

Step 2   Divide each element of the matrix by its column total.

	Comfort		
	Car A	Car B	Car C
Car A	8/13	12/19	8/15
Car B	4/13	6/19	6/15
Car C	1/13	1/19	1/15

Note: All columns in the normalized pairwise comparison matrix now have a sum of 1.

Step 3   Average the elements in each row. (The values in the normalized pairwise comparison matrix have been converted to decimal form.)

	Comfort			
	Car A	Car B	Car C	**Row Average**
Car A	0.615	0.632	0.533	0.593
Car B	0.308	0.316	0.400	0.341
Car C	0.077	0.053	0.067	0.066
			Total	1.000

This synthesis provides the relative priorities for the three cars with respect to the comfort criterion. Thus, considering comfort, the most preferred car is car A (with a priority of 0.593). Car B (with a priority of 0.341) is second, followed by car C (with a priority of 0.066). We write the priority vector showing the relative priorities of car A, car B, and car C with respect to the comfort criterion as

$$\begin{bmatrix} 0.593 \\ 0.341 \\ 0.066 \end{bmatrix}$$

You should be able to set up the pairwise comparison matrix and determine priorities. Try Problem 12.

Consistency

A key step in AHP is the establishment of priorities through the use of the pairwise comparison procedure just described. An important consideration in terms of the quality of the ultimate decision relates to the *consistency* of judgments that the decision maker demonstrated during the series of pairwise comparisons.

Realize that perfect consistency is difficult to achieve and that some lack of consistency is expected to exist in almost any set of pairwise comparisons. To handle the consistency question, AHP provides a method for measuring the degree of consistency among the pairwise judgments provided by the decision maker. If the degree of consistency is acceptable, the decision process can continue. However, if the degree of consistency is unacceptable, the decision maker should reconsider and possibly revise the pairwise comparison judgments before proceeding with the analysis.

AHP provides a measure of the consistency of pairwise comparison judgments by computing a *consistency ratio*. This ratio is designed in such a way that values of the ratio exceeding 0.10 are indicative of inconsistent judgments; in such cases, the decision maker would probably want to revise the original values in the pairwise comparison matrix. Values of the consistency ratio of 0.10 or less are considered to be a reasonable level of consistency in the pairwise comparisons.

Although the exact mathematical computation of the consistency ratio is beyond the scope of this text, an approximation of the ratio can be obtained. We will illustrate this computational procedure for the car-selection problem by considering Diane Payne's pairwise comparisons for the comfort criterion.

Estimating the Consistency Ratio

Step 1   Multiply each value in the first column of the pairwise comparison matrix by the relative priority of the first item considered; multiply each value in the second column of the matrix by the relative priority of the second item considered; multiply each value in the third column of the matrix by the relative priority of the third item considered. Sum the values across the rows to obtain a vector of values labeled "weighted sum." This computation for the car-selection problem is

$$0.593 \begin{bmatrix} 1 \\ 1/2 \\ 1/8 \end{bmatrix} + 0.341 \begin{bmatrix} 2 \\ 1 \\ 1/6 \end{bmatrix} + 0.066 \begin{bmatrix} 8 \\ 6 \\ 1 \end{bmatrix} = \begin{bmatrix} 0.593 \\ 0.297 \\ 0.074 \end{bmatrix} + \begin{bmatrix} 0.682 \\ 0.341 \\ 0.057 \end{bmatrix} + \begin{bmatrix} 0.528 \\ 0.396 \\ 0.066 \end{bmatrix}$$

$$= \begin{bmatrix} 1.803 \\ 1.034 \\ 0.197 \end{bmatrix} \quad \text{Weighted sum vector}$$

Step 2   Divide the elements of the vector of weighted sums obtained in step 1 by the corresponding priority value. For the car-selection problem, we obtain

$$\frac{1.803}{0.593} = 3.040$$

$$\frac{1.034}{0.341} = 3.032$$

$$\frac{0.197}{0.066} = 2.985$$

Step 3   Compute the average of the values found in step 2; this average is denoted λ_{max}. For the car-selection problem, we obtain

$$\lambda_{max} = \frac{3.040 + 3.032 + 2.985}{3} = 3.019$$

Step 4   Compute the consistency index (CI), which is defined as

$$CI = \frac{\lambda_{max} - n}{n - 1}$$

where

$$n = \text{the number of items being compared}$$

For the car-selection problem with $n = 3$, we obtain

$$CI = \frac{3.019 - 3}{2} = 0.010$$

Step 5   Compute the consistency ratio (CR), which is defined as

$$CR = \frac{CI}{RI}$$

where RI, the random index, is the consistency index of a randomly generated pairwise comparison matrix. The RI, which depends on the number of elements being compared, takes on the following values:

n	3	4	5	6	7	8
RI	0.58	0.90	1.12	1.24	1.32	1.41

Thus, for the car-selection problem with $n = 3$ and RI $= 0.58$, we obtain the following consistency ratio:

$$CR = \frac{0.01}{0.58} = 0.017$$

As mentioned previously, a consistency ratio of 0.10 or less is considered acceptable. Our example shows a consistency ratio of 0.017, so the degree of consistency exhibited in the pairwise comparison matrix for comfort is acceptable.

You should now be able to determine whether judgments are consistent. Try Problem 16.

Other Pairwise Comparisons for the Car-Selection Problem

Continuing with the AHP analysis of the car-selection problem, we need to use the pairwise comparison procedure to determine the priorities of the three cars in terms of the purchase price, MPG, and style criteria. This requires that Diane Payne express pairwise comparison preferences for the cars, considering these criteria one at a time. Assume that she has done so and that her preferences are summarized in the pairwise comparison matrices shown in Table 15.4.

Following the same synthesis procedure that we used for the comfort criterion, we can compute the priority vectors for these criteria. Table 15.5 shows the result of this synthesis. Interpreting these priorities, we note that car C is the most preferable in terms of purchase price (0.557) and miles per gallon (0.639). Car B is the most preferable in terms of style (0.655). No car is the most preferred with respect to all the criteria. Thus, before a final decision can be made, we must assess the relative importance of the criteria.

In addition to the pairwise comparisons for the decision alternatives, we must use the same pairwise comparison procedure to set priorities for all four criteria in terms of the importance of each in contributing toward the overall goal of selecting the best car. To develop this final pairwise comparison matrix, Payne would have to specify the importance of each criterion compared to each of the other criteria. To do so, she has to make six pairwise judgments:

> Purchase price compared to MPG
> Purchase price compared to comfort
> Purchase price compared to style
>
> MPG compared to comfort
> MPG compared to style
>
> Comfort compared to style

Table 15.4

Pairwise Comparison Matrices for Price, MPG, and Style in the Car-Selection Problem

Price	Car A	Car B	Car C
Car A	1	1/3	1/4
Car B	3	1	1/2
Car C	4	2	1

MPG	Car A	Car B	Car C
Car A	1	1/4	1/6
Car B	4	1	1/3
Car C	6	3	1

Style	Car A	Car B	Car C
Car A	1	1/3	4
Car B	3	1	7
Car C	1/4	1/7	1

Table 15.5

Priority Vectors for Price, MPG, and Style in the Car-Selection Problem

Price	MPG	Style
$\begin{bmatrix} 0.123 \\ 0.320 \\ 0.557 \end{bmatrix}$	$\begin{bmatrix} 0.087 \\ 0.274 \\ 0.639 \end{bmatrix}$	$\begin{bmatrix} 0.265 \\ 0.655 \\ 0.080 \end{bmatrix}$

For example, in the pairwise comparison of the purchase price and MPG, Payne indicates that purchase price is *moderately* more important than MPG. Using the AHP 9-point numerical rating scale (see Table 15.2), a value of 3 is recorded to show the higher importance of the purchase price criterion. Table 15.6 shows the summary of the pairwise comparison matrix preferences for the four criteria.

We can now use the synthesization process described earlier in this section to convert the pairwise comparison information into the priorities for the four criteria:

Priorities for the Four Criteria	
Price	0.398
MPG	0.085
Comfort	0.218
Style	0.299

The purchase price (0.398) is the highest-priority, or most important, criterion in the car-selection decision. Style (0.299) and comfort (0.218) rank next in importance. Miles per gallon (0.085) is a relatively unimportant criterion in terms of the overall goal of selecting the best car. In the next section we show how AHP uses the priority information generated here to develop an overall priority ranking for the three cars.

Table 15.6
....
Pairwise Comparison Matrix for the Four Criteria in the Car-Selection Problem

| | Criterion | | | |
	Price	MPG	Comfort	Style
Price	1	3	2	2
MPG	1/3	1	1/4	1/4
Comfort	1/2	4	1	1/2
Style	1/2	4	2	1

Table 15.7
....
The Priority Matrix for the Car-Selection Problem

	Price	MPG	Comfort	Style
Car A	0.123	0.087	0.593	0.265
Car B	0.320	0.274	0.341	0.655
Car C	0.557	0.639	0.066	0.080

15.5 Using AHP to Develop an Overall Priority Ranking

In the preceding section we showed how to use a pairwise comparison matrix to develop a prioritized ranking of the items being compared. Now we will show how to combine the criterion priorities and the priorities of each decision alternative relative to each criterion to develop an overall priority ranking of the decision alternatives. Table 15.7 summarizes the priorities for each car in terms of each criterion as computed in Section 15.4. We will refer to this matrix as the *priority matrix*.

The procedure used to compute the overall priorities for each decision alternative can best be understood if we think of the priority for each criterion as a weight that reflects its importance. The overall priority for each decision alternative is obtained by summing the products of the criterion priority times the priority of its decision alternative. Recall that the criterion priorities were found to be 0.398 for purchase price, 0.085 for MPG, 0.218 for comfort, and 0.299 for style. Thus, the computation of the overall priority for car A is as follows:

$$\text{Overall car A priority} = 0.398(0.123) + 0.085(0.087) + 0.218(0.593) + 0.299(0.265)$$
$$= 0.265$$

Repeating this calculation for cars B and C provides their overall priorities:

$$\text{Overall car B priority} = 0.398(0.320) + 0.085(0.274) + 0.218(0.341) + 0.299(0.655)$$
$$= 0.421$$

$$\text{Overall car C priority} = 0.398(0.557) + 0.085(0.639) + 0.218(0.066) + 0.299(0.080)$$
$$= 0.314$$

You should now be able to use AHP to determine overall priority ranking. Try Problem 20.

Ranking these priority values, we have the AHP ranking of the decision alternatives:

Alternative	Priority
Car A	0.265
Car B	0.421
Car C	0.314
Total	1.000

These results provide a basis for Diane Payne to make a decision regarding the purchase of a car. Based on the AHP priorities, she should select car B. Whether she actually decides to purchase car B based on the AHP analysis is still her decision to make. If Payne believes that the judgments she has made regarding the importance of the criteria and her preferences for the cars in terms of the criteria are valid, the AHP priorities show that car B is the preferred car. Whether Payne actually decides to purchase car B may not be as important as the additional understanding that she gained through the AHP analysis. That is, the process may be as helpful to her as the actual decision recommendation itself.

15.6 Using Expert Choice to Implement AHP

Expert Choice (EC), a software package marketed by Decision Support Software, provides a user-friendly procedure for implementing AHP on a microcomputer. In this section we provide an introduction to this software package by using it to compute the priorities for the car-selection problem.

Expert Choice enables the user to construct a graphical representation of the hierarchy easily. For example, to create the hierarchy for the car-selection problem, the user selects the option to develop a new application: what appears on the computer's monitor is a request to define the overall goal. After the user defines the overall goal—select the best car—a rectangular box, or node, appears on the screen with this goal description written directly above it. The user selects the Edit pull-down menu and then the Insert option; another rectangular box or node appears below the goal node, and the user now types the name of a criterion, such as price, which will be entered inside the box. This process continues until the user has specified all four criterion nodes, including MPG, comfort, and style. Figure 15.8 shows the partial hierarchy appearing on the computer screen after the four criteria have been entered.

Figure 15.8 shows that, in addition to the names of each criterion, the criterion nodes also contain the decimal value .250. This value represents the initial weight, or priority, given to each criterion at the start of the EC session. The user can now continue to use the Insert option to define the decision alternative nodes associated with each of the criterion nodes. Figure 15.9 shows the result of defining the decision alternative nodes of car A, car B, and car C for the price criterion; note that since there are three alternatives, the initial priorities are .333. Similar sets of decision alternatives are then identified for the other three criteria.

Now that the hierarchy has been input to EC, the user is ready to begin developing the pairwise comparisons needed to establish priorities for the decision alternatives. To illustrate the type of approach used, we moved back to the goal node and then selected the

Figure 15.8

Partial Hierarchy Showing Criteria with Initial Priorities Equal to 0.250

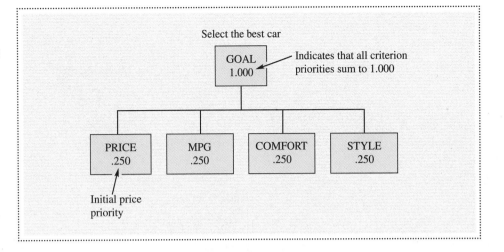

Figure 15.9

Partial Hierarchy Showing the Price Criterion with Initial Priorities for Cars A, B, and C

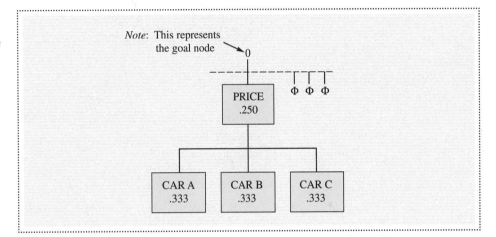

Compare pull-down menu. After selecting the option to make comparisons based on the importance of the decision criteria, the EC system begins to go through the pairwise comparison analysis.

First, EC asks the user if PRICE and MPG are equally important. A no response leads EC to ask if PRICE is more important than MPG; a yes response leads to a new screen on which the user specifies the comparative importance of PRICE and MPG, as shown in Figure 15.10. Note that PRICE is moderately more important than MPG. This process continues until all the entries in the pairwise comparison matrix for criteria have been developed. Figure 15.11 shows the priorities that EC obtained after synthesization.[2]

Pairwise preferences for the cars relative to each criterion were entered in a similar manner. The overall decision was then arrived at by selecting the Synthesis pull-down menu and selecting the Distributive Mode option to obtain an overall prioritization

---

[2]The priorities computed by EC differ slightly from those we obtained previously. The reason is that the method we used was an approximation to the EC synthesization procedure, which involves the computation of eigenvalues and eigenvectors.

Figure 15.10 **Determining the Rating for the Price and MPG Pairwise Comparison**

Goal: Select the best car

with respect to

```
GOAL
```

PRICE
 is EQUAL to MODERATELY more IMPORTANT than
MPG:

```
EXTREME-------------

VERY STRONG---------

STRONG--------------

MODERATE------------

EQUAL---------------    <--  <---
```

System initially positions
pointer here because we
said price and mileage are
not equally important.

PRICE
 is MODERATELY more IMPORTANT than
MPG:

```
EXTREME-------------

VERY STRONG---------

STRONG--------------

MODERATE------------<--  <---

EQUAL---------------
```

User moves the arrow to
the position that best
describes the relationship.

Figure 15.11

**The Hierarchy Showing Priorities
for the Criteria**

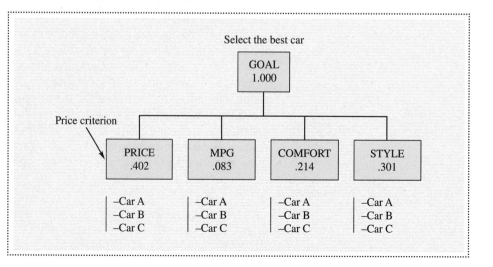

658

Figure 15.12 **AHP Final Results for the Car-Selection Problem**

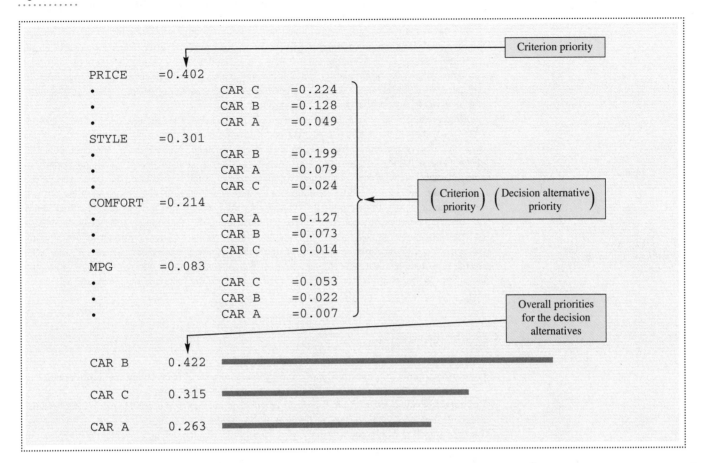

of the decision alternatives. Figure 15.12 shows the results. Note that the final priority for car B, the most preferable, is 0.422.

The EC system is much more powerful and comprehensive than our brief introduction can begin to show. It is extremely helpful in performing the multicriteria decision analysis of AHP. In addition to providing the overall priorities for the decision alternatives, EC is capable of performing sensitivity analyses, whereby the decision maker can begin to learn how the overall priorities for the decision alternatives are affected by changes in the preference input data.

Summary

In this chapter we used goal programming to solve problems with multiple goals within the linear programming framework. We showed that the goal programming model contains one or more goal equations and an objective function designed to minimize deviations from the goals. In situations where resource capacities or other restrictions affect the achievement of the goals, the model will contain constraints that are formulated and treated in the same manner as constraints in an ordinary linear programming model.

In goal programming problems with preemptive priorities, priority level 1 goals are treated first in an objective function to identify a solution that will best satisfy these goals. This solution is then revised by considering an objective function involving only the priority level 2 goals; solution modifications are considered only if they do not degrade the solution obtained for the priority level 1 goals. This process continues until all priority levels have been considered.

We showed how a variation of the linear programming graphical solution procedure can be used to solve goal programming problems with two decision variables. Specialized goal programming computer packages are available for solving the general goal programming problem, but such computer codes are not as readily available as are general purpose linear programming computer packages. As a result, we showed how a general linear programming package such as LINDO/PC can be used to solve a goal programming problem.

We presented an approach to multicriteria decision making called the analytic hierarchy process (AHP). We showed that a key part of AHP is the development of judgments concerning the relative importance of, or preference for, the elements being compared. A consistency ratio is computed to determine the degree of consistency exhibited by the decision maker in making the pairwise comparisons. Values of the consistency ratio less than or equal to 0.10 are considered acceptable.

Once the set of all pairwise comparisons has been developed, a process referred to as synthesization is used to determine the priorities for the elements being compared. The final step of the analytic hierarchy process is an overall synthesization, in which the priority levels established for the decision alternatives relative to each criterion are multiplied by the priority levels reflecting the importance of the criteria themselves; the sum of these products over all the criteria is the overall priority level for the decision alternative. We concluded the chapter with a brief introduction to Expert Choice, a software package designed to perform the computational steps of AHP.

Glossary

Goal programming A linear programming approach to problems involving multicriteria whereby the objective function is designed to minimize the deviations from goals.

Preemptive priorities Priorities assigned to goals that ensure that the satisfaction of a higher level goal cannot be traded for the satisfaction of a lower level goal.

Target value The value specified in the statement of the goal. Based on the context of the problem, management will want the solution to the goal programming problem to result in a value for the goal that is less than, equal to, or greater than the target value.

Goal equation An equation whose right-hand side is the target value for the goal; the left-hand side of the goal equation consists of (1) a function representing the level of achievement and (2) deviation variables representing the difference between the target value for the goal and the level achieved.

Deviation variables Variables that are added to the goal equation to allow the solution to deviate from the goal's target value.

Analytic hierarchy process (AHP) An approach to multicriteria decision making based in part on pairwise comparisons for elements in a hierarchy.

Hierarchy A diagram that shows the levels of a problem in terms of the overall goal, the criteria, and the decision alternatives.

Pairwise comparison matrix A matrix that consists of the preference, or relative importance, ratings provided during a series of pairwise comparisons.

Synthesization A mathematical process that uses the preference or relative importance values in the pairwise comparison matrix to develop priorities.

Normalized pairwise comparison matrix The matrix obtained by dividing each element of the pairwise comparison matrix by its column total. This matrix is computed as an intermediate step in the synthesization of priorities.

Consistency A concept developed to assess the quality of the judgments made during a series of pairwise comparisons. It is a measure of the internal consistency of these comparisons.

Consistency ratio A numerical measure of the degree of consistency in a series of pairwise comparisons. Values less than or equal to 0.10 are considered acceptable.

Expert Choice (EC) A computer software package that performs the computations required by the analytic hierarchy process.

Problems

1. The RMC Corporation blends three raw materials to produce two products: a fuel additive and a solvent base. Each ton of fuel additive is a mixture of 2/5 ton of material 1 and 3/5 ton of material 3. A ton of solvent base is a mixture of 1/2 ton of material 1, 1/5 ton of material 2, and 3/10 ton of material 3. RMC's production is constrained by a limited availability of the three raw materials. For the current production period, RMC has the following quantities of each raw material: material 1, 20 tons; material 2, 5 tons; material 3, 21 tons. Management wants to achieve the following P_1 priority level goals.

Goal 1: Produce at least 30 tons of fuel additive.

Goal 2: Produce at least 15 tons of solvent base.

Assume that there are no other goals.

a. Is it possible for management to achieve both P_1 level goals given the constraints on the amounts of each material available? Explain.
b. Treating the amounts of each material available as constraints, formulate a goal programming model to determine the optimal product mix. Assume that both P_1 priority level goals are equally important to management.
c. Use the graphical goal programming procedure to solve the model formulated in part (b).
d. If goal 1 is twice as important as goal 2, what is the optimal product mix?

2. **SELF Test** DJS Investment Services must develop an investment portfolio for a new client. As an initial investment strategy, the new client would like to restrict the portfolio to a mix of two stocks:

Stock	Price/Share	Estimated Annual Return (%)
AGA Products	$ 50	6
Key Oil	100	10

The client has $50,000 to invest and has established the following two investment goals.

Priority Level 1 Goal

Goal 1: Obtain an annual return of at least 9%.

Priority Level 2 Goal

Goal 2: Limit the investment in Key Oil, the riskier investment, to no more than 60% of the total investment.

a. Formulate a goal programming model for the DJS Investment problem.
b. Use the graphical goal programming procedure to obtain a solution.

3. The L. Young & Sons Manufacturing Company produces two products, which have the following profit and resource requirement characteristics.

Characteristic	Product 1	Product 2
Profit/unit	$4	$2
Dept. A hours/unit	1	1
Dept. B hours/unit	2	5

Last month's production schedule used 350 hours of labor in department A and 1000 hours of labor in department B.

Young's management has been experiencing work force morale and labor union problems during the past 6 months because of monthly departmental work load fluctuations. New hiring, layoffs, and interdepartmental transfers have been common because the firm has not attempted to stabilize work-load requirements.

Management would like to develop a production schedule for the coming month that will achieve the following goals.

Goal 1:   Use 350 hours of labor in department A.

Goal 2:   Use 1000 hours of labor in department B.

Goal 3:   Earn a profit of at least $1300.

a. Formulate a goal programming model for this problem, assuming that goals 1 and 2 are P_1 level goals and goal 3 is a P_2 level goal; assume that goals 1 and 2 are equally important.

b. Solve the model formulated in part (a) using the graphical goal programming procedure.

c. Suppose that the firm ignores the work-load fluctuations and considers the 350 hours in department A and the 1000 hours in department B as the maximum available. Formulate and solve a linear programming problem to maximize profit subject to these constraints.

d. Compare the solutions obtained in parts (b) and (c). Discuss which approach you favor, and why.

e. Reconsider part (a), assuming that the priority level 1 goal is goal 3 and the priority level 2 goals are goals 1 and 2; as before, assume that goals 1 and 2 are equally important. Solve this revised problem using the graphical goal programming procedure and compare your solution to the one obtained for the original problem.

4. Industrial Chemicals produces two adhesives used in the manufacturing process for airplanes. The two adhesives, which have different bonding strengths, require different amounts of production time: the IC-100 adhesive requires 20 minutes of production time per gallon of finished product, and the IC-200 adhesive uses 30 minutes of production time per gallon. Both products use 1 pound of a highly perishable resin for each gallon of finished product. There are 300 pounds of the resin in inventory, and more can be obtained if necessary. However, because of the shelf life of the material, any amount not used in the next 2 weeks will be discarded.

The firm has existing orders for 100 gallons of IC-100 and 120 gallons of IC-200. Under normal conditions, the production process operates 8 hours per day, 5 days per week. Management wants to schedule production for the next 2 weeks to achieve the following goals.

Priority Level 1 Goals

Goal 1:   Avoid underutilization of the production process.

Goal 2:   Avoid overtime in excess of 20 hours for the 2 weeks.

Priority Level 2 Goals

Goal 3:   Satisfy existing orders for the IC-100 adhesive; that is, produce at least 100 gallons of IC-100.

Goal 4:   Satisfy existing orders for the IC-200 adhesive; that is, produce at least 120 gallons of IC-200.

Priority Level 3 Goal

Goal 5:   Use all the available resin.

a. Formulate a goal programming model for the Industrial Chemicals problem. Assume that both priority level 1 goals and that both priority level 2 goals are equally important.

b. Use the graphical goal programming procedure to develop a solution for the model formulated in part (a).

5. Reconsider the RMC data presented in Problem 1. Assume that the two P_1 priority level goals remain the same and that both goals are equally important to management. Suppose that management has learned that additional amounts of material 3 can be obtained from another RMC plant. Although management wants to obtain a solution that satisfies their production goals using the 21 tons of material 3 currently available, it is willing to consider using additional amounts of material 3 from the other plant. With this new goal as a P_2 priority level goal, the problem goals can now be restated.

Priority Level 1 Goals

Goal 1: Produce at least 30 tons of fuel additive.

Goal 2: Produce at least 15 tons of solvent base.

Priority Level 2 Goal

Goal 3: Use no more than 21 tons of material 3.

a. Treat the amounts of materials 1 and 2 available as problem constraints and formulate a goal programming model for this problem.
b. Use the goal programming computer procedure illustrated in Section 15.2 to solve the model formulated in part (a).
c. How many tons of material 3 need to be obtained from RMC's other plant?

6. Michigan Motors Corporation (MMC) has just introduced a new luxury touring sedan. As part of its promotional campaign, the marketing department has decided to send personalized invitations to test drive the new sedan to two target groups: (1) current owners of an MMC luxury automobile and (2) owners of luxury cars manufactured by one of MMC's competitors. The cost of sending a personalized invitation to each customer is estimated to be $1 per letter. Based on previous experience with this type of advertising, MMC estimates that 25% of the customers contacted from group 1 and 10% of the customers contacted from group 2 will test drive the new sedan. As part of this campaign, MMC has set the following goals.

Goal 1: Get at least 10,000 customers from group 1 to test drive the new sedan.

Goal 2: Get at least 5000 customers from group 2 to test drive the new sedan.

Goal 3: Limit the expense of sending out the invitations to $70,000.

Assume that goals 1 and 2 are P_1 priority level goals and that goal 3 is a P_2 priority level goal.

a. Suppose that goals 1 and 2 are equally important; formulate a goal programming model of the MMC problem.
b. Use the goal programming computer procedure illustrated in Section 15.2 to solve the model formulated in part (a).
c. If management believes that contacting customers from group 2 is twice as important as contacting customers from group 1, what should MMC do?

7. A committee in charge of promoting a Ladies Professional Golf Association tournament is trying to determine how best to advertise the event during the 2 weeks prior to the tournament. The committee obtained the following information about the three advertising media they are considering using.

Category	Audience Reached Per Advertisement	Cost Per Advertisement	Maximum Number of Advertisements
TV	200,000	$2500	10
Radio	50,000	$ 400	15
Newspaper	100,000	$ 500	20

The last column in this table shows the maximum number of advertisements that can be run during the next 2 weeks; these values should be treated as constraints. The committee has established the following goals for the campaign.

Priority Level 1 Goal

Goal 1: Reach at least 4 million people.

Priority Level 2 Goal

Goal 2: The number of television advertisements should be at least 30% of the total number of advertisements.

Priority Level 3 Goal

Goal 3: The number of radio advertisements should not exceed 20% of the total number of advertisements.

Priority Level 4 Goal

Goal 4: Limit the total amount spent for advertising to $20,000.

a. Formulate a goal programming model for this problem.
b. Use the goal programming computer procedure illustrated in Section 15.2 to solve the model formulated in part (a).

8. Morley Company is attempting to determine the best location for a new machine in an existing layout of three machines. The existing machines are located at the following x_1, x_2 coordinates on the shop floor.

$$\text{Machine 1:} \quad x_1 = 1, x_2 = 7$$

$$\text{Machine 2:} \quad x_1 = 5, x_2 = 9$$

$$\text{Machine 3:} \quad x_1 = 6, x_2 = 2$$

a. Develop a goal programming model that can be solved to minimize the total distance of the new machine from the three existing machines. The distance is to be measured rectangularly. For example, if the location of the new machine is $(x_1 = 3, x_2 = 5)$, it is considered to be a distance of $|3 - 1| + |5 - 7| = 2 + 2 = 4$ from machine 1. *Hint:* In the goal programming formulation, let

x_1 = first coordinate of the new machine location

x_2 = second coordinate of the new machine location

d_i^+ = amount by which the x_1 coordinate of the new machine exceeds the x_1 coordinate of machine i ($i = 1, 2, 3$)

d_i^- = amount by which the x_1 coordinate of machine i exceeds the x_1 coordinate of the new machine ($i = 1, 2, 3$)

e_i^+ = amount by which the x_2 coordinate of the new machine exceeds the x_2 coordinate of machine i ($i = 1, 2, 3$)

e_i^- = amount by which the x_2 coordinate of machine i exceeds the x_2 coordinate of the new machine ($i = 1, 2, 3$)

b. What is the optimal location for the new machine?

9. A fast-food chain is attempting to determine the best location of a new outlet. Management wants to determine the best location for drawing customers from three population centers.

Letting (x_1, x_2) represent the map coordinates of the three population centers, we can show their locations as

$$\text{Population center 1: } x_1 = 2, x_2 = 8$$

$$\text{Population center 2: } x_1 = 6, x_2 = 6$$

$$\text{Population center 3: } x_1 = 1, x_2 = 1$$

If the new outlet were located at coordinates $(x_1 = 3, x_2 = 2)$, it would be $(3 - 1) + (2 - 1) = 3$ miles from population center 3 (distance is measured as the sum of the east–west and north–south differences in coordinates).

a. Formulate and solve a goal programming model to determine the location for the new outlet that will minimize the total distance from the three population centers. (*Hint:* Let (x_1, x_2) represent the coordinates of the new location.)

b. Population center 1 is four times as large as center 3, and center 2 is twice as large as center 3. Management believes that the importance of locating near a population center is proportional to its population. Develop and solve a new goal programming model in which the weights for the deviation variables reflect this importance.

10. Use the pairwise comparison matrix for the price criterion shown in Table 15.4 to verify that the priorities after synthesization are 0.123, 0.320, and 0.557. Compute the consistency ratio and comment on its acceptability.

11. Use the pairwise comparison matrix for the MPG criterion shown in Table 15.4 to verify that the priorities after synthesization are 0.087, 0.274, and 0.639. Compute the consistency ratio and comment on its acceptability.

12. **SELFTest** Use the pairwise comparison matrix for the style criterion as shown in Table 15.4 to verify that the priorities after synthesization are 0.265, 0.655, and 0.080. Compute the consistency ratio and comment on its acceptability.

13. Dan Joseph was considering entering one of two graduate schools of business to pursue studies for an MBA degree. When asked how he compared the two schools with respect to reputation, he responded that he preferred school A strongly to very strongly to school B.
a. Set up the pairwise comparison matrix for this problem.
b. Determine the priorities for the two schools relative to this criterion.

14. An organization was investigating relocating its corporate headquarters to one of three possible cities. The following pairwise comparison matrix shows the president's judgments regarding the desirability for the three cities.

	City 1	City 2	City 3
City 1	1	5	7
City 2	1/5	1	3
City 3	1/7	1/3	1

a. Determine the priorities for the three cities.
b. Is the president consistent in terms of the judgments provided? Explain.

15. The following pairwise comparison matrix contains the judgments of an individual regarding the fairness of two proposed tax programs, A and B.

	A	B
A	1	3
B	1/3	1

    a. Determine the priorities for the two programs.
    b. Are the individual's judgments consistent? Explain.

16. **SELF**Test Asked to compare three soft drinks with respect to flavor, an individual stated that

    A is moderately more preferable than B,

    A is equally to moderately more preferable than C, and

    B is strongly more preferable than C.

    a. Set up the pairwise comparison matrix for this problem.
    b. Determine the priorities for the soft drinks with respect to the flavor criterion.
    c. Compute the consistency ratio. Are the individual's judgments consistent? Explain.

17. Refer to Problem 16. Suppose that the individual had stated the following judgments instead of those given in Problem 16.

    A is strongly more preferable than C.

    B is equally to moderately more preferable than A.

    B is strongly more preferable than C.

Answer parts (a), (b), and (c) as stated in Problem 16.

18. The national sales director for Jones Office Supplies needs to determine the best location for the next national sales meeting. Three locations have been proposed: Dallas, San Francisco, and New York. One criterion considered important in the decision is the desirability of the location in terms of restaurants, entertainment, and so on. The national sales manager made the following judgments with regard to this criterion.

    New York is very strongly more preferred than Dallas.

    New York is moderately more preferred than San Francisco.

    San Francisco is moderately to strongly more preferred than Dallas.

    a. Set up the pairwise comparison matrix for this problem.
    b. Determine the priorities for the desirability criterion.
    c. Compute the consistency ratio. Are the sales manager's judgments consistent? Explain.

19. A study comparing four personal computers resulted in the following pairwise comparison matrix for the performance criterion.

	1	2	3	4
1	1	3	7	1/3
2	1/3	1	4	1/4
3	1/7	1/4	1	1/6
4	3	4	6	1

    a. Determine the priorities for the four computers relative to the performance criterion.
    b. Compute the consistency ratio. Are the judgments regarding performance consistent? Explain.

20. **SELF**Test An individual was interested in determining which of two stocks to invest in, Central Computing Company (CCC) or Software Research, Inc. (SRI). The criteria thought to be most relevant in making the decision are the potential yield of the stock and the risk associated with the investment. The pairwise comparison matrices for this problem are

Criterion	Yield	Risk
Yield	1	2
Risk	1/2	1

Yield	CCI	SRI
CCI	1	3
SRI	1/3	1

Risk	CCI	SRI
CCI	1	1/2
SRI	2	1

a. Draw the hierarchy for this problem.
b. Compute the priorities for each of the pairwise comparison matrices.
c. Determine the overall priority for the two investments.

21. The vice-president of Harling Equipment needs to select a new director of marketing. The two possible candidates are Bill Jacobs and Sue Martin, and the criteria thought to be most relevant in the selection are leadership ability (L), personal skills (P), and administrative skills (A). The following pairwise comparison matrices were obtained.

Criterion	L	P	A
L	1	1/3	1/4
P	3	1	2
A	4	1/2	1

Leadership	Jacobs	Martin
Jacobs	1	4
Martin	1/4	1

Personal	Jacobs	Martin
Jacobs	1	1/3
Martin	3	1

Administrative	Jacobs	Martin
Jacobs	1	2
Martin	1/2	1

a. Draw the hierarchy for this problem.
b. Compute the priorities for each of the pairwise comparison matrices.
c. Determine an overall priority for each of the candidates.

22. A woman considering the purchase of a custom sound stereo system for her car looked at three different systems (A, B, and C) that varied in terms of price (P), sound quality (Q), and FM reception (FM). The following pairwise comparison matrices were developed.

Criterion	P	Q	FM
P	1	3	4
Q	1/3	1	3
FM	1/4	1/3	1

Price	A	B	C
A	1	4	2
B	1/4	1	1/3
C	1/2	3	1

Quality	A	B	C
A	1	1/2	1/4
B	2	1	1/3
C	4	3	1

FM Reception	A	B	C
A	1	4	2
B	1/4	1	1
C	1/2	1	1

a. Draw the hierarchy for this problem.
b. Compute the priorities for each of the pairwise comparison matrices.
c. Determine an overall priority for each of the systems.

Case Problem: Production Scheduling

EZ Trailers, Inc., manufactures a variety of general purpose trailers, including a complete line of boat trailers. Two of their best-selling boat trailers are the EZ-190 and the EZ-250; the EZ-190 is designed for boats up to 19 feet in length, and the EZ-250 can be used for boats up to 25 feet in length.

EZ Trailers would like to schedule production for the next 2 months for these two models. Each unit of the EZ-190 requires 4 hours of production time, and each unit of the EZ-250 uses 6 hours of production time. The following orders have been received for March and April.

Model	March	April
EZ-190	800	600
EZ-250	1100	1200

The ending inventory from February was 200 units of the EZ-190 and 300 units of the EZ-250. The total number of hours of production time used in February was 6300 hours.

The management of EZ Trailers is concerned about being able to satisfy existing orders for the EZ-250 for both March and April. In fact, it believes that this is the most important goal that a production schedule should meet. Next in importance is satisfying existing orders for the EZ-190. In addition, management doesn't want to implement any production schedule that would involve significant labor fluctuations from month to month. In this regard, its goal is to develop a production schedule that would limit fluctuations in labor-hours used to a maximum of 1000 hours from one month to the next.

Managerial Report

Perform an analysis of EZ Trailers' production scheduling problem, and prepare a report for EZ's president that summarizes your findings. Include a discussion and analysis of the following items in your report.

1. The production schedule that best achieves the goals as specified by management.
2. Suppose that EZ Trailers' storage facilities would accommodate only a maximum of 300 trailers in any one month. What effect would this have on the production schedule?
3. Suppose that EZ Trailers can store only a maximum of 300 trailers in any one month. In addition, suppose management would like to have an ending inventory in April of at least 100 units of each model. What effect would both of these changes have on the production schedule?
4. What changes would occur in the production schedule if the labor fluctuation goal was the highest-priority goal?

CHAPTER sixteen

Forecasting

An essential aspect of managing any organization is planning for the future. Indeed, the long-run success of an organization is closely related to how well management is able to foresee the future and develop appropriate strategies. Good judgment, intuition, and an awareness of the state of the economy may give a manager a rough idea or "feeling" of what is likely to happen in the future. However, it is often difficult to convert this feeling into a number that can be used as next quarter's sales volume or next year's raw material cost per unit. The purpose of this chapter is to introduce several forecasting methods.

Suppose we have been asked to provide quarterly forecasts of the sales volume for a particular product during the coming 1-year period. Production schedules, raw material purchasing plans, inventory policies, and sales quotas will all be affected by the quarterly forecasts that we provide. Consequently, poor forecasts may result in increased costs for the firm. How should we go about providing the quarterly sales volume forecasts?

We will certainly want to review the actual sales data for the product in past periods. Suppose we have actual sales data for each quarter over the past 3 years. Using these historical data, we can identify the general level of sales and determine whether there is any trend, such as an increase or decrease in sales volume over time. A further review of the data might reveal a seasonal pattern, such as peak sales occurring in the third quarter of each year and sales volume bottoming out during the first quarter. By reviewing historical data over time, we can often develop a better understanding of the pattern of past sales; often this can lead to better predictions of future sales for the product.

The historical sales data form a *time series*. A time series is a set of observations of a variable measured at successive points in time or over successive periods of time. In this chapter we will introduce several procedures for analyzing a time series. The objective of such analyses is to provide good *forecasts* or predictions of future values of the time series.

Forecasting methods can be classified as quantitative or qualitative. Quantitative forecasting methods can be used when (1) past information about the variable being forecast is available; (2) the information can be quantified; and (3) a reasonable assumption is that the pattern of the past will continue into the future. In such cases, a forecast can be developed using a time series method or a causal method.

Figure 16.1

An Overview of Forecasting Methods

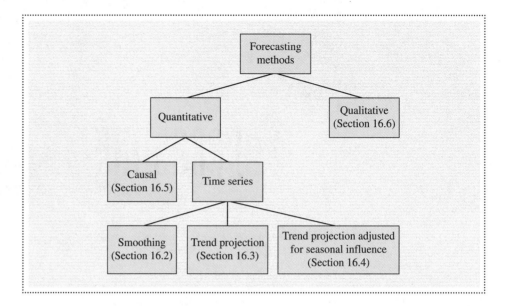

If the historical data are restricted to past values of the variable that we are trying to forecast, the forecasting procedure is called a time series method. The objective of time series methods is to discover a pattern in the historical data and then extrapolate this pattern into the future; the forecast is based solely on past values of the variable that we are trying to forecast and/or on past forecast errors. In this chapter we discuss three time series methods: smoothing (moving averages, weighted moving averages, and exponential smoothing), trend projection, and trend projection adjusted for seasonal influence.

Causal forecasting methods are based on the assumption that the variable that we are trying to forecast exhibits a cause–effect relationship with one or more other variables. In this chapter we discuss the use of regression analysis as a causal forecasting method. For instance, the sales volume for many products is influenced by advertising expenditures, so regression analysis may be used to develop an equation showing how these two variables are related. Then, once the advertising budget has been set for the next period, we could substitute this value into the equation to develop a prediction or forecast of the sales volume for that period. Note that if a time series method had been used to develop the forecast, advertising expenditures would not even have been considered; that is, a time series method would have based the forecast solely on past sales.

Qualitative methods generally involve the use of expert judgment to develop forecasts. For instance, a panel of experts might develop a consensus forecast of the prime rate for a year from now. An advantage of qualitative procedures is that they can be applied when the information on the variable being forecast cannot be quantified and when historical data either are not applicable or available. Figure 16.1 provides an overview of the types of forecasting methods.

16.1 The Components of a Time Series

The pattern or behavior of the data in a time series has several components. The usual assumption is that four separate components—trend, cyclical, seasonal, and irregular—combine to provide specific values for the time series. Let us look more closely at each of these components.

Figure 16.2
....

Linear Trend of Camera Sales

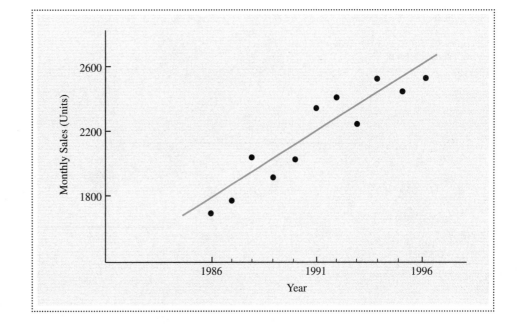

Trend Component
....

In time series analysis, the measurements may be taken every hour, day, week, month, or year, or at any other regular interval.[1] Although time series data generally exhibit random fluctuations, the time series may still show gradual shifts or movements, to relatively higher or lower values over a longer period of time. The gradual shifting of the time series is referred to as the *trend* in the time series; this shifting or trend is usually due to long-term factors such as changes in the population, in demographic characteristics of the population, in technology, and in consumer preferences.

For example, a manufacturer of photographic equipment may see substantial month-to-month variability in the number of cameras sold. However, in reviewing the sales over the past 10–15 years, this manufacturer may find a gradual increase in the annual sales volume. Suppose the sales volume was approximately 1700 cameras per month in 1986, 2300 cameras per month in 1991, and 2500 cameras per month in 1996. While actual month-to-month sales volumes may vary substantially, this gradual growth in sales over time shows an upward trend for the time series. Figure 16.2 shows a straight line that may be a good approximation of the trend in camera sales. Although the trend for camera sales appears to be linear and increasing over time, sometimes the trend in a time series is better described by other patterns.

Figure 16.3 shows some other possible time series trend patterns. In part (a) we see a nonlinear trend; in this case, the time series shows very little growth initially, followed by a period of rapid growth, and then a leveling off. This trend pattern might be a good approximation of sales for a product from introduction through a growth period and into a period of market saturation. The linear decreasing trend in part (b) is useful for time series displaying a steady decrease over time. The horizontal line in part (c) represents a time series that has no consistent increase or decrease over time and thus no trend.

---

[1] We restrict our attention here to time series where the values of the series are recorded at equal intervals. Treatment of cases where the observations are not made at equal intervals is beyond the scope of this text.

Figure 16.3

....

Examples of Some Possible Time Series Trend Patterns

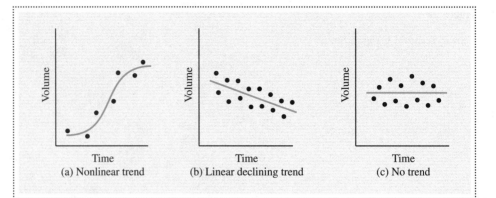

Figure 16.4

....

Trend and Cyclical Components of a Time Series with Data Points 1 Year Apart

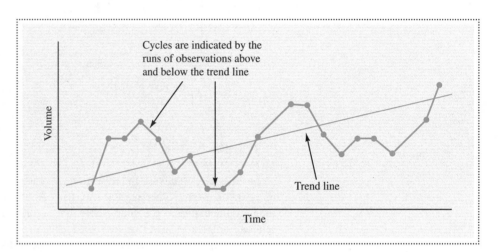

Cyclical Component

....

Although a time series may exhibit a trend over long periods of time, all future values of the time series will not fall exactly on the trend line. In fact, time series often show alternating sequences of points below and above the trend line. Any recurring sequence of points above and below the trend line lasting more than 1 year can be attributed to the *cyclical component* of the time series. Figure 16.4 shows the graph of a time series with an obvious cyclical component. The observations are taken at intervals of 1 year.

Many time series exhibit cyclical behavior with regular runs of observations below and above the trend line. Generally, this component of the time series is due to multiyear cyclical movements in the economy. For example, periods of modest inflation followed by periods of rapid inflation can lead to many time series that alternate below and above a generally increasing trend line (e.g., a time series for housing costs). Many time series in the early 1980s displayed this type of behavior.

Seasonal Component

....

Whereas the trend and cyclical components of a time series are identified by analyzing multiyear movements in historical data, many time series show a regular pattern over 1-year periods. For example, a manufacturer of swimming pools expects low sales activity in the fall and winter months, with peak sales occurring in the spring and summer months. Manufacturers of snow removal equipment and heavy clothing, however, expect just the opposite yearly pattern. Not surprisingly, the component of the time series that represents the variability in the data due to seasonal influences is called the *seasonal component.* Although we generally think of seasonal movement in a time series as occurring within 1 year, the seasonal component also may be used to represent any regularly repeating pattern that is less than 1 year in duration. For example, daily traffic volume data show within-the-day "seasonal" behavior, with peak levels during rush hours, moderate flow during the rest of the day and early evening, and light flow from midnight to early morning.

Irregular Component

The *irregular component* of the time series is the residual or "catchall" factor that accounts for the deviations of the actual time series values from what we would expect given the effects of the trend, cyclical, and seasonal components. It accounts for the random variability in the time series. The irregular component is caused by the short-term, unanticipated, and nonrecurring factors that affect the time series. Because this component accounts for the random variability in the time series, it is unpredictable. We cannot attempt to predict its impact on the time series.

16.2   Smoothing Methods

In this section we discuss three forecasting methods: moving averages, weighted moving averages, and exponential smoothing. Since the objective of each of these methods is to "smooth out" the random fluctuations caused by the irregular component of the time series, they are referred to as smoothing methods. Smoothing methods are appropriate for a stable time series—that is, one that exhibits no significant trend, cyclical, or seasonal effects—since they adapt well to changes in the level of the time series. However, without modification, they do not work as well when a significant trend and/or seasonal variation are present.

Smoothing methods are easy to use and generally provide a high level of accuracy for short-range forecasts, such as a forecast for the next time period. One of the methods, exponential smoothing, has minimal data requirements and thus is a good method to use when forecasts are required for large numbers of items.

Moving Averages

The *moving averages* method uses the average of the *most recent n* data values in the time series as the forecast for the next period. Mathematically,

$$\text{Moving average} = \frac{\Sigma(\text{most recent } n \text{ data values})}{n} \qquad (16.1)$$

The term *moving* indicates that as a new observation becomes available for the time series, it replaces the oldest observation in equation (16.1), and a new average is computed. As a result, the average will change, or move, as new observations become available.

Table 16.1

Gasoline Sales Time Series Data

Week	Sales (1000s of gallons)
1	17
2	21
3	19
4	23
5	18
6	16
7	20
8	18
9	22
10	20
11	15
12	22

You should now be able to use moving averages to compute a forecast. Try Problem 1.

Figure 16.5

Gasoline Sales Time Series

To illustrate the moving averages method, consider the 12 weeks of data presented in Table 16.1 and Figure 16.5. These data show the number of gallons of gasoline sold by a gasoline distributor in Bennington, Vermont, over the past 12 weeks. Figure 16.5 indicates that, although random variability is present, the time series appears to be stable over time. Thus, the smoothing methods of this section are applicable.

To use moving averages to forecast gasoline sales, we must first select the number of data values to be included in the moving average. For example, let us compute forecasts using a 3-week moving average. The moving average calculation for the first 3 weeks of the gasoline sales time series is

$$\text{Moving average (weeks 1--3)} = \frac{17 + 21 + 19}{3} = 19$$

We then use this moving average value as the forecast for week 4. The actual value observed in week 4 is 23, so the forecast error in week 4 is $23 - 19 = 4$. In general, the error associated with a forecast is the difference between the observed value of the time series and the forecast.

The calculation for the second 3-week moving average is

$$\text{Moving average (weeks 2--4)} = \frac{21 + 19 + 23}{3} = 21$$

Hence, the forecast for week 5 is 21, and the error associated with this forecast is $18 - 21 = -3$. Thus, the forecast error may be positive or negative, depending on whether the forecast is too low or too high. A complete summary of the 3-week moving average calculations for the gasoline sales time series is shown in Table 16.2 and Figure 16.6.

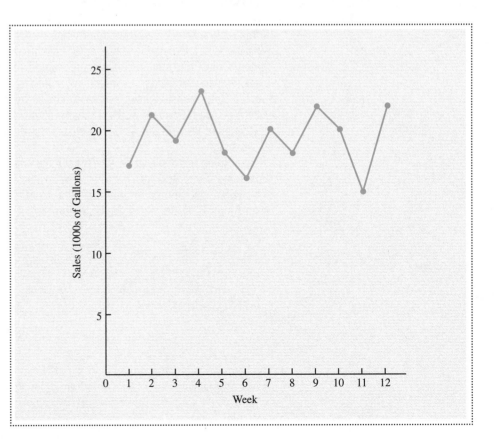

Table 16.2
. . . .
Summary of 3-Week Moving Average Calculations

Week	Time Series Value	Moving Average Forecast	Forecast Error	Squared Forecast Error
1	17			
2	21			
3	19			
4	23	19	4	16
5	18	21	−3	9
6	16	20	−4	16
7	20	19	1	1
8	18	18	0	0
9	22	18	4	16
10	20	20	0	0
11	15	20	−5	25
12	22	19	3	9
			Totals 0	92

Figure 16.6
. . . .
Gasoline Sales Time Series and 3-Week Moving Average Forecasts

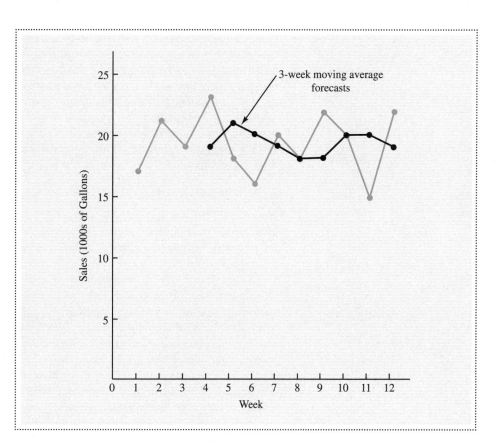

Forecast Accuracy   An important consideration in selecting a forecasting method is the accuracy of the forecast. Clearly, we want forecast errors to be small. The last two columns of Table 16.2, which contain the forecast errors and the forecast errors squared, can be used to develop measures of forecast accuracy.

For the gasoline sales time series, we can use the last column of Table 16.2 to compute the average of the sum of the squared errors. Doing so, we obtain

$$\text{Average of the sum of squared errors} = \frac{92}{9} = 10.22$$

This average of the sum of squared errors is commonly referred to as the *mean squared error* (MSE). The MSE is an often-used measure of the accuracy of a forecasting method and is the one we use in this chapter.

As we indicated previously, to use the moving averages method, we must first select the number of data values to be included in the moving average. Not surprisingly, for a particular time series, different lengths of moving averages will affect the accuracy of the forecast. One possible approach to choosing the number of values to be included is to use trial and error to identify the length that minimizes the MSE. Then, if we assume that the length that is best for the past will also be best for the future, we would forecast the next value in the time series using the number of data values that minimized the MSE for the historical time series.

You should now be able to use MSE as a measure of forecast accuracy. Try Problem 2.

Weighted Moving Averages

In the moving averages method, each observation in the calculation receives the same weight. One possible variation, known as *weighted moving averages,* involves selecting different weights for each data value and then computing a weighted mean as the forecast. In most cases, the most recent observation receives the most weight, and the weight decreases for older data values. For example, we can use the gasoline sales time series to illustrate the computation of a weighted 3-week moving average, with the most recent observation receiving a weight three times as great as that given the oldest observation, and the next oldest observation receives a weight twice as great as the oldest. For week 4 the computation is

Weighted moving averages forecast for week 4 = $\frac{3}{6}(19) + \frac{2}{6}(21) + \frac{1}{6}(17) = 19.33$

Note that for the weighted moving average the sum of the weights is equal to 1. This was also true for the simple moving average, where each weight was $\frac{1}{3}$. However, recall that the simple or unweighted moving average provided a forecast of 19.

Forecast Accuracy   To use the weighted moving averages method we must first select the number of data values to be included in the weighted moving average and then choose weights for each of the data values. In general, if we believe that the recent past is a better predictor of the future than the distant past, larger weights should be given to the more recent observations. However, when the time series is highly variable, selecting approximately equal weights for each data value may be best. The only requirement in selecting the weights is that their sum must equal 1. To determine whether one particular combination of number of data values and weights provides a more accurate forecast than another combination, we will continue to use the MSE criterion as the measure of forecast accuracy. That is, if we assume that the combination that is best for the past will also be best for the future, we would use the combination of number of data values and weights that minimized MSE for the historical time series to forecast the next value in the time series.

Exponential Smoothing

Exponential smoothing uses a weighted average of past time series values as the forecast; it is a special case of the weighted moving averages method in which we select only one weight—the weight for the most recent observation. The weights for the other data values are automatically computed and get smaller and smaller as the observations move farther into the past. The basic exponential smoothing model is

$$F_{t+1} = \alpha Y_t + (1 - \alpha)F_t \tag{16.2}$$

where

$$F_{t+1} = \text{forecast of the time series for period } t + 1$$

$$Y_t = \text{actual value of the time series in period } t$$

$$F_t = \text{forecast of the time series for period } t$$

$$\alpha = \text{smoothing constant } (0 \leq \alpha \leq 1)$$

Equation (16.2) shows that the forecast for period $t + 1$ is a weighted average of the actual value in period t and the forecast for period t; note in particular that the weight given to the actual value in period t is α and that the weight given to the forecast in period t is $1 - \alpha$. We can demonstrate that the exponential smoothing forecast for any period also is a weighted average of *all the previous actual values* for the time series with a time series consisting of three periods of data: Y_1, Y_2, and Y_3. To start the calculations, we let F_1 equal the actual value of the time series in period 1; that is, $F_1 = Y_1$. Hence, the forecast for period 2

$$F_2 = \alpha Y_1 + (1 - \alpha)F_1$$
$$= \alpha Y_1 + (1 - \alpha)Y_1$$
$$= Y_1$$

Thus, the exponential smoothing forecast for period 2 is equal to the actual value of the time series in period 1.

The forecast for period 3 is

$$F_3 = \alpha Y_2 + (1 - \alpha)F_2 = \alpha Y_2 + (1 - \alpha)Y_1$$

Finally, substituting this expression for F_3 in the expression for F_4, we obtain

$$F_4 = \alpha Y_3 + (1 - \alpha)[\alpha Y_2 + (1 - \alpha)Y_1]$$
$$= \alpha Y_3 + \alpha(1 - \alpha)Y_2 + (1 - \alpha)^2 Y_1$$

Hence, F_4 is a weighted average of the first three time series values. The sum of the coefficients or weights for Y_1, Y_2, and Y_3 equals 1. A similar argument can be made to show that any forecast F_{t+1} is a weighted average of all the previous time series values.

Despite the fact that exponential smoothing provides a forecast that is a weighted average of all past observations, all the past data do not need to be saved in order to compute the forecast for the next period. In fact, once the *smoothing constant* α has been selected, only two pieces of information are required to compute the forecast for the next period. Equation (16.2) shows that with a given α we can compute the forecast for period $t + 1$ simply by knowing the actual and forecast time series values for period t—that is, Y_t and F_t.

To illustrate the exponential smoothing approach to forecasting, consider the gasoline sales time series presented previously in Table 16.1 and Figure 16.5. As indicated, the exponential smoothing forecast for period 2 is equal to the actual value of the time series in period 1. Thus, with $Y_1 = 17$, we set $F_2 = 17$ to get the exponential smoothing computations started. From the time series data in Table 16.1, we find an actual time series value in period 2 of $Y_2 = 21$. Thus, period 2 has a forecast error of $21 - 17 = 4$.

Table 16.3

Summary of the Exponential Smoothing Forecasts and Forecast Errors for Gasoline Sales with Smoothing Constant $\alpha = 0.2$

Week (t)	Time Series Value (Y_t)	Exponential Smoothing Forecast (F_t)	Forecast Error $(Y_t - F_t)$
1	17		
2	21	17.00	4.00
3	19	17.80	1.20
4	23	18.04	4.96
5	18	19.03	−1.03
6	16	18.83	−2.83
7	20	18.26	1.74
8	18	18.61	−0.61
9	22	18.49	3.51
10	20	19.19	0.81
11	15	19.35	−4.35
12	22	18.48	3.52

Continuing with the exponential smoothing computations using $\alpha = 0.2$, we obtain the following forecast for period 3:

$$F_3 = 0.2Y_2 + 0.8F_2 = 0.2(21) + 0.8(17) = 17.8$$

Once the actual time series value in period 3, $Y_3 = 19$, is known, we can generate a forecast for period 4 as follows:

$$F_4 = 0.2Y_3 + 0.8F_3 = 0.2(19) + 0.8(17.8) = 18.04$$

By continuing the exponential smoothing calculations, we are able to determine the weekly forecast values and the corresponding weekly forecast errors, as shown in Table 16.3. Note that we have not shown an exponential smoothing forecast or the forecast error for period 1 because F_1 was set equal to Y_1 in order to begin the smoothing computations. For week 12, we have $Y_{12} = 22$ and $F_{12} = 18.48$. Can you use this information to generate a forecast for week 13 before the actual value of week 13 becomes known? Using the exponential smoothing model, we have

$$F_{13} = 0.2Y_{12} + 0.8F_{12} = 0.2(22) + 0.8(18.48) = 19.18$$

You should now be able to develop forecasts using exponential smoothing. Try Problem 4.

Thus, the exponential smoothing forecast of the amount sold in week 13 is 19.18, or 19,180 gallons of gasoline. With this forecast, the firm can make plans and decisions accordingly. The accuracy of the forecast will not be known until the firm conducts its business through week 13.

Figure 16.7 shows the plot of the actual and the forecast time series values. Note in particular how the forecasts "smooth out" the irregular fluctuations in the time series.

Forecast Accuracy   In the preceding exponential smoothing calculations, we used a smoothing constant of $\alpha = 0.2$. Although any value of α between 0 and 1 is acceptable, some values will yield better forecasts than others. Insight into choosing a good value for α can be obtained by rewriting the basic exponential smoothing model as follows:

$$F_{t+1} = \alpha Y_t + (1 - \alpha)F_t$$

$$F_{t+1} = \alpha Y_t + F_t - \alpha F_t \tag{16.3}$$

$$F_{t+1} = F_t + \alpha \underbrace{(Y_t - F_t)}$$

Forecast
in period t

Forecast error
in period t

Figure 16.7

**Actual and Forecast Gasoline Sales
Time Series with Smoothing
Constant $\alpha = 0.2$**

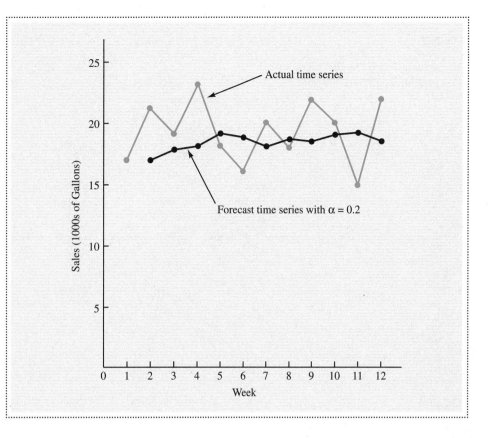

Thus, the new forecast F_{t+1} is equal to the previous forecast F_t plus an adjustment, which is α times the most recent forecast error, $Y_t - F_t$. That is, the forecast in period $t + 1$ is obtained by adjusting the forecast in period t by a fraction of the forecast error. If the time series contains substantial random variability, a small value of the smoothing constant is preferred. The reason for this choice is that since much of the forecast error is due to random variability, we do not want to overreact and adjust the forecasts too quickly. For a time series with relatively little random variability, larger values of the smoothing constant have the advantage of quickly adjusting the forecasts when forecasting errors occur and therefore allowing the forecast to react faster to changing conditions.

The criterion we will use to determine a desirable value for the smoothing constant α is the same as the criterion we proposed earlier for determining the number of periods of data to include in the moving averages calculation. That is, we choose the value of α that minimizes the mean squared error. A summary of the MSE calculations for the exponential smoothing forecast of gasoline sales with $\alpha = 0.2$ is shown in Table 16.4. Note that there is one less squared error term than the number of periods because we had no past values with which to make a forecast for period 1. Would a different value of α have provided better results in terms of a lower MSE value? Perhaps the most straightforward way to answer this question is simply to try another value for α. We will then compare its mean squared error with the MSE value of 8.98, obtained using a smoothing constant of 0.2.

The exponential smoothing results with $\alpha = 0.3$ are shown in Table 16.5. With MSE = 9.35, we see that for the current data set a smoothing constant of $\alpha = 0.3$ results in less forecast accuracy than a smoothing constant of $\alpha = 0.2$. Thus, in making a choice between $\alpha = 0.2$ and $\alpha = 0.3$, we would be inclined to use the original smoothing constant

For a given set of data, you should now be able to determine whether moving averages or exponential smoothing provides the best forecasts. Try Problem 5.

Table 16.4

Mean Squared Error Computations for Forecasting Gasoline Sales with $\alpha = 0.2$

Week (t)	Time Series Value (Y_t)	Forecast (F_t)	Forecast Error ($Y_t - F_t$)	Squared Forecast Error ($Y_t - F_t)^2$
1	17			
2	21	17.00	4.00	16.00
3	19	17.80	1.20	1.44
4	23	18.04	4.96	24.60
5	18	19.03	−1.03	1.06
6	16	18.83	−2.83	8.01
7	20	18.26	1.74	3.03
8	18	18.61	−0.61	0.37
9	22	18.49	3.51	12.32
10	20	19.19	0.81	0.66
11	15	19.35	−4.35	18.92
12	22	18.48	3.52	12.39

Total   98.80

$$\text{MSE} = \frac{98.80}{11} = 8.98$$

Table 16.5

Mean Squared Error Computations for Forecasting Gasoline Sales with $\alpha = 0.3$

Week (t)	Time Series Value (Y_t)	Forecast (F_t)	Forecast Error ($Y_t - F_t$)	Squared Forecast Error ($Y_t - F_t)^2$
1	17			
2	21	17.00	4.00	16.00
3	19	18.20	0.80	0.64
4	23	18.44	4.56	20.79
5	18	19.81	−1.81	3.28
6	16	19.27	−3.27	10.69
7	20	18.29	1.71	2.92
8	18	18.80	−0.80	0.64
9	22	18.56	3.44	11.83
10	20	19.59	0.41	0.17
11	15	19.71	−4.71	22.18
12	22	18.30	3.70	13.69

Total   102.83

$$\text{MSE} = \frac{102.83}{11} = 9.35$$

of 0.2. Using a trial-and-error calculation with other values of α, a "good" value for the smoothing constant can be found. This value can be used in the exponential smoothing model to provide forecasts for the future. At a later date, after a number of new time series observations have been obtained, it is good practice to analyze the newly collected time series data to see if the smoothing constant should be revised to provide better results.

NOTES & comments

1. Another commonly used measure of forecast accuracy is the *mean absolute deviation* (MAD). This measure is simply the average of the sum of the absolute values of all the forecast errors. Using the errors given in Table 16.2, we obtain

$$\text{MAD} = \frac{4 + 3 + 4 + 1 + 0 + 4 + 0 + 5 + 3}{9} = 2.67$$

One major difference between the MSE and the MAD is that the MSE measure is much more influenced by large forecast errors than by small errors (since for the MSE measure, the errors are squared). The selection of the best measure of forecasting accuracy is not a simple matter. Indeed, forecasting experts often disagree as to which measure should be used. We will use the MSE measure in this chapter.

2. Spreadsheet packages are an effective aid in choosing a good value of α for exponential smoothing and selecting weights for the weighted moving averages method. With the time series data and the forecasting formulas in a spreadsheet, you can experiment with different values of α (or moving average weights) and choose the value(s) providing the smallest MSE or MAD. In the chapter appendix we show how this can be done.

16.3 Trend Projection

Table 16.6

Bicycle Sales Data

Year (t)	Sales (1000s) (Y_t)
1	21.6
2	22.9
3	25.5
4	21.9
5	23.9
6	27.5
7	31.5
8	29.7
9	28.6
10	31.4

In this section we show how to forecast the values of a time series that exhibits a long-term linear trend. The type of time series for which the trend projection method is applicable shows a consistent increase or decrease over time; it is not stable, so the smoothing methods described in the preceding section are not applicable.

Consider the time series for bicycle sales for a particular manufacturer over the past 10 years, as shown in Table 16.6 and Figure 16.8. Note that 21,600 bicycles were sold in year 1, 22,900 were sold in year 2, and so on; in year 10, the most recent year, 31,400 bicycles were sold. Although Figure 16.8 shows some up-and-down movement over the past 10 years, the time series clearly has an upward trend.

We do not want the trend component of a time series to follow each and every "up" and "down" movement. Rather, the trend component should reflect the gradual shifting—in our case, growth—of the time series values. After we view the time series data in Table 16.6 and the graph in Figure 16.8, we might agree that a linear trend as shown in Figure 16.9 has the potential of providing a reasonable description of the long-run movement in the series.

We use the bicycle sales data to illustrate the calculations involved in applying regression analysis to identify a linear trend. For a linear trend, the estimated sales volume expressed as a function of time is

$$T_t = b_0 + b_1 t \tag{16.4}$$

Figure 16.8

Bicycle Sales Time Series

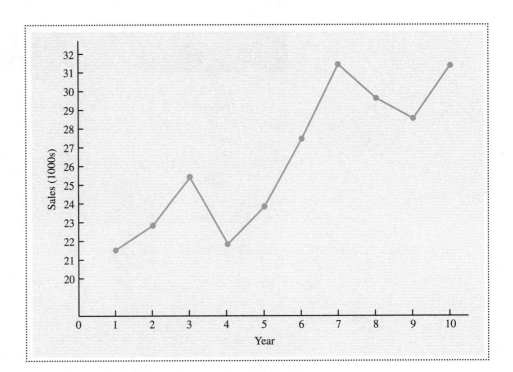

Figure 16.9

Trend Represented by a Linear Function for Bicycle Sales

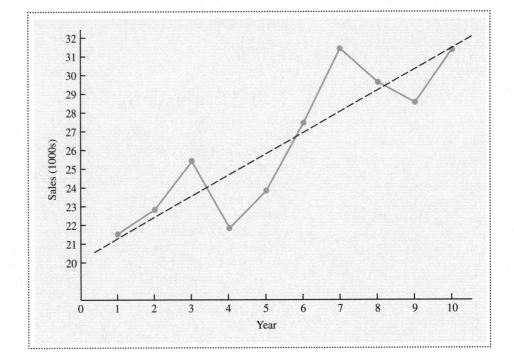

where

T_t = trend value for bicycle sales in period t

b_0 = intercept of the trend line

b_1 = slope of the trend line

Note that for the time series on bicycle sales, $t = 1$ corresponds to the oldest time series value and $t = 10$ corresponds to the most recent time series value. Formulas for computing b_1 and b_0 are:

$$b_1 = \frac{\Sigma t Y_t - (\Sigma t \Sigma Y_t)/n}{\Sigma t^2 - (\Sigma t)^2/n} \tag{16.5}$$

$$b_0 = \overline{Y} - b_1 \overline{t} \tag{16.6}$$

where

Y_t = actual value of the time series in period t

n = number of periods

$\overline{Y}$ = average value of the time series; that is, $\overline{Y} = \Sigma Y_t/n$

$\overline{t}$ = average value of t; that is, $\overline{t} = \Sigma t/n$

Using these relationships for b_0 and b_1 and the bicycle sales data of Table 16.6, we have the following calculations:

t	Y_t	tY_t	t^2
1	21.6	21.6	1
2	22.9	45.8	4
3	25.5	76.5	9
4	21.9	87.6	16
5	23.9	119.5	25
6	27.5	165.0	36
7	31.5	220.5	49
8	29.7	237.6	64
9	28.6	257.4	81
10	31.4	314.0	100
Totals 55	264.5	1545.5	385

$$\overline{t} = \frac{55}{10} = 5.5$$

$$\overline{Y} = \frac{264.5}{10} = 26.45$$

$$b_1 = \frac{1545.5 - (55)(264.5)/10}{385 - (55)^2/10} = 1.10$$

$$b_0 = 26.45 - 1.10(5.5) = 20.4$$

Therefore,

$$T_t = 20.4 + 1.1t \tag{16.7}$$

You should now be able to develop the equation for the linear trend component for a time series. Try Problem 14.

is the expression for the linear trend component for the bicycle sales time series.

The slope of 1.1 in the trend equation indicates that over the past 10 years the firm has experienced an average growth in sales of around 1100 units per year. If we assume that the past 10-year trend in sales is a good indicator of the future, then equation (16.7) can be used to project the trend component of the time series. For example, substituting $t = 11$ into equation (16.7) yields next year's trend projection, T_{11}:

$$T_{11} = 20.4 + 1.1(11) = 32.5$$

Figure 16.10

Some Possible Functional Forms for Nonlinear Trend Patterns

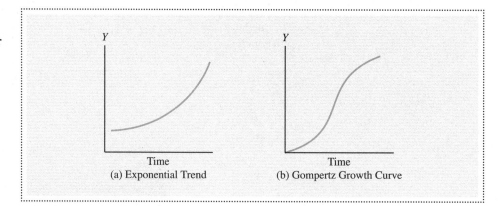

(a) Exponential Trend   (b) Gompertz Growth Curve

Thus, the trend component yields a sales forecast of 32,500 bicycles for next year.

We can also use the trend line to forecast sales farther into the future. For instance, using equation (16.7), we develop forecasts for an additional 2 and 3 years into the future:

$$T_{12} = 20.4 + 1.1(12) = 33.6$$

$$T_{13} = 20.4 + 1.1(13) = 34.7$$

The use of a linear function to model the trend is common. However, as we discussed earlier, sometimes time series exhibit a curvilinear, or nonlinear, trend similar to those shown in Figure 16.10. More advanced texts discuss in detail how to develop models for these more complex relationships.

16.4 Trend and Seasonal Components

We have shown how to forecast the values of a time series that had a trend component. In this section we extend the discussion by showing how to forecast the values of a time series that has both trend and seasonal components.

Many situations in business and economics involve period-to-period comparisons. For instance, we might be interested to learn that unemployment is up 2% compared to last month, steel production is up 5% over last month, or that the production of electric power is down 3% from the previous month. Care must be exercised in using such information, however, because whenever a seasonal influence is present, such comparisons usually are not very meaningful. For instance, the fact that electric power consumption is down by 3% from August to September might be due to the seasonal effect associated with a decrease in the use of air conditioning and not because of a long-term decline in the use of electric power. Indeed, after adjusting for the seasonal effect, we might even find that the use of electric power has increased.

Removing the seasonal effect from a time series is known as deseasonalizing the time series. After we do so, period-to-period comparisons are more meaningful and can help identify whether a trend exists. The approach we take in this section is appropriate in situations when only seasonal effects are present or in situations when both seasonal and trend components are present. The first step is to compute seasonal indexes and use them to deseasonalize the data. Then, if a trend is apparent in the deseasonalized data, we use regression analysis on the deseasonalized data to estimate the trend.

Figure 16.11

Quarterly Television Set Sales Time Series

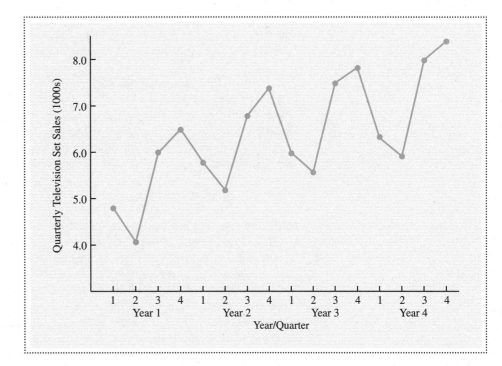

The Multiplicative Model

In addition to a trend component T and a seasonal component S, we will assume that the time series also has an irregular component I. The irregular component accounts for the random effects in the time series that cannot be explained by the trend and seasonal components. Using T_t, S_t, and I_t to identify the trend, seasonal, and irregular components at time t, we will assume that the actual time series value, denoted by Y_t, can be described by the following *multiplicative time series model*:

$$Y_t = T_t \times S_t \times I_t \tag{16.8}$$

In this model, T_t is the trend measured in units of the item being forecast. However, the S_t and I_t components are measured in relative terms, with values above 1.00 indicating effects above the trend, and values below 1.00 indicating effects below the trend.

We illustrate the use of the multiplicative model with trend, seasonal, and irregular components by working with the quarterly data presented in Table 16.7 and Figure 16.11. These data show the television set sales (in thousands of units) for a particular manufacturer over the past 4 years. We begin by showing how to identify the seasonal component of the time series.

Calculating the Seasonal Indexes

Figure 16.11 indicates that sales are lowest in the second quarter of each year, followed by higher sales levels in quarters 3 and 4. Thus, we conclude that a seasonal pattern exists for the television set sales. We begin the computational procedure used to identify each quarter's seasonal influence by computing a moving average to isolate the combined seasonal and irregular components, S_t and I_t.

Table 16.7

Quarterly Data for Television Set Sales

Year	Quarter	Sales (1000s)
1	1	4.8
	2	4.1
	3	6.0
	4	6.5
2	1	5.8
	2	5.2
	3	6.8
	4	7.4
3	1	6.0
	2	5.6
	3	7.5
	4	7.8
4	1	6.3
	2	5.9
	3	8.0
	4	8.4

To do this, we use 1 year of data in each calculation. Because we are working with a quarterly series, we will use four data values in each moving average. The moving average calculation for the first 4 quarters of the television set sales data is

$$\text{First moving average} = \frac{4.8 + 4.1 + 6.0 + 6.5}{4} = \frac{21.4}{4} = 5.35$$

Note that the moving average calculation for the first 4 quarters yields the average quarterly sales over the first year of the time series. Continuing the moving average calculation, we next add the 5.8 value for the first quarter of year 2 and drop the 4.8 for the first quarter of year 1. Thus, the second moving average is

$$\text{Second moving average} = \frac{4.1 + 6.0 + 6.5 + 5.8}{4} = \frac{22.4}{4} = 5.6$$

Similarly, the third moving average calculation is (6.0 + 6.5 + 5.8 + 5.2)/4 = 5.875.

Before we proceed with the moving average calculations for the entire time series, we return to the first moving average calculation, which resulted in a value of 5.35. The 5.35 value represents an average quarterly sales volume (across all seasons) for year 1. As we look back at the calculation of the 5.35 value, perhaps it makes sense to associate 5.35 with the "middle" quarter of the moving average group. Note, however, that some difficulty in identifying the middle quarter is encountered; with 4 quarters in the moving average, there is no middle quarter. The 5.35 value corresponds to the last half of quarter 2 and the first half of quarter 3. Similarly, if we go to the next moving average value of 5.60, the middle corresponds to the last half of quarter 3 and the first half of quarter 4.

Recall that the reason we are computing moving averages is to isolate the combined seasonal and irregular components. However, the moving average values we have computed do not correspond directly to the original quarters of the time series. We can resolve this difficulty by using the midpoints between successive moving average values. For example, since 5.35 corresponds to the first half of quarter 3 and 5.60 corresponds to the last half of quarter 3, we will use (5.35 + 5.60)/2 = 5.475 as the moving average value for quarter 3. In a similar manner, we associate a moving average value of (5.60 + 5.875)/2 = 5.738 with quarter 4. The result is a *centered moving average*. Table 16.8 shows a complete summary of the moving average and centered moving average calculations for the television set sales data.

If the number of data points in a moving average calculation is an odd number, the middle point will correspond to one of the periods in the time series. In such cases, we would not have to center the moving average values to correspond to a particular time period, as we did in the calculations in Table 16.8.

What does the centered moving averages in Table 16.8 tell us about this time series? Figure 16.12 shows plots of the actual time series values and the corresponding centered moving average. Note particularly how the centered moving average values tend to "smooth out" both the seasonal and irregular fluctuations in the time series. The moving average values computed for 4 quarters of data do not include the fluctuations due to seasonal influences because the seasonal effect has been averaged out. Each point in the centered moving average represents what the value of the time series would be if there were no seasonal or irregular influence.

By dividing each time series observation by the corresponding centered moving average value, we can identify the seasonal–irregular effect in the time series. For example, the third quarter of year 1 shows 6.0/5.475 = 1.096 as the combined seasonal–irregular component. The resulting seasonal–irregular values for the entire time series are summarized in Table 16.9.

Consider the third quarter. The results from years 1, 2, and 3 show third-quarter values of 1.096, 1.075, and 1.109, respectively. Thus, in all cases the seasonal–irregular

Table 16.8
....

Moving Average Calculations for the Television Set Sales Time Series

Year	Quarter	Sales (1000s)	4-Quarter Moving Average	Centered Moving Average
1	1	4.8		
	2	4.1		
			5.350	
	3	6.0		5.475
			5.600	
	4	6.5		5.738
			5.875	
2	1	5.8		5.975
			6.075	
	2	5.2		6.188
			6.300	
	3	6.8		6.325
			6.350	
	4	7.4		6.400
			6.450	
3	1	6.0		6.538
			6.625	
	2	5.6		6.675
			6.725	
	3	7.5		6.763
			6.800	
	4	7.8		6.838
			6.875	
4	1	6.3		6.938
			7.000	
	2	5.9		7.075
			7.150	
	3	8.0		
	4	8.4		

Figure 16.12
....

Quarterly Television Set Sales Time Series and Centered Moving Average

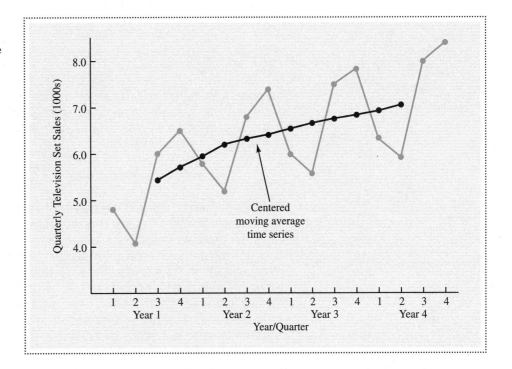

Table 16.9

Seasonal–Irregular Factors for the Television Set Sales Time Series

Year	Quarter	Sales (1000s)	Centered Moving Average	Seasonal–Irregular Component
1	1	4.8		
	2	4.1		
	3	6.0	5.475	1.096
	4	6.5	5.738	1.133
2	1	5.8	5.975	0.971
	2	5.2	6.188	0.840
	3	6.8	6.325	1.075
	4	7.4	6.400	1.156
3	1	6.0	6.538	0.918
	2	5.6	6.675	0.839
	3	7.5	6.763	1.109
	4	7.8	6.838	1.141
4	1	6.3	6.938	0.908
	2	5.9	7.075	0.834
	3	8.0		
	4	8.4		

Table 16.10

Seasonal Index Calculations for the Television Set Sales Time Series

Quarter	Seasonal–Irregular Component Values $(S_t I_t)$			Seasonal Index (S_t)
1	0.971	0.918	0.908	0.93
2	0.840	0.839	0.834	0.84
3	1.096	1.075	1.109	1.09
4	1.133	1.156	1.141	1.14

component appears to have an above average influence in the third quarter. The fluctuations over the 3 years can be attributed to the irregular component, so we can average the computed values to eliminate the irregular influence and obtain an estimate of the third-quarter seasonal influence:

$$\text{Seasonal effect of third quarter} = \frac{1.096 + 1.075 + 1.109}{3} = 1.09$$

We refer to 1.09 as the *seasonal index* for the third quarter. In Table 16.10 we summarize the calculations involved in computing the seasonal indexes for the television set sales time series. Thus, we see that the seasonal indexes for all 4 quarters are as follows: quarter 1, 0.93; quarter 2, 0.84; quarter 3, 1.09; and quarter 4, 1.14.

Interpretation of the values in Table 16.10 provides some observations about the "seasonal" component in television set sales. The best sales quarter is the fourth quarter, with sales averaging 14% above the average quarterly value. The worst, or slowest, sales quarter is the second quarter, with its seasonal index at 0.84, showing the sales average 16% below the average quarterly sales. The seasonal component corresponds nicely to the intuitive expectation that television viewing interest and thus television purchase patterns tend to peak in the fourth quarter, around Christmas. The low second-quarter sales reflect the reduced television interest resulting from the spring and presummer activities of the potential customers.

You should now be able to compute and interpret seasonal indexes for a time series. Try Problem 27.

One final adjustment is sometimes necessary in obtaining the seasonal indexes. The multiplicative model requires that the average seasonal index equal 1.00; that is, the sum of the four seasonal indexes in Table 16.10 must equal 4.00. In other words, the seasonal effects must even out over the year. The average of the seasonal indexes in our example is equal to 1.00, and hence, this type of adjustment is not necessary. In other cases, a slight adjustment may be necessary. To make the adjustment, multiply each seasonal index by the number of seasons divided by the sum of the unadjusted seasonal indexes. For instance, for quarterly data, multiply each seasonal index by 4/(sum of the unadjusted seasonal indexes). Some of the problems at the end of the chapter will require this adjustment.

Deseasonalizing the Time Series

The purpose of finding seasonal indexes is to remove the seasonal effects from a time series. This process is referred to as *deseasonalizing* the time series. Economic time series adjusted for seasonal variations (deseasonalized time series) are often reported in publications such as the *Survey of Current Business, The Wall Street Journal,* and *Business Week.* Using the notation of the multiplicative model, we have

$$Y_t = T_t \times S_t \times I_t$$

By dividing each time series observation by the corresponding seasonal index, we will remove the effect of season from the time series. The deseasonalized time series for television set sales is summarized in Table 16.11. A graph of the deseasonalized television set sales time series is shown in Figure 16.13.

Table 16.11

Deseasonalized Values for the Television Set Sales Time Series

Year	Quarter	Sales (1000s) (Y_t)	Seasonal Index (S_t)	Deseasonalized Sales $(Y_t/S_t = T_tI_t)$
1	1	4.8	0.93	5.16
	2	4.1	0.84	4.88
	3	6.0	1.09	5.50
	4	6.5	1.14	5.70
2	1	5.8	0.93	6.24
	2	5.2	0.84	6.19
	3	6.8	1.09	6.24
	4	7.4	1.14	6.49
3	1	6.0	0.93	6.45
	2	5.6	0.84	6.67
	3	7.5	1.09	6.88
	4	7.8	1.14	6.84
4	1	6.3	0.93	6.77
	2	5.9	0.84	7.02
	3	8.0	1.09	7.34
	4	8.4	1.14	7.37

Figure 16.13

Deseasonalized Television Set Sales Time Series

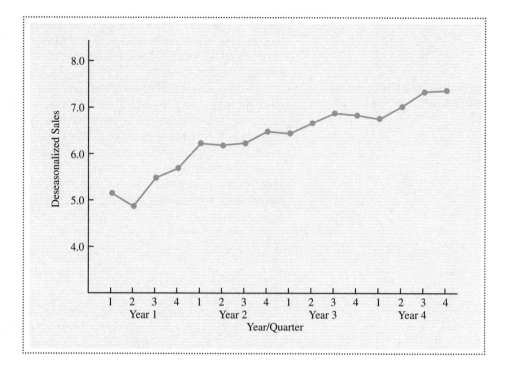

Using the Deseasonalized Time Series to Identify Trend

Although the graph in Figure 16.13 shows some up-and-down movement over the past 16 quarters, the time series seems to have an upward linear trend. To identify this trend, we will use the same procedure as in the preceding section; however, in this case, the data used are quarterly deseasonalized sales values. Thus, for a linear trend, the estimated sales volume expressed as a function of time is

$$T_t = b_0 + b_1 t$$

where

T_t = trend value for television set sales in period t

b_0 = intercept of the trend line

b_1 = slope of the trend line

As before, $t = 1$ corresponds to the time of the first observation for the time series, $t = 2$ corresponds to the time of the second observation, and so on. Thus, for the deseasonalized television set sales time series, $t = 1$ corresponds to the first deseasonalized quarterly sales value, and $t = 16$ corresponds to the most recent deseasonalized quarterly sales value. The formulas for computing the values of b_0 and b_1 are

$$b_1 = \frac{\Sigma t Y_t - (\Sigma t \Sigma Y_t)/n}{\Sigma t^2 - (\Sigma t)^2/n}$$

$$b_0 = \overline{Y} - b_1 \overline{t}$$

Note, however, that Y_t now refers to the deseasonalized time series value at time t and not to the actual value of the time series. Using the given relationships for b_0 and b_1 and the deseasonalized sales data of Table 16.11, we have the following calculations:

t	Y_t (deseasonalized)	tY_t	t^2
1	5.16	5.16	1
2	4.88	9.76	4
3	5.50	16.50	9
4	5.70	22.80	16
5	6.24	31.20	25
6	6.19	37.14	36
7	6.24	43.68	49
8	6.49	51.92	64
9	6.45	58.05	81
10	6.67	66.70	100
11	6.88	75.68	121
12	6.84	82.08	144
13	6.77	88.01	169
14	7.02	98.28	196
15	7.34	110.10	225
16	7.37	117.92	256
Totals 136	101.74	914.98	1496

$$\bar{t} = \frac{136}{16} = 8.5$$

$$\bar{Y} = \frac{101.74}{16} = 6.359$$

$$b_1 = \frac{914.98 - (136)(101.74)/16}{1496 - (136)^2/16} = 0.148$$

$$b_0 = 6.359 - 0.148(8.5) = 5.101$$

Therefore,

$$T_t = 5.101 + 0.148t$$

is the equation for the linear trend component of the time series.

The slope of 0.148 indicates that over the past 16 quarters the firm has experienced an average deseasonalized growth in sales of around 148 sets per quarter. If we assume that the past 16-quarter trend in sales data is a reasonably good indicator of the future, then this equation can be used to project the trend component of the time series for future quarters. For example, substituting $t = 17$ into the equation yields next quarter's trend projection, T_{17}:

$$T_{17} = 5.101 + 0.148(17) = 7.617$$

Using the trend component only, we would forecast sales of 7617 television sets for the next quarter. In a similar fashion, if we use the trend component only, we would forecast sales of 7765, 7913, and 8061 television sets in quarters 18, 19, and 20, respectively.

Table 16.12
. . . .
**Quarterly Forecasts for the
Television Set Sales Time Series**

Year	Quarter	Trend Forecast	Seasonal Index (see Table 16.10)	Quarterly Forecast
5	1	7617	0.93	(7617)(0.93) = 7084
	2	7765	0.84	(7765)(0.84) = 6523
	3	7913	1.09	(7913)(1.09) = 8625
	4	8061	1.14	(8061)(1.14) = 9190

Seasonal Adjustments

The final step in developing the forecast when both trend and seasonal components are present is to use the seasonal index to adjust the trend projection. Returning to the television set sales example, we have a trend projection for the next 4 quarters. Now we must adjust the forecast for the seasonal effect. The seasonal index for the first quarter of year 5 ($t = 17$) is 0.93, so we obtain the quarterly forecast by multiplying the forecast based on trend ($T_{17} = 7617$) times the seasonal index (0.93). Thus, the forecast for the next quarter is $7617(0.93) = 7084$. Table 16.12 shows the quarterly forecast for quarters 17–20. The forecasts show the high-volume fourth quarter with a 9190-unit forecast and the low-volume second quarter with a 6523-unit forecast.

Models Based on Monthly Data

In the preceding television set sales example we used quarterly data to illustrate the computation of seasonal indexes. However, many businesses use monthly rather than quarterly forecasts. In such cases, the procedures introduced in this section can be applied with minor modifications. First, a 12-month moving average replaces the 4-quarter moving average; second, 12 monthly seasonal indexes, rather than the 4 quarterly indexes, need to be computed. Other than these changes, the computational and forecasting procedures are identical.

Cyclical Component

Mathematically, the multiplicative model of equation (16.8) can be expanded to include a cyclical component as follows:

$$Y_t = T_t \times C_t \times S_t \times I_t \qquad (16.9)$$

As with the seasonal component, the cyclical component is expressed as a percentage of trend. This component, mentioned in Section 16.1, is attributable to multiyear cycles in the time series. It is analogous to the seasonal component, but over a longer period of time. However, because of the length of time involved, it is often difficult to obtain enough relevant data to estimate the cyclical component. Another difficulty is that the length of cycles usually varies. We leave further discussion of the cyclical component to texts on forecasting methods.

16.5   Forecasting Using Regression Models

Regression analysis is a statistical technique that can be used to develop a mathematical equation showing how variables are related. In regression terminology, the variable that is being predicted is called the *dependent* or *response* variable. The variable or variables that predict the value of the dependent variable are called the *independent* or *predictor* variables. Regression analysis involving one independent variable and one dependent variable for which the relationship between the variables is approximated by a straight line is called *simple linear regression*. Regression analysis involving two or more independent variables is called *multiple regression analysis.*

In Section 16.3 we utilized simple linear regression to fit a linear trend to the bicycle sales time series. Recall that we developed a linear equation relating bicycle sales to the time period. The number of bicycles sold isn't actually causally related to time; instead, time is a surrogate for variables to which the number of bicycles sold is actually related but which are either unknown or too difficult or costly to measure. Thus, the use of regression analysis for trend projection is not a causal forecasting method because only past values of sales, the variable being forecast, were used.

When we use regression analysis to relate the variable we want to forecast to other variables that are supposed to influence or explain that variable, it becomes a causal forecasting method. The Management Science in Action: Spare Parts Forecasting at American Airlines explains why that company uses regression analysis as a causal forecasting method to estimate the demand for spare parts.

MANAGEMENT SCIENCE in action

Spare Parts Forecasting at American Airlines[*]

American Airlines developed the Rotables Allocation and Planning System (RAPS) to provide demand forecasts for spare parts, assist in allocating spare parts to airports, and calculate the availability level of each spare part. The demand forecasting module of RAPS provides monthly demand forecasts for more than 5000 parts, ranging from coffee makers to landing gears. The average price for parts covered by RAPS is approximately $5000.

Prior to RAPS, American Airlines used time series methodology to forecast spare parts demand. The time series methodology was slow to respond to external factors such as changes in aircraft utilization and major fleet expansions. To correct for these deficiencies, the forecasting component of RAPS involves the use of regression analysis "to establish a relationship between monthly part removals and various functions of monthly flying hours." The RAPS system generates the monthly demand forecasts in less than an hour.

Nearly all the parts covered by the RAPS system are essential to the operation of an aircraft. A part shortage can even result in cancellation of a flight, so the cost can be substantial. The materials management group at American Airlines estimated "that using RAPS has provided a one-time savings of $7 million and recurring annual savings of nearly $1 million."

. . . .

*Based on Tedone, Mark J., "Repairable Part Management."
Interfaces, vol. 19, no. 4, July–August 1989, pp. 61–68.

Using Regression Analysis When Time Series Data Are Not Available

· ·

Regression analysis also may be used to develop forecasts when time series data are not available. To illustrate how regression analysis is used in this context, we consider the sales forecasting problem faced by Armand, Inc., a chain of Italian restaurants doing business in a five-state area. Armand's most successful locations have been near college campuses. Before opening a new restaurant, management requires a forecast of sales revenues. Such an estimate is used in planning restaurant capacity, making initial staffing decisions, and deciding whether the potential revenue justifies the cost of operation. No historical data are available on sales at a new store, so Armand cannot use time series data to develop the forecast.

Management believes that quarterly sales is related to the size of the student population on the nearby campus. Intuitively, management believes that restaurants located near large campuses generate more sales than those located near small campuses. If a relationship can be established between sales and the size of the campus population, Armand can use the size of the campus population to predict revenues for the new restaurant. To evaluate the relationship between quarterly sales y and student population x, Armand collected data from a sample of 10 of its restaurants located near college campuses. These data are summarized in Table 16.13. For example, we see that restaurant 1, with $y = 58$ and $x = 2$, has quarterly sales of $58,000 and is located near a campus with 2000 students.

Figure 16.14 shows graphically the data presented in Table 16.13. The size of the student population is shown on the horizontal axis, with quarterly sales on the vertical axis. A graph such as this is known as a *scatter diagram*. Usually the independent variable is plotted on the horizontal axis, and the dependent variable is plotted on the vertical axis. The advantage of a scatter diagram is that it provides an overview of the data and enables us to draw preliminary conclusions about a possible relationship between the variables.

What preliminary conclusions can we draw from Figure 16.14? Sales appear to be higher at campuses with larger student populations. Also, it appears that the relationship between the two variables can be approximated by a straight line. In Figure 16.15 we have drawn a straight line through the data that appears to provide a good linear approximation of the relationship between the variables. Observe that the relationship is not perfect. Indeed, few, if any, of the data items fall exactly on the line. However, if we

Table 16.13
· · · · · · · · · · ·
Data on Quarterly Sales and Student Population for 10 Restaurants

Restaurant	y = Quarterly Sales ($1000s)	x = Student Population (1000s)
1	58	2
2	105	6
3	88	8
4	118	8
5	117	12
6	137	16
7	157	20
8	169	20
9	149	22
10	202	26

Figure 16.14

Scatter Diagram of Quarterly Sales Versus Student Population

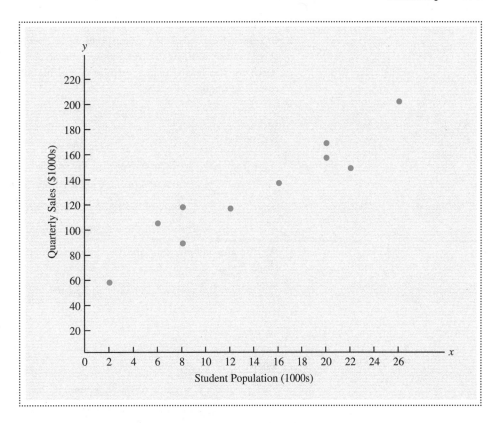

Figure 16.15

Straight-Line Approximation for Data on Quarterly Sales and Student Population

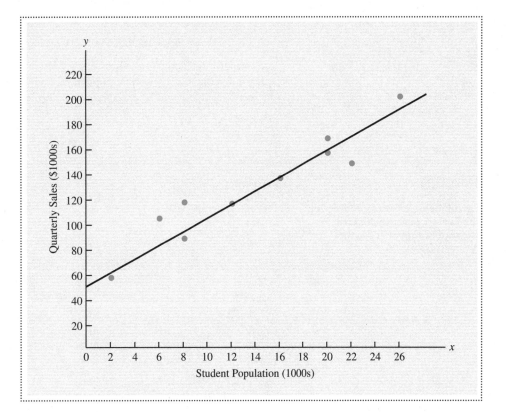

can develop the mathematical expression for this line, we may be able to use it to predict or forecast the value of y corresponding to each possible value of x. We will refer to the resulting equation of the line as the *estimated regression equation.*

Using the least-squares method of estimation, we develop the following estimated regression equation:

$$\hat{y} = b_0 + b_1 x \qquad (16.10)$$

where

$\hat{y}$ = estimated value of the dependent variable (quarterly sales)

b_0 = intercept of the estimated regression equation

b_1 = slope of the estimated regression equation

x = value of the independent variable (student population)

We use the sample data and the following expression to compute the intercept b_0 and slope b_1:

$$b_1 = \frac{\Sigma x_i y_i - (\Sigma x_i \, \Sigma y_i)/n}{\Sigma x_i^2 - (\Sigma x_i)^2/n} \qquad (16.11)$$

$$b_0 = \bar{y} - b_1 \bar{x} \qquad (16.12)$$

where

x_i = value of the independent variable for the ith observation

y_i = value of the dependent variable for the ith observation

$\bar{x}$ = mean value for the independent variable

$\bar{y}$ = mean value for the dependent variable

n = total number of observations

Some of the calculations necessary to develop the least-squares estimated regression equation for the data on student population and annual sales are shown in Table 16.14. In our example there are 10 restaurants or observations; hence $n = 10$. Using equations

Table 16.14

Calculations Necessary to Develop the Least-Squares Estimated Regression Equation for the Armand Data

Restaurant (i)	y_i	x_i	$x_i y_i$	x_i^2
1	58	2	116	4
2	105	6	630	36
3	88	8	704	64
4	118	8	944	64
5	117	12	1,404	144
6	137	16	2,192	256
7	157	20	3,140	400
8	169	20	3,380	400
9	149	22	3,278	484
10	202	26	5,252	676
Totals	1300	140	21,040	2528

(16.11) and (16.12), we can now compute the slope and intercept of the estimated regression equation. The calculation of the slope b_1 proceeds as follows:

$$b_1 = \frac{\Sigma x_i y_i - (\Sigma x_i \, \Sigma y_i)/n}{\Sigma x_i^2 - (\Sigma x_i)^2/n}$$

$$= \frac{21,040 - (140)(1300)/10}{2528 - (140)^2/10}$$

$$= \frac{2840}{568} = 5$$

We then calculate the intercept b_0 as follows:

$$\bar{x} = \frac{\Sigma x_i}{n} = \frac{140}{10} = 14$$

$$\bar{y} = \frac{\Sigma y_i}{n} = \frac{1300}{10} = 130$$

$$b_0 = \bar{y} - b_1 \bar{x}$$

$$= 130 - 5(14) = 60$$

Thus, the estimated regression equation found by using the method of least squares is

$$\hat{y} = 60 + 5x$$

We show the graph of this equation in Figure 16.16.

Figure 16.16

The Estimated Regression Equation for the Armand Data

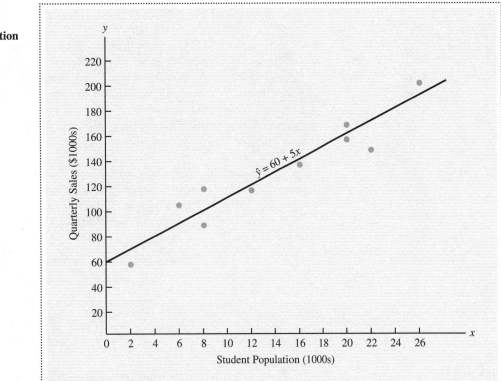

The slope of the estimated regression equation ($b_1 = 5$) is positive, implying that as student population increases, quarterly sales increase. In fact, we can conclude (since sales are measured in thousands of dollars and student population in thousands) that an increase in the student population of 1000 is associated with an increase of $5000 in expected quarterly sales; that is, sales are expected to increase by $5 per student.

If we believe that the least-squares estimated regression equation adequately describes the relationship between x and y, then it would seem reasonable to use the estimated regression equation to forecast the value of y for a given value of x. For example, if we wanted to forecast quarterly sales for a new restaurant location near a campus with 16,000 students, we would compute

$$\hat{y} = 60 + 5(16) = 140$$

You should now be able to use regression analysis to develop a forecast when time series data are not available. Try Problem 35.

Hence we would forecast sales of $140,000 per quarter.

The sales forecasting problem faced by Armand, Inc., illustrates how simple linear regression analysis can be used to develop forecasts when time series data are not available. Multiple regression analysis can also be applied in these situations provided additional data for other independent variables are available. For example, suppose that management of Armand, Inc., also believes that the number of competitors near the college campus is related to the quarterly sales. On an intuitive basis, management believes that restaurants located near campuses where there are fewer competitors generate more sales revenue than those located near campuses where there are more competitors. Given these additional data, multiple regression analysis could be used to develop an equation relating annual sales to the size of the student population and the number of competitors.

Using Regression Analysis with Time Series Data

In Section 16.3 we fit a linear trend to the bicycle sales time series to show how simple linear regression analysis can be used to forecast future values of a time series when past values of the time series are available. Recall that for this problem the annual sales in year t was treated as the dependent variable and the year t was treated as the independent variable. The inherent complexity of most real problems necessitates the consideration of more than one independent variable to predict the dependent variable. Let us consider how multiple regression analysis is used to develop forecasts when time series data are available.

To use multiple regression analysis, we need a sample of observations for the dependent variable and all independent variables. In time series analysis, the n periods of time series data provide a sample of n observations for each variable. To describe the wide variety of regression-based models that can be developed, we will use the following notation:

$$Y_t = \text{actual value of the time series in period } t$$
$$x_{1t} = \text{value of independent variable 1 in period } t$$
$$x_{2t} = \text{value of independent variable 2 in period } t$$
$$\cdot$$
$$\cdot$$
$$\cdot$$
$$x_{kt} = \text{value of independent variable } k \text{ in period } t$$

The n periods of data necessary to develop the estimated regression equation would appear as follows:

Period	Time Series Value (Y_t)	Value of Independent Variables						
		x_{1t}	x_{2t}	x_{3t}	.	.	.	x_{kt}
1	Y_1	x_{11}	x_{21}	x_{31}	.	.	.	x_{k1}
2	Y_2	x_{12}	x_{22}	x_{32}	.	.	.	x_{k2}
.	.	.	.	.	.	.	.	.
.	.	.	.	.	.	.	.	.
.	.	.	.	.	.	.	.	.
n	Y_n	x_{1n}	x_{2n}	x_{3n}	.	.	.	x_{kn}

As you might imagine, there are a number of choices for the independent variables in a forecasting model. One possible choice is simply time. This is the choice we made in Section 16.3 when we estimated the trend of the time series using a linear function of the independent variable time. Letting

$$x_{1t} = t$$

we obtain an estimated regression equation of the form

$$\hat{Y}_t = b_0 + b_1 t$$

where $\hat{Y}_t$ is the estimate of the time series value Y_t and where b_0 and b_1 are the estimated regression coefficients. In a more complex model, additional terms could be added corresponding to time raised to other powers. For example, if

$$x_{2t} = t^2$$

and

$$x_{3t} = t^3$$

the estimated regression equation would then become

$$\hat{Y}_t = b_0 + b_1 x_{1t} + b_2 x_{2t} + b_3 x_{3t}$$

$$= b_0 + b_1 t + b_2 t^2 + b_3 t^3$$

Note that this model provides a forecast of a time series with curvilinear characteristics over time.

Other regression-based forecasting models employ a mixture of economic and demographic independent variables. For example, in forecasting the sale of refrigerators, we might select independent variables such as the following:

x_{1t} = price in period t

x_{2t} = total industry sales in period $t - 1$

x_{3t} = number of building permits for new houses in period $t - 1$

x_{4t} = population forecast for period t

x_{5t} = advertising budget for period t

According to the usual multiple regression procedure, an estimated regression equation with five independent variables would be used to develop forecasts.

Whether a regression approach provides a good forecast depends largely on how well we are able to identify and obtain data for independent variables that are closely related to the time series. Generally, during the development of an estimated regression equation, we will want to consider many possible sets of independent variables. Thus, part of the regression analysis procedure should focus on the selection of the set of independent variables that provides the best forecasting model.

In the chapter introduction we stated that *causal forecasting models* utilized time series related to the one being forecast in an effort to better explain the cause of a time series' behavior. Regression analysis is the tool most often used in developing these causal models. The related time series become the independent variables, and the time series being forecast is the dependent variable.

Another type of regression-based forecasting model occurs whenever the independent variables are all previous values of the *same* time series. For example, if the time series values are denoted by $Y_1, Y_2, \ldots, Y_n$, we might try to find an estimated regression equation relating Y_t to the most recent time series values, Y_{t-1}, Y_{t-2}, and so on. For instance, using the actual values of the time series for the three most recent periods as independent variables, the estimated regression equation would be

$$\hat{Y}_t = b_0 + b_1 Y_{t-1} + b_2 Y_{t-2} + b_3 Y_{t-3}$$

Regression models such as this, where the independent variables are previous values of the time series, are referred to as *autoregressive models*.

Finally, another regression-based forecasting approach is one that incorporates a mixture of the independent variables previously discussed. For example, we might select a combination of time variables, some economic/demographic variables, and some previous values of the time series variable itself.

16.6 Qualitative Approaches to Forecasting

In the previous sections we discussed several types of quantitative forecasting methods. Most of these techniques require historical data on the variable of interest, so they cannot be applied when no historical data are available. Furthermore, even when such data are available, a significant change in environmental conditions affecting the time series may make the use of past data questionable in predicting future values of the time series. For example, a government-imposed gasoline rationing program would cause one to question the validity of a gasoline sales forecast based on historical data. Qualitative forecasting techniques offer an alternative in these and other cases.

Delphi Method

One of the most commonly used qualitative forecasting methods is the *Delphi approach*. This technique, originally developed by a research group at the Rand Corporation, attempts to develop forecasts through "group consensus." In the usual application of this technique, the members of a panel of experts—all of whom are physically separated from and unknown to each other—are asked to respond to a series of questionnaires. The responses from the first questionnaire are tabulated and used to prepare a second questionnaire that contains information and opinions of the whole group. Each respondent is then asked to reconsider and possibly revise his or her previous response in light of the group information provided. This process continues until the coordinator feels that some degree of consensus has been reached. The goal of the Delphi method is not to produce a single answer as output, but to produce a relatively narrow spread of opinions within which the majority of experts concur.

Expert Judgment

Qualitative forecasts often are based on the judgment of a single expert or represent the consensus of a group of experts. For example, each year a group of experts at Merrill Lynch gather to forecast the level of the Dow Jones Industrial Average and the prime rate for the next year. In doing so, the experts individually consider information that they believe will influence the stock market and interest rates; then, they combine their conclusions into a forecast. No formal model is used, and no two experts are likely to consider the same information in the same way.

Expert judgment is a forecasting method that is often recommended when conditions in the past are not likely to hold in the future. Even though no formal quantitative model is used, expert judgment has provided good forecasts in many situations. The MS in Action: The *Business Week* Industry Outlook shows that the magazine provides a good 1-year forecast of industry prospects.

Scenario Writing

The qualitative procedure referred to as *scenario writing* consists of developing a conceptual scenario of the future based on a well-defined set of assumptions. Different sets of assumptions lead to different scenarios. The job of the decision maker is to decide how likely each scenario is and then to make decisions accordingly.

MANAGEMENT SCIENCE in action

The *Business Week* Industry Outlook[*]

The *Business Week* industry outlook survey is a qualitative approach to forecasting based on expert judgment. It combines information from hundreds of interviews with industry leaders with the expertise of the magazine's editors who follow the industries daily to provide a judgment on the prospects for the next year. Steven Schnaars and Iris Mohr conducted a study to evaluate the accuracy of the *Business Week* forecasts for five industries (autos, steel, chemicals, computers, and energy) over a 9-year period (1978–1986).

Schnaars and Mohr evaluated *Business Week*'s approach in terms of its ability to predict correctly the general direction for the industry (getting better or getting worse) and the accuracy of specific forecasts (e.g., sales and profit). They found that "nearly 80 percent of the outlooks correctly foresaw the overall direction in which the industry would move in the coming year." And, when comparing the *Business Week* forecast with a naive forecast of no change in the coming year, the *Business Week* forecast clearly was better. The authors conclude that judgmental forecasting can work well for forecasting the general direction of change.

....

*Schnaars, Steven P., and Iris Mohr, "The Accuracy of *Business Week's* Industry Outlook Survey." *Interfaces,* vol. 18, no. 5, September–October 1988, pp. 31–38.

Intuitive Approaches

Intuitive approaches are based on the ability of the human mind to process a variety of information that, in most cases, is difficult to quantify. These techniques are often used in group work, wherein a committee or panel seeks to develop new ideas or solve complex problems through a series of "brainstorming sessions." In such sessions, individuals are freed from the usual group restrictions of peer pressure and criticism because they can present any idea or opinion without regard to its relevancy and, even more importantly, without fear of criticism.

Summary

In this chapter we discussed how forecasts can be developed to help management develop appropriate strategies for the future. We began by defining a time series as a set of observations of a variable measured at successive points in time or over successive periods of time. A time series may involve four separate components: trend, seasonal, irregular, and cyclical. By isolating these components and measuring their apparent effects, future values of the time series can be forecast.

Quantitative forecasting methods include time series methods and causal methods. A time series method is appropriate when the historical data are restricted to past values of the variable being forecast. The three time series methods discussed in the chapter are smoothing (moving averages, weighted moving averages, and exponential smoothing), trend projection, and trend projection adjusted for seasonal influence.

Smoothing methods are appropriate for a stable time series, that is, one that exhibits no significant trend, cyclical, or seasonal effects. The moving averages approach consists of computing an average of past values and then using this average as the forecast for the next period. The weighted moving averages method allows for the possibility of unequal weights for the data; thus, the moving averages method is a special case of the weighted moving averages method in which all the weights are equal. Exponential smoothing is a special case of the weighted moving averages method involving only one weight: the weight for the most recent observation.

When a time series consists of random fluctuations around a long-term trend line, a linear equation may be used to estimate the trend. When seasonal effects are present, seasonal indexes can be computed and used to deseasonalize the data and to develop forecasts. When both seasonal and long-term trend effects are present, a trend line is fitted to the deseasonalized data; the seasonal indexes are then used to adjust the trend projections.

Causal forecasting methods are based on the assumption that the variable being forecast exhibits a cause–effect relationship with one or more other variables. A causal forecasting method is one that relates the variable being forecast to other variables thought to influence or explain it. Regression analysis as a causal forecasting method can be used to develop forecasts when time series data are not available.

Qualitative forecasting methods may be used when little or no historical data are available. Qualitative forecasting methods also are considered most appropriate when the historical pattern of the time series is not expected to continue into the future.

Glossary

Time series A set of observations measured at successive points in time or over successive periods of time.

Forecast A projection or prediction of future values of a time series.

Trend The long-run shift or movement in the time series observable over several periods of data.

Cyclical component The component of the time series model that results in periodic above-trend and below-trend behavior of the time series lasting more than 1 year.

Seasonal component The component of the time series model that shows a periodic pattern over 1 year or less.

Irregular component The component of the time series model that reflects the random variation of the actual time series values beyond what can be explained by the trend, cyclical, and seasonal components.

Moving averages A method of forecasting or smoothing a time series by averaging each successive group of data points. The moving averages method can be used to isolate the seasonal component of the time series.

Mean squared error (MSE) One approach to measuring the accuracy of a forecasting model. This measure is the average of the sum of the squared differences between the forecasted values and the actual time series values.

Weighted moving averages A method of forecasting or smoothing a time series by computing a weighted average of past time series values. The sum of the weights must equal 1.

Exponential smoothing A forecasting technique that uses a weighted average of past time series values to arrive at smoothed time series values that can be used as forecasts.

Smoothing constant A parameter of the exponential smoothing model that provides the weight given to the most recent time series value in the calculation of the forecast.

Multiplicative time series model A model that assumes that the separate components of the time series can be multiplied together to identify the actual time series value. When the four components of trend, cyclical, seasonal, and irregular are assumed present, we obtain $Y_t = T_t \times C_t \times S_t \times I_t$. When cyclical effects are not modeled, we obtain $Y_t = T_t \times S_t \times I_t$.

Deseasonalized time series A time series that has had the effect of season removed by dividing each original time series observation by the corresponding seasonal index.

Regression analysis A statistical technique that can be used to develop a mathematical equation showing how variables are related.

Causal forecasting methods Forecasting methods that relate a time series to other variables believed to explain or cause its behavior.

Autoregressive model A time series model that uses a regression relationship based on historical time series values to predict the future time series values.

Delphi approach A qualitative forecasting method that obtains forecasts through group consensus.

Scenario writing A qualitative forecasting method that consists of developing a conceptual scenario of the future based on a well-defined set of assumptions.

Problems

1. **SELF Test** Consider the following time series data.

Week	1	2	3	4	5	6
Value	8	13	15	17	16	9

   a. Develop a 3-week moving average for this time series. What is the forecast for week 7?
   b. Compute the MSE for the 3-week moving average.
   c. Use $\alpha = .2$ to compute the exponential smoothing values for the time series. What is the forecast for week 7?
   d. Compare the 3-week moving average forecast with the exponential smoothing forecast using $\alpha = .2$. Which appears to provide the better forecast?
   e. Use a smoothing constant of .4 to compute the exponential smoothing values. Does a smoothing constant of .2 or .4 appear to provide the better forecast? Explain.

2. **SELF Test** Refer to the gasoline sales time series data in Table 16.1.

   a. Compute 4- and 5-week moving averages for the time series.
   b. Compute the MSE for the 4- and 5-week moving average forecasts.
   c. What appears to be the best number of weeks of past data to use in the moving average computation? Remember that the MSE for the 3-week moving average is 10.22.

3. Refer again to the gasoline sales time series data in Table 16.1.
   a. Using a weight of $\frac{1}{2}$ for the most recent observation, $\frac{1}{3}$ for the second most recent, and $\frac{1}{6}$ for third most recent, compute a 3-week weighted moving average for the time series.
   b. Compute the MSE for the weighted moving average in part (a). Do you prefer this weighted moving average to the unweighted moving average? Remember that the MSE for the unweighted moving average is 10.22.
   c. Suppose you are allowed to choose any weights as long as they sum to 1. Could you always find a set of weights that would make the MSE smaller for a weighted moving average than for an unweighted moving average? Why or why not?

4. **SELFTest** With the gasoline time series data from Table 16.1, show the exponential smoothing forecasts using $\alpha = 0.1$. Applying the MSE criterion, would you prefer a smoothing constant of $\alpha = 0.1$ or $\alpha = 0.2$?

5. **SELFTest** The following data show the monthly percentages of all shipments that were received on time over the past 12 months.

   80   82   84   83   83   84   85   84   82   83   84   83

   a. Compare a 3-month moving average forecast with an exponential smoothing forecast using $\alpha = 0.2$. Which provides the better forecasts?
   b. What is the forecast for next month?

6. With a smoothing constant of $\alpha = 0.2$, equation (16.2) shows that the forecast for the 13th week of the gasoline sales data from Table 16.1 is given by $F_{13} = 0.2Y_{12} + 0.8F_{12}$. However, the forecast for week 12 is given by $F_{12} = 0.2Y_{11} + 0.8F_{11}$. Thus, we could combine these two results to show that the forecast for the 13th week can be written

   $$F_{13} = 0.2Y_{12} + 0.8(0.2Y_{11} + 0.8F_{11}) = 0.2Y_{12} + 0.16Y_{11} + 0.64F_{11}$$

   a. Making use of the fact that $F_{11} = 0.2Y_{10} + 0.8F_{10}$ (and similarly for F_{10} and F_9), continue to expand the expression for F_{13} until it is written in terms of the past data values $Y_{12}, Y_{11}, Y_{10}, Y_9,$ and Y_8, and the forecast for period 8.
   b. Refer to the coefficients or weights for the past data values $Y_{12}, Y_{11}, Y_{10}, Y_9,$ and Y_8; what observation do you make about how exponential smoothing weights past data values in arriving at new forecasts? Compare this weighting pattern with the weighting pattern of the moving averages method.

7. Alabama building contracts for a 12-month period are shown here. Data are in millions of dollars.

   240   350   230   260   280   320   220   310   240   310   240   230

   a. Compare a 3-month moving average forecast with an exponential smoothing forecast using $\alpha = 0.2$. Which provides the better forecasts?
   b. What is the forecast for the next month?

8. The following time series shows the sales of a particular product over the past 12 months:

Month	Sales	Month	Sales
1	105	7	145
2	135	8	140
3	120	9	100
4	105	10	80
5	90	11	100
6	120	12	110

a. Use $\alpha = 0.3$ to compute the exponential smoothing values for the time series.

b. Use a smoothing constant of 0.5 to compute the exponential smoothing values. Does a smoothing constant of 0.3 or 0.5 appear to provide the better forecasts?

9. The Dow Jones Industrial Average is based on common stock prices of 30 industrial stocks. This average is used to describe what is happening in the stock market. The following data show weekly closing levels of the Dow Jones average for 12 weeks.

Week	Dow Jones	Week	Dow Jones
1	2480	7	2520
2	2470	8	2470
3	2475	9	2440
4	2510	10	2480
5	2500	11	2530
6	2480	12	2550

a. Compute the exponential smoothing forecasts using $\alpha = 0.2$.

b. Compute the exponential smoothing forecasts using $\alpha = 0.3$.

c. Which exponential smoothing model provides the better forecasts? What is the forecast of the Dow Jones Industrial Average for week 13?

10. The following data show the number of component parts used in a production process during the last 10 weeks.

Week	Parts	Week	Parts
1	200	6	210
2	350	7	280
3	250	8	350
4	360	9	290
5	250	10	320

Using a smoothing constant of 0.25, develop the exponential smoothing values for this time series. Indicate your forecast for week 11.

11. A chain of grocery stores experienced the following weekly demand (cases) for a particular brand of automatic-dishwasher detergent:

Week	Demand	Week	Demand
1	22	6	24
2	18	7	20
3	23	8	19
4	21	9	18
5	17	10	21

Use exponential smoothing with $\alpha = 0.2$ to develop a forecast for week 11.

12. United Dairies, Inc., supplies milk to several independent grocers throughout Dade County, Florida. The management of United Dairies would like to develop a forecast of the number of half-gallons of milk sold per week. Sales data for the past 12 weeks are as follows:

Week	Sales (Units)	Week	Sales (Units)
1	2750	7	3300
2	3100	8	3100
3	3250	9	2950
4	2800	10	3000
5	2900	11	3200
6	3050	12	3150

Using exponential smoothing with $\alpha = 0.4$, develop a forecast of demand for week 13.

13. Ten weeks of data on the Commodity Futures Index are shown here.

$$7.35 \quad 7.40 \quad 7.55 \quad 7.56 \quad 7.60 \quad 7.52 \quad 7.52 \quad 7.70 \quad 7.62 \quad 7.55$$

a. Compute the exponential smoothing forecasts using $\alpha = 0.2$.
b. Compute the exponential smoothing forecasts using $\alpha = 0.3$.
c. Which exponential smoothing model provides the better forecasts? What is the forecast for week 11?

14. SELF**Test**   The following data show enrollment (1000s) for a state college for the past 6 years.

Year	1	2	3	4	5	6
Enrollment	20.5	20.2	19.5	19.0	19.1	18.8

Develop the equation for the linear trend component for this time series. Comment on what is happening to enrollment at this institution.

15. The following time series data show the retail price index of consumer goods and services over a 9-year period.

Year	Price Index	Year	Price Index
1	66.9	6	94.6
2	74.8	7	97.8
3	81.2	8	101.9
4	85.0	9	106.9
5	89.2		

Use trend projection to forecast the retail price index for years 10 and 11.

16. Average attendance figures at home football games for a major university show the following pattern for the past 7 years:

Year	1	2	3	4	5	6	7
Attendance	28,000	30,000	31,500	30,400	30,500	32,200	30,800

Develop the equation for the linear trend component (equation (16.4)) for this time series.

17. Automobile sales at B. J. Scott Motors, Inc., provided the following 10-year time series:

Year	Sales	Year	Sales
1	400	6	260
2	390	7	300
3	320	8	320
4	340	9	340
5	270	10	370

Plot the time series, and comment on the appropriateness of a linear trend. What type of functional form do you believe would be most appropriate for the trend pattern of this time series?

18. The president of a small manufacturing firm has been concerned about the continual growth in manufacturing costs over the past several years. The following time series data show the cost per unit for the firm's leading product over the past 8 years.

Year	Cost Per Unit ($)	Year	Cost Per Unit ($)
1	20.00	5	26.60
2	24.50	6	30.00
3	28.20	7	31.00
4	27.50	8	36.00

a. Show a graph of this time series. Does a linear trend appear to exist?
b. Develop the equation for the linear trend component for the above time series. What is the average cost increase that the firm has been realizing per year?

19. Earnings per share (in dollars) for the Walgreen Company for a 10-year period are as follows:

0.84   0.73   0.94   1.14   1.33   1.53   1.67   1.68   2.10   2.50

a. Use a linear trend projection to forecast this time series for the coming year.
b. What does this time series analysis tell you about the Walgreen Company? Do the historical data indicate the Walgreen Company is a good investment?

20. The gross revenue data for Delta Airlines for a 10-year period are shown here. Data are in millions of dollars.

Year	Revenue	Year	Revenue
1	2428	6	4264
2	2951	7	4738
3	3533	8	4460
4	3618	9	5318
5	3616	10	6915

a. Develop a linear trend expression for this time series. Comment on what the expression tells about the gross revenue for Delta Airlines for the 10-year period.
b. Provide the forecasts of gross revenue for years 11 and 12.

21. The vacancy rate for office rentals is reported in terms of the percentage of available offices that are not rented. Office vacancy rates for downtown Philadelphia over an 8-year period are as follows:

Year	Vacancy Rate	Year	Vacancy Rate
1	5.9	5	9.2
2	4.6	6	9.5
3	6.4	7	10.8
4	9.5	8	11.0

   a. Develop a linear trend for this time series.

   b. Provide forecasts of the vacancy rate for years 9, 10, and 11.

   c. Should city planners be concerned with the forecasts of office vacancy? What conclusion should be reached, and what possible actions should the city planners consider?

22. Canton Supplies, Inc., is a service firm that employs approximately 100 individuals. Because of the necessity of meeting monthly cash obligations, the management of Canton Supplies would like to develop a forecast of monthly cash requirements. Because of a recent change in operating policy, only the past 7 months of data were considered to be relevant. Use the historical data shown below to develop a forecast of cash requirements for each of the next 2 months using trend projection.

Month	1	2	3	4	5	6	7
Cash Required ($1000s)	205	212	218	224	230	240	246

23. The following data show the time series of the most recent quarterly capital expenditures in billions of dollars for the 1000 largest manufacturing firms.

      24 25 23 24 22 26 28 31 29 32 37 42

   a. Develop a linear trend expression for the above time series.

   b. Show a graph of the time series and the linear trend expression.

   c. Using the time series, what appears to be happening to the capital expenditures? What is the forecast 1 year or 4 quarters into the future?

24. The Costello Music Company has been in business for 5 years. During this time, the sale of electric organs has grown from 12 units in the first year to 76 units in the most recent year. Fred Costello, the firm's owner, would like to develop a forecast of organ sales for the coming year. The historical data are shown below.

Year	1	2	3	4	5
Sales	12	28	34	50	76

   a. Show a graph of this time series. Does a linear trend appear to exist?

   b. Develop the equation for the linear trend component for the above time series. What is the average increase in sales that the firm has been realizing per year?

25. Hudson Marine has been an authorized dealer for C&D marine radios for the past 7 years. The number of radios sold each year is shown here.

Year	1	2	3	4	5	6	7
Number Sold	35	50	75	90	105	110	130

   a. Show a graph of this time series. Does a linear trend appear to exist?

   b. Develop the equation for the linear trend component for the above time series.

   c. Use the linear trend developed in part (b) to prepare a forecast for annual sales in year 8.

26. Aggregate personal income data (in billions of dollars) by month are as follows:

January	3.92	July	4.05
February	3.96	August	4.08
March	4.00	September	4.10
April	4.01	October	4.12
May	4.02	November	4.18
June	4.04	December	4.22

a. Develop a linear trend expression for the above time series. What was happening to aggregate personal income during the year?

b. Provide estimates of aggregate personal income for the first 6 months of the coming year.

c. Assume that in June of the coming year, the actual level of aggregate personal income turned out to be 4.41. Comment on the forecasting error based on your trend projection.

27. **SELF Test** The quarterly sales data (number of copies sold) for a college textbook over the past 3 years are as follows:

Quarter	Year 1	Year 2	Year 3
1	1690	1800	1850
2	940	900	1100
3	2625	2900	2930
4	2500	2360	2615

a. Show the 4-quarter moving average values for this time series. Plot both the original time series and the moving averages on the same graph.

b. Compute seasonal indexes for the 4 quarters.

c. When does the textbook publisher experience the largest seasonal index? Does this appear reasonable? Explain.

28. Identify the monthly seasonal indexes for the following 3 years of expenses for a 6-unit apartment house in southern Florida. Use a 12-month moving average calculation.

Month	Year 1	Year 2	Year 3
January	170	180	195
February	180	205	210
March	205	215	230
April	230	245	280
May	240	265	290
June	315	330	390
July	360	400	420
August	290	335	330
September	240	260	290
October	240	270	295
November	230	255	280
December	195	220	250

29. Air pollution control specialists in southern California monitor the amount of ozone, carbon dioxide, and nitrogen dioxide in the air on an hourly basis. The hourly time series data exhibit seasonality, with the levels of pollutants showing similar patterns over the hours in the day. On July 15, 16, and 17, the observed levels of nitrogen dioxide in a city's downtown area for the 12 hours from 6:00 A.M. to 6:00 P.M. were as follows:

July 15	25	28	35	50	60	60	40	35	30	25	25	20
July 16	28	30	35	48	60	65	50	40	35	25	20	20
July 17	35	42	45	70	72	75	60	45	40	25	25	25

a. Identify the hourly seasonal indexes for the 12-hour daily readings.
b. Using the seasonal indexes from part (a), the trend equation developed for the deseasonalized data is $T_t = 32.983 + 0.3922t$. Using the trend component only, develop forecasts for the 12 hours for July 18.
c. Use the seasonal indexes from part (a) to adjust the trend forecasts developed in part (b).

30. Refer to Problem 25. Suppose the quarterly sales values for the 7 years of historical data are as follows:

Year	Quarter 1	Quarter 2	Quarter 3	Quarter 4	Total Sales
1	6	15	10	4	35
2	10	18	15	7	50
3	14	26	23	12	75
4	19	28	25	18	90
5	22	34	28	21	105
6	24	36	30	20	110
7	28	40	35	27	130

a. Show the 4-quarter moving average values for this time series. Plot both the original time series and the moving averages on the same graph.
b. Compute the seasonal indexes for the 4 quarters.
c. When does Hudson Marine experience the largest seasonal effect? Does this seem reasonable? Explain.

31. Consider the Costello Music Company scenario presented in Problem 24. The quarterly sales data are shown below.

Year	Quarter 1	Quarter 2	Quarter 3	Quarter 4	Total Yearly Sales
1	4	2	1	5	12
2	6	4	4	14	28
3	10	3	5	16	34
4	12	9	7	22	50
5	18	10	13	35	76

a. Compute the seasonal indexes for the 4 quarters.
b. When does Costello Music experience the largest seasonal effect? Does this appear reasonable? Explain.

32. Refer to the Hudson Marine data presented in Problem 30.
a. Deseasonalize the data, and use the deseasonalized time series to identify the trend.
b. Use the results of part (a) to develop a quarterly forecast for next year based on trend.
c. Use the seasonal indexes developed in Problem 30 to adjust the forecasts developed in part (b) to account for the effect of season.

33. Consider the Costello Music Company time series presented in Problem 31.
   a. Deseasonalize the data, and use the deseasonalized time series to identify the trend.
   b. Use the results of part (a) to develop a quarterly forecast for next year based on trend.
   c. Use the seasonal indexes to adjust the forecasts developed in part (b) to account for the effect of season.

34. Electric power consumption is measured in kilowatt-hours (kWh). The local utility company has an interrupt program whereby commercial customers that participate receive favorable rates but must agree to cut back consumption if the utility requests them to do so. Timko Products cut back consumption at 12:00 noon Thursday. To assess the savings, the utility must estimate Timko's usage without the interrupt. The period of interrupted service was from noon to 8:00 P.M. Data on electric power consumption for the past 72 hours are avaiable.

Time Period	Monday	Tuesday	Wednesday	Thursday
12–4 A.M.	—	19,281	31,209	27,330
4–8 A.M.	—	33,195	37,014	32,715
8–12 noon	—	99,516	119,968	152,465
12–4 P.M.	124,299	123,666	156,033	
4–8 P.M.	113,545	111,717	128,889	
8–12 midnight	41,300	48,112	73,923	

   a. Is there a seasonal effect over the 24-hour period? Compute seasonal indexes for the six 4-hour periods.
   b. Use trend adjusted for seasonal indexes to estimate Timko's normal usage over the period of interrupted service.

35. **SELFTest** Eddie's Restaurants collected the following data on the relationship between advertising and sales at a sample of five restaurants:

Advertising Expenditures ($1000s)	1.0	4.0	6.0	10.0	14.0
Sales ($1000s)	19.0	44.0	40.0	52.0	53.0

   a. Let x equal advertising expenditures and y equal sales. Use the method of least squares to develop a straight-line approximation to the relationship between the two variables.
   b. Use the equation developed in part (a) to forecast sales for an advertising expenditure of $8000.

36. The management of a chain of fast-food restaurants would like to investigate the relationship between the daily sales volume of a company restaurant and the number of competitor restaurants within a 1-mile radius of the firm's restaurant. The following data have been collected:

Number of Competitors Within 1 Mile	Sales ($)
1	3600
1	3300
2	3100
3	2900
3	2700
4	2500
5	2300
5	2000

a. Develop the least-squares estimated regression equation that relates daily sales volume to the number of competitor restaurants within a 1-mile radius.

b. Use the estimated regression equation developed in part (a) to forecast the daily sales volume for a particular company restaurant that has four competitors within a 1-mile radius.

37. In a manufacturing process, the assembly-line speed (feet/minute) was thought to affect the number of defective parts found during the inspection process. To test this theory, management devised a situation where the same batch of parts was inspected visually at a variety of line speeds. The following data were collected:

Line Speed	Number of Defective Parts Found
20	21
20	19
40	15
30	16
60	14
40	17

a. Develop the estimated regression equation that relates line speed to the number of defective parts found.

b. Use the equation developed in part (a) to forecast the number of defective parts found for a line speed of 50 feet per minute.

Case Problem: Forecasting Sales

The Vintage Restaurant is located on Captiva Island, a resort community located near Fort Meyers, Florida. The restaurant, which is owned and operated by Karen Payne, has just completed its third year of operation. During this time, Karen has sought to establish a reputation for the restaurant as a high-quality dining establishment that specializes in fresh seafood. The efforts made by Karen and her staff have proved successful, and her restaurant has become one of the best and fastest-growing restaurants on the island.

Karen has concluded that in order to plan better for the growth of the restaurant in the future, it is necessary to develop a system that will enable her to forecast food and beverage sales by month for up to 1 year in advance. Karen has the following data available on the total food and beverage sales that were realized during the previous 3 years of operation.

Food and Beverage Sales for the Vintage Restaurant ($1000s)

Month	First Year	Second Year	Third Year
January	242	263	282
February	235	238	255
March	232	247	265
April	178	193	205
May	184	193	210
June	140	149	160
July	145	157	166
August	152	161	174
September	110	122	126
October	130	130	148
November	152	167	173
December	206	230	235

Managerial Report

Perform an analysis of the sales data for the Vintage Restaurant. Prepare a report for Karen that summarizes your findings, forecasts, and recommendations. Include information on the following:

1. A graph of the time series.
2. An analysis of the seasonality of the data. Include the seasonal indexes for each month, and comment on the high seasonal and low seasonal sales months. Do the seasonal indexes make intuitive sense? Discuss.
3. Forecast sales for January through December of the fourth year.
4. Assume that January sales for the fourth year turned out to be $295,000. What was your forecast error? If this is a large error, Karen may be puzzled as to why there is such a difference between your forecast and the actual sales value. What can you do to resolve her uncertainty in the forecasting procedure?
5. Develop recommendations as to when the system that you have developed should be updated to account for new sales data that will occur.
6. Include any detailed calculations of your analysis in the appendix of your report.

Case Problem: Forecasting Lost Sales

The Carlson Department Store suffered heavy damage when a hurricane struck on August 31, 1992. The store was closed for 4 months (September 1992 through December 1992), and Carlson is now involved in a dispute with its insurance company about the amount of lost sales during the time the store was closed. Two key issues must be resolved: (1) the amount of sales Carlson would have made if the hurricane had not struck and (2) whether Carlson is entitled to any compensation for excess sales due to increased business activity after the storm. More than $8 billion in federal disaster relief and insurance money came into the county, resulting in increased sales at department stores and numerous other businesses.

Table 16.15 gives Carlson's sales data for the 48 months preceding the storm. Table 16.16 reports the U.S. Department of Commerce data on total sales for the 48 months preceding the storm for all department stores in the county, as well as the total sales in the county for the 4 months the Carlson Department Store was closed. Carlson's managers have asked you to analyze these data and develop estimates of the lost sales at the Carlson Department Store for the months of September through December 1992. They also have asked you to determine whether a case can be made for excess storm-related sales during the same period. If such a case can be made, Carlson is entitled to compensation for excess sales it would have earned in addition to ordinary sales.

Table 16.15

Sales for Carlson Department Store, September 1988 Through August 1992 (Millions of Dollars)

Month	1988	1989	1990	1991	1992
January		1.45	2.31	2.31	2.56
February		1.80	1.89	1.99	2.28
March		2.03	2.02	2.42	2.69
April		1.99	2.23	2.45	2.48
May		2.32	2.39	2.57	2.73
June		2.20	2.14	2.42	2.37
July		2.13	2.27	2.40	2.31
August		2.43	2.21	2.50	2.23
September	1.71	1.90	1.89	2.09	
October	1.90	2.13	2.29	2.54	
November	2.74	2.56	2.83	2.97	
December	4.20	4.16	4.04	4.35	

Table 16.16

....

Department Store Sales for the County, September 1988 Through December 1992 (Millions of Dollars)

Month	1988	1989	1990	1991	1992
January		46.8	46.8	43.8	48.0
February		48.0	48.6	45.6	51.6
March		60.0	59.4	57.6	57.6
April		57.6	58.2	53.4	58.2
May		61.8	60.6	56.4	60.0
June		58.2	55.2	52.8	57.0
July		56.4	51.0	54.0	57.6
August		63.0	58.8	60.6	61.8
September	55.8	57.6	49.8	47.4	69.0
October	56.4	53.4	54.6	54.6	75.0
November	71.4	71.4	65.4	67.8	85.2
December	117.6	114.0	102.0	100.2	121.8

Managerial Report

....

Prepare a report for the managers of the Carlson Department Store that summarizes your findings, forecasts, and recommendations. Include the following information:

1. An estimate of sales had there been no hurricane.
2. An estimate of countywide department store sales had there been no hurricane.
3. An estimate of lost sales for the Carlson Department Store for September through December 1992.

In addition, use the countywide actual department stores sales for September through December 1992 and the estimate in part (2) to make a case for or against excess storm-related sales.

APPENDIX 16.1   Forecasting with Spreadsheets

....

In this Appendix we show how Excel can be used to develop forecasts using three forecasting methods: moving averages, exponential smoothing, and trend projection.

Moving Averages

....

To show how Excel can be used to develop forecasts using the moving averages method, we will develop a forecast for the gasoline sales time series in Table 16.1 and Figure 16.5. We assume that the user has entered the sales data for the 12 weeks into worksheet rows 1 through 12 of column A. The following steps can be used to produce a 3-week moving average.

Step 1   Select the **Tools** pull-down menu

Step 2   Select the **Data Analysis** option

Step 3   When the Analysis Tools dialog box appears, choose **Moving Average**

Step 4   When the Moving Average dialog box appears:
Enter A1:A12 in the **Input Range** box
Enter 3 in the **Interval** box
Enter B1 in the **Output Range** box
Select **OK**

The 3-week moving average forecasts will appear in column B of the worksheet. Note that forecasts for periods of other length can be computed easily by entering a different value in the Interval box.

Exponential Smoothing
....

To show how Excel can be used for exponential smoothing, we again develop a forecast for the gasoline sales time series in Table 16.1 and Figure 16.5. We assume that the user has entered the sales data for the 12 weeks into worksheet rows 1 through 12 of column A and that the smoothing constant is $\alpha = .2$. The following steps can be used to produce a forecast.

Step 1   Select the **Tools** pull-down menu

Step 2   Select the **Data Analysis** option

Step 3   When the Analysis Tools dialog box appears, choose **Exponential Smoothing**

Step 4   When the Exponential Smoothing dialog box appears:
Enter A1:A12 in the **Input Range** box
Enter .8 in the **Damping factor** box
Enter B1 in the **Output Range** box
Select **OK**

The exponential smoothing forecasts will appear in column B of the worksheet. Note that the value we entered in the Damping factor box is $1 - \alpha$; forecasts for other smoothing constants can be computed easily by entering a different value for $1 - \alpha$ in the Damping factor box.

Trend Projection
....

To show how Excel can be used for trend projection, we develop a forecast for the bicycle sales time series in Table 16.8 and Figure 16.8. We assume that the user has entered the year $(1-10)$ for each observation into worksheet rows 1 through 10 of column A and the sales values into worksheet rows 1 through 10 of column B. The following steps can be used to produce a forecast for year 11 by trend projection.

Step 1   Select an empty cell in the worksheet

Step 2   Select the **Insert** pull-down menu

Step 3   Choose the **Function** option

Step 4   When the Function Wizard—Step 1 of 2 dialog box appears:
Choose **Statistical** in the Function Category box
Choose **Forecast** in the Function Name box
Select **Next**

Step 5   When the Function Wizard—Step 2 of 2 dialog box appears:
Enter 11 in the x box
Enter B1:B10 in the **Known y's** box
Enter A1:A10 in the **Known x's** box
Select **Finish**

The forecast for year 11, in this case 32.5, will appear in the cell selected in Step 1.

The Cincinnati Gas & Electric Company*
Cincinnati, Ohio

The Cincinnati Gas Light and Coke Company was chartered by the state of Ohio on April 3, 1837. Under this charter, the company manufactured gas by distillation of coal and sold it for lighting purposes. During the last quarter of the 19th century, the company successfully marketed gas for lighting, heating, and cooking and as fuel for gas engines.

In 1901 the Cincinnati Gas Light and Coke Company and the Cincinnati Electric Light Company merged to form The Cincinnati Gas & Electric Company (CG&E). This new company was able to shift from manufactured gas to natural gas and adopt the rapidly emerging technologies in generating and distributing electricity. CG&E operated as a subsidiary of the Columbia Gas Electric Company from 1909 until 1944.

Today CG&E is a privately owned public utility serving approximately 420,000 gas customers and 700,000 electric customers. The company's service area covers approximately 3000 square miles in and around the Greater Cincinnati area.

Forecasting at CG&E

As in any modern company, forecasting at CG&E is an integral part of operating and managing the business. Depending on the decision to be made, the forecasting techniques used range from judgment and graphical trend projections to sophisticated multiple regression models.

Forecasting in the utility industry offers some unique perspectives. Since there are no finished-goods or in-process inventories of electricity, this product must be generated to meet the instantaneous requirements of the customers. Electrical shortages are not just lost sales, but "brownouts" or "blackouts." This situation places an unusual burden on the utility forecaster. On the positive side, the demand for energy and the sale of energy are more predictable than for many other products. Also, unlike the situation in a multiproduct firm, a great amount of forecasting effort and expertise can be concentrated on the two products: gas and electricity.

Forecasting Electric Energy and Peak Loads

The two types of forecasts discussed in this section are the long-range forecasts of electric peak load and electric energy. The largest observed electric demand for any given period, such as an hour, a day, a month, or a year, is defined as the peak load. The cumulative amount of energy generated and used over the period of an hour is referred to as electric energy.

Until the mid-1970s the seasonal patterns of both electric energy and electric peak load were very regular; the time series for both of these exhibited a fairly steady exponential growth. Business cycles had little noticeable effect on either. Perhaps the most serious shift in the behavior of these time series came from the increasing installation of air conditioning units in the Greater Cincinnati area, which caused an accelerated growth in the trend component and also in the relative magnitude of the summer peaks. Nevertheless, the two time series were regular and generally quite predictable.

Trend projection was the most popular method used to forecast electric energy and electric peak load. The forecast accuracy was acceptable and even enviable when compared to forecast errors experienced in other industries.

A New Era in Forecasting

In the mid-1970s a variety of actions by the government, the off-and-on energy shortages, and price signals to the consumer began to affect the consumption of electric energy. The behavior of the peak load and electric energy time series became less predictable, and a simple trend projection forecasting model was no longer adequate. As a result, a special forecasting model—referred to as an econometric model—was developed by CG&E to better account for the behavior of these time series.

The purpose of the econometric model is to forecast the annual energy consumption by residential, commercial, and industrial classes of service. These forecasts are then used to develop forecasts of summer and winter peak loads. First, energy consumption in the industrial and commercial classes is forecast. For an assumed level of economic activity, the projection of electric energy is made along with a forecast of employment in the area. The employment forecast is converted to a forecast of adult population through the use of unemployment rates and labor force participation rates. Household forecasts are then developed through the use of demographic statistics on the average number of persons per household. The resulting forecast of households is used as an indicator of residential customers.

—Continued on next page

—*Continued from previous page*

At this point, a comparison is made with the demographic projections for the area population. The differences between the residential customers forecast and the population forecast are reconciled to produce the final forecast of residential customers. This forecast becomes the principal independent variable in forecasting residential electric energy.

Summer and winter peak loads are then forecast by applying class peak contribution factors to the energy forecasts. The contributions that each class makes toward the peak are summed to establish the peak forecast.

A number of economic and demographic time series are used in the construction of the econometric model. Simply speaking, the entire forecasting system is a compilation of several statistically verified multiple regression equations.

Impact and Value of the Forecasts

The forecast of the annual electric peak load guides the timing decisions for constructing future generating units, and the financial impact of these decisions is great. For example, a large generating unit built by the company cost nearly $600 million, and the interest rate on a recent first mortgage bond was 16%. At this rate, annual interest costs would be nearly $100 million. Obviously, a timing decision that leads to having the unit available no sooner than necessary is crucial.

The energy forecasts are important in other ways also. For example, purchases of coal as fuel for the generating units are based on the forecast levels of energy needed. The revenue from the electric operations of the company is determined from forecasted sales, which in turn enters into the planning of rate changes and external financing. These planning and decision-making processes are among the most important management activities in the company. It is imperative that the decision makers have the best forecast information available to assist them in arriving at these decisions.

Questions

1. Describe some of the unique perspectives associated with forecasting in the utility industry as compared with other industries.
2. What type of forecasting procedure was used by CG&E into the mid-1970s? What necessitated a change?
3. Briefly describe CG&E's current approach to forecasting.
4. What are the benefits of accurate forecasts for CG&E?

....

The authors are indebted to Dr. Richard Evans, The Cincinnati Gas & Electric Company, Cincinnati, Ohio, for providing this application.

seventeen

Markov Processes

Markov process models are useful in studying the evolution of systems over repeated trials. The repeated trials are often successive time periods where the state of the system in any particular period cannot be determined with certainty. Rather, transition probabilities are used to describe the manner in which the system makes transitions from one period to the next. Hence, we are interested in the probability of the system being in a particular state at a given time period.

Markov process models have been used to describe the probability that a machine that is functioning in one period will continue to function or will break down in the next period. They have also been used to describe the probability that a consumer purchasing brand A in one period will purchase brand B in the next period. In this chapter we present a marketing application that involves an analysis of the store-switching behavior of supermarket customers. As a second illustration, we will consider an accounting application that is concerned with the transitioning of accounts receivable dollars to different account-aging categories.

Since an in-depth treatment of Markov processes is beyond the scope of this text, the analysis in both illustrations will be restricted to situations in which there are a finite number of states, the transition probabilities remain constant over time, and the probability of being in a particular state at any one time period depends only on the state in the immediately preceding time period. Such Markov processes are referred to as Markov chains with stationary transition probabilities.

17.1 Market Share Analysis

Suppose that we are interested in analyzing the market share and customer loyalty for Murphy's Foodliner and Ashley's Supermarket, the only two grocery stores in a small town. We focus on the sequence of shopping trips of one customer, and assume that the customer makes one shopping trip each week to either Murphy's Foodliner or Ashley's Supermarket, but not both.

Using the terminology of Markov processes, we refer to the weekly periods or shopping trips as the *trials of the process*. Thus, at each trial, the customer will shop at either Murphy's Foodliner or Ashley's Supermarket. The particular store selected in a given week is referred to as the *state of the system* in that period. Since the customer has two shopping alternatives at each trial, we say the system has two states, and since the number of states is finite, we can identify each state as follows:

State 1   The customer shops at Murphy's Foodliner
State 2   The customer shops at Ashley's Supermarket

If we say the system is in state 1 at trial 3, we are simply saying that the customer shops at Murphy's during the third weekly shopping period.

As we continue the shopping trip process into the future, we cannot say for certain where the customer will shop during a given week or trial. In fact, we realize that during any given week, the customer may be either a Murphy's customer or an Ashley's customer. However, using a Markov process model, we will be able to compute the probability that the customer shops at each store during any period. For example, we may find there is a 0.6 probability that the customer will shop at Murphy's during a particular week and a 0.4 probability that the customer will shop at Ashley's.

To determine the probabilities of the various states occurring at successive trials of the Markov process, we need information on the probability that a customer remains with the same store or switches to the competing store as the process continues from trial to trial or week to week.

Suppose as part of a market research study we collect data from 100 shoppers over a 10-week period. Suppose further that these data show each customer's weekly shopping trip pattern in terms of the sequence of visits to Murphy's and Ashley's. To develop a Markov process model for the sequence of weekly shopping trips, we need to express the probability of selecting each store (state) in a given period solely in terms of the store (state) that was selected during the previous period. In reviewing the data, suppose we find that of all customers who shopped at Murphy's in a given week, 90% shopped at Murphy's the following week while 10% switched to Ashley's. Suppose that similar data for the customers who shopped at Ashley's in a given week show that 80% shopped at Ashley's the following week while 20% switched to Murphy's. Probabilities based on these data are shown in Table 17.1. Since these are the probabilities that a customer moves, or makes a transition, from a state in a given period to each state in the following period, these probabilities are called *transition probabilities*.

An important property of the table of transition probabilities is that the sum of the entries in each row is 1; this indicates that each row of the table provides a probability distribution. For example, a customer who shops at Murphy's one week must shop at either Murphy's or Ashley's the next week. The entries in row 1 give the probabilities associated with each of these events. The 0.9 and 0.8 probabilities in Table 17.1 can be interpreted as measures of store loyalty in that they indicate the probability of a repeat

Table 17.1

Transition Probabilities for Murphy's and Ashley's Grocery Stores

Current Weekly Shopping Period	Next Weekly Shopping Period	
	Murphy's Foodliner	Ashley's Supermarket
Murphy's Foodliner	0.9	0.1
Ashley's Supermarket	0.2	0.8

visit to the same store. Similarly, the 0.1 and 0.2 probabilities are measures of the store-switching characteristics of the customers.

It is important to realize that in developing a Markov process model for this problem, we are assuming that the transition probabilities will be the same for any customer and that the transition probabilities will not change over time.

Note that Table 17.1 has one row and one column for each state of the system. We will use the symbol p_{ij} to represent the transition probabilities and the symbol P to represent the matrix of transition probabilities; that is,

$$p_{ij} = \text{probability of making a transition from state } i \text{ in a given}$$
$$\text{period to state } j \text{ in the next period}$$

For the supermarket problem, we have

$$P = \begin{bmatrix} p_{11} & p_{12} \\ p_{21} & p_{22} \end{bmatrix} = \begin{bmatrix} 0.9 & 0.1 \\ 0.2 & 0.8 \end{bmatrix}$$

Using the matrix of transition probabilities, we can now determine the probability that a customer will be a Murphy's customer or an Ashley's customer at some period in the future. Let us begin by assuming that we have a customer whose last weekly shopping trip was to Murphy's. What is the probability that this customer will shop at Murphy's on the next weekly shopping trip, period 1? In other words, what is the probability that the system will be in state 1 after the first transition? The matrix of transition probabilities indicates that this probability is $p_{11} = 0.9$.

Now let us consider the state of the system in period 2. A useful way of depicting what can happen on the second weekly shopping trip is to draw a tree diagram of the possible outcomes (see Figure 17.1). Using this tree diagram, we see that the probability that the customer shops at Murphy's during both the first and the second weeks is $(0.9)(0.9) = 0.81$. Also, note that the probability of the customer switching to Ashley's on the first trip and then switching back to Murphy's on the second trip is $(0.1)(0.2) = 0.02$. Since these are the only two ways that the customer can be in state 1 (shopping at Murphy's) during the second period, the probability of the system being in state 1 during the second period is $0.81 + 0.02 = 0.83$. Similarly, the probability of the system being in state 2 during the second period is $0.09 + 0.08 = 0.17$.

As desirable as the tree diagram approach may be from an intuitive point of view, this approach becomes cumbersome when we want to extend the analysis to three or more periods. Fortunately, there is an easier way to calculate the probabilities of the system being in state 1 or state 2 for any subsequent period. First, we introduce notation that will allow us to represent these probabilities for any given period. Let

$$\pi_i(n) = \text{probability that the system is in state } i \text{ in period } n$$

Index denotes the state ↗ ↖ Denotes the time period or number of transitions

For example, $\pi_1(1)$ denotes the probability of the system being in state 1 in period 1, while $\pi_2(1)$ denotes the probability of the system being in state 2 in period 1. Since $\pi_i(n)$ is the probability that the system is in state i in period n, this probability is referred to as a *state probability*.

The terms $\pi_1(0)$ and $\pi_2(0)$ will denote the probability of the system being in state 1 or state 2 at some initial or starting period. Week 0 represents the most recent period, when we are beginning the analysis of a Markov process. If we set $\pi_1(0) = 1$ and $\pi_2(0) = 0$, we are saying that as an initial condition the customer shopped last week at Murphy's; alternatively, if we set $\pi_1(0) = 0$ and $\pi_2(0) = 1$, we would be starting the

Figure 17.1

Tree Diagram Depicting Two Weekly Shopping Trips of a Customer Who Shopped Last at Murphy's

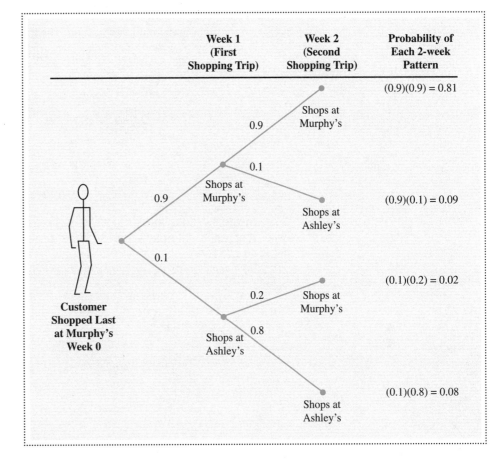

system with a customer who shopped last week at Ashley's. In the tree diagram of Figure 17.1, we consider the situation where the customer shopped last at Murphy's. Thus,

$$[\pi_1(0) \quad \pi_2(0)] = [1 \quad 0]$$

is a vector that represents the initial state probabilities of the system. In general, we use the notation

$$\Pi(n) = [\pi_1(n) \quad \pi_2(n)]$$

to denote the vector of state probabilities for the system in period n. In the example, $\Pi(1)$ is a vector representing the state probabilities for the first week, $\Pi(2)$ is a vector representing the state probabilities for the second week, and so on.

Using this notation, we can find the state probabilities for period $n + 1$ by simply multiplying the known state probabilities for period n by the transition probability matrix. Using the vector of state probabilities and the matrix of transition probabilities, the multiplication[1] can be expressed as follows:

$$\Pi(\text{next period}) = \Pi(\text{current period})P$$

or

$$\Pi(n + 1) = \Pi(n)P \tag{17.1}$$

---

[1] Appendix E provides the step-by-step procedure for vector and matrix multiplication.

Beginning with the system in state 1 at period 0, we have $\Pi(0) = [1\ 0]$. We can compute the state probabilities for period 1 as follows:

$$\Pi(1) = \Pi(0)P$$

or

$$[\pi_1(1)\quad \pi_2(1)] = [\pi_1(0)\quad \pi_2(0)]\begin{bmatrix} p_{11} & p_{12} \\ p_{21} & p_{22} \end{bmatrix}$$

$$= [1\quad 0]\begin{bmatrix} 0.9 & 0.1 \\ 0.2 & 0.8 \end{bmatrix}$$

$$= [0.9\quad 0.1]$$

The state probabilities $\pi_1(1) = 0.9$ and $\pi_2(1) = 0.1$ are the probabilities that a customer who shopped at Murphy's during week 0 will shop at Murphy's or at Ashley's during week 1.

Using equation (17.1), we can compute the state probabilities for the second week as follows:

$$\Pi(2) = \Pi(1)P$$

or

$$[\pi_1(2)\quad \pi_2(2)] = [\pi_1(1)\quad \pi_2(1)]\begin{bmatrix} p_{11} & p_{12} \\ p_{21} & p_{22} \end{bmatrix}$$

$$= [0.9\quad 0.1]\begin{bmatrix} 0.9 & 0.1 \\ 0.2 & 0.8 \end{bmatrix}$$

$$= [0.83\quad 0.17]$$

We see that the probability of shopping at Murphy's during the second week is 0.83, while the probability of shopping at Ashley's during the second week is 0.17. These same results were previously obtained using the tree diagram of Figure 17.1. By continuing to apply equation (17.1), we can compute the state probabilities for any future period; that is,

$$\Pi(3) = \Pi(2)P$$
$$\Pi(4) = \Pi(3)P$$
$$\vdots \qquad \vdots$$
$$\Pi(n + 1) = \Pi(n)P$$

Table 17.2 shows the result of carrying out these calculations for ten periods.

The vectors $\Pi(1), \Pi(2), \Pi(3), \ldots$ contain the probabilities that a customer who started out as a Murphy customer will be in state 1 or state 2 in the first period, the second period,

Table 17.2

State Probabilities for Future Periods Beginning Initially with a Murphy's Customer

| State Probability | \multicolumn{11}{c}{Period (n)} |
	0	1	2	3	4	5	6	7	8	9	10
$\pi_1(n)$	1	0.9	0.83	0.781	0.747	0.723	0.706	0.694	0.686	0.680	0.676
$\pi_2(n)$	0	0.1	0.17	0.219	0.253	0.277	0.294	0.306	0.314	0.320	0.324

the third period, and so on. In Table 17.2 we see that after a few periods these probabilities do not change much from one period to the next.

If we had started with 1000 Murphy customers—that is, 1000 consumers who last shopped at Murphy's—our analysis indicates that during the fifth weekly shopping period, 723 would be customers of Murphy's and 277 would be customers of Ashley's. Moreover, during the tenth weekly shopping period, 676 would be customers of Murphy's and 324 customers of Ashley's.

Now let us repeat the analysis, but this time we will begin the process with a customer who shopped last at Ashley's. Thus,

$$\Pi(0) = [\pi_1(0) \quad \pi_2(0)] = [0 \quad 1]$$

Using equation (17.1), the probability of the system being in state 1 or state 2 in period 1 is given by

$$\Pi(1) = \Pi(0)P$$

or

$$[\pi_1(1) \quad \pi_2(1)] = [\pi_1(0) \quad \pi_2(0)] \begin{bmatrix} p_{11} & p_{12} \\ p_{12} & p_{22} \end{bmatrix}$$

$$= [0 \quad 1] \begin{bmatrix} 0.9 & 0.1 \\ 0.2 & 0.8 \end{bmatrix}$$

$$= [0.2 \quad 0.8]$$

Proceeding as before, we can calculate subsequent state probabilities. Doing so, we obtain the results shown in Table 17.3.

In the fifth shopping period, the probability that the customer will be shopping at Murphy's is 0.555, and the probability that the customer will be shopping at Ashley's is 0.445. In the tenth period, the probability that a customer will be shopping at Murphy's is 0.648, and the probability that a customer will be shopping at Ashley's is 0.352.

As we continue the Markov process, we will find that the probability of the system being in a particular state after a large number of periods is independent of the beginning state of the system. The probabilities that we approach after a large number of transitions are referred to as the *steady-state probabilities*. We shall denote the steady-state probability for state 1 with the symbol π_1 and the steady-state probability for state 2 with the symbol π_2. In other words, in the steady-state case, we simply omit the period designation from $\pi_i(n)$ since it is no longer necessary.

The analysis of Tables 17.2 and 17.3 indicates that as n gets larger, the difference between the state probabilities for the nth period and the $(n + 1)$th period becomes increasingly smaller. This leads us to the conclusion that as n gets large, the state probabilities at the $(n + 1)$th period are very close to those at the nth period. This observation provides the basis for a simple method for computing the steady-state probabilities without having to actually carry out a large number of calculations.

Table 17.3

State Probabilities for Future Periods Beginning Initially with an Ashley's Customer

State Probability	Period (n)										
	0	1	2	3	4	5	6	7	8	9	10
$\pi_1(n)$	0	0.2	0.34	0.438	0.507	0.555	0.589	0.612	0.628	0.640	0.648
$\pi_2(n)$	1	0.8	0.66	0.562	0.493	0.445	0.411	0.388	0.372	0.360	0.352

In general, we know from equation (17.1) that

$$[\pi_1(n+1) \quad \pi_2(n+1)] = [\pi_1(n) \quad \pi_2(n)] \begin{bmatrix} p_{11} & p_{12} \\ p_{21} & p_{22} \end{bmatrix}$$

Since for sufficiently large n the difference between $\Pi(n+1)$ and $\Pi(n)$ is negligible, we see that in the steady state $\pi_1(n+1) = \pi_1(n) = \pi_1$, and $\pi_2(n+1) = \pi_2(n) = \pi_2$. Thus, we have

$$[\pi_1 \quad \pi_2] = [\pi_1 \quad \pi_2] \begin{bmatrix} p_{11} & p_{12} \\ p_{21} & p_{22} \end{bmatrix}$$

$$= [\pi_1 \quad \pi_2] \begin{bmatrix} 0.9 & 0.1 \\ 0.2 & 0.8 \end{bmatrix}$$

After carrying out the multiplications, we obtain

$$\pi_1 = 0.9\pi_1 + 0.2\pi_2 \tag{17.2}$$

and

$$\pi_2 = 0.1\pi_1 + 0.8\pi_2 \tag{17.3}$$

However, we also know the steady-state probabilities must sum to 1 with

$$\pi_1 + \pi_2 = 1 \tag{17.4}$$

Using equation (17.4) to solve for π_2 and substituting the result in equation (17.2), we obtain

$$\pi_1 = 0.9\pi_1 + 0.2(1 - \pi_1)$$

$$\pi_1 = 0.9\pi_1 + 0.2 - 0.2\pi_1$$

$$\pi_1 - 0.7\pi_1 = 0.2$$

$$0.3\pi_1 = 0.2$$

$$\pi_1 = \tfrac{2}{3}$$

Then, using equation (17.4), we can conclude that $\pi_2 = 1 - \pi_1 = \tfrac{1}{3}$. Thus, using equations (17.2) and (17.4), we can solve for the steady-state probabilities directly. You can check for yourself that we could have obtained the same result using equations (17.3) and (17.4).[2]

Thus, if we have 1000 customers in the system, the Markov process model tells us that in the long run, with steady-state probabilities $\pi_1 = \tfrac{2}{3}$ and $\pi_2 = \tfrac{1}{3}$, $\tfrac{2}{3}(1000) = 667$ customers will be Murphy's and $\tfrac{1}{3}(1000) = 333$ customers will be Ashley's. The steady-state probabilities can be interpreted as the market shares for the two stores.

Market share information is often quite valuable in decision making. For example, suppose Ashley's Supermarket is contemplating an advertising campaign to attract more of Murphy's customers to its store. Let us suppose further that Ashley's believes this promotional strategy will increase the probability of a Murphy's customer switching to Ashley's from 0.10 to 0.15. The revised transition probabilities are given in Table 17.4.

---

[2] Even though equations (17.2) and (17.3) provide two equations and two unknowns, we must include equation (17.4) when solving for π_1 and π_2 to ensure that the sum of steady-state probabilities will equal 1.

Table 17.4	Current Weekly Shopping Period	Next Weekly Shopping Period	
		Murphy's Foodliner	Ashley's Supermarket
Revised Transition Probabilities for Murphy's and Ashley's Grocery Stores	Murphy's Foodliner	0.85	0.15
	'Ashley's Supermarket	0.20	0.80

Given the new transition probabilities, we can modify equations (17.2) and (17.4) to solve for the new steady-state probabilities or market shares. Thus, we obtain

$$\pi_1 = 0.85\pi_1 + 0.20\pi_2$$

Substituting $\pi_2 = 1 - \pi_1$ from equation (17.4), we have

$$\pi_1 = 0.85\pi_1 + 0.20(1 - \pi_1)$$

$$\pi_1 = 0.85\pi_1 + 0.20 - 0.20\pi_1$$

$$\pi_1 - 0.65\pi_1 = 0.20$$

$$0.35\pi_1 = 0.20$$

$$\pi_1 = 0.57$$

and

$$\pi_2 = 1 - 0.57 = 0.43$$

You should now be able to compute the steady-state probabilities for Markov processes with two states. Problem 3 provides an application.

We see that the proposed promotional strategy will increase Ashley's market share from $\pi_2 = 0.33$ to $\pi_2 = 0.43$. Suppose that the total market consists of 6000 customers per week. The new promotional strategy will increase the number of customers doing their weekly shopping at Ashley's from 2000 to 2580. If the average weekly profit per customer is $10, the proposed promotional strategy can be expected to increase Ashley's profits by $5800 per week. If the cost of the promotional campaign is less than $5800 per week, Ashley should consider implementing the strategy.

With three states, the steady-state probabilities are found by solving three equations for the three unknown steady-state probabilities. Try Problem 7 as a slightly more difficult problem involving three states.

This is one illustration of how a Markov analysis of a firm's market share can be useful in decision making. Suppose that instead of trying to attract customers from Murphy's Foodliner, Ashley's directed a promotional effort at increasing the loyalty of its own customers. In this case, p_{22} would increase, and p_{21} would decrease. Once we knew the amount of the change, we could calculate new steady-state probabilities and compute the impact on profits.

NOTES & comments

1. The Markov processes presented in this section have what is called the *memoryless* property: the current state of the system together with the transition probabilities contains all the information necessary to predict the future behavior of the system. The prior states of the system do not have to be considered. Such Markov processes are considered first-order Markov processes. Higher-order Markov processes are ones in which future states of the system depend on two or more previous states.

—Continued on next page

—*Continued from previous page*

2. Analysis of a Markov process model is not intended to optimize any particular aspect of a system. Rather, the analysis predicts or describes the future and steady-state behavior of the system. For instance, in the grocery store example, the analysis of the steady-state behavior provided a forecast or prediction of the market shares for the two competitors. In other applications, management scientists have extended the study of Markov processes to what are called *Markov decision processes*. In these models, decisions can be made at each period that affect the transition probabilities and hence influence the future behavior of the system. Markov decision processes have been used in analyzing machine breakdown and maintenance operations, planning the movement of patients in hospitals, developing inspection strategies, determining newspaper subscription duration, and analyzing equipment replacement.

17.2 Accounts Receivable Analysis

An accounting application in which Markov processes have produced useful results involves the estimation of the allowance for doubtful accounts receivable. This allowance is an estimate of the amount of accounts receivable that will ultimately prove to be uncollectible (i.e., bad debts).

Let us consider the accounts receivable situation for Heidman's Department Store. Heidman's has two aging categories for its accounts receivable: (1) accounts that are classified as 0–30 days old and (2) accounts that are classified as 31–90 days old. If any portion of an account balance exceeds 90 days, that portion is written off as a bad debt. Heidman's follows the procedure of aging the total balance in any customer's account according to the oldest unpaid bill. For example, suppose one customer's account balance on September 30 is as follows:

Date of Purchase	Amount Charged
August 15	$25
September 18	10
September 28	50
Total	$85

An aging of accounts receivable on September 30 would assign the total balance of $85 to the 31–90-day category because the oldest unpaid bill of August 15 is 46 days old. Let us assume that one week later, October 7, the customer pays the August 15 bill of $25. The remaining total balance of $60 would now be placed in the 0–30-day category since the oldest unpaid amount, corresponding to the September 18 purchase, is less than 31 days old. This method of aging accounts receivable is called the *total balance method* since the total account balance is placed in the age category corresponding to the oldest unpaid amount.

Note that under the total balance method of aging accounts receivable, dollars appearing in a 31–90-day category at one point in time may appear in a 0–30-day category at a later point in time. In the preceding example, this was true for $60 of September billings, which shifted from a 31–90-day to a 0–30-day category after the August bill had been paid.

Let us assume that on December 31 Heidman's shows a total of $3000 in its accounts receivable and that the firm's management would like an estimate of how much of the $3000 will eventually be collected and how much will eventually result in bad debts. The estimated amount of bad debts will appear as an allowance for doubtful accounts in the year-ending financial statements.

Let us see how we can view the accounts receivable operation as a Markov process. First, concentrate on what happens to *one* dollar currently in accounts receivable. As the firm continues to operate into the future, we can consider each week as a trial of a Markov process with a dollar existing in one of the following states of the system:

State 1   Paid category

State 2   Bad debt category

State 3   0–30-day category

State 4   31–90-day category

Thus, we can track the week-by-week status of one dollar by using a Markov analysis to identify the state of the system at a particular week or period.

Using a Markov process model with the above states, we define the transition probabilities as follows:

p_{ij} = probability of a dollar in state i in one week moving to state j in the next week

Based on historical transitions of accounts receivable dollars, the following matrix of transition probabilities, P, has been developed for Heidman's Department Store:

$$P = \begin{bmatrix} p_{11} & p_{12} & p_{13} & p_{14} \\ p_{21} & p_{22} & p_{23} & p_{24} \\ p_{31} & p_{32} & p_{33} & p_{34} \\ p_{41} & p_{42} & p_{43} & p_{44} \end{bmatrix} = \begin{bmatrix} 1.0 & 0.0 & 0.0 & 0.0 \\ 0.0 & 1.0 & 0.0 & 0.0 \\ 0.4 & 0.0 & 0.3 & 0.3 \\ 0.4 & 0.2 & 0.3 & 0.1 \end{bmatrix}$$

Note that the probability of a dollar in the 0–30-day category (state 3) moving to the paid category (state 1) in the next period is 0.4. Also, there is a 0.3 probability that this dollar will remain in the 0–30-day category (state 3) one week later, while there is a 0.3 probability that it will be in the 31–90-day category (state 4) one week later. Note also that a dollar in a 0–30-day account cannot make the transition to a bad debt (state 2) in one week.

An important property of the Markov process model for Heidman's accounts receivable situation is the presence of *absorbing states*. For example, once a dollar makes a transition to state 1, the paid state, the probability of making a transition to any other state is zero. Similarly, once a dollar is in state 2, the bad debt state, the probability of a transition to any other state is zero. Thus, once a dollar reaches state 1 or state 2, the system will remain in this state indefinitely. This leads us to conclude that all accounts receivable dollars will eventually be absorbed into either the paid or the bad debt state, and hence the name *absorbing state*.

The Fundamental Matrix and Associated Calculations

Whenever a Markov process has absorbing states, we do not compute steady-state probabilities because each unit ultimately ends up in one of the absorbing states. With absorbing states present, we are interested in knowing the probability that a unit will end up in each of the absorbing states. For the Heidman's Department Store problem, we want to know the probability that a dollar currently in the 0–30-day age category will end up paid (absorbing state 1) as well as the probability that a dollar in this age category will end up a bad debt (absorbing state 2). We also want to know these absorbing-state probabilities for dollars currently in the 31–90-day age category.

The computation of the absorbing-state probabilities requires the determination and use of what is called a *fundamental matrix*. The mathematical logic underlying the fundamental matrix is beyond the scope of this text. However, as we will see, the fundamental matrix is derived from the matrix of transition probabilities and is relatively easy to compute for Markov processes with a small number of states. In the following example, we show the computation of the fundamental matrix and the determination of the absorbing-state probabilities for Heidman's Department Store.

We begin the computations by partitioning the matrix of transition probabilities into the following four parts:

$$
P = \begin{bmatrix} 1.0 & 0.0 & | & 0.0 & 0.0 \\ 0.0 & 1.0 & | & 0.0 & 0.0 \\ \text{---} & \text{---} & | & \text{---} & \text{---} \\ 0.4 & 0.0 & | & 0.3 & 0.3 \\ 0.4 & 0.2 & | & 0.3 & 0.1 \end{bmatrix} = \begin{bmatrix} 1.0 & 0.0 & | & 0.0 & 0.0 \\ 0.0 & 1.0 & | & 0.0 & 0.0 \\ \text{---} & \text{---} & | & \text{---} & \text{---} \\ & R & | & & Q \end{bmatrix}
$$

where

$$
R = \begin{bmatrix} 0.4 & 0.0 \\ 0.4 & 0.2 \end{bmatrix} \qquad Q = \begin{bmatrix} 0.3 & 0.3 \\ 0.3 & 0.1 \end{bmatrix}
$$

A matrix N, called a *fundamental matrix*, can be calculated using the following formula:

$$
N = (I - Q)^{-1} \tag{17.5}
$$

where I is an identity matrix with 1's on the main diagonal and 0's elsewhere. The superscript -1 is used to indicate the inverse of the matrix $(I - Q)$. In Appendix E we present formulas for finding the inverse of a matrix with two rows and two columns.

Before proceeding, we note that to use equation (17.5), the identity matrix I must be chosen such that it has the *same size or dimensionality* as the matrix Q. In our example problem, Q has two rows and two columns, so we must choose

$$
I = \begin{bmatrix} 1.0 & 0.0 \\ 0.0 & 1.0 \end{bmatrix}
$$

Let us now continue with the example problem by computing the fundamental matrix.

$$
I - Q = \begin{bmatrix} 1.0 & 0.0 \\ 0.0 & 1.0 \end{bmatrix} - \begin{bmatrix} 0.3 & 0.3 \\ 0.3 & 0.1 \end{bmatrix}
$$

$$
= \begin{bmatrix} 0.7 & -0.3 \\ -0.3 & 0.9 \end{bmatrix}
$$

and (see Appendix E)

$$
N = (I - Q)^{-1} = \begin{bmatrix} 1.67 & 0.56 \\ 0.56 & 1.30 \end{bmatrix}
$$

If we multiply the fundamental matrix N times the R portion of the P matrix, we obtain the probabilities that accounts receivable dollars initially in states 3 or 4 will eventually reach each of the absorbing states. The multiplication of N times R for the Heidman's

Department Store problem provides the following results (again, see Appendix E for the steps of this matrix multiplication):

$$NR = \begin{bmatrix} 1.67 & 0.56 \\ 0.56 & 1.30 \end{bmatrix} \begin{bmatrix} 0.4 & 0.0 \\ 0.4 & 0.2 \end{bmatrix} = \begin{bmatrix} 0.89 & 0.11 \\ 0.74 & 0.26 \end{bmatrix}$$

The first row of the product NR is the probability that a dollar in the $0-30$-day age category will end up in each of the absorbing states. Thus, we see that there is a 0.89 probability that a dollar in the $0-30$-day category will eventually be paid and a 0.11 probability that it will become a bad debt. Similarly, the second row shows the probabilities associated with a dollar in the $31-90$-day category; that is, a dollar in the $31-90$-day category has a 0.74 probability of eventually being paid and a 0.26 probability of proving to be uncollectible. Using this information, we can predict the amount of money that will be paid and the amount that will be lost as bad debts.

Establishing the Allowance for Doubtful Accounts

Let B represent a two-element vector that contains the current accounts receivable balances in the $0-30$-day and the $31-90$-day age categories; that is,

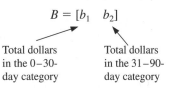

$$B = [b_1 \quad b_2]$$

Total dollars in the $0-30$-day category   Total dollars in the $31-90$-day category

Suppose that the December 31 balance of accounts receivable for Heidman's shows $1000 in the $0-30$-day category (state 3) and $2000 in the $31-90$-day category (state 4).

$$B = [1000 \quad 2000]$$

We can multiply B times NR to determine how much of the $3000 will be collected and how much will be lost. For example

$$BNR = [1000 \quad 2000] \begin{bmatrix} 0.89 & 0.11 \\ 0.74 & 0.26 \end{bmatrix}$$

$$= [2370 \quad 630]$$

Thus, we see that $2370 of the accounts receivable balances will be collected and $630 will be written off as a bad debt expense. Based on this analysis, the accounting department would set up an allowance for doubtful accounts of $630.

The matrix multiplication of BNR is simply a convenient way of computing the eventual collections and bad debts of the accounts receivable. Recall that the NR matrix showed a 0.89 probability of collecting dollars in the $0-30$-day category and a 0.74 probability of collecting dollars in the $31-90$-day category. Thus, as was shown by the BNR calculation, we expect to collect a total of $(1000)0.89 + (2000)0.74 = 890 + 1480 = \$2370$.

Suppose that on the basis of the previous analysis Heidman's would like to investigate the possibility of reducing the amount of bad debts. Recall that the analysis indicated that a 0.11 probability or 11% of the amount in the $0-30$-day age category and 26% of the amount in the $31-90$-day age category will prove to be uncollectible. Let us assume that Heidman's is considering instituting a new credit policy involving a discount for prompt payment.

Management believes that the policy under consideration will increase the probability of a transition from the 0–30-day age category to the paid category and decrease the probability of a transition from the 0–30-day to the 31–90-day age category. Let us assume that a careful study of the effects of this new policy leads management to conclude that the following transition matrix would be applicable:

$$P = \begin{bmatrix} 1.0 & 0.0 & | & 0.0 & 0.0 \\ 0.0 & 1.0 & | & 0.0 & 0.0 \\ -- & -- & -- & -- & -- \\ 0.6 & 0.0 & | & 0.3 & 0.1 \\ 0.4 & 0.2 & | & 0.3 & 0.1 \end{bmatrix}$$

We see that the probability of a dollar in the 0–30-day age category making a transition to the paid category in the next period has increased to 0.6 and that the probability of a dollar in the 0–30-day age category making a transition to the 31–90-day category has decreased to 0.1. To determine the effect of these changes on bad debt expense, we must calculate N, NR, and BNR. We begin by using equation (17.5) to calculate the fundamental matrix N:

$$N = (I - Q)^{-1} = \left\{ \begin{bmatrix} 1.0 & 0.0 \\ 0.0 & 1.0 \end{bmatrix} - \begin{bmatrix} 0.3 & 0.1 \\ 0.3 & 0.1 \end{bmatrix} \right\}^{-1}$$

$$= \begin{bmatrix} 0.7 & -0.1 \\ -0.3 & 0.9 \end{bmatrix}^{-1}$$

$$= \begin{bmatrix} 1.5 & 0.17 \\ 0.5 & 1.17 \end{bmatrix}$$

By multiplying N times R, we obtain the new probabilities that the dollars in each age category will end up in the two absorbing states:

$$NR = \begin{bmatrix} 1.5 & 0.17 \\ 0.5 & 1.17 \end{bmatrix} \begin{bmatrix} 0.6 & 0.0 \\ 0.4 & 0.2 \end{bmatrix}$$

$$= \begin{bmatrix} 0.97 & 0.03 \\ 0.77 & 0.23 \end{bmatrix}$$

We see that with the new credit policy we would expect only 3% of the funds in the 0–30-day age category and 23% of the funds in the 31–90-day age category to prove to be uncollectible. If, as before, we assume that there is a current balance of $1000 in the 0–30-day age category and $2000 in the 31–90-day age category, we can calculate the total amount of accounts receivable that will end up in the two absorbing states by multiplying B times NR. We obtain

$$BNR = \begin{bmatrix} 1000 & 2000 \end{bmatrix} \begin{bmatrix} 0.97 & 0.03 \\ 0.77 & 0.23 \end{bmatrix}$$

$$= \begin{bmatrix} 2510 & 490 \end{bmatrix}$$

Problem 11, which provides a variation of Heidman's Department Store problem, will give you practice in analyzing Markov processes with absorbing states.

Thus, the new credit policy shows a bad debt expense of $490. Under the previous credit policy, we found the bad debt expense to be $630. Thus, a savings of $630 − $490 = $140 could be expected as a result of the new credit policy. Given the total accounts receivable balance of $3000, this is a 4.7% reduction in bad debt expense. After considering the costs involved, management can evaluate the economics of adopting the new credit policy. If the cost, including discounts, is less than 4.7% of the accounts receivable balance, we would expect the new policy to lead to increased profits for Heidman's Department Store.

Summary

In this chapter we have presented Markov process models as well as examples of their application. We saw that a Markov analysis could provide helpful decision-making information about a situation that involves a sequence of repeated trials with a finite number of possible states on each trial. A primary objective is obtaining information about the probability of each state after a large number of transitions or time periods.

A market share application showed the computational procedure for determining the steady-state probabilities that could be interpreted as market shares for two competing supermarkets. In an accounts receivable application, we introduced the notion of absorbing states; for the two absorbing states, referred to as the paid and bad debt categories, we showed how to determine the percentage of an accounts receivable balance that would be absorbed in each of these states.

Glossary

Trials of the process The events that trigger transitions of the system from one state to another. In many applications, successive time periods represent the trials of the process.

State of the system The condition of the system at any particular trial or time period.

Transition probability Given the system is in state i during one period, the transition probability p_{ij} is the probability that the system will be in state j during the next period.

State probability The probability that the system will be in any particular state. (That is, $\pi_i(n)$ is the probability of the system being in state i in period n.)

Steady-state probability The probability that the system will be in any particular state after a large number of transitions. Once steady state has been reached, the state probabilities do not change from period to period.

Absorbing state A state is said to be absorbing if the probability of making a transition out of that state is zero. Thus, once the system has made a transition into an absorbing state, it will remain there.

Fundamental matrix A matrix necessary for the computation of probabilities associated with absorbing states of a Markov process.

Problems

1. In the market share analysis of Section 17.1, suppose that we are considering the Markov process associated with the shopping trips of one customer, but we do not know where the customer shopped during the last week. Thus, we might make the assumption that there is a 0.5 probability that the customer shopped at Murphy's and a 0.5 probability that the customer shopped at Ashley's at period 0; that is, $\pi_1(0) = 0.5$ and $\pi_2(0) = 0.5$. Given these initial state probabilities, develop a table similar to Table 17.2 showing the probability of each state in future periods. What do you observe about the long-run probabilities of each state?

2. Management of the New Fangled Softdrink Company believes that the probability of a customer purchasing Red Pop or the company's major competition, Super Cola, is based on the customer's most recent purchase. Suppose the following transition probabilities are appropriate:

	To	
From	Red Pop	Super Cola
Red Pop	0.9	0.1
Super Cola	0.1	0.9

a. Show the two-period tree diagram for a customer who last purchased Red Pop. What is the probability that this customer purchases Red Pop on the second purchase?

b. What is the long-run market share for each of these two products?

c. A Red Pop advertising campaign is being planned to increase the probability of attracting Super Cola customers. Management believes that the new campaign will increase the probability of a customer switching from Super Cola to Red Pop is 0.15. What is the projected effect of the advertising campaign on the market shares?

3. **SELFTest** The computer center at Rockbottom University has been experiencing computer downtime. Let us assume that the trials of an associated Markov process are defined as 1-hour periods and that the probability of the system being in a running state or a down state is based on the state of the system in the previous period. Historical data show the following transition probabilities:

	To	
From	Running	Down
Running	0.90	0.10
Down	0.30	0.70

a. If the system is initially running, what is the probability of the system being down in the next hour of operation?

b. What are the steady-state probabilities of the system being in the running state and in the down state?

4. One cause of the downtime in Problem 3 was traced to a specific piece of computer hardware. Management believes that switching to a different hardware component will result in the following transition probabilities:

	To	
From	Running	Down
Running	0.95	0.05
Down	0.60	0.40

a. What are the steady-state probabilities of the system being in the running and down states?

b. If the cost of the system being down for any period is estimated to be $500 (including lost profits for time down and maintenance), what is the breakeven cost for the new hardware component on a time-period basis?

5. A major traffic problem in the Greater Cincinnati area involves traffic attempting to cross the Ohio River from Cincinnati to Kentucky using Interstate I-75. Let us assume that the probability of no traffic delay in one period, given no traffic delay in the preceding period, is 0.85 and that the probability of finding a traffic delay in one period, given a delay in the preceding period, is 0.75. Traffic is classified as having either a delay or a no-delay state, and the period considered is 30 minutes.

a. Assuming you are a motorist entering the traffic system and receive a radio report of a traffic delay, what is the probability that for the next 60 minutes (two time periods) the system will be in the delay state? Note that this is the probability of being in the delay state for two consecutive periods.

b. What is the probability that in the long run the traffic will not be in the delay state?

c. An important assumption of the Markov process models presented in this chapter has been the constant or stationary transition probabilities as the system operates in the future. Do you believe this assumption should be questioned for this traffic problem? Explain.

6. Data collected from selected major metropolitan areas in the eastern United States show that 2% of individuals living within the city limits move to the suburbs during a 1-year period while 1% of individuals living in the suburbs move to the city during a 1-year period. Answer the following questions assuming this process is modeled by a Markov process with two states: city and suburbs.
   a. Show the matrix of transition probabilities.
   b. Compute the steady-state probabilities.
   c. In a particular metropolitan area, 40% of the population live in the city and 60% of the population live in the suburbs. What population changes do your steady-state probabilities project for this metropolitan area?

7. **SELF Test** Assume a third grocery store, Quick Stop Groceries, enters the market share and customer loyalty situation described in Section 17.1. Quick Stop Groceries is smaller than either Murphy's Foodliner or Ashley's Supermarket. However, Quick Stop's convenience with faster service and gasoline for automobiles can be expected to attract some customers who currently make weekly shopping visits to either Murphy's or Ashley's. Assume the transition probabilities are as follows:

	To		
From	Murphy's	Ashley's	Quick Stop
Murphy's Foodliner	0.85	0.10	0.05
Ashley's Supermarket	0.20	0.75	0.05
Quick Stop	0.15	0.10	0.75

   a. Compute the steady-state probabilities for this three-state Markov process.
   b. What market share will Quick Stop obtain?
   c. With 1000 customers, the original two-state Markov process in Section 17.1 projected 667 weekly customer trips to Murphy's Foodliner and 333 weekly customer trips to Ashley's Supermarket. What impact will Quick Stop have on the customer visits at Murphy's and Ashley's? Explain.

8. The purchase patterns of two brands of toothpaste can be expressed as a Markov process with the following transition probabilities:

	To	
From	Special B	MDA
Special B	0.90	0.10
MDA	0.05	0.95

   a. Which brand appears to have the most loyal customers? Explain.
   b. What are the projected market shares for the two brands?

9. Suppose that in Problem 8 a new toothpaste brand enters the market such that the following transition probabilities exist:

	To		
From	Special B	MDA	T-White
Special B	0.80	0.10	0.10
MDA	0.05	0.75	0.20
T-White	0.40	0.30	0.30

What are the new long-run market shares? Which brand will suffer most from the introduction of the new brand of toothpaste?

10. Given the following transition matrix with states 1 and 2 as absorbing states, what is the probability that units in states 3 and 4 end up in each of the absorbing states?

$$P = \begin{bmatrix} 1.0 & 0.0 & 0.0 & 0.0 \\ 0.0 & 1.0 & 0.0 & 0.0 \\ 0.2 & 0.1 & 0.4 & 0.3 \\ 0.2 & 0.2 & 0.1 & 0.5 \end{bmatrix}$$

11. **SELF Test** In the Heidman's Department Store problem of Section 17.2, suppose the following transition matrix is appropriate:

$$P = \begin{bmatrix} 1.0 & 0.0 & 0.0 & 0.0 \\ 0.0 & 1.0 & 0.0 & 0.0 \\ 0.5 & 0.0 & 0.25 & 0.25 \\ 0.5 & 0.2 & 0.05 & 0.25 \end{bmatrix}$$

If Heidman's has $4000 in the 0–30-day age category and $5000 in the 31–90-day age category, what is your estimate of the amount of bad debts the company will experience?

12. The KLM Christmas Tree Farm owns a plot of land with 5000 evergreen trees. Each year KLM allows retailers of Christmas trees to select and cut trees for sale to individual customers. KLM protects small trees (usually less than 4 feet tall) so that they will be available for sale in future years. Currently 1500 trees are classified as protected trees, while the remaining 3500 are available for cutting. However, even though a tree is available for cutting in a given year, it may not be selected for cutting until future years. While most trees not cut in a given year live until the next year, some diseased trees are lost every year.

In viewing the KLM Christmas tree operation as a Markov process with yearly periods, we define the following four states:

State 1   Cut and sold
State 2   Lost to disease
State 3   Too small for cutting
State 4   Available for cutting but not cut and sold

The following transition matrix is appropriate:

$$P = \begin{bmatrix} 1.0 & 0.0 & 0.0 & 0.0 \\ 0.0 & 1.0 & 0.0 & 0.0 \\ 0.1 & 0.2 & 0.5 & 0.2 \\ 0.4 & 0.1 & 0.0 & 0.5 \end{bmatrix}$$

How many of the farm's 5000 trees will be sold eventually, and how many will be lost?

13. A large corporation has collected data on the reasons both middle managers and senior managers leave the company. Some managers eventually retire, but others leave the company prior to retirement for personal reasons including more attractive positions with other firms. Assume that the following matrix of 1-year transition probabilities applies with the four states of the Markov process being retirement, leaves prior to retirement for personal reasons, stays as a middle manager, stays as a senior manager.

	Retirement	Leaves— Personal	Middle Manager	Senior Manager
Retirement	1.00	0.00	0.00	0.00
Leaves—Personal	0.00	1.00	0.00	0.00
Middle Manager	0.03	0.07	0.80	0.10
Senior Manager	0.08	0.01	0.03	0.88

a. What states are considered absorbing states? Why?
b. Interpret the transition probabilities for the middle managers.
c. Interpret the transition probabilities for the senior managers.
d. What percentage of the current middle managers will eventually retire from the company? What percentage will leave the company for personal reasons?
e. The company currently has 920 managers: 640 middle managers and 280 senior managers. How many of these managers will eventually retire from the company? How many will leave the company for personal reasons?

14. Data for the progression of college students at a particular college are summarized in the following matrix of transition probabilities.

	Graduate	Dropout	Freshmen	Sophomore	Junior	Senior
Graduate	1.00	0.00	0.00	0.00	0.00	0.00
Dropout	0.00	1.00	0.00	0.00	0.00	0.00
Freshmen	0.00	0.20	0.15	0.65	0.00	0.00
Sophomore	0.00	0.15	0.00	0.10	0.75	0.00
Junior	0.00	0.10	0.00	0.00	0.05	0.85
Senior	0.90	0.05	0.00	0.00	0.00	0.05

a. What states are absorbing states?
b. Interpret the transition probabilities for a sophomore.
c. Use The Management Scientist software package to compute the probabilities that a sophomore will graduate and that a sophomore will drop out.
d. In an address to the incoming class of 600 freshmen, the dean asks the students to look around the auditorium and realize that about 50% of the freshmen present today will not make it to graduation day. Does your Markov process analysis support the dean's statement? Explain.
e. Currently, the college has 600 freshmen, 520 sophomores, 460 juniors, and 420 seniors. What percentage of the 2000 students attending the college will eventually graduate?

MANAGEMENT SCIENCE in practice

U.S. General Accounting Office*
Washington, D.C.

The U.S. General Accounting Office (GAO) is an independent, nonpolitical audit organization in the legislative branch of the federal government. The GAO was created by the Budget and Accounting Act of 1921 and has three basic purposes:

1. To assist Congress, its committees, and its members in carrying out their legislative and oversight responsibilities, consistent with its role as an independent, nonpolitical agency.
2. To audit and evaluate the programs, activities, and financial operations of federal departments and agencies and to make recommendations toward more efficient and effective operations.
3. To carry out financial control and other functions with respect to federal government programs and operations including accounting, legal, and claims settlement work.

GAO evaluators, the main occupation in the GAO, determine the effectiveness of existing or proposed federal programs and

—Continued on next page

—Continued from previous page

the efficiency, economy, legality, and effectiveness with which federal agencies carry out their responsibilities. These evaluations culminate in reports to the Congress and to the heads of federal departments and agencies. Such reports typically include recommendations to Congress concerning the need for enabling or remedial legislation and suggestions to agencies concerning the need for changes in programs or operations to improve their economy, efficiency, and effectiveness.

GAO evaluators analyze policies and practices and the use of resources within and among federal programs, identify problem areas and deficiencies in meeting program goals, develop and analyze alternative solutions to problems of program execution, and develop and recommend changes to enable the programs to better conform to congressional goals and legislative intent. To effectively carry out their duties, evaluators must be proficient in interviewing, data processing, records review, legislative research, management science, and statistical analysis techniques.

Impact of Services on the Well-being of Older People

GAO evaluators obtained data from a random sample of noninstitutionalized persons aged 65 and older living in Cleveland, Ohio. The health conditions of the sampled individuals in the 65- to 69-year-old groups were defined by the following three states:

■ **Best.** Individual able to perform 13 identified activities of daily living without help.

■ **Next best.** Individual able to perform the same 13 activities, but required help for at least one activity.

■ **Worst.** Individual unable to perform the same 13 activities even with help.

Using a 2-year period, GAO evaluators developed estimates of the year-to-year transition probabilities for individuals in the 65- to 69-year-old group. These estimates were then used to develop a transition probability matrix such as shown in Table 17.5. Note that a death state has been added as an absorbing state.

Using the transition probabilities, a Markov process analysis can be used to determine the state probabilities for any number of periods (years) into the future. To verify the appropriateness of the Markov process model, GAO evaluators used the

transition probabilities to determine the state probabilities for the 65- to 69-year-old age group 5 years into the future. The resulting state probabilities were compared with the health states of individuals in a known 70- to 74-year-old age group. There was no statistically significant difference between the probabilities provided by the model and the actual state probabilities of the 70- to 74-year-old group.

Estimating the Likely Effects of Health Care Programs

The individuals in the original study were subdivided into two groups: those receiving appropriate health care and those not receiving appropriate health care. For the purpose of the study, a person was classified as receiving appropriate health care if the person was taking medication and/or treatment for each illness present and if the person was receiving help to perform each of the 13 activities of daily living as specifically needed. As a result, GAO evaluators developed two matrices of transition probabilities: one for individuals receiving appropriate health care and one for individuals not receiving appropriate health care.

For any individuals not receiving appropriate help, the kind of additional help needed was determined, and the cost of that help was estimated. Then those persons were artificially aged using the transition probabilities to establish the likely benefits in terms of improved health states for the individuals. Over a 20-year period, there was a net savings for the health care program provided all other factors remained equal. That is, the increased cost to provide sufficient appropriate help to all persons was eventually offset by individuals either improving their health state or by not spending as much time in a worse state. Although benefits of health care are often proclaimed theoretically, the Markov process model provided evidence that indicated benefits would be achieved with the health care program.

This type of Markov analysis was also conducted for economic, social, and life view status as well as for the health status. In some instances, the Markov model showed that additional help and/or programs did not result in net savings over time.

Questions

1. Suppose the transition probabilities in Table 17.5 were as follows:

$$\begin{bmatrix} 0.80 & 0.10 & 0.06 & 0.04 \\ 0.05 & 0.75 & 0.15 & 0.05 \\ 0.00 & 0.05 & 0.75 & 0.20 \\ 0.00 & 0.00 & 0.00 & 1.00 \end{bmatrix}$$

Assume a particular city has 1000 individuals in the best state, 2000 in the next best state, and 500 in the worst state. Estimate how many of each of these individuals will be in each state 2 years from now.

2. How might health care programs affect the matrix of transition probabilities in question (1)? What effect would you expect to see in the distribution of individuals across the four states 2 years from now?

. . . .

The authors are indebted to Bill Ammann, U.S. General Accounting Office, Washington, D.C., for providing this application.

Table 17.5

Transition Probability Matrix for the Health Condition of Individuals 65–69 Years Old

Current Year Condition	Following Year Condition			
	Best	Next Best	Worst	Death
Best	p_{11}	p_{12}	p_{13}	p_{14}
Next Best	p_{21}	p_{22}	p_{23}	p_{24}
Worst	p_{31}	p_{32}	p_{33}	p_{34}
Death	0	0	0	1

eighteen
CHAPTER

Dynamic Programming

Dynamic programming **is an** approach to problem solving that decomposes a large problem that may be difficult to solve into a number of smaller problems that are usually much easier to solve. Moreover, the dynamic programming approach allows us to break up a large problem such that once all the smaller problems have been solved, we have an optimal solution to the large problem. We shall see that each of the smaller problems is identified with a *stage* of the dynamic programming solution procedure. As a consequence, the technique has been applied to decision problems that are multistage in nature. Often, multiple stages are created because a sequence of decisions must be made over time. For example, a problem of determining an optimal decision over a 1-year horizon might be broken into 12 smaller stages, where each stage requires an optimal decision over a 1-month horizon. In most cases, each of these smaller problems cannot be considered to be completely independent of the others, and this is where dynamic programming is helpful. Let us begin by showing how to solve a shortest-route problem using dynamic programming.

18.1 A Shortest-Route Problem

In Chapter 9 we studied a labeling algorithm for solving the shortest-route problem. Let us now illustrate the dynamic programming approach by using it to solve a shortest-route problem. Consider the network presented in Figure 18.1. Assuming that the numbers above each arc denote the direct distance in miles between two nodes, find the shortest route from node 1 to node 10.

Before attempting to solve this problem, let us note an important characteristic of shortest-route problems. This characteristic is actually a restatement of Richard Bellman's famous *principle of optimality* as it applies to the shortest-route problem.[1]

---

[1]S. Dreyfus, *Dynamic Programming and the Calculus of Variations* (New York: Academic Press, 1965).

The Principle of Optimality

If a particular node is on the optimal route, then the shortest path from that node to the end is also on the optimal route.

The dynamic programming approach to the shortest-route problem essentially involves treating each node as if it were on the optimal route and making calculations accordingly. In doing so, we will work backward by starting at the terminal node, node 10, and calculating the shortest route from each node to node 10 until we reach the origin, node 1. At this point, we will have solved the original problem of finding the shortest route from node 1 to node 10.

As we stated in the introduction to this chapter, dynamic programming decomposes the original problem into a number of smaller problems that are much easier to solve. In the shortest-route problem for the network in Figure 18.1, the smaller problems that we will create define a four-stage dynamic programming problem. The first stage begins with nodes that are exactly one arc away from the destination and ends at the destination node. Note from Figure 18.1 that only nodes 8 and 9 are exactly one arc away from node 10. In dynamic programming terminology, nodes 8 and 9 are considered to be the input nodes for stage 1, and node 10 is considered to be the output node for stage 1.

The second stage begins with all nodes that are exactly two arcs away from the destination and ends with all nodes that are exactly one arc away. Hence, nodes 5, 6, and 7 are the input nodes for stage 2, and nodes 8 and 9 are the output nodes for stage 2. Note that the output nodes for stage 2 are the input nodes for stage 1. The input nodes for the third-stage problem are all nodes that are exactly three arcs away from the destination— that is, nodes 2, 3, and 4. The output nodes for stage 3, all of which are one arc closer to the destination, are nodes 5, 6, and 7. Finally, the input node for stage 4 is node 1, and the output nodes are 2, 3, and 4. The decision problem we shall want to solve at each stage is, Which arc is best to travel over in moving from each particular input node to an output node? Let us consider the stage 1 problem.

We arbitrarily begin the stage 1 calculations with node 9. Since there is only one way to travel from node 9 to node 10, this is obviously the shortest route and requires us to

Figure 18.1

Network for the Shortest-Route Problem

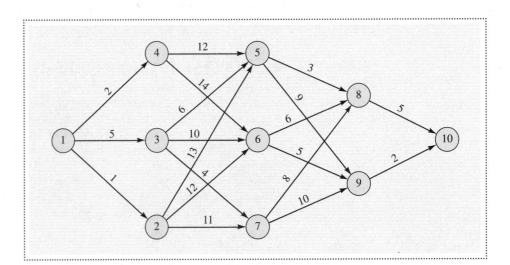

travel a distance of 2 miles. Similarly, there is only one path from node 8 to node 10. The shortest route from node 8 to the end is thus the length of that route, or 5 miles. The stage 1 decision problem is solved. For each input node, we have identified an optimal decision—that is, the best arc to travel over to reach the output node. The stage 1 results are summarized below:

Stage 1		
Input Node	Arc (decision)	Shortest Distance to Node 10
8	8–10	5
9	9–10	2

To begin the solution to the stage 2 problem, we move to node 7. (We could have selected node 5 or 6; the order of the nodes selected at any stage is arbitrary.) There are two arcs that leave node 7 and are connected to input nodes for stage 1. These are arc 7–8, which has a length of 8 miles, and arc 7–9, which has a length of 10 miles. If we select arc 7–8, we will have a distance from node 7 to node 10 of 13 miles; i.e., the length of arc 7–8, 8 miles, plus the shortest distance to node 10 from node 8, 5 miles. Thus, the decision to select arc 7–8 has a total associated distance of $8 + 5 = 13$ miles. With a distance of 10 miles for arc 7–9 and stage 1 results showing a distance of 2 miles from node 9 to node 10, the decision to select arc 7–9 has an associated distance of $10 + 2 = 12$ miles. Thus, given we are at node 7, we should select arc 7–9 since it is on the path that will reach node 10 in the shortest distance (12 miles). By performing similar calculations for nodes 5 and 6, we can generate the following stage 2 results:

Stage 2			
Input Node	Arc (decision)	Output Node	Shortest Distance to Node 10
5	5–8	8	8
6	6–9	9	7
7	7–9	9	12

In Figure 18.2 the number in the square by each node considered so far indicates the length of the shortest route from that node to the end. We have completed the solution to the first two subproblems (stages 1 and 2). We now know the shortest route from nodes 5, 6, 7, 8, and 9 to node 10.

To begin the third stage, let us start with node 2. Note that there are three arcs that connect node 2 to the stage 2 input nodes. Thus, to find the shortest route from node 2 to node 10, we must make three calculations. If we select arc 2–7 and then follow the shortest route to the end, we will have a distance of $11 + 12 = 23$ miles. Similarly, selecting arc 2–6 requires $12 + 7 = 19$ miles, and selecting arc 2–5 requires $13 + 8 = 21$ miles. Thus, the shortest route from node 2 to node 10 is 19 miles, which indicates that arc 2–6 is the best decision, given that we are at node 2. Similarly, we find that the shortest route from node 3 to node 10 is given by Min $\{4 + 12, 10 + 7, 6 + 8\} = 14$; the shortest route from node 4 to node 10 is given by Min $\{14 + 7, 12 + 8\} = 20$. This completes the stage 3 calculations with the following results:

Figure 18.2

Intermediate Solution to the
Shortest-Route Problem Using
Dynamic Programming

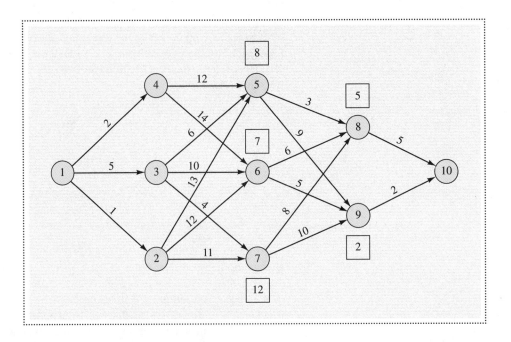

	Stage 3		
Input Node	Arc (decision)	Output Node	Shortest Distance to Node 10
2	2–6	6	19
3	3–5	5	14
4	4–5	5	20

In solving the stage 4 subproblem, we find that the shortest route from node 1 to node 10 is given by Min $\{1 + 19, 5 + 14, 2 + 20\} = 19$. Thus, the optimal decision at stage 4 is the selection of arc 1–3. By moving through the network from stage 4 to stage 3 to stage 2 to stage 1, we can identify the best decision at each stage and therefore the shortest route from node 1 to node 10. This is as follows:

Stage	Arc (decision)
4	1–3
3	3–5
2	5–8
1	8–10

Thus, the shortest route is through nodes 1–3–5–8–10 with a distance of $5 + 6 + 3 + 5 = 19$ miles.

Figure 18.3

Final Solution to the Shortest-Route Problem Using Dynamic Programming

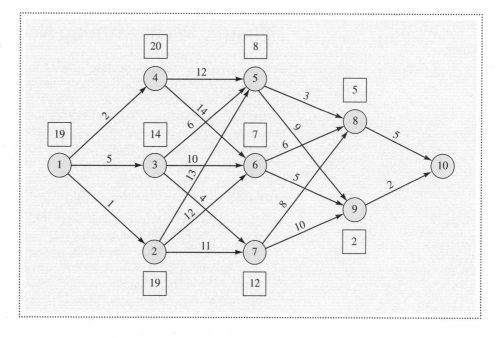

Note how the calculations at each successive stage make use of the calculations at prior stages. This characteristic is an important part of the dynamic programming procedure. Figure 18.3 illustrates the final network calculations. Note that in working back through the stages we have now determined the shortest route from every node to node 10.

Dynamic programming, while enumerating or evaluating several paths at each stage, does not require us to enumerate all possible paths from node 1 to node 10. Returning to the stage 4 calculations, we consider three alternatives for leaving node 1. The complete route associated with each of these alternatives is presented below.

Arc Alternatives at Node 1	Complete Path to Node 10	Distance	
1–2	1–2–6–9–10	20	
1–3	1–3–5–8–10	19 ◄—— Selected as best
1–4	1–4–5–8–10	22	

Try Problem 2, part (a), for practice solving a shortest-route problem using dynamic programming.

When you realize that there are a total of 16 alternate routes from node 1 to node 10, you can see that dynamic programming has provided substantial computational savings over a total enumeration of all possible solutions.

The fact that we did not have to evaluate all the paths at each stage as we moved backward from node 10 to node 1 is illustrative of the power of dynamic programming. Using dynamic programming, we need only make a small fraction of the number of calculations that would be required using total enumeration. If the example network had been larger, the computational savings provided by dynamic programming would have been even greater.

18.2 Dynamic Programming Notation

Perhaps one of the most difficult aspects of learning to apply dynamic programming involves understanding the notation. The notation we will use is the same as that used by Nemhauser[2] and is fairly standard.

The *stages* of a dynamic programming solution procedure are formed by decomposing the original problem into a number of subproblems. Associated with each subproblem is a stage in the dynamic programming solution procedure. For example, the shortest-route problem introduced in the preceding section was solved using a four-stage dynamic programming solution procedure. We had four stages because we decomposed the original problem into the following four subproblems:

1. **Stage 1 Problem:** Where should we go from nodes 8 and 9 so that we will reach node 10 along the shortest route?
2. **Stage 2 Problem:** Using the results of stage 1, where should we go from nodes 5, 6, and 7 so that we will reach node 10 along the shortest route?
3. **Stage 3 Problem:** Using the results of stage 2, where should we go from nodes 2, 3, and 4 so that we will reach node 10 along the shortest route?
4. **Stage 4 Problem:** Using the results of stage 3, where should we go from node 1 so that we will reach node 10 along the shortest route?

Let us look closely at what occurs at the stage 2 problem. Consider the following representation of this stage:

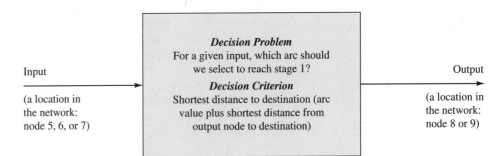

Using dynamic programming notation, we define

x_2 = input to stage 2; represents the location in the network at the beginning of stage 2 (node 5, 6, or 7).

d_2 = decision variable at stage 2 (the arc selected to move to stage 1).

x_1 = output for stage 2; represents the location in the network at the end of stage 2 (node 8 or 9).

Using this notation, the stage 2 problem can be represented as follows:

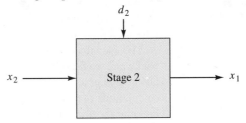

---

[2]G. L. Nemhauser, *Introduction to Dynamic Programming* (New York: Wiley, 1966).

Recall that using dynamic programming to solve the shortest-route problem, we worked backward through the stages, beginning at node 10. When we reached stage 2, we did not know x_2 because the stage 3 problem had not yet been solved. The approach used was to consider *all* alternatives for the input x_2. Then we determined the best decision d_2 for each of the inputs x_2. Later, when we moved forward through the system to recover the optimal sequence of decisions, we saw that the stage 3 decision provided a specific x_2, node 5, and from our previous analysis we knew the best decision (d_2) to make as we continued on to stage 1.

Let us consider a general dynamic programming problem with N stages and adopt the following general notation:

$$x_n = \text{input to stage } n \text{ (output from stage } n + 1)$$

$$d_n = \text{decision variable at stage } n$$

The general N-stage problem is decomposed as follows:

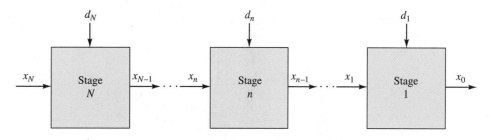

The four-stage shortest-route problem can be represented as follows:

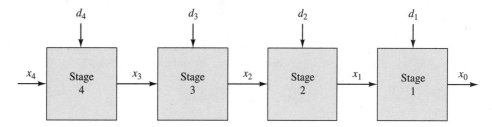

The values of the input and output variables x_4, x_3, x_2, x_1, and x_0 are important because they join the four subproblems together. At any stage, we will ultimately need to know the input x_n to make the best decision d_n. These x_n variables can be thought of as defining the *state* or condition of the system as we move from stage to stage. Accordingly, these variables are referred to as the *state variables* of the problem. In the shortest-route problem, the state variables represented the location in the network at each stage (i.e., a particular node).

At stage 2 of the shortest-route problem, we considered the input x_2 and made the decision d_2 that would provide the shortest distance to the destination. The output x_1 was based on a combination of the input and the decision; that is, x_1 was a function of x_2 and d_2. In dynamic programming notation, we write

$$x_1 = t_2(x_2, d_2)$$

where $t_2(x_2, d_2)$ is the function that determines the stage 2 output. Since $t_2(x_2, d_2)$ is the function that "transforms" the input to the stage into the output, this function is referred to as the *stage transformation function*.

The general expression for the stage transformation function is

$$x_{n-1} = t_n(x_n, d_n) \qquad (18.1)$$

The mathematical form of the stage transformation function is dependent on the particular dynamic programming problem. In the shortest-route problem, the transformation function was based on a tabular calculation. For example, Table 18.1 shows the stage transformation function $t_2(x_2, d_2)$ for stage 2. The possible values of d_2 are the arcs selected in the body of the table.

Each stage also has a return associated with it. In the shortest-route problem, the return was the arc distance traveled in moving from an input node to an output node. For example, if node 7 were the input state for stage 2 and we selected arc 7–9 as d_2, the return for that stage would be the arc length, 10 miles. The return at a stage, which may be thought of as the payoff or value for a stage, is represented by the general notation $r_n(x_n, d_n)$.

Using the stage transformation function and the *return function,* the shortest-route problem can be shown as follows.

Table 18.1

Stage Transformation $x_1 = t_2(x_2, d_2)$ for Stage 2 with the Value of x_1 Corresponding to Each Value of x_2

x_2 Input State	x_1 Output State 8	x_1 Output State 9
5	5–8	5–9
6	6–8	6–9
7	7–8	7–9

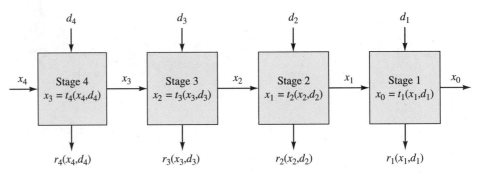

If we view a system or a process as consisting of N stages, we can represent a dynamic programming formulation as follows:

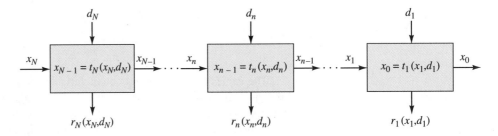

Each of the rectangles in the diagram represents a stage in the process. As indicated, there are two inputs to each stage: the state variable and the decision variable. There are also two outputs: a new value for the state variable and a return for the stage. The new value for the state variable is determined as a function of the inputs using $t_n(x_n, d_n)$. The value of the return for a stage is also determined as a function of the inputs using $r_n(x_n, d_n)$.

In addition, we will use the notation $f_n(x_n)$ to represent the optimal total return from stage n and all remaining stages, given an input of x_n to stage n. For example, in the shortest-route problem, $f_2(x_2)$ represents the optimal total return (i.e., the minimum distance) from stage 2 and all remaining stages, given an input of x_2 to stage 2. Thus, we see from Figure 18.3 that $f_2(x_2 = \text{node } 5) = 8, f_2(x_2 = \text{node } 6) = 7$, and $f_2(x_2 = \text{node } 7) = 12$. These are just the values in the squares at nodes 5, 6, and 7.

NOTES & comments

1. The primary advantage of dynamic programming is its "divide and conquer" solution strategy. Using dynamic programming, a large, complex problem can be divided into a sequence of smaller interrelated problems. By solving the smaller problems sequentially, the optimal solution to the larger problem is found. Dynamic programming is a general approach to problem solving; it is not a specific technique such as linear programming, which can be applied in the same fashion to a variety of problems. Although there are some common characteristics of all dynamic programming problems, each application requires some degree of creativity, insight, and expertise to recognize how the larger problems can be broken into a sequence of interrelated smaller problems.

2. Dynamic programming has been applied to a wide variety of problems including inventory control, production scheduling, capital budgeting, resource allocation, equipment replacement, and maintenance. In many of these applications, periods such as days, weeks, and months, provide the sequence of interrelated stages for the larger multiperiod problem.

18.3 The Knapsack Problem

The basic idea of the knapsack problem is that there are N different types of items that can be put into a knapsack. Each item has a certain weight associated with it as well as a value. The problem is to determine how many units of each item to place in the knapsack to maximize the total value. A constraint is placed on the maximum weight permissible.

To provide a practical application of the knapsack problem, consider a manager of a manufacturing operation who must make a biweekly selection of jobs from each of 4 categories to process during the following 2-week period. A list showing the number of jobs waiting to be processed is presented in Table 18.2. The estimated time required for completion and the value rating associated with each job are also shown.

The value rating assigned to each job category is a subjective score assigned by the manager. A scale from 1 to 20 is used to measure the value of each job, where 1

Table 18.2

Job Data for the Manufacturing Operation

Job Category	Number of Jobs to Be Processed	Estimated Completion Time Per Job (days)	Value Rating Per Job
1	4	1	2
2	3	3	8
3	2	4	11
4	2	7	20

represents jobs of the least value, and 20 represents jobs of most value. The value of a job depends on such things as expected profit, length of time the job has been waiting to be processed, priority, and so on. In this situation, we would like to select certain jobs during the next 2 weeks such that all the jobs selected can be processed within 10 working days and the total value of the jobs selected is maximized. In knapsack problem terminology, we are in essence selecting the best jobs for the 2-week (10 working days) knapsack, where the knapsack has a capacity equal to the 10-day production capacity. Let us formulate and solve this problem using dynamic programming.

This problem can be formulated as a dynamic programming problem involving four stages. At stage 1, we must decide how many jobs from category 1 to process; at stage 2, we must decide how many jobs from category 2 to process; and so on. Thus, we let

d_n = number of jobs processed from category n (decision variable at stage n)

x_n = number of days of processing time remaining at the beginning of stage n (state variable for stage n)

Thus, with a 2-week production period, $x_4 = 10$ represents the total number of days available for processing jobs. The stage transformation functions are as follows:

$$\text{Stage 4} \quad x_3 = t_4(x_4, d_4) = x_4 - 7d_4$$

$$\text{Stage 3} \quad x_2 = t_3(x_3, d_3) = x_3 - 4d_3$$

$$\text{Stage 2} \quad x_1 = t_2(x_2, d_2) = x_2 - 3d_2$$

$$\text{Stage 1} \quad x_0 = t_1(x_1, d_1) = x_1 - 1d_1$$

The return at each stage is based on the value rating of the associated job category and the number of jobs selected from that category. The return functions are as follows:

$$\text{Stage 4} \quad r_4(x_4, d_4) = 20d_4$$

$$\text{Stage 3} \quad r_3(x_3, d_3) = 11d_3$$

$$\text{Stage 2} \quad r_2(x_2, d_2) = 8d_2$$

$$\text{Stage 1} \quad r_1(x_1, d_1) = 2d_1$$

Figure 18.4 shows a schematic of the problem.

Figure 18.4

Dynamic Programming Formulation of the Job Selection Problem

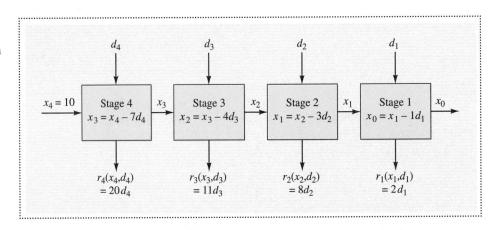

As with the shortest-route problem in Section 18.1, we will apply a backward solution procedure; that is, we will begin by assuming that decisions have already been made for stages 4, 3, and 2 and that the final decision remains (how many jobs from category 1 to select at stage 1). A restatement of the principle of optimality can be made in terms of this problem. That is, regardless of whatever decisions have been made at previous stages, if the decision at stage n is to be part of an optimal overall strategy, the decision made at stage n must necessarily be optimal for all remaining stages.

Let us set up a table that will help us calculate the optimal decisions for stage 1.

Stage 1 Note that stage 1's input (x_1), the number of days of processing time available at stage 1, is unknown because we have not yet identified the decisions at the previous stages. Therefore, in our analysis at stage 1, we will have to consider all possible values of x_1 and identify the best decision d_1 for each case; $f_1(x_1)$ will be the total return after decision d_1 is made. The possible values of x_1 and the associated d_1 and $f_1(x_1)$ values are as follows:

x_1	d_1^*	$f_1(x_1)$
0	0	0
1	1	2
2	2	4
3	3	6
4	4	8
5	4	8
6	4	8
7	4	8
8	4	8
9	4	8
10	4	8

The d_1^* column gives the optimal values of d_1 corresponding to a particular value of x_1, where x_1 can range from 0 to 10. The specific value of x_1 will depend on how much processing time has been used by the jobs in the other categories selected in stages 2, 3, and 4. Since each stage 1 job requires 1 day of processing time and has a positive return of 2 per job, we always select as many jobs at this stage as possible. The number of category 1 jobs selected will depend on the processing time available, but cannot exceed four.

Recall that $f_1(x_1)$ represents the value of the optimal total return from stage 1 and all remaining stages, given an input of x_1 to stage 1. Therefore, $f_1(x_1) = 2x_1$ for values of $x_1 \leq 4$, and $f_1(x_1) = 8$ for values of $x_1 > 4$. The optimization of stage 1 is accomplished. *us now move on to stage 2 and carry out the optimization at that stage.*

Stage 2 Again, we will use a table to help identify the optimal decision. Since stage 2's input (x_2), is unknown, we have to consider all possible values from 0 to 10. Also, we have to consider all possible values of d_2 (i.e., 0, 1, 2, or 3). The entries under the heading $r_2(x_2, d_2) + f_1(x_1)$ represent the total return that will be forthcoming from the final two stages, given the input of x_2 and the decision of d_2. For example, if stage 2 were entered with $x_2 = 7$ days of processing time remaining, and if a decision were made to select two jobs from category 2 (i.e., $d_2 = 2$), the total return for stages 1 and 2 would be 18.

| d_2 | $r_2(x_2, d_2) + f_1(x_1)$ | | | | | | $x_1 = t_2(x_2, d_2^*)$ |
x_2	0	1	2	3	d_2^*	$f_2(x_2)$	$= x_2 - 3d_2^*$
0	⓪	—	—	—	0	0	0
1	②	—	—	—	0	2	1
2	④	—	—	—	0	4	2
3	6	⑧	—	—	1	8	0
4	8	⑩	—	—	1	10	1
5	8	⑫	—	—	1	12	2
6	8	14	⑯	—	2	16	0
7	8	16	⑱	—	2	18	1
8	8	16	⑳	—	2	20	2
9	8	16	22	㉔	3	24	0
10	8	16	24	㉖	3	26	1

The return for stage 2 would be $r_2(x_2, d_2) = 8d_2 = 8(2) = 16$, and with $x_2 = 7$ and $d_2 = 2$, we would have $x_1 = x_2 - 3d_2 = 7 - 6 = 1$. From the previous table, we see that the optimal return from stage 1 with $x_1 = 1$ is $f_1(1) = 2$. Thus, the total return corresponding to $x_2 = 7$ and $d_2 = 2$ is given by $r_2(7,2) + f_1(1) = 16 + 2 = 18$. Similarly, with $x_2 = 5$, and $d_2 = 1$, we get $r_2(5,1) + f_1(2) = 8 + 4 = 12$. Note that some combinations of x_2 and d_2 are not feasible. For example, with $x_2 = 2$ days, $d_2 = 1$ is infeasible because category 2 jobs each require 3 days to process. The infeasible solutions are indicated by a dash.

After all the total returns in the rectangle have been calculated, we can determine an optimal decision at this stage for each possible value of the input or state variable x_2. For example, if $x_2 = 9$, there are four possible values we can select for d_2: 0, 1, 2, or 3. Clearly $d_3 = 3$ with a value of 24 yields the maximum total return for the last two stages. Therefore, we record this value in the d_2^* column. For additional emphasis, we circle the element inside the rectangle corresponding to the optimal return. The optimal total return, given that we are in state $x_2 = 9$ and must pass through two more stages, is thus 24, and we record this value in the $f_2(x_2)$ column. Given that we enter stage 2 with $x_2 = 9$ and make the optimal decision there of $d_2^* = 3$, we will enter stage 1 with $x_1 = t_2(9, 3) = x_2 - 3d_2 = 9 - 3(3) = 0$. This value is recorded in the last column in the table. We can now go on to stage 3.

Stage 3   The table we construct here is much the same as for stage 2. The entries under the heading $r_2(x_3, d_3) + f_2(x_2)$ represent the total return over stages 3, 2, and 1 for all possible inputs x_3 and all possible decisions d_3.

x_3 \ d_3	$r_3(x_3,d_3)+f_2(x_2)$			d_3^*	$f_3(x_3)$	$x_2=t_3(x_3,d_3^*)$ $=x_3-4d_3^*$
	0	1	2			
0	(0)	—	—	0	0	0
1	(2)	—	—	0	2	1
2	(4)	—	—	0	4	2
3	(8)	—	—	0	8	3
4	10	(11)	—	1	11	0
5	12	(13)	—	1	13	1
6	(16)	15	—	0	16	6
7	18	(19)	—	1	19	3
8	20	21	(22)	2	22	0
9	(24)	23	(24)	0,2	24	9,1
10	26	(27)	26	1	27	6

There are some features of interest in this table that were not present at stage 2. We note that if the state variable $x_3 = 9$, then there are two decisions that will lead to an optimal total return from stages 1, 2, and 3; that is, we may elect to process no jobs from category 3, in which case, we will obtain no return from stage 3, but will enter stage 2 with $x_2 = 9$. Since $f_2(9) = 24$, the selection of $d_3 = 0$ would result in a total return of 24. However, a selection of $d_3 = 2$ also leads to a total return of 24. We obtain a return of $11(d_3) = 11(2) = 22$ for stage 3 and a return of 2 for the remaining two stages since $x_2 = 1$. To show that there are alternative optimal solutions at this stage, we have placed two entries in the d_3^* and $x_2 = t_3(x_3, d_3^*)$ columns. The other entries in this table are calculated in the same manner as at stage 2. Let us now move on to the last stage.

Stage 4   Since we know that there are 10 days available in the planning period, the input to stage 4 is $x_4 = 10$. Thus, we have to consider only one row in the table, corresponding to stage 4.

x_4 \ d_4	$r_4(x_4,d_4)+f_3(x_3)$		d_4^*	$f_4(x_4)$	$x_3=t_4(x_4,d_4^*)$ $=10-7d_4^*$
	0	1			
10	27	(28)	1	28	3

The optimal decision, given $x_4 = 10$, is $d_4^* = 1$.

We have completed the dynamic programming solution of this problem. To identify the overall optimal solution, we must now trace back through the tables, beginning at stage 4, the last stage considered. The optimal decision at stage 4 is $d_4^* = 1$. Thus, $x_3 = 10 - 7d_4^* = 3$, and we enter stage 3 with 3 days available for processing. With $x_3 = 3$, we see that the best decision at stage 3 is $d_3^* = 0$. Thus, we enter stage 2 with $x_2 = 3$. The optimal decision at stage 2 with $x_2 = 3$ is $d_2^* = 1$, resulting in $x_1 = 0$. Finally, the decision at stage 1 must be $d_1^* = 0$. The optimal strategy for the manufacturing operation is as follows:

Decision	Return
$d_1^* = 0$	0
$d_2^* = 1$	8
$d_3^* = 0$	0
$d_4^* = 1$	20
Total	28

We should schedule one job from category 2 and one job from category 4 for processing over the next 10 days.

Another advantage of the dynamic programming approach can now be illustrated. Suppose we wanted to schedule the jobs to be processed over an 8-day period only. We can solve this new problem simply by making a recalculation at stage 4. The new stage 4 table would appear as follows:

d_4 x_4	$r_4(x_4,d_4) + f_3(x_3)$					$x_3 = t_4(x_4, d_4^*)$
	0	1	d_4^*	$f_4(x_4)$	$= 8 - 7d_4^*$
8	(22)	(22)	0,1	22	8,1

Actually, we are testing the sensitivity of the optimal solution to a change in the total number of days available for processing. We have here the case of alternative optimal solutions. One solution can be found by setting $d_4^* = 0$ and tracing through the tables. Doing so, we obtain the following:

Decision	Return
$d_1^* = 0$	0
$d_2^* = 0$	0
$d_3^* = 2$	22
$d_4^* = 0$	0
Total	22

A second optimal solution can be found by setting $d_4^* = 1$ and tracing back through the tables. Doing so, we obtain another solution (which has exactly the same total return):

Decision	Return
$d_1^* = 1$	2
$d_2^* = 0$	0
$d_3^* = 0$	0
$d_4^* = 1$	20
Total	22

You should now be able to solve a knapsack problem using dynamic programming. Try Problem 3.

From the shortest-route and the knapsack examples you should be familiar with the stage-by-stage solution procedure of dynamic programming. In the next section we show how dynamic programming can be used to solve a production and inventory control problem.

18.4 A Production and Inventory Control Problem

Suppose we have developed forecasts of the demand for a particular product over several periods and we would like to decide on a production quantity for each of the periods so that demand can be satisfied at a minimum cost. There are two costs to be considered: production costs and holding costs. We will assume that one production setup will be made each period; thus, setup costs will be constant. As a result, setup costs are not considered in the analysis.

We will allow the production and holding costs to vary across periods. This makes the model more flexible since it also allows for the possibility of using different facilities for production and storage in different periods. Production and storage capacity constraints, which may vary across periods, will be included in the model. We adopt the following notation:

N = number of periods (stages in the dynamic programming formulation)

D_n = demand during stage n; $n = 1, 2, \ldots, N$

x_n = a state variable representing the amount of inventory on hand at the beginning of stage n; $n = 1, 2, \ldots, N$

d_n = production quantity for stage n; $n = 1, 2, \ldots, N$

P_n = production capacity in stage n; $n = 1, 2, \ldots, N$

W_n = storage capacity at the end of stage n; $n = 1, 2, \ldots, N$

C_n = production cost per unit in stage n; $n = 1, 2, \ldots, N$

H_n = holding cost per unit of ending inventory for stage n; $n = 1, 2, \ldots, N$

We will develop the dynamic programming solution for a problem covering 3 months of operation. The data for the problem are presented in Table 18.3. We can think of each month as a stage in a dynamic programming formulation. Figure 18.5 shows a schematic of such a formulation. Note that the beginning inventory in January is one unit.

In Figure 18.5 we have numbered the periods backward; that is, stage 1 corresponds to March, stage 2 corresponds to February, and stage 3 corresponds to January. The stage transformation functions take the form of ending inventory = beginning inventory + production − demand. Thus, we have

$$x_3 = 1$$
$$x_2 = x_3 + d_3 - D_3 = x_3 + d_3 - 2$$
$$x_1 = x_2 + d_2 - D_2 = x_2 + d_2 - 3$$
$$x_0 = x_1 + d_1 - D_1 = x_1 + d_1 - 3$$

Table 18.3

Production and Inventory Control Problem Data

		Capacity		Cost Per Unit	
Month	Demand	Production	Storage	Production	Holding
January	2	3	2	$175	$30
February	3	2	3	150	30
March	3	3	2	200	40

The beginning inventory for January is one unit.

Figure 18.5

Production and Inventory Control Problem as a Three-Stage Dynamic Programming Problem

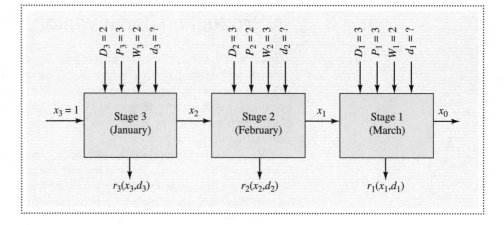

The return functions for each stage represent the sum of production and holding costs for the month. For example, in stage 1 (March), $r_1(x_1, d_1) = 200d_1 + 40(x_1 + d_1 - 3)$ represents the total production and holding costs for the period. The production costs are \$200 per unit, and the holding costs are \$40 per unit of ending inventory. The other return functions are

$$r_2(x_2, d_2) = 150d_2 + 30(x_2 + d_2 - 3) \qquad \text{Stage 2, February}$$

$$r_3(x_3, d_3) = 175d_3 + 30(x_3 + d_3 - 2) \qquad \text{Stage 3, January}$$

This problem is particularly interesting because there are three constraints that must be satisfied at each stage as we perform the optimization procedure. The first constraint is that the ending inventory must be less than or equal to the warehouse capacity. Mathematically, we have

$$x_n + d_n - D_n \le W_n$$

or

$$x_n + d_n \le W_n + D_n \qquad (18.2)$$

The second constraint is that the production level in each period may not exceed the production capacity. Mathematically, we have

$$d_n \le P_n \qquad (18.3)$$

In order to satisfy demand, the third constraint is that the beginning inventory plus production must be greater than or equal to demand. Mathematically, this constraint can be written as

$$x_n + d_n \ge D_n \qquad (18.4)$$

Let us now begin the stagewise solution procedure. At each stage, we want to minimize $r_n(x_n, d_n) + f_{n-1}(x_{n-1})$ subject to the constraints given by equations (18.2), (18.3), and (18.4).

Stage 1   The stage 1 problem is as follows:

$$\text{Min} \quad r_1(x_1, d_1) = 200d_1 + 40(x_1 + d_1 - 3)$$

s.t.

$$x_1 + d_1 \le 5 \qquad \text{Warehouse constraint}$$

$$d_1 \le 3 \qquad \text{Production constraint}$$

$$x_1 + d_1 \ge 3 \qquad \text{Satisfy demand constraint}$$

Combining terms in the objective function, we can rewrite the problem:

$$\text{Min} \quad r_1(x_1, d_1) = 240d_1 + 40x_1 - 120$$

s.t.

$$x_1 + d_1 \leq 5$$
$$d_1 \leq 3$$
$$x_1 + d_1 \geq 3$$

Following the tabular approach we adopted in Section 18.3, we will consider all possible inputs to stage 1 (x_1) and make the corresponding minimum-cost decision. Since we are attempting to minimize cost, we will want the decision variable d_1 to be as small as possible and still satisfy the demand constraint. Thus, the table for stage 1 is as follows:

	x_1	d_1^*		$f_1(x_1)=r_1(x_1, d_1^*)$ $240d_1+40x_1-120$
	0	3		600
	1	2		400
	2	1	Production	200
	3	0	capacity of 3 for stage 1 limits d_1	0

Warehouse capacity of 3 from stage 2 limits value of x_1

Demand constraint: $x_1 + d_1 \geq 3$

Now let us proceed to stage 2.

Stage 2

$$\text{Min} \quad r_2(x_2, d_2) + f_1(x_1) = 150d_2 + 30(x_2 + d_2 - 3) + f_1(x_1)$$
$$= 180d_2 + 30x_2 - 90 + f_1(x_1)$$

s.t.

$$x_2 + d_2 \leq 6$$
$$d_2 \leq 2$$
$$x_2 + d_2 \geq 3$$

The stage 2 calculations are summarized in the table below:

d_2	$r_2(x_2, d_2) + f_1(x_1)$			Production capacity of 2 for stage 2		
x_2	0	1	2	d_2^*	$f_2(x_2)$	$x_1 = x_2 + d_2^* - 3$
0	—	—	—	—	M	—
1	—	—	(900)	2	900	0
2	—	750	(730)	2	730	1

Warehouse capacity of 2 from stage 3

Check demand constraint $x_2 + d_2 \geq 3$ for each x_2, d_2 combination (– indicates an infeasible solution)

The detailed calculations for $r_2(x_2, d_2) + f_1(x_1)$ when $x_2 = 1$ and $d_2 = 2$ are as follows:

$$r_2(1,2) + f_1(0) = 180(2) + 30(1) - 90 + 600 = 900$$

For $r_2(x_2, d_2) + f_1(x_1)$ when $x_2 = 2$ and $d_2 = 1$, we have

$$r_2(2,1) + f_1(0) = 180(1) + 30(2) - 90 + 600 = 750$$

For $x_2 = 2$ and $d_2 = 2$, we have

$$r_2(2,2) + f_1(1) = 180(2) + 30(2) - 90 + 400 = 730$$

Note that an arbitrarily high cost M is assigned to the $f_2(x_2)$ column for $x_2 = 0$. Since an input of 0 to stage 2 does not provide a feasible solution, the M cost associated with the $x_2 = 0$ input will prevent $x_2 = 0$ from occurring in the optimal solution.

Stage 3

$$\text{Min} \quad r_3(x_3, d_3) + f_2(x_2) = 175d_3 + 30(x_3 + d_3 - 2) + f_2(x_2)$$
$$= 205d_3 + 30x_3 - 60 + f_2(x_2)$$

s.t.

$$x_3 + d_3 \leq 4$$
$$d_3 \leq 3$$
$$x_3 + d_3 \geq 2$$

With $x_3 = 1$ already defined by the beginning inventory level, the table for stage 3 becomes

d_3		$r_3(x_3,d_3)+f_2(x_2)$			Production capacity of 3 at stage 3		
x_3	0	1	2	3	d_3^*	$f_3(x_3)$	$x_2 = x_3 + d_3^* - 2$
1	—	M	(1280)	1315	2	1280	1

Thus, we find that the total cost associated with the optimal production and inventory policy is $1280. To find the optimal decisions and inventory levels for each period, we trace back through each stage and identify x_n and d_n^* as we go. Table 18.4 summarizes the optimal production and inventory policy.

Try Problem 10 for practice using dynamic programming to solve a production and inventory control problem.

Table 18.4

Optimal Production and Inventory Control Policy

Month	Beginning Inventory	Production	Production Cost	Ending Inventory	Holding Cost	Total Monthly Cost
January	1	2	$ 350	1	$30	$ 380
February	1	2	300	0	0	300
March	0	3	600	0	0	600
Totals			$1250		$30	$1280

NOTES & comments

1. With dynamic programming, as with other management science techniques, the computer can be a valuable computational aid. However, since dynamic programming is a general approach with stage decision problems differing substantially from application to application, no one algorithm or computer software package is available for solving dynamic programs. Some software packages exist for specific types of problems; however, most new applications of dynamic programming will require specially designed software if a computer solution is to be obtained.

2. The introductory illustrations of dynamic programming presented in this chapter are deterministic and involve a finite number of decision alternatives and a finite number of stages. For problems such as these, computations can be organized and carried out in a tabular form. With this structure, the optimization problem at each stage can usually be solved by total enumeration of all possible outcomes. More complex dynamic programming models may include probabilistic components, continuous decision variables, and/or an infinite number of stages. In cases where the optimization problem at each stage involves continuous decision variables, linear programming or calculus-based procedures may be needed to obtain an optimal solution.

Summary

Dynamic programming is an attractive approach to problem solving when it is possible to break a large problem up into interrelated smaller problems. The solution procedure then proceeds recursively, solving one of the smaller problems at each stage. Dynamic programming is not a specific algorithm, but rather an approach to problem solving. Thus, the recursive optimization may be carried out differently for different problems. In any case, it is almost always easier to solve a series of smaller problems than one large one. This is how dynamic programming obtains its power.

Glossary

Dynamic programming An approach to problem solving that permits decomposing a large problem that may be difficult to solve into a number of interrelated smaller problems that are usually easier to solve.

Principle of optimality Regardless of the decisions that have been made at the previous stages, if the decision made at stage n is to be part of an overall optimal solution, the decision made at stage n must be optimal for all remaining stages.

Stages When a large problem is decomposed into a number of subproblems, the dynamic programming solution approach creates a stage to correspond to each of the subproblems.

State variables x_n and x_{n-1} An input state variable x_n and an output state variable x_{n-1} together define the condition of the process at the beginning and end of stage n.

Decision variable d_n A variable representing the possible decisions that can be made at stage n.

Stage transformation function $t_n(x_n, d_n)$ The rule or equation that relates the output state variable x_{n-1} for stage n to the input state variable x_n and the decision variable d_n.

Return function $r_n(x_n, d_n)$ A value (such as profit or loss) associated with making decision d_n at stage n for a specific value of the input state variable x_n.

Knapsack problem Finding the number of N items, each of which has a different weight and value, that can be placed in a knapsack with limited weight capacity so as to maximize the total value of the items placed in the knapsack.

Problems

1. In Section 18.1 we solved a shortest-route problem using dynamic programming. Find the optimal solution to this problem by total enumeration; that is, list all 16 possible routes from the origin, node 1, to the destination, node 10, and pick the one with the smallest value. Explain why dynamic programming results in fewer computations for this problem.

2. 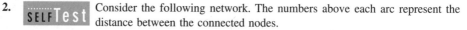 Consider the following network. The numbers above each arc represent the distance between the connected nodes.

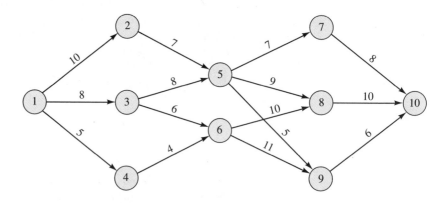

   a. Find the shortest route from node 1 to node 10 using dynamic programming.
   b. What is the shortest route from node 4 to node 10?
   c. Enumerate all possible routes from node 1 to node 10. Explain how dynamic programming has reduced the number of computations to fewer than the number required by total enumeration.

3. 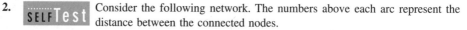 A charter pilot has additional capacity for 2000 pounds of cargo on a flight from Dallas to Seattle. A transport company has four types of cargo in Dallas to be delivered to Seattle. The number of units of each cargo type, the weight per unit, and the delivery fee per unit are shown.

Cargo Type	Units Available	Weight Per Unit (100 pounds)	Delivery Fee ($100)
1	2	8	22
2	2	5	12
3	4	3	7
4	3	2	3

a. Use dynamic programming to find how many units of each cargo type the pilot should contract to deliver.

b. Suppose the pilot agrees to take another passenger and the additional cargo capacity is reduced to 1800 pounds. How does your recommendation change?

4. A firm has just hired eight new employees and would like to determine how to allocate their time to four activities. The firm has prepared the following table, which gives the estimated profit for each activity as a function of the number of new employees allocated to it:

	Number of New Employees								
Activities	0	1	2	3	4	5	6	7	8
1	22	30	37	44	49	54	58	60	61
2	30	40	48	55	59	62	64	66	67
3	46	52	56	59	62	65	67	68	69
4	5	22	36	48	52	55	58	60	61

a. Use dynamic programming to determine the optimal allocation of new employees to the activities.

b. Suppose only six new employees were hired. Which activities would you assign to these employees?

5. A sawmill receives logs in 20-foot lengths, cuts them to smaller lengths, and then sells these smaller lengths to a number of manufacturing companies. The company has orders for the following lengths:

$$l_1 = 3 \text{ ft}$$
$$l_2 = 7 \text{ ft}$$
$$l_3 = 11 \text{ ft}$$
$$l_4 = 16 \text{ ft}$$

The sawmill currently has an inventory of 2000 logs in 20-foot lengths and would like to select a cutting pattern that will maximize the profit made on this inventory. Assuming the sawmill has sufficient orders available, its problem becomes one of determining the cutting pattern that will maximize profits. The per-unit profit for each of the smaller lengths is as follows:

Length (feet)	3	7	11	16
Profit ($)	1	3	5	8

Any cutting pattern is permissible as long as

$$3d_1 + 7d_2 + 11d_3 + 16d_4 \leq 20$$

where d_i is the number of pieces of length l_i cut, $i = 1, 2, 3, 4$.

a. Set up a dynamic programming model of this problem, and solve it. What are your decision variables? What is your state variable?

b. Explain briefly how this model can be extended to find the best cutting pattern in cases where the overall length l can be cut into N lengths, $l_1, l_2, \ldots, l_N$.

6. A large manufacturing company has a well-developed management training program. Each trainee is expected to complete a four-phase program, but there are a number of different assignments that each trainee can be given at each phase of the training program. The

following assignments are available with their estimated completion times in months at each phase of the program.

Phase I	Phase II	Phase III	Phase IV
A–13	E–3	H–12	L–10
B–10	F–6	I–6	M–5
C–20	G–5	J–7	N–13
D–17		K–10	

Assignments made at subsequent phases depend on the previous assignment. For example, a trainee who completes assignment A at phase I may only go on to assignment F or G at phase II—that is, there is a precedence relationship for each assignment.

Assignment	Feasible Succeeding Assignments	Assignment	Feasible Succeeding Assignments
A	F, G	H	L, M
B	F	I	L, M
C	G	J	M, N
D	E, G	K	N
E	H, I, J, K	L	Finish
F	H, K	M	Finish
G	J, K	N	Finish

a. The company would like to determine the sequence of assignments that will minimize the time in the training program. Formulate and solve this as a dynamic programming problem. (*Hint*: Develop a network representation of the problem where each node represents completion of an activity.)

b. If a trainee has just completed assignment F and would like to complete the remainder of the training program in the shortest possible time, which assignment should be chosen next?

7. Crazy Robin, the owner of a small chain of Robin Hood Sporting Goods stores in Des Moines and Cedar Rapids, Iowa, has just purchased a new supply of 500 dozen top-line golf balls. Because she was willing to purchase the entire amount of a production overrun, Robin was able to buy the golf balls at one-half the usual price.

   Three of Robin's stores do a good business in the sale of golf equipment and supplies, and, as a result, Robin has decided to retail the balls at these three stores. Thus, Robin is faced with the problem of determining how many dozen balls to allocate to each store. The following estimates show the expected profit from allocating 100, 200, 300, 400, or 500 dozen to each store:

	Number of Dozens of Golf Balls				
Store	100	200	300	400	500
1	$600	$1100	$1550	$1700	$1800
2	500	1200	1700	2000	2100
3	550	1100	1500	1850	1950

Assuming the lots cannot be broken into any sizes smaller than 100 dozen each, how many dozen golf balls should Crazy Robin send to each store?

8. The Max X. Posure Advertising Agency is conducting a 10-day advertising campaign for a local department store. The agency has determined that the most effective campaign would possibly include placing ads in four media: daily newspaper, Sunday newspaper, radio, and television. A total of $8000 has been made available for this campaign, and the agency would like to distribute this in $1000 increments across the media in such a fashion that an advertising exposure index is maximized. Research that has been conducted by the agency permits the following estimates to be made of the exposure per each $1000 expenditure in each of the media.

Media	Thousands of Dollars Spent							
	1	2	3	4	5	6	7	8
Daily newspaper	24	37	46	59	72	80	82	82
Sunday newspaper	15	55	70	75	90	95	95	95
Radio	20	30	45	55	60	62	63	63
Television	20	40	55	65	70	70	70	70

a. How much should the agency spend on each medium to maximize the department store's exposure?
b. How would your answer change if only $6000 were budgeted?
c. How would your answers in parts (a) and (b) change if television were not considered as one of the media?

9. Suppose we have a three-stage process where the yield for each stage is a function of the decision made. In mathematical notation, we may state our problem as follows:

$$\text{Max} \quad r_1(d_1) + r_2(d_2) + r_3(d_3)$$

s.t.

$$d_1 + d_2 + d_3 \leq 1000$$

The possible values the decision variables may take on at each stage and the corresponding returns are as follows:

Stage 1		Stage 2		Stage 3	
d_1	$r_1(d_1)$	d_2	$r_2(d_2)$	d_3	$r_3(d_3)$
0	0	100	120	100	175
100	110	300	400	500	700
200	300	500	650		
300	400	600	700		
400	425	800	975		

a. Use total enumeration to list all feasible sequences of decisions for this problem. Which one is optimal (i.e., maximizes $r_1(d_1) + r_2(d_2) + r_3(d_3)$)?
b. Use dynamic programming to solve this problem.

10. **SELFTest** Recall the production and inventory control problem of Section 18.4. Mills Manufacturing Company has just such a production and inventory control

problem for an armature the company manufactures as a component for a generator. The available data for the next 3-month planning period are as follows:

Month	Demand	Capacity Production	Capacity Warehouse	Cost Per Unit Production	Cost Per Unit Holding
1	20	30	40	$2.00	$0.30
2	30	20	30	1.50	0.30
3	30	30	20	2.00	0.20

Use dynamic programming to find the optimal production quantities and inventory levels in each period for the Mills Manufacturing Company. Assume there is an inventory of 10 units on hand at the beginning of month 1 and production runs are completed in multiples of 10 units (i.e., 10, 20, or 30 units).

11. A chemical processing plant is considering introducing a new product. However, before making a final decision, management has requested that you provide estimates of profits associated with different process designs. The general flow process is represented:

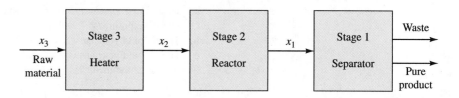

Raw material is fed into a heater at the rate of 4500 pounds per week. The heated material is then routed to a reactor where a portion of the raw material is converted to pure product. A separator then withdraws the finished product for sale. The unconverted material is discarded as waste.

Profit considerations are to be based on a 2-year payback period on investments; that is, all capital expenditures must be recovered in 2 years (100 weeks). All calculations will be based on weekly operations. Raw material costs are expected to stay fixed at $1 per pound, and it has been forecast that the finished product will sell for $6 per pound.

It is your responsibility to determine the process design that will yield maximum profit per week. You and your co-workers have collected the following preliminary data.

One heater with an initial cost of $12,000 is being considered at stage 3. Two temperatures, 700°F and 800°F, are feasible. The operating costs for the heater depend directly on the temperature to be attained. These costs are as follows:

	Operating Costs at Stage 3	
	Decisions at Stage 3	
Input x_3	700°F	800°F
4500 lb	$280/week	$380/week

Stage 3's output x_2, which is also the input to stage 2, may be expressed as 4500 pounds of raw material heated to either 700°F or 800°F. One of the decisions you must make is to what temperature the raw material should be heated.

A reactor, which can operate with either of two catalysts, C1 or C2, is to be used for stage 2. The initial cost of this reactor is $50,000. The operating costs of this reactor are independent of the input x_2 and depend only on the catalyst selected. The costs of the catalysts are included in the operating costs. The output will be expressed in pounds of converted (or pure) material. The percentage of material converted depends on the incoming temperature and the catalyst used. The following tables summarize the pertinent information. Thus, a second decision you must make is to specify which catalyst should be used.

Percent Conversion

	Decisions at Stage 2	
x_2	C1	C2
(4500 lb, 700°F)	20	40
(4500 lb, 800°F)	40	60

Operating Costs
Decision at Stage 2

C1	C2
$450/week	$650/week

One of two separators, S1 or S2, will be purchased for stage 1. The S1 separator has an initial cost of $20,000 and a weekly operating cost of $0.10 per pound of pure product to be separated. Comparatively, S2 has an initial cost of $5000 and a weekly operating cost of $0.20. Included in these operating costs is the expense of discarding the unconverted raw material as waste.

Develop a dynamic programming model for this problem. What is your recommendation for the best temperature for the heater? The best catalyst to use with the reactor? The best separator to purchase? What is the maximum weekly profit?

MANAGEMENT SCIENCE in practice

U.S. Environmental Protection Agency*
Washington, D.C.

The U.S. Environmental Protection Agency (EPA) is an independent agency of the executive branch of the federal government. Fifteen components of five executive departments and independent agencies were consolidated to form the EPA on December 2, 1970, under Reorganization Plan No. 3 by President Nixon. Today, the EPA administers comprehensive environmental protection laws related to the following areas:

- Water pollution control, water quality, and drinking water
- Air pollution and radiation
- Pesticides and toxic substances
- Solid and hazardous waste including emergency spill response and Superfund site remediation

Program offices for each of these media support the EPA administrator through policy development, standards and criteria development, and support and evaluation of regional activities. The ten regional offices implement and enforce standards, conduct monitoring and surveillance programs, and provide technical and financial assistance to state and local governments.

Functional activities at EPA headquarters, which transcend all media, include planning and management, enforcement, and research and development. Management science techniques are used extensively in the experimental design of research studies, providing quality assurance of monitoring surveys and enforcement actions, as well as environmental modeling and simulation studies to evaluate the cost effectiveness of alternative environmental policies, regulations, and control technologies.

The EPA's Office of Research and Development serves as the primary source of scientific and technical support to the agency's operating programs and regional offices by conducting in-house and extramural research at 14 locations throughout the country. Research activities focus on analytical methods, development and quality assurance, environmental processes and effects research, health effects research, and environmental engineering. Environmental modeling is conducted for all media at many of these research locations. The Office of Research and Development maintains a Center for Water Quality Modeling at its laboratory in Athens, Georgia. The following dynamic programming application was developed by the Municipal Environmental Research Laboratory in Cincinnati, Ohio, as part of an effort to evaluate the usefulness of seasonal discharge permits in reducing the cost of wastewater treatment while maintaining water quality.

Water-Quality Management Program

The EPA administers programs designed to maintain acceptable water-quality conditions for rivers and streams throughout theUnited States. To guard against polluted rivers and streams, the government requires companies to obtain a discharge permit from federal or state authorities before any form of pollutants can be discharged into a body of water. These permits specifically notify each discharger as to the amount of legally dischargeable waste that can be placed in the river or stream. The discharge limits are determined by ensuring that water-quality criteria are met even in unusually dry seasons when the river or stream has a critically low flow condition. Most often, this condition is based on the lowest flow recorded over the past ten years. By ensuring that water quality is maintained under the low-flow conditions, there is a high degree of reliability that the water-quality criteria can be maintained throughout the year.

At different seasons of the year, water will flow at different rates in the various rivers and streams. With these seasonal variations, seasonal discharge permits can be issued that allow different discharge limits at the different times of the year. As a result, companies can take advantage of higher stream flow rates to reduce treatment requirements and to lower the discharge treatment costs. A goal of the EPA is to establish seasonal discharge limits that enable lower treatment costs while maintaining water-quality standards at a prescribed level of reliability.

A Dynamic Programming Model for Seasonal Discharge Limits

A dynamic programming model has been formulated for establishing the allowable waste discharge load during the various seasons of the year. The periods or stages of the model correspond to different seasons considered during the year; there is a separate stage for each season. The return function at each stage is the cost of the treatment for waste discharged during that stage. The decision variable at each stage is the design streamflow for the body of water receiving the waste. Once the design streamflow has been established, an allowable waste discharge and its associated treatment cost can be determined. The design streamflow decisions at each stage interact to determine the overall reliability that the annual water-quality conditions will be maintained. In this regard, the decision variable choice at any one stage, or period, is affected by the decision variable choices at the other stages.

....

*The authors are indebted to John Convery, Environmental Protection Agency, for providing this application.

—Continued on next page

—Continued from previous page

The probability that there will be no water-quality violations over the entire year is the product of the seasonal probabilities of no violations. To maintain reliability standards, the probability of no violation during the year must exceed a certain value. Suppose we let $P_j(q_j)$ represent the probability of no violation during season j when the design streamflow is q_j. Then the probability of no water-quality violation over the entire year is given by

$$\prod_{j=1}^{N} P_j(q_j) = \text{probability of no violation}$$

where N is the number of seasons during the year.

The reliability requirement is satisfied when this probability is sufficiently high. Suppose α is the minimal acceptable probability. The water-quality constraint is then

$$\prod_{j=1}^{N} P_j(q_j) \geq \alpha$$

By taking the logarithm of both sides, this constraint can be written as

$$\sum_{j=1}^{N} \log P_j(q_j) \geq \log \alpha$$

The state variable at stage j is then defined to be

$$s_j = \sum_{k=1}^{j} P_k(q_k)$$

The design streamflows (the decision variables) are chosen to minimize treatment cost subject to requirements that the allowable waste discharge be within given limits and that the state variable ensure sufficient reliability of no water-quality violations.

The solution to the model provides the design streamflows for each seasonal period. These streamflows combine with the water-quality criterion to establish the seasonal waste discharge load. With the return function measuring treatment cost, the model obtains the minimum-cost solution that will maintain the EPA water-quality standards.

1. Suppose there are four seasons and the probabilities of a water-quality violation in each season are 0.01, 0.05, 0.02, and 0.01, respectively. What is the probability that there will be no water-quality violation over the entire year?
2. Let P_j = the probability of no water-quality violation in season j. Suppose there are three seasons. Write a constraint specifying that the minimal acceptable probability of no violation over the three seasons is 0.90.

Appendixes

APPENDIX A: Areas for the Standard Normal Distribution

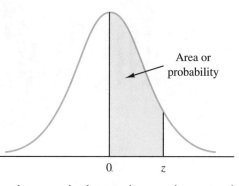

Area or probability

Entries in the table give the area under the curve between the mean and z standard deviations above the mean. For example, for $z = 1.25$ the area under the curve between the mean and z is 0.3944.

z	0.00	0.01	0.02	0.03	0.04	0.05	0.06	0.07	0.08	0.09
0.0	0.0000	0.0040	0.0080	0.0120	0.0160	0.0199	0.0239	0.0279	0.0319	0.0359
0.1	0.0398	0.0438	0.0478	0.0517	0.0557	0.0596	0.0636	0.0675	0.0714	0.0753
0.2	0.0793	0.0832	0.0871	0.0910	0.0948	0.0987	0.1026	0.1064	0.1103	0.1141
0.3	0.1179	0.1217	0.1255	0.1293	0.1331	0.1368	0.1406	0.1443	0.1480	0.1517
0.4	0.1554	0.1591	0.1628	0.1664	0.1700	0.1736	0.1772	0.1808	0.1844	0.1879
0.5	0.1915	0.1950	0.1985	0.2019	0.2054	0.2088	0.2123	0.2157	0.2190	0.2224
0.6	0.2257	0.2291	0.2324	0.2357	0.2389	0.2422	0.2454	0.2486	0.2518	0.2549
0.7	0.2580	0.2612	0.2642	0.2673	0.2704	0.2734	0.2764	0.2794	0.2823	0.2852
0.8	0.2881	0.2910	0.2939	0.2967	0.2995	0.3023	0.3051	0.3078	0.3106	0.3133
0.9	0.3159	0.3186	0.3212	0.3238	0.3264	0.3289	0.3315	0.3340	0.3365	0.3389
1.0	0.3413	0.3438	0.3461	0.3485	0.3508	0.3531	0.3554	0.3577	0.3599	0.3621
1.1	0.3643	0.3665	0.3686	0.3708	0.3729	0.3749	0.3770	0.3790	0.3810	0.3830
1.2	0.3849	0.3869	0.3888	0.3907	0.3925	0.3944	0.3962	0.3980	0.3997	0.4015
1.3	0.4032	0.4049	0.4066	0.4082	0.4099	0.4115	0.4131	0.4147	0.4162	0.4177
1.4	0.4192	0.4207	0.4222	0.4236	0.4251	0.4265	0.4279	0.4292	0.4306	0.4319
1.5	0.4332	0.4345	0.4357	0.4370	0.4382	0.4394	0.4406	0.4418	0.4429	0.4441
1.6	0.4452	0.4463	0.4474	0.4484	0.4495	0.4505	0.4515	0.4525	0.4535	0.4545
1.7	0.4554	0.4564	0.4573	0.4582	0.4591	0.4599	0.4608	0.4616	0.4625	0.4633
1.8	0.4641	0.4649	0.4656	0.4664	0.4671	0.4678	0.4686	0.4693	0.4699	0.4706
1.9	0.4713	0.4719	0.4726	0.4732	0.4738	0.4744	0.4750	0.4756	0.4761	0.4767
2.0	0.4772	0.4778	0.4783	0.4788	0.4793	0.4798	0.4803	0.4808	0.4812	0.4817
2.1	0.4821	0.4826	0.4830	0.4834	0.4838	0.4842	0.4846	0.4850	0.4854	0.4857
2.2	0.4861	0.4864	0.4868	0.4871	0.4875	0.4878	0.4881	0.4884	0.4887	0.4890
2.3	0.4893	0.4896	0.4898	0.4901	0.4904	0.4906	0.4909	0.4911	0.4913	0.4916
2.4	0.4918	0.4920	0.4922	0.4925	0.4927	0.4929	0.4931	0.4932	0.4934	0.4936
2.5	0.4938	0.4940	0.4941	0.4943	0.4945	0.4946	0.4948	0.4949	0.4951	0.4952
2.6	0.4953	0.4955	0.4956	0.4957	0.4959	0.4960	0.4961	0.4962	0.4963	0.4964
2.7	0.4965	0.4966	0.4967	0.4968	0.4969	0.4970	0.4971	0.4972	0.4973	0.4974
2.8	0.4974	0.4975	0.4976	0.4977	0.4977	0.4978	0.4979	0.4979	0.4980	0.4981
2.9	0.4981	0.4982	0.4982	0.4983	0.4984	0.4984	0.4985	0.4985	0.4986	0.4986
3.0	0.4986	0.4987	0.4987	0.4988	0.4988	0.4989	0.4989	0.4989	0.4990	0.4990

APPENDIX B: Random Digits

63271	59986	71744	51102	15141	80714	58683	93108	13554	79945
88547	09896	95436	79115	08303	01041	20030	63754	08459	28364
55957	57243	83865	09911	19761	66535	40102	26646	60147	15702
46276	87453	44790	67122	45573	84358	21625	16999	13385	22782
55363	07449	34835	15290	76616	67191	12777	21861	68689	03263
69393	92785	49902	58447	42048	30378	87618	26933	40640	16281
13186	29431	88190	04588	38733	81290	89541	70290	40113	08243
17726	28652	56836	78351	47327	18518	92222	55201	27340	10493
36520	64465	05550	30157	82242	29520	69753	72602	23756	54935
81628	36100	39254	56835	37636	02421	98063	89641	64953	99337
84649	38968	75215	75498	49539	74240	03466	49292	36401	45525
63291	11618	12613	75055	43915	26488	41116	64531	56827	30825
70502	53225	03655	05915	37140	57051	48393	91322	25653	06543
06426	24771	59935	49801	11082	66762	94477	02494	88215	27191
20711	55609	29430	70165	45406	78484	31639	52009	18873	96927
41990	70538	77191	25860	55204	73417	83920	69468	74972	38712
72452	36618	76298	26678	89334	33938	95567	29380	75906	91807
37042	40318	57099	10528	09925	89773	41335	96244	29002	46453
53766	52875	15987	46962	67342	77592	57651	95508	80033	69828
90585	58955	53122	16025	84299	53310	67380	84249	25348	04332
32001	96293	37203	64516	51530	37069	40261	61374	05815	06714
62606	64324	46354	72157	67248	20135	49804	09226	64419	29457
10078	28073	85389	50324	14500	15562	64165	06125	71353	77669
91561	46145	24177	15294	10061	98124	75732	00815	83452	97355
13091	98112	53959	79607	52244	63303	10413	63839	74762	50289
73864	83014	72457	22682	03033	61714	88173	90835	00634	85169
66668	25467	48894	51043	02365	91726	09365	63167	95264	45643
84745	41042	29493	01836	09044	51926	43630	63470	76508	14194
48068	26805	94595	47907	13357	38412	33318	26098	82782	42851
54310	96175	97594	88616	42035	38093	36745	56702	40644	83514
14877	33095	10924	58013	61439	21882	42059	24177	58739	60170
78295	23179	02771	43464	59061	71411	05697	67194	30495	21157
67524	02865	39593	54278	04237	92441	26602	63835	38032	94770
58268	57219	68124	73455	83236	08710	04284	55005	84171	42596
97158	28672	50685	01181	24262	19427	52106	34308	73685	74246
04230	16831	69085	30802	65559	09205	71829	06489	85650	38707
94879	56606	30401	02602	57658	70091	54986	41394	60437	03195
71446	15232	66715	26385	91518	70566	02888	79941	39684	54315
32886	05644	79316	09819	00813	88407	17461	73925	53037	91904
62048	33711	25290	21526	02223	75947	66466	06232	10913	75336

This table is reproduced with permission from The Rand Corporation, *A Million Random Digits,* The Free Press, New York, 1955 and 1983.

APPENDIX C: Values of $e^{-\lambda}$

λ	$e^{-\lambda}$	λ	$e^{-\lambda}$	λ	$e^{-\lambda}$
0.05	0.9512	2.05	0.1287	4.05	0.0174
0.10	0.9048	2.10	0.1225	4.10	0.0166
0.15	0.8607	2.15	0.1165	4.15	0.0158
0.20	0.8187	2.20	0.1108	4.20	0.0150
0.25	0.7788	2.25	0.1054	4.25	0.0143
0.30	0.7408	2.30	0.1003	4.30	0.0136
0.35	0.7047	2.35	0.0954	4.35	0.0129
0.40	0.6703	2.40	0.0907	4.40	0.0123
0.45	0.6376	2.45	0.0863	4.45	0.0117
0.50	0.6065	2.50	0.0821	4.50	0.0111
0.55	0.5769	2.55	0.0781	4.55	0.0106
0.60	0.5488	2.60	0.0743	4.60	0.0101
0.65	0.5220	2.65	0.0707	4.65	0.0096
0.70	0.4966	2.70	0.0672	4.70	0.0091
0.75	0.4724	2.75	0.0639	4.75	0.0087
0.80	0.4493	2.80	0.0608	4.80	0.0082
0.85	0.4274	2.85	0.0578	4.85	0.0078
0.90	0.4066	2.90	0.0550	4.90	0.0074
0.95	0.3867	2.95	0.0523	4.95	0.0071
1.00	0.3679	3.00	0.0498	5.00	0.0067
1.05	0.3499	3.05	0.0474	5.05	0.0064
1.10	0.3329	3.10	0.0450	5.10	0.0061
1.15	0.3166	3.15	0.0429	5.15	0.0058
1.20	0.3012	3.20	0.0408	5.20	0.0055
1.25	0.2865	3.25	0.0388	5.25	0.0052
1.30	0.2725	3.30	0.0369	5.30	0.0050
1.35	0.2592	3.35	0.0351	5.35	0.0047
1.40	0.2466	3.40	0.0334	5.40	0.0045
1.45	0.2346	3.45	0.0317	5.45	0.0043
1.50	0.2231	3.50	0.0302	5.50	0.0041
1.55	0.2122	3.55	0.0287	5.55	0.0039
1.60	0.2019	3.60	0.0273	5.60	0.0037
1.65	0.1920	3.65	0.0260	5.65	0.0035
1.70	0.1827	3.70	0.0247	5.70	0.0033
1.75	0.1738	3.75	0.0235	5.75	0.0032
1.80	0.1653	3.80	0.0224	5.80	0.0030
1.85	0.1572	3.85	0.0213	5.85	0.0029
1.90	0.1496	3.90	0.0202	5.90	0.0027
1.95	0.1423	3.95	0.0193	5.95	0.0026
2.00	0.1353	4.00	0.0183	6.00	0.0025
				7.00	0.0009
				8.00	0.000335
				9.00	0.000123
				10.00	0.000045

APPENDIX D: Matrix Notation and Operations

Matrix Notation

A matrix is a rectangular arrangement of numbers. For example, consider the following matrix which we have named D:

$$D = \begin{bmatrix} 1 & 3 & 2 \\ 0 & 4 & 5 \end{bmatrix}$$

The matrix D is said to consist of six elements, where each element of D is a number. In order to identify a particular element of a matrix, we have to specify its location. To do this, we introduce the concepts of rows and columns.

All elements across some horizontal line in a matrix are said to be in a row of the matrix. For example, elements 1, 3, and 2 in D are in the first row, and elements 0, 4, and 5 are in the second row. By convention, we refer to the top row as row 1, the second row from the top as row 2, and so on.

All elements along some vertical line are said to be in a column of the matrix. Elements 1 and 0 in D are elements in the first column, elements 3 and 4 are elements of the second column, and elements 2 and 5 are elements of the third column. By convention, we refer to the leftmost column as column 1, the next column to the right as column 2, and so on.

We can identify a particular element in a matrix by specifying its row and column position. For example, the element in row 1 and column 2 of D is the number 3. This is written as

$$d_{12} = 3$$

In general, we use the following notation to refer to specific elements of D:

$$d_{ij} = \text{element located in the } i\text{th row and } j\text{th column of } D$$

We always use capital letters for the names of matrices and the corresponding lowercase letters with two subscripts to denote the elements.

The *size* of a matrix is the number of rows and columns in the matrix and is written as the number of rows × the number of columns. Thus, the size of D is 2×3.

Frequently we will encounter matrices that have only one row or one column. For example,

$$G = \begin{bmatrix} 6 \\ 4 \\ 2 \\ 3 \end{bmatrix}$$

is a matrix that has only one column. Whenever a matrix that has only one column, we call the matrix a column vector. In a similar manner, any matrix that has only one row is called a row vector. Using our previous notation for the elements of a matrix, we would refer to specific elements in G by writing g_{ij}. However, since G has only one column, the column position is unimportant, and we need only specify the row the element of interest is in. That is, instead of referring to elements in a vector using g_{ij}, we specify only one subscript, which denotes the position of the element in the vector. For example,

$$g_1 = 6 \qquad g_2 = 4 \qquad g_3 = 2 \qquad g_4 = 3$$

Matrix Operations

Matrix Transpose

The transpose of a matrix is formed by making the rows in the original matrix the columns in the transpose matrix, and by making the columns in the original matrix the rows in the transpose matrix. For example, if the transpose of the matrix

$$D = \begin{bmatrix} 1 & 3 & 2 \\ 0 & 4 & 5 \end{bmatrix}$$

is

$$D^t = \begin{bmatrix} 1 & 0 \\ 3 & 4 \\ 2 & 5 \end{bmatrix}$$

Note that we use the superscript t to denote the transpose of a matrix.

Matrix Multiplication

We will demonstrate how to perform two types of matrix multiplication: (1) multiplying two vectors, and (2) multiplying a matrix times a matrix.

The product of a row vector of size $1 \times n$ times a column vector of size $n \times 1$ is the number obtained by multiplying the first element in the row vector times the first element in the column vector, the second element in the row vector times the second element in the column vector, and continuing on through the last element in the row vector times the last element in the column vector, and then summing the products. Suppose, for example, that we wanted to multiply the row vector H times the column vector G, where

$$H = \begin{bmatrix} 2 & 1 & 5 & 0 \end{bmatrix} \text{ and } G = \begin{bmatrix} 6 \\ 4 \\ 2 \\ 3 \end{bmatrix}$$

The product HG, referred to as a vector product, is given by

$$HG = 2(6) + 1(4) + 5(2) + 0(3) = 26$$

The product of a matrix of size $p \times n$ and a matrix of size $n \times m$ is a new matrix of size $p \times m$. The element in the ith row and jth column of the new matrix is given by the vector product of the ith row of the $p \times n$ matrix times the jth column of the $n \times m$ matrix. Suppose, for example, that we want to multiply D times A, where

$$D = \begin{bmatrix} 1 & 3 & 2 \\ 0 & 4 & 5 \end{bmatrix} \quad A = \begin{bmatrix} 1 & 3 & 5 \\ 2 & 0 & 4 \\ 1 & 5 & 2 \end{bmatrix}$$

Let $C = DA$ denote the product of D times A. The element in row 1 and column 1 of C is given by the vector product of the first row of D times the first column of A. Thus

$$c_{11} = \begin{bmatrix} 1 & 3 & 2 \end{bmatrix} \begin{bmatrix} 1 \\ 2 \\ 1 \end{bmatrix} = 1(1) + 3(2) + 2(1) = 9$$

The element in row 2 and column 1 of C is given by the vector product of the second row of D times the first column of A. Thus,

$$c_{21} = \begin{bmatrix} 0 & 4 & 5 \end{bmatrix} \begin{bmatrix} 1 \\ 2 \\ 1 \end{bmatrix} = 0(1) + 4(2) + 5(1) = 13$$

Calculating the remaining elements of C in a similar fashion, we obtain

$$C = \begin{bmatrix} 9 & 13 & 21 \\ 13 & 25 & 26 \end{bmatrix}$$

Clearly, the product of a matrix and a vector is just a special case of multiplying a matrix times a matrix. For example, the product of a matrix of size $m \times n$ and a vector of size $n \times 1$ is a new vector of size $m \times 1$. The element in the ith position of the new vector is given by the vector product of the ith row of the $m \times n$ matrix times the $n \times 1$ column vector. Suppose, for example, that we want to multiply D times K, where

$$D = \begin{bmatrix} 1 & 3 & 2 \\ 0 & 4 & 5 \end{bmatrix} \quad K = \begin{bmatrix} 1 \\ 4 \\ 2 \end{bmatrix}$$

The first element of DK is given by the vector product of the first row of D times K. Thus,

$$\begin{bmatrix} 1 & 3 & 2 \end{bmatrix} \begin{bmatrix} 1 \\ 4 \\ 2 \end{bmatrix} = 1(1) + 3(4) + 2(2) = 17$$

The second element of DK is given by the vector product of the second row of D and K. Thus,

$$\begin{bmatrix} 0 & 4 & 5 \end{bmatrix} \begin{bmatrix} 1 \\ 4 \\ 2 \end{bmatrix} = 0(1) + 4(4) + 5(2) = 26$$

Hence, we see that the product of the matrix D times the vector K is given by

$$DK = \begin{bmatrix} 1 & 3 & 2 \\ 0 & 4 & 5 \end{bmatrix} \begin{bmatrix} 1 \\ 4 \\ 2 \end{bmatrix} = \begin{bmatrix} 17 \\ 26 \end{bmatrix}$$

Can any two matrices be multiplied? The answer is no. In order to multiply two matrices, the number of the columns in the first matrix must equal the number of rows in the second. If this property is satisfied, the matrices are said to conform for multiplication. Thus, in our example, D and K could be multiplied because D had three columns and K had three rows.

Matrix Inverse   The inverse of any square matrix A consisting of two rows and two columns, denoted by A^{-1}, is computed as follows:

$$A = \begin{bmatrix} a_{11} & a_{12} \\ a_{21} & a_{22} \end{bmatrix}$$

$$A^{-1} = \begin{bmatrix} a_{22}/d & -a_{12}/d \\ -a_{21}/d & a_{11}/d \end{bmatrix}$$

where $d = a_{11}a_{22} - a_{21}a_{12}$ is the determinant of the 2×2 matrix A. For example, if

$$A = \begin{bmatrix} 0.7 & -0.3 \\ -0.3 & 0.9 \end{bmatrix}$$

then

$$d = (0.7)(0.9) - (-0.3)(-0.3) = 0.54$$

and

$$A^{-1} = \begin{bmatrix} 0.9/0.54 & 0.3/0.54 \\ 0.3/0.54 & 0.7/0.54 \end{bmatrix} = \begin{bmatrix} 1.67 & 0.56 \\ 0.56 & 1.30 \end{bmatrix}$$

APPENDIX E: References and Bibliography

The Role and Nature of Management Science (Chapter 1)

Churchman, C. W., R. L. Ackoff, and E. L. Arnoff, *Introduction to Operations Research.* New York: Wiley, 1957.

Forgionne, G. A., "Corporate Management Science Activities: An Update." *Interfaces,* vol. 13, no. 3, 1983, pp. 20–23.

Hillier, F., and G. J. Lieberman, *Introduction to Operations Research,* 4th ed. San Francisco: Holden-Day, 1986.

Ledbetter, W. and J. Cox, "Are OR Techniques Being Used?" *Industrial Engineering,* vol. 9, 1977, pp. 19–21.

Shannon, R. E., S. S. Long, and B. P. Buckles, "Operations Research Methodologies in Industrial Engineering: A Survey." *AIIE Transactions,* vol. 12, no. 4, 1980, pp. 364–367.

Thomas, G., and J. DaCosta, "A Sample Survey of Corporate Operations Research." *Interfaces,* August 1979.

Thomas G., and M. Mitchell, "OR in the U.S. Marine Corps: A Characterization." *Interfaces,* June 1983.

Linear Programming, Transportation, Assignment and Transshipment Problems (Chapters 2 to 7)

Bazarra, M. S., J. J. Jarvis and H. D. Sherali, *Linear Programming and Network Flows,* 2d ed. New York: Wiley, 1990.

Bradley, S. P., A. C. Hax, and T. L. Magnanti, *Applied Mathematical Programming.* Reading, Mass.: Addison-Wesley, 1977.

Charnes, A., W. W. Cooper, and E. Rhodes, "Measuring Efficiency of Decision Making Units." *European Journal of Operations Research,* vol. 2, 1978, pp. 429–449.

Dantzig, G. B., *Linear Programming and Extensions.* Princeton, N.J.: Princeton University Press, 1963.

Hillier, F., and G. J. Lieberman, *Introduction to Operations Research,* 4th ed. San Francisco: Holden-Day, 1986.

Hooker, J. N., "Karmarkar's Linear Programming Algorithm." *Interfaces,* vol. 16, no. 4, 1986, pp. 75–90.

Lewin, A. Y., and R. C. Morey, "Measuring the Relative Efficiency and Output Potential of Public Sector Organizations: An Application of Data Envelopment Analysis." *International Journal of Policy Analysis and Information Systems,* vol. 5, no. 4, 1981, pp. 267–285.

Schrage, L., *LINDO: An Optimization Modeling System,* 4th ed. South San Francisco, Calif.: Scientific Press, 1986.

Schrage, L., *User's Manual for Linear, Integer, and Quadratic Programming with LINDO.* Redwood City, Calif.: Scientific Press, 1989.

Sherman, H. D., "Hospital Efficiency Measurement and Evaluation." *Medical Care,* vol. 22, no. 10, October 1984, pp. 922–938.

Winston, W. L., *Operations Research: Applications and Algorithms,* 3rd. ed. Belmont, Calif.: Duxbury Press, 1994.

Integer Linear Programming (Chapter 8)

Garfinkel, R. S., and G. L. Nemhauser, *Integer Programming.* New York: Wiley, 1972.

Nemhauser, G. L., and L. A. Wolsey, *Integer and Combinatorial Optimization.* New York: Wiley, 1988.

Parker, G., and R. Rardin, *Discrete Optimization.* San Diego: Academic Press, 1988.

Salkin, H. M., *Integer Programming.* Reading, Mass.: Addison-Wesley, 1975.

Winston, W. L., *Operations Research: Applications and Algorithms,* 3rd ed. Belmont, Calif.: Duxbury Press, 1994.

Network Models (Chapter 9)

Bazarra, M. S., J. J. Jarvis, and H. D. Sherali, *Linear Programming and Network Flows,* 2d ed. New York: Wiley, 1977.

Glover, F., and D. Klingman, "Network Application in Industry and Government." *AIIE Transactions,* December 1977.

Ford, L. R., and D. R. Fulkerson, *Flows and Networks.* Princeton, N.J.: Princeton University Press, 1962.

Jensen, P., and J. W. Barnes, *Network Flow Programming.* New York: Wiley, 1980.

Minieka, Edward, and J. R. Evans, *Optimization Algorithms for Networks and Graphs,* 2d ed. New York: Marcel Dekker, 1992.

Project Scheduling: PERT/CPM (Chapter 10)

Evarts, H. F., *Introduction to PERT.* Boston: Allyn & Bacon, 1964.

Moder, J. J., and C. R. Phillips, *Project Management with CPM and PERT,* 2d ed. New York: Van Nostrand, 1970.

Wasil, E. A., and A. A. Assad, "Project Management on the PC: Software, Applications, and Trends," *Interfaces,* vol. 18, no. 2, March–April 1988, pp. 75–84.

Wiest, J., and F. Levy, *Management Guide to PERT-CPM,* 2d ed. Englewood Cliffs, N.J.: Prentice-Hall, 1977.

Inventory Models (Chapter 11)

Buffa, E. S., and W. Taubert, *Production-Inventory Systems: Planning and Control,* 3rd ed. Homewood, Ill.: Richard D. Irwin, 1979.

Davis, E. W., *Case Studies in Material Requirements Planning.* Washington, D.C.: APICS, 1978.

Fogarty, D. W., J. H. Blackstone, Jr., and T. R. Hoffman, *Production and Inventory Management.* Cincinnati: SouthWestern, 1991.

Hadley, G., and T. M. Whitin, *Analysis of Inventory Systems.* Englewood Cliffs, N.J.: Prentice-Hall, 1963.

Hillier, F., and G. J. Lieberman, *Introduction to Operations Research,* 4th ed. San Francisco: Holden-Day, 1986.

Narasimhan, S., D. W. McLeavey, and P. Billington, *Production Planning and Inventory Control,* 2d ed. Englewood Cliffs, N.J.: Prentice-Hall, 1995.

Orlicky, J., *Material Requirements Planning.* New York: McGraw-Hill, 1975.

Plossl, G. W., *Manufacturing Control: The Last Frontier for Profits.* Reston, Va.: Reston, 1973.

Vollman, T. E., W. L. Berry, and D. C. Whybark, *Manufacturing Planning and Control Systems,* 3rd ed. Homewood, Ill.: Richard D. Irwin, 1992.

Waiting Lines (Chapter 12)

Cooper, R. B., *Introduction to Queueing Theory,* 2d ed. New York: North-Holland, 1981.

Cox, D. R., and W. L. Smith, *Queues.* New York: Wiley, 1965.

Gross, D., and C. M. Harris, *Fundamentals of Queueing Theory,* 2d ed. New York: Wiley, 1985.

Hall, R., *Queuing Methods for Service and Manufacturing.* Englewood Cliffs, N.J.: Prentice-Hall, 1991.

Hillier, F., and G. J. Lieberman, *Introduction to Operations Research,* 4th ed. San Francisco: Holden-Day, 1986.

Simulation (Chapter 13)

Banks, J., and J. Carson, Discrete-Event System Simulation. Englewood Cliffs, N.J.: Prentice-Hall, 1984.

Christy, D. P., and H. J. Watson, "The Application of Simulation: A Survey of Industry Practice." *Interfaces,* October 1983.

Fishman, George S., *Principles of Discrete Event Simulation.* New York: Wiley, 1978.

Law, A. M., and W. D. Kelton, *Simulation Modeling and Analysis,* 2d ed. New York: McGraw-Hill, 1991.

Naylor, T. H., *Computer Simulation Experiments with Models of Economic Systems.* New York: Wiley, 1971.

Naylor, T. H., J. L. Balintfy, D. S. Burdick, and K. Chu, *Computer Simulation Techniques.* New York: Wiley, 1968.

Schmidt, J. W., and R. E. Taylor, *Simulation and Analysis of Industrial Systems.* Homewood, Ill.: Richard D. Irwin, 1970.

Thesen, A. and L. Travis, *Simulation for Decision Making.* St Paul: West Publishing, 1992.

Decision Analysis (Chapter 14)

Behn, R. D., and J. W. Vaupel, *Quick Analysis for Busy Decision Makers.* New York: Basic Books, 1982.

Berger, J. O., *Statistical Decision Theory and Bayesian Analysis,* 2d ed. New York: Springer-Verlag, 1985.

Bunn, D., *Applied Decision Analysis.* New York: McGraw-Hill, 1984.

Chernoff, H., and L. E. Moses, *Elementary Decision Theory.* New York: Wiley, 1959.

Fishburn, P. C., "Foundations of Decision Analysis: Along the Way." *Management Science,* vol. 35, no. 4, April 1989, pp. 387–405.

French, S., *Decision Theory.* New York: Wiley, 1986.

Keeney, R. L., and H. Raiffa, *Decisions with Multiple Objectives: Preferences and Value Trade Offs.* New York: Wiley, 1976.

Raiffa, H., *Decision Analysis: Introductory Lectures on Choices Under Uncertainty.* Reading, Mass.: Addison-Wesley, 1968.

Samson, D., *Managerial Decision Analysis.* Homewood, Ill.: Irwin, 1988.

Schlaifer, R., *Analysis of Decisions under Uncertainty.* New York: McGraw-Hill, 1969.

Winkler, R. L., *An Introduction to Bayesian Inference and Decision.* New York: Holt, Rinehart & Winston, 1972.

Winkler, R. L., and W. L. Hays, *Statistics: Probability, Inference and Decision,* 2d ed. New York: Holt, Rinehart & Winston, 1975.

Multicriteria Decision Problems (Chapter 15)

Baird, B. F., *Managerial Decisions Under Uncertainty.* New York: Wiley, 1989.

Bunn, D. W., *Analysis for Optimal Decisions.* New York: Wiley, 1982.

Dyer, J. S., "A Clarification of Remarks on the Analytic Hierarchy Process." *Management Science,* vol. 36, no. 3, March 1990, pp. 274–275.

Dyer, J. S., "Remarks on the Analytic Hierarchy Process." *Management Science,* vol. 36, no. 3, March 1990, pp. 249–258.

Harker, P. T., and L. G. Vargas, "The Theory of Ratio Scale Estimation: Saaty's Analytic Hierarchy Process." *Management Science,* vol. 33, no. 11, November 1987, pp. 1383–1403.

Harker, P. T., and L. G. Vargas, "Reply to Remarks on the Analytic Hierarchy Process by J. S. Dyer." *Management Science,* vol. 36, no. 3, March 1990, pp. 269–273.

Ignizio, J. P., *Goal Programming and Extensions.* Lexington, Mass.: D. C. Heath, 1976.

Keeney, R. L., and H. Raiffa, *Decisions with Multiple Objectives: Preferences and Value Tradeoffs.* New York: Wiley, 1976.

Lee, S. M., *Goal Programming for Decision Analysis.* Philadelphia: Auerbach, 1972.

Saaty, T., *The Analytic Hierarachy Process.* Pittsburgh, Pa.: 1988.

Saaty, T. L., "An Exposition of the AHP in Reply to the Paper Remarks on the Analytic Hierarchy Process." *Management Science,* Vol. 36, No. 3, March 1990, pp. 259–268.

Saaty, T. L., "Rank Generation, Preservation, and Reversal in the Analytic Hierarchy Decision Process." *Decision Sciences,* vol. 18, 1987, pp. 157–177.

Weiss, E. N., and V. R. Rao, "AHP Design Issues for Large-Scale Systems." *Decision Sciences,* vol. 18, 1987, pp. 43–61.

Winkler, R. L., "Decision Modeling and Rational Choice: AHP and Utility Theory." *Management Science,* vol. 36, no. 3, March 1990, pp. 247–248.

Zahedi, F., "Analytic Hierarchy Process—A Survey of the Method and its Applications." *Interfaces,* vol. 16, no. 4, August 1986, pp. 96–108.

Forecasting (Chapter 16)

Bowerman, B. L., and R. T. O'Connell, *Time Series Forecasting,* 2d ed. Boston: PWS-Kent, 1987.

Box, G. E. P., and G. M. Jenkins, *Time Series Analysis: Forecasting and Control,* rev. ed. San Francisco: Holden-Day, 1976.

Gilchrist, W. G., *Statistical Forecasting.* New York: Wiley, 1976.

Hanke, J. E., and A. G. Reitsch, *Business Forecasting,* 2d ed. Boston: Allyn & Bacon, 1986.

Makridakis, S., S. C. Wheelwright, and Victor E. McGee, *Forecasting: Methods and Applications.* 2d ed. New York: Wiley, 1983.

Nelson, C. R., *Applied Time Series Analysis.* San Francisco: Holden-Day, 1973.

Thomopoulos, N. T., *Applied Forecasting Methods.* Englewood Cliffs, N.J.: Prentice-Hall, 1980.

Wheelwright, S. C., and S. Makridakis, *Forecasting Models for Management,* 4th ed. New York: Wiley, 1985.

Wilson, J. H., and B. Keating, *Business Forecasting.* Homewood, Ill.: Richard D. Irwin, 1990.

Markov Processes (Chapter 17)

Bhat, N., *Elements of Applied Stochastic Processes,* 2d ed. New York: Wiley, 1985.

Howard, R. A., *Dynamic Programming and Markov Processes.* Cambridge, Mass.: M.I.T. Press, 1960.

Kemeny, J. G., and J. L. Snell, *Finite Markov Chains.* Englewood Cliffs, N.J.: Prentice-Hall, 1960.

Dynamic Programming (Chapter 18)

Bersetkas, *Dynamic Programming,* Englewood Cliffs, N.J.: Prentice Hall, 1987.

Bellman, R., *Dynamic Programming.* Princeton, N.J.: Princeton University Press, 1957.

Dreyfus, S., and A. M. Law, *The Art and Theory of Dynamic Programming.* New York: Academic Press, 1977.

Nemhauser, G. L., *Introduction to Dynamic Programming.* New York: Wiley, 1967.

APPENDIX F: Answers to Even-Numbered Problems

Chapter 1

2. Methodological developments based on research advances in computer technology

4. The problem is large, complex, important, new, and repetitive

6. Iconic—scale model of a new building
   Analog—barometer
   Mathematical—inventory cost equation

8. **a.** Max $10x + 5y$
   s.t.
   $$5x + 2y \leq 40$$
   $$x \geq 0, y \geq 0$$
   b. Controllable inputs: x and y
   Uncontrollable inputs: profit, labor-hours per unit, and total labor-hours available
   d. $x = 0, y = 20$, profit $= \$100$

10. If $a = 3$, $x = 13\frac{1}{3}$ and profit $= \$133$
    If $a = 4$, $x = 10$ and profit $= \$100$
    If $a = 5$, $x = 8$ and profit $= \$80$
    If $a = 6$, $x = 6\frac{2}{3}$ and profit $= \$67$

12. A deterministic model with $d =$ distance, $m =$ miles per gallon, and $c =$ cost per gallon, where total cost $= (2d/m)c$

14. Quicker to formulate, easier to solve, and/or more easily understood

16. **a.** 4706
    b. Loss $12,000
    c. $23
    d. $11,800

18. **a.** Max $6x + 4y$
    b. $50x + 30y \leq 80,000$
    $50x \qquad \leq 50,000$
    $\qquad 30y \leq 45,000$

Chapter 2

6. $-\frac{7}{10}, -\frac{3}{2}, \frac{4}{7}$

10. $x_1 = 100, x_2 = 50, z = 750$

12. **a.** $x_1 = 3, x_2 = 1.5, z = 13.5$

14. **a.** Feasible region consists of a line segment
    b. (5,1) and (2,4)
    c. $x_1 = 2, x_2 = 4$

16. **a.** $x_1 = 300, x_2 = 420, z = 10,560$
    b. $x_1 = 708, x_2 = 0, z = 14,160$
    c. Sewing constraint is redundant; optimal solution is still $x_1 = 540, x_2 = 252$

20. **b.** $x_1 = \frac{20}{3}, x_2 = \frac{8}{3}, z = 30\frac{2}{3}$
    c. $s_1 = \frac{28}{3}, s_2 = 0, s_3 = 0$

22. **a.** Max $5x_1 + 8x_2$
    s.t.
    $$1x_1 + \tfrac{3}{2}x_2 \leq 900$$
    $$\tfrac{1}{2}x_1 + \tfrac{1}{3}x_2 \leq 300$$
    $$\tfrac{1}{8}x_1 + \tfrac{1}{4}x_2 \leq 100$$
    $$x_1, x_2 \geq 0$$
    b. $x_1 = 500, x_2 = 150$
    c. $3700
    d. 725, 300, 100
    e. 175, 0, 0

24. **a.** Max $50x_1 + 80x_2$
    s.t.
    $$x_1 + x_2 = 1000$$
    $$x_1 \qquad \geq 250$$
    $$\qquad x_2 \geq 250$$
    $$x_1 - 2x_2 \geq 0$$
    $$x_1, x_2 \geq 0$$
    b. $x_1 = 333.33, x_2 = 666.67, z = 70,000.10$

26. **a.** Max $1x_1 + 1.25x_2$
    s.t.
    $$5x_1 + 7x_2 \leq 4480$$
    $$3x_1 + 1x_2 \leq 2080$$
    $$2x_1 + 2x_2 \leq 1600$$
    $$x_1, x_2 \geq 0$$
    d. $x_1 = 560, x_2 = 240, z = 860$

28. **b.** $x_1 = 158\frac{1}{3}, x_2 = 25$, profit $= 7583$
    c. $1x_2 \geq 1x_1$ or $-1x_1 + 1x_2 \geq 0$
    d. $x_1 = 75, x_2 = 75$, profit $= 6750$

30.

Extreme Points	Objective Function Value	Surplus Demand	Surplus Total Production	Slack Processing Time
(250, 100)	800	125	—	—
(125, 225)	925	—	—	125
(125, 350)	1300	—	125	—

32. **b.** $(4, 1), (2\frac{1}{4}, \frac{9}{4})$
    c. $x_1 = 4, x_2 = 1$

34. 15 ounces of Bark Bits, $\frac{5}{2}$ ounces of Canine Chow, $z = 1.025$

36. **a.** Min $2.5A + 2B$
    s.t.
    $$2A + 1.5B \geq 1.7$$
    $$2A + 3B \leq 2.8$$
    $$4A + 3B \leq 3.6$$
    $$A + B = 1$$
    $$A, B \geq 0$$
    b. $A = 0.6, B = 0.4, z = \$0.022$
    c. .1, .4, 0, 0
    d. $0.176

38. $x_1 = 30$, $x_2 = 25$, cost = \$55
40. Infeasibility
42. a. $x_1 = {}^{30}\!/_{16}$, $x_2 = {}^{30}\!/_{16}$, $z = {}^{60}\!/_{16}$
　　b. $x_1 = 0$, $x_2 = 3$, $z = 6$
　　c. Max $x_1 + {}^5\!/_3\, x_2$
44. a. 180, 20
　　b. Alternative optimal solutions
　　c. 120, 80
46. Solution becomes infeasible
48. a. No feasible solution
　　b. 1.5 additional tons of material 3
50. $20 \leq c_2 \leq 50$
52. a. $x_1 = 3$, $x_2 = 7$, $z = 27$
　　b. $1 \leq c_1 \leq 3$
　　c. $2 \leq c_2 \leq 6$
　　d. Same solution is optimal
　　e. New optimal solution has alternate optima
54. a. $x_1 = 1$, $x_2 = 3$, $z = 4$
　　b. $\frac{1}{2} \leq c_1 \leq 2$
　　c. $\frac{1}{2} \leq c_2 \leq 2$
　　d. Same solution is optimal
　　e. New optimal solution is $x_1 = 0$, $x_2 = 5$
56. a. $x_1 = 7$, $x_2 = 7$
　　b. $3 \leq c_1 \leq 10.5$
　　c. ${}^{10}\!/_3 \leq c_2 \leq {}^{35}\!/_3$
　　d. New optimal solution is $x_1 = 0$, $x_2 = 10$; the value is 70
　　e. Same solution is optimal
58. a. Optimal solution does not change
　　b. $x_1 = 6$, $x_2 = 4$, $z = 26$
60. $x_1 = 65.45$, $x_2 = 261.82$, $z = \$45{,}818$
62. $x_1 = 384$, $x_2 = 80$
64. a. Max $160\, x_1 + 345 x_2$
　　　s.t.

$$
\begin{aligned}
x_1 + \quad x_2 &\leq 15 \\
x_2 &\leq 10 \\
x_1 \qquad\quad &\geq 5 \\
x_2 &\geq 5 \\
40x_1 + \quad 50x_2 &\leq 1000 \\
x_1, x_2 &\geq 0
\end{aligned}
$$

　　b. $x_1 = 12.5$, $x_2 = 10$

Chapter 3

2. a. $4 \leq c_1 \leq 12$　　$3.33 \leq c_2 \leq 10$
　　c.

Min RHS	Max RHS
725	No upper limit
133.33	400
75	135

　　d. \$560

4. a. More than \$7.00
　　b. More than \$3.50
　　c. None
6. a. $x_1 = 4000$, $x_2 = 10{,}000$; total risk = 62,000
　　b. $3.75 \leq c_1 \leq$ No upper limit
　　　No lower limit $\leq c_2 \leq 6.4$
　　c. \$60,000
　　d. 5%
　　e. .057 risk units
　　f. 5.7%
8. a. $x_1 = 0$, $x_2 = 25$, $x_3 = 125$, $x_4 = 0$; $z = 525$
　　b. A and C
　　c. B; 425 hours
　　d. Yes
10. a. $x_1 = 7.30$, $x_2 = 0$, $x_3 = 1.89$, $z = 139.73$
　　b. Two and three
　　c. 0, -3.41, and -4.43
　　d. Decrease the right-hand side of constraint 3 from 20 to 19
12. a. All Pro: 1000; College: 200; High School: 0
　　b. Sewing and minimum All Pro production requirement
　　c. 4000 minutes of unused cutting and dyeing time; all the sewing time is being used; 5200 minutes of unused inspection and packaging time; only the minimum number of All Pro models is being produced
　　d. No lower limit $< c_1 \leq 5$
　　　$5 \leq c_2 <$ No upper limit
　　　No lower limit $< c_3 \leq 4$
14. a. $x_1 = 25$, $x_2 = 0$, $x_3 = 25$, profit = 1250
　　b. Machine 1: 31.25, machine 2: 37.50
　　c. \$12.50
　　d. $x_1 = 24$, $x_2 = 8$, $x_3 = 16$, profit = \$1440
16. a. 333.3, 0, 833.3, 2500; risk = 14,666.7, return = 18,000 (9%)
　　b. 1000, 0, 0, 2500; risk = 18,000, return = 22,000 (11%)
　　c. \$4000
18. RS = 20,000, RT = 180,000, SS = 75,000, ST = 0, $z = 1{,}401{,}000$
20. a. Relevant
　　b. $x_1 = 10{,}000$, $x_2 = 6000$, $x_3 = 4{,}000$, $z = \$29{,}000$
　　c. \$2.90 is the maximum premium (over the normal price of \$1.00) that LaJolla Beverage Products should be willing to pay to obtain one additional gallon of wine.
　　d. No
　　e. Requiring 50% plus one gallon of white wine would reduce profit by \$2.40.
22. a. $x_1 = 4181$, $x_2 = 41{,}806$, $x_3 = 30{,}000$
　　c. Total cost will decrease by \$0.2210

Chapter 4

2. a. $x_1 = 77.89$, $x_2 = 63.16$, \$3284.21
　　b. Department A \$15.79; department B \$47.37
　　c. $x_1 = 87.21$, $x_2 = 65.12$, \$3341.34
　　　Department A 10 hours; department B 3.2 hours

4. a. $x_1 = 500$, $x_2 = 300$, $x_3 = 200$, \$550

   b. \$0.55

   c. Aroma 75; taste 84.4

   d. \$0.60

6. 50 units of product 1; 0 units of product 2

   300 hours department A; 600 hours department B

8. Schedule 19 officers as follows:

   3 begin at 8:00 A.M.; 3 begin at noon; 7 begin at 4:00 P.M.; 4 begin at midnight; 2 begin at 4:00 A.M.

10.

Product	Modern Line	Old Line
1	500	0
2	300	400

   Cost = \$3850

12. a. Purchase 5000 bases

   b. Same solution with objective function increased by \$80

   c. Yes; total cost = \$24,293.33; FCP = 1333 and FCM = 1667

14. b.

Quarter	Production	Ending Inventory
1	4000	2100
2	3000	1100
3	2000	100
4	1900	500

16. x_1 = number of 10-inch rolls processed by cutting alternative i

   a. $x_1 = 0$, $x_2 = 125$, $x_3 = 500$, $x_4 = 1500$, $x_5 = 0$, $x_6 = 0$, $x_7 = 0$; 2125 rolls with waste of 750 inches

   b. 2500 rolls with no waste; however, 1½ inch size is overproduced by 3000 units

18. a. 5 super, 2 regular, and 3 econotankers

   b. Total cost \$583,000; monthly operating cost \$4650

20. Produce 10,250 units in March, 10,250 units in April, and 12,000 units in May

22. $x_1 = 48$, $x_2 = 96$, \$456

   Assembler times: 480, 480, and 456

24. Investment strategy: 45.8% of A and 100% of B

   Objective function = \$4340.40

   Savings/Loan Schedule

	Period			
	1	*2*	*3*	*4*
Savings	242.11	—	—	341.04
Funds from loan	—	200.00	127.58	—

26. b. Solution does not indicate that General Hospital is relatively inefficient.

28. c. No; E = 1 indicates that the amount of resources used by Hospital E are required to produce the outputs of Hospital E.

Chapter 5

2. a. Max $x_1 + 2x_2$

   s.t.

$$x_1 + 5x_2 + s_1 \qquad\quad = 10$$
$$2x_1 + 6x_2 \qquad + s_2 = 16$$
$$x_1, x_2, s_1, s_2 \geq 0$$

   b. 2

   c. $x_1 = 0$, $x_2 = 0$, $s_1 = 10$, $s_2 = 16$; feasible

     $x_1 = 0$, $x_2 = 2$, $s_1 = 0$, $s_2 = 4$; feasible

     $x_1 = 0$, $x_2 = 8/3$, $s_1 = -10/3$, $s_2 = 0$; not feasible

     $x_1 = 10$, $x_2 = 0$, $s_1 = 0$, $s_2 = -4$; not feasible

     $x_1 = 8$, $x_2 = 0$, $s_1 = 2$, $s_2 = 0$; feasible

     $x_1 = 5$, $x_2 = 1$, $s_1 = 0$, $s_2 = 0$; feasible

   d. $x_1 = 8$, $x_2 = 0$; value = 8

4. a. Max $60x_1 + 90x_2$

   s.t.

$$15x_1 + 45x_2 + s_1 \qquad\quad = 90$$
$$5x_1 + 5x_2 \qquad + s_2 = 20$$
$$x_1, x_2, s_1, s_2 \geq 0$$

   b.

x_1	x_2	s_1	s_2	
60	90	0	0	
15	45	1	0	90
5	5	0	1	20

6. a.

z_j	0	0	0	0	0	0	0
$c_j - z_j$	5	20	25	0	0	0	

   b. Max $5x_1 + 20x_2 + 25x_3 + 0s_1 + 0s_2 + 0s_3$

   s.t.

$$2x_1 + 1x_2 \qquad\quad + 1s_1 \qquad\qquad = 40$$
$$2x_2 + 1x_3 \qquad + 1s_2 \qquad = 30$$
$$3x_1 \qquad - \tfrac{1}{2}x_3 \qquad\qquad + 1s_3 = 15$$
$$x_1, x_2, x_3, s_1, s_2, s_3 \geq 0$$

   c. s_1, s_2, s_3; it is the origin

   d. 0

   e. x_3 enters, s_2 leaves

   f. 30, 750

   g. $x_1 = 10$ $s_1 = 20$

     $x_2 = 0$ $s_2 = 0$ Value = 800

     $x_3 = 30$ $s_3 = 0$

8. a. $x_1 = 540$, $x_2 = 252$

   b. \$7668

   c. 630, 480, 708, 117

   d. 0, 120, 0, 18

10. $x_2 = 250$, $x_3 = 150$, $s_2 = 4000$

   Value = 4850

12. A = 0, B = 0, C = 33⅓; profit = 500

14. a. $x_1 = 0$, $x_2 = 50$, $x_3 = 75$; profit = \$210

   c. Grade B grapes and labor

16.

Max $-4x_1 - 5x_2 - 3x_3 + 0s_1 + 0s_2 + 0s_4 - Ma_1 - Ma_2 - Ma_3$

s.t.

$$
\begin{array}{llllll}
4x_1 & + 2x_3 - 1s_1 & & + 1a_1 & & = 20 \\
- 1x_2 + 1x_3 & - 1s_2 & & + 1a_2 & & = 8 \\
-1x_1 + 2x_2 & & & + 1a_3 & & = 5 \\
2x_1 + 1x_2 + 1x_3 & + 1s_4 & & & & = 12
\end{array}
$$

$$x_1, x_2, x_3, s_1, s_2, s_4, a_1, a_2, a_3 \geq 0$$

18. $x_2 = 60$, $x_3 = 60$, $s_3 = 20$; value = 2040

20. 2400 boxes of 33 gallon bags
Profit = $480

22. $x_1 = 480$, $x_4 = 480$, $x_6 = 800$; value: 46,400

24. Alternative optimal solution: $x_1 = 4$, $x_2 = 4$
$x_1 = 8$, $x_2 = 0$

26. Alternative opitmal solution: $x_1 = 4$, $x_2 = 0$, $x_3 = 0$
$x_1 = 0$, $x_2 = 0$, $x_3 = 8$

28. Infeasible

30. a. Infeasible solution; not enough sewing time

   b. Alternative optimal solutions $x_1 = 1000$, $x_2 = 0$, $x_3 = 250$ or
$x_1 = 1000$, $x_2 = 200$, $x_3 = 0$
Profit = $4000

Chapter 6

2. a. $31.25 \leq c_2 \leq 83.33$

   b. $-43.33 \leq c_{s_2} \leq 8.75$

   c. $c_{s_3} \leq 26/5$

   d. Variables do not change; value = $1920

4. a. $100 \leq b_1 \leq 150$

   b. $40 \leq b_2 \leq 60$

   c. $b_3 \leq 110$

6. a. $6.3 \leq c_1 \leq 13.5$

   b. $6\frac{2}{3} \leq c_2 \leq 14\frac{2}{7}$

   c. Variables do not change; value = $7164

   d. Below $6\frac{2}{3}$ or above $14\frac{2}{7}$

   e. $x_1 = 300$, $x_2 = 420$; value = $9300

8. a. $x_1 = 5220/11$, $x_2 = 3852/11$; value = 86,868/11

   b. No, s_1 would enter the basis

10. a. Increase in profit

   b. No

12. a. $14 \leq b_1 \leq 21\frac{1}{2}$

   b. $4 \leq b_2$

   c. $18\frac{3}{4} \leq b_3 \leq 30$

   d. Dual price = 400/9; range: $18\frac{3}{4} \leq b_3 \leq 30$

14. a. $400/3 \leq b_1 \leq 800$

   b. $275 \leq b_2$

   c. $275/2 \leq b_3 \leq 625$

16. a. $x_1 = 4000$, $x_2 = 10,000$; total risk = 62,000

   b. Increase it by 2.167 per unit

   c. $48,000 \leq b_2 \leq 102,000$

   d. $x_1 = 5667$, $x_2 = 9167$; total risk = 72,833

   e. Variables do not change; total risk = 66,000

18. Max $5u_1 + 5u_2 + 24u_3$

s.t.

$$
\begin{array}{llll}
15u_1 + 4u_2 + 12u_3 & \leq 2800 \\
15u_1 + 8u_2 & \leq 6000 \\
u_1 & + 8u_3 \leq 1200 \\
u_1, u_2, u_3 \geq 0
\end{array}
$$

20. a. Max $30u_1 + 20u_2 + 80u_3$

s.t.

$$
\begin{array}{lll}
u_1 & + u_3 \leq 1 \\
u_2 & + 2u_3 \leq 1 \\
u_1, u_2, u_3 \geq 0
\end{array}
$$

   b. $x_1 = 30$, $x_2 = 25$

   c. Reduce cost by $0.50

22. a. Max $10x_1 + 5x_2$

s.t.

$$
\begin{array}{lll}
x_1 & \geq 20 \\
x_2 & \geq 20 \\
x_1 & \leq 100 \\
x_2 & \leq 100 \\
3x_1 + x_2 & \leq 175 \\
x_1, x_2 \geq 0
\end{array}
$$

   b. Min $-20u_1 - 20u_2 + 100u_3 + 100u_4 + 175u_5$

s.t.

$$
\begin{array}{lll}
-u_1 & + u_3 & + 3u_5 \geq 10 \\
- u_2 & + u_4 + u_5 \geq 5 \\
u_1, u_2, u_3, u_4, u_5 \geq 0
\end{array}
$$

Solution: $u_4 = 5/3$, $u_5 = 10/3$

   c. $x_1 = 25$, $x_2 = 100$; commission = $750

24. Check both constraints with $x_1 = 10$, $x_2 = 30$, $x_3 = 15$
Both constraints are satisfied; solution remains optimal.

Chapter 7

2. a. Min $14x_{11} + 9x_{12} + 7x_{13} + 8x_{21} + 10x_{22} + 5x_{23}$

s.t.

$$
\begin{array}{llll}
x_{11} + x_{12} + x_{13} & & \leq 30 \\
& x_{21} + x_{22} + x_{23} & \leq 20 \\
x_{11} & + x_{21} & = 25 \\
x_{12} & + x_{22} & = 15 \\
x_{13} & + x_{23} & = 10
\end{array}
$$

$$x_{11}, x_{12}, x_{13}, x_{21}, x_{22}, x_{23} \geq 0$$

   b. $x_{11} = 5$, $x_{12} = 15$, $x_{13} = 10$, $x_{21} = 20$

4. b. $x_{12} = 300$, $x_{21} = 100$, $x_{22} = 100$, $x_{23} = 300$, $x_{31} = 100$
Cost = 10,400

6. b. Seattle–Denver   4000; Seattle–Los Angeles   5000;
Columbus–Mobile   4000; New York–Pittsburgh   3000;
New York–Mobile   1000; New York–Los Angeles 1000;
New York–Washington   3000
Cost = $150,000

   c. Seattle–Denver   4000; Seattle–Los Angeles   5000;
Columbus–Mobile   5000; New York–Pittsburgh   4000;
New York–Los Angeles 1000; New York–Washington   3000
Cost actually decreases by $9000

8. Clifton–D_2 4000; Clifton–D_4 1000;
   Danville–D_1 2000; Danville–D_4 1000
   Customer 2 has a shortfall of 1000; customer 3's demand is not satisfied

10. 1–A 300; 1–C 1200; 2–A 1200; 3–A 500; 3–B 500

12. **b.** Jackson–2, Ellis–1, Smith–3 Total completion time = 64

14. **b.** Bostock–Southwest, Miller–Northwest

16. **b.** Toy–2, auto parts–4, housewares–3 video–1; profit = 61

18. 1–B, 2–C, 3–A, 4–D; 74 hours required

20. A to MS, B to Ph.D., C to MBA, D to undergrad
    Maximum total rating = 3.3

22. **a.**

	Supplier					
Division	*1*	*2*	*3*	*4*	*5*	*6*
1	614	660	534	680	590	630
2	603	639	702	693	693	630
3	865	830	775	850	900	930
4	532	553	511	581	595	553
5	720	648	684	693	657	747

b. Optimal Solution:

Supplier 1–Division 2	$603
Supplier 2–Division 5	648
Supplier 3–Division 3	775
Supplier 5–Division 1	590
Supplier 6–Division 4	553
Total	$3169

24. **c.** $x_{14} = 320$, $x_{25} = 600$, $x_{47} = 300$, $x_{49} = 20$, $x_{56} = 300$, $x_{58} = 300$, $x_{39} = 380$
    Cost = $11,220

26. **c.** Optimal Solution:

Variable	Value	Variable	Value
x_{13}	50	x_{36}	0
x_{14}	250	x_{37}	150
x_{23}	100	x_{45}	150
x_{24}	0	x_{46}	100
x_{35}	0	x_{47}	0

Objective function = 4300

28.

Optimal Solution	Units Shipped	Cost
Muncie–Cincinnati	1	6
Cincinnati–Concord	3	84
Brazil–Louisville	6	18
Louisville–Macon	2	88
Louisville–Greenwood	4	136
Xenia–Cincinnati	5	15
Cincinnati–Chatham	3	72
Total		419

Two rail cars must be held at Muncie until a buyer is found

32. **c.** Regular–month 1: 275; overtime–month 1: 25; inventory–end of month 1: 150
    Regular–month 2: 200; overtime–month 2: 50; inventory–end of month 2: 150
    Regular–month 3: 100; overtime–month 3: 50; inventory–end of month 3: 0

34. **a.** San Jose–Los Angeles 100; Las Vegas–Los Angeles 100;
    Las Vegas–San Diego 200; Tucson–San Francisco 300
    Cost = $7800

   b. Initial solution is optimal

   c. San Jose–San Francisco 100; Las Vegas–Los Angeles 200;
    Las Vegas–San Diego 100; Tucson–San Francisco 200;
    Tucson–San Diego 100
    Cost = $7800

   d. San Jose–San Francisco 100; Las Vegas–Los Angeles 200;
    Las Vegas–San Francisco 100; Tucson–San Francisco 100;
    Tucson–San Diego 200
    Cost = $8000

36. See Problem 4

40. See Problem 12

42. Terry 2; Carle 3; McClymonds 1; Higley usassigned
    Time = 26 days

44. Toy–2; auto–4; housewares–3; video–1

Chapter 8

2. **b.** $x_1 = 1.43$, $x_2 = 4.29$; value = 41.47
    Rounded: $x_1 = 1$, $x_2 = 4$; value = 37

   c. $x_1 = 0$, $x_2 = 5$; value = 40
    Not the same

4. **a.** $x_1 = 3.67$, $x_2 = 0$; value = 36.7
    Rounded: $x_1 = 3$, $x_2 = 0$; value = 30
    Lower bound = 30; upper bound = 36.7

   b. $x_1 = 3$, $x_2 = 2$; value = 36

   c. Alternative optimal solutions: $x_1 = 0$, $x_2 = 5$
                                          $x_1 = 2$, $x_2 = 4$

6. **b.** $x_1 = 1.96$, $x_2 = 5.48$; value = 7.44
    Rounded: $x_1 = 1.96$, $x_2 = 5$; value = 6.96
    Lower bound = 6.96; upper bound = 7.44

   c. $x_1 = 1.29$, $x_2 = 6$; value = 7.29

8. **a.** $x_3 = 1$, $x_4 = 1$, $x_6 = 1$; value = 17,500

   b. Add $x_1 + x_2 \leq 1$

   c. Add $x_3 - x_4 = 0$

10. **a.** $z = 100 x_1 + 150x_2 + 250x_3 + 400x_4$
             $x_1 + x_2 + x_3 + x_4 = 1$

   b. $z = 100x_1 + 150x_2 + 250x_3 + 400x_4$
             $x_1 + x_2 + x_3 + x_4 \leq 1$

12. **b.** Choose locations B and E

14. **a.** $x_1 \leq 15 + 15y_1$
            $x_2 \leq 15 + 15y_2$
            $x_3 \leq 15 + 15y_3$
            $y_1 + y_2 + y_3 \leq 1$

   b. $x_1 = 15$, $x_2 = 15$, $x_3 = 30$
            $y_1 = 0$, $y_2 = 0$, $y_3 = 1$; value = 50

16. b. Modernize plants 1 and 3 or plants 4 and 5

    d. Modernize plants 1 and 3

18. b. Use all part-time employees

    Bring on as follows: 9:00 A.M.–6, 11:00 A.M.–2, 12:00 noon–6, 1:00 P.M.–1, 3:00 P.M.–6

    Cost = $672

    c. Same as in part (b)

    d. New solution is to bring on 1 full-time employee at 9:00 A.M., 4 more at 11:00 A.M. and part-time employees as follows: 9:00 A.M.–5, 12:00 noon–5, and 3:00 P.M.–2

20. a. New objective function: Min $25x_1 + 40x_2 + 40x_3 + 40x_4 + 25x_5$

    b. $x_4 = x_5 = 1$; modernize the Ohio and California plants

    c. Add the constraint $x_2 + x_3 = 1$

    d. $x_1 = x_3 = 1$

22. $x_1 + x_2 + x_3 = 3y_1 + 5y_2 + 7y_3$

    $y_1 + y_2 + y_3 = 1$

Chapter 9

2.

	Shortest	
Node	Route from Node 7	Distance
1	7–6–5–3–1	22
2	7–4–2	11
3	7–6–5–3	12
4	7–4	5
5	7–5–6	8
6	7–6	6

4. 1–4–5–6–8; distance = 10

6.

	Shortest	
Node	Route from Node C	Distance
1	C–1	35
2	C–2	20
3	C–3	20
4	C–4	30
5	C–3–5	55
6	C–3–6	50
7	C–3–8–7	100
8	C–3–8	80
9	C–4–10–9	85
10	C–4–10	70

8. 1–2–8–10–11

10. 1–6, 6–7, 7–8, 7–10, 10–9, 9–4, 9–3, 3–2, 4–5, 7–11, 8–13, 14–15, 15–12, 14–13

    Total = 37

12. 1–2, 2–5, 5–6, 6–3, 6–8, 3–4, 8–7

    Total length = 2900 feet

14. 1–4, 2–3, 3–4, 4–5, 4–6, 6–7, 7–8, 8–9, 9–11, 11–10

    Minimum length = 28 miles

16. Maximal flow = 11,000 vehicles per hour

18. a. 10 hours; 10,000 gallons per hour

    b. 11.1 hours; flow reduced to 9000 gallons per hour

20. Maximal flow = 23 gallons/minute

    From steps 2 and 5, we see that the total flow from 3 to 5 must be 5 gallons/minute

Chapter 10

2.

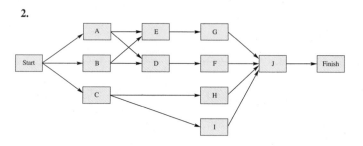

4. a. A–D–G

    b. No; time = 15 months

6. a. A–D–F–H

    b. 22 weeks

    c. No, it is a critical activity

    d. Yes, 2 weeks

    e. ES = 3, LS = 4, EF = 10, LF = 11

8. b. B–C–E–F–H

    d. Yes, time = 49 weeks

10. a.

Activity	Time	Variance
A	5.00	0.11
B	9.00	0.11
C	8.00	0.44
D	8.83	0.25
E	7.17	0.25
F	6.00	0.11

    b. 23.83, 0.47

12. a. A–D–H–I

    b. 25.66 days

    c. 0.2578

14. a. A–D–F–G

    b. 1.5 days

    c. 29.5, 2.36

    d. 0.6293

16. a.

E(T)	Variance
16	3.92
13	2.03
10	1.27

    b. 0.9783, approximately 1.00, approximately 1.00

18. **c.** A–B–D–G–H–I, 14.17 weeks
    d. Yes, P(13 weeks completion) = 0.0951
20. **b.** Crash B(1 week), D(2 weeks), E(1 week), F(1 week),
    G(1 week)
    Total cost = $2427
    c. All activities are critical
22. **b.** Crash C(1 day) and E(1 day)
    c. $9300
24. **c.** A–B–C–F, 31 weeks
    d. Crash A(2 weeks), B(2 weeks), C(1 week), D(1 week),
    E(1 week)
    e. All activities are critical
    f. $112,500

Chapter 11

2. $164.32 for each; total cost = $328.64
4. **a.** 1095.45
   b. 240
   c. 22.82 days
   d. $273.86 for each; total cost = $547.72
6. **a.** 15.95
   b. $2106
   c. 15.04
   d. 16.62 days
8. $Q^* = 11.73$, use 12
   5 classes per year
   $225,200
10. $Q^* = 1414.21$
    $T = 28.28$ days
    Production runs of 7.07 days
12. $Q^* = 1000$; total cost = $1200
    Yes, the change saves $300 per year
14. New $Q^* = 4509$
16. 135.55; $r = dm - S$; less than
18. 64, 24.44
20. $Q^* = 100$; total cost = $3,601.50
22. $Q^* = 300$; savings = $480
24. **a.** 500
    b. 580.4
26. **a.** 397
    b. 0.70
    c. 489, 0.35
28. **a.** 440
    b. 0.60
    c. 710
    d. $c_u = 17
30. **a.** 13.68 (14)
    b. 17.83 (18)
    c. 2, $10; 6, $30
32. **a.** 31.62
    b. 19.86 (20); 0.2108
    c. 5, $15

34. **a.** 243
    b. 93, $54.87
    c. 613
    d. 163, $96.17
    e. Yes, added cost only $41.30 per year
    f. Yes, added cost would be $4,130 per year
36. **a.** 40
    b. 62.25; 7.9
    c. 54
    d. 36
38. Engines   10
    Air cleaners   7
    Filter housings   2
40. Base assemblies   13
    Wheel subassemblies   9
    Tires   4

Chapter 12

2. **a.** 0.4512
   b. 0.6988
   c. 0.3012
4. 0.3333, 0.2222, 0.1481, 0.0988, 0.1976
6. **a.** 0.3333
   b. 1.3333
   c. 0.1111 hours
   d. 0.6667
8. 0.20, 3.2, 4, 3.2, 4, 0.80
   Slightly poorer service
10. **a.** New: 1.3333, 2, 0.6667, 1, 0.6667
        Experienced: 0.50, 1, 0.25, 0.50, 0.50
    b. New $74; experienced $50; hire experienced
12. **a.** 0.25, 2.25, 3, 0.15 hours, 0.20 hours, 0.75
    b. The service needs improvement
14. **a.** 0.1667
    b. 5
    c. 0.4167 hours
    d. 0.8333
    e. No
16. **a.** 0.50
    b. 0.50
    c. 0.10 hours
    d. 0.20 hours
18. **a.** 0.5385
    b. 0.0593
    c. 0.0099 hours
    d. 0.1099 hours
    e. 0.1384
20. **a.** 0.2360, 0.1771, 1.5771, 0.0127 hours, 0.1127 hours
    b. P(wait) = 0.2023; prefer 3-channel system

22.

Characteristic		A	B	C
a.	P_0	0.2000	0.5000	0.4286
b.	L_q	3.2000	0.5000	0.1524
c.	L	4.0000	1.0000	0.9524
d.	W_q	0.1333	0.0200	0.0063
e.	W	0.1667	0.0417	0.0397
f.	P_w	0.8000	0.5000	0.2286

(System C provides the best service)

24. a. 0.0466, 0.05
   b. 1.4
   c. 11:00 A.M.

26. a. 0.2668, 10 minutes, 0.6667
   b. 0.0667, 7 minutes, 0.4669
   c. $25.33; $33.34; one-channel

28. a. 10, 9.6
   b. Design A with $\mu = 10$
   c. 0.05, 0.01
   d. A: 0.5, 0.3125, 0.8125, 0.0625, 0.1625, 0.5
      B: 0.4792, 0.2857, 0.8065, 0.0571, 0.1613, 0.5208
   e. Design B is slightly better

30. a. 0.1460, 0.3066, 0.3220, 0.2254
   b. 0.2254
   c. 1.6267
   d. 4; 0.1499

32. a. 31.04%
   b. 27.58%
   c. 0.2758, 0.1092, 0.0351
   d. 3, 10.92%

34. a. 0.4790
   b. 0.3110
   c. 0.8320
   d. 2.9846 minutes
   e. 7.9846 minutes
   f. 95.8 minutes; 35.8 minutes
   g. Yes

Chapter 13

2. a.

Number of Breakdowns	0	1	2	3	4
Probability	0.12	0.24	0.37	0.19	0.08

   b. 1.87
   c. 0, 2, 1

4. a.

Number Absent	1	2	3	4	5	6
Probability	0.10	0.20	0.35	0.15	0.10	0.10

   b. 1, 6, 3, 3, 2, 3, 3, 2, 2, 2
   c. Because different random numbers can be generated, a variety of answers is possible.

6. $4532
8. Because different random numbers can be generated, a variety of answers is possible.
10. The answer depends upon the random numbers used.
12. Because different random numbers can be generated, a variety of answers is possible.
14. a. $5
   b. $7
   c,d. Because different random numbers can be generated, a variety of answers is possible.
16. Because different random numbers can be generated, a variety of answers is possible.
18. An order size of 200 is preferred.
20. Because different random numbers can be generated, a variety of answers is possible.
22. Because different random numbers can be generated, a variety of answers is possible.
24. a,b. Because different random numbers can be generated, a variety of answers is possible.
26. Because different random numbers can be generated, a variety of answers is possible.

Chapter 14

2. a. Optimistic: d_1
   Conservative: d_3
   Minimax regret: d_3
   c. Optimistic: d_1
   Conservative: d_2 or d_3
   Minimax regret: d_2
4. Optimistic: d_2
   Conservative: d_1
   Minimax regret: d_2
6. a. d_1 **b.** d_4
8. $p = 0.25$
10. a. If $p > 0.44$, location A; if $p < 0.44$, location C
   b. Location A because $0.65 > 0.44$
12. a. If s_1, then d_1; if s_2, then d_1 or d_2; if s_3, then d_2
   b. 192.5
   c. d_1; 182.5
   d. 10
14. 0.1905, 0.2381, 0.5714
16. a. 0.56, 0.44
   b. 0.57143, 0.42857, 0.18182, 0.81818
   c. If I_1, then d_2; if I_2, then d_1; EV = 292
18. b. Optimistic: d_3
   Conservative: d_1
   Minimax regret: d_2
   c. d_2
   d. 195
   e. If I_1, then d_2; if I_2, then d_2; if I_3, then d_3
   f. $38,500
   g. $195,000, 19.7%

20. c. Yes

  e. Purchase blade attachment

  f. $2150

22. a. St. Louis

  b. $0 \le p < 0.67$, d_1; when $p = 0.67$, d_1 or d_2, $0.67 < p \le 1$, d_2

  c. $200

  d. If I_1, then d_1; if I_2, then d_1

  e. 0.57

  f. 0%

24. a. d_1

  b. If $p < 0.75$, then d_2; if $p = 0.75$, d_1 or d_2; if $p > 0.75$, d_1

  c. Yes

  d. If I_1, then d_1; if I_2, then d_1; if I_3, then d_2

  f. 60%

26. a. 0, 125, 250, 375

  b. Yes

  d. 0, 0.048, 0.092, 0.133

  e. 0, 0.159, 0.488, 0.353

  f. Yes

  g. $24.25

28. $20, $30

30. a. d_2; $EV(d_2) = 52.5$

  b. A—d_3; 6.0

  B—d_1; 4.45

  c. Different attitudes toward risk

32. a. d_2; $EV(d_2) = \$5,000$

  b. p = probability of a $0 cost

  $1 - p$ = probability of a $200,000 cost

  c. d_1; $EV(d_1) = 9.9$

  d. Expected utility approach

34. a. Route B; $EV = 58.5$

  b. p = probability of a 45-minute travel time

  $1 - p$ = probability of a 90-minute travel time

  c. Route A; $EV = 7.6$; risk-avoider strategy

36. a.

	Win	Lose
Bet	350	− 10
Do not bet	0	0

  b. d_2

  c. Between 0 and 0.26

Chapter 15

  a. Min $P_1(d_1^-) + P_2(d_2^+)$

  s.t.

$$
\begin{aligned}
50x_1 + 100x_2 &\le 50{,}000 \\
3x_1 + 10x_2 - d_1^+ + d_1^- &= 4500 \\
x_2 - d_2^+ + d_2^- &= 300 \\
x_1, x_2, d_1^+, d_1^-, d_2^+, d_2^- &\ge 0
\end{aligned}
$$

  b. $x_1 = 250$, $x_2 = 375$

4. a. Min $P_1(d_1^-) + P_1(d_2^+) + P_2(d_3^-) + P_2(d_4^+) + P_5(d_5^-)$

  s.t.

$$
\begin{aligned}
20x_1 + 30x_2 - d_1^+ + d_1^- &= 1800 \\
20x_1 + 30x_2 - d_2^+ + d_2^- &= 6000 \\
x_1 - d_3^+ + d_3^- &= 100 \\
x_2 - d_4^+ + d_4^- &= 120 \\
x_1 + x_2 - d_5^+ + d_5^- &= 300
\end{aligned}
$$

  x_1, x_2, all deviation variables ≥ 0

  b. $x_1 = 120$, $x_2 = 120$

6. a. Let x_1 = number of letters mailed to group 1 customers

  x_2 = number of letters mailed to group 2 customers

  Min $P_1(d_1^-) + P_1(d_2^-) + P_2(d_3^+)$

  s.t.

$$
\begin{aligned}
x_1 - d_1^+ + d_1^- &= 40{,}000 \\
x_2 - d_2^+ + d_2^- &= 50{,}000 \\
x_1 + x_2 - d_3^+ + d_3^- &= 70{,}000
\end{aligned}
$$

  x_1, x_2, all deviation variables ≥ 0

  b. $x_1 = 40{,}000$, $x_2 = 50{,}000$

  c. Optimal solution does not change

8. a. Min $d_1^- + d_1^+ + e_1^- + e_1^+ + d_2^- + d_2^+ + e_2^- + e_2^+ + d_3^- + d_3^+ + e_3^- + e_3^+$

  s.t.

$$
\begin{aligned}
x_1 + d_1^- - d_1^+ &= 1 \\
x_2 + e_1^- - e_1^+ &= 7 \\
x_1 + d_2^- - d_2^+ &= 5 \\
x_2 + e_2^- - e_2^+ &= 9 \\
x_1 + d_3^- - d_3^+ &= 6 \\
x_2 + e_3^- - e_3^+ &= 2
\end{aligned}
$$

  all variables ≥ 0

  b. $x_1 = 5$, $x_2 = 7$

10. Since CR = 0.017 is less than 0.10, the degree of consistency exhibited in the pairwise comparison matrix is acceptable

12. Since CR = 0.029 is less than 0.10, the degree of consistency exhibited in the pairwise comparison matrix is acceptable

14. a. 0.723, 0.193, 0.083

  b. Since CR = 0.055 is less than 0.10, the degree of consistency exhibited in the pairwise comparison matrix is acceptable

16. a.

	A	B	C
A	1	3	2
B	1/3	1	5
C	1/2	1/5	1

  b. 0.503, 0.348, 0.149

  c. Since CR = 0.417 is greater than 0.10, the individual's judgments are not consistent

18. a.

	D	S	N
D	1	1/4	1/7
S	4	1	1/3
N	7	3	1

  b. 0.080, 0.265, 0.655

c. Since CR = 0.029 is less than 0.10, the manager's judgments are consistent

20. b. Criterion: 0.667, 0.333

Yield: 0.75, 0.25

Risk: 0.333, 0.667

c. CCI: 0.611; SRI: 0.389

22. b. Criterion: 0.608, 0.272, 0.120

Price: 0.557, 0.123, 0.320

Quality: 0.137, 0.240, 0.623

FM reception: 0.579, 0.187, 0.234

c. A: 0.445, B: 0.163, C: 0.392

Chapter 16

2. a.

Week	4-Week	5-Week
10	19.00	18.80
11	20.00	19.20
12	18.75	19.00

b. 9.65, 7.41

c. 5-week

4. Weeks 10, 11, and 12: 18.48, 18.63, 18.27

MSE = 9.25; $\alpha = 0.2$ is better

6. b. The more recent data receives the greater weight or importance in determining the forecast

8. a. Month 13: 106.4; MSE = 510.29

b. Month 13: 104.62; MSE = 540.55

Conclusion: a smoothing constant of 0.3 is better

10. Forecast for weeks 8, 9, 10, and 11: 258.64, 281.48, 283.61, and 292.71

12. 3117

14. $T_t = 20,746.67 - 351.429t$

Enrollment appears to be decreasing by an average of 351 students per year

16. $T_t = 28,800 + 421.429t$

18. a. Linear trend appears to be reasonable

b. $T_t = 19.993 + 1.774t$

Average cost increase of $1.77 per unit per year

20. a. $T_t = 1997.6 + 397.545t$

b. 6371; 6768

22. $T_8 = 252.28$; $T_9 = 259.10$

24. a. A linear trend appears to exist

b. $T_t = -5 + 15t$

Average increase in sales is 15 units per year

26. a. $T_t = 3.9041 + .0236t$

Personal income increasing at an average of 0.0236 per month

b. 4.21, 4.23, 4.26, 4.28, 4.31, 4.33

c. Actual 4.41 is above the forecast 4.33

28. 0.707, 0.777, 0.827, 0.966, 1.016, 1.305, 1.494, 1.225, 0.976, 0.986, 0.936, 0.787

30. Selected centered moving averages for t = 5, 10, 15, and 20 are 11.125, 18.125, 22.875, and 27.000

b. 0.899, 1.362, 1.118, 0.621

c. Quarter 2, prior to summer boating season

32. a. $T_t = 6.329 + 1.055t$

b. 36.92, 37.98, 39.03, 40.09

c. 33.23, 51.65, 43.71, 24.86

34. a. Yes

b. 12–4: 166,761.13

4–8: 146,052.99

36. a. $\hat{y} = 37.666 - 3.222t$

b. $3444

Chapter 17

2. b. $\pi_1 = 0.5$, $\pi_2 = 0.5$

c. $\pi_1 = 0.6$, $\pi_2 = 0.4$

4. a. $\pi_1 = 0.92$, $\pi_2 = 0.08$

b. $85

6. a.

	City	Suburbs
City	0.98	0.02
Suburbs	0.01	0.99

b. $\pi_1 = 0.333$, $\pi_2 = 0.667$

c. City will decrease from 40% to 33%; suburbs will increase from 60% to 67%

8. a. MDA

b. $\pi_1 = \frac{1}{3}$, $\pi_2 = \frac{2}{3}$

10. $3 - 1(0.59)$, $4 - 1(0.52)$

12. 1420 will be lost

14. a. Graduate and drop out

b. P(Drop out) = 0.15, P(Sophomore) = 0.10, P(Junior) = 0.75

c. 0.706, 0.294

d. Yes; P(Graduate) = 0.54

P(Drop out) = 0.46

e. 1479 (74%) will graduate

Chapter 18

2. a. 1–4–6–9–10

b. 4–6–9–10

c.

Route	Value	Route	Value
(1–2–5–7–10)	32	(1–3–6–8–10)	34
(1–2–5–8–10)	36	(1–3–6–9–10)	31
(1–2–5–9–10)	28	(1–4–6–8–10)	29
(1–3–5–7–10)	31	(1–4–6–9–10)	26
(1–3–5–8–10)	35		
(1–3–5–9–10)	27		

4. a. Alternative optimal solutions—value = 186
   Solution 1: A1–3, A2–2, A3–0, A4–3
   Solution 2: A1–2, A2–3, A3–0, A4–3
b. A1–1, A2–2, A3–0, A4–3
6. a. A–G–J–M
b. Choose H

8. a. Daily News–1, Sunday news–3, radio–1, TV–3; max exposure = 169
b. 1, 2, 1, 2; max exposure = 139
c. For part (a): 2, 3, 3; max exposure = 152
   For part (b): 2, 3, 1; max exposure = 127
10. Monthly production: 20, 20, 30

APPENDIX G: Solutions to Self-Test Problems

CHAPTER 1

4. A quantitative approach may be considered for the following reasons:

   a. the problem is large and complex

   b. the problem is very important

   c. the problem is new and no past experience exists

   d. the problem is repetitive

8. a. Max $10x + 5y$

     s.t. $5x + 2y \leq 40$

            $x \geq 0, y \geq 0$

  b. Controllable inputs: x and y

     Uncontrollable inputs: profit (10,5), labor-hours (5,2) and labor-hour availability (40)

  c. See Figure G1.8c

  d. $x = 0$, $y = 20$; profit = \$100

    (Solution by trial and error)

15. a. $TC = 1000 + 30x$

  b. $P = 40x - (1000 + 30x) = 10x - 1000$

  c. Breakeven when $P = 0$

    Thus $10x - 1000 = 0$

            $10x = 1000$

              $x = 100$

CHAPTER 2

1. Parts (a), (b), and (e) are acceptable linear programming relationships.

Part (c) is not acceptable because of $-2x_2^2$.

Part (d) is not acceptable because of $3\sqrt{x_1}$.

Part (f) is not acceptable because of $1x_1x_2$.

Parts (c), (d), and (f) could not be found in a linear programming model because they have the above nonlinear terms.

2. a.

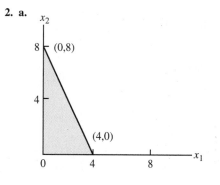

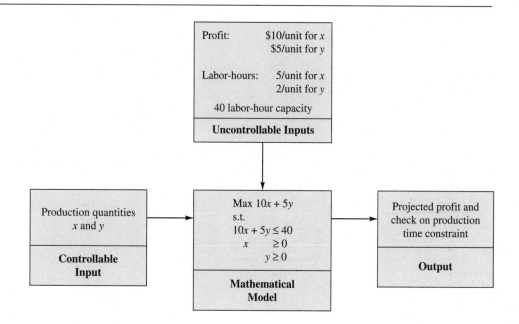

FIGURE G1.8c

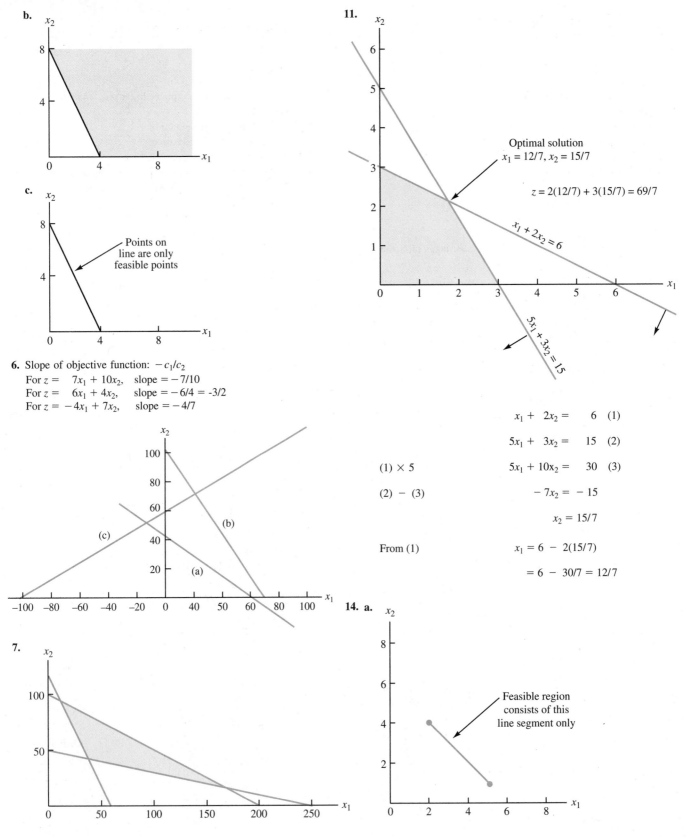

b.

c.

Points on
line are only
feasible points

11.

Optimal solution
$x_1 = 12/7$, $x_2 = 15/7$

$z = 2(12/7) + 3(15/7) = 69/7$

$x_1 + 2x_2 = 6$

$5x_1 + 3x_2 = 15$

6. Slope of objective function: $-c_1/c_2$

For $z = 7x_1 + 10x_2$, slope $= -7/10$

For $z = 6x_1 + 4x_2$, slope $= -6/4 = -3/2$

For $z = -4x_1 + 7x_2$, slope $= -4/7$

$$x_1 + 2x_2 = 6 \quad (1)$$

$$5x_1 + 3x_2 = 15 \quad (2)$$

$(1) \times 5$ \qquad $5x_1 + 10x_2 = 30 \quad (3)$

$(2) - (3)$ \qquad\qquad $-7x_2 = -15$

$$x_2 = 15/7$$

From (1) \qquad $x_1 = 6 - 2(15/7)$

$$= 6 - 30/7 = 12/7$$

7.

14. a.

Feasible region
consists of this
line segment only

b. The extreme points are (5,1) and (2,4)

c.

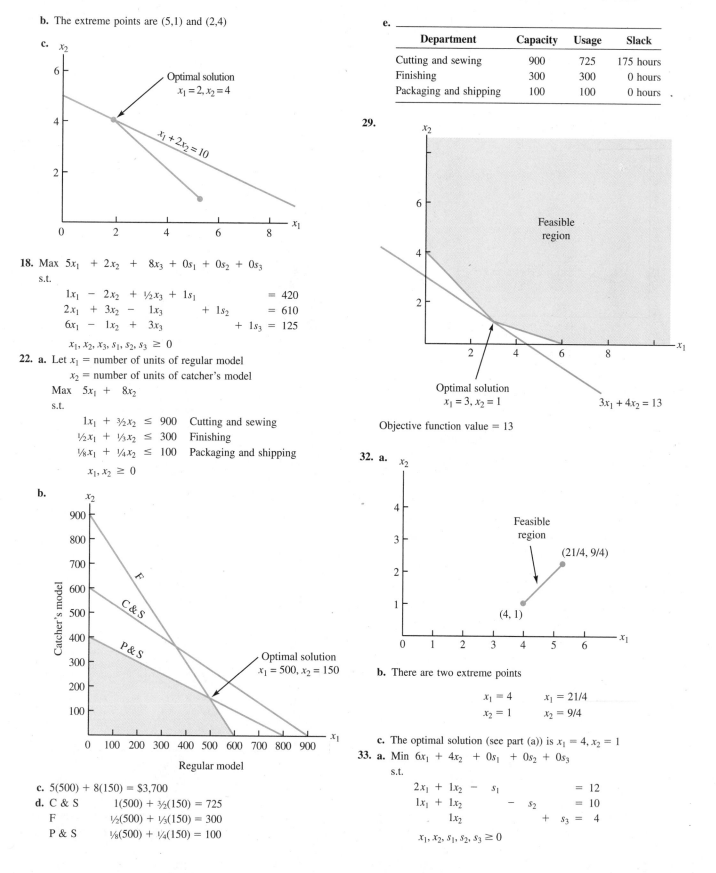

18. Max $5x_1 + 2x_2 + 8x_3 + 0s_1 + 0s_2 + 0s_3$

s.t.

$$1x_1 - 2x_2 + \tfrac{1}{2}x_3 + 1s_1 \qquad\qquad = 420$$
$$2x_1 + 3x_2 - 1x_3 \qquad + 1s_2 \qquad = 610$$
$$6x_1 - 1x_2 + 3x_3 \qquad\qquad + 1s_3 = 125$$

$$x_1, x_2, x_3, s_1, s_2, s_3 \geq 0$$

22. a. Let x_1 = number of units of regular model

x_2 = number of units of catcher's model

Max $5x_1 + 8x_2$

s.t.

$$1x_1 + \tfrac{3}{2}x_2 \leq 900 \quad \text{Cutting and sewing}$$
$$\tfrac{1}{2}x_1 + \tfrac{1}{3}x_2 \leq 300 \quad \text{Finishing}$$
$$\tfrac{1}{8}x_1 + \tfrac{1}{4}x_2 \leq 100 \quad \text{Packaging and shipping}$$

$$x_1, x_2 \geq 0$$

b.

c. $5(500) + 8(150) = \$3,700$

d. C & S $\quad 1(500) + \tfrac{3}{2}(150) = 725$

F $\qquad \tfrac{1}{2}(500) + \tfrac{1}{3}(150) = 300$

P & S $\quad \tfrac{1}{8}(500) + \tfrac{1}{4}(150) = 100$

e.

Department	Capacity	Usage	Slack
Cutting and sewing	900	725	175 hours
Finishing	300	300	0 hours
Packaging and shipping	100	100	0 hours

29.

Objective function value = 13

32. a.

b. There are two extreme points

$$x_1 = 4 \qquad x_1 = 21/4$$
$$x_2 = 1 \qquad x_2 = 9/4$$

c. The optimal solution (see part (a)) is $x_1 = 4, x_2 = 1$

33. a. Min $6x_1 + 4x_2 + 0s_1 + 0s_2 + 0s_3$

s.t.

$$2x_1 + 1x_2 - s_1 \qquad\qquad = 12$$
$$1x_1 + 1x_2 \qquad - s_2 \qquad = 10$$
$$1x_2 \qquad\qquad + s_3 = 4$$

$$x_1, x_2, s_1, s_2, s_3 \geq 0$$

b. The optimal solution is $x_1 = 6$, $x_2 = 4$

c. $s_1 = 4$, $s_2 = 0$, $s_3 = 0$

40.

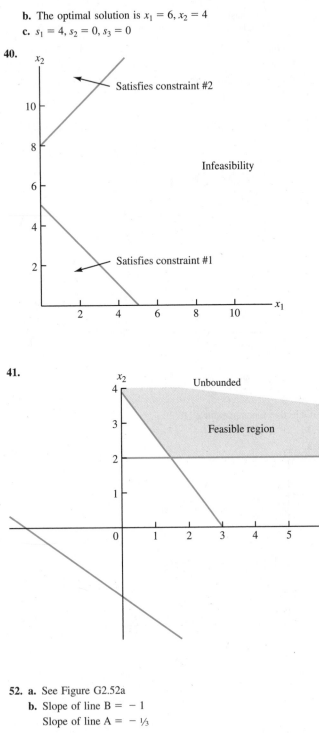

41.

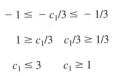

52. a. See Figure G2.52a

b. Slope of line B $= -1$

   Slope of line A $= -\frac{1}{3}$

$$-1 \le -c_1/3 \le -1/3$$

$$1 \ge c_1/3 \quad c_1/3 \ge 1/3$$

$$c_1 \le 3 \quad c_1 \ge 1$$

   Range: $1 \le c_1 \le 3$

FIGURE **G**2.52a

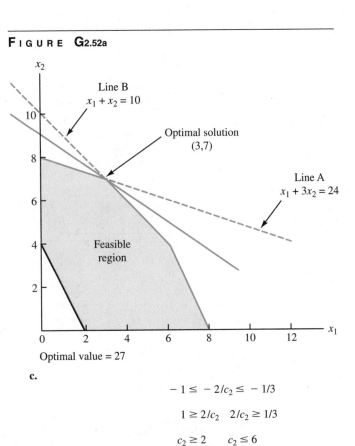

Optimal value = 27

c.

$$-1 \le -2/c_2 \le -1/3$$

$$1 \ge 2/c_2 \quad 2/c_2 \ge 1/3$$

$$c_2 \ge 2 \quad c_2 \le 6$$

Range: $2 \le c_2 \le 6$

d. Since this change leaves c_1 in its range of optimality, the same solution ($x_1 = 3$, $x_2 = 7$) is optimal

e. This change moves c_2 outside its range of optimality; the new optimal solution is shown here:

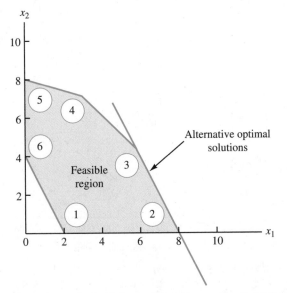

Alternative optimal solutions exist; extreme points 2 and 3 and all points on the line segment between them are optimal

53. By making a small increase in the right-hand side of constraint 1 and resolving, we find a dual price of 1.5 for the constraint; thus, the objective function will improve at the rate of 1.5 per unit increase in the right-hand side.

Since constraint 2 is not binding, its dual price is zero.

To determine the range over which these dual prices are applicable, one must obtain the range of feasibility.

CHAPTER 3

1. a. $x_1 = 500$; $x_2 = 150$; value = 3700

b. The finishing, packaging, and shipping constraints are binding; there is no slack

c. Cutting and sewing   = 0
Finishing   = 3
Packaging and shipping = 28
Additional finishing time is worth $3 per unit, and additional packaging and shipping time is worth $28 per unit

d. In the packaging and shipping department; each additional hour is worth $28

2. a. $4 \leq c_1 \leq 12$
  $3.33 \leq c_2 \leq 10$

b. As long as the profit contribution for the regular glove is between $4.00 and $12.00, the current solution is optimal. As long as the profit contribution for the catcher's mitt stays between $3.33 and $10.00, the current solution is optimal. The optimal solution is not sensitive to small changes in the profit contributions for the gloves.

c. The dual prices for the resources are applicable over the following ranges:

Constraint	Min RHS	Max RHS
Cutting and sewing	725	No upper limit
Finishing	133.33	400
Packaging and shipping	75	135

d. Amount of increase = (28)(20) = $560

6. a. $x_1 = 4000$
$x_2 = 10,000$
Total risk = 62,000

b. $3.75 \leq c_1 <$ No upper limit
No lower limit $< c_2 \leq 6.4$

c. 5(4000) + 4(10,000) = $60,000

d. 60,000/1,200,000 = 0.05 or 5%

e. 0.057 risk units

f. 0.057(100) = 5.7%

8. a. $x_1 = 0$; $x_2 = 25$; $x_3 = 125$; $x_4 = 0$
Value of solution = 525.0

b. The constraints on machine A and machine C hours are binding

c. Machine B has 425 hours of excess capacity

d. Yes, the allowable increase is only 0.05

9. a. No lower limit $< c_1 \leq 4.05$
$5.923 \leq c_2 \leq 9$
$2 \leq c_3 \leq 12$
No lower limit $< c_4 \leq 4.5$

b. The allowable decrease for c_1 is ∞; thus, the percentage decrease is 0%

$$\frac{1.5}{3.0} + \frac{1}{3.5} = 0.79$$

The accumulated percentage of allowable increases and decreases is 79%; since this is less than 100%, the optimal solution will not change

c.

Constraint	Min RHS	Max RHS
Machine A hours	133.33	800
Machine B hours	275	No upper limit
Machine C hours	137.5	825

d. Yes, because that is outside the range of feasibility

CHAPTER 4

1. a. Let x_1 = number of television advertisements
x_2 = number of radio advertisements
x_3 = number of newspaper advertisements

Max $100,000x_1 + 18,000x_2 + 40,000x_3$
s.t.

$$2,000x_1 + 300x_2 + 600x_3 \leq 18,200 \text{ Budget}$$
$$x_1 \leq 10 \text{ Max TV}$$
$$x_2 \leq 20 \text{ Max radio}$$
$$x_3 \leq 10 \text{ Max news}$$
$$-0.5x_1 + 0.5x_2 - 0.5x_3 \leq 0 \text{ Max 50\% radio}$$
$$0.9x_1 - 0.1x_2 - 0.1x_3 \geq 0 \text{ Min 10\% TV}$$
$$x_1, x_2, x_3, \geq 0$$

                    Budget $
Solution: $x_1 = 4$ $ 8,000
          $x_2 = 14$ 4,200
          $x_3 = 10$ 6,000
                  $18,200   Audience = 1,052,000

b. The dual price for the budget constraint is 51.30. Thus, a $100 increase in the budget should provide an increase in audience coverage of approximately 5130. The range of feasibility for the right-hand side of the budget constraint will show this interpretation is correct.

9. Let x_1 = number of shares of stock A
x_2 = number of shares of stock B
x_3 = number of shares of stock C
x_4 = number of shares of stock D

a. To get data on a per-share basis, multiply price by rate of return or risk measure value

Min $10x_1 + 3.5x_2 + 4x_3 + 3.2x_4$

s.t.

$$100x_1 + 50x_2 + 80x_3 + 40x_4 = 200,000$$
$$12x_1 + 4x_2 + 4.8x_3 + 4x_4 \geq 18,000 \text{ (9\% of 200,000)}$$
$$100x_1 \leq 100,000$$
$$50x_2 \leq 100,000$$
$$80x_3 \leq 100,000$$
$$40x_4 \leq 100,000$$

$$x_1, x_2, x_3, x_4 \geq 0$$

Solution: $x_1 = 333.3$, $x_2 = 0$, $x_3 = 833.3$, $x_4 = 2500$

Risk: 14,666.7

Return: 18,000 (9%) from constraint 2

b. Max $12x_1 + 4x_2 + 4.8x_3 + 4x_4$

s.t.

$$100x_1 + 50x_2 + 80x_3 + 40x_4 = 200,000$$
$$100x_1 \leq 100,000$$
$$50x_2 \leq 100,000$$
$$80x_3 \leq 100,000$$
$$40x_4 \leq 100,000$$

$$x_1, x_2, x_3, x_4 \geq 0$$

Solution: $x_1 = 1000$, $x_2 = 0$, $x_3 = 0$, $x_4 = 2500$

Risk: $10x_1 + 3.5x_2 + 4x_3 + 3.2x_4 = 18,000$

Return: 22,000 (11%)

c. The return in part (b) is $4000 or 2% greater, but the risk index has increased by 3333.

Obtaining a reasonable return with a lower risk is a preferred strategy in many financial firms. The more speculative, higher return investments are not always preferred because of their associated higher risk.

15. Let x_{11} = gallons of crude 1 used to produce regular
x_{12} = gallons of crude 1 used to produce high octane
x_{21} = gallons of crude 2 used to produce regular
x_{22} = gallons of crude 2 used to produce high octane

Min $0.10x_{11} + 0.10x_{12} + 0.15x_{21} + 0.15x_{22}$

s.t.

Each gallon of regular must have at least 40% A

$x_{11} + x_{21}$ = amount of regular produced

$0.4(x_{11} + x_{21})$ = amount of A required for regular

$0.2x_{11} + 0.50x_{21}$ = amount of A in $(x_{11} + x_{21})$ gallons of regular gas

$$\therefore 0.2x_{11} + 0.50x_{21} \geq 0.4x_{11} + +0.40x_{21}$$

$$\therefore -0.2x_{11} + 0.10x_{21} \geq 0$$

Each gallon of high octane can have at most 50% B

$x_{12} + x_{22}$ = amount high octane

$0.5(x_{12} + x_{22})$ = amount of B required for high octane

$0.60x_{12} + 0.30x_{22}$ = amount of B in $(x_{12} + x_{22})$ gallons of high octane

$$\therefore 0.60x_{12} + 0.30x_{22} \leq 0.5x_{12} + 0.5x_{22}$$
$$\therefore 0.1x_{12} - 0.2x_{22} \leq 0$$
$$x_{11} + x_{21} \geq 800,000$$
$$x_{12} + x_{22} \geq 500,000$$

$$x_{11}, x_{12}, x_{21}, x_{22} \geq 0$$

Optimal solution: $x_{11} = 266,667$, $x_{12} = 333,333$, $x_{21} = 533,333$, $x_{22} = 166,667$

Cost = \$165,000

19. a. Let x_{11} = amount of men's model in month 1
x_{21} = amount of women's model in month 1
x_{12} = amount of men's model in month 2
x_{22} = amount of women's model in month 2
s_{11} = inventory of men's model at end of month 1
s_{21} = inventory of women's model at end of month 1
s_{12} = inventory of men's model at end of month 2
s_{22} = inventory of women's model at end of month 2

Min $120x_{11} + 90x_{21} + 120x_{12} + 90x_{22} + 2.4s_{11} + 1.8s_{21} + 2.4s_{12} + 1.8s_{22}$

s.t.

$$\left.\begin{array}{l} x_{11} - s_{11} = 130 \\ x_{21} - s_{21} = 95 \\ s_{11} + x_{12} - s_{12} = 200 \\ s_{21} + x_{22} - s_{22} = 150 \end{array}\right\} \text{Satisfy demand}$$

$$\left.\begin{array}{l} s_{12} \geq 25 \\ s_{22} \geq 25 \end{array}\right\} \text{Ending inventory requirement}$$

Labor-hours: Men's $2.0 + 1.5 = 3.5$
Women's $1.6 + 1.0 = 2.6$

$$\left.\begin{array}{l} 3.5x_{11} + 2.6x_{21} \geq 900 \\ 3.5x_{11} + 2.6x_{21} \leq 1100 \\ 3.5x_{11} + 2.6x_{21} - 3.5x_{21} - 2.6x_{22} \leq 100 \\ 3.5x_{11} - 2.6x_{21} + 3.5x_{21} + 2.6x_{22} \leq 100 \end{array}\right\} \text{Labor smoothing}$$

$$x_{11}, x_{12}, x_{21}, x_{22}, s_{11}, s_{12}, s_{21}, s_{22} \geq 0$$

Solution: $x_{11} = 193$; $x_{21} = 95$; $x_{12} = 162$; $x_{22} = 175$

Total cost = \$67,156

Inventory levels: $s_{11} = 63$; $s_{12} = 25$; $s_{21} = 0$; $s_{22} = 25$

Labor levels: Previous   1000 hours
Month 1   922.25 hours
Month 2   1022.25 hours

b. To accommodate the new policy, the right-hand sides of the four labor-smoothing constraints must be changed to 950, 1050, 50, and 50 respectively. The new total cost is \$67,175.

CHAPTER 5

1. a. With $x_1 = 0$, we have

$$x_2 = 6$$
$$4x_2 + x_3 = 12$$

From (1), we have $x_2 = 6$; substituting for x_2 in (2) yields

$$4(6) + x_3 = 12$$
$$x_3 = 12 - 24 = -12$$

Basic solution: $x_1 = 0, x_2 = 6, x_3 = -12$

b. With $x_2 = 0$, we have

$$3x_1 = 6$$
$$2x_1 + x_3 = 12$$

From (3), we find $x_1 = 2$; substituting for x_1 in (4) yields

$$2(2) + x_3 = 12$$
$$x_3 = 12 - 4 = 8$$

Basic solution: $x_1 = 2, x_2 = 0, x_3 = 8$

c. With $x_3 = 0$, we have

$$3x_1 + x_2 = 6$$
$$2x_1 + 4x_2 = 12$$

Multiplying (6) by $\frac{3}{2}$ and subtracting from (5) yields

$$3x_1 + x_2 = 6$$
$$\underline{- (3x_1 + 6x_2) = -18}$$
$$-5x_2 = -12$$
$$x_2 = \frac{12}{5}$$

Substituting $x_2 = \frac{12}{5}$ into (5) yields

$$3x_1 + \frac{12}{5} = 6$$
$$3x_1 = \frac{18}{5}$$
$$x_1 = \frac{6}{5}$$

Basic solution: $x_1 = \frac{6}{5}, x_2 = \frac{12}{5}, x_3 = 0$

d. The basic solutions found in parts (b) and (c) are basic feasible solutions. The one in part (a) is not because $x_3 = -12$.

4. a. Standard form:

Max $60x_1 + 90x_2$

s.t.

$$15x_1 + 45x_2 + s_1 \qquad = 90$$
$$5x_1 + 5x_2 \qquad + s_2 = 20$$
$$x_1, x_2, s_1, s_2 \geq 0$$

b. Partial initial simplex tableau:

	x_1	x_2	s_1	s_2	
(1)	60	90	0	0	
(2)	15	45	1	0	**90**
	5	5	0	1	**20**

5. a. Initial tableau:

Basis	c_B	x_1 5	x_2 9	s_1 0	s_2 0	
s_1	0	10	9	1	0	90
s_2	0	-5	3	0	1	15
z_j		0	0	0	0	0
$c_j - z_j$		5	9	0	0	

b. We would introduce x_2 at the first iteration

c. Max $5x_1 + 9x_2$

s.t.

$$10x_1 + 9x_2 \leq 90$$
$$-5x_1 + 3x_2 \leq 15$$
$$x_1, x_2 \geq 0$$

15.

Max $4x_1 + 2x_2 - 3x_3 + 5x_4 + 0s_1 - Ma_1 + 0s_2 - Ma_3$

s.t.

$$2x_1 - 1x_2 + 1x_3 + 2x_4 - 1s_1 + 1a_1 \qquad\qquad = 50$$
$$3x_1 \qquad - 1x_3 + 2x_4 \qquad\qquad + 1s_2 \qquad = 80$$
$$1x_1 + 1x_2 \qquad + 1x_4 \qquad\qquad\qquad + 1a_3 = 60$$
$$x_1, x_2, x_3, x_4, s_1, s_2, a_1, a_3 \geq 0$$

17. Converting to a max problem and solving using the simplex method, the final simplex tableau is

Basis	c_B	x_1 -3	x_2 -4	x_3 -8	s_1 0	s_2 0	
x_1	-3	1	0	-1	$-\frac{1}{4}$	$\frac{1}{8}$	1
x_2	-4	0	1	2	0	$-\frac{1}{4}$	4
z_j		-3	-4	-5	$\frac{3}{4}$	$\frac{5}{8}$	-19
$c_j - z_j$		0	0	-3	$-\frac{3}{4}$	$-\frac{5}{8}$	

23. Final simplex tableau:

Basis	c_B	x_1 4	x_2 8	s_1 0	s_2 0	a_2 -M	
x_2	8	1	1	$\frac{1}{2}$	0	0	5
a_2	-M	-2	0	$-\frac{1}{2}$	-1	1	3
z_j		$8 + 2M$	8	$4 + M/2$	$+M$	$-M$	$40 - 3M$
$c_j - z_j$		$-4 - 2M$	0	$-4 - M/2$	$-M$	0	

Infeasible; optimal solution condition is reached with the artificial variable a_2 still in the solution

24. Alternative optimal solutions:

Basis	c_B	x_1 -3	x_2 -3	s_1 0	s_2 0	s_3 0	
s_2	0	0	0	$-4/3$	1	$1/6$	4
x_1	-3	1	0	$-2/3$	0	$1/12$	4
x_2	-3	0	1	$2/3$	0	$-1/3$	4
z_j		-3	-3	0	0	$3/4$	-24
$c_j - z_j$		0	0	0	0	$-3/4$	

$\uparrow$

Indicates alternative optimal solutions exist:
$x_1 = 4$, $x_2 = 4$, $z = 24$
$x_1 = 8$, $x_2 = 0$, $z = 24$

25. Unbounded solution:

Basis	c_B	x_1 1	x_2 1	s_1 0	s_2 0	s_3 0	
s_3	0	$8/3$	0	$-1/3$	0	1	4
s_2	0	4	0	-1	1	0	36
x_2	1	$4/3$	1	$-1/6$	0	0	4
z_j		$4/3$	1	$-1/6$	0	0	4
$c_j - z_j$		$-1/3$	0	$1/6$	0	0	

$\uparrow$
Incoming
column

CHAPTER 6

1. a. Recomputing the $c_j - z_j$ values for the nonbasic variables with c_1 as the coefficient of x_1 leads to the following inequalities that must be satisfied:

For x_2, we get no inequality since there is a zero in the x_2 column for the row in which x_1 is a basic variable

For s_1, we get

$$0 + 4 - c_1 \leq 0$$

$$c_1 \geq 4$$

For s_2, we get

$$0 - 12 + 2c_1 \leq 0$$

$$2c_1 \leq 12$$

$$c_1 \leq 6$$

Range: $4 \leq c_1 \leq 6$

b. Since x_2 is nonbasic, we have

$$c_2 \leq 8$$

c. Since s_1 is nonbasic, we have

$$c_{s_1} \leq 1$$

3. a. It is the z_j value for s_1; dual price = 1
b. It is the z_j value for s_2; dual price = 2
c. It is the z_j value for s_3; dual price = 0
d.
$$s_3 = 80 + 5(-2) = 70$$
$$x_3 = 30 + 5(-1) = 25$$
$$x_1 = 20 + 5(1) = 25$$
$$\text{Value} = 220 + 5(1) = 225$$
e.
$$s_3 = 80 - 10(-2) = 100$$
$$x_3 = 30 - 10(-1) = 40$$
$$x_1 = 20 - 10(1) = 10$$
$$\text{Value} = 220 - 10(1) = 210$$

4. a.
$$80 + \Delta b_1(-2) \geq 0 \qquad \Delta b_1 \leq 40$$
$$30 + \Delta b_1(-1) \geq 0 \qquad \Delta b_1 \leq 30$$
$$20 + \Delta b_1(1) \geq 0 \qquad \Delta b_1 \geq -20$$
$$-20 \leq \Delta b_1 \leq 30$$
$$100 \leq b_1 \leq 150$$
b.
$$80 + \Delta b_2(7) \geq 0 \qquad \Delta b_2 \geq -80/7$$
$$30 + \Delta b_2(3) \geq 0 \qquad \Delta b_2 \geq -10$$
$$20 + \Delta b_2(-2) \geq 0 \qquad \Delta b_2 \leq 10$$
$$-10 \leq \Delta b_2 \leq 10$$
$$40 \leq b_2 \leq 60$$
c.
$$80 - \Delta b_3(1) \geq 0 \rightarrow \Delta b_3 \leq 80$$
$$30 - \Delta b_3(0) \geq 0$$
$$20 - \Delta b_3(0) \geq 0$$
$$\Delta b_3 \leq 80$$
$$b_3 \leq 110$$

17. a. The dual is given by:

Min $550u_1 + 700u_2 + 200u_3$
s.t.

$$1.5u_1 + 4u_2 + 2u_3 \geq 4$$
$$2u_1 + 1u_2 + 3u_3 \geq 6$$
$$4u_1 + 2u_2 + 1u_3 \geq 3$$
$$3u_1 + 1u_2 + 2u_3 \geq 1$$
$$u_1, u_2, u_3, \geq 0$$

b. Optimal solution: $u_1 = 3/10$; $u_2 = 0$, $u_3 = 54/30$
The z_j values for the four surplus variables of the dual show $x_1 = 0$, $x_2 = 25$, $x_3 = 125$, and $x_4 = 0$.
c. Since $u_1 = 3/10$, $u_2 = 0$, and $u_3 = 54/30$, machines A and C $(u_j > 0)$ are operating at capacity; machine C is the priority machine since each hour is worth 54/30.

18. The dual is given by

Max $5u_1 + 5u_2 + 24u_3$
s.t.

$$15u_1 + 4u_2 + 12u_3 \leq 2800$$
$$15u_1 + 8u_2 \leq 6000$$
$$u_1 + 8u_3 \leq 1200$$
$$u_1, u_2, u_3 \geq 0$$

19. The canonical form is

Max $3x_1 + x_2 + 5x_3 + 3x_4$

s.t.

$$
\begin{aligned}
3x_1 + 1x_2 + 2x_3 &\leq 30 \\
-3x_1 - 1x_2 - 2x_3 &\leq -30 \\
-2x_1 - 1x_2 - 3x_3 - x_4 &\leq -15 \\
2x_2 + 3x_4 &\leq 25
\end{aligned}
$$

$$x_1, x_2, x_3, x_4 \geq 0$$

The dual is

Min $30u_1' - 30u_1'' - 15u_2 + 25u_3$

s.t.

$$
\begin{aligned}
3u_1' - 3u_1'' - 2u_2 &\geq 3 \\
u_1' - u_1'' - u_2 + 2u_3 &\geq 1 \\
2u_1' - 2u_1'' - 3u_2 &\geq 5 \\
- u_2 + 3u_3 &\geq 3
\end{aligned}
$$

$$u_1', u_1'', u_2, u_3 \geq 0$$

CHAPTER 7

1.

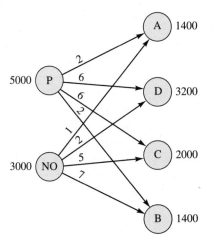

2. a. Let x_{11} = amount shipped from Jefferson City to Des Moines
x_{12} = amount shipped from Jefferson City to Kansas City

.
.
.

x_{23} = amount shipped from Omaha to St. Louis

Min $14x_{11} + 9x_{12} + 7x_{13} + 8x_{21} + 10x_{22} + 5x_{23}$

s.t.

$$
\begin{aligned}
x_{11} + x_{12} + x_{13} &\leq 30 \\
x_{21} + x_{22} + x_{23} &\leq 20 \\
x_{11} + x_{21} &= 25 \\
x_{12} + x_{22} &= 15 \\
x_{13} + x_{23} &= 10
\end{aligned}
$$

$$x_{11}, x_{12}, x_{13}, x_{21}, x_{22}, x_{23} \geq 0$$

b. _____

Optimal Solution	Amount	Cost
Jefferson City–Des Moines	5	70
Jefferson City–Kansas City	15,	135
Jefferson City–St. Louis	10	70
Omaha–Des Moines	20	160
	Total	435

8. The network model, the linear programming formulation and the optimal solution are shown. Note that the third constraint corresponds to the dummy origin; the variables x_{31}, x_{32}, x_{33}, and x_{34} are the amounts shipped out of the dummy origin and do not appear in the objective function since they are given a coefficient of zero.

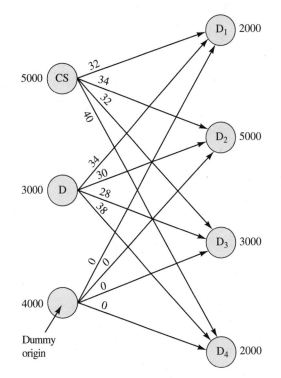

Max $32x_{11} + 34x_{12} + 32x_{13} + 40x_{14} + 34x_{21} + 30x_{22} + 28x_{23} + 38x_{24}$

s.t.

$$
\begin{aligned}
x_{11} + x_{12} + x_{13} + x_{14} &\leq 5000 \\
x_{21} + x_{22} + x_{23} + x_{24} &\leq 3000 \\
x_{31} + x_{32} + x_{33} + x_{34} &\leq 4000 \\
x_{11} + x_{21} + x_{31} &= 2000 \\
x_{12} + x_{22} + x_{32} &= 5000 \\
x_{13} + x_{23} + x_{33} &= 3000 \\
x_{14} + x_{24} + x_{34} &= 2000
\end{aligned}
$$

$$x_{ij} \geq 0 \quad \text{for all } i, j$$

Optimal Solution	Units	Cost
Clifton Springs–D_2	4000	$136,000
Clifton Springs–D_4	1000	40,000
Danville–D_1	2000	68,000
Danville–D_4	1000	38,000
	Total	$282,000

Customer 2 demand has a shortfall of 1000; customer 3 demand of 3000 is not satisfied

12. a.

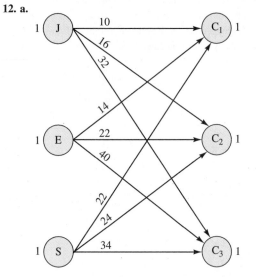

b.

$$\text{Min } 10x_{11} + 16x_{12} + 32x_{13} + 14x_{21} + 22x_{22} + 40x_{23} + 22x_{31} + 24x_{32} + 34x_{33}$$
s.t.

$$
\begin{aligned}
x_{11} + x_{12} + x_{13} &\leq 1 \\
x_{21} + x_{22} + x_{23} &\leq 1 \\
x_{31} + x_{32} + x_{33} &\leq 1 \\
x_{11} \quad + x_{21} \quad + x_{31} &= 1 \\
x_{12} \quad + x_{22} \quad + x_{32} &= 1 \\
x_{13} \quad + x_{23} \quad + x_{33} &= 1 \\
x_{ij} \geq 0 \quad \text{for all } i, j &
\end{aligned}
$$

Solution $x_{12} = 1$, $x_{21} = 1$, $x_{33} = 1$; total completion time = 64

23. a.

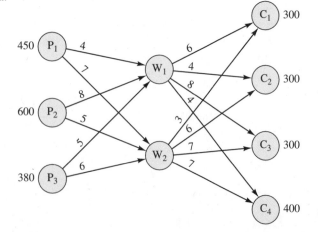

b.

$$\text{Min } 4x_{14} + 7x_{15} + 8x_{24} + 5x_{25} + 5x_{34} + 6x_{35} + 6x_{46} + 4x_{47} + 8x_{48} + 4x_{49} + 3x_{56} + 6x_{57} + 7x_{58} + 7x_{59}$$

$$
\begin{aligned}
x_{14} + x_{15} &\leq 450 \\
x_{24} + x_{25} &\leq 600 \\
x_{34} + x_{35} &\leq 380 \\
-x_{14} \quad -x_{24} \quad -x_{34} \quad + x_{46} + x_{47} + x_{48} + x_{49} &= 0 \\
-x_{15} \quad -x_{25} \quad -x_{35} \quad + x_{56} + x_{57} + x_{58} + x_{59} &= 0 \\
x_{46} \quad + x_{56} &= 300 \\
x_{47} \quad + x_{57} &= 300 \\
x_{48} \quad + x_{58} &= 300 \\
x_{49} \quad + x_{59} &= 300
\end{aligned}
$$

c.

	Warehouse	
Plant	1	2
1	450	—
2	—	600
3	250	—

Total cost = $11,850

	Customer			
Warehouse	1	2	3	4
1	—	300	—	400
2	300	—	300	—

34. a. An initial solution is

	Los Angeles	San Francisco	San Diego
San Jose	4 \ 100	10	6
Las Vegas	8 \ 100	16	6 \ 200
Tucson	14	18 \ 300	10

Total cost = $7800

b. Note that the initial solution is degenerate because there are only 4 occuped cells; a zero is assigned to the cell in row 3 and column 1 so that the row and column indices can be computed

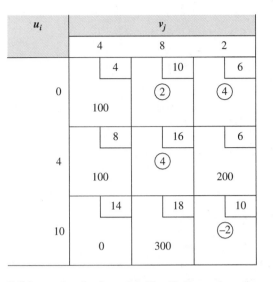

Cell in row 3 and column 3 is identified as an incoming cell. However, 0 units can be added to this cell. Initial solution remains optimal.

c.

San Jose–San Francisco:	100
Las Vegas–Los Angeles:	200
Las Vegas–San Diego:	100
Tucson–San Francisco:	200
Tucson–San Diego	100
Total Cost = $7800	

Note that this total cost is the same as for part (a); thus, we have alternative optima.

d. The final transportation tableau is shown; the total transportation cost is $8000, an increase of $200 over the solution to part (a)

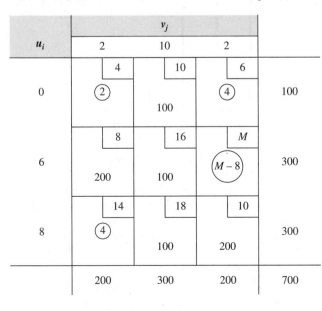

40. Substract 10 from row 1, 14 from row 2, and 22 from row 3 to obtain:

	1	2	3
Jackson	0	6	22
Ellis	0	8	26
Smith	0	2	12

Subtract 0 from column 1, 2 from column 2, and 12 from column 3 to obtain:

	1	2	3
Jackson	0	④	10
Ellis	0	6	14
Smith	0	0	0

Two lines cover the zeros; the minimum unlined element is 4; Step 3 yields:

	1	2	3
Jackson	0	[0]	6
Ellis	[0]	2	10
Smith	0	0	[0]

Optimal solution: Jackson—2
Ellis—1
Smith—3

Time requirement is 64 days

43. We start with the opportunity loss matrix:

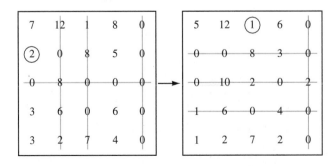

	1	2	3	4	D*
Shoe	4	11	0	5	[0]
Toy	0	[0]	8	3	1
Auto	0	10	2	[0]	3
Houseware	1	6	[0]	4	1
Video	[0]	1	6	1	0

*D = Dummy

	Optimal Solution	Profit
Toy:	2	18
Auto:	4	16
Houseware:	3	13
Video:	1	14
	Total	61

Chapter 8

1. a. This is a mixed-integer linear program. Its LP Relaxation is

Max $30x_1 + 25x_2$
s.t.
$$3x_1 + 1.5x_2 \le 400$$
$$1.5x_1 + 2x_2 \le 250$$
$$x_1 + x_2 \le 150$$
$$x_1, x_2 \ge 0$$

b. This is an all-integer linear progam; its LP Relaxation just requires dropping the words "and integer" from the last line
c. This is a mixed-integer linear program; its LP Relaxation is obtained by dropping the integer requirement on x_1
d. This is an all-integer linear program; its LP Relaxation is obtained by dropping the integer requirement on all the variables
e. This is a linear program; no variables are required to be integer

2. a.

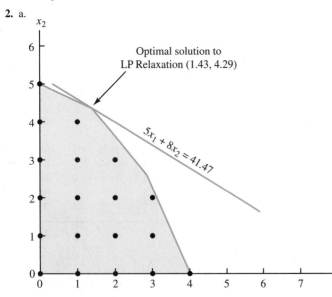

b. The optimal solution to the LP Relaxation is given by $x_1 = 1.43$, $x_2 = 4.29$ with an objective function value of 41.47. Rounding down gives the feasible integer solution $x_1 = 1$, $x_2 = 4$; its value is 37

c.

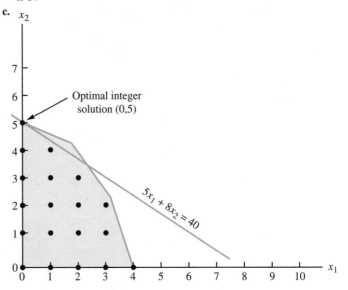

The optimal solution is given by $x_1 = 0$, $x_2 = 5$; its value is 40
This is not the same solution as that found by rounding down; it provides a 3-unit increase in the value of the objective function

5. a. The feasible mixed-integer solutions are indicated by the boldface vertical lines in the graph

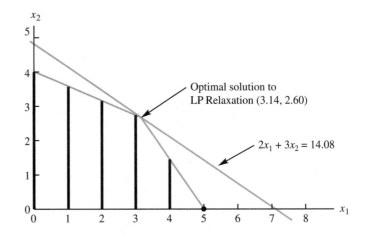

b. The optimal solution to the LP Relaxation is given by $x_1 = 3.14$, $x_2 = 2.60$; its value is 14.08
Rounding the value of x_1 down to find a feasible mixed-integer solution yields $x_1 = 3$, $x_2 = 2.60$ with a value of 13.8; this solution is clearly not optimal; with $x_1 = 3$, x_2 can be made larger without violating the constraints
c. The optimal solution to the MILP is given by $x_1 = 3$, $x_2 = 2.67$; its value is 14. See Figure G8.5c

Figure G8.5c

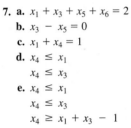

Optimal mixed-integer solution (3, 2.67)

$2x_1 + 3x_2 = 14$

7. a. $x_1 + x_3 + x_5 + x_6 = 2$
   b. $x_3 - x_5 = 0$
   c. $x_1 + x_4 = 1$
   d. $x_4 \leq x_1$
      $x_4 \leq x_3$
   e. $x_4 \leq x_1$
      $x_4 \leq x_3$
      $x_4 \geq x_1 + x_3 - 1$

15. a. Add the following multiple choice constraint to the problem

$$y_2 + y_2 = 1$$

New optimal solution: $y_1 = 1$, $y_3 = 1$, $x_{12} = 10$, $x_{31} = 30$, $x_{52} = 10$, $x_{53} = 20$
Value = 940

   b. Since one plant is already located in St. Louis, add only the following constraint to the model in Section 8.3:

$$y_3 + y_4 \leq 1$$

Optimal solution: Same as in Figure 8.5

CHAPTER 9

1.

Node	Shortest Route from Node 1	Distance
2	1–2	7
3	1–3	9
4	1–2–5–6–4	17
5	1–2–5	12
6	1–2–5–6	14
7	1–2–5–6–7	17

10.

Connect	Distant
1–6	2
6–7	3
7–8	1
7–10	2
10–9	3
9–4	2
9–3	3
3–2	1
4–5	3
7–11	4
8–13	4
14–15	2
15–12	3
14–13	4
Total	37

15.

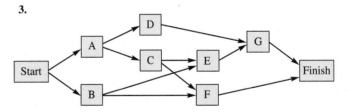

Maximum flow 9000 vehicles per hour

CHAPTER 10

3.

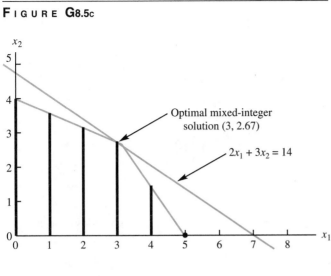

6. a. Critical path: A-D-F-H
   b. 22 weeks
   c. No, it is a critical activity
   d. Yes, 2 weeks
   e. Schedule for activity E:

Earliest start	3
Latest start	4
Earliest finish	10
Latest finish	11

10. a.

Activity	Optimistic	Most Probable	Pessimistic	Expected Times	Variance
A	4	5	6	5.00	0.11
B	8	9	10	9.00	0.11
C	7	7.5	11	8.00	0.44
D	6	9	10	8.83	0.25
E	6	7	9	7.17	0.25
F	5	6	7	6.00	0.11

b. Critical activities: B–D–F

Expected project completion time: $9.00 + 8.83 + 6.00 = 23.83$

Variance of projection completion time: $0.11 + 0.25 + 0.11 + = 0.47$

13.

Activity	Expected Time	Variance
A	5	0.11
B	3	0.03
C	7	0.11
D	6	0.44
E	7	0.44
F	3	0.11
G	10	0.44
H	8	1.78

From Problem 6, A–D–F–H is the critical path, so

$$E(T) = 5 + 6 + 3 + 8 = 22$$

$$\sigma^2 = 0.11 + 0.44 + 0.11 + 1.78 = 2.44$$

$$z = \frac{\text{Time} - E(T)}{\sigma} = \frac{\text{Time} - 22}{\sqrt{2.44}}$$

a. Time = 21:

		Area
	$z = -0.64$	0.2389
$P(21 \text{ weeks}) = 0.5000 - 0.2389 = 0.2611$		

b. Time = 22:

		Area
	$z = 0$	0.0000
$P(22 \text{ weeks}) = 0.5000$		

c. Time = 25:

		Area
	$z = +1.92$	0.4726
$P(22 \text{ weeks}) = 0.5000 + 0.4726 = 0.9726$		

21. a.

Activity	Earliest Start	Latest Start	Earliest Finish	Latest Finish	Slack	Critical Activity
A	0	0	3	3	0	Yes
B	0	1	2	3	1	
C	3	3	8	8	0	Yes
D	2	3	7	8	1	
E	8	8	14	14	0	Yes
F	8	10	10	12	2	
G	10	12	12	14	2	

Critical path: A–C–E

Project completion time $= t_A + t_C + t_E = 3 + 5 + 6 = 14$ days

b. Total cost = $8400

22. a.

Activity	Max Crash Days	Crash Cost/Day
A	1	600
B	1	700
C	2	400
D	2	400
E	2	500
F	1	400
G	1	500

$$\text{Min } 600Y_A + 700Y_B + 400Y_C + 400Y_D + 500Y_E + 400Y_F + 400Y_G$$

s.t.

$$X_A + Y_A \geq 3$$
$$X_B + Y_B \geq 2$$
$$-X_A + X_C + Y_C \geq 5$$
$$-X_B + X_D + Y_D \geq 5$$
$$-X_C + X_E + Y_E \geq 6$$
$$-X_D + X_E + Y_E \geq 6$$
$$-X_C + X_F + Y_F \geq 2$$
$$-X_D + X_F + Y_F \geq 2$$
$$-X_F + X_G + Y_G \geq 2$$
$$-X_E + X_{FIN} \geq 0$$
$$-X_G + X_{FIN} \geq 0$$
$$X_{FIN} \leq 12$$
$$Y_A \leq 1$$
$$Y_B \leq 1$$
$$Y_C \leq 2$$
$$Y_D \leq 2$$
$$Y_E \leq 2$$
$$Y_F \leq 1$$
$$Y_G \leq 1$$
$$\text{All } X, Y \geq 0$$

b. Solution of the linear programming model in part (a) that shows

Activity	Crash	Crashing Cost
C	1 day	$400
E	1 day	500
	Total	$900

c. Total cost = Normal cost + Crashing cost

$$= \$8400 + \$900 = \$9300$$

CHAPTER 11

1. a. $Q^* = \sqrt{\dfrac{2DC_0}{C_h}} = \sqrt{\dfrac{2(3600)(20)}{0.25(3)}} = 438.18$

b. $r = dm = \dfrac{3600}{250}(5) = 72$

c. $T = \dfrac{250Q^*}{D} = \dfrac{250(438.18)}{3600} = 30.43$ days

d. $TC = \dfrac{1}{2}QC_h + \dfrac{D}{Q}C_0$

$= \dfrac{1}{2}(438.18)(0.25)(3) + \dfrac{3600}{438.18}(20) = \$328.63$

13. a. $Q^* = \sqrt{\dfrac{2DC_0}{(1-D/P)C_h}}$

$= \sqrt{\dfrac{2(7200)(150)}{(1-7200/25,000)(0.18)(14.50)}} = 1078.12$

b. Number of production runs $= \dfrac{D}{Q^*} = \dfrac{7200}{1078.12} = 6.68$

c. $T = \dfrac{250Q}{D} = \dfrac{250(1078.12)}{7200} = 37.43$ days

d. Production run length $= \dfrac{Q}{P/250} = \dfrac{1078.12}{25,000/250} = 10.78$ days

e. Maximum inventory $= \left(1 - \dfrac{D}{P}\right)Q$

$= \left(1 - \dfrac{7200}{25,000}\right)(1078.12) = 767.62$

f. Holding cost $= \dfrac{1}{2}\left(1-\dfrac{D}{P}\right)QC_h$

$= \dfrac{1}{2}\left(1 - \dfrac{7200}{25,000}\right)(1078.12)(0.18)(14.50)$

$= \$1001.74$

Ordering cost $= \dfrac{D}{Q}C_0 = \dfrac{7200}{1078.12}(150) = \$1001.74$

Total cost $= \$2003.48$

g. $r = dm = \left(\dfrac{D}{250}\right)m = \dfrac{7200}{250}(15) = 432$

15. a. $Q^* = \sqrt{\dfrac{2DC_0}{C_h}\left(\dfrac{C_h + C_b}{C_b}\right)} =$

$\sqrt{\dfrac{2(12,000)(25)}{0.50}\left(\dfrac{0.50 + 5}{0.50}\right)} = 1148.91$

b. $S^* = Q^*\left(\dfrac{C_h}{C_h + C_b}\right) = 1148.91\left(\dfrac{0.50}{0.50 + 5}\right) = 104.45$

c. Max inventory $= Q^* - S^* = 1044.46$

d. $T = \dfrac{250Q^*}{D} = \dfrac{250(1148.91)}{12,000} = 23.94$ days

e. Holding $= \dfrac{(Q - S)^2}{2Q}C_h = \$237.38$

Ordering $= \dfrac{D}{Q}C_0 = 261.12$

Backorder $= \dfrac{S^2}{2Q}C_b = 23.74$

Total Cost $= \$522.24$

The total cost for the EOQ model in Problem 4 was \$547.72; allowing backorders reduces the total cost

21. $Q = \sqrt{\dfrac{2DC_0}{C_h}}$

$Q_1 = \sqrt{\dfrac{2(500)(40)}{0.20(10)}} = 141.42$

$Q_2 = \sqrt{\dfrac{2(500)(40)}{0.20(9.7)}} = 143.59$

Since Q_1 is over its limit of 99 units, Q_1 cannot be optimal (see Problem 23); use $Q_2 = 143.59$ as the optimal order quantity

Total cost $= \dfrac{1}{2}QC_h + \dfrac{D}{Q}C_0 + DC$

$= 139.28 + 139.28 + 4850.00 = \$5128.56$

25. a.

$c_o = 80 - 50 = 30$

$c_u = 125 - 80 = 45$

$P(D \le Q^*) = \dfrac{c_u}{c_u + c_o} = \dfrac{45}{45 + 30} = 0.60$

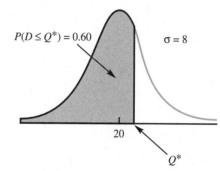

$P(D \le Q^*) = 0.60$ $\sigma = 8$

20

Q^*

For an area of 0.60 below Q^*, $z = 0.25$

$Q^* = 20 + 0.25(8) = 22$

b. $P(\text{Sell all}) = P(D \ge Q^*) = 1 - 0.60 = 0.40$

29. a. $r = dm = (200/250)15 = 12$

b. $\dfrac{D}{Q} = \dfrac{200}{25} = 8$ orders/year

The limit of 1 stockout per year means that

$P(\text{Stockout/cycle}) = 1/8 = 0.125$

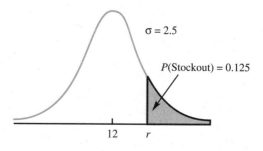

$\sigma = 2.5$

$P(\text{Stockout}) = 0.125$

12   r

For area in tail = 0.125, $z = 1.15$

$$z = \frac{r - 12}{2.5} = 1.15$$

or

$$r = 12 + 1.15(2.5) = 14.875 \approx 15$$

  c. Safety stock = 3 units
     Added cost = 3($5) = $15/year

33. a. 1/52 = 0.0192
   b. $M = \mu + z\sigma = 60 + 2.07(12) = 85$
   c. $M = 35 + (0.9808)(85 - 35) = 84$

37. Quantity of snowblowers to be produced: 5000

Gross requirements, engines:	5000
Engines in inventory:	2000
Net requirements, engines:	3000
Gross requirements, air cleaners:	3000
Air cleaners in inventory:	1500
Net requirements, air cleaners:	1500
Gross requirements, filter housings:	1500
Filter housings in inventory:	1000
Net requirements, filter housing:	500

Chapter 12

5. a. $P_0 = 1 - \dfrac{\lambda}{\mu} = 1 - \dfrac{10}{12} = 0.1667$

   b. $L_q = \dfrac{\lambda^2}{\mu(\mu - \lambda)} = \dfrac{10^2}{12(12 - 10)} = 4.1667$

   c. $W_q = \dfrac{L_q}{\lambda} = 0.4167$ hour

   d. $W = W_q + \dfrac{1}{\mu} = 0.5$ hour (30 minutes)

   e. $P_w = \dfrac{\lambda}{\mu} = \dfrac{10}{12} = 0.8333$

11. a. $\lambda = 2.5;\quad \mu = \dfrac{60}{10} = 6$ customers per hour

$$L_q = \frac{\lambda^2}{\mu(\mu - \lambda)} = \frac{(2.5)^2}{6(6 - 2.5)} = 0.2976$$

$$L = L_q + \frac{\lambda}{\mu} = 0.7143$$

$$W_q = \frac{L_q}{\lambda} = 0.1190 \text{ hours (7.14 minutes)}$$

$$W = W_q + \frac{1}{\mu} = 0.2857 \text{ hours}$$

$$P_w = \frac{\lambda}{\mu} = \frac{2.5}{6} = 0.4167$$

   b. No; $W_q = 7.14$ minutes; firm should increase the mean service rate (μ) for the consultant or hire a second consultant

   c. $\mu = \dfrac{60}{8} = 7.5$ customers per hour

$$L_q = \frac{\lambda^2}{\mu(\mu - \lambda)} = \frac{(2.5)^2}{7.5(7.5 - 2.5)} = 0.1667$$

$$W_q = \frac{L_q}{\lambda} = 0.0667 \text{ hour (4 minutes)}$$
The service goal is being met

19. a. $k = 2;\quad \lambda/\mu = 14/10 = 1.4$
   From table, $P_0 = 0.1765$

   b. $L_q = \dfrac{(\lambda/\mu)^2 \lambda\mu}{1!(2\mu - \lambda)^2}P_0 = \dfrac{(1.4)^2(14)(10)}{(20 - 14)^2}(0.1765) = 1.3453$

$$L = L_q + \frac{\lambda}{\mu} = 1.3453 + \frac{14}{10} = 2.7453$$

   c. $W_q = \dfrac{L_q}{\lambda} = \dfrac{1.3453}{14} = 0.961$ hours

   d. $W = W_q + \dfrac{1}{\mu} = 0.0961 + \dfrac{1}{10} = 0.1961$ hours

   e. $P_0 = 0.1765$

$$P_1 = \frac{(\lambda/\mu)^1}{1!}P_0 = \frac{14}{10}(0.1765) = 0.2471$$

$$P(\text{wait}) = P(n \geq 2) = 1 - P(n \leq 1)$$
$$= 1 - 0.4236 = 0.5764$$

21. From Problem 11, a service time of 8 minutes has $\mu = 60/8 = 7.5$

$$L_q = \frac{\lambda^2}{\mu(\mu - \lambda)} = \frac{(2.5)^2}{7.5(7.5 - 2.5)} = 0.1667$$

$$L = L_q + \frac{\lambda}{\mu} = 0.50$$

Total cost = $25L + $16
$$= 25(0.50) + 16 = \$28.50$$

Two channels: $\lambda = 2.5;\quad \mu = 60/10 = 6$

Using equation (12.11) and $P_0 = 0.6552$, we get

$$L_q = \frac{(\lambda/\mu)^2 \lambda\mu}{1!(2\mu - \lambda)^2}P_0 = 0.0189$$

$$L = L_q + \frac{\lambda}{\mu} = 0.4356$$

Total cost = $25(0.4356) + 2(16) = \$42.89$

Use the one consultant with an 8-minute service time

25. $\lambda = 4, W = 10$ minutes
   a. $\mu = \frac{1}{2} = 0.5$
   b. $W_q = W - 1/\mu = 10 - 1/0.5 = 8$ minutes
   c. $L = \lambda W = 4(10) = 40$

27. a. $\frac{2}{8}$ hours = 0.25 per hour
   b. 1/3.2 hours = 0.3125 per hour

   c. $L_q = \dfrac{\lambda^2\sigma^2 + (\lambda/\mu)^2}{2(1 - \lambda/\mu)} = \dfrac{(0.25)^2(2)^2 + (0.25/0.3125)^2}{2(1 - 0.25/0.3125)} = 2.225$

   d. $W_q = \dfrac{L_q}{\lambda} = \dfrac{2.225}{0.25} = 8.9$ hours

   e. $W = W_q + \dfrac{1}{\mu} = 8.9 + \dfrac{1}{0.3125} = 12.1$ hours

   f. Same at $P_w = \dfrac{\lambda}{\mu} = \dfrac{0.25}{0.3125} = 0.80$

   80% of the time the welder is busy

30. a. $\lambda = 42$; $\mu = 20$

i	$(\lambda/\mu)^i/i!$
0	1.0000
1	2.1000
2	2.2050
3	1.5435
Total	6.8485

j	P_j	
0	1/6.8485	= 0.1460
1	2.1/6.8485	= 0.3066
2	2.2050/6.8485	= 0.3220
3	1.5435/6.8485	= 0.2254
		1.0000

b. 0.2254

c. $L = \lambda/\mu(1 - P_k) = 42/20(1 - 0.2254) = 1.6267$

d. Four lines will be necessary; the probability of denied access is 0.1499

34. $N = 5$; $\lambda = 0.025$; $\mu = 0.20$; $\lambda/\mu = 0.125$

a.

n	$\dfrac{N!}{(N-n)!}\left(\dfrac{\lambda}{\mu}\right)^n$
0	1.0000
1	0.6250
2	0.3125
3	0.1172
4	0.0293
5	0.0037
Total	2.0877

$P_0 = 1/2.0877 = 0.4790$

b. $L_q = N - \left(\dfrac{\lambda + \mu}{\lambda}\right)(1 - P_0) = 5 - \left(\dfrac{0.225}{0.025}\right)(1 - 0.4790)$
   $= 0.3110$

c. $L = L_q + (1 - P_0) = 0.3110 + (1 - 0.4790) = 0.8320$

d. $W_q = \dfrac{L_q}{(N - L)\lambda} = \dfrac{0.3110}{(5 - 0.8320)(0.025)} = 2.9846$ minutes

e. $W = W_q + \dfrac{1}{\mu} = 2.9846 + \dfrac{1}{0.20} = 7.9846$ minutes

f. Trips/day = (8 hours)(60 minutes/hour)(λ)
   $= (8)(60)(0.025) = 12$ trips

Time at copier: $12 \times 7.9846 = 95.8$ minutes/day
Wait time at copier: $12 \times 2.9846 = 35.8$ minutes/day

g. Yes, five secretaries $\times$ 35.8 = 179 minutes (3 hours/day), so 3 hours per day are lost to waiting
$(35.8/480)(100) = 7.5\%$ of each secretary's day is spent waiting for the copier

CHAPTER 13

1. a. An estimate of the probability distribution of sales is shown here:

Sales	Probability
0	4/50=0.08
1	6/50=0.12
2	14/50=0.28
3	12/50=0.24
4	7/50=0.14
5	5/50=0.10
6	2/50=0.04
Total	1.00

b. E(Sales) = 0(.08) + 1(.12) + 2(.28) + 3(.24) + 4(.14) + 5(.10) + 6(.04) = 2.70

c. Use the following table to generate sales values.

Sales	Interval of Random Numbers
0	0.00 but less than 0.08
1	0.08 but less than 0.20
2	0.20 but less than 0.48
3	0.48 but less than 0.72
4	0.72 but less than 0.86
5	0.86 but less than 0.96
6	0.96 but less than 1.00

Using the 10 random numbers provided, the sales for the first ten days of operation are as follows:

Day	1	2	3	4	5	6	7	8	9	10
Sales	2	2	3	4	3	2	4	0	3	2

d. The average sales for the 10-day period is 2.5; this value is close to the value computed in (b).

3. a. The following table shows the relative frequencies and associated intervals of random numbers used to generate demand.

Rental Demand	Probability	Interval of Random Numbers
7	0.08	0.00 but less than 0.08
8	0.20	0.08 but less than 0.28
9	0.32	0.28 but less than 0.60
10	0.28	0.60 but less than 0.88
11	0.12	0.88 but less than 1.00
	1.00	

Day	Random Number	Simulated Demand
1	.15	8
2	.48	9
3	.71	10
4	.56	9
5	.90	11

b. Note that no more than nine cars can be rented each day because only nine are available.

$$\text{Average rentals} = \frac{8 + 9 + 9 + 9 + 9}{d} = \frac{44}{5} = 8.8 \text{ cars}$$

c. There will be one lost on day 3 and two lost on day 5. Total lost = 3.

d. Average daily demand $= \dfrac{8 + 9 + 10 + 9 + 11}{5} = \dfrac{47}{5} = 9.4$ cars

e. Because different random numbers can be generated, a variety of answers is possible.

6. Account balances $= a + r(b-a) = 2000 + r(8000 - 2000) = 2000 + 6000(r)$

Customer	Random Number	Account Balance
1	0.14	2000 + 6000(0.14) = 2840
2	0.56	2000 + 6000(0.56) = 5360
3	0.08	2000 + 6000(0.08) = 2480
4	0.89	2000 + 6000(0.89) = 7340
5	0.44	2000 + 6000(0.44) = 4640

Average account balance = (2840 + 5360 + 2480 + 7340 + 4640)/5 = 22,660/5 = 4532

8. Because different random numbers can be generated, a variety of answers is possible.

15. a. If the last purchase is at Super Z, the following table can be used to generate the store at which the next purchase is made.

Next Purchase	Probability	Interval of Random Numbers
Super Z	0.70	0.00 but less than 0.70
Devco	0.10	0.70 but less than 0.80
Floorgreen	0.20	0.80 but less than 1.00

If the last purchase is at Devco, the following table can be used to generate the store at which the next purchase is made.

Next Purchase	Probability	Interval of Random Numbers
Super Z	0.30	0.00 but less than 0.30
Devco	0.55	0.30 but less than 0.85
Floorgreen	0.15	0.85 but less than 1.00

If the last purchase is at Floorgreen, the following table can be used to generate the store at which the next purchase is made.

Next Purchase	Probability	Interval of Random Numbers
Super Z	0.10	0.00 but less than 0.10
Devco	0.10	0.10 but less than 0.20
Floorgreen	0.80	0.20 but less than 1.00

If Hatcher's last purchase had been made at Super Z, the store at which his next purchase is made is as follows:

Random Number	0.42	0.81	0.16	0.57
Next Purchase	Super Z	Floorgreen	Devco	Devco

b. If Hatcher's last purchase had been made at Devco, the store at which his next purchase is made is as follows:

Random Number	0.42	0.81	0.16	0.57
Next Purchase	Devco	Devco	Super Z	Super Z

c. It definitely is not. We did not see any purchases from Floorgreen for the results in part (b). Simulation for 1000 periods or more will show Floorgreen with the largest market share at approximately 48% of the purchases. Super Z has approximately 34% with Devco approximately 18%. The four-period simulation is not enough.

CHAPTER 14

1. a.

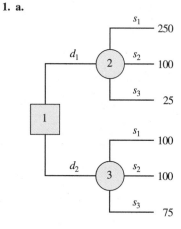

b.

Decision	Maximum Profit	Minimum Profit
d_1	250	25
d_2	100	75

Optimistic approach: Select d_1
Conservative approach: Select d_2
Regret or opportunity loss table:

Decision	s_1	s_2	s_3
d_1	0	0	50
d_2	150	0	0

Maximum regret: 50 for d_1 and 150 for d_2; select d_1

5. $EV(d_1) = 0.65(250) + 0.15(100) + 0.20(25) = 182.5$
$EV(d_2) = 0.65(100) + 0.15(100) + 0.20(75) = 95$
The optimal decision is d_1

8. $EV(d_1) = p(10) + (1 - p)(1) = 9p + 1$
$\quad EV(d_2) = p(4) + (1 - p)(3) = 1p + 3$

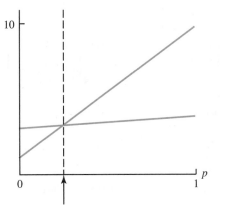

Value of p for
which EVs are equal

$9p + 1 = 1p + 3$ and hence $p = 0.25$

12. a. if s_1, then d_1; if s_2, then d_1 or d_2; if s_3, then d_2
  b. EVwPI $= 0.65(250) + 0.15(100) + 0.20(75) = 192.5$
  c. From the solution to Problem 5, we know that $EV(d_1) = 182.5$
    and $EV(d_2) = 95$; thus, recommended decision is d_1; hence,
    EVwoPI $= 182.5$
  d. EVPI $=$ EVwPI $-$ EVwoPI $= 192.5 - 182.5 = 10$

14.

State of Nature	$P(s_j)$	$P(I|s_j)$	$P(I \cap s_j)$	$P(s_j|I)$
s_1	0.2	0.10	0.020	0.1905
s_2	0.5	0.05	0.025	0.2381
s_3	0.3	0.20	0.060	0.5714
	1.0		$P(I) = 0.105$	1.0000

28. Risk-avoider, at \$20 payoff $p = 0.70$
  EV(Lottery) $= 0.70(100) + 0.30(-100) = \$40$
  Will Pay $40 - 20 = \$20$
  Risk-taker, at \$20 payoff $p = 0.45$
  EV(Lottery $= 0.45(100) + 0.55(-100) = -\$10$
  Will Pay $20 - (-10) = \$30$

30. a. $EV(d_1) = 0.40(100) + 0.30(25) + .30(0) = 47.5$
$\qquad EV(d_2) = 0.40(75) + 0.30(50) + 0.30(25) = 52.5 \,\Big\}\, d_2$
$\qquad EV(d_3) = 0.40(50) + 0.30(50) + 0.30(50) = 50.0$

  b. Using utilities

Decision Maker A	Decision Maker B
EU(d_1) = 4.9	EU(d_1) = 4.45 Best
EU(d_2) = 5.9	EU(d_2) = 3.75
EU(d_3) = 6.0 Best	EU(d_3) = 3.00

c. Difference in attitude toward risk; decision maker A tends to
avoid risk, whereas decision maker B tends to take a risk for the
opportunity of a large payoff

CHAPTER 15

2. a. Let $x_1 =$ number of shares of AGA Products purchased
$\qquad x_2 =$ number of shares of Key Oil purchased
To obtain an annual return of exactly 9%:

$$0.06(50)x_1 + 0.10(100)x_2 = 0.09(50,000)$$

$$3x_1 + 10x_2 = 4500$$

To have exactly 60% of the total investment in Key Oil:

$$100x_2 = 0.60(50,000)$$

$$x_2 = 300$$

Therefore, we can write the goal programming model as
follows:

Min $P_1(d_1^-) + P_2(d_2^+)$
s.t.

$50x_1 +$	$100x_2$		$\leq 50,000$	funds available
$3x_1 +$	$10x_2 - d_1^+ + d_1^-$	$=$	$4,500$	P_1 goal
	$x_2 - d_2^+ + d_2^-$	$=$	300	P_2 goal

$\qquad x_1, x_2, d_1^+, d_1^-, d_2^+, d_2^- \geq 0$

  b. In the graphical solution shown below, $x_1 = 250$ and $x_2 = 375$

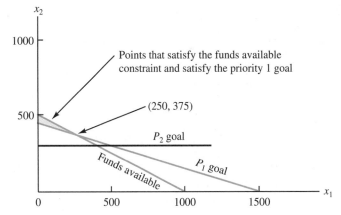

12. *Synthesization*
Step 1: Column totals are 17/4, 31/21, and 12
Step 2:

Style	Style Car A	Car B	Car C
Car A	4/17	7/31	4/12
Car B	12/17	21/31	7/12
Car C	1/17	3/31	1/12

Step 3:

Style	Style			
	Car A	Car B	Car C	Row Average
Car A	0.235	0.226	0.333	0.265
Car B	0.706	0.677	0.583	0.655
Car C	0.059	0.097	0.083	0.080

Consistency Ratio

Step 1:

$$0.265 \begin{bmatrix} 1 \\ 3 \\ 1/4 \end{bmatrix} + 0.655 \begin{bmatrix} 1/3 \\ 1 \\ 1/7 \end{bmatrix} + 0.080 \begin{bmatrix} 4 \\ 7 \\ 1 \end{bmatrix}$$

Weighted Sum

$$\begin{bmatrix} 0.265 \\ 0.795 \\ 0.066 \end{bmatrix} + \begin{bmatrix} 0.218 \\ 0.655 \\ 0.094 \end{bmatrix} + \begin{bmatrix} 0.320 \\ 0.560 \\ 0.080 \end{bmatrix} = \begin{bmatrix} 0.803 \\ 2.010 \\ 0.240 \end{bmatrix}$$

Step 2:   0.803/0.265 = 3.030
        2.010/0.655 = 3.069
        0.240/0.080 = 3.000

Step 3: λ_{max} = (3.030 + 3.069 + 3.000)/3 = 3.033
Step 4: CI = (3.033 − 3)/2 = 0.017
Step 5: CR = 0.017/0.58 = 0.29
Since CR = 0.029 is less than 0.10, the degree of consistency exhibited in the pairwise comparison matrix for style is acceptable

16. a.

Flavor	Flavor		
	A	B	C
A	1	3	2
B	1/3	1	5
C	1/2	1/5	1

b. Step 1: Column totals are 11/6, 21/5, and 8

Step 2:

Flavor	Flavor		
	A	B	C
A	6/11	15/21	2/8
B	2/11	5/21	5/8
C	3/11	1/21	1/8

Step 3:

Flavor	Flavor			
	A	B	C	Row Average
A	0.545	0.714	0.250	0.503
B	0.182	0.238	0.625	0.348
C	0.273	0.048	0.125	0.149

c. Step 1:

$$0.503 \begin{bmatrix} 1 \\ 1/3 \\ 1/2 \end{bmatrix} + 0.348 \begin{bmatrix} 3 \\ 1 \\ 1/5 \end{bmatrix} + 0.149 \begin{bmatrix} 2 \\ 5 \\ 1 \end{bmatrix}$$

Weighted Sum

$$\begin{bmatrix} 0.503 \\ 0.168 \\ 0.252 \end{bmatrix} + \begin{bmatrix} 1.044 \\ 0.348 \\ 0.070 \end{bmatrix} + \begin{bmatrix} 0.298 \\ 0.745 \\ 0.149 \end{bmatrix} = \begin{bmatrix} 1.845 \\ 1.261 \\ 0.471 \end{bmatrix}$$

Step 2: 1.845/0.503 = 3.668
       1.261/0.348 = 3.624
       0.471/0.149 = 3.161
Step 3: λ_{max} = (3.668 + 3.624 + 3.161)/3 = 3.484
Step 4: CI = (3.484 − 3)/2 = 0.242
Step 5: CR = 0.242/0.58 = 0.417
Since CR = 0.417 is greater than 0.10, the individual's judgments are not consistent

20. a.

Overall Goal

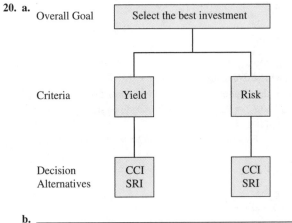

b.

Criterion	Yield		Risk	
Yield: 0.667	CCI: 0.750		CCI: 0.333	
Risk: 0.333	SRI: 0.250		SRI: 0.667	

c.

Alternative	Criterion	
	Yield	Risk
CCI	0.750	0.333
SRI	0.250	0.667

Overall priority for CCI:

    0.667(0.750) + 0.333(0.333) = 0.500 + 0.111 = 0.611

Overall priority for SRI:

    0.667(0.250) + 0.333(0.667) = 0.167 + 0.222 = 0.389

CHAPTER 16

1. a.

Week	Time Series Value	Forecast	Forecast Error	Squared Forecast Error
1	8			
2	13			
3	15			
4	17	12	5	25
5	16	15	1	1
6	9	16	−7	49
			Total	75

Forecast for week 7 is $(17 + 16 + 9)/3 = 14$

b. MSE = 75/3 = 25

c.

Week (t)	Time Series Value (Y_t)	Forecast F_t	Forecast Error $Y_t - F_t$	Squared Error $(Y_t - F_t)^2$
1	8			
2	13	8.00	5.00	25.00
3	15	9.00	6.00	36.00
4	17	10.20	6.80	46.24
5	16	11.56	4.44	19.71
6	9	12.45	−3.45	11.90
			Total	138.85

Forecast for week 7 is $.2(9) + .8(12.45) = 11.76$

d. For the $\alpha = .2$ exponential smoothing forecast

$$\text{MSE} = \frac{138.85}{5} = 27.77$$

Since the 3-week moving average has a smaller MSE, it appears to provide the better forecasts

e.

Week (t)	Time Series Value (Y_t)	Forecast F_t	Forecast Error $Y_t - F_t$	Squared Error $(Y_t - F_t)^2$
1	8			
2	13	8.0	5.0	25.00
3	15	10.0	5.0	25.00
4	17	12.0	5.0	25.00
5	16	14.0	2.0	4.00
6	9	14.8	−5.8	33.64
			Total	112.64

$$\text{MSE} = \frac{112.64}{5} = 22.53$$

A smoothing constant of .4 appears to provide the better forecasts; for week 7 the forecasts using $\alpha = .4$ is $.4(9) + .6(14.8) = 12.48$

2. a.

Week	Time Series Value	4-Week Moving Average Forecast	(Error)^2	5-Week Moving Average Forecast	(Error)^2
1	17				
2	21				
3	19				
4	23				
5	18	20.00	4.00		
6	16	20.25	18.06	19.60	12.96
7	20	19.00	1.00	19.40	0.36
8	18	19.25	1.56	19.20	1.44
9	22	18.00	16.00	19.00	9.00
10	20	19.00	1.00	18.80	1.44
11	15	20.00	25.00	19.20	17.64
12	22	18.75	10.56	19.00	9.00
		Totals	77.18		51.84

b. MSE(4-week) = 77.18/8 = 9.65
MSE(5-week) = 51.84/7 = 7.41

c. For the limited data provided, the 5-week moving average provides the smallest MSE

4.

Week	Time Series Value	Forecast	Error	(Error)^2
1	17			
2	21	17.00	4.00	16.00
3	19	17.40	1.60	2.56
4	23	17.56	5.44	29.59
5	18	18.10	−0.10	0.01
6	16	18.09	−2.09	4.37
7	20	17.88	2.12	4.49
8	18	18.10	−0.10	0.01
9	22	18.09	3.91	15.29
10	20	18.48	1.52	2.31
11	15	18.63	−3.63	13.18
12	22	18.27	3.73	13.91
			Total	101.72

$$\text{MSE} = 101.72/11 = 9.25$$

$\alpha = 0.2$ provided a lower MSE; therefore $\alpha = 0.2$ is better than $\alpha = 0.1$

5. a.

Month	Y_t	3-Month Moving Averages Forecast	(Error)^2	$\alpha = 2$ Forecast	(Error)^2
1	80				
2	82			80.00	4.00
3	84			80.40	12.96
4	83	82.00	1.00	81.12	3.53
5	83	83.00	0.00	81.50	2.25
6	84	83.33	0.45	81.80	4.84
7	85	83.33	2.79	82.24	7.62
8	84	84.00	0.00	82.79	1.46
9	82	84.33	5.43	83.03	1.06
10	83	83.67	0.45	82.83	0.03
11	84	83.00	1.00	82.86	1.30
12	83	83.00	0.00	83.09	0.01
		Totals	11.12		39.06

MSE(3-month) = 11.12/9 = 1.24

MSE($\alpha = 0.2$) = 39.06/11 = 3.55

Use 3-month moving averages

b. $(83 + 84 + 83)/3 = 83.3$

14. $\Sigma t = 21$; $\Sigma t^2 = 91$; $\Sigma Y_t = 117{,}100$;

$\Sigma t Y_t = 403{,}700$; $n = 6$

$$b_1 = \frac{\Sigma t Y_t - (\Sigma t \Sigma Y_t)/n}{\Sigma t^2 - (\Sigma t)^2/n}$$

$$= \frac{403{,}700 - (21)(117{,}100)/6}{91 - (21)^2/6}$$

$$= \frac{-6{,}150}{17.5} = -351.429$$

$b_0 = \bar{Y} - b_1 \bar{t} = 19{,}516.667 - (-351.429)(3.5) = 20{,}746.67$

$T_t = 20{,}746.67 - 351.429t$

Conclusion: enrollment appears to be decreasing by an average of approximately 351 students per year

27. a. Four-quarter moving averages beginning with

$(1690 + 940 + 2625 + 2500)/4 = 1938.75$

Other moving averages are

1966.25	2002.50
1956.25	2052.50
2025.00	2060.00
1990.00	2123.75

b.

Quarter	Seasonal-Irregular Component Values		Seasonal Index	Adjusted Seasonal Index
1	0.904	0.900	0.9020	0.900
2	0.448	0.526	0.4970	0.486
3	1.344	1.453	1.3985	1.396
4	1.275	1.164	1.2195	1.217
		Total	4.0070	

c. Third quarter (1.396) which corresponds to the back-to-school months.

Note: Adjustment for seasonal index = 4.000/4.007 = 0.9983

35.

Restaurant

(i)	x_i	y_i	$x_i y_i$	x_i^2
1	1	19	19	1
2	4	44	176	16
3	6	40	240	36
4	10	52	520	100
5	14	53	742	196
Totals	35	208	1697	349

$$\bar{x} = \frac{35}{5} = 7$$

$$\bar{y} = \frac{208}{5} = 41.6$$

$$b_1 = \frac{\Sigma x_i y_i - (\Sigma x_i \Sigma y_i)/n}{\Sigma x_i^2 - (\Sigma x_i)^2/n}$$

$$= \frac{1697 - (35)(208)/5}{349 - (35)^2/5}$$

$$= \frac{241}{104} = 2.317$$

$b_0 = \bar{y} - b_1 \bar{x} = 41.6 - 2.317(7) = 25.381$

$\hat{y} = 25.381 + 2.317x$

b. $\hat{y} = 25.381 + 2.317(8) = 43.917$ or $43{,}917

CHAPTER 17

3. a. 0.10 as given by the transition probability

  b. $\pi_1 = 0.90\pi_1 + 0.30\pi_2$ (1)

   $\pi_2 = 0.10\pi_1 + 0.70\pi_2$ (2)

   $\pi_1 + \pi_2 = 1$ (3)

Using (1) and (3),

$$0.10\pi_1 - 0.30\pi_2 = 0$$

$$0.10\pi_1 - 0.30(1 - \pi_1) = 0$$

$$0.10\pi_1 - 0.30 + 0.30\pi_1 = 0$$

$$0.40\pi_1 = 0.30$$

$$\pi_1 = 0.75$$

$$\pi_2 = (1 - \pi_1) = 0.25$$

7. a.

$$\pi_1 = 0.85\pi_1 + 0.20\pi_2 + 0.15\pi_3 \qquad (1)$$

$$\pi_2 = 0.10\pi_1 + 0.75\pi_2 + 0.10\pi_3 \qquad (2)$$

$$\pi_3 = 0.05\pi_1 + 0.05\pi_2 + 0.75\pi_3 \qquad (3)$$

$$\pi_1 + \pi_2 + \pi_3 = 1 \qquad (4)$$

Using (1), (2), and (4) provides three equations with three unknowns; solving provides $\pi_1 = 0.548$, $\pi_2 = 0.286$, and $\pi_3 = 0.166$

b. 16.6% as given by π_3

c. Quick Stop should take

$$667 - 0.548(1000) = 119 \text{ Murphy's customers}$$

$$\text{and } 333 - 0.286(1000) = \underline{47} \text{ Ashley's customers}$$

$$\text{Total} \quad 166 \text{ Quick Stop customers}$$

11.

$$I = \begin{bmatrix} 1 & 0 \\ 0 & 1 \end{bmatrix} \qquad Q = \begin{bmatrix} 0.25 & 0.25 \\ 0.05 & 0.25 \end{bmatrix} \qquad (I - Q) = \begin{bmatrix} 0.75 & -0.25 \\ -0.05 & 0.75 \end{bmatrix}$$

$$N = (I - Q)^{-1} = \begin{bmatrix} 1.3636 & 0.4545 \\ 0.0909 & 1.3636 \end{bmatrix}$$

$$NR = \begin{bmatrix} 1.3636 & 0.4545 \\ 0.0909 & 1.3636 \end{bmatrix} \begin{bmatrix} 0.5 & 0.0 \\ 0.5 & 0.2 \end{bmatrix} = \begin{bmatrix} 0.909 & 0.091 \\ 0.727 & 0.273 \end{bmatrix}$$

$$BNR = \begin{bmatrix} 4000 & 5000 \end{bmatrix} \begin{bmatrix} 0.909 & 0.091 \\ 0.727 & 0.273 \end{bmatrix} = \begin{bmatrix} 7271 & 1729 \end{bmatrix}$$

Estimate $1729 in bad debts

CHAPTER 18

2. a. The numbers in the squares above each node represent the shortest route from that node to node 10

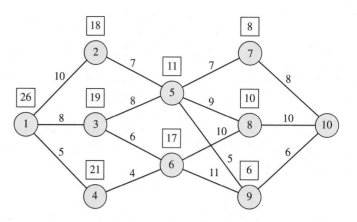

The shortest route is given by the sequence of nodes (1–4–6–9–10)

b. The shortest route from node 4 to node 10 is given by (4–6–9–10)

c.

Route	Value	Route	Value
(1–2–5–7–10)	32	(1–3–6–8–10)	34
(1–2–5–8–10)	36	(1–3–6–9–10)	31
(1–2–5–9–10)	28	(1–4–6–8–10)	29
(1–3–5–7–10)	31	(1–4–6–9–10)	26
(1–3–5–8–10)	35		
(1–3–5–9–10)	27		

3. Use four stages; one for each type of cargo. Let the state variable represent the amount of cargo space remaining.

a. In hundreds of pounds, we have up to 20 units of capacity available.

Stage 1 (Cargo Type 1):

x_1	0	1	2	d_1^*	$f_1(x_1)$	x_0
0–7	0	—	—	0	0	0–7
8–15	0	22	—	1	22	0–7
16–20	0	22	44	2	44	0–4

Stage 2 (Cargo Type 2):

x_2	0	1	2	d_2^*	$f_2(x_2)$	x_1
0–4	0	—	—	0	0	0–4
5–7	0	12	—	1	12	0–2
8–9	22	12	—	0	22	8–9
10–12	22	12	24	2	24	0–2
13–15	22	34	24	1	34	8–10
16–17	44	34	24	0	44	16–17
18–20	44	34	46	2	46	8–10

Stage 3 (Cargo Type 3):

x_3	0	1	2	3	4	d_3^*	$f_3(x_3)$	x_2
0–2	0	—	—	—	—	0	0	0–2
3–4	0	7	—	—	—	1	7	0–1
5	12	7	—	—	—	0	12	5
6–7	12	7	14	—	—	2	14	0–1
8	22	19	14	—	—	0	22	8
9	22	19	14	21	—	0	22	9
10	24	19	14	21	—	0	24	10
11	24	29	26	21	—	1	29	8
12	24	29	26	21	28	1	29	9
13	34	31	26	21	28	0	34	13
14–15	34	31	36	33	28	2	36	8–9
16	44	41	38	33	28	0	44	16
17	44	41	38	43	40	0	44	17
18	46	41	38	43	40	0	46	18
19	46	51	48	45	40	1	51	16
20	46	51	48	45	50	1	51	17

Stage 4 (Cargo Type 4):

x_4	0	1	2	3	d_4^*	$f_4(x_4)$	x_3
20	51	49	50	45	0	51	20

Tracing back through the tables, we find

Stage	State Variable Entering	Optimal Decision	State Variable Leaving
4	20	0	20
3	20	1	17
2	17	0	17
1	17	2	1

Load 1 unit of cargo type 3 and 2 units of cargo type 1 for a total return of $5100

b. Only the calculations for stage 4 need to be repeated; the entering value for the state variable is 18

x_4	0	1	2	3	d_4^*	$f_4(x_4)$	x_3
18	46	47	42	38	1	47	16

Optimal solution: $d_4 = 1$, $d_3 = 0$, $d_2 = 0$, $d_1 = 2$
Value $= 47$

10. The optimal production schedule is given below:

Month	Beginning Inventory	Production	Ending Inventory
1	10	20	10
2	10	20	0
3	0	30	0

Index

n after a page number = footnote